THE K&W GUIDE TO
COLLEGE PROGRAMS & SERVICES

FOR STUDENTS WITH LEARNING DISABILITIES OR ATTENTION DEFICIT HYPERACTIVITY DISORDER

11TH EDITION

Good luck on your journey...and the K&W Guide will help you find the school that fits!!

Richard D Lavoie, M.A., M.Ed., EdD. (Hon)

Vitally important is learning what universities are offering in terms of services and who is providing these services. The K and W Guide is an exemplary first step in discovering the answers to these questions.

Marsha A. Glines, Ph.D., Dean
Institute for Achievement and Learning, Lynn University

One of the wonderful things about this K & W Guide is that it helps students and their parents plan the best ways to find and use help. With this Guide you can map out new, essential connections: with colleges and universities who understand your needs; with appropriate support services on campus; with departments and faculty members who will understand, challenge and respect you. Use this guide to start planning now, and to further develop your ability to find and use help.

Ed Hallowell, ¹The Hallowell Center, Sudbury, MA

K &W is a "godsend."

Dodge Johnson
College Planning
Malvern, PA

The authors gratefully acknowledge the time and effort of all the parents, high school staff, professionals, and service providers at the colleges and universities who give these students encouragement and support. It is these individuals and others like them who are willing to work closely with students with learning disabilities, believe in empowering students to articulate their needs, and help students to become independent and successful learners as they pursue a college education and life beyond college. Those who believe in the merit of helping these individuals should reach out to those who do not understand. Those who do not understand should open their minds to the fact that learning disabilities are neurological and are life-long; they do not go away. The authors of this guide applaud these students. No children choose to be born with a learning disability or ADHD. However, if they hold fast to their dreams and aspirations, look beyond the imperfections and hidden handicaps, they can make things happen for themselves.

Marybeth Kravets and Imy Wax
Co-authors of the K&W Guide.

The Princeton Review®

PrincetonReview.com

THE K&W GUIDE TO COLLEGE PROGRAMS & SERVICES

FOR STUDENTS WITH LEARNING DISABILITIES OR ATTENTION DEFICIT HYPERACTIVITY DISORDER

11TH EDITION

MARYBETH KRAVETS, MA

AND IMY F. WAX, MS

RANDOM HOUSE, INC.

NEW YORK

The Princeton Review, Inc.
111 Speen Street, Suite 550
Framingham, MA 01701
E-mail: bookeditor@review.com

ISBN: 978-0-307-94507-5
ISSN: 1934-4775

Printed in the United States of America on partially recycled paper.

9 8 7 6 5 4 3 2 1

11th Edition

DEDICATION

This book is a labor of love. It is written to help individuals throughout the world who have been identified as having learning disabilities or Attention Deficit Hyperactivity Disorder and who are seeking the right match and fit for life after high school. Just as important, the K&W Guide is for those students who have never been officially identified as having a disability. It is an educational tool for all of the families, professionals, and friends who know someone who has a learning disability or Attention Deficit/Hyperactivity Disorder or other learning issues who have hopes and dreams.

ACKNOWLEDGMENTS

To the families of Marybeth Kravets and Imy F. Wax for their patience and support in this endeavor: Alan, Wendy, Steve, Allison, Connor, Isabel, Mark, Sara, David, Robert, Bennett, Cathy (in loving memory), Dan, Andrea, Benjamin, Matthew, Howard, Lisa, Bill, Niaya, Ellis, Gary, Tamar, Jordan, Debrah, Greg, Jamie and Joey

To all of the colleges who provide services and programs to promote the educational endeavors and dreams of students with learning disabilities or attention deficit disorder. To all of the contributors in the K&W Guide who share their thoughts and experiences with learning disabilities and attention deficit/hyperactivity disorder.

To Stephanie Gordon, transition counselor and Learning disability specialist, Deerfield High School, Deerfield, Illinois, for her professional assistance. To Karen Rodgers Photography for the authors' pictures on the back cover of the book. karenrodgersphot@sbcglobal.net

CONTENTS

FOREWORD

Dr. Richard D. Lavoie

"You will do OK for yourself....but not BY yourself"

In the classic 1960's film The Graduate, one scene is among the most memorable in movie history. Dustin Hoffman plays a young man at his college graduation party. An inebriated guest approaches him and pulls him into a corner. The guest says that he is going to give him a word that is the key to his future.

He leans into Dustin and whispers emphatically into his ear, "PLASTICS!"

I had such a "plastic moment" as an undergraduate student in a Classroom Management course over thirty-five years ago. The professor said, "If you want a well-managed and well-behaved classroom, remember this one all important word: TRANSITIONS!

Very sage advice. Research supports the premise that the overwhelming number of classroom "crises" occur during times of transition.   Students with learning disorders have significant difficulty dealing with changes, modifications, or interruptions to routines and adjustments. In short, "transitions".

As any experienced teacher or parent will attest, children with special needs find transitions to be anxiety producing and confusing. Even small transitions (moving from one class to another, unexpected visitors at home, eating in restaurants, etc.) can cause great angst and puzzlement for these students. If these minor adjustments are troubling for them...imagine how difficult it must be to make the major transition from the relative cocoon of high school to the world of work or the college campus.

Enter Imy Wax and Marybeth Kravets. In the 11th edition of their invaluable K&W Guide to Colleges for Students with LD/ADHD they provide updated information and data to assist families with this challenging transition. The Guide has become an invaluable road map and compass for parents, professionals and students as they search for appropriate post secondary placements. The authors' knowledge and extensive first hand experience with "the search" makes them informed and sensitive guides on this journey.....a voyage that requires a supportive responsive team.

When I was a young camp counselor many years ago, I worked with a wonderful adolescent named Jimmy. He would be identified in today's special education parlance as "multiply handicapped" or "comorbid". That is, he was fighting the battle on several fronts. He had significant physical disabilities, cognitive problems and perceptual limitations. He used a specialized wheelchair and his speech was garbled and nearly unintelligible. Despite his difficulties, he had a great and dynamic spirit and humbled – and inspired – us all with his joy and nonstop celebration of life.

On the back of his wheelchair, he had affixed a 10 X 12 brightly colored poster with a quote from a classic rock anthem:

"I GET BY WITH A LITTLE HELP FROM MY FRIENDS"

Very wise, Jimmy. This wonderful kid recognized that his day-to-day successes and victories required a cadre of supporters ......a circle of friends who understood and cared for Jimmy's needs. He knew that he would "make it". But he also recognized that he could not do it alone. A blazing insight.

When a student moves from high school to postsecondary programs, it is important to remember Jimmy's counsel. One of the most important steps in the Transition Process is the development of an effective, efficient and responsive Support System.   Quite simply, the success of the Transition is greatly dependent on the establishment of this Support System. In fact, I am hard pressed to recall a single successful transitioning student who did not have a functioning "team" behind him.

Throughout my career I have counseled and advised young people who are setting out for a major life transition. Below are some of the suggestions that I make to students in anticipation of these transitions.

Consider. As adults, we all have (and need!) a functioning Support System. My personal/professional Support System sits next to me on my desk as I write this. It consists of a battered and worn Business Card file that I have had for over thirty years. I studiously update the file by adding new cards and making necessary changes in the contact information on the individual cards. This file represents my Support System...the individuals who provide me with the support that I need "to get by".

Let's look at a couple of the dozens of cards that I have placed in the file.

One card is my longtime colleague, Psychologist,, Dr. Robert Brooks. Bob's area of expertise is anxiety and resilience and he is widely published in both areas. Bob is also a cherished and loyal friend and his card contains his business and home contact information.

Another equally important card is for "Wally". I do not know Wally's last name or where he lives. But he is the only mechanic within fifty miles of my home who truly understand the care-and-feeding of my 1972 air-cooled Volkswagen Kharmann Ghia. He is a magician and has been invaluable to me for twenty summers and I endeavor to keep my Ghia in working order.

Both of these men are part of my support system. Bob plays a role in my personal and professional support systems. Wally's role is related only to his profession, but my daily existence would be somewhat diminished if either of these people were to leave my "team". Each plays a uniquely important role in my life.

Let us refer to Bob and Wally as we explore the importance of your Support System.

It is relatively simple to establish a Support System. You merely make a list of the people upon whom you depend. However, the real challenge is maintaining that support system. How do you keep it functioning and effective?

In order to maintain the "Team", you must be diligent in four specific areas:

• Selection
• Reciprocation
• Maintenance
• Responsiveness

SELECTION

As a transitioning student, you must become aware of the different roles that individuals play in your system. Each has a specific function or purpose.

For example, if I were unable to start my car, I would contact Wally. It would be inappropriate and ineffective to call Dr. Bob with that problem. Conversely, if I were consulting with a client with significant anxiety problems that I did not understand, a call to Wally would be fruitless. Rather, I would reach out to Bob for his advice and counsel.

As a transitioning student, it is crucial that you understand this concept. For years, your parents have been the core of your Support System...and they will continue to play a very important role on your Team. But if you are having difficulty with your dormitory roommate, there is little that Mom can do when she is 200 miles from campus. It would be more appropriate to access your school-based support system by discussing the issue with friends or with dormitory personnel.

It is critical that you come to recognize the roles and functions of the individuals on our team and that you bring issues or problems to the appropriate members of your "safety net". If you continually access the "wrong" person by asking for advice or assistance that is beyond their scope, those members will become increasingly reluctant to assist you.

If I called Dr. Bob every time my Volkswagen sputtered, he would soon begin to separate himself from me...and with good reason!

When you are faced with a problem or concern, carefully examine your Support System and select the person who would be the most appropriate to ask for counsel, advice or assistance.

It is important to remember the nature of the relationships that you have with your Team members. For example, I said that Bob plays a dual role in my system. He is a colleague and a friend. Wally, however, plays a singular role. I am fond of him.... but he is not my friend. He is an acquaintance.

Therefore, when my brother was having serious health problems, I sought comfort and solace from Bob. I did not mention my brother's illness to Wally...and it would have been inappropriate to do so.

At times, students with learning problems do not understand these boundaries and they discuss intimate or personal matter and with people whose "role" is not befitting such personal communication. Wally would find it odd and off-putting if I brought my personal problems to him while he was changing my oil!

RECIPROCATION

When I was Director of a Residential School in Massachusetts, we received a phone call from the parents of a student from Texas. Sadly, the boy's grandfather had passed away, and we were asked to get him to the airport to fly home to Houston for the funeral services.

The boy was fourteen and was truly a wonderful kid. But he was somewhat immature and self-involved and a bit dramatic in his demeanor.

"Michael" was taken from class, informed of the death and taken to his room to pack for the trip home. He was then brought to the lobby outside of my office to wait for his ride to the airport.

Mike sat in the lobby wailing and sobbing loudly.   The secretaries were making him tea and attempting to comfort him, but he was inconsolable.

I thought that I would take a chance. I called him into my office.

"Mike", I began. "It is very sad about our grandfather. I met him when he visited campus last year and I liked him very much. I am sorry for your loss and I know that you must be very sad today."

"But, Michael, this weekend is not about you. It's really about your grandmother who has lost her husband...and your Dad who lost his father. Your family has always been wonderfully supportive of you...and now comes your opportunity to return that support.

Your Mom and Dad want you home because they need you now. They need your support, your comfort...and your love. You're a young man now. You are part of their support system. It's not about you, Mike."

Michael looked at me with a combination of shock and bewilderment. He had never considered that HE should (or could!) play a supportive role for another person. He had been making "withdrawals" from his Support System for years. Now it was time to make some "deposits".

Our little talk must have worked. His Dad called me after Mike returned to campus and raved about how mature, helpful and sensitive Michael was during that weekend. He never left his grandmother's side during the services and was seen fetching coffee for the older relatives during the gathering that evening. Nice.

If you are going to maintain your Support System, it is crucial that you reciprocate. Dir. Bob always takes my calls when I contact him or makes certain that he returns my calls as soon as possible.... and he knows that I am equally responsive to him. But, suppose I stopped taking his calls and failed to respond when he contacted me for advice or assistance? Eventually, he would become less responsive to my contacts because of my failure to reciprocate.

"Support" is a two-way street. You must give and take in order to keep your Team functioning.

MAINTENANCE

It is inappropriate or ineffective to contact Team members only when they are needed. It is important to nurture the relationships by "feeding" them once in awhile.

For example, whenever I run across a piece of interesting research on anxiety, I forward it to Bob...and he does the same with me. Bob and I are rabid Boston Red Sox fans, and we often email one another after a crucial or particularly noteworthy game. I saw a classic 1950's Volkswagen in California recently, and I sent a photo to Wally. These small acts of kindness and consideration are very effective in keeping the relationship solid and lasting.

RESPONSIVENESS

Once during a question/answer session at a speaking engagement, a father challenged me on a comment that I had made during the seminar.

"You said that we should say, 'Thank you' to our kids for doing their chores and being cooperative and helpful around the house, " he said. "I don't agree. If you thank them for doing routine things that they should be doing anyway, they will expect you to thank them all the time."

I was hard-pressed to give him a response. I could not understand why anyone would object to that suggestion. I think that living in a home where people expressed their gratitude and appreciation in courteous ways would be pretty enjoyable, wouldn't you?

Responsiveness means never taking a relationship for granted. My wife and I have been married for forty years. I still open the car door for her...and she thanks me every time. Relationships begin to unravel and fray when responsiveness wanes.

Be mindful of this and be careful to reinforce the acts of your Team by showing genuine gratitude and appreciation for their efforts on your behalf.

In closing, it is so important to develop and nurture your own personal "safety net" as you undertake this major – and very exciting – transition in your life. Don't hesitate to ask for support when you need it.... and provide support when it is needed, as well.

And - speaking of support - you, your parents and your counselors will be able to use this book as a source of support as well. The information in these pages will assist you in making informed choices as you search for a school or a program for your postsecondary experience.

There are no "bad" schools profiled in this book. You see, there are no "good" or "bad" schools....there are just some schools that "fit". A school that is "just right" for you might be inappropriate for one of your classmates. For example, suppose I am shopping for shoes and find a great pair of fine imported shoes.....well-made, size 9, fashionable and "on sale". Well, they ARE fine shoes and at a great price....but I have a size 10 foot !! They just won't fit.

Good luck on your journey...and the K&W Guide will help you find the school that fits !!

Richard D Lavoie, M.A., M.Ed., EdD. (Hon)

Author, *It's So Much Work to Be Your Friend: Helping the Child with Learning Disabilities Find Social Success*

Executive Producer, The F.A.T. City Workshop

It is a great honor to have Rick Lavoie write the Introduction to the K & W Guide.

THOUGHTS FROM . . .

THOUGHTS FROM . . .

MICHAEL BARRON, ASSISTANT PROVOST FOR ENROLLMENT MANAGEMENT AND EXECUTIVE DIRECTOR OF ADMISSIONS, UNIVERSITY OF IOWA

Over four decades ago when I first became an admission officer, my mentors and colleagues suggested that I would encounter applicants who had not performed very well in high school. I was told to expect that some of those students would "claim" to have a reading problem and others would actually use the term dyslexia. It seems that many of my admission colleagues were somewhat dubious about the true extent of such a disability. I sadly shake my head now when I look back on those times when many of us simply discounted such students as just being lazy, dumb, or under-prepared.

We are blessed today with greater knowledge about such matters, and more importantly, with compassionate understanding of those individuals who cope with one or more of the growing list of what we now call learning disabilities. Often these students exhibit strong to superior intellectual capacity, but lack the ability to mark the appropriate bubble or write an answer on paper in the prescribed time period. They are a resource that should not be overlooked or swept aside by our application of some of the more odious and inappropriate labels used in the past.

Educational institutions must take risks along with these students in order to help them develop their potential. We have learned that there are many disorders that impact an individual's ability to learn, but do not impair their intellectual capacity. I am pleased to say that now there are many more of my colleagues who understand these needs and, working carefully with disabilities specialists and faculty, are developing ways to provide these students with the opportunity for higher education.

At Iowa, staff in the Office of Admissions has taken the time to study and understand these conditions and carefully provide a holistic review of all factors in a student's background when considering their application for admission. When appropriate, we consult with professionals such as those who work in our Student Disability Services office to ensure that we have a clear understanding of the current thinking and research regarding the ability of students with learning disabilities to accommodate their disability and pursue their education.

When students with learning disabilities apply for admission and self-identify, we look closely for those who have used the resources available to them to their fullest potential.

A diverse student body with a variety of talents, interests, and backgrounds is necessary in a university. Iowa welcomes applications from students with documented learning disabilities and/or attention deficit disorders. . We keep in mind that we are looking for students with the ability to do college work that is reflected in the strength of the courses they have taken, as well as the compensatory strategies that they have employed during their high school years.

Some students fulfill all of our regular admission requirements despite documented learning disabilities. This does not mean that they no longer need compensatory strategies or a special office to assist them in advising faculty of their special needs. They do. We have also had excellent success at Iowa with students with learning disabilities who do not meet our regular admission requirements, and data suggest that with proper attention, as many as eight out of ten such students succeed at the university. Faculty members are recruited to be partners in this process.

We recognize that the decision for students to self-identify as learning disabled is a personal choice. A student's decision not to self-identify is respected. However, it has been our experience that students with learning disabilities who acknowledge the existence of a disability and seek assistance early are more likely to achieve academic success than those who wait for problems to develop. It was not too long ago that such students probably would never graduate from high school. Even if they did, they could not look forward to a future with very many options for employment.

Thankfully, we are making breakthroughs for many of these students, and are now providing them with access to and opportunities for higher education. While there are intervention and support programs like Iowa's that are beginning to achieve success, we have by no means provided a paradigm that is consistently accepted and used throughout the country. That will only come through public discussion of the successes and failures of those of us who have met the challenge and taken the risk. This book, The K&W Guide to Colleges for Students with Learning Disabilities or Attention Deficit Disorders, is certainly one of the resources I hope will be widely used in that effort.

While we are working to educate our colleagues, to modify our systems to accommodate these students, and to provide them with the opportunity to obtain the education that they desire, we also must begin to work as partners with industry. It will not be enough to provide an environment where an individual can complete a university degree and yet fail miserably in the world of work because of its lack of understanding and inappropriate job placement procedures. Our experience at Iowa is that these students desperately want to succeed, and they want to stand on the merits of their own achievements. To deny them the opportunity to be an asset at the highest level of their ability is to squander a valuable human resource, creating an unnecessary and unwanted liability for society. I urge students with learning disabilities and their families to use available law to firmly request the services they need and to be patient with those of us in the education establishment as we seek to understand. I also encourage educators at all levels to be sensitive to and aware of these individuals as a resource not to be wasted, and to work diligently to provide educational opportunity to all..

THOUGHTS FROM . . .
DR. MARSHA GLINES, DEAN OF THE INSTITUTE FOR ACHIEVEMENT AND LEARNING, LYNN UNIVERSITY

With every new edition of this guide, with changes in the Americans with Disabilities Act (now amended), and with court or judicial decisions regarding who qualifies for accommodations in higher education and how those accommodations are determined new information emerges. Declining budget dollars, reductions in support staff and ongoing changes in university and college academic programs in terms of majors and specific needs require that we must keep current if we hope to help our children make an appropriate and successful transition from high school to post-secondary institutions. This is a mighty challenge. Vitally important is learning what universities are offering in terms of services and who is providing these services. The K and W Guide is an exemplary first step in discovering the answers to these questions.

Without a doubt, visiting campuses can be a determining factor in choosing a college. Sitting in the cafeteria and watching the interaction among students (and faculty and staff) is critical. Also the location and size of a campus, public versus private, and the areas of academic expertise offered by colleges need to be considered. Be sure to review the literature about campus life, residence living and the study abroad options. Properly reviewing all these considerations are equally challenging.

Countless students have struggled with learning challenges and/or ADHD executive functioning problems throughout their K-12 years; and many of those students may not yet have been recognized for their strengths, passions, affinities or POTENTIAL. However, there is good news. The choices in post-secondary programs are tremendous. Think about all the institutions represented in this publication. Those of us who began working in this field 40 years ago remember how limited the choices of where children could attend college were. More importantly, many universities are becoming more accepting and understanding of students who, at 18, have not yet come into their own.

This is a time of more creative thinking in terms of teaching pedagogy. We, in higher education, should constantly be asking, "How do we connect with approximately 80% of the already academically disengaged high school seniors?" Many universities are beginning to offer their instructors professional development in neurology and learning. We have begun, as professionals in higher education, to realize the need for coaches-not only life coaches but also professionals certified in ADHD coaching.

The world of knowledge regarding learning continues to explode. As educators and parents we are continually offered new research to help us understand the importance of working memory, retrieval of information, meaningfulness of information in terms of memory storage, coherency and learning for understanding (to borrow a term from David Perkins, Harvard Graduate School of Education) and to understand our children's learning. We know how important it is for students to make connections to facts and new information in order to "understand" rather than to simply "know" something. Universities and colleges are challenging themselves with revisiting traditional teaching strategies and expanding into creative, timely pedagogy.

While we live in a technology-based world, even Apple says technology isn't the answer to learning, it is to ENHANCE learning and some universities are adapting Apple's challenge based learning model and the academic supportive iTunes U.

No two students are wired the same. Our brains function in wildly unique and wondrous ways. We are in a time of neurological research acknowledgement. Why should we care or pay attention to new studies about learning? What have we learned?

1. Every prospective college student possesses some potential although that potential may not have been previously acknowledged. If a student has not been proficient in the areas of verbal linguistic and logical mathematical skills, that student has already been in a disadvantaged learning environment. Students need to understand their "cognitive clusters" of strengths prior to matriculation to college.

2. The more students understand their learning profile, the more they can develop strategies for learning. (Levine)

3. Failure of a student in college, not due to an inability intellectually or academically, may be due to a lack of understanding the meaningfulness of a course(s) to the student, negative self-messages from previous unsuccessful school experiences, feelings of hopelessness, fear of failure, underdeveloped problem solving skills, lack of understanding of learning challenges, and/or the inability to seek resources or self-advocate appropriately. Parents can be most helpful in preparing their children for the college experience by helping them learn to articulate their challenges and needs and by encouraging students as they matriculate to new college campuses to utilize all support services made available to them.

4. Working memory, attention and executive functioning challenges pose difficulties for many students and may be diagnosed as a "reading disorder". In fact there are strategies that have been discovered that address working memory, coherence, and attention that can lead to increased comprehension ability.

5. Making the transition from high school to a college campus means not only adapting to a new environment BUT ALSO learning a new culture and developing a new sense of self within this environment.

It is amazing to see a student discover that learning can provide the most exciting moments—the "ah ha" moments. These are powerful and have the capability of changing children and young adults forever. Search for a higher education institution that will provide opportunities for learning for understanding, institutions that will support and encourage your learner, and those that will help your child identify and connect to a passion or interest leading to a major and ultimately satisfying life work.

The message to parents and what is required of parents is this:

1. It is imperative that you teach your children to articulate for themselves what their learning disabilities or disorders are and what and how they are to request (not demand) accommodations from higher education institutions.

2. Students also need to know how to illustrate the history of accommodations that have been granted prior to matriculation onto a college campus.

3. Finally, my advice to parents is that you prepare your children for the college experience by FOSTERING INDEPENDENCE THROUGH SELF UNDERSTANDING AND FACILITATING---not doing or enabling. Students who have not experienced this sense of independence, that feeling they can be successful without a parent advocating, struggle in college on their own. As you assist in the search for the right match for our future college students, help them identify their passions---something that "makes their heart sing." Encourage them to pursue their interests and passions as long as it brings them pleasure and a sense of challenge. It is NEVER too early to guide them to identify their metacognitive skills and study strengths as they develop their sense of self.

THOUGHTS FROM . . .
DR. LILLIAN A. O'CONNELL, DIRECTOR OF STUDENT ACCESSIBILITY AND DISABILITY SERVICES, EDGEWOOD COLLEGE
A PROGRAMS FOR STUDENTS WITH INTELLECTUAL AND DEVELOPMENTAL DISABILITIES

In the ever changing landscape of post-secondary education (PSE) one of the newer developments is the emergence of programs for students with significant intellectual and developmental disabilities (ID/DD), that is students who in the past would not have been included in the traditional PSE environment of college. PSE institutions are responding to an emerging need for such programs that stems from a number of factors: an increasing number of students with significant disabilities who receive special education services in K-12, very limited success in terms of independent living and employment for students with ID/DD after leaving Public Education (usually at age 21), and increased understanding of what is possible for people with ID after leaving secondary school.

Further, the view of PSE is expanding from simply that of attaining a degree to one that emphasizes the transformational experience that college is for those who attend. College is a place where students become adults, developing values and skills (academic and non- academic) that help to make them more productive and independent members of society. Such skills are essential regardless of whether or not a student attains a college degree. Increasing numbers of PSE institutions are recognizing the value of providing educational opportunities to all students and are developing a more inclusive attitude and creating programs designed to provide educational and vocational experiences to other groups not traditionally seen on college campuses. One of those groups is students with ID/DD.

Another factor that may be helping to drive this change is the natural progression for a generation of students with ID/DD who have been integrated and educated with their non-disabled peers in mainstream elementary and high schools. It should come as no surprise that these students and their parents would like to see similar opportunities to develop intellectually and socially continue beyond high school. Like any parents, parents of students with ID/DD want their children to grow and develop, and to live as productive and independent lives as possible. College attendance is correlated with better employment outcomes for those who attend. Students with ID/DD historically have had

poor employment outcomes and limited independent living success and options. In this emerging area, there is little empirical data regarding the outcomes for students with ID/DD enrolled in these programs. However, there have been some very promising preliminary findings from ongoing research indicating that students who have participated in such programs have improved outcomes in terms of employment and educational attainment.

Although relatively small in numbers, there are many more programs available now that there have been in even recent years. However, there are differences among the programs, and parents and students should search carefully among the options in order to find the best fit for individual students. In general, these programs have a separate admissions process from the general admissions process for the institution in which they are housed. The process can vary amongst programs and are often highly individualized. Typically, these programs offer a mix of academic and life skills classes and programming. Many of the programs offer housing, though the housing options can vary. At some of the schools, students are housed separately from the general population, while others offer a more inclusive model wherein students are housed in the residence halls with general admissions students. Parents and students should also investigate the level and types of support that are available to students in the program. In most cases, students with ID/DD will need a great deal of support in order to be successful on a college campus. Things to look for can include the amount and types of individual academic support offered. Some programs offer individual support in the classroom, which can be very important for some students. Another consideration is the areas of study that are available to students. Since these programs are often highly individualized, there is sometimes the flexibility to design a program around the specific interests of students. Further, parents and students should inquire about career and vocational components to the programs. Financial aid is also an important consideration. Factors such as age and status within the public school system will determine sources for financial support. Likewise, funding eligibility may also vary with the type of program.

As with any other college search, students and their parents should visit the campuses and meet with the staff of the individual programs to determine that best option. The biggest consideration is often location, as for most ID/DD students, parents remain an important source of support. Some programs may expect some involvement from parents. And, being able to get to campus with relative ease and speed may be beneficial if the student experiences any difficulties. Visits to campus should be scheduled for times when students are on campus, rather than during breaks, in order to get a feel for the campus culture. Meeting should also include meetings with program staff and faculty, as well as with students enrolled the program. Typically, these programs offer a combination of academic and life skills classes.

A very good place to start is at: www.thinkcollege.net , which is the website of Think College, an initiative of the Institute for Community Inclusion at the University of Massachusetts Boston. This website, as well as the initiative's publications offers a wealth of information for parents and students looking for PSE options for students with ID/DD. Visitors to the site can search for and compare programs. As of January 2012, the site listed 168 programs, located in 38 U.S. state and 2 Canadian Provinces. Their book Think College – Postsecondary Education Options for Students with Intellectual Disabilities, by Meg Grigal and Debra Hart provides much useful information and many

tools, such as assessments and checklists to help families find the best program for individual students. As with students, these programs vary quite a bit, and matching individual student needs with what specific programs have to offer can only aid in a good transition and successful participation in collegiate life for students with ID/DD.

THOUGHTS FROM . . .
MATTHEW COHEN, ESQ., ATTORNEY, CHICAGO ILLINOIS
OBTAINING ACCOMMODATIONS FOR COLLEGE STUDENTS WITH DISABILITIES

Many children with disabilities have the potential to be highly successful in post-secondary school and beyond, particularly if provided the appropriate accommodations that they need to function within the school environment. Whether trade school, junior college, Liberal Arts College or major university, educational institutions are required to provide reasonable accommodations to students that are able to document the presence of a disability and the need for accommodation. However, the procedures for obtaining accommodations are very different in relation to getting into and participating in higher education than they are in elementary and high school. In the public school system, the responsibility lies with the school district to identify children suspected of having disabilities, to evaluate them (with parent consent), and to develop and implement individualized educational programs (IEPs) or Section 504 plans designed to meet their unique needs. Unfortunately, the law governing special education, the Individuals with Disabilities Education Act (IDEA) does not apply to higher education.

Further, while Section 504 applies to many colleges and universities, the rules for how it applies are different than within public elementary and high schools. Eligibility under the IDEA or Section 504 in public school does NOT automatically ensure that a student will be eligible for accommodations in college or, if eligible, will automatically qualify for the same services or accommodations. In order to maximize the likelihood that the student will receive appropriate accommodations in college, planning by the parents, the student, and the school district must begin well before the child applies for college. Some of these steps will be briefly highlighted below.

The Right to Accommodations

Two different federal laws govern the right to accommodations in relation to higher education. The first is the Americans with Disabilities Act of 1990 (the ADA), which has two different sections that are relevant to higher education. Title II of the ADA regulates local and state governmental entities, which includes community colleges, state colleges and universities. Title III of the ADA regulates what are called places of public accommodation. All private colleges and universities are places of public accommodation. However, those colleges that are religiously controlled are exempt from the coverage of the ADA.

In addition to regulating the provision of "reasonable accommodations" within colleges and universities, the ADA also provides the right to reasonable accommodations from agencies that administer the tests that are used for college and graduate admissions and for licensing upon graduation. Thus, the ACT, SAT, MCAT, LSAT and the like are all operated by organizations that are required to comply with the requirements of the ADA.

The second law, which governs the right to reasonable accommodations in higher education, is Section 504 of the Rehabilitation Act of 1973. Section 504 provides very similar protections as the ADA, but has two significant differences. In order for Section 504 to be applicable, the organization must be a recipient of federal financial assistance. As there is no exception under Section 504 for colleges that are religiously controlled, those religiously controlled colleges that do accept federal funds must adhere to the Section 504 disability regulations even though the ADA does not apply. While most colleges and universities do receive federal financial assistance, and are therefore governed by Section 504, not all do. Thus, the non-discrimination laws apply to all colleges and universities except those that are religiously controlled and do not take federal financial assistance.

What Needs to Happen during High School?

First, all students in special education should have a transition plan in place starting at the age of 16 (or earlier, based on state law or individual need). This plan should include the student's input about their long-term goals; assessment of the student's continuing needs, and the development and implementation of a plan to facilitate the student's accomplishment of realistic post-secondary goals. Notably, the first step in the transition planning process is to conduct a transition assessment, including age appropriate assessment of the student's functioning and needs in relation to training, education, employment and independent living skills. 34 CFR 300.320(b). This plan must include the course of study necessary to reach the student's measurable post-secondary goals. This plan, when done right, can often provide important support for the student to prepare them for college, before they even get there. Notably, the transition plan can address not only academic and vocational goals, but also life skills, organizational or executive functioning needs, social deficits and a variety of other issues that may impact a student's ability to function successfully in college even if they meet the college's admissions criteria.

Second, the student needs to identify what colleges may be appropriate, given the student's disability (ies). The K&W Guide and consultation with college counselors can be invaluable in helping to determine whether particular colleges or even types of colleges are realistic for the student, with or without the provision of accommodations. If the student is going to take the SAT and/or ACT, the school and the family must take the necessary steps to secure accommodations on those tests as well.

For those students who do badly on such tests, it is worth investigating schools that place less emphasis on those tests or don't require them at all, a trend that has been gathering momentum recently.(www.fairtest.org)

Third, before a student receiving special education graduates, the school district is now required to complete a document called a Summary of Performance.   According to the IDEA, when a student's special education eligibility is terminated due to graduation or aging out of school, the school must provide a summary of the child's "academic achievement, functional performance and recommendations on how to assist the child in meeting their post-secondary goals." 34 CFR 300.305. (e)(3).   This document can be of enormous value both in documenting the nature of the child's disability and in providing support for the provision of particular accommodations. As the Summary of Performance statement is a relatively new requirement of the special education system and not all schools are fully familiar with it, parents should be sure that this is provided before the student graduates.

Who is Entitled to Accommodations Under the Disability Rights Laws?

Under both the ADA and Section 504, a person is entitled to reasonable accommodations if they meet a number of criteria. First, the person must have a physical or mental impairment that substantially limits a major life activity. There are a variety of different major life activities, but some of the most important, for purposes of accommodations in college, are learning, reading, concentrating, thinking and communicating. Second, the person must meet the general qualifications for participation in the program or activity that they are applying for, either with or without accommodations. Third, they must establish that they: a) have a physical or mental impairment, b)need specific accommodations and c) that these accommodations are "reasonable."

It is important to note that the burden is on the student to identify themselves as having a disability, provide documentation supporting this, and request accommodations. Unlike in elementary and high school, the burden is on the student to tell the college they have a disability and seek accommodations, not on the college to figure it out for themselves. The student is not obligated to disclose the disability, either in the application process or after admission, but they are not entitled to accommodations unless they make the disclosure and document the need for assistance.   This is generally done by communication with the college or university's Disability Services Office.

Thankfully, these court decisions were reversed by the Americans with Disabilities Act Amendments of 2008, which substantially expanded the grounds for a person to be determined to have a disability and eligible for accommodations, by overturning a number of court cases that had dramatically restricted the eligibility criteria.

With regard to the eligibility criteria, the 2008 amendments provided as follows:

The ADA Amendments define a person as being person with a disability if they have:

(A)   a physical or mental impairment that substantially limits one or more major life activities of such individual;

(B)   a record of such an impairment, or

(C)   being regarded as having such impairment as described in paragraph (3).

The Amendments defined "Major life activities" as including but not being limited to, caring for oneself, performing manual tasks, seeing, bending, speaking, breathing, learning, reading, concentrating, thinking, communicating and working.

They also defined A major life activity to include the operation of a major bodily function, including but not limited to, functions of the immune system, normal cell growth, digestive, bowel, bladder, neurological, brain, respiratory, circulatory, endocrine and reproductive functions.....

An impairment that substantially limits one major life activity need not limit other major life activities in order to be considered a disability.

Further, an impairment that is episodic or in remission is a disability if it would substantially limit a major life activity when active.

One of the most important changes made by the 1998 amendments was the elimination of the use of mitigating measures as a basis for concluding that a person did not have a protected disability. This means that individuals that rely on special equipment, supports or accommodations that allow them to function at a level that is not regarded as impaired are still eligible as people with disabilities despite the use of these mitigating measures. Examples of mitigating measures provided in the law include:

(I)   medication, medical supplies, equipment, or appliances, low-vision devices (which do not include ordinary eyeglasses or contact lenses), prosthetics including limbs and devices, hearing aids and cochlear implants or other implantable hearing devices, mobility devices, or oxygen therapy equipment and supplies;

(II)   use of assistive technology;

(III)   reasonable accommodations or auxiliary aids or services; or

(IV)   learned behavioral or adaptive neurological modifications.

These new standards reinstate the original and far broader reach of the ADA (and by parallel interpretation, Section 504). However, these criteria are very different than those used under the IDEA for children in special education Again, however, unlike the public schools, where the responsibility lies with the school to identify, evaluate and plan a program for children suspected of having a disability, the ADA and Section 504 give the responsibility for establishing the presence of a disability to the student seeking the accommodation. In other words, if the student wants reasonable accommodations, they must come forward, identify that they have a disability, document the disability and the need for accommodation and specifically request the provision of such accommodations. In fact, under these laws, the colleges may not ask questions about disability in the application/admissions process and the student need not disclose the existence of a disability at that stage.

Students seeking information about how a particular college will respond to the student's disability and whether it will have appropriate services to meet the student's needs can and should contact the school's Office of Disability Services (different colleges use different names). The Disability Services staff will be able to share information about the types of services that are provided, the types of students that are effectively served by the college or university, and help the student to determine when and what information to share (pre or post-application) in securing accommodations.

Although this is less often an issue, it should also be pointed out that under both laws, students are protected from discrimination if they have a history of disability or are perceived to have a disability. Thus, a school could not discriminate against an individual who is HIV Positive but has no symptoms, simply because of their HIV-Positive status. This would be discrimination based on the student being regarded as having a disability, even though they were not at that time actually disabled.

The Need for Documentation

Because the burden rests with the student to document that they actually have a disability, it is important that the student carefully document the existence of the impairment. This requires several different kinds of documentation. First, the colleges and universities are interested in the student's history in relation to their disability. Clinical reports which provide the diagnosis and which track the progression of the disorder are useful in establishing that the disability has been present on a long-standing basis. Second, schools are interested in current evaluations, typically at least within the past three years if not more current. Often, evaluations can be obtained from the school districts during this period, which may provide the necessary information. However, under some circumstances, the student may need to obtain outside clinical evaluations. This may be necessary for several reasons. First, if the student does not have a current school district evaluation, the outside evaluation may be the only option for obtaining current diagnostic material. Second, and particularly for students who are high functioning or even gifted, or who have more subtle disabilities, more sophisticated private testing may provide data that offers support for the presence of a disability that is not present in the public school's testing.

In addition to clinical material, the colleges and universities are very interested in whether the student has been receiving special education and/or Section 504 services. Colleges tend to be more receptive to the provision of accommodations when the student has a history of having received special education or Section 504 accommodations for a long period of time. Colleges tend to be more skeptical of the student's entitlement to accommodations if the student went through most or all of school without assistance and only became eligible for services late in high school. Unfortunately, there is a sense that some students deliberately seek eligibility around the junior year of high school for the primary purpose of obtaining accommodations on the SAT and ACT and for purposes of accommodations in college. While this may sometimes happen, there are also many students whose disability does not become a major problem or become obvious until the rigors of high school expose the problems that the student had previously been able to cope with successfully. Nonetheless, providing documentation of a prior history of accommodations is very useful in establishing both general eligibility for accommodations and justifying the need for the particular accommodations being requested. The graduate exam administrators (for the MCAT, LSAT, etc.) also look closely at whether there is a history of accommodation in high school and college, so these processes have a domino effect as the student progresses through college.

While students with late – diagnosed disabilities are not excluded from being considered for accommodations, either for college board testing, or once admitted, there is no question that those students are viewed with greater scrutiny and may need even more documentation to establish that they have areal impairment and require accommodations. Notably, recent research has suggested that the criteria for diagnosing AD/HD may be modified to allow for diagnosis based on symptoms that manifest themselves in adolescence, rather than in childhood, because of growing information that suggests that not all students with AD/HD meet criteria in elementary school. This may make it easier for some late-diagnosed students to make the case for eligibility.

Obtaining Accommodations After Admission

As indicated, the college may not ask questions that directly or indirectly seek to identify whether a student has a disability during the application process. However, some students may choose to share information about their disability during the application process or even use the disability as material in application essays for sharing ways that they have coped with adversity or otherwise. Whether and what to share in the application process is a difficult decision, which typically should be made with the benefit of consultation from parents, college counselors and even the disabilities services staff at the college the student is interested in attending.

Once the student has been admitted, however, if the student wants accommodations, they must contact the Office of Disability Services, present their documentation of disability and formally request accommodations. A wide variety of accommodations are available, from preferential seating to extra time for assignments or tests, to use of a note-taker, to use of a tape recorder or word processor for completion of assignments. The nature of potential accommodations is extensive, in that there is no specified list. Instead, accommodations are developed to respond to the needs of the particular individual. On the other hand, just because a student seeks a particular accommodation, or even received that accommodation previously in public school, does not mean that the college or university is obligated to provide it.

In particular, unlike special education, the college or university is not obligated to provide individual tutoring or 1-1 aides. If they elect to do so, as some do, they may charge extra for those services. The colleges must make their own judgment as to whether a request for a particular accommodation is "unduly burdensome," rather than reasonable. That determination will be based on a variety of factors, including but not limited to the quality of the student's documentation supporting the need for the accommodation, whether the student has a history of receiving the accommodation, the size of the college and its ability to provide the accommodation, and whether the college feels the accommodation simply goes beyond what is reasonable for the student to be accommodated.

In addition, the college has the right to refuse requested accommodations if the college believes and can establish that the proposed accommodation will "fundamentally alter" the basic mission, organization or mode of operation of the school. This comes up most often in circumstances when the student is requesting a total waiver of a particular requirement for graduation, such as exemption from math or foreign language requirements. Under some circumstances, alternatives to these requirements can be agreed upon which will work for the student and satisfy the college, but this is not always the case.

What To Do if the Accommodation is Denied or is not Being provided?

Unlike public school, where the school district is charged with the responsibility for insuring compliance with the IEP or 504 plan, there is less direct responsibility for enforcement placed on the college or university. At the outset, colleges handle the process of alerting faculty of the accommodation plan in a variety of ways. In some, the Office of Disability Services takes initial responsibility for notifying the faculty, while in others the burden is put on the student to bring the accommodations plan to the attention of the faculty member. Once the plan has been presented, the staff person is supposed to carry the plan out, but implementation often varies with the personality, understanding, and sensitivity of the individual staff member. Where there is a problem with compliance, the student generally is well advised to follow a series of steps:

1) Try to work it out directly with the faculty member
2) Seek the help of the Office of Disability Services staff
3) Seek to work things out with higher ups in the particular department or Dean's Office
4) Determine what the school's internal grievance procedure is. Typically, colleges have two sets of grievance procedures, a general grievance procedure relating to any problem involving a student, and a specific grievances procedure for handling disability related complaints. In consultation with the Office of Disability Services staff, parents, and perhaps private counsel, the student may opt to use the disability grievance procedure, the general grievance procedure or both. In either event, the student should be aware that there are typically specific timelines and documentation requirements contained in the grievance procedures.
5) If these efforts are unsuccessful, or if the problem is sufficiently severe to warrant more serious action, the student may file complaints with the US Department of Education, Office for Civil Rights or the US Department of Justice, for violation of Section 504 or the ADA respectively.

Obviously, these are last resort measures and students are best off resolving matters informally and amicably within the school structure wherever possible.

When seeking to obtain reasonable accommodations, documentation is critical. As indicated above, the ADAA of 2008 provides more expansive standards for demonstrating that the individual has a disability that substantially limits major life functions. Even given this important expansion of the scope of these laws, parents and students should be thorough in gathering as much information about the student's difficulties, both historically and currently, as possible. School records, clinical data, anecdotal information and evidence of the actual impact of the impairment are all critical to receiving recognition as a person with a disability and obtaining the desired accommodations. If a student is late diagnosed, it is even more important to seek information showing the historical presence of the disability (unless it is based on a recent medical condition or accident). This can include information about extra tutorial or therapeutic help the student received outside of school, informal accommodations that were provided by the teachers, staff or parents, anecdotal or report card information documenting that the student was having difficulties early on, even though they were not identified as related to a disability, and statements by the student and parents describing the ways that the disability adversely affected the student's functioning, even if they were able to progress academically or were not formally diagnosed. Once the accommodations have been secured, the student must develop and judiciously implement self-advocacy skills to insure that the accommodations are provided as intended and as needed. When in doubt, students should seek assistance from their Office of Disability Services, or if necessary, from outside agencies such as OCR,(www.ed.gov./about/offices/list/ocr and www.hhs.gov.ocr) or from knowledgeable lawyers. Students and parents can obtain more information about disability rights in higher education and the process of securing accommodations at two excellent websites: www.heath.gwu.edu and www.ahead.org.

Matt Cohen has represented children and adults with disabilities in regard to public and higher education for approximately 30 years. He regularly writes on disability law topics and lectures regularly on these subjects throughout the United States. His law firm, based in Chicago, has represented children, college students and adults throughout the United States.

Matt Cohen, Esq.
Matthew Cohen & Associates, Chicago IL
312-961-4179

THOUGHTS FROM . . .
DR. MIRIAM PIKE, HEAD OF WOLCOTT SCHOOL FOR STUDENTS WITH SPECIAL NEEDS

As students with specific learning disabilities and ADHD transition from high school to college, accessing appropriate accommodations at the college level is a critical step in the process. Students should apply for accommodations once they have been admitted so they have sufficient time to submit the required documentation and to provide any additional information that may be needed. If students wait until they begin their first semester to apply, they may not have sufficient time to gain approval before they need to use their accommodations.

Students should also inquire about the procedures the college or university has in place for accessing accommodations once they are approved. In some schools students have to follow a series of specific steps each time they use their accommodations, while in other schools the process may be more streamlined. Being informed of the procedures may promote a smoother transition.

Since IEPs and 504 plans are considered temporary records they may only be available at the high school for five years following graduation. Many students find it beneficial to request a copy of their most recent plan and the most recent evaluation report prior to high school graduation. These documents can be stored in a secure location at home in case they are needed in the future. Students and families should be aware that once the student turns 18, they are the only ones who may request copies of their confidential school records.

Miriam Pike, Ph.D. Head of School, Wolcott School, Chicago, IL

GENERAL GUIDELINES FOR REQUESTING ACCOMMODATIONS DUE TO A LEARNING DISABILITY

Introduction

Students requesting accommodations are required to submit documentation to determine eligibility in accordance with Section 504 of the Rehabilitation Act of 1973 and the Americans with Disabilities Act (ADA). A diagnosis of a learning disability does not necessarily qualify a student for academic accommodations under the law. To establish that a student is covered under Section 504 and the ADA, the documentation must indicate that the disability substantially limits some major life activity, including learning. Individual colleges or universities will determine eligibility and appropriate services, case by case, based on the quality, current testing and completeness of the documentation submitted.

Requirements of the components of documentation

A Qualified Professional Must Conduct the Evaluation: The assessment must be administered by a trained and qualified (i.e., certified and/or licensed) professional.

Documentation Must be Current: Reasonable accommodations are based on the current impact of the disability on academic performance. A diagnostic evaluation should be age appropriate and relevant to the student's learning environment, and show the student's current level of functioning.

Documentation Must Include a Specific Diagnosis: The report must include a clear and direct statement that a learning disability does or does not exist and must rule out alternative explanations of learning problems. Terms such as "learning difficulty", "appears", "suggests", or "probable" do not support a conclusive diagnosis.

Documentation Must be Comprehensive: It must include a summary containing relevant historical information, instructional interventions, related services, and age of initial diagnosis. The documentation must also include objective data regarding aptitude, achievement and information processing. Test scores (standard scores, percentiles, and grade equivalents) must be included in the documentation. A description of the student's functional limitations as a result of the disability must be included.

Recommendations for Accommodations: A diagnostic report may include specific recommendations for accommodations. Prior history of an accommodation, without a demonstration of a current need, does not in and of itself warrant the provision of a like accommodation. Each accommodation recommended should include a rationale and the evaluation should support the recommendations with specific test results or clinical observations.

Examples of Typical Measures Used in Adult Assessment of Learning Disabilities (this is intended to serve only as a guide for clinicians)

Aptitude

a. Wechsler Adult Intelligence Scale-4th Edition (WAIS-IV) b. Stanford Binet Intelligence Scale-4th and 5th Edition (SB IV, V) c. Woodcock-Johnson Psycho educational Battery-3rd Edition: Tests of Cognitive Ability d. Kaufman Adolescent and Adult Intelligence Test

Achievement

a. Wechsler Individual Achievement Tests II (WIAT II) b. Wechsler Individual Achievement Test

(WIAT) c. Woodcock-Johnson Psycho educational Battery-3rd Edition: Tests of Achievement (WJ-III) d. Stanford Test of Academic Skills (TASK) e. Scholastic Abilities Test for Adults (SATA)

Assessments such as the **Wide Range Achievement Test (WRAT-III)** are not considered a comprehensive measure of achievement and must be accompanied by a comprehensive measure such as one of those listed above. All instruments selected to measure these areas must be age appropriate.

Information Processing

a. Subtests of the WAIS-R or WAIS-IV b. Subtests of the Woodcock-Johnson Psycho educational Battery: Tests of Cognitive Ability c. Wechsler Memory Scales IV-Revised or 3rd Edition.

GENERAL GUIDELINES FOR REQUESTING ACCOMMODATIONS DUE TO ATTENTION DEFICIT HYPERACTIVITY DISORDER

Students requesting accommodations or services because of AD/HD are required to submit documentation to determine eligibility in accordance with Section 504 of the Rehabilitation Act of 1973 and the Americans with Disabilities Act (ADA). A diagnosis of AD/HD does not necessarily qualify a student for academic accommodations under the law. To establish that a student is covered under Section 504 and the ADA, the documentation must indicate that the disability substantially limits some major life activity, including learning. For students previously diagnosed who have not continuously received medical and educational support, a comprehensive evaluation may be necessary to determine whether academic accommodations are appropriate

Requirements of the components of documentation

A Qualified Professional Must Conduct the Evaluation: The assessment must be administered by a trained and qualified (i.e., certified and/or licensed) professional, who has had direct experience with adolescents and adults with AD/HD.

Documentation Must Include a Specific Diagnosis: The report must include a specific diagnosis of AD/HD based on the DSM-V (2011) diagnostic criteria. It is recommended that the diagnostic criteria used to support the diagnosis be included. The diagnosis must avoid the use of terms such as "suggests," "is indicative of" or "attentional problems."

Documentation Must Include Evidence of Current Impairment Statement of Presenting Problem: A history of the individual's presenting attentional symptoms including evidence of ongoing hyperactive-impulsive or inattentive behaviors that significantly impair functioning in an academic setting. Diagnostic Interview Information from a structured interview may include: - Family history - Educational history - Developmental history - Medical history - Social history - Review of prior psycho-educational reports - Description of current functional limitations pertaining to an educational setting - Relevant history of therapeutic treatment

Documentation Must Be Current: Reasonable accommodations are based on the current impact of the disability on academic performance. In most cases, this means that a diagnostic evaluation should be age appropriate and relevant to the students learning environment, and show the students' current level of functioning.

Documentation Must Include Relevant Testing Information

Psycho-educational assessments help determine the current impact of the disorder on the individual's ability to function in an academic setting. The report must include objective data, which might include, but not be limited to psychological assessments, educational assessments, rating scales, memory function tests, attention or tracking tests, or continuous performance tests. The report should include a score report page(s) presenting the tests, sub tests, standard scores, and percentiles.

Current Plan for Treatment and Effects of Medication

Plans should summarize current treatment including the use of medications. The report should indicate whether or not the individual was evaluated while on medication, and whether the use of medications mitigates the impact of the disorder on the individual's ability to function in an academic setting.

Recommendations for Accommodations

A diagnostic report may include specific recommendations for accommodation(s). It is important to note that a prior history of an accommodation, without demonstrating a current need, may not warrant the provision of similar accommodation. Each accommodation recommended should include a rationale. The evaluation should also support the recommendations with specific test results or clinical observations. Each college will make the final determination of what accommodations are appropriate based on documentation provided.

THE JOURNEY

Edward M. Hallowell, M.D. and David Keevil, Psy.D., The Hallowell Center[1]:

Going to college is a rite of passage. The time for college finally arrives, and with considerable fanfare our children go: they go away from home, friends, and family, and go toward a "grown up" life of freedom and independence.

As this time arrives, parents and children often have powerful and competing urges on both sides: to hold on tight and never let go, or to sever all connections and begin anew. Of course many parents tend toward the former urge, while their adolescents yearn for the latter.

When you're a parent, so many instincts protest against letting go. The world is often a cruel and dangerous place, and you are all too aware of your child's newness – their youth and fragility. When you're young, it's blissful to dream of a new life that is entirely yours. And so much in our world supports that dream: songs, sitcoms, the exalted fables of popular culture.

If your child has ADHD or LD, you may feel even more acutely the urge to hold tight. Your child may be impulsive; he or she may seem emotionally unprepared for the challenges ahead, and may have only a vague understanding of the sometimes tedious and always disciplined work required at college. You may be particularly aware of all the effort "behind the scenes" that went into getting your child even this far – the homework assistance, the teachers meetings, the evaluations and treatments – the countless hours of "extra help" along the way.

Your child with ADHD or LD may yearn particularly for the independence of college life. He or she may be awfully tired of feeling dependent on all the help you and others have offered. College may feel like a chance to "throw off the yoke" and finally succeed on one's own, free of dependence.

This tension – between the urge to hold on and the urge to let go – is very real for all of us who are parents, and it is very real for our children. I suppose the good and bad news is that this tension is life-long: we never really outgrow these competing urges. They just take on different shapes and sizes as we all continue to grow and mature.

What I want to tell you here – something I'm sure you already understand – is that the way to resolve this conflict is not to choose one side or the other – not to hold on even tighter, or pull away so hard that you are impossible to hold – but to mix them together, to balance them. In order to do this,

---

1 The Hallowell Center, Sudbury, MA, is dedicated to promoting cognitive and emotional well being in children and adults. www.DrHallowell.com

you need to stay connected.

What do I mean by "stay connected"? I mean three things. First, hold on to what you have. Second, stay flexible. And third, grow new connections. Let me tell you a little more about each of these ideas.

Hold on to what you have.

Maybe it looks as if I'm saying that you shouldn't let go. Actually, some letting go will be essential, for both parent and child. Parents will probably unpack the car, move things into their child's room, get a last hug, and drive away. Students will spend their first night in a college dorm, go to their first campus party, register for classes, and set their own study schedule. But in the midst of all this necessary letting go, remember to hold on to what's important from the past as well.

What is important from the past? Every new college student will have his or her own list, but I hope most lists will include these headlines:

- Your parents love you, and will continue to love you no matter what;
- You have a home to return to, where you are welcome;
- You have friends who care about you;
- You have specific strengths and abilities you carry with you;
- You have learned many essential skills for coping with your ADHD or LD, and college is a tremendous opportunity to learn and use many more.

Here's an idea for parents: as your child with ADHD or LD prepares for college, devote some time to making a detailed, truthful, loving, and relentlessly supportive list of what your child will "carry" to college, and offer it to your child as a gift. And here's an idea for new college students with ADHD or LD: make your own list of what you will carry with you, as a personal, intimate reminder of what is strong and sustaining in your life.

Each list is a testament to the connections that will endure and sustain.

Stay Flexible

In nature, the best connections – the strongest and most sustaining – are flexible. Think of how a tree sways in the wind, allowing it to stay connected both to the ground and to the air, through its branches and leaves. Connections that are rigid tend to snap and crack apart under strain. Flexibility allows us to grow and flourish.

What does this mean for parents, and for their child with ADHD or LD? It means not to attach too rigidly to any one thing – to any one expectation, to any one vision of the future, to any one marker of "success." Think "trial and error"; think "a different drummer"; think "two steps forward, one and a half steps back."

One of the exciting and dismaying things about people with ADHD is that we do not always follow the pack. We may act impulsively, or "forget" to act at all. We may make associative connections between seven different ideas, but drop the one that's on next Monday's test. These and many other behaviors can lead to difficulty and risk. And they can lead to creativity and discovery.

Parents: if your child goes off to college and marches through in four years with a high grade point average, then good for your child! But this may well not happen. And if you tie your happiness to such expectations – if your expectations are too rigid – then you may well be disappointed, or unhappy, or angry, or dismissive. As a result, the connection between you and your child, and between your child and his or her positive self-understanding, may snap and crack apart. And that's not a good thing for anyone. Keep the connections flexible, pliant, and resilient. Cut each other slack, practice forgiveness, and keep your sense of humor.

And expect surprises. Life is always a dress rehearsal, and people flub their lines and miss their cues all the time. People with ADHD or LD may play a love scene when we expected tragedy, or start tap-dancing during the soliloquy. There's nothing to be gained by throwing them off the stage. Rather, find out how your script might be re-written, and how they can accustom themselves to the action around them. Stay flexible!

Grow New Connections

Many adolescents with ADHD or LD who head off to college have already received a great deal of help over the years. They may be sick of help! But if they avoid help at college they will be missing one of the most important lessons college has to teach: how to find and use help. Think of preparing for college as preparing to find and use help: from teachers, from tutors, from other students, from administrators, from friends and family.

Finding and using help is not the same thing as offering excuses, or getting others to do your work. It is the same thing as growing new connections. College is a community of learners. The vast majority of human beings learn best in community – we learn from others and with others. A student who has something to prove by "going it alone" is mistaking a lack of connections for maturity.

One of the wonderful things about this K & W Guide is that it helps students and their parents plan the best ways to find and use help. With this Guide you can map out new, essential connections: with colleges and universities who understand your needs; with appropriate support services on campus; with departments and faculty members who will understand, challenge and respect you. Use this guide to start planning now, and to further develop your ability to find and use help. Ask yourself: what kind of help might I need? How will I recognize when I need it? How will I go about finding it? How will I ask, and who will I ask? The answers you discover will change and grow as you change and grow. Remember, stay connected, and stay flexible!

In Closing

Bon voyage! You have an exciting trip ahead of you, climbing to the top of your own particular mountain. If you have ADHD or LD the path may be particularly challenging, and the air particularly thin at times. But you will get there. The people who love and respect you will not stand on the summit with you – that is yours alone. But I hope and trust they will help you along the paths you choose (and the paths that choose you), by remaining connected with you, assisting you in ways you find helpful, and sharing with you the wonder and excitement of your discoveries.

GETTING READY

The purpose of The K&W Guide is to help students with learning disabilities or attention deficit disorder acquire the basic knowledge necessary to begin the college exploration process and get ready to make appropriate college selections.

To get ready students need to:
- Understand their strengths and weaknesses.
- Be able to articulate the nature of their learning disabilities.
- Understand the compensatory skills developed to accommodate the learning differences.
- Describe the services they received in high school.
- Identify short-term and long-term goals.
- Select appropriate college choices to match individual needs.

GUIDELINES FOR THE SEARCH AND SELECTION PROCESS

Self-Assessment
- What is the student's disability?
- When was the disability diagnosed?
- What is the student's level of performance in high school?
- Is the student enrolled in college-prep courses, modified courses, or individualized, special-education courses?
- What are the student's individual strengths and weaknesses?
- Is it easier for the student to learn from a lecture, reading the material, or having the material read to her?
- Does the student perform better on written assignments or oral presentations?
- Which subjects are easier, and which are more difficult?
- What are the student's favorite and least favorite courses and why?
- What are the student's short-term and long-term goals?
- Are these goals realistic?
- Is the student striving to improve in academic areas?
- What accommodations are being provided?
- Is the student actively utilizing resource assistance and learning compensatory strategies?
- What does the student plan to study in college?
- What skills and competencies are required for the career goals being pursued?
- When were the last diagnostic tests given?
- What level of services/accommodations is needed in college? Structured programs, comprehensive services, or basic services?

Articulation
- Does the student understand the disability?
- Can the student describe the disability?
- Does the student comprehend how the disability impacts learning?
- Can the student explain the nature of the disability?
- Can the student explain the accommodations being utilized as well as any curriculum modifications received?
- Can the student explain necessary accommodations to teachers?

ACADEMIC ASSESSMENT

Does the student have difficulty with written language?
- using appropriate words
- organizing thoughts
- writing lengthy compositions
- using correct punctuation and sentence structure
- expressing thoughts clearly

Does the student have trouble with verbal expression?
- retrieving appropriate words
- understanding what others are saying
- using words in the correct context
- carrying on conversations

Does the student have a problem with hand-eye coordination?
- finding certain information on a page
- performing tasks that require fine motor coordination

Does the student get frustrated reading?
- decoding unfamiliar words
- understanding reading assignments
- completing reading assignments within a time frame

Does the student often misspell words?
- mix up the sequence of letters
- become confused when spelling irregular words

Does the student experience difficulty performing mathematics?
- multiplication table and fractions
- sequencing of steps of various mathematical questions

Does the student have difficulty concentrating?
- fidgets or squirms
- distracted by noises
- difficulty following instructions
- difficulty finishing assignments

What are the student's study habits?
- attentive in class for an extended period of time
- easily distracted
- needs extra time to respond to questions
- note-taking skills
- memory
- time management
- time orientation
- organization

How is the student's handwriting ability?

- assignments are difficult to read
- appropriate capitalization used
- stays within the lines when writing
- leaves enough space between words

EXPLORATION AND TIMELINES

SOPHOMORE YEAR

- Explore options.
- Consider taking the PLAN (if available) - request appropriate testing accommodations
- Meet with counselor and case manager.
- Review testing and documentation.
- Review course registration for junior year
- Students considering four year colleges/universities should be enrolled in as many mainstreamed, college preparatory courses as possible.
- Use college web sites to explore for information.
- Register online as a prospective student
- Contact the service providers on the college campus.
- Work on developing good self-advocacy skills
- Understand learning style and strengths and challenges
- Understand the disability

JUNIOR YEAR

- Consider taking the PSAT- request appropriate testing accommodations
- Review achievement level.
- Review course registration for senior year
- Students considering four year colleges/universities should be enrolled in as many mainstreamed, college preparatory courses as possible.
- Use college web sites to explore for information
- Review the level of services in high school.
- Identify the level of services needed in college.
- Be able to articulate the disability.
- Be comfortable asking for support and accommodations.
- Participate in the IEP process and be actively involved in the IEP meeting.
- Be involved in writing your Summary of Performance (SOP)
- Visit colleges.
- Register for the ACT/SAT, standardized or non-standardized.
- Request necessary updated psycho-educational testing. (Including the WAIS-IV)

SENIOR YEAR

- Submit general applications.
- Submit special applications (if required).
- Schedule interviews (if appropriate).
- Write a personal statement and self-disclose the disability.
- Answer essay questions (if required).
- Release current psycho-educational testing if required for a Support Program; otherwise release after determining what college the student will attend
- Release documentation of other health-related disabilities once it has been determined what college the student will attend.
- Be sure that the documentation includes a description of the disability and recommended accommodations.
- Be sure to get copies of the entire special education file including testing assessments and IEP summaries to have in your personal files after graduation.
- Students under the age of eighteen must have their parents' signature to release documentation to each of the colleges.

CAMPUS VISITS

- The student should call to make an arrangement for a visit.
- Visit while classes are in session.
- Meet with admissions and special support service providers.
- Take a guided tour.
- Attend a class.
- Eat a meal on campus.
- Drive around the boundaries of the campus.
- Take pictures, take notes, and talk to students on campus.
- Take parents or family members along (but not in the interview).
- Get available information on disability services
- Write thank-you notes.

INTERVIEWS

To prepare for interviews, students should know:
- Strengths and weaknesses
- The accommodations needed
- How to describe learning disability

If an interview is required prior to an admission decision:
- View the interview as an opportunity.
- Prepare a list of questions.
- Know that interviews, if required, are either required of all applicants or required for a special program or special admission practice.

QUESTIONS THE DIRECTOR OF SUPPORT SERVICES MAY ASK:

- When was the learning disability first diagnosed?
- What type of assistance has the student been receiving in high school?
- What kind of accommodations will the student need in college?
- Can the student describe the learning difficulties?
- Can the student articulate strengths and weaknesses?
- How has the disability affected the student's learning?
- What high school courses were easy (or more difficult)?
- Is the student comfortable with the learning disability?
- Can the student self-advocate?
- What does the student plan to choose as a major?
- Is the student motivated?

QUESTIONS STUDENTS AND/OR PARENTS MAY ASK:

- What are the admission requirements?
- Is there any flexibility in admission policy? Course substitutions? GPA?
- What is the application procedure?
- Is a special application required?
- What auxiliary testing is required?
- Are there extra charges or fees for the special programs or services?
- Are there remedial or developmental courses?
- What is the procedure for requesting waivers or substitutions?
- Who is the contact person for learning disabilities?
- What are the academic qualifications of the individual who provides services to students with learning disabilities?
- What services and accommodations are available: Testing accommodations? Note takers? Books on tape? Skills classes? Support groups? Priority registration? Professional tutors? Peer tutors? Advising? Computer-aided technology? Scribes? Proctors? Oral tests? Use of computers and spell-checker in class? Use of calculators in class? Distraction-free environment for tests? Learning disability specialists? Advocacy with professors? Faculty in-services?
- How long has the program been in existence?
- How many students are receiving services?
- How long can students access services?
- What is the success rate of students receiving services?

FOR A SUCCESSFUL INTERVIEW:

- Develop a list of questions.
- Know the accommodations needed.
- Provide new information.
- Practice interviewing.
- Be able to describe strengths and weaknesses.
- Talk about extracurricular activities.
- Take notes.
- Get the business card of the interviewer.
- Try to relax.
- Have fun!

Letters of Recommendation

- Obtain descriptive letters from counselors, teachers, and case managers.
- Have recommenders address learning style, degree of motivation, level of achievement, abilities, attitudes, self-discipline, determination, creativity, mastery of subject matter, academic risks, and growth.
- Have a teacher describe the challenge in a difficult course.
- Advise recommenders when letters are due.

We have just highlighted some of the areas of importance. Now it is time to begin to use the information in this guide that describes the various programs and services at various colleges and universities in the United States.

COLLEGE INTERVIEW PREPARATION FORM FOR STUDENTS WITH LEARNING DISABILITIES/ADHD

NAME: _____ DATE: _____

ADDRESS: _____

PHONE: _____

Description of Disability:

_____

_____

When Diagnosed:

_____

_____

Special Help Received:

Tutoring_____

LD Resource _____

Remedial Reading_____

Study Skills _____

Other _____

Which were helpful and why?

_____

_____

_____

_____

Current high school:

_____

Describe this school:

_____

_____

_____

GPA _____

SAT _____

ACT _____

Comment on your abilities in the following areas and describe them:

_____

_____

Memory:

_____

Attention:

_____

Time management:

_____

Time orientation:

_____

Describe strategies you have used to compensate for your learning disability:

_____

Why were these strategies successful/unsuccessful for you?

_____

_____

_____

When was your last diagnostic testing?

_____

_____

What is taking these kinds of tests like for you?

_____

_____

Describe your skills in the following areas. If your learning disability interferes in any of these areas, describe strategies you have used to compensate:

_____

Reading

_____

Writing

_____

Spelling

_____

Math

_____

Test-taking

_____

Note-taking

_____

What is your favorite subject? Least favorite?

_____

_____

_____

How would your favorite teacher describe you?

_____

_____

_____

How would your least favorite teacher describe you?

_____

_____

_____

What do you see as your own personal strengths?

_____

_____

What are your weaknesses?

_____

_____

What kinds of activities are you involved in?

_____

_____

_____

What do you hope to get out of college?

_____

_____

What do you want in an LD college program?

_____

_____

Which of the following services will be appropriate for you?

Extended Time Tests   _____

Distraction Reduced
Environment for Tests   _____

Taped Texts   _____

LD Specialist   _____

Skills Courses in Time
Management/Test Taking/
Organization/Note taking   _____

Tutors   _____

Note takers   _____

Counseling   _____

Reduced Course Load   _____

Study Skills   _____

Support Group   _____

What are your career interests?

_____

_____

_____

HOW TO USE THIS GUIDE

The K&W Guide to Colleges for Students with Learning Disabilities or Attention Deficit Disorderr includes information on colleges and universities that offer services to students with learning disabilities. No two colleges are identical in the programs or services they provide, but there are some similarities. For the purpose of this guide, the services and programs at the various colleges have been grouped into three categories.

STRUCTURED PROGRAMS (SP)

Colleges with Structured Programs offer the most comprehensive services for students with learning disabilities. The director and/or staff are certified in learning disabilities or related areas. The director is actively involved in the admission decision and, often, the criteria for admission may be more flexible than general admission requirements. Services are highly structured and students are involved in developing plans to meet their particular learning styles and needs. Often students in Structured Programs sign a contract agreeing to actively participate in the program. There is usually an additional fee for the enhanced services. Students who have participated in a Structured Program or Structured Services in high school such as the Learning Disabilities Resource Program, individualized or modified coursework, tutorial assistance, academic monitoring, note-takers, test accommodations, or skill classes might benefit from exploring colleges with Structured Programs or Coordinated Services.

COORDINATED SERVICES (CS)

Coordinated Services differ from Structured Programs in that the services are not as comprehensive. These services are provided by at least one certified learning disability specialist. The staff is knowledgeable and trained to provide assistance to students to develop strategies for their individual needs. The director of the program or services may be involved in the admission decision, be in a position to offer recommendations to the admissions office on the potential success of the applicant, or to assist the students with an appeal if denied admission to the college. Receiving these services generally requires specific documentation of the learning disability – students are encouraged to self-identify prior to entry. Students voluntarily request accommodations or services in the Coordinated Services category, and there may be specific skills courses or remedial classes available or required for students with learning disabilities who are admitted probationally or conditionally. High school students who may have enrolled in some modified or remedial courses, utilized test accommodations, or required tutorial assistance, but who typically requested services only as needed, might benefit from exploring colleges with Coordinated Services or Services.

SERVICES (S)

Services are the least comprehensive of the three categories. Colleges offering Services generally are complying with the federal mandate requiring reasonable accommodations to all students with appropriate and current documentation. These colleges routinely require documentation of the disability in order for the students with LD/ADHD to receive accommodations. Staff and faculty actively support the students by providing basic services to meet the needs of the students. Services are requested on a voluntarily basis, and there may be some limitations as to what is reasonable and the degree of services available. Sometimes, just the small size of the student body allows for the necessary personal attention to help students with learning disabilities succeed in college. High school students who require minimum accommodations, but who would find comfort in knowing that services are available, knowing who the contact person is, and knowing that this person is sensitive to students with learning disabilities, might benefit from exploring colleges providing Services or Coordinated Services.

CATEGORIES USED TO DESCRIBE THE PROGRAMS AND SERVICES AT COLLEGES AND UNIVERSITIES

The categories on the following pages describe the topics of information used in this guide. Each college in the book is covered on two pages, beginning with pertinent information describing the learning disability program or services. This is followed by special admission procedures, specific information about services offered, and concludes with general college information. Please note the statement preceding the section on services and accommodations which states "Services and Accommodations are determined individually for each student based on current and appropriate documentation." Some categories are answered with: N/A (not applicable) because not all colleges were able to fit into every category included in this guide; NR (not reported) because some colleges were unable to provide the information we requested; and Y/N (Yes/No) because the answer is dependent on individual situations. The authors have made a conscientious effort to provide the most current information possible. However, names, costs, dates, policies, and other information are always subject to change, and colleges of particular interest or importance to the reader should be contacted directly for verification of the data.

JACKSONVILLE STATE UNIVERSITY

700 Pelham Road North, Jacksonville, AL 36265
Phone: 256-782-5268 • Fax: 256-782-5953
E-mail: info@jsu.edu • Web: www.jsu.edu
Support: CS • Institution: 4-year public

PROGRAMS OR SERVICES FOR STUDENTS WITH LD

Disability Support Services (DSS) offers services for students with learning disabilities and ADHD. It is an inclusive service community that promotes academic excellence and empowers students for success. Once students have been admitted, DSS assists the qualified student with a documented disability in receiving academic support services. Accommodations are based solely on the supporting documentation. Required documents for a student with learning disabilities may include current intelligence tests, current achievement tests, certified professional validation of the LD and high school records that document prior identification and/or services. Each student with appropriate documentation of a learning disability will develop an individualized postsecondary program (IPP). The IPP is prepared from the documentation received, input from the student, and the staff in support services. Copies of the IPP are given to the student who is responsible for identifying himself or herself and giving a copy to each instructor.

ADMISSION INFORMATION FOR STUDENTS WITH LD/ADHD

College entrance tests required: Yes
Interview required: No
Essay recommended: No
What documentation required for LD: Psycho Ed evaluation to include: relevant historical info, instructional interventions, related services, age diagnosed, objective data (aptitude, achievement, info processing), test scores (standard, percentile and grade equivalents) and describe functional limitations.
With general application: No
To receive services after enrolling: Yes
What documentation required for ADHD: Diagnosis based on DSM-V; history of behaviors impairing functioning in academic setting; diagnostic interview; history of symptoms; evidence of ongoing behaviors.

With general application: No
To receive services after enrolling: Yes
Submitted to: Support Program/Services
Special Ed. HS course work accepted: Yes
Specific course requirements for all applicants: Yes
Separate application required: Request for Services (Applying to DSS) can be completed online or printable version available
# of LD applications submitted each year: 100
# of LD applications accepted yearly: 100
Total # of students receiving LD services: 100
Acceptance into program means acceptance into college: Students must be admitted and enrolled in the university first and then request services.

ADMISSIONS

All applicants must meet the general entrance requirements. Unconditional admission ACT 20+ or SAT 950+ (Critical Reading and Math combined). The middle 50 percent of the applicants have an ACT of 18–22. All students must have at least 3 years of English, and no more than 4 of the 15 required courses in high school may be in vocational courses. Interviews are recommended but not required. Students with an ACT between 14–16 may enter through successful completion of a summer bridge program. The program, Experiencing Success in Education and Life, offers skill-building classes. Students with an ACT between 17 and 19 or SAT between 830–940 are conditionally admitted.

ADDITIONAL INFORMATION

Disability Support Services will provide services to any student with LD/ADHD with appropriate documentation, and accommodations are based solely on the supporting documentation. DSS requires formal documentation (current— within the past 3 years), and the academic accommodations needed are determined from this documentation. Services available may include note-takers, readers, scribes, priority registration, assistive technology, testing modifications, distraction-free environment for tests, and an Individualized Postsecondary Program. Academic Success Skills offers skills classes in time management, test strategies, organizational skills, as well as other areas. These courses are offered for college credit. All students have access to tutoring, supplemental instruction, structured study sessions, and online tutorials.

LEARNING DISABILITY PROGRAMS OR SERVICES

Contact Information
Name of program or department: Disability Support Services
  Telephone: 256-782-8380
  Fax: 256-782-8383

LEARNING DISABILITY SERVICES

Accommodations are decided upon an individual basis after a thorough review of appropriate, current documentation. The accommodations requested must be supported through the documentation provided and must be logically linked to the current impact of the condition on academic functioning.

Allowed in exams
  Calculator: Yes
  Dictionary: Yes
  Computer: Yes
  Spellchecker: Yes
Extended test time: Yes
Scribes: Yes
Proctors: Yes
Oral exams: Yes
Note-takers: Yes

Distraction-reduced environment: Yes
Tape recording in class: Yes
Electronic texts: Yes
Accommodations for students with ADHD: Yes
Kurzweil Reader: Yes
Other assistive technology: Yes
Priority registration: Yes

Added costs for services: No
LD specialists: Yes
Professional tutors: No
Peer tutors: 40, ACE Program
Max. hours/wk. for services: Weekdays and evenings
How professors are notified of LD/ADHD: Copy of IPP is provided to student to disclose to professors.

GENERAL ADMISSIONS INFORMATION

Office of Admission: 256-782-5268

ENTRANCE REQUIREMENTS

Freshman Applicants must submit an official high school transcript showing course work through the junior year at the time of application and submit a final high school transcript after graduation showing graduation date and diploma type. JSU requires students to complete high school with an acceptable diploma type, and GED is accepted. For unconditional admission, students must score 20 or above (composite) on the ACT or 950 or above (combined Critical Reading and Math) on the SAT. For conditional admission, scores are 17–19 (composite) on the ACT, and 830 - 940 (combined Critical Reading and Math) on the SAT. TOEFL required of all international applicants: minimum paper TOEFL 500, minimum computer TOEFL 173, minimum internet-based TOEFL 61.

Application deadline: None
Notification: Rolling
Average GPA: 3.03
ACT Composite middle 50% range: 18–22

SAT Math middle 50% range: 420–510
SAT Critical Reading middle 50% range: 410–520
SAT Writing middle 50% range: NR

Graduated top 10% of class: 19%
Graduated top 25% of class: 42%
Graduated top 50% of class: 74%

COLLEGE GRADUATION REQUIREMENTS

Course waivers allowed: Yes
In what course: Individual case-by-case decisions
Course substitutions allowed: Yes
In what course: Individual case-by-case decisions

ADDITIONAL INFORMATION

Environment: Located in a small town about 75 miles from Birmingham.

Student Body
  Undergrad enrollment: 8,199
  Women: 59%
  Men: 41%
  Percent out-of-state: 19%

Cost Information
  In-state tuition: $7,650
  Out-of-state tuition: $15,300
  Room & board: $6,328
  Housing Information
    University housing: Yes
    Percent living on campus: 20%

Greek System
  Fraternity: Yes
  Sorority: Yes
Athletics: Division I

THE U. OF ALABAMA IN HUNTSVILLE

301 Sparkman Drive, Huntsville, AL 35899
Phone: 256-824-6070 • Fax: 256-824-6073
E-mail: admitme@uah.edu • Web: www.uah.edu
Support: S • Institution type: 4-year public

PROGRAMS OR SERVICES FOR STUDENTS WITH LD

The Office of Student Development Services offers a variety of services and accommodations to assist students with disabilities in eliminating barriers they encounter in pursuing higher education. The office's main objective is to provide access to academic, social, cultural, recreational, and housing opportunities at the university. A student is considered registered with Disability Support Services (DSS) when they have completed all application paperwork, their intake/registration paperwork has been approved, and they have had an interview with a 504 Coordinator. The services offered through this office encourage students to achieve and maintain autonomy.

ADMISSION INFORMATION FOR STUDENTS WITH LD/ADHD

College entrance tests required: Yes
Interview required: No
Essay recommended: No
What documentation required for LD: Psycho Ed evaluation to include: relevant historical info, instructional interventions, related services, age diagnosed, objective data (aptitude, achievement, info processing), test scores (standard, percentile and grade equivalents) and describe functional limitations.
With general application: No
To receive services after enrolling: Yes
What documentation required for ADHD: Diagnosis based on DSM-V; history of behaviors impairing functioning in academic setting; diagnostic interview; history of symptoms; evidence of ongoing behaviors.
With general application: No
To receive services after enrolling: Yes

Submitted to: Disability Support Services
Special Ed. HS course work accepted: Yes
Specific course requirements for all applicants: Yes
Separate application required: Yes
# of LD applications submitted each year: NR
# of LD applications accepted yearly: NR
Total # of students receiving LD services: 150
Acceptance into program means acceptance into college: Students must be admitted and enrolled in the university first and then request services.

ADMISSIONS

Admission is based on grades and test scores. Additionally, applicants should have 4 years of English, 3 years of social studies, 3 years of math, 2 years of science, and a total of 20 Carnegie units. Dificiences must be removed within one year.

ACT	SAT	GPA
17 or below	700 or below	3.25
18	740	3.00
19	790	2.75
20–21	860	2.50
22	920	2.25
23	970	2.00
24 or above	1010 or above	1.15

There is no special LD admission process. If a student becomes subject to academic suspension, the suspension is for a minimum of one term, and the student must petition the Admissions Committee for approval to reenroll.

ADDITIONAL INFORMATION

Students should forward their documentation to Disability Support Services. Disability Support Services provides the mandated services, including testing accommodations, reduced distraction environments for tests, readers, proctors, scribes, note-takers, and specialized adaptive computers, Institution organized Peer Assisted Study Sessions (PASS), covering math, chemistry classes along with many others are available to all students. In addition the Student Success Center provides centralized access to academic coaching, tutorial services, and the writing center to all students on campus. All students have access to skills classes in time management, test-taking strategies, and study skills. Services and accommodations are available for undergraduate and graduate students.

LEARNING DISABILITY PROGRAMS OR SERVICES

Contact Information
Name of program or department: Student Development Services
 Telephone: 256-824-6203
 Fax: 256-824-6672

LEARNING DISABILITY SERVICES

Accommodations are decided upon an individual basis after a thorough review of appropriate, current documentation. The accommodations requested must be supported through the documentation provided and must be logically linked to the current impact of the condition on academic functioning.

Allowed in exams
 Calculator: Yes
 Dictionary: Yes
 Computer: Yes
 Spellchecker: Yes
Extended test time: Yes
Scribes: Yes
Proctors: Yes
Oral exams: Yes
Note-takers: Yes

Distraction-reduced environment: Yes
Tape recording in class: Yes
Electronic texts: Yes
Accommodations for students with
 ADHD: Yes
Kurzweil Reader: Yes
Other assistive technology: Yes
Priority registration: Yes

Added costs for services: No
LD specialists: No
Max. hours/wk. for services: Unlimited
How professors are notified of LD/ADHD: By both student and director

GENERAL ADMISSIONS INFORMATION

Office of Admission: 256-824-6070

ENTRANCE REQUIREMENTS

Academic units required: 4 English, 3 math, 3 science, 4 social studies, 6 academic electives. High school diploma is required, and GED is accepted. ACT with or without writing component accepted. TOEFL required of all international applicants: minimum paper TOEFL 500, minimum computer TOEFL 173.

Application deadline: 8/22
Notification: Rolling
Average GPA: 3.62
ACT Composite middle 50% range: 22–29

SAT Math middle 50% range: 520–670
SAT Critical Reading middle 50% range: 500–630
SAT Writing middle 50% range: NR

Graduated top 10% of class: 29%
Graduated top 25% of class: 50%
Graduated top 50% of class: 80%

COLLEGE GRADUATION REQUIREMENTS

Course waivers allowed: Yes
In what course: Individual case-by-case decisions
Course substitutions allowed: Yes
In what course: Individual case-by-case decisions

ADDITIONAL INFORMATION

Environment: The university is located on 337 acres 100 miles north of Birmingham and 100 miles south of Nashville.

Student Body
 Undergrad enrollment: 6,005
 Women: 46%
 Men: 54%
 Percent out-of-state: 10%

Cost Information
 In-state tuition: $8,094
 Out-of-state tuition: $19,424
 Room & board: $7,930
Housing Information
 University housing: Yes
 Percent living on campus: 20%

Greek System
 Fraternity: Yes
 Sorority: Yes
Athletics: Division II

THE U. OF ALABAMA AT TUSCALOOSA

Box 870132, Tuscaloosa, AL 35487-0132
Phone: 205-348-5666 • Fax: 205-348-9046
E-mail: admissions@ua.edu • Web: www.ua.edu
Support: S • Institution: 4-year public

PROGRAMS OR SERVICES FOR STUDENTS WITH LD

Any student enrolled with a documented physical or mental condition that substantially limits one or more major life activities may be eligible for services and accommodations. Those seeking services for LD and/or ADHD must provide documentation including a narrative report of a psychoeducational or neuropsychological evaluation; a summary of areas of testing; actual test scores; overall summary and diagnosis; and recommendations and suggested strategies for students, professors, and academic advisors. The Office of Disability Services may request further testing. Complete documentation requirements can be found at www.ods.ua.edu.

ADMISSION INFORMATION FOR STUDENTS WITH LD/ADHD

College entrance tests required: Yes
Interview required: No
Essay required: N/A
What documentation required for LD: Psycho Ed evaluation to include: relevant historical info, instructional interventions, related services, age diagnosed, objective data (aptitude, achievement, info processing), test scores (standard, percentile and grade equivalents) and describe functional limitations.
With general application: No
To receive services after enrolling: Yes
What documentation required for ADHD: Diagnosis based on DSM-V; history of behaviors impairing functioning in academic setting; diagnostic interview; history of symptoms; evidence of ongoing behaviors.

With general application: No
Submitted to: Support Program/Services
Special Ed. HS course work accepted: No
Specific course requirements for all applicants: Yes
Separate application required for program services: Yes
# of LD applications submitted each year: NR
# of LD applications accepted yearly: NR
Total # of students receiving LD services: 465
Acceptance into program means acceptance into college: Separate application required after student has enrolled

ADMISSIONS

All students must meet regular entrance requirements 4 English, 4 social studies, 3 math, 3 science, 1 foreign language, 5 electives. An interview with the Office of Disabilities is recommended. ACT with Writing or SAT (use Critical Reading and Math).

ADDITIONAL INFORMATION

Accommodations are tailored to individual needs according to diagnostic testing. Accommodations include early registration; testing modifications; academic aids such as taping lectures and the use of calculators, dictionaries, spellcheckers, note-takers, and taped materials; and reading assistance. The Center for Academic Succeses (CAS) Independent Study Lab is available for all students. Students can use videotapes, computer software, and other self-paced materials for review of math, chemistry, physics, biology, statistics, and other selected classes; study and reading skills; and graduate entrance exam preparation. Individual tutoring is offered for select classes. Math review and help sessions offered through small group review sessions. The CAS offers reading comprehension workshops, as well as workshops in study skills and time management. The Writing Center is staffed by instructors from the University of Alabama's English Department who provide individual assistance in developing the composition skills necessary to complete university course work.

PROGRAM FOR DISABILITY SERVICES

Contact Information
Name of program or department: Office of Disability Services
  Telephone: 205-348-4285
  Fax: 205-348-0804

LEARNING DISABILITY SERVICES

Accommodations are decided upon an individual basis after a thorough review of appropriate, current documentation. The accommodations requested must be supported through the documentation provided and must be logically linked to the current impact of the condition on academic functioning.

Allowed in exams
  Calculator: Yes
  Dictionary: Yes
  Computer: Yes
  Spellchecker: Yes
Extended test time: Yes
Scribes: Yes
Proctors: Yes
Oral exams: Yes
Note-takers: Yes

Distraction-reduced environment: Yes
Tape recording in class: Yes
Electronic texts: Yes
Accommodations for students with ADHD: Yes
Kurzweil Reader: Alternative text formats available
Other assistive technology: E-text conversion; training in the use of certain assistive technology programs.

Priority registration: Yes
Added costs for services: No
LD specialists: No
Professional tutors: No
Max. hours/wk. for services: NR
How professors are notified of LD/ADHD: Student

GENERAL ADMISSIONS INFORMATION

Office of Admission: 205-348-5666

ENTRANCE REQUIREMENTS
Academic units required: 4 English, 3 mathematics, 3 science, (2 science labs), 1 foreign language, 4 social studies, 1 history, 5 academic electives. **Academic units recommended:** 4 English, 3 mathematics, 3 science, (2 science labs), 1 foreign language, 4 social studies, 1 history, 5 academic electives. High school diploma is required and GED is accepted. SAT or ACT required; ACT with Writing component required. TOEFL required of all international applicants; minimum paper TOEFL 500, minimum computer TOEFL 173, minimum web-based TOEFL 61.

Application deadline: NR
Notification: Rolling
Average GPA: 3.54
ACT Composite middle 50% range: 22–29

SAT Math middle 50% range: 495–640
SAT Critical Reading middle 50% range: 500–620
SAT Writing middle 50% range: 490–610

Graduated top 10% of class: 42.7%
Graduated top 25% of class: 62.3%
Graduated top 50% of class: 82.8%

COLLEGE GRADUATION REQUIREMENTS

Course waivers allowed: No
Course substitutions allowed: Yes
In what course: Substitutions are sometimes granted, but no courses are waived. Courses cannot be substituted if doing so would substantially alter the nature of the program or if the course is required as part of the student's major or for any type of certification.

ADDITIONAL INFORMATION

Environment: The university is located 55 miles from the city of Birmingham.
Student Body
  Undergrad enrollment: 26,234
  Women: 53.2%
  Men: 46.8%
  Percent out-of-state: 34.9%

Cost Information
  In-state tuition: $8,600
  Out-of-state tuition: $21,900
  Room and board: $8,564
Housing Information
  University housing: Yes
  Percent living on campus: 27.8%

Greek System
  Fraternity: Yes
  Sorority: Yes
Athletics: Division I

UNIVERSITY OF ALASKA—ANCHORAGE

3211 Providence Drive, Anchorage, AK 99508-8046
Phone: 907-786-1480 • Fax: 907-786-4888
E-mail: enroll@uaa.alaska.edu • Web: www.uaa.alaska.edu
Support: S • Institution type: 4-year public

AK
Anchorage ★
Gulf of Alaska

PROGRAMS OR SERVICES FOR STUDENTS WITH LD

The University of Alaska—Anchorage provides equal opportunities for students who have disabilities. Academic support services are available to students with learning disabilities. Staff trained to work with students with disabilities coordinate these services. To allow time for service coordination, students are encouraged to contact the Disability Support Services (DSS) office several weeks before the beginning of each semester. Ongoing communication with the staff throughout the semester is encouraged.

ADMISSION INFORMATION FOR STUDENTS WITH LD/ADHD

College entrance tests required: Yes
Interview required: No
Essay recommended: No
What documentation required for LD: Psycho Ed evaluation to include: relevant historical info, instructional interventions, related services, age diagnosed, objective data (aptitude, achievement, info processing), test scores (standard, percentile and grade equivalents) and describe functional limitations.
With general application: No
To receive services after enrolling: Yes
What documentation required for ADHD: Diagnosis based on DSM-V; history of behaviors impairing functioning in academic setting; diagnostic interview; history of symptoms; evidence of ongoing behaviors.

With general application: No
Submitted to: Disability Support Services
Special Ed. HS course work accepted: Yes
Specific course requirements for all applicants: NR
Separate application required: No
# of LD applications submitted each year: NR
# of LD applications accepted yearly: NR
Total # of students receiving LD services: 90 plus
Acceptance into program means acceptance into college: The University of Alaska—Anchorage has open enrollment; students are accepted to the university and then may request services.

ADMISSIONS

All students must meet the same admission requirements. The university has an open enrollment policy. However, admission to specific programs of study may have specific course work or testing criteria that all students will have to meet. While formal admission is encouraged, the university has an open enrollment policy that allows students to register for courses in which they have the adequate background. Open enrollment does not guarantee subsequent formal admission to certificate or degree programs. Individuals with learning disabilities are admitted via the standard admissions procedures that apply to all students submitting applications for formal admission. Students with documentation of a learning disability are eligible to receive support services once they are enrolled in the university. LD students who self-disclose during the admission process are referred to DSS for information about services and accommodations.

ADDITIONAL INFORMATION

Classes are available for all students in the areas of vocabulary building and study skills. There is no separate tutoring for students with learning disabilities. Tutorial help is available for all students in the reading and writing labs and the Learning Resource Center. With appropriate documentation, students with LD or ADHD may have access to accommodations such as testing modifications, distraction-free testing environments, scribes, proctors, note-takers, calculators, dictionaries, and computers in exams, and access to assistive technology. Services and accommodations are available for undergraduate and graduate students.

LEARNING DISABILITY PROGRAMS OR SERVICES

Contact Information
Name of program or department: Disability Support Services
  Telephone: 907-786-4530
  Fax: 907-786-4531

LEARNING DISABILITY SERVICES

Accommodations are decided upon an individual basis after a thorough review of appropriate, current documentation. The accommodations requested must be supported through the documentation provided and must be logically linked to the current impact of the condition on academic functioning.

Allowed in exams
  Calculator: Yes
  Dictionary: Yes
  Computer: Yes
  Spellchecker: Yes
Extended test time: Yes
Scribes: Yes
Proctors: Yes
Oral exams: Yes
Note-takers: Yes

Distraction-reduced environment: Yes
Tape recording in class: Yes
Electronic texts: Yes
**Accommodations for students with
  ADHD:** Yes
Kurzweil Reader: Yes
Other assistive technology: Yes
Priority registration: Yes

Added costs for services: No
LD specialists: No
Professional tutors: No
Peer tutors: Yes
Max. hours/wk. for services:
  Unlimited
**How professors are notified of
  LD/ADHD:** By student initiated letters
  sent through Disability Support

GENERAL ADMISSIONS INFORMATION

Office of Admission: 907-786-1480

ENTRANCE REQUIREMENTS

Academic units recommended: 4 English, 2 math, 3 science, 1 foreign language, 3 social studies, 1 history. High school diploma is required, and GED is accepted. TOEFL required of all international applicants: minimum paper TOEFL 450.

Application deadline: 7/1
Notification: Rolling
Average GPA: 2.95
ACT Composite middle 50% range:
  18–25

SAT Math middle 50% range:
  450–570
**SAT Critical Reading middle 50%
  range:** 470–620
SAT Writing middle 50% range: NR

Graduated top 10% of class: 11%
Graduated top 25% of class: 29%
Graduated top 50% of class: 59%

COLLEGE GRADUATION REQUIREMENTS

Course waivers allowed: Yes
In what course: Individual case-by-case decisions
Course substitutions allowed: Yes
In what course: Individual case-by-case decisions

ADDITIONAL INFORMATION

Environment: The University of Alaska is an urban campus on 350 acres 7 miles from downtown Anchorage.

Student Body
  Undergrad enrollment: 17,597
  Women: 60%
  Men: 40%
  Percent out-of-state: 7%

Cost Information
  In-state tuition: $5,300
  Out-of-state tuition: $15,550
  Room & board: $9,500
Housing Information
  University housing: Yes
  Percent living on campus: 5%

Greek System
  Fraternity: Yes
  Sorority: Yes
Athletics: Division II

University of Alaska—Fairbanks

PO Box 757480, Fairbanks, AK 99775-7480
Phone: 907-474-7500 • Fax: 907-474-5379
E-mail: admissions@uaf.edu • Web: www.uaf.edu
Support: S • Institution type: 4-year public

PROGRAMS OR SERVICES FOR STUDENTS WITH LD

The University of Alaska is committed to providing equal opportunity to students with disabilities. Disability Services at The University of Alaska—Fairbanks provides assistance to students with documented disabilities. The purpose of Disability Services (DS) is to provide equal access to higher education for students with disabilities. Campus services include the Academic Advising Center, which is responsible for advising incoming freshmen and students with undeclared majors. It provides explanations of programs and their requirements and assists students with choosing majors, selecting electives, and choosing classes consistent with their academic and career goals. Student Support Services provides academic and personal support, including developmental classes and tutoring for students who are economically disadvantaged, do not have a parent who graduated from college, or have a documented disability. Disabled Students of UAF is an organizations that provides peer support groups for UAF students experiencing disabilities. The Student Development and Learning Center provides tutoring, individual instruction in basic skills and counseling, career-planning services, and assessment testing. Disability Services welcomes inquiries and seeks to make the college experience a success for students with disabilities.

ADMISSION INFORMATION FOR STUDENTS WITH LD/ADHD

College entrance tests required: Yes
Interview required: No
Essay recommended: No
What documentation required for LD: Psycho Ed evaluation to include: relevant historical info, instructional interventions, related services, age diagnosed, objective data (aptitude, achievement, info processing), test scores (standard, percentile and grade equivalents) and describe functional limitations.
With general application: No
To receive services after enrolling: Yes
What documentation required for ADHD: Diagnosis based on DSM-V; history of behaviors impairing functioning in academic setting; diagnostic interview; history of symptoms; evidence of ongoing behaviors.

With general application: No
Submitted to: Disability Services
Special Ed. HS course work accepted: Yes
Specific course requirements for all applicants: Yes
Separate application required: No
# of LD applications submitted each year: NR
# of LD applications accepted yearly: NR
Total # of students receiving LD services: 30–40
Acceptance into program means acceptance into college: Students must be admitted and enrolled in the university first and then request services.

ADMISSIONS

To enter as a freshman for a baccalaureate degree there are two options: 1) high school diplomas, 2.5 in core courses and EPA 3.0 and no cut-off on ACT/SAT. 2) high school diploma, 2.5 in core courses, a minimum 2.5 GPA and ACT 18 or SAT 1290. Core curriculum 4 years English, 3 years math, 3 years social sciences, and 3 years natural or physical sciences. Foreign languages are recommended. Students can be provisionally accepted if they make up course deficiencies with a C or better in each of the developmental or university courses and complete nine credits of general degree requirements with a C or better.

ADDITIONAL INFORMATION

Services include individual counseling to determine necessary accommodations; arrangements for special services such as readers, scribes, and note-takers; advocacy with faculty and staff; assistance to faculty and staff in determining appropriate accommodations; help in determining specific needs for students with learning disabilities; and referral to campus and community agencies for additional services. Basic study-skills classes are offered for all students and may be taken for credit. Services and accommodations are provided for any student registered for at least 1 credit.

LEARNING DISABILITY PROGRAMS OR SERVICES

Contact Information
Name of program or department: Disability Services
　Telephone: 907-474-5655
　Fax: 907-474-5688

LEARNING DISABILITY SERVICES

Accommodations are decided upon an individual basis after a thorough review of appropriate, current documentation. The accommodations requested must be supported through the documentation provided and must be logically linked to the current impact of the condition on academic functioning.

Allowed in exams	Note-takers: Yes	Added costs for services: No
Calculator: No	Distraction-reduced environment: Yes	LD specialists: No
Dictionary: Yes	Tape recording in class: Yes	Professional tutors: No
Computer: Yes	Electronic texts: Yes	Peer tutors: No
Spellchecker: Yes	Accommodations for students with	Max. hours/wk. for services: N/A
Extended test time: Yes	ADHD: Yes	How professors are notified of
Scribes: Yes	Kurzweil Reader: Yes	LD/ADHD: By student
Proctors: Yes	Other assistive technology: Yes	
Oral exams: Yes	Priority registration: No	

GENERAL ADMISSIONS INFORMATION

Office of Admission: 907-474-7500

ENTRANCE REQUIREMENTS

Academic units required: 4 English, 3 math, 3 science (1 science lab), 3 social studies, 3 academic electives.
Academic units recommended: 2 foreign language. High school diploma is required, and GED is not accepted. ACT with or without Writing component accepted. TOEFL required of all international applicants: minimum paper TOEFL 550, minimum computer TOEFL 213.

Application deadline: 7/1	SAT Math middle 50% range:	Graduated top 10% of class: 15%
Notification: Rolling	500–580	Graduated top 25% of class: 35%
Average GPA: 3.19	SAT Critical Reading middle 50%	Graduated top 50% of class: 64%
ACT Composite middle 50% range:	range: 520–580	
17–24	SAT Writing middle 50% range:	
	430–540	

COLLEGE GRADUATION REQUIREMENTS

Course waivers allowed: No
In what course: N/A
Course substitutions allowed: Yes
In what course: Depends on documentation

ADDITIONAL INFORMATION

Environment: The university is located in the city of Fairbanks.

Student Body	Cost Information	Greek System
Undergrad enrollment: 8,652	In-state tuition: $5,580	Fraternity: Yes
Women: 57%	Out-of-state tuition: $17,600	Sorority: Yes
Men: 43%	Room & board: $7,000	Athletics: Division II
Percent out-of-state: 9%	Housing Information	
	University housing: Yes	
	Percent living on campus: 27%	

ARIZONA STATE UNIVERSITY

PO Box 870112, Tempe, AZ 85287-0112
Phone: 480-965-7788 • Fax: 480-965-3610
E-mail: ugradinq@asu.edu • Web: www.asu.edu
Support: CS • Institution type: 4-year public

PROGRAMS OR SERVICES FOR STUDENTS WITH LD

The Arizona State University (ASU) Disability Resource Centers (DRC) on each ASU campus facilitate access to educational, social, and career opportunities for qualified ASU students with disabilities, including but not limited to students with learning disabilities and attention deficit hyperactivity disorder. Qualified DRC professional staff on each ASU campus are recommending and implementing reasonable and effective disability accommodations, resources, services, and auxiliary aids upon student request to facilitate student access. DRC services and accommodations are recommended individually for each student. DRC students are provided with self-advocacy training and academic resources and referrals, e.g., Student Success Centers, Writing Centers, Career Services, Enrollment Services, Student Financial Assistance, academic advising referrals, TRiO Student Support Services (for qualified applicants), etc., and encouraged to seek out methods for attaining the highest possible goals and achievement. All DRC services and accommodations are recommended and provided on an individual basis upon request as appropriate for qualified/eligible students. DRC is an access facilitator assisting qualified students in becoming academically and socially independent. DRC professional staff provides and facilitates a wide range of academic support services and accommodations for qualified students in addition to faculty and staff education and training. The Centers also provide ASU pre-entry consultation regarding disability accommodations eligibility upon request.

ADMISSION INFORMATION FOR STUDENTS WITH LD/ADHD

College entrance tests required: Yes
Interview required: Contact individual colleges
Essay recommended: In some cases; contact department directly
What documentation required for LD: Yes, for disability documentation requirements visitL: www.asu.edu/studentaffairs/ed/drc/qualification.htm
With general application: No
To receive services after enrolling: Yes
What documentation required for ADHD: Diagnosis based on DSM-V; history of behaviors impairing functioning in academic setting; diagnostic interview; history of symptoms; evidence of ongoing behaviors.
With general application: No

Submitted to: The ASU Disability Resource Center (DRC) on the campus of the major
Special Ed. HS course work accepted: Yes
Specific course requirements for all applicants: Yes
Separate application required: No
# of LD applications submitted each year: Varies
# of LD applications accepted yearly: All students who qualify for admissions to ASU are admissible. Any student who does not meet the admissions requirements can appeal their admissions decision due to special circumstances.
Total # of students receiving LD services: Over 800
Acceptance into program means acceptance into college: N/A

ADMISSIONS

Students with LD submit the ASU application, self-disclose and submit documentation. Courses required: 4 English, 4 math, 3 science, 2 social science, 2 foreign language and 1 fine arts. Applicants must meet at least one of the following: Top 25% or 3.0 GPA or 22 ACT (24 ACT non-resident) or SAT 1040 (1110 non-resident). All applicants not meeting these standards are evaluated through an Individual Review process. To appeal a denial write a letter "Why ASU", describe ability for success, send 3 recommendations demonstrating motivation and perseverance, and gradual upward trend in courses and grades. Admissions and disability support personnel review appeals. If applicants are denied after an appeal students may become a non-degree-seeking applicant.. Transcripts not required. Non-degree candidates may live in residential housing at ASU and attend local community college. After 24 credits and 2.0, GPA students may apply for regular admission at ASU.

ADDITIONAL INFORMATION

Academic support accommodations include consultation, individualized program recommendations, registration information and advisement referrals, academic tutoring, Computer Tech Center, learning strategies instruction, library research assistance, supplemental readers, mastery of Alternative Learning Techniques Lab, note-taking, testing accommodations, and diagnostic testing referrals. DSR will accept current diagnosis of ADHD based on appropriate diagnostic information that includes a clinical history, instruments used for the diagnosis, narrative, DSM–IV diagnosis, and recommendations for accommodations.

LEARNING DISABILITY PROGRAMS OR SERVICES

Contact Information
Name of program or department: ASU Disability Resource Centers
  Telephone (Tempe Campus): 480-965-1234   **(Downtown Phoenix Campus):** 602-496-4321
  Fax (Tempe Campus): 480-965-0441   **(Downtown Phoenix Campus):** 602-496-0384
  Telephone (Polytechnic Campus): 480-727-1039   **(West Campus):** 602-543-8145
  Fax (Polytechnic Campus): 480-727-1904   **(West Campus):** 602-543-8169

LEARNING DISABILITY SERVICES

Accommodations are decided upon an individual basis after a thorough review of appropriate, current documentation. The accommodations requested must be supported through the documentation provided and must be logically linked to the current impact of the condition on academic functioning.

Allowed in exams
  Calculator: Yes
  Dictionary: Yes
  Computer: Yes
  Spellchecker: Yes
Extended test time: Yes
Scribes: Yes
Proctors: Yes
Oral exams: Yes
Note-takers: Yes

Distraction-reduced environment: Yes
Tape recording in class: Yes
Electronic texts: Yes
**Accommodations for students with
  ADHD:** Yes
Kurzweil Reader: Yes
Other assistive technology: Yes
Priority registration: Yes

Added costs for services: No
LD specialists: Yes
Professional tutors: No
Peer tutors: Yes
Max. hours/wk. for services: 3
**How professors are notified of
  LD/ADHD:** By student

GENERAL ADMISSIONS INFORMATION

Office of Admission: 480-965-7788

ENTRANCE REQUIREMENTS
Academic units required: 4 English, 4 math, 3 science (3 science labs), 2 foreign language, 1 social studies, 1 history, 1 fine arts. High school diploma is required, and GED is accepted. ACT without Writing component accepted. TOEFL required of all international applicants: minimum paper TOEFL 500, minimum computer TOEFL 173.

Application deadline: NR
Notification: Rolling
Average GPA: 3.30
ACT Composite middle 50% range:
  21–27

SAT Math middle 50% range:
  490–630
**SAT Critical Reading middle 50%
  range:** 480–610
SAT Writing middle 50% range: NR

Graduated top 10% of class: 28%
Graduated top 25% of class: 55%
Graduated top 50% of class: 83%

COLLEGE GRADUATION REQUIREMENTS

Course waivers allowed: N/A
In what course: N/A
Course substitutions allowed: N/A
In what course: N/A

ADDITIONAL INFORMATION

Environment: Arizona State University has 4 campuses that are located across the Metropolitan Valley.

Student Body
  Undergrad enrollment: 58,404
  Women: 52%
  Men: 48%
  Percent out-of-state: 30%

Cost Information
  In-state tuition: $9,208
  Out-of-state tuition: $21,807
  Room & board: $11,436
Housing Information
  University housing: Yes
Percent living on campus: 19%

Greek System
  Fraternity: Yes
  Sorority: Yes
Athletics: Division I

NORTHERN ARIZONA UNIVERSITY

PO Box 4084, Flagstaff, AZ 86011-4084
Phone: 928-523-5511 • Fax: 928-523-0226
E-mail: undergraduate.admissions@nau.edu • Web: www.nau.edu
Support: S • Institution type: 4-year public

PROGRAMS OR SERVICES FOR STUDENTS WITH LD

Disability Resources promotes educational opportunities for students with disabilities at Northern Arizona University. DSS assists students in their persistence to graduate by providing resources, services, and auxiliary aids so that they may realize their life goals. The goal of Disability Resources is to assist students in achieving their academic goals while at the same time creating an environment conducive to learning and building students' self-esteem. The belief is that by receiving supportive assistance, the student will become an independent learner and self-advocate.

ADMISSION INFORMATION FOR STUDENTS WITH LD/ADHD

College entrance tests required: Yes
Interview required: No
Essay recommended: No
What documentation required for LD: Psycho Ed evaluation to include: relevant historical info, instructional interventions, related services, age diagnosed, objective data (aptitude, achievement, info processing), test scores (standard, percentile and grade equivalents) and describe functional limitations.
With general application: No
To receive services after enrolling: Yes
What documentation required for ADHD: Diagnosis based on DSM-V; history of behaviors impairing functioning in academic setting; diagnostic interview; history of symptoms; evidence of ongoing behaviors.

With general application: No
Submitted to: Disability Resources
Special Ed. HS course work accepted: Yes
Specific course requirements for all applicants: Yes
Separate application required: No
# of LD applications submitted each year: NR
# of LD applications accepted yearly: NR
Total # of students receiving LD services: 117
Acceptance into program means acceptance into college: Students must be admitted and enrolled in the university first and then request services.

ADMISSIONS

There are no special admissions criteria for students with learning disabilities. General admission requirements for unconditional admission include: 4 years of English, 4 years of math; 2 years of social science with 1 year being American history; 2–3 years of science lab with additional requirements; 1 year of fine arts; and 2 years of a foreign language. (Students may be admitted conditionally with course deficiencies, but not in both math and science). In-state residents should have a 2.5 GPA, be in the top 50 percent of their high school class (a 3.0 GPA or being in the upper 25 percent of their graduating class is required for non-residents), or earn an SAT combined score of 930 (1010 for non-residents) or an ACT score of 22 (24 for non-residents). Conditional admissions is possible with a 2.5–2.99 GPA or being in the top 50 percent of their graduating class and strong ACT/SAT scores. Exceptional admission may be offered to 10 percent of the new freshmen applicants or transfer applicants. The Writing section of the ACT is not required.

ADDITIONAL INFORMATION

Skills classes are available in note-taking, study techniques, reading, memory and learning, overcoming math anxiety, speed reading, time management, test-taking strategies. The university offers the following courses: How to Make Math Easy, How to Get Started Writing, How to Edit Writing, and How to Prepare for Final Exams. All services and accommodations are available for undergraduate and graduate students.

LEARNING DISABILITY PROGRAMS OR SERVICES

Contact Information
Name of program or department: Disability Resources
  Telephone: 928-523-8773
  Fax: 928-523-8747

LEARNING DISABILITY SERVICES

Accommodations are decided upon an individual basis after a thorough review of appropriate, current documentation. The accommodations requested must be supported through the documentation provided and must be logically linked to the current impact of the condition on academic functioning.

Allowed in exams	**Distraction-reduced environment:** Yes	**Added costs for services:** No
Calculator: Yes	**Tape recording in class:** Yes	**LD specialists:** No
Dictionary: Yes	**Electronic texts:** Yes	**Professional tutors:** No
Computer: Yes	**Accommodations for students with**	**Peer tutors:** 100
Spellchecker: Yes	**ADHD:** Yes	**Max. hours/wk. for services:**
Extended test time: Yes	**Kurzweil Reader:** Yes	Unlimited
Scribes: Yes	**Other assistive technology:** Yes	**How professors are notified of**
Proctors: Yes	**Priority registration:** Yes	**LD/ADHD:** By student
Oral exams: Yes		
Note-takers: Yes		

GENERAL ADMISSIONS INFORMATION

Office of Admission: 928-523-6053

ENTRANCE REQUIREMENTS

Academic units required: 4 English, 4 math, 3 science (1 science lab), 2 foreign language, 2 social studies, 1 history, 1 fine arts. High school diploma is required, and GED is accepted. TOEFL required of all international applicants: minimum paper TOEFL 525, minimum computer TOEFL 195.

Application deadline: None	**SAT Math middle 50% range:**	**Graduated top 10% of class:** 19%
Notification: Rolling	480–590	**Graduated top 25% of class:** 48%
Average GPA: 3.40	**SAT Critical Reading middle 50%**	**Graduated top 50% of class:** 82%
ACT Composite middle 50% range:	**range:** 470–590	
20–25	**SAT Writing middle 50% range:**	
	460–570	

COLLEGE GRADUATION REQUIREMENTS

Course waivers allowed: No
Course substitutions allowed: Yes
In what course: There is a math substitution (not waiver) program for individuals with a math learning disability. It only applies to the liberal studies math requirement.

ADDITIONAL INFORMATION

Environment: The university is located on 320 acres in an urban area 2 hours from Phoenix.

Student Body	Cost Information	Greek System
Undergrad enrollment: 20,750	**In-state tuition:** $8,800	**Fraternity:** Yes
Women: 58%	**Out-of-state tuition:** $21,000	**Sorority:** Yes
Men: 42%	**Room & board:** $8,474	**Athletics:** Division I
Percent out-of-state: 24%	**Housing Information**	
	University housing: Yes	
	Percent living on campus: 32%	

UNIVERSITY OF ARIZONA

PO Box 210040, Tucson, AZ 85721-0040
Phone: 520-621-3237 • Fax: 520-621-9799
E-mail: appinfo@arizona.edu • Web: www.arizona.edu
Support: SP • Institution type: 4-year public

PROGRAMS OR SERVICES FOR STUDENTS WITH LD

The SALT Center (Strategic Alternative Learning Techniques) is a fee-based academic support program that provides a comprehensive range of enhanced services to University of Arizona students who have learning and/or attention challenges. The SALT Center's innovative approach is recognized nationwide as one of the most successful for empowering students in the university setting. The range of services in the SALT Center facilitates student learning, self-advocacy, and independence. Students take ownership of their education through working with a Strategic Learning Specialist to create an Individualized Learning Plan; engaging in strategies for time management, organization, reading and writing; utilizing tutoring by peer tutors who are internationally certified by the College Reading and Learning Association; and accessing assistive technology in the SALT Center's technology lab.

ADMISSION INFORMATION FOR STUDENTS WITH LD/ADHD

College entrance tests required: Yes
Interview required: No
Essay recommended: Yes
What documentation required for LD: Psycho Ed evaluation to include: relevant historical info, instructional interventions, related services, age diagnosed, objective data (aptitude, achievement, info processing), test scores (standard, percentile and grade equivalents) and describe functional limitations.
With general application: Yes if requested as part of Structured Program application
To receive services after enrolling: Yes
What documentation required for ADHD: Diagnosis based on DSM-V; history of behaviors impairing functioning in academic setting; diagnostic interview; history of symptoms; evidence of ongoing behaviors.

With general application: Yes if requested as part of Structured Program application
To receive services after enrolling: Yes
Submitted to: NR
Special Ed. HS course work accepted: NR
Separate application required: NR
# of LD applications submitted each year: NR
# of LD applications accepted yearly: NR
Total # of students receiving LD services: NR
Acceptance into program means acceptance into college: NR

ADMISSIONS

Students must submit a general application to the University and a SALT application. Students may check the box on the general application indicating they are interested in SALT. Students are admitted to the University and then reviewed by SALT. General admission criteria include: 4 English, 4 math, 3 science, 2 social studies, 2 foreign language, 1 fine art. Deficiencies can be made up in English with ACT sub score of 21, Math ACT sub score 24 and science ACT sub score 20. Most applicants are admissible with required courses and either 24 ACT (22 ACT resident) or SAT 1110) SAT 1040 resident) or top ¼ of the class. SALT application should be submitted early in the process. All SALT applicants should answer 3 essay questions 1) Why are you applying to SALT and how do you plan to use the services 2) Describe a difficult situation you have encountered in your life, and tell how you handled the situation 3) Tell about your strengths, skills and talents. Students can submit documentation of a disability to Admissions and to SALT or answer SALT question #4 which asks for a description of academic challenges and the support services used to manage those challenges.

ADDITIONAL INFORMATION

SALT provides Strategic Learning Specialists who help students create an Individualized Learning Plan and meet with students weekly. Students have access to tutoring services with one-to –one tutoring. They also have a computer resource lab with Kurzweil 3000, Inspiration and Dagon Naturally Speaking. Workshops are offered in reading, writing, organization, tie management, test prep and test taking strategies. There is a special orientation for SALT students before freshman year. The fee for SALT is $2450 per semester. All accommodations and services (such as testing accommodations, note taker, scribe) for students with documented disabilities are provided through the Disability Resource Center (no fee).

LEARNING DISABILITY PROGRAMS OR SERVICES

Contact Information
Name of program or department: SALT Center (Strategic Alternative Learning Techniques)
   Telephone: 520-621-8493
   Fax: 520-626-3260

LEARNING DISABILITY SERVICES

Accommodations are decided upon an individual basis after a thorough review of appropriate, current documentation. The accommodations requested must be supported through the documentation provided and must be logically linked to the current impact of the condition on academic functioning.

Allowed in exams	Distraction-reduced environment: NR	Added costs for services: $2,450 per
Calculator: NR	Tape recording in class: NR	semester
Dictionary: NR	Electronic texts: NR	LD specialists: NR
Computer: NR	Accommodations for students with	Professional tutors: NR
Spellchecker: NR	ADHD: NR	Peer tutors: NR
Extended test time: NR	Kurzweil Reader: NR	Max. hours/wk. for services: NR
Scribes: NR	Other assistive technology: NR	How professors are notified of
Proctors: NR	Priority registration: NR	LD/ADHD: NR
Oral exams: NR		
Note-takers: NR		

GENERAL ADMISSIONS INFORMATION

Office of Admission: 520-621-3237

ENTRANCE REQUIREMENTS

Academic units required: 4 years English, 4 years math, 3 years lab science, 2 years of the same second language, 2 years of social studies (1 year American history), 1 year fine arts. High school diploma is required, and GED is accepted.

Application deadline: 5/1	**SAT Math middle 50% range:** NR	**Graduated top 10% of class:** 34%
Notification: Rolling	**SAT Critical Reading middle 50%**	**Graduated top 25% of class:** 62%
Average GPA: 3.39	**range:** NR	**Graduated top 50% of class:** 87%
ACT Composite middle 50% range:	**SAT Writing middle 50% range:** NR	
NR		

COLLEGE GRADUATION REQUIREMENTS

Course waivers allowed: No
Course substitutions allowed: Yes
In what course: Course substitutions are typically in math or second language; approval must come from college/major department.

ADDITIONAL INFORMATION

Environment: Situated in downtown Tucson on 325 acres, the university is surrounded by the Santa Catalina Mountain range in the Sonora Desert.

Student Body	Cost Information	Greek System
Undergrad enrollment: 30,665	In-state tuition: $9,286	Fraternity: Yes
Women: 52%	Out-of-state tuition: $25,494	Sorority: Yes
Men: 48%	Room & board: $8,540	Athletics: Division I
Percent out-of-state: 32%	Housing Information	
	University housing: Yes	
	Percent living on campus: 22%	

U. OF ARKANSAS—FAYETTEVILLE

232 Silas Hunt Hall, Fayetteville, AR 72701
Phone: 479-575-5346 • Fax: 479-575-7515
E-mail: uofa@uark.edu • Web: www.uark.edu
Support: S • Institution type: 4-year public

PROGRAMS OR SERVICES FOR STUDENTS WITH LD

The Center for Educational Access (CEA) is the office responsible for facilitating campus access and accommodations for students with disabilities. The philosophy of the CEA is to provide an environment in which students are encouraged to develop independence, the ability to self-advocate, and knowledge of resources that will enable them to take advantage of opportunities available in the modern world. The Enhanced Learning Center offers tutoring services to all University of Arkansas students free of charge. Supplemental Instruction (SI) is an academic enrichment program that increases student performance and retention. SI offers enrolled students regularly scheduled, out-of-class review sessions in historically difficult courses. Sessions are led by experienced students who excel in the difficult subject matter. SI is free to all UA students.

ADMISSION INFORMATION FOR STUDENTS WITH LD/ADHD

College entrance tests required: Yes
Interview required: No
Essay recommended: No
What documentation required for LD: Psycho Ed evaluation to include: relevant historical info, instructional interventions, related services, age diagnosed, objective data (aptitude, achievement, info processing), test scores (standard, percentile and grade equivalents) and describe functional limitations.
With general application: No
To receive services after enrolling: Yes
What documentation required for ADHD: Diagnosis based on DSM-V; history of behaviors impairing functioning in academic setting; diagnostic interview; history of symptoms; evidence of ongoing behaviors.

With general application: No
Submitted to: Center for Educational Access
Specific course requirements of all applicants: Yes
Separate application required: No
# of LD applications submitted each year: NR
# of LD applications accepted yearly: NR
Total # of students receiving LD services: NR
Acceptance into program means acceptance into college: Students must be admitted and enrolled prior to requesting services.

ADMISSIONS

Guaranteed general admission to the University of Arkansas requires a minimum GPA of 3.0 and an ACT score of 20 (or SAT of 930). Students who do not meet qualifications may be admitted on the basis of individual review of their application portfolios. Course requirements include: 4 years of English, 4 years of math, 3 years of social studies, 3 years of science, and 2 electives to be chosen from English, foreign languages, oral communication, mathematics, computer science, natural sciences, and social studies.

ADDITIONAL INFORMATION

The University of Arkansas is committed to ensuring student success through a powerful convergence of programs and services. While at the university, we help students meet their challenges confidently. SSS has a friendly, resourceful, and helpful staff committed to helping students succeed.

LEARNING DISABILITY PROGRAM/SERVICES

Contact Information
Name of program or department: Center for Educational Access
 Telephone: 479-575-3104
 Fax: 479-575-7445

LEARNING DISABILITY SERVICES

Accommodations are decided upon an individual basis after a thorough review of appropriate, current documentation. The accommodations requested must be supported through the documentation provided and must be logically linked to the current impact of the condition on academic functioning.

Allowed in exams
 Calculator: Yes
 Dictionary: Yes
 Computer: Yes
 Spellchecker: Yes
Extended test time: Yes
Scribes: Yes
Proctors: Yes
Oral exams: No
Notetakers: Yes

Distraction-reduced environment: Yes
Tape recording in class: Yes
Electronic texts: Yes
Accommodations for students with
 ADHD: Yes
Kurzweil Reader: Yes
Other assistive technology: Yes
Priority registration: Yes

Added costs for services: No
LD specialists: No
Professional tutors: No
Peer tutors: Yes
Max. hours/wk. for services: N/A
How professors are notified of
 LD/ADHD: Student

GENERAL ADMISSIONS INFORMATION

Office of Admission: 479-575-53

ENTRANCE REQUIREMENTS

Academic units required: 4 English, 4 math, 3 science (2 science labs), 3 social studies, 2 academic electives. Academic units recomended: 2 foreign language. High school diploma is required, and GED is accepted. ACT with or without Writing component accepted. TOEFL required of all international applicants: minimum paper TOEFL 550, minimum computer TOEFL 213.

Application deadline: 8/15
Notification: Rolling
Average GPA: 3.56
ACT Composite middle 50% range:
 23–28

SAT Math middle 50% range:
 520–630
SAT Critical Reading middle 50% range: 500–610
SAT Writing middle 50% range:
 NR

Graduated top 10% of class: 31%
Graduated top 25% of class: 58%
Graduated top 50% of class: 87%

COLLEGE GRADUATION REQUIREMENTS

Course waivers allowed: N/A
Course substitutions allowed: N/A

ADDITIONAL INFORMATION

Environment: Urban area about 200 miles northwest of Little Rock.

Student Body
 Undergrad enrollment: 19,027
 Women: 49%
 Men: 51%
 Percent out-of-state: 33%

Cost Information
 In-state tuition: $7,175
 Out-of-state tuition: $17,600
 Room & board: $8,200
Housing Information
 University housing: Yes
 Percent living on campus: 33%

Greek System
 Fraternity: Yes
 Sorority: Yes
Athletics: Division I

UNIVERSITY OF THE OZARKS

415 N College Avenue, Clarksville, AR 72830
Phone: 800-264-8636 • Fax: 479-979-1417
E-mail: admiss@ozarks.edu • Web: www.ozarks.edu
Support: SP • Institution: 4-year private

PROGRAMS OR SERVICES FOR STUDENTS WITH LD

The Jones Learning Center believes that students with specific learning disabilities are entitled to services that allow them to successfully compete with other students. The Learning Center program emphasizes a total and interactive learning environment, enabling bright college students to pursue challenging course work in a uniquely supportive environment. Enhanced services include individualized programming; a technology unit; centralized accessibility; and a supportive atmosphere with a 4:1 student to-staff ratio, which provides students even greater opportunity to realize their true academic potential. This program is very comprehensive in every area. At the beginning of each semester the course load and needs of the student are assessed to determine what services will be needed. Jones Learning Center comprehensive services are provided for an additional fee.

ADMISSION INFORMATION FOR STUDENTS WITH LD/ADHD

College entrance tests required: Yes
Interview required: Yes
Essay required: No
What documentation required for LD: Psycho Ed evaluation to include: relevant historical info, instructional interventions, related services, age diagnosed, objective data (aptitude, achievement, info processing), test scores (standard, percentile and grade equivalents) and describe functional limitations.
With general application: Yes if requested as part of Structured Program application
To receive services after enrolling: Yes
What documentation required for ADHD: Diagnosis based on DSM-V; history of behaviors impairing functioning in academic setting; diagnostic interview; history of symptoms; evidence of ongoing behaviors.

With general application: Yes if requested as part of Structured Program application
To receive services after enrolling: Yes
Submitted to: Support Program/Services
Special Ed. HS course work accepted: Yes
Specific course requirements for all applicants: No
Separate application required for program services: Yes
# of LD applications submitted each year: 150–250
# of LD applications accepted yearly: 25–30
Total # of students receiving LD services: 55–70
Acceptance into program means acceptance into college: Separate application is part of admissions process

ADMISSIONS

Students complete a special application. Applicants must be 18 or older; complete high school or obtain a GED; demonstrate average or above-average I.Q.; have a learning disability or Attention Deficit Disorder as a primary disability; provide diagnostic information from previous evaluations; complete the admissions packet and visit campus. If the psychoeducational evaluation is not current, applicants may choose to update the documentation during a two-day campus visit. The this evaluation is offered for an additional fee. Applicants with some areas of concern for the admissions committee may be admitted on a one-year trial basis. This conditional admission is only available to students applying to the Jones Learning Center. There are no specific high school courses and no minimum ACT/SAT score value or grade point average required for admission. Motivation is a key factor in the admission decision. Students are encouraged to begin application to the Jones Learning Center during the spring semester of their junior year or early in the senior year. The JLC has a rolling admission policy. Once students are admitted into the JLC they are automatically admitted to the university.

ADDITIONAL INFORMATION

Students are assigned to a program coordinator who meets daily with the student and assists in the individualized planning of the students' program of study, acts as an advocate, and monitors the students' progress. Students receive help in understanding their learning styles, utilizing their strengths, circumventing deficits and building skills, and becoming independent learners and self-advocates. Skills classes are offered in study skills/writing (for credit), and math (for credit). Enhanced services include testing accommodations; one-to-one administration of a test with a reader and staff to take dictation, if needed; assistive technology available throughout the building; peer tutoring; and note-takers. Developmental services include opportunities to improve basic skills in writing and math. Students with ADD and/or LD may receive services from the Learning Center. In an effort to better serve students who are diagnosed with Autism Spectrum Disorder, the Jones Learning Center (JLC) will pilot an additional premium residential program, the Living and Learning Community (LLC), beginning in Fall 2012.

PROGRAM FOR DISABILITY SERVICES

Contact Information
Name of program or department: Student Support Services/Jones Learning Center
  Telephone: 479-979-1403
  Fax: 479-979-1429

LEARNING DISABILITY SERVICES

Accommodations are decided upon an individual basis after a thorough review of appropriate, current documentation. The accommodations requested must be supported through the documentation provided and must be logically linked to the current impact of the condition on academic functioning.

Allowed in exams	**Distraction-reduced environment:** Yes	**Added costs for services:** Yes
Calculator: Yes	**Tape recording in class:** Yes	**LD specialists:** Yes
Dictionary: No	**Electronic texts:** Yes	**Professional tutors:** 15
Computer: Yes	**Accommodations for students with**	**Peer tutors:** 100–125
Spellchecker: Yes	**ADHD:** Yes	**Max. hours/wk. for services:**
Extended test time: Yes	**Kurzweil Reader:** Yes	Unlimited
Scribes: Yes	**Other assistive technology:** The	**How professors are notified of**
Proctors: Yes	Kurzweil Reader and Dragon Naturally	**LD/ADHD:** Both student and director
Oral exams: Yes	Speaking have been installed on the	
Note-takers: Yes	majority of computers in the building.	
	Priority registration: Yes	

GENERAL ADMISSIONS INFORMATION

Office of Admission: 800-264-8636

ENTRANCE REQUIREMENTS

Academic units recommended: 4 English, 4 mathematics, 3 science, (2 science labs), 2 foreign language, 1 social studies, 2 history. High school diploma is required and GED is accepted. SAT or ACT required; TOEFL required of all international applicants; minimum paper TOEFL 500, minimum computer TOEFL 173.

Application deadline: None	**SAT Math middle 50% range:**	**Graduated top 10% of class:** 19%
Notification: Rolling	443–560	**Graduated top 25% of class:** 37%
Average GPA: 3.39	**SAT Critical Reading middle 50%**	**Graduated top 50% of class:** 77%
ACT Composite middle 50% range:	**range:** 450–570	
19–25	**SAT Writing middle 50% range:** NR	

COLLEGE GRADUATION REQUIREMENTS

Course waivers allowed: No
Course substitutions allowed: Yes
In what course: College algebra and foreign language

ADDITIONAL INFORMATION

Environment: The university is located on 56 acres, 100 miles northwest of Little Rock. Clarksville is a town of 7,500 residents in the Arkansas River Valley.

Student Body	**Cost Information**	**Greek System**
Undergrad enrollment: 623	**Tuition:** $22,650	**Fraternity:** No
Women: 52%	**Room and board:** $7,000	**Sorority:** No
Men: 48%	**Housing Information**	**Athletics:** Division III
Percent out-of-state: 32%	**University housing:** Yes	
	Percent living on campus: 71%	

CALIFORNIA POLYTECHNIC STATE UNIVERSITY—SAN LUIS OBISPO

Admissions Office, Cal Poly, San Luis Obispo, CA 93407-0031
Phone: 805-756-2311 • Fax: 805-756-5400
E-mail: admissions@calpoly.edu • Web: www.calpoly.edu
Support: CS • Institution: 4-year public

PROGRAMS OR SERVICES FOR STUDENTS WITH LD

The goal of the program is to ensure students with learning disabilities have equal access and opportunity. The Disability Resource Center (DRC) assists students with disabilities in achieving access to higher education, promotes personal and educational success, and increases the awareness and responsiveness of the campus community. DRC is actively involved with students and faculty to keep the University population aware of who it is and what it does. Incoming students are encouraged to meet with college advisors, in conjunction with DRC staff, to receive assistance in the planning of class schedules. This allows for the selection of appropriate classes to fit particular needs and personal goals. It is the responsibility of each student seeking accommodations and services to provide a written, comprehensive psychological and/or medical evaluation verifying the diagnosis. The Cal Poly Student Learning Outcomes model promotes student personal growth and the development of self-advocacy for full inclusion of qualified stuedents with verified disabilities. The promotion of student self-reliance and responsibility are necessary adjuncts to educational development. For learning disabilities the assessments must be done by a licensed educational psychologist, psychologist, neurologist, or LD specialist.

ADMISSION INFORMATION FOR STUDENTS WITH LD/ADHD

College entrance tests required: Yes
Interview required: No
Essay required: N/A
What documentation required for LD: Psycho Ed evaluation
to include: relevant historical info, instructional interventions, related services, age diagnosed, objective data (aptitude, achievement, info processing), test scores (standard, percentile and grade equivalents) and describe functional limitations.
With general application: No
To receive services after enrolling: Yes
What documentation required for ADHD: Diagnosis based on DSM-V; history of behaviors impairing functioning in academic setting; diagnostic interview; history of symptoms; evidence of ongoing behaviors.

With general application: No
Submitted to: Support Program/Services
Special Ed. HS course work accepted: Yes
Specific course requirements for all applicants: Yes
Separate application required for program services: N/A
# of LD applications submitted each year: 60–70
# of LD applications accepted yearly: 50–70
Total # of students receiving LD services: 150–200
Acceptance into program means acceptance into college: Separate application required after student has been admitted.

ADMISSIONS
Students with LD must meet the same admission criteria as all applicants, and should submit a general admission application to the Admissions Office. General requirements include: four years English, three years math, one year U.S. history or government, one year lab science, two years foreign language, one year fine arts, and three years electives. On a case-by-case basis, foreign language substitutions may be allowed. All documentation should be sent directly to the Disability Resource Center, and students who self-disclose will receive information. Admission decisions are made by the Admissions Office.

ADDITIONAL INFORMATION
Incoming students are strongly urged to contact the DRC if disability related assistance is required. Academic accommodations are designed to meet a student's disabiity-related needs without fundamentally altering the nature of the instructional program, and are not intended to provide remediation. Supportive services may include: alternative format materials, assistive listening devices, note-taking, audio textbooks, test accommodations, and writing assistance. DRC may recommend the services of the Academic Skills Center of Student Academic Services and enrollment in English and math classes offering additional support. Students requesting accommodations, which include using a computer, dictionary, or spellchecker during an exam, will have a discussion with the instructor to ensure that the accommodation doesn't fundementally alter the exam. The unviersity cannot provide psychoeducational assessment services. Services and accommodations are available to undergraduate and graduate students.

PROGRAM FOR DISABILITY SERVICES

Contact Information
Name of program or department: Disability Resource Center(DRC)
Telephone: 805-756-1395
Fax: 805-756-5451

LEARNING DISABILITY SERVICES

Accommodations are decided upon an individual basis after a thorough review of appropriate, current documentation. The accommodations requested must be supported through the documentation provided and must be logically linked to the current impact of the condition on academic functioning.

Allowed in exams
Calculator: Maybe
Dictionary: Maybe
Computer: Maybe
Spellchecker: Maybe
Extended test time: Yes
Scribes: Yes
Proctors: Yes
Oral exams: Rarely
Note-takers: Yes

Distraction-reduced environment: Yes
Tape recording in class: Yes
Electronic texts: Yes
Accommodations for students with ADHD: Yes
Kurzweil Reader: Yes
Other assistive technology: Adaptive computer technology (Kurzweil, JAWS, Dragon), Read & Write Gold, smart pens
Priority registration: Sometimes

Added costs for services: No
LD specialists: No
Professional tutors: 0
Peer tutors: NR
Max. hours/wk. for services: NR
How professors are notified of LD/ADHD: Student

GENERAL ADMISSIONS INFORMATION

Office of Admission: 805-756-2311

ENTRANCE REQUIREMENTS
Academic units required: 4 English, 3 mathematics, 3 science, (1 science labs), 2 foreign language, 2 social studies, 1 history, 1 visual/performing arts, 1 academic electives. **Academic units recommended:** 5 English, 4 mathematics, 4 science, (2 science labs), 3 foreign language, 2 social studies, 1 history, 1 visual/performing arts. High school diploma is required and GED is accepted. SAT or ACT required; TOEFL required of all international applicants; minimum paper TOEFL 550, minimum computer TOEFL 213, minimum web-based TOEFL 80.

Application deadline: 11/30
Notification: 4/1
Average GPA: 3.84
ACT Composite middle 50% range: 25–29

SAT Math middle 50% range: 580–690
SAT Critical Reading middle 50% range: 540–640
SAT Writing middle 50% range: NR

Graduated top 10% of class: 46%
Graduated top 25% of class: 83%
Graduated top 50% of class: 98%

COLLEGE GRADUATION REQUIREMENTS

Course waivers allowed: No
Course substitutions allowed: Yes
In what course: On a case-by-case basis, individuals may be granted course substitutions (not waivers) in quantitative reasoning (in very limited non-math related majors) by the VP of Academic Affairs and foreign language substitutions with department approval.

ADDITIONAL INFORMATION

Environment: The campus is located 100 miles north of Santa Barbara.

Student Body
Undergrad enrollment: 17,725
Women: 44%
Men: 56%
Percent out-of-state: 8%

Cost Information
In-state tuition: $7,920
Out-of-state tuition: $19,000
Room and board: $10,444
Housing Information
University housing: Yes
Percent living on campus: 38%

Greek System
Fraternity: Yes
Sorority: Yes
Athletics: Division I

CALIFORNIA STATE POLYTECHNIC UNIVERSITY—POMONA

3801 West Temple Avenue, Pomona, CA 91768
Phone: 909-869-3210 • Fax: 909-869-4529
E-mail: admissions@csupomona.edu • Web: www.csupomona.edu
Support: CS • Institution: 4-year public

PROGRAMS OR SERVICES FOR STUDENTS WITH LD

The Disability Resource Center (DRC) in collaboration with the campus community advocates for the equal access and opportunity for individuals with disabilities to be enfranchised in all aspects of university life by supporting personal, academic, and career development. DRC furthers seeks to empower students to fulfill their potential through self-determination, life-long learning, and growth. The DRC's primary aim is to create an equitable learning and testing environment by way of identifying reasonable academic accommodations without altering the fundamental requirements of university programs and courses.

ADMISSION INFORMATION FOR STUDENTS WITH LD/ADHD

College entrance tests required: Yes
Interview required: No
Essay required: N/A
What documentation required for LD: Report with scores for aptitude and achievement testing. Visit Documentation Standards for LD at:
www.dsa.csupomona.edu/drc/forms.asp
What documentation required for ADHD: Diagnostic information and historical data should be summarized in a report. Visit Documentation Standards for ADD at:
www.dsa.csupomona.edu/drc/forms.asp

Submitted to: Support Program/Services
Special Ed. HS course work accepted: No
Specific course requirements for all applicants: Yes
Separate application required for program services: No
# of LD applications submitted each year: NR
# of LD applications accepted yearly: NR
Total # of students receiving LD services: 173
Acceptance into program means acceptance into college: No

ADMISSIONS

Students must meet the university's regular entrance requirements, including C or better in the subject requirements of 4 years of English, 3 years of math, 1 year of U.S. history, 2 years of science lab, 2 years of a foreign language, 1 year of visual or performing arts, and 3 years of academic electives and a qualifiable eligibility index based on high school GPA and scores on either ACT or SAT. Special admits are very limited. Applicants with LD are encouraged to complete college-prep courses. However, if students are unable to fulfill a specific course requirement because of a learning disability, alternative college-prep courses may be substituted. Substitutions may be granted in foreign language, science lab, and math. Substitutions may be authorized on an individual basis after review and recommendation by applicant's guidance counselor in consultation with the Director of DSS. Course substitutions could limit access to some majors. Students are encouraged to self-disclose a learning disability if it would help to explain lower grades. Students who self-disclose are reviewed by DSS, which provides a recommendation to admissions.

ADDITIONAL INFORMATION

Support services include counseling, advocacy services, registration, note-takers, readers, tutors, testing accommodations, and specialized equipment. Skills classes are not offered through DSS, but are available in other departments in the areas of reading skills, test preparation, test-taking strategies, and study skills. Services and accommodations are available to undergraduate and graduate students. Cal Poly offers a summer program for any high school student.

PROGRAM FOR DISABILITY SERVICES

Contact Information
Name of program or department: Disability Resource Center (DRC)
Telephone: 909-869-3333
Fax: 909-869-3271

LEARNING DISABILITY SERVICES

Accommodations are decided upon an individual basis after a thorough review of appropriate, current documentation. The accommodations requested must be supported through the documentation provided and must be logically linked to the current impact of the condition on academic functioning.

Allowed in exams
 Calculator: Yes
 Dictionary: Yes
 Computer: Yes
 Spellchecker: Yes
Extended test time: Yes
Scribes: Yes
Proctors: Yes
Oral exams: Yes
Note-takers: Yes

Distraction-reduced environment: Yes
Tape recording in class: Yes
Electronic texts: Yes
Accommodations for students with
 ADHD: Yes
Kurzweil Reader: Yes
Other assistive technology: We have an excellent assistive technology lab that will help students learn and use adaptive technology.
Priority registration: Yes

Added costs for services: No
LD specialists: Yes
Professional tutors: 0
Peer tutors: 10–15
Max. hours/wk. for services: 2 per course
How professors are notified of LD/ADHD: Student

GENERAL ADMISSIONS INFORMATION

Office of Admission: 909-869-3258

ENTRANCE REQUIREMENTS

Academic units required: 4 English, 3 mathematics, 2 science, (2 science labs), 2 foreign language, 1 social studies, 1 history, 1 visual/performing arts, 1 academic electives. **Academic units recommended:** 4 mathematics. High school diploma is required and GED is accepted. SAT or ACT required; TOEFL required of all international applicants; minimum paper TOEFL 525, minimum computer TOEFL 195.

Application deadline: 11/30
Notification: Rolling
Average GPA: 3.32
ACT Composite middle 50% range: 19–25

SAT Math middle 50% range: 480–620
SAT Critical Reading middle 50% range: 450–560
SAT Writing middle 50% range: NR

Graduated top 10% of class: NR
Graduated top 25% of class: NR
Graduated top 50% of class: NR

COLLEGE GRADUATION REQUIREMENTS

Course waivers allowed: No
Course substitutions allowed: Yes
In what course: On a case-by-case basis, individuals may be granted course substitutions (not waivers) in quantitative reasoning (in very limited non-math related majors) and foreign language substitutions by the AVP of Academic Affairs.

ADDITIONAL INFORMATION

Environment: The university is located on 1,437 acres in a suburban area 30 miles east of Los Angeles.

Student Body
 Undergrad enrollment: 19,399
 Women: 43%
 Men: 57%
 Percent out-of-state: 1%

Cost Information
 In-state tuition: $5,513
 Out-of-state tuition $16,700
 Room and board: $12,500
Housing Information
 University housing: Yes
 Percent living on campus: 13%

Greek System
 Fraternity: Yes
 Sorority: Yes
 Athletics: Division II

CALIFORNIA STATE U.—FULLERTON

800 North State College Boulevard, Fullerton, CA 92834-6900
Phone: 657-773-2370 • Fax: 657-278-2356
E-mail: admissions@fullerton.edu • Web: www.fullerton.edu
Support: CS • Institution type: 4-year public

PROGRAMS OR SERVICES FOR STUDENTS WITH LD

The Student Support Services Program is a wide network of support services that help ensure academic and personal success in college. The program is designed to increase retention and graduation rates for underrepresented students. Students are encouraged to fulfill their academic and career potential by participating in an exceptional support environment. Each participant is teamed with an academic counselor for one-on-one mentoring and advisement. The emphasis is on providing students with personal attention and access to support services that include academic advisement; tutoring (referrals for individual and group tutoring including review sessions in select courses and development of study group); co-curricular events; peer mentoring for first-time freshmen; workshops and study-skills courses in reading, writing, math and other subjects, as well as time management; counseling; and an introduction to campus resources.

ADMISSION INFORMATION FOR STUDENTS WITH LD/ADHD

College entrance tests required: Yes
Interview required: No
Essay recommended: No
What documentation required for LD: Psycho Ed evaluation to include: relevant historical info, instructional interventions, related services, age diagnosed, objective data (aptitude, achievement, info processing), test scores (standard, percentile and grade equivalents) and describe functional limitations.
With general application: No
To receive services after enrolling: Yes
What documentation required for ADHD: Diagnosis based on DSM-V; history of behaviors impairing functioning in academic setting; diagnostic interview; history of symptoms; evidence of ongoing behaviors.

With general application: No
Submitted to: Disabled Student Services
Special Ed. HS course work accepted: No
Specific course requirements of all applicants: Yes
Separate application required: No
# of LD applications submitted each year: NR
# of LD applications accepted yearly: NR
Total # of students receiving LD services: NR
Acceptance into program means acceptance into college: Students must be admitted and enrolled prior to requesting services.

ADMISSIONS

Students are admitted on an eligibility index based on high school GPA in college-prep courses and scores on ACT or SAT. Lower GPA requires higher scores on the test. Other factors such as impaction and residency status are also considered. The foreign language requirement may be waived in rare cases when supported by the testing data supporting a relevant learning disability. ACT or SAT Reasoning Test required. All applicants must have 2 social science, 4 English, 3 math, 2 science (science with a lab, 1 biological and 1 physical), and 2 foreign language. The GPA is calculated based on the college-prep courses completed in grades 10, 11, and if available, 12. Students must have at least a C in these courses. Grades of D or less cannot be validated by a higher second semester grade in any of the following disciplines: social science/history, English, laboratory science, visual/performing arts, and electives. Students must have C or higher in all semesters of English, other lab sciences than chemistry, social sciences/history, and visual/performing arts to have the course counted toward the required preparatory units. Applicants within the local area will be required to meet the minimum eligibility requirement of 2900 based on GPA and SAT result or a 694 based on GPA and ACT result. Students outside of the local area should not anticipate receiving an admissions decision until late January or February.

ADDITIONAL INFORMATION

The Intensive Learning Experience (ILE) program is designed to monitor the progress of any students fulfilling remedial compliance requirements and help students make successful progress in fulfilling the graduation requirements. ILE staff helps students on class planning, study skills, transfer work, campus resources, time management, and campus organizations. If not exempt from the English Placement Test (EPT) and Entry Level Mathematics (ELM), freshman must pass the EPT and/or ELM to move into the GE-level mathematics and English courses. If students do not pass they must take a developmental English and/or math course to fulfill the remedial compliance requirements. ILE provides students with an accommodation letter for professors each semester.

LEARNING DISABILITY PROGRAMS OR SERVICES

Contact Information
Name of program or department: Student Support Services
  Telephone: 657-278-3112
  Fax: 657-278-2408

LEARNING DISABILITY SERVICES

Accommodations are decided upon an individual basis after a thorough review of appropriate, current documentation. The accommodations requested must be supported through the documentation provided and must be logically linked to the current impact of the condition on academic functioning.

Allowed in exams	**Distraction-reduced environment:** Yes	**Added costs for services:** No
Calculator: Yes	**Tape recording in class:** Yes	**LD specialists:** Yes
Dictionary: Yes	**Electronic texts:** Yes	**Professional tutors:** No
Computer: Yes	**Accommodations for students with**	**Peer tutors:** No
Spellchecker: Yes	**ADHD:** Yes	**Max. hours/wk. for services:** Varies
Extended test time: Yes	**Kurzweil Reader:** Yes	**How professors are notified of**
Scribes: Yes	**Other assistive technology:** Yes	**LD/ADHD:** By student
Proctors: Yes	**Priority registration:** Yes	
Oral exams: Yes		
Note-takers: Yes		

GENERAL ADMISSIONS INFORMATION

Office of Admission: 657-773-2370

ENTRANCE REQUIREMENTS

Academic units required: 4 English, 3 math, 2 science (2 science labs), 2 foreign language, 2 history, 1 academic elective, 1 visual/performing arts. High school diploma is required, and GED is accepted. TOEFL required of all international applicants: minimum paper TOEFL 500, minimum computer TOEFL 173.

Application deadline: 11/30	**SAT Math middle 50% range:**	**Graduated top 10% of class:** 16%
Notification: Rolling	460–570	**Graduated top 25% of class:** 55%
Average GPA: 3.37	**SAT Critical Reading middle 50%**	**Graduated top 50% of class:** 92%
ACT Composite middle 50% range:	**range:** 450–550	
19–24	**SAT Writing middle 50% range:** NR	

COLLEGE GRADUATION REQUIREMENTS

Course waivers allowed: No
Course substitutions allowed: Yes
In what course: Those students with a documented severe math disbility may be allowed a substitution for the math general education requirement.

ADDITIONAL INFORMATION

Environment: The university is located 35 miles from Los Angeles.

Student Body	**Cost Information**	**Greek System**
Undergrad enrollment: 30,782	**In-state tuition:** $6,130	**Fraternity:** Yes
Women: 56%	**Out-of-state tuition:** $17,300	**Sorority:** Yes
Men: 44%	**Room & board:** $10,600	**Athletics:** Division I
Percent out-of-state: 1%	**Housing Information**	
	University housing: Yes	
	Percent living on campus: 7%	

CALIFORNIA STATE U.—LONG BEACH

1250 Bellflower Boulevard, Long Beach, CA 90840
Phone: 562-985-5471 • Fax: 562-985-4973
E-mail: eslb@csulb.edu • Web: www.csulb.com
Support: CS • Institution type: 4-year public

PROGRAMS OR SERVICES FOR STUDENTS WITH LD

The Office of Disabled Student Services (DSS) is a student support program within the Division of Student Services. Its mission is to assist students with disabilities as they secure their university degrees at California State University—Long Beach (CSULB). They provide services to over 1,300 students each semester. Over 3,000 students with disabilities have graduated from CSULB with support from the program. The program staff are committed to helping students with disabilities build a better future. To meet this goal, the Disabled Student Services program provides support services for in-classroom activities, career development resources, use of and training on adaptive computer equipment and access devices, disability related counseling, and academic advisement. If you have any questions, please contact the DSS office at 562-985-5401.

ADMISSION INFORMATION FOR STUDENTS WITH LD/ADHD

College entrance tests required: Yes
Interview required: No
Essay recommended: Yes
What documentation required for LD: Psycho Ed evaluation to include: relevant historical info, instructional interventions, related services, age diagnosed, objective data (aptitude, achievement, info processing), test scores (standard, percentile and grade equivalents) and describe functional limitations.
With general application: No
To receive services after enrolling: Yes
What documentation required for ADHD: Diagnosis based on DSM-V; history of behaviors impairing functioning in academic setting; diagnostic interview; history of symptoms; evidence of ongoing behaviors.

With general application: No
Submitted to: Both Admissions and Disabled Student Services
Special Ed. HS course work accepted: N/A
Specific course requirements of all applicants: Yes
Separate application required: Yes
# of LD applications submitted each year: 50–100
# of LD applications accepted yearly: 20–40
Total # of students receiving LD services: 300–400
Acceptance into program means acceptance into college: Students must be admitted and enrolled prior to requesting services.

ADMISSIONS

Freshmen applicants must have completed each of the courses in the comprehensive pattern of college-preparatory subject requirements with a grade of C or higher prior to high school graduation and must have a qualifiable index based on their high school GPA in approved college-preparatory courses taken in the 10th through 12th grades and test scores. There is a special admission process for California residents who may not meet the regular admission requirements due to a disability but who are otherwise qualified. These students may appeal for special consideration. The Stephen Benson Program (SBP) facilitates this process by providing additional information about the applicant's circumstances to admissions. SBP evaluates documentation of the learning disability, and decisions are made by the Admissions Office. A student wishing to be considered for special admission must apply through regular admission procedures. California residents should submit the following information to SBP: personal statement letter describing interest in attending, two letters of recommendation, transcripts (unofficial accepted), a copy of SAT or ACT or transcripts of 60 transferable units from a community college, verification of specific learning disability, photograph of applicant, and a completed Special Admission Information Form and checklist of these requirements.

ADDITIONAL INFORMATION

The Stephen Benson Program for Students with LD was created to serve the needs of CSULB students who have a diagnosed learning disability. SBP provides a support system to assist students in attaining academic goals. The program provides counseling for clarification of issues related to learning disabilities, makes recommendations for accommodations, and fosters self-advocacy in students. Students with documented disabilities are entitled to one hour of tutoring per class, per week. All of the tutoring is done through the Learning Assistance Center. Special testing accommodation for course-related examinations are arranged through the Support Services Program. These accommodations include readers, writers, monitors, extended time, and alternative testing locations. Additional support services could include note-taking, readers, and registration assistance if appropriate.

LEARNING DISABILITY PROGRAMS OR SERVICES

Contact Information
Name of program or department: Disabled Student Services
Telephone: 562-985-5401
Fax: 562-985-7183

LEARNING DISABILITY SERVICES

Accommodations are decided upon an individual basis after a thorough review of appropriate, current documentation. The accommodations requested must be supported through the documentation provided and must be logically linked to the current impact of the condition on academic functioning.

Allowed in exams	**Distraction-reduced environment:** Yes	**Added costs for services:** No
Calculator: Yes	**Tape recording in class:** Yes	**LD specialists:** Yes
Dictionary: Yes	**Electronic texts:** Yes	**Professional tutors:** No
Computer: Yes	**Accommodations for students with**	**Peer tutors:** 4–7
Spellchecker: Yes	**ADHD:** Yes	**Max. hours/wk. for services:** NR
Extended test time: Yes	**Kurzweil Reader:** Yes	**How professors are notified of**
Scribes: Yes	**Other assistive technology:** Yes	**LD/ADHD:** By student
Proctors: Yes	**Priority registration:** Yes	
Oral exams: Yes		
Note-takers: Yes		

GENERAL ADMISSIONS INFORMATION

Office of Admission: 562-985-5471

ENTRANCE REQUIREMENTS

Academic units recommended: 4 English, 3 math, 2 science (2 science labs), 2 foreign language, 1 social study, 1 history, 1 academic elective, 1 fine arts. High school diploma is required, and GED is accepted. ACT with or without Writing component accepted. TOEFL required of all international applicants: minimum paper TOEFL 525.

Application deadline: 11/30	**SAT Math middle 50% range:**	**Graduated top 25% of class:** NR
Notification: Rolling	460–590	**Graduated top 25% of class:** 84%
Average GPA: 3.43	**SAT Critical Reading middle 50%**	**Graduated top 50% of class:** 100%
ACT Composite middle 50% range:	**range:** 440–560	
18–24	**SAT Writing middle 50% range:** NR	

COLLEGE GRADUATION REQUIREMENTS

Course substitutions allowed: Yes
In what course: Math and other general education courses as needed, on a case-by-case basis by way of an appeal through Academic Affairs.

ADDITIONAL INFORMATION

Environment: The campus is located south of Los Angeles.

Student Body	**Cost Information**	**Greek System**
Undergrad enrollment: 29,287	**In-state tuition:** $6,130	**Fraternity:** Yes
Women: 60%	**Out-of-state tuition:** $16,600	**Sorority:** Yes
Men: 40%	**Room & board:** $11,300	**Athletics:** Division I
Percent out-of-state: 1%	**Housing Information**	
	University housing: Yes	
	Percent living on campus: 7%	

CALIFORNIA STATE U.—NORTHRIDGE

18111 Nordhoff Street, Northridge, CA 91330-8365
Phone: 818-677-2684 • Fax: 818-677-4932
E-mail: lorraine.newlon@csun.edu • Web: www.csun.edu
Support: S • Institution type: 4-year public

PROGRAMS OR SERVICES FOR STUDENTS WITH LD

Disability Resources and Education Services recognizes that students with learning disabilities can be quite successful in a university setting if appropriate educational support services are offered to them. In an effort to assist students with learning disabilities in reaching their full potential, the program offers a comprehensive and well-coordinated system of educational support services that allow students to be judged on the basis of their ability rather than disability. The program employs academic coaches who work under the direction of the professional staff and assist students with study skills, time management procedures, test-taking techniques, and other individualized programs.

ADMISSION INFORMATION FOR STUDENTS WITH LD/ADHD

College entrance tests required: Yes
Interview required: No
Essay recommended: No
What documentation required for LD: The documentation should contain a specific diagnosis and a concise description of the functional limitations imposed by the disability; a diagnostic interview, an assessment of aptitude, academic achievement, and information processing as well as a diagnosis with functional limitations are recommended.
What documentation required for ADHD:
Neuropsychological assessment signed by your physician, other licensed health care professional, or rehabilitation counselor, with a specific diagnosis that indicates a concise description of the functional limitations.

Submitted to: Disability Resources and Educational Services
Special Ed. HS course work accepted: Yes, if college level
Specific course requirements of all applicants: Yes
Separate application required: No
# of LD applications submitted each year: NR
# of LD applications accepted yearly: 120–125
Total # of students receiving LD services: 280–300
Acceptance into program means acceptance into college: Students must be admitted and enrolled in the university first and then request services.

ADMISSIONS
There is no special admission process. Students must get a C or better in 4 years of English, 3 years of math, 2 years of social science/U.S. history/government, 2 years of science, 2 years of a foreign language, 1 year of visual/performing arts, and 1 year of academic electives. An eligibility index combining GPA and a score on either the ACT or SAT is used. Index is calculated by multiplying GPA by 800 and adding SAT or multiplying GPA by 200 and adding 10 times the ACT. California residents need an index of 2900 using SAT or 694 using ACT. Nonresidents must have a minimum index of 3200 (SAT) or 740 (ACT).

ADDITIONAL INFORMATION
Services and accommodations are available to students with appropriate documentation: calculators, dictionary, computer and spellchecker for tests, extended testing time, scribes, proctors, oral exams, note-takers, distraction-free testing environments, tape recorder in class, e-texts, and priority registration. Testing accommodations may be arranged without the integrity of the test being sacrificed. The Computer Access Lab provides computers along with professional assistance. The program and the CSUN Career Center work cooperatively to assist students with LD in planning and attaining career goals. Referrals for diagnostic testing are available for students who suspect they may have a learning disability. Counselors are available to assist students with social/emotional needs as well as academic requirements. Assistance in developing appropriate learning strategies is provided on an individual basis. There are also workshops, academic coaching, and technologies to enhance learning. Services and accommodations are available for undergraduate and graduate students.

LEARNING DISABILITY PROGRAMS OR SERVICES

Contact Information
Name of program or department: Disability Resources and Educational Services
   Telephone: 818-677-2684
   Fax: 818-677-4932

LEARNING DISABILITY SERVICES

Accommodations are decided upon an individual basis after a thorough review of appropriate, current documentation. The accommodations requested must be supported through the documentation provided and must be logically linked to the current impact of the condition on academic functioning.

Allowed in exams	**Distraction-reduced environment:** Yes	**Added costs for services:** No
Calculator: Yes	**Tape recording in class:** Yes	**LD specialists:** No
Dictionary: No	**Electronic texts:** Yes	**Professional tutors:** No
Computer: Yes	**Accommodations for students with**	**Peer tutors:** Yes (academic coaches)
Spellchecker: Yes	**ADHD:** Yes	**Max. hours/wk. for services:** N/A
Extended test time: Yes	**Kurzweil Reader:** Yes	**How professors are notified of**
Scribes: Yes	**Other assistive technology:** Yes	**LD/ADHD:** By student
Proctors: Yes	**Priority registration:** Yes	
Oral exams: Yes		
Note-takers: Yes		

GENERAL ADMISSIONS INFORMATION

Office of Admission: 818-677-3700

ENTRANCE REQUIREMENTS

Academic units required: 4 English, 3 math, 2 science (with lab), 2 foreign language, 2 history, 1 academic elective, 1 visual/performing arts. High school diploma is required, and GED is accepted. TOEFL required of all international applicants: minimum paper TOEFL 500.

Application deadline: 11/30	**SAT Math middle 50% range:** NR	**Graduated top 25% of class:** NR
Notification: Rolling	**SAT Critical Reading middle 50%**	**Graduated top 25% of class:** NR
Average GPA: 3.10	**range:** NR	**Graduated top 50% of class:** NR
ACT Composite middle 50% range: NR	**SAT Writing middle 50% range:** NR	

COLLEGE GRADUATION REQUIREMENTS

Course waivers allowed: No
In what course: N/A
Course substitutions allowed: Yes
In what course: Individual case-by-case decisions

ADDITIONAL INFORMATION

Environment: The university has a large suburban campus in the San Fernando Valley northwest of Los Angeles.

Student Body	**Cost Information**	**Greek System**
Undergrad enrollment: 35,250	**In-state tuition:** $6,488	**Fraternity:** Yes
Women: 58%	**Out-of-state tuition:** $17,600	**Sorority:** Yes
Men: 42%	**Room & board:** $12,300	**Athletics:** Division I
Percent out-of-state: 8%	**Housing Information**	
	University housing: Yes	
	Percent living on campus: 5%	

CAL. STATE U.—SAN BERNARDINO

5500 University Parkway, San Bernardino, CA 92407-2397
Phone: 909-537-5188 • Fax: 909-537-7034
E-mail: moreinfo@mail.csusb.edu • Web: www.csusb.edu
Support: CS • Institution type: 4-year public

PROGRAMS OR SERVICES FOR STUDENTS WITH LD

The Learning Disability Program is dedicated to assuring each student an opportunity to experience equity in education. Each student must complete an assessment, and then the staff helps to develop compensatory methods for handling assignments and classroom projects. Careful attention is paid to helping the student acquire learning skills and formulating and implementing specific strategies for note-taking and management of written materials. Recommendations are designed for each student as a result of a psychometric assessment, personal interview, and academic requirements. The emphasis of the plan is to assist the students with a learning disability in finding techniques to deal with it in college and in the job market.

ADMISSION INFORMATION FOR STUDENTS WITH LD/ADHD

College entrance tests required: Yes
Interview required: Yes
Essay recommended: No
What documentation required for LD: Psycho Ed evaluation to include: relevant historical info, instructional interventions, related services, age diagnosed, objective data (aptitude, achievement, info processing), test scores (standard, percentile and grade equivalents) and describe functional limitations.
With general application: No
To receive services after enrolling: Yes
What documentation required for ADHD: Diagnosis based on DSM-V; history of behaviors impairing functioning in academic setting; diagnostic interview; history of symptoms; evidence of ongoing behaviors.

With general application: No
Submitted to: Services for Students with Disabilities
Special Ed. HS course work accepted: No
Specific course requirements of all applicants: Yes
Separate application required: Yes
# of LD applications submitted each year: 75–101
# of LD applications accepted yearly: 45–66
Total # of students receiving LD services: 140–156
Acceptance into program means acceptance into college: Students must be admitted and enrolled in the university first and then request services.

ADMISSIONS

Applicants with learning disabilities must follow the same application procedure as all students. Entrance requirements include a minimum GPA of 2.0; 4 years of English, 3 years of math, 1 year of U.S. history, 1 year of science, 2 years of a foreign language, 1 year of visual/performing arts, and 3 years of electives from any of the previous areas (including agriculture). The middle 50 percent have an ACT of 15–19 and SAT of 800–1020. Special admission may be requested through the Learning Disability Program if the student has a deficiency in course entrance requirements. The Director of the LD Program provides recommendations on the admissibility of those students who do not meet regular admissions requirements. Occasionally, the special admit will consider students who are below the required GPA or test scores. These requirements can be substituted, and the student can make up the deficiency on campus once enrolled.

ADDITIONAL INFORMATION

Services and accommodations for students with appropriate documentation could include the following: the use of calculators, dictionaries, computers, or spellchecker during exams; extended time on tests; distraction-free testing environments; oral exams; note-takers; proctors; scribes; tape recorders in class; books on tape; assisting technology; and priority registration. Specific services include assessment counseling and testing accommodations. Students on academic probation have two quarters to raise their GPA to a 2.0. The LD Program provides continual academic support.

LEARNING DISABILITY PROGRAMS OR SERVICES

Contact Information
Name of program or department: Services to Students with Disabilities
   Telephone: 909-537-5238
   Fax: 909-537-7090

LEARNING DISABILITY SERVICES

Accommodations are decided upon an individual basis after a thorough review of appropriate, current documentation. The accommodations requested must be supported through the documentation provided and must be logically linked to the current impact of the condition on academic functioning.

Allowed in exams
   Calculator: Yes
   Dictionary: No
   Computer: Yes
   Spellchecker: Yes
Extended test time: Yes
Scribes: Yes
Proctors: Yes
Oral exams: Yes
Note-takers: Yes

Distraction-reduced environment: Yes
Tape recording in class: Yes
Electronic texts: Yes
Accommodations for students with ADHD: Yes
Kurzweil Reader: Yes
Other assistive technology: Yes
Priority registration: Yes

Added costs for services: No
LD specialists: Yes
Professional tutors: No
Peer tutors: No
Max. hours/wk. for services: N/A
How professors are notified of LD/ADHD: By student

GENERAL ADMISSIONS INFORMATION

Office of Admission: 909-537-5188

ENTRANCE REQUIREMENTS
Academic units required: 4 English, 3 math, 2 science (2 science labs), 2 foreign language, 2 social studies, 1 academic elective, 1 visual/performing arts. High school diploma is required, and GED is accepted. ACT without Writing component accepted. TOEFL required of undergraduate international applicants: minimum paper TOEFL 500, minimum computer TOEFL 173.

Application deadline: None
Notification: Rolling
Average GPA: 3.22
ACT Composite middle 50% range: 16–20

SAT Math middle 50% range: 400–499
SAT Critical Reading middle 50% range: 390–499
SAT Writing middle 50% range: 400–499

Graduated top 10% of class: 18%
Graduated top 25% of class: 35%
Graduated top 50% of class: 90%

COLLEGE GRADUATION REQUIREMENTS

Course waivers allowed: No
Course substitutions allowed: Yes
In what course: General education, math

ADDITIONAL INFORMATION

Environment: The university is located in a suburban area in the foothills of the San Bernadino Mountains.

Student Body
   Undergrad enrollment: 14,732
   Women: 62%
   Men: 38%
   Percent out-of-state: 0.5%

Cost Information
   In-state tuition: $5,190
   Out-of-state tuition: $17,600
   Room & board: $12,300
Housing Information
   University housing: Yes
   Percent living on campus: 9%

Greek System
   Fraternity: Yes
   Sorority: Yes
Athletics: Division II

COLLEGE OF THE SISKIYOUS

800 College Avenue, Weed, CA 96094
Phone: 530-938-5555 • Fax: 530-938-5367
E-mail: registration@siskiyous.edu • Web: www.siskiyous.edu
Support: CS • Institution type: 2-year public

PROGRAMS OR SERVICES FOR STUDENTS WITH LD

The Disabled Student Programs and Services Office (DSP&S) is dedicated to meeting the needs of students with disabilities. The goal of DSP&S is to assist students to overcome barriers to allow access to the college's regular programs and activities. Support services are provided for students with a wide variety of disabilities. Any student who has a documented disability and demonstrates a need for a service that is directly related to the educational limitation is eligible for support services.

ADMISSION INFORMATION FOR STUDENTS WITH LD/ADHD

College entrance tests required: Yes
Interview required: No
Essay recommended: No
What documentation required for LD: Psycho Ed evaluation to include: relevant historical info, instructional interventions, related services, age diagnosed, objective data (aptitude, achievement, info processing), test scores (standard, percentile and grade equivalents) and describe functional limitations.
With general application: No
To receive services after enrolling: Yes
What documentation required for ADHD: Diagnosis based on DSM-V; history of behaviors impairing functioning in academic setting; diagnostic interview; history of symptoms; evidence of ongoing behaviors.

With general application: No
Submitted to: Disabled Student Programs and Services
Special Ed. HS course work accepted: No
Specific course requirements of all applicants: No
Separate application required: Yes
# of LD applications submitted each year: 30
# of LD applications accepted yearly: 20
Total # of students receiving LD services: 50
Acceptance into program means acceptance into college: Students must be admitted and enrolled in the college first and then request services.

ADMISSIONS

Students with LD/ADHD who self-disclose during the admission process may receive advice from DSP&S during the admission process. Basically, this advice would provide descriptions of appropriate courses the students may take and the services and accommodations they may be eligible to receive. There are not any minimum admission requirements for a specific class rank, GPA, or ACT/SAT score. Applicants must have a high school diploma or equivalent certification.

ADDITIONAL INFORMATION

There is an LD specialist available in the Disabled Students Programs and Services Office. There are support services available for students who have a documented disability and demonstrate a need for a service that is directly related to their educational limitations. They may include academic advising, registration assistance, an LD assessment, tutoring, readers, note-takers, testing accommodations, and adaptive educational equipment. The COS High Tech Center is designed to provide computer access and technology to students with disabilities to educate and prepare them for academic success and today's work force. In addition, all students have access to skills classes in areas such as time management, organization, study strategies, and test-taking strategies.

LEARNING DISABILITY PROGRAMS OR SERVICES

Contact Information
Name of program or department: Disabled Student Programs and Services
 Telephone: 530-938-5297
 Fax: 530-938-5375

LEARNING DISABILITY SERVICES

Accommodations are decided upon an individual basis after a thorough review of appropriate, current documentation. The accommodations requested must be supported through the documentation provided and must be logically linked to the current impact of the condition on academic functioning.

Allowed in exams
 Calculator: No
 Dictionary: No
 Computer: Yes
 Spellchecker: No
Extended test time: Yes
Scribes: Yes
Proctors: Yes
Oral exams: Yes
Note-takers: Yes

Distraction-reduced environment: Yes
Tape recording in class: Yes
Electronic texts: Yes
Accommodations for students with
 ADHD: Yes
Kurzweil Reader: Yes
Other assistive technology: Yes
Priority registration: No

Added costs for services: No
LD specialists: Yes
Professional tutors: No
Peer tutors: Yes
Max. hours/wk. for services:
 Unlimited
How professors are notified of
 LD/ADHD: By student

GENERAL ADMISSIONS INFORMATION

Office of Admission: 530-938-5555

ENTRANCE REQUIREMENTS

There are no specific requirements for courses, GPA, class rank, or test scores. TOEFL required of all international applicants: minimum paper TOEFL 470, minimum computer TOEFL 150.

Application deadline: None
Notification: Rolling
Average GPA: NR
ACT Composite middle 50% range:
 NR

SAT Math middle 50% range: NR
SAT Critical Reading middle 50%
 range: NR
SAT Writing middle 50% range: NR

Graduated top 10% of class: NR
Graduated top 25% of class: NR
Graduated top 50% of class: NR

COLLEGE GRADUATION REQUIREMENTS

Course waivers allowed: No
Course substitutions allowed: Yes
In what course: Students can petition for a substitute course.

ADDITIONAL INFORMATION

Environment: The college is located at the base of Mt. Shasta.

Student Body
 Undergrad enrollment: 4,587
 Women: 53%
 Men: 44%
 Percent out-of-state: 27%

Cost Information
 In-state tuition: $46 per unit
 Out-of-state tuition: $2,600
 Room & board: $8,000
Housing Information
 College housing: Yes
 Percent living on campus: 3%

Greek System
 Fraternity: No
 Sorority: No
Athletics: Intercollegiate

LOYOLA MARYMOUNT UNIVERSITY

One LMU Drive, Suite 100, Los Angeles, CA 90045
Phone: 310-338-2750 • Fax: 310-338-2797
E-mail: admissions@lmu.edu • Web: www.lmu.edu
Support: S • Institution: 4-year private

PROGRAMS OR SERVICES FOR STUDENTS WITH LD

The Office of Disability Support Services (DSS) provides specialized assistance and resources that enable students with physical, perceptual, emotional, and learning disabilities to achieve maximum independence while they pursue their educational goals. Assisted by staff specialists from all areas of the University, the DSS Office works to eliminate physical and attitudinal barriers. To be eligible for services, students must provide documentation of the disability from a licensed professional. At the Academic Resource Center, students can receive tutoring in over 250 LMU classes, attend workshops, and access assistance in writing, reading, and math with LRC specialists.

ADMISSION INFORMATION FOR STUDENTS WITH LD/ADHD

College entrance tests required: Yes
Interview required: No
Essay required: N/A
What documentation required for LD: Psycho Ed evaluation to include: relevant historical info, instructional interventions, related services, age diagnosed, objective data (aptitude, achievement, info processing), test scores (standard, percentile and grade equivalents) and describe functional limitations.
With general application: No
To receive services after enrolling: Yes
What documentation required for ADHD: Diagnosis based on DSM-V; history of behaviors impairing functioning in academic setting; diagnostic interview; history of symptoms; evidence of ongoing behaviors.

With general application: No
Submitted to: Disability Support Services
Special Ed. HS course work accepted: Yes
Specific course requirements for all applicants: NR
Separate application required for program services: Yes
# of LD applications submitted each year: NR
# of LD applications accepted yearly: NR
Total # of students receiving LD services: 117
Acceptance into program means acceptance into college: Separate application required after student has enrolled

ADMISSIONS

There is no special admissions process for students with Learning Disabilities or Attention Deficit Hyperactive Disorder. The admission decision will be based upon the student's grade point average, SAT/ACT scores, strength of curriculum, the application essay, letters of recommendation, and extracurricular activities. Enrolled students have an average GPA of 3.3, 25 ACT, and 1800 SAT. Students are encouraged to have completed four years English, three years social sciences, three years foreign language, three years math (four years for engineering and science), and one year elective.

ADDITIONAL INFORMATION

There is a, Academic Resource Center where all students can find specialists and tutors. There is course-specific tutoring, study skills programs (which include learning time management, overcoming test anxiety, conquering math word problems, mastering the textbook, preparing for exams, and studying efficiently), and other academic support programs with full-time professional staff members prepared to assist with writing, reading, math, ESL, and Disability Support Services. Assistive technology includes: equipment that enlarges print, Kurzweil 3000, JAWS, and Dragon Dictate. Specific accommodations for LD students with appropriate documentation could include: priority registration, note-takers, readers, transcribers, alternate testing conditions, taped books, and advocacy, extended time on testing.

PROGRAM FOR DISABILITY SERVICES

Contact Information
Name of program or department: Office of Disability Support Services (DSS)
  Telephone: 310-338-4216
  Fax: 310-338-5344

LEARNING DISABILITY SERVICES

Accommodations are decided upon an individual basis after a thorough review of appropriate, current documentation. The accommodations requested must be supported through the documentation provided and must be logically linked to the current impact of the condition on academic functioning. .

Allowed in exams
  Calculator: Yes
  Dictionary: Yes
  Computer: Yes
  Spellchecker: Yes
Extended test time: Yes
Scribes: Yes
Proctors: Yes
Oral exams: Yes
Note-takers: Yes

Distraction-reduced environment: Yes
Tape recording in class: Yes
Electronic texts: Yes
Accommodations for students with ADHD: Yes
Kurzweil Reader: Yes
Other assistive technology: CTV Machines, JAWS, Kurzweil 3000, Zoomtext.
Priority registration: Yes

Added costs for services: No
LD specialists: No
Professional tutors: No
Peer tutors: 80
Max. hours/wk. for services: 1 per subject
How professors are notified of LD/ADHD: Student

GENERAL ADMISSIONS INFORMATION

Office of Admission: 310-338-4216

ENTRANCE REQUIREMENTS

Academic units recommended: 4 English, 3 mathematics, 2 science, (2 science labs), 3 foreign language, 3 social studies, 1 academic electives. High school diploma is required and GED is accepted. SAT or ACT required; TOEFL required of all international applicants; minimum paper TOEFL 550, minimum computer TOEFL 213.

Application deadline: 1/15
Notification: Rolling
Average GPA: 3.6
ACT Composite middle 50% range: 23–28

SAT Math middle 50% range: 540–640
SAT Critical Reading middle 50% range: 530–630
SAT Writing middle 50% range: NR

Graduated top 10% of class: 30%
Graduated top 25% of class: 66%
Graduated top 50% of class: 99%

COLLEGE GRADUATION REQUIREMENTS

Course waivers allowed: No
Course substitutions allowed: No

ADDITIONAL INFORMATION

Environment: The university is located on 125 acres in a suburban setting, with stunning views of the Pacific Ocean and downtown Los Angeles.
Student Body
  Undergrad enrollment: 5,952
  Women: 58%
  Men: 42%
  Percent out-of-state: 26%

Cost Information
  Tuition: $37,000
  Room and board: $13,300
Housing Information
  University housing: Yes
  Percent living on campus: 53%

Greek System
  Fraternity: Yes
  Sorority: Yes
Athletics: Division I

MENLO COLLEGE

1000 El Camino Real, Atherton, CA 94027
Phone: 650-543-3753 • Fax: 650-543-4496
E-mail: admissions@menlo.edu • Web: www.menlo.edu
Support: CS • Institution type: 4-year private

PROGRAMS OR SERVICES FOR STUDENTS WITH LD

The Menlo College Academic Success Center (ASC) welcomes all students including those with learning, psychological, and attention challenges. In its new configuration with the Bowman Library, now the Learning Community Commons, services have broadened to include library staff and resources. Students who present proper documentation of a disability may qualify for accommodations. All students are welcome to utilize the services of the Academic Success Center.

ADMISSION INFORMATION FOR STUDENTS WITH LD/ADHD

College entrance tests required: Yes
Interview required: No
Essay recommended: Yes
What documentation required for LD: Psycho Ed evaluation
   to include: relevant historical info, instructional interventions,
   related services, age diagnosed, objective data (aptitude,
   achievement, info processing), test scores (standard,
   percentile and grade equivalents) and describe functional
   limitations.
With general application: No
To receive services after enrolling: Yes
What documentation required for ADHD: Diagnosis based
   on DSM-V; history of behaviors impairing functioning in
   academic setting; diagnostic interview; history of symptoms;
   evidence of ongoing behaviors.

With general application: No
Submitted to: Academic Success Center
Special Ed. HS course work accepted: No
Specific course requirements for all applicants: No
Separate application required: No
# of LD applications submitted each year: NR
# of LD applications accepted yearly: NR
Total # of students receiving LD services: 200
Acceptance into program means acceptance into
   college: Students must be admitted and enrolled prior to
   requesting services.

ADMISSIONS

Students are admitted to Menlo College on their own merits, without regard to disability. If students choose to self-disclose their learning challenges, they are encouraged to meet with the Academic Success Center in advance of their arrival to arrange for early set-up of accommodations. Menlo values the individual strengths and diversity that students bring to Menlo, so we choose not to follow a specific formula when making our admission decisions. Each applicant is reviewed individually, and the acceptance decisions are based on many factors including the strength of your course curriculum, the school you attend(ed), and your grades and test scores. In addition, we consider your extracurricular activities, community involvement, employment, and leadership roles. Menlo College is most interested in the quality of students' activities, rather than the quantity. Essay required regarding either 1) Academic strengths or weaknesses, or 2) Reasons for seeking college education, or 3) Learning experiences you hope to have, or 4) Why Menlo Counselor teacher ecommendation, ACT/SAT.

ADDITIONAL INFORMATION

The Academic Success Center provides a 'one-stop' center for information and resources that are key to academic and career success. The services include: Advising, advocacy, assistive technology, note takers, books on tape, tutoring lab and writing center.

LEARNING DISABILITY PROGRAMS OR SERVICES

Contact Information
Name of program or department: Academic Success Center
  Telephone: 650-543-3854
  Fax: 650-543-4120

LEARNING DISABILITY SERVICES

Accommodations are decided upon an individual basis after a thorough review of appropriate, current documentation. The accommodations requested must be supported through the documentation provided and must be logically linked to the current impact of the condition on academic functioning.

Allowed in exams
  Calculator: Yes
  Dictionary: Yes
  Computer: Yes
  Spellchecker: Yes
  Extended test time: Yes
  Scribes: Yes
  Proctors: Yes
  Oral exams: No
  Note-takers: Yes

Distraction-reduced environment: Yes
Tape recording in class: Yes
Electronic texts: Yes
Accommodations for students with
  ADHD: Yes
Kurzweil Reader: Yes
Other assistive technology: Yes
Priority registration: No

Added costs for services: No
LD specialists: Yes
Professional tutors: No
Peer tutors: 6–10
Max. hours/wk. for services: N/A
How professors are notified of
  LD/ADHD: By both student and director

GENERAL ADMISSIONS INFORMATION

Office of Admission: 650-543-3753

ENTRANCE REQUIREMENTS

Academic units recommended: 4 English, 3 math, 3 science (1 science lab), 2 foreign language, 3 social studies, 3 history. Recommendation from teacher or counselor and a student essay required. High school diploma is required, and GED is accepted. ACT with or without Writing component accepted. TOEFL required of all international applicants: minimum paper TOEFL 500, minimum computer TOEFL 173.

Application deadline: None
Notification: Rolling
Average GPA: NR
ACT Composite middle 50% range:
  17–22

SAT Math middle 50% range:
  430–550
SAT Critical Reading middle 50%
  range: 420–520
SAT Writing middle 50% range:
  400–500

Graduated top 10% of class: NR
Graduated top 25% of class: NR
Graduated top 50% of class: NR

COLLEGE GRADUATION REQUIREMENTS

Course waivers allowed: No
Course substitutions allowed: Yes
In what course: Math, foreign language

ADDITIONAL INFORMATION

Environment: Menlo College is within easy reach of the San Francisco Bay Area.

Student Body
  Undergrad enrollment: 594
  Women: 39%
  Men: 61%
  Percent out-of-state: 22%

Cost Information
  Tuition: $34,500
  Room & board: $13,330
Housing Information
  University housing: Yes
  Percent living on campus: 58%

Greek System
  Fraternity: No
  Sorority: No
  Athletics: Division III

OCCIDENTAL COLLEGE

1600 Campus Road, Office of Admission, Los Angeles, CA 90041
Phone: 323-259-2700 • Fax: 323-341-4875
E-mail: admission@oxy.edu • Web: www.oxy.edu
Support: S • Institution type: 4-year private

PROGRAMS OR SERVICES FOR STUDENTS WITH LD

The Dean's office coordinates academic support services for all students, including those with disabilities, who want to enhance their academic success. Students who have a documented disability requiring academic accommodation and who wish to apply for academic accommodation in addition to the general academic support services need to make an appointment with the Dean's office as far in advance of the semester of enrollment as possible. The purpose of this meeting is to acquaint the student with the available resources, determine the accommodations required by the student, and complete appropriate forms requesting services. If relevant documentation has not been previously submitted to the Dean's office, students should bring it to this meeting. The documentation should support assessments completed within the past 3 years. Accommodations for students with documented disabilities are determined by individual student needs.

ADMISSION INFORMATION FOR STUDENTS WITH LD/ADHD

College entrance tests required: Yes
Interview required: N/A
Essay recommended: N/A
What documentation required for LD: Psycho Ed evaluation to
   include: relevant historical info, instructional interventions,
   related services, age diagnosed, objective data (aptitude,
   achievement, info processing), test scores (standard, percentile
   and grade equivalents) and describe functional limitations.
With general application: No
To receive services after enrolling: Yes
What documentation required for ADHD: Diagnosis based
   on DSM-V; history of behaviors impairing functioning in
   academic setting; diagnostic interview; history of symptoms;
   evidence of ongoing behaviors.

With general application: No
Submitted to: Dean's office
Special Ed. HS course work accepted: NR
Specific course requirements for all applicants: NR
Separate application required: N/A
# of LD applications submitted each year: NR
# of LD applications accepted yearly: NR
Total # of students receiving LD services: NR
Acceptance into program means acceptance into
   college: Students must be admitted and enrolled prior to
   requesting services.

ADMISSIONS

There are no special admissions criteria for students with learning disabilities. The college will assess and balance a variety of academic factors to determine the overall scholastic strength of each applicant. An applicant who wishes to have his or her disability considered as a factor in the admission process must identify the disability and provide an explanation of why it is a factor at the time of application. If the applicant wishes the disability to be considered a factor, it may be necessary to provide appropriate documentation of the disability at the time of application for admission.

ADDITIONAL INFORMATION

The most typically successful student at Occidental College is a self-advocate who understands and can explain his or her academic needs, when appropriate, to professors and others providing academic assistance. The student seeks assistance related to the disability, as needed, from the CAE coordinator. If concerns or questions arise, the student contacts the coordinator of the CAE to resolve or clarify. If extended time for exams, note-taking, alternative formats to text, or other academic accommodations are needed, the student carries out his or her responsibilities for receiving these accommodations, including timely scheduling of exam proctoring appointments, communicating with professors, seeking out student note-takers, and notifying the CAE of assigned readings. Alternative courses to the foreign language requirement are offered on a case-by case basis and with presentation of psychoeducational documentation that specifically justifies the need in the area of foreign language. In such cases, the student will make arrangements through the coordinator of Academic Support Services. Occidental College does not provide daily support and consultation for learning disabled students. Students are encouraged to find fellow students as note-takers, and the college will make available two-ply paper for use by volunteer note-takers and will honor volunteer note-takers with bookstore gift certificates. Students enrolled at Occidental College who have not been previously diagnosed and who have reason to suspect they may have a learning disability or ADHD are encouraged to meet with the coordinator of Academic Support Services to determine appropriate action. Occidental College does not administer diagnostic assessments, but will assist students in making arrangements to be tested by a qualified professional. The cost of the evaluation is the responsibility of the student.

LEARNING DISABILITY PROGRAMS OR SERVICES

Contact Information
Name of program or department: Occidental College Dean of Students Office
  Telephone: 323-259-2969
  Fax: 323-341-4927

LEARNING DISABILITY SERVICES

Accommodations are decided upon an individual basis after a thorough review of appropriate, current documentation. The accommodations requested must be supported through the documentation provided and must be logically linked to the current impact of the condition on academic functioning.

Allowed in exams
  Calculator: Yes
  Dictionary: Yes
  Computer: Yes
  Spellchecker: Yes
Extended test time: Yes
Scribes: Yes
Proctors: Yes
Oral exams: No
Note-takers: Yes

Distraction-reduced environment: Yes
Tape recording in class: Yes
Electronic texts: NR
Accommodations for students with ADHD: Yes
Kurzweil Reader: Yes
Other assistive technology: Yes
Priority registration: N/A

Added costs for services: No
LD specialists: No
Professional tutors: 6
Peer tutors: 43
Max. hours/wk. for services: NR
How professors are notified of LD/ADHD: By student

GENERAL ADMISSIONS INFORMATION

Office of Admission: 323-259-2700

ENTRANCE REQUIREMENTS

Academic units recommended: 4 English, 4 math, 3 science (2 science labs), 3 foreign language, 2 social studies, 2 history, 2 academic electives. High school diploma is required, and GED is accepted. ACT with or without Writing component accepted. TOEFL required of all international applicants: minimum paper TOEFL 600, minimum computer TOEFL 250.

Application deadline: 1/10
Notification: 4/01
Average GPA: 3.57
ACT Composite middle 50% range: 27–31

SAT Math middle 50% range: 610–690
SAT Critical Reading middle 50% range: 600–700
SAT Writing middle 50% range: 600–700

Graduated top 10% of class: 60%
Graduated top 25% of class: 91%
Graduated top 50% of class: 100%

COLLEGE GRADUATION REQUIREMENTS

Course waivers allowed: No
Course substitutions allowed: Yes
In what course: Foreign language

ADDITIONAL INFORMATION

Environment: Occidental College is located in northeast Los Angeles.

Student Body
  Undergrad enrollment: 2,123
  Women: 57%
  Men: 43%
  Percent out-of-state: 54%

Cost Information
  Tuition: $42,900
  Room & board: $11,900
Housing Information
  University housing: Yes
  Percent living on campus: 80%

Greek System
  Fraternity: Yes
  Sorority: Yes
Athletics: Division III

REEDLEY COLLEGE

995 North Reed Avenue, Reedley, CA 93654
Phone: 559-638-3641 • Fax: 559-638-5040
E-mail: emerzian@sccd.org • Web: www.reedleycollege.com
Support: CS • Institution type: 2-year public

PROGRAMS OR SERVICES FOR STUDENTS WITH LD

The Disabled Student Program and Services (DSP&S) focuses on abilities, not disabilities. DSP&S offers services to students with learning disabilities beyond those provided by conventional programs at the college and enables students to pursue their individual educational, vocational, and personal goals successfully. The Learning Disabilities Program assesses the needs and skill levels of each student, tailoring a specific educational course of study designed to bring out the best in an individual at a college level. The instructional program in reading, writing, math, and other academics prepares students to function in the classroom, in their vocation, and throughout life. The LD Program provides special instruction and attention for students with specific educational needs not available in mainstream classes.

ADMISSION INFORMATION FOR STUDENTS WITH LD/ADHD

College entrance tests required: No
Interview required: Yes
Essay recommended: No
What documentation required for LD: Psycho Ed evaluation to include: relevant historical info, instructional interventions, related services, age diagnosed, objective data (aptitude, achievement, info processing), test scores (standard, percentile and grade equivalents) and describe functional limitations.
With general application: No
To receive services after enrolling: Yes
What documentation required for ADHD: Diagnosis based on DSM-V; history of behaviors impairing functioning in academic setting; diagnostic interview; history of symptoms; evidence of ongoing behaviors.

With general application: No
Submitted to: Disabled Student Program and Services
Special Ed. HS course work accepted: Yes
Specific course requirements of all applicants: No
Separate application required: No
# of LD applications submitted each year: NR
# of LD applications accepted yearly: NR
Total # of students receiving LD services: 200
Acceptance into program means acceptance into college: Students must be admitted and enrolled in the university first and then request services.

ADMISSIONS

Reedley is an open-door admission college. Students present a high school diploma, certificate of high school completion equivalent, or LD/special education test results. There is no minimum GPA or required courses required for admission. ACT/SAT tests are not required for admission. There is a separate application to access services for students with learning disabilities. This application, however, is submitted after admission.

ADDITIONAL INFORMATION

The LD Program services includes 3 main service components of testing, accommodations and instruction: LD assessments, learning strategies instruction from an LD specialist, small class sessions, adaptive instruction, matriculation and integration with mainstream classes, individualized student contact, and specialized educational counseling. In addition, students can access the following accommodations if they provide appropriate documentation: the use of calculators, dictionaries, computers, or spellchecker in exams; extended time on tests; scribes; proctors; oral exams; note-takers; tape recorder in class; books on tape; assistive technology; and priority registration. American Sign Language may be substituted for foreign language, and students are responsible for providing information about their disability to their professors.

LEARNING DISABILITY PROGRAMS OR SERVICES

Contact Information
Name of program or department: Disabled Students Program and Services (DSP&S)
   Telephone: 559-638-0332
   Fax: 559-638-0382

LEARNING DISABILITY SERVICES

Accommodations are decided upon an individual basis after a thorough review of appropriate, current documentation. The accommodations requested must be supported through the documentation provided and must be logically linked to the current impact of the condition on academic functioning.

Allowed in exams
   Calculator: Yes
   Dictionary: Yes
   Computer: Yes
   Spellchecker: Yes
Extended test time: Yes
Scribes: Yes
Proctors: Yes
Oral exams: Yes
Note-takers: Yes

Distraction-reduced environment: Yes
Tape recording in class: Yes
Electronic texts: Yes
Accommodations for students with ADHD: Yes
Kurzweil Reader: Yes
Other assistive technology: Yes
Priority registration: Yes

Added costs for services: No
LD specialists: Yes
Professional tutors: No
Peer tutors: Yes
Max. hours/wk. for services: Unlimited
How professors are notified of LD/ADHD: By student

GENERAL ADMISSIONS INFORMATION

Office of Admission: 559-638-3641

ENTRANCE REQUIREMENTS
High school diploma is required, and GED is accepted.

Application deadline: None
Notification: Rolling
Average GPA: NR
ACT Composite middle 50% range: NR

SAT Math middle 50% range: NR
SAT Critical Reading middle 50% range: NR
SAT Writing middle 50% range: NR

Graduated top 10% of class: NR
Graduated top 25% of class: NR
Graduated top 50% of class: NR

COLLEGE GRADUATION REQUIREMENTS

ADDITIONAL INFORMATION

Environment: The college is located 30 miles southeast of Fresno.

Student Body
   Undergrad enrollment: 7,718
   Women: 61%
   Men: 39%
   Percent out-of-state: 1%

Cost Information
   In-state tuition: $20 per unit
   Out-of-state tuition: $201 per unit
   Room & board: $5,650
Housing Information
   University housing: Yes
   Percent living on campus: 18%

Greek System
   Fraternity: No
   Sorority: No
Athletics: NJCAA

SAN DIEGO STATE UNIVERSITY

5500 Campanile Drive, San Diego, CA 92182
Phone: 619-594-6336 • Fax: 619-594-1250
E-mail: admissions@sdsu.edu • Web: www.sdsu.edu
Support: CS • Institution: 4-year public

PROGRAMS OR SERVICES FOR STUDENTS WITH LD

The Learning Disability Program at San Diego State is part of Student Disability Services. The LD Program is designed to provide assessment, accommodations, and advocacy. Students must provide documentation prior to receiving services. Students with learning disabilities may be assessed using nationally standardized batteries. The university believes that students with learning disabilities can be successful at San Diego State and will provide the appropriate services to foster their success.

ADMISSION INFORMATION FOR STUDENTS WITH LD/ADHD

College entrance tests required: Yes
Interview required: No
What documentation required for LD: Psycho Ed evaluation to include: relevant historical info, instructional interventions, related services, age diagnosed, objective data (aptitude, achievement, info processing), test scores (standard, percentile and grade equivalents) and describe functional limitations.
With general application: No
To receive services after enrolling: Yes
What documentation required for ADHD: Diagnosis based on DSM-V; history of behaviors impairing functioning in academic setting; diagnostic interview; history of symptoms; evidence of ongoing behaviors.

With general application: No
Submitted to: Support Program/Services
Special Ed. HS course work accepted: No
Specific course requirements for all applicants: Yes
Separate application required for program services: Yes
# of LD applications submitted each year: NR
# of LD applications accepted yearly: NR
Total # of students receiving LD services: 233
Acceptance into program means acceptance into college: Separate application required after student has been admitted to college.

ADMISSIONS

Students with disabilities must meet the university's admissions criteria. Under exceptional circumstances, students who are denied admission may appeal the decision. If the circumstances involve disability, contact Student Disability Services.

ADDITIONAL INFORMATION

Students are encouraged to get volunteer note-takers from among other students enrolled in the class. Limited tutoring is available based on documented functional limitations related to subject matter. Tutoring, when authorized, is available at no charge. Students with learning disabilities may request permission to tape a lecture. Students will also need permission from the professor to use a calculator, dictionary, computer, or spellchecker in exams. High Tech Center is an assistive technology center available to students with disabilities. Services and accommodations are available for undergraduates and graduate students.

PROGRAM FOR DISABILITY SERVICES

Contact Information
Name of program or department: Student Disability Services
  Telephone: 619-594-6473
  Fax: 619-594-4315

LEARNING DISABILITY SERVICES

Accommodations are decided upon an individual basis after a thorough review of appropriate, current documentation. The accommodations requested must be supported through the documentation provided and must be logically linked to the current impact of the condition on academic functioning. .

Allowed in exams
  Calculator: Yes
  Dictionary: No
  Computer: Yes
  Spellchecker: Yes
Extended test time: Yes
Scribes: Yes
Proctors: Yes
Oral exams: No
Note-takers: Yes

Distraction-reduced environment: Yes
Tape recording in class: Yes
Electronic texts: Yes
Accommodations for students with ADHD: Yes
Kurzweil Reader: Yes
Other assistive technology: Screen readers (Kurzweil 3000), e-text, voice recognition, word prediction software, Inspiration, etc., depending on functional limitation documented by professional
Priority registration: Yes

Added costs for services: No
LD specialists: Yes
Professional tutors: 2
Peer tutors: 1–20
Max. hours/wk. for services: As needed
How professors are notified of LD/ADHD: Student

GENERAL ADMISSIONS INFORMATION

Office of Admission: 619-594-6336

ENTRANCE REQUIREMENTS
Academic units required: 4 English, 3 mathematics, 2 science, (2 science labs), 2 foreign language, 1 social studies, 1 history, 1 visual/performing arts, 1 academic electives. **Academic units recommended:** 4 mathematics. High school diploma is required and GED is accepted. SAT or ACT required; TOEFL required of all international applicants; minimum paper TOEFL 550, minimum computer TOEFL 213.

Application deadline: 11/30
Notification: 3/1
Average GPA: 3.62
ACT Composite middle 50% range: 20–25

SAT Math middle 50% range: 470–600
SAT Critical Reading middle 50% range: 460–570
SAT Writing middle 50% range: NR

Graduated top 10% of class: NR
Graduated top 25% of class: NR
Graduated top 50% of class: NR

COLLEGE GRADUATION REQUIREMENTS

Course substitutions allowed: Yes
In what course: Varies; must be directly related to disability

ADDITIONAL INFORMATION

Environment: San Diego State is located on 300 acres 12 miles from the ocean, in a large, Southern California urban area.

Student Body
  Undergrad enrollment: 24,590
  Women: 57%
  Men: 43%
  Percent out-of-state: 8%

Cost Information
  In-state tuition: $6,578
  Out-of-state tuition: $17,738
  Room & board: $12,240
Housing Information
  University housing: Yes
  Percent living on campus: 10%

Greek System
  Fraternity: Yes
  Sorority: Yes
Athletics: Division I

SAN FRANCISCO STATE UNIVERSITY

1600 Holloway Avenue, San Francisco, CA 94132
Phone: 415-338-6486 • Fax: 415-338-7196
E-mail: ugadmit@sfsu.edu • Web: www.sfsu.com
Support: CS • Institution type: 4-year public

PROGRAMS OR SERVICES FOR STUDENTS WITH LD

The Disability Program and Resource Center (DPRC) is available to promote and provide equal access to the classroom and campus-related activities. A full range of support services is provided so that students may define and achieve personal autonomy at SFSU. The staff is sensitive to the diversity of disabilities, including those only recently recognized as disabilities requiring reasonable accommodations. Confidential support services are available. All students registered with DPRC are eligible for disability management advising. This consists of helping students access services from DPRC; manage DPRC services and school in general; problem-solve conflicts/concerns that are disability-related with individuals, programs, and services on campus; and understand "reasonable accommodation" under the law. Generally, the campus community is sensitive, but if an oversight occurs, students do have protection under Section 504 and the ADA. Students are encouraged to contact DPRC for guidance in pursuing a grievance. Resolution of a violation can often be achieved informally without completing the formal grievance procedure.

ADMISSION INFORMATION FOR STUDENTS WITH LD/ADHD

College entrance tests required: Yes
Interview required: Yes
Essay recommended: No
What documentation required for LD: Psycho Ed evaluation to include: relevant historical info, instructional interventions, related services, age diagnosed, objective data (aptitude, achievement, info processing), test scores (standard, percentile and grade equivalents) and describe functional limitations.
With general application: No
To receive services after enrolling: Yes
What documentation required for ADHD: Diagnosis based on DSM-V; history of behaviors impairing functioning in academic setting; diagnostic interview; history of symptoms; evidence of ongoing behaviors.

With general application: No
Submitted to: Disability Program and Resource Center (DPRC)
Special Ed. HS course work accepted: Yes
Specific course requirements of all applicants: Yes
Separate application required: Yes
# of LD applications submitted each year: NR
# of LD applications accepted yearly: NR
Total # of students receiving LD services: 250
Acceptance into program means acceptance into college: Students must be admitted and enrolled in the university first and then request services.

ADMISSIONS

Students with LD apply to the university through the regular application process. If the student is not eligible for regular admission for a disability-related reason, DPRC can provide special admissions assistance. To obtain special admissions assistance, students need to register with the DPRC office, provide verification of the disability, and notify the Admissions Office that the DPRC has the appropriate verification. When these steps have been taken, the Admissions Office will consult with the DPRC before making a decision. The admissions contact person can request substitutions of high school courses in math, foreign language, and science. Students with LD who are judged unable to fulfill specific requirements may take course substitutions. Substitutions are authorized on an individual basis after review and recommendation by the high school or community college counselor. Students taking substitutions must have 15 units of college-prep study. High school case managers may write summaries and provide a clinical judgment. The DPRC wants information about achievement deficits and may require the student to attend an admissions interview.

ADDITIONAL INFORMATION

The DPRC offers a drop-in center with available tutorial services. The DPRC can also arrange for test accommodations and note-takers and will advocate for the student. The staff is very involved and offers comprehensive services through a team approach. There are no developmental courses offered at the university. However, there are skills classes. Students with documented LD may request assistance in locating tutors. Other services may include registration assistance, campus orientation, note-takers, readers, test-taking assistance, tutoring, disability-related counseling, and referral information.

LEARNING DISABILITY PROGRAMS OR SERVICES

Contact Information
Name of program or department: Disability Programs and Resource Center
  Telephone: 415-338-2472
  Fax: 415-338-1041

LEARNING DISABILITY SERVICES

Accommodations are decided upon an individual basis after a thorough review of appropriate, current documentation. The accommodations requested must be supported through the documentation provided and must be logically linked to the current impact of the condition on academic functioning.

Allowed in exams
  Calculator: Yes
  Dictionary: Yes
  Computer: Yes
  Spellchecker: Yes
Extended test time: Yes
Scribes: Yes
Proctors: Yes
Oral exams: Yes
Note-takers: Yes

Distraction-reduced environment: Yes
Tape recording in class: Yes
Electronic texts: Yes
Accommodations for students with
  ADHD: Yes
Kurzweil Reader: Yes
Other assistive technology: Yes
Priority registration: Yes

Added costs for services: No
LD specialists: Yes
Professional tutors: No
Peer tutors: Yes
Max. hours/wk. for services: Limited
How professors are notified of
  LD/ADHD: By student

GENERAL ADMISSIONS INFORMATION

Office of Admission: 415-338-2037

ENTRANCE REQUIREMENTS

Academic units required: 4 English, 3 math, 2 science (2 science labs), 2 foreign language, 1 social studies, 1 history, 1 visual/performing arts. **Academic units recommended:** 1 academic elective. High school diploma is required, and GED is accepted. ACT with or without Writing component accepted. TOEFL required of all international applicants: minimum paper TOEFL 550, minimum computer TOEFL 173.

Application deadline: 11/30
Notification: Rolling
Average GPA: 3.12
ACT Composite middle 50% range:
  18–24

SAT Math middle 50% range:
  450–570
SAT Critical Reading middle 50% range: 440–570
SAT Writing middle 50% range:
  450–560

Graduated top 10% of class: NR
Graduated top 25% of class: NR
Graduated top 50% of class: NR

COLLEGE GRADUATION REQUIREMENTS

Course waivers allowed: Yes
In what course: Individual case-by-case decisions
Course substitutions allowed: Yes
In what course: Individual case-by-case decisions in subjects where impact of disability is evident.

ADDITIONAL INFORMATION

Environment: The school is located in downtown San Francisco on a 130-acre campus.

Student Body
  Undergrad enrollment: 24,378
  Women: 59%
  Men: 41%
  Percent out-of-state: 2%

Cost Information
  Tuition: $16,828
  Room & board: $11,408
Housing Information
  University housing: Yes
  Percent living on campus: 15%
Greek System

Fraternity: Yes
Sorority: Yes
Athletics: Division II

SAN JOSE STATE UNIVERSITY

One Washington Square, San Jose, CA 95112-0001
Phone: 408-283-7500 • Fax: 408-924-2050
E-mail: contact@sjsu.edu • Web: www.sjsu.com
Support: CS • Institution type: 4-year public

PROGRAMS OR SERVICES FOR STUDENTS WITH LD

The goal of the Disability Resource Center (DRC) is to provide appropriate academic adjustments and support services to students with disabilities while teaching them to become self-advocates and develop maximum independence. The DRC provides services to students and consultation to faculty to educate every department so that they best serve students with disabilities. To request services students must self identify and meet with a DRC counselor to create a confidential student file. Documentation of the disability should verify a disability and support the requests for accommodations or academic adjustments.

ADMISSION INFORMATION FOR STUDENTS WITH LD/ADHD

College entrance tests required: No
Interview required: No
Essay recommended: No
What documentation required for LD: Psycho Ed evaluation to include: relevant historical info, instructional interventions, related services, age diagnosed, objective data (aptitude, achievement, info processing), test scores (standard, percentile and grade equivalents) and describe functional limitations.
With general application: No
To receive services after enrolling: Yes
What documentation required for ADHD: Diagnosis based on DSM-V; history of behaviors impairing functioning in academic setting; diagnostic interview; history of symptoms; evidence of ongoing behaviors.

With general application: No
Submitted to: Disability Resource Center
Special Ed. HS course work accepted: No
Specific course requirements of all applicants: Yes
Separate application required: No
# of LD applications submitted each year: NR
# of LD applications accepted yearly: NR
Total # of students receiving LD services: 652
Acceptance into program means acceptance into college: Students must be admitted and enrolled in the university first and then request services.

ADMISSIONS

Students with LD apply directly to the Admissions Office; there is no special handling of the student's applications through the DRC. All assessments and disability verifications go direct to DRC for establishment of a confidential file. (The assessment should include the WJ–R Parts 1 and 2 or the WAIS–IV and WJ–R Part 2 and other skills tests.) California resident entering freshman applicants must have at least a 2.0 GPA, and a sliding scale is used combining GPA and test scores. Only courses from grades 10–12 are used to compute GPA. High school courses required include 4 years of English, 3 years of math, 1 year of biological science lab, 2 year of U.S. history/social sciences, 2 years of a foreign language, 1 year of visual/performing arts, and 3 years of academic electives. Those students not meeting general entrance criteria can petition the Admissions Appeal Committee of the Admissions Office. These students must submit a personal statement and two letters of recommendation, plus disclosure of their learning disability, to be eligible for special consideration. The Admissions Committee has a representative from Disabled Student Services.

ADDITIONAL INFORMATION

No skills courses are offered by the DRC, nor is tutoring offered by the DRC. Referral for skills courses and tutoring is made to regular university services. Recent changes in SJSU policy require that any remediation needed in math and English be cleared during students' first years. Transfer students must have completed oral communication, English 1A equivalent, critical thinking, and math past intermediate algebra. Students who request the use of a calculator in an exam will need to secure permission from the professor, as well as have appropriate documentation identifying that this is a necessary accommodation to compensate for the disability. Some accommodations include note-taking, priority registration, test accommodations, adaptive technology, disability management, learning disability assessment, readers, academic counseling, and faculty and staff consultation to assist with access and recommended accommodations. Students who are transferring to San Jose State University from another campus in California do not need to provide new documentation of the learning disability.

LEARNING DISABILITY PROGRAMS OR SERVICES

Contact Information
Name of program or department: Disability Resource Center
 Telephone: 408-924-6000
 Fax: 408-924-5999

LEARNING DISABILITY SERVICES

Accommodations are determined on an individual basis after a thorough review of appropriate, current documentation. The accommodations requested must be supported through the documentation provided and must be logically linked to the current impact of the condition on academic functioning.

Allowed in exams
 Calculator: Case-by-case basis
 Dictionary: Yes
 Computer: Yes
 Spellchecker: Yes
Extended test time: Yes
Scribes: Yes
Proctors: Yes
Oral exams: Yes
Note-takers: Yes

Distraction-reduced environment: Yes
Tape recording in class: Yes
Electronic texts: Yes
Accommodations for students with ADHD: Yes
Kurzweil Reader: Yes
Other assistive technology: Yes
Priority registration: Yes

Added costs for services: No
LD specialists: Yes
Professional tutors: No
Peer tutors: No
Max. hours/wk. for services: Case-by-case basis
How professors are notified of LD/ADHD: Case-by-case basis

GENERAL ADMISSIONS INFORMATION

Office of Admission: 408-924-2550

ENTRANCE REQUIREMENTS

Academic units required: 4 English, 3 math, 2 science (2 science labs), 2 foreign language, 1 social studies, 1 history, 1 academic elective, 1 visual/performing arts. **Academic units recommended:** 4 math, 3 science. High school diploma is required, and GED is accepted. ACT with Writing component required. TOEFL required of all international applicants: minimum paper TOEFL 550, minimum computer TOEFL 213.

Application deadline: 11/30
Notification: Rolling
Average GPA: NR
ACT Composite middle 50% range: NR

SAT Math middle 50% range: NR
SAT Critical Reading middle 50% range: NR
SAT Writing middle 50% range: NR

Graduated top 10% of class: NR
Graduated top 25% of class: NR
Graduated top 50% of class: NR

COLLEGE GRADUATION REQUIREMENTS

Course waivers allowed: Yes
In what course: General education quantitative reasoning substitutions made on case-by-case basis.
Course substitutions allowed: Yes
In what course: General education quantitative reasoning substitutions made on case-by-case basis; must be disability related.

ADDITIONAL INFORMATION

Environment: The university is located on 117 acres in an urban area in the center of San Jose.

Student Body
 Undergrad enrollment: 24,794
 Women: 52%
 Men: 48%
 Percent out-of-state: 1%

Cost Information
 In-state tuition: $6,828
 Out-of-state tuition: $16,214
 Room & board: $10,733
Housing Information
 University housing: Yes
 Percent living on campus: 7%

Greek System
 Fraternity: Yes
 Sorority: Yes
Athletics: Division I

SANTA CLARA UNIVERSITY

500 El Camino Real, Santa Clara, CA 95053
Phone: 408-554-4700 • Fax: 408-554-5255
E-mail: ugadmissions@scu.edu • Web: www.scu.edu
Support: CS • Institution: 4-year private

PROGRAMS OR SERVICES FOR STUDENTS WITH LD

The Primary mission of Disabilities Resources is to enhance academic progress and build bridges connecting the various services of the university for all students. This goal is met by providing academic intervention programs and opportunities to increase students' personal understanding of their disability. Disabilities Resources is a resource area that helps to ensure equal access to all academic and programmatic activities for students with disabilities. This goal is met through the provision of Academic Support Services, contact with other university offices, educational programming on disability issues for the university, and, most importantly, assistance in teaching students effective self-advocacy skills. Students with disabilities must have documentation of their disability from a qualified professional.

Students must submit proper documentation to obtain services through the Office of Disabilities Resources. The documentation needs to have been completed within the past four years to be valid and must include a diagnostic statement; the date of the disability's onset, if appropriate; what procedures and measures (formal and informal) were used to assess the condition; what functional limitations there are and how they will affect academics; if appropriate, all psychometric testing results (standard scores or percentile scores); and what the examiners' recommendations are for specific academic accommodations for a documented disability or attention deficit hyperactivity disorder, a narrative listing in history of ADD/ADHD, must be completed by a certified medical professional addressing treatment plan.

ADMISSION INFORMATION FOR STUDENTS WITH LD/ADHD

College entrance tests required: Yes
Interview required: No
Essay required: No
What documentation required for LD: Psycho Ed evaluation to include: relevant historical info, instructional interventions, related services, age diagnosed, objective data (aptitude, achievement, info processing), test scores (standard, percentile and grade equivalents) and describe functional limitations.
With general application: No
To receive services after enrolling: Yes
What documentation required for ADHD: Diagnosis based on DSM-V; history of behaviors impairing functioning in academic setting; diagnostic interview; history of symptoms; evidence of ongoing behaviors.

With general application: No
Submitted to: Disability Resources
Special Ed. HS course work accepted: No
Specific course requirements for all applicants: No
Separate application required for program services: Yes
# of LD applications submitted each year: NR
# of LD applications accepted yearly: NR
Total # of students receiving LD services: 156
Acceptance into program means acceptance into college: No

ADMISSIONS

All students submit the same general application. Santa Clara takes pride in the personal nature of its admission process. All applicants are carefully reviewed. Freshman applicants are offered admission based upon (1) high school record; (2) ACT/SAT; (3) recommendations; and (4) personal factors. Applicants submitting a nonstandardized ACT/SAT are encouraged to write a personal statement to assist the admission committee in evaluating the application.

ADDITIONAL INFORMATION

The Disabilities Resources staff meets individually with students. Some of the academic accommodations provided by DR include note-taking and test accommodations. Other support services may include priority registration, tutoring or academic counseling, and self-advocacy. Graduate students with learning disabilities are offered the same services and accommodations as those provided for undergraduate students. All lower-division students have access to peer-tutoring, drop-in math lab, and a drop-in writing center. Some other accommodations will need to be approved by the professor.

PROGRAM FOR DISABILITY SERVICES

Contact Information
Name of program or department: Disability Resources (DR)
  Telephone: 408-554-4111
  Fax: 408-554-2709

LEARNING DISABILITY SERVICES

Accommodations are decided upon an individual basis after a thorough review of appropriate, current documentation. The accommodations requested must be supported through the documentation provided and must be logically linked to the current impact of the condition on academic functioning. .

Allowed in exams
  Calculator: Yes
  Dictionary: Yes
  Computer: Yes
  Spellchecker: Yes
Extended test time: Yes
Scribes: Yes
Proctors: Yes
Oral exams: No
Note-takers: Yes

Distraction-reduced environment: Yes
Tape recording in class: Yes
Electronic texts: Yes
Accommodations for students with ADHD: Yes
Kurzweil Reader: Yes
Other assistive technology: Certain of the above accommodations marked "yes" would be with the professor's approval.
Priority registration: No

Added costs for services: No
LD specialists: Yes
Professional tutors: No
Peer tutors: 50
Max. hours/wk. for services: Varies
How professors are notified of LD/ADHD: Student responsibility with director approval

GENERAL ADMISSIONS INFORMATION

Office of Admission: 408-554-5251

ENTRANCE REQUIREMENTS
Academic units required: 4 English, 3 mathematics, 2 science, 2 foreign language, 3 social studies, 1 academic electives. **Academic units recommended:** 4 English, 4 mathematics, 3 science, 3 foreign language, 3 social studies, 1 visual/performing arts, 1 academic electives. High school diploma is required and GED is not accepted. SAT or ACT required; TOEFL required of all international applicants; minimum paper TOEFL 550, minimum computer TOEFL 213.

Application deadline: 1/7
Notification: 4/1
Average GPA: 3.61
ACT Composite middle 50% range: 27–31

SAT Math middle 50% range: 600–690
SAT Critical Reading middle 50% range: 570–680
SAT Writing middle 50% range: NR

Graduated top 10% of class: 42%
Graduated top 25% of class: 75%
Graduated top 50% of class: 93%

COLLEGE GRADUATION REQUIREMENTS

Course waivers allowed: No
Course substitutions allowed: Yes
In what course: Foreign language

ADDITIONAL INFORMATION

Environment: The university is located 1 hour south of San Francisco in Silicon Valley, 3 miles from San Jose airport.

Student Body
  Undergrad enrollment: 5,229
  Women: 51%
  Men: 49%
  Percent out-of-state: 36%

Cost Information
  Tuition: $39,048
  Room and board: $11,997
Housing Information
  University housing: Yes
  Percent living on campus: 50%

Greek System
  Fraternity: No
  Sorority: No
Athletics: Division I

SANTA MONICA COLLEGE

1900 Pico Boulevard, Santa Monica, CA 90405
Phone: 310-434-4000 • Fax: 310-434-3645
E-mail: admission@smc.edu • Web: www.smc.edu
Support: CS • Institution type: 2-year public

PROGRAMS OR SERVICES FOR STUDENTS WITH LD

The college is dedicated to helping students with LD achieve their goals by assisting them in becoming independent, college students. These goals are met by screening, testing, and certifying learning disabilities; developing individual plans and recommending appropriate academic accommodations to provide academic equity; and teaching compensatory learning strategies and fostering self-awareness of learning strengths and weaknesses. Students must be evaluated to determine eligibility for the program. This evaluation is achieved in an 8-week assessment workshop where students discover their learning strengths and weaknesses through a series of tasks. Academic and thinking skills are assessed. Test results will be compared to guidelines provided by the State of California, to determine whether a student qualifies for ongoing support services student with LD. The LD specialist interprets test results and makes individual recommendations on how to improve learning and study strategies.

ADMISSION INFORMATION FOR STUDENTS WITH LD/ADHD

College entrance tests required: No
Interview required: No
Essay recommended: No
What documentation required for LD: Psycho Ed evaluation to include: relevant historical info, instructional interventions, related services, age diagnosed, objective data (aptitude, achievement, info processing), test scores (standard, percentile and grade equivalents) and describe functional limitations.
With general application: No
To receive services after enrolling: Yes
What documentation required for ADHD: Diagnosis based on DSM-V; history of behaviors impairing functioning in academic setting; diagnostic interview; history of symptoms; evidence of ongoing behaviors.

With general application: No
Submitted to: Center for Students with Disabilities
Special Ed. HS course work accepted: Yes
Specific course requirements for all applicants: No
Separate application required: No
# of LD applications submitted each year: 120
# of LD applications accepted yearly: 100
Total # of students receiving LD services: 300
Acceptance into program means acceptance into college: Students must be admitted and enrolled in the university first and then request services.

ADMISSIONS

Students may enroll at Santa Monica College if they have graduated from high school, are 18 or 16 years and submit a Student Score Report for passing the California High School Proficiency examination. Assessment tests are required to enroll in English or math courses unless the student meets the exemption criteria. Orientations can be completed in person or online. After the orientation, the student will be able to proceed with enrollment. Submission of the printed application will result in a significantly lower priority date for enrollment than online applications.

ADDITIONAL INFORMATION

After the assessment process, an individual plan is developed with recommendations for needed skills training and appropriate accommodations. Services that students may be eligible for as indicated in the personal plan: study-strategies workshops, drop-in tutoring appointments, and long-term tutoring. The LD program has help in math and English. Additional accommodations or services could include test proctoring, if recommended as an appropriate accommodation on the Student Educational Contract, which will provide a quiet, distraction-free environment; priority registration for fall and spring only; volunteer note-takers for students who have difficulty listening and taking notes at the same time; tape-recording lectures (but it is also possible to request the assistance of a student in the class who is a good note-taker and willing to volunteer); books on tape for students who have severe reading difficulties; access to the High Tech Training Center, which includes assistive technology training, word-processing classes, computer-assisted instruction, introduction to the Internet, and open lab times to get help or work on an assignment; academic advisement; and on- and off-campus referrals.

LEARNING DISABILITY PROGRAMS OR SERVICES

Contact Information
Name of program or department: Learning Disability Program/Center for Students with Disabilities
  Telephone: 310-434-4265
  Fax: 310-434-4272

LEARNING DISABILITY SERVICES

Accommodations are decided upon an individual basis after a thorough review of appropriate, current documentation. The accommodations requested must be supported through the documentation provided and must be logically linked to the current impact of the condition on academic functioning.

Allowed in exams	**Distraction-reduced environment:** Yes	**Added costs for services:** No
Calculator: Yes	**Tape recording in class:** Yes	**LD specialists:** Yes
Dictionary: Yes	**Electronic texts:** Yes	**Professional tutors:** No
Computer: Yes	**Accommodations for students with**	**Peer tutors:** Yes
Spellchecker: Yes	**ADHD:** Yes	**Max. hours/wk. for services:** N/A
Extended test time: Yes	**Kurzweil Reader:** Yes	**How professors are notified of**
Scribes: No	**Other assistive technology:** Yes	**LD/ADHD:** By student
Proctors: Yes	**Priority registration:** Yes	
Oral exams: Yes		
Note-takers: Yes		

GENERAL ADMISSIONS INFORMATION

Office of Admission: 310-434-4000

ENTRANCE REQUIREMENTS

Academic units recommended: 16 total (4 English, 3 math, 3 science, 4 social studies, and 2 foreign language). No ACT/SAT required. High school diploma or GED accepted. TOEFL required of all international applicants: minimum paper TOEFL 450, minimum computer TOEFL 133.

Application deadline: None	**SAT Math middle 50% range:** NR	**Graduated top 10% of class:** NR
Notification: Rolling	**SAT Critical Reading middle 50%**	**Graduated top 25% of class:** NR
Average GPA: NR	**range:** NR	**Graduated top 50% of class:** NR
ACT Composite middle 50% range:	**SAT Writing middle 50% range:** NR	
NR		

COLLEGE GRADUATION REQUIREMENTS

Course waivers allowed: Yes
In what course: Math proficiency exam
Course substitutions allowed: Yes
In what course: Math proficiency exam

ADDITIONAL INFORMATION

Environment: Santa Monica College is located in West Los Angeles.

Student Body	**Cost Information**	**Greek System**
Undergrad enrollment: 21,976	**In-state tuition:** $36 per unit	**Fraternity:** No
Women: 57%	**Out-of-state tuition:** $275 per unit	**Sorority:** No
Men: 43%	**Housing Information**	**Athletics:** NJCAA
Percent out-of-state: NR	**University housing:** Yes, off campus	

SANTA ROSA JUNIOR COLLEGE

Santa Rosa Campus: 1501 Mendocino Avenue, Santa Rosa, CA 95401
Phone: 707-527-4685 • Fax: 707-527-4798
Petaluma Campus: 680 Sonoma Mtn. Parkway, Petaluma, CA 94954
Phone: 707-527-4685 • Fax: 707-527-4798
E-mail: admininfo@santarosa.edu • Web: www.santarosa.edu
Support: CS • Institution type: 2-year public

PROGRAMS OR SERVICES FOR STUDENTS WITH LD

The Disability Resources Department provides students with disabilities equal access to a community college education by providing academic accommodations, support services, and advocacy services. Santa Rosa Junior College is a state supported community college that accepts all students who apply for and meet the state eligibility criteria for general admission to the college. In order to receive disability services, valid documentation that verifies a learning disability must be submitted. Learning disabilities testing must have been completed by a licensed, qualified professional using appropriate standardized testing. Santa Rosa Junior College creates a campus climate in which diverse learning styles and equal access for students with disabilities can be realized.

ADMISSION INFORMATION FOR STUDENTS WITH LD/ADHD

College entrance tests required: No
Interview required: No
Essay recommended: No
What documentation required for LD: Psycho Ed evaluation to include: relevant historical info, instructional interventions, related services, age diagnosed, objective data (aptitude, achievement, info processing), test scores (standard, percentile and grade equivalents) and describe functional limitations.
With general application: No
To receive services after enrolling: Yes
What documentation required for ADHD: Diagnosis based on DSM-V; history of behaviors impairing functioning in academic setting; diagnostic interview; history of symptoms; evidence of ongoing behaviors.

With general application: No
Submitted to: Disability Resources
Special Ed. HS course work accepted: Yes
Specific course requirements of all applicants: No
Separate application required: No
# of LD applications submitted each year: 150–200
# of LD applications accepted yearly: 125–175
Total # of students receiving LD services: 500
Acceptance into program means acceptance into college: Students must be admitted and enrolled in the college first and then request services.

ADMISSIONS

Admission to Santa Rosa is open to students with a high school diploma or a GED, or are 18 years of age or older. Students with learning disabilities must meet state eligibility requirements verifying a learning disability to qualify for services. Students must demonstrate: average to above-average intellectual ability, adequate measured achievement in at least one academic area or employment setting, a severe processing deficit in one or more areas, and a severe discrepancy between aptitude and achievement in one or more academic areas. All students must demonstrate appropriate behavior and an ability to benefit from the instructional program.

ADDITIONAL INFORMATION

The Learning Skills Program offers limited specialized classes. Support services include limited assessment for learning disabilities, advising, assistive technology, alternate media, and liaison. Services are also provided to students with medical verification of other disabilities, such as blind/low-vision, deaf/hearing impaired, physical disabilities, psychological disabilities, chronic health impaired, etc.

LEARNING DISABILITY PROGRAMS OR SERVICES

Contact Information
Name of program or department: Disability Resources Department
Santa Rosa Campus: Telephone: 707-527-4278   **Petaluma Campus:Telephone:** 707-778-2492
Fax: 707-524-1768   **Fax:** 707-778-2497

LEARNING DISABILITY SERVICES

Accommodations are decided upon an individual basis after a thorough review of appropriate, current documentation. The accommodations requested must be supported through the documentation provided.

Allowed in exams
  Calculator: Yes
  Dictionary: Yes
  Computer: Yes
  Spellchecker: Yes
Extended test time: Yes
Scribes: Yes
Proctors: Yes
Oral exams: Yes
Note-takers: Yes

Distraction-reduced environment: Yes
Tape recording in class: Yes
Electronic texts: Yes
Accommodations for students with ADHD: Yes
Kurzweil Reader: NR
Other assistive technology: NR
Priority registration: Yes

Added costs for services: No
LD specialists: Yes
Professional tutors: NR
Peer tutors: NR
Max. hours/wk. for services: NR
How professors are notified of LD/ADHD: NR

GENERAL ADMISSIONS INFORMATION

Office of Admission: 707-527-4685

ENTRANCE REQUIREMENTS

The college has an open-door admissions policy. GED or high school diploma required. **Academic units recommended:** 16 total (4 English, 3 math, 3 science, 4 social studies, and 2 foreign language.) TOEFL required of all international applicants: minimum paper TOEFL 475, minimum IBT TOEFL 53.

Application deadline: None
Notification: Rolling
Average GPA: NR
ACT Composite middle 50% range: NR

SAT Math middle 50% range: NR
SAT Critical Reading middle 50% range: NR
SAT Writing middle 50% range: NR

Graduated top 10% of class: NR
Graduated top 25% of class: NR
Graduated top 50% of class: NR

COLLEGE GRADUATION REQUIREMENTS

Course waivers allowed: Yes
In what course: Student must attempt math course/s before a waiver is granted.
Course substitutions allowed: No

ADDITIONAL INFORMATION

Environment: The college is located on 93 acres with easy access to San Francisco.

Student Body
  Santa Rosa enrollment: 35,000
  Petaluma enrollment: 6,000
  Women: 60%
  Men: 40%
  Percent out-of-state: 2%

Cost Information
  In-state tuition: $36 per unit
  Out-of-state tuition: $212 per unit
Housing Information
  University housing: No
  Percent living on campus: NR

Greek System
  Fraternity: No
  Sorority: No
Athletics: Intercollegiate

SIERRA COLLEGE

5000 Rocklin Road, Rocklin, CA 95677
Phone: 916-789-0553 • Fax: 916-789-2967
E-mail: gmodder@sierracollege.edu • Web: www.sierracollege.edu
Support: CS • Institution type: 2-year public

PROGRAMS OR SERVICES FOR STUDENTS WITH LD

The goals of the program are to assist students with learning disabilities in reaching their academic/vocational goals, help the students strengthen and develop their perceptual skills, and provide the support needed to maximize student success. Sierra College subscribes to the psychometric-evaluation model established by the California Community College System. This six-step process includes intake screening, measured achievement, ability level, processing deficit, aptitude-achievement discrepancy, and eligibility recommendation. Students are evaluated individually through the Learning Disabilities Orientation course. This is a mainstreamed program with no special classes, but it does provide support and accommodations for students with learning disabilities.

ADMISSION INFORMATION FOR STUDENTS WITH LD/ADHD

College entrance tests required: No
Interview required: No
Essay recommended: No
What documentation required for LD: Psycho Ed evaluation to include: relevant historical info, instructional interventions, related services, age diagnosed, objective data (aptitude, achievement, info processing), test scores (standard, percentile and grade equivalents) and describe functional limitations.
With general application: No
To receive services after enrolling: Yes
What documentation required for ADHD: Diagnosis based on DSM-V; history of behaviors impairing functioning in academic setting; diagnostic interview; history of symptoms; evidence of ongoing behaviors.

With general application: No
Submitted to: Disabled Student Program and Services
Special Ed. HS course work accepted: Yes
Specific course requirements for all applicants: NR
Separate application required: No
# of LD applications submitted each year: NR
# of LD applications accepted yearly: NR
Total # of students receiving LD services: 350
Acceptance into program means acceptance into college: Students must be admitted and enrolled in the university first and then request services.

ADMISSIONS

Sierra College has an open admissions policy for those students who meet the regular entrance requirements. ACT/SAT are not required, and there are no cutoffs for GPA, class rank, or test scores. Additionally, no specific courses are required for admission. Any student who holds a high school diploma or GED is admitted. Services are provided to all enrolled students with appropriate documentation.

ADDITIONAL INFORMATION

To receive services and accommodations, students must meet the eligibility requirements set forth by the state of California for students with learning disabilities. Skills courses are available in reading, math, writing, study strategies, English as a second language, and spelling. These skills classes are offered for college credit. In addition, students can get assistance in test-taking techniques, priority registration, and peer tutoring. Other services include assessment and evaluation of learning disabilities, individual education plans, identification of students' learning styles and modalities, perceptual training programs, test-taking facilitation, compensatory learning strategies/techniques, computer-assisted instruction, and classroom accommodations.

LEARNING DISABILITY PROGRAMS OR SERVICES

Contact Information
Name of program or department: Learning Opportunities Center/Disabled Student Programs and Services (DSP&S)
Telephone: 916-789-2939

LEARNING DISABILITY SERVICES

Accommodations are decided upon an individual basis after a thorough review of appropriate, current documentation. The accommodations requested must be supported through the documentation provided and must be logically linked to the current impact of the condition on academic functioning.

Allowed in exams
Calculator: Yes
Dictionary: Yes
Computer: Yes
Spellchecker: Yes
Extended test time: Yes
Scribes: No
Proctors: Yes
Oral exams: Yes
Note-takers: Yes

Distraction-reduced environment: Yes
Tape recording in class: Yes
Electronic texts: Yes
Accommodations for students with ADHD: Yes
Kurzweil Reader: No
Other assistive technology: Yes
Priority registration: Yes

Added costs for services: No
LD specialists: Yes
Professional tutors: No
Peer tutors: Approximately 100
Max. hours/wk. for services: Unlimited
How professors are notified of LD/ADHD: By student

GENERAL ADMISSIONS INFORMATION

Office of Admission: 916-781-0430

ENTRANCE REQUIREMENTS

The college has an open admissions policy. High school diploma or GED is accepted. ACT/SAT are not required for admission.

Application deadline: None
Notification: Rolling
Average GPA: NR
ACT Composite middle 50% range: NR

SAT Math middle 50% range: NR
SAT Critical Reading middle 50% range: NR
SAT Writing middle 50% range: NR

Graduated top 10% of class: NR
Graduated top 25% of class: NR
Graduated top 50% of class: NR

COLLEGE GRADUATION REQUIREMENTS

Course waivers allowed: Yes
In what course: Waivers are provided on an individual basis.
Course substitutions allowed: Yes
In what course: Substitutions are provided on an individual basis.

ADDITIONAL INFORMATION

Environment: The school is located on a 327-acre campus in a rural setting with easy access to Sacramento.

Student Body
Undergrad enrollment: 13,403
Women: 56%
Men: 44%
Percent out-of-state: 1%

Cost Information
In-state tuition: $36 per unit
Out-of-state tuition: $216 per unit
Room & board: $6,700
Housing Information
University housing: Yes
Percent living on campus: 1% (150 students)

Greek System
Fraternity: No
Sorority: No
Athletics: Intercollegiate

SONOMA STATE UNIVERSITY

1801 East Cotati Avenue, Rohnert Park, CA 94928
Phone: 707-664-2778 • Fax: 707-664-2060
Web: www.sonoma.edu
Support: S • Institution type: 4-year public

PROGRAMS OR SERVICES FOR STUDENTS WITH LD

After admission to Sonoma State University, students are encouraged to register with DSS by contacting the office and providing documentation of their disability. Students with disabilities who register with DSS are eligible for a variety of services and accommodations. All accommodations are determined on an individual basis and will vary from one student to the next depending on disability verification and professional judgment. Services may include disability management advising, classroom accommodations, test-taking accommodations, alternate media, and assistive technology. Visit www.sonoma.edu/lss/ for more information about the Learning Center and www.sonoma.edu/writingcenter/ for more information about the Writing Center.

ADMISSION INFORMATION FOR STUDENTS WITH LD/ADHD

College entrance tests required: Yes
Interview required: No
Essay recommended: No
What documentation required for LD: Psycho Ed evaluation to include: relevant historical info, instructional interventions, related services, age diagnosed, objective data (aptitude, achievement, info processing), test scores (standard, percentile and grade equivalents) and describe functional limitations.
With general application: No
To receive services after enrolling: Yes
What documentation required for ADHD: Diagnosis based on DSM-V; history of behaviors impairing functioning in academic setting; diagnostic interview; history of symptoms; evidence of ongoing behaviors.

With general application: No
Submitted to: Disability Services for Students (DSS)
Special Ed. HS course work accepted: No
Specific course requirements of all applicants: Yes
Separate application required: No
# of LD applications submitted each year: 60
# of LD applications accepted yearly: 60
Total # of students receiving LD services: 460 (Services are provided to all students with disabilities who are registered with DSS. DSS is not a program specific to students with LD and/or ADHD.)
Acceptance into program means acceptance into college: Students must be admitted and enrolled in the university first and then request services.

ADMISSIONS

Admission is based on a combination of high school GPA, test scores, and college-preparatory classes. Courses include 4 years of English, 3 years of math, 1 year of social studies, 2 years of science, 2 years of a foreign language, 1 year of visual/performing arts, and 3 years of academic electives. SAT/ACT score requirements depend on the GPA. However, a 2.0 GPA is the absolute minimum. Students with learning disabilities submit a general application. If a limited number of required courses are missing, students can be granted a conditional admission, and these courses must be made up in college. Students not meeting either regular or conditional admissions may initiate a request for special admissions by writing a letter to the DSS director providing information about strengths, weaknesses, and why special admission is needed. LD diagnostic evaluation and two letters of recommendations are also required for conditional admission. All special admission applicants are interviewed in person or by phone. Special admission is only available to designated groups of students. Special admissions applicants need to submit a letter to Linda Lipps describing what subject areas are missing or if the GPA or SAT/ACT are low. The staff of DSS makes recommendations, but the final decision is made by the Office of Admissions.

ADDITIONAL INFORMATION

DSS does not offer skills classes or tutoring. Reading, writing, and math are offered through the Learning Skills Services. Tutorial assistance is available in the Tutorial Center. There are no LD specialists in the DSS; however, there are disability management advisors who authorize accommodations. With appropriate documentation, some of the services or accommodations offered include the use of calculators, dictionaries, computers, or spellchecker during exams; extended time on tests; scribes; proctors; oral exams; note-takers; distraction-free testing environments; tape recorder in class; taped text; and priority registration.

LEARNING DISABILITY PROGRAMS OR SERVICES

Contact Information
Name of program or department: Disability Services for Students (DSS)
  Telephone: 707-664-2958
  Fax: 707-664-3330

LEARNING DISABILITY SERVICES

All services and accommodations are determined on an individual basis and will vary from one student to the next depending on disability verification and professional judgment.

Allowed in exams (determined on a case-by-case basis)
  Calculator: Yes
  Dictionary: Yes
  Computer: Yes
  Spellchecker: Yes
Extended test time: Yes
Scribes: Yes
Proctors: Yes
Oral exams: Yes
Note-takers: Yes

Distraction-reduced environment: Yes
Tape recording in class: Yes
Electronic texts: Yes
Accommodations for students with ADHD: Yes
Kurzweil Reader: Yes
Other assistive technology: Yes
Priority registration: Yes

Added costs for services: No
LD specialists: No
Professional tutors: No
Peer tutors: In the tutorial program
Max. hours/wk. for services: NR
How professors are notified of LD/ADHD: By student via accomodation letter

GENERAL ADMISSIONS INFORMATION

Office of Admission: 707-664-2778

ENTRANCE REQUIREMENTS

Academic units required: 4 English, 3 math, 2 science (1 science lab), 2 foreign language, 2 history, 1 visual/performing arts, 1 U.S. government. High school diploma is required, and GED is accepted. TOEFL required of all international applicants: minimum paper TOEFL 500, minimum computer TOEFL 173.

Application deadline: 11/30
Notification: Rolling
Average GPA: NR
ACT Composite middle 50% range: NR

SAT Math middle 50% range: NR
SAT Critical Reading middle 50% range: NR
SAT Writing middle 50% range: NR

Graduated top 10% of class: NR
Graduated top 25% of class: NR
Graduated top 50% of class: NR

COLLEGE GRADUATION REQUIREMENTS

Course waivers allowed: No
Course substitutions allowed: Yes
In what course: TBD

ADDITIONAL INFORMATION

Environment: The school is located on 220 acres with easy access to San Francisco.

Student Body
  Undergrad enrollment: 8,000
  Women: 63%
  Men: 37%
  Percent out-of-state: 1%

Cost Information
  In-state tuition: $6,174
  Out-of-state tuition: $17,334
  Room & board: $10,961
Housing Information
  University housing: Yes
  Percent living on campus: 35%

Greek System
  Fraternity: Yes
  Sorority: Yes
Athletics: Division II

STANFORD UNIVERSITY

Office of Undergraduate Admission, Montag Hall, Stanford, CA 94305-3020
Phone: 650-723-2091 • Fax: 650-723-6050
E-mail: admission@stanford.edu • Web: www.stanford.edu
Support: CS • Institution type: 4-year private

PROGRAMS OR SERVICES FOR STUDENTS WITH LD

The Office of Accessible Education (OAE) provides services and resources to students with disabilities. Students who may be eligible for services have a variety of disabilities, including mobility impairments, chronic illness, sensory disabilities, learning disabilities, and psychological disabilities. The center's goal is to enable students with disabilities to participate fully in the educational experience at Stanford while meeting the academic standards maintained by the University. The Schwab Learning Center, affiliated with the OAE, offers enhanced services specifically for students with learning disabilities and attention deficit hyperactivity disorder. The center was established in 2002 by an endowment from Charles and Helen Schwab. Services may include screening assessments for learning disabilities, individual learning strategy sessions, individual tutoring in various academic disciplines, workshops for faculty and teaching staff, as well as community outreach programs. The funding support provided by Mr. and Mrs. Schwab allows Stanford University to offer services and resources above and beyond what is required by federal and state disability laws.

ADMISSION INFORMATION FOR STUDENTS WITH LD/ADHD

College entrance tests required: Yes
Interview required: No
Essay recommended: No
What documentation required for LD: Psycho Ed evaluation to include: relevant historical info, instructional interventions, related services, age diagnosed, objective data (aptitude, achievement, info processing), test scores (standard, percentile and grade equivalents) and describe functional limitations.
With general application: No
To receive services after enrolling: Yes
What documentation required for ADHD: Diagnosis based on DSM-V; history of behaviors impairing functioning in academic setting; diagnostic interview; history of symptoms; evidence of ongoing behaviors.

With general application: No
Submitted to: Office of Accessible Education
Special Ed. HS course work accepted: No
Specific course requirements: NR
Specific course requirements of all applicants: Yes
Separate application required: No
# of LD applications submitted each year: NR
# of LD applications accepted yearly: NR
Total # of students receiving LD services: 253 (LD and AD/HD)
Acceptance into program means acceptance into college: Students must be admitted and enrolled prior to requesting services.

ADMISSIONS

Stanford seeks to enroll students with excellent academic records who show evidence of personal achievement outside the classroom and who have used the resources available to them to their fullest potential. The policy on the admissions of students with learning disabilities makes clear there is no separate academic program. Students should take a strong college-preparatory curriculum, including honors and Advanced Placement courses. Applicants must submit the ACT with Writing or the SAT Reasoning Test, plus three SAT Subject Tests. The university will look at ACT/SAT test scores in context of the learning disability. Students must release all tests taken. Typically, applicants to Stanford rank in the top 10 percent from a public high school or the top 20–30 percent in a private high school. Stanford has a "Single Choice Early Action" policy. This means a student can apply Early Action to Stanford but can not submit any other Early Action or Early Decision applications. Students applying "SCEA" may apply regular decision to other colleges.

ADDITIONAL INFORMATION

Students seeking services or accommodations for specific learning disabilities or attention deficit hyperactivity disorder must submit psychoeducational evaluations that are recent enough to reflect current levels of functioning. There are no skill courses offered. Tutoring is available through the SLC and on campus through the Center for Teaching and Learning. A peer support group is available. Other accommodations can include note-taking services, typist/scribe services, course materials in alternate format, letters to professors for course/exam accommodations, and exam room accommodation. Services and accommodations are offered to undergraduate and graduate students.

LEARNING DISABILITY PROGRAMS OR SERVICES

Contact Information
Name of program or department: Office of Accessible Education and Schwab Learning Center
 Telephone: 650-723-1066, 650-723-1067
 Fax: 650-725-5301

LEARNING DISABILITY SERVICES

Accommodations are decided upon an individual basis after a thorough review of appropriate, current documentation. The accommodations requested must be supported through the documentation provided and must be logically linked to the current impact of the condition on academic functioning. Note: Accommodations provided must not fundamentally alter what the instructor is assessing.

Allowed in exams
 Calculator: Yes
 Dictionary: NR
 Computer: Yes
 Spellchecker: Yes
Extended test time: Yes
Scribes: Yes
Proctors: No (honor code)
Oral exams: Considered
Note-takers: Yes

Distraction-reduced environment: Yes
Tape recording in class: Yes
Electronic texts: Yes
Accommodations for students with
 ADHD: Yes
Kurzweil Reader: Yes
Other assistive technology: Yes
Priority registration: No

Added costs for services: No
LD specialists: Yes
Professional tutors: Yes
Peer tutors: Yes
Max. hours/wk. for services: Varies
How professors are notified of
 LD/ADHD: By student

GENERAL ADMISSIONS INFORMATION

Office of Admission: 650-723-2091

ENTRANCE REQUIREMENTS

Academic units recommended: 4 English, 4 math, 3 science (3 science labs), 3 foreign language, 2 social studies, 1 history. High school diploma is required, and GED is accepted.

Application deadline: 1/1
Notification: 4/1
Average GPA: Nr
ACT Composite middle 50% range:
 30–34

SAT Math middle 50% range:
 690–780
SAT Critical Reading middle 50%
 range: 67–770
SAT Writing middle 50% range:
 680–780

Graduated top 10% of class: 92%
Graduated top 25% of class: 98%
Graduated top 50% of class: 100%

COLLEGE GRADUATION REQUIREMENTS

Course waivers allowed: No
Course substitutions allowed: Considered

ADDITIONAL INFORMATION

Environment: Stanford University is located about 30 minutes south of San Francisco.

Student Body
 Undergrad enrollment: 6,988
 Women: 49%
 Men: 51%
 Percent out-of-state: 55%

Cost Information
 Tuition: $40,050
 Room & board: $12,291
Housing Information
 University housing: Yes
 Percent living on campus: 91%

Greek System
 Fraternity: Yes
 Sorority: Yes
Athletics: Division I

U. OF CALIFORNIA—BERKELEY

Office of Undergraduate Admissions, 110 Sproul Hall #5800,
Berkeley, CA 94720-5800 • Phone: 510-642-3175 • Fax: 510-642-7333
E-mail: ouars@uclink.berkeley.edu • Web: www.berkeley.edu
Support: CS • Institution type: 4-year public

PROGRAMS OR SERVICES FOR STUDENTS WITH LD

The Disabled Student Program (DSP) seeks to ensure that students with disabilities have equal access to educational opportunities and student life at UC—Berkeley. DSP works to sustain a supportive environment that provides appropriate and necessary disability-related accommodations, enables students to demonstrate their knowledge and skills, facilitates students' success in academic pursuits, and promotes independence. DSP's services assist students as they develop their skills and the qualities needed to meet their educational, personal, and professional goals. DSP also works to support the efforts of the campus community to ensure full participation of students with disabilities in every aspect of university life. DSP is a recipient of a TRIO Student Support Services Grant. Funds are used to provide a variety of services for students, helping them to achieve academic success, complete graduation requirements and plan successful post-graduation educations or careers. For services, DSP must have verification of the disability on file. Students with LD must submit a psychoeducational evaluation completed by a qualified professional. Students with ADHD must submit a letter from a qualified professional who has an expertise in diagnosing ADHD in adults. Additional testing may be requested if it is deemed necessary for the planning and provision of appropriate accommodations and services. Information on the DSP and documentation requirements are available at dsp.berkeley.edu.

ADMISSION INFORMATION FOR STUDENTS WITH LD/ADHD

College entrance tests required: Yes
Interview required: No
Essay recommended: Yes
What documentation required for LD: Psycho Ed evaluation to include: relevant historical info, instructional interventions, related services, age diagnosed, objective data (aptitude, achievement, info processing), test scores (standard, percentile and grade equivalents) and describe functional limitations.
With general application: No
To receive services after enrolling: Yes
What documentation required for ADHD: Diagnosis based on DSM-V; history of behaviors impairing functioning in academic setting; diagnostic interview; history of symptoms; evidence of ongoing behaviors.

With general application: No
Submitted to: Disabled Student Program
Special Ed. HS course work accepted: No
Specific course requirements of all applicants: Yes
Separate application required: No
# of LD applications submitted each year: NR
# of LD applications accepted yearly: NR
Total # of students receiving LD services: 242
Acceptance into program means acceptance into college: Students must be admitted and enrolled in the university first and then request services.

ADMISSIONS

An LD and admission specialist are available to meet applicants with LD interested in UC Berkeley. Specialists will review the transcript and give advice on how to proceed with the application. DSP works closely with Admissions. There are two tiers for admission: Tier I is an automatic admission; Tier II applicants may need other criteria to be admitted. The impact of a disability could be a factor in an admission for a Tier II applicant. When an applicant self-discloses a disability, DSP requests documentation, and a statement about the impact of the disability. DSP uses this information to answer questions about the applicant from the Admissions Office. In general, applicants have 4 English, 2 social science, 3 math (4 years recommended), 2 science (3 recommended), 2 foreign language (3 years recommended), 1 visual/performing arts, and 1 year academic elective from previous areas.

ADDITIONAL INFORMATION

DSP provides academic accommodations; consulting with instructors about accommodations; academic strategies and study skills; academic advising, adaptive technology, support groups, and a course "Facilitating Success" for students with LD/ADHD that centers on understanding learning differences, maximizing strengths, academic planning, research, writing, exam preparation, and using university resources; priority registration; specialists to help in problem-solving strategies and solutions to difficult problems; informational workshops on topics like understanding disabilities and individual learning styles; reading, writing, and research efficiency; memory strategies, self-advocacy; computer applications that facilitate learning; and career or graduate school planning.

LEARNING DISABILITY PROGRAMS OR SERVICES

Contact Information
Name of program or department: Disabled Students' Program
 Telephone: 510-642-0518
 Fax: 510-643-9686

LEARNING DISABILITY SERVICES

Accommodations are decided upon an individual basis after a thorough review of appropriate, current documentation. The accommodations requested must be supported through the documentation provided and must be logically linked to the current impact of the condition on academic functioning.

Allowed in exams	**Distraction-reduced environment:** Yes	**Added costs for services:** No
Calculator: Yes	**Tape recording in class:** Yes	**LD specialists:** Yes
Spellchecker: Yes	**Electronic texts:** Yes	**Professional tutors:** No
Extended test time: Yes	**Accommodations for students with**	**Peer tutors:** Some individual tutoring is
Scribes: Yes	**ADHD:** Yes	available through the TRIO grant.
Proctors: Yes	**Kurzweil Reader:** Yes	**max. hours/wk. for services:** NR
Oral exams: No	**Other assistive technology:** Yes	**How professors are notified of**
Note-takers: Yes	**Priority registration:** Yes	**LD/ADHD:** By student

GENERAL ADMISSIONS INFORMATION

Office of Admission: 510-642-3175

ENTRANCE REQUIREMENTS
Academic units required: 4 English, 3 math, 2 science (2 science labs), 2 foreign language, 2 social studies, 2 history, 1 academic elective, 1 visual/performing arts. **Academic units recommended:** 4 English, 4 math, 3 science (3 science labs), 3 foreign language, 2 social studies, 2 historys, 1 academic elective, 1 visual/performing arts. High school diploma is required, and GED is accepted. SAT Reasoning or ACT with Writing component required plus 2 SAT Subject Tests. TOEFL required of all international applicants: minimum paper TOEFL 550, minimum computer TOEFL 213.

Application deadline: 11/30	**SAT Math middle 50% range:**	**Graduated top 10% of class:** 98%
Notification: Decisions available on	650–770	**Graduated top 25% of class:** 100%
website by 3/31	**SAT Critical Reading middle 50%**	**Graduated top 50% of class:** 100%
Average GPA: 3.84	**range:** 600–720	
ACT Composite middle 50% range:	**SAT Writing middle 50% range:**	
28–33	620–740	

COLLEGE GRADUATION REQUIREMENTS

Course waivers allowed: Yes
In what course: Math waivers are considered on a case-by-case basis.
Course substitutions allowed: Yes
In what course: Foreign language requirement can be substituted with cultural courses on a case-by-case basis.

ADDITIONAL INFORMATION

Environment: The 1,232-acre campus is in an urban area 10 miles east of San Francisco.

Student Body	**Cost Information**	**Greek System**
Undergrad enrollment: 25,885	**In-state tuition:** $11,220	**Fraternity:** Yes
Women: NR	**Out-of-state tuition:** $34,098	**Sorority:** Yes
Men: NR	**Room & board:** $14,990	**Athletics:** Division I
Percent out-of-state: 10%	**Housing Information**	
	University housing: Yes	
	Percent living on campus: 35%	

U. OF CALIFORNIA—LOS ANGELES

1147 Murphy Hall, Box 951436, Los Angeles, CA 90095-1436
Phone: 310-825-3101 • Fax: 310-206-1206
E-mail: ugadm@saonet.ucla.edu • Web: www.ucla.edu
Support: CS • Institution type: 4-year public

PROGRAMS OR SERVICES FOR STUDENTS WITH LD

UCLA complies with state, federal, and university guidelines that mandate full access for students with disabilities, including learning disabilities. UCLA complies with the requirement to provide reasonable accommodations for documented students to allow them to participate in their academic program to the greatest extent possible. Students with other documented types of learning disabilities, including attention deficit hyperactive disorder and traumatic brain injury, are also served by the LD program. The UCLA LD program is coordinated by a full-time learning disabilities specialist and offers a full range of accommodations and services. Services are individually designed and include counseling, special test arrangements, note-taker services, readers, priority enrollment, adaptive technology, and individual tutoring. An active support group provides opportunities for students to discuss mutual concerns and enhance learning strategies. Workshops and speakers address skill development and topics of interest. In the Peer Mentor Program, continuing students with learning disabilities serve as resources to entering students.

ADMISSION INFORMATION FOR STUDENTS WITH LD/ADHD

College entrance tests required: Yes
Interview required: No
Essay recommended: Yes
What documentation required for LD: Psycho Ed evaluation to include: relevant historical info, instructional interventions, related services, age diagnosed, objective data (aptitude, achievement, info processing), test scores (standard, percentile and grade equivalents) and describe functional limitations.
With general application: No
To receive services after enrolling: Yes
What documentation required for ADHD: Diagnosis based on DSM-V; history of behaviors impairing functioning in academic setting; diagnostic interview; history of symptoms; evidence of ongoing behaviors.

With general application: No
Submitted to: Office for Students with Disabilities
Special Ed. HS course work accepted: No
Specific course requirements of all applicants: Yes
Separate application required: No
# of LD applications submitted each year: NR
# of LD applications accepted yearly: NR
Total # of students receiving LD services: 225–300
Acceptance into program means acceptance into college: Students must be admitted and enrolled in the university first and then request services.

ADMISSIONS

There are no special admissions criteria for students with learning disabilities. In an academic review, the university will assess and balance a variety of academic factors to determine the overall scholastic strength of each applicant. UCLA does not use a formula. The comprehensive review includes the remainder of the freshman applicants after the academic review. While commitment to intellectual development and academic progress continues to be of primary importance, the personal statement also forms an integral part of this review. All applicants are required to submit the SAT or ACT and SAT Subject Tests (including the Writing Test, Mathematics Level I or II, and either English Literature, Foreign Language, Science, or Social Studies). To be competitive, students usually score in the high 20s on the ACT or high 1100s on the SAT I and between 500–600 on each of the SAT Subject Tests. Required high school courses are 4 years of English, 2 years of history/social science, 3 years of math, 2 years of a foreign language (3 years recommended), 2 years of science lab (3 years recommended), and 2 years of electives. Additional criteria are based on an eligibility index using test scores and class rank. Selected students are admitted for winter. Admissions readers pay attention to significant obstacles and challenges related in personal statements. The LD specialists provide disability-related information to admissions staff.

ADDITIONAL INFORMATION

The LD Program includes tutors for individual classes, peer mentors, support group meetings, learning skills workshops, advocacy, referrals to campus resources, priority enrollment, orientation program, LD screening, and disability management counseling by four LD specialists including disability awareness, learning, and time management strategies, self-advocacy skills, and interpretation of evaluation reports. Accommodations could include alternatives in printed materials: (taped textbooks, computerized voice synthesizer, and Learning Ally); test-taking procedures (extended time, proctor to assist with reading and writing, distraction-free test area, computer for essay exams, or spellchecker); note-taking (note-takers or taped lectures); writing essays and papers (word processors with voice synthesizers or composition tutors); reduced course load; extended time to complete a program.

LEARNING DISABILITY PROGRAMS OR SERVICES

Contact Information
Name of program or department: Office for Students with Disabilities
  Telephone: 310-825-1501
  Fax: 310-825-9656

LEARNING DISABILITY SERVICES

Accommodations are decided upon an individual basis after a thorough review of appropriate, current documentation. The accommodations requested must be supported through the documentation provided and must be logically linked to the current impact of the condition on academic functioning.

Allowed in exams
  Calculator: Yes
  Dictionary: Yes
  Computer: Yes
  Spellchecker: Yes
Extended test time: Yes
Scribes: Yes
Proctors: Yes
Oral exams: No
Note-takers: Yes

Distraction-reduced environment: Yes
Tape recording in class: Yes
Electronic texts: Yes
Accommodations for students with ADHD: Yes
Kurzweil Reader: Yes
Other assistive technology: Yes
Priority registration: Yes

Added costs for services: No
LD specialists: Yes
Professional tutors: No
Peer tutors: Yes
Max. hours/wk. for services: Unlimited
How professors are notified of LD/ADHD: By both student and director

GENERAL ADMISSIONS INFORMATION

Office of Admission: 310-825-3101

ENTRANCE REQUIREMENTS

Academic units required: 4 English, 3 math, 2 science (2 science labs), 2 foreign language, 2 history, 1 academic elective, 1 visual/performing arts. **Academic units recommended:** 4 English, 4 math, 3 science (3 science labs), 3 foreign language, 2 historys, 1 academic elective, 1 visual/performing arts. High school diploma is required, and GED is accepted. SAT Reasoning or ACT with Writing component required plus 2 SAT Subject Tests. TOEFL required of all international applicants: minimum paper TOEFL 550, minimum computer TOEFL 220.

Application deadline: 11/30
Notification: 3/31
Average GPA: 4.22
ACT Composite middle 50% range: 25–31

SAT Math middle 50% range: 610–740
SAT Critical Reading middle 50% range: 560–690
SAT Writing middle 50% range: 590–710

Graduated top 10% of class: 97%
Graduated top 25% of class: 100%
Graduated top 50% of class: 100%

COLLEGE GRADUATION REQUIREMENTS

Course waivers allowed: No
Course substitutions allowed: Yes
In what course: Foreign language and math as appropriate based on documentation, history, and recommendation.

ADDITIONAL INFORMATION

Environment: The university is located on 419 acres in an urban area of Los Angeles.

Student Body
  Undergrad enrollment: 27,199
  Women: 55%
  Men: 45%
  Percent out-of-state: 5%

Cost Information
  In-state tuition: $16,508
  Out-of-state tuition: $39,386
  Room & board: $13,968
Housing Information
  University housing: Yes
  Percent living on campus: 45%

Greek System
  Fraternity: Yes
  Sorority: Yes
Athletics: Division I

U. OF CALIFORNIA—SAN DIEGO

9500 Gilman Drive, La Jolla, CA 92093-0021
Phone: 858-534-4831 • Fax: 858-534-5629
E-mail: admissionsreply@ucsd.edu • Web: www.ucsd.edu
Support: CS • Institution type: 4-year public

PROGRAMS OR SERVICES FOR STUDENTS WITH LD

The primary objective of the Office for Students with Disabilities (OSD) is to integrate mainstream students with learning disabilities into campus programs, services, and activities. Academic accommodations are designed to meet disability related needs without fundamentally altering the program; and may include part-time enrollment, exception to minimum academic progress requirements, substitution of course work required for graduation, and alternative test formats. This program is not intended to provide remediation. Students seeking accommodations must provide a comprehensive written evaluation that meets the following requirements: Assessments, including test scores and sub-test scores, must be provided. Testing must be current, valid, reliable, and appropriate for college age students. A narrative report needs to discuss the student's educational, medical and family histories and any presenting concerns related to learning disabilities. If co-occurring conditions exist, they need to be discussed within the context of a DSM IV diagnosis on all 5 axes. A discussion of the student's current and functional limitations needs to occur. The assessment should include aptitude testing (WAIS IV with scaled scores and percentiles and/or the W-J III Tests of Cognitive Ability with standard scores and percentiles; achievement testing (WJ-III Tests of Achievement along with specific tests such as the Nelson Denny Reading Test); Information Processing (WAIS IV or WJ-III); and a narrative report explaining that the student's difficulties are not the result of other factors such as educational under preparation, sensory impairment, cultural differences, etc.

ADMISSION INFORMATION FOR STUDENTS WITH LD/ADHD

College entrance tests required: Yes
Interview required: No
Essay recommended: Yes
What documentation required for LD: Psycho Ed evaluation to include: relevant historical info, instructional interventions, related services, age diagnosed, objective data (aptitude, achievement, info processing), test scores (standard, percentile and grade equivalents) and describe functional limitations.
With general application: No
To receive services after enrolling: Yes
What documentation required for ADHD: Diagnosis based on DSM-V; history of behaviors impairing functioning in academic setting; diagnostic interview; history of symptoms; evidence of ongoing behaviors.

With general application: No
Submitted to: Office for Students with Disabilities
Special Ed. HS course work accepted: NR
Specific course requirements of all applicants: Yes
Separate application required: Yes
# of LD applications submitted each year: NA
# of LD applications accepted yearly: NA
Total # of students receiving LD services: 100
Acceptance into program means acceptance into college: Student must be admitted and enrolled in the university first and then reviewed for LD services.

ADMISSIONS
There is no special admissions process for students with learning disabilities. All applicants must meet the same admission criteria. Students must satisfy subject, GPA, and examination requirements. 15 units of high school courses must be completed to fulfill the subject requirements. At least 7 of those 15 units must be taken in the last 2 years of high school and a grade of "C" or greater must be earned: History (2 years), English (4 years), Math (3 years, although 4 years are recommended), Lab science (2 years, although 3 years are recommended), Language other than English (2 years although 3 years are recommended), Visual and Performing Arts (1 year), College Prep Electives (1 year). Students need to earn a minimum GPA based on "a-g" courses taken in the 10th and 11th grades. California residents with a 3.0 GPA or above satisfy the minimum scholarship requirement if they achieve a correlating score on the SAT/ACT tests listed in the UC Admissions Index; Non-California residents must have a 3.4 GPA or higher in "a-g" courses and achieve a correlating score in the UC Admissions Index. The UC Admissions Index may be found at: http://www.universityofcalifornia.edu/admissions/freshman/california-residents/admissions-index/index.html

ADDITIONAL INFORMATION
Depending upon the current functional limitations imposed by the diagnosed disability, accommodations may include the following: extended test time, note-taking, permission to tape record lectures, priority registration, calculators, etc.

LEARNING DISABILITY PROGRAMS OR SERVICES

Contact Information
Name of program or department: Office for Students with Disabilities (OSD)
  Telephone: 858-534-4382
  Fax: 858-534-4650

LEARNING DISABILITY SERVICES

Accommodations are decided upon an individual basis after a thorough review of appropriate, current documentation. The accommodations requested must be supported through the documentation provided and must be logically linked to the current impact of the condition on academic functioning.

Allowed in exams
  Calculator: Yes
  Dictionary: Yes
  Computer: Yes
  Spellchecker: Yes
Extended test time: Yes
Scribes: Yes
Proctors: Yes
Oral exams: Yes
Note-takers: Yes

Distraction-reduced environment: Yes
Tape recording in class: Yes
Electronic texts: Yes
Accommodations for students with ADHD: Yes
Kurzweil Reader: Yes
Other assistive technology: Yes
Priority registration: Yes

Added costs for services: No
LD specialists: Yes
Professional tutors: No
Peer tutors: Offered through OASIS program
Max. hours/wk. for services: Unlimited
How professors are notified of LD/ADHD: By student

GENERAL ADMISSIONS INFORMATION

Office of Admission: 858-534-4831

ENTRANCE REQUIREMENTS
Academic units required: 4 English, 3 math, 2 science labs, 2 foreign language, 2 history, 1 academic elective, 1 visual/performing arts. **Academic units recommended:** 4 English, 4 math, 3 science labs, 3 foreign language, 2 history, 1 academic elective, 1 visual/performing arts. See admissions website for additional information: http://ucsd.edu/prospective-students/index.html.

Application deadline: 11/30
Notification: 3/31
Average GPA: 3.96
ACT Composite middle 50% range: 24–30

SAT Math middle 50% range: 610–720
SAT Critical Reading middle 50% range: 540–660
SAT Writing middle 50% range: 560–680

Graduated top 10% of class: 100%
Graduated top 25% of class: 100%
Graduated top 50% of class: 100%

COLLEGE GRADUATION REQUIREMENTS

Course waivers allowed: Yes
In what course: Course waivers are dependent on college and major requirements.
Course substitutions allowed: Yes
In what course: Course substitution is dependent on college and major requirements.

ADDITIONAL INFORMATION

Environment: The university has a suburban campus north of downtown San Diego.

Student Body
  Undergrad enrollment: 23,663
  Women: 51%
  Men: 49%
  Percent out-of-state: 3%

Cost Information
  In-state tuition: $13,284
  Out-of-state tuition: $36,112
  Room & board: $11,684
Housing Information
  University housing: Yes
  Percent living on campus: 39.4%

Greek System
  Fraternity: Yes
  Sorority: Yes
Athletics: Division II

U. OF CALIFORNIA—SANTA BARBARA

1210 Cheadle Hall, U. of California, Santa Barbara, CA 93106-2014
Phone: 805-893-2881 • Fax: 805-893-2676
E-mail: admissions@sa.ucsb.edu • Web: www.ucsb.edu
Support: CS • Institution type: 4-year public

PROGRAMS OR SERVICES FOR STUDENTS WITH LD

The Disabled Student Program (DSP) is a department within the Division of Student Affairs that works to increase the retention and graduation ratio of students with temporary and permanent disabilities, assure equal access to all educational and academic programs, and foster student independence. The university is strongly committed to maintaining an environment that guarantees students with disabilities full access to educational programs and activities. The DSP office serves as a campus liaison regarding issues and regulations related to students with disabilities. DSP provides reasonable accommodations to students with disabilities; specific accommodations are determined on an individual basis. Admitted students should upload documentation to the DSP online system following the completion of an online application. The online system can be accessed at http://dsp.sa.ucsb.edu. Students enter the program via the DSP portal using their NetID and password following admission to the university. When students are set to a status of 'Ready for Meeting' they should schedule an appointment with a disabilities specialist. Accommodations and academically related services are not designed to provide remediation, but to accommodate a disorder that impairs the student's ability to acquire, process, or communicate information. Each accommodation will be made available to the extent that it does not compromise the academic integrity of the student's academic program.

ADMISSION INFORMATION FOR STUDENTS WITH LD/ADHD

College entrance tests required: Yes
Interview required: No
Essay recommended: Yes
What documentation required for LD: Documentation is not submitted with an application to the university. Documentation is required when students apply to the Disabled Students Program.
With general application: No
To receive services after enrolling: Yes
What documentation required for ADHD: Documentation is not submitted with an application to the university. Documentation is required when students apply to the Disabled Students Program.
With general application: No

Submitted to: Disabled Student Program following admission to the university
Special Ed. HS course work accepted: No
Specific course requirements of all applicants: Yes
Separate application required: No
# of LD applications submitted each year: NR
# of LD applications accepted yearly: NR
Total # of students receiving LD services: 294 (LD and ADHD)
Acceptance into program means acceptance into college: No, students must be admitted and enrolled at the University before requesting academic support services.

ADMISSIONS

There is no additional application for students with learning disabilities or AD/HD. All students with disabilities must meet the same admission criteria as the general student population. However, students may self-disclose the existence of a disability in their personal statements. They may address how they have coped with it in high school, indicate the compensatory strategies they have learned and note accommodations they have used. Each essay is reviewed by three readers who assign a score and consider achievements within the context of the student's circumstances. Once a student is admitted to the University, they may apply to the Disabled Students Program using an online system (http://dsp.sa.ucsb.edu) They enter the DSP portal using their UCSB NetID and password. General admission requirements include 4 years of English, 3 years of math, 1 year of world history, 1 year of U.S. history, 2 years of science labs, 2 years of a foreign language, 1 year of Visual and Performing Arts and 1 years of academic electives. The ACT or SAT is required.

ADDITIONAL INFORMATION

Non-remedial individualized and group tutoring, as well as study skills workshops are offered through the campus tutoring center (Campus Learning Assistance Services) for all university students. Academic support services include priority registration; reading and note taking services, adaptive technology and exam accommodations including extended time, an alternate setting and test proctoring. Incoming DSP students are strongly encouraged to attend a fall orientation program.

LEARNING DISABILITY PROGRAMS OR SERVICES

Contact Information
Name of program or department: Disabled Student Program (DSP)
  Telephone: 805-893-2182
  Fax: 805-893-7127

LEARNING DISABILITY SERVICES

Following the submission of an application to DSP, the student uploads their documentation to the DSP online system. Upon receiving disability documentation, the Documentation Review Committee reviews such and determines eligibility for services. Students are informed of their DSP status via email. Once they are set for 'Ready for Meeting', an intake appointment is made. Based on the committee's review of documentation, the intake interview, and the students' requests for accommodations, services are approved. The accommodations requested must be supported by complete and current documentation provided and must be logically linked to the current impact of the condition on academic functioning.

Allowed in exams
  Calculator: Yes
  Dictionary: No
  Computer: Yes
  Spellchecker: Yes
Extended test time: Yes
Scribes: Yes
Proctors: Yes
Oral exams: No

Note-takers: Yes
Distraction-reduced environment: Yes
Tape recording in class: Yes, with
  instructor's permission
Electronic texts: Yes
**Accommodations for students with
  ADHD:** Yes
Kurzweil Reader: Yes
Other assistive technology: Yes

Priority registration: Yes
Added costs for services: No
LD specialists: Yes
Professional tutors: No
Max. hours/wk. for services: 1 hr
  through CLAS
**How professors are notified of
  LD/ADHD:** Via online system once
  student requests instructor letters

GENERAL ADMISSIONS INFORMATION

Office of Admission: 805-893-2881

ENTRANCE REQUIREMENTS

Academic units required: Complete a minimum of 15 college-preparatory courses, with at least 11 finished prior to the beginning of your senior year (see http://www.universityofcalifornia.edu/admissions/freshman/requirements/a-g-requirements/index.html for list); earn a grade point average (GPA) of 3.0 or better (3.4 for nonresidents) in these courses with no grade lower than a C; meet the examination requirement by taking the ACT With Writing or the SAT Reasoning Test by December of your senior year. We do not require SAT Subject Tests, but certain programs recommend them, and subject tests with particular scores can be used to satisfy the "a-g" requirements listed above. The TOEFL exam is required of all international applicants: a minimum score of 80 is required.

Application deadline: 11/30
Notification: No later than 3/30
Average GPA: 3.92
ACT Composite middle 50% range:
  25–30

SAT Math middle 50% range:
  560–680
**SAT Critical Reading middle 50%
  range:** 540–650
SAT Writing middle 50% range:
  540–660

Graduated top 10% of class: 96%
Graduated top 25% of class: 98%
Graduated top 50% of class: 100%

COLLEGE GRADUATION REQUIREMENTS

Course waivers allowed: No
Course substitutions allowed: No
ADDITIONAL INFORMATION

Environment: The university is located on 813 acres in a small city 10 miles west of Santa Barbara.

Student Body
  Undergrad enrollment: 19,186
  Women: 53%
  Men: 47%
  Percent out-of-state: 3%

Cost Information
  In-state tuition: $12,192
  Out-of-state tuition: $34,213
  Room & board: $13,345
Housing Information
  University housing: Yes
  Percent living on campus: 33%

Greek System
  Fraternity: Yes
  Sorority: Yes
Athletics: Division I

UNIVERSITY OF REDLANDS

1200 East Colton Avenue, Redlands, CA 92373
Phone: 909-793-2121 • Fax: 909-793-2029
E-mail: admissions@redlands.edu • Web: www.redlands.edu
Support: S • Institution type: 4-year private

PROGRAMS OR SERVICES FOR STUDENTS WITH LD

Students identified as learning disabled are eligible for tutoring and individual assistance from Academic Success and Disability Services. While the university does not have a formal program for students with learning disabilities, the goal is to help students succeed in college once they are enrolled. Although the services and accommodations offered are minimal, they do comply with the mandates of Section 504 of the Rehabilitation Act of 1973. Academic Success and Disability Services is sensitive to the needs of students with disabilities and strives to provide the services and accommodations that are identified in the professional documentation.

ADMISSION INFORMATION FOR STUDENTS WITH LD/ADHD

College entrance tests required: Yes
Interview required: No
Essay recommended: Yes
What documentation required for LD: Psycho Ed evaluation to include: relevant historical info, instructional interventions, related services, age diagnosed, objective data (aptitude, achievement, info processing), test scores (standard, percentile and grade equivalents) and describe functional limitations.
With general application: No
To receive services after enrolling: Yes
What documentation required for ADHD: Diagnosis based on DSM-V; history of behaviors impairing functioning in academic setting; diagnostic interview; history of symptoms; evidence of ongoing behaviors.

With general application: No
Submitted to: Academic Success and Disability Services
Special Ed. HS course work accepted: No
Specific course requirements of all applicants: Yes
Separate application required: No
# of LD applications submitted each year: N/A
# of LD applications accepted yearly: 30–50
Total # of students receiving LD services: 190
Acceptance into program means acceptance into college: Students must be admitted and enrolled in the university first and then request services.

ADMISSIONS

Students with learning disabilities are required to submit the general application form and meet the same admission standards as all applicants. Redlands strongly recommends a college-preparatory program that includes 4 years of English and 2 or 3 years each of foreign language, science labs, and social studies. Three years of math up to and including Algebra II is required. The middle 50 percent of the class has between 1060 and 1240 SAT Reasoning Test and between 22 and 27 ACT. Faculty admits are for those students whose GPAs or SAT/ACT scores do not meet admissions standards, but who show promise of success in college. The Assistant Dean of Academics and Student Life is involved in the admission decision for students with learning disabilities.

ADDITIONAL INFORMATION

Each service provided by Academic Success and Disability Services encourages students to take personal responsibility for their academic success. A study skills and learning strategies course is available and students have access to tutoring on a one-on-one basis. The peer tutoring program provides friendly, supportive assistance for most academic subjects. Peer tutors must have faculty recommendations in the subjects they wish to tutor and at least a 3.0 GPA in the area they tutor. The Assistant Dean of Academics and Student Life will work with students to assist them in identifying their needs and securing appropriate accommodations. Additionally, students may make individual appointments for assistance with time management and study skills. However, it is the students' responsibility to seek out help and request assistance.

LEARNING DISABILITY PROGRAMS OR SERVICES

Contact Information
Name of program or department: Academic Success and Disability Services
 Telephone: 909-748-8108
 Fax: 909-335-5296

LEARNING DISABILITY SERVICES

Accommodations are decided upon an individual basis after a thorough review of appropriate, current documentation. The accommodations requested must be supported through the documentation provided and must be logically linked to the current impact of the condition on academic functioning.

Allowed in exams
 Calculator: Yes
 Dictionary: Yes
 Computer: Yes
 Spellchecker: Yes
Extended test time: Yes
Scribes: Yes
Proctors: Yes
Oral exams: Yes
Note-takers: Yes

Distraction-reduced environment: Yes
Tape recording in class: Yes
Electronic texts: Yes
Accommodations for students with ADHD: Yes
Kurzweil Reader: Yes
Other assistive technology: Yes
Priority registration: Case-by-case basis

Added costs for services: No
LD specialists: No
Professional tutors: No
Peer tutors: 50–80
Max. hours/wk. for services: Unlimited
How professors are notified of LD/ADHD: By both student and Disability Services

GENERAL ADMISSIONS INFORMATION

Office of Admission: 909-748-8074

ENTRANCE REQUIREMENTS

Academic units required: 4 English, 3 math, 2 science (1 science lab), 2 foreign language, 2 social studies.
Academic units recommended: 4 English, 4 math, 3 science (1 science lab), 3 foreign language, 2 social studies, 1 history. High school diploma is required, and GED is accepted. ACT without Writing component accepted. TOEFL required of all international applicants: minimum paper TOEFL 550, minimum computer TOEFL 213.

Application deadline: 2/1
Notification: Rolling
Average GPA: 3.58
ACT Composite middle 50% range: 22–27

SAT Math middle 50% range: 520–620
SAT Critical Reading middle 50% range: 520–620
SAT Writing middle 50% range: NR

Graduated top 10% of class: 35%
Graduated top 25% of class: 37%
Graduated top 50% of class: 91%

COLLEGE GRADUATION REQUIREMENTS

Course waivers allowed: No
Course substitutions allowed: Yes
In what course: Math and foreign language

ADDITIONAL INFORMATION

Environment: The university is located on 130 acres in a small town 60 miles east of Los Angeles.

Student Body
 Undergrad enrollment: 2,302
 Women: 56%
 Men: 44%
 Percent out-of-state: 23%

Cost Information
 Tuition: $39,038
 Room & board: $11,924
Housing Information
 University housing: Yes
 Percent living on campus: 70%

Greek System
 Fraternity: Yes
 Sorority: Yes
Athletics: Division III

UNIVERSITY OF SAN FRANCISCO

2130 Fulton Street, San Francisco, CA 94117
Phone: 415-422-6563 • Fax: 415-422-2217
E-mail: admission@usfca.edu • Web: www.usfca.edu
Support: CS • Institution type: 4-year private

PROGRAMS OR SERVICES FOR STUDENTS WITH LD

The University of San Francisco believes that students with learning disabilities are capable of succeeding and becoming contributing members of the university community and society. To this end, USF provides educational support and assistance to those students whose goals are successful completion of college and who take an active participatory role in their own education. Services provided enable students to achieve grades that accurately reflect their ability, promote healthy self-images, remediate deficit areas, and promote USF's LD program by conducting in-services for faculty, admissions, and other staff; providing brochures and advertising services; and working closely with faculty to provide accommodations to students with learning disabilities. USF does not provide diagnostic testing for LD or ADHD. However, students can request a screening or consultation.

ADMISSION INFORMATION FOR STUDENTS WITH LD/ADHD

College entrance tests required: Yes
Interview required: No
Essay recommended: No
What documentation required for LD: Psycho Ed evaluation to include: relevant historical info, instructional interventions, related services, age diagnosed, objective data (aptitude, achievement, info processing), test scores (standard, percentile and grade equivalents) and describe functional limitations.
With general application: No
To receive services after enrolling: Yes
What documentation required for ADHD: Diagnosis based on DSM-V; history of behaviors impairing functioning in academic setting; diagnostic interview; history of symptoms; evidence of ongoing behaviors.

With general application: No
Submitted to: Student Disability Services
Special Ed. HS course work accepted: Yes
Specific course requirements for all applicants: NR
Separate application required: No
# of LD applications submitted each year: 100
# of LD applications accepted yearly: 80
Total # of students receiving LD services: 200
Acceptance into program means acceptance into college: Students must be admitted and enrolled in the university first and then request services.

ADMISSIONS

All applicants must meet the entrance requirements (examples: GPA, ACT, SAT, letters of recommendation). Once a student is admitted, disclosure of a disability will allow the student to work with faculty, staff, and Student Disability Services (SDS) to obtain reasonable accommodations. If a student who is a borderline admit self-discloses on the regular application form, the Director of Student Disability Services reviews the documentation and gives an evaluation before an admission decision is made. The final decision is made jointly between the Director of Student Disability Services and the Office of Admissions.

ADDITIONAL INFORMATION

Services include trained tutors, instruction in study skills and coping strategies, academic advising, maintaining regular contact with the LD coordinator, diagnostic testing, individual or small group instruction for educational building, and helping students improve their understanding of their learning disability. Assistive technology includes Kurzweil, Dragon Naturally Speaking, and so on. Extended time for course examinations may be a reasonable accommodation for students with specific types of disabilities. SDS reviews the documentation submitted by the student as part of the intake process and indicates extended time on a letter of accommodation when appropriate. Students with attention deficit hyperactivity disorder request services through SDS. A comprehensive neuropsychological or psychoeducational assessment report by a qualified professional clearly stating the presence of this disorder is required. The University of San Francisco's Learning and Writing Center aims to help all students to connect with one another and with professional staff members to achieve their academic best. Services in the Learning Center include tutors, academic workshops, and opportunities for study group information, and computer and other learning resources. The Writing Center provides professional writing assistance. For a complete and comprehensive listing of documentation guidelines and how to access services, please visit the website: www.usfca.edu/acadserv/academic/services/sds.

LEARNING DISABILITY PROGRAMS OR SERVICES

Contact Information
Name of program or department: Student Disability Services
  Telephone: 415-422-2613
  Fax: 415-422-5906

LEARNING DISABILITY SERVICES

Accommodations are decided upon an individual basis after a thorough review of appropriate, current documentation. The accommodations requested must be supported through the documentation provided and must be logically linked to the current impact of the condition on academic functioning.

Allowed in exams
  Calculator: Yes
  Dictionary: Yes
  Computer: Yes
  Spellchecker: Yes
Extended test time: Yes
Scribes: Yes
Proctors: Yes
Oral exams: Yes

Note-takers: Yes
Distraction-reduced environment: Yes
Tape recording in class: Yes
Electronic texts: Yes
Accommodations for students with
  ADHD: Yes
Kurzweil Reader: Yes
Other assistive technology: Yes
Priority registration: Yes

Added costs for services: No
LD specialists: Yes
Professional tutors: 3
Peer tutors: 100
Max. hours/wk. for services: 3
How professors are notified of
  LD/ADHD: By student

GENERAL ADMISSIONS INFORMATION

Office of Admission: 415-422-6563

ENTRANCE REQUIREMENTS

Academic units recommended: 4 English, 3 math, 2 science (2 science labs), 2 foreign language, 3 social studies, 6 academic electives, 1 chemistry, and 1 biology or physics is required of nursing and science applicants. High school diploma is required, and GED is accepted. ACT with Writing component required. TOEFL required of all international applicants: minimum paper TOEFL 550, minimum internet TOEFL 79.

Application deadline: 1/15
Notification: Rolling
Average GPA: 3.53
ACT Composite middle 50% range:
  22–27

SAT Math middle 50% range:
  520–620
SAT Critical Reading middle 50%
  range: 510–620
SAT Writing middle 50% range:
  510–620

Graduated top 10% of class: 21%
Graduated top 25% of class: 59%
Graduated top 50% of class: 91%

COLLEGE GRADUATION REQUIREMENTS

Course waivers allowed: Yes
Course substitutions allowed: Yes
In what course: Foreign language, math

ADDITIONAL INFORMATION

Environment: The University of San Francisco is located on 55 acres in the heart of the city.

Student Body
  Undergrad enrollment: 5,761
  Women: 64%
  Men: 36%
  Percent out-of-state: 30%

Cost Information
  Tuition: $37,424
  Room & board: $12250
Housing Information
  University housing: Yes
  Percent living on campus: 48%

Greek System
  Fraternity: Yes
  Sorority: Yes
Athletics: Division I

UNIVERSITY OF SOUTHERN CALIFORNIA

Admissions Office: Student Administrative Services, 700 Childs Way,
Los Angeles, CA 90089-0911 • Phone: 213-740-1111 • Fax: 213-740-6364
E-mail: admitusc@usc.edu • Web: www.usc.edu
Support: CS • Institution type: 4-year private

PROGRAMS OR SERVICES FOR STUDENTS WITH LD

Disability Services and Programs is responsible for delivery of services to students with learning disabilities. It offers a comprehensive support program in the areas of educational therapy, content area tutoring, study skills instruction, special exam administration, liaison with textbook-taping services, advocacy, and network referral system. The learning specialists, graduate assistants, and learning assistants are available to students for academic therapy. A computer lab is available for computer-assisted learning and for word processing when working with a staff person. After admission, students with LD are counseled by advisors who dialogue with the learning specialist and who are sensitive to special needs. Educational counseling is done by the learning specialist. Off-campus referrals are made to students desiring comprehensive diagnostic testing. The support structure for students with documented learning disabilities is one that is totally individualized; there is no special program per se. Support is given at the request of the student. The learning disabilities specialist and/or grad assistants at USC are prepared to act as advocates when appropriate for any student experiencing academic problems that are related to the learning disability. USC aims to assure close, personal attention to its students even though it is a large campus.

ADMISSION INFORMATION FOR STUDENTS WITH LD/ADHD

College entrance tests required: Yes
Interview required: No
Essay recommended: Yes
What documentation required for LD: Psycho Ed evaluation to include: relevant historical info, instructional interventions, related services, age diagnosed, objective data (aptitude, achievement, info processing), test scores (standard, percentile and grade equivalents) and describe functional limitations.
With general application: No
To receive services after enrolling: Yes
What documentation required for ADHD: Diagnosis based on DSM-V; history of behaviors impairing functioning in academic setting; diagnostic interview; history of symptoms; evidence of ongoing behaviors.

With general application: No
Submitted to: Disability and Services and Programs
Special Ed. HS course work accepted: Yes
Specific course requirements of all applicants: Yes
Separate application required: NR
# of LD applications submitted each year: NR
# of LD applications accepted yearly: NR
Total # of students receiving LD services: 350
Acceptance into program means acceptance into college: Students must be admitted and enrolled in the university first and then request services.

ADMISSIONS

There are no special admissions for students with learning disabilities. Course requirements include 4 years of English, 3 years of math, 2 years of natural science, 2 years of social studies, 2 years of a foreign language, and 4 year-long electives. (The foreign language requirement is not waived in the admission process). It is helpful for comparison purposes to have both timed and untimed SAT or ACT test results. Transfer students are admitted on the basis of their college course work as well as the high school record. It is the student's responsibility to provide recent educational evaluations for documentation as part of the admissions application process. Testing must be current within 3 years, or 5 years for transfer or returning students.

ADDITIONAL INFORMATION

The services provided are modifications that are determined to be appropriate for students with LD. During the first 3 weeks of each semester, students are seen on a walk-in basis by the staff in the LD Support Services. Students requesting assistance must have a planning appointment with an LD specialist or grad assistant; provide a copy of the current class schedule; and be sure that eligibility has been determined by documenting specific learning disabilities. Learning assistance most often involves one-on-one attention for academic planning, scheduling, organization, and methods of compensation. Students may have standing appointments with learning assistants and subject tutors. After one "no-show" or three canceled appointments, standing appointments will be canceled. Course accommodations could include taping of lectures, note-taking, extended time for tests, use of word processor, proofreader, limiting scheduling of consecutive exams, and advocacy. Other services include support groups, counseling, and coaching.

LEARNING DISABILITY PROGRAMS OR SERVICES

Contact Information
Name of program or department: Disability Services and Programs
  Telephone: 213-740-0776
  Fax: 213-740-8216

LEARNING DISABILITY SERVICES

Accommodations are decided upon an individual basis after a thorough review of appropriate, current documentation. The accommodations requested must be supported through the documentation provided and must be logically linked to the current impact of the condition on academic functioning.

Allowed in exams
  Calculator: NR
  Dictionary: NR
  Computer: Yes
  Spellchecker: Yes
Extended test time: Yes
Scribes: Yes
Proctors: Yes
Oral exams: No
Note-takers: Yes

Distraction-reduced environment: Yes
Tape recording in class: Yes
Electronic texts: Yes
Accommodations for students with ADHD: Yes
Kurzweil Reader: Yes
Other assistive technology: Yes
Priority registration: No

Added costs for services: No
LD specialists: Yes
Professional tutors: Yes
Peer tutors: 15
Max. hours/wk. for services: 2
How professors are notified of LD/ADHD: By both student and director

GENERAL ADMISSIONS INFORMATION

Office of Admission: 213-740-6753

ENTRANCE REQUIREMENTS

Academic units required: 4 English, 3 math, 2 science (2 science labs), 2 foreign language, 2 social studies, 4 academic electives. **Academic units recommended:** 4 English, 4 math, 3 science (3 science labs), 3 foreign language, 3 social studies, 4 academic electives. High school diploma is required, and GED is not accepted. ACT with Writing component required.

Application deadline: 1/10
Notification: 4/1
Average GPA: 3.71
ACT Composite middle 50% range: 29–33

SAT Math middle 50% range: 670–770
SAT Critical Reading middle 50% range: 610–720
SAT Writing middle 50% range: 650–740

Graduated top 10% of class: 88%
Graduated top 25% of class: 97%
Graduated top 50% of class: 100%

COLLEGE GRADUATION REQUIREMENTS

Course waivers allowed: No
Course substitutions allowed: Yes
In what course: Students may petition for substitution for foreign language. LD specialist decides if appeal is valid and writes a letter recommending course substitutions. Course valid for substitutions include literature in translation, linguistics, and classics.

ADDITIONAL INFORMATION

Environment: The university is located on 150 acres in an urban area, 2 miles south of downtown Los Angeles.

Student Body
  Undergrad enrollment: 17,414
  Women: 50%
  Men: 50%
  Percent out-of-state: 35%

Cost Information
  Tuition: $42,162
  Room & board: $11,580
Housing Information
  University housing: Yes
  Percent living on campus: 38%

Greek System
  Fraternity: Yes
  Sorority: Yes
Athletics: Division I

UNIVERSITY OF THE PACIFIC

3601 Pacific Avenue, Stockton, CA 95211
Phone: 209-946-2211 • Fax: 209-946-2413
E-mail: admissions@pacific.edu • Web: www.pacific.edu
Support: S • Institution type: 4-year private

PROGRAMS OR SERVICES FOR STUDENTS WITH LD

There is no special program for students with learning disabilities, but the university does have a Learning Disabilities Support Program. This program offers assistance through tutoring, study skills classes, support groups, and testing accommodations. Documentation for LD must include psychoeducational evaluations from a professional. The documentation for ADHD must be from a medical doctor. Documentation should be sent to the Director of the Office of Services for Students with Disabilities. Students register for services after admission by contacting the Office of Services for Students with Disabilities. Student confidentiality is protected. The ultimate goal is for the student to earn a degree that is unmodified and unflagged. Faculty and staff are dedicated to providing students with learning disabilities all reasonable accommodations so that they may enjoy academic success. The LD Support Program helps keep University of the Pacific in compliance with the Americans with Disabilities Act and Section 504 of the Rehabilitation Act. Compliance is accomplished without compromising University of the Pacific standards, placing undue financial or administrative burden on the university, fundamentally altering the nature of programs, or extending unreasonable accommodations.

ADMISSION INFORMATION FOR STUDENTS WITH LD/ADHD

College entrance tests required: Yes
Interview required: No
Essay recommended: Yes
What documentation required for LD: Psycho Ed evaluation to include: relevant historical info, instructional interventions, related services, age diagnosed, objective data (aptitude, achievement, info processing), test scores (standard, percentile and grade equivalents) and describe functional limitations.
With general application: No
To receive services after enrolling: Yes
What documentation required for ADHD: Diagnosis based on DSM-V; history of behaviors impairing functioning in academic setting; diagnostic interview; history of symptoms; evidence of ongoing behaviors.

With general application: No
Submitted to: Office of Services for Students with Disabilities
Special Ed. HS course work accepted: Yes
Specific course requirements for all applicants: NR
Separate application required: No
# of LD applications submitted each year: NR
# of LD applications accepted yearly: NR
Total # of students receiving LD services: 140–160
Acceptance into program means acceptance into college: Students must be admitted and enrolled in the university first and then request services.

ADMISSIONS

UOP welcomes students with learning disabilities. Although there is no special admission procedure, students are given special consideration. There is no minimum ACT/SAT requirement. There are two alternative methods for admissions: (1) probationary admissions for the marginal student—C/D average with no special requirements, but the university advisor is notified of status; no required test score; and no quota regarding the number of students admitted; and (2) special admissions—students who begin college courses in the summer prior to freshman year and receive at least a C average in two courses and one study skills class (can take those courses at any local community college).

ADDITIONAL INFORMATION

All admitted students are eligible for LD services with the appropriate assessment documentation. Academic Support Services offers services to improve learning opportunities for students with LD and are provided within reasonable limits. These services could include diagnostic assessment, accommodations for academic needs, electronic books and alternate formatting, readers, tutorials for academic courses, and referrals to appropriate resources. Skills courses for credit are available in reading, study skills, writing, and math. Services and accommodations are available for undergraduate and graduate students.

LEARNING DISABILITY PROGRAMS OR SERVICES

Contact Information
Name of program or department: Office of Services for Students with Disabilities
 Telephone: 209-946-3221
 Fax: 209-946-2278

LEARNING DISABILITY SERVICES

Accommodations are decided upon an individual basis after a thorough review of appropriate, current documentation. The accommodations requested must be supported through the documentation provided and must be logically linked to the current impact of the condition on academic functioning.

Allowed in exams
 Calculator: Yes
 Dictionary: Yes
 Computer: Yes
 Spellchecker: Yes
Extended test time: Yes
Scribes: Yes
Proctors: Yes
Oral exams: Yes
Note-takers: Yes

Distraction-reduced environment: Yes
Tape recording in class: Yes
Electronic texts: Yes
Accommodations for students with
 ADHD: Yes
Kurzweil Reader: Yes
Other assistive technology: Yes
Priority registration: Yes

Added costs for services: No
LD specialists: No
Professional tutors: No
Peer tutors: 80
Max. hours/wk. for services: 2
How professors are notified of
 LD/ADHD: By director

GENERAL ADMISSIONS INFORMATION

Office of Admission: 209-946-2211

ENTRANCE REQUIREMENTS

Academic units recommended: 4 English, 3 math, 2 science lab, 2 foreign language, 3 social studies, 3 academic electives, 1 fine arts/performing arts. High school diploma is required, and GED is accepted. TOEFL required of all international applicants: minimum paper TOEFL 475, minimum computer TOEFL 150.

Application deadline: Early 11/5, regular 1/5
Notification: Rolling
Average GPA: 3.46
ACT Composite middle 50% range: 23–29

SAT Math middle 50% range: NR
SAT Critical Reading middle 50% range: NR
SAT Writing middle 50% range: NR

Graduated top 10% of class: 42%
Graduated top 25% of class: 72%
Graduated top 50% of class: 93%

COLLEGE GRADUATION REQUIREMENTS

Course waivers allowed: Yes
Course substitutions allowed: Yes

ADDITIONAL INFORMATION

Environment: The university is located on 150 acres 90 miles east of San Francisco.

Student Body
 Undergrad enrollment: 3,757
 Women: 55%
 Men: 45%
 Percent out-of-state: 21%

Cost Information
 Tuition: $36,390
 Room & board: $11,688
Housing Information
 University housing: Yes
 Percent living on campus: 69%

Greek System
 Fraternity: Yes
 Sorority: Yes
Athletics: Division I

WHITTIER COLLEGE

13406 Philadelphia Street, Whittier, CA 90608
Phone: 562-907-4238 • Fax: 562-907-4870
E-mail: admission@whittier.edu • Web: www.whittier.edu
Support: S • Institution type: 4-year private

PROGRAMS OR SERVICES FOR STUDENTS WITH LD

The Director of Disability Services provides assistance to students with documented disabilities. Accommodation requests are made through the director's office. Students with disabilities must make their needs known to the Director of Learning Support Services (LSS) to receive accommodations. To arrange for services, students must self-disclose the disability and make an individual appointment to discuss their accommodation requests with the director. Learning Support Services offers additional services: peer tutoring, workshops on study skills, and basic English and math skills assistance. These services are provided at no cost.

ADMISSION INFORMATION FOR STUDENTS WITH LD/ADHD

College entrance tests required: Yes
Interview required: No
Essay recommended: No
What documentation required for LD: Psycho Ed evaluation to include: relevant historical info, instructional interventions, related services, age diagnosed, objective data (aptitude, achievement, info processing), test scores (standard, percentile and grade equivalents) and describe functional limitations.
With general application: No
To receive services after enrolling: Yes
What documentation required for ADHD: Diagnosis based on DSM-V; history of behaviors impairing functioning in academic setting; diagnostic interview; history of symptoms; evidence of ongoing behaviors.

With general application: No
Submitted to: Disability Services
Special Ed. HS course work accepted: NR
Specific course requirements of all applicants: Yes
Separate application required: No
# of LD applications submitted each year: 25–30
# of LD applications accepted yearly: NR
Total # of students receiving LD services: 22
Acceptance into program means acceptance into college: Student must be admitted and enrolled in the university first and then reviewed for LD services.

ADMISSIONS
There is no special admissions process for students with disabilities. All applicants are expected to meet the same admission criteria. Students must submit the ACT or SAT Reasoning and have a minimum of a 2.0 GPA; the recommended courses include 4 years of English, 3–4 years of math, 2–3 years of a foreign language, 2–3 years of social studies, and 2–3 years of science labs.

ADDITIONAL INFORMATION
The use of calculators, dictionaries, computers, or spellcheckers in exams would be considered on a case-by-case basis, depending on appropriate documentation and student needs. Students with appropriate documentation will have access to note-takers, readers, extended exam times, alternative exam locations, proctors, scribes, oral exams, books on tape, and priority registration. All students have access to a Math Lab, a Writing Center, a Learning Lab, and academic counseling.

LEARNING DISABILITY PROGRAMS OR SERVICES

Contact Information
Name of program or department: Disability Services
  Telephone: 562-907-4840
  Fax: 562-907-4827

LEARNING DISABILITY SERVICES

Accommodations are decided upon an individual basis after a thorough review of appropriate, current documentation. The accommodations requested must be supported through the documentation provided and must be logically linked to the current impact of the condition on academic functioning.

Allowed in exams	**Distraction-reduced environment:** Yes	**Added costs for services:** No
Calculator: Yes	**Tape recording in class:** Yes	**LD specialists:** No
Dictionary: Yes	**Electronic texts:** Yes	**Professional tutors:** No
Computer: Yes	**Accommodations for students with**	**Peer tutors:** 15–30
Spellchecker: Yes	**ADHD:** Yes	**Max. hours/wk. for services:**
Extended test time: Yes	**Kurzweil Reader:** Yes	Unlimited
Scribes: Yes	**Other assistive technology:** Yes	**How professors are notified of**
Proctors: Yes	**Priority registration:** Yes	**LD/ADHD:** By both student and
Oral exams: No		director
Note-takers: Yes		

GENERAL ADMISSIONS INFORMATION

Director of Admissions: Kieron Miller

ENTRANCE REQUIREMENTS

Academic units required: 3 English, 3 math, 2 science (2 science lab), 2 foreign language, 2 social studies.
Academic units recommended: 4 English, 3 math, 3 science (3 science labs), 3 foreign language, 4 social studies. High school diploma is required, and GED is accepted. ACT with Writing component required. TOEFL required of all international applicants: minimum paper TOEFL 550, minimum computer TOEFL 230.

Application deadline: None	**SAT Math middle 50% range:**	**Graduated top 10% of class:** 27%
Notification: Rolling	460–580	**Graduated top 25% of class:** 57%
Average GPA: 3.4	**SAT Critical Reading middle 50%**	**Graduated top 50% of class:** 88%
ACT Composite middle 50% range:	range: 470–580	
21–25	**SAT Writing middle 50% range:**	
	460–580	

COLLEGE GRADUATION REQUIREMENTS

Course waivers allowed: Yes
In what course: Foreign language, math
Course substitutions allowed: Yes
In what course: Foreign language as an admissions requirement

ADDITIONAL INFORMATION

Environment: The college is on a suburban campus 20 miles southeast of Los Angeles.

Student Body	**Cost Information**	**Greek System**
Undergrad enrollment: 1,617	**Tuition:** $38,280	**Fraternity:** Yes
Women: 55%	**Room & board:** $10,948	**Sorority:** Yes
Men: 45%	**Housing Information**	**Athletics:** Division III
Percent out-of-state: 30%	**University housing:** Yes	
	Percent living on campus: 60%	

COLORADO STATE U.—PUEBLO

Admissions, 2200 Bonforte Boulevard, Pueblo, CO 81001
Phone: 719-549-2461 • Fax: 719-549-2419
E-mail: info@colostate-pueblo.edu • Web: www.colostate-pueblo.edu
Support: S • Institution type: 4-year public

PROGRAMS OR SERVICES FOR STUDENTS WITH LD

The Mission of the Disability Resource Office at Colorado State University—Pueblo is to ensure provision of reasonable academic accommodations and support, designed to enhance academic effectiveness and promote independence in students with documented disabilities.

ADMISSION INFORMATION FOR STUDENTS WITH LD/ADHD

College entrance tests required: Yes
Interview required: No
Essay recommended: No
What documentation required for LD: Psycho Ed evaluation to include: relevant historical info, instructional interventions, related services, age diagnosed, objective data (aptitude, achievement, info processing), test scores (standard, percentile and grade equivalents) and describe functional limitations.
With general application: No
To receive services after enrolling: Yes
What documentation required for ADHD: Diagnosis based on DSM-V; history of behaviors impairing functioning in academic setting; diagnostic interview; history of symptoms; evidence of ongoing behaviors.

With general application: No
Submitted to: Disability Resource Office
Special Ed. HS course work accepted: NR
Specific course requirements for all applicants: NR
Separate application required: No
# of LD applications submitted each year: NR
# of LD applications accepted yearly: NR
Total # of students receiving LD services: NR
Acceptance into program means acceptance into college: Students must be admitted and enrolled in the university first and then request services.

ADMISSIONS
Colorado State University—Pueblo's admission process is designed to promote diversity within the student population and to assure equal access to qualified applicants. The final admission decision is based on the applicant's potential for attaining a degree at the university. All first-time freshmen must submit their high school transcripts with GPA and ACT/SAT scores along with CSU—Pueblo's application. Applicants who do not meet admission standards are encouraged to submit personal statements explaining their circumstances and to show academic progress throughout high school.

ADDITIONAL INFORMATION
Skills classes are offered in note-taking strategies, study skills, and textbook-reading strategies. The request for the use of a dictionary, computer, or spellchecker during exams will depend on the student's documented needs and permission from the professor. Students with specific needs are encouraged to provide documentation that specifically identifies the disability and the accommodations needed. Services and accommodations are available for undergraduate and graduate students.

LEARNING DISABILITY PROGRAMS OR SERVICES

Contact Information
Name of program or department: Disability Resource Office
  Telephone: 719-549-2648
  Fax: 719-549-2195

LEARNING DISABILITY SERVICES

Accommodations are decided upon an individual basis after a thorough review of appropriate, current documentation. The accommodations requested must be supported through the documentation provided.

Allowed in exams
  Calculator: Yes
  Dictionary: Yes
  Computer: Yes
  Spellchecker: Yes
Extended test time: Yes
Scribes: Yes
Proctors: Yes
Oral exams: Yes
Note-takers: Yes

Distraction-reduced environment: Yes
Tape recording in class: Yes
Electronic texts: Yes
Accommodations for students with ADHD: Yes
Kurzweil Reader: Yes
Other assistive technology: Yes
Priority registration: No

Added costs for services: No
LD specialists: No
Professional tutors: No
Peer tutors: No
Max. hours/wk. for services: As needed
How professors are notified of LD/ADHD: By student

GENERAL ADMISSIONS INFORMATION

Office of Admission: 719-549-2462

ENTRANCE REQUIREMENTS

Academic units required: 4 English, 4 math, 3 science (2 science labs), 1 foreign language, 3 social studies/history, 2 academic electives. High school diploma is required, and GED is accepted. ACT Writing component not required. TOEFL required of all international applicants: minimum paper TOEFL 500, minimum computer TOEFL 173.

Application deadline: 8/1
Notification: Rolling
Average GPA: 3.10
ACT Composite middle 50% range: 18–23

SAT Math middle 50% range: 420–550
SAT Critical Reading middle 50% range: 420–530
SAT Writing middle 50% range: NR

Graduated top 10% of class: 2%
Graduated top 25% of class: 7%
Graduated top 50% of class: 30%

COLLEGE GRADUATION REQUIREMENTS

Course substitutions allowed: Yes
In what course: Possibly math with appropriate documentation

ADDITIONAL INFORMATION

Environment: The university is located in an urban area 100 miles south of Denver.

Student Body
  Undergrad enrollment: 5,250
  Women: 54%
  Men: 46%
  Percent out-of-state: 10%

Cost Information
  In-state tuition: $5,722
  Out-of-state tuition: $14,179
  Room & board: $8,300
Housing Information
  University housing: Yes
  Percent living on campus: 22%

Greek System
  Fraternity: Yes
  Sorority: Yes
Athletics: Division II

REGIS UNIVERSITY

3333 Regis Boulevard, A-12, Denver, CO 80221-1099
Phone: 303-458-4900 • Fax: 303-964-5534
E-mail: regisadm@regis.edu/college.asp • Web: www.regis.edu
Support: CS • Institution type: 4-year private

PROGRAMS OR SERVICES FOR STUDENTS WITH LD

The Commitment Program, created in 1976, provides learning support courses, peer mentoring, study groups, and priority advising and registration for approximately 50 freshmen who are provisionally admitted to the University. Commitment students may not participate in varsity sports or off-campus employment during their freshman year, and are obliged to make regular use of academic support provided by the Program. Two Commitment study rooms are available all day every day, and weekly Forum meetings offer career counseling, study skills, time management, and other first-year enrichment services. LS courses (including critical reading and writing, and math and science learning strategies) apply toward elective credit. The Director of the Program works closely with the Office of Disability Services to support students in need of specific accommodations. In keeping with the Jesuit Mission of "educating men and women in the service others," Commitment students work throughout the academic year in a variety of Father Woody Service Projects.

ADMISSION INFORMATION FOR STUDENTS WITH LD/ADHD

College entrance tests required: Yes
Interview required: No
Essay recommended: No
What documentation required for LD: Psycho Ed evaluation to include: relevant historical info, instructional interventions, related services, age diagnosed, objective data (aptitude, achievement, info processing), test scores (standard, percentile and grade equivalents) and describe functional limitations.
With general application: No
To receive services after enrolling: Yes
What documentation required for ADHD: Diagnosis based on DSM-V; history of behaviors impairing functioning in academic setting; diagnostic interview; history of symptoms; evidence of ongoing behaviors.

With general application: No
Submitted to: Disability Services
Special Ed. HS course work accepted: NR
Specific course requirements for all applicants: NR
Separate application required: No
# of LD applications submitted each year: 90
# of LD applications accepted yearly: 20
Total # of students receiving LD services: 1–150
Acceptance into program means acceptance into college: Students are reviewed by Freshman Commitment and a recommendation is provided to the Admissions Committee for a final decision.

ADMISSIONS

There is no special admission for students with LD. Interview not required. Minimum GPA 2.56, SAT of 930, or ACT of 20 and 15 academic units. Students may be considered with 17 ACT or 810 SAT and 2.3 GPA. Students need to show sufficient evidence of motivation and ability to succeed in college, even though they may not have the required GPA or test scores. Recommendations and extracurricular activities will be considered. Students admitted on probation typically have stronger test scores and lower GPAs and are admitted on one semester probation. They need a 2.0 GPA to return the second semester. Other students may be admitted into the Freshman Commitment Program. These students usually have lower test scores and C-plus average. Probationary admission is for two semesters.

ADDITIONAL INFORMATION

Disability Services provides self-advocacy training; test-taking and learning strategies assistance; academic monitoring; note-takers; readers; scribes; extended testing time; and course substitutions. Students in the Commitment Program remain for one year and, with successful completion, are officially admitted to the college. They must pass all required commitment courses with a C or better, not fall below a 2.0 GPA in non-Commitment courses, and agree not to participate in varsity sports or other activities that interfere with class attendance while in the program. There are learning support courses, study groups, and tutorials. Tutors available and all students must pass 3 hours of math. There is a math learning support course or a remedial math class available prior to taking the regular college algebra class. Learning support classes in reading skills, writing skills, and study skills apply toward elective credit. Special advising, tutoring, diagnostic academic testing, and study and testing assistance are other services offered.

LEARNING DISABILITY PROGRAMS OR SERVICES

Contact Information
Name of program or department: Disability Services
  Telephone: 303-458-3572
  Fax: 303-458-3566

LEARNING DISABILITY SERVICES

Accommodations are decided upon an individual basis after a thorough review of appropriate, current documentation. The accommodations requested must be supported through the documentation provided and must be logically linked to the current impact of the condition on academic functioning.

Allowed in exams (with appropriate documentation)	**Note-takers:** Yes	**Added costs for services:** No
Calculator: Yes	**Distraction-reduced environment:** Yes	**LD specialists:** No
Dictionary: Yes	**Tape recording in class:** Yes	**Professional tutors:** No
Computer: Yes	**Electronic texts:** Yes	**Peer tutors:** Varies
Spellchecker: Yes	**Accommodations for students with ADHD:** Yes	**Max. hours/wk. for services:** Unlimited
Extended test time: Yes	**Kurzweil Reader:** Yes	**How professors are notified of LD/ADHD:** By student
Scribes: Yes	**Other assistive technology:** Yes	
Proctors: Yes	**Priority registration:** No	
Oral exams: Yes		

GENERAL ADMISSIONS INFORMATION

Office of Admission: 303-458-4900

ENTRANCE REQUIREMENTS

Academic units recommended: 4 English, 2 math, 2 science, 2 foreign language, 2 social studies, 1 history. High school diploma is required, and GED is accepted. TOEFL required of all international applicants: minimum paper TOEFL 550, minimum computer TOEFL 213.

Application deadline: 8/1	**SAT Math middle 50% range:** 460–570	**Graduated top 10% of class:** 21%
Notification: Rolling	**SAT Critical Reading middle 50% range:** 480–590	**Graduated top 25% of class:** 47%
Average GPA: 3.24	**SAT Writing middle 50% range:** NR	**Graduated top 50% of class:** 79%
ACT Composite middle 50% range: 20–26		

COLLEGE GRADUATION REQUIREMENTS

Course waivers allowed: Yes
In what course: All students must take 3 hours of math. Foreign culture courses are substituted for foreign language if the documentation verifies a disability.
Course substitutions allowed: Yes
In what course: All students must take 3 hours of math. Foreign culture courses are substituted for foreign language if the documentation verifies a disability.

ADDITIONAL INFORMATION

Environment: The university is on a 90-acre campus in a suburban area of Denver.

Student Body	**Cost Information**	**Greek System**
Undergrad enrollment: 1,734	**Tuition:** $29,988	**Fraternity:** No
Women: 57%	**Room & board:** $9,300	**Sorority:** No
Men: 43%	**Housing Information**	**Athletics:** Division II
Percent out-of-state: 43%	**University housing:** Yes	
	Percent living on campus: 8%	

U. OF COLORADO—BOULDER

552 UCB, Boulder, CO 80309-0552
Phone: 303-492-6301 • Fax: 303-492-7115
E-mail: • Web: www.colorado.edu/
Support: CS • Institution: 4-year public

PROGRAMS OR SERVICES FOR STUDENTS WITH LD

Disability Services supports students with disabilities who request accommodations and services at the university. Students with LD and/or ADHD are encouraged to submit documentation according to the guidelines posted online. Disability Services' mission is "to ensure that students with disabilities receive reasonable accommodations and services to participate fully in the academic environment. DS expects and coaches the campus community to embrace and embody a fully accessible and culturally sensitive campus." Inherent within this philosophy is the importance of the student understanding his/her disability profile. The goal is for the student to take ownership and responsibility for the learning process at this research intensive academic environment.

ADMISSION INFORMATION FOR STUDENTS WITH LD/ADHD

College entrance tests required: Yes
Interview required: No
What documentation required for LD: Psycho Ed evaluation to include: relevant historical info, instructional interventions, related services, age diagnosed, objective data (aptitude, achievement, info processing), test scores (standard, percentile and grade equivalents) and describe functional limitations.
With general application: No
To receive services after enrolling: Yes
What documentation required for ADHD: Diagnosis based on DSM-V; history of behaviors impairing functioning in academic setting; diagnostic interview; history of symptoms; evidence of ongoing behaviors.

With general application: No
Submitted to: Disability Services
Specific course requirements for all applicants: Yes
Separate application required for program services: No
# of LD applications submitted each year: NR
# of LD applications accepted yearly: NR
Total # of students receiving LD services: 800–850
Acceptance into program means acceptance into college: Students must be admitted and enrolled in the university first and then reviewed for Disability Services.

ADMISSIONS
There is not a special admission process for students with disabilities. All students are considered under the same competitive admissions criteria. All application information should be submitted to admissions, but documentation should be submitted directly to Disability Services. Mid 50% GPA for Arts and Science is 3.2. -3.85, ACT 23-28 class rank 59%-89%. Guaranteed admission to Arts and Science is top 10% or 3.8 GPA or 3.5 GPA and 1150 SAT or 25 ACT or 3.25 GPA and 1260 SAT or 28 ACT. Mid 50% for College of Engineering is 3.7-4.0 GPA, 27-32 CT, rank 80%-97%. Guaranteed admission to College of Engineering is top 5% or 3.8 HPA or 1280 SAT (Critical Reading 610 and Math 670)) or 29 English and 30 Math on ACT. Guaranteed admission to School of Business rank in top 10% or GPA 3.6 and SAT Critical Reading 580 and Math 620 or ACT English 25 and ACT Math 27. Graduation requirements are not waived. Students with documented LD/ADHD with questions about the foreign language requirement should contact Disability Services.

ADDITIONAL INFORMATION
Services provided through Disability Services include an opportunity to meet with a disability specialist to identify appropriate accommodations, campus resources , advocacy, and short-term academics strategies. The Disability Specialist provides individualized support to students with all kinds of disabilities. This support can take many forms including informal academic advising, advocacy, and letters to professors designating reasonable accommodation, if appropriate. Disability Specialists assist students in developing strategies for time management, organization, study skills, test preparation, and transition to and beyond life at the university. Generally, the Disability Specialist will conduct an intake with new students. If tutoring is needed, the disability specialist can refer the student to the appropriate resources, but the student pays for the service. Early registration is provided only if it relates to the disability.

PROGRAM FOR DISABILITY SERVICES

Contact Information
Name of program or department: Disability Services
  Telephone: 303-492-8671
  Fax: 303-492-5601

LEARNING DISABILITY SERVICES

Accommodations are decided upon an individual basis after a thorough review of appropriate, current documentation. The accommodations requested must be supported through the documentation provided and must be logically linked to the current impact of the condition on academic functioning. .

Allowed in exams
  Calculator: Yes
  Dictionary: No
  Computer: Yes
  Spellchecker: Yes
Extended test time: Yes
Scribes: Yes
Proctors: Yes
Oral exams: No
Note-takers: Yes

Distraction-reduced environment: Yes
Tape recording in class: Yes
Electronic texts: Yes
Accommodations for students with
  ADHD: Yes
Kurzweil Reader: No
Other assistive technology: Assistive Technology Lab includes a variety of supportive technology.
Priority registration: Yes

Added costs for services: No
LD specialists: Yes
Professional tutors: No
Peer tutors: No
Max. hours/wk. for services: Varies
How professors are notified of LD/ADHD: Student

GENERL ADMISSIONS INFORMATION

Office of Admission: 303-492-8671

ENTRANCE REQUIREMENTS
Academic units required: 4 English, 4 mathematics, 3 science, (2 science labs), 3 foreign language, 3 social studies, 1 history, 1 geography. High school diploma is required and GED is accepted. SAT or ACT required; TOEFL required of all international applicants; minimum paper TOEFL 500, minimum computer TOEFL 173, minimum web-based TOEFL 61.

Application deadline: 1/15
Notification: 4/1
Average GPA: 3.55
ACT Composite middle 50% range:
  24–28

SAT Math middle 50% range:
  540–650
SAT Critical Reading middle 50% range: 520–630
SAT Writing middle 50% range: NR

Graduated top 10% of class: 24%
Graduated top 25% of class: 54%
Graduated top 50% of class: 89%

COLLEGE GRADUATION REQUIREMENTS

Course waivers allowed: No
Course substitutions allowed: Yes
In what course: Foreign language. Decisions on academic requirements are within the domain of the academic deans. Decisions are made on an individualized basis.

ADDITIONAL INFORMATION

Environment: The school is located at the base of the Rocky Mountains, 45 minutes from Denver.

Student Body
  Undergrad enrollment: 26,325
  Women: 47%
  Men: 53%
  Percent out-of-state: 35

Cost Information
  In-state tuition: $7,672
  Out-of-state tuition: $28,850
  Room and board: $11,278
Housing Information
  University housing: Yes
  Percent living on campus: 28%

Greek System
  Fraternity: Yes
  Sorority: Yes
Athletics: Division I

UNIVERSITY OF COLORADO—COLORADO SPRINGS

1420 Austin Bluffs Parkway, Colorado Springs, CO 80918
Phone: 719-255-3383 • Fax: 719-255-3116
E-mail: admrec@uccs.edu • Web: www.uccs.edu
Support: CS • Institution type: 4-year public

PROGRAMS OR SERVICES FOR STUDENTS WITH LD

University of Colorado—Colorado Springs is committed to providing equal educational opportunity for all students who meet the academic admission requirements. The purpose of Disability Services is to provide comprehensive support to meet the individual needs of students with disabilities. Students are expected to utilize the resources of Disability Services to the degree they determine necessary.

ADMISSION INFORMATION FOR STUDENTS WITH LD/ADHD

College entrance tests required: Yes
Interview required: No
Essay recommended: No
What documentation required for LD: Psycho Ed evaluation to include: relevant historical info, instructional interventions, related services, age diagnosed, objective data (aptitude, achievement, info processing), test scores (standard, percentile and grade equivalents) and describe functional limitations.
With general application: No
To receive services after enrolling: Yes
What documentation required for ADHD: Diagnosis based on DSM-V; history of behaviors impairing functioning in academic setting; diagnostic interview; history of symptoms; evidence of ongoing behaviors.

With general application: No
Submitted to: Disability Services
Special Ed. HS course work accepted: No
Specific course requirements of all applicants: Yes
Separate application required: No
# of LD applications submitted each year: NR
# of LD applications accepted yearly: NR
Total # of students receiving LD services: 40
Acceptance into program means acceptance into college: Student must be admitted and enrolled in the university first and then reviewed for LD services.

ADMISSIONS

An applicant's learning disability is not considered in an admission decision. All applicants are required to meet the Minimum Academic Preparation Standards (MAPS), including 4 years of English, 3 years of math (4 years for engineering and business), 3 years of natural science, 2 years of social science, 2 years of a foreign language, and 1 year of an elective; fine and performing arts are encouraged. Courses taken before 9th grade are accepted as long as the documentation provided shows that the courses were completed. American Sign Language is a qualified substitute for a foreign language.Successfully completing 2 years of a foreign language will satisfy the foreign language requirement regardless of whether the courses were taken before the 9th grade. Students with deficiencies may be admitted to the university provided they meet the other admission standards of test scores, rank in class, and GPA (minimum of 2.8), provided they make up any deficiencies in the MAPS prior to graduation.

ADDITIONAL INFORMATION

Students with learning disabilities receive information in their acceptance letter about contacting Disability Services if they wish to request accommodations or services. Students must request services and submit appropriate documentation. Students must meet with Disability Services to discuss support services and/or accommodations that are appropriate. Strategy development is offered in study skills, reading, test performance, stress reduction, time management, and writing skills. Disability Services offers the use of volunteers who use carbonless paper provided by the support services. Services and accommodations are available for undergraduate and graduate students with learning disabilities. Tutors are available for all university students in labs; tutors are also provided for students with disabilities.

LEARNING DISABILITY PROGRAMS OR SERVICES

Contact Information
Name of program or department: Disability Services
  Telephone: 719-262-3354
  Fax: 719-262-3195

LEARNING DISABILITY SERVICES

Accommodations are decided upon an individual basis after a thorough review of appropriate, current documentation. The accommodations requested must be supported through the documentation provided and must be logically linked to the current impact of the condition on academic functioning.

Allowed in exams
  Dictionary: Yes
  Computer: Yes
  Spellchecker: Yes
Extended test time: Yes
Scribes: Yes
Proctors: Yes
Oral exams: Yes
Note-takers: No

Distraction-reduced environment: Yes
Tape recording in class: Yes
Electronic texts: Yes
Accommodations for students with ADHD: Yes
Kurzweil Reader: Yes
Other assistive technology: Yes
Priority registration: No

Added costs for services: No
LD specialists: Yes
Professional tutors: No
Peer tutors: No
Max. hours/wk. for services: N/A
How professors are notified of LD/ADHD: By student

GENERAL ADMISSIONS INFORMATION

Office of Admission: 719-255-3383

ENTRANCE REQUIREMENTS

Academic units required: 4 English, 3 math, 3 science (2 science labs), 2 foreign language, 2 social studies, 1 academic elective. **Academic units recommended:** 4 English, 4 math, 3 science (2 science labs), 2 foreign language, 2 social studies, 1 academic elective. High school diploma is required, and GED is accepted. ACT with or without Writing component accepted. TOEFL required of all international applicants: minimum paper TOEFL 550, minimum computer TOEFL 213.

Application deadline: 8/1
Notification: Rolling
Average GPA: 3.36
ACT Composite middle 50% range: 21–26

SAT Math middle 50% range: 470–610
SAT Critical Reading middle 50% range: 470–600
SAT Writing middle 50% range: 450–560

Graduated top 10% of class: 16%
Graduated top 25% of class: 42%
Graduated top 50% of class: 78%

COLLEGE GRADUATION REQUIREMENTS

Course waivers allowed: No
In what course: N/A
Course substitutions allowed: Yes
In what course: American Sign Language is accepted as a foreign language.

ADDITIONAL INFORMATION

Environment: The university has an urban campus 70 miles south of Denver.

Student Body
  Undergrad enrollment: 12,022
  Women: 57%
  Men: 43%
  Percent out-of-state: 11%

Cost Information
  In-state tuition: $7,893
  Out-of-state tuition: $17,413
  Room & board: $9,300
Housing Information
  University housing: Yes
  Percent living on campus: 10%

Greek System
  Fraternity: No
  Sorority: Yes
Athletics: Division II

UNIVERSITY OF DENVER

Office of Admission, 2197 South University Boulevard, Denver, CO 80208
Phone: 303-871-2036 • Fax: 303-871-3301
E-mail: admission@du.edu • Web: www.du.edu/admission
Support: SP • Institution type: 4-year private

PROGRAMS OR SERVICES FOR STUDENTS WITH LD

The Learning Effectiveness Program (LEP) is a comprehensive program structured to provide individualized support to students with learning disabilities, ADHD or a history of learning differences. LEP counselors work one-on-one with students to determine their learning strengths and develop skills that will make them successful university students. Three crucial areas of skill development are encouraged: self-advocacy, articulation of strengths and weaknesses, and independent learning strategies. Cognitive strategy development is a basic part of individual sessions with a LED counselor. Students participate in regular course work and do not take special classes. Another major focus of the LEP is reducing anxiety about learning in a college environment. Students are also taught nontraditional study skills designed to increase reading, writing, and memory. Students are treated as responsible adults and are expected to participate in the program willingly. LEP also provides subject specific tutoring and an organizational specialist.

ADMISSION INFORMATION FOR STUDENTS WITH LD/ADHD

College entrance tests required: Yes
Interview required: No
Essay recommended: Yes
What documentation required for LD: Psycho Ed evaluation to include: relevant historical info, instructional interventions, related services, age diagnosed, objective data (aptitude, achievement, info processing), test scores (standard, percentile and grade equivalents) and describe functional limitations.
With general application: Yes if requested as part of Structured Program application
To receive services after enrolling: Yes
What documentation required for ADHD: Diagnosis based on DSM-V; history of behaviors impairing functioning in academic setting; diagnostic interview; history of symptoms; evidence of ongoing behaviors.

With general application: Yes if requested as part of Structured Program application
To receive services after enrolling: Yes
Submitted to: Learning Effectiveness Program
Special Ed. HS course work accepted: No
Specific course requirements for all applicants: NR
Separate application required: Yes
# of LD applications submitted each year: 300
# of LD applications accepted yearly: 95
Total # of students receiving LD services: NR
# of students in LEP: 220
Acceptance into program means acceptance into college: Student must be admitted first to the university to enroll in the LEP.

ADMISSIONS

Admission to the LEP program is contingent upon admission to the university. An enrollment form for the LEP can be found on line. Students applying to LEP must also provide appropriate documentation of LD/ADHD or a history of learning differences. A campus visit is welcomed and recommended, but not required.

ADDITIONAL INFORMATION

The LEP is a fee-for-service program and services are only provided to those enrolled in the program. LEP provides services beyond those mandated under section 504 provided by the Disabilities Services Program at the university. The fee for the LEP is $3,300 a year for the academic year (Fall, Winter, and Spring) and an additional $1,100 for summer. Students who feel that they need only basic accommodations and do not wish to participate in the comprehensive LEP, should contact the Disability Services Program (DSP) at 303-871-2278 to make those arrangements. DSP website is www.du.edu/disability/dsp. The following are accommodations that may be granted to students, however, requests will be evaluated individually based on appropriate and current documentation: use of calculator, computer, spell check, extended time testing, scribe, oral exams, note taker, distraction reduced environment, alternate format text, priority registration, and foreign language substitution.

LEARNING DISABILITY PROGRAMS OR SERVICES

Contact Information
Name of program or department: Learning Effectiveness Program
  Telephone: 303-871-4393
  Fax: 303-871-3939

LEARNING DISABILITY SERVICES

Accommodations are decided upon an individual basis after a thorough review of appropriate, current documentation. The accommodations requested must be supported through the documentation provided and must be logically linked to the current impact of the condition on academic functioning.

Allowed in exams
  Calculator: Yes
  Computer: Yes
  Spellchecker: No
Extended test time: Yes
Scribes: Yes
Proctors: Yes
Oral exams: Yes
Note-takers: Yes

Distraction-reduced environment: Yes
Tape recording in class: Yes
Electronic texts: Yes
Accommodations for students with
  ADHD: Yes
Kurzweil Reader: Yes
Other assistive technology: Yes
Priority registration: Yes

Added costs for services: Yes
LD specialists: Yes
Professional tutors: 30
Peer tutors: Yes
Max. hours/wk. for services:
  Unlimited
How professors are notified of
  LD/ADHD: By student

GENERAL ADMISSIONS INFORMATION

Office of Admission: 303-871-3383

ENTRANCE REQUIREMENTS

Academic units recommended: 4 English, 4 math, 4 science (2 science labs), 3 foreign language, 2 social studies, 2 history. Interview required. Essay required. High school diploma is required, and GED is accepted. ACT with or without Writing component accepted. TOEFL required of all international applicants: minimum paper TOEFL 525, minimum computer TOEFL 193.

Application deadline: 1/15
Notification: 3/15
Average GPA: 3.71
ACT Composite middle 50% range:
  25–30

SAT Math middle 50% range:
  560–670
SAT Critical Reading middle 50%
  range: 550–660
SAT Writing middle 50% range:
  540–640

Graduated top 10% of class: 44%
Graduated top 25% of class: 81%
Graduated top 50% of class: 97%

COLLEGE GRADUATION REQUIREMENTS

Course waivers allowed: No
Course substitutions allowed: Yes
In what course: In the area of foreign language, students may qualify to take substitution courses that still expose them to new cultures and identities but do not have the intensive grammar component.

ADDITIONAL INFORMATION

Environment: The university has a 230-acre campus 7 miles southeast of Denver.

Student Body
  Undergrad enrollment: 5,455
  Women: 56%
  Men: 44%
  Percent out-of-state: 50%

Cost Information
  Tuition: $37,833
  Room & board: $10,440
Housing Information
  University housing: Yes
  Percent living on campus: 44%

Greek System
  Fraternity: Yes
  Sorority: Yes
Athletics: Division I

UNIVERSITY OF NORTHERN COLORADO

UNC Admissions Office, Campus Box 10, Greeley, CO 80639
Phone: 970-351-2881 • Fax: 970-351-2984
E-mail: admissions.help@unco.edu • Web: www.unco.edu
Support: S • Institution type: 4-year public

PROGRAMS OR SERVICES FOR STUDENTS WITH LD

Although the university does not offer a formal LD program, individual assistance is provided whenever possible. The Disability Support Services (DSS) provides access, accommodations, and advocacy for UNC students who have documented disabilities. Academic needs are determined by the documentation and a student interview. Students with disabilities have an equal opportunity to pursue their educational goals. DSS provides test accommodations, adaptive hardware and software, learning strategies, organizational skills, and a reader program. Students requesting accommodations at UNC must provide test instruments from a certified professional that measures general intellect, aptitude, and more specific information processing tests; academic and vocational measures of achievement; and a clinical interview, which is the primary measure of previous educational and psychological functioning. Suggestions of reasonable accommodations that may be appropriate at the postsecondary level are encouraged. These recommendations should be supported by the diagnosis. Students with ADHD must provide a medical or clinical diagnosis from a developmental pediatrician, neurologist, and psychiatrist, licensed clinical or educational psychologist, family physician, or a combination of such professionals.

ADMISSION INFORMATION FOR STUDENTS WITH LD/ADHD

College entrance tests required: Yes
Interview required: Yes
Essay recommended: No
What documentation required for LD: Psycho Ed evaluation to include: relevant historical info, instructional interventions, related services, age diagnosed, objective data (aptitude, achievement, info processing), test scores (standard, percentile and grade equivalents) and describe functional limitations.
With general application: No
To receive services after enrolling: Yes
What documentation required for ADHD: Diagnosis based on DSM-V; history of behaviors impairing functioning in academic setting; diagnostic interview; history of symptoms; evidence of ongoing behaviors.

With general application: No
Submitted to: Disability Support Services
Special Ed. HS course work accepted: Yes
Specific course requirements of all applicants: Yes
Separate application required: No
# of LD applications submitted each year: 75
# of LD applications accepted yearly: NR
Total # of students receiving LD services: 100
Acceptance into program means acceptance into college: Students must be admitted and enrolled in the university first and then request services.

ADMISSIONS

There is no special admission process for students with learning disabilities. All students with disabilities are admitted to UNC under the standard admission requirements of the university. The university uses class rank, GPA, and test scores to determine a selection index. UNC requires 3 years of math, and the classes must be college-prep. Pre-Algebra does not count. UNC recommends 4 years of English, 3 years of history/social sciences, and 3 years of natural science. When UNC evaluates a transcript for admissions, they only look at the math. The UNC has a special window for admitting students who do not meet UNC's freshman admission requirements but want to earn full admission into a degree program. Students wishing to participate in this program need to call the Admissions Office. Each applicant is judged on an individual basis. Students do not need to be LD to apply for this DSS program but must have a documented disability. To assist in determining eligibility for the program, current medical/clinical information is necessary. To receive services, students must request accommodations upon arrival at UNC. Students enrolled in the Challenge Program must take 12 hours of college credit and earn a GPA of 2.0 after one or two semesters to remain at UNC.

ADDITIONAL INFORMATION

Services for individuals with LD/ADHD includes learning strategies, organizational skills, and advocacy skills; reader program; test accommodations; assistance in arranging for note-takers; and assistive technology, including voice synthesizers, screen readers, screen enlargers, scanners, voice-recognition computer systems, large monitors, and word processing with spellchecker. Workshops are offered in student skills, organizational skills, study strategies, and time management. These workshops are electives and are not for credit. Services and accommodations are available for undergraduate and graduate students.

LEARNING DISABILITY PROGRAMS OR SERVICES

Contact Information
Name of program or department: Disability Support Services
  Telephone: 970-351-2289
  Fax: 970-351-4166

LEARNING DISABILITY SERVICES

Accommodations are decided upon an individual basis after a thorough review of appropriate, current documentation. The accommodations requested must be supported through the documentation provided and must be logically linked to the current impact of the condition on academic functioning.

Allowed in exams	**Distraction-reduced environment:** Yes	**Added costs for services:** No
Calculator: Yes	**Tape recording in class:** Yes	**LD specialists:** No
Dictionary: Yes	**Electronic texts:** Yes	**Professional tutors:** No
Computer: Yes	**Accommodations for students with**	**Peer tutors:** 20
Spellchecker: Yes	**ADHD:** Yes	**Max. hours/wk. for services:** Varies
Extended test time: Yes	**Other assistive technology:** Yes	**How professors are notified of**
Scribes: Yes	**Priority registration:** Yes	**LD/ADHD:** By student
Proctors: Yes		
Readers: Yes		
Note-takers: Yes		

GENERAL ADMISSIONS INFORMATION

Office of Admission: 970-351-2881

ENTRANCE REQUIREMENTS

Academic units required: 3 math. **Academic units recommended:** 4 English, 3 science (1 science lab), 3 social studies. High school diploma is required, and GED is accepted. ACT with or without Writing component accepted. TOEFL required of all international applicants: minimum paper TOEFL 520, minimum computer TOEFL 190.

Application deadline: None	**SAT Math middle 50% range:**	**Graduated top 10% of class:** 14%
Notification: Rolling	450–580	**Graduated top 25% of class:** 38%
Average GPA: 3.22	**SAT Critical Reading middle 50%**	**Graduated top 50% of class:** 70%
ACT Composite middle 50% range:	**range:** 460–580	
19–25	**SAT Writing middle 50% range:** NR	

COLLEGE GRADUATION REQUIREMENTS

Course waivers allowed: No
Course substitutions allowed: No

ADDITIONAL INFORMATION

Environment: The university is located on 240 acres in a small town 50 miles north of Denver.

Student Body	**Cost Information**	**Greek System**
Undergrad enrollment: 10,090	**In-state tuition:** $5,300	**Fraternity:** Yes
Women: 61%	**Out-of-state tuition:** $16,822	**Sorority:** Yes
Men: 39%	**Room & board:** $9,750	**Athletics:** Division I
Percent out-of-state: 10%	**Housing Information**	
	University housing: Yes	
	Percent living on campus: 29%	

WESTERN STATE COLLEGE OF COLORADO

600 North Adams Street, Gunnison, CO 81231
Phone: 800-876-5309 • Fax: 970-943-2363
E-mail: admissions@western.edu • Web: www.western.edu
Support: S• Institution type: 4-year public

PROGRAMS OR SERVICES FOR STUDENTS WITH LD

Disability Services, located in Western's Academic Resource Center, coordinates support services for all qualified students with disabilities. We offer a variety of resources and accommodations to assist students as they pursue their academic and career goals. While providing a supportive environment, we encourage students to develop independence and take responsibility for their academic experiences. Personal consultation and workshops are available to help students improve learning, problem-solving, and self-advocacy skills.

ADMISSION INFORMATION FOR STUDENTS WITH LD/ADHD

College entrance tests required: Yes
Interview required: No
Essay recommended: No
What documentation required for LD: Psycho Ed evaluation to include: relevant historical info, instructional interventions, related services, age diagnosed, objective data (aptitude, achievement, info processing), test scores (standard, percentile and grade equivalents) and describe functional limitations.
With general application: No
To receive services after enrolling: Yes
What documentation required for ADHD: Diagnosis based on DSM-V; history of behaviors impairing functioning in academic setting; diagnostic interview; history of symptoms; evidence of ongoing behaviors.

With general application: No
Submitted to: Disability Services
Special Ed. HS course work accepted: Yes
Specific course requirements of all applicants: Yes
Separate application required: No
# of LD applications submitted each year: NR
# of LD applications accepted yearly: NR
Total # of students receiving LD services: NR
Acceptance into program means acceptance into college: Students must be admitted and enrolled prior to requesting services.

ADMISSIONS

Admission to Western depends on academic performance and background, standardized test scores, and personal attributes. In addition to general admissions requirements, Western State recommends a personal essay and recommendations from teachers, counselors, or others who know the student's academic ability. The college tries to admit those students who have demonstrated their ability to succeed. Normally, students are admitted if they meet the following criteria: graduate from an accredited high school; have a cumulative GPA of 2.5 or better (on a 4.0 scale of college-prep courses) and/or rank in the upper two-thirds of the student's graduating class; and score 20 or higher on the ACT or 950 on the SAT. Western recommends 4 years of English, 3 years of mathematics to include Algebra II, 2 years of natural science, and 2 years of social science. Modern language and computer science units are also important.

ADDITIONAL INFORMATION

Students who choose to register for Learning Disability Program/Services typically do so soon after acceptance to Western. All accepted students will receive information regarding the Academic Resource Center, including Disability Services and the registration link (www.western.edu/dsinfo). Once registered, all students will go through an intake session with Disability Services staff to review policies, procedures, resources, and accommodations. Some of the services used by students include, but are not limited to, test accommodations, taped textbooks, readers, scribes, note-takers, and assistance with academic advising and course registration. Individual learning skills assistance is availalble through appointments and workshops, our staff works with students to help them develop effective learning skills and study strategies in areas such as reading, memory, test taking, note-taking, organization, and time management. We encourage students who wish to enhance motivation, develop an understanding of individual learning styles, and improve academic performance to use the Academic Resource Center's resources.

LEARNING DISABILITY PROGRAMS OR SERVICES

Contact Information
Name of program or department: Disability Services
  Telephone: 970.943.7056
  Fax: 970.943.3409

LEARNING DISABILITY SERVICES

Accommodations are decided upon an individual basis after a thorough review of appropriate, current documentation. The accommodations requested must be supported through the documentation provided and must be logically linked to the current impact of the condition on academic functioning.

Allowed in exams
  Calculator: Yes
  Dictionary: No
  Computer: Yes
  Spellchecker: Yes
Extended test time: Yes
Scribes: Yes
Proctors: Yes
Oral exams: Yes
Note-takers: Yes

Distraction-reduced environment: Yes
Tape recording in class: Yes
Electronic texts: Yes
**Accommodations for students with
  ADHD:** Yes
Kurzweil Reader: Yes
Other assistive technology: Yes
Priority registration: Yes

Added costs for services: No
LD specialists: No
Professional tutors: No
Peer tutors: NR
Max. hours/wk. for services: NR
**How professors are notified of
  LD/ADHD:** By student

GENERAL ADMISSIONS INFORMATION

Office of Admission: 970-943-2119

ENTRANCE REQUIREMENTS
Academic units required: 4 English, 3 math, 2 science (2 science labs), 2 social studies, 2 history, 3 academic electives. **Academic units recommended:** 4 English, 4 math, 3 science, 2 foreign language, 3 social studies, 3 history. High school diploma is required, and GED is accepted. ACT with or without Writing component accepted. TOEFL required of all international applicants: minimum paper TOEFL 550, minimum computer TOEFL 213.

Application deadline: 8/1
Notification: Rolling
Average GPA: 3.00
ACT Composite middle 50% range:
  19–24

SAT Math middle 50% range:
  460–550
**SAT Critical Reading middle 50%
  range:** 450–550
SAT Writing middle 50% range:
  450–550

Graduated top 10% of class: 9%
Graduated top 25% of class: 25%
Graduated top 50% of class: 54%

COLLEGE GRADUATION REQUIREMENTS

Course waivers allowed: No
Course substitutions allowed: Yes
In what course: Math substitutions may be approved for students with documented math learning disabilities, when appropriate.

ADDITIONAL INFORMATION

Environment: Western State College of Colorado is located in the heart of the Rocky Mountains.

Student Body
  Undergrad enrollment: 2,169
  Women: 40%
  Men: 60%
  Percent out-of-state: 24%

Cost Information
  In-state tuition: $4,627
  Out-of-state tuition: $14,496
  Room & board: $8,688
Housing Information
  University housing: Yes
  Percent living on campus: 36%

Greek System
  Fraternity: Yes
  Sorority: Yes
  Athletics: Division II

FAIRFIELD UNIVERSITY

1073 North Benson Road, Fairfield, CT 06824-5195
Phone: 203-254-4100 • Fax: 203-254-4199
E-mail: admis@mail.fairfield.edu • Web: www.fairfield.edu
Support: CS • Institution type: 4-year private

PROGRAMS OR SERVICES FOR STUDENTS WITH LD

The university provides services for students with disabilities through Student Support Services. There is no learning disability program, only services that are available for all students with disabilities. These services are designed to provide equal access to the learning environment. Students are supported while being encouraged to be self-advocates. Students with learning disabilities must provide documentation from an appropriate testing agent. Students with ADHD must have documentation from appropriate professionals who can provide behavior rating scales, ruling out other disabilities, and showing the onset of the ADHD between ages 7–12. All documentation should be submitted to Student Support Services.

ADMISSION INFORMATION FOR STUDENTS WITH LD/ADHD

College entrance tests required: Yes
Interview required: No
Essay recommended: No
What documentation required for LD: Psycho Ed evaluation to
  include: relevant historical info, instructional interventions,
  related services, age diagnosed, objective data (aptitude,
  achievement, info processing), test scores (standard, percentile
  and grade equivalents) and describe functional limitations.
With general application: No
To receive services after enrolling: Yes
What documentation required for ADHD: Diagnosis based
  on DSM-V; history of behaviors impairing functioning in
  academic setting; diagnostic interview; history of symptoms;
  evidence of ongoing behaviors.

With general application: No
Submitted to: Student Support Services
Special Ed. HS course work accepted: Yes
Specific course requirements of all applicants: Yes
Separate application required: No
# of LD applications submitted each year: NR
# of LD applications accepted yearly: NR
Total # of students receiving LD services: 150
Acceptance into program means acceptance into
  college: Students must be admitted and enrolled in the
  university first and then request services.

ADMISSIONS

There is no special admissions process for students with learning disabilities. Admission criteria include ranking in top 40 percent of graduating class or better; maintaining a B average; scoring 25 ACT; counselor recommendations; and college-prep courses including 4 years of English, 3–4 years of math, 2–4 years of a foreign language, 1–3 years of science lab, and 2–3 years of history. Courses taken in the Special Education Department may be acceptable. The mid 50 percent SAT Reasoning Test scores are 1120–1270, and ACT scores are 26–29. Once students have been admitted and have enrolled, they may initiate contact for services.

ADDITIONAL INFORMATION

Skills courses are offered in study skills, note-taking strategies, time management skills, and strategies for success. These skills courses are not for credit. Students are offered meetings with a professional who has a background in teaching students with disabilities. Letters are sent to professors on students' request. All students have access to content tutoring and a Writing Center. Services and accommodations are available for undergraduate and graduate students.

LEARNING DISABILITY PROGRAMS OR SERVICES

Contact Information
Name of program or department: Student Support Services
 Telephone: 203-254-4000 ext. 2615
 Fax: 203-254-5542

LEARNING DISABILITY SERVICES

Accommodations are decided upon an individual basis after a thorough review of appropriate, current documentation. The accommodations requested must be supported through the documentation provided and must be logically linked to the current impact of the condition on academic functioning.

Allowed in exams
 Calculator: Yes
 Dictionary: Yes
 Computer: Yes
 Spellchecker: Yes
Extended test time: Yes
Scribes: Yes
Proctors: Yes
Oral exams: Yes
Note-takers: Yes

Distraction-reduced environment: Yes
Tape recording in class: Yes
Electronic texts: Yes
Accommodations for students with
 ADHD: Yes
Kurzweil Reader: Yes
Other assistive technology: Yes
Priority registration: No

Added costs for services: No
LD specialists: Yes
Professional tutors: No
Peer tutors: 90–120
Max. hours/wk. for services:
 Unlimited
How professors are notified of
 LD/ADHD: By student

GENERAL ADMISSIONS INFORMATION

Office of Admission: 203-254-4100

ENTRANCE REQUIREMENTS
Academic units required: 4 English, 3 math, 2 science (2 science labs), 2 foreign language, 2 social studies, 2 history, 1 academic elective. **Academic units recommended:** 4 English, 4 math, 3 science (2 science labs), 4 foreign language, 2 social studies, 2 history, 1 academic elective. High school diploma is required, and GED is not accepted. ACT with or without Writing component accepted. TOEFL required of all international applicants: minimum paper TOEFL 550, minimum computer TOEFL 213.

Application deadline: 1/15
Notification: 4/1
Average GPA: 3.47
ACT Composite middle 50% range:
 23–27

SAT Math middle 50% range:
 540–630
SAT Critical Reading middle 50%
 range: 520–610
SAT Writing middle 50% range:
 540–630

Graduated top 10% of class: 12%
Graduated top 25% of class: 26%
Graduated top 50% of class: 98%

COLLEGE GRADUATION REQUIREMENTS

Course substitutions allowed: Yes
In what course: Foreign language, math (must have severe impairment)

ADDITIONAL INFORMATION

Environment: The university is located on 200 acres in a suburban area 60 miles northeast of New York City.
Student Body
 Undergrad enrollment: 3,948
 Women: 58%
 Men: 42%
 Percent out-of-state: 76%

Cost Information
 Tuition: $39,990
 Room & board: $12,210
Housing Information
 University housing: Yes
 Percent living on campus: 67%

Greek System
 Fraternity: No
 Sorority: No
 Athletics: Division I

MITCHELL COLLEGE

437 Pequot Avenue, New London, CT 06320
Phone: 860-701-5011 • Fax: 860-444-1209
E-mail: admissions@mitchell.edu • Web: www.mitchell.edu
Support: SP • Institution type: 2-year and 4-year private

PROGRAMS OR SERVICES FOR STUDENTS WITH LD

Mitchell College is dedicated to providing a student-centered, supportive learning environment that addresses the educational needs of all students, including those with disabilities. The Duques Academic Success Center offers academic and other supports through five functions—the Tutoring Center offers professional tutoring to all students; the Career Center helps students investigate and pursue career options; the Academic Advising Center offers professional academic advising: Disability Student Services (DSS) determines eligibility for services and arranges accommodations; and the Bentsen Learning Resource Center (LRC) for students with documented learning disabilities and ADHD. The LRC offers two levels of academic support. Students participating at Level 1 work with a LRC Specialist 4 times a week. An individualized program of support is developed based on a student's learning strengths, challenges, and goals. Close individual attention, frequent contact, and structured follow up are the main components of the fee-based program. Level 2 is an enhanced support program offering less-involved and less-directed assistance on an individual and/or small group basis, with up to 2 scheduled appointments a week. In addition, the LRC offers Academic Coaching for Empowerment designed for students with ADHD or executive functioning issues. Students direct the session, tell the coach what short term goals they hope to accomplish, and formulate an action plan for achieving these goals. The frequent check ins with a coach provide the structure and feedback to keep students on track and develop planning and organizational skills in a nonjudgmental environment.

ADMISSION INFORMATION FOR STUDENTS WITH LD/ADHD

College entrance tests required: No
Interview required: Yes
Essay recommended: Yes
What documentation required for LD: Psycho Ed evaluation to include: relevant historical info, instructional interventions, related services, age diagnosed, objective data (aptitude, achievement, info processing), test scores (standard, percentile and grade equivalents) and describe functional limitations.
With general application: Yes if requested as part of Structured Program application
To receive services after enrolling: Yes
What documentation required for ADHD: Diagnosis based on DSM-V; history of behaviors impairing functioning in academic setting; diagnostic interview; history of symptoms; evidence of ongoing behaviors.

With general application: Yes if requested as part of Structured Program application
To receive services after enrolling: Yes
Submitted to: DSS
Special Ed. HS course work accepted: NR
Specific course requirements for all applicants: No
Separate application required: Submittal of documentation currently constitutes application for eligibility determination.
# of LD applications submitted each year: 550
# of LD applications accepted yearly: 300
Total # of students receiving LD services: 300

ADMISSIONS

Students must first apply and be accepted into Mitchell College. Application requirements are listed on www.mitchell.edu and include the application itself, transcripts, at least one recommendation, a written personal statement, as well as an interview. Standardized tests are currently optional. A high school diploma or GED is required for admission. Applicants are evaluated holistically and admitted based on their potential. Generally, students who complete a college preparatory curriculum with a GPA of 2.0 or higher are admitted. Approximately 95% of those who are admitted receive financial aid, which can be applied to supplemental fees for services offered by the LRC. Students who are interested in participating in the LRC program need to complete a Request for Services Application. In addition, students need to submit documentation of a learning disability and or AD/HD to Disability Student Services. Only students with a definitive diagnosis of LD or AD/HD will be considered for the program.

ADDITIONAL INFORMATION

Mitchell College also has the "Thames Academy," a post-grad (PG) or pre-college transitional experience. It is a year of academic preparation that students take between the end of their high school education and the start of their college studies. Unlike traditional post-grad programs at prep schools, Thames Academy at Mitchell College provides college-level courses for credit. Located on Mitchell College Campus, the Academy provides a structured residential program within a collegiate environment and co-curricular interaction with two- and four-year students. Please contact Tammy Vuksinic at viksinic_t@mitchell.edu for more information.

LEARNING DISABILITY PROGRAMS OR SERVICES

Contact Information
Name of program or department: Bentsen Learning Resource Center
 Telephone: 860-701-5145
 Fax: 860-701-5090

LEARNING DISABILITY SERVICES

Accommodations are decided upon an individual basis after a thorough review of appropriate, current documentation. The accommodations requested must be supported through the documentation provided and must be logically linked to the current impact of the condition on academic functioning.

Allowed in exams	**Distraction-reduced environment:** Yes	**Added costs for services:** Yes
Calculator: Yes	**Tape recording in class:** Yes	**LD specialists:** Yes
Dictionary: Yes	**Electronic texts:** Yes	**Professional tutors:** 10–12
Computer: Yes	**Accommodations for students with**	**Peer tutors:** No
Spellchecker: Yes	ADHD: Yes	**Max. hours/wk. for services:** 4
Extended test time: Yes	**Kurzweil Reader:** Yes	**How professors are notified of**
Scribes: Yes	**Other assistive technology:** Yes	LD/ADHD: By student
Proctors: Yes	**Priority registration:** N/A	
Oral exams: Yes		
Note-takers: Yes		

GENERAL ADMISSIONS INFORMATION

Office of Admission: 860-701-5011

ENTRANCE REQUIREMENTS

Academic units recommended: 4 English, 3 math, 3 science, 2 social studies, 2 history, 2 academic electives. High school diploma is required, and GED is accepted. TOEFL required of all international applicants: minimum paper TOEFL 500.

Application deadline: None	**SAT Math middle 50% range:** NR	**Graduated top 10% of class:** NR
Notification: Rolling	**SAT Critical Reading middle 50%**	**Graduated top 25% of class:** NR
Average GPA: 2.80	range: NR	**Graduated top 50% of class:** NR
ACT Composite middle 50% range:	**SAT Writing middle 50% range:** NR	
NR		

COLLEGE GRADUATION REQUIREMENTS

Course waivers allowed: No
Course substitutions allowed: Yes
In what course: Varies based on the student's history with the subject area and the school policies and procedures.

ADDITIONAL INFORMATION

Environment: The 65-acre campus sits on a former estate located in a safe and quiet residential area of historic New London.

Student Body	**Cost Information**	**Greek System**
Undergrad enrollment: 992	Tuition: $27,714	Fraternity: No
Women: 47%	Room & board: $12,492	Sorority: No
Men: 53%	**Housing Information**	Athletics: Division III
Percent out-of-state: 45%	University housing: Yes	
	Percent living on campus: 60%	

SOUTHERN CONNECTICUT STATE U.

SCSU—Admissions House, 131 Farnham Ave., New Haven, CT 06515-1202
Phone: 203-392-5644 • Fax: 203-392-5727
E-mail: adminfo@scsu.ctstateu.edu • Web: www.southernct.edu
Support: CS • Institution type: 4-year public

PROGRAMS OR SERVICES FOR STUDENTS WITH LD

The purpose of the Disability Resource Center (DRC) is to ensure educational equity for students with disabilities. The DRO works to provide access to full participation in all aspects of campus life. The DRC assists students in arranging for individualized accommodations and support services. The DRC is a resource for students, faculty, and the university at large. Use of DRC services is voluntary and confidential. The DRC provides academic, career, and personal support for all university students with disabilities, including students with specific learning disabilities and Attention Deficit Hyperactivity Disorder.

ADMISSION INFORMATION FOR STUDENTS WITH LD/ADHD

College entrance tests required: Yes
Interview required: No
Essay recommended: No
What documentation required for LD: Psycho Ed evaluation to include: relevant historical info, instructional interventions, related services, age diagnosed, objective data (aptitude, achievement, info processing), test scores (standard, percentile and grade equivalents) and describe functional limitations.
With general application: No
To receive services after enrolling: Yes
What documentation required for ADHD: Diagnosis based on DSM-V; history of behaviors impairing functioning in academic setting; diagnostic interview; history of symptoms; evidence of ongoing behaviors.

With general application: No
Submitted to: Disability Resource Center
Special Ed. HS course work accepted: Yes
Specific course requirements of all applicants: Yes
Separate application required: No
# of LD applications submitted each year: NR
# of LD applications accepted yearly: NR
Total # of students receiving LD services: 559
Acceptance into program means acceptance into college: Students must be admitted and enrolled in the university first and then request services.

ADMISSIONS

There is no special admissions process for students with learning disabilities. All applicants must meet the same criteria. Course requirements include 4 years of English, 3 years of math, 2 years of science, 2 years of a foreign language, 2 years of social studies, and 2 years of history.

ADDITIONAL INFORMATION

The DRC assists students in arranging for individualized accommodations and support services. Current students should make an appointment with the office and bring educational documentation, including achievement testing and psychoeducational evaluation, or medical documentation. Services include course selection and registration assistance; course and testing accommodations; support in developing time management and study skills, identifying strengths and weaknesses, and acquiring compensatory strategies; contact with faculty and university departments; and advocacy and self-advocacy information and training. Services and accommodations are available for undergraduate and graduate students.

LEARNING DISABILITY PROGRAMS OR SERVICES

Learning Disability Services: Disability Resource Center (DRC)
Telephone: 203-392-6828
Fax: 203-392-6829

LEARNING DISABILITY SERVICES

Accommodations are decided upon an individual basis after a thorough review of appropriate, current documentation. The accommodations requested must be supported through the documentation provided and must be logically linked to the current impact of the condition on academic functioning.

Allowed in exams
Calculator: Yes
Computer: Yes
Spellchecker: Yes
Extended test time: Yes
Scribes: Yes
Proctors: Yes
Note-takers: Yes

Distraction-reduced environment: Yes
Tape recording in class: Yes
Electronic texts: Yes
Accommodations for students with ADHD: Yes
Kurzweil Reader: Yes
Other assistive technology: Yes
Priority registration: No

Added costs for services: No
LD specialists: Yes
Professional tutors: No
Max. hours/wk. for services: 1.5
How professors are notified of LD/ADHD: By student

GENERAL ADMISSIONS INFORMATION

Office of Admission: 203-392-5656

ENTRANCE REQUIREMENTS

Academic units required: 4 English, 3 math, 2 science (1 science lab), 2 foreign language, 2 social studies, 2 history. **Academic units recommended:** 4 math, 3 foreign language. High school diploma is required, and GED is accepted. ACT with Writing component required. TOEFL required of all international applicants: minimum paper TOEFL 525, minimum computer TOEFL 1.

Application deadline: 4/1
Notification: Rolling
Average GPA: NR
ACT Composite middle 50% range: NR

SAT Math middle 50% range: 420–520
SAT Critical Reading middle 50% range: 430–530
SAT Writing middle 50% range: NR

Graduated top 10% of class: 6%
Graduated top 25% of class: 22%
Graduated top 50% of class: 64%

COLLEGE GRADUATION REQUIREMENTS

Course waivers allowed: No
Course substitutions allowed: Yes
In what course: Foreign language

ADDITIONAL INFORMATION

Environment: The university is located in an urban area 35 miles south of Hartford and 90 miles from New York City.

Student Body
Undergrad enrollment: 8,778
Women: 65%
Men: 35%
Percent out-of-state: 6%

Cost Information
In-state tuition: $8,248
Out-of-state tuition: $18,872
Room & board: $10,232
Housing Information
University housing: Yes
Percent living on campus: 31%

Greek System
Fraternity: Yes
Sorority: Yes
Athletics: Division II

UNIVERSITY OF CONNECTICUT

2131 Hillside Road, Unit 3088, Storrs, CT 06268-3088
Phone: 860-486-3137 • Fax: 860-486-1476
E-mail: beahusky@uconn.edu • Web: www.uconn.edu
Support: CS • Institution type: 4-year public

PROGRAMS OR SERVICES FOR STUDENTS WITH LD

The major goal of the University Program for College Students with LD (UPLD) is to assist qualified students with LD to become independent and successful learners within the regular university curriculum. The program is designed to complement and support, but not to duplicate, the university's existing campus services and programs. Three types of program services are offered along a continuum leading to independence: direct instruction, in which students meet with learning specialists weekly to learn compensatory skills to strengthen learning strategies; monitoring for students who need periodic contact; and consultation with UPLD staff on a student-initiated basis. Most students find that it is beneficial to access services at the direct instruction level and progress at an individual rate through the UPLD Continuum as they experience increasing confidence and competence. UPLD staff is available to help student's access additional campus resources. Staff of UPLD is not qualified to serve as academic advisors. In cases where the disability does not include a specific LD, such as ADHD, students can receive support services from the Center for Students with Disabilities (CSD). Students diagnosed with LD and ADHD have services coordinated through UPLD and CSD.

ADMISSION INFORMATION FOR STUDENTS WITH LD/ADHD

College entrance tests required: Yes
Interview required: No
Essay recommended: No
What documentation required for LD: Psycho Ed evaluation to include: relevant historical info, instructional interventions, related services, age diagnosed, objective data (aptitude, achievement, info processing), test scores (standard, percentile and grade equivalents) and describe functional limitations.
With general application: No
To receive services after enrolling: Yes
What documentation required for ADHD: Diagnosis based on DSM-V; history of behaviors impairing functioning in academic setting; diagnostic interview; history of symptoms; evidence of ongoing behaviors.

With general application: No
Submitted to: University Program for College Students with LD
Special Ed. HS course work accepted: NR
Specific course requirements of all applicants: Yes
Separate application required: No
# of LD applications submitted each year: 40
# of LD applications accepted yearly: 40
Total # of students receiving LD services: 150
Acceptance into program means acceptance into college: Students must be admitted and enrolled in the university first and then request services.

ADMISSIONS

There is no separate application or process for students with LD, and they must meet regular admissions criteria. The typical profile is rank in top third of class; 3.2 GPA in college-prep courses; 4 English, 3 math, 2 social studies, 2 foreign language, 2 science, 3 electives; and SAT 1100-plus or ACT 24, UConn will super score ACT/SAT. To access services, students must refer themselves to UPLD and submit documentation of a specific LD. There must be clear and specific evidence and identification of an LD. Actual test scores must be provided, including interpretation of the results. A written summary about relevant educational, medical, and family histories that relate to LD must be included. Recommendations for accommodations should be based on objective evidence of a current substantial limitation to learning, and descriptions of any accommodation and/or auxiliary aid used in high school or college should be discussed. IEPs and Section 504 plans are useful but not sufficient.

ADDITIONAL INFORMATION

Trained staff works with students on developing learning strategies and offers individual structured sessions. Learning specialists help students develop self-advocacy, identify and monitor needs, and develop individualized goals. Reasonable accommodations are determined on a case-by-case basis. The CSD coordinates requests for proctors or scribes and provides services to students with ADHD without a diagnosed LD. The university has a formal course substitution policy for students with LD that requires current, valid diagnostic evidence that the nature and severity of the LD precludes completion of courses in foreign language or math despite the provision of accommodations. A waiver of a subject in high school does not guarantee a substitution at the university.

LEARNING DISABILITY PROGRAMS OR SERVICES

Contact Information
Name of program or department: University Program for College Students with LD
  Telephone: 860-486-0178
  Fax: 860-486-5799

LEARNING DISABILITY SERVICES

Accommodations are decided upon an individual basis after a thorough review of appropriate, current documentation. The accommodations requested must be supported through the documentation provided and must be logically linked to the current impact of the condition on academic functioning.

Allowed in exams
  Calculator: Yes
  Dictionary: Yes
  Computer: Yes
  Spellchecker: Yes
Extended test time: Yes
Scribes: Yes
Proctors: Yes
Oral exams: Yes
Note-takers: Yes

Distraction-reduced environment: Yes
Tape recording in class: Yes
Electronic texts: Yes
**Accommodations for students with
  ADHD:** Yes
Kurzweil Reader: Yes
Other assistive technology: Yes
Priority registration: Yes

Added costs for services: No
LD specialists: Yes
Professional tutors: No
Peer tutors: No
Max. hours/wk. for services: 2
**How professors are notified of
  LD/ADHD:** By student

GENERAL ADMISSIONS INFORMATION

Office of Admission: 860-486-3137

ENTRANCE REQUIREMENTS

Academic units required: 4 English, 3 math, 2 science (2 science labs), 2 foreign language, 2 social studies, 3 academic electives. **Academic units recommended:** 3 foreign language. High school diploma is required, and GED is accepted. ACT with Writing component required. TOEFL required of all international applicants: minimum paper TOEFL 550, minimum computer TOEFL 213.

Application deadline: 2/1
Notification: Rolling
Average GPA: NR
ACT Composite middle 50% range:
  24–28

SAT Math middle 50% range:
  570–660
**SAT Critical Reading middle 50%
  range:** 540–630
SAT Writing middle 50% range:
  550–640

Graduated top 10% of class: 38%
Graduated top 25% of class: 81%
Graduated top 50% of class: 98%

COLLEGE GRADUATION REQUIREMENTS

Course waivers allowed: No
Course substitutions allowed: Yes
In what course: Based on documented evidence of significant impairment, some students qualify for course substitutions in foreign language or math courses.

ADDITIONAL INFORMATION

Environment: The University of Connecticut is located 30 miles northeast of Hartford.

Student Body
  Undergrad enrollment: 17,346
  Women: 50%
  Men: 50%
  Percent out-of-state: 33%

Cost Information
  In-state tuition: $10,670
  Out-of-state tuition: $27,566
  Room & board: $11,050
Housing Information
  University housing: Yes
  Percent living on campus: 71%

Greek System
  Fraternity: Yes
  Sorority: Yes
Athletics: Division I

UNIVERSITY OF HARTFORD

200 Bloomfield Avenue, West Hartford, CT 06117
Phone: 860-768-4296 • Fax: 860-768-4961
E-mail: admissions@mail.hartford.edu • Web: www.hartford.edu
Support: CS • Institution type: 2-year and 4-year private

PROGRAMS OR SERVICES FOR STUDENTS WITH LD

The Learning Plus department (L+) facilitates disability services and accommodations for eligible students in all seven colleges who have well-documented learning or attention disabilities (LD or ADHD), acquired brain injuries (ABI), or disabilities on the autism spectrum (ASD). Program objectives include helping students understand their learning strengths and weaknesses; providing direct learning strategy instruction; helping students develop accountability and self-advocacy skills; connecting students with other campus resources; facilitating test accommodations; providing information to faculty, parents, and students about disability- related issues including legal rights and responsibilities. Please note: all disability information is confidential. Eligible students who wish to access approved accommodations are required to self-disclose directly to the faculty member by submitting a Letter of Disclosure obtained from Learning Plus. Letters of Disclosure must be renewed and submitted to faculty each semester. Accommodations and services are determined on a case-by-case basis taking a variety of factors into consideration including the nature and extent of the disability, semester standing, course curricula, and other concerns. First Year and Transfer Students are eligible for weekly, one-to-one appointments with professional Learning Specialists. Skills taught during the appointments address the following areas: time management; organization; any step of the writing process; college-level reading and research; note taking; self-advocacy; and personal accountability. Second Year Students are eligible for direct strategy instruction once every other week. Drop-In appointments are available on a first-come, first-served basis. There are a limited number of appointments available. Learning Plus does not tutor in content. However, Learning Specialists will refer students needing content tutoring to other resources on campus that provide such. Please check the Learning Plus website for current documentation guidelines www.hartford.edu/Learning_Plus.

ADMISSION INFORMATION FOR STUDENTS WITH LD/ADHD

College entrance tests required: Yes
Interview required: No
Essay recommended: No
What documentation required for LD: See
   www.hartford.edu/Learning-Plus
With general application: No
To receive services after enrolling: Yes
What documentation required for ADHD: Same as above
With general application: No
Submitted to: Learning Plus
Special Ed. HS course work accepted: NR

Specific course requirements of all applicants: Yes
Separate application required: No
# of LD applications submitted each year: NR
# of LD applications accepted yearly: NR
Total # of students receiving LD services: 125–400
Acceptance into program means acceptance into
   college: Students must be admitted and enrolled in one of
   the 7 colleges in the university first and then request
   services.

ADMISSIONS

Students who have been diagnosed with LD, ADHD, ABI, ASD do not apply to the Learning Plus department per se. Students apply to one of the 7 colleges within the university. Once admitted and after depositing, the student who has been diagnosed with LD, ADHD, ABI, ASD may then elect to request disability services by submitting documentation to Learning Plus. The Admissions Committee pays particular attention to the student's individual talents and aspirations, especially as they relate to the programs available at the university.

ADDITIONAL INFORMATION

Learning Plus is voluntary. Eligible students may elect to access one or all of their approved disability services and accommodations. However, students who have disabilities are not required to access any services or accommodations. Regardless of disability, all students are expected to meet the same academic and comportment standards as their nondisabled peers.

LEARNING DISABILITY PROGRAMS OR SERVICES

Contact Information
Name of program or department: Learning Plus
  Web: www.hartford.edu/Learning-Plus
  Telephone: 860-768-4312

LEARNING DISABILITY SERVICES

Accommodations are decided on an individual basis after a thorough review of appropriate, current documentation. The accommodations requested must be supported through the documentation provided and must be logically linked to the functional limitations as posed by the disability.

Allowed in exams	**Distraction-reduced environment:** Yes	**Added costs for services:** No
Calculator: Yes, when appropriate	**Tape recording in class:** Yes	**LD specialists:** Yes
Dictionary: No	**Electronic texts:** No	**Professional tutors:** NR
Computer: Yes, when appropriate	**Accommodations for students with**	**Peer tutors:** No
Spellchecker: Yes, when appropriate	**ADHD:** Yes	**Max. hours/wk. for services:** NR
Extended test time: Yes	**Kurzweil Reader:** No	**How professors are notified of**
Scribes: Yes	**Other assistive technology:** Yes	**LD/ADHD:** By student
Proctors: Yes	**Priority registration:** No	
Oral exams: NR		
Note-takers: Yes, peers in class		

GENERAL ADMISSIONS INFORMATION

Office of Admission: 860-768-4296

ENTRANCE REQUIREMENTS
Academic units required: 4 English, 3 math, 2 science, 2 social studies, 2 history, 4 academic electives.
Academic units recommended: 3.5 math, 3 science, 2 foreign language, 3 social studies. High school diploma is required, and GED is accepted. TOEFL required of all international applicants: minimum paper TOEFL 550, minimum computer TOEFL 213.

Application deadline: None	**SAT Math middle 50% range:**	**Graduated top 10% of class:** NR
Notification: Rolling	490–590	**Graduated top 25% of class:** NR
Average GPA: NR	**SAT Critical Reading middle 50%**	**Graduated top 50% of class:** NR
ACT Composite middle 50% range:	range: 480–580	
21–25	**SAT Writing middle 50% range:**	
	540–630	

COLLEGE GRADUATION REQUIREMENTS

Course substitutions allowed: Yes, on occasion
In what course: Depends on degree program/major, possibly foreign language

ADDITIONAL INFORMATION

Environment: The university is located on 320 acres in a residential section of West Hartford, 90 minutes from Boston.

Student Body	**Cost Information**	**Greek System**
Undergrad enrollment: 5,449	**Tuition:** $28,582	**Fraternity:** Yes
Women: 52%	**Room & board:** $12,114	**Sorority:** Yes
Men: 48%	**Housing Information**	**Athletics:** Division I
Percent out-of-state: 74%	**University housing:** Yes	
	Percent living on campus: 66%	

UNIVERSITY OF NEW HAVEN

300 Boston Post Road, West Haven, CT 06516
Phone: 203-932-7319 • Fax: 203-931-6093
E-mail: adminfo@newhaven.edu • Web: www.newhaven.edu
Support: S • Institution type: 4-year private

PROGRAMS OR SERVICES FOR STUDENTS WITH LD

The primary responsibility of Campus Access Services (CAS) is to provide services and support that promote access to the university's educational programs and services for students with disabilities. Students must self-identify and submit documentation of a disability and the need for accommodations. Documentation should be submitted once the student is accepted to the university along with a signed DSR Intake form to request accommodations. Students must also follow the established policies and procedures for making arrangements for accommodations each semester. Staff members act as advocates, liaisons, planners, and troubleshooters. Staff is responsible for assuring access, but at the same time, they avoid creating an artificial atmosphere of dependence on services that cannot reasonably be expected after graduation. The Center for Learning Resources (CLR) offers free tutoring for all students, including students with disabilities. The Office of Academic Services offers academic assistance to all students. Academic skills counselors work one-on-one with students to strengthen their abilities and develop individualized study strategies, which focus on reading, note-taking, time management, learning/memory, and test-taking skills.

ADMISSION INFORMATION FOR STUDENTS WITH LD/ADHD

College entrance tests required: Yes
Interview required: No
Essay recommended: No
What documentation required for LD: Psycho Ed evaluation to include: relevant historical info, instructional interventions, related services, age diagnosed, objective data (aptitude, achievement, info processing), test scores (standard, percentile and grade equivalents) and describe functional limitations.
With general application: No
To receive services after enrolling: Yes
What documentation required for ADHD: Diagnosis based on DSM-V; history of behaviors impairing functioning in academic setting; diagnostic interview; history of symptoms; evidence of ongoing behaviors.

With general application: No
Submitted to: Campus Access Services
Special Ed. HS course work accepted: Yes
Specific course requirements for all applicants: Yes
Separate application required: No
# of LD applications submitted each year: NR
# of LD applications accepted yearly: NR
Total # of students receiving LD services: NR
Acceptance into program means acceptance into college: Students must be admitted and enrolled in the university first and then request services.

ADMISSIONS

All applicants must meet the same admission requirements. SAT or ACT required. Students must submit a personal essay, and letter of recommendation. Foreign language is not required for admission. Students with learning disabilities may self-disclose if they feel that it would positively affect the admissions decision. Students admitted as a conditional admit are limited to four classes for the first semester.

ADDITIONAL INFORMATION

CAS provides services that include the coordination of classroom accommodations, such as extended time for exams; use of a tape recorder, calculator, note-takers, and so on; access to readers, scribes, or books on tape; assistance during the course registration process; proctoring of tests when accommodations cannot be arranged for in the classroom; proctoring of English course post-tests and the Writing Proficiency Exam; and training in time management, organization, and test anxiety management. The office includes testing rooms and a mini computer lab with some adaptive software. The Center for Learning Resources has a Math Lab, Writing Lab, and Computer Lab. The CLR presents free workshops on preparing resumes and preparing for the Writing Proficiency Exam. The Office of Academic Services presents free workshops on improving study skills, such as getting organized, textbook and lecture note-taking techniques, and test preparation and strategies.

LEARNING DISABILITY PROGRAMS OR SERVICES

Contact Information
Name of program or department: Campus Access Services
  Telephone: 203-932-7332
  Fax: 203-931-6082

LEARNING DISABILITY SERVICES

Accommodations are decided upon an individual basis after a thorough review of appropriate, current documentation. The accommodations requested must be supported through the documentation provided and must be logically linked to the current impact of the condition on academic functioning.

Allowed in exams
  Calculator: Yes
  Dictionary: Yes
  Computer: Yes
  Spellchecker: Yes
Extended test time: Yes
Scribes: Yes
Proctors: Yes
Oral exams: No
Note-takers: Yes
	Distraction-reduced environment: Yes
	Tape recording in class: Yes
	Electronic texts: Yes
	Accommodations for students with
	  ADHD: Yes
	Kurzweil Reader: Yes
	Other assistive technology: Yes
	Priority registration: No
		Added costs for services: No
		LD specialists: No
		Professional tutors: No
		Peer tutors: N/A
		Max. hours/wk. for services:
		  Unlimited
		How professors are notified of
		  LD/ADHD: By student

GENERAL ADMISSIONS INFORMATION

Office of Admission: 203-932-7319

ENTRANCE REQUIREMENTS

Academic units required: 4 English, 3 math, 2 science, 2 history, 3 academic electives. **Academic units recommended:** 2 foreign language, 2 social studies. High school diploma is required, and GED is accepted. TOEFL required of all international applicants: minimum paper TOEFL 520, minimum computer TOEFL 190.

Application deadline: Early Action
  I–11/15; Early Action II–1/15
Notification: Rolling
Average GPA: 3.3
ACT Composite middle 50% range:
  20–25
	SAT Math middle 50% range:
	  480–580
	SAT Critical Reading middle 50%
	  range: 470–570
	SAT Writing middle 50% range:
	  470–560
		Graduated top 10% of class: NR
		Graduated top 25% of class: NR
		Graduated top 50% of class: NR

COLLEGE GRADUATION REQUIREMENTS

Course waivers allowed: No
Course substitutions allowed: Yes
In what course: Courses that are not essential to the student's program of study

ADDITIONAL INFORMATION

Environment: The campus is located close to New Haven and 75 miles from New York City.

Student Body
  Undergrad enrollment: 4,203
  Women: 50%
  Men: 50%
  Percent out-of-state: 47%
	Cost Information
	  Tuition: $31,500
	  Room & board: $13,230
	Housing Information
	  University housing: Yes
	  Percent living on campus: 57%
		Greek System
		  Fraternity: Yes
		  Sorority: Yes
		Athletics: Division II

WESTERN CONNECTICUT STATE U.

Undergraduate Admissions Office, 181 White St., Danbury, CT 06810-6855
Phone: 203-837-9000 • Fax: 203-837-8338
E-mail: admissions@wcsu.edu • Web: www.wcsu.edu
Support: CS • Institution type: 4-year public

PROGRAMS OR SERVICES FOR STUDENTS WITH LD

Two primary purposes of Students with Disabilities Services are to provide the educational development of disabled students and improve understanding and support in the campus environment. Students with learning disabilities will be assisted in receiving the services necessary to achieve their goals. Western Connecticut recognizes your right to reasonable accommodations and necessary services as a student qualified to be enrolled at this university. The Office of Disability Services directs and coordinates such services for students with disabilities that impact their educational experience. We provide advocacy, early registration, confidential counseling, empowerment counseling, complaint processing, accommodation planning, accommodation referrals, referrals to other university services, exam proctoring, accessibility, and other important services that are of value and consequence to students.

ADMISSION INFORMATION FOR STUDENTS WITH LD/ADHD

College entrance tests required: Yes
Interview required: No
Essay recommended: No
What documentation required for LD: Psycho Ed evaluation to include: relevant historical info, instructional interventions, related services, age diagnosed, objective data (aptitude, achievement, info processing), test scores (standard, percentile and grade equivalents) and describe functional limitations.
With general application: No
To receive services after enrolling: Yes
What documentation required for ADHD: Diagnosis based on DSM-V; history of behaviors impairing functioning in academic setting; diagnostic interview; history of symptoms; evidence of ongoing behaviors.

With general application: No
Submitted to: Disability Services
Special Ed. HS course work accepted: Yes
Specific course requirements of all applicants: Yes
Separate application required: No
# of LD applications submitted each year: NR
# of LD applications accepted yearly: NR
Total # of students receiving LD services: NR
Acceptance into program means acceptance into college: Students must be admitted and enrolled in the university first and then request services.

ADMISSIONS

Students with learning disabilities submit the general application form. No alternative admission policies are offered. Students should have a 2.5 GPA (C-plus or better), with the average SAT of 894 (ACT may be substituted). Courses required include 4 years of English, 3 years of math, 2 years of science, 2 science labs, 2 years of a foreign language (3 years of a foreign language recommended), 1 year of social studies, 1 year of history, and 3 years of electives. Students are encouraged to self-disclose their disability on the application and submit documentation to be used after admission to determine services and accommodations.

ADDITIONAL INFORMATION

Services include priority registration, tutoring, testing accommodations, and advocacy and counseling. The university does not offer any skills classes. The university offers a special summer program for precollege freshmen with learning disabilities. Services and accommodations are available for undergraduate and graduate students.

LEARNING DISABILITY PROGRAMS OR SERVICES

Contact Information
Name of program or department: Disability Services
   Telephone: 203-837-8946
   Fax: 203-837-8848

LEARNING DISABILITY SERVICES

Accommodations are decided upon an individual basis after a thorough review of appropriate, current documentation. The accommodations requested must be supported through the documentation provided and must be logically linked to the current impact of the condition on academic functioning.

Allowed in exams
   Calculator: Yes
   Dictionary: No
   Computer: Yes
   Spellchecker: Yes
Extended test time: Yes
Scribes: Yes
Proctors: Yes
Oral exams: Yes
Note-takers: Yes

Distraction-reduced environment: Yes
Tape recording in class: Yes
Electronic texts: Yes
Accommodations for students with ADHD: Yes
Kurzweil Reader: No
Other assistive technology: Yes
Priority registration: Yes

Added costs for services: No
LD specialists: Yes
Professional tutors: 1
Peer tutors: N/A
Max. hours/wk. for services: N/A
How professors are notified of LD/ADHD: By both student and director

GENERAL ADMISSIONS INFORMATION

Office of Admission: 203-837-9000

ENTRANCE REQUIREMENTS

Academic units required: 4 English, 3 math, 2 science (2 science labs), 2 foreign language, 1 social studies, 1 history. **Academic units recommended:** 3 foreign language. High school diploma is required, and GED is accepted. TOEFL required of all international applicants: minimum paper TOEFL 550, minimum computer TOEFL 213.

Application deadline: None
Notification: Rolling
Average GPA: NR
ACT Composite middle 50% range:
   NR

SAT Math middle 50% range:
   440–550
SAT Critical Reading middle 50% range: 440–540
SAT Writing middle 50% range:
   440–530

Graduated top 10% of class: 4%
Graduated top 25% of class: 24%
Graduated top 50% of class: 62%

COLLEGE GRADUATION REQUIREMENTS

Course waivers allowed: Yes
In what course: As required depending on the student's disability
Course substitutions allowed: Yes
In what course: As required depending on the student's disability

ADDITIONAL INFORMATION

Environment: The university is located on 315 acres, 60 miles from New York City.

Student Body
   Undergrad enrollment: 11,127
   Women: 54%
   Men: 46%
   Percent out-of-state: 10%

Cost Information
   In-state tuition: $7,909
   Out-of-state tuition: $18,274
   Room & board: $9,970
Housing Information
   University housing: Yes
   Percent living on campus: 34%

Greek System
   Fraternity: Yes
   Sorority: Yes
Athletics: Division III

UNIVERSITY OF DELAWARE

210 South College Avenue, Newark, DE 19716
Phone: 302-831-8123 • Fax: 302-831-6905
Web: www.udel.edu/admissions
Support: CS • Institution type: 4-year independent, state-related

PROGRAMS OR SERVICES FOR STUDENTS WITH LD

Eligibility for reasonable accommodations is determined on a case-by-case basis upon receipt of appropriate documentation in order to determine that a disability exists and results in a functional limitation. Requested accommodations must be supported by the documentation and be logically linked to the current impact of the disability. Accommodations are provided in order to provide equal access to University course work, activities and programs. Accommodations may not interfere with or alter the essential skills of course curriculum.

ADMISSION INFORMATION FOR STUDENTS WITH LD/ADHD

College entrance tests required: Yes
Interview required: No
Essay recommended: Yes
What documentation required for LD: Yes, after admission
With general application: No
To receive services after enrolling: Yes
What documentation required for ADHD: Yes, after admission
With general application: No
Submitted to: Academic Success Services

Special Ed. HS course work accepted: NR
Specific course requirements of all applicants: Yes
Separate application required: NR
# of LD applications submitted each year: NR
# of LD applications accepted yearly: NR
Total # of students receiving LD services: NR
Acceptance into program means acceptance into college: Student must be admitted and enrolled in the university prior to requesting accommodation(s).

ADMISSIONS

Students must be otherwise qualified to admissions. Applicants are typically admitted to their first choice major if admitted to the university. Only list a second major if there is active interest. Courses required include 4 English, 3 math, 3 science, 4 social studies, 2 foreign language, and 2 electives. Foreign language taken prior to 9th grade is not counted. The university looks for academic rigor; grades in college prep classes, and highly recommends that applicants be enrolled in 5 academic core courses each semester. Essays are important and students must submit at least one recommendation from an academic source. Most students submit more recommendations. ACT with writing or SAT required and they will super score. Once admitted and committed to attending the university, students are encouraged to self-disclose their disability to the Office of Disability Support Services (DSS).

ADDITIONAL INFORMATION

DSS reviews documentation and provides appropriate accommodations such as: assistive technology, note takers, notification to faculty, test accommodations, tutoring in conjunction with the Academic Enrichment Program in the Academic Enrichment Center. Support includes: individual and group tutoring, study skills workshops and classes and one-on-one academic assistance. The Summer Enrichment Program (SEP) is an academically intensive five-week residential program for incoming freshmen. Students can earn seven credits in math, English and a college transition course. Placement is determined by ACT/SAT. These students also participate in a variety of academic support meetings, cultural enrichment events, and personal, social and recreational activities. Participants are encouraged to participate in Office of Academic Enrichment activities throughout their freshman year and beyond.

LEARNING DISABILITY PROGRAMS OR SERVICES

Contact Information
Name of program or department: Disability Support Services (DSS)
  Telephone: 302-831-4643
  Fax: 302-8313261

LEARNING DISABILITY SERVICES

Accommodations are decided upon an individual basis after a thorough review of appropriate, current documentation. The accommodations requested must be supported through the documentation provided and must be logically linked to the current impact of the condition on academic functioning. The following are possible accommodations.

Allowed in exams
  Calculator: Yes
  Dictionary: No
  Computer: Yes
  Spellchecker: Yes
Extended test time: Yes
Scribes: Yes
Proctors: Yes
Oral exams: No
Note-takers: Yes

Distraction-reduced environment: Yes
Tape recording in class: Yes
Electronic texts: Yes
Accommodations for students with ADHD: Yes
Kurzweil Reader: Yes
Other assistive technology: Yes
Priority registration: Yes

Added costs for services: No
LD specialists: Yes
Professional tutors: No
Peer tutors: 150
Max. hours/wk. for services: N/A
How professors are notified of LD/ADHD: By both student and DSS

GENERAL ADMISSIONS INFORMATION

Office of Admission: 302-831-8123

ENTRANCE REQUIREMENTS

Academic units required: 4 years English, 3 years Math, 3 years Science (2 must include lab), 4 years History/Social Sciences (at least 2 must be history, and one of those must be world history), 2 years (same) Foreign Language, 2 units of Academic Electives. **Academic units recommended:** 4 years English, 4 years Math, 4 years Science (3 with lab), 4 years History/Social Sciences, 4 years (same) Foreign Language, 2 units of Academic Electives.

Application deadline: 1/15
Notification: 3/15
Average GPA: 3.62
ACT Composite middle 50% range: 25–28

SAT Math middle 50% range: 560–650
SAT Critical Reading middle 50% range: 540–640
SAT Writing middle 50% range: 550–650

Graduated top 10% of class: 38%
Graduated top 25% of class: 79%
Graduated top 50% of class: 98%

COLLEGE GRADUATION REQUIREMENTS

Course waivers allowed: No
Course substitutions allowed: Yes
In what course: Math and foreign language course substitution decisions are made on a case-by-case basis. Students are asked to attempt the class and work closely with a tutor before submitting a petition for a substitution.

ADDITIONAL INFORMATION

Environment: The 1,100-acre campus is in a small town 12 miles southwest of Wilmington and midway between Philadelphia and Baltimore.

Student Body
  Undergrad enrollment: 17,892
  Women: 57%
  Men: 43%
  Percent out-of-state: 68%

Cost Information
  In-state tuition: $9,670
  Out-of-state tuition: $25,942
  Room & board: $10,196
Housing Information
  University housing: Yes

Percent living on campus: 44%
Greek System
  Fraternity: Yes
  Sorority: Yes
Athletics: Division I

AMERICAN UNIVERSITY

4400 Massachusetts Avenue, Northwest, Washington, DC 20016-8001
Phone: 202-885-6000 • Fax: 202-885-1025
E-mail: admissions@american.edu • Web: www.american.edu
Support: SP • Institution type: 4-year private

PROGRAMS OR SERVICES FOR STUDENTS WITH LD

The Academic Support Center (ASC) provides extensive support for students with documented learning disabilities and ADHD. Any student whose documentation meets university guidelines can access approved accommodations, work with a learning specialist, meet with the assistive technology specialist, use the Writing Lab, request peer tutors, and take advantage of group workshops. The Learning Services Program (LSP), within the ASC, is a mainstream freshman transition program offering additional support for students who apply to the program with learning disabilities that impact writing. There is a one-time fee for this program, and students must apply at the time they apply to the university. Disability services continue to be available until graduation.

ADMISSION INFORMATION FOR STUDENTS WITH LD/ADHD

College entrance tests required: Yes, test optional applications are possible
Interview required: No
Essay recommended: Yes
What documentation required for LD: Psycho Ed evaluation to include: relevant historical info, instructional interventions, related services, age diagnosed, objective data (aptitude, achievement, info processing), test scores (standard, percentile and grade equivalents) and describe functional limitations.
With general application: Yes if requested as part of Structured Program application
To receive services after enrolling: Yes
What documentation required for ADHD: Diagnosis based on DSM-V; history of behaviors impairing functioning in academic setting; diagnostic interview; history of symptoms; evidence of ongoing behaviors.

With general application: Yes if requested as part of Structured Program application
To receive services after enrolling: Yes
Submitted to: Academic Support Center
Special Ed. HS course work accepted: Yes
Specific course requirements of all applicants: Yes
Separate application required: Yes for LSP
# of LD applications submitted each year: 65–80 for LSP
# of LD applications accepted yearly: 40–50 for LSP
Total # of students receiving LD services: 300–350
Acceptance into program means acceptance into college: Student must be admitted and enrolled in the university first and then reviewed for LSP.

ADMISSIONS

Students with LD must be admitted to the university and then to the Learning Services Program. Students who wish to have program staff consult with the Admissions Office about their LD during the admissions process must submit a supplemental application to the Learning Services Program that requires documentation of the LD. Students should indicate interest in the program on their application. Special education courses taken in high school may be accepted if they meet the criteria for the Carnegie Units. The academic credentials of successful applicants with LD fall within the range of regular admissions criteria: the mean GPA is 2.9 for LD admits and 3.2 for regularly admitted students; ACT ranges from 24–29 for regular admits and 24–28 for LD admits or SAT 1110–1270 for regular admits and 1131 for LD admits. American Sign Language is an acceptable substitution for foreign language. The admission decision is made by a special Admissions Committee and is based on the high school record, recommendations, and all pertinent diagnostic reports.

ADDITIONAL INFORMATION

All students work with an academic advisor in their school or college; students in the Learning Services Program have an advisor who consults on their learning disability. Students in the program meet weekly with a learning specialist for individual sessions that help them further develop college-level reading, writing, and study strategies—and with a writing tutor. Peer tutors assist with course content tutoring. Accommodations are based on diagnostic testing. Students are held to the same academic standards as all students but may meet these standards through nontraditional means.

LEARNING DISABILITY PROGRAMS OR SERVICES

Contact Information
Name of program or department: Academic Support Center
  Telephone: 202-885-3360
  Fax: 202-885-1042

LEARNING DISABILITY SERVICES

Accommodations are decided upon an individual basis after a thorough review of appropriate, current documentation. The accommodations requested must be supported through the documentation provided and must be logically linked to the current impact of the condition on academic functioning.

Allowed in exams
  Calculator: Yes
  Dictionary: Yes
  Computer: Yes
  Spellchecker: Yes
Extended test time: Yes
Scribes: Yes
Proctors: Yes
Oral exams: Rarely
Note-takers: Yes

Distraction-reduced environment: Yes
Tape recording in class: Yes
Electronic texts: Yes
Accommodations for students with
  ADHD: Yes
Kurzweil Reader: Yes
Other assistive technology: Yes
Priority registration: Yes

Added costs for services: LSP only
LD specialists: Yes
Professional tutors: No
Peer tutors: Yes
Max. hours/wk. for services:
  Unlimited
How professors are notified of
  LD/ADHD: By student

GENERAL ADMISSIONS INFORMATION

Office of Admission: 202-885-6000

ENTRANCE REQUIREMENTS
Academic units required: 4 English, 3 math, 2 science (2 science labs), 2 foreign language, 2 social studies, 3 academic electives. **Academic units recommended:** 4 English, 4 math, 4 science, 3 foreign language, 4 social studies, 4 academic electives. High school diploma is required, and GED is accepted. ACT with Writing component required. TOEFL required of all international applicants: minimum paper TOEFL 590, minimum computer TOEFL 213.

Application deadline: 1/15
Notification: 4/1
Average GPA: 3.8
ACT Composite middle 50% range:
  26–30

SAT Math middle 50% range:
  570–670
SAT Critical Reading middle 50%
  range: 600–700
SAT Writing middle 50% range:
  580–680

Graduated top 10% of class: 45%
Graduated top 25% of class: 81%
Graduated top 50% of class: 98%

COLLEGE GRADUATION REQUIREMENTS

Course waivers allowed: No
Course substitutions allowed: No

ADDITIONAL INFORMATION

Environment: The university is located on 77 acres close to the Capitol.

Student Body
  Undergrad enrollment: 7,212
  Women: 60%
  Men: 40%
  Percent out-of-state: 84%

Cost Information
  Tuition: $37,554
  Room & board: $13,648
Housing Information
  University housing: Yes
  Percent living on campus: 75%

Greek System
  Fraternity: Yes
  Sorority: Yes
  Athletics: Division I

THE CATHOLIC U. OF AMERICA

Office of Undergraduate Admissions, 620 Michigan Avenue, NE, Washington
Phone: 202-319-5305 • Fax: 202-319-6533
E-mail: cua-admissions@cua.edu • Web: www.cua.edu
Support: CS • Institution: 4-year private

PROGRAMS OR SERVICES FOR STUDENTS WITH LD

The Office of Disability Support Services (DSS) supports the missions of the Dean of Students and the university by providing programs and services designed to support and encourage the integration of students with disabilities into the mainstream of the university community. DSS assists in creating an accessible university community where students with disabilities have an equal opportunity to fully participate in all aspects of the educational environment. We cooperate through partnerships with students, faculty, and staff to promote students' independence and to ensure recognition of their abilities, not disabilities. Essential to the larger mission of the university, DSS promotes universally designed environments and facilitates full access through reasonable accommodations, training, collaboration and innovative programming. The university recognizes that student disability records contain confidential information and are to be treated as such. Therefore, documentation of a student's disability is maintained in a confidential file in DSS and is considered part of the student's education record. Information related to a disability may be disclosed only with the permission of the student or as permitted by the university's student records policy and federal law. At the same time, however, a students' right to privacy must still be balanced against the university's need to know the information in order to provide requested and recommended services and accommodations. Therefore, in the interest of serving the needs of the student, the provision of services may involve DSS staff disclosing disability information provided by the student to appropriate university personnel participating in the accommodation process. The amount of information that may be released is determined on a case-by-case basis, and will be made in accordance with the university's policy on student records.

ADMISSION INFORMATION FOR STUDENTS WITH LD/ADHD

College entrance tests required: Yes
Interview required: No
What documentation required for LD: Psycho Ed evaluation to include: relevant historical info, instructional interventions, related services, age diagnosed, objective data (aptitude, achievement, info processing), test scores (standard, percentile and grade equivalents) and describe functional limitations.
With general application: No
To receive services after enrolling: Yes
What documentation required for ADHD: Diagnosis based on DSM-V; history of behaviors impairing functioning in academic setting; diagnostic interview; history of symptoms; evidence of ongoing behaviors.

With general application: No
Special Ed. HS course work accepted: Yes
Specific course requirements for all applicants: NR
Separate application required for program services: No
# of LD applications submitted each year: NR
# of LD applications accepted yearly: NR
Total # of students receiving LD services: 200
Acceptance into program means acceptance into college: Separate application required after student has enrolled

ADMISSIONS

The Office of Undergraduate Admissions reviews each application on its own merits. Students with disabilities must meet the same standards as all other applicants. Documentation of your disability should not be sent with your application. Prospective students with disabilities are encouraged to write an additional personal statement.

ADDITIONAL INFORMATION

A key component of becoming a successful college student lies within the transition from high school to college. Students who come to CUA with an understanding of their disability, strengths, limitations, interests and who have a willingness to seek out resources and additional help are much more likely to succeed than those students who do not. DSS emphasizes the importance for parents and students to understand the following aspect of transition: Academic demands in college are much more intense than in high school. Therefore, students with disabilities MUST be able to advocate for their needs, are expected to ask for help when necessary, and must meet the same academic standards as students who do not have disabilities. DSS works with each student on a case-by-case basis to determine and implement appropriate accommodations based on documentation and personal interview. Some typical accommodations for students with learning disabilities and ADHD include: note-takers, alternative testing arrangements such as extra time, books in alternative formats, assistive technology, foreign language substitution, and separate testing areas.

PROGRAM FOR DISABILITY SERVICES

Contact Information
Name of program or department: Disability Support Services
   Telephone: 202-319-5211
   Fax: 202-319-5126

LEARNING DISABILITY SERVICES

Accommodations are decided upon an individual basis after a thorough review of appropriate, current documentation. The accommodations requested must be supported through the documentation provided and must be logically linked to the current impact of the condition on academic functioning.

Allowed in exams	**Distraction-reduced environment:** Yes	**Added costs for services:** Yes
Calculator: Yes	**Tape recording in class:** Yes	**LD specialists:** Yes
Dictionary: Yes	**Electronic texts:** Yes	**Professional tutors:** No
Computer: Yes	**Accommodations for students with**	**Peer tutors:** 55–100
Spellchecker: Yes	**ADHD:** Yes	**Max. hours/wk. for services:** 3
Extended test time: Yes	**Kurzweil Reader:** Yes	**How professors are notified of**
Scribes: Yes	**Other assistive technology:** Yes	**LD/ADHD:** Student
Proctors: Yes	**Priority registration:** Yes	
Oral exams: Yes		
Note-takers: Yes		

GENERAL ADMISSIONS INFORMATION

Office of Admission: 202-319-5305

ENTRANCE REQUIREMENTS

Academic units recommended: 4 English, 3 mathematics, 3 science, (1 science labs), 2 foreign language, 4 social studies, 1 fine arts or humanities. High school diploma is required and GED is accepted. SAT Subject Tests recommended; SAT or ACT required; ACT or SAT with Writing component required. TOEFL required of all international applicants; minimum paper TOEFL 550, minimum computer TOEFL 213, minimum web-based TOEFL 80.

Application deadline: 2/15	**SAT Math middle 50% range:** 580	**Graduated top 10% of class:** NA
Notification: Mid-March	**SAT Critical Reading middle 50%**	**Graduated top 25% of class:** NA
Average GPA: 3.5	**range:** 580	**Graduated top 50% of class:** NA
ACT Composite middle 50% range:	**SAT Writing middle 50% range:** 1170	
26	Math/Verbal combined	

COLLEGE GRADUATION REQUIREMENTS

Course substitutions allowed: Yes
In what course: Foreign language and math

ADDITIONAL INFORMATION

Environment: The university is situated in northeast Washington, DC, within minutes of the Capitol.

Student Body	**Cost Information**	**Greek System**
Undergrad enrollment: 3,500	**Tuition:** $35,260	**Fraternity:** Yes
Women: 55%	**Room & board:** $13,800	**Sorority:** Yes
Men: 45%	**Housing Information**	**Athletics:** Division III
Percent out-of-state: 99%	**University housing:** Yes	
	Percent living on campus: 80%	

THE GEORGE WASHINGTON UNIVERSITY

2121 I Street Northwest, Suite 201, Washington, DC 20052
Phone: 202-994-6040 • Fax: 202-994-0325
E-mail: gwadm@gwu.edu • Web: www.gwu.edu
Support: CS • Institution type: 4-year private

PROGRAMS OR SERVICES FOR STUDENTS WITH LD

Disability Support Services (DSS) was established to provide support to learning disabled students so that they might participate fully in university life, derive the greatest benefit from their educational experiences, and achieve maximum personal success. There is no LD program at GWU with a fee for service. Students with LD/ADHD are served through DSS. Services are designed to eliminate competitive disadvantages in an academic environment while preserving academic integrity. The staff is committed to providing student-centered services that meet the individual needs of each student. The ultimate goal of DSS is to assist students with disabilities as they gain knowledge to recognize strengths, accommodate differences, and become strong self-advocates. Staff are available to discuss issues such as course load, learning strategies, academic accommodations, and petitions for course waivers or substitutions. DSS offers individual assistance in addressing needs not provided through routine services. Students with LD must provide documentation, including a comprehensive diagnostic interview, psychoeducational evaluation, and a treatment plan; test scores and an interpretation of overall intelligence, information processing, executive functioning, spatial ability, memory, motor ability, achievement skills, reading, writing, and math; and a specific diagnosis and description of the student's functional limitations in an educational setting.

ADMISSION INFORMATION FOR STUDENTS WITH LD/ADHD

College entrance tests required: Yes
Interview required: No
Essay recommended: N/A
What documentation required for LD: Psycho Ed evaluation to include: relevant historical info, instructional interventions, related services, age diagnosed, objective data (aptitude, achievement, info processing), test scores (standard, percentile and grade equivalents) and describe functional limitations.
With general application: No
To receive services after enrolling: Yes
What documentation required for ADHD: Diagnosis based on DSM-V; history of behaviors impairing functioning in academic setting; diagnostic interview; history of symptoms; evidence of ongoing behaviors.

With general application: No
Submitted to: Disability Support Services
Special Ed. HS course work accepted: No
Specific course requirements for all applicants: Yes
Separate application required: No
# of LD applications submitted each year: NR
# of LD applications accepted yearly: NR
Total # of students receiving LD services: 258
Acceptance into program means acceptance into college: Student must be admitted and enrolled in the university and then reviewed for services with Disability Support Services.

ADMISSIONS

GWU does not discriminate on the basis of disability in the recruitment and admission of students. There are no separate admissions procedures or criteria for disabled students. The minimal course requirements include 2 years of math (4 recommended), 4 years of English, 2 years of a foreign language (4 recommended), 2–3 years of social sciences (4 recommended), and 2–3 years of science (4 recommended). The score range for the ACT is 28-31 and for the SAT 1900–2100. The SAT Subject Tests are optional. Since there is no automatic referral from admissions or other campus offices, students are encouraged to contact DSS directly prior to or at the time of admission.

ADDITIONAL INFORMATION

To be eligible, a student must provide to DSS documentation that substantiates the need for such services in compliance with Section 504 of the Rehabilitation Act and the Americans with Disabilities Act (ADA). Services provided without charge to students may include registration assistance, reading services, assistive technology, learning specialist services, note-taking assistance, test accommodations, and referrals. DSS does not provide content tutoring, although it is available on a fee basis from other campus resources.

LEARNING DISABILITY PROGRAMS OR SERVICES

Contact Information
Name of program or department: Disability Support Services
   Telephone: 202-994-8250
   Fax: 202-994-7610

LEARNING DISABILITY SERVICES

Accommodations are decided upon an individual basis after a thorough review of appropriate, current documentation. The accommodations requested must be supported through the documentation provided and must be logically linked to the current impact of the condition on academic functioning.

Allowed in exams	**Distraction-reduced environment:** Yes	**Added costs for services:** No
Calculator: Yes	**Tape recording in class:** Yes	**LD specialists:** Yes
Dictionary: Yes	**Electronic texts:** Yes	**Professional tutors:** No
Computer: Yes	**Accommodations for students with**	**Peer tutors:** No
Spellchecker: Yes	**ADHD:** Yes	**Max. hours/wk. for services:** NR
Extended test time: Yes	**Kurzweil Reader:** Yes	**How professors are notified of**
Scribes: Yes	**Other assistive technology:** Yes	**LD/ADHD:** By student
Proctors: Yes	**Priority registration:** Yes	
Oral exams: Yes		
Note-takers: Yes		

GENERAL ADMISSIONS INFORMATION

Office of Admission: 202-994-6040

ENTRANCE REQUIREMENTS

Academic units required: 4 English, 2 math, 2 science (1 science lab), 2 foreign language, 2 social studies.
Academic units recommended: 4 English, 4 math, 4 science, 4 foreign language, 4 social studies. High school diploma is required, and GED is not accepted. ACT with or without Writing component accepted. Essay, teacher and counselor recommendations are required. TOEFL required of all international applicants: minimum paper TOEFL 550, minimum computer TOEFL 213, minimum, internet 80.

Application deadline: 1/10	**SAT Math middle 50% range:**	**Graduated top 10% of class:** 78%
Notification: 4/1	610–700	**Graduated top 25% of class:** NR
Average GPA: B+/A–	**SAT Critical Reading middle 50%**	**Graduated top 50% of class:** NR
ACT Composite middle 50% range:	**range:** 600–690	
27–31	**SAT Writing middle 50% range:**	
	620–700	

COLLEGE GRADUATION REQUIREMENTS

Course waivers allowed: No
Course substitutions allowed: Yes
In what course: Determination is made on a case-by-case basis, primarily in the areas of math and foreign language.

ADDITIONAL INFORMATION

Environment: The university has an urban campus three blocks from the White House.

Student Body	**Cost Information**	**Greek System**
Undergrad enrollment: 10,558	**Tuition:** $42,905	**Fraternity:** Yes
Women: 55%	**Room & board:** $10,325	**Sorority:** Yes
Men: 45%	**Housing Information**	**Athletics:** Division I
Percent out-of-state: 99%	**University housing:** Yes	
	Percent living on campus: 75%	

BARRY UNIVERSITY

11300 North East Second Avenue, Miami Shores, FL 33161-6695
Phone: 305-899-3100 • Fax: 305-899-2971
E-mail: Des-forms@mail.barry.edu • Web: www.barry.edu
Support: SP • Institution type: 4-year private

PROGRAMS OR SERVICES FOR STUDENTS WITH LD

Barry University offers a fee-for-service support program for students with LD. The Center for Advanced Learning (CAL) Program is a comprehensive, intensive, structured, and individualized approach to assisting students with LD throughout their college careers. It is designed to move students gradually toward increasing self-direction in academic, personal, and career activities. This program affirms Barry University's commitment to expand college opportunities to students with LD and provide the specialized services that can enhance college success. Services and admission details are found on the CAL website at: www.barry.edu/CAL.

ADMISSION INFORMATION FOR STUDENTS WITH LD/ADHD

College entrance tests required: Yes
Interview required: Yes
Essay recommended: Yes
What documentation required for LD: Psycho Ed evaluation to include: relevant historical info, instructional interventions, related services, age diagnosed, objective data (aptitude, achievement, info processing), test scores (standard, percentile and grade equivalents) and describe functional limitations.
With general application: Yes if requested as part of Structured Program application
To receive services after enrolling: Yes
What documentation required for ADHD: Diagnosis based on DSM-V; history of behaviors impairing functioning in academic setting; diagnostic interview; history of symptoms; evidence of ongoing behaviors.

With general application: Yes if requested as part of Structured Program application
To receive services after enrolling: Yes
Submitted to: CAL—Garner Building
Special Ed. HS course work accepted: Yes
Specific course requirements of all applicants: Yes
Separate application required: No
# of LD applications submitted each year: 80
# of LD applications accepted yearly: 45
Total # of students receiving LD services: 50
Acceptance into program means acceptance into college: Student must be admitted and enrolled in the university first and then request services from CAL.

ADMISSIONS

Students with learning disabilities must meet the regular admission criteria for the university, which includes 2.0 GPA, ACT of 17 or above, or SAT of 800 or above, and 4 years of English, 3–4 years of math, 3 years of natural science, and 3–4 years of social science. There is a process of individual review by learning disability professionals for those students who have a diagnosed disability and who do not meet the general admission criteria. These students must provide appropriate and current LD documentation and be interviewed by the Director of the CAL Program. Students admitted are expected to meet all requirements established for them and those of the specific university program in which they enroll.

ADDITIONAL INFORMATION

The CAL Program includes a full range of professionally managed and intensive support services that includes the following: Review of diagnostic information allowing for development of a personalized educational plan; intensive scheduled classes to improve math, reading, and written and oral communication skills; individual and small-group subject-area tutoring; instruction in learning and study strategies; academic advising; assistance in developing interpersonal skills; individual and small-group personal, academic, and career counseling; assistance in obtaining study aids and training in the use of assistive technology; computer access; special test administration services; advocacy with faculty. Additionally, all students have access to a math lab, reading and writing centers, and selected educational seminars. All instructional staff hold advanced degrees in their area of specialization. Services are available for both undergraduate and graduate students.

LEARNING DISABILITY PROGRAMS OR SERVICES

Contact Information
Name of program or department: Office of Disability Services in R. Kirk London Building. CAL Program in Garner Building
   Telephone: 305-899-3488
   Fax: 305-899-3056

LEARNING DISABILITY SERVICES

Accommodations are decided upon an individual basis after a thorough review of appropriate, current documentation. The accommodations requested must be supported through the documentation provided and must be logically linked to the current impact of the condition on academic functioning.

Allowed in exams	**Distraction-reduced environment:** Yes	**Added costs for services:** Yes
Calculator: Yes	**Tape recording in class:** Yes	**LD specialists:** Yes
Dictionary: Yes	**Electronic texts:** Yes	**Professional tutors:** 13
Computer: Yes	**Accommodations for students with**	**Peer tutors:** No
Spellchecker: Yes	**ADHD:** Yes	**Max. hours/wk. for services:**
Extended test time: Yes	**Kurzweil Reader:** Yes	Unlimited
Scribes: Yes	**Other assistive technology:** Yes	**How professors are notified of**
Proctors: Yes	**Priority registration:** No	**LD/ADHD:** By both student and
Oral exams: Yes		director
Note-takers: Yes		

GENERAL ADMISSIONS INFORMATION

Office of Admission: 305-899-3100

ENTRANCE REQUIREMENTS

Academic units recommended: 4 English, 3 math, 3 science, 3 social studies. High school diploma is required, and GED is accepted. ACT with or without Writing component accepted. TOEFL required of all international applicants: minimum paper TOEFL 550, minimum computer TOEFL 213.

Application deadline: None	**SAT Math middle 50% range:**	**Graduated top 10% of class:** NR
Notification: Rolling	420–520	**Graduated top 25% of class:** NR
Average GPA: 3.14	**SAT Critical Reading middle 50%**	**Graduated top 50% of class:** 100%
ACT Composite middle 50% range:	**range:** 440–520	
18–22	**SAT Writing middle 50% range:** NR	

COLLEGE GRADUATION REQUIREMENTS

Course waivers allowed: No
Course substitutions allowed: No

ADDITIONAL INFORMATION

Environment: The university is located seven miles from Miami.		
Student Body	**Cost Information**	**Greek System**
Undergrad enrollment: 5,088	**Tuition:** $28,160	**Fraternity:** Yes
Women: 69%	**Room & board:** $9,300	**Sorority:** Yes
Men: 31%	**Housing Information**	**Athletics:** Division II
Percent out-of-state: 26%	**University housing:** Yes	
	Percent living on campus: 35%	

BEACON COLLEGE

105 E. Main Street, Leesburg, FL 34748
Phone: 855-220-5376 • Fax: 352-787-0721
E-mail: admissions@beaconcollege.edu • Web: www.beaconcollege.edu
Support: SP • Institution: private

PROGRAMS OR SERVICES FOR STUDENTS WITH LD

The mission of Beacon College is to offer BA- and A.A. degrees exclusively for students with dyslexia, AD/HD, or other specific learning disabilities. The College provides a quality undergraduate education that is supplemented by appropriate accommodations. Beacon College is accredited by the Comission on Colleges of the Southern Association of Colleges and Schools to award Bachelor and Associate of Arts degrees.

ADMISSION INFORMATION FOR STUDENTS WITH LD/ADHD

College entrance tests required: No
Interview required: No
Essay required: No
What documentation required for LD: Psycho Ed evaluation to include: relevant historical info, instructional interventions, related services, age diagnosed, objective data (aptitude, achievement, info processing), test scores (standard, percentile and grade equivalents) and describe functional limitations.
With general application: Yes if requested as part of Structured Program application
To receive services after enrolling: Yes
What documentation required for ADHD: Diagnosis based on DSM-V; history of behaviors impairing functioning in academic setting; diagnostic interview; history of symptoms; evidence of ongoing behaviors.

With general application: Yes if requested as part of Structured Program application
To receive services after enrolling: Yes
Submitted to: Admissions
Special Ed. HS coursework accepted: Yes
Specific course requirements for all applicants: Standard High School Diploma
Separate application required for program services: No
# of LD applications submitted each year: 146
# of LD applications accepted yearly: 85
Total # of students receiving LD services: 100%
Acceptance into program means acceptance into college: NR

ADMISSIONS

In order to be considered for admissions to Beacon College, an applicant must submit: a completed application, non-refundable $50.00 application fee, and psychoeducational evaluation (completed within three years) that documents a learning disability, or AD/HD. The evaluation must include a complete WAIS with sub-test scores and assessments in reading and math. Official high school transcripts showing successful completion of a standard high school diploma or GED is also required. Beacon College does not place heavy emphasis on SAT/ACT scores. Interviews are preferred and provide a better understanding of the applicant.

ADDITIONAL INFORMATION

Beacon College provides a comprehensive educational support services for students with learning disabilities or ADHD. Beacon serves a culturally diverse group of men and women from across the United States and internationally. Out-of-state students make up 65% of the student population at Beacon College. The average age of students ranges from 20–24 years of age, and 45% of students transfer to Beacon from another college or university. In order to meet the needs of our students, the average class size is approximately 12–15 students. The cornerstone of educational support services at Beacon College is our Academic Mentoring Program. In order to foster success, each student receives one-to-one academic mentoring services, which are designed to enhance academic performance and develop skills for life-long learning. The Field Placement Program allows students to complete supervised hours in the workplace to enhance their resumes and further their employment skills. The Cultural Studies Abroad Program gives students the opportunity to experience the life, history, culture, cuisine, architecture, music, and literature of exotic places. During the past ten years, students and professors have traveled to Italy, Greece, France, Spain, Australia, Russia, Sweden, Austria, England, and Ireland.

PROGRAM FOR DISABILITY SERVICES

Contact Information
 Telephone: 855-220-5376
 Fax: 352-787-0796

LEARNING DISABILITY SERVICES

Accommodations are decided upon an individual basis after a thorough review of appropriate, current documentation. The accommodations requested must be supported through the documentation provided and must be logically linked to the current impact of the condition on academic functioning.

Allowed in exams
 Calculator: Yes
 Dictionary: Yes
 Computer: Yes
 Spellchecker: Yes
Extended test time: Yes
Scribes: Yes
Proctors: Yes
Oral exams: Yes
Notetakers: Yes

Distraction-reduced environment: Yes
Tape recording in class: Yes
Electronic texts: Yes
Accommodations for students with ADHD: Yes
Kurzweil Reader: Yes
Other assistive technology: Various voice-activated dictation software, WordQ, Inspiration, and computerized reading programs.
Priority registration: N/A

Added costs for services: No
LD specialists: Yes
Professional tutors: Yes
Max. hours/wk. for services: Based on need.
How professors are notified of LD/ADHD: Both Student and Director

GENERAL ADMISSIONS INFORMATION

Office of Admission: 855-220-5376

ENTRANCE REQUIREMENTS

Academic units required: 4 English, 1 mathematics, 1 science, 1 social studies, 2 history, 3 academic electives, standard High school diploma is required and GED is accepted. TOEFL required of all international applicants; minimum paper TOEFL 525.

Application deadline: 8/1
Notification: Rolling
Average GPA: 2.8
ACT Composite middle 50% range: NR

SAT Math middle 50% range: NR
SAT Critical Reading middle 50% range: NR
SAT Writing middle 50% range: NR

Graduated top 10% of class: NR
Graduated top 25% of class: NR
Graduated top 50% of class: NR

COLLEGE GRADUATION REQUIREMENTS

Course waivers allowed: Yes
In what course: Math
Course substitutions allowed: Yes
In what course: Math

ADDITIONAL INFORMATION

Environment: The college is located in the city of Leesburg, 1 hour from Orlando.

Student Body
 Undergrad enrollment: 162
 Women: 40%
 Men: 60%
 Percent out-of-state: 74%

Cost Information
 Tuition: $28,650
 Room and board: $8,350
Housing Information
 University housing: Yes
 Percent living on campus: 95

Greek System
 Fraternity: Yes
 Sorority: Yes
 Athletics: NR

FLORIDA A&M UNIVERSITY

Suite G-9, Foote-Hilyer Administration Center, Tallahassee, FL 32307
Phone: 850-599-3796 • Fax: 850-599-3069
E-mail: admission@famu.edu • Web: www.famu.edu
Support: SP • Institution: 4-year public

PROGRAMS OR SERVICES FOR STUDENTS WITH LD

The Center for Disability Access and Resources (CeDAR) at Florida A & M University provides comprehensive services and accommodations to FAMU students with disabilities. As an advocate for students with disabilities, the CeDAR collaborates with faculty, staff, and community partners to provide accommodations for the unique needs of students both in and out of the classroom. The mission is to provide enriching support programs, services, and reasonable accommodations. CeDAR hopes to foster a sense of empowerment in students with disabilities by educating them about their legal rights and responsibilities so that they can make informed choices, be critical thinkers, and self advocates. The goal is to ensure students with disabilities have access to the same programs, opportunities, and activities available to all FAMU students. The team works to celebrate and reward the unique backgrounds, viewpoints, skills, and talents of all CeDAR students.

ADMISSION INFORMATION FOR STUDENTS WITH LD/ADHD

College entrance tests required: Yes
Interview required: No
Essay required: Yes
What documentation required for LD: Psycho Ed evaluation to include: relevant historical info, instructional interventions, related services, age diagnosed, objective data (aptitude, achievement, info processing), test scores (standard, percentile and grade equivalents) and describe functional limitations.
With general application: Yes if requested as part of Structured Program application
To receive services after enrolling: Yes
What documentation required for ADHD: Diagnosis based on DSM-V; history of behaviors impairing functioning in academic setting; diagnostic interview; history of symptoms; evidence of ongoing behaviors.

With general application: Yes if requested as part of Structured Program application
To receive services after enrolling: Yes
Submitted to: Support Program/Services
Special Ed. HS course work accepted: No
Specific course requirements for all applicants: Yes
Separate application required for program services: Yes
# of LD applications submitted each year: 40–50
# of LD applications accepted yearly: 40–60
Total # of students receiving LD services: 144
Acceptance into program means acceptance into college: Separate application required after student has enrolled

ADMISSIONS

CeDAR helps applicants who do not meet standard admission criteria to be admitted to FAMU under alternate criteria when appropriate based on the applicant's disability. Students are reviewed under alternate criteria. In implementing this procedure, the CeDAR shall not compromise academic or admission standards in any way. Students requesting an alternate review must request this review in writing and provide documentation certifying the existence of a disability; and verifying functional limitations imposed. These applicants are forwarded to CeDAR by admissions and a review confirms that the applicant's disability necessitates using alternate criteria. CeDAR will make a recommendation to admissions. Students may be required to attend the CeDAR College Study Skills Institute held during the summer prior to entrance before a recommendation to admit is completed. General admission includes GPA 2.55-2.99 (extra weight for AP/IB and Honors). FAMU uses the highest sub scores of ACT or SAT and does not use the ACT composite or SAT total score. Requires 4 English.

ADDITIONAL INFORMATION

The CeDAR offers a six-week summer transition program (CSSI; required attendance for some incoming students with a disability who request special admissions consideration)to students who will be graduating or have graduated from high school. This program provides students a chance to focus on remediation of skill deficits, technology, and researching their area of disability. There are no fees for services provided.

PROGRAM FOR DISABILITY SERVICES

Contact Information
Name of program or department: Center for Disability Access and Resources (CeDAR)
  Telephone: 850-599-3180
  Fax: 850-561-2513

LEARNING DISABILITY SERVICES

Accommodations are decided upon an individual basis after a thorough review of appropriate, current documentation. The accommodations requested must be supported through the documentation provided and must be logically linked to the current impact of the condition on academic functioning.

Allowed in exams
  Calculator: Yes
  Dictionary: Yes
  Computer: Yes
  Spellchecker: Yes
Extended test time: Yes
Scribes: Yes
Proctors: Yes
Oral exams: Yes
Note-takers: Yes

Distraction-reduced environment: Yes
Tape recording in class: Yes
Electronic texts: Yes
Accommodations for students with
  ADHD: Yes
Kurzweil Reader: Yes
Other assistive technology:
  Quicktionary(hand held tool that scans
  a word, comparable to a dictionary),
  software, and image magifier
Priority registration: No

Added costs for services: Yes
LD specialists: Yes
Professional tutors: NR
Peer tutors: 4
Max. hours/wk. for services: 45
How professors are notified of
  LD/ADHD: Both student and director

GENERAL ADMISSIONS INFORMATION

Office of Admission: 850-599-3796

ENTRANCE REQUIREMENTS
Academic units required: 4 English, 3 mathematics, 3 science, (1 science labs), 2 foreign language, 3 social studies, 3 academic electives. **Academic units recommended:** 4 English, 3 mathematics, 3 science, 2 foreign language, 3 social studies, 3 academic electives. High school diploma is required and GED is accepted. SAT or ACT required; TOEFL required of all international applicants; minimum paper TOEFL 500, minimum computer TOEFL 173, minimum web-based TOEFL 80.

Application deadline: 5/9
Notification: NR
Average GPA: Rolling
ACT Composite middle 50% range:
  17–21

SAT Math middle 50% range:
  410–500
SAT Critical Reading middle 50%
  range: 410–500
SAT Writing middle 50% range: NR

Graduated top 10% of class: %
Graduated top 25% of class: %
Graduated top 50% of class: %

COLLEGE GRADUATION REQUIREMENTS

Course waivers allowed: Yes
In what course: Math and foreign language
Course substitutions allowed: Yes
In what course: Varies; it depends on the major. Substitutions used rather than waivers when possible.

ADDITIONAL INFORMATION

Environment: The university is located in Tallahassee, Florida.

Student Body
  Undergrad enrollment: 11,289
  Women: 57%
  Men: 43%
  Percent out-of-state: 24%

Cost Information
  In-state tuition: $5,910
  Out-of-state tuition: $20,700
    Room and board: $10,700
  Housing Information
    University housing: Yes
    Percent living on campus: 75%

Greek System
  Fraternity: Yes
  Sorority: Yes
Athletics: Division I

FLORIDA ATLANTIC UNIVERSITY

777 Glades Road, PO Box 3091, Boca Raton, FL 33431-0991
Phone: 561-297-3040 • Fax: 561-297-2758
E-mail: UGRecruitment@fau.edu • Web: www.fau.edu
Support: CS • Institution type: 4-year public

PROGRAMS OR SERVICES FOR STUDENTS WITH LD

The Office for Students with Disabilities (OSD) offers equal access to a quality education by providing reasonable accommodations to qualified students. Students who have a documented LD may receive strategy tutoring from an LD specialist by appointment. Students are expected to be self-sufficient and strong self-advocates. There is a Counseling Center with professionally trained staff to help students with interpersonal conflicts and concerns, test anxiety, poor concentration, and guidance services.

ADMISSION INFORMATION FOR STUDENTS WITH LD/ADHD

College entrance tests required: Yes
Interview required: No
Essay recommended: No
What documentation required for LD: Psycho Ed evaluation to include: relevant historical info, instructional interventions, related services, age diagnosed, objective data (aptitude, achievement, info processing), test scores (standard, percentile and grade equivalents) and describe functional limitations.
With general application: No
To receive services after enrolling: Yes
What documentation required for ADHD: Diagnosis based on DSM-V; history of behaviors impairing functioning in academic setting; diagnostic interview; history of symptoms; evidence of ongoing behaviors.

With general application: No
Submitted to: Office for Students with Disabilities
Special Ed. HS course work accepted: Yes
Specific course requirements of all applicants: Yes
Separate application required: Yes
# of LD applications submitted each year: NR
# of LD applications accepted yearly: NR
Total # of students receiving LD services: NR
Acceptance into program means acceptance into college: Student must be admitted and enrolled in the university first (they can appeal a denial) and then request services.

ADMISSIONS

There is no special application process for students with LD. However, students with LD may be eligible to substitute for certain admission requirements. Students not meeting admission criteria may be admitted by a faculty admission committee if they possess the potential to succeed in university studies or will enhance the university. Supporting documentation explaining circumstances that adversely affected the student's past academic performances will be required. An admissions counselor will assess each applicant in developing supporting materials to be presented to the committee by the Director of Admissions. Students are expected to have a minimum ACT of 21 or SAT of 1450. A sliding scale is used with GPA and test scores. Students who self-disclose and are admitted are then reviewed for services. In some cases, these students are reviewed by the OSD, which provides a recommendation to admissions. Typical courses required for admission include 4 years of English, 4 years of math (Algebra I and higher), 3 years of science, 2 years of a foreign language, 3 years of social studies, and 2 electives.

ADDITIONAL INFORMATION

Students must provide documentation including an aptitude (WAIS preferred) and achievement battery. In the case of ADHD, the diagnostician's report must indicate standardized assessment measures of attention, reported history, and corroboration of current symptoms using two rating scales. With appropriate documentation, students may receive the following accommodations or services: the use of calculators, dictionaries, computers, or spellchecker during exams; extended time on tests; distraction-free environment for tests; oral exams; proctors; scribes; tape recorders in class; textbooks in alternate format; note-takers; and course substitutions. Learning Strategy classes are offered in study skill techniques and organizational strategies. There are occasionally instances where a student is unable to master a particular course because of a disability. In those cases, course substitutions may be permitted if the course in question is not essential to the degree program or related to a licensing requirement. If a student feels he or she may be eligible for a course substitution, the student must first contact OSD for information regarding the substitution process.

LEARNING DISABILITY PROGRAMS OR SERVICES

Contact Information
Name of program or department: Office for Students with Disabilities (OSD)
  Telephone: 561-297-3880
  Fax: 561-297-2184

LEARNING DISABILITY SERVICES

Accommodations are decided upon an individual basis after a thorough review of appropriate, current documentation. The accommodations requested must be supported through the documentation provided and must be logically linked to the current impact of the condition on academic functioning.

Allowed in exams
  Calculator: Yes
  Dictionary: No
  Computer: Yes
  Spellchecker: Yes
Extended test time: Yes
Scribes: Yes
Proctors: Yes
Oral exams: Yes
Note-takers: Yes

Distraction-reduced environment: Yes
Tape recording in class: Yes
Electronic texts: Yes
Accommodations for students with ADHD: Yes
Kurzweil Reader: Yes
Other assistive technology: Yes
Priority registration: No

Added costs for services: No
LD specialists: Yes
Professional tutors: NR
Peer tutors: 1–10
Max. hours/wk. for services: Unlimited
How professors are notified of LD/ADHD: By letters of recommendation presented by student

GENERAL ADMISSIONS INFORMATION

Office of Admission: 561-297-3040

ENTRANCE REQUIREMENTS

Academic units required: 4 English, 4 math, 3 science (2 science labs), 2 foreign language, 3 social studies, 2 academic electives. High school diploma is required, and GED is accepted. SAT or ACT with Writing component required. TOEFL required of all international applicants: minimum paper TOEFL 550, minimum computer TOEFL 300.

Application deadline: 5/1
Notification: Rolling
Average GPA: 3.2–3.8
ACT Composite middle 50% range: 22–25

SAT Composite middle 50% range: 1510–1720

Graduated top 10% of class: NR
Graduated top 25% of class: NR
Graduated top 50% of class: NR

COLLEGE GRADUATION REQUIREMENTS

Course waivers allowed: Yes
In what course: Substitutions rather than waivers when possible for math and foreign language requirements (depending on major)
Course substitutions allowed: Yes
In what course: Varies; it depends on the major requirements and the disability. Substitutions used rather than waivers when possible.

ADDITIONAL INFORMATION

Environment: The university is located on 1,000 acres one and a half miles from the ocean and in proximity to Miami and Fort Lauderdale.

Student Body
  Undergrad enrollment: 23,107
  Women: 58%
  Men: 42%
  Percent out-of-state: 9%

Cost Information
  In-state tuition: $5,372
  Out-of-state tuition: $19,715
  Room & board: $10,940
Housing Information
  University housing: Yes
  Percent living on campus: 17%

Greek System
  Fraternity: Yes
  Sorority: Yes
Athletics: Division I

FLORIDA STATE UNIVERSITY

PO Box 3062400, Tallahassee, FL 32306-2400
Phone: 850-644-6200 • Fax: 850-644-0197
E-mail: admissions@admin.fsu.edu • Web: www.disabilitycenter.fsu.edu
Support: CS • Institution type: 4-year public

PROGRAMS OR SERVICES FOR STUDENTS WITH LD

The Student Disability Resource Center (SDRC) is the primary office of support for students with disabilities. The center works with faculty and staff to provide accommodations unique to the needs of students both in and out of the classroom. Staff meet individually with students who have LD/ADHD, or other types of disabilities. FSU is noted for its sensitivity to students with disabilities. By providing support services at no cost to students with disabilities, the Student Disability Resource Center offers an opportunity for students to achieve their academic and personal goals. Students who self-disclose their disability must complete a request for services form and participate in the accommodation determination process by meeting with a staff member (intake) to receive accommodations. LD documentation must be current, adult-normed, and provided by a qualified professional (e.g. licensed psychologist).

ADMISSION INFORMATION FOR STUDENTS WITH LD/ADHD

College entrance tests required: Yes
Interview required: No
Essay recommended: Yes
What documentation required for LD: Psycho Ed evaluation to include: relevant historical info, instructional interventions, related services, age diagnosed, objective data (aptitude, achievement, info processing), test scores (standard, percentile and grade equivalents) and describe functional limitations.
With general application: No
To receive services after enrolling: Yes
What documentation required for ADHD: Diagnosis based on DSM-V; history of behaviors impairing functioning in academic setting; diagnostic interview; history of symptoms; evidence of ongoing behaviors.

With general application: No
Submitted to: Admissions Office (only if appealing initial decision) and Student Disability Resource Center
Special Ed. HS course work accepted: No
Specific course requirements of all applicants: Yes
Separate application required: Yes
# of LD applications submitted each year: NR
# of LD applications accepted yearly: NR
Total # of students receiving LD services: 638
Acceptance into program means acceptance into college: Students must be admitted and enrolled in the university first and then request services.

ADMISSIONS

The University application does not address disabilities, and if a student self-discloses the information, it will not be used in the initial review process. Students denied admission to the University may appeal that decision in writing and provide a recent psycho-educational evaluation, or other medical documentation relating to the disability, to supplement the basis for their appeal. Most freshman applicants accepted to the University present at least a 3.7 (B+/A-) average in all academic subjects (grades 9-12) and test scores of at least 26 (composite) on the ACT or 1740 (total) on the SAT. In addition to academic grade point average and test scores, a variety of additional factors are considered. These include an essay, the pattern and quality of courses and curriculum, grade trends, class rank, and educational objectives. Applicants should take both the ACT and SAT since Florida State uses the best composite/total score for admission purposes. Applicants taking the ACT must also submit the ACT Combined English/Writing Test. They should also take each exam more than once since the highest subscores are used to create the ACT composite and SAT total. In addition to the overall composite on the ACT or total score on the SAT, the following minimum subscores are required: Writing: 21 on the ACT English or 21 on the ACT English/writing or 500 on the SAT writing; Math: 21 on the ACT math or 500 on the SAT math; and Reading: 22 on the ACT reading or 500 on the SAT critical reading. Auditions are required of all applicants wishing to major in music, dance, or the bachelor of fine arts (BFA) degree program in theatre.

ADDITIONAL INFORMATION

Students who choose to disclose their disability to receive accommodations must complete a Request for Services form provided by the SDRC. For an LD, documentation must be current (normed to the adult population) and provided by a qualified professional (Licensed psychologist.) Staff members assist students in exploring their needs and determining the necessary services and accommodations. Academic accommodations include alternate text formats, alternative testing location, extended time, reader and/or scribe, and inclass note-takers. Staff members meet individually with students with LD/ADHD. Services include teaching study skills, memory enhancement techniques, organizational skills, test-taking strategies, stress management techniques, ways to structure tutoring for best results, and skills for negotiating accommodations with instructors. Student Disability Union (SDU) act as a support group for students with disabilities.

LEARNING DISABILITY PROGRAMS OR SERVICES

Contact Information
Name of program or department: Student Disability Resource Center
   Telephone: 850-644-9566
   Fax: 850-644-7164

LEARNING DISABILITY SERVICES

Accommodations are decided upon an individual basis after a thorough review of appropriate, current documentation. The accommodations requested must be supported through the documentation provided and must be logically linked to the current impact of the condition on academic functioning.

Allowed in exams
   Calculator: Yes
   Dictionary: Yes
   Computer: Yes
   Spellchecker: Yes
Extended test time: Yes
Scribes: Yes
Proctors: Yes
Oral exams: No
Note-takers: Yes

Distraction-reduced environment: Yes
Tape recording in class: Yes
Electronic texts: Yes
**Accommodations for students with
   ADHD:** Yes
Electronic Reading Software: Yes
Other assistive technology: Yes
Priority registration: Yes

Added costs for services: No
LD specialists: Yes
Professional tutors: NR
Peer tutors: No
Max. hours/wk. for services: N/A
**How professors are notified of
   LD/ADHD:** By student

GENERAL ADMISSIONS INFORMATION

Office of Admission: 850-644-6200

ENTRANCE REQUIREMENTS

Academic units required: 4 English, 4 math, 3 science, 2 sequential units of the same foreign language, 3 social studies, 2 academic electives. **Academic units recommended:** High school diploma is required, and GED is accepted. ACT with Writing component required. Official English language proficiency results are required of all international applicants whose native language is not English. 80 on Internet based TOEFL (IBTOEFL); 550 on paper based TOEFL; 77 on Michigan English Language Assessment Battery (MELAB); and 6.5 on International English Language Testing System (IELTS).

Application deadline: 1/14
Notification: 2/19, 3/20
Average GPA: 3.9
ACT Composite middle 50% range:
   25–29

SAT Math middle 50% range:
   560–650
**SAT Critical Reading middle 50%
   range:** 570–660
SAT Writing middle 50% range:
   570–650

Graduated top 10% of class: 40%
Graduated top 25% of class: 78%
Graduated top 50% of class: 97%

COLLEGE GRADUATION REQUIREMENTS

Course waivers allowed: No
In what course: N/A
Course substitutions allowed: Yes
In what course: Foreign language, math.

ADDITIONAL INFORMATION

Environment: Suburban campus in Tallahassee

Student Body
   Undergrad enrollment: 32,201
   Women: 55%
   Men: 45%
   Percent out-of-state: 9%

Cost Information
   In-state tuition: $5,825
   Out-of-state tuition: $20,992
   Room & board: $9,324
Housing Information
   University housing: Yes
   Percent living on campus: 15%

Greek System
   Fraternity: Yes
   Sorority: Yes
Athletics: Division I

LYNN UNIVERSITY

3601 North Military Trail, Boca Raton, FL 33431-5598
Phone: 561-237-7900 • Fax: 561-237-7100
E-mail: admission@lynn.edu • Web: www.lynn.edu
Support: SP • Institution: 4-year private

PROGRAMS OR SERVICES FOR STUDENTS WITH LD

The Comprehensive Support Program has experts in the field of learning pedagogy and nontraditional methodology providing extensive academic support for students with learning differences. This program includes group and individual tutoring, testing accommodations, an alternative testing environment, specialized classes, expert instructors who teach in a multimodality instruction and assessment format, workshops on anxiety and testing, progress updates, mid-term grades, and more. The coaching component of the program uses a diagnostic coaching model to addresses specific executive functioning issues such as organizational skills, procrastination, impulsivity, focus and attention, and study skills, etc.

ADMISSION INFORMATION FOR STUDENTS WITH LD/ADHD

College entrance tests required: Yes
Interview required: No
What documentation required for LD: Psycho Ed evaluation to include: relevant historical info, instructional interventions, related services, age diagnosed, objective data (aptitude, achievement, info processing), test scores (standard, percentile and grade equivalents) and describe functional limitations.
With general application: Yes if requested as part of Structured Program application
To receive services after enrolling: Yes
What documentation required for ADHD: Diagnosis based on DSM-V; history of behaviors impairing functioning in academic setting; diagnostic interview; history of symptoms; evidence of ongoing behaviors.

With general application: Yes if requested as part of Structured Program application
To receive services after enrolling: Yes
Submitted to: Support Program/Services
Special Ed. HS course work accepted: Yes
Specific course requirements for all applicants: NR
Separate application required for program services: No
# of LD applications submitted each year: 750
# of LD applications accepted yearly: 300
Total # of students receiving LD services: 350
Acceptance into program means acceptance into college: Student must be admitted and enrolled in the university first and then offered services through IAL.

ADMISSIONS

Students should submit the general application to Lynn University. Admissions criteria are dependent on the level of services required. Students needing the least restrictive services should have taken college-prep high school courses. Some students may be admitted provisionally after submitting official information. Typically, these students have an ACT of 18 or lower or an SAT of 850 or lower and 2.5 GPA.

ADDITIONAL INFORMATION

The IAL (Institute for Achievement and Learning) program features include: individual and group tutoring; study strategy sessions to enhance study and organizational skills; test anxiety sessions; faculty progress reports; extended time exams and alternative testing procedures; academic coaching and schedule planning; selected core courses offered through IAL trained faculty who teach students in a multimodality style in order to meet students' individual needs; communicative intervention with faculty and thematic instruction. The program uses a diagnostic coaching model to address behavioral issues such as organization skills, prioritizing of assignments and daily activities, strategies for procrastination, time management skills, coping with impulsivity, strategies to aid with focus and attention in and out of the classroom and study skills.

PROGRAM FOR DISABILITY SERVICES

Contact Information
Name of program or department: Institute for Achievement and Learning
  Telephone: 561-237-7064
  Fax: 561-237-7873

LEARNING DISABILITY SERVICES

Accommodations are decided on an individual basis after a thorough review of appropriate, current documentation. Accommodations requested must be supported through the documentation provided and must be logically linked to the current impact of the condition on academic functioning.

Allowed in exams	**Distraction-reduced environment:** Yes	**Added costs for services:** Yes
Calculator: Yes	**Tape recording in class:** Yes	**LD specialists:** Yes
Dictionary: Yes	**Electronic texts:** Yes	**Professional tutors:** 46
Computer: Yes	**Accommodations for students with**	**Peer tutors:** No
Spellchecker: Yes	**ADHD:** Yes	**Max. hours/wk. for services:**
Extended test time: Yes	**Kurzweil Reader:** Yes	Unlimited
Scribes: Yes	**Other assistive technology:** CCTV,	**How professors are notified of**
Proctors: Yes	Kurzweil Reader, Books on tape,	**LD/ADHD:** Student
Oral exams: Yes	Dragon Naturally Speak	
Note-takers: No	**Priority registration:** Yes	

GENERAL ADMISSIONS INFORMATION

Office of Admission: 561-237-7304

ENTRANCE REQUIREMENTS
Academic units required: 4 English, 4 mathematics, 4 science, 2 social studies, 2 history. High school diploma is required and GED is accepted. SAT or ACT required; ACT with Writing component recommended. TOEFL required of all international applicants; minimum paper TOEFL 525, minimum computer TOEFL 197, minimum web-based TOEFL 71.

Application deadline: None	**SAT Math middle 50% range:**	**Graduated top 10% of class:** 7%
Notification: Rolling	410–520	**Graduated top 25% of class:** 23%
Average GPA: 2.85	**SAT Critical Reading middle 50%**	**Graduated top 50% of class:** 51%
ACT Composite middle 50% range:	**range:** 370–510	
18–21	**SAT Writing middle 50% range:** NR	

COLLEGE GRADUATION REQUIREMENTS

Course waivers allowed: No
Course substitutions allowed: No
In what course: Foreign language

ADDITIONAL INFORMATION

Environment: The university is located on 123 acres in a suburban area on Florida's Gold Coast.

Student Body	**Cost Information**	**Greek System**
Undergrad enrollment: 1,619	**Tuition:** $30,100	**Fraternity:** Yes
Women: 51%	**Room and board:** $10,900	**Sorority:** Yes
Men: 49%	**Housing Information**	**Athletics:** Division II
Percent out-of-state: 70%	**University housing:** Yes	
	Percent living on campus: 53%	

UNIVERSITY OF CENTRAL FLORIDA

PO Box 160111, Orlando, FL 32816-0111
Phone: 407-823-3000 • Fax: 407-823-5625
E-mail: admission@mail.ucf.edu • Web: www.ucf.edu
Support: CS • Institution type: 4-year public

PROGRAMS OR SERVICES FOR STUDENTS WITH LD

The Office of Student Disability Services provides information and individualized services consistent with the student's documented disability. To be eligible for disability-related services, individuals must have a documented disability as defined by applicable federal and state laws. Individuals seeking services are required to provide recent documentation from an appropriate health care provider or professional. See www.sds.ucf.edu for specific documentation required.

ADMISSION INFORMATION FOR STUDENTS WITH LD/ADHD

College entrance tests required: Yes
Interview required: No
Essay recommended: No
What documentation required for LD: Psycho Ed evaluation to include: relevant historical info, instructional interventions, related services, age diagnosed, objective data (aptitude, achievement, info processing), test scores (standard, percentile and grade equivalents) and describe functional limitations.
With general application: No
To receive services after enrolling: Yes
What documentation required for ADHD: Diagnosis based on DSM-V; history of behaviors impairing functioning in academic setting; diagnostic interview; history of symptoms; evidence of ongoing behaviors.

With general application: No
Submitted to: Admissions Office
Special Ed. HS course work accepted: No
Specific course requirements of all applicants: Yes
Separate application required: No
# of LD applications submitted each year: NR
# of LD applications accepted yearly: NR
Total # of students receiving LD services: NR
Acceptance into program means acceptance into college: Students must be admitted and enrolled prior to requesting services.

ADMISSIONS

Admission to the University of Central Florida requires graduation from an accredited high school with certain high school academic units, a cumulative high school GPA in those academic units, and SAT or ACT test scores. Course requirements include 4 years of English (at least 3 with substantial writing requirements); 3 years of mathematics (Algebra I and above); 3 years of natural science (at least 2 with labs); 3 years of social science; 2 sequential years of the same foreign language; 3 elective years (preferably from English, mathematics, natural science, social science, or foreign language areas). Students with disabilities who have not taken a foreign language in high school must submit, along with appropriate documentation, a letter from a school official verifying that not taking a foreign language was an accommodation for the disability. If a student needs special admission consideration based on a disability, the student should send the requested appropriate documentation to the Undergraduate Admissions Office. Satisfying minimum requirements does not guarantee admission to UCF since preference will be given to those students whose credentials indicate the greatest promise of academic success.

ADDITIONAL INFORMATION

The University Writing Center (UWC) provides free writing support to all undergraduates and graduates at the University of Central Florida. The Student Academic Resource Center (SARC) provides high-quality academic support programs, including tutoring and supplemental instruction, retention programs, academic advising programs, and various other academic programs and services. The Math Lab provides tutoring for students enrolled in mathematics courses.

LEARNING DISABILITY PROGRAMS OR SERVICES

Contact Information
Name of program or department: Student Disibility Services
  Telephone: 407-823-2371
  Fax: 407-823-2372

LEARNING DISABILITY SERVICES

Accommodations are decided upon an individual basis after a thorough review of appropriate, current documentation. The accommodations requested must be supported through the documentation provided and must be logically linked to the current impact of the condition on academic functioning.

Allowed in exams
  Calculator: Yes
  Dictionary: Yes
  Computer: Yes
  Spellchecker: Yes
Extended test time: Yes
Scribes: Yes
Proctors: Yes
Oral exams: No
Note-takers: Yes

Distraction-reduced environment: Yes
Tape recording in class: Yes
Electronic texts: Yes
Accommodations for students with
  ADHD: Yes
Kurzweil Reader: No
Other assistive technology: Yes
Priority registration: Yes

Added costs for services: No
LD specialists: Yes
Professional tutors: No
Peer tutors: N/A
Max. hours/wk. for services: Varies
How professors are notified of
  LD/ADHD: By student

GENERAL ADMISSIONS INFORMATION

Office of Admission: 407-823-3000

ENTRANCE REQUIREMENTS

Academic units required: 4 English, 3 math, 3 science (2 science labs), 2 foreign language, 3 social studies, 4 academic electives. High school diploma is required, and GED is accepted. ACT with Writing component required. TOEFL required of all international applicants: minimum paper TOEFL 550, minimum computer TOEFL 213.

Application deadline: 5/1
Notification: Rolling
Average GPA: 3.9
ACT Composite middle 50% range:
  24–28

SAT Math middle 50% range:
  560–650
SAT Critical Reading middle 50%
  range: 530–630
SAT Writing middle 50% range:
  510–610

Graduated top 10% of class: 34%
Graduated top 25% of class: 72%
Graduated top 50% of class: 96%

COLLEGE GRADUATION REQUIREMENTS

Course waivers allowed: No
Course substitutions allowed: Yes
In what course: With appropriate documentation, math and foreign language may be substituted with selected other courses.

ADDITIONAL INFORMATION

Environment: The main campus of UCF is located 13 miles east of Orlando.

Student Body
  Undergrad enrollment: 49,900
  Women: 54%
  Men: 46%
  Percent out-of-state: 5%

Cost Information
  In-state tuition: $5,584
  Out-of-state tuition: $21,063
  Room & board: $9,063
Housing Information
  University housing: Yes
  Percent living on campus: 15%

Greek System
  Fraternity: Yes
  Sorority: Yes
Athletics: Division I

UNIVERSITY OF FLORIDA

201 Criser Hall, Box 114000, Gainesville, FL 32611-4000
Phone: 352-392-1365 • Fax: 904-392-3987
E-mail: • Web: www.ufl.edu
Support: CS • Institution: 4-year public

PROGRAMS OR SERVICES FOR STUDENTS WITH LD

The University of Florida offers a full range of support services designed to assist students with learning disabilities. Support services are individually tailored to each student's needs and those supports may be modified to meet the specific demands and requirements of individual courses. Advisement and support services are available to students on an as-needed basis. Assistance can be provided regarding registration, learning strategies, classroom accommodations, and the University of Florida petition process.

ADMISSION INFORMATION FOR STUDENTS WITH LD/ADHD

College entrance tests required: Yes
Interview required: No
Essay required: N/A
What documentation required for LD: Psycho Ed evaluation to include: relevant historical info, instructional interventions, related services, age diagnosed, objective data (aptitude, achievement, info processing), test scores (standard, percentile and grade equivalents) and describe functional limitations.
With general application: No
To receive services after enrolling: Yes
What documentation required for ADHD: Diagnosis based on DSM-V; history of behaviors impairing functioning in academic setting; diagnostic interview; history of symptoms; evidence of ongoing behaviors.

With general application: No
Submitted to: Admissions
Special Ed. HS course work accepted: Yes
Specific course requirements for all applicants: Yes
Separate application required for program services: No
# of LD applications submitted each year: NR
# of LD applications accepted yearly: NR
Total # of students receiving LD services: 850
Acceptance into program means acceptance into college: Students must be admitted and enrolled in the university first (they can appeal a denial) and then request services.

ADMISSIONS

The student with learning disabilities applies to the university under the same guidelines as all other students. However, students with learning disabilities may request a separate review. Students should check the box on the general application to request information and submit a personal statement describing how their learning disabilities may have had an impact or an effect on their grade point average or standardized test scores, if applicable. The required SAT or ACT varies according to the student's GPA. Students denied admission may petition for a review of their application. This review process petition should be directed to the Office of Admissions.

ADDITIONAL INFORMATION

The Dean of Students Office sponsors "Preview," a mandatory registration and orientation program. A student who can not meet the minimum credit hour per semester standard set by his/her major, college or the university due to impact of a disability could be granted a Reduced Course Load (RCL) accommodation.

PROGRAM FOR DISABILITY SERVICES

Contact Information
Name of program or department: Disability Resource Center
  Telephone: 352-392-8565 ext 200
  Fax: 352-392-8570

LEARNING DISABILITY SERVICES

Accommodations are decided upon an individual basis after a thorough review of appropriate, current documentation. The accommodations requested must be supported through the documentation provided and must be logically linked to the current impact of the condition on academic functioning.

Allowed in exams
  Calculator: Yes
  Dictionary: Yes
  Computer: Yes
  Spellchecker: Yes
Extended test time: Yes
Scribes: Yes
Proctors: Yes
Oral exams: Yes
Note-takers: Yes

Distraction-reduced environment: Yes
Tape recording in class: Yes
Electronic texts: Yes
Accommodations for students with
  ADHD: Yes
Kurzweil Reader: Yes
Other assistive technology: Kurzweil, Inspiration, Dragon Naturally Speaking, ZoomText, JAWS, OpenBook
Priority registration: Yes

Added costs for services: No
LD specialists: Yes
Professional tutors: No
Peer tutors: No
Max. hours/wk. for services: N/A
How professors are notified of
  LD/ADHD: Student

GENERAL ADMISSIONS INFORMATION

Office of Admission: 352-392-1365

ENTRANCE REQUIREMENTS
Academic units required: 4 English, 3 mathematics, 3 science, (2 science labs), 2 foreign language, 3 social studies, 0 history, 3 academic electives. High school diploma is required and GED is accepted. SAT or ACT required; ACT with Writing component required. .

Application deadline: 11/1
Notification: Rolling
Average GPA: 4.2
ACT Composite middle 50% range:
  26–30

SAT Math middle 50% range:
  600–690
SAT Critical Reading middle 50%
  range: 570–670
SAT Writing middle 50% range: NR

Graduated top 10% of class: 76%
Graduated top 25% of class: 92%
Graduated top 50% of class: 98%

COLLEGE GRADUATION REQUIREMENTS

Course waivers allowed: Yes
In what course: Foreign language and math
Course substitutions allowed: Yes
In what course: Students may petition for substitutions in foreign language and math courses. Substituted courses are decided on a case-by-case basis.

ADDITIONAL INFORMATION

Environment: The university is located on 2,000 acres 115 miles north of Orlando.

Student Body
  Undergrad enrollment: 32,660
  Women: 55%
  Men: 45%
  Percent out-of-state: 2.5

Cost Information
  In-state tuition: $5,656
  Out-of-state tuition: $27,933
  Room and board: $8,800
  Housing Information
    University housing: Yes
    Percent living on campus: 23%

Greek System
  Fraternity: Yes
  Sorority: Yes
Athletics: Division I

Brenau University

500 Washington St SE, Gainesville, GA 30501
Phone: 770-534-6100 • Fax: 770-538-4306
E-mail: wcadmissions@lib.brenau.edu • Web: www.brenau.edu
Support: SP • Institution: 4-year private

PROGRAMS OR SERVICES FOR STUDENTS WITH LD

The Brenau Learning Center is a program for students with a diagnosed learning disability or Attention Deficit Disorder. Students must also have average to above average academic aptitude with an adequate high school preparation for college studies. The program is designed to provide support services for students as they attend regular college courses. It also offers a more structured learning environment as well as the freedom associated with college living. Full-time students enroll in four or five courses per semester. Learning Center students receive academic advising from the college, as well as the Director of the program. Students have the opportunity to register early, which allows them to take required courses at the appropriate time in their college career. Many students become inactive in the program as they experience success and require less assistance. They may re-enter the program at any time. Brenau University attempts to offer a more personalized caring approach to college education. Faculty are very supportive of students who request extra help. So, in addition to receiving special services from the Learning Center, staff, and tutors, the student is being educated in an environment conducive to learning.

ADMISSION INFORMATION FOR STUDENTS WITH LD/ADHD

College entrance tests required: Yes
Interview required: No
Essay required: N/A
What documentation required for LD: Psycho Ed evaluation to include: relevant historical info, instructional interventions, related services, age diagnosed, objective data (aptitude, achievement, info processing), test scores (standard, percentile and grade equivalents) and describe functional limitations.
With general application: Yes if requested as part of Structured Program application
To receive services after enrolling: Yes
What documentation required for ADHD: Diagnosis based on DSM-V; history of behaviors impairing functioning in academic setting; diagnostic interview; history of symptoms; evidence of ongoing behaviors.

With general application: Yes if requested as part of Structured Program application
To receive services after enrolling: Yes
Submitted to: Admissions
Special Ed. HS course work accepted: Yes
Specific course requirements for all applicants: NR
Separate application required for program services: Yes
# of LD applications submitted each year: 10–15
# of LD applications accepted yearly: 12
Total # of students receiving LD services: 40
Acceptance into college means acceptance into program: Yes

ADMISSIONS

Regular admission criteria include an SAT score of 900-plus (Critical Reading and Math combined) or ACT score of 19-plus, and a GPA of 2.5-plus. Applicants with an LD not meeting regular admissions requirements may be referred to an admissions committee for special consideration. Both the Director of the LC and the Director of Admissions make a decision after reviewing SAT/ACT scores, academic performance and preparation, counselor's recommendation and other letters of reference, test results contained in the psychological evaluation, and a campus interview.

ADDITIONAL INFORMATION

Learning Center students can register early and receive regular academic advising from the Director of the program. Study skills and computer skills courses are offered for credit. Other campus-life skills are taught in the University 101 class. At all service levels students may take tests in an extended-time format where oral assistance is available. Learning Center students begin tutoring with professional tutors during the first week of the term and contract to regularly attend tutoring sessions throughout the semester. All LC students may receive one free hour of educational support per week in addition to scheduled tutoring. Students may be tutored in one to four academic classes per semester. LD services and accommodations are available for undergraduate and graduate students.

PROGRAM FOR DISABILITY SERVICES

Contact Information
Name of program or department: Learning Center (LC)
  Telephone: 770-534-6134
  Fax: 770-297-5883

LEARNING DISABILITY SERVICES

Accommodations are decided upon an individual basis after a thorough review of appropriate, current documentation. The accommodations requested must be supported through the documentation provided and must be logically linked to the current impact of the condition on academic functioning.

Allowed in exams
  Calculator: Yes
  Dictionary: Yes
  Computer: Yes
  Spellchecker: Yes
  Extended test time: Yes
  Scribes: Yes
  Proctors: Yes
  Oral exams: Yes
  Note-takers: Yes

Distraction-reduced environment: Yes
Tape recording in class: Yes
Electronic texts: Yes
Accommodations for students with ADHD: Yes
Kurzweil Reader: Yes
Other assistive technology: Learning Center computers with additional software applications.
Priority registration: Yes

Added costs for services: Yes, some for tutoring
LD specialists: Yes
Professional tutors: 8
Peer tutors: 0
Max. hours/wk. for services: 9
How professors are notified of LD/ADHD: Both student and director

GENERAL ADMISSIONS INFORMATION

Office of Admission: 770-538-4704

ENTRANCE REQUIREMENTS
High school diploma is required and GED is accepted. SAT or ACT required; TOEFL required of all international applicants; minimum paper TOEFL 550, minimum computer TOEFL 173.

Application deadline: None
Notification: Rolling
Average GPA: NR
ACT Composite middle 50% range: 19–21

SAT Math middle 50% range: 440–540
SAT Critical Reading middle 50% range: 455–565
SAT Writing middle 50% range: 440–545

Graduated top 10% of class: NR
Graduated top 25% of class: NR
Graduated top 50% of class: NR

COLLEGE GRADUATION REQUIREMENTS

Course waivers allowed: No
Course substitutions allowed: No

ADDITIONAL INFORMATION

Environment: Brenau University is in a small city setting in the foothills of the Blue Ridge Mountains 50 miles northeast of Atlanta.

Student Body
  Undergrad enrollment: 830
  Women: 100%
  Percent out-of-state: 8%

Cost Information
  Tuition: $21,124
  Room and board: $10,366
Housing Information
  University housing: Yes
  Percent living on campus: 32%

Greek System
  Fraternity: No
  Sorority: Yes
  Athletics: NAIA

EMORY UNIVERSITY

Emory University, Oxford Road Building, Atlanta, GA 30322
Phone: 404-727-6036 • Fax: 404-727-4303
E-mail: admiss@emory.edu • Web: www.emory.edu
Support: S • Institution: 4-year private

PROGRAMS OR SERVICES FOR STUDENTS WITH LD

Emory University is committed to access for all. The Office of Access, Disability Services and   Resources (ADSR) is the administrative unit responsible for "access" management, appropriation of reasonable accommodations, and sustainment of Emory's commitment to access, equity, and systemic change in support of full and rich living, learning, and working experiences.

ADMISSION INFORMATION FOR STUDENTS WITH LD/ADHD

College entrance tests required: Yes
Interview required: No
Essay required: N/A
What documentation required for LD: Psycho Ed evaluation to include: relevant historical info, instructional interventions, related services, age diagnosed, objective data (aptitude, achievement, info processing), test scores (standard, percentile and grade equivalents) and describe functional limitations.
With general application: No
To receive services after enrolling: Yes
What documentation required for ADHD: Diagnosis based on DSM-V; history of behaviors impairing functioning in academic setting; diagnostic interview; history of symptoms; evidence of ongoing behaviors.

With general application: No
Submitted to: Support Program/Services
Special Ed. HS course work accepted: No
Specific course requirements for all applicants: Yes
Separate application required for program services: No
# of LD applications submitted each year: NR
# of LD applications accepted yearly: NR
Total # of students receiving LD services: NR
Acceptance into program means acceptance into college: Students must be admitted and enrolled in the university first and then request services.

ADMISSIONS
Students with learning disabilities are required to submit everything requested by the Office of Admissions for regular admissions. Teacher and/or counselor recommendations may be weighted more heavily in the admissions process. Each student with a disability is evaluated individually and admitted based on potential for success in the Emory environment. Please do not send documentation to the Admissions office. Documentation is required for access to accommodations and services, not admissions. Once admitted, the Admissions Office sends a self-identification form in the acceptance packet to all admitted students.

ADDITIONAL INFORMATION
The needs of students with learning disabilities are met through academic accommodations and a variety of support services. Tutoring is offered by Emory College in most subjects on a one-on-one basis or in small groups. ADSR staff provides information for students about how to access specific accommodation needs once the student is accepted and begins his or her academic work. Information can be obtained about ADSR at www.ods.emory.edu.

PROGRAM FOR DISABILITY SERVICES

Contact Information
Name of program or department: Office of Disablility Services
 Telephone: 404-727-9877
 Fax: 404-727-1126

LEARNING DISABILITY SERVICES

Accommodations are decided upon an individual basis after a thorough review of appropriate, current documentation. The accommodations requested must be supported through the documentation provided and must be logically linked to the current impact of the condition on academic functioning.

Allowed in exams	**Distraction-reduced environment:** Yes	**Added costs for services:** No
Calculator: Yes	**Tape recording in class:** Yes	**LD specialists:** No
Dictionary: Yes	**Electronic texts:** Yes	**Professional tutors:** Yes
Computer: Yes	**Accommodations for students with**	**Peer tutors:** Yes
Spellchecker: Yes	**ADHD:** Yes	**Max. hours/wk. for services:** 2
Extended test time: Yes	**Kurzweil Reader:** No	**How professors are notified of**
Scribes: Yes	**Other assistive technology:** N/A	**LD/ADHD:** Student
Proctors: Yes	**Priority registration:** Yes	
Oral exams: Yes		
Note-takers: Yes		

GENERAL ADMISSIONS INFORMATION

Office of Admission: 404-727-6036

ENTRANCE REQUIREMENTS

Academic units required: 4 English, 3 mathematics, 2 science, (2 science labs), 2 foreign language, 2 social studies, 2 history, 1 visual/performing arts, 2 academic electives. **Academic units recommended:** 4 mathematics, 3 science, 3 foreign language. High school diploma is required and GED is not accepted. SAT or ACT required; ACT with Writing component required. TOEFL required of all international applicants; minimum paper TOEFL 600, minimum computer TOEFL 250.

Application deadline: 1/15	**SAT Critical Reading middle 50%**	**Graduated top 10% of class:** 87%
Notification: 4/1	**range:** 650–740	**Graduated top 25% of class:** 98%
Average GPA: 3.86	**SAT Math middle 50% range:**	**Graduated top 50% of class:** 100%
ACT Composite middle 50% range:	670–770	
30–33	**SAT Writing middle 50% range:**	
	660–750	

COLLEGE GRADUATION REQUIREMENTS

Course waivers allowed: No
In what course: Decisions made on a case-by-case basis
Course substitutions allowed: No
In what course: Decisions made on a case-by-case basis

ADDITIONAL INFORMATION

Environment: The 631-acre campus is in a suburban section 5 miles northeast of Atlanta.

Student Body	**Cost Information**	**Greek System**
Undergrad enrollment: 7,441	**Tuition:** $40,600	**Fraternity:** Yes
Women: 55%	**Room and board:** $11,628	**Sorority:** Yes
Men: 45%	**Housing Information**	**Athletics:** Division III
Percent out-of-state: 72%	**University housing:** Yes	
	Percent living on campus: 70%	

GEORGIA SOUTHERN UNIVERSITY

PO Box 8024, Statesboro, GA 30460
Phone: 912-681-5391 • Fax: 912-486-7240
E-mail: admissions@georgiasouthern.edu • Web: www.georgiasouthern.edu
Support: CS • Institution type: 4-year public

PROGRAMS OR SERVICES FOR STUDENTS WITH LD

Georgia Southern University wants all students to have a rewarding and pleasant college experience. The university offers a variety of services specifically tailored to afford students with learning disabilities an equal opportunity for success. These services are in addition to those provided to all students and to the access provided by campus facilities. Opportunities available through the Student Disability Resource Center, include special registration, which allows students to complete the course registration process without going through the standard procedure, and academic/personal assistance for students who are having difficulty with passing a class and need help with time management, note-taking skills, study strategies, and self-confidence. The university has a support group designed to help students with disabilities deal with personal and academic problems related to their disability.

ADMISSION INFORMATION FOR STUDENTS WITH LD/ADHD

College entrance tests required: Yes
Interview required: No
Essay recommended: No
What documentation required for LD: Psycho Ed evaluation to include: relevant historical info, instructional interventions, related services, age diagnosed, objective data (aptitude, achievement, info processing), test scores (standard, percentile and grade equivalents) and describe functional limitations.
With general application: No
To receive services after enrolling: Yes
What documentation required for ADHD: Diagnosis based on DSM-V; history of behaviors impairing functioning in academic setting; diagnostic interview; history of symptoms; evidence of ongoing behaviors.

With general application: No
Submitted to: Student Disability Resource Center
Special Ed. HS course work accepted: Yes
Specific course requirements of all applicants: Yes
Separate application required: No
# of LD applications submitted each year: NR
# of LD applications accepted yearly: NR
Total # of students receiving LD services: 236
Acceptance into program means acceptance into college: Students must be admitted and enrolled in the university first and then request services.

ADMISSIONS

There is no special admission procedure for students with LD. All applicants must meet the same minimum requirements. Courses required include 4 English, 4 math, 3 science, 2 foreign language, and 3 social studies. The minimum SAT is 1010 or ACT 21. State minimum requirements for each portion of the SAT/ACT are 430 Critical reading, 400 Math/17 English, 17 Math. The minimum GPA is 2.0. Students not meeting the general admission requirements may be admitted through the Eagle Incentive Program (IEP). EIP is a summer program for students provisionally accepted for fall. Students who pass all summer courses and earn a "C" or better GPA. Students must have a minimum 920-1000 SAT or 20 ACT and meet state minimums for SAT Critical Reading and Math and ACT English and Math and complete the college prep curriculum required for general admission Students will be denied admission for fall if their EIP GPA is below a 2.0 or they fail one or more of the summer courses or they do not complete the required 8 summer credit hours.

ADDITIONAL INFORMATION

The Learning Support Program provides students admitted with inadequate skills in reading, composition, and/or math the opportunity to develop those skills to entry-level competency for regular freshman credit hours. If results of the placement tests reflect a need for assistance in developing academic skills of those who qualify for admission, students will be enrolled in a portion or in the entire Learning Support curriculum. Students may carry a maximum of 15 hours (including any Learning Support courses) except in their third semester when they are limited to 12 hours. Learning Support students are assigned an advisor in the Academic Success Center and must see this advisor for drop/add and registration (even if the student has declared a major). Students are not allowed to drop any required Learning Support classes. The only way a student can withdraw from a required Learning Support course is to withdraw from school.

LEARNING DISABILITY PROGRAMS OR SERVICES

Contact Information
Name of program or department: Student Disability Resource Center
Telephone: 912-871-1566
Fax: 912-871-1419

LEARNING DISABILITY SERVICES

Accommodations are decided upon an individual basis after a thorough review of appropriate, current documentation. The accommodations requested must be supported through the documentation provided and must be logically linked to the current impact of the condition on academic functioning.

Allowed in exams	**Distraction-reduced environment:** Yes	**Added costs for services:** No
Calculator: Yes	**Tape recording in class:** Yes	**LD specialists:** Yes
Dictionary: Yes	**Electronic texts:** Yes	**Professional tutors:** No
Computer: Yes	**Accommodations for students with**	**Peer tutors:** Yes
Spellchecker: Yes	**ADHD:** Yes	**Max. hours/wk. for services:**
Extended test time: Yes	**Kurzweil Reader:** No	Unlimited
Scribes: Yes	**Other assistive technology:** No	**How professors are notified of**
Proctors: Yes	**Priority registration:** Yes	**LD/ADHD:** By student
Oral exams: Yes		
Note-takers: Yes		

GENERAL ADMISSIONS INFORMATION

Office of Admission: 912-681-5533

ENTRANCE REQUIREMENTS

Academic units required: 4 English, 4 math, 3 science (2 science labs), 2 foreign language, 3 social studies. High school diploma is required, and GED is not accepted. ACT with or without Writing component accepted. TOEFL required of all international applicants: minimum paper TOEFL 500, minimum computer TOEFL 173.

Application deadline: 5/1	**SAT Math middle 50% range:**	**Graduated top 10% of class:** 14%
Notification: Rolling	510–600	**Graduated top 25% of class:** 38%
Average GPA: 3.14	**SAT Critical Reading middle 50%**	**Graduated top 50% of class:** 68%
ACT Composite middle 50% range:	**range:** 510–590	
21–24	**SAT Writing middle 50% range:** NR	

COLLEGE GRADUATION REQUIREMENTS

Course waivers allowed: No
Course substitutions allowed: Yes
In what course: Substitutions have only been granted in foreign language and a deficit area.

ADDITIONAL INFORMATION

Environment: The campus is in a small town close to Savannah.

Student Body	**Cost Information**	**Greek System**
Undergrad enrollment: 17,044	**In-state tuition:** $4,734	**Fraternity:** Yes
Women: 48%	**Out-of-state tuition:** $16,710	**Sorority:** Yes
Men: 52%	**Room & board:** $9,020	**Athletics:** Division I
Percent out-of-state: 4%	**Housing Information**	
	University housing: Yes	
	Percent living on campus: 26%	

GEORGIA STATE UNIVERSITY

PO Box 4009, Atlanta, GA 30302-4009
Phone: 404-651-2365 • Fax: 404-651-4811
E-mail: admissions@gsu.edu • Web: www.gsu.edu
Support: CS • Institution type: 4-year public

PROGRAMS OR SERVICES FOR STUDENTS WITH LD

Georgia State University is committed to helping each student, including those students with disabilities; realize his or her full potential. This commitment is fulfilled through the provision of reasonable accommodations to ensure equitable access to its programs and services for all qualified students with disabilities. In general, the university will provide accommodations for students with disabilities on an individualized and flexible basis. It is the student's responsibility to seek available assistance and make his or her needs known. All students are encouraged to contact the Office of Disability Services and/or Student Support Services in the early stages of their college planning. The pre-admission services include information regarding admission requirements and academic support services. Students should register with both services before classes begin. This will assure that appropriate services are in place prior to the first day of classes. As a rule, the university does not waive academic requirements because of any disability. Therefore, the student should carefully evaluate degree requirements early in his or her studies. The only exception to this policy is if there is a documented learning disability that would hinder the learning of a foreign language, in which case a student may petition for a substitution in the foreign language requirement.

ADMISSION INFORMATION FOR STUDENTS WITH LD/ADHD

College entrance tests required: Yes
Interview required: No
Essay recommended: No
What documentation required for LD: Psycho Ed evaluation to include: relevant historical info, instructional interventions, related services, age diagnosed, objective data (aptitude, achievement, info processing), test scores (standard, percentile and grade equivalents) and describe functional limitations.
With general application: No
To receive services after enrolling: Yes
What documentation required for ADHD: Diagnosis based on DSM-V; history of behaviors impairing functioning in academic setting; diagnostic interview; history of symptoms; evidence of ongoing behaviors.

With general application: No
Submitted to: Office of Disability Services
Special Ed. HS course work accepted: No
Specific course requirements of all applicants: Yes
Separate application required: No
# of LD applications submitted each year: NR
# of LD applications accepted yearly: NR
Total # of students receiving LD services: 163
Acceptance into program means acceptance into college: Students must be admitted and enrolled in the university first and then request services.

ADMISSIONS

Students with LD must meet the same admission criteria as all other applicants. The university uses a predicted GPA of 2.1 for admission to a degree program or a GPA of 1.8 for admission to Learning Support Systems. This is determined by the ACT/SAT score and the high school GPA. The higher the GPA, the lower the ACT/SAT can be and vice versa. Course requirements include 4 years of English, 3 years of science, 3 years of math, 3 years of social science, and 2 years of a foreign language. (Substitutions are allowed for foreign language if the student has documentation that supports the substitution). Students may appeal an admission decision if they are denied and could be offered a probationary admission. If a student contacts the Office of Disability Services and provides documentation of an LD, the office will write the Admissions Office and verify the existence of the LD.

ADDITIONAL INFORMATION

To receive LD services, students must submit documentation that evaluates intelligence; academic achievement in reading, math, and written language; auditory/phonological processing; language skills; visual-perceptual-spatial-constructural capabilities; attention; memory; executive function; motor skills; and social-emotional behavior. Student Support Services provides individual and group counseling, tutoring, advocacy, taped texts, advising, readers, learning lab, computer training, and referral for diagnosis of LD. The University Counseling Center provides study skills training; test-taking strategies; note-taking skills; textbook-reading skills; test anxiety and stress management, time management, and organizational techniques; thesis and dissertation writing; and personal counseling. Passport is a special section of the Personal and Academic Development Seminar Class offered through the Learning Support Program and is specifically designed for students with LD. The Office of Disability Services offers advisement, a study lab, readers, and testing accommodations.

LEARNING DISABILITY PROGRAMS OR SERVICES

Contact Information
Name of program or department: Margaret A. Staton Office of Disability Services
   Telephone: 404-463-9044
   Fax: 404-463-9049

LEARNING DISABILITY SERVICES

Accommodations are decided upon an individual basis after a thorough review of appropriate, current documentation. The accommodations requested must be supported through the documentation provided and must be logically linked to the current impact of the condition on academic functioning.

Allowed in exams
  Calculator: Yes
  Dictionary: Yes
  Computer: Yes
  Spellchecker: Yes
Extended test time: Yes
Scribes: No
Proctors: Yes
Oral exams: No
Note-takers: Yes

Distraction-reduced environment: Yes
Tape recording in class: Yes
Electronic texts: Yes
Accommodations for students with
  ADHD: Yes
Kurzweil Reader: Yes
Other assistive technology: Yes
Priority registration: Yes

Added costs for services: No
LD specialists: Yes
Professional tutors: No
Peer tutors: No
Max. hours/wk. for services: Based on need and availability of space and staff
How professors are notified of LD/ADHD: By student

GENERAL ADMISSIONS INFORMATION

Office of Admission: 404-651-2365

ENTRANCE REQUIREMENTS

Academic units required: 4 English, 4 math, 3 science (2 science labs), 2 foreign language, 2 social studies, 1 history. High school diploma is required, and GED is not accepted. ACT with Writing component required. TOEFL required of all international applicants: minimum paper TOEFL 525, minimum computer TOEFL 213.

Application deadline: 3/1
Notification: Rolling
Average GPA: 3.33
ACT Composite middle 50% range:
  21–25

SAT Math middle 50% range:
  490–590
SAT Critical Reading middle 50% range: 490–590
SAT Writing middle 50% range: NR

Graduated top 10% of class: NR
Graduated top 25% of class: NR
Graduated top 50% of class: NR

COLLEGE GRADUATION REQUIREMENTS

Course waivers allowed: Yes
Course substitutions allowed: Yes
In what course: Foreign language course substitutions, not waivers, are approved by appeal in a limited number of cases based on psychological evaluation and finding of significant language disability.

ADDITIONAL INFORMATION

Environment: The university's campus is in an urban area in Atlanta.

Student Body
  Undergrad enrollment: 23,359
  Women: 60%
  Men: 40%
  Percent out-of-state: 4%

Cost Information
  In-state tuition: $9,410
  Out-of-state tuition: $27,600
  Room & board: $12,880
  Housing Information
    University housing: Yes
    Percent living on campus: 13%

Greek System
  Fraternity: Yes
  Sorority: Yes
Athletics: Division I

REINHARDT COLLEGE

7300 Reinhardt College Circle, Waleska, GA 30183
Phone: 770-720-5526 • Fax: 770-720-5899
E-mail: www.reinhardt.edu • Web: www.reinhardt.edu
Support: SP • Institution: 4-year private

PROGRAMS OR SERVICES FOR STUDENTS WITH LD

The Academic Support Office (ASO) provides assistance to students with specific learning abilities or attention deficit disorders. Students are enrolled in regular college courses. The program focuses on compensatory skills and provides special services in academic advising, group tutoring, assistance in writing assignments, note-taking, testing accommodations, and coordination of assistive learning technologies. Reinhardt's ASO was established in 1982 to provide assistance to students with learning disabilities who meet regular college entrance requirements, have a diagnosed LD, and may or may not have received any LD services in the past due to ineligibility for high school services, or a recent diagnosis.

ADMISSION INFORMATION FOR STUDENTS WITH LD/ADHD

College entrance tests required: Yes
Interview required: Yes
Essay required: N/A
What documentation required for LD: Psycho Ed evaluation to include: relevant historical info, instructional interventions, related services, age diagnosed, objective data (aptitude, achievement, info processing), test scores (standard, percentile and grade equivalents) and describe functional limitations.
With general application: Yes if requested as part of Structured Program application
To receive services after enrolling: Yes
What documentation required for ADHD: Diagnosis based on DSM-V; history of behaviors impairing functioning in academic setting; diagnostic interview; history of symptoms; evidence of ongoing behaviors.

With general application: Yes if requested as part of Structured Program application
To receive services after enrolling: Yes
Submitted to: Admissions
Special Ed. HS course work accepted: No
Specific course requirements for all applicants: Yes
Separate application required for program services: Yes
# of LD applications submitted each year: 70
# of LD applications accepted yearly: 30
Total # of students receiving LD services: 70
Acceptance into program means acceptance into college: Separate application required after student has enrolled

ADMISSIONS

Applicants with learning disabilities should request an ASO admission packet from Admissions; if they choose to self-disclose upon application, they should complete the regular application; note an interest in Academic Support; fill out the supplemental form from ASO; provide IEPs from as many years of high school, psychological evaluations documenting the disability, and three references addressing aptitude, motivation, ability to set realistic goals, interpersonal skills, and readiness for college; and submit SAT/ACT scores. Students applying to the ASO program may be asked to interview with the ASO faculty. Admission decisions are made by the Admission Office. Students choosing not to self-disclose upon application should request information from the ASO Director.

ADDITIONAL INFORMATION

The ASO is staffed by three full-time faculty members. Additional tuition is required for students enrolled in ASO tutorials. A generous financial aid program is available to all qualified students. Academic Support Services include: faculty-led tutorials (for fee); academic advisement and counseling; accommodative services for students with documented LD/ADD such as individualized testing, note-takers, and the coordination of assistive technology. All students admitted and enrolled in the ASO Program attend a regular student orientation program plus have an interview and orientation with the faculty from the ASO Program.

PROGRAM FOR DISABILITY SERVICES

Contact Information
Name of program or department: Academic Support Office (ASO)
  Telephone: 770-720-5567
  Fax: 770-720-5602

LEARNING DISABILITY SERVICES

Accommodations are decided upon an individual basis after a thorough review of appropriate, current documentation. The accommodations requested must be supported through the documentation provided and must be logically linked to the current impact of the condition on academic functioning.

Allowed in exams
  Calculator: Yes
  Dictionary: No
  Computer: Yes
  Spellchecker: Yes
Extended test time: Yes
Scribes: Yes
Proctors: Yes
Oral exams: Yes
Note-takers: Yes

Distraction-reduced environment: Yes
Tape recording in class: Yes
Electronic texts: Yes
Accommodations for students with ADHD: Yes
Kurzweil Reader: Yes
Other assistive technology: Yes
Priority registration: Yes

Added costs for services: Yes
LD specialists: Yes
Professional tutors: 3
Peer tutors: No
Max. hours/wk. for services: Unlimited
How professors are notified of LD/ADHD: Both student and director

GENERAL ADMISSIONS INFORMATION

Office of Admission: 770-720-5524

ENTRANCE REQUIREMENTS
Academic units required: 4 English, 4 mathematics, 3 science, 3 social studies. **Academic units recommended:** 2 foreign language. High school diploma is required and GED is accepted. SAT or ACT required; TOEFL required of all international applicants; minimum paper TOEFL 500, minimum computer TOEFL 150.

Application deadline: None
Notification: Rolling
Average GPA: 3.02
ACT Composite middle 50% range: 17–22

SAT Math middle 50% range: 430–530
SAT Critical Reading middle 50% range: 410–520
SAT Writing middle 50% range: 410–520

Graduated top 10% of class: NR
Graduated top 25% of class: NR
Graduated top 50% of class: 63%

COLLEGE GRADUATION REQUIREMENTS

Course waivers allowed: No
Course substitutions allowed: No

ADDITIONAL INFORMATION

Environment: The college is located on a 600-acre campus in a small town 40 miles north of Atlanta.

Student Body
  Undergrad enrollment: 1,035
  Women: 60%
  Men: 40%
  Percent out-of-state: 27%

Cost Information
  Tuition: $18,000
  Room and board: $7,000
Housing Information
  University housing: Yes
  Percent living on campus: 43%

Greek System
  Fraternity: No
  Sorority: No
Athletics: NAIA

UNIVERSITY OF GEORGIA

Undergraduate Admissions, Terrell Hall, Athens, GA 30602
Phone: 706-542-8776 • Fax: 706-542-1466
E-mail: undergrad@admissions.uga.edu • Web: www.uga.edu
Support: CS • Institution type: 4-year public

PROGRAMS OR SERVICES FOR STUDENTS WITH LD

The Disability Resource Center (DRC) assists the University in fulfilling its commitment to educate and serve students with disabilities who qualify for admissions. The DRC coordinates and provides a variety of academic and support services to students, including students with learning disabilities (LD) and attention deficit disorder (ADHD). The mission is to promote equal educational opportunities and a welcoming environment for students with disabilities at the University of Georgia. The DRC staff members are dedicated professionals with a wide variety of expertise in disability related issues. These encompass disability specific accommodations, universal design, program access, assistive technology, alternative text, architectural access, and disability law. Staff can hold regular meetings with students to discuss and monitor academic progress, assist students in understanding their disability, make referrals to other campuses and community resources, and consult with faculty as needed. Documentation for a specific learning disability must meet the following criteria: current within the past 3 years; average broad cognitive abilities; specific cognitive processing deficits; significant achievement deficits relative to documented potential in the areas of written expression, reading, and or math; oral language assessment; social emotional assessment that doesn't suggest a primary emotional basis for results; and utilization of assessment instruments with appropriate age norms. All standardized measures must be represented by standard scores or percentile ranks based on published norms.

ADMISSION INFORMATION FOR STUDENTS WITH LD/ADHD

College entrance tests required: Yes
Interview required: No
Essay recommended: Yes
Documentation required for LD: Yes, see www.drc.uga.edu under "Disabilities"
Documentation required for ADHD: Yes
Submitted to: Disability Resource Center
Special Ed. HS course work accepted: No

Specific course requirements of all applicants: Yes
Separate application required: No
# of LD applications submitted each year: N/A
# of LD applications accepted yearly: N/A
Total # of students receiving LD services: 350–400
Acceptance into program means acceptance into college: No LD program. Students must first be admitted. However, students can submit DRC registration information and appropriate LD documentation for review during the application process. Upon review, the students will be notified if their documentation meets UGA criteria to receive accommodation if the student is accepted to UGA.

ADMISSIONS

Students with and without disabilities must meet the eligibility requirements set fourth in the Admission Guidelines. The mid-50% range for GPA: 3.74-4.04 (this is the GPA that UGA calculates based on the core courses taken in high school, and looking at the actual grades on the transcript). The mid-50% range for the SAT Critical Reading and Math is 1190-1360 and SAT Writing is 580-690. The mid-50% range for the ACT is 27-31.The average number of AP/IB courses are approximately 6.

ADDITIONAL INFORMATION

Specialists help with learning strategies for courses. Students meet with LD specialists to register quarterly and design a schedule that considers their LD along with curriculum requirements. Students are assisted in communicating their disabilities and learning needs with their instructors. Course substitutions for foreign language may be approved with appropriate documentation. Modifications for assignments and tests are designed to meet students' specific needs. Skills classes for college credit are offered to all students at UGA in study techniques, time management, problem-solving, research paper writing, and career selection. Students with ADHD are serviced by Disability Services.

LEARNING DISABILITY PROGRAMS OR SERVICES

Contact Information
Name of program or department: Disability Resource Center, Clark Howell Hall
  Telephone: 706-542-8719
  Fax: 706-542-7719

LEARNING DISABILITY SERVICES

Requests for service and accommodations are evaluated individually based on appropriate and current documentation. For more information, go to www.drc.uga.edu under 'Disabilities'.

Allowed in exams
  Calculator: Yes
  Dictionary: No
  Computer: Yes
  Spellchecker: Yes
Extended test time: Yes
Scribes: Yes
Proctors: Yes
Oral exams: Yes
Note-takers: Yes

Distraction-reduced environment: Yes
Tape recording in class: Yes
Electronic texts: Yes
Accommodations for students with ADHD: Yes
Kurzweil Reader: Yes
Other assistive technology: Yes
Priority registration: Yes

Added costs for services: No
LD specialists: Yes
Professional tutors: No
Peer tutors: No
Max. hours/wk. for services: N/A
How professors are notified of LD/ADHD: By student

GENERAL ADMISSIONS INFORMATION

Office of Admission: 706-542-8776

ENTRANCE REQUIREMENTS

Academic units required: 4 English, 4 math, 4 science (2 science labs), 2 foreign language, 3 social studies.
Academic units recommended: As above.

Application deadline: 1/15
Notification: Rolling
Average GPA: 3.83
ACT Composite middle 50% range: 26–30

SAT Math middle 50% range: 580–670
SAT Critical Reading middle 50% range: 580–690
SAT Writing middle 50% range: 560–650

Graduated top 10% of class: 47%
Graduated top 25% of class: 89%
Graduated top 50% of class: 98%

COLLEGE GRADUATION REQUIREMENTS

Course waivers allowed: No
Course substitutions allowed: Yes
In what course: Foreign language

ADDITIONAL INFORMATION

Environment: The university is located on a large campus 80 miles from Atlanta.

Student Body
  Undergrad enrollment: 25,947
  Women: 58%
  Men: 42%
  Percent out-of-state: 12%

Cost Information
  In-state tuition: $9,472
  Out-of-state tuition: $27,682
  Room & board: $9,786
Housing Information
  University housing: Yes
  Percent living on campus: 27%

Greek System
  Fraternity: Yes
  Sorority: Yes
Athletics: Division I

UNIVERSITY OF IDAHO

UI Admissions Office, PO Box 444264, Moscow, ID 83844-4264
Phone: 208-885-6326 • Fax: 208-885-9119
E-mail: admappl@uidaho.edu • Web: www.uihome.uidaho.edu/uihome
Support: S • Institution type: 4-year public

PROGRAMS OR SERVICES FOR STUDENTS WITH LD

Disability Support Services (DSS) provides services and support to all students with documented disabilities. Tutoring and Academic Assistance Program (TAAP) provides additional academic support services offered through Student Support Services (SSS) and Tutoring and Learning Services (TLS) which many students with disabilities find helpful. SSS provides 1-1 assistance with a professional academic counselor and individualized tutoring in one-two courses per semester. The Learning Disabilities Specialist is the primary staff member who works with students with disabilities that affect academic achievement, memory, concentration or cognition (LD, ADHD, or Psychological Disabilities).The TLS Learning Specialist offers in-depth help with learning strategies and basic academic skill development. TLS can help students develop reading and writing skills, as well as learn new approaches to memorizing, note-taking and test preparation. TLS also provides small group tutoring in many introductory courses, primarily in sciences, engineering and foreign languages.

ADMISSION INFORMATION FOR STUDENTS WITH LD/ADHD

College entrance tests required: Yes
Interview required: No
Essay recommended: No
What documentation required for LD: Psycho Ed evaluation to include: relevant historical info, instructional interventions, related services, age diagnosed, objective data (aptitude, achievement, info processing), test scores (standard, percentile and grade equivalents) and describe functional limitations.
With general application: No
To receive services after enrolling: Yes
What documentation required for ADHD: Diagnosis based on DSM-V; history of behaviors impairing functioning in academic setting; diagnostic interview; history of symptoms; evidence of ongoing behaviors.

With general application: No
Submitted to: Student Support Services
Special Ed. HS course work accepted: NR
Specific course requirements of all applicants: Yes
Separate application required: NR
# of LD applications submitted each year: NR
# of LD applications accepted yearly: NR
Total # of students receiving LD services: 100
Acceptance into program means acceptance into college: Student must be admitted and enrolled in the university first and then reviewed for LD services.

ADMISSIONS
Students must meet the general admission requirements. The following index is used : 3.0 GPA and any ACT/SAT; 2.6-2.9 and ACT 15+/SAT 790+; 2.5-2.59 and ACT 17+/SAT 870+; 2.4-2.49 AND ACT 19+/SAT 930+; 2.3-2.39 and ACT 21+/SAT 1000+; 2.2-2.29 and ACT 23/SAT 1030+; and 2.0 GPA in 4 English, 3 math, 1 humanities or foreign language, 2.5 social science, 3 science, plus electives. A freshman student seeking "provisional admission" must submit e recommendations and a written statement addressing goals, educational and/or professional objectives, an explanation of past academic performance, information and/or documentation regarding any extenuating circumstances, and other information pertinent to the request. These files are reviewed by admissions and SSS and admitted students must complete 14 credits in four core areas over three semesters.

ADDITIONAL INFORMATION
The LD Specialist offers academic coaching as well as help with learning strategies and basic academic skill development, personal planning and development, educational and career planning, support with transition issues and problem management, advocacy, and referral to campus and community resources. Accommodations are based upon functional limitations related to a disability. Documentation must be submitted that supports the need for accommodations. In addition, Tutoring Academic Assistance Program (TAAP) provides additional academic support services offered through SSS and TLS which many students with disabilities find helpful.

LEARNING DISABILITY PROGRAMS OR SERVICES

Contact Information
Name of program or department: Student Support Services
  Telephone: 208-885-7200
  Fax: 208-885-9404

LEARNING DISABILITY SERVICES

Accommodations are decided upon an individual basis after a thorough review of appropriate, current documentation. The accommodations requested must be supported through the documentation provided and must be logically linked to the current impact of the condition on academic functioning.

Allowed in exams	**Distraction-reduced environment:** Yes	**Added costs for services:** No
Calculator: Yes	**Tape recording in class:** Yes	**LD specialists:** No
Dictionary: Yes	**Electronic texts:** Yes	**Professional tutors:** No
Computer: Yes	**Accommodations for students with**	**Peer tutors:** Yes
Spellchecker: Yes	**ADHD:** Yes	**Max. hours/wk. for services:** NR
Extended test time: Yes	**Kurzweil Reader:** No	**How professors are notified of**
Scribes: Yes	**Other assistive technology:** Yes	**LD/ADHD:** By student
Proctors: Yes	**Priority registration:** Yes	
Oral exams: Yes		
Note-takers: Yes		

GENERAL ADMISSIONS INFORMATION

Office of Admission: 208-885-7616

ENTRANCE REQUIREMENTS
Academic units required: 4 English, 3 math, 3 science (1 science lab), 1 foreign language, 2 social studies, 1 academic elective. High school diploma is required, and GED is accepted. ACT with or without Writing component accepted. TOEFL required of all international applicants: minimum paper TOEFL 525, minimum computer TOEFL 193.

Application deadline: 8/1	**SAT Math middle 50% range:**	**Graduated top 10% of class:** 20%
Notification: Rolling	490–610	**Graduated top 25% of class:** 45%
Average GPA: 3.36	**SAT Critical Reading middle 50%**	**Graduated top 50% of class:** 77%
ACT Composite middle 50% range:	range: 480–600	
19–26	**SAT Writing middle 50% range:**	
	460–570	

COLLEGE GRADUATION REQUIREMENTS

Course waivers allowed: No
Course substitutions allowed: Yes
In what course: Math and foreign language: Students must request substitutions by petition.

ADDITIONAL INFORMATION

Environment: The university is located on a 800-acre campus in a small town 90 miles south of Spokane, Washington.

Student Body	**Cost Information**	**Greek System**
Undergrad enrollment: 9,343	**In-state tuition:** $5,856	**Fraternity:** Yes
Women: 46%	**Out-of-state tuition:** $18,376	**Sorority:** Yes
Men: 54%	**Room & board:** $7,304	**Athletics:** Division I
Percent out-of-state: 38%	**Housing Information**	
	University housing: Yes	
	Percent living on campus: 90%	

DePaul University

One East Jackson Boulevard, Chicago, IL 60604-2287
Phone: 312-362-8300 • Fax: 312-362-5749
E-mail: admitdpu@depaul.edu • Web: www.depaul.edu
Support: CS • Institution type: 4-year private

PROGRAMS OR SERVICES FOR STUDENTS WITH LD

The Center for Students with Disabilities (CSD) is designed to service and support students with learning disabilities, attention deficit hyperactivity disorder, and all other disabilities. The immediate goals are to provide learning strategies based on students' strengths and weaknesses to assist students in the completion of course work. The ultimate goal is to impart academic and study skills that will enable the students to function independently in the academic environment and competitive job market. CSD provides intensive help on a one-on-one basis. It is designed to assist with regular college courses, improve learning deficits, and help the student learn compensatory skills. Students can choose to work with learning disability specialists with whom they can meet for up to 2 hours per week.

ADMISSION INFORMATION FOR STUDENTS WITH LD/ADHD

College entrance tests required: Yes
Interview required: Yes
Essay recommended: No
What documentation required for LD: Psycho Ed evaluation to include: relevant historical info, instructional interventions, related services, age diagnosed, objective data (aptitude, achievement, info processing), test scores (standard, percentile and grade equivalents) and describe functional limitations.
With general application: No
To receive services after enrolling: Yes
What documentation required for ADHD: Diagnosis based on DSM-V; history of behaviors impairing functioning in academic setting; diagnostic interview; history of symptoms; evidence of ongoing behaviors.

With general application: No
Submitted to: Center for Students with Disabilities (CSD)
Special Ed. HS course work accepted: Yes
Specific course requirements of all applicants: Yes
Separate application required: Yes
# of LD applications submitted each year: 100–120
# of LD applications accepted yearly: 100–120
Total # of students receiving LD services: 350–400
Acceptance into program means acceptance into college: Students must be admitted and enrolled in the university first and then request services.

ADMISSIONS

There is no separate process for students with learning disabilities who wish to be considered for admission to the University. Students with learning disabilities must be first accepted to DePaul University before they can be accepted to the Center for Students with Disabilities (CSD). University admission requirements include a completed application, official high school transcripts, counselor recommendation, ACT/SAT score or responses to supplemental essay questions, and an application fee. In 2011, DePaul implemented a test-optional policy for students applying for freshman admission. Students can choose to apply with or without ACT or SAT scores. For more information regarding requirements and the process please visit: http://www.depaul.edu/admission.

ADDITIONAL INFORMATION

DePaul's Center for Students with Disabilities (CSD) coordinates DePaul University's provision of accommodations and other services to students pursuant to the Americans with Disabilities Act and Section 504 of the Rehabilitation Act of 1973. CSD provides support services for all enrolled students at DePaul; part-time and full-time, undergraduate and graduate, and across all Schools/Colleges within DePaul for all campuses. Recommendations for accommodations are determined by CSD staff after reviewing the documentation provided and an interview with the student. CSD follows the guidelines of the newly updated Americans with Disabilities Act (ADA) and related legislation to determine the most appropriate accommodations for the students. CSD provides appropriate accommodations and services for students related to the nature of their disability.

LEARNING DISABILITY PROGRAMS OR SERVICES

Contact Information
Name of program or department: Center for Students with Disabilities
Telephone: 773-325-1677
Fax: 773-325-3720

LEARNING DISABILITY SERVICES

Accommodations are decided upon an individual basis after a thorough review of appropriate, current documentation. The accommodations requested must be supported through the documentation aligned with ADA guidelines provided and must be logically linked to the current impact of the condition on academic functioning.

Allowed in exams
Calculator: Yes
Dictionary: Yes
Computer: Yes
Spellchecker: Yes
Extended test time: Yes
Scribes: Yes
Proctors: Yes
Oral exams: Yes
Note-takers: No

Distraction-reduced environment: Yes
Tape recording in class: Yes
Electronic texts: Yes
Accommodations for students with ADHD: Yes
Kurzweil Reader: Yes
Other assistive technology: Yes
Priority registration: Yes

Added costs for services: No
LD specialists: Yes
Professional tutors: No
Peer tutors: No
Max. hours/wk. for services: 2
How professors are notified of LD/ADHD: By student

GENERAL ADMISSIONS INFORMATION

Office of Admission: 312-362-8300

ENTRANCE REQUIREMENTS

Academic units required: 4 English, 3 math, 3 science (2 science labs), and 2 social science. High school diploma is required, and GED is accepted. ACT/SAT (with or without Writing component). TOEFL or ACT/SAT required of all international applicants.

Application deadline: Early Action 11/15; Regular 3/15
Notification: 1/15; 3/15
Average GPA: 3.55
ACT Composite middle 50% range: 23–28

SAT Math middle 50% range: 520–620
SAT Critical Reading middle 50% range: 520–650
SAT Writing middle 50% range: NR

Graduated top 10% of class: 25%
Graduated top 25% of class: 54%
Graduated top 50% of class: 86%

COLLEGE GRADUATION REQUIREMENTS

Course waivers allowed: Yes
In what course: Foreign language (LD and ADHD)
Course substitutions allowed: Yes
In what course: Foreign language (LD and ADHD)

ADDITIONAL INFORMATION

Environment: DePaul has a three-acre urban campus located in Chicago's Lincoln Park area three miles north of the downtown area, as well as a Loop campus in downtown Chicago.

Student Body
Undergrad enrollment: 16,384
Women: 55%
Men: 45%
Percent out-of-state: 18%

Cost Information
Tuition: $30,000
Room & board: $11,335
Housing Information
University housing: Yes
Percent living on campus: 16%

Greek System
Fraternity: Yes
Sorority: Yes
Athletics: Division I

EASTERN ILLINOIS UNIVERSITY

600 Lincoln Avenue, Charleston, IL 61920
Phone: 217-581-2223 • Fax: 217-581-7060
E-mail: admissions@eiu.edu • Web: www.eiu.edu
Support: S • Institution: 4-year public

PROGRAMS OR SERVICES FOR STUDENTS WITH LD

EIU will provide services as deemed effective and reasonable to assist students with LD to obtain access to the proper university programs. Students applying to the university who are requesting support services and/or accommodations from the Office of Disability Services are required to submit documentation to verify eligibility under Section 504. The assessment and diagnosis of specific LD must be conducted by a qualified professional. The written diagnostic evaluation report should include the following information: diagnostic report clearly stating the LD and the rationale for the diagnosis; the tests administered and the specific scores including grade level scores, standard scores, and percentile scores; descriptive written text beyond that which is provided on a typical IEP and including qualitative information about the student's abilities; recommendations for accommodations that include specific suggestions based on the diagnostic evaluation results and supported by the diagnosis; and identifying information about the evaluator/diagnostician. The diagnostic tests should be adult normed; they should be comprehensive and include a battery of more than one test and/or subtest. They should also include at least one instrument to measure aptitude or cognitive ability; and should include at least one measurement in reading, written language, and math.

ADMISSION INFORMATION FOR STUDENTS WITH LD/ADHD

College entrance tests required: Yes
Interview required: No
Essay required: N/A
What documentation required for LD: Psycho Ed evaluation to include: relevant historical info, instructional interventions, related services, age diagnosed, objective data (aptitude, achievement, info processing), test scores (standard, percentile and grade equivalents) and describe functional limitations.
With general application: No
To receive services after enrolling: Yes
What documentation required for ADHD: Diagnosis based on DSM-V; history of behaviors impairing functioning in academic setting; diagnostic interview; history of symptoms; evidence of ongoing behaviors.

With general application: No
Submitted to: Support Program/Services
Special Ed. HS course work accepted: Yes
Specific course requirements for all applicants: Yes
Separate application required for program services: No
# of LD applications submitted each year: NR
# of LD applications accepted yearly: NR
Total # of students receiving LD services: NR
Acceptance into program means acceptance into college: NR

ADMISSIONS
All applicants must meet the same admission criteria. Once admitted, students with LD or ADHD must provide appropriate documentation in order to access services and accommodations.

ADDITIONAL INFORMATION
Students should meet with the Office of Disability Services to discuss accommodations or make further arrangements as needed. Some services provided include priority registration, alternate format for classroom materials, note-takers, and testing accommodations. Skills classes can be arranged in time management, note-taking, test-taking, and study strategies.

PROGRAM FOR DISABILITY SERVICES

Contact Information
Name of program or department: Office of Disability Services
  Telephone: 217-581-6583
  Fax: 217-581-7208

LEARNING DISABILITY SERVICES

Accommodations are decided upon an individual basis after a thorough review of appropriate, current documentation. The accommodations requested must be supported through the documentation provided and must be logically linked to the current impact of the condition on academic functioning.

Allowed in exams	**Distraction-reduced environment:** Yes	**Added costs for services:** No
Calculator: Yes	**Tape recording in class:** Yes	**LD specialists:** No
Dictionary: Yes	**Electronic texts:** N/A	**Professional tutors:** NR
Computer: Yes	**Accommodations for students with**	**Peer tutors:** NR
Spellchecker: Yes	**ADHD:** Yes	**Max. hours/wk. for services:** NR
Extended test time: Yes	**Kurzweil Reader:** Yes	**How professors are notified of**
Scribes: Yes	**Other assistive technology:** JAWS,	**LD/ADHD:** Student
Proctors: Yes	Dragon Naturally Speaking, Universal	
Oral exams: Yes	Reader, Kurzweil 3000	
Note-takers: Yes	**Priority registration:** Yes	

GENERAL ADMISSIONS INFORMATION

Office of Admission: 217-581-2223

ENTRANCE REQUIREMENTS
Academic units required: 4 English, 3 mathematics, 3 science, (3 science labs), 3 social studies, 2 academic electives. **Academic units recommended:** 2 foreign language. High school diploma is required and GED is accepted. SAT or ACT required; TOEFL required of all international applicants; minimum paper TOEFL 500, minimum web-based TOEFL 61.

Application deadline: None	**SAT Math middle 50% range:** NR	**Graduated top 10% of class:** 11%
Notification: Rolling	**SAT Critical Reading middle 50%**	**Graduated top 25% of class:** 30%
Average GPA: 3.10	**range:** NR	**Graduated top 50% of class:** 66%
ACT Composite middle 50% range: 19–23	**SAT Writing middle 50% range:** NR	

COLLEGE GRADUATION REQUIREMENTS

Course waivers allowed: No

ADDITIONAL INFORMATION

Environment: The university is in a small town 50 miles south of the University of Illinois.

Student Body	**Cost Information**	**Greek System**
Undergrad enrollment: 9,657	**In-state tuition:** $8,070	**Fraternity:** Yes
Women: 59%	**Out-of-state tuition:** $24,210	**Sorority:** Yes
Men: 41%	**Room and board:** $8,884	**Athletics:** Division I
Percent out-of-state: 2%	**Housing Information**	
	University housing: Yes	
	Percent living on campus: 49%	

ILLINOIS STATE UNIVERSITY

Admissions Office, Campus Box 2200, Normal, IL 61790-2200
Phone: 309-438-2181 • Fax: 309-438-3932
E-mail: admissions@ilstu.edu • Web: www.ilstu.edu
Support: CS • Institution: 4-year public

PROGRAMS OR SERVICES FOR STUDENTS WITH LD

The mission of the Disability Concerns office is to ensure the full and equal participation for persons with disabilities in the university community through empowering individuals, promoting equal access, encouraging self-advocacy, reducing attitudinal and communication barriers, and providing appropriate accommodation. The Disability Concerns program is designed to work with students who have learning disabilities on becoming academically and socially successful while attending Illinois State University. After a review of the appropriate documentation by our Documentation Review Committee, accommodations can then be determined based on the needs of the individual. Students with LD must provide a complete psychoeducational evaluation and a report that includes: a complete adult aptitude assessment (WAIS-III or IV preferred); individual achievement testing (WIAT preferred); measures that assess information processing such as short and long-term memory, sequential memory, auditory and visual perception, and processing speed; and comprehensive background information including a developmental and educational history, and a review of any past evaluations and services received; and finally the diagnosis indicating the impact the disability has on academic performance and recommended accommodations pertinent to the testing results. Students with ADHD must provide the same information as for LD plus the diagnosis with the DSM–IV–TR criteria and information relating to prescribed medication, including information on the side effects and the impact of medication changes.

ADMISSION INFORMATION FOR STUDENTS WITH LD/ADHD

College entrance tests required: Yes
Interview required: No
Documentation required for LD: Adult nonmed
  Psychoeducational evaluation
Documentation required for ADHD: Yes
Submitted to: Support Program/Services
Special Ed. HS course work accepted: Yes

Specific course requirements for all applicants: Yes
Separate application required for program services: No
# of LD applications submitted each year: NR
# of LD applications accepted yearly: NR
Total # of students receiving LD services: 92
Acceptance into program means acceptance into
  college: Students must be admitted and enrolled in the
  university first and then request services.

ADMISSIONS

Admissions criteria for students with learning disabilities are the same as for other students. Of freshman admitted fall 2011, one half earned composite ACT scores of 22 to 26, and the average GPA was 3.43 on a 4.0 scale. High school courses required include: four years English, three years math (algebra, geometry, algebra II), two years social science, two years natural science with laboratories, two years of one foreign language or two years of fine arts, and two years of electives. Students with LD/ADHD who are denied admission may self-disclose and submit a letter of appeal. That appeal is then reviewed by the Office of Admissions. The appeal process is available to all students who are denied admission, but have special circumstances that need consideration.

ADDITIONAL INFORMATION

The following are options for accommodations based on appropriate documentation and needs: note-takers; readers; e-text; scribes; computers; testing accommodations; conference with LD/ADHD specialist; and quiet study rooms. Skills courses are offered to all students in time management, test taking strategies, and study skills. Additionally, there is a writing center, math lab, and tutorial assistance for all students.

PROGRAM FOR DISABILITY SERVICES

Contact Information
Name of program or department: Disability Concerns
  Telephone: 309-438-5853
  Fax: 309-438-7713

LEARNING DISABILITY SERVICES

Accommodations are decided upon an individual basis after a thorough review of appropriate, current documentation. The accommodations requested must be supported through the documentation provided and must be logically linked to the current impact of the condition on academic functioning.

Allowed in exams
  Calculator: Yes
  Dictionary: No
  Computer: Yes
  Spellchecker: Yes
Extended test time: Yes
Scribes: Yes
Proctors: Yes
Oral exams: Yes
Note-takers: Yes

Distraction-reduced environment: Yes
Tape recording in class: Yes
Electronic texts: Yes
Accommodations for students with ADHD: Yes
Kurzweil Reader: No
Other assistive technology: Electronic text is available to students who qualify. Electronic text is used in place of books on tape.
Priority registration: No

Added costs for services: No
LD specialists: Yes
Professional tutors: No
Peer tutors: 30–40
Max. hours/wk. for services: NR
How professors are notified of LD/ADHD: Student

GENERAL ADMISSIONS INFORMATION

Office of Admission: 309-438-2181

ENTRANCE REQUIREMENTS
Academic units required: 4 English, 3 mathematics, 2 science, (2 science labs), 2 foreign language or 2 fine arts, 2 social studies, 2 academic electives. High school diploma is required and GED is accepted. SAT or ACT required; TOEFL required of all international applicants whose native language is not English; minimum paper TOEFL 550, minimum computer TOEFL 213.

Application deadline: 3/1
Notification: Rolling
Average GPA: 3.43
ACT Composite middle 50% range: 22–26

SAT Math middle 50% range: NR
SAT Critical Reading middle 50% range: NR
SAT Writing middle 50% range: NR

Graduated top 10% of class: NR
Graduated top 25% of class: NR
Graduated top 50% of class: NR

COLLEGE GRADUATION REQUIREMENTS

Course waivers allowed: No
Course substitutions allowed: Yes
In what course: Determined on individual basis

ADDITIONAL INFORMATION

Environment: The university is located on 850 acres in a small town 125 miles south of Chicago and 180 miles north of St. Louis.

Student Body
  Undergrad enrollment: 18,314
  Women: 56%
  Men: 44%
  Percent out-of-state: 7%

Cost Information
  In-state tuition: $9,030
  Out-of-state tuition: $15,570
  Room and board: $9,726
Housing Information
  University housing: Yes
  Percent living on campus: 30%
Greek System
  Fraternity: Yes

Sorority: Yes
Athletics: Division I

LINCOLN COLLEGE

300 Keokuk Street, Lincoln, IL 62656
Phone: 800-569-0556 • Fax: 217-732-7715
E-mail: admission@lincolncollege.com • Web: www.lincolncollege.edu
Support: CS • Institution type: 2-year private

PROGRAMS OR SERVICES FOR STUDENTS WITH LD

Lincoln College is committed to enhancing student achievement through a campus-wide approach to supportive services in combination with parental involvement. The college offers personal attention and a number of supportive services to assist students. All incoming first-year students are highly encouraged to take a one credit First Year Experience course to aid with their transition to college. All students have access to free tutoring in all subject areas through the Academic Success Center. Students can receive additional help as needed in the math lab, which is staffed by full-time math faculty 8 hours per week, and the writing lab. Students diagnosed with AD/HD, or whose disability negatively impacts them in areas of time management, organization, or planning, can participate in the ACCESS Program which is a fee-based program that consists of a five-day intensive transition course before the fall semester begins, academic coaching sessions (at least two per week), academic advising, and ongoing communication between ACCESS coaches, parents, and instructors. The cost of the program is $2,250 per semester (in addition to regular tuition and fees) and students can enroll at any point during their academic career.

ADMISSION INFORMATION FOR STUDENTS WITH LD/ADHD

College entrance tests required: Yes
Interview required: Possibly, depends on ACT score, GPA, and highschool curriculum
Essay recommended: Same as above
What documentation required for LD: Psycho Ed evaluation to include: relevant historical info, instructional interventions, related services, age diagnosed, objective data (aptitude, achievement, info processing), test scores (standard, percentile and grade equivalents) and describe functional limitations.
With general application: No
To receive services after enrolling: Yes
What documentation required for ADHD: Diagnosis based on DSM-V; history of behaviors impairing functioning in academic setting; diagnostic interview; history of symptoms; evidence of ongoing behaviors.

With general application: No
Submitted to: Office of Disability Services
Special Ed. HS course work accepted: Yes
Specific course requirements of all applicants: NR
Separate application required: No
# of LD applications submitted each year: NR
# of LD applications accepted yearly: NR
Total # of students receiving LD services: NR
Acceptance into program means acceptance into college: Students are admitted and enrolled at the college and then reviewed for supportive services.

ADMISSIONS

There is no special admissions process for students with learning disabilities. Students must submit the application for admission to Lincoln College, along with an official high school and/or college transcript, and ACT/ SAT score. Students who do not initially meet the ACT/SAT or GPA requirements may be asked to submit a personal essay and letters of recommendation, and attend an on-campus interview with the Academic Review Committee to complete the admissions process.

ADDITIONAL INFORMATION

Lincoln College offers the Academic Development Seminar for students the week before fall semester starts. Students learn writing and speaking skills, effective library skills, and science lab orientation. They develop effective student techniques; lab and field orientation; methods to evaluate social science graphs, charts, and maps; and concepts and values in the humanities. The Academic Writing Seminar is also offered one week in the summer to cover crucial college skills such as writing skill development, note-taking techniques, exam tips, speaking skills, writing to define and classify, college expectations, analytical thinking and writing, and writing to understand and evaluate. Lincoln also has a special program for students with ADHD. The Academy for Collegiate Collaboration for Effective Student Success (ACCESS) is designed for students with ADHD to receive services from private coaches trained to support students. Tuition is $1,000 per semester plus $500 for ACCESS prep course prior to the fall semester.

LEARNING DISABILITY PROGRAMS OR SERVICES

Contact Information
Name of program or department: The Office for Disability Services; The ACCESS Program
  Telephone: 800-569-0556
  Fax: 217-735-4902

LEARNING DISABILITY SERVICES

Accommodations are decided upon an individual basis after a thorough review of appropriate, current documentation. The accommodations requested must be supported through the documentation provided and must be logically linked to the current impact of the condition on academic functioning.

Allowed in exams	**Distraction-reduced environment:** Yes	**Added costs for services:** Yes for
Calculator: Yes	**Tape recording in class:** Yes	ACCESS Program
Dictionary: No	**Electronic texts:** Yes	**LD specialists:** Yes
Computer: Yes	**Accommodations for students with**	**Professional tutors:** 15
Spellchecker: Yes	**ADHD:** Yes	**Peer tutors:** No
Extended test time: Yes	**Kurzweil Reader:** No	**Max. hours/wk. for services:**
Scribes: No	**Other assistive technology:** Yes	Unlimited
Proctors: Yes	**Priority registration:** Yes	**How professors are notified of**
Oral exams: Yes		**LD/ADHD:** By student
Note-takers: No		

GENERAL ADMISSIONS INFORMATION

Office of Admission: 800-569-0556 ext. 252

ENTRANCE REQUIREMENTS

4 years of English, 3 years of math, 3 years of science, 3 years of social studies, and 2 years of foreign language are recommended. ACT of 16 or higher and a cumulative GPA of 2.0 or higher admitted without restriction. Those with an ACT of 15 or lower or any student with less than a 2.0 GPA may be admitted upon review by the Academic Review Committee. TOEFL required of all international applicants, minimum paper TOEFL 480, minimum computer TOEFL 157.

Application deadline: 1 week prior to start of semester	**SAT Math middle 50% range:** NR	**Graduated top 10% of class:** 5
Notification: Rolling	**SAT Critical Reading middle 50% range:** NR	**Graduated top 25% of class:** 10
Average GPA: 2.47	**SAT Writing middle 50% range:** NR	**Graduated top 50% of class:** 65
ACT Composite middle 50% range: NR		

COLLEGE GRADUATION REQUIREMENTS

Course waivers allowed: Case-by-case basis
Course substitutions allowed: Case-by-case basis

ADDITIONAL INFORMATION

Environment: The college has a suburban campus in Normal, Illinois and a small town campus in Lincoln.

Student Body	Cost Information	Greek System
Undergrad enrollment: 700	**Tuition:** $17,500	**Fraternity:** No
Women: 56%	**Room & board:** $7,000	**Sorority:** No
Men: 44%	**Housing Information**	**Athletics:** NJCAA Div. I and Div. II
Percent out-of-state: 11%	**University housing:** Yes	
	Percent living on campus: 88%	

LOYOLA UNIVERSITY—CHICAGO

820 North Michigan Avenue, Chicago, IL 60611
Phone: 312-915-6500 • Fax: 312-915-7216
E-mail: admission@luc.edu • Web: www.luc.edu
Support: S • Institution type: 4-year private

PROGRAMS OR SERVICES FOR STUDENTS WITH LD

Every student with a disability is unique and his or her requests for services will be considered on a case-by-case basis. Services for Students with Disabilities (SSWD) work closely with several Loyola departments and outside agencies to ensure that their educational needs are met. The goal of SSWD is to maximize each student's potential by assisting him or her to develop and maintain independence. Our philosophy encourages self-awareness, self-determination, self-advocacy, and independence in an accessible learning environment. Encouragement is given to all students to visit the Services for Students with Disabilities office to explore the services available.

ADMISSION INFORMATION FOR STUDENTS WITH LD/ADHD

College entrance tests required: Yes

Interview required: No
Essay recommended: No
What documentation required for LD: Psycho Ed evaluation to include: relevant historical info, instructional interventions, related services, age diagnosed, objective data (aptitude, achievement, info processing), test scores (standard, percentile and grade equivalents) and describe functional limitations.
With general application: No
To receive services after enrolling: Yes
What documentation required for ADHD: Diagnosis based on DSM-V; history of behaviors impairing functioning in academic setting; diagnostic interview; history of symptoms; evidence of ongoing behaviors.

With general application: No
Submitted to: Services for Students with Disabilities
Special Ed. HS course work accepted: Yes
Specific course requirements of all applicants: Yes
Separate application required: No
# of LD applications submitted each year: NR
# of LD applications accepted yearly: NR
Total # of students receiving LD services: NR
Acceptance into program means acceptance into college: Students must be admitted and enrolled prior to requesting services.

ADMISSIONS

There is no special admissions procedure for students with disabilities. All admission applications are handled on a case-by-case basis by the Admissions Office for the Undergraduate Admissions. The following units or courses are suggested for admission to Loyola University—Chicago: 4 years of English (required), 3–4 years of math, 3 years of social science, 2 or more years of a foreign language, and 3–4 years of natural or physical science. Each application is reviewed individually and thoroughly. The writing sample, counselor recommendations (up to 3 reommendations), student activities, grades (minimum 3.2 GPA), and standardized test scores are all considered to determine if Loyola will be a good academic match for the strengths and abilities of the applicant. Loyola does not require or use the new written sections on the SAT and ACT for admission or placement.

ADDITIONAL INFORMATION

"Students are encouraged to meet with a staff member in the Services for Students with Disabilities office early on to determine accommodations and services for the upcoming semester. Documentation should provide a clear description of the recommended accommodations, connect these to the impact of the condition, provide possible alternatives to the recommended accommodations, and include a statement regarding the level of need for accommodations."

LEARNING DISABILITY PROGRAMS OR SERVICES

Contact Information
Name of program or department: Services for Students with Disabilities (SSWD)
   Telephone: 773-508-3700
   Fax: 773-508-3810

LEARNING DISABILITY SERVICES

Accommodations are decided upon an individual basis after a thorough review of appropriate, current documentation. The accommodations requested must be supported through the documentation provided and must be logically linked to the current impact of the condition on academic functioning.

Allowed in exams	**Distraction-reduced environment:** Yes	**Added costs for services:** N/A
Calculator: Yes	**Tape recording in class:** Yes	**LD specialists:** No
Dictionary: Yes	**Electronic texts:** Yes	**Professional tutors:** No
Computer: Yes	**Accommodations for students with**	**Peer tutors:** Yes
Spellchecker: Yes	**ADHD:** Yes	**Max. hours/wk. for services:** NR
Extended test time: Yes	**Kurzweil Reader:** No	**How professors are notified of**
Scribes: Yes	**Other assistive technology:** Yes	**LD/ADHD:** SSWD accommodation
Proctors: Yes	**Priority registration:** Yes	letter
Oral exams: Yes		
Note-takers: Yes		

GENERAL ADMISSIONS INFORMATION

Office of Admission: 773-508-3079

ENTRANCE REQUIREMENTS

Academic units required: 4 English, 3 math, 3 science, 3 social studies, 1 history, 1 academic elective.
Academic units recommended: 4 English, 4 math, 4 science, 2 foreign language, 3 social studies, 2 history, 3 academic electives. High school diploma is required, and GED is accepted. ACT with or without Writing component accepted. TOEFL required of all international applicants: minimum paper TOEFL 550, minimum computer TOEFL 213.

Application deadline: None	**SAT Math middle 50% range:**	**Graduated top 10% of class:** 32%
Notification: Rolling	540–650	**Graduated top 25% of class:** 65%
Average GPA: 3.73	**SAT Critical Reading middle 50%**	**Graduated top 50% of class:** 93%
ACT Composite middle 50% range:	**range:** 540–660	
25–29	**SAT Writing middle 50% range:**	
	530–640	

COLLEGE GRADUATION REQUIREMENTS

Course waivers allowed: Yes
In what course: Waiver for math and foreign language if documentation supports the request.
Course substitutions allowed: Yes
In what course: Substitution for math and foreign language if documentation supports the request.

ADDITIONAL INFORMATION

Environment: The campus is located in downtown Chicago, just east of Lake Michigan.

Student Body	**Cost Information**	**Greek System**
Undergrad enrollment: 9,856	**Tuition:** $33,810	**Fraternity:** Yes
Women: 65%	**Room & board:** $12,010	**Sorority:** Yes
Men: 35%	**Housing Information**	**Athletics:** Division I
Percent out-of-state: 35%	**University housing:** Yes	
	Percent living on campus: 38%	

NATIONAL LOUIS UNIVERSITY

122 South Michigan Avenue, Chicago, IL 60603
Phone: 312-261-3550
E-mail: nlnuinfo@wheeling1.nl.edu • Web: www.nl.edu
Support: SP • Institution type: 4-year private

PROGRAMS OR SERVICES FOR STUDENTS WITH LD

The Learning & Library Center is designed to assist students with learning disabilities to pursue and complete a college education. It is a supportive program for students admitted by the university and enrolled in regular and developmental college courses. While the total services furnished in this program are provided by the university to all students who might experience difficulty with a regular college curriculum, emphasis is placed on individual program planning, tutoring, monitoring, arranged counseling, and special testing for the learning disabled. The Center provides peer tutoring, contact with faculty, academic advising, and career and emotional counseling for students who make reasonable progress toward a degree in one of the college programs.

ADMISSION INFORMATION FOR STUDENTS WITH LD/ADHD

College entrance tests required: Yes
Interview required: No
Essay recommended: No
What documentation required for LD: Psycho Ed evaluation to include: relevant historical info, instructional interventions, related services, age diagnosed, objective data (aptitude, achievement, info processing), test scores (standard, percentile and grade equivalents) and describe functional limitations.
With general application: Yes if requested as part of Structured Program application
To receive services after enrolling: Yes
What documentation required for ADHD: Diagnosis based on DSM-V; history of behaviors impairing functioning in academic setting; diagnostic interview; history of symptoms; evidence of ongoing behaviors.

With general application: Yes if requested as part of Structured Program application
To receive services after enrolling: Yes
Submitted to: Center for Academic Development
Special Ed. HS course work accepted: No
Specific course requirements of all applicants: NR
Separate application required: No
# of LD applications submitted each year: NR
# of LD applications accepted yearly: NR
Total # of students receiving LD services: 25
Acceptance into program means acceptance into college: Students must be admitted and enrolled in the university first and then request services.

ADMISSIONS

Students must meet regular admission requirements of a 2.0 GPA in college prep classes and be in top 50% of class. . Minimum 19 ACT/750 SAT. Some may be admitted on a provisional basis as summer admits or as high-potential students. Criteria used in determining admissibility could include work experience, demonstrated leadership in community or extracurricular activities, motivation and attitude toward learning, and career objectives. In addition, an interview and letters of recommendation may be requested. Interested applicants should indicate interest and submit documentation to admission with permission to share with Learning Specialist. Applicants will meet with Learning Specialists for an informal assessment. Student documentation should highlight the ability to function at college level.

ADDITIONAL INFORMATION

The Learning & Library Center is staffed by specialists. Services include: Summer Bridge Program, developmental reading, writing, and math courses; advising; individualized tutoring and monitoring; organizational skills training; and modification of course presentation and exams if appropriate. Pace is a 2 year, post-secondary certificate program offered by NLU. The Program is designed to meet the transitional needs of students with multiple LD. Generally students have a range of cognitive and processing difficulties, a high probability of difficulty with a regular college curriculum, and sufficient emotional stability to adjust to all aspects of the program. Students get work experience as teacher aides or in human resources. 80% of the graduates are employed.

LEARNING DISABILITY PROGRAMS OR SERVICES

Contact Information
Name of program or department: Learning & Library Center
  Telephone: 847-947-5491
  Fax: 847-947-5610

LEARNING DISABILITY SERVICES

Accommodations are decided upon an individual basis after a thorough review of appropriate, current documentation. The accommodations requested must be supported through the documentation provided and must be logically linked to the current impact of the condition on academic functioning.

Allowed in exams
  Calculator: Yes
  Dictionary: Yes
  Computer: Yes
  Spellchecker: Yes
Extended test time: Yes
Scribes: Yes
Proctors: Yes
Oral exams: No
Note-takers: Yes

Distraction-reduced environment: Yes
Tape recording in class: Yes
Electronic texts: No
**Accommodations for students with
  ADHD:** Yes
Kurzweil Reader: No
Other assistive technology: Yes
Priority registration: Yes

Added costs for services: Yes for
  P.A.C.E. Program
LD specialists: Yes
Professional tutors: 5
Peer tutors: 5
Max. hours/wk. for services: 2
**How professors are notified of
  LD/ADHD:** By both student and
  director

GENERAL ADMISSIONS INFORMATION

Office of Admission: 847-465-0575

ENTRANCE REQUIREMENTS
Academic units recommended: 4 English, 3 math, 2 science (1 science lab), 2 foreign language, 3 social studies. High school diploma is required, and GED is accepted.

Application deadline: None
Notification: Rolling
Average GPA: NR
ACT Composite middle 50% range:
  15–20

SAT Math middle 50% range: NR
**SAT Critical Reading middle 50%
  range:** NR
SAT Writing middle 50% range: NR

Graduated top 10% of class: 0%
Graduated top 25% of class: 29%
Graduated top 50% of class: 89%

COLLEGE GRADUATION REQUIREMENTS

Course waivers allowed: No
Course substitutions allowed: Yes

ADDITIONAL INFORMATION

Environment: There are five locations in the Chicago area.

Student Body
  Undergrad enrollment: 1,701
  Women: 78%
  Men: 28%
  Percent out-of-state: 1%

Cost Information
  Tuition: $15,735
  Room & board: NR
Housing Information
  University housing: Yes
  Percent living on campus: 5%

Greek System
  Fraternity: No
  Sorority: No
Athletics: Division I

NORTHERN ILLINOIS UNIVERSITY

Office of Admissions, Williston Hall 101, NIU, DeKalb, IL 60115-2857
Phone: 815-753-0446 • Fax: 815-753-1783
E-mail: admissions-info@niu.edu • Web: www.reg.niu.edu
Support: CS • Institution type: 4-year public

PROGRAMS OR SERVICES FOR STUDENTS WITH LD

The mission of the Center for Access-Ability Resources (CAAR) is to create an accessible, inclusive, sustainable learning environment, where disability is recognized as an aspect of diversity that is integral to the campus community and to society. The goals and objectives of the Center for Access-Ability Resources are to: promote and facilitate access through creative outreach and training, collaborative partnerships, innovative programs, and proactive solutions; create inclusive environments by engaging and supporting the campus community in progressive system change; increase the recruitment, transition, retention and graduation of students with disabilities; consult regarding reducing barriers for persons with disabilities; and ensure the effective delivery of accommodations. The CAAR staff work with all students with disabilities, in an inclusive, educational environment. Students with Learning Disabilities have the same opportunities to engage with and interact with CAAR staff as other students with disabilities. Students seeking resources from the CAAR should contact the Center to schedule an informational interview. During an informational interview, students will meet with a CAAR staff member to discuss barriers that are being encountered and how those barriers may be reduced, such as through reasonable and appropriate accommodations. During the informational interview students will typically share written documentation of their disability.

ADMISSION INFORMATION FOR STUDENTS WITH LD/ADHD

College entrance tests required: Yes
Interview required: No
Essay recommended: No
What documentation required for LD: See website:
  www.niu.edu/caar
With general application: No
To receive services after enrolling: Yes
What documentation required for ADHD: See website:
  www.niu.edu/caar
With general application: No
Submitted to: Center for Access Ability Resources

Special Ed. HS course work accepted: No
Specific course requirements of all applicants: Yes
Separate application required: No
# of LD applications submitted each year: NR
# of LD applications accepted yearly: NR
Total # of students receiving LD services: 175–200
Acceptance into program means acceptance into college: Students admitted may request services. Students denied admission may appeal the decision, and once admitted, they may request services.

ADMISSIONS
General admission requires class rank 50-99% and 19 ACT or 34-49% and 23 ACT. Courses required include: 4 English, 3 math, 3 science, 3 social studies and 1-2 foreign language, art, or music. Substitutions allowed with appropriate documentation. A freshmen applicant with LD who does not meet admission standards can self-disclose and request "special consideration" with the general application for admission. Students should include a letter requesting this special consideration based on a diagnosed disability and describe the disability. Admissions will forward the application to the Center for Access-Ability Resources (CAAR). Students will need to provide documentation, 3 letters of recommendation from people who have worked with the student in an academic setting and any other pertinent information CAAR will make a recommendation to admissions and students may be asked to interview with CAAR prior to a decision.

ADDITIONAL INFORMATION
Academic resources include priority registration, exam accommodations, limited tutoring, individualized study-skill learning strategy advisement and instruction by LD specialists, and a reading and study techniques course taught by LD specialists. Foreign language substitution allowed with appropriate documentation. Other substitution requests are reviewed individually.

LEARNING DISABILITY PROGRAMS OR SERVICES

Contact Information
Name of program or department: Center for Access-Ability Resources
  Telephone: 815-753-1303
  Fax: 815-753-9570

LEARNING DISABILITY SERVICES

Accommodations are determined on an individualized, student by student basis. Requests for accommodations should be related to the impact of the student's disability, should be supported by educational experience and documentation, and should not alter essential elements of the educational experience. Following are examples of accommodations that may be provided:

Allowed in exams	**Distraction-reduced environment:** Yes	**Added costs for services:** No
Calculator: Yes	**Tape recording in class:** Yes	**LD specialists:** Yes
Dictionary: Yes	**Electronic texts:** Yes	**Professional tutors:** NR
Computer: Yes	**Accommodations for students with**	**Peer tutors:** No
Spellchecker: Yes	**ADHD:** Yes	**Max. hours/wk. for services:**
Extended test time: Yes	**Kurzweil Reader:** Yes	Unlimited
Scribes: Yes	**Other assistive technology:** Yes	**How professors are notified of**
Proctors: Yes	**Priority registration:** Yes	**LD/ADHD:** By student
Oral exams: Yes		
Note-takers: Yes		

GENERAL ADMISSIONS INFORMATION

Office of Admission: 815-753-0446

ENTRANCE REQUIREMENTS

Academic units required: 4 English, 2 math, 2 science (1 science lab), 1 foreign language, 2 social studies, 1 history. **Academic units recommended:** 4 math, 4 science (2 science labs), 2 foreign language, 3 social studies. High school diploma is required, and GED is accepted. TOEFL required of all international applicants: minimum paper TOEFL 525, minimum computer TOEFL 1.

Application deadline: 8/1	**SAT Math middle 50% range:** NR	**Graduated top 10% of class:** 9%
Notification: Rolling	**SAT Critical Reading middle 50%**	**Graduated top 25% of class:** 34%
Average GPA: NR	**range:** NR	**Graduated top 50% of class:** 74%
ACT Composite middle 50% range:	**SAT Writing middle 50% range:** NR	
19–24		

COLLEGE GRADUATION REQUIREMENTS

Course waivers allowed: No
Course substitutions allowed: Yes
In what course: Primarily for foreign language if disability severely impacts the learning of foreign language. Substitutions are not given for core competency math classes (general education).

ADDITIONAL INFORMATION

Environment: The school is located on 460 acres in a small town 65 miles from Chicago.

Student Body	**Cost Information**	**Greek System**
Undergrad enrollment: 17,306	**In-state tuition:** $9,390	**Fraternity:** Yes
Women: 51%	**Out-of-state tuition:** $16,650	**Sorority:** Yes
Men: 47%	**Room & board:** $8,112	**Athletics:** Division I
Percent out-of-state: 3%	**Housing Information**	
	University housing: Yes	
	Percent living on campus: 33%	

NORTHWESTERN UNIVERSITY

PO Box 3060, 1801 Hinman Avenue, Evanston, IL 60204-3060
Phone: 847-491-7271
E-mail: ug-admission@northwestern.edu • Web: www.northwestern.edu
Support: CS • Institution: 4-year private

PROGRAMS OR SERVICES FOR STUDENTS WITH LD

The Office of Services for Students with Disabilities (SSD) is the campus resource that provides students with LD, ADHD and all other disabilities the tools, reasonable accommodations and support services needed to participate fully in the University Environment. A wide range of services are provided to students with disabilities enrolled in undergraduate, graduate, or professional schools, allowing them full access to programs and activities at Northwestern University. It is the responsibility of the student to provide documentation of disability, to inform the SSD office and to request accommodations and services if needed. A student who has a disability but has not registered with SSD is not entitled to services or accommodations.

ADMISSION INFORMATION FOR STUDENTS WITH LD/ADHD

College entrance tests required: Yes
Interview required: No
Essay recommended: Yes
What documentation required for LD: Psycho Ed evaluation to include: relevant historical info, instructional interventions, related services, age diagnosed, objective data (aptitude, achievement, info processing), test scores (standard, percentile and grade equivalents) and describe functional limitations.
With general application: No
To receive services after enrolling: Yes
What documentation required for ADHD: Diagnosis based on DSM-V; history of behaviors impairing functioning in academic setting; diagnostic interview; history of symptoms; evidence of ongoing behaviors.

With general application: No
Submitted to: Services for Students with Disabilities
Special Ed. HS course work accepted: No
Specific course requirements of all applicants: NR
Separate application required: No
# of LD applications submitted each year: NR
# of LD applications accepted yearly: NR
Total # of students receiving LD services: 280
Acceptance into program means acceptance into college: Students must be admitted and enrolled in the university first and then request services.

ADMISSIONS

There is no special admissions procedure for students with learning disabilities or ADHD. All applicants must meet the general admission criteria. Most students have taken AP and honors courses in high school and been very successful in these competitive college-prep courses. ACT/SAT tests are required, and SAT Subject Tests are recommended. Foreign-language substitutions may be allowed and are decided on a case-by-case basis.

ADDITIONAL INFORMATION

Some students who received disability-related services in high school may decide to try taking their Northwestern courses without any accommodations or services. SSD recommends that those students nonetheless provide documentation of their disability. In this way, the SSD office can easily serve the student if he or she later finds that accommodations are needed. SSD maintains confidentiality of information, meaning that records contained in SSD files are housed only in the SSD office and are not part of the student's academic file. Support services may include testing accommodations, such as extended time and alternative test environment, note-taking services, materials in e-text and audio format, access to adaptive equipment and software, scribe, study strategy assistance, access to a computer to type exam responses, sign language interpreter, C-Print and assistance in activity relocation.

PROGRAM FOR DISABILITY SERVICES

Contact Information
Name of program or department: Services for Students with Disabilities
  Telephone: 847-467-5530
  Fax: 847-467-5531

LEARNING DISABILITY SERVICES

Accommodations are decided upon an individual basis after a thorough review of appropriate, current documentation. The accommodations requested must be supported through the documentation provided and must be logically linked to the current impact of the condition on academic functioning.

Allowed in exams
  Calculator: Yes
  Dictionary: Yes
  Computer: Yes
  Spellchecker: Yes
Extended test time: Yes
Scribes: Yes
Proctors: Yes
Oral exams: Yes
Note-takers: Yes

Distraction-reduced environment: Yes
Tape recording in class: Yes
Electronic texts: Yes
**Accommodations for students with
  ADHD:** Yes
Kurzweil Reader: Yes
Other assistive technology: Yes
Priority registration: Yes

Added costs for services: No
LD specialists: Yes
Professional tutors: No
Peer tutors: No
Max. hours/wk. for services: Usually
  1 hour
**How professors are notified of
  LD/ADHD:** Student

GENERAL ADMISSIONS INFORMATION

Office of Admission: 847-491-7271

ENTRANCE REQUIREMENTS

Academic units recommended: 4 English, 3 mathematics, 2 science, (2 science labs), 2 foreign language, 2 social studies, 1 academic electives. High school diploma or equivalent is not required. SAT or ACT required; ACT with Writing component required. TOEFL required of all international applicants; minimum paper TOEFL 600, minimum computer TOEFL 250.

Application deadline: 1/1
Notification: 4/1 or earlier
Average GPA: NR
ACT Composite middle 50% range:
  31–33

SAT Math middle 50% range:
  700–780
**SAT Critical Reading middle 50%
  range:** 680–770
SAT Writing middle 50% range:
  680–770

Graduated top 10% of class: 91%
Graduated top 25% of class: 98%
Graduated top 50% of class: 100%

COLLEGE GRADUATION REQUIREMENTS

Course waivers allowed: No
Course substitutions allowed: Yes
In what course: On a case-by-case basis

ADDITIONAL INFORMATION

Environment: The Evanston campus, which houses the undergraduate schools, is located approximately 15 miles from downtown Chicago.

Student Body
  Undergrad enrollment: 8,367
  Women: 52%
  Men: 48%
  Percent out-of-state: 75%

Cost Information
  Tuition: $41,592
  Room and board: $12,780
Housing Information
  University housing: Yes
  Percent living on campus: 60%

Greek System
  Fraternity: Yes
  Sorority: Yes
Athletics: Division I

ROOSEVELT UNIVERSITY

430 South Michigan Avenue, Chicago, IL 60605
Phone: 312-341-3515 • Fax: 312-341-3523
E-mail: applyRU@roosevelt.edu • Web: www.roosevelt.edu
Support: CS • Institution type: 4-year private

PROGRAMS OR SERVICES FOR STUDENTS WITH LD

The goal of the Learning and Support Services Program (LSSP) is to provide a highly individualized support system designed to assist students in their pursuit of a college education. The staff works with each student individually in a variety of different ways with the objective of developing compensatory skills and strategies to become independent, successful college students. Topics typically addressed but not limited to include: reading comprehension, writing skills, note-taking, study skills, time management skills, self-advocacy and test-taking skills.

Roosevelt's small classroom size provides a unique opportunity for students to work closely with professors and an added benefit to students who learn best with more direct instruction. The program is for students who would otherwise experience difficulty with a regular college curriculum. Emphasis is placed on individual program planning, development of self advocacy skills, tutoring, arranged counseling, and alternative test-taking.

ADMISSION INFORMATION FOR STUDENTS WITH LD/ADHD

College entrance tests required: Yes
Interview required: Yes
Essay recommended: Yes
What documentation required for LD: Psycho Ed evaluation to include: relevant historical info, instructional interventions, related services, age diagnosed, objective data (aptitude, achievement, info processing), test scores (standard, percentile and grade equivalents) and describe functional limitations.
With general application: No
To receive services after enrolling: Yes
What documentation required for ADHD: Diagnosis based on DSM-V; history of behaviors impairing functioning in academic setting; diagnostic interview; history of symptoms; evidence of ongoing behaviors.

With general application: No
Submitted to: Learning and Support Services Program
Special Ed. HS course work accepted: No
Specific course requirements of all applicants: Yes
Separate application required: No
# of LD applications submitted each year: NR
# of LD applications accepted yearly: NR
Total # of students receiving LD services: 25–30
Acceptance into program means acceptance into college: Students must be admitted through the regular university admissions process, and once enrolled, may request services.

ADMISSIONS

There is not a separate admissions process through LSSP. However, it is recommended that students write a letter to the LSSP director to request services and state the purpose and reason for seeking help. After reviewing the letter, LSSP staff holds an informal interview assessment with the student. Applicants send reports to the LSSP with authorization for release of information. These reports should include the following: (1) most recent transcript and confidential records; (2) health and academic history; (3) test results and reports, including achievements, individual IQ, or other measurements of academic performance; and (4) the latest IEP. The LSSP staff will evaluate the reports and a meeting will be held to determine eligibility into LSSP.

ADDITIONAL INFORMATION

The Learning and Support Services Program is available to students with learning disabilities, attention disorders, traumatic brain injury, and any other condition that presents learning disorders. Assistance is available in course selection, required course readings, assignments, and more. Depending on individual needs, tutoring assistance may include course-related training, time management, organizational skills, to name a few. Students are highly encouraged to utilize other appropriate resources, such as counseling, career development, campus life and tutoring center. Services and accommodations are available to undergraduate and graduate students.

LEARNING DISABILITY PROGRAMS OR SERVICES

Contact Information
Name of program or department: Learning and Support Services Program
  Telephone: 312-341-3810
  Fax: 312-341-2471

LEARNING DISABILITY SERVICES

Accommodations are decided upon an individual basis after a thorough review of appropriate, current documentation. The accommodations requested must be supported through the documentation provided and must be logically linked to the current impact of the condition on academic functioning.

Allowed in exams	**Distraction-reduced environment:** Yes	**Added costs for services:** Yes
Calculator: Yes	**Tape recording in class:** Yes	**LD specialists:** Yes
Dictionary: Yes	**Electronic texts:** Yes	**Professional tutors:** 3
Computer: Yes	**Accommodations for students with**	**Peer tutors:** Yes
Spellchecker: Yes	**ADHD:** Yes	**Max. hours/wk. for services:** NR
Extended test time: Yes	**Kurzweil Reader:** No	**How professors are notified of**
Scribes: Yes	**Other assistive technology:** Yes	**LD/ADHD:** By student
Proctors: Yes	**Priority registration:** No	
Oral exams: Yes		
Note-takers: Yes		

GENERAL ADMISSIONS INFORMATION

Office of Admission: 877-277-5978

ENTRANCE REQUIREMENTS

Academic units required: 4 English, 3 math, 2 science (2 science labs), 2 social studies, 1 history, 2 academic electives. **Academic units recommended:** 4 English, 4 math, 3 science (2 science labs), 2 foreign language, 3 social studies, 2 history, 2 academic electives. High school diploma is required, and GED is accepted. ACT with or without Writing component accepted. TOEFL required of all international applicants: minimum score of 80 (internet based TOEFL) with at least 18 on the writing section, or 213 (computer based TOEFL); some departments may require a minimum score on the writing section of the TOEFL.

Application deadline: 9/1	**SAT Math middle 50% range:**	**Graduated top 10% of class:** 2%
Notification: Rolling	450–600	**Graduated top 25% of class:** 10%
Average GPA: 3.10	**SAT Critical Reading middle 50%**	**Graduated top 50% of class:** 35%
ACT Composite middle 50% range:	**range:** 510–600	
20–25	**SAT Writing middle 50% range:**	
	490–600	

COLLEGE GRADUATION REQUIREMENTS

Course waivers allowed: Yes
In what course: Varies. Each request is considered individually and subject to department approval.
Course substitutions allowed: Yes
In what course: Varies. Each request is considered individually and subject to department approval.

ADDITIONAL INFORMATION

Environment: Roosevelt University is located in an urban area in downtown Chicago and in Schaumburg, Illinois, which is 20 miles west of Chicago.

Student Body	**Cost Information**	**Greek System**
Undergrad enrollment: 4,264	**Tuition:** $25,000	**Fraternity:** Yes
Women: 66%	**Room & board:** $11,600	**Sorority:** Yes
Men: 34%	**Housing Information**	**Athletics:** Division III
Percent out-of-state: 30%	**University housing:** Yes	
	Percent living on campus: 15%	

SHIMER COLLEGE

Shimer College, 3424 South State Street, Chicago, IL 60616
Phone: 312-235-3500 • Fax: 312-235-3501
E-mail: admission@shimer.edu • Web: www.shimer.edu
Support: S • Institution type: 4-year private

PROGRAMS OR SERVICES FOR STUDENTS WITH LD

Shimer has no specific program for students with learning disabilities. Some students with relatively mild learning disabilities who have been unsuccessful in other settings have been successful at Shimer because of the unusual approach to education. Shimer offers an integrated curriculum where students read original sources and not textbooks. Students gather to discuss the books in small groups. Many students with learning disabilities who are motivated to seek the kind of education offered by Shimer have been successful. Students are responsible for seeking the supportive help they want. Class sizes vary from 8 to 12 students, and a great deal of individual attention is available to all students.

ADMISSION INFORMATION FOR STUDENTS WITH LD/ADHD

College entrance tests required: No
Interview required: Yes
Essay recommended: Yes
What documentation required for LD: Psycho Ed evaluation to include: relevant historical info, instructional interventions, related services, age diagnosed, objective data (aptitude, achievement, info processing), test scores (standard, percentile and grade equivalents) and describe functional limitations.
With general application: No
To receive services after enrolling: Yes
What documentation required for ADHD:
  Neuropsychological or psychoeducational assessment
With general application: No
Submitted to: Dean of students

Special Ed. HS course work accepted: Yes
Specific course requirements of all applicants: NR
Separate application required: No
# of LD applications submitted each year: NR
# of LD applications accepted yearly: NR
Total # of students receiving LD services: NR
Acceptance into program means acceptance into college: Students must be admitted and enrolled in the university first and then request services.

ADMISSIONS

The goal of Shimer is to select students who will benefit from and contribute to its intellectual community. Each applicant is considered on an individual basis. Motivation, intellectual curiosity, and commitment to a rigorous and integrative educational program are important qualifications. Shimer will consider the application of any individual who has the potential to perform well. Admission standards are the same for all students. Once admitted, students with learning disabilities work with the Dean of Students office to document disability, request reasonable accommodation, and determine the level of support the college is able to provide. Students are required to have a personal interview, which can be conducted by telephone; write a personal essay; provide ACT/SAT scores (if available); and submit letters of recommendation to the Admission Office. There is no minimum GPA or specific high school courses required. ACT/SAT scores are considered in the admission decision, but they are not required. Writing samples and other personal contact will be used by the Admission Committee to make an evaluation. A campus visit is strongly encouraged. The essay portion of the application asks the applicant to provide an analysis of academic experience and offers the opportunity to demonstrate creative talent. These essays are major criteria in determining candidacy for admission. Shimer will accept a limited number of students on a threshold basis. These students often lack specific evidence of academic achievement, but they are able to convince the Admission Committee of their commitment and potential. These students receive additional mentoring and support from faculty. Continuation after one semester is dependent on academic achievement.

ADDITIONAL INFORMATION

Classes, except in a rare instance, are never larger than 12 students. All courses are conducted through discussion, and all course reading is from original sources. Because of Shimer's faculty/student ratio, all students receive individualized attention from faculty, staff, and other students.

LEARNING DISABILITY PROGRAMS OR SERVICES

Contact Information
Name of program or department: Dean of Students Office
  Telephone: 312-235-3511
  Fax: 312-235-3051

LEARNING DISABILITY SERVICES

Accommodations are decided upon an individual basis after a thorough review of appropriate, current documentation. The accommodations requested must be supported through the documentation provided and must be logically linked to the current impact of the condition on academic functioning. Determination of accommodations may require an on-campus meeting.

Allowed in exams
  Calculator: Yes
  Dictionary: Yes
  Computer: Yes
  Spellchecker: Yes
Extended test time: Yes
Scribes: No
Proctors: No
Oral exams: Yes
Note-takers: No

Distraction-reduced environment: Yes
Tape recording in class: Yes
Electronic texts: Yes
Accommodations for students with ADHD: Yes
Kurzweil Reader: No
Other assistive technology: No
Priority registration: No

Added costs for services: No
LD specialists: No
Professional tutors: Yes
Peer tutors: 1–3
Max. hours/wk. for services: Unlimited
How professors are notified of LD/ADHD: Dean of Students Office

GENERAL ADMISSIONS INFORMATION

Office of Admission: 312-235-3500

ENTRANCE REQUIREMENTS

Academic units recommended: 4 English, 4 math, 3 science (1 science lab), 3 foreign language, 1 social studies, 2 history, 3 academic electives. High school diploma or equivalent is not required. ACT without Writing component accepted. TOEFL required of all international applicants: minimum paper TOEFL 625, minimum computer TOEFL 263.

Application deadline: None
Notification: Rolling
Average GPA: 3.10
ACT Composite middle 50% range: NR

SAT Math middle 50% range: NR
SAT Critical Reading middle 50% range: NR
SAT Writing middle 50% range: NR

Graduated top 10% of class: NR
Graduated top 25% of class: NR
Graduated top 50% of class: NR

COLLEGE GRADUATION REQUIREMENTS

Course waivers allowed: No
Course substitutions allowed: No

ADDITIONAL INFORMATION

Environment: Shimer is located in Chicago on the campus of the Illinois Institute of Technology.

Student Body
  Undergrad enrollment: 127
  Women: 52%
  Men: 48%
  Percent out-of-state: 56%

Cost Information
  Tuition: $26,510
  Room & board: $10,626
Housing Information
  University housing: Yes
  Percent living on campus: 17%

Greek System
  Fraternity: No
  Sorority: No
  Athletics: Intramural

SOUTHERN ILLINOIS U.—CARBONDALE

Southern Illinois University Carbondale MC 4710, Carbondale, IL 62901-45
Phone: 618-536-4405 • Fax: 618-453-4609
E-mail: joinsiuc@siu.edu • Web: www.siuc.edu
Support: SP • Institution: 4-year public

PROGRAMS OR SERVICES FOR STUDENTS WITH LD

The Achieve Program has been successfully providing academic assistance to SIU Carbondale students for over 33 years. A fee-for-service program, it specializes in academic support services for students with learning disabilities, attention deficits, and other learning differences. Interested students must submit a completed Achieve Program application with supporting documentation and attend an assessment interview session with Achieve Program staff. The applicant is evaluated on the basis of academic, cognitive and social-emotional appropriateness for college-level achievement.

ADMISSION INFORMATION FOR STUDENTS WITH LD/ADHD

College entrance tests required: Yes
Interview required: Yes
Essay required: No
What documentation required for LD: Psycho Ed evaluation to include: relevant historical info, instructional interventions, related services, age diagnosed, objective data (aptitude, achievement, info processing), test scores (standard, percentile and grade equivalents) and describe functional limitations.
With general application: Yes if requested as part of Structured Program application
To receive services after enrolling: Yes
What documentation required for ADHD: Diagnosis based on DSM-V; history of behaviors impairing functioning in academic setting; diagnostic interview; history of symptoms; evidence of ongoing behaviors.

With general application: Yes if requested as part of Structured Program application
To receive services after enrolling: Yes
Submitted to: Support Program/Services
Special Ed. HS course work accepted: No
Specific course requirements for all applicants: Yes
Separate application required for program services: Yes
# of LD applications submitted each year: 200
# of LD applications accepted yearly: 50
Total # of students receiving LD services: 130
Acceptance into program means acceptance into college: Separate application is part of admissions process

ADMISSIONS

Application to the University and the Achieve Program are separate. Applicants must apply to both. Applicants to the Achieve Program are required to provide: Achieve Program application, $50.00 application fee, Professional Reference form, and documentation of disability. Visit the Achieve Program webpage (http://achieveprogram.siuc.edu/) for downloadable application materials. The Achieve Program application can be submitted after completion of junior year of high school. For admission to the University please visit the admissions website: http://admissions.siu.edu/.

ADDITIONAL INFORMATION

Achieve Program students are required to complete the same core curriculum requirements as all other students. The Achieve Program does teach its own sections of UCOL 101, a required course for all first semester freshmen. First year Achieve students are required to spend a minimum of five hours per week at the Achieve Program facilities either working independently, with a general tutor or course specific tutor. The student resource and math labs are staffed with peer tutors to assist with studying and preparing for exams, homework assignments, projects, and written work. Note-takers are assigned for some classes when instructor-provided course notes, PowerPoint presentations, and relevant information are unavailable. Students are encouraged to take their exams at the Achieve offices and may receive extended time as well as a reader or scribe if needed. Audio books are available for students with a demonstrated need, and the Achieve Program has a site license for Kurzweil software. Graduate assistants and staff work with students as case managers so that students have individualized attention and support. All staff is trained to assist students with organization and time management skill building. The Achieve Program has a private computer lab for Achieve students as well as wireless rooms.

PROGRAM FOR DISABILITY SERVICES

Contact Information
Name of program or department: The Achieve Program
  Telephone: 618-453-6155
  Fax: 618-453-3711

LEARNING DISABILITY SERVICES

Accommodations are decided upon an individual basis after a thorough review of appropriate, current documentation. The accommodations requested must be supported through the documentation provided and must be logically linked to the current impact of the condition on academic functioning.

Allowed in exams
  Calculator: Yes, if allowed by instructor
  Dictionary: Yes
  Computer: Yes
  Spellchecker: Yes
Extended test time: Yes
Scribes: Yes
Proctors: Yes
Oral exams: Yes
Note-takers: Yes

Distraction-reduced environment: Yes
Tape recording in class: Recording devices of many types generally permitted
Electronic texts: Yes
Accommodations for students with ADHD: Yes
Kurzweil Reader: Yes
Other assistive technology: SIUC has a long history of providing support for students with disabilities. .

Priority registration: Yes
Added costs for services: Yes
LD specialists: Yes
Professional tutors: 10 (Achieve Staff)
Peer tutors: 40–80
Max. hours/wk. for services: N/A
How professors are notified of LD/ADHD: Both student and supervisor

GENERAL ADMISSIONS INFORMATION

Office of Admission: 618-536-4405

ENTRANCE REQUIREMENTS
Academic units required: 4 English, 3 mathematics, 3 science, 3 social studies, 2 academic electives. High school diploma is required and GED is accepted. SAT or ACT required; TOEFL required of all international applicants; minimum paper TOEFL 520, minimum computer TOEFL 190.

Application deadline: None
Notification: Rolling
Average GPA: NR
ACT Composite middle 50% range:
  19–24

SAT Math middle 50% range:
  440–590
SAT Critical Reading middle 50% range: 420–570
SAT Writing middle 50% range:
  410–520

Graduated top 10% of class: 9%
Graduated top 25% of class: 29%
Graduated top 50% of class: 62%

COLLEGE GRADUATION REQUIREMENTS

Course waivers allowed: Yes
In what course: Waivers or substitutions are granted by committee within the student's department.
Course substitutions allowed: Yes
In what course: Waivers or substitutions are granted by committee within the student's department. Individual decisions are made for each student request regarding curriculum. Achieve will provide input for the committee's review.

ADDITIONAL INFORMATION

Environment: The campus lies at the edge of the Shawnee National Forest 6 hours south of Chicago.

Student Body
  Undergrad enrollment: 18,442
  Women: 43%
  Men: 57%
  Percent out-of-state: 6%

Cost Information
  In-state tuition: $9,794; in-state tuition for surrounding states
  Out-of-state tuition: $19,485
  Room and board: $8,648
Housing Information
  University housing: Yes
  Percent living on campus: 30%

Greek System
  Fraternity: Yes
  Sorority: Yes
Athletics: Division I

SOUTHERN ILLINOIS U.—EDWARDSVILLE

PO Box 1600, Edwardsville, IL 62026-1080
Phone: 618-650-3705 • Fax: 618-650-5013
E-mail: admissions@siue.edu • Web: www.siue.edu
Support: CS • Institution type: 4-year public

PROGRAMS OR SERVICES FOR STUDENTS WITH LD

SIUE's philosophy is to assist students in becoming as independent as possible, and every effort has been made to eliminate barriers to learning. SIUE offers a full range of resources to support students with disabilities and help them attain their educational goals. Students are encouraged to contact Disability Support Services (DSS) as soon as they decide to enroll at the university in order to plan academic accommodations. SIUE does not have special classes for students with learning disabilities; however, the university does offer academic development classes for students who need to develop their math, readying, and writing skills. New Horizons is an organization for students, faculty, and staff who are concerned with issues faced by students with disabilities on campus. New Horizons' activities include disability awareness events, fund-raising, guest speakers, and social activities.

ADMISSION INFORMATION FOR STUDENTS WITH LD/ADHD

College entrance tests required: Yes
Interview required: No
Essay recommended: No
What documentation required for LD: Psycho Ed evaluation to include: relevant historical info, instructional interventions, related services, age diagnosed, objective data (aptitude, achievement, info processing), test scores (standard, percentile and grade equivalents) and describe functional limitations.
With general application: No
To receive services after enrolling: Yes
What documentation required for ADHD: Diagnosis based on DSM-V; history of behaviors impairing functioning in academic setting; diagnostic interview; history of symptoms; evidence of ongoing behaviors.

With general application: No
Submitted to: Disability Support Services
Special Ed. HS course work accepted: NR
Specific course requirements of all applicants: Yes
Separate application required: No
# of LD applications submitted each year: NR
# of LD applications accepted yearly: NR
Total # of students receiving LD services: 136
Acceptance into program means acceptance into college: Student must be admitted and enrolled in the university first and then reviewed for LD services.

ADMISSIONS

Students with learning disabilities are required to submit the same general application form as all other students. Students should submit documentation of their learning disability in order to receive services once enrolled. This documentation should be sent to DSS. Regular admissions criteria recommended: 4 years of English, 3 years of math, 3 years of science, 3 years of social science, 2 years of a foreign language or electives (students with deficiencies need to check with the Office of Admissions); grade point average of 2.5/4.0 and an ACT minimum of 18 (the average is 22.4) or SAT of 860-890. Students not meeting this criteria are encouraged to apply and may be subject to additional review; Students denied admission may appeal the decision.

ADDITIONAL INFORMATION

The Learning Disability Specialist is available to help students with disabilities improve their time management skills and develop effective study strategies. Current resources include advocacy, priority registration, books in alternate format, extended time testing (double time), assistance in writing/ready exams, and volunteer note takers. In addition, the DSS staff members act as liaisons with faculty and staff regarding learning disabilities and accommodations needed by students. Services and accommodations are available for undergraduate and graduate students.

LEARNING DISABILITY PROGRAMS OR SERVICES

Contact Information
Name of program or department: Disability Support Services
  Telephone: 618-650-3726
  Fax: 618-650-5691

LEARNING DISABILITY SERVICES

Accommodations are decided upon an individual basis after a thorough review of appropriate, current documentation. The accommodations requested must be supported through the documentation provided and must be logically linked to the current impact of the condition on academic functioning.

Allowed in exams	**Distraction-reduced environment:** Yes	**Added costs for services:** No
Calculator: Yes	**Tape recording in class:** Yes	**LD specialists:** Yes
Dictionary: Yes	**Electronic texts:** Yes	**Professional tutors:** No
Computer: Yes	**Accommodations for students with**	**Peer tutors:** No
Spellchecker: Yes	**ADHD:** Yes	**Max. hours/wk. for services:** 43
Extended test time: Yes	**Kurzweil Reader:** Yes	**How professors are notified of**
Scribes: Yes	**Other assistive technology:** Yes	**LD/ADHD:** By student
Proctors: Yes	**Priority registration:** Yes	
Oral exams: Yes		
Note-takers: Yes		

GENERAL ADMISSIONS INFORMATION

Office of Admission: 618-650-3705

ENTRANCE REQUIREMENTS

Academic units required: 4 English, 3 math, 3 science (3 science labs), 3 social studies, 2 academic electives.
Academic units recommended: 2 foreign language. High school diploma is required, and GED is accepted. TOEFL required of all international applicants: minimum paper TOEFL 550, minimum computer TOEFL 213.

Application deadline: 5/1	**SAT Math middle 50% range:** NR	**Graduated top 10% of class:** 18%
Notification: Rolling	**SAT Critical Reading middle 50%**	**Graduated top 25% of class:** 44%
Average GPA: NR	**range:** NR	**Graduated top 50% of class:** 79%
ACT Composite middle 50% range:	**SAT Writing middle 50% range:** NR	
20–25		

COLLEGE GRADUATION REQUIREMENTS

Course waivers allowed: No
In what course: N/A
Course substitutions allowed: Yes
In what course: Math

ADDITIONAL INFORMATION

Environment: The university is located on 2,664 acres 18 miles northeast of St. Louis.

Student Body	Cost Information	Greek System
Undergrad enrollment: 11,428	**In-state tuition:** $8,401	**Fraternity:** Yes
Women: 53%	**Out-of-state tuition:** $17,703	**Sorority:** Yes
Men: 47%	**Room & board:** $7,821	**Athletics:** Division I
Percent out-of-state: 10%	**Housing Information**	
	University housing: Yes	
	Percent living on campus: 31%	

U. OF ILLINOIS AT URBANA-CHAMPAIGN

901 West Illinois Street, Urbana, IL 61801
Phone: 217-333-0302 • Fax: 217-244-0903
E-mail: ugradadmissions@illinois.edu • Web: www.illinois.edu
Support: CS • Institution: 4-year public

PROGRAMS OR SERVICES FOR STUDENTS WITH LD

The Division of Disability Resources and Educational Services (DRES) assists qualified students with disabilities in the pursuit of their higher education objectives. DRES assists students with disabilities in gaining access to and benefiting from all the related experiences that are an integral part of a University of Illinois education. Professional staff, including an LD specialist, two clinical psychologists, a career specialist, and an assistive information technology specialist, are available at DRES to assist students in the following areas: planning and implementing academic accommodations, developing compensatory strategies, coaching, for organization and time management, assistive information technology, test accommodations, counseling, and priority registration. Students who receive an offer of admission should submit their documentation to DRES. This documentation should include: diagnostic interviews (developmental, medical, family histories); WAIS, Woodcock-Johnson Tests of Cognitive Ability, Academic Achievement Battery, and a specific LD diagnosis by a qualified professional. ADHD documentation should include: evidence of early impairment, an extensive interview, developmental history, consideration of alternative causes, all appropriate neuropsych tests, extensive clinical summary, and specific DSM-IV diagnosis.

ADMISSION INFORMATION FOR STUDENTS WITH LD/ADHD

College entrance tests required: Yes
Interview required: No
Essay required: N/A
What documentation required for LD: Psycho Ed evaluation to include: relevant historical info, instructional interventions, related services, age diagnosed, objective data (aptitude, achievement, info processing), test scores (standard, percentile and grade equivalents) and describe functional limitations.
With general application: No
To receive services after enrolling: Yes
What documentation required for ADHD: Diagnosis based on DSM-V; history of behaviors impairing functioning in academic setting; diagnostic interview; history of symptoms; evidence of ongoing behaviors.

With general application: No
Submitted to: Support Program/Services
Special Ed. HS course work accepted: Yes
Specific course requirements for all applicants: NR
Separate application required for program services: Yes
# of LD applications submitted each year: NR
# of LD applications accepted yearly: NR
Total # of students receiving LD services: 205
Acceptance into program means acceptance into college: Separate application required after student has enrolled at the University

Admissions

Applicants with LD/ADHD are expected to meet the same admission criteria as all other applicants. Any tests for undergraduate and graduate admissions taken with accommodations are considered as competitive. Applicants whose qualifications are slightly below a college's admission guidelines are encouraged to use the first essay on the application to provide additional information that could be useful in understanding the student's academic history. The university admits students to particular colleges on the basis of class rank, GPA, ACT/SAT scores, extracurricular activities, two application essays, achievements, and challenge of curriculum. Prospective students should contact the appropriate college for complete course requirements. Required courses include four years English, three to three and a half years math, two years foreign language, two years social science, two years lab science, and two courses from any of the five subject categories.

Additional Information

Accommodations are individually student-centered. The student is expected to declare and document all concurrent disabilities for which services are expected. The design and implementation of accommodations depend on the student's perspective of his/her functional limitations relative to the academic requirements of each course. Timely communication to the learning disability specialist of any situations that are projected to need accommodations during the semester is essential. Individual inquiries and early contacts prior to campus residency strengthen the process of accommodation. Students with LD/ADHD work with specialists to develop learning and compensatory strategies and access accommodation and services. Reading and Study Skills Workshops and Writer's Workshops are available for all O of I students. Test preparation and test taking workshops are provided to all students with disabilities registered with DRES by the LD Specialist. Individual therapy, support groups, and coaching are available for students with learning disabilities and ADHD. Coaching involves one-on-one meetings to help with organization, time management, prioritizing, and motivation.

PROGRAM FOR DISABILITY SERVICES

Contact Information
Name of program or department: Division of Disability Resources and Educational Services (DRES)
  Telephone: 217-333-4603
  Fax: 217-333-0248

LEARNING DISABILITY SERVICES

Accommodations are decided upon an individual basis after a thorough review of appropriate, current documentation. The accommodations requested must be supported through the documentation provided and must be logically linked to the current impact of the condition on academic functioning.

Allowed in exams
  Calculator: Yes
  Dictionary: Yes
  Computer: Yes
  Spellchecker: Yes
Extended test time: Yes
Scribes: Yes
Proctors: Yes
Oral exams: Yes
Note-takers: Yes

Distraction-reduced environment: Yes
Tape recording in class: Yes
Electronic texts: Yes
Accommodations for students with
  ADHD: Yes
Kurzweil Reader: Yes
Other assistive technology: Yes
Priority registration: Yes

Added costs for services: No
LD specialists: Yes
Max. hours/wk. for services:
  Unlimited
How professors are notified of
  LD/ADHD: Student

GENERAL ADMISSIONS INFORMATION

Office of Admission: 217-333-0302

ENTRANCE REQUIREMENTS
Academic units required: 4 English, 3 mathematics, 2 science, (2 science labs), 2 foreign language, 2 social studies, 2 academic electives, 3.5 years of mathematics including trigonometry are required in the Agricultural program. High school diploma is required and GED is accepted. SAT or ACT required; ACT with Writing component required. TOEFL required of all international applicants; minimum paper TOEFL 550, minimum computer TOEFL 213, minimum web-based TOEFL 79.

Application deadline: 1/2
Notification: 2/15
Average GPA: NR
ACT Composite middle 50% range:
  26–31

SAT Math middle 50% range:
  680–770
SAT Critical Reading middle 50%
  range: 530–660
SAT Writing middle 50% range:
  570–670

Graduated top 10% of class: 56%
Graduated top 25% of class: 93%
Graduated top 50% of class: 99%

COLLEGE GRADUATION REQUIREMENTS

Course waivers allowed: No
Course substitutions allowed: Yes
In what course: Course substitutions for foreign language and math are available via a petition process through the student's college.

ADDITIONAL INFORMATION

Environment: The university has an urban campus 130 miles south of Chicago.

Student Body
  Undergrad enrollment: 31,540
  Women: 45%
  Men: 55%
  Percent out-of-state: 15%

Cost Information
  In-state tuition: $11,104
  Out-of-state tuition: $25,246
  Room and board: $10,080
Housing Information
  University housing: Yes
  Percent living on campus: 50%

Greek System
  Fraternity: Yes
  Sorority: Yes
Athletics: Division I

WESTERN ILLINOIS UNIVERSITY

1 University Circle, 115 Sherman Hall, Macomb, IL 61455-1390
Phone: 309-298-3157 • Fax: 309-298-3111
E-mail: wiuadm@wiu.edu • Web: www.wiu.edu
Support: CS • Institution: 4-year public

PROGRAMS OR SERVICES FOR STUDENTS WITH LD

Western Illinois University is committed to justice, equity, and diversity. Providing equal opportunities for students with disabilities is a campus-wide responsibility. Disability Resource Center is the office that coordinates academic accommodations for students with diagnosed disabilities who self-identify to the office. Remedial assisstance or a specialized curriculum is not available at WIU. Students requesting accommodations must provide current documentation verifying the specific disability.

ADMISSION INFORMATION FOR STUDENTS WITH LD/ADHD

College entrance tests required: Yes
Interview required: No
Essay required: N/A
What documentation required for LD/ADHD: Students are the best source of information DRC needs. While DRC staff do rely on third-party documentation, it is imperative that DRC staff speak with students regarding their experiences in the educational environment. When DRC reviews third-party information, they are looking for two key elements: the information is provided by an evaluator who is qualified to diagnose the condition, and documentation supports the requested accommodations.
With general application: No
To receive services after enrolling: Yes

Submitted to: Support Program/Services
Special Ed. HS course work accepted: N/A
Specific course requirements for all applicants: NR
Separate application required for program services: Yes
# of LD applications submitted each year: NR
# of LD applications accepted yearly: NR
Total # of students receiving LD services: NR
Acceptance into program means acceptance into college: Separate application required after student has enrolled

ADMISSIONS

Students with learning disabilities must meet the same admission criteria as all applicants, which includes four years English, three years social studies, three years math, three years science, and two years electives. Applicants must also have a ACT 20/SAT 920 and a 2.5 GPA. Students not meeting these standards may be considered for alternative admission. The application should be supported by a letter of recommendation from the counselor and a letter of appeal from the student. The Academic Services Program provides an opportunity for admission to a limited number of students yearly who do not meet the regular WIU admissions. Students considered for alternative admissions must have an ACT of 16 and a high school cummulative GPA of 2.2. Students admitted in the Academic Services Program are chosen on the basis of demonstrated academic potential for success. Several criteria are considered including, but not limited to high school academic GPA, grade patterns, references, and student letter expressing interest in the program.

ADDITIONAL INFORMATION

The purpose of the DRC exam service is to modify aspects of the testing environment in a manner that allows for accurate assessment of achievement. Exam Accommodations include but are not limited to extended time, a reduced-distraction test environment, readers, scribes, and a computer for essay and short answer exams. While instructors may provide these accommodations to students if they wish, DRC offers an exam service for faculty who do not have the resources to provided necessary modifications within their respective departments. Students who plan to take exams using the DRC exam service, will meet with a DRC staff member to schedule exams. The University may allow course substitutions for students receiving DRC services, based on strong documentation of a weakness in a specific area. A student must write a letter of appeal to the Council on Admission, Graduation and Academic Standards (CAGAS). The student should send a copy of the appeal letter to Disability Resource Center. The letter of appeal should contain at least the following.: The student's name, address, identification number, and major; the type of request; an explanation of the student's disability; the rationale for the request; a history of any previous attempts to complete courses that satisfy current requirements; and any history of similar requests granted by any college, university or high school. A letter from DRC should accompany the student's request verifying the disability, when they notified DRC of their disability, and an indication of how long the student has had the disability.

PROGRAM FOR DISABILITY SERVICES

Contact Information
Name of program or department: Disability Support Services (DSS)
  Telephone: 309-298-2512
  Fax: 309-298-2361

LEARNING DISABILITY SERVICES

Accommodations are decided upon an individual basis after a thorough review of appropriate, current documentation. The accommodations requested must be supported through the documentation provided and must be logically linked to the current impact of the condition on academic functioning.

Allowed in exams
  Calculator: Yes
  Dictionary: Yes
  Computer: Yes
  Spellchecker: Yes
Extended test time: Yes
Scribes: Yes
Proctors: Yes
Oral exams: Yes
Note-takers: Yes

Distraction-reduced environment: Yes
Tape recording in class: Yes
Electronic texts: No
Accommodations for students with
  ADHD: Yes
Kurzweil Reader: No
Other assistive technology: Yes
Priority registration: Yes

Added costs for services: No
LD specialists: Yes
Professional tutors: No
Peer tutors: 3
Max. hours/wk. for services: N/A
How professors are notified of
  LD/ADHD: Student

GENERAL ADMISSIONS INFORMATION

Office of Admission: 309-298-1968

ENTRANCE REQUIREMENTS

Academic units recommended: 4 English, 3 mathematics, 3 science, 3 social studies. High school diploma is required and GED is accepted. SAT or ACT required; TOEFL required of all international applicants; minimum paper TOEFL 550, minimum computer TOEFL 213.

Application deadline: 5/15
Notification: Rolling
Average GPA: 2.99
ACT Composite middle 50% range:
  18–23

SAT Math middle 50% range: NR
SAT Critical Reading middle 50%
  range: NR
SAT Writing middle 50% range: NR

Graduated top 10% of class: 8%
Graduated top 25% of class: 26%
Graduated top 50% of class: 57%

COLLEGE GRADUATION REQUIREMENTS

Course waivers allowed: No
In what course: N/A
Course substitutions allowed: Yes
In what course: Students may submit a request for course subsitutions to the Council on Admission, Graduation, and Academic Standards for review.

ADDITIONAL INFORMATION

Environment: The university is located in a rural area 75 miles from Peoria.

Student Body
  Undergrad enrollment: 10,520
  Women: 47%
  Men: 53%
  Percent out-of-state: 6%

Cost Information
  In-state tuition: $8,867
  Out-of-state tuition: $12,347
  Room & board: $8,460
Housing Information
  University housing: Yes
  Percent living on campus: 44%

Greek System
  Fraternity: Yes
  Sorority: Yes
Athletics: Division I

ANDERSON UNIVERSITY

1100 East Fifth Street, Anderson, IN 46012
Phone: 800-428-6414 • Fax: 765-641-4091
E-mail: info@anderson.edu • Web: www.anderson.edu
Support: CS • Institution type: 4-year private

PROGRAMS OR SERVICES FOR STUDENTS WITH LD

It is the philosophy of Anderson University that those students who are qualified and have a sincere motivation to complete a college education should be given every opportunity to work toward that goal. Students with specific learning disabilities may be integrated into any of the many existing services at the Kissinger Learning Center or more individual programming may be designed. Students receive extensive personal contact through the program. The director of the program schedules time with each student to evaluate personal learning style in order to assist in planning for the most appropriate learning environment. One of the most successful programs is individual or small group tutorial assistance. Adjustment and emotional support is also provided. The college strives to provide the maximum amount of services necessary to assist students with learning disabilities in their academic endeavors, while being careful not to create an overdependency.

ADMISSION INFORMATION FOR STUDENTS WITH LD/ADHD

College entrance tests required: Yes
Interview required: Yes
Essay recommended: Yes
What documentation required for LD: Psycho Ed evaluation to include: relevant historical info, instructional interventions, related services, age diagnosed, objective data (aptitude, achievement, info processing), test scores (standard, percentile and grade equivalents) and describe functional limitations.
With general application: No
To receive services after enrolling: Yes
What documentation required for ADHD: Diagnosis based on DSM-V; history of behaviors impairing functioning in academic setting; diagnostic interview; history of symptoms; evidence of ongoing behaviors.

With general application: No
Submitted to: Disability Services for Students
Special Ed. HS course work accepted: N/A
Specific course requirements of all applicants: Yes
Separate application required: No
# of LD applications submitted each year: 8–15
# of LD applications accepted yearly: 7–11
Total # of students receiving LD services: 48
Acceptance into program means acceptance into college: The final decision is made by Admissions.

ADMISSIONS

Students with specific learning disabilities who apply to Anderson do so through the regular admission channels. The university recommends that students have the following courses in their high school background: 4 years of English, 3 years of mathematics, 2 years of a foreign language, 3 years of science, and 3 years of social studies. Also considered in the evaluation of each application is the student's seriousness of purpose; personality and character; expressed willingness to live within the standards of the Anderson University community; and service to school, church, and community. Documentation of a specific learning disability must be included with the application. We encourage students to self-disclose because they may qualify for special consideration and be admitted through the LD program. Failure to disclose could result in nonacceptance based on standardized class scores, GPA, etc. Upon request for consideration for the program, prospective students are expected to make an on-campus visit, at which time a personal interview is arranged with the program director. All applicants are considered on an individual basis.

ADDITIONAL INFORMATION

Freshmen enrolled in the program are typically limited to 12–13 credit hours of course work during the first semester, including a 2-hour study skills class. As students become more independent and demonstrate the ability to deal with increased hours, an additional course load may be considered. There are currently 48 students with LD and 10 students with ADHD receiving accommodations or services. Depending on the specific needs of the student, all or a selected number of services may be provided including: assistance with advising, study skills instruction, time management, career counseling, alternative testing situations, and advocacy/liaison. The Kissinger Learning Center offers a variety of services, including a writing assistance program directed by a faculty member of the English Department. Students are fully integrated into the university and are expected to meet the same academic standards as all other students.

LEARNING DISABILITY PROGRAMS OR SERVICES

Contact Information
Name of program or department: Disability Services for Students, Kissinger Learning Center
  Telephone: 765-641-4223 or 4226
  Fax: 765-641-3851

LEARNING DISABILITY SERVICES

Accommodations are decided upon an individual basis after a thorough review of appropriate, current documentation. The accommodations requested must be supported through the documentation provided and must be logically linked to the current impact of the condition on academic functioning.

Allowed in exams	**Distraction-reduced environment:** Yes	**Added costs for services:** No
Calculator: NR	**Tape recording in class:** Yes	**LD specialists:** Yes
Dictionary: Yes	**Electronic texts:** Yes	**Professional tutors:** 2
Computer: Yes	**Accommodations for students with**	**Peer tutors:** 46
Spellchecker: Yes	**ADHD:** Yes	**Max. hours/wk. for services:**
Extended test time: Yes	**Kurzweil Reader:** Yes	Unlimited
Scribes: Yes	**Other assistive technology:** Yes	**How professors are notified of**
Proctors: Yes	**Priority registration:** No	**LD/ADHD:** Students self-identify
Oral exams: Yes		
Note-takers: Yes		

GENERAL ADMISSIONS INFORMATION

Office of Admission: 765-641-4084 or 800-428-6414

ENTRANCE REQUIREMENTS
Academic units required: 4 English, 3 math, 3 science (3 science labs), 2 foreign language, 1 social studies, 1 history.
Academic units recommended: 4 English, 4 math, 4 science (4 science labs), 3 foreign language, 3 social studies, 2 history, 5 academic electives. High school diploma is required, and GED is not accepted. ACT with Writing component required. TOEFL required of all international applicants: minimum paper TOEFL 547, minimum computer TOEFL 210.

Application deadline: None	**SAT Math middle 50% range:**	**Graduated top 10% of class:** 22%
Notification: Rolling	460–580	**Graduated top 25% of class:** 46%
Average GPA: 3.33	**SAT Critical Reading middle 50%**	**Graduated top 50% of class:** 78%
ACT Composite middle 50% range:	**range:** 460–570	
20–25	**SAT Writing middle 50% range:** NR	

COLLEGE GRADUATION REQUIREMENTS

Course waivers allowed: No
Course substitutions allowed: No

ADDITIONAL INFORMATION

Environment: Anderson University is located on 100 acres 40 miles northeast of Indianapolis.

Student Body	**Cost Information**	**Greek System**
Undergrad enrollment: 2,022	**Tuition:** $25,400	**Fraternity:** No
Women: 57%	**Room & board:** $8,860	**Sorority:** No
Men: 43%	**Housing Information**	**Athletics:** Division III
Percent out-of-state: 31%	**University housing:** Yes	
	Percent living on campus: 70%	

INDIANA UNIVERSITY

300 North Jordan Avenue, Bloomington, IN 47405-1106
Phone: 812-855-0661 • Fax: 812-855-5102
E-mail: iuadmit@indiana.edu • Web: www.iub.edu
Support: CS • Institution type: 4-year public

PROGRAMS OR SERVICES FOR STUDENTS WITH LD

The goal of the Office of Disability Services for Students (DSS) is to provide services that enable students with disabilities to participate in, and benefit from all university programs and activities. There is no specific program for students with LD. However there is a Learning Disabilities Coordinator who provides supportive services necessary to help students pursue their academic objectives. The Briscoe Academic Support Center offers free assistance to all IU students, night and day. During the day, the center is used for study groups, meetings, and advising, and in the evenings it provides free tutoring, advising, and academic support to assist with course assignments and studying. No appointments are necessary. Students with LD must provide current and appropriate psychoeducational evaluations that address: aptitude; achievement; information processing; clear and specific evidence and identification of an LD; test scores/data must be included; evaluations must be done by a qualified professional; and current IEPs are helpful. Students with ADHD must provide documentation that includes: a clear statement of ADHD with a current diagnosis, including a description of supporting symptoms; current testing, preferably within 3 years; a summary of assessment procedures and evaluations used; a summary supporting diagnosis; medical history; suggestions of reasonable accommodations; and current IEP is helpful.

ADMISSION INFORMATION FOR STUDENTS WITH LD/ADHD

College entrance tests required: Yes
Interview required: No
Essay recommended: No
What documentation required for LD: Psycho Ed evaluation to include: relevant historical info, instructional interventions, related services, age diagnosed, objective data (aptitude, achievement, info processing), test scores (standard, percentile and grade equivalents) and describe functional limitations.
With general application: No
To receive services after enrolling: Yes
What documentation required for ADHD: Diagnosis based on DSM-V; history of behaviors impairing functioning in academic setting; diagnostic interview; history of symptoms; evidence of ongoing behaviors.

With general application: No
Submitted to: Office of Disability Services for Students
Special Ed. HS course work accepted: No
Specific course requirements of all applicants: Yes
Separate application required: Yes
# of LD applications submitted each year: NR
# of LD applications accepted yearly: NR
Total # of students receiving LD services: NR
Acceptance into program means acceptance into college: Students must be admitted and enrolled in the university first and then request services.

ADMISSIONS

There is no special admission process for students with learning disabilities. Each applicant is reviewed individually. IU is concerned with the strength of the college-prep program, including senior year, grade trends, and the student's class rank. Students falling below the minimum standards may receive serious consideration for admission if their grades have been steadily improving in a challenging college-prep program. Conversely, declining grades and/or a program of less demanding courses are often reasons to deny admission. 4 years English, 3 years math, 1 year science, 2 years social science, 2 years foreign language, plus additional courses in math, science, social science and/or foreign language to be competitive for admission. Indiana residents must complete Core 40 which includes a minimum of 28 semesters of college-prep courses. Nonresidents must complete a minimum of 32 semester college-prep classes. All students should be enrolled in at least 4 college-prep courses each semester. Students usually rank in the top one-third out-of-state and top half in-state. Students must take either the ACT with Writing or the SAT Reasoning.

ADDITIONAL INFORMATION

Accommodations can be made to provide: test modifications, referrals to tutors, peer note-takers, books on tape, adaptive technology, and priority registration for students needing books on tape. Students must provide appropriate documentation and submit request for services. Students need to request a letter from DSS to give to their professors. No course requirements are waived automatically. Students who have difficulty with math or foreign language should discuss with DSS. The Student Academic Center offers workshops, courses for credit, and individualized academic assesments. No fees.

LEARNING DISABILITY PROGRAMS OR SERVICES

Contact Information
Name of program or department: Disability Services for Students (DSS)
  Telephone: 812-855-7578
  Fax: 812-855-7650

LEARNING DISABILITY SERVICES

Accommodations are decided upon an individual basis after a thorough review of appropriate, current documentation. The accommodations requested must be supported through the documentation provided and must be logically linked to the current impact of the condition on academic functioning.

Allowed in exams	**Distraction-reduced environment:** Yes	**Added costs for services:** No
Calculator: Yes	**Tape recording in class:** Yes	**LD specialists:** Yes
Dictionary: Yes	**Electronic texts:** Yes	**Professional tutors:** No
Computer: Yes	**Accommodations for students with**	**Peer tutors:** Yes
Spellchecker: Yes	**ADHD:** Yes	**Max. hours/wk. for services:** Varies
Extended test time: Yes	**Kurzweil Reader:** Yes	**How professors are notified of**
Scribes: Yes	**Other assistive technology:** Yes	**LD/ADHD:** By student
Proctors: Yes	**Priority registration:** Yes	
Oral exams: Yes		
Note-takers: Yes		

GENERAL ADMISSIONS INFORMATION

Office of Admission: 812-855-0661

ENTRANCE REQUIREMENTS

Academic units required: 4 English, 3 math, 1 science (1 science lab), 2 social studies, 4 academic electives.
Academic units recommended: 4 math, 3 science, 3 foreign language, 3 social studies. High school diploma is required, and GED is accepted. ACT with Writing component required.

Application deadline: None	**SAT Math middle 50% range:**	**Graduated top 10% of class:** 27%
Notification: Rolling	530–640	**Graduated top 25% of class:** 61%
Average GPA: 3.50	**SAT Critical Reading middle 50%**	**Graduated top 50% of class:** 95%
ACT Composite middle 50% range:	**range:** 510–620	
23–29	**SAT Writing middle 50% range:** NR	

COLLEGE GRADUATION REQUIREMENTS

Course waivers allowed: No
Course substitutions allowed: Yes
In what course: There are processes to request accommodations and substitutions in regard to math and foreign language for eligible students with LD. Students are required to attempt the course.

ADDITIONAL INFORMATION

Environment: The university is located in a small town 45 minutes from Indianapolis.

Student Body	**Cost Information**	**Greek System**
Undergrad enrollment: 32,300	**In-state tuition:** $9,525	**Fraternity:** Yes
Women: 50%	**Out-of-state tuition:** $29,540	**Sorority:** Yes
Men: 50%	**Room & board:** $8,520	**Athletics:** Division I
Percent out-of-state: 37%	**Housing Information**	
	University housing: Yes	
	Percent living on campus: 36%	

INDIANA WESLEYAN UNIVERSITY

4201 South Washington Street, Marion, IN 46953-4974
Phone: 765-677-2138 • Fax: 765-677-2333
E-mail: admissions@indwes.edu • Web: www.indwes.edu
Support: S • Institution type: 4-year private

PROGRAMS OR SERVICES FOR STUDENTS WITH LD

The services offered at IWU are designed to assist students who have documented Learning Disabilities through advocacy and provision of appropriate accommodations. The Center for Student Success (CSS) provides academic and tutoring support, counseling, disability accommodation services, and testing. CSS is available to all students who seek assistance with raising the quality of their academic work; however, documentation of diagnosed disability is required to receive accommodation for academic coursework. Developmental Critical Reading, English Composition, and Math courses are required for some students based on low entrance and/or placement test scores.

ADMISSION INFORMATION FOR STUDENTS WITH LD/ADHD

College entrance tests required: Yes
Interview required: No
Essay recommended: No
What documentation required for LD: Psycho Ed evaluation to include: relevant historical info, instructional interventions, related services, age diagnosed, objective data (aptitude, achievement, info processing), test scores (standard, percentile and grade equivalents) and describe functional limitations.
With general application: No
To receive services after enrolling: Yes
What documentation required for ADHD: Diagnosis based on DSM-V; history of behaviors impairing functioning in academic setting; diagnostic interview; history of symptoms; evidence of ongoing behaviors.

With general application: No
Submitted to: The Center for Student Success
Special Ed. HS course work accepted: Yes, with a diploma meeting university admissions standards
Specific course requirements of all applicants: NR
Separate application required: No
# of LD applications submitted each year: NR
# of LD applications accepted yearly: NR
Total # of students receiving LD services: 40
Acceptance into program means acceptance into college: Students are admitted to the university and are eligible to receive services at time of enrollment.

ADMISSIONS

The Office of Admissions seeks students with at least a 2.6 GPA and an ACT of 18 or SAT Reasoning Test of 880. Students not meeting these requirements may be accepted on a conditional status and be required to enroll in a student success program designed to enhance their academic skills. Students with learning disabilities may self-disclose their LD or ADHD through a personal statement attached to the application for admission. There is a separate application for requesting services/accommodations for disabilities that is submitted after a student has been accepted and enrolled.

ADDITIONAL INFORMATION

Students with Reading scores below SAT 460 or below ACT 20 are required to take the COMPASS Reading placement test during new student registration as the opportunity to be exempt from the ENG101 Critical Reading and Study Skills course in their first semester. With appropriate documentation, students with LD/ADHA may be eligible for some of the following services of accommodations: use of calculator, computer, or spellchecker in exams; extended time on tests; note-takers; distraction-free testing; recording device in class; books and tests in electronic format; assistive technology; and priority registration. Workshops for time management test-taking skills, reading, and stress management are also available. The Center for Student Support Services offers academic and personal counseling services for students at the university. Course-specific small group tutoring is available in which groups of up to five students are placed with student tutors for weekly tutoring sessions that run the length of the semester. Additionally there are monthly academic 'check-ups' for students under probationary status. Other services available through the center include study skills assessment and help, test anxiety strategies, personal counseling, short-term assessment and counseling for students with mental health issues, crisis intervention, referral facilitation for medication management/long-term therapy, and tips for recognizing and addressing typical student mental health concerns.

LEARNING DISABILITY PROGRAMS OR SERVICES

Contact Information
Name of program or department: The Center for Student Success
 Telephone: 765-677-2257
 Fax: 765-677-2140

LEARNING DISABILITY SERVICES

Accommodations are decided upon an individual basis after a thorough review of appropriate, current documentation. The accommodations requested must be supported through the documentation provided and must be logically linked to the current impact of the condition on academic functioning.

Allowed in exams
 Calculator: Yes
 Dictionary: Yes
 Computer: Yes
 Spellchecker: Yes
Extended test time: Yes
 Scribes: Yes
 Proctors: Yes
 Oral exams: Yes
 Note-takers: Yes

Distraction-reduced environment: Yes
Tape recording in class: Yes
Electronic texts: Yes
Accommodations for students with
 ADHD: Yes
Kurzweil Reader: Yes
Other assistive technology: Yes
Priority registration: Yes

Added costs for services: No
LD specialists: No
Professional tutors: No
Peer tutors: 230
Max. hours/wk. for services: NR
How professors are notified of
 LD/ADHD: By student

GENERAL ADMISSIONS INFORMATION

Office of Admission: 765-677-2138

ENTRANCE REQUIREMENTS

Academic units recommended: 4 English, 3 math, 3 science, 2 foreign language, 3 social studies, 5 academic electives, 1 health/physical education. High school diploma is required, and GED is accepted. ACT without Writing component accepted. TOEFL required of all international applicants: minimum paper TOEFL 550, minimum computer TOEFL 213.

Application deadline: 8/1
Notification: Rolling
Average GPA: 3.55
ACT Composite middle 50% range:
 21–27

SAT Math middle 50% range:
 470–590
SAT Critical Reading middle 50%
 range: 470–590
SAT Writing middle 50% range:
 460–570

Graduated top 10% of class: 27%
Graduated top 25% of class: 54%
Graduated top 50% of class: 85%

COLLEGE GRADUATION REQUIREMENTS

Course waivers allowed: Yes
In what course: Dependent on course of study and specific disability. Assessed on an individual basis.
Course substitutions allowed: Yes
In what course: Dependent on course of study and specific disability. Assessed on an individual basis.

ADDITIONAL INFORMATION

Environment: The university is located on a 50-acre campus in a rural city 65 miles from Indianapolis and 50 miles south of Fort Wayne.

Student Body
 Undergrad enrollment: 2,582
 (residential)
 Women: 63%
 Men: 37%
 Percent out-of-state: 52%

Cost Information
 Tuition: $23,164
 Room & board: $7,412
Housing Information
 University housing: Yes
 Percent living on campus: 78%

Greek System
 Fraternity: No
 Sorority: No
 Athletics: NAIA

MANCHESTER COLLEGE

604 East College Avenue, North Manchester, IN 46962
Phone: 260-982-5055 • Fax: 260-982-5239
E-mail: admitinfo@manchester.edu • Web: www.manchester.edu
Support: CS • Institution type: 4-year private

PROGRAMS OR SERVICES FOR STUDENTS WITH LD

Manchester College does not have a specific program for students with learning disabilities. The college is, however, very sensitive to all students. The key word at Manchester College is "success," which means graduating in 4 years. The college wants all students to be able to complete their degree in 4 years. The college does provide support services to students identified as disabled to allow them to be successful. The goal is to assist students in their individual needs.

ADMISSION INFORMATION FOR STUDENTS WITH LD/ADHD

College entrance tests required: Yes
Interview required: Yes
Essay recommended: No
What documentation required for LD: Psycho Ed evaluation to include: relevant historical info, instructional interventions, related services, age diagnosed, objective data (aptitude, achievement, info processing), test scores (standard, percentile and grade equivalents) and describe functional limitations.
With general application: No
To receive services after enrolling: Yes
What documentation required for ADHD: Diagnosis based on DSM-V; history of behaviors impairing functioning in academic setting; diagnostic interview; history of symptoms; evidence of ongoing behaviors.

With general application: No
Submitted to: Learning Support Services
Special Ed. HS course work accepted: Yes
Specific course requirements of all applicants: Yes
Separate application required: No
# of LD applications submitted each year: NR
# of LD applications accepted yearly: NR
Total # of students receiving LD services: 20–30
Acceptance into program means acceptance into college: Students must be admitted and enrolled in the university first and then request services.

ADMISSIONS

Students with learning disabilities submit the regular application form, and are required to meet the same admission criteria as all other applicants. Course requirements include 4 years of English, 2 years of math (3 years recommended), 2 years of science (3 years recommended), 2 years of science labs (3 years of science labs recommended), 2 years of a foreign language required, 2 years of social studies, 1 year of history (2 years recommended), and 1 year of an elective (2 years recommended). Average ACT is 22 or SAT Reasoning 990. Students are admitted to the college and use the support services as they choose. If special consideration for admission is requested, it is done individually, based on potential for graduation from the college. Manchester considers a wide range of information in making individual admission decisions. Students are encouraged to provide information beyond what is required on the application form if they believe it will strengthen their application or help the college to understand the students' performance or potential. Students who self-disclose the existence of a learning disability and are denied can ask to appeal the decision and have their application reviewed in a "different" way. The key question that will be asked is if the student can graduate in 4 years or, at the most, 5 years.

ADDITIONAL INFORMATION

The Success Center provides tutoring for all students at the college. A course is offered presenting college level study skills with opportunities for students to apply these skills in their current course texts. Specific topics include time management, note-taking, vocabulary, text study techniques, test-taking, and memory strategies. Other topics include: college expectations, learning styles and assessments, self-management, and educational and career planning.

LEARNING DISABILITY PROGRAMS OR SERVICES

Contact Information
Name of program or department: Academic Success
 Telephone: 260-982-5076
 Fax: 260-982-5888

LEARNING DISABILITY SERVICES

Accommodations are decided upon an individual basis after a thorough review of appropriate, current documentation. The accommodations requested must be supported through the documentation provided and must be logically linked to the current impact of the condition on academic functioning.

Allowed in exams
 Calculator: Yes
 Dictionary: No
 Computer: Yes
 Spellchecker: Yes
Extended test time: Yes
Scribes: Yes
Proctors: Yes
Oral exams: Yes
Note-takers: Yes

Distraction-reduced environment: Yes
Tape recording in class: Yes
Electronic texts: Yes
Accommodations for students with
 ADHD: Yes
Kurzweil Reader: No
Other assistive technology: Yes
Priority registration: No

Added costs for services: No
LD specialists: Yes
Professional tutors: No
Peer tutors: Yes
Max. hours/wk. for services:
 Unlimited
How professors are notified of
 LD/ADHD: By both student and
 director

GENERAL ADMISSIONS INFORMATION

Office of Admission: 260-982-5055

ENTRANCE REQUIREMENTS

Academic units required: 4 English, 2 math, 2 science (2 science labs), 2 foreign language, 2 social studies, 1 history, 1 academic elective. **Academic units recommended:** 4 English, 3 math, 3 science (3 science labs), 2 foreign language, 2 social studies, 2 history, 2 academic electives. High school diploma is required, and GED is accepted. ACT with or without Writing component accepted. TOEFL required of all international applicants: minimum paper TOEFL 550, minimum computer TOEFL 213.

Application deadline: None
Notification: Rolling
Average GPA: NR
ACT Composite middle 50% range:
 19–24

SAT Math middle 50% range:
 470–580
SAT Critical Reading middle 50%
 range: 440–550
SAT Writing middle 50% range:
 430–540

Graduated top 10% of class: NR
Graduated top 25% of class: NR
Graduated top 50% of class: NR

COLLEGE GRADUATION REQUIREMENTS

Course waivers allowed: No
Course substitutions allowed: No

ADDITIONAL INFORMATION

Environment: The college is located in North Manchester, 35 miles southwest of Fort Wayne.

Student Body
 Undergrad enrollment: 1,320
 Women: 51%
 Men: 49%
 Percent out-of-state: 11%

Cost Information
 Tuition: $25,970
 Room & board: $9,100
Housing Information
 University housing: Yes
 Percent living on campus: 74%

Greek System
 Fraternity: No
 Sorority: No
Athletics: Division III

UNIVERSITY OF INDIANAPOLIS

1400 East Hanna Avenue, Indianapolis, IN 46227-3697
Phone: 317-788-3216 • Fax: 317-788-3300
E-mail: admissions@uindy.edu • Web: www.uindy.edu
Support: SP • Institution type: 4-year private

PROGRAMS OR SERVICES FOR STUDENTS WITH LD

The University of Indianapolis offers a full support system for students with learning disabilities called BUILD (Baccalaureate for University of Indianapolis Learning Disabled). The goal of this program is to help students with learning disabilities reach their academic potential. All students with disabilities at the University have reasonable modifications available to them at no extra charge. The BUILD program offers accommodations significantly more in depth than just minimal requirements. Services are comprehensive, and the staff is knowledgeable about learning disabilities.

ADMISSION INFORMATION FOR STUDENTS WITH LD/ADHD

College entrance tests required: Yes
Interview required: Yes
Essay recommended: No
What documentation required for LD: Psycho Ed evaluation to include: relevant historical info, instructional interventions, related services, age diagnosed, objective data (aptitude, achievement, info processing), test scores (standard, percentile and grade equivalents) and describe functional limitations.
With general application: Yes if requested as part of Structured Program application
To receive services after enrolling: Yes
What documentation required for ADHD: Diagnosis based on DSM-V; history of behaviors impairing functioning in academic setting; diagnostic interview; history of symptoms; evidence of ongoing behaviors.

With general application: Yes if requested as part of Structured Program application
To receive services after enrolling: Yes
Submitted to: BUILD
Special Ed. HS course work accepted: No
Specific course requirements of all applicants: Yes
Separate application required: Yes
# of LD applications submitted each year: 50
# of LD applications accepted yearly: 30
Total # of students receiving LD services: 80
Acceptance into program means acceptance into college: Students must be admitted by the university and then admitted to BUILD. If not accepted by admissions, a committee confers.

ADMISSIONS

Admission to the BUILD program occurs after a student has been accepted to the university. Students with LD must meet the university admissions requirements. However, consideration is given for individual strengths and weaknesses. The student must submit the following to the Office of Admissions: university application for admission, high school transcript, SAT or ACT scores (if not on the high school transcript), and $25 application fee (the fee is waived if the student applies on-line at www.uindy.edu.). The student must submit the following to the BUILD Program: current documentation regarding I.Q. scores, reading and math proficiency level, primary learning style, and major learning difficulty. After BUILD reviews the information, interviews will be arranged for those applicants being considered for final selection into the BUILD Program. Acceptance into BUILD is determined by the program director.

ADDITIONAL INFORMATION

The director assigns tutors to each student in BUILD. All students must have at least 2 hours per week of individualized tutoring. Books on CD, test modifications, and group study are also provided. Course substitution is a possibility. BUILD offers three special courses to meet university requirements for English and math proficiency, all other classes are regular classes. Students are limited to 12 hours each semester until they can demonstrate academic success indicating they can handle the demands of a heavier course load. Other services include: a specialized study skills course; specialized note-taking paper; test-taking arrangements; private study area; advice with course selection and career planning; possible course substitution; diagnostic testing referrals; and other aids such as books on tape, compressed-time tape recorders, and computers.

LEARNING DISABILITY PROGRAMS OR SERVICES

Contact Information
Name of program or department: Baccalaureate for University of Indianapolis Learning Disabled (BUILD)
Telephone: 317-788-3536
Fax: 317-788-3585

LEARNING DISABILITY SERVICES

Accommodations are decided upon an individual basis after a thorough review of appropriate, current documentation. The accommodations requested must be supported through the documentation provided and must be logically linked to the current impact of the condition on academic functioning.

Allowed in exams	**Distraction-reduced environment:** Yes	**Added costs for services:** Yes
Calculator: Yes	**Tape recording in class:** Yes	**LD specialists:** Yes
Dictionary: Yes	**Electronic texts:** No	**Professional tutors:** 25
Computer: Yes	**Accommodations for students with**	**Peer tutors:** No
Spellchecker: Yes	**ADHD:** Yes	**Max. hours/wk. for services:**
Extended test time: Yes	**Kurzweil Reader:** Yes	Unlimited
Scribes: Yes	**Other assistive technology:** Yes	**How professors are notified of**
Proctors: Yes	**Priority registration:** No	**LD/ADHD:** By both student and
Oral exams: Yes		director
Note-takers: No		

GENERAL ADMISSIONS INFORMATION

Office of Admission: 317-788-3216.

ENTRANCE REQUIREMENTS

Academic units required: 4 English, 3 math, 2 science (1 science lab), 1 social studies, 1 history, 3 academic electives. **Academic units recommended:** 4 English, 4 math, 3 science (2 science labs), 2 foreign language, 1 social studies, 1 history, 3 academic electives. High school diploma is required, and GED is accepted. ACT with or without Writing component accepted. TOEFL required of all international applicants: minimum paper TOEFL 500, minimum computer TOEFL 173.

Application deadline: Recommended by 12/1	**SAT Math middle 50% range:** 460–570	**Graduated top 10% of class:** 27%
Notification: Rolling	**SAT Critical Reading middle 50% range:** 450–560	**Graduated top 25% of class:** 56%
Average GPA: 3.4		**Graduated top 50% of class:** 88%
ACT Composite middle 50% range: 19–25	**SAT Writing middle 50% range:** 440–550	

COLLEGE GRADUATION REQUIREMENTS

Course waivers allowed: No
Course substitutions allowed: Yes
In what course: Modern language requirements

ADDITIONAL INFORMATION

Environment: The 70-acre campus in a suburban neighborhood is located 10 miles south of downtown Indianapolis.

Student Body	**Cost Information**	**Greek System**
Undergrad enrollment: 3,590	Tuition: $22,790	Fraternity: No
Women: 69%	Room & board: $8,730	Sorority: No
Men: 31%	**Housing Information**	Athletics: Division II
Percent out-of-state: 12%	University housing: Yes	
	Percent living on campus: 48%	

UNIVERSITY OF NOTRE DAME

220 Main Building, Notre Dame, IN 46556
Phone: 574-631-7505 • Fax: 574-631-8865
E-mail: admissions@nd.edu • Web: www.nd.edu
Support: S • Institution type: 4-year private

PROGRAMS OR SERVICES FOR STUDENTS WITH LD

The Coordinator of Disability Services provides reasonable accommodations for qualified students with disabilities. To become eligible for accommodations, a student must register with the office by providing recent documentation of their disability. Registered students are responsible for requesting accommodations each semester. The mission of the office is to provide or coordinate reasonable accommodations. A reasonable accommodation is a modification or adjustment to a course, program, or activity that enables a qualified student with a disability to obtain equal access. The accommodations provided are in response to a student's perceived barrier to access. In other words, a student must, at a minimum, identify how their disability is preventing them from having access. Therefore, the services and accommodations provided are intended to reasonable remove a barrier. The office does not provide treatment or teach students how to minimize the impact of their disability. Instead, reasonable modifications are made to a course, program, or facility to allow the same access as experienced by students without disabilities. An accommodation is considered reasonable only if it does not significantly alter the essential components of a course or program.

ADMISSION INFORMATION FOR STUDENTS WITH LD/ADHD

College entrance tests required: Yes
Interview required: No
Essay recommended: No
What documentation required for LD: Psycho Ed evaluation to include: relevant historical info, instructional interventions, related services, age diagnosed, objective data (aptitude, achievement, info processing), test scores (standard, percentile and grade equivalents) and describe functional limitations.
With general application: No
To receive services after enrolling: Yes
What documentation required for ADHD: Diagnosis based on DSM-V; history of behaviors impairing functioning in academic setting; diagnostic interview; history of symptoms; evidence of ongoing behaviors.

With general application: No
Submitted to: Office for Students with Disabilities
Special Ed. HS course work accepted: N/A
Specific course requirements of all applicants: Yes
Separate application required: No
# of LD applications submitted each year: NR
# of LD applications accepted yearly: NR
Total # of students receiving LD services: 0–75
Acceptance into program means acceptance into college: Students must be admitted and enrolled in the university first and then request services.

ADMISSIONS

The university does not have a special admission process for students with learning disabilities. All students submit the same application and are expected to meet the same admission criteria. Admission to the university is highly competitive. The university seeks to enroll an exceptionally distinguished student body from among its broadly diverse and richly talented applicant pool. The Admissions Office prides itself on reviewing each application individually and with care. Students are expected to have 4 years of English, 4 years of math, 4 years of science, 2 years of a foreign language, 2 years of social studies, and 3 years of additional courses from these mentioned areas.

ADDITIONAL INFORMATION

At the start of each semester students must meet with the Coordinator to discuss their needs for the semester. Current documentation must be on file at the Disability Services office to be eligible for accommodations. The accommodations that are used the most include testing accommodations, note takers, textbooks and course material in audio, large print, or electronic format, and foreign language substitution. In many situations, information provided by Disability Services to a professor will open a dialogue with the office, student, and professor so that appropriate accommodations can be discussed and implemented. Information from a doctor must be provided to be eligible for services and reasonable accommodations. Documentation must be no older than three years when entering the University. It must include a diagnosis of a disability and describe the functional limitations caused by it. Guidelines for documentation of a learning disability or attention deficit hyperactivity disorder can be found at: www.ets.org/disability/index.html. It is the student's responsibility to identify his or her disability and request accommodations. Once documentation is on file at Disability Services the student must meet with the Coordinator at the start of each semester to request services.

LEARNING DISABILITY PROGRAMS OR SERVICES

Contact Information
Name of program or department: Disability Services
  Telephone: 574-631-7157
  Fax: 574-631-2133

LEARNING DISABILITY SERVICES

Accommodations are decided upon an individual basis after a thorough review of appropriate, current documentation. The accommodations requested must be supported through the documentation provided and must be logically linked to the current impact of the condition on academic functioning.

Allowed in exams	**Distraction-reduced environment:** Yes	**Added costs for services:** No
Calculator: If reasonable	**Tape recording in class:** Yes	**LD specialists:** No
Dictionary: If reasonable	**Electronic texts:** Yes	**Professional tutors:** NR
Computer: Yes	**Accommodations for students with**	**Peer tutors:** No
Spellchecker: Yes	**ADHD:** Yes	**Max. hours/wk. for services:**
Extended test time: Yes	**Kurzweil Reader:** Yes	Unlimited
Scribes: Yes	**Other assistive technology:** Yes	**How professors are notified of**
Proctors: Yes	**Priority registration:** Yes	**LD/ADHD:** By student
Oral exams: If reasonable		
Note-takers: Yes		

GENERAL ADMISSIONS INFORMATION

Office of Admission: 574-631-7505

ENTRANCE REQUIREMENTS

Academic units required: 4 English, 4 math, 4 science, 2 foreign language, 2 social studies, 3 academic electives.
Academic units recommended: 4 English, 4 math, 4 science, 4 foreign language, 4 social studies. High school diploma is required, and GED is not accepted. ACT with or without Writing component accepted. TOEFL required of all international applicants: minimum paper TOEFL 600, minimum computer TOEFL 250.

Application deadline: 12/31	**SAT Math middle 50% range:**	**Graduated top 10% of class:** 89%
Notification: 4/10	680–770	**Graduated top 25% of class:** 97%
Average GPA: NR	**SAT Critical Reading middle 50%**	**Graduated top 50% of class:** 99%
ACT Composite middle 50% range:	**range:** 660–750	
32–34	**SAT Writing middle 50% range:**	
	650–740	

COLLEGE GRADUATION REQUIREMENTS

Course waivers allowed: No
Course substitutions allowed: Yes
In what course: Students with supportive documentation can receive a substitution course for the foreign language requirement.

ADDITIONAL INFORMATION

Environment: The university is located in a suburban area about 1.5 hours from Chicago.

Student Body	**Cost Information**	**Greek System**
Undergrad enrollment: 8,452	**Tuition:** $42,464	**Fraternity:** No
Women: 47%	**Room & board:** $11,394	**Sorority:** No
Men: 53%	**Housing Information**	**Athletics:** Division I
Percent out-of-state: 91%	**University housing:** Yes	
	Percent living on campus: 81%	

UNIVERSITY OF SAINT FRANCIS (IN)

2701 Spring Street, Fort Wayne, IN 46808
Phone: 260-399-8065 • Fax: 260-399-8161
E-mail: admis@sf.edu • Web: www.sf.edu
Support: CS • Institution type: 4-year private

PROGRAMS OR SERVICES FOR STUDENTS WITH LD

Student Academic Support Services (SASS) provides reasonable academic accommodations for students with diagnosed and documented disabilities. Students are self-advocates and develop skills to become independent learners. SASS provides accommodations to ensure students have access to the college environment. Students are encouraged to meet with the Director of SASS prior to the start of the semester to discuss accommodations available to provide the most opportunity for the student as the semester begins. SASS offers coordinated services to students with documentation but no formal program is available.

ADMISSION INFORMATION FOR STUDENTS WITH LD/ADHD

College entrance tests required: ACT or SAT
Interview required: No
Essay recommended: Not due to disability but may be for other admissions requirements
Documentation required for LD: The most recent psychological evaluation and the most recent individual education plan.
Documentation required for ADHD: Yes
Submitted to: Academic Support Services
Special Ed. HS course work accepted: No

Specific course requirements of all applicants: Nothing based on disability
Separate application required: No
# of LD applications submitted each year: NR
# of LD applications accepted yearly: NR
Total # of students receiving LD services: Varies by semester
Acceptance into program means acceptance into college: Students must be admitted and enrolled in the university first and then request services. Coordinated services are offered; not a specific LD/ADHD program.

ADMISSIONS
There is no special admission process for students with learning disabilities. Entrance is based on an overall evaluation of the student's high school transcript, recommendations, and test scores. Automatic admission is granted for students with a HS GPA of 2.3 or higher and either 21 on ACT or 1000 on SAT. Some students may be asked to write a personal statement or essay based on admissions criteria below the automatic admission level—disability is not a factor in this process. Students may be listed as full admit, admit MAP, or admit part-time.

ADDITIONAL INFORMATION
Incoming students may be required to take placement exams in reading, English, math, and computers to determine appropriate entry level courses. Skills developing courses are offered based on student placement. All university students are encouraged to access available tutoring. We offer both in person and online tutoring to all USF students. Disability accommodations are determined after documentation evaluation and student intake interview. Some regular accommodations include but are not limited to: alternative testing location, extended time, note-taking assistance (when the student is in class), books in alternative formats, reading of exams, and others as determined on a case by case basis. Students are encouraged to meet with Assistant Director (or designee) weekly or as needed for assistance with organization, time management, and other study skills beneficial in college.

LEARNING DISABILITY PROGRAMS OR SERVICES

Contact Information
Name of program or department: Student Academic Support Services
  Telephone: 260-339-8065
  Fax: 260-339-8161

LEARNING DISABILITY SERVICES

Accommodations are decided upon an individual basis after a thorough review of appropriate, current documentation. The accommodations requested must be supported through the documentation provided and must be logically linked to the current impact of the condition on academic functioning.

Allowed in exams (When supported through documentation, determined on a case by case basis)
Calculator: Yes
Dictionary: Yes
Computer: Yes
Spellchecker: Yes
Extended test time: Yes
Scribes: Yes
Proctors: Yes
Oral exams: Yes
Note-takers: Yes

Distraction-reduced environment: Yes
Tape recording in class: Yes, when student is present in class
Electronic texts: As available
Accommodations for students with ADHD: Yes, based on documentation
Kurzweil Reader: Yes
Other assistive technology: Yes
Priority registration: No

Added costs for services: No
LD specialists: No
Professional tutors: Yes
Peer tutors: Yes
Max. hours/wk. for services: Predominantly during business hours but no limit per student per week.
How professors are notified of LD/ADHD: Confidential student summary latter delivered by student

GENERAL ADMISSIONS INFORMATION

Office of Admission: 260-399-8000 **Toll Free:** 800-729-4732

ENTRANCE REQUIREMENTS

Academic units recommended: 4 English, 3 math, 2 science (2 science labs), 2 foreign language, 2 social studies. High school diploma is required. TOEFL required of all international applicants.

Application deadline: Rolling
Notification: Rolling
Average GPA: 3.22
ACT Composite middle 50% range: 18–24

SAT Math middle 50% range: 430–540
SAT Critical Reading middle 50% range: 430–540
SAT Writing middle 50% range: 410–520

Graduated top 10% of class: 10%
Graduated top 25% of class: 42%
Graduated top 50% of class: 78%

COLLEGE GRADUATION REQUIREMENTS

Course waivers allowed: Yes, in some courses
Course substitutions allowed: Yes, in some courses

ADDITIONAL INFORMATION

Environment: The 70-acre campus is located west of Fort Wayne.

Student Body
Undergrad enrollment: 1,857
Women: 69%
Men: 31%
Percent out-of-state: 17%

Cost Information
Tuition: $23, 950
Room & board: $7,666
Housing Information
University housing: Yes
Percent living on campus: 16%

Greek System
Fraternity: No
Sorority: No
Athletics: NAIA

UNIVERSITY OF SOUTHERN INDIANA

8600 University Boulevard, Evansville, IN 47712
Phone: 812-464-1765 • Fax: 812-465-7154
E-mail: enroll@usi.edu • Web: www.usi.edu
Support: S • Institution: 4-year public

PROGRAMS OR SERVICES FOR STUDENTS WITH LD

Counseling Center staff provide resources to assist students with disabilities so they can participate in educational programming. This is accomplished by offering student support and advocacy, being available for student and faculty consultation, and providing specific accommodation resources. Students must have a professionally diagnosed disabilty to qualify for use disability resources.

ADMISSION INFORMATION FOR STUDENTS WITH LD/ADHD

College entrance tests required: Yes
Interview required: N/A
Essay required: Yes
Documentation required for LD: USI's Verification of Disability Form filled out by the appropriate professional, including a complete diagnostic report. Testing older than three years may not be accepted.
Documentation required for ADHD: USI's Verification of Disability Form filled out by the appropriate professional, including a complete diagnostic report or diagnostic narrative. Testing older than three years may not be accepted.
Submitted to: Counseling Center

Special Ed. HS course work accepted: Yes
Specific course requirements for all applicants: NR
Separate application required for program services: Yes
# of LD applications submitted each year: 50–60
# of LD applications accepted yearly: 50–60
Total # of students receiving LD services: 62
Acceptance into program means acceptance into college: Separate application required after student has enrolled

ADMISSIONS

Admissions criteria are the same for all students; however, the admissions office will always work with students on an individual basis if needed. In general, students with a 3.6 GPA or higher are admitted with honors. Students with a 2.0–3.5 GPA are admitted in good standing, and students with a GPA below a 2.0 are accepted conditionally. The conditional admissions procedure is for new freshmen who earned below a 2.0 in English, math, science, and social studies. The following are required for those admitted conditionally: freshman seminar; 2.0 GPA; registration through the University Division rather than a specific major; enrollment in no more than 12 credit hours. ACT/SAT scores are used for placement purposes.

ADDITIONAL INFORMATION

In order to use resources for a disability, professional documentation of a disability attached to the university's Verification of Disability form must be provided by the student. Skills classes are offered in basic grammar, algebra review, reading, and study skills. Credit is given for the hours, but the grades are Pass/No Pass. There are no paid note-takers, but special supplies and copy services are provided at no charge to allow the students to get copies of other students'notes. Other services include: assistance obtaining alternative format textbooks; test accommodations; and advocacy and counseling. Services and accommodations are available for undergraduate and graduate students.

PROGRAM FOR DISABILITY SERVICES

Contact Information
Name of program or department: Program/Services for Special Need Students Counseling Center
  Telephone: 812-464-1867
  Fax: 812-461-5288

LEARNING DISABILITY SERVICES

Accommodations are decided upon an individual basis after a thorough review of appropriate, current documentation. The accommodations requested must be supported through the documentation provided and must be logically linked to the current impact of the condition on academic functioning.

Allowed in exams
  Calculator: Yes
  Dictionary: No
  Computer: Yes
  Spellchecker: Yes
Extended test time: Yes
Scribes: Yes
Proctors: Yes
Oral exams: Yes
Note-takers: Yes

Distraction-reduced environment: Yes
Tape recording in class: Yes
Electronic texts: Yes
Accommodations for students with
  ADHD: Yes
Kurzweil Reader: No
Other assistive technology: special
  requests for AT considered
Priority registration: Yes

Added costs for services: No
LD specialists: No
Professional tutors: NR
Peer tutors: 25–50
Max. hours/wk. for services:
  Unlimited
How professors are notified of
  LD/ADHD: Student

GENERAL ADMISSIONS INFORMATION

Office of Admission: 812-464-1765

ENTRANCE REQUIREMENTS

Academic units recommended: 4 English, 4 mathematics, 2 science, 2 foreign language, 2 social studies, 2 history, 2 academic electives. High school diploma is required and GED is accepted. SAT or ACT required; ACT with Writing component required. TOEFL required of all international applicants; minimum paper TOEFL 525, minimum computer TOEFL 197, minimum web-based TOEFL 71.

Application deadline: 8/15
Notification: Rolling
Average GPA: 3.02
ACT Composite middle 50% range:
  18–23

SAT Math middle 50% range:
  420–540
SAT Critical Reading middle 50%
  range: 420–530
SAT Writing middle 50% range:
  410–510

Graduated top 10% of class: 12%
Graduated top 25% of class: 31%
Graduated top 50% of class: 64%

COLLEGE GRADUATION REQUIREMENTS

Course waivers allowed: No
Course substitutions allowed: Yes
In what course: Math and physical education courses are considered for substitution when detailed documentation and a written request is submitted through the student's advisor.

ADDITIONAL INFORMATION

Environment: The university is located on 300 acres in a suburban area 150 miles south of Indianapolis.

Student Body
  Undergrad enrollment: 17,846
  Women: 61%
  Men: 39%
  Percent out-of-state: 7%

Cost Information
  In-state tuition: $5,740r
  Out-of-state tuition: $3,386
  Room and board: $7,200
Housing Information
  University housing: Yes
  Percent living on campus: 28%

Greek System
  Fraternity: Yes
  Sorority: Yes
Athletics: Division II

VINCENNES UNIVERSITY

1002 North First Street, Vincennes, IN 47591
Phone: 800-742-9198 • Fax: 812-888-8888
E-mail: vuadmit@vinu.edu • Web: www.vinu.edu
Support: SP • Institution type: 4-year public

PROGRAMS OR SERVICES FOR STUDENTS WITH LD

Students Transition into Education Program (STEP) is a LD support program for students in the mainstream. Students' strengths are the emphasis; compensatory techniques rather than remediation are the thrust. STEP is designed to develop unique abilities, achieve academic potential, and develop a sense of self-worth and skills to function and learn independently. Students take four semesters in STEP I–IV: The course teaches requisite social, study, and self-awareness skills and serves as a support group. The curriculum is practical and emphasizes active thinking, independent learning, student accountability, and the acquisition of specific strategies proven to improve academic performance. STEP I addresses self-advocacy, compensatory techniques, coping, adaptation, stress, and socialization; II emphasizes socialization and metacognitive skills; III further develops social skills and solidifies study skills; IV emphasizes career planning, job-search, and social skills, and includes the STEP retreat. COPE Student Support Services (seperate from STEP) is a Trio Program requiring that the student meet one of three requirements: first generation college student, low income, or disabled.

ADMISSION INFORMATION FOR STUDENTS WITH LD/ADHD

College entrance tests required: No
Interview required: No
Essay recommended: No
What documentation required for LD: Psycho Ed evaluation to include: relevant historical info, instructional interventions, related services, age diagnosed, objective data (aptitude, achievement, info processing), test scores (standard, percentile and grade equivalents) and describe functional limitations.
With general application: Yes if requested as part of Structured Program application
To receive services after enrolling: Yes
What documentation required for ADHD: Diagnosis based on DSM-V; history of behaviors impairing functioning in academic setting; diagnostic interview; history of symptoms; evidence of ongoing behaviors.

With general application: Yes if requested as part of Structured Program application
To receive services after enrolling: Yes
Submitted to: STEP
Special Ed. HS course work accepted: Yes
Specific course requirements of all applicants: NR
Separate application required: Yes
# of LD applications submitted each year: 200
# of LD applications accepted yearly: 40
Total # of students receiving LD services: 100–120
Acceptance into program means acceptance into college: Students must apply separately to the university and STEP or Cope. Students will be accepted to the university first and then to the STEP or Cope.

ADMISSIONS

Students with learning disabilities must submit the general application. SAT and ACT scores are not required for other majors, however they are used for placement in course levels appropriate to a student's academic preparation. If students have not taken the SAT or ACT, they will be required to take a placement test before they can register for classes. Students with learning disabilities must apply separately to STEP: Send the STEP application; psychological evaluation; and letters of recommendation from LD specialists, counselors, or teachers. The transcript is less important and recommendations more important. Admission is based on determination of student eligibility, available funding, and space remaining. Early application is important. Students applying to Cope should apply separately to the university prior to applying to STEP.

ADDITIONAL INFORMATION

STEP benefits include an LD specialist for individualized tutoring/remediation, professional/peer tutoring, specialized remedial and/or support classes, weekly academic monitoring, special classes, reduced class load, auditing class before taking test modifications, papers rather than tests, and alternative ways to demonstrate competency. STEP does not exempt students from classes, class requirements, or provide taped books and note-takers. Cope provides individual counselor to assist with needs; tutoring; progress reports; academic advising; appropriate accommodations; academic support groups; and workshops on study skills, test anxiety, self-esteem, and interview skills. The Study Skills Center is open to all students.

LEARNING DISABILITY PROGRAMS OR SERVICES

Contact Information
Name of program or department: Students Transition into Education Program (STEP)
 Telephone: 812-888-4212
 Fax: 812-888-5531

LEARNING DISABILITY SERVICES

Accommodations are decided upon an individual basis after a thorough review of appropriate, current documentation. The accommodations requested must be supported through the documentation provided and must be logically linked to the current impact of the condition on academic functioning.

Allowed in exams
 Calculator: Yes
 Dictionary: Yes
 Computer: Yes
 Spellchecker: Yes
Extended test time: Yes
Scribes: Yes
Proctors: Yes
Oral exams: Yes
Note-takers: Yes

Distraction-reduced environment: Yes
Tape recording in class: Yes
Electronic texts: Yes
Accommodations for students with ADHD: Yes
Kurzweil Reader: Yes
Other assistive technology: Yes
Priority registration: Yes

Added costs for services: $425 per semester
LD specialists: Yes
Professional tutors: 10–20
Peer tutors: 25–45
Max. hours/wk. for services: N/A
How professors are notified of LD/ADHD: By both student and director

GENERAL ADMISSIONS INFORMATION

Office of Admission: 800-742-9198

ENTRANCE REQUIREMENTS:

ACT/SAT not required for admission.

Application deadline: None
Notification: Rolling
Average GPA: NR
ACT Composite middle 50% range: NR

SAT Math middle 50% range: NR
SAT Critical Reading middle 50% range: NR
SAT Writing middle 50% range: NR

Graduated top 10% of class: NR
Graduated top 25% of class: NR
Graduated top 50% of class: NR

COLLEGE GRADUATION REQUIREMENTS

Course waivers allowed: NR
Course substitutions allowed: NR

ADDITIONAL INFORMATION

Environment: The school is located on 95 acres 45 minutes south of Terre Haute.

Student Body
 Undergrad enrollment: 8,848
 Women: 40%
 Men: 60%
 Percent out-of-state: 36%

Cost Information
 In-state tuition: $13,573
 Out-of-state tuition: $19,990
 Room & board: Included
Housing Information
 University housing: Yes
 Percent living on campus: 44%

Greek System
 Fraternity: Yes
 Sorority: Yes
Athletics: NJCAA

DRAKE UNIVERSITY

2507 University Avenue, Des Moines, IA 50311-4505
Phone: 515-271-3181 • Fax: 515-271-2831
E-mail: admission@drake.edu • Web: www.choose.drake.edu
Support: S • Institution type: 4-year private

PROGRAMS OR SERVICES FOR STUDENTS WITH LD

The Student Disability Services' purpose is to facilitate and enhance the opportunity for students with any type of disability to successfully complete their postsecondary education. The SDS is committed to enriching the academic experience of Drake students with disabilities through individualized assessment of accommodations and resource needs. To initiate a request for services, students should contact the SDS. An appointment will be made with a staff member to begin the registration process. Students are encouraged to meet with a SDS counselor each semester to identify accommodations that are needed. It is the students' responsibility to self-identify that they have a learning disability; to provide professional documentation of their disability; and to request the accommodations that they need. The SDS office maintains a collection of information on disabilities, and there are many sources on the instruction and evaluation of students with disabilities. SDS encourages faculty, staff, and students to contact the office if they are interested in this type of information.

ADMISSION INFORMATION FOR STUDENTS WITH LD/ADHD

College entrance tests required: Yes
Interview required: No
Essay recommended: No
What documentation required for LD: Psycho Ed evaluation to include: relevant historical info, instructional interventions, related services, age diagnosed, objective data (aptitude, achievement, info processing), test scores (standard, percentile and grade equivalents) and describe functional limitations.
With general application: No
To receive services after enrolling: Yes
What documentation required for ADHD: Diagnosis based on DSM-V; history of behaviors impairing functioning in academic setting; diagnostic interview; history of symptoms; evidence of ongoing behaviors.

With general application: No
Submitted to: Student Disability Services
Special Ed. HS course work accepted: Yes
Specific course requirements of all applicants: Yes
Separate application required: No
# of LD applications submitted each year: NR
# of LD applications accepted yearly: NR
Total # of students receiving LD services: NR
Acceptance into program means acceptance into college: Student must be admitted and enrolled in the university first and then reviewed for LD services.

ADMISSIONS

There is no special admission process for students with learning disabilities. All applicants are expected to meet the same admission criteria, including 16 academic college-prep courses with a minimum of 4 years of English, 2 years of math, 2 years of science, 2 years of social studies, 1 year of history, and 2 years of a foreign language; 21 ACT or 970 SAT; and a minimum of a 2.0 GPA. Students must be admitted and enrolled in the university prior to seeking accommodations or services for a learning disability.

ADDITIONAL INFORMATION

The SDS can offer students appointments at the pre-admission and pre-enrollment stages; review of Drake's policies and procedures regarding students with disabilities; identification and coordination of classroom accommodations; assessment of service needs; note-takers, scribes, and readers; referral to appropriate campus resources; advocacy and liaison with the university community; and training on the use of assistive technology. Services provided by the SDS do not lower any course standards or change any requirements of a particular degree. The services are intended to allow equal access and provide an opportunity for students with disabilities to demonstrate their abilities.

LEARNING DISABILITY PROGRAMS OR SERVICES

Contact Information
Name of program or department: Student Disability Services
Telephone: 515-271-1835
Fax: 515-271-1855

LEARNING DISABILITY SERVICES

Accommodations are decided upon an individual basis after a thorough review of appropriate, current documentation. The accommodations requested must be supported through the documentation provided and must be logically linked to the current impact of the condition on academic functioning.

Allowed in exams
   Calculator: Yes
   Dictionary: Yes
   Computer: Yes
   Spellchecker: Yes
Extended test time: Yes
Scribes: Yes
Proctors: Yes
Oral exams: Yes
Note-takers: Yes

Distraction-reduced environment: Yes
Tape recording in class: Yes
Electronic texts: Yes
Accommodations for students with ADHD: Yes
Kurzweil Reader: Yes
Other assistive technology: Yes
Priority registration: No

Added costs for services: No
LD specialists: No
Professional tutors: No
Peer tutors: 30–40
Max. hours/wk. for services: Unlimited
How professors are notified of LD/ADHD: By student

GENERAL ADMISSIONS INFORMATION

Office of Admission: 515-271-3182

ENTRANCE REQUIREMENTS

Academic units recommended: 4 English, 3 math, 2 science, 2 foreign language, 4 social studies. High school diploma is required, and GED is accepted. ACT with or without Writing component accepted. TOEFL required of all international applicants: minimum paper TOEFL 545, minimum computer TOEFL 252.

Application deadline: None
Notification: Rolling
Average GPA: 3.7
ACT Composite middle 50% range: 25–29

SAT Math middle 50% range: 580–680
SAT Critical Reading middle 50% range: 530–650
SAT Writing middle 50% range: NR

Graduated top 10% of class: 42%
Graduated top 25% of class: 75%
Graduated top 50% of class: 95%

COLLEGE GRADUATION REQUIREMENTS

Course waivers allowed: No
Course substitutions allowed: Yes
In what course: Documentation must be provided and is considered on a case-by-case basis.

ADDITIONAL INFORMATION

Environment: The campus is located in the suburbs of Des Moines.

Student Body
   Undergrad enrollment: 3,438
   Women: 56%
   Men: 44%
   Percent out-of-state: 62%

Cost Information
   Tuition: $29,410
   Room & board: $8,680
Housing Information
   University housing: Yes
   Percent living on campus: 71%

Greek System
   Fraternity: Yes
   Sorority: Yes
Athletics: Division I

GRAND VIEW UNIVERSITY

1200 Grandview Avenue, Des Moines, IA 50316-1599
Phone: 515-263-2810 • Fax: 515-263-2974
E-mail: admissions@grandview.edu • Web: www.admissions.grandview.edu
Support: CS • Institution type: 4-year private

PROGRAMS OR SERVICES FOR STUDENTS WITH LD

The Academic Success Program is available for all students on campus. The objective of the program is to provide a variety of learning environments and teaching techniques. Academic Success provides academic support programs, services and courses designed to optimize student performance. Students who participate in these services make a smoother transition to Grand View, develop social and academic networks essential to their success, and benefit from informal student-faculty-staff interactions. Grand View is committed to enriching the academic experience of every qualified student with LD and endorses reasonable accommodations for participation in all programs and activities. Students are encouraged to make an appointment in the Academic and Career Center to review college policies and procedures, request accommodations, develop an accommodation plan, or discuss personal advocacy issues.

ADMISSION INFORMATION FOR STUDENTS WITH LD/ADHD

College entrance tests required: Yes
Interview required: No
Essay recommended: No
Documentation required for LD: Verification of learning disabilities by licensed psychologist required.
Documentation required for ADHD: Verification of learning disabilities by licensed psychologist required.
Submitted to: Academic Success
Special Ed. HS course work accepted: Yes

Specific course requirements of all applicants: No
Separate application required: No
# of LD applications submitted each year: NR
# of LD applications accepted yearly: NR
Total # of students receiving LD services: 15
Acceptance into program means acceptance into college: Students must be admitted and enrolled prior to requesting services.

ADMISSIONS

There is no special admissions process for students with LD and ADHD. There is a provisional admit for students who do not have sufficient preparation to undertake college work but show potential for success in college. Grand View has a personalized admission and enrollment policy. Consideration may be given to: class rank and test scores; quality of high school curriculum completed; co-curricular achievement; and maturity and seriousness of purpose as displayed through church, community, school, work, and family activities. Students planning to attend Grand View University are encouraged to pursue a college-preparatory course of study in high school. It is recommended that students complete: Four years of English, three years of math, three years of science, three years of social science and two years of foreign language. Admission to a particular program or major may be governed by different standards.

ADDITIONAL INFORMATION

Academic Success provides resources which complement classroom instruction enabling students to optimize their academic experience. Students can receive help with reading comprehension, study skills, organizational skills, developing a personal management plan, test-taking strategies, writing skills, personalized instruction in math, and peer tutoring. The Career Center provides services, resources, and educational opportunities by assisting students in developing, evaluating, initiating, and implementing personal career and life plans. Faculty members serve as academic advisors. Core courses can have substitutions options. Other services or accommodations offered for students with appropriate documentation include the use of calculators, computers, or spellcheckers; extended testing time; scribes; proctors; oral exams; note-takers; a distraction-free environment for taking tests; tape-recording of lectures; and services for students with ADHD.

LEARNING DISABILITY PROGRAMS OR SERVICES

Contact Information
Name of program or department: Academic Success
   Telephone: 515-263-2971
   Fax: 515-263-2824

LEARNING DISABILITY SERVICES

Accommodations are decided upon an individual basis after a thorough review of appropriate, current documentation. The accommodations requested must be supported through the documentation provided and must be logically linked to the current impact of the condition on academic functioning.

Allowed in exams	**Distraction-reduced environment:** Yes	**Added costs for services:** No
Calculator: Yes	**Tape recording in class:** Yes	**LD specialists:** Yes
Dictionary: Yes	**Electronic texts:** Yes	**Professional tutors:** 1
Computer: Yes	**Accommodations for students with**	**Peer tutors:** NR
Spellchecker: Yes	**ADHD:** Yes	**Max. hours/wk. for services:**
Extended test time: Yes	**Kurzweil Reader:** Yes	Unlimited
Scribes: Yes	**Other assistive technology:** Yes	**How professors are notified of**
Proctors: Yes	**Priority registration:** Yes	**LD/ADHD:** By student in collaboration
Oral exams: Yes		with the director
Note-takers: Yes		

GENERAL ADMISSIONS INFORMATION

Office of Admission: 515-263-2810

ENTRANCE REQUIREMENTS

Academic units recommended: 4 English, 3 math, 3 science, 2 foreign language, 3 social studies. High school diploma is required, and GED is accepted. ACT without Writing component accepted. TOEFL required of all international applicants: minimum paper TOEFL 550, minimum computer TOEFL 77.

Application deadline: Rolling	**SAT Math middle 50% range:**	**Graduated top 10% of class:** 11%
Notification: Rolling	420–490	**Graduated top 25% of class:** 29%
Average GPA: 3.14	**SAT Critical Reading middle 50%**	**Graduated top 50% of class:** 63%
ACT Composite middle 50% range:	**range:** 380–450	
18–23	**SAT Writing middle 50% range:**	
	350–450	

COLLEGE GRADUATION REQUIREMENTS

Course waivers allowed: No
Course substitutions allowed: Yes
In what course: Substitutions/options vary.

ADDITIONAL INFORMATION

Environment: Located in Des Moines		
Student Body	**Cost Information**	**Greek System**
Undergrad enrollment: 2,195	**Tuition:** $22,088	**Fraternity:** No
Women: 58%	**Room & board:** $7,316	**Sorority:** No
Men: 42%	**Housing Information**	**Athletics:** NAIA
Percent out-of-state: 10%	**University housing:** Yes	
	Percent living on campus: 36%	

GRINNELL COLLEGE

1103 Park Street, Grinnell, IA 50112-1690
Phone: 641-269-3600 • Fax: 641-269-4800
E-mail: askgrin@grinnell.edu • Web: www.grinnell.edu
Support: S • Institution type: 4-year private

PROGRAMS OR SERVICES FOR STUDENTS WITH LD

Grinnell College is dedicated to educating young people whose achievements show a high level of intellectual capacity, initiative, and maturity. Every year, this highly qualified group of students includes people with learning disabilities. Grinnell is committed to providing academic adjustments and reasonable accommodations for students with disabilities who are otherwise qualified for admission. Many of Grinnell's characteristics make it a positive educational environment for all students: an open curriculum, small classes, easy access to professors, and openness to diversity. The Academic Advising Office coordinates services for students with LD, arranges for academic accommodations, acts as a liaison to the faculty, and offers personal, individual assistance. Once students are admitted and they accept the offer of admission, Grinnell likes to plan with them for any reasonable accommodation they will need in order to enjoy a successful experience. Students have the responsibility to make their needs known. The most important factors for college success are seeking help early and learning to be self-advocates. Students are encouraged to notify the Academic Advising Office about their needs before they arrive for the first semester. For planning purposes, sooner is always better.

ADMISSION INFORMATION FOR STUDENTS WITH LD/ADHD

College entrance tests required: Yes
Interview required: No
Essay recommended: Yes
What documentation required for LD: Psycho Ed evaluation to include: relevant historical info, instructional interventions, related services, age diagnosed, objective data (aptitude, achievement, info processing), test scores (standard, percentile and grade equivalents) and describe functional limitations.
With general application: No
To receive services after enrolling: Yes
What documentation required for ADHD: Diagnosis based on DSM-V; history of behaviors impairing functioning in academic setting; diagnostic interview; history of symptoms; evidence of ongoing behaviors.

With general application: No
Submitted to: Academic Advising.
Special Ed. HS course work accepted: N/A
Specific course requirements of all applicants: Yes
Separate application required: No
# of LD applications submitted each year: NR
# of LD applications accepted yearly: NR
Total # of students receiving LD services: 40
Acceptance into program means acceptance into college: Students must be admitted and enrolled in the college first and then request services.

ADMISSIONS

Grinnell welcomes applications from students with learning disabilities. The same admission standards apply to all students. However students are advised to document their needs in the application for admission and how learning disabilities may have affected their high school performance. Interviews are encouraged on or off campus. Grinnell is looking for a strong scholastic record from high school, recommendations, satisfactory results on the ACT/SAT, and college prep courses including 4 years English, 3 years math, 3 years social studies, 3 years science and 3 years of a foreign language. Applicants with appropriate documentation may substitute for some entrance requirements such as foreign language. The middle 50% range for ACT is 28-32 and SAT 1210-1430. Over 85% of the admitted students are from the top 20% of their class.

ADDITIONAL INFORMATION

Students need to meet with their faculty advisor and the Academic Advising Office to plan for their individual needs. The Academic Advising Office coordinates services for students and arranges for academic accommodations and assists students with LD to develop effective academic strategies. The Reading Lab helps students improve reading speed, vocabulary, and reading comprehension. The Science Learning Center and Math Lab provide instruction for students who want to strengthen their background in these areas. Individual tutoring and supplemental instruction is available in all subjects at no charge. Additional resources include referral for LD testing, reduced course loads, extended time for exams, personal counseling, an books in auditory (electronic) format. Skills classes for credit are offered in reading, writing, math and science.

LEARNING DISABILITY PROGRAMS OR SERVICES

Contact Information
Name of program or department: Academic Advising Office
  Telephone: 641-269-3702
  Fax: 641-269-3710

LEARNING DISABILITY SERVICES

Accommodations are decided upon an individual basis after a thorough review of appropriate, current documentation. The accommodations requested must be supported through the documentation provided and must be logically linked to the current impact of the condition on academic functioning.

Allowed in exams	**Distraction-reduced environment:** Yes	**Added costs for services:** No
Calculator: Yes	**Tape recording in class:** Yes	**LD specialists:** No
Dictionary: Yes	**Electronic texts:** Yes	**Professional tutors:** 7
Computer: Yes	**Accommodations for students with**	**Peer tutors:** 50
Spellchecker: Yes	**ADHD:** Yes	**Max. hours/wk. for services:**
Extended test time: Yes	**Kurzweil Reader:** Yes	Unlimited
Scribes: Yes	**Other assistive technology:** Yes	**How professors are notified of**
Proctors: Yes	**Priority registration:** No	**LD/ADHD:** By both student and
Oral exams: Yes		director
Note-takers: Yes		

GENERAL ADMISSIONS INFORMATION

Office of Admission: 641-269-3600

ENTRANCE REQUIREMENTS

Academic units recommended: 4 English, 4 math, 4 science (3 science labs), 4 foreign language, 4 social studies. High school diploma is required, and GED is accepted. ACT with or without Writing component accepted. TOEFL required of all international applicants: minimum paper TOEFL 550, minimum computer TOEFL 220.

Application deadline: 1/15	**SAT Math middle 50% range:**	**Graduated top 10% of class:** 62%
Notification: 4/1	610–710	**Graduated top 25% of class:** 88%
Average GPA: NR	**SAT Critical Reading middle 50%**	**Graduated top 50% of class:** 99%
ACT Composite middle 50% range:	**range:** 600–720	
28–32	**SAT Writing middle 50% range:** NR	

COLLEGE GRADUATION REQUIREMENTS

Course waivers allowed: No
Course substitutions allowed: No

ADDITIONAL INFORMATION

Environment: The college is located on 95 acres in a small town 55 miles east of Des Moines.

Student Body	**Cost Information**	**Greek System**
Undergrad enrollment: 1,693	**Tuition:** $39,810	**Fraternity:** No
Women: 54%	**Room & board:** $9,335	**Sorority:** No
Men: 46%	**Housing Information**	**Athletics:** Division III
Percent out-of-state: 88%	**University housing:** Yes	
	Percent living on campus: 88%	

INDIAN HILLS COMMUNITY COLLEGE

623 Indian Hills Drive, Building 12, Ottumwa, IA 52501
Phone: 800-726-2585 • Fax: 641-683-5263
E-mail: disabilityservices@indianhills.edu • Web: www.indianhills.edu
Support: CS • Institution type: 2-year public

PROGRAMS OR SERVICES FOR STUDENTS WITH LD

Disability Services provides academic and physical accommodations and services for students with disabilities based on documented needs. Students with a documented learning disability or attention deficit hyperactivity disorder must provide current documentation which has been completed by a qualified professional such as a school counselor, physician, psychologist, or other health care professional. Statements must include: a description of the disability, a statement of how the disability prohibits one or more major life activities and is a barrier to the student's full participation in the program, and a description of the specific accommodations which might be provided. All requests for accommodations should be made as far in advance as possible. Students enrolling in credit programs are encouraged to make their requests for accommodations at the time they are applying for admission and preferably no later than 6 weeks prior to the beginning of each academic term. All student requests are dealt with in a confidential manner.

ADMISSION INFORMATION FOR STUDENTS WITH LD/ADHD

College entrance tests required: Compass
Interview required: No
Essay recommended: No
What documentation required for LD: Psycho Ed evaluation to include: relevant historical info, instructional interventions, related services, age diagnosed, objective data (aptitude, achievement, info processing), test scores (standard, percentile and grade equivalents) and describe functional limitations.
With general application: No
To receive services after enrolling: Yes
What documentation required for ADHD: Diagnosis based on DSM-V; history of behaviors impairing functioning in academic setting; diagnostic interview; history of symptoms; evidence of ongoing behaviors.

With general application: No
Submitted to: Disability Services
Special Ed. HS course work accepted: Yes
Specific course requirements of all applicants: NR
Separate application required: No
# of LD applications submitted each year: N/A
# of LD applications accepted yearly: N/A
Total # of students receiving LD services: N/A
Acceptance into program means acceptance into college: Students must be admitted and enrolled in the college first and then request services.

ADMISSIONS

Indian Hills Community College is an "open-door" institution. All students must present a high school diploma or GED or must earn one while enrolled in order to receive a college degree. ACT/SAT tests are not required, and there are no specific high school courses required for admission.

ADDITIONAL INFORMATION

Student Support Services is a Trio program and will provide services to students with disabilities. Trio will assist in securing admission and financial aid for enrollment in four-year institutions. The cornerstone of Student Support Services is guidance and counseling. Trio offers tutoring both on an individual and/or group basis. All services are free of charge for eligible students. The Success Center services include: Skill-Building Courses, Disability Services, tutoring, computer labs, supplemental instruction and resources, and access to online SUCCESS Center resources. The Success Center offers pre-enrollment workshops to review basic academic skills and become familiar with the college community.

LEARNING DISABILITY PROGRAMS OR SERVICES

Contact Information
Name of program or department: Disability Services
  Telephone: 641-683-5749
  Fax: 641-683-5263

LEARNING DISABILITY SERVICES

Accommodations are decided upon an individual basis after a thorough review of appropriate, current documentation. The accommodations requested must be supported through the documentation provided and must be logically linked to the current impact of the condition on academic functioning. The following accommodations are determined on a case-by-case basis.

Allowed in exams
  Calculator: Yes
  Dictionary: Yes
  Computer: Yes
  Spellchecker: Yes
Extended test time: Yes
Scribes: Yes
Proctors: Yes
Oral exams: Yes
Note-takers: Yes

Distraction-reduced environment: Yes
Tape recording in class: Yes
Electronic texts: Yes
Accommodations for students with ADHD: Yes
Kurzweil Reader: Yes
Other assistive technology: Yes
Priority registration: No

Added costs for services: No
LD specialists: No
Professional tutors: 9
Peer tutors: 20–30
Max. hours/wk. for services: Unlimited
How professors are notified of LD/ADHD: Disability Services shares accommodatiions

GENERAL ADMISSIONS INFORMATION

Office of Admission: 800-726-2585

ENTRANCE REQUIREMENTS

Academic Units Recommended: 4 English, 3 math, 3 science, 4 social studies, 2 foreign language. Some majors require specific math courses. Open admissions. High school diploma or GED equivalent accepted.

Application deadline: None
Notification: Rolling
Average GPA: NR
ACT Composite middle 50% range: NR

SAT Math middle 50% range: NR
SAT Critical Reading middle 50% range: NR
SAT Writing middle 50% range: NR

Graduated top 10% of class: NR
Graduated top 25% of class: NR
Graduated top 50% of class: NR

COLLEGE GRADUATION REQUIREMENTS

Course waivers allowed: No
Course substitutions allowed: No

ADDITIONAL INFORMATION

Environment: The college is located on 400 acres about 2 hours east of Iowa City or west of Des Moines.

Student Body
  Undergrad enrollment: 8,065
  Women: 56%
  Men: 44%
  Percent out-of-state: 5%

Cost Information
  In-state tuition: $137 per credit
  Out-of-state tuition: $206 per credit
  Room & board: $5,380–$5,820
Housing Information
  University housing: Yes
  Percent living on campus: NR

Greek System
  Fraternity: No
  Sorority: No
Athletics: NJCAA

IOWA STATE UNIVERSITY

100 Enrollment Services Center, Ames, IA 50011-2011
Phone: 515-294-5836 • Fax: 515-294-2592
E-mail: admissions@iastate.edu • Web: www.iastate.edu
Support: CS • Institution type: 4-year public

PROGRAMS OR SERVICES FOR STUDENTS WITH LD

ISU is committed to providing equal opportunities and facilitating the personal growth and development of all students. Staff from the Student Disability Resources Office assists students with issues relating to the documented disability. A thorough review of most current LD evaluation and documentation is completed to determine the possible accommodations needed. SDR staff also offers assistance in articulating needs to faculty and staff, and may serve as a liaison in student/staff negotiations. Documentation should include current diagnosis, functional limitations, and relevant information about the student and examiner's qualifications; behavioral observation of the way students present themselves, verbal and nonverbal communication, interpersonal skills and behavior during testing; a narrative describing developmental and educational history; a description of the effect of the disability on learning is required. Recommendations concerning possible accommodations is welcomed.

ADMISSION INFORMATION FOR STUDENTS WITH LD/ADHD

College entrance tests required: Yes
Interview required: No
Essay recommended: No
What documentation required for LD: Psycho Ed evaluation to include: relevant historical info, instructional interventions, related services, age diagnosed, objective data (aptitude, achievement, info processing), test scores (standard, percentile and grade equivalents) and describe functional limitations.
With general application: No
To receive services after enrolling: Yes
What documentation required for ADHD: Diagnosis based on DSM-V; history of behaviors impairing functioning in academic setting; diagnostic interview; history of symptoms; evidence of ongoing behaviors.

With general application: No
Submitted to: Student Disability Resources
Special Ed. HS course work accepted: No
Specific course requirements of all applicants: Yes
Separate application required: N/A
# of LD applications submitted each year: NR
# of LD applications accepted yearly: NR
Total # of students receiving LD services: NR
Acceptance into program means acceptance into college: Students must be admitted and enrolled in the university first and then request services.

ADMISSIONS

Students with documented disabilities are held to Iowa State's regular freshman admission requirements (listed below). Those who feel their academic record does not accurately reflect their ability to succeed and, therefore, wish to be considered for admission on an individual basis are asked to submit additional documentation explaining their circumstances. This documentation should include: 1) A letter from the applicant requesting special consideration. This letter should identify the disability and include a description of how the disability impacts academic performance. 2) Information pertaining to accommodations and services used in high school or the most recent educational setting. 3) A recent typed report prepared by a qualified provider that contains a specific current diagnosis, treatment history, and existing functional impact as it relates to one's participation at Iowa State University. Please refer to www.dso.iastate.edu/dr/ for more details on documentation requirements. Freshman applicants are considered for admission based on their Regent Admission Index (RAI) score which is based on the following equation: RAI = (2 x ACT composite score) + (1 x percentile high school rank) + (20 x high school grade point average) + (5 x number of years of high school courses completed in the core subject areas) Students who achieve at least a 245 RAI and who meet the University's minimum high school course requirements will automatically qualify for admission. Students who achieve less than a 245 RAI will be considered for admission on an individual basis.

ADDITIONAL INFORMATION

The Academic Learning Lab is a "learning-how-to-learn" center designed to help all students. Counselors work one-on-one to evaluate and identify problem study habits and devise strategies to improve them. The Learning Lab and Tutoring and Student Support Services are in one area called the Academic Success Center (ASC). ASC coordinates services including counseling, teaching reading, and study skills, and provides a list of tutors. The Writing Center is available to all students. The LD specialist provides information about readers, note-takers, and scribes. Peer Supplemental Instruction (SI) is an academic assistance program attached to very difficult courses. SI leaders attend classes and conduct biweekly sessions to help students learn and study the course material. Student Support Services is a federally funded program for students with LD and others qualified to receive academic support in the form of free tutoring and skill-building workshops.

LEARNING DISABILITY PROGRAMS OR SERVICES

Contact Information
Name of program or department: Student Disability Resources
  Telephone: 515-294-7220
  Fax: 515-294-2397

LEARNING DISABILITY SERVICES

Accommodations are decided upon an individual basis after a thorough review of appropriate, current documentation. The accommodations requested must be supported through the documentation provided and must be logically linked to the current impact of the condition on academic functioning.

Allowed in exams
  Calculator: Yes
  Dictionary: Yes
  Computer: Yes
  Spellchecker: Yes
Extended test time: Yes
Scribes: Yes
Proctors: Yes
Oral exams: No
Note-takers: Yes

Distraction-reduced environment: Yes
Tape recording in class: Yes
Electronic texts: Yes
Accommodations for students with
  ADHD: Yes
Kurzweil Reader: Yes
Other assistive technology: Yes
Priority registration: No

Added costs for services: No
LD specialists: Yes
Professional tutors: No
Peer tutors: Varies
Max. hours/wk. for services: 0.5
How professors are notified of
  LD/ADHD: By student

GENERAL ADMISSIONS INFORMATION

Office of Admission: 515-294-5836

ENTRANCE REQUIREMENTS
Academic units required: 4 English, 3 math, 3 science (2 science labs), 2 foreign language, 2 social studies.
Academic units recommended: 4 English, 4 math, 4 science (3 science labs), 3 foreign language, 4 social studies. High school diploma is required, and GED is accepted. ACT with or without Writing component accepted. TOEFL required of all international applicants: minimum paper TOEFL 500, minimum computer TOEFL 173.

Application deadline: 7/1
Notification: Rolling
Average GPA: 3.50
ACT Composite middle 50% range:
  22–27

SAT Math middle 50% range:
  550–680
SAT Critical Reading middle 50%
  range: 490–650
SAT Writing middle 50% range: NR

Graduated top 10% of class: 25%
Graduated top 25% of class: 55%
Graduated top 50% of class: 90%

COLLEGE GRADUATION REQUIREMENTS

Course waivers allowed: NR
Course substitutions allowed: NR

ADDITIONAL INFORMATION

Environment: Iowa State University is located on a 1,000-acre campus about 30 miles north of Des Moines.

Student Body
  Undergrad enrollment: 24,343
  Women: 44%
  Men: 56%
  Percent out-of-state: 33%

Cost Information
  In-state tuition: $7,486
  Out-of-state tuition: $19,357
  Room & board: $7,982
Housing Information
  University housing: Yes
  Percent living on campus: 37%

Greek System
  Fraternity: Yes
  Sorority: Yes
Athletics: Division I

LORAS COLLEGE

1450 Alta Vista, Dubuque, IA 52001
Phone: 800-245-6727 • Fax: 563-588-7071
E-mail: admissions@loras.edu • Web: www.loras.edu
Support: SP • Institution: 4-year private

PROGRAMS OR SERVICES FOR STUDENTS WITH LD

Loras College provides a supportive, comprehensive program for the motivated individual with a learning disability or ADHD. Students can be successful in Loras' competitive environment if they have had adequate preparation, are willing to work with program staff, and take responsibility for their own learning. The Enhanced Program staff has three specialists to serve as guides and advocates, encouraging and supporting students to become independent learners. Students with LD or ADHD who are enrolled in college-preparatory courses in high school are the most appropriate candidates for the Loras program. Often high school students who previously were in support programs, but are not currently receiving services, are excellent candidates for the program if they have taken challenging classes.

ADMISSION INFORMATION FOR STUDENTS WITH LD/ADHD

College entrance tests required: Yes
Interview required: Yes
Essay required: Yes
What documentation required for LD: Psycho Ed evaluation to include: relevant historical info, instructional interventions, related services, age diagnosed, objective data (aptitude, achievement, info processing), test scores (standard, percentile and grade equivalents) and describe functional limitations.
With general application: Yes if requested as part of Structured Program application
To receive services after enrolling: Yes
What documentation required for ADHD: Diagnosis based on DSM-V; history of behaviors impairing functioning in academic setting; diagnostic interview; history of symptoms; evidence of ongoing behaviors.

With general application: Yes if requested as part of Structured Program application
To receive services after enrolling: Yes
Submitted to: Support Program/Services
Special Ed. HS course work accepted: N/A
Specific course requirements for all applicants: NR
Separate application required for program services: Yes
# of LD applications submitted each year: 50–60
# of LD applications accepted yearly: 20–30
Total # of students receiving LD services: 50–60
Acceptance into program means acceptance into college: Separate application required after student has enrolled

ADMISSIONS
Students may contact program staff as early as their junior year and request an assessment of their chances for admission; the admission process will be explained. Students may apply for regular admission online and the Enhanced Program simultaneously (access the Enhanced Program's application materials from our website: http://depts.loras.edu/lods/). Students should arrange for an evaluation documenting their learning disability (if their current evaluation is more than three years old) to include the WAIS or other IQ testing, as well as achievement/diagnostic tests of reading, written expression, and math and send the evaluation when completed.

ADDITIONAL INFORMATION
The Lynch Office of Disability Services provides two levels of service: an Enhanced Program and Accommodation Services. The Enhanced Program for first-year students includes a two-credit class, Learning Strategies (both semesters of the first year), an individual meeting with program staff each week and tutors, as needed. Students continuing after the first year, and transfer students, receive the same support with the exception of the class. The students in the Enhanced Program are also eligible to receive Accommodation Services, which include note-takers, texts in alternative formats, other assistive technology (including screen readers and speech recognition software), and extended time and/or distraction-reduced testing rooms. Students in the Enhanced Program are charged a fee for services(first year $4,225; all others $3,725 per year, 2011–2012. Accommodation Services are provided at no cost. Students with the Learning Strategies class who want Accommodation Services only are not required to self-disclose their need for services until after they are accepted to Loras. However, those who want the more comprehensive Enhanced Program should apply simultaneously to the college and the Enhanced Program. The deadline for the Enhanced Program is February 15. Note: Accommodation Services are available to all students with documented disabilities who need accommodations.

PROGRAM FOR DISABILITY SERVICES

Contact Information
Name of program or department: Enhanced Program
  Telephone: 563-588-7134
  Fax: 563-588-7071

LEARNING DISABILITY SERVICES

Accommodations are decided upon an individual basis after a thorough review of appropriate, current documentation. The accommodations requested must be supported through the documentation provided and must be logically linked to the current impact of the condition on academic functioning.

Allowed in exams
  Calculator: Yes
  Dictionary: Yes
  Computer: Yes
  Spellchecker: Yes
Extended test time: Yes
Scribes: Yes
Proctors: Yes
Oral exams: Yes
Note-takers: Yes

Distraction-reduced environment: Yes
Tape recording in class: Yes
Electronic texts: Yes
Accommodations for students with ADHD: Yes
Kurzweil Reader: Yes
Other assistive technology: Kurzweil 3000, Dragon Naturally Speaking.
Priority registration: Yes

Added costs for services: Yes
LD specialists: Yes
Professional tutors: No
Peer tutors: 5–15
Max. hours/wk. for services: Unlimited
How professors are notified of LD/ADHD: Student

GENERAL ADMISSIONS INFORMATION

Office of Admission: 563-588-7829

ENTRANCE REQUIREMENTS

Academic units recommended: 4 English, 3 mathematics, 3 science, 0 foreign language, 3 social studies, 3 history. High school diploma is required and GED is accepted. SAT or ACT required; TOEFL required of all international applicants; minimum paper TOEFL 550, minimum computer TOEFL 213.

Application deadline: None
Notification: Rolling
Average GPA: 3.22
ACT Composite middle 50% range: 19–26

SAT Math middle 50% range: 453–575
SAT Critical Reading middle 50% range: 503–625
SAT Writing middle 50% range: NR

Graduated top 10% of class: 13%
Graduated top 25% of class: 34%
Graduated top 50% of class: 65%

COLLEGE GRADUATION REQUIREMENTS

Course waivers allowed: Yes
In what course: Waivers are possible for math after attempting math course work; no foreign language waivers are necessary because there is no foreign language requirement.
Course substitutions allowed: N/A

ADDITIONAL INFORMATION

Environment: The college is located on 66 hilltop acres in northeast Iowa overlooking the Mississippi River.

Student Body
  Undergrad enrollment: 1,530
  Women: 49%
  Men: 51%
  Percent out-of-state: 50%

Cost Information
  Tuition: $27,258
  Room and board: $7,524
Housing Information
  University housing: Yes
  Percent living on campus: 60%

Greek System
  Fraternity: Yes
  Sorority: Yes
Athletics: Division III

MORNINGSIDE COLLEGE

1501 Morningside Avenue, Sioux City, IA 51106-1751
Phone: 712-274-5511 • Fax: 712-274-5101
E-mail: mscadm@morningside.edu • Web: www.morningside.edu
Support: CS • Institution type: 4-year private

PROGRAMS OR SERVICES FOR STUDENTS WITH LD

Students with learning disabilities can and do succeed in college. However, students with different learning styles may need assistance in order to be truly successful students. Morningside College will require supportive data to verify that a disability exists. These may include, but are not necessarily limited to, the following: high school records; specific plans recommended by qualified professionals and/or consultants; and satisfactory medical determination as required.

ADMISSION INFORMATION FOR STUDENTS WITH LD/ADHD

College entrance tests required: Yes
Interview required: Yes
Essay recommended: Yes
What documentation required for LD: Psycho Ed evaluation to include: relevant historical info, instructional interventions, related services, age diagnosed, objective data (aptitude, achievement, info processing), test scores (standard, percentile and grade equivalents) and describe functional limitations.
With general application: No
To receive services after enrolling: Yes
What documentation required for ADHD: Diagnosis based on DSM-V; history of behaviors impairing functioning in academic setting; diagnostic interview; history of symptoms; evidence of ongoing behaviors.

With general application: No
Submitted to: Associate Dean for Academic Affairs
Special Ed. HS course work accepted: N/A
Specific course requirements of all applicants: NR
Separate application required: Yes
# of LD applications submitted each year: N/A
# of LD applications accepted yearly: N/A
Total # of students receiving LD services: 15–20
Acceptance into program means acceptance into college: Students must be admitted and enrolled prior to requesting services.

ADMISSIONS

Morningside's selective admissions program is based on the following criteria: class rank, college preparatory course work, GPA, ACT or SAT, essay participation recommended but not required, character, and personal abilities. Students with ACT of 20 or SAT of 1410, and either ranked in the top half of their class or have achieved a high school GPA of 2.5 meet the academic standards for admissions. First-year students who have been out of high school more than 5 years are not required to submit ACT or SAT test scores but are required to take math and/or English placement assessments. Students who have not completed high school may be admitted on the basis of a GED score.

ADDITIONAL INFORMATION

Examples of potential reasonable accommodations for students might include the following: note-taking, copies of instructor's notes, tape-recording of class, reasonable equipment modification, preferential seating, books on tape, test-taking accommodations, word processor adaptations, and reader service. The Academic Support Center is open to all students. Academic Support Center staff helps students improve or strengthen their academics by providing free assistance in writing techniques. Writing specialists are available to help students with the basics as well as help proficient writers who want assistance for particular writing assignments or projects. The specialists do not proofread, but they can help students see the strengths and weaknesses of their paper. Staff and student tutors are available in the Academic Support Center for students who want help in areas such as accounting, biology, chemistry, economics, history, math, science, religion, and sociology.

LEARNING DISABILITY PROGRAMS OR SERVICES

Contact Information
Name of program or department: Academic Support Center
  Telephone: 800-831-0806, ext. 5388
  Fax: 712-274-5358

LEARNING DISABILITY SERVICES

Accommodations are decided upon an individual basis after a thorough review of appropriate, current documentation. The accommodations requested must be supported through the documentation provided and must be logically linked to the current impact of the condition on academic functioning.

Allowed in exams
  Calculator: Yes
  Dictionary: Yes
  Computer: Yes
  Spellchecker: Yes
Extended test time: Yes
Scribes: Yes
Proctors: Yes
Oral exams: Yes
Note-takers: Yes

Distraction-reduced environment: Yes
Tape recording in class: Yes
Electronic texts: Yes
Accommodations for students with ADHD: Yes
Kurzweil Reader: No
Other assistive technology: No
Priority registration: No

Added costs for services: No
LD specialists: No
Professional tutors: 5–10
Peer tutors: 5–15
Max. hours/wk. for services: Unlimited
How professors are notified of LD/ADHD: Associate Dean

GENERAL ADMISSIONS INFORMATION

Office of Admission: 712-274-5511

ENTRANCE REQUIREMENTS

Academic units recommended: 3 English, 2 math, 2 science, 3 social studies. High school diploma is required, and GED is accepted. ACT with or without Writing component accepted. TOEFL required of all international applicants: minimum paper TOEFL 450, minimum computer TOEFL 133.

Application deadline: None
Notification: Rolling
Average GPA: 3.38
ACT Composite middle 50% range: 21–26

SAT Math middle 50% range: NR
SAT Critical Reading middle 50% range: NR
SAT Writing middle 50% range: NR

Graduated top 10% of class: 19%
Graduated top 25% of class: 46%
Graduated top 50% of class: 78%

COLLEGE GRADUATION REQUIREMENTS

Course waivers allowed: No
Course substitutions allowed: No

ADDITIONAL INFORMATION

Environment: Morningside College is located in Sioux City, Iowa, 90 miles north of Omaha, Nebraska, and 75 miles south of Sioux Falls, South Dakota.

Student Body
  Undergrad enrollment: 1,269
  Women: 53%
  Men: 47%
  Percent out-of-state: 36%

Cost Information
  Tuition: $22,880
  Room & board: $7,500
Housing Information
  University housing: Yes
  Percent living on campus: 64%

Greek System
  Fraternity: Yes
  Sorority: Yes
Athletics: NAIA

SAINT AMBROSE UNIVERSITY

518 West Locust Street, Davenport, IA 52803-2898
Phone: 563-333-6300 • Fax: 563-333-6297
E-mail: admit@sau.edu • Web: www.sau.edu
Support: CS • Institution: 4-year private

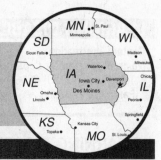

PROGRAMS OR SERVICES FOR STUDENTS WITH LD

Student Disability Services at St. Ambrose University has two primary goals. The first goal is to provide qualified students with disabilities services or reasonable accommodations intended to reduce the effects that a disability may have on their performance in a traditional academic setting. Services do not lower course standards or significantly alter degree requirements, but instead give students a better chance to demonstrate their academic abilities. The second goal of the office is to assist students with disabilities in developing learning strategies to compensate for their disability and to become independent learners. Any student can initiate a request for services by registering with Student Disability Services, and providing information that documents the disability.

ADMISSION INFORMATION FOR STUDENTS WITH LD/ADHD

College entrance tests required: Yes

Interview required: No
Essay required: N/A
What documentation required for LD: Psycho Ed evaluation to include: relevant historical info, instructional interventions, related services, age diagnosed, objective data (aptitude, achievement, info processing), test scores (standard, percentile and grade equivalents) and describe functional limitations.
With general application: No
To receive services after enrolling: Yes
What documentation required for ADHD: Diagnosis based on DSM-V; history of behaviors impairing functioning in academic setting; diagnostic interview; history of symptoms; evidence of ongoing behaviors.
With general application: No

Submitted to: Support Program/Services
Special Ed. HS course work accepted: Yes
Specific course requirements for all applicants: NR
Separate application required for program services: No
# of LD applications submitted each year: 70
# of LD applications accepted yearly: 40
Total # of students receiving LD services: 60–70
Acceptance into program means acceptance into college: Students mus be admitted and enrolled in the university first and then request services.

ADMISSIONS

Students meeting minimum admission requirements are not required to send additional information for admission purposes, but it is helpful in providing effective services. The general admission criteria include minimum ACT 20 or minimum 950 SAT; 2.5 GPA; with specific course requirements. Students who have completed junior year in high school may attend the Summer Transition Program to assess their ability for regular admission. Students who do not meet the criteria are encouraged to contact the Director for additional consideration.

ADDITIONAL INFORMATION

Through Student Disability Services students may have access to the following services: academic advising; advocacy; alternate exam arrangements including extended time, large print, separate testing room, readers, scribes, or use of a computer; books in alternative format; assitive technology; equipment loans; LD specialist to provide one-to-one learning skills instruction; liaison with outside agencies; screening and referral for diagnosis of learning disabilities; and other accommodations to meet appropriate needs. A four-week Summer Transition Program is available for college-bound students with learning disabilities, Asperger's and/or ADHD who have completed their junior year in high school. Students do not have to be admitted to St. Ambrose to participate in this program, and completion of the program does not guarantee admission to St. Ambrose University. Students take either Intro to Psychology or Intro to Sociology, and engage in sessions where they receive instruction on study skills, note-taking, textbook reading, memorization strategies, and test preparation. Additional sessions are also required where students are engaged in informal discussion groups on topics such as rights and responsibilities of students with disabilities, selecting accommodations, understanding their disability, and self-advocacy. Learning disability specialists attend the psych class and assist students in applying learning skills to their course work.

PROGRAM FOR DISABILITY SERVICES

Contact Information
Name of program or department: Student Disability Services
  Telephone: 563-333-6275
  Fax: 563-333-6248

LEARNING DISABILITY SERVICES

Accommodations are decided upon an individual basis after a thorough review of appropriate, current documentation. The accommodations requested must be supported through the documentation provided and must be logically linked to the current impact of the condition on academic functioning.

Allowed in exams
  Calculator: Yes
  Dictionary: Yes
  Computer: Yes
  Spellchecker: Yes
Extended test time: Yes
Scribes: Yes
Proctors: Yes
Oral exams: Yes
Note-takers: Yes

Distraction-reduced environment: Yes
Tape recording in class: Yes
Electronic texts: Yes
Accommodations for students with ADHD: Yes
Kurzweil Reader: Yes
Other assistive technology: Voice to text software, FM systems, 4-track tape recorders/digital CD players to check out
Priority registration: Yes

Added costs for services: No
LD specialists: Yes
Professional tutors: NR
Peer tutors: No
Max. hours/wk. for services: Unlimited
How professors are notified of LD/ADHD: Both student and director

GENERAL ADMISSIONS INFORMATION

Office of Admission: 563-333-6311

ENTRANCE REQUIREMENTS

Academic units recommended: 4 English, 3 mathematics, 2 science, (2 science labs), 1 foreign language, 1 social studies, 1 history, 4 academic electives. High school diploma is required and GED is accepted. SAT or ACT required; TOEFL required of all international applicants; minimum paper TOEFL 500, minimum computer TOEFL 213.

Application deadline: None
Notification: Rolling
Average GPA: 3.19
ACT Composite middle 50% range: 20–25

SAT Math middle 50% range: NR
SAT Critical Reading middle 50% range: NR
SAT Writing middle 50% range: NR

Graduated top 10% of class: 19%
Graduated top 25% of class: 37%
Graduated top 50% of class: 65%

COLLEGE GRADUATION REQUIREMENTS

Course waivers allowed: Yes
In what course: Physical education activity courses
Course substitutions allowed: Yes
In what course: Foreign language, physical education

ADDITIONAL INFORMATION

Environment: The campus is located in an urban area 180 miles west of Chicago.

Student Body
  Undergrad enrollment: 2,752
  Women: 61%
  Men: 39%
  Percent out-of-state: 58%

Cost Information
  Tuition: $25,730
  Room and board: $9,195
Housing Information
  University housing: Yes
  Percent living on campus: 57%

Greek System
  Fraternity: No
  Sorority: No
  Athletics: NAIA

UNIVERSITY OF DUBUQUE

2000 University Avenue, Dubuque, IA 52001-5050
Phone: 563-589-3200 • Fax: 563-589-3690
E-mail: admssns@dbq.edu • Web: www.dbq.edu
Support: CS • Institution: 4-year private

PROGRAMS OR SERVICES FOR STUDENTS WITH LD

The University of Dubuque meets the requirements of the American Disability Act and provides reasonable accommodations for qualified students. The goal of the Academic Success Center is to assist all students to achieve success in college. Those wishing to receive accommodations need to meet with the Disabilities Services Coordinator. A written formal request must be submitted. Documentation regarding the disability must be provided.

ADMISSION INFORMATION FOR STUDENTS WITH LD/ADHD

College entrance tests required: Varies
Interview required: No
What documentation required for LD: Psycho Ed evaluation to include: relevant historical info, instructional interventions, related services, age diagnosed, objective data (aptitude, achievement, info processing), test scores (standard, percentile and grade equivalents) and describe functional limitations.
With general application: No
To receive services after enrolling: Yes
What documentation required for ADHD: Diagnosis based on DSM-V; history of behaviors impairing functioning in academic setting; diagnostic interview; history of symptoms; evidence of ongoing behaviors.

With general application: No
Submitted to: Disability Services Coordinator
Special Ed. HS course work accepted: Yes
Specific course requirements for all applicants: Yes; some substitutions available
Separate application required for program services: Yes
# of LD applications submitted each year: NR
# of LD applications accepted yearly: NR
Total # of students receiving LD services: 36
Acceptance into program means acceptance into college: Students must be admitted and enrolled prior to requesting services.

ADMISSIONS

An applicant for admission to the University of Dubuque should be a graduate of a high school or have an equivalent (GED). Applicants should have a minimum of 15 high school units of which 10 should be from academic fields (English, social studies, natural science, mathematics, foreign language). Preference is given to students in the upper one-half of their graduating class and who have an ACT score of 18 or higher. A limited number of students may be granted provisional admittance based on counselor recommendations and evidence of potential for college success. These students are admitted to the University of Dubuque "Bridge" Program. The "Bridge" Program provides consistent tutoring and grade monitoring in a welcoming environment.

ADDITIONAL INFORMATION

The Academic Success Center provides help for all University of Dubuque students and seminary students needing one-on-one assistance with course work, writing, study skills, and other academic matters. Students can improve their grades and study habits with the assistance of tutors, who help with a variety of subjects. The Academic Support Center's professional tutors and peer tutors have combined expertise in almost all academic areas taught. Specific accommodations for students with learning disabilities include the following: textbooks on CD and numerous resource materials, supplemental note-takers, test monitoring for students who are overly anxious about time constraints on regular classroom testing, tests read aloud to students when necessary, monitoring of progress by the Director of the Academic Success Center, and advocacy for students with academic disabilities. The Academic Support Center is dedicated to helping students get the most out of college. It offers free supplemental and supportive assistance for students in all majors and at all grade-point levels. The hours for walk-in tutoring or tutoring by appointment are Monday–Thursday 9am–9pm, Fridays 9am–5pm, and varied weekend hours (determined semester to semester.)

PROGRAM FOR DISABILITY SERVICES

Contact Information
Name of program or department: Academic Success Center
  Telephone: 563-589-3757
  Fax: 563-589-3722

LEARNING DISABILITY SERVICES

Accommodations are decided upon an individual basis after a thorough review of appropriate, current documentation. The accommodations requested must be supported through the documentation provided and must be logically linked to the current impact of the condition on academic functioning.

Allowed in exams	**Distraction-reduced environment:** Yes	**Priority registration:** N/A
Calculator: Yes	**Tape recording in class:** Yes	**Added costs for services:** No
Dictionary: Yes	**Electronic texts:** Yes	**LD specialists:** Yes
Computer: Yes	**Accommodations for students with**	**Professional tutors:** 10
Spellchecker: Yes	**ADHD:** Yes	**Peer tutors:** 17
Extended test time: Yes	**Kurzweil Reader:** No	**Max. hours/wk. for services:**
Scribes: Yes	**Other assistive technology:** Textaloud	Unlimited
Proctors: Yes	software which allows students to scan	**How professors are notified of**
Oral exams: Yes	pages of textbooks and listen to the	**LD/ADHD:** Student
Note-takers: Yes	pages being read aloud, Dragon	
	Naturally Speaking, Kindles, audio	
	recorder, and limited number of smart	
	pens.	

GENERAL ADMISSIONS INFORMATION

Office of Admission: 563-589-3214

ENTRANCE REQUIREMENTS
Academic units required: 4 English, 3 mathematics, 3 science, 3 social studies, 3 academic electives. **Academic units recommended:** 4 English, 3 mathematics, 3 science, 3 social studies, 3 academic electives. High school diploma is required and GED is accepted. SAT or ACT required; TOEFL required of all international applicants; minimum paper TOEFL 500, minimum computer TOEFL 275.

Application deadline: None	**SAT Math middle 50% range:**	**Graduated top 10% of class:** 8%
Notification: Rolling	400–520	**Graduated top 25% of class:** 25%
Average GPA: 3.0	**SAT Critical Reading middle 50%**	**Graduated top 50% of class:** 54%
ACT Composite middle 50% range:	**range:** 410–470	
18–23	**SAT Writing middle 50% range:** NR	

COLLEGE GRADUATION REQUIREMENTS

Course waivers allowed: No
Course substitutions allowed: No

ADDITIONAL INFORMATION

Environment: The University of Dubuque is located in Dubuque, Iowa, on the Mississippi River.

Student Body	**Cost Information**	**Greek System**
Undergrad enrollment: 1,674	**Tuition:** $22,000	**Fraternity:** Yes
Women: 43%	**Room and board:** $7,580	**Sorority:** Yes
Men: 57%	**Housing Information**	**Athletics:** Division III
Percent out-of-state: 52%	**University housing:** Yes	
	Percent living on campus: 42%	

University of Iowa

107 Calvin Hall, Iowa City, IA 52242
Phone: 319-335-3847 • Fax: 319-333-1535
E-mail: admissions@uiowa.edu • Web: www.uiowa.edu
Support: CS • Institution type: 4-year public

PROGRAMS OR SERVICES FOR STUDENTS WITH LD

The mission of LD/ADHD Services in the University of Iowa's Student Disability Services (SDS) is to facilitate individualized academic accommodations for eligible students. Each student has an assigned staff adviser who assists the student in identifying appropriate course accommodations, communicating classroom needs to faculty, accessing other related services and resources. Students with LD/ADHD who believe they will need disability services in order to have an equal educational opportunity are encouraged to self-disclose their disability to SDS as soon as possible. "Prospective students are encouraged to schedule an on-campus interview with the LD/ADHD coordinator to learn more about disability services for students with LD/ADHD and about the university.

ADMISSION INFORMATION FOR STUDENTS WITH LD/ADHD

College entrance tests required: Yes
Interview required: No
Essay recommended: No
What documentation required for LD: Psycho Ed evaluation to include: relevant historical info, instructional interventions, related services, age diagnosed, objective data (aptitude, achievement, info processing), test scores (standard, percentile and grade equivalents) and describe functional limitations.
With general application: No
To receive services after enrolling: Yes
What documentation required for ADHD: Diagnosis based on DSM-V; history of behaviors impairing functioning in academic setting; diagnostic interview; history of symptoms; evidence of ongoing behaviors.

With general application: No
Submitted to: Student Disability Services
Special Ed. HS course work accepted: Yes
Specific course requirements of all applicants: Yes
Separate application required: No
# of LD applications submitted each year: NR
# of LD applications accepted yearly: NR
Total # of students receiving LD services: 326
Acceptance into program means acceptance into college: Students must be admitted and enrolled in the university first and then request services.

ADMISSIONS

General admissions require 4 years of English, 3 years of math, 3 years of social studies, 3 years of science, and 2 years of a foreign language. Iowa Residents must present a Regent Admission Index (RAI) score of 245 or above; residents of other states must present an RAI of 255 or above. RAI combines four factors: ACT or SAT, high school rank, high school cumulative grade point average and the number of completed high school core courses. The College of Engineering requires successful completion of High School Course Requirements, including demonstrated success (As or Bs) in math and science courses; and present ACT math and composite scores of 25 or above and present a Regent Admission Index score of 265 or higher. There is a "special considerations" procedure for students not meeting general admission requirements who do not believe their academic record accurately reflects their ability to do college work. Students must submit a general application, transcript, and test scores; a letter disclosing the disability and requesting "special consideration," describing how the disability affected academic performance and what accommodations and compensation strategies are used to strengthen performance in deficit areas; a description of resources used and a statement explaining why the student may not have completed high school requirements, if applicable; letters from two people, not related, who can attest to the applicant's ability to be successful; and a diagnostic report verifying the disability and providing information about both the process and findings of the diagnostic assessment. The report should contain specific recommendations concerning the eligible academic accommodations, including whether the student qualifies for foreign language or math substitutions, and be signed by a licensed professional with the license number.

ADDITIONAL INFORMATION

Students requesting services and resources from Student Disability Services must self-disclose and provide satisfactory evidence of their disability-related eligibility for services. It is the responsibility of each student to determine whether or not to utilize services for which he or she is eligible. Services available through SDS for which students may be eligible on a case-by-case basis include the following: pre-admission information, new student orientation, assistance in communicating with faculty and administrators, note-taking assistance, alternative examination services, obtaining audiotapes of required reading materials, referrals to other university resources for counseling, tutoring, study skills development, and time management training. SDS notes that due to the high demand for tutoring at the university, tutors are not always available for all courses.

LEARNING DISABILITY PROGRAMS OR SERVICES

Contact Information
Name of program or department: Student Disability Services (SDS)
 Telephone: 319-335-1462
 Fax: 319-335-3973

LEARNING DISABILITY SERVICES

Accommodations are decided upon an individual basis after a thorough review of appropriate, current documentation. The accommodations requested must be supported through the documentation provided and must be logically linked to the current impact of the condition on academic functioning.

Allowed in exams	**Distraction-reduced environment:** Yes	**Added costs for services:** No
Calculator: Yes	**Tape recording in class:** Yes	**LD specialists:** Yes
Dictionary: Yes	**Electronic texts:** Yes	**Professional tutors:** NR
Computer: Yes	**Accommodations for students with**	**Peer tutors:** 50–60
Spellchecker: Yes	**ADHD:** Yes	**Max. hours/wk. for services:** 1
Extended test time: Yes	**Kurzweil Reader:** Yes	**How professors are notified of**
Scribes: Yes	**Other assistive technology:** Yes	**LD/ADHD:** By student
Proctors: Yes	**Priority registration:** Yes	
Oral exams: No		
Note-takers: Yes		

GENERAL ADMISSIONS INFORMATION

Office of Admission: 319-335-3847

ENTRANCE REQUIREMENTS
Academic units required: 4 English, 3 math, 3 science, 2 foreign language, 3 social studies. **Academic units recommended:** 4 foreign language. High school diploma is required, and GED is accepted. ACT without Writing component accepted. TOEFL required of all international applicants: minimum paper TOEFL 530, 80 on the Internet-based test, with no subscore lower than 17.

Application deadline: 4/1	**SAT Math middle 50% range:**	**Graduated top 10% of class:** 24%
Notification: Rolling	540–630	**Graduated top 25% of class:** 56%
Average GPA: 3.61	**SAT Critical Reading middle 50%**	**Graduated top 50% of class:** 92%
ACT Composite middle 50% range:	range: 450–630	
23–28	**SAT Writing middle 50% range:** NR	

COLLEGE GRADUATION REQUIREMENTS

Course waivers allowed: No
Course substitutions allowed: Yes
In what course: High school math deficiency, general education foreign language requirement, or both

ADDITIONAL INFORMATION

Environment: The university is on a 1,900-acre campus in a small city 180 miles east of Des Moines.

Student Body	**Cost Information**	**Greek System**
Undergrad enrollment: 21,564	**In-state tuition:** $7,765	**Fraternity:** Yes
Women: 52%	**Out-of-state tuition:** $25,099	**Sorority:** Yes
Men: 48%	**Room & board:** $8,750	**Athletics:** Division I
Percent out-of-state: 38%	**Housing Information**	
	University housing: Yes	
	Percent living on campus: 29%	

UNIVERSITY OF NORTHERN IOWA

1227 West 27th Street, Cedar Falls, IA 50614-0018
Phone: 319-273-2281 • Fax: 319-273-2885
E-mail: admissions@uni.edu • Web: www.uni.edu
Support: S • Institution: 4-year public

PROGRAMS OR SERVICES FOR STUDENTS WITH LD

Student Disability Services is dedicated to serving the special needs of students at the University of Northern Iowa. Student Disability Services works with students to ensure that all persons with disabilities have access to university activities, programs, and services. Specialized services are provided to enhance the overall academic, career, and personal development of each person with a physical, psychological, or learning disability. Services are available to currently enrolled students, who must apply for services, and provide appropriate documentation to substantiate the claimed disability.

ADMISSION INFORMATION FOR STUDENTS WITH LD/ADHD

College entrance tests required: Yes
Interview required: N/A
What documentation required for LD: Psycho Ed evaluation to include: relevant historical info, instructional interventions, related services, age diagnosed, objective data (aptitude, achievement, info processing), test scores (standard, percentile and grade equivalents) and describe functional limitations.
With general application: No
To receive services after enrolling: Yes
What documentation required for ADHD: Diagnosis based on DSM-V; history of behaviors impairing functioning in academic setting; diagnostic interview; history of symptoms; evidence of ongoing behaviors.

With general application: No
Submitted to: Admissions
Special Ed. HS course work accepted: Yes
Specific course requirements for all applicants: Yes
Separate application required for program services: No
# of LD applications submitted each year: NR
# of LD applications accepted yearly: NR
Total # of students receiving LD services: 149
Acceptance into program means acceptance into college: Students must be admiteed and enrolled in the university first and then request services.

ADMISSIONS

There is no special admission process for students with learning disabilities. Students with disabilities are considered for admission on the same basis as all other applicants, and must meet the same academic standards. Students must have four years English, three years math, three years science, three years social studies, two years academic elective (can be foreign language). The university will accept college-preparatory courses taken through the special education department of the high school. Class rank and either the ACT or the SAT are considered.

ADDITIONAL INFORMATION

Services available include individualized pre-enrollment interview and orientation to disability services; preferred registration; list of students interested in serving as academic aides; alternative testing arrangements; auxiliary aides. Academic services are available to all students at UNI who wish to receive additional academic support outside of the classroom. The Academic Learning Center provides students with a variety of supportive services that will enhance academic achievement and success. Students may access help in Writing Assistance in any of their classes. Students may schedule a single appointment to work on a specific assignment or a regular appointment to work on a variety of assignments. Assistance with math skills is also available in the Math Lab. Services include one-to-one and small group instruction; individual instruction and practice through a variety of self-instructional modes; and review lessons to support the development and practice of concepts/skills taught in math courses. Drop-in hours are available.

PROGRAM FOR DISABILITY SERVICES

Contact Information
Name of program or department: Student Disability Services
  Telephone: 319-273-2677
  Fax: 319-273-7576

LEARNING DISABILITY SERVICES

Accommodations are decided upon an individual basis after a thorough review of appropriate, current documentation. The accommodations requested must be supported through the documentation provided and must be logically linked to the current impact of the condition on academic functioning.

Allowed in exams
  Calculator: Yes
  Dictionary: Yes
  Computer: Yes
  Spellchecker: Yes
Extended test time: Yes
Scribes: Yes
Proctors: No
Oral exams: Yes
Note-takers: Yes

Distraction-reduced environment: Yes
Tape recording in class: Yes
Electronic texts: Yes
Accommodations for students with
  ADHD: Yes
Kurzweil Reader: No
Other assistive technology: Yes
Priority registration: Yes

Added costs for services: No
LD specialists: No
Professional tutors: No
Peer tutors: Yes
Max. hours/wk. for services: 1
How professors are notified of
  LD/ADHD: Both student and director

GENERAL ADMISSIONS INFORMATION

Office of Admission: 319-273-2281

ENTRANCE REQUIREMENTS
Academic units required: 4 English, 3 mathematics, 3 science, 3 social studies, 2 academic electives. **Academic units recommended:** (1 science labs), 2 foreign language. High school diploma is required and GED is accepted. SAT recommended; SAT or ACT required; ACT recommended; TOEFL required of all international applicants; minimum paper TOEFL 550, minimum web-based TOEFL 79.

Application deadline: 8/15
Notification: Rolling
Average GPA: 3.45
ACT Composite middle 50% range:
  21–25

SAT Math middle 50% range:
  440–590
SAT Critical Reading middle 50%
  range: 460–580
SAT Writing middle 50% range: NR

Graduated top 10% of class: 18.9%
Graduated top 25% of class: 46%
Graduated top 50% of class: 84%

COLLEGE GRADUATION REQUIREMENTS

Course waivers allowed: Yes
In what course: The university has guidelines for waiver/substitutions in math and foreign language.
Course substitutions allowed: Yes
In what course: Case-by-case basis for math and foreign language.

ADDITIONAL INFORMATION

Environment: The campus is in a small college town about one and a half hours from Des Moines.

Student Body
  Undergrad enrollment: 13,391
  Women: 57%
  Men: 43%
  Percent out-of-state: 8%

Cost Information
  In-state tuition: $7,350
  Out-of-state tuition: $16,106
  Room and board: $7,462
Housing Information
  University housing: Yes
  Percent living on campus: 39%

Greek System
  Fraternity: Yes
  Sorority: Yes
Athletics: Division I

WALDORF COLLEGE

106 South Sixth Street, Forest City, IA 50436
Phone: 641-585-8112 • Fax: 641-585-8125
E-mail: admissions@waldorf.edu • Web: www.waldorf.edu
Support: SP • Institution type: 4-year private

PROGRAMS OR SERVICES FOR STUDENTS WITH LD

The Learning Disabilities Program (LDP) fully integrates students with learning disabilities into mainstream courses. The program features a special orientation session, academic advising, tutoring, specialized services, and developmental courses. The LDP takes a holistic approach to address the social, emotional, and academic needs of the person with a learning disability. The LDP is learning strategies based. Students are accepted as individuals with the potential to succeed in college. The students have the opportunity to participate fully in college life and to experience academic success. Students benefit from a 12:1 student/instructor ratio; each student is provided a laptop computer to use while in attendance. To be eligible for the Waldorf LDP, students must meet the following criteria: have psychological and achievement test results, preferably no more than 2 years old; have been involved with intervention on some level during high school; and exhibit a positive attitude and potential for good college success when appropriate learning strategies and coping skills are used.

ADMISSION INFORMATION FOR STUDENTS WITH LD/ADHD

College entrance tests required: Yes
Interview required: Maybe
Essay recommended: NR
What documentation required for LD: Psycho Ed evaluation to include: relevant historical info, instructional interventions, related services, age diagnosed, objective data (aptitude, achievement, info processing), test scores (standard, percentile and grade equivalents) and describe functional limitations.
With general application: Yes if requested as part of Structured Program application
To receive services after enrolling: Yes
What documentation required for ADHD: Diagnosis based on DSM-V; history of behaviors impairing functioning in academic setting; diagnostic interview; history of symptoms; evidence of ongoing behaviors.

With general application: Yes if requested as part of Structured Program application
To receive services after enrolling: Yes
Submitted to: Learning Disability Program
Special Ed. HS course work accepted: Yes
Specific course requirements of all applicants: NR
Separate application required: NR
# of LD applications submitted each year: NR
# of LD applications accepted yearly: NR
Total # of students receiving LD services: 30
Acceptance into program means acceptance into college: Students are either admitted directly into the college and then must request LDP or are reviewed by Admissions and Academic Progress committee and a decision is made on acceptance.

ADMISSIONS

There is no special admissions process for students with learning disabilities. LDP students go through the regular admission procedures. General admission requirements include 4 years of English, 2 years of math and science; ACT 18 minimum; and a 2.0 GPA. There is a probationary admission for some students not meeting the regular criteria. These students will be asked to participate in a special interview, either by phone or in person, in order to be considered for LDP. The number of spaces in LDP is limited.

ADDITIONAL INFORMATION

Services in the LDP include the following: specialized academic advising regarding schedules and academic classes; priority time and scheduling with the learning specialist; counseling services available upon referral or request; special orientation for LDP students at the beginning of the academic year, tutor time above and beyond the regular services available to all students; academic coaches who work one-on-one with students; specialized materials and/or technology for LD students; priority registration for developmental and study skills classes; as-needed academic testing with a learning-style emphasis; instructor notification of learning disability; and academic progress monitoring that will be shared with the student, and parents if permission is given. There are skills classes for credit in study skills, math/pre-algebra, reading, and writing.

LEARNING DISABILITY PROGRAMS OR SERVICES

Contact Information
Name of program or department: Learning Disability Program
  Telephone: 641-585-8207
  Fax: 641-584-8194

LEARNING DISABILITY SERVICES

Accommodations are decided upon an individual basis after a thorough review of appropriate, current documentation and meeting with the student. The accommodations requested must be supported through the documentation provided and must be logically linked to the current impact of the condition on academic functioning.

Allowed in exams
  Calculator: Yes
  Dictionary: Yes
  Computer: Yes
  Spellchecker: Yes
Extended test time: Yes
Scribes: Yes
Proctors: Yes
Oral exams: Yes
Note-takers: Yes

Distraction-reduced environment: Yes
Tape recording in class: Yes
Electronic texts: Yes
Accommodations for students with ADHD: Yes
Kurzweil Reader: Yes
Other assistive technology: Yes
Priority registration: Yes

Added costs for services: Yes
LD specialists: Yes
Professional tutors: 8–10
Peer tutors: 25
Max. hours/wk. for services: Unlimited
How professors are notified of LD/ADHD: By director and student letters

GENERAL ADMISSIONS INFORMATION

Office of Admission: 641-585-8112

ENTRANCE REQUIREMENTS

Academic units recommended: 4 English, 3 math, 3 science, 2 foreign language, 4 history. High school diploma is required, and GED is accepted. TOEFL required of all international applicants: minimum paper TOEFL 500, minimum computer TOEFL 173.

Application deadline: None
Notification: Rolling
Average GPA: NR
ACT Composite middle 50% range: 18–22

SAT Math middle 50% range: NR
SAT Critical Reading middle 50% range: NR
SAT Writing middle 50% range: NR

Graduated top 10% of class: NR
Graduated top 25% of class: NR
Graduated top 50% of class: NR

COLLEGE GRADUATION REQUIREMENTS

Course waivers allowed: No
Course substitutions allowed: Yes
In what course: NR

ADDITIONAL INFORMATION

Environment: The campus is in a small town 2.5 hours from Des Moines.

Student Body
  Undergrad enrollment: 643
  Women: 48%
  Men: 52%
  Percent out-of-state: 42%

Cost Information
  Tuition: $19,694
  Room & board: $6,370
Housing Information
  University housing: Yes
  Percent living on campus: 71%

Greek System
  Fraternity: No
  Sorority: No
  Athletics: NAIA

KANSAS STATE UNIVERSITY

119 Anderson Hall, Manhattan, KS 66506
Phone: 785-532-6250 • Fax: 785-532-6393
E-mail: kstate@ksu.edu • Web: www.consider.k-state.edu
Support: CS • Institution type: 4-year public

PROGRAMS OR SERVICES FOR STUDENTS WITH LD

Kansas State provides a broad range of support services to students with learning disabilities through Disability Support Services (DSS), as well as through numerous other university departments. The goals of the program are to recommend and provide accommodations and assistance tailored to the students' needs. Faculty and staff are sensitive to the special needs of the students and will work with them in their pursuit of educational goals. DSS works with students to plan accommodations that best aid the students to overcome areas of difficulty. DSS does not modify or reduce the content of courses. Rather, DSS helps to set up ways for students to demonstrate academic knowledge without interference from the disability. To qualify for services students must provide DSS with documentation of a learning disability that includes: a complete record of all testing administered; a signed statement from a professional documenting LD; and information about strengths and weaknesses to help plan accommodations best suited to the student's needs. Many of the services provided take time to arrange. Consequently, students are encouraged to apply for services early in the process of planning for college.

ADMISSION INFORMATION FOR STUDENTS WITH LD/ADHD

College entrance tests required: Yes
Interview required: No
Essay recommended: No
What documentation required for LD: Psycho Ed evaluation to include: relevant historical info, instructional interventions, related services, age diagnosed, objective data (aptitude, achievement, info processing), test scores (standard, percentile and grade equivalents) and describe functional limitations.
With general application: No
To receive services after enrolling: Yes
What documentation required for ADHD: Diagnosis based on DSM-V; history of behaviors impairing functioning in academic setting; diagnostic interview; history of symptoms; evidence of ongoing behaviors.

With general application: No
Submitted to: Disability Support Services
Special Ed. HS course work accepted: Yes
Specific course requirements of all applicants: NR
Separate application required: No
# of LD applications submitted each year: 268
# of LD applications accepted yearly: NR
Total # of students receiving LD services: 380–421
Acceptance into program means acceptance into college: Students must be admitted and enrolled in the university first and then request services.

ADMISSIONS

There is no special admissions process for students with learning disabilities. Applicants must either have a 21 on the ACT or 980 SAT Reasoning, rank in the top third of their senior class, or have a 2.0 GPA (2.5 GPA for out-of-state students) in the Kansas precollege curriculum. If applicants don't meet these criteria, they may be admitted as an exception. Exceptions option: If students have encountered unusual situations that keep them from meeting the requirements they should contact the Office of Admissions. As many as 10 percent of new freshmen may be offered admission based on other measures of their ability to succeed at K-State. High schools may recommend approval of course substitutions to the Regents. Special consideration may be given when requested. The Director of Disability Support Services may be asked to consult with admissions on individual applicants.

ADDITIONAL INFORMATION

To access support services students must provide DSS with verification of LD. Specific information about strengths and weaknesses help DSS plan accommodations best suited to students' needs. Students should contact DSS for services. Many services take time to arrange so early applications are encouraged. Students with LD may be eligible for services such as test-taking accommodations, readers, assistance in obtaining alternative text, note-takers. Tutoring is offered in some freshman/sophomore classes. All students may attend an orientation meeting prior to registration freshman year. Special courses are offered in Enhanced University Experience to learn note-taking, textbook-reading, and test-taking skills; math review for students experiencing difficulty with arithmetic computations; intermediate algebra; and college algebra. Services are available for undergrads and graduate students.

LEARNING DISABILITY PROGRAMS OR SERVICES

Contact Information
Name of program or department: Disability Support Services (DSS)
  Telephone: 785-532-6441
  Fax: 785-532-6457

LEARNING DISABILITY SERVICES

Accommodations are decided upon an individual basis after a thorough review of appropriate, current documentation. The accommodations requested must be supported through the documentation provided and must be logically linked to the current impact of the condition on academic functioning.

Allowed in exams
  Calculator: Yes
  Dictionary: Yes
  Computer: Yes
  Spellchecker: Yes
Extended test time: Yes
Scribes: Yes
Proctors: Yes
Oral exams: Yes
Note-takers: Yes

Distraction-reduced environment: Yes
Tape recording in class: Yes
Electronic texts: Yes
Accommodations for students with ADHD: Yes
Kurzweil Reader: Yes
Other assistive technology: Yes
Priority registration: Yes

Added costs for services: No
LD specialists: Yes
Professional tutors: No
Peer tutors: Yes
Max. hours/wk. for services: 3
How professors are notified of LD/ADHD: By both student and Disability Support Services

GENERAL ADMISSIONS INFORMATION

Office of Admission: 785-532-6250

ENTRANCE REQUIREMENTS

Academic units recommended: 4 English, 3 math, 3 science, 2 social studies, 1 history, 1 computer technology. High school diploma is required, and GED is accepted. ACT with or without Writing component accepted.

Application deadline: None
Notification: Rolling
Average GPA: 3.42
ACT Composite middle 50% range: 21–27

SAT Math middle 50% range: NR
SAT Critical Reading middle 50% range: NR
SAT Writing middle 50% range: NR

Graduated top 10% of class: 20%
Graduated top 25% of class: 45%
Graduated top 50% of class: 73%

COLLEGE GRADUATION REQUIREMENTS

Course waivers allowed: Yes
In what course: Substitutions only. No waivers. Math and foreign language are most frequently requested.
Course substitutions allowed: Yes
In what course: Substitutions only. No waivers. Math and foreign language are most frequently requested.

ADDITIONAL INFORMATION

Environment: The university is located on 664 acres in a suburban area 125 miles west of Kansas City.

Student Body
  Undergrad enrollment: 19,385
  Women: 48%
  Men: 52%
  Percent out-of-state: 16%

Cost Information
  In-state tuition: $6,936
  Out-of-state tuition: $18,402
  Room & board: $7,198
Housing Information
  University housing: Yes
  Percent living on campus: 24%

Greek System
  Fraternity: Yes
  Sorority: Yes
Athletics: Division I

PITTSBURG STATE UNIVERSITY

1701 South Broadway, Pittsburg, KS 66762
Phone: 620-235-4251 • Fax: 620-235-6003
E-mail: psuadmit@pittstate.edu • Web: www.pittstate.edu
Support: CS • Institution: 4-year public

PROGRAMS OR SERVICES FOR STUDENTS WITH LD

The Center for Student Accommodations at Pittsburg State University is committed to providing appropriate educational and related services to students with LD. PSU works hard to help meet the transition needs of new students with identified LD. The specific type of assistance is determined on an individual basis. Previous records and an interview determine the type and degree of assistance appropriate for the student. The main purpose of the LD Assistance Team is to assist students in understanding and preparing assignments and completing tests. They provide a minimum amount of tutoring, but look to respective departments to provide these services. The key to their services is assistance. They do not provide content, information, or answers that do not reflect knowledge obtained by the student. Bright, highly motivated students with LD who are confident that they can succeed with hard work and supervision are welcomed to explore the educational possibilities at PSU.

ADMISSION INFORMATION FOR STUDENTS WITH LD/ADHD

College entrance tests required: No
Interview required: No
What documentation required for LD: Psycho Ed evaluation to include: relevant historical info, instructional interventions, related services, age diagnosed, objective data (aptitude, achievement, info processing), test scores (standard, percentile and grade equivalents) and describe functional limitations.
With general application: No
To receive services after enrolling: Yes
What documentation required for ADHD: Diagnosis based on DSM-V; history of behaviors impairing functioning in academic setting; diagnostic interview; history of symptoms; evidence of ongoing behaviors.

With general application: No
Submitted to: Support Program/Services
Special Ed. HS course work accepted: Yes
Specific course requirements for all applicants: NR
Separate application required for program services: Yes
# of LD applications submitted each year: NR
# of LD applications accepted yearly: NR
Total # of students receiving LD services: 65–70
Acceptance into program means acceptance into college: Students must be admitted and enrolled in the university first and then request services.

ADMISSIONS

Students must meet the regular admissions criteria to the university. Upon acceptance, they should visit the campus in the spring, request to visit with a member of the coordinator of the Center for Student Accommodations, attend a summer orientation program on campus, and forward a copy of the most recent Individualized Education Plan or documentation from the high school or doctor stating the nature of the LD. Once on campus, contact the team for an appointment to plan your study schedule at the Center for Student Accommodations.

ADDITIONAL INFORMATION

Specific assistance is determined on an individual basis based on documentation and an interview. Services provided by the Learning Disabilities Assistance Team include: academic advising and planning; study skills strategies; testing modifications include extended time for tests, reading multiple choice and true-false tests verbatim, reading and defining words on a test (if the definition of that word does not give the student an unfair advantage in answering questions), reading and explaining what is being asked on short answer and essay tests; reading and helping the student understand the notes they took in class or the notes they took from their tape-recorded lectures; writing or typing a tape recorded assignment prepared by the student; and reading and explaining the assignment to the student. They will also monitor student's class attendance, study schedule, and free time schedule.

PROGRAM FOR DISABILITY SERVICES

Contact Information
Name of program or department: The Center for Student Accommodations
 Telephone: 620-235-6584
 Fax: 620-235-4455

LEARNING DISABILITY SERVICES

Accommodations are decided upon an individual basis after a thorough review of appropriate, current documentation. The accommodations requested must be supported through the documentation provided and must be logically linked to the current impact of the condition on academic functioning.

Allowed in exams
 Calculator: Yes
 Dictionary: Yes
 Computer: Yes
 Spellchecker: Yes
Extended test time: Yes
Scribes: Yes
Proctors: Yes
Oral exams: Yes
Note-takers: Yes

Distraction-reduced environment: Yes
Tape recording in class: Yes
Electronic texts: No
**Accommodations for students with
 ADHD:** Yes
Kurzweil Reader: No
Other assistive technology: N/A
Priority registration: No

Added costs for services: No
LD specialists: Yes
Professional tutors: 2
Peer tutors: 2
Max. hours/wk. for services: 40
**How professors are notified of
 LD/ADHD:** Director

GENERAL ADMISSIONS INFORMATION

Office of Admission: 620-235-4251

ENTRANCE REQUIREMENTS
Academic units recommended: 4 English, 3 mathematics, 3 science, 3 social studies. High school diploma is required and GED is accepted. ACT required; TOEFL required of all international applicants; minimum paper TOEFL 520, minimum computer TOEFL 190, minimum web-based TOEFL 68.

Application deadline: None
Notification: Rolling
Average GPA: 3.3
ACT Composite middle 50% range:
 19–24

SAT Math middle 50% range: NR
SAT Writing middle 50% range:
 NR
ACT Composite middle 50% range:
 NR

Graduated top 10% of class: 18%
Graduated top 25% of class: 43%
Graduated top 50% of class: 72%

COLLEGE GRADUATION REQUIREMENTS

Course waivers allowed: No
Course substitutions allowed: No

ADDITIONAL INFORMATION

Environment: 120 miles from Kansas City and Tulsa

Student Body
 Undergrad enrollment: 7,000
 Women: 47%
 Men: 53%
 Percent out-of-state: 24%

Cost Information
 In-state tuition: $5,162
 Out-of-state tuition: $14,166
 Room and board: $6,016
Housing Information
 University housing: Yes
 Percent living on campus: 15%

Greek System
 Fraternity: Yes
 Sorority: Yes
Athletics: Division II

UNIVERSITY OF KANSAS

Office of Admissions and Scholarships, 1502 Iowa Street, Lawrence, KS 66
Phone: 785-864-3911 • Fax: 785-864-5017
E-mail: adm@ku.edu • Web: www.ku.edu
Support: CS • Institution: 4-year public

PROGRAMS OR SERVICES FOR STUDENTS WITH LD

The university accommodates the students with LD by understanding the student's ability and individualizing academic accommodations throughout a student's career. Disability Resources also serves as a referral agent to other resources at the university and in the Lawrence community. Current documentation is necessary and should include a recent diagnostic report of LD.

ADMISSION INFORMATION FOR STUDENTS WITH LD/ADHD

College entrance tests required: Yes
Interview required: No
What documentation required for LD: Psycho Ed evaluation
  to include: relevant historical info, instructional interventions,
  related services, age diagnosed, objective data (aptitude,
  achievement, info processing), test scores (standard,
  percentile and grade equivalents) and describe functional
  limitations.
With general application: No
To receive services after enrolling: Yes
What documentation required for ADHD: Diagnosis based
  on DSM-V; history of behaviors impairing functioning in
  academic setting; diagnostic interview; history of symptoms;
  evidence of ongoing behaviors.

With general application: No
Submitted to: Disability Resources
Special Ed. HS course work accepted: Yes
Specific course requirements for all applicants: NR
Separate application required for program services: No
# of LD applications submitted each year: NR
# of LD applications accepted yearly: NR
Total # of students receiving LD services: 256
Acceptance into program means acceptance into
  college: Student must be admitted and enrolled in the
  university first (they can appeal a denial) and then request
  services.

ADMISSIONS

All applicants are admitted using the same criteria. Students unable to meet admission criteria because of LD should submit a personal statement providing additional information, such as no foreign language taken in high school because of the LD. Applicants should contact Disability Resources for information and an early assessment of needs. It is important to include recent documentation or diagnosis, samples of students' work, and parent and student statements regarding educational history. Regular in-state admission requires either: (1) complete the Kansas Board of Regents Qualified Admission Curriculum with a 2.0 or higher; or (2) achieve an ACT score of 21 or hgher or SAT of 990 or above; or (3) rank in the top third of your high school class. Regular out-of state admissions requires either: (1) complete the Kansas Board of Regents Qualified Admission Curriculum with a 2.5 or higher; or (2) achieve an ACT score of 24 or higher or SAT of 1090; or (3) rank in the top third of your high school class. The university is very concerned that a student with LD be competitive in this academic environment. If admission criteria are not met because of LD, the applicant should submit documentation and counselor recommendation.

ADDITIONAL INFORMATION

Skill workshops are available in study skills, time management,stress management,and preparing for exams. Disability Resources also serves as an advocate or liaison for students. Tutoring services for students who meet qualifications are available through Supportive Educational Services at no cost. Tutoring Services offered through the Academic Achievement and Access Center are also available in most challenging entry level courses for a fee. Services and accommodations are available for undergraduate and graduate students.

PROGRAM FOR DISABILITY SERVICES

Contact Information
Name of program or department: Disability Resources
  Telephone: 785-864-2620
  Fax: 785-864-2817

LEARNING DISABILITY SERVICES

Accommodations are decided upon an individual basis after a thorough review of appropriate, current documentation. The accommodations requested must be supported through the documentation provided and must be logically linked to the current impact of the condition on academic functioning.

Allowed in exams
  Calculator: Yes
  Dictionary: Yes
  Computer: Yes
  Spellchecker: Yes
Extended test time: Yes
Scribes: Yes
Proctors: Yes
Oral exams: Yes
Note-takers: Yes

Distraction-reduced environment: Yes
Tape recording in class: Yes
Electronic texts: Yes
Accommodations for students with
  ADHD: Yes
Kurzweil Reader: Yes
Other assistive technology: Electronic text via e-mail or CD in text or MP3 file format
Priority registration: Yes

Added costs for services: No
LD specialists: Yes
Professional tutors: NR
Peer tutors: 100
Max. hours/wk. for services: Unlimited
How professors are notified of LD/ADHD: Both student and director

GENERAL ADMISSIONS INFORMATION

Office of Admission: 785-864-3911

ENTRANCE REQUIREMENTS
Academic units required: 4 English, 3 mathematics, 3 science, 3 social studies. **Academic units recommended:** 4 English, 4 mathematics, 3 science, 2 foreign language, 3 social studies. High school diploma is required and GED is accepted. SAT or ACT required.

Application deadline: 4/1
Notification: Rolling
Average GPA: 3.5
ACT Composite middle 50% range: 22–28

SAT Math middle 50% range: NR
SAT Critical Reading middle 50% range: NR
SAT Writing middle 50% range: NR

Graduated top 10% of class: 27%
Graduated top 25% of class: 57%
Graduated top 50% of class: 87%

COLLEGE GRADUATION REQUIREMENTS

Course waivers allowed: No
Course substitutions allowed: Yes
In what course: Math

ADDITIONAL INFORMATION

Environment: The 1,000-acre campus is located in a small city 40 miles west of Kansas City, with many cultural amenities and a pleasant climate.

Student Body
  Undergrad enrollment: 19,852
  Women: 49%
  Men: 51%
  Percent out-of-state: 21%

Cost Information
  In-state tuition: $8,364
  Out-of-state tuition: $21,750
  Room and board: $7,080
Housing Information
  University housing: Yes
  Percent living on campus: 22%

Greek System
  Fraternity: Yes
  Sorority: Yes
Athletics: Division I

BLUEGRASS COMMUNITY AND TECHNICAL COLLEGE

103 Oswald Building, Cooper Drive, Lexington, KY 40506
Phone: 859-246-6530 • Fax: 859-246-4678
E-mail: bl-dss@kctcs.edu • Web: www.bluegrass.kctcs.edu
Support: S • Institution type: 2-year public

PROGRAMS OR SERVICES FOR STUDENTS WITH LD

Bluegrass Community and Technical College (BCTC) has made a firm commitment to providing high-quality postsecondary education to persons with disabilities. Disability Support Services staff seek to ensure equal access and full participation for persons with disabilities in postsecondary education, and empower students to obtain the life skills necessary for a fulfilling, productive lifestyle after leaving BCTC. Students can request services by visiting Disability Support Services (DSS). Full participation in the DSS program is encouraged from the initial admission contact throughout the student's academic career. Positive peer contacts as well as guidance from the DSS staff also play a major role in encouraging participation in the DSS program.

ADMISSION INFORMATION FOR STUDENTS WITH LD/ADHD

College entrance tests required: No
Interview required: No
Essay recommended: No
What documentation required for LD: Psycho Ed evaluation
  to include: relevant historical info, instructional interventions,
  related services, age diagnosed, objective data (aptitude,
  achievement, info processing), test scores (standard,
  percentile and grade equivalents) and describe functional
  limitations.
With general application: No
To receive services after enrolling: Yes
What documentation required for ADHD: Diagnosis based
  on DSM-V; history of behaviors impairing functioning in
  academic setting; diagnostic interview; history of symptoms;
  evidence of ongoing behaviors.

With general application: No
Submitted to: Disability Support Services
Special Ed. HS course work accepted: Yes
Specific course requirements of all applicants: NR
Separate application required: No
# of LD applications submitted each year: NR
# of LD applications accepted yearly: NR
Total # of students receiving LD services: NR
Acceptance into program means acceptance into
  college: Students must be admitted and enrolled at LCC and
  then may request services.

ADMISSIONS

BCTC offers open-door admission to all applicants who meet the following requirements: proof of a high school diploma or the GED; ACT for placement not admission; 4 years of English, Algebra I and II, biology, chemistry or physics, U.S. history, and geometry. Any areas of deficiency can be made up at BCTC before enrolling in college courses; there is no required GPA or class rank. However, if a student scored below an 18 ACT in English, 20 Reading, or 21 Math the student must take the Comapss test. There is an articulation agreement between BCTC and the University of Kentucky.

ADDITIONAL INFORMATION

DSS provides a full range of services, including academic advising, career counseling, supportive counseling, specialized computer software, recorded textbooks, note-takers, writers/scribes, tutors, and testing accommodation. The DSS coordinator serves as student liaison with college faculty, staff, and administrators; vocational rehabilitational counselors; and various other social service agencies. Study Strategies is offered for college credit. The Athena Club is a student organization created to assume an advocacy role on behalf of students with disabilities at BCTC through education, recruiting, support groups, and social opportunities.

LEARNING DISABILITY PROGRAMS OR SERVICES

Contact Information
Name of program or department: Disability Support Services
  Telephone: 859-246-6530
  Fax: 859-246-4678

LEARNING DISABILITY SERVICES

Accommodations are decided upon an individual basis after a thorough review of appropriate, current documentation. The accommodations requested must be supported through the documentation provided and must be logically linked to the current impact of the condition on academic functioning.

Allowed in exams
  Calculator: Yes
  Dictionary: No
  Computer: Yes
  Spellchecker: Yes
Extended test time: Yes
Scribes: Yes
Proctors: Yes
Oral exams: Yes
Note-takers: Yes

Distraction-reduced environment: Yes
Tape recording in class: Yes
Electronic texts: Yes
Accommodations for students with
  ADHD: Yes
Kurzweil Reader: Yes
Other assistive technology: Yes
Priority registration: Yes

Added costs for services: No
LD specialists: No
Professional tutors: No
Peer tutors: Yes
Max. hours/wk. for services: 2
How professors are notified of
  LD/ADHD: By director

GENERAL ADMISSIONS INFORMATION

Office of Admission: 859-246-6210

ENTRANCE REQUIREMENTS

Academic units recommended: 4 English, 3 math, 3 science, 3 U.S. history. Course deficiencies can be made up at BCTC. Open admissions. High school diploma or GED accepted. ACT is used for placement but not for admissions. GPA and class rank are not required.

Application deadline: Yes
Notification: Yes
Average GPA: NR
ACT Composite middle 50% range: NR

SAT Math middle 50% range: NR
SAT Critical Reading middle 50% range: NR
SAT Writing middle 50% range: NR

Graduated top 10% of class: NR
Graduated top 25% of class: NR
Graduated top 50% of class: NR

COLLEGE GRADUATION REQUIREMENTS

Course waivers allowed: No
Course substitutions allowed: Yes
In what course: Students may request subsitutions for courses with the approriate documentation.

ADDITIONAL INFORMATION

Environment: The college is located on the campus of the University of Kentucky.

Student Body
  Undergrad enrollment: 12,143
  Women: 58%
  Men: 42%
  Percent out-of-state: 5%

Cost Information
  In-state tuition: $135 per credit
  Out-of-state tuition: $465 per credit
  Room & board: $6,139
Housing Information
  University housing: Yes
  Percent living on campus: 1%

Greek System
  Fraternity: No
  Sorority: No
Athletics: Intramural

EASTERN KENTUCKY UNIVERSITY

SSB CPO 54, 521 Lancaster Ave., Richmond, KY 40475
Phone: 859-622-2106 • Fax: 859-622-8024
E-mail: admissions@eku.edu • Web: www.eku.edu
Support: CS • Institution: 4-year public

PROGRAMS OR SERVICES FOR STUDENTS WITH LD

The mission of Project SUCCESS is to respond effectively and efficiently to the individual educational needs of eligible university students with learning disabilities through a cost-effective, flexible program of peer tutors, academic coaching, focus groups, and assistive technology. Upon admittance Project SUCCESS develops an individualized program of services that serve to enhance the academic success of each student. The services a student utilizes will be determined in a conference between the student and the program director. EKU also offers a summer transition program for students with learning disabilities. The program is designed to smooth the transition between high school and college. To apply for participation in Project SUCCESS, students are encouraged to visit both the campus and the Office of Services for Individuals with Disabilities (OSID). The student will be asked to fill out an application and provide appropriate, current documentation of the disability.

ADMISSION INFORMATION FOR STUDENTS WITH LD/ADHD

College entrance tests required: Yes
Interview required: Yes
Essay required: No
What documentation required for LD: Psycho Ed evaluation to include: relevant historical info, instructional interventions, related services, age diagnosed, objective data (aptitude, achievement, info processing), test scores (standard, percentile and grade equivalents) and describe functional limitations.
With general application: No
To receive services after enrolling: Yes
What documentation required for ADHD: Diagnosis based on DSM-V; history of behaviors impairing functioning in academic setting; diagnostic interview; history of symptoms; evidence of ongoing behaviors.

With general application: No
Submitted to: OSID
Special Ed. HS course work accepted: Yes
Specific course requirements for all applicants: Yes
Separate application required for program services: Yes
# of LD applications submitted each year: 100
# of LD applications accepted yearly: 80
Total # of students receiving LD services: 250
Acceptance into program means acceptance into college: No

ADMISSIONS

To be granted full admission you must have graduated from an accredited high school, and earned a minimum cumulative high school grade point average of 2.0 on a 4.0 scale, or received a G.E.D., or completed an EKU-approved home-school or distance learning high school program; AND met the Kentucky Pre-College Curriculum, and submitted an official copy of final H.S. transcript or GED results. If you do not meet the admission requirements as outlined above, you may apply to attend Eastern Kentucky University through a retention support program by applying for special admission. Enrollment at the University will be contingent on selection into this category. Continued enrollment will require full participation and success in identified support programs and coursework as approved through special admissions. Collaborating retention support programs may include: Bridge Program/First Step to College Success, NOVA, Project Success, HCOP, Education Pays Center, Center on Deafness, Academic Monitoring through Multicultural Student Services, and the Student Athlete WIN Program. Retention support programs will be reviewed and approved yearly based on their retention successes.

ADDITIONAL INFORMATION

Project SUCCESS services provided include academic coaching, one-on-one tutoring, note-taking services, e-texts, test accommodations, advocacy, weekly seminars. Skills classes are offered in study skills, reading skills, weekly workshops in transition, time management, learning and study strategies, test-taking skills, developmental math, developmental reading, and developmental writing. Planning to Win is a summer transitions program specifically designed for high school juniors and graduating seniors with learning disabilities, attention deficit hyperactivity disorder, and other cognitive disorders. The program is geared towards high school students who are planning to attend college in the fall, as well as those who are only exploring postsecondary educational options at any college. Students will attend 3 days of educational and inspiring workshops and fellowship with current college students, and spend the night in an EKU residence hall. All services and accommodations are available for undergraduate and graduate students.

LEARNING DISABILITY PROGRAMS OR SERVICES

Contact Information
Name of program or department: Office of Services for Individuals with Disabilities
Telephone: 859-622-2933
Fax: 859-622-6794

LEARNING DISABILITY SERVICES

Accommodations are decided upon an individual basis after a thorough review of appropriate, current documentation. The accommodations requested must be supported through the documentation provided and must be logically linked to the current impact of the condition on academic functioning.

Allowed in exams
  Calculator: Yes
  Dictionary: Yes
  Computer: Yes
  Spellchecker: Yes
Extended test time: Yes
Scribes: Yes
Proctors: Yes
Oral exams: Possibly
Note-takers: Yes

Distraction-reduced environment: Yes
Tape recording in class: Yes
Electronic texts: Yes
Accommodations for students with ADHD: Yes
Kurzweil Reader: No
Other assistive technology: Digital books (e-texts), assistive technology software including Zoomtext, Read and Write Gold, Inspiration, Window Eyes, JAWS

Priority registration: Yes
Added costs for services: Yes
LD specialists: Yes
Professional tutors: No
Peer tutors: 35
Max. hours/wk. for services: 6
How professors are notified of LD/ADHD: Student

GENERAL ADMISSIONS INFORMATION

Office of Admission: 859-622-2106

ENTRANCE REQUIREMENTS
Academic units required: 4 English, 3 mathematics, 3 science, (1 science labs), 2 foreign language, 3 social studies, 5 academic electives, 0.5 Health, Physical Ed. 0.5 and Art 1. High school diploma is required and GED is accepted. SAT or ACT required; TOEFL required of all international applicants; minimum paper TOEFL 500, minimum computer TOEFL 173.

Application deadline: 8/1
Notification: Rolling
Average GPA: NR
ACT Composite middle 50% range: 18–24

SAT Math middle 50% range: 440–450
SAT Critical Reading middle 50% range: 440–550
SAT Writing middle 50% range: 420–430

Graduated top 10% of class: NR
Graduated top 25% of class: NR
Graduated top 50% of class: NR

COLLEGE GRADUATION REQUIREMENTS

Course waivers allowed: Yes
In what course: Waivers and substitutions are determined on a case-by-case basis.
Course substitutions allowed: Yes
In what course: Waivers and substitutions are determined on a case-by-case basis.

ADDITIONAL INFORMATION

Environment: The university is located on 350 acres in a small town 20 miles south of Lexington.

Student Body
  Undergrad enrollment: 14,396
  Women: 57%
  Men: 43%
  Percent out-of-state: 15%

Cost Information
  In-state tuition: $6,960
  Out-of-state tuition: $19,056
    Room and board: $7,012
  Housing Information
    University housing: Yes
    Percent living on campus: 29%

Greek System
  Fraternity: Yes
  Sorority: Yes
Athletics: Division I

THOMAS MORE COLLEGE

333 Thomas More Parkway, Crestview Hill, KY 41017-3495
Phone: 859-344-3332 • Fax: 859-344-3444
E-mail: admissions@thomasmore.edu • Web: www.thomasmore.edu
Support: S • Institution type: 4-year private

PROGRAMS OR SERVICES FOR STUDENTS WITH LD

Thomas More College's Student Support Services program is committed to the individual academic, personal, cultural/social, and financial needs of the student. It is committed to promoting sensitivity and cultural awareness of the population served and to promoting varied on/off campus services and events that enhance the student's educational opportunities. A variety of support services are offered, including developmental courses, peer tutoring, and individual counseling. Students with deficits in speech/language, study skills, written expression, ongoing additional skills, perceptual skills, reading, speaking, math, fine motor, and ADHD with or without LD are admissible. Students may need 5 years to graduate. The college offers small classes, excellent faculty, and solid preparation for the future.

ADMISSION INFORMATION FOR STUDENTS WITH LD/ADHD

College entrance tests required: Yes
Interview required: No
Essay recommended: No
What documentation required for LD: Psycho Ed evaluation to include: relevant historical info, instructional interventions, related services, age diagnosed, objective data (aptitude, achievement, info processing), test scores (standard, percentile and grade equivalents) and describe functional limitations.
With general application: No
To receive services after enrolling: Yes
What documentation required for ADHD: Diagnosis based on DSM-V; history of behaviors impairing functioning in academic setting; diagnostic interview; history of symptoms; evidence of ongoing behaviors.

With general application: No
Submitted to: Student Support Services
Special Ed. HS course work accepted: Yes
Specific course requirements of all applicants: Yes
Separate application required: No
# of LD applications submitted each year: NR
# of LD applications accepted yearly: NR
Total # of students receiving LD services: 10
Acceptance into program means acceptance into college: Students must be admitted and enrolled in the university first and then request services.

ADMISSIONS

There is no separate application required for an applicant with learning disabilities. All students must submit the general application for admission. A Student Support Services staff person is part of the Admissions Committee. Students with learning disabilities may be conditionally admitted so that they can receive extra support. General admission criteria include a recommendation for 4 years of English, 2 years of math, 2 years of science, 2 years of social studies, and 2 years of a foreign language. Foreign language, and possibly math requirements, may be substituted for: ACT 19–23 or 950 SAT; rank in top half of class; and a B-minus average. The college can waive ACT/SAT scores after considering the student's LD status. A WAIS–R is not required, but diagnostic testing is encouraged before enrolling, as it is required to be on file before students can access services.

ADDITIONAL INFORMATION

Students with learning disabilities could be limited to 12–13 hours the first semester. Student progress will be monitored. Some students may be required to take developmental courses based on the college's assessment of reading, writing, and math skills. Skills classes are paired with World History, and there is college credit for skill classes in study skills, reading, and math. Some students are admitted on a conditional status and are given additional support through Student Support Services.

LEARNING DISABILITY PROGRAMS OR SERVICES

Contact Information
Name of program or department: Student Support Services
   Telephone: 606-344-3521
   Fax: 606-433-3638

LEARNING DISABILITY SERVICES

Accommodations are decided upon an individual basis after a thorough review of appropriate, current documentation. The accommodations requested must be supported through the documentation provided and must be logically linked to the current impact of the condition on academic functioning.

Allowed in exams
   Calculator: Per accommodations
   Dictionary: NR
   Computer: Per accommodations
   Spellchecker: No
Extended test time: Yes
Scribes: Yes
Proctors: Yes
Oral exams: Yes
Note-takers: Yes

Distraction-reduced environment: Yes
Tape recording in class: Yes
Electronic texts: Yes
Accommodations for students with ADHD: Yes
Kurzweil Reader: Yes
Other assistive technology: Per accommodations
Priority registration: No

Added costs for services: No
LD specialists: No
Professional tutors: 2
Peer tutors: 40
Max. hours/wk. for services: Unlimited
How professors are notified of LD/ADHD: By student

GENERAL ADMISSIONS INFORMATION

Office of Admission: 859-344-3332

ENTRANCE REQUIREMENTS

Academic units required: 4 English, 3 math, 3 science (1 science lab), 2 foreign language, 3 social studies.
Academic units recommended: 2 arts appreciation and computer literacy. High school diploma is required, and GED is accepted. TOEFL required of all international applicants: minimum paper TOEFL 515, minimum computer TOEFL 187.

Application deadline: 8/15
Notification: Rolling
Average GPA: 2.88
ACT Composite middle 50% range: 19–25

SAT Math middle 50% range: 460–570
SAT Critical Reading middle 50% range: 440–570
SAT Writing middle 50% range: NR

Graduated top 10% of class: 7%
Graduated top 25% of class: 31%
Graduated top 50% of class: 85%

COLLEGE GRADUATION REQUIREMENTS

Course waivers allowed: Yes
In what course: Foreign language and math
Course substitutions allowed: No

ADDITIONAL INFORMATION

Environment: The college is located on a 160-acre campus 8 miles from Cincinnati.

Student Body
   Undergrad enrollment: 1,397
   Women: 54%
   Men: 46%
   Percent out-of-state: 49%

Cost Information
   Tuition: $25,000
   Room & board: $6,790
Housing Information
   University housing: Yes
   Percent living on campus: 20%

Greek System
   Fraternity: No
   Sorority: No
Athletics: Division III

UNIVERSITY OF KENTUCKY

100 Funkhouser Building, Lexington, KY 40506
Phone: 859-257-2000 • Fax: 859-257-3823
E-mail: admissions@uky.edu • Web: www.uky.edu
Support: S • Institution: 4-year public

PROGRAMS OR SERVICES FOR STUDENTS WITH LD

The goal of the Disability Resource Center is to provide equal access to students who are eligible. We advocate for reasonable accommodations, removal of barriers, and acceptance of different learning methods. In partnership with students, faculty, and staff, our purpose is to achieve an accessible educational environment where students with disabilities have an equal opportunity to fully participate in all aspects of the university community. Students with learning disabilities may find the transition to college challenging. Typical concerns may include one or more of the following: slow reading/processing rate; poor memory skills; problems organizing and sequencing ideas; frequent spelling errors; difficulty taking notes; low math reasoning; problems with basic math operations; poor study skills; difficulty organizing, planning, and completing tasks. With reasonable classroom accommodations and individualized learning strategies, students can generally learn to compensate for these problems and manage their academic expectations competently. It is recommended that students with learning disabilities who are preparing to enter University of Kentucky register with the Disability Resource Center (DRC) soon after acceptance. The DRC can play a vital role in providing students with information, strategies, other campus resources, and support to improve their efforts in making these transitions and completing their educational degree programs. Students must provide a current psychological assessment or medical assessment using adult measures and complete results as documentation of their diagnosis to the DRC, and schedule an appointment to discuss their accommodation needs. IEPs or 504 Plans or Transition Plans are useful but cannot be used to document a disability.

ADMISSION INFORMATION FOR STUDENTS WITH LD/ADHD

College entrance tests required: Yes
Interview required: No
Essay required: N/A
What documentation required for LD: Psycho Ed evaluation
to include: relevant historical info, instructional interventions,
related services, age diagnosed, objective data (aptitude,
achievement, info processing), test scores (standard,
percentile and grade equivalents) and describe functional
limitations.
With general application: No
To receive services after enrolling: Yes
What documentation required for ADHD: Diagnosis based
on DSM-V; history of behaviors impairing functioning in
academic setting; diagnostic interview; history of symptoms;
evidence of ongoing behaviors.

With general application: No
Submitted to: Disability Resource Center
Special Ed. HS course work accepted: No
Specific course requirements for all applicants: Yes
Separate application required for program services: No
# of LD applications submitted each year: 200–250
# of LD applications accepted yearly: 200–250
Total # of students receiving LD services: 550–600
**Acceptance into program means acceptance into
college:** Students must be admitted and enrolled prior to
requesting services.

ADMISSIONS
The University of Kentucky subscribes to a selective admission policy. The academic criteria are established by a faculty committee of the University Senate. The admission decision is based on factors, including cumulative high school grade point average, completion of the precollege curriculum, ACT or SAT Reasoning score results, and special talents and abilities. High school minimum GPA is 2.0 to 2.49 with an average of 3.55. High school courses required: 4 English, 3 math, 3 science, 2 foreign language, 3 social studies, 5 academic electives, 1 health/physical education, and 1 visual/performing arts.

ADDITIONAL INFORMATION
The Academic Enhancement Program, referred to as The Study, helps students reach their academic goals. The Study includes academic study groups, tutoring, and learning skills workshops. Programs are purposefully designed to foster interactions that promote learning strategies and attitudes toward academic life that are characteristic of successful college students. The Writing Center offers free individual or group consultations for students, faculty, and staff. The Writing Center provides help for many kinds of writing: class assignments, creative writing, dissertations, scholarly monographs, grant applications, reports, articles, scholarship applications, and more. The Math Resource Center (Mathskeller) is specifically designed for students studying mathematics courses at the University of Kentucky, and tutors are free and available.

PROGRAM FOR DISABILITY SERVICES

Contact Information
Name of program or department: Disability Resource Center
  Telephone: 859-257-2754
  Fax: 859-257-1980

LEARNING DISABILITY SERVICES

Accommodations are decided on an individual basis after a thorough review of appropriate, current documentation. The accommodations requested must be supported through the documentation provided and must be logically linked to the current impact of the condition on academic functioning.

Allowed in exams
  Calculator: No
  Dictionary: No
  Computer: Yes
  Spellchecker: No
Extended test time: Yes
Scribes: Yes
Proctors: Yes
Oral exams: Yes
Note-takers: No

Distraction-reduced environment: Yes
Tape recording in class: Yes
Electronic texts: Yes
Accommodations for students with
  ADHD: Yes
Kurzweil Reader: Yes
Other assistive technology: Yes
Priority registration: Yes

Added costs for services: No
LD specialists: Yes
Professional tutors: NR
Peer tutors: N/A
Max. hours/wk. for services: As needed
How professors are notified of
  LD/ADHD: Student

GENERAL ADMISSIONS INFORMATION

Office of Admission: 859-257-2754

ENTRANCE REQUIREMENTS
Academic units required: 4 English, 3 mathematics, 3 science, 2 foreign language, 3 social studies, 5 academic electives, 2 fine or performing arts, (.5) health, and (.5) physical ed. **Academic units recommended:** 4 English, 4 mathematics, 4 science, 2 foreign language, 3 social studies, 3 academic electives, 2 fine or performing arts, (.5) health, and (.5) physical ed. High school diploma is required and GED is accepted. SAT or ACT required; TOEFL required of all international applicants; minimum paper TOEFL 527, minimum computer TOEFL 197.

Application deadline: 2/15
Notification: Rolling
Average GPA: 3.46
ACT Composite middle 50% range: 22–27

SAT Math middle 50% range: 500–630
SAT Critical Reading middle 50% range: 490–620
SAT Writing middle 50% range: 480–590

Graduated top 10% of class: 32%
Graduated top 25% of class: 60%
Graduated top 50% of class: 87%

COLLEGE GRADUATION REQUIREMENTS

Course substitutions allowed: Yes
In what course: Possibly in math, statistics, logic, and foreign language, depending on individual circumstances and a student's documentation.

ADDITIONAL INFORMATION

Environment: The university is located on 687 acres in the city of Lexington.

Student Body
  Undergrad enrollment: 19,927
  Women: 50%
  Men: 50%
  Percent out-of-state: 20%

Cost Information
  In-state tuition: $8,228
  Out-of-state tuition: $18,740
  Room and board: $9,439
Housing Information
  University housing: Yes
  Percent living on campus: 27%

Greek System
  Fraternity: Yes
  Sorority: Yes
Athletics: Division I

WESTERN KENTUCKY UNIVERSITY

Potter Hall 117, 1906 College Heights Blvd., Bowling Green, KY 42101-107
Phone: 270-745-2551 • Fax: 270-745-6133
E-mail: admission@wku.edu • Web: www.wku.edu
Support: CS • Institution: 4-year public

PROGRAMS OR SERVICES FOR STUDENTS WITH LD

The goal of the Office of Student Disability Services is to foster the full and self-directed participation of persons with disabilities attending the university. The service is established to facilitate the participation of students at Western Kentucky University by providing information on services, acting as liaison with faculty and staff for reasonable accommodation, and providing learning disability services. Office for Student Disability Services (SDS) coordinates support services so that students can be self-sufficient and can develop to their maximum academic potential. Our offices are located in the Student Success Center and just opened in our new building in 2006. To be eligible for SDS services, documentation from a licensed professional must be provided. This documentation must be no more than three years old, state the nature of the disability, and clearly describe the kinds of accommodations recommended. Once accepted students should provide the documentation; discuss the disability and ways to accommodate special needs; arrange to take placement tests and register for classes early; contact instructors to learn what each instructor will require in terms of grading criteria, amount of weekly reading, and number and types of homework assignments and tests; order books on tape; and request alternative testing conditions, note-takers, and readers. Students needing specialized help beyond that offered by the university may need to seek financial assistance.

ADMISSION INFORMATION FOR STUDENTS WITH LD/ADHD

College entrance tests required: Yes
Interview required: Yes
Essay required: N/A
What documentation required for LD: Psycho Ed evaluation to include: relevant historical info, instructional interventions, related services, age diagnosed, objective data (aptitude, achievement, info processing), test scores (standard, percentile and grade equivalents) and describe functional limitations.
With general application: No
To receive services after enrolling: Yes
What documentation required for ADHD: Diagnosis based on DSM-V; history of behaviors impairing functioning in academic setting; diagnostic interview; history of symptoms; evidence of ongoing behaviors.

With general application: No
Submitted to: Support Program/Services
Special Ed. HS course work accepted: Yes
Specific course requirements for all applicants: Yes
Separate application required for program services: No
# of LD applications submitted each year: 100
# of LD applications accepted yearly: 100
Total # of students receiving LD services: 380
Acceptance into program means acceptance into college: No

ADMISSIONS

There is no special admissions process for students with learning disabilities. All applicants must meet the same admission criteria. High school courses required include: four years English, three years math, two years social science, and two years lab science (biology, physics and chemistry). In-state residents must have a minimum 2.5 GPA or 20 ACT; factors considered for admission are ACT/SAT; high school performance; any post-secondary record; recommendations; personal qualifications and conduct; interview; and complete and accurate information listed on the application for admission. Students can be admitted by exception through the Director of Admissions. Western Kentucky University's Community College will admit students who do not meet high school course requirements.

ADDITIONAL INFORMATION

The program for students with LD offers students: adapted test administrations; textbooks in alternative format; short-term loan of special equipment; reading referral services; faculty liaison; peer tutoring; academic, personal, and career counseling; and assistance with the Reading and Learning Labs. Academic advisors assist students in course selection. The university combines intensive academic advisement with special seminars to provide support during the freshman year. The University Counseling Services Center provides assistance in personal, social, emotional, and intellectual development. Skills classes are offered in math, reading, vocabulary, study skills, and English through the Community College. College credit is given for these classes. Services and accommodations are available for undergraduate and graduate students. Students work directly with a counselor and meet twice weekly during the intital semester. Testing may be completed in the SDS facilities.

PROGRAM FOR DISABILITY SERVICES

Contact Information
Name of program or department: Office for Student Disability Services
  Telephone: 502-745-5004
  Fax: 502-745-6289

LEARNING DISABILITY SERVICES

Accommodations are decided upon an individual basis after a thorough review of appropriate, current documentation. The accommodations requested must be supported through the documentation provided and must be logically linked to the current impact of the condition on academic functioning.

Allowed in exams
  Calculator: Yes
  Dictionary: N/A
  Computer: Yes
  Spellchecker: Yes
Extended test time: Yes
Scribes: Yes
Proctors: Yes
Oral exams: Yes
Note-takers: Yes

Distraction-reduced environment: Yes
Tape recording in class: Yes
Electronic texts: Yes
Accommodations for students with
  ADHD: Yes
Kurzweil Reader: No
Other assistive technology: Captioning
Priority registration: Yes

Added costs for services: No
LD specialists: Yes
Professional tutors: 25
Peer tutors: 20
Max. hours/wk. for services: 20
How professors are notified of
  LD/ADHD: Both student and director

GENERAL ADMISSIONS INFORMATION

Office of Admission: 270-745-2551

ENTRANCE REQUIREMENTS
Academic units required: 4 English, 3 mathematics, 3 science, (1 science labs), 2 foreign language, 3 social studies, 1.5 credits each: health and PE, history, performing arts. High school diploma is required and GED is accepted. SAT or ACT required; TOEFL required of all international applicants; minimum paper TOEFL 525, minimum computer TOEFL 197.

Application deadline: 8/1
Notification: Rolling
Average GPA: 3.15
ACT Composite middle 50% range:
  18–24

SAT Math middle 50% range:
  430–590
SAT Critical Reading middle 50%
  range: 440–580
SAT Writing middle 50% range: NR

Graduated top 10% of class: 18%
Graduated top 25% of class: 40%
Graduated top 50% of class: 68%

COLLEGE GRADUATION REQUIREMENTS

Course waivers allowed: Yes
In what course: Courses that can be substituted are handled on a case-by-case basis.
Course substitutions allowed: Yes
In what course: NR

ADDITIONAL INFORMATION

Environment: The university is located on 200 acres in a suburban area 65 miles north of Nashville.

Student Body
  Undergrad enrollment: 17,970
  Women: 58%
  Men: 42%
  Percent out-of-state: 15%

Cost Information
  In-state tuition: $8,084
  Out-of-state tuition: $20,016
  Room and board: $7,320
Housing Information
  University housing: Yes
  Percent living on campus: 29%

Greek System
  Fraternity: Yes
  Sorority: Yes
Athletics: Division I

LOUISIANA COLLEGE

1140 College Drive, PO Box 566, Pineville, LA 71359-0560
Phone: 318-487-7259 • Fax: 318-487-7550
E-mail: admissions@lacollege.edu • Web: www.lacollege.edu
Support: SP • Institution type: 4-year private

PROGRAMS OR SERVICES FOR STUDENTS WITH LD

The goal of the Program to Assist Student Success (PASS) is to facilitate the academic success of students with disabilities and to serve as an advocate for the students. This highly individualized, limited enrollment program provides support services and personal attention to students who need special academic counseling, tutoring, or classroom assistance. Three levels of services are provided. Level I students are required to attend weekly individual counseling and tutoring sessions; the emphasis at this level is to provide individualized help to ensure the student's successful transition to college and to compensate for any identifiable disability. Level II students have, at a minimum, completed 24 hours of college credit at Louisiana College with at least a 2.5 GPA. Regularly scheduled individual counseling sessions continue to be provided; all other services continue to be available to the student as needed. Level III students have learned to compensate for their disability and are independently achieving college success; these students will have their progress monitored by the staff, and tutoring will continue to be available. Any student not maintaining a 2.5 GPA must remain in or return to Level I.

ADMISSION INFORMATION FOR STUDENTS WITH LD/ADHD

College entrance tests required: Yes
Interview required: Yes
Essay recommended: Yes
What documentation required for LD: Psycho Ed evaluation to include: relevant historical info, instructional interventions, related services, age diagnosed, objective data (aptitude, achievement, info processing), test scores (standard, percentile and grade equivalents) and describe functional limitations.
With general application: Yes if requested as part of Structured Program application
To receive services after enrolling: Yes
What documentation required for ADHD: Diagnosis based on DSM-V; history of behaviors impairing functioning in academic setting; diagnostic interview; history of symptoms; evidence of ongoing behaviors.

With general application: Yes if requested as part of Structured Program application
To receive services after enrolling: Yes
Submitted to: Program to Assist Student Services
Special Ed. HS course work accepted: Yes
Specific course requirements of all applicants: NR
Separate application required: Yes
# of LD applications submitted each year: 15–20
# of LD applications accepted yearly: 8–13
Total # of students receiving LD services: 44
Acceptance into program means acceptance into college: Student must be admitted and enrolled in the university first and then request admission to PASS.

ADMISSIONS

All qualified applicants to PASS must submit the regular application, meet the general criteria for admission to Louisiana College, and have a diagnosed learning or physical disability. Successful applicants must have the intellectual potential (average to superior), the appropriate academic foundation (class standing and/or ACT/SAT scores), and the personal desire and motivation to succeed. The PASS director and staff make the final decision about admission to the program after reviewing the following: 20 or above on ACT or 930 or above on SAT; 4 years of English, 3 years of science, 3 years of social studies, and 3 years of math; 2.0 GPA; counselor's recommendation and other letters of reference; psychological or medical reports; and an essay outlining why the student feels he or she can succeed in college. At least one personal interview with student and parent(s) is required. Students are encouraged to apply early and there is an application evaluation fee of $25. Students may appeal to the Appeals Board if they are denied admission.

ADDITIONAL INFORMATION

Tutoring sessions are conducted in most subjects taken by Level I students. Additional tutorial help is available at the higher levels as needed. The PASS staff will carefully work with individual professors and the student's academic advisor to coordinate and accommodate the student's learning needs. Students admitted to PASS will remain in the program as long as they are at Louisiana College. Noncompliance with any component of the program may result in a student's dismissal from the program. Skills classes are offered in study techniques, test-taking strategies, and time management through orientation, and private tutoring from a PASS staff member. Incoming freshmen are encouraged to attend one summer session (5 weeks) to become familiar with the campus and college life.

LEARNING DISABILITY PROGRAMS OR SERVICES

Contact Information
Name of program or department: Program to Assist Student Success (PASS)
 Telephone: 318-487-7629

LEARNING DISABILITY SERVICES

Accommodations are decided upon an individual basis after a thorough review of appropriate, current documentation. The accommodations requested must be supported through the documentation provided and must be logically linked to the current impact of the condition on academic functioning.

Allowed in exams	**Distraction-reduced environment:** Yes	**Added costs for services:** Yes
Calculator: Yes	**Tape recording in class:** Yes	**LD specialists:** Yes
Dictionary: Yes	**Electronic texts:** Yes	**Professional tutors:** 3
Computer: Yes	**Accommodations for students with**	**Peer tutors:** 50–60
Spellchecker: Yes	**ADHD:** Yes	**Max. hours/wk. for services:** 10
Extended test time: Yes	**Kurzweil Reader:** Yes	**How professors are notified of**
Scribes: Yes	**Other assistive technology:** Yes	**LD/ADHD:** By both student and
Proctors: Yes	**Priority registration:** No	director
Oral exams: Yes		
Note-takers: Yes		

GENERAL ADMISSIONS INFORMATION

Office of Admission: 318-487-7259

ENTRANCE REQUIREMENTS

Academic units required: 4 English, 3 math, 3 science (2 science labs), 2 social studies, 1 history, 4 academic electives. **Academic units recommended:** 2 foreign language. High school diploma is required, and GED is accepted. TOEFL required of all international applicants: minimum paper TOEFL 550, minimum computer TOEFL 213.

Application deadline: 8/15	**SAT Math middle 50% range:**	**Graduated top 10% of class:** 23%
Notification: Rolling	420–600	**Graduated top 25% of class:** 47%
Average GPA: 3.40	**SAT Critical Reading middle 50%**	**Graduated top 50% of class:** 78%
ACT Composite middle 50% range:	**range:** 530–600	
17–24	**SAT Writing middle 50% range:**	
	400–600	

COLLEGE GRADUATION REQUIREMENTS

Course waivers allowed: No
Course substitutions allowed: Yes
In what course: Appeals for substitutions must be made to special committee.

ADDITIONAL INFORMATION

Environment: The college is located on 81 acres in a small town, 1 mile northeast of Alexandria.

Student Body	**Cost Information**	**Greek System**
Undergrad enrollment: 1,032	**Tuition:** $11,850	**Fraternity:** No
Women: 49%	**Room & board:** $4,720	**Sorority:** No
Men: 51%	**Housing Information**	**Athletics:** Division III
Percent out-of-state: 8%	**University housing:** Yes	
	Percent living on campus: 56%	

LOUISIANA STATE UNIVERSITY

110 Thomas Boyd Hall, Baton Rouge, LA 70803
Phone: 225-578-1175 • Fax: 225-578-4433
E-mail: admissions@lsu.edu • Web: www.lsu.edu
Support: CS • Institution type: 4-year public

PROGRAMS OR SERVICES FOR STUDENTS WITH LD

The purpose of Disability Services (DS) is to assist any student who finds his or her disability to be a barrier to achieving educational and/or personal goals. The office provides support services to students with learning disabilities. These services are provided to encourage students with LD/ADHD to achieve success in college. The consequences of a disability may include specialized requirements; therefore, the particular needs of each student are considered on an individual basis. DS dedicates its efforts to meeting both the needs of students with disabilities and the interests of faculty, staff, and the university as a whole. It is the practice of DS that issues concerning accommodations of students with disabilities in academic and other programs and activities be resolved between the student requesting the accommodation and the university employee representing the department within which the academic program or service is located. After intervention, if the student does not find the provision of an accommodation satisfactory, the student may file a formal grievance.

ADMISSION INFORMATION FOR STUDENTS WITH LD/ADHD

College entrance tests required: Yes
Interview required: No
Essay recommended: No
What documentation required for LD: Psycho Ed evaluation
  to include: relevant historical info, instructional interventions,
  related services, age diagnosed, objective data (aptitude,
  achievement, info processing), test scores (standard,
  percentile and grade equivalents) and describe functional
  limitations.
With general application: No
To receive services after enrolling: Yes
What documentation required for ADHD: Diagnosis based
  on DSM-V; history of behaviors impairing functioning in
  academic setting; diagnostic interview; history of symptoms;
  evidence of ongoing behaviors.

With general application: No
Submitted to: Disability Services
Special Ed. HS course work accepted: No
Specific course requirements of all applicants: Yes
Separate application required: Yes
# of LD applications submitted each year: NR
# of LD applications accepted yearly: NR
Total # of students receiving LD services: 475
Acceptance into program means acceptance into
  college: Students must be admitted and enrolled in the
  university first and then request services.

ADMISSIONS

There is no special admissions process for students with learning disabilities. All applicants must meet the general admission requirements, including: 4 years of English, 3 years of math (including Algebra I and II and an advanced math), 3 sciences in biology, chemistry, and physics, 3 social studies in American and world history or world geography or History of Western Civilization and 1 additional social studies, 2 years of a foreign language, 0.5 years of computers, and 1.5 academic electives, plus 1 additional math/science elective. ACT 20 or above or SAT 910 or above, (exact scores are dependent on an individual student record); 2.3 GPA. LSU will consider the total high school record: rigor of courses completed, grades, test scores, educational objectives, school leadership, and breadth of experiences in and out of the classroom. Minimum expectations for consideration for admission are 3.0 academic on 18 units of college-preparatory high school courses as outlined in the LSU Core, a 1030 SAT (Critical Reading and Math), and a 22 Composite ACT. If an applicant does not meet the general admission criteria but is borderline, the student can be admitted through the Access Program.

ADDITIONAL INFORMATION

Specialized support services are based on individual disability-based needs. Services available include disability management counseling; adaptive equipment loan; note-takers; referral for tutoring; assistance with enrollment and registration; liaison assistance and referral to on-campus and off-campus resources; supplemental orientation to the campus; and advocacy on behalf of students with campus faculty, staff, and students. Learning Assistance Center is open to all students on campus. Computer labs, science tutoring, math lab, learning-skills assistance, supplemental instruction, and skills classes in time management, test-taking strategies, note-taking skills, reading skills, and study skills are available. The decision to provide accommodations and services is made by the SSD after reviewing documentation. Currently there are 175 students with LD and 300 students with ADHD receiving services and accommodations.

LEARNING DISABILITY PROGRAMS OR SERVICES

Contact Information
Name of program or department: Disability Services (DS)
Telephone: 225-578-4401
Fax: 225-578-4560

LEARNING DISABILITY SERVICES

Accommodations are decided upon an individual basis after a thorough review of appropriate, current documentation. The accommodations requested must be supported through the documentation provided and must be logically linked to the current impact of the condition on academic functioning.

Allowed in exams
Calculator: Yes
Dictionary: Yes
Computer: Yes
Spellchecker: Yes
Extended test time: Yes
Scribes: Yes
Proctors: Yes
Oral exams: Yes
Note-takers: Yes

Distraction-reduced environment: Yes
Tape recording in class: Yes
Electronic texts: Yes
Accommodations for students with ADHD: Yes
Kurzweil Reader: Yes
Other assistive technology: Yes
Priority registration: Yes

Added costs for services: No
LD specialists: Yes
Professional tutors: No
Peer tutors: No
Max. hours/wk. for services: Unlimited
How professors are notified of LD/ADHD: By student

GENERAL ADMISSIONS INFORMATION

Office of Admission: 225-578-1175

ENTRANCE REQUIREMENTS
Academic units required: 4 English, 3 math, 3 science, 2 foreign language, 3 social studies, 3 academic electives.
Academic units recommended: 4 math. High school diploma is required, and GED is accepted. ACT with Writing component required. TOEFL required of all international applicants: minimum paper TOEFL 550, minimum computer TOEFL 213.

Application deadline: 4/15
Notification: Rolling
Average GPA: 3.45
ACT Composite middle 50% range: 23–28

SAT Math middle 50% range: 530–630
SAT Critical Reading middle 50% range: 500–610
SAT Writing middle 50% range: NR

Graduated top 10% of class: 24%
Graduated top 25% of class: 51%
Graduated top 50% of class: 81%

COLLEGE GRADUATION REQUIREMENTS

Course waivers allowed: No
Course substitutions allowed: No

ADDITIONAL INFORMATION

Environment: The campus is in an urban area in Baton Rouge.

Student Body
Undergrad enrollment: 23,977
Women: 51%
Men: 49%
Percent out-of-state: 20%

Cost Information
In-state tuition: $4,558
Out-of-state tuition: $17,566
Room & board: $8,670
Housing Information
University housing: Yes
Percent living on campus: 24%

Greek System
Fraternity: Yes
Sorority: Yes
Athletics: Division I

NICHOLLS STATE UNIVERSITY

PO Box 2004, Thibodaux, LA 70310
Phone: 985-449-7194 • Fax: 985-448-4478
E-mail: nicholls@nicholls.edu • Web: www.nicholls.edu
Support: S • Institution type: 4-year public

PROGRAMS OR SERVICES FOR STUDENTS WITH LD

The Louisiana Center for Dyslexia and Related Learning Disorders offers assistance to serious, capable students with learning disabilities at Nicholls State University who seek to earn an undergraduate degree. They believe that everyone has the right and the obligation to pursue the fulfillment of their learning potential. The center's programs are data driven, goal oriented, and committed to change. The center has close ties with leading scholars and researchers in dyslexia. The center is impressed with multisensory, linguistic, and direct instructional approaches, but to maintain its own integrity, it projects an orientation that is objective, open-minded, and directed toward the future. The goals of the center are focused on the need to increase the understanding of dyslexia and to upgrade and improve the accessibility and quality of the services that individuals with dyslexia depend upon to help them to become self-sufficient, well-adjusted, and contributing members of society.

ADMISSION INFORMATION FOR STUDENTS WITH LD/ADHD

College entrance tests required: Yes
Interview required: Yes
Essay recommended: NR
What documentation required for LD: Psycho Ed evaluation
  to include: relevant historical info, instructional interventions,
  related services, age diagnosed, objective data (aptitude,
  achievement, info processing), test scores (standard,
  percentile and grade equivalents) and describe functional
  limitations.
With general application: No
To receive services after enrolling: Yes
What documentation required for ADHD: Diagnosis based
  on DSM-V; history of behaviors impairing functioning in
  academic setting; diagnostic interview; history of symptoms;
  evidence of ongoing behaviors.

With general application: No
Submitted to: LA Center for Dyslexia
Special Ed. HS course work accepted: Yes
Separate application required: Yes
# of LD applications submitted each year: 0–60
# of LD applications accepted yearly: 0–50
Total # of students receiving LD services: 0–150
**Acceptance into program means acceptance into
  college:** Student must be admitted and enrolled in the
  university first and then request to be reviewed for services.

ADMISSIONS

There is no special admissions process for students with learning disabilities. The college has a selective admissions policy; refer to www.nicholls.edu for admission requirements. There are a limited number of openings in the center, and students should apply early to assure space. The program seeks highly motivated students who have been diagnosed as having a learning disability. Admission decisions are made after careful review of all submitted documentation. The final decision is based on selecting the option best suited to providing a successful experience at NSU for the student.

ADDITIONAL INFORMATION

The Dyslexia Center provides a support system; equipment; remediation; academic planning; resources; and assistance. Accommodation forms with appropriate classroom and testing accommodations are given to professors. Typical accommodations may include but are not limited to extended time; use of an electronic dictionary; oral reader; or use of a computer. Students are enrolled in regular college classes. Other campus services for students with disabilities include the Office for Students with Disabilities; the Testing Center for special testing accommodations such as extended time or a quiet room; the Tutorial and Academic Enhancement Center for tutoring assistance; the university Counseling Center, which provides counseling directed at self-encouragement, self-esteem, assertiveness, stress management, and test anxiety; and the computer lab for assistance with written assignments. Assessment is available for a fee for students applying to the university.

LEARNING DISABILITY PROGRAMS OR SERVICES

Contact Information
Name of program or department: Office of Disability Services
 Telephone: 985-448-4430

LEARNING DISABILITY SERVICES

Accommodations are decided upon an individual basis after a thorough review of appropriate, current documentation. The accommodations requested must be supported through the documentation provided and must be logically linked to the current impact of the condition on academic functioning.

Allowed in exams
 Calculator: Yes
 Dictionary: Yes
 Computer: Yes
 Spellchecker: Yes
Extended test time: Yes
Scribes: Yes
Proctors: Yes
Oral exams: Yes
Note-takers: Yes

Distraction-reduced environment: Yes
Tape recording in class: Yes
Electronic texts: Yes
Accommodations for students with
 ADHD: Yes
Kurzweil Reader: Yes
Other assistive technology: Yes
Priority registration: Yes

Added costs for services: No
LD specialists: No
Professional tutors: No
Peer tutors: No
Max. hours/wk. for services: N/A
How professors are notified of
 LD/ADHD: By student

GENERAL ADMISSIONS INFORMATION

Office of Admission: 985-448-4510

ENTRANCE REQUIREMENTS

Academic units required: 4 English, 3 math, 3 science, 2 foreign language, 3 social studies, 2 history, 1 academic elective. High school diploma is required, and GED is accepted. ACT with or without Writing component accepted. TOEFL required of all international applicants: minimum paper TOEFL 500, minimum computer TOEFL 173.

Application deadline: None
Notification: Rolling
Average GPA: 3.11
ACT Composite middle 50% range:
 20–24

SAT Math middle 50% range: NR
SAT Critical Reading middle 50%
 range: NR
SAT Writing middle 50% range: NR
Graduated top 10% of class: 37%

Graduated top 25% of class: 46%
Graduated top 50% of class: 61%

COLLEGE GRADUATION REQUIREMENTS

Course waivers allowed: No
Course substitutions allowed: No

ADDITIONAL INFORMATION

Environment: The university is in a small town 1 hour from New Orleans.

Student Body
 Undergrad enrollment: 7,093
 Women: 61%
 Men: 39%
 Percent out-of-state: 4%

Cost Information
 In-state tuition: $4,736
 Out-of-state tuition: $12,686
 Room & board: $8,236
Housing Information
 University housing: Yes
 Percent living on campus: 18%

Greek System
 Fraternity: Yes
 Sorority: Yes
Athletics: Division I

UNIVERSITY OF NEW ORLEANS

AD 103, Lakefront, New Orleans, LA 70148
Phone: 504-280-6595 • Fax: 504-280-5522
E-mail: admissions@uno.edu • Web: www.uno.edu
Support: S • Institution type: 4-year public

PROGRAMS OR SERVICES FOR STUDENTS WITH LD

The University of New Orleans is committed to providing all students with equal opportunities for academic and extracurricular success. The Office of Disability Services (ODS) coordinates all services and programs. In addition to serving its primary function as a liaison between the student and the university, the office provides a limited number of direct services to students with all kinds of permanent and temporary disabilities. Services begin when a student registered with the university contacts the ODS office, provides documentation of the disability, and requests assistance. ODS encourages student independence, program accessibility, and a psychologically supportive environment, so students may achieve their educational objectives. ODS also seeks to educate the campus community about disability issues.

ADMISSION INFORMATION FOR STUDENTS WITH LD/ADHD

College entrance tests required: Yes
Interview required: No
Essay recommended: No
What documentation required for LD: Psycho Ed evaluation
to include: relevant historical info, instructional interventions,
related services, age diagnosed, objective data (aptitude,
achievement, info processing), test scores (standard,
percentile and grade equivalents) and describe functional
limitations.
With general application: No
To receive services after enrolling: Yes
What documentation required for ADHD: Diagnosis based
on DSM-V; history of behaviors impairing functioning in
academic setting; diagnostic interview; history of symptoms;
evidence of ongoing behaviors.

With general application: No
Submitted to: Office of Disability Services
Special Ed. HS course work accepted: Yes
Specific course requirements of all applicants: Yes
Separate application required: Yes
# of LD applications submitted each year: NR
# of LD applications accepted yearly: NR
Total # of students receiving LD services: NR
**Acceptance into program means acceptance into
college:** Students must be admitted and enrolled in the
university first and then request services.

ADMISSIONS

UNO does not have any special admissions process for students with LD. Students with LD should submit the general application form and are expected to meet the same admission standards as all other applicants. Students who graduate from state-approved high schools must complete an academic core curriculum and require no remedial coursework. 4 English, 4 math, 4 science (Biology, chemistry and either physics, earth science, environmental science, anatomy and physiology, or agriscience) 4 social studies, 2 foreign language or 2 speech and 1 fine art. Other courses may be acceptable as substitutes for courses in the core curriculum. A minimum score at or above 19 Math (460 SAT); 18 English (450 SAT) is required to avoid remedial classes; Plus one of the following:
ACT composite score of 23 or greater (SAT 1060) or High School core GPA of 2.5 or greater; Students with less than 2.0 will not be admitted. Out-of-State and Homeschool students who do not meet the core ¬curriculum must have a composite ACT score of 26 or greater (SAT I Math + Critical Reading combined score of 1170 or greater) and require no remedial course.

ADDITIONAL INFORMATION

ODS provides support services to students who self identify. Students must submit appropriate documentation of disability and of the disability-related need for any specific accommodations being requested. Accommodations are decided case-by-case basis and may include: taped lectures, note-taker, alternate format text books, extended testing time in a distraction-reduced environment, reader, scribe, and use of spellchecker for exams. Accommodations for students with ADHD are also decided case-by-case and could include: extended time for tests, writing directly on tests without a scantron; distraction-reduced environment; taped lectures; and note-taker. Drop-in tutoring for math and writing in the Learning Resource Center and testing centers.. Developmental courses are offered in math and English, and skills classes are available for assistance in study techniques. PREP START is a special summer outreach program for recent high school graduates to gain admission to UNO.

LEARNING DISABILITY PROGRAMS OR SERVICES

Contact Information
Name of program or department: Office of Disability Services
  Telephone: 504-280-6222
  Fax: 504-280-3975

LEARNING DISABILITY SERVICES

Accommodations are decided upon an individual basis after a thorough review of appropriate, current documentation. The accommodations requested must be supported through the documentation provided and must be logically linked to the current impact of the condition on academic functioning.

Allowed in exams
  Calculator: Yes
  Dictionary: Yes
  Computer: Yes
  Spellchecker: Yes
Extended test time: Yes
Scribes: Yes
Proctors: Yes
Oral exams: Yes
Note-takers: Yes

Distraction-reduced environment: Yes
Tape recording in class: Yes
Electronic texts: Yes
Accommodations for students with
  ADHD: Yes
Kurzweil Reader: No
Other assistive technology: Yes
Priority registration: No

Added costs for services: No
LD specialists: No
Professional tutors: No
Peer tutors: No
Max. hours/wk. for services: Referred to Learning Resource Center
How professors are notified of LD/ADHD: By both student and director

GENERAL ADMISSIONS INFORMATION

Office of Admission: 504-280-6595

ENTRANCE REQUIREMENTS

Academic units required: 4 English, 4 math, 4 science, 2 foreign language, 4 social studies, 1 art. High school diploma is required, and GED is accepted. ACT with or without Writing component accepted. TOEFL required of all international applicants: minimum paper TOEFL 525, minimum computer TOEFL 195.

Application deadline: 7/1
Notification: NR
Average GPA: 3.03
ACT Composite middle 50% range:
  19–24

SAT Math middle 50% range:
  460–590
SAT Critical Reading middle 50% range: 480–590
SAT Writing middle 50% range: NR

Graduated top 10% of class: 12%
Graduated top 25% of class: 30%
Graduated top 50% of class: 61%

COLLEGE GRADUATION REQUIREMENTS

Course waivers allowed: No
Course substitutions allowed: Yes
In what course: Foreign language and math substitutions may be requested through individual colleges with appropriate documentation.

ADDITIONAL INFORMATION

Environment: The university is located on 345 acres in downtown New Orleans.

Student Body
  Undergrad enrollment: 8,345
  Women: 52%
  Men: 48%
  Percent out-of-state: 4%

Cost Information
  In-state tuition: $5,198
  Out-of-state tuition: $16,722
  Room and board: $8,236
Housing Information
  University housing: Yes
  Percent living on campus: 8%

Greek System
  Fraternity: Yes
  Sorority: Yes
Athletics: Division I

SOUTHERN MAINE COMM. COLLEGE

2 Fort Road, South Portland, ME 04106
Phone: 207-741-5800 • Fax: 207-741-5760
E-mail: madmissions@smccme.edu • Web: www.smccme.edu
Support: S • Institution type: 2-year public

PROGRAMS OR SERVICES FOR STUDENTS WITH LD

The Disability Services program is designed to offer academic support to students through various individualized services. Students can get professional faculty tutoring in their most difficult courses; learn about their specific learning style; improve concentration and memory; study more efficiently for tests; learn how to better manage their time; learn the basic skills that are the foundation of their specific technology; and use a computer toward processing, Internet research, and other computer applications.

ADMISSION INFORMATION FOR STUDENTS WITH LD/ADHD

College entrance tests required: Yes, SAT or Accuplacer
Interview required: No
Essay recommended: No
What documentation required for LD: Psycho Ed evaluation to include: relevant historical info, instructional interventions, related services, age diagnosed, objective data (aptitude, achievement, info processing), test scores (standard, percentile and grade equivalents) and describe functional limitations.
With general application: No
To receive services after enrolling: Yes
What documentation required for ADHD: Diagnosis based on DSM-V; history of behaviors impairing functioning in academic setting; diagnostic interview; history of symptoms; evidence of ongoing behaviors.

With general application: No
Submitted to: Disability Services
Special Ed. HS course work accepted: Yes
Specific course requirements of all applicants: No
Separate application required: No
# of LD applications submitted each year: NR
# of LD applications accepted yearly: NR
Total # of students receiving LD services: 150
Acceptance into program means acceptance into college: Students must be admitted and enrolled in the university first and then request services.

ADMISSIONS

All students must meet the same admission criteria. There is no special admissions process for students with learning disabilities. All students have access to disability services, including those with a diagnosed learning disability. Some students are required to take the Accuplacer tests for placement into many courses. Students are exempt from the English portion with an SAT Critical Reading score of 450+ or ACT of 21. Students are exempt from Math portion of Accuplacer with SAT 490 Math or ACT 21.

ADDITIONAL INFORMATION

Students with diagnosed LD, as well as any student with academic needs, are provided with tutoring by faculty and students; access to resources in study skills in the form of personal advising/counseling, skill inventories, and study guides; and for LD, access to academic accommodations such as extended time on exams, testing in a quiet area, and note-takers or readers. Other services are learning assessments; faculty consulting; preparation of materials to assist students in all courses; study skills counseling; academic advising; counseling and support for students with learning disabilities; and access to multimedia self-teaching materials including computer-assisted instruction, videotapes. The college administers the Accuplacer test to any student who has not provided scores from the ACT or SAT.

LEARNING DISABILITY PROGRAMS OR SERVICES

Contact Information
Name of program or department: Disability Services
   Telephone: 207-741-5629
   Fax: 207-741-5653

LEARNING DISABILITY SERVICES

Accommodations are decided upon an individual basis after a thorough review of appropriate, current documentation. The accommodations requested must be supported through the documentation provided and must be logically linked to the current impact of the condition on academic functioning.

Allowed in exams
  Calculator: Yes
  Dictionary: Yes
  Computer: Yes
  Spellchecker: Yes
Extended test time: Yes
Scribes: Yes
Proctors: Yes
Oral exams: Yes
Note-takers: Yes

Distraction-reduced environment: Yes
Tape recording in class: Yes
Electronic texts: Yes
Accommodations for students with ADHD: Yes
Kurzweil Reader: Yes
Other assistive technology: Yes
Priority registration: Yes

Added costs for services: No
LD specialists: No
Professional tutors: 3
Peer tutors: 3
Max. hours/wk. for services: 3
How professors are notified of LD/ADHD: By both student and director

GENERAL ADMISSIONS INFORMATION

Office of Admission: 207-741-5800

ENTRANCE REQUIREMENTS
Academic units recommended: 4 English, 3 math, 1 lab science. High school diploma is required, and GED is accepted.

Application deadline: None
Notification: Rolling
Average GPA: NR
ACT Composite middle 50% range: NR

SAT Math middle 50% range: NR
SAT Critical Reading middle 50% range: NR
SAT Writing middle 50% range: NR

Graduated top 10% of class: NR
Graduated top 25% of class: NR
Graduated top 50% of class: NR

COLLEGE GRADUATION REQUIREMENTS

Course waivers allowed: Yes
In what course: Limited
Course substitutions allowed: Yes
In what course: Limited

ADDITIONAL INFORMATION

Environment: The college, part of the Maine Community College System, is located on a 80-acre campus.

Student Body
  Undergrad enrollment: 7,500
  Women: 49%
  Men: 51%
  Percent out-of-state: 6%

Cost Information
  In-state tuition: $86 per credit
  Out-of-state tuition: $172 per credit
  Room & board: $8,300
Housing Information
  University housing: Yes

  Percent living on campus: 4%
Greek System
  Fraternity: No
  Sorority: No
Athletics: USCAA

UNITY COLLEGE

PO Box 532, Unity, ME 04988-0532
Phone: 207-948-3131 • Fax: 207-948-6277
E-mail: admissions@unity.edu • Web: www.unity.edu
Support: CS • Institution type: 4-year private

PROGRAMS OR SERVICES FOR STUDENTS WITH LD

Unity College offers services for students with LD and encourages freshmen to attend the Summer Institute. The institute provides an opportunity to become familiar with the college and prepare for college course work. The Learning Resource Center (LRC) provides a program for highly motivated students. Students with LD follow a coordinated program combining regular course work, supportive services, and intensive individual work on academic course support. The LD specialist meets regularly with students, monitoring progress and ensuring personal contact. The LRC's staff is composed of faculty, LD specialist, and peer tutors. Staff helps students develop effective learning strategies, with special emphasis placed on individual student needs. The LRC gives necessary attention to each student's academic and personal growth.

ADMISSION INFORMATION FOR STUDENTS WITH LD/ADHD

College entrance tests required: Yes
Interview required: Yes
Essay recommended: NR
What documentation required for LD: Psycho Ed evaluation
  to include: relevant historical info, instructional interventions,
  related services, age diagnosed, objective data (aptitude,
  achievement, info processing), test scores (standard,
  percentile and grade equivalents) and describe functional
  limitations.
With general application: No
To receive services after enrolling: Yes
What documentation required for ADHD: Diagnosis based
  on DSM-V; history of behaviors impairing functioning in
  academic setting; diagnostic interview; history of symptoms;
  evidence of ongoing behaviors.

With general application: No
Submitted to: Learning Resource Center
Special Ed. HS course work accepted: Yes
Specific course requirements of all applicants: Yes
Separate application required: No
# of LD applications submitted each year: NR
# of LD applications accepted yearly: NR
Total # of students receiving LD services: 60–75
**Acceptance into program means acceptance into
  college:** Student must be admitted and enrolled in the
  university prior to requesting services from the Learning
  Resource Center.

ADMISSIONS
Students with LD submit the general college application and the results of recent diagnostic tests including a WAIS–IV, and other diagnostic materials indicating their level of functioning. SAT/ACT scores are not required; two letters of recommendation and transcript are required. Admissions may require an on campus interview or testing. Students may request an interview with the director of Student Support Services. Other admission for the fall.. Other factors used in the admission decision include special talents, leadership, activities, and personality. Students not regularly admissible are reviewed by the LD specialist, who provides a recommendation to admissions, and a joint decision is made.

ADDITIONAL INFORMATION
Unity College offers services to assist students who need additional academic support or accommodations. During an initial consultation with the learning specialist, a student's eligibility for services is determined. Students must submit documentation no more than 3 years old. The high school IEP, is not sufficient for determining eligibility for services in college. The Summer Institute ($1,495), required of some incoming freshmen, is a 4-week pre college program offering basic academic skills in writing, math, study strategies, computers, credit and noncredit courses and individual tutorial assistance. Students meet with academic advisors and pre-register for fall LD specialist is on staff. Services during the school year include academic advising, support groups, taped texts, tutoring one-on-one or in small groups, and skills remediation in reading, math, spelling, written language, and learning techniques. Special courses, mostly for credit, are offered in composition, math, reading, college survival skills, and study skills.

LEARNING DISABILITY PROGRAMS OR SERVICES

Contact Information
Name of program or department: Learning Resource Center (LRC)
  E-mail: jreed@unity.edu
  Telephone: 207-948-3131, ext. 241

LEARNING DISABILITY SERVICES

Accommodations are decided upon an individual basis after a thorough review of appropriate, current documentation. The accommodations requested must be supported through the documentation provided and must be logically linked to the current impact of the condition on academic functioning.

Allowed in exams
  Calculator: Yes
  Dictionary: Yes
  Computer: Yes
  Spellchecker: Yes
Extended test time: Yes
Scribes: Yes
Proctors: Yes
Oral exams: Yes
Note-takers: Yes

Distraction-reduced environment: Yes
Tape recording in class: Yes
Electronic texts: Yes
Accommodations for students with
  ADHD: Yes
Kurzweil Reader: No
Other assistive technology: No
Priority registration: Yes

Added costs for services: Yes,
  summer institute
LD specialists: Yes
Professional tutors: Yes
Peer tutors: Yes
Max. hours/wk. for services:
  Unlimited
How professors are notified of
  LD/ADHD: By both student and
  director

GENERAL ADMISSIONS INFORMATION

Office of Admission: 207-948-3131

ENTRANCE REQUIREMENTS

Academic units required: 4 English, 2 science. **Academic units recommended:** 4 math, 2 foreign language, 4 social studies. High school diploma is required, and GED is accepted. TOEFL required of all international applicants: minimum paper TOEFL 500, minimum computer TOEFL 1.

Application deadline: None
Notification: Rolling
Average GPA: 2.70
ACT Composite middle 50% range:
  NR

SAT Math middle 50% range:
  500–510
SAT Critical Reading middle 50%
  range: 480–500
SAT Writing middle 50% range: NR

Graduated top 10% of class: 3%
Graduated top 25% of class: 13%
Graduated top 50% of class: 48%

COLLEGE GRADUATION REQUIREMENTS

Course waivers allowed: Yes
In what course: Waivers are handled on an individual basis.
Course substitutions allowed: Yes
In what course: Substitutions are handled on an individual basis.

ADDITIONAL INFORMATION

Environment: The college is located on 185-acres in a rural community about 20 miles from Waterville.

Student Body
  Undergrad enrollment: 584
  Women: 43%
  Men: 57%
  Percent out-of-state: 80%

Cost Information
  Tuition: $22,440
  Room & board: $8,380
Housing Information
  University housing: Yes
  Percent living on campus: 90%

Greek System
  Fraternity: Yes
  Sorority: Yes
Athletics: NAIA

UNIVERSITY OF MAINE AT MACHIAS

Office of Admissions, Nine O'Brien Avenue, Machias, ME 04654
Phone: 207-255-1318 • Fax: 207-255-1363
E-mail: ummadmissions@maine.edu • Web: www.umm.maine.edu
Support: S • Institution type: 4-year public

PROGRAMS OR SERVICES FOR STUDENTS WITH LD

The University of Maine at Machias offers a personal approach to education. Students with documented disabilities may request modifications, accommodations, or auxiliary aids that will enable them to participate in and benefit from all postsecondary educational programs and activities. Students must provide current documentation completed within the past 3 years. This documentation should be submitted to Disability Services Coordinator who works one-on-one with any student who needs academic support. This support takes the form of working with methods specific to the LD. All accommodation requests must be processed through the Disability Services Coordinator.

ADMISSION INFORMATION FOR STUDENTS WITH LD/ADHD

College entrance tests required: Yes
Interview required: No
Essay recommended: No
What documentation required for LD: Psycho Ed evaluation to include: relevant historical info, instructional interventions, related services, age diagnosed, objective data (aptitude, achievement, info processing), test scores (standard, percentile and grade equivalents) and describe functional limitations.
With general application: No
To receive services after enrolling: Yes
What documentation required for ADHD: Diagnosis based on DSM-V; history of behaviors impairing functioning in academic setting; diagnostic interview; history of symptoms; evidence of ongoing behaviors.

With general application: No
Submitted to: Both Admissions and Disability Services
Special Ed. HS course work accepted: Yes
Specific course requirements of all applicants: Yes
Separate application required: No
# of LD applications submitted each year: NR
# of LD applications accepted yearly: NR
Total # of students receiving LD services: NR
Acceptance into program means acceptance into college: Students must be admitted and enrolled in the university first and then request services.

ADMISSIONS

There is no special admissions process for students with LD and ADHD. An interview is strongly suggested. Applicants in general have a 1000 on the SAT or 21 ACT, rank in the top 50% of class, and have a 3.0 GPA in college prep courses. These courses include: 4 English, 3 Math, 3 Lab Sciences, 2 Social Studies, 2 Foreign Language recommended, Computer Competency. Business majors can take business classes in high school for credit towards admission. ACT/SAT scores used for college English and Math placement. Students seeking admission to an associate's degree program should have a C average and rank in the top two-thirds of their senior class.

ADDITIONAL INFORMATION

One-on-one services are available on request. One-on-one assistance is offered in the following areas: learning style and learning strategies, time management skills, organizing and writing papers, basic study skills, anxiety management, major and career focus, assistance using the library, information and/or referrals, advocacy, and peer tutoring. For a student to obtain a waiver or substitution of a course, a Disabilities Committee meets to evaluate the student's documentation and make a recommendation to the Vice President of Academic Affairs.

LEARNING DISABILITY PROGRAMS OR SERVICES

Contact Information
Name of program or department: Disability Services
  Telephone: 207-255-1228
  Fax: 208-255-4864

LEARNING DISABILITY SERVICES

Accommodations are decided upon an individual basis after a thorough review of appropriate, current documentation. The accommodations requested must be supported through the documentation provided and must be logically linked to the current impact of the condition on academic functioning.

Allowed in exams	**Distraction-reduced environment:** Yes	**Added costs for services:** No
Calculator: Yes	**Tape recording in class:** Yes	**LD specialists:** No
Dictionary: Yes	**Electronic texts:** Yes	**Professional tutors:** No
Computer: Yes	**Accommodations for students with**	**Peer tutors:** 14
Spellchecker: Yes	**ADHD:** Yes	**Max. hours/wk. for services:**
Extended test time: Yes	**Kurzweil Reader:** No	Unlimited
Scribes: Yes	**Other assistive technology:** Yes	**How professors are notified of**
Proctors: Yes	**Priority registration:** Yes	**LD/ADHD:** By director
Oral exams: Yes		
Note-takers: Yes		

GENERAL ADMISSIONS INFORMATION

Office of Admission: 207-255-1318

ENTRANCE REQUIREMENTS

Academic units required: 4 English, 3 math, 3 science (2 science labs), 2 social studies. **Academic units recommended:** 2 foreign language, 3 academic electives. High school diploma is required, and GED is accepted. ACT with or without Writing component accepted. TOEFL required of all international applicants: minimum paper TOEFL 500, minimum computer TOEFL 173.

Application deadline: 8/15	**SAT Math middle 50% range:**	**Graduated top 10% of class:** 15%
Notification: Rolling	410–540	**Graduated top 25% of class:** 31%
Average GPA: 2.80	**SAT Critical Reading middle 50%**	**Graduated top 50% of class:** 69%
ACT Composite middle 50% range:	range: 420–580	
16–25	**SAT Writing middle 50% range:**	
	400–530	

COLLEGE GRADUATION REQUIREMENTS

Course waivers allowed: Yes
In what course: The student's petition for a waiver goes through a Disabilities Committee who make recommendation to the Vice President of Academic Affairs for final determination.
Course substitutions allowed: Yes
In what course: The student's petition for a substitution goes through a Disabilities Committee who make recommendation to the Vice President of Academic Affairs for final determination.

ADDITIONAL INFORMATION

Environment: The rural campus is located 85 miles east of Bangor.

Student Body	**Cost Information**	**Percent living on campus:** 43%
Undergrad enrollment: 964	**In-state tuition:** $6,330	**Greek System**
Women: 72%	**Out-of-state tuition:** $17,610	**Fraternity:** Yes
Men: 38%	**Room & board:** $7,282	**Sorority:** Yes
Percent out-of-state: 25%	**Housing Information**	**Athletics:** NAIA
	University housing: Yes	

UNIVERSITY OF NEW ENGLAND

11 Hills Beach Road, Biddeford, ME 04005-9599
Phone: 207-602-2297 • Fax: 207-602-5900
E-mail: admissions@une.edu • Web: www.une.edu
Support: S • Institution: 4-year private

PROGRAMS OR SERVICES FOR STUDENTS WITH LD

The University of New England's Disabiity Services exists to ensure that the university fulfills the part of its mission that seeks to promote respect for individual differences and to ensure that no one person who meets the academic and technical standards requisite for admission to, and the continued enrollment at, the university is denied benefits or subjected to discrimination at UNE solely by reason of the disability. Toward this end, and in conjunction with federal and state laws, the university both accepts and provides reasonable accommodations for qualified students. Students with learning disabilities or attention deficit disorder must provide current documentation that identifies the specific disability. All documentation should be submitted to Disability Services.

ADMISSION INFORMATION FOR STUDENTS WITH LD/ADHD

College entrance tests required: Yes
Interview required: N/A
Essay required: N/A
What documentation required for LD: Psycho Ed evaluation
  to include: relevant historical info, instructional interventions,
  related services, age diagnosed, objective data (aptitude,
  achievement, info processing), test scores (standard,
  percentile and grade equivalents) and describe functional
  limitations.
With general application: No
To receive services after enrolling: Yes
What documentation required for ADHD: Diagnosis based
  on DSM-V; history of behaviors impairing functioning in
  academic setting; diagnostic interview; history of symptoms;
  evidence of ongoing behaviors.

With general application: No
Submitted to: Support Program/Services
Special Ed. HS course work accepted: Yes
Specific course requirements for all applicants: Yes
Separate application required for program services: No
# of LD applications submitted each year: NR
# of LD applications accepted yearly: NR
Total # of students receiving LD services: NR
**Acceptance into program means acceptance into
  college:** Separate application required after student has
  enrolled

ADMISSIONS

All applicants must meet the same admission criteria. There is no separate process for students with LD/ADHD. General admission criteria include four years English, two to four years math, two to four years social studies, two to four years science, and two to four years foreign language. It is recommended that students submit an essay and have an interview. Interviews are especially helpful for borderline applicants. After being admitted, students may submit documentation to Disability Services in order to request accommodations and services.

ADDITIONAL INFORMATION

Documentation requirements have been established by Disability Services. Students with learning disabilities should submit psychoeducational assessment reports based on adult-normed tests of ability and achievement. Students with ADHD must also submit appropriate documentation from a qualified professional. Services could include priority registration, note-takers, scribes, proctors, and alternative format of required print materials. Accommodations could include the use of a calculator, dictionary, computer, or spellchecker in exams; reduced-distraction site for exams; extended time on tests; and assistive technology. All students have access to tutoring.

PROGRAM FOR DISABILITY SERVICES

Contact Information
Name of program or department: Disability Services
Telephone: 207-602-2815
Fax: 207-602-5971

LEARNING DISABILITY SERVICES

Accommodations are decided upon an individual basis after a thorough review of appropriate, current documentation. The accommodations requested must be supported through the documentation provided and must be logically linked to the current impact of the condition on academic functioning.

Allowed in exams	**Distraction-reduced environment:** Yes	**Added costs for services:** No
Calculator: Yes	**Tape recording in class:** Yes	**LD specialists:** No
Dictionary: Yes	**Electronic texts:** Yes	**Professional tutors:** 5
Computer: Yes	**Accommodations for students with**	**Peer tutors:** 20
Spellchecker: Yes	**ADHD:** Yes	**Max. hours/wk. for services:**
Extended test time: Yes	**Kurzweil Reader:** Yes	Unlimited
Scribes: Yes	**Other assistive technology:** N/A	**How professors are notified of**
Proctors: Yes	**Priority registration:** Yes	**LD/ADHD:** Student
Oral exams: No		
Note-takers: Yes		

GENERAL ADMISSIONS INFORMATION

Office of Admission: 207-602-2297

ENTRANCE REQUIREMENTS
Academic units required: 4 English, 3 mathematics, 3 science, (2 science labs), 2 social studies, 2 history.
Academic units recommended: 4 mathematics, 4 science, (3 science labs), 2 foreign language, 4 social studies, 4 history, 4 academic electives. High school diploma is required and GED is accepted. SAT or ACT required; TOEFL required of all international applicants; minimum paper TOEFL 550, minimum computer TOEFL 213.

Application deadline: 2/15	**SAT Math middle 50% range:**	**Graduated top 10% of class:** 17%
Notification: Rolling	470–590	**Graduated top 25% of class:** 49%
Average GPA: 3.2	**SAT Critical Reading middle 50%**	**Graduated top 50% of class:** 86%
ACT Composite middle 50% range:	**range:** 480–570	
NR	**SAT Writing middle 50% range:** NR	

COLLEGE GRADUATION REQUIREMENTS

Course waivers allowed: No
Course substitutions allowed: Yes
In what course: Substitutions on a case-by-case basis only after a reasonable attempt has been made to succeed in any given course.

ADDITIONAL INFORMATION

Environment: The 121-acre campus is in a coastal area 20 miles south of Portland, Maine.

Student Body	**Cost Information**	**Greek System**
Undergrad enrollment: 3,000	**Tuition:** $30,500	**Fraternity:** No
Women: 60%	**Room and board:** $12,020	**Sorority:** No
Men: 40%	**Housing Information**	**Athletics:** Division III
Percent out-of-state: 60%	**University housing:** Yes	
	Percent living on campus: 66%	

FROSTBURG STATE UNIVERSITY

FSU, 101 Braddock Road, Frostburg, MD 21532
Phone: 301-687-4201 • Fax: 301-687-7074
E-mail: fsuadmissions@frostburg.edu • Web: www.frostburg.edu
Support: S • Institution type: 4-year public

PROGRAMS OR SERVICES FOR STUDENTS WITH LD

Frostburg State University provides comprehensive support services for students with disabilities to assist them in achieving their potential. To be eligible for the services, admitted students must provide recent and appropriate documentation relating to their disability. Some of the services provided are extended time for testing, note takers, advocacy, electronic texts, priority registration, readers and scribes, and assistive technology. The goal of the program is to provide appropriate support services to enhance learning and to strive for student self-advocacy and understanding of and independence in their learning styles.

ADMISSION INFORMATION FOR STUDENTS WITH LD/ADHD

College entrance tests required: Yes
Interview required: No
Essay recommended: No
What documentation required for LD: Psycho Ed evaluation to include: relevant historical info, instructional interventions, related services, age diagnosed, objective data (aptitude, achievement, info processing), test scores (standard, percentile and grade equivalents) and describe functional limitations.
With general application: No
To receive services after enrolling: Yes
What documentation required for ADHD: Diagnosis based on DSM-V; history of behaviors impairing functioning in academic setting; diagnostic interview; history of symptoms; evidence of ongoing behaviors.

With general application: No
Submitted to: Disability Support Services
Special Ed. HS course work accepted: Yes
Specific course requirements of all applicants: Yes
Separate application required: No
# of LD applications submitted each year: NR
# of LD applications accepted yearly: NR
Total # of students receiving LD services: 250
Acceptance into program means acceptance into college: Students must be admitted and enrolled in the university first and then request services. There is an appeal procedure for students who are denied admission.

ADMISSIONS

There is no special admission procedure for students with learning disabilities. All students must complete the mainstream program in high school and meet all of the requirements for the university and the state. There is a Student Support Services/Disabled Student Services information form that must be completed by students to enroll in these programs. Admission to FSU is determined by the Admissions Office, which assesses an applicant's likelihood of success in a regular college program with support service assistance. Course requirements include 4 English, 3 math, 3 science, 2 science lab, 2 foreign language, and 3 social studies. If you have not taken the required courses, you may be admitted to the university with the understanding that courses in the deficient area(s) must be completed during the first year if you want to continue your studies. The average SAT Reasoning is 980 or ACT 21.

ADDITIONAL INFORMATION

Students with LD or ADHD must provide current and appropriate documentation to receive support services. Tutoring is available to all FSU students through the tutoring center. Other services are offered through the PASS office such as time management, study techniques, developmental math and reading, organizational skills, and test-taking strategies.

LEARNING DISABILITY PROGRAMS OR SERVICES

Contact Information
Name of program or department: Disability Support Services
  Telephone: 301-687-4483
  Fax: 301-687-4671

LEARNING DISABILITY SERVICES

Accommodations are decided upon an individual basis after a thorough review of appropriate, current documentation. The accommodations requested must be supported through the documentation provided and must be logically linked to the current impact of the condition on academic functioning.

Allowed in exams
  Calculator: Yes
  Dictionary: Yes
  Computer: Yes
  Spellchecker: Yes
Extended test time: Yes
Scribes: Yes
Proctors: Yes
Oral exams: Yes
Note-takers: Yes

Distraction-reduced environment: Yes
Tape recording in class: Yes
Electronic texts: Yes
Accommodations for students with ADHD: Yes
Kurzweil Reader: Yes
Other assistive technology: Yes
Priority registration: Yes, when applicable

Added costs for services: No
LD specialists: No
Professional tutors: 7
Peer tutors: Yes
Max. hours/wk. for services: Varies
How professors are notified of LD/ADHD: By student

GENERAL ADMISSIONS INFORMATION

Office of Admission: 301-687-4201

ENTRANCE REQUIREMENTS

Academic units required: 4 English, 3 math, 3 science (2 science labs), 2 foreign language, 3 social studies. High school diploma is required, and GED is accepted. ACT with or without Writing component accepted. TOEFL required of all international applicants: minimum paper TOEFL 550, minimum computer TOEFL 213.

Application deadline: None
Notification: Rolling
Average GPA: 3.06
ACT Composite middle 50% range: 17–21

SAT Math middle 50% range: 440–540
SAT Critical Reading middle 50% range: 440–540
SAT Writing middle 50% range: 420–520

Graduated top 10% of class: 11%
Graduated top 25% of class: 29%
Graduated top 50% of class: 67%

COLLEGE GRADUATION REQUIREMENTS

Course waivers allowed: No
Course substitutions allowed: Yes
In what course: Students may appeal for any course to be substituted. Appeals are determined on a case-by-case basis.

ADDITIONAL INFORMATION

Environment: The university in located on 260 acres in the Appalachian Highlands in a small town 150 miles northwest of Baltimore.

Student Body
  Undergrad enrollment: 4,731
  Women: 49%
  Men: 51%
  Percent out-of-state: 8%

Cost Information
  In-state tuition: $7,436
  Out-of-state tuition: $17,624
  Room & board: $9,012
Housing Information
  University housing: Yes
  Percent living on campus: 33%

Greek System
  Fraternity: Yes
  Sorority: Yes
Athletics: Division III

McDaniel College

Two College Hill, Westminster, MD 21157
Phone: 410-857-2230 • Fax: 410-857-2757
E-mail: admissions@mcdaniel.edu • Web: www.mcdaniel.edu
Support: SP • Institution type: 4-year private

PROGRAMS OR SERVICES FOR STUDENTS WITH LD

The Academic Skills Program is wet up similar to a resource room in high school and is an optional service that is primarily for students with Learning disabilities and ADHD. However, there may be other students with disabilities who have a documented need for this service. The Academic Skills Center (ASC) provides three levels of services: Within Level ! (no fee), students receive appropriate accommodations, tutoring, and access to monthly support groups, and for two hours a semester, students meet with an ASC coordinator. During Level II ($1,000 fee), the ASC provides Level I services and prescheduling of courses, consulting with an ASC coordinator, access to a study lab, and assignment to an ASC mentor. At Level III ($,1500 fee), the ASC provides services from Level I and Level II and diagnostic testing, planning, developmental implementation, and evaluation of a yearly-individualized academic program plus 1 hour per week of one-to-one tutoring. Student Academic Support Services works with each student on a case-by-case basis to determine and implement appropriate accommodations based on documentation.

ADMISSION INFORMATION FOR STUDENTS WITH LD/ADHD

College entrance tests required: Yes
Interview required: No
Essay recommended: Yes
What documentation required for LD: Psycho Ed evaluation
  to include: relevant historical info, instructional interventions,
  related services, age diagnosed, objective data (aptitude,
  achievement, info processing), test scores (standard,
  percentile and grade equivalents) and describe functional
  limitations.
With general application: No
To receive services after enrolling: Yes
What documentation required for ADHD: Diagnosis based
  on DSM-V; history of behaviors impairing functioning in
  academic setting; diagnostic interview; history of symptoms;
  evidence of ongoing behaviors.

With general application: No
Submitted to: Academic Skills Center
Special Ed. HS course work accepted: No
Specific course requirements of all applicants: Yes
Separate application required: Yes
# of LD applications submitted each year: N/A
# of LD applications accepted yearly: N/A
Total # of students receiving LD services: 165
**Acceptance into program means acceptance into
  college:** Students must be admitted and enrolled in the
  university first and then request services.

ADMISSIONS

The admission process is the same for all applicants. General admission criteria include a minimum 2.75 GPA in core academic courses including 4 years English, 3 years math, 3 years science, 3 years social studies and 3 years of a foreign language (substitutions are allowed in foreign language if appropriate). Students with a 3.5 GPA do not have to submit an ACT or SAT. The average ACT is 21 and average SAT is 1000. Any documentation for LD or ADHD should be sent to ASC to be used after a student is admitted and enrolled.

ADDITIONAL INFORMATION

If there is sufficient support for a foreign language substitution, a recommendation is made to the provost of the college. If approved, cross-cultural studies courses may be suggested. Students will have 2 advisors, the ASC coordinator and a faculty advisor. Some typical accommodations for various disabilities include, but are not limited to Learning Disabilities (including ADD, ADHD, and TBI): note takers, alternative testing arrangements such as extra time, books on tape, computer with speech input, separate testing room, tape recorder, foreign language substitution, math substitution. Content tutors on campus are available and skills' tutoring with a Grad Assistant is also available on a limited basis. If there is sufficient support for a foreign language substitution, a recommendation is made to the provost of the college. If approved, cross-cultural studies courses may be suggested. Students will have 2 advisors, the ASC coordinator and a faculty advisor.

LEARNING DISABILITY PROGRAMS OR SERVICES

Contact Information
Name of program or department: Academic Skills Center
  Telephone: 410-857-2504
  Fax: 410-386-4617

LEARNING DISABILITY SERVICES

Accommodations are decided upon an individual basis after a thorough review of appropriate, current documentation. The accommodations requested must be supported through the documentation provided and must be logically linked to the current impact of the condition on academic functioning.

Allowed in exams
  Calculator: Yes
  Dictionary: Yes
  Computer: Yes
  Spellchecker: Yes
Extended test time: Yes
Scribes: Yes
Proctors: Yes
Oral exams: Yes
Note-takers: Yes

Distraction-reduced environment: Yes
Tape recording in class: Yes
Electronic texts: Yes
Accommodations for students with
  ADHD: Yes
Kurzweil Reader: Yes
Other assistive technology: Yes
Priority registration: Yes

Added costs for services: Yes
LD specialists: Yes
Professional tutors: Yes
Peer tutors: 10
Max. hours/wk. for services:
  Unlimited
How professors are notified of
  LD/ADHD: By student

GENERAL ADMISSIONS INFORMATION

Office of Admission: 410-857-2273

ENTRANCE REQUIREMENTS

Academic units required: 4 English, 3 math, 3 science (3 science labs), 3 foreign language, 3 social studies, 2 history. **Academic units recommended:** 4 English, 4 math, 4 science (3 science labs), 4 foreign language, 3 social studies, 3 history. High school diploma is required, and GED is accepted. ACT with or without Writing component accepted. TOEFL required of all international applicants: minimum paper TOEFL 550, minimum computer TOEFL 213.

Application deadline: 2/15
Notification: 3/8
Average GPA: 3.49
ACT Composite middle 50% range:
  21–26

SAT Math middle 50% range:
  510–610
SAT Critical Reading middle 50%
  range: 500–620
SAT Writing middle 50% range: NR

Graduated top 10% of class: 29%
Graduated top 25% of class: 56%
Graduated top 50% of class: 91%

COLLEGE GRADUATION REQUIREMENTS

Course waivers allowed: Yes
In what course: Foreign language
Course substitutions allowed: Yes
In what course: Foreign language

ADDITIONAL INFORMATION

Environment: The college is located on 160 acres in a small town 30 miles northwest of Baltimore.

Student Body
  Undergrad enrollment: 1,600
  Women: 53%
  Men: 47%
  Percent out-of-state: 41%

Cost Information
  Tuition: $34,780
  Room & board: $7,380
Housing Information
  University housing: Yes
  Percent living on campus: 80%

Greek System
  Fraternity: Yes
  Sorority: Yes
Athletics: Division III

TOWSON UNIVERSITY

8000 York Road, Towson, MD 21252-0001
Phone: 410-704-2113 • Fax: 410-704-3030
E-mail: admissions@towson.edu • Web: www.new.towson.edu
Support: CS • Institution type: 4-year public

PROGRAMS OR SERVICES FOR STUDENTS WITH LD

Towson University offers many services to students with disabilities, but it does not have a separate program for students with learning disabilities and/or attention deficit hyperactivity disorder. Eligibility for services is determined individually by the Disability Support Services (DSS) office based on documented need and personal interview. Students are encouraged to register with DSS as soon as possible after admission to the University to ensure timely provision of services. Once registered with Disability Support Services, students are issued a memo listing their accommodations that students are expected to present to professors. Towson University also offers all students tutorial services and a writing lab not affiliated with Disability Support Services.

ADMISSION INFORMATION FOR STUDENTS WITH LD/ADHD

College entrance tests required: Yes
Interview required: No
Essay recommended: Yes
What documentation required for LD: Psycho Ed evaluation to include: relevant historical info, instructional interventions, related services, age diagnosed, objective data (aptitude, achievement, info processing), test scores (standard, percentile and grade equivalents) and describe functional limitations.
With general application: No
To receive services after enrolling: Yes
What documentation required for ADHD: Diagnosis based on DSM-V; history of behaviors impairing functioning in academic setting; diagnostic interview; history of symptoms; evidence of ongoing behaviors.

With general application: No
Submitted to: Disability Support Services
Special Ed. HS course work accepted: Yes
Specific course requirements of all applicants: Yes
Separate application required: No
# of LD applications submitted each year: NR
# of LD applications accepted yearly: NR
Total # of students receiving LD services: NR
Acceptance into program means acceptance into college: Students must be admitted and enrolled in the university first and then request services.

ADMISSIONS

There is no question on the application that inquires about a learning disability. Students with learning disabilities who want to request services after they are admitted should provide documentation and information about their learning disability to the office of Disability Support Services only after they have been accepted to the university. The mid 50 percent SAT range for applicants (combined reading, math, and writing) is 1560-1770. Priority admission is granted to applicants with GPA of 3.0 and 4 years of English, 3 years of social science, 3 years of science lab, 3 years of math, and 2 years of a foreign language (waived with appropriate documentation). Courses taken in special education may be considered. Applicants with lower GPAs and test scores will be considered after their seventh semester grades on a space available basis, with priority given to those with the highest GPA.

ADDITIONAL INFORMATION

Towson University provides students with learning disabilities with necessary accommodations based on recent psycho-educational evaluations. The Academic Achievement Center and Writing Lab provide assistance for students who need tutoring and help with writing skills regardless of disability. Additionally, Disability Support Services provides note-takers; a Testing Center to be used for a quiet place to take a test; extended test time and other testing arrangements as appropriate; student advocacy; assistance with the implementation of reasonable accommodations; scribes and readers; short-term instructional support in time management, study, and test-taking strategies; assistive technology; orientation and help with transition; help with course load and selection; priority registration; alternate formats for printed materials; and referrals for other services.

LEARNING DISABILITY PROGRAMS OR SERVICES

Contact Information
Name of program or department: Disability Support Services
  Telephone: 410-704-2638
  Fax: 410-704-4247

LEARNING DISABILITY SERVICES

Accommodations are decided upon an individual basis after a thorough review of appropriate, current documentation, and a personal interview. The accommodations requested must be supported through the documentation provided and must be logically linked to the current impact of the condition on academic functioning.

Allowed in exams
  Calculator: Yes
  Dictionary: No
  Computer: Yes
  Spellchecker: Yes
Extended test time: Yes
Scribes: Yes
Proctors: Yes
Oral exams: Yes
Note-takers: Yes

Distraction-reduced environment: Yes
Tape recording in class: Yes
Electronic texts: Yes
**Accommodations for students with
  ADHD:** Yes
Kurzweil Reader: Yes
Other assistive technology: Yes
Priority registration: Yes

Added costs for services: No
LD specialists: Yes
Professional tutors: No
Peer tutors: No
Max. hours/wk. for services: Varies
**How professors are notified of
  LD/ADHD:** By student

GENERAL ADMISSIONS INFORMATION

Office of Admission: 410-704-2113

ENTRANCE REQUIREMENTS

Academic units required: 4 English, 3 math, 3 science (3 science labs), 2 foreign language, 3 social studies, 6 academic electives. **Academic units recommended:** 4 English, 4 math, 3 science (3 science labs), 4 foreign language, 4 social studies. High school diploma is required, and GED is accepted. ACT with Writing component required. TOEFL required of all international applicants: minimum paper TOEFL 500, minimum computer TOEFL 173.

Application deadline: 2/15
Notification: Rolling
Average GPA: 3.5
ACT Composite middle 50% range:
  20–24

SAT Math middle 50% range:
  490–590
**SAT Critical Reading middle 50%
  range:** 480–570
SAT Writing middle 50% range:
  500–590

Graduated top 10% of class: 9.2%
Graduated top 25% of class: 22.6%
Graduated top 50% of class: 40.3%

COLLEGE GRADUATION REQUIREMENTS

Course waivers allowed: No
Course substitutions allowed: Yes
In what course: Course substitutions are based on individual need and current documentation.

ADDITIONAL INFORMATION

Environment: The school is located on 328 landscaped and wooded acres minutes from downtown Baltimore.

Student Body
  Undergrad enrollment: 17,517
  Women: 60%
  Men: 40%
  Percent out-of-state: 29%

Cost Information
  In-state tuition: $7,906
  Out-of-state tuition: $19,418
  Room & board: $9,942
Housing Information
  University housing: Yes
  Percent living on campus: NR

Greek System
  Fraternity: Yes
  Sorority: Yes
Athletics: Division I

U. OF MARYLAND—COLLEGE PARK

Mitchell Building, College Park, MD 20742-5235
Phone: 301-314-8385 • Fax: 301-314-9693
E-mail: um-admit@uga.umd.edu • Web: www.maryland.edu
Support: CS • Institution: 4-year public

PROGRAMS OR SERVICES FOR STUDENTS WITH LD

The goal of the Disability Support Service is to coordinate services which ensure individuvals with disabilities equal access to university programs. This goal is accomplished by: 1) providing and coordinating individually tailored direct services to students, faculty and staff, and campus visitors who have disabilities; 2) providing consultation to university staff regarding the individualized accommodation needs of students and staff who have disabilities; 3) providing support and information to students and staff which promotes the development of advocacy and negotiation skills.

ADMISSION INFORMATION FOR STUDENTS WITH LD/ADHD

College entrance tests required: Yes
Interview required: No
Essay required: N/A
What documentation required for LD: Psycho Ed evaluation to include: relevant historical info, instructional interventions, related services, age diagnosed, objective data (aptitude, achievement, info processing), test scores (standard, percentile and grade equivalents) and describe functional limitations.
With general application: No
To receive services after enrolling: Yes
What documentation required for ADHD: Diagnosis based on DSM-V; history of behaviors impairing functioning in academic setting; diagnostic interview; history of symptoms; evidence of ongoing behaviors.

With general application: No
Submitted to: Disability Support Service
Special Ed. HS course work accepted: Yes
Specific course requirements for all applicants: Yes
Separate application required for program services: No
# of LD applications submitted each year: NR
# of LD applications accepted yearly: NR
Total # of students receiving LD services: 450
Acceptance into program means acceptance into college: Students must be admitted and enrolled in the university first and then request program services.

ADMISSIONS

There is no special admissions or alternative admissions process for students with learning disabilities. Applicants with learning disabilities must meet general admissions criteria. The admission decision is based on courses taken in high school, which include: four years English, three years of history or social studies, three years of science including two years lab science, three years math, and two years foreign language; GPA; SAT/ACT; class rank; personal statement; recommendations; and the psychoeducational evaluation. The mid 50 percent range for the ACT is 28–31 and SAT 1250–1400. All freshmen applicants must submit a personal statement for admissions. The student may submit supporting documentation, which will be considered during the decision-making process. The admissions decision rests with the Office of Admissions.

ADDITIONAL INFORMATION

There is a math lab and writing center available for all students. There is no centralized tutoring service. However, limited free tutoring is available through departments. For most tutoring needs, students need to hire their own tutors. There are approximately 800 students with either LD or ADHD currently receiving services or accommodations on campus. Note-takers are volunteers and could be students enrolled in the course. There is a mentoring program and support programs for students with disabilities. Priority registration is available. Services and accommodations are available to undergraduate and graduate students. There are summer programs for high school students. While they are not specifically for those with learning disabilities, students with learning disabilities could benefit from the program.

PROGRAM FOR DISABILITY SERVICES

Contact Information
Name of program or department: Disability Support Service (DSS)
Telephone: 301-314-7682
Fax: 301-405-0813

LEARNING DISABILITY SERVICES

Accommodations are decided upon an individual basis after a thorough review of appropriate, current documentation. The accommodations requested must be supported through the documentation provided and must be logically linked to the current impact of the condition on academic functioning.

Allowed in exams
  Calculator: Yes
  Dictionary: Yes
  Computer: Yes
  Spellchecker: Yes
Extended test time: Yes
Scribes: Yes
Proctors: Yes
Oral exams: Yes
Note-takers: Yes

Distraction-reduced environment: Yes
Tape recording in class: Yes
Electronic texts: Yes
Accommodations for students with ADHD: Yes
Kurzweil Reader: Yes
Other assistive technology: Inspiration; magnification hardware; scanning/copying; Braille and tactile graphics
Priority registration: Yes

Added costs for services: No
LD specialists: Yes
Professional tutors: No
Peer tutors: Yes
Max. hours/wk. for services: Unlimited
How professors are notified of LD/ADHD: Student

GENERAL ADMISSIONS INFORMATION

Office of Admission: 301-314-8350

ENTRANCE REQUIREMENTS
Academic units required: 4 English, 3 mathematics, 3 science, (2 science labs), 2 foreign language, 3 social studies.
Academic units recommended: 4 mathematics. High school diploma is required and GED is accepted. SAT or ACT required; ACT with Writing component required. TOEFL required of all international applicants; minimum paper TOEFL 575.

Application deadline: 1/20
Notification: 4/1
Average GPA: 4.01
ACT Composite middle 50% range: NR

SAT Math middle 50% range: 610–710
SAT Critical Reading middle 50% range: 580–680
SAT Writing middle 50% range: NR

Graduated top 10% of class: 71%
Graduated top 25% of class: 91%
Graduated top 50% of class: 100%

COLLEGE GRADUATION REQUIREMENTS

Course waivers allowed: No
Course substitutions allowed: Yes
In what course: Math, foreign language

ADDITIONAL INFORMATION

Environment: The university is in a small town setting within proximity to Washington, D.C., and Baltimore.

Student Body
  Undergrad enrollment: 26,876
  Women: 49%
  Men: 53%
  Percent out-of-state: 23%

Cost Information
  In-state tuition: $8,655
  Out-of-state tuition: $26,026
  Room and board: $9,942
Housing Information
  University housing: Yes
  Percent living on campus: 44%

Greek System
  Fraternity: Yes
  Sorority: Yes
Athletics: Division I

U. OF MARYLAND—EASTERN SHORE

Office of Admissions, Backbone Road, Princess Anne, MD 21853
Phone: 410-651-6410 • Fax: 410-651-7922
E-mail: ccmills@mail.umes.edu • Web: www.umes.edu
Support: CS • Institution type: 4-year public

PROGRAMS OR SERVICES FOR STUDENTS WITH LD

The Office of Services for Students with Disabilities (OSSD) assures the commitment of the University to provide access and equal opportunities to the students with disabilities. There is no special curriculum for students with disabilities. OSSD maintains a comprehensive support network for students with disabilities. The office provides consultation with university staff, faculty, administrators, and student body to increase awareness of the needs of students with disabilities and eliminate accessibility barriers. The OSSD's focus is on supporting the positive development of students with disabilities.

ADMISSION INFORMATION FOR STUDENTS WITH LD/ADHD

College entrance tests required: Yes
Interview required: No
Essay recommended: Yes
What documentation required for LD: Psycho Ed evaluation to include: relevant historical info, instructional interventions, related services, age diagnosed, objective data (aptitude, achievement, info processing), test scores (standard, percentile and grade equivalents) and describe functional limitations.
With general application: No
To receive services after enrolling: Yes
What documentation required for ADHD: Diagnosis based on DSM-V; history of behaviors impairing functioning in academic setting; diagnostic interview; history of symptoms; evidence of ongoing behaviors.

With general application: No
Submitted to: Disabled Student Services
Special Ed. HS course work accepted: Yes
Specific course requirements of all applicants: Yes
Separate application required: No
# of LD applications submitted each year: 30–40
# of LD applications accepted yearly: NR
Total # of students receiving LD services: 25–35
Acceptance into program means acceptance into college: Students must be admitted and enrolled in the university first and then request services.

ADMISSIONS

There is no special admissions process for students with disabilities. All applicants must meet the same criteria. General admission requirements include 4 English, 3 math, 2 foreign language, and 3 social studies; minimum SAT of 750 and minimum GPA of 2.5 are recommended. In-state students who have a high school diploma and minimum C average may be admitted on the basis on the predictive index weighing SAT scores and GPA. The PACE Summer Program is a 6-week residential program designed to provide basic skills enhancement and college orientation for any applicant whose high school GPAs and/or SAT scores do not meet the criteria for admission to the university. For those who do not meet regular admission standards, participation and success in the program is required as a preliminary step to admission to the university. The program offers students an opportunity to enhance their proficiency in the following fundamental skills areas: math, science, reading/study skills, writing, and college orientation. Upon successful completion of the summer program, students may be admitted to the university. Evaluation of student performance in the program will include the successful completion of math, writing, and science components, as well as the student's positive social development and adjustment to university life.

ADDITIONAL INFORMATION

Tutoring is available in every subject for all students. Developmental skills classes are extensions of the university's academic program. Students can get instructional assistance in reading, study skills, math, and writing skills. These tutorials are taught and directed by professional staff specialists. The emphasis will be on assisting students to master college-level basic skills as required in their academic programs. As a result of placement tests, many students are required to successfully complete the fundamental classes of reading/study skills, math, or writing. Additional accommodations for students with LD could include tape recorders; test proctoring; recorded materials; recorded text; note-takers; and an LD support group.

LEARNING DISABILITY PROGRAMS OR SERVICES

Contact Information
Name of program or department: Office of Services for Students with Disabilities
  Telephone: 410-651-6461
  Fax: 410-651-6322

LEARNING DISABILITY SERVICES

Accommodations are decided upon an individual basis after a thorough review of appropriate, current documentation. The accommodations requested must be supported through the documentation provided and must be logically linked to the current impact of the condition on academic functioning.

Allowed in exams
  Calculator: Yes
  Dictionary: Yes
  Computer: Yes
  Spellchecker: Yes
Extended test time: Yes
Scribes: Yes
Proctors: Yes
Oral exams: Yes
Note-takers: Yes

Distraction-reduced environment: Yes
Tape recording in class: Yes
Electronic texts: Yes
Accommodations for students with ADHD: Yes
Kurzweil Reader: No
Other assistive technology: No
Priority registration: No

Added costs for services: No
LD specialists: Yes
Professional tutors: No
Peer tutors: No
Max. hours/wk. for services: Unlimited
How professors are notified of LD/ADHD: By student

GENERAL ADMISSIONS INFORMATION

Office of Admission: 410-651-6410

ENTRANCE REQUIREMENTS

Academic units required: 4 English, 3 math, 2 science (2 science labs), 2 foreign language, 3 social studies, 6 academic electives. High school diploma is required with 2.5 GPA, and GED is accepted. TOEFL required of all international applicants: minimum paper TOEFL 500, minimum computer TOEFL 1.

Application deadline: 7/15
Notification: Rolling
Average GPA: 2.68
ACT Composite middle 50% range: 14–17

SAT Math middle 50% range: 360–450
SAT Critical Reading middle 50% range: 370–460
SAT Writing middle 50% range: 380–460

Graduated top 10% of class: NR
Graduated top 25% of class: NR
Graduated top 50% of class: NR

COLLEGE GRADUATION REQUIREMENTS

Course waivers allowed: Yes
In what course: All pending core course requirements
Course substitutions allowed: Yes
In what course: Foreign language, math

ADDITIONAL INFORMATION

Environment: The university is located on a 600-acre campus in a rural area 15 miles south of Salisbury.

Student Body
  Undergrad enrollment: 3,967
  Women: 60%
  Men: 40%
  Percent out-of-state: 29%

Cost Information
  In-state tuition: $6,482
  Out-of-state tuition: $14,263
  Room & board: $7,758
Housing Information
  University housing: Yes
  Percent living on campus: 56%

Greek System
  Fraternity: Yes
  Sorority: Yes
Athletics: Division I

AMERICAN INTERNATIONAL COLLEGE

1000 State Street, Springfield, MA 01109-3184
Phone: 413-205-3201 • Fax: 413-205-3051
E-mail: inquiry@www.aic.edu • Web: www.aic.edu
Support: SP • Institution type: 4-year private

PROGRAMS OR SERVICES FOR STUDENTS WITH LD

American International College believes that individuals who have LD can compensate for their difficulties and achieve success in the college environment. AIC feels that the Supportive Learning Services Program (SLSP) has all of the components necessary to allow for a successful college career for a student with LD. The college models compensatory techniques and teaching strategies to enable students to be effective in college and plan for their future. Students receiving supportive learning services may elect to participate in the comprehensive services offered by the Curtis Blake Center. Metacognitive strategies are taught to help students use their intellect more efficiently. Students are mainstreamed and may receive a minimum of 2 hours of tutoring/studying strategies weekly. Students create an IEP with their tutor freshman year and may take as few as four courses each semester. Students generally stay in the program for 4 years. In addition to comprehensive services, AIC also offers a limited services component that allows students with LD to reserve 5–10 hours of professional tutoring to be used over the semester. Additional hours can also be arranged for a fee.

ADMISSION INFORMATION FOR STUDENTS WITH LD/ADHD

College entrance tests required: Yes
Interview required: Yes
Essay recommended: No
What documentation required for LD: Psycho Ed evaluation to include: relevant historical info, instructional interventions, related services, age diagnosed, objective data (aptitude, achievement, info processing), test scores (standard, percentile and grade equivalents) and describe functional limitations.
With general application: Yes if requested as part of Structured Program application
To receive services after enrolling: Yes
What documentation required for ADHD: Diagnosis based on DSM-V; history of behaviors impairing functioning in academic setting; diagnostic interview; history of symptoms; evidence of ongoing behaviors.

With general application: Yes if requested as part of Structured Program application
To receive services after enrolling: Yes
Submitted to: Supportive Learning Services Program
Special Ed. HS course work accepted: No
Specific course requirements of all applicants: Yes
Separate application required: No
# of LD applications submitted each year: 300
# of LD applications accepted yearly: 35
Total # of students receiving LD services: 95
Acceptance into program means acceptance into college: Simultaneous admission decisions are made by the program and admissions.

ADMISSIONS

In addition to submitting an application to admissions, students interested in applying for the support program must also contact the coordinator of SLSP. Applicants must schedule an on-campus interview with admissions and SLSP. Applicants must submit the results of the WAIS and accompanying report, relevant diagnostic material, and information about supportive assistance in the past. The college requires a high school transcript and ACT/SAT scores. There should be a strong indication of achievement and motivation in the fields of knowledge studied. The majority of applicants have a GPA of 2.0–3.0. Courses required include 16 academic units from English, math, science, and social studies. Foreign language is not required. The admission decision is made simultaneously between admissions and SLSP.

ADDITIONAL INFORMATION

At the heart of the services provided is a minimum of 2 hours of regularly scheduled direct, one-to-one assistance provided by a learning specialist. The specialist develops a tailored support program based on a student's needs. Priority is given to practical assistance to help students negotiate demands of the curriculum. Provisions can be made for more basic remediation of the student's learning difficulties. Specialists assist in course selection, organizing work and study schedules, and as a resource. Students have access to skills seminars in many areas. Classes in reading, spelling, math, study strategies, time management, written language, and handwriting are offered. Services and accommodations are available to undergraduate and graduate students.

LEARNING DISABILITY PROGRAMS OR SERVICES

Contact Information
Name of program or department: Supportive Learning Services Program
  Telephone: 413-205-3426   **Telephone:** 413-205-3426
  Fax: 413-205-3908   **Fax:** 413-205-3908

LEARNING DISABILITY SERVICES

Accommodations are decided upon an individual basis after a thorough review of appropriate, current documentation. The accommodations requested must be supported through the documentation provided and must be logically linked to the current impact of the condition on academic functioning.

Allowed in exams
  Calculator: Yes
  Dictionary: No
  Computer: Yes
  Spellchecker: Yes
Extended test time: Yes
Scribes: Yes
Proctors: Yes
Oral exams: Yes
Note-takers: No

Distraction-reduced environment: Yes
Tape recording in class: Yes
Books on CD from RFBD: Yes
Electronic texts: Yes
Accommodations for students with
  ADHD: Yes
Kurzweil Reader: Yes
Other assistive technology: Yes
Priority registration: Yes

Added costs for services: Yes
LD specialists: Yes
Professional tutors: 9
Peer tutors: No
Max. hours/wk. for services: 5
How professors are notified of
  LD/ADHD: By both student and director

GENERAL ADMISSIONS INFORMATION

Office of Admission: 413-205-3201

ENTRANCE REQUIREMENTS

Academic units required: 4 English, 2 math, 2 science, 1 science lab, 1 social studies, 1 history, 5 academic electives. **Academic units recommended:** 4 English, 3 math, 2 science (1 science lab), 2 foreign language, 1 social studies, 1 history, 3 academic electives. High school diploma is required, and GED is accepted. ACT with or without Writing component accepted. TOEFL required of all international applicants: minimum paper TOEFL 500, minimum computer TOEFL 173.

Application deadline: None
Notification: Rolling
Average GPA: 2.90
ACT Composite middle 50% range:
  17–23

SAT Math middle 50% range:
  420–520
SAT Critical Reading middle 50%
  range: 420–510
SAT Writing middle 50% range:
  420–500

Graduated top 10% of class: 15%
Graduated top 25% of class: 25%
Graduated top 50% of class: 70%

COLLEGE GRADUATION REQUIREMENTS

Course waivers allowed: No
Course substitutions allowed: No

ADDITIONAL INFORMATION

Environment: The school is located on 58 acres in Springfield, 75 miles west of Boston and 30 miles north of Hartford.

Student Body
  Undergrad enrollment: 1,750
  Women: 59%
  Men: 41%
  Percent out-of-state: 51%

Cost Information
  Tuition: $27,900
  Room & board: $13,500
Housing Information
  University housing: Yes
  Percent living on campus: 55%

Greek System
  Fraternity: Yes
  Sorority: Yes
Athletics: Division II

BOSTON COLLEGE

140 Commonwealth Ave., Devlin Hall 208, Chestnut Hill, MA 02467-3809
Phone: 617-552-3100 • Fax: 617-552-0798
E-mail: ugadmis@bc.edu• Web: www.bc.edu
Support: CS • Institution type: 4-year private

PROGRAMS OR SERVICES FOR STUDENTS WITH LD

There is no specific program at Boston College for students with LD. The Connors Family Learning Center (CFLC) offers instructional support to faculty and graduate students, special services to students with LD, and tutoring and skills workshops to all Boston College students. The CFLC provides academic support to more that 250 BC students with LD. The CFLC aims to help students with LD to become independent learners who understand their abilities and disabilities and can act effectively as self-advocates. The CFLC also offers free tutoring to all students at BC. All tutors receive training and must be recommended or approved by the chair of the department for which the student will tutor. Students who are seeking support services are required to submit documentation to verify eligibility. Testing must be current, comprehensive, and performed by a certified LD specialist or licensed psychologist, and there must be clear and specific evidence of an LD. Educational recommendations regarding the impact of the disability and accommodations recommended at the postsecondary level must be included. Documentation for ADHD must include an in depth evaluation from the psychiatrist/psychologist/physician who made the diagnosis as well as specific educational recommendations.

ADMISSION INFORMATION FOR STUDENTS WITH LD/ADHD

College entrance tests required: Yes
Interview required: No
Essay recommended: Yes
Documentation required for LD: Psychoeducational
  evaluation (optional for admissions)
Documentation required for ADHD: Yes
Submitted to: Admissions Office
Special Ed. HS course work accepted: No

Specific course requirements of all applicants: NR
Separate application required: No
# of LD applications submitted each year: NR
# of LD applications accepted yearly: NR
Total # of students receiving LD services: NR
**Acceptance into program means acceptance into
  college:** Students must be admitted and enrolled in the
  university first and then request services.

ADMISSIONS

Students with LD who self-disclose during the admission process may receive a second review by the Committee on Learning Disabilities. Some students may be given the option of a summer admit into a transition program for the summer prior to freshman year. General admission requirements for BC are very competitive. SAT Subject Tests are required in Writing, Math, and one additional subject. It is recommended that students have 4 years of English, 4 years of a foreign language, 4 years of math, 3 years of science, and 3 years of social studies. All students must submit an essay. Students with LD who may be deficient in foreign language or math skills should provide documentation and request a substitution for these courses. Documentation of the LD should be sent to the Office of Admissions. Students are encouraged to self-disclose during the admission process.

ADDITIONAL INFORMATION

Services offered by the CFLC include the option to take summer courses prior to entrance, individual consultations with a learning specialist, letters to faculty confirming and explaining the LD, reduced course load during the academic year combined with summer school, access to textbooks on CD, testing in a distraction-free room, workshops on study skills and time management, and small group seminars on learning strategies.

LEARNING DISABILITY PROGRAMS OR SERVICES

Contact Information
Name of program or department: Connors Family Learning Center
   Telephone: 617-552-8055
   Fax: 617-552-6075

LEARNING DISABILITY SERVICES

Accommodations are decided upon an individual basis after a thorough review of appropriate, current documentation. The accommodations requested must be supported through the documentation provided and must be logically linked to the current impact of the condition on academic functioning.

Allowed in exams
   Calculator: NR
   Dictionary: NR
   Computer: Yes
   Spellchecker: Yes
Extended test time: Yes
Scribes: Yes
Proctors: Yes
Oral exams: No
Note-takers: Yes

Distraction-reduced environment: Yes
Tape recording in class: Yes
Electronic texts: No
Accommodations for students with ADHD: Yes
Kurzweil Reader: No
Other assistive technology: Yes
Priority registration: Yes

Added costs for services: No
LD specialists: Yes
Professional tutors: No
Peer tutors: Yes
Max. hours/wk. for services: N/A
How professors are notified of LD/ADHD: By both student and director

GENERAL ADMISSIONS INFORMATION

Office of Admission: 617-552-3100

ENTRANCE REQUIREMENTS

Academic units recommended: 4 English, 4 math, 3 science (3 science labs), 4 foreign language, 3 social studies. High school diploma is required, and GED is accepted. ACT with Writing component required. TOEFL required of all international applicants: minimum paper TOEFL 600, minimum computer TOEFL 250.

Application deadline: 1/1
Notification: 4/15
Average GPA: NR
ACT Composite middle 50% range: 29–32

SAT Math middle 50% range: 640–730
SAT Critical Reading middle 50% range: 620–710
SAT Writing middle 50% range: 630–730

Graduated top 10% of class: 82%
Graduated top 25% of class: 95%
Graduated top 50% of class: 99%

COLLEGE GRADUATION REQUIREMENTS

Course waivers allowed: No
Course substitutions allowed: Yes
In what course: Foreign language

ADDITIONAL INFORMATION

Environment: The campus is located six miles from downtown Boston.

Student Body
   Undergrad enrollment: 9,099
   Women: 52%
   Men: 48%
   Percent out-of-state: 73%

Cost Information
   Tuition: $41,480
   Room & board: $12,324
Housing Information
   University housing: Yes
   Percent living on campus: 85%

Greek System
   Fraternity: No
   Sorority: No
Athletics: Division I

BOSTON UNIVERSITY

121 Bay State Road, Boston, MA 02215
Phone: 617-353-2300 • Fax: 617-353-9695
E-mail: admissions@bu.edu • Web: www.bu.edu
Support: CS • Institution type: 4-year private

PROGRAMS OR SERVICES FOR STUDENTS WITH LD

Boston University recognizes that many students with a learning disability, attention deficit hyperactivity disorder, or psychiatry disability (including autism spectrum diagnoses) can succeed in a university if they are provided with support services and appropriate accommodations. The Office of Disability Services (ODS) is committed to assisting individuals with disabilities in achieving fulfillment and success in all aspects of university life. The primary objective of ODS is to foster academic excellence, personal responsibility, and leadership growth in students with disabilities through vigorous programming and the provision of reasonable accommodations. We further this commitment through the promotion of independence and self-advocacy in students with LD, ADHD, or other disabilities. The university does not waive program requirements or permit substitutions for required courses. Several degree programs have foreign language or mathematics requirements. The university considers these degree requirements essential to its programs.

ADMISSION INFORMATION FOR STUDENTS WITH LD/ADHD

College entrance tests required: Yes
Interview required: No
Essay recommended: No
What documentation required for LD: Psycho Ed evaluation to include: relevant historical info, instructional interventions, related services, age diagnosed, objective data (aptitude, achievement, info processing), test scores (standard, percentile and grade equivalents) and describe functional limitations.
With general application: No
To receive services after enrolling: Yes
What documentation required for ADHD: Diagnosis based on DSM-V; history of behaviors impairing functioning in academic setting; diagnostic interview; history of symptoms; evidence of ongoing behaviors.

With general application: No
Submitted to: Office of Disability Services
Special Ed. HS course work accepted: No
Specific course requirements of all applicants: Yes
Separate application required: No
# of LD applications submitted each year: NR
# of LD applications accepted yearly: NR
Total # of students receiving LD services: 550
Acceptance into program means acceptance into college: Students must be admitted and enrolled in the university first and then request to be considered for services.

ADMISSIONS

All admissions decisions are made on an individual basis by the Office of Admissions. BU expects that students with disabilities, including those with LD, will meet the same competitive admissions criteria as their peers without disabilities. Thus, there are no special admissions procedures for applicants with LD. The Office of Disability Services does not participate in any way in the application process or in admissions decisions. Admissions is based on the strength of a student's secondary school record. For most programs at BU, the minimum requirements for consideration include 4 years of English, 3 years of mathematics (through precalculus), 3 years of history and/or social science, 3 years of science (with laboratory components), and 2 years of a foreign language. Teacher and counselor recommendations and other personal qualifications as demonstrated by extracurricular activities are evaluated and weighed before admission decisions are made. The essay is considered a significant part of the application process. Activities in and out of school are important, and it is helpful if there is a match between the student's experiences or academic interests and the opportunities available at Boston University. ACT with writing or SAT Reasoning and 2 SAT subject tests. For the College of General Studies either ACT or SAT Reasoning subject tests are recommended.

ADDITIONAL INFORMATION

ODS offers support services to students with LD/ADHD, including access to academic accommodations for which the student is eligible, academic counseling and support in self-advocacy, access to assistive technology, and professional referrals for assessment and treatment. Students are required to be active in the accommodation process and must notify faculty about the implementation of approved accommodations.

LEARNING DISABILITY PROGRAMS OR SERVICES

Contact Information
Name of program or department: Office of Disability Services
 Telephone: 617-353-3658
 Fax: 617-353-9646

LEARNING DISABILITY SERVICES

Accommodations are decided upon an individual basis after a thorough review of appropriate, current documentation. The accommodations requested must be supported through the documentation provided and must be logically linked to the current impact of the condition on academic functioning.

Allowed in exams
 Calculator: No
 Dictionary: No
 Computer: Yes
 Spellchecker: Yes
Extended test time: Yes
Scribes: Yes
Proctors: Yes
Oral exams: Yes
Note-takers: Yes

Distraction-reduced environment: Yes
Tape recording in class: Yes
Electronic texts: Yes
**Accommodations for students with
 ADHD:** Yes
Kurzweil Reader: No
Other assistive technology: Yes
Priority registration: No

Added costs for services: Yes
LD specialists: Yes
Professional tutors: None
Peer tutors: No
Max. hours/wk. for services: N/A
**How professors are notified of
 LD/ADHD:** By student

GENERAL ADMISSIONS INFORMATION

Office of Admission: 617-353-2300

ENTRANCE REQUIREMENTS

Academic units required: 4 English, 3 math, 3 science (3 science labs), 2 foreign language, 3 social studies.
Academic units recommended: 4 English, 4 math, 4 science (4 science labs), 4 foreign language, 4 social studies. High school diploma is required, and GED is accepted. ACT with Writing component required or SAT Reasoning and 2 SAT subject tests. TOEFL required of all international applicants: minimum paper TOEFL 550, minimum computer TOEFL 215.

Application deadline: 1/1
Notification: 4/15
Average GPA: 3.46
ACT Composite middle 50% range:
 25–30

SAT Math middle 50% range:
 600–690
**SAT Critical Reading middle 50%
 range:** 580–670
SAT Writing middle 50% range:
 590–680

Graduated top 10% of class: 53%
Graduated top 25% of class: 87%
Graduated top 50% of class: 99%

COLLEGE GRADUATION REQUIREMENTS

Course waivers allowed: No
Course substitutions allowed: No

ADDITIONAL INFORMATION

Environment: The university is located on a 131-acre campus in an urban area.

Student Body
 Undergrad enrollment: 16,683
 Women: 60%
 Men: 40%
 Percent out-of-state: 80%

Cost Information
 Tuition: $40,850
 Room & board: $12,520
Housing Information
 University housing: Yes
 Percent living on campus: 66%

Greek System
 Fraternity: Yes
 Sorority: Yes
Athletics: Division I

CLARK UNIVERSITY

950 Main Street, Worcester, MA 01610-1477
Phone: 508-793-7431 • Fax: 508-793-8821
E-mail: admissions@clarku.edu • Web: www.clarku.edu
Support: CS • Institution type: 4-year private

PROGRAMS OR SERVICES FOR STUDENTS WITH LD

The learning disabilities services at Clark University, based within the Academic Advising Center (AAC), was developed to advocate and support the needs of the student with learning disabilities in a college environment. Strategies are developed to help the student with learning disabilities cope with the increased demands of the college curriculum. Resources are available to students who experience difficulties and who may require some support or wish to learn more about their own learning styles. Support services in the AAC are coordinated with services offered by the university's Writing Center, Math Clinic, and Dean of Students. The most successful students are the ones who accept their disability, develop good self-advocacy skills, and are capable of good time management. The ultimate goal of special services is to help students improve their self-awareness and self-advocacy skills and assist them in being successful and independent in college.

ADMISSION INFORMATION FOR STUDENTS WITH LD/ADHD

College entrance tests required: Yes
Interview required: No
Essay recommended: No
What documentation required for LD: Psycho Ed evaluation to include: relevant historical info, instructional interventions, related services, age diagnosed, objective data (aptitude, achievement, info processing), test scores (standard, percentile and grade equivalents) and describe functional limitations.
With general application: No
To receive services after enrolling: Yes
What documentation required for ADHD: Diagnosis based on DSM-V; history of behaviors impairing functioning in academic setting; diagnostic interview; history of symptoms; evidence of ongoing behaviors.

With general application: No
Submitted to: Academic Advising Center
Special Ed. HS course work accepted: N/A
Specific course requirements of all applicants: Yes
Separate application required: No
# of LD applications submitted each year: NR
# of LD applications accepted yearly: NR
Total # of students receiving LD services: 550
Acceptance into program means acceptance into college: Students must be admitted and enrolled in the university first and then request services.

ADMISSIONS

Special Services and the Office of Undergraduate Admissions work together in considering students for admission. Admission is based on ability rather than disability. Applicants must meet standard admissions requirements. An interview with Clark's Special Services Office is highly recommended. If a student requires any classroom accommodations or support services, a diagnostic assessment completed within the past 2 years must be submitted, documenting the learning disability. This documentation is needed to evaluate the applicant's needs and determine what services the university can provide. The university looks at a student's upward trend in high school, as well as the challenge of the curriculum and the number of mainstream courses the student has taken. Some special education courses in freshman year may be allowed if they have been followed by a college-prep curriculum during the rest of high school. The Director of Special Services makes a recommendation to the Admissions Office about the applicant, but the final decision rests with the Office of Admissions. The university values diversity in their applicants, but most students have taken 4 years of English, 3 years of mathematics, 3 years of science, 2 years of both a social science and a foreign language, and other credit electives, including the arts, recognized in the curriculum. The university feels that successful candidates for admission should have a strong senior-year course load (at least four, preferably five, solid academic courses).

ADDITIONAL INFORMATION

An early orientation program 2 days prior to general orientation is designed to meet the needs of entering students with LD. This program is highly recommended as it provides intensive exposure to academic services on campus. Students take a reading comprehension and writing exam, and results are used to match students to the most appropriate academic program. Graduate students work with students on time management and organizational skills. Although note-takers are available, Special Services supplements this accommodation with the taping of lectures and highly recommends that students use a cassette recorder with a count. It is also recommended that freshmen students take only three courses in their first semester. All students must complete one math course in basic algebra prior to graduating. The overall GPA of freshmen receiving services from Special Services is a 2.7. Clark offers space to an outside LD specialist who will provide tutoring and services for a fee. Services and accommodations are available to undergrads and graduates.

LEARNING DISABILITY PROGRAMS OR SERVICES

Contact Information
Name of program or department: Academic Advising Center
  Telephone: 508-793-7468
  Fax: 508-421-3700

LEARNING DISABILITY SERVICES

Accommodations are decided upon an individual basis after a thorough review of appropriate, current documentation. The accommodations requested must be supported through the documentation provided and must be logically linked to the current impact of the condition on academic functioning.

Allowed in exams	**Distraction-reduced environment:** Yes	**Added costs for services:** No
Calculator: Yes	**Tape recording in class:** Yes	**LD specialists:** Yes
Dictionary: Yes	**Electronic texts:** No	**Professional tutors:** No
Computer: Yes	**Accommodations for students with**	**Peer tutors:** No
Spellchecker: Yes	**ADHD:** Yes	**Max. hours/wk. for services:** N/A
Extended test time: Yes	**Kurzweil Reader:** No	**How professors are notified of**
Scribes: No	**Other assistive technology:** Yes	**LD/ADHD:** By both student and
Proctors: Yes	**Priority registration:** No	director
Oral exams: No		
Note-takers: Yes		

GENERAL ADMISSIONS INFORMATION

Office of Admission: 508-793-7431

ENTRANCE REQUIREMENTS

Academic units recommended: 4 English, 3 math, 3 science (2 science labs), 2 foreign language, 2 social studies, 2 history. High school diploma is required, and GED is accepted. ACT with or without Writing component accepted. TOEFL required of all international applicants: minimum paper TOEFL 550, minimum computer TOEFL 213.

Application deadline: 1/15	**SAT Math middle 50% range:**	**Graduated top 10% of class:** 30%
Notification: 4/1	540–650	**Graduated top 25% of class:** 73%
Average GPA: 3.48	**SAT Critical Reading middle 50%**	**Graduated top 50% of class:** 95%
ACT Composite middle 50% range:	**range:** 540–660	
23–29	**SAT Writing middle 50% range:**	
	540–650	

COLLEGE GRADUATION REQUIREMENTS

Course waivers allowed: No
Course substitutions allowed: NR

ADDITIONAL INFORMATION

Environment: The university is located on 45 acres in a small city 38 miles west of Boston.

Student Body	**Cost Information**	**Greek System**
Undergrad enrollment: 2,311	**Tuition:** $38,100	**Fraternity:** No
Women: 60%	**Room & board:** $7,320	**Sorority:** No
Men: 40%	**Housing Information**	**Athletics:** Division III
Percent out-of-state: 59%	**University housing:** Yes	
	Percent living on campus: 71%	

CURRY COLLEGE

1071 Blue Hill Avenue, Milton, MA 02186
Phone: 617-333-2210 • Fax: 617-333-2114
E-mail: curryadm@curry.edu • Web: www.curry.edu
Support: SP • Institution type: 4-year private

PROGRAMS OR SERVICES FOR STUDENTS WITH LD

The Program for Advancement of Learning (PAL) at Curry College is a comprehensive individualized program for students with specific learning disabilities and ADHD. Students in PAL participate fully in Curry College course work and extracurricular activities. The goal of PAL is to facilitate students' understanding of their individual learning styles and help them achieve independence as learners. Students' empowerment is developed via intensive study of their own strengths, needs, and learning styles. PAL is a place where students are honored for the strengths and talents they bring to the learning process and are given the chance to demonstrate their abilities. PAL students are leaders on campus. The PAL summer program is a 3-week course that is strongly recommended for new students to ease the transition to college and provide excellent preparation.

ADMISSION INFORMATION FOR STUDENTS WITH LD/ADHD

College entrance tests required: No
Interview required: No, but strongly recommended
Essay recommended: Yes
What documentation required for LD: Psycho Ed evaluation to include: relevant historical info, instructional interventions, related services, age diagnosed, objective data (aptitude, achievement, info processing), test scores (standard, percentile and grade equivalents) and describe functional limitations.
With general application: Yes if requested as part of Structured Program application
To receive services after enrolling: Yes
What documentation required for ADHD: Diagnosis based on DSM-V; history of behaviors impairing functioning in academic setting; diagnostic interview; history of symptoms; evidence of ongoing behaviors.

With general application: Yes if requested as part of Structured Program application
To receive services after enrolling: Yes
Submitted to: Program for the Advancement of Learning (PAL)
Special Ed. HS course work accepted: Yes
Specific course requirements of all applicants: NR
Separate application required: Yes
# of LD applications submitted each year: 900
# of LD applications accepted yearly: 400
Total # of students receiving LD services: 275
Acceptance into program means acceptance into college: Yes

ADMISSIONS

For regular admission to the college, applicants must submit the application fee, their official transcript, SAT or ACT (recommended) scores, and counselor or teacher recommendations. Courses required for general admission include 4 English, 3 math, 2 science, 2 science lab, 1 social studies, 1 history, and 5 electives. For admission into the Program of the Advancement of Learning, applicants must submit a recent diagnostic evaluation describing a Specific Learning Disability and/or ADHD. Diagnostic evaluations must be less than three years old and contain the results of cognitive (preferably WAIS or Woodcock-Johnson) and achievement tests (preferably Woodcock-Johnson or Wechsler Individual Achievement Test). In addition, an IEP or its equivalent is requested, if available. On-campus interviews are strongly recommended and may be required of some applicants. Space is limited for the program. Students applying to PAL are not required to submit SAT or ACT. Admission decisions are made jointly by PAL and the Office of Admissions.

ADDITIONAL INFORMATION

PAL students must commit to the program for at least 1 year and have the option to continue with full or partial support beyond the first year. A 3-week 3-credit summer PAL summer session is strongly recommended. Students meet regularly with their own PAL instructor who is a learning specialist. The focus is on using the student's strengths to improve skills in areas such as listening, speaking, reading, writing, organization and time management, note-taking, and test-taking. Students also receive help with readings, papers, and assignments for classes as the basis for learning about their unique learning style. The specialist reviews diagnostic testing to help the student understand the profile of strengths and needs. Students earn three credits toward graduation for the first year. Skills classes, for credit, are offered through the Academic Enrichment Center in developmental reading, writing, and math. Another special offering is diagnostic testing, which available through the Educational Diagnostic Center at PAL at 617-333-2314.

LEARNING DISABILITY PROGRAMS OR SERVICES

Contact Information
Name of program or department: Program for Advancement of Learning (PAL)
 Telephone: 617-333-2250
 Fax: 617-333-2018

LEARNING DISABILITY SERVICES

Accommodations are decided upon an individual basis after a thorough review of appropriate, current documentation. The accommodations requested must be supported through the documentation provided and must be logically linked to the current impact of the condition on academic functioning.

Allowed in exams
 Calculator: Yes
 Dictionary: Yes
 Computer: Yes
 Spellchecker: Yes
Extended test time: Yes
Scribes: Yes
Proctors: Yes
Oral exams: NR
Note-takers: NR

Distraction-reduced environment: Yes
Tape recording in class: Yes
Electronic texts: Yes
Accommodations for students with
 ADHD: Yes
Kurzweil Reader: Yes
Other assistive technology: Yes
Priority registration: No

Added costs for services: Yes
LD specialists: Yes
Professional tutors: Yes
Peer tutors: Yes
Max. hours/wk. for services: 2.5
How professors are notified of
 LD/ADHD: By student

GENERAL ADMISSIONS INFORMATION

Office of Admission: 617-333-2210

ENTRANCE REQUIREMENTS

Academic units required: 4 English, 3 math, 2 science (2 science labs), 1 social studies, 1 history, 5 academic electives. High school diploma is required, and GED is accepted. ACT with or without Writing component accepted. TOEFL required of all international applicants: minimum paper TOEFL 500, minimum computer TOEFL 173.

Application deadline: 4/1
Notification: Rolling
Average GPA: 2.30
ACT Composite middle 50% range:
 NR

SAT Math middle 50% range:
 470–550
SAT Critical Reading middle 50%
 range: 470–590
SAT Writing middle 50% range: NR

Graduated top 10% of class: 5%
Graduated top 25% of class: 22%
Graduated top 50% of class: 65%

COLLEGE GRADUATION REQUIREMENTS

Course waivers allowed: No
Course substitutions allowed: Yes
In what course: Varies

ADDITIONAL INFORMATION

Environment: Curry's 120-acre campus is minutes from metropolitan Boston.

Student Body
 Undergrad enrollment: 2,832
 Women: 58%
 Men: 42%
 Percent out-of-state: 37%

Cost Information
 Tuition: $29,300
 Room & board: $11,650
Housing Information
 University housing: Yes
 Percent living on campus: 60%

Greek System
 Fraternity: No
 Sorority: No
Athletics: Division III

DEAN COLLEGE

Office of Admission, 99 Main Street, Franklin, MA 02038-1994
Phone: 508-541-1508 • Fax: 508-541-8726
E-mail: admission@dean.edu • Web: www.dean.edu
Support: SP • Institution: 2-year and 4-year private

PROGRAMS OR SERVICES FOR STUDENTS WITH LD

The Learning Center offers student academic support and assistance through the Writing Center, Disability Support Services, and course-specific tutoring. Personalized Learning Services (PLS) offers a comprehensive system of support for students with documented learning disabilities. Academic Coaches work with students to develop customized programs that address the skills and knowledge that create a foundation for success in future academic and professional settings. The goal of PLS is to assist students in becoming confident, successful, independent learners and to help all students achieve their academic goals. The Dean College Arch Learning Community (a two-semester first year program) is for students with diagnosed learning disabilities and/or other learning challenges such as attention and memory difficulties who need additional intensive academic skill development. Through individual tutoring, smaller-sized Arch-designated courses and specialized academic advising, students will acquire the necessary skills to be successful in their degree programs. The Pathway Learning Community (a one semester first year program) is designed to provide support for students with or without learning disabilities through smaller sized courses, individualized advising, and professional tutoring support. The Advising Center provides comprehensive assistance and students are assigned a personal advisor to guide them as they move through the academic year.

ADMISSION INFORMATION FOR STUDENTS WITH LD/ADHD

College entrance tests required: Yes
Interview required: No
What documentation required for LD: Psycho Ed evaluation to include: relevant historical info, instructional interventions, related services, age diagnosed, objective data (aptitude, achievement, info processing), test scores (standard, percentile and grade equivalents) and describe functional limitations.
With general application: Yes if requested as part of Structured Program application
To receive services after enrolling: Yes
What documentation required for ADHD: Diagnosis based on DSM-V; history of behaviors impairing functioning in academic setting; diagnostic interview; history of symptoms; evidence of ongoing behaviors.

With general application: Yes if requested as part of Structured Program application
To receive services after enrolling: Yes
Submitted to: Support Program/Services
Special Ed. HS course work accepted: Yes
Specific course requirements for all applicants: NR
Separate application required for program services: Yes
# of LD applications submitted each year: 125
# of LD applications accepted yearly: 50
Total # of students receiving LD services: 100
Acceptance into program means acceptance into college: No

ADMISSIONS

There is no special admission process for students with learning disabilities. All students submit the same general application. Every application is carefully reviewed by admissions, and students are selected based on their academic performance in high school, recommendations, and personal accomplishments. There is no simple formula applied to an application. Dean strives to make the best match between what it offers as an institution and each student's skills, interests, and abilities. Students should have college-prep courses including four years English and three years math. Interviews are not required, but they are highly recommended, and students must submit a counselor's recommendation. SAT/ACT are required.

ADDITIONAL INFORMATION

Accommodations may include, but are not limited to, electronic texts, access to computers, scribes and note-takers, and extended time for testing. The Learning Center provides free academic assistance and support services for all students through tutoring, workshops, and study groups. Professional and peer tutors are available to assist students in developing writing, math, and study skills, and to provide course-specific tutoring. Personalized Learning Services (PLS) offers tutorial support to students. Students may meet weekly with a learning, writing, or math academic coach one-to-one or in small groups. Learning and study strategies taught by specialist include test-taking; test preparation; note-taking skills; time management; academic organization; reading comprehension; research and writing skills; and self-awareness and advocacy. The fee for PLS is $800–$4,000 per semester. The fee for ARCH is $3,500 per semester. The fee for Pathway is $2,500 per semester.

PROGRAM FOR DISABILITY SERVICES

Contact Information
Name of program or department: Disability Support Services
Telephone: 508-541-1768
Fax: 508-541-1829

LEARNING DISABILITY SERVICES

Accommodations are decided upon an individual basis after a thorough review of appropriate, current documentation. The accommodations requested must be supported through the documentation provided and must be logically linked to the current impact of the condition on academic functioning.

Allowed in exams	**Distraction-reduced environment:** Yes	**Added costs for services:** Yes, $3,500 Arch (per semester), $2,500 Pathway (per semester)
Calculator: Yes	**Tape recording in class:** Yes	
Dictionary: No	**Electronic texts:** No	
Computer: Yes	**Accommodations for students with ADHD:** Yes	**LD specialists:** Yes
Spellchecker: Yes		**Professional tutors:** 35
Extended test time: Yes	**Kurzweil Reader:** Yes	**Peer tutors:** 12–18
Scribes: Yes	**Other assistive technology:** Microsoft Speak, a word processing dictation program; Kurzweil reader	**Max. hours/wk. for services:** NR
Proctors: Yes		**How professors are notified of LD/ADHD:** Student
Oral exams: No		
Note-takers: Yes	**Priority registration:** No	

GENERAL ADMISSIONS INFORMATION

Office of Admission: 508-541-1768

ENTRANCE REQUIREMENTS
Academic units required: 3 English, 1 mathematics, 1 science, (1 science labs), 0 foreign language, 1 social studies, 1 history, 0 academic electives. **Academic units recommended:** 4 English, 2 mathematics, 2 science, (1 science labs), 1 foreign language, 2 social studies, 2 history, 1 academic electives. High school diploma is required and GED is accepted. SAT or ACT required.

Application deadline: None	**SAT Math middle 50% range:** 390–490	**Graduated top 10% of class:** NR
Notification: Rolling	**SAT Critical Reading middle 50% range:** 380–490	**Graduated top 25% of class:** NR
Average GPA: 2.2		**Graduated top 50% of class:** NR
ACT Composite middle 50% range: 15–20	**SAT Writing middle 50% range:** NR	

COLLEGE GRADUATION REQUIREMENTS

Course waivers allowed: No
Course substitutions allowed: No

ADDITIONAL INFORMATION

Environment: The campus is in a small town near both Boston, Massachusetts, and Providence, Rhode Island.

Student Body	**Cost Information**	**Greek System**
Undergrad enrollment: 1,147	**Tuition:** $31,900	**Fraternity:** No
Women: 49%	**Room & board:** $13,600	**Sorority:** No
Men: 51%	**Housing Information**	**Athletics:** NJCAA
Percent out-of-state: 42%	**University housing:** Yes	
	Percent living on campus: 88%	

EMERSON COLLEGE

120 Boylston Street, Boston, MA 02116-4624
Phone: 617-824-8600 • Fax: 617-824-8609
E-mail: admission@emerson.edu • Web: www.emerson.edu
Support: CS • Institution: 4-year private

PROGRAMS OR SERVICES FOR STUDENTS WITH LD

Emerson College is committed to providing equal access to its academic programs and social activities for all qualified students with disabilities. While upholding this commitment, we maintain the high standards of achievement that are essential to the integrity of the College's programs and services. One of the primary goals of the DSO is to foster a welcoming and accessible environment for students across the campus. The school's philosophy is that students are independent and self-determined, and that students with disabilities—just like all students—have control over their lives at Emerson and they are ultimately responsible for making their own decisions. Emerson's Disability Services Office (DSO) offers academic accommodations and related services to qualified students with documented physical, medical, visual, hearing, learning, and psychological disabilities. Students with disabilities are not required to register with the DSO, but in order to receive accommodations they must self-identify to the DSO and request accommodations. Recommendations regarding accommodations for students with disabilities are determined on an individual basis. As part of the request process, students must provide recent documentation of their disabilities and have an interview with staff in the DSO. The documentation, prepared by a qualified professional, must substantiate the nature of the disability and its relationship to the requested accommodation.

ADMISSION INFORMATION FOR STUDENTS WITH LD/ADHD

College entrance tests required: Yes
Interview required: No
Documentation required for LD: Yes
Documentation required for ADHD: Yes
Submitted to: Disability Services Office
Special Ed. HS course work accepted: N/A

Specific course requirements for all applicants: Yes
Separate application required for program services: No
# of LD applications submitted each year: NR
# of LD applications accepted yearly: NR
Total # of students receiving LD services: NR
Acceptance into program means acceptance into college: Student must be admitted and enrolled in the college to request services.

ADMISSIONS
Emerson College accepts the Common Application with a required Supplement. Admission is competitive. In choosing candidates for the entering class, we look for students who present academic promise in their secondary school record, recommendations, and writing competency, as well as personal qualities as seen in extracurricular activities, community involvement, and demonstrated leadership. There is no separate application for students with learning disabilities.

ADDITIONAL INFORMATION
Emerson College offers academic support services, free of charge, to all undergraduate and graduate Emerson students. The College's Writing & Academic Resource Center (WARC) consists of three full-time professionals, graduate assistant writing tutors, and peer tutors. The professional staff provides academic counseling and support with study strategies and time management to individuals seeking academic support. Graduate writing tutors guide students in becoming more effective writers, and peer tutors assist students with course content. The center also offers grammar tutorials across the curriculum.

PROGRAM FOR DISABILITY SERVICES

Contact Information
Name of program or department: Disability Services Office
  Telephone: 617-824-8592
  Fax: 617-824-8941

LEARNING DISABILITY SERVICES

Accommodations are decided on an individual basis after a review of current documentation and an interview conducted by a DSO staff member. The College reserves the right to determine the adequacy of the documentation and may request additional assessments and materials.

Allowed in exams
  Calculator: Yes
  Dictionary: Yes
  Computer: Yes
  Spellchecker: Yes
Extended test time: Yes
Scribes: Yes
Proctors: Yes
Oral exams:
Note-takers: Yes

Distraction-reduced environment: Yes
Tape recording in class: Yes
Electronic texts: No
Accommodations for students with ADHD: Yes
Kurzweil Reader: Yes
Other assistive technology: Print to Speech; JAWS; other adaptive software and hardware.
Priority registration: N/A

Added costs for services: No
LD specialists: Yes
Professional tutors: No
Peer tutors: Yes
Max. hours/wk. for services: 4
How professors are notified of LD/ADHD: Student.

GENERAL ADMISSIONS INFORMATION

Office of Admission: 617-824-8600

ENTRANCE REQUIREMENTS
Academic units required: 4 English, 3 mathematics, 3 science, 3 foreign language, 3 social studies. **Academic units recommended:** 4 English, 3 mathematics, 3 science, 3 foreign language, 3 social studies, 4 academic electives. High school diploma is required and GED is accepted. SAT or ACT required; ACT with Writing component required. TOEFL required of all international applicants; minimum paper TOEFL 550, minimum computer TOEFL 213, minimum web-based TOEFL 80.

Application deadline: 1/15
Notification: 4/1
Average GPA: 3.5
ACT Composite middle 50% range: 25–29

SAT Math middle 50% range: 550–640
SAT Critical Reading middle 50% range: 580–680
SAT Writing middle 50% range: 580–670

Graduated top 10% of class: 42.4%
Graduated top 25% of class: 76.6%
Graduated top 50% of class: 98%

COLLEGE GRADUATION REQUIREMENTS

Course waivers allowed: Yes
In what course: Quantitative reasoning (math) , world languages.
Course substitutions allowed: No
In what course: Students can choose to take American Sign Language to fulfill the World Language requirement.

ADDITIONAL INFORMATION

Environment: Emerson's campus is located on Boston Common in the heart of the city's theater district.

Student Body
  Undergrad enrollment: 3,453
  Women: 57%
  Men: 43%
  Percent out-of-state: 82%

Cost Information
  Tuition: $32,128
  Room and board: $13,422
Housing Information
  University housing: Yes
  Percent living on campus: 48%

Greek System
  Fraternity: Yes
  Sorority: Yes
  Athletics: Division III

FITCHBURG STATE UNIVERSITY

160 Pearl Street, Fitchburg, MA 01420-2697
Phone: 978-665-3144 • Fax: 800-705-9692
E-mail: admissions@fitchburgstate.edu • Web: www.fitchburgstate.edu
Support: S • Institution type: 4-year public

PROGRAMS OR SERVICES FOR STUDENTS WITH LD

The Disability Services Office provides individually tailored support services and programs for students with disabilities. Disability Services empowers eligible students to succeed by striving to assure equal access and opportunity of curricular and extracurricular activities. Student autonomy is encouraged through the provision of reasonable accommodations, services, and training in the use of assistive technology, self-advocacy, and leadership. Disability Services is responsible for verifying student eligibility for accommodations and for coordinating accommodations across campus. Students must request services themselves and must provide appropriate documentation to support the need for such services. Once students have obtained copies of their disability documentation from their high school (or medical provider who is most familiar with their needs and their disabilities, they should complete and sign the Statement of Learning Needs and Release of Information forms. Documentation must clearly state the diagnosis, describe the symptoms that impact the student's ability to function in the educational environment, and provide specific recommendations for accommodations.

ADMISSION INFORMATION FOR STUDENTS WITH LD/ADHD

College entrance tests required: Yes
Interview required: No
Essay recommended: No
What documentation required for LD: Psycho Ed evaluation to include: relevant historical info, instructional interventions, related services, age diagnosed, objective data (aptitude, achievement, info processing), test scores (standard, percentile and grade equivalents) and describe functional limitations.
With general application: No
To receive services after enrolling: Yes
What documentation required for ADHD: Diagnosis based on DSM-V; history of behaviors impairing functioning in academic setting; diagnostic interview; history of symptoms; evidence of ongoing behaviors.

With general application: No
Submitted to: Disability Services Office
Special Ed. HS course work accepted: Yes
Specific course requirements of all applicants: Yes
Separate application required: No
# of LD applications submitted each year: NR
# of LD applications accepted yearly: NR
Total # of students receiving LD services: 280
Acceptance into program means acceptance into college: Students must be admitted and enrolled in the college prior to requesting services.

ADMISSIONS

The Admissions Office forwards folders for students with documented disabilities who have waived the ACT/SAT or foreign language entrance requirement or have requested evaluation by the Admissions Advocacy Committee for Students with Disabilities. Students may opt to have an interview with the Office of Disability Services. Review by the Admissions Advocacy Committee can be requested by the candidate. General admission requirements include 4 English, 3 math, 3 science, 2 social science, 2 foreign language, and 2 electives. GPA is based on all college-prep courses and weighs honors and Advanced Placement courses. The college looks for a minimum weighted GPA of 3.0. However, the Admissions Committee will consider applicants with GPAs between 2.0 and 2.99 if they submit SAT/ACT scores meeting the sliding scale requirements. Applicants who do not meet the sliding scale requirements will be considered on an individual basis for a limited number of admission exceptions. Meeting the minimum GPA and SAT/ACT requirements does not guarantee admission to the college. Applicants who meet the 3.0 GPA requirements do not have to use the sliding scale for admission, but still must submit competitive SAT/ACT scores if they are applying within 3 years of high school graduation.

ADDITIONAL INFORMATION

Disability Services provides individually tailored support services, programs, and academic accommodations for students with documented disabilities. Services available include: an adaptive computer lab, tape recorders, testing accommodations, note-takers, readers, interpreters, support groups, coaching, and consultation with the faculty. The adaptive computer lab houses a Braille printer, Kurzweil 3000 reading program, Dragon Dictate, scanner with print recognition, screen enlargement programs, a closed circuit television, and speech synthesizers. Students with disabilities needing testing accommodations for placement exams or other standardized tests must submit requests for accommodations. Extended-time, out-of-classroom testing, oral exams, and other alternative testing are options offered to students with disabilities. Reduced courseload waivers may be available to students with disabilities who need the accommodation of taking below 12 credits per semester. Waivers are granted by the Dean of Student and Academic Life.

LEARNING DISABILITY PROGRAMS OR SERVICES

Contact Information
Name of program or department: Disability Services
  Telephone: 978-665-3427
  Fax: 978-665-4786

LEARNING DISABILITY SERVICES

Accommodations are decided upon an individual basis after a thorough review of appropriate, current documentation. The accommodations requested must be supported through the documentation provided and must be logically linked to the current impact of the condition on academic functioning.

Allowed in exams
  Calculator: Yes
  Dictionary: Yes
  Computer: Yes
  Spellchecker: Yes
Extended test time: Yes
Scribes: Yes
Proctors: Yes
Oral exams: Yes
Note-takers: Yes
	Distraction-reduced environment: Yes
	Tape recording in class: Yes
	Electronic texts: Yes
	Accommodations for students with
	  ADHD: Yes
	Kurzweil Reader: Yes
	Other assistive technology: Yes
	Priority registration: Yes
		Added costs for services: No
		LD specialists: No
		Professional tutors: 1
		Peer tutors: Yes
		Max. hours/wk. for services:
		  Unlimited
		How professors are notified of
		  LD/ADHD: By student

GENERAL ADMISSIONS INFORMATION

Office of Admission: 978-665-3144

ENTRANCE REQUIREMENTS

Academic units required: 4 English, 3 math, 3 science (2 science labs), 2 foreign language, 1 social studies, 1 history, 2 academic electives. **Academic units recommended:** 4 math. High school diploma is required, and GED is accepted. TOEFL required of all international applicants: minimum paper TOEFL 550, minimum computer TOEFL 213.

Application deadline: None
Notification: Rolling
Average GPA: 2.95
ACT Composite middle 50% range:
  18–23
	SAT Math middle 50% range:
	  460–560
	SAT Critical Reading middle 50%
	  range: 440–550
	SAT Writing middle 50% range:
	  450–540
		Graduated top 10% of class: NR
		Graduated top 25% of class: NR
		Graduated top 50% of class: NR

COLLEGE GRADUATION REQUIREMENTS

Course waivers allowed: No
In what course: Varies
Course substitutions allowed: Yes

ADDITIONAL INFORMATION

Environment: 45-acre campus is located 50 miles from Boston.

Student Body
  Undergrad enrollment: 3,858
  Women: 54%
  Men: 46%
  Percent out-of-state: 11%
	Cost Information
	  In-state tuition: $16,640
	  Out-of-state tuition: $22,720
	  Room & board: $10,450
	Housing Information
	  University housing: Yes
	  Percent living on campus: 41%
		Greek System
		  Fraternity: Yes
		  Sorority: Yes
		Athletics: Division III

MOUNT IDA COLLEGE

777 Dedham Street, Newton, MA 02459
Phone: 617-928-4553 • Fax: 617-928-4507
E-mail: admissions@mountida.edu • Web: www.mountida.edu
Support: SP • Institution type: 4-year private

PROGRAMS OR SERVICES FOR STUDENTS WITH LD

The Learning Opportunities Program (LOP) provides additional academic support for students with LD. The program focuses on developing and strengthening individual learning styles that create successful, independent learners. Students are mainstreamed in a regular degree curriculum. Mount Ida goes the extra mile for all its students, and the LOP is a natural extension of this philosophy. Students discover a supportive environment where a positive, successful experience is the goal. An important component of the LOP is the mentoring relationship with individual learning specialists.

ADMISSION INFORMATION FOR STUDENTS WITH LD/ADHD

College entrance tests required: Yes
Interview required: No
Essay recommended: Yes
What documentation required for LD: Psycho Ed evaluation to include: relevant historical info, instructional interventions, related services, age diagnosed, objective data (aptitude, achievement, info processing), test scores (standard, percentile and grade equivalents) and describe functional limitations.
With general application: Yes if requested as part of Structured Program application
To receive services after enrolling: Yes
What documentation required for ADHD: Diagnosis based on DSM-V; history of behaviors impairing functioning in academic setting; diagnostic interview; history of symptoms; evidence of ongoing behaviors.

With general application: Yes if requested as part of Structured Program application
To receive services after enrolling: Yes
Submitted to: Admissions
Special Ed. HS course work accepted: Yes
Specific course requirements of all applicants: Yes
Separate application required: Yes
# of LD applications submitted each year: 100
# of LD applications accepted yearly: 70–90
Total # of students receiving LD services: 150
Acceptance into program means acceptance into college: Students are admitted first to the college and then to the LOP.

ADMISSIONS

There is no special admissions process for students with learning disabilities. Open admissions is available. ACT/SAT are required for admission. An interview is strongly recommended. Students with disabilities should submit the WAIS–R, a test indicating appropriate reading grade level, and evaluative documentation of the learning disability.

ADDITIONAL INFORMATION

In the Learning Skills Laboratory, students have the opportunity to work with Mount Ida faculty and students to improve study skills. Tutoring provided by professional tutors who are learning specialists is available two times per week. Each tutoring session is private and strategy based. These meetings focus on developing self-advocacy skills and independent learning skills. Other services include reduced course load; enrollment in basic English, if needed; extended testing times; diagnostic testing; and counseling. Study skills courses in math and English are available. Additional support and content tutoring are offered in the Academic Success Center. The college also runs a Freshman Experience course that focuses on building the skills necessary to facilitate student success specifically for students who may be under prepared for college. Students work to identify and strengthen their individual learning styles.

LEARNING DISABILITY PROGRAMS OR SERVICES

Contact Information
Name of program or department: Learning Opportunities Program (LOP)
  Telephone: 617-928-4648
  Fax: 617-928-4648

LEARNING DISABILITY SERVICES

Accommodations are decided upon an individual basis after a thorough review of appropriate, current documentation. The accommodations requested must be supported through the documentation provided and must be logically linked to the current impact of the condition on academic functioning.

Allowed in exams
  Calculator: Yes
  Dictionary: Yes
  Computer: No
  Spellchecker: Yes
Extended test time: Yes
Scribes: No
Proctors: No
Oral exams: Yes
Note-takers: No

Distraction-reduced environment: Yes
Tape recording in class: Yes
Electronic texts: Yes
Accommodations for students with ADHD: Yes
Kurzweil Reader: Yes
Other assistive technology: Yes
Priority registration: No

Added costs for services: Yes
LD specialists: Yes
Professional tutors: 7–10
Peer tutors: No
Max. hours/wk. for services: 2
How professors are notified of LD/ADHD: By student

GENERAL ADMISSIONS INFORMATION

Office of Admission: 617-928-4553

ENTRANCE REQUIREMENTS

Academic units required: 4 English. **Academic units recommended:** 3 math, 3 science, 2 foreign language, 2 social studies, 2 history. High school diploma is required, and GED is accepted. ACT without Writing component accepted. TOEFL required of all international applicants: minimum paper TOEFL 525, minimum computer TOEFL 197.

Application deadline: None
Notification: Rolling
Average GPA: 2.0–2.9
ACT Composite middle 50% range: 15–20

SAT Math middle 50% range: 380–490
SAT Critical Reading middle 50% range: 390–490
SAT Writing middle 50% range: 400–500

Graduated top 10% of class: NR
Graduated top 25% of class: NR
Graduated top 50% of class: NR

COLLEGE GRADUATION REQUIREMENTS

Course waivers allowed: No
In what course: No foreign language requirement
Course substitutions allowed: Yes, under special conditions
In what course: Depends on the major and the learning style issues; not a usual accommodation

ADDITIONAL INFORMATION

Environment: Mount Ida's 85-acre campus is in a suburban neighborhood eight miles west of Boston.

Student Body
  Undergrad enrollment: 1,491
  Women: 67%
  Men: 33%
  Percent out-of-state: 40%

Cost Information
  Tuition: $25,915
  Room & board: $12,500
Housing Information
  University housing: Yes
  Percent living on campus: 64%

Greek System
  Fraternity: No
  Sorority: No
Athletics: Division III

NORTHEASTERN UNIVERSITY

360 Huntington Avenue, 510 International Village, Boston, MA 02115
Phone: 617-373-2200 • Fax: 617-373-8780
E-mail: admissions@neu.edu • Web: www.northeastern.edu
Support: SP • Institution type: 4-year private

PROGRAMS OR SERVICES FOR STUDENTS WITH LD

For students with documented learning disabilities and/or ADHD, Northeastern offers both a comprehensive program and basic support services. The Learning Disabilities Program (LDP) is a comprehensive program for students with LD and/or ADHD. Students meet with a LD specialist for two regularly-scheduled one hour appointments each week. Content for meetings includes time management, organization, reading comprehension, expository writing, research and study skills, and self advocacy. The LDP is a fee-based service and requires an additional application and interview. The Disability Resource Center (DRC) offers accommodations to students with disabilities, including exam accommodations, notetaking services, and alternate format text. Students registered with the DRC may also meet with a LD specialist for support in using accommodations and for other disability-related needs. There is no charge for basic support services through the DRC.

ADMISSION INFORMATION FOR STUDENTS WITH LD/ADHD

College entrance tests required: Yes
Interview required: Yes, for LDP
Essay recommended: No
What documentation required for LD: Psycho Ed evaluation to include: relevant historical info, instructional interventions, related services, age diagnosed, objective data (aptitude, achievement, info processing), test scores (standard, percentile and grade equivalents) and describe functional limitations.
With general application: Yes if requested as part of Structured Program application
To receive services after enrolling: Yes
What documentation required for ADHD: Diagnosis based on DSM-V; history of behaviors impairing functioning in academic setting; diagnostic interview; history of symptoms; evidence of ongoing behaviors.

With general application: Yes if requested as part of Structured Program application
To receive services after enrolling: Yes
Submitted to: Disability Resource Center
Special Ed. HS course work accepted: N/A
Specific course requirements of all applicants: Yes
Separate application required: Yes, for LDP
# of LD applications submitted each year: N/A
# of LD applications accepted yearly: N/A
Total # of students receiving LD services: 400
Acceptance into program means acceptance into college: Student must be admitted and enrolled in the university first and then request accommodations from DRC or admission to the LD program.

ADMISSIONS

There is no separate or different admissions process for students with learning disabilities or ADHD. However, students who are interested in the Learning Disabilities Program (LDP), must apply to the LDP as well as to the University. Students are encouraged to submit an application to the LDP immediately upon their decision to attend the University. The LDP also requires an interview for admission to the program. LDP application and additional information about the program are available at www.northeastern.edu/uhcs/idp.

ADDITIONAL INFORMATION

Students who are interested in basic services, including accommodations, are encouraged to provide documentation to the DRC while their applications are being reviewed by the Admissions Office. In this way, the DRC can provide feedback on the documentation as soon as the student is accepted to NU. Please see the DRC's website at www.northeastern.edu/drc.

LEARNING DISABILITY PROGRAMS OR SERVICES

Contact Information
Name of program or department: Learning Disabilities Program
  Telephone: 617-373-4525
  Fax: 617-373-4142

LEARNING DISABILITY SERVICES

Accommodations are decided upon an individual basis after a thorough review of appropriate, current documentation. The accommodations requested must be supported through the documentation provided and must be logically linked to the current impact of the condition on academic functioning.

Allowed in exams
  Calculator: Yes
  Dictionary: Yes
  Computer: Yes
  Spellchecker: Yes
Extended test time: Yes
Scribes: Yes
Proctors: Yes
Oral exams: Yes

Note-takers: Yes
Distraction-reduced environment: Yes
Tape recording in class: Yes
Electronic texts: Yes
Accommodations for students with
  ADHD: Yes
Kurzweil Reader: Yes
Other assistive technology: Yes
Priority registration: N/A

Added costs for services: Yes, for LDP
LD specialists: Yes
Professional tutors: No
Peer tutors: Yes
Max. hours/wk. for services:
  Unlimited
How professors are notified of
  LD/ADHD: By student

GENERAL ADMISSIONS INFORMATION

Office of Admission: 617-373-2200

ENTRANCE REQUIREMENTS

Academic units required: 4 English, 3 math, 3 science (2 science labs), 2 foreign language, 3 social studies, 2 history. **Academic units recommended:** 4 math, 4 science (4 science labs), 4 foreign language. High school diploma is required, and GED is accepted. SAT or ACT required. TOEFL, IELTS, APIEL is required for students whose native language is not English and who score below 550 on the Critical Reading SAT/ACT equivalent. TOEFL-passing score of 223 on the computer-based test, 563 on the paper-based test, 84 on the Internet-based test, and a passing score of 6.5 on the International English Language Testing System (IELTS).

Application deadline: 1/15
Notification: 4/1
Average GPA: NR
ACT Composite middle 50% range:
  28–32

SAT Math middle 50% range:
  640–730
SAT Critical Reading middle 50%
  range: 610–700
SAT Writing middle 50% range:
  600–700

Graduated top 10% of class: 56%
Graduated top 25% of class: 83%
Graduated top 50% of class: 96%

COLLEGE GRADUATION REQUIREMENTS

Course waivers allowed: No
Course substitutions allowed: Yes
In what course: Foreign language course substitutions are available with approval from the learning disabilities specialist.

ADDITIONAL INFORMATION

Environment: The school is located on 73 acres in the city of Boston.

Student Body
  Undergrad enrollment: 16,385
  Women: 50%
  Men: 50%
  Percent out-of-state: 64%

Cost Information
  Tuition: $37,840
  Room & board: $12,760
Housing Information
  University housing: Yes
  Percent living on campus: 53%

Greek System
  Fraternity: Yes
  Sorority: Yes
Athletics: Division I

PINE MANOR COLLEGE

400 Heath Street, Chestnut Hill, MA 02467-2332
Phone: 617-731-7104 • Fax: 617-731-7102
E-mail: admission@pmc.edu • Web: www.pmc.edu
Support: CS • Institution type: 2-year and 4-year private

PROGRAMS OR SERVICES FOR STUDENTS WITH LD

The Learning Resource Center (LRC) is an expression of the college's strong commitment to the individual learning experience. The LRC supports and challenges students to realize their maximum academic potential in the way that best suits their individual learning styles. There are four full-time and three part-time professional tutors—writing tutors, math tutors, learning specialists, and the director—who provide tutoring that is individually tailored to the learning style and needs of the student. The tutoring is not content-oriented, but rather strategy-based and process-oriented. The LRC hopes that students with learning disabilities enter college with some compensatory techniques and study skills. The tutors furnish guidance and academic skills assistance to students whose learning disabilities create a gap between their true capacity and daily performance. The LRC serves the whole college population free of charge, whether or not a student has a documented learning disability.

ADMISSION INFORMATION FOR STUDENTS WITH LD/ADHD

College entrance tests required: Yes
Interview required: No
Essay recommended: Yes
What documentation required for LD: Psycho Ed evaluation to include: relevant historical info, instructional interventions, related services, age diagnosed, objective data (aptitude, achievement, info processing), test scores (standard, percentile and grade equivalents) and describe functional limitations.
With general application: No
To receive services after enrolling: Yes
What documentation required for ADHD: Diagnosis based on DSM-V; history of behaviors impairing functioning in academic setting; diagnostic interview; history of symptoms; evidence of ongoing behaviors.

With general application: No
Submitted to: Learning Resource Center
Special Ed. HS course work accepted: Yes
Specific course requirements of all applicants: NR
Separate application required: No
# of LD applications submitted each year: NR
# of LD applications accepted yearly: NR
Total # of students receiving LD services: 35–50
Acceptance into program means acceptance into college: Students must be admitted and enrolled at the college prior to requesting services from the LRC.

ADMISSIONS

All applicants submit the same general application. Although not required, an interview is highly recommended. The average ACT is 19, and the average SAT is 820. Courses required are 4 years of English, 3 years of math, 2 years of science, and 4 years of social studies. Courses taken in special education are accepted. Admissions decisions are made by the Office of Admissions. However, the director of the LRC assists in interpreting testing and documentation and makes a recommendation to the Office of Admissions. Students are encouraged to self-disclose during the admission process. There is a special optional response form that is used by the LRC after the student is accepted.

ADDITIONAL INFORMATION

LRC staff work with students on a regular, once- or twice-a-week, basis or on a drop-in basis. Students also work closely with their academic advisors. LRC tutors offer assessment and support for students in academic difficulty, enrichment for successful students, and assistance to faculty and staff. The LRC can also obtain recorded textbooks and arrange for tutors and diagnostic testing. In addition, allowing for the following accommodations has proved useful to students with disabilities: reduced course loads each semester; additional time to complete exams, quizzes, or written assignments; and separate, distraction-free room for examinations. Basic skills classes are offered in reading, math, learning strategies, written language, study strategies, and time management.

LEARNING DISABILITY PROGRAMS OR SERVICES

Contact Information
Name of program or department: Learning Resource Center (LRC)
  Telephone: 617-731-7181
  Fax: 617-731-7631

LEARNING DISABILITY SERVICES

Accommodations are decided upon an individual basis after a thorough review of appropriate, current documentation. The accommodations requested must be supported through the documentation provided and must be logically linked to the current impact of the condition on academic functioning.

Allowed in exams	**Distraction-reduced environment:** Yes	**Added costs for services:** No
Calculator: Yes	**Tape recording in class:** Yes	**LD specialists:** Yes
Dictionary: Yes	**Electronic texts:** No	**Professional tutors:** 5
Computer: Yes	**Accommodations for students with**	**Peer tutors:** No
Spellchecker: Yes	**ADHD:** Yes	**Max. hours/wk. for services:** 3
Extended test time: Yes	**Kurzweil Reader:** No	**How professors are notified of**
Scribes: Yes	**Other assistive technology:** Yes	**LD/ADHD:** By both student and
Proctors: Yes	**Priority registration:** No	director
Oral exams: Yes		
Note-takers: Yes		

GENERAL ADMISSIONS INFORMATION

Office of Admission: 617-731-7167

ENTRANCE REQUIREMENTS

Academic units recommended: 4 English, 3 math, 2 science, 2 foreign language, 4 social studies. High school diploma is required, and GED is accepted. ACT with or without Writing component accepted. TOEFL required of all international applicants: minimum paper TOEFL 500, minimum computer TOEFL 173.

Application deadline: None	**SAT Math middle 50% range:**	**Graduated top 10% of class:** 0%
Notification: Rolling	340–450	**Graduated top 25% of class:** 23%
Average GPA: 2.98	**SAT Critical Reading middle 50%**	**Graduated top 50% of class:** 49%
ACT Composite middle 50% range:	range: 340–450	
15–17	**SAT Writing middle 50% range:** NR	

COLLEGE GRADUATION REQUIREMENTS

Course waivers allowed: Yes
In what course: Mathematics
Course substitutions allowed: Yes
In what course: Mathematics

ADDITIONAL INFORMATION

Environment: Pine Manor is located on a 79-acre campus in Chestnut Hill, five miles west of Boston.

Student Body	**Cost Information**	**Greek System**
Undergrad enrollment: 450	**Tuition:** $22,042	**Fraternity:** No
Women: 99%	**Room & board:** $12,500	**Sorority:** No
Percent out-of-state: 26%	**Housing Information**	**Athletics:** Division III
	University housing: Yes	
	Percent living on campus: 74%	

SMITH COLLEGE

Seven College Lane, Northampton, MA 01063
Phone: 413-585-2500 • Fax: 413-585-2527
E-mail: admission@smith.edu • Web: www.smith.edu
Support: S • Institution type: 4-year private

PROGRAMS OR SERVICES FOR STUDENTS WITH LD

Smith College does not have a formal LD program. However, the college is both philosophically committed and legally required to enable students with documented disabilities to participate in college programs by providing reasonable accommodations for them. The Office of Disabilities Services (ODS) facilitates the provision of services and offers services aimed to eliminate barriers through modification of the program when necessary. A student may voluntarily register with ODS by completing a disability identification form and providing documentation of the disability, after which proper accommodations will be determined. Students with disabilities who need academic services are asked to make their needs known and file timely request forms for accommodations in course work each semester with ODS. The college cannot make retroactive accommodations. Students are encouraged to tell professors about the accommodations needed. The college is responsible for providing that, within certain limits, students are not denied the opportunity to participate in college programs on the basis of a disability. The college will provide support services to students with appropriate evaluations and documentation. Students should contact the ODS for consultation and advice.

ADMISSION INFORMATION FOR STUDENTS WITH LD/ADHD

College entrance tests required: Yes
Interview required: Yes
Essay recommended: Yes
What documentation required for LD: Psycho Ed evaluation
  to include: relevant historical info, instructional interventions,
  related services, age diagnosed, objective data (aptitude,
  achievement, info processing), test scores (standard,
  percentile and grade equivalents) and describe functional
  limitations.
With general application: No
To receive services after enrolling: Yes
What documentation required for ADHD: Diagnosis based
  on DSM-V; history of behaviors impairing functioning in
  academic setting; diagnostic interview; history of symptoms;
  evidence of ongoing behaviors.

With general application: No
Submitted to: Office of Disability Services
Special Ed. HS course work accepted: No
Specific course requirements of all applicants: NR
Separate application required: Yes
# of LD applications submitted each year: NR
# of LD applications accepted yearly: NR
Total # of students receiving LD services: 80
Acceptance into program means acceptance into
  college: Students must be admitted to and enrolled in the
  university first and then request services.

ADMISSIONS

There is no special admissions procedure for students with learning disabilities. ACT/SAT are optional. Students may release scores at their discretion. Leniency may be granted in regard to a high school's waiving of foreign language requirements due to a learning disability. High school courses recommended are 4 years of English composition and literature, 3 years of a foreign language (or 2 years in each of 2 languages), 3 years of math, 2 years of science, and 2 years of history. Essays are required and help them understand how the student thinks, writes and what they are about. Recommendations are required. Interviews are highly recommended.

ADDITIONAL INFORMATION

College and departmental requirements are implemented for sound academic reasons, and Smith College does not provide waivers for required courses for students with LD. The support services assist students to meet their requirements through modifications to programs when necessary. Courses are available in quantitative skills, study skills, and time management skills. The Special Needs Action Group for Support is a cross-disability, student-led group that meets regularly to provide support and peer mentoring and plan activities. Support services include readers, note-takers, scribes, assistive listening devices, typists, computing software and hardware, books on tape, writing counseling (more and/or longer appointments), peer tutoring, and time management/study skills training. If peer tutors are not available, other tutorial services may be sought. The college will not provide services that create an undue burden for the college.

LEARNING DISABILITY PROGRAMS OR SERVICES

Contact Information
Name of program or department: Office of Disability Services (ODS)
  Telephone: 413-585-2071
  Fax: 413-585-2206

LEARNING DISABILITY SERVICES

Accommodations are decided upon an individual basis after a thorough review of appropriate, current documentation. The accommodations requested must be supported through the documentation provided and must be logically linked to the current impact of the condition on academic functioning.

Allowed in exams
  Calculator: Yes
  Dictionary: No
  Computer: Yes
  Spellchecker: Yes
Extended test time: Yes
Scribes: Yes
Proctors: No
Oral exams: Yes
Note-takers: Yes

Distraction-reduced environment: Yes
Tape recording in class: Yes
Electronic texts: Yes
Accommodations for students with ADHD: Yes
Kurzweil Reader: Yes
Other assistive technology: Yes
Priority registration: Yes

Added costs for services: No
LD specialists: No
Professional tutors: 2
Peer tutors: Yes
Max. hours/wk. for services: Unlimited
How professors are notified of LD/ADHD: By both student and director

GENERAL ADMISSIONS INFORMATION

Office of Admission: 413-585-2500

ENTRANCE REQUIREMENTS

Academic units recommended: 4 English, 3 math, 3 science (3 science labs), 3 foreign language, 2 history. High school diploma or equivalent is not required. ACT with or without Writing component accepted. TOEFL required of all international applicants: minimum paper TOEFL 600, minimum computer TOEFL 250.

Application deadline: 1/15
Notification: 4/1
Average GPA: 4.00
ACT Composite middle 50% range: 25–31

SAT Math middle 50% range: 570–680
SAT Critical Reading middle 50% range: 600–710
SAT Writing middle 50% range: 590–700

Graduated top 10% of class: 61%
Graduated top 25% of class: 91%
Graduated top 50% of class: 100%

COLLEGE GRADUATION REQUIREMENTS

Course waivers allowed: No
Course substitutions allowed: Yes
In what course: Foreign language

ADDITIONAL INFORMATION

Environment: The 204-acre campus is located in a small city 85 miles west of Boston and 15 minutes from Amherst.

Student Body
  Undergrad enrollment: 2,610
  Women: 100%
  Percent out-of-state: 83%

Cost Information
  Tuition: $44,190
  Room & board: $13,860
Housing Information
  University housing: Yes
  Percent living on campus: 88%

Greek System
  Fraternity: No
  Sorority: No
Athletics: Division III

SPRINGFIELD COLLEGE

263 Alden Street, Springfield, MA 01109
Phone: 413-748-3136 • Fax: 413-748-3694
E-mail: admissions@spfldcol.edu • Web: www.springfieldcollege.edu
Support: CS • Institution type: 4-year private

PROGRAMS OR SERVICES FOR STUDENTS WITH LD

Springfield College is committed to providing an equal educational opportunity and full participation in college activities for persons with disabilities. The Office of Learning Support Services provides services that ensure that students with disabilities are given an equal educational opportunity and the opportunity for full participation in all college programs and activities. In addition to supporting students with disabilities, Learning Support Services works with students who are having academic difficulty. Students can receive services by meeting with the director of Learning Support Services to verify eligibility for services, identify student needs, and determine appropriate services and accommodations. To receive services, students must provide documentation of their learning disabilities; the documentation must be current and comprehensive and contain specific evidence and identification of a learning disability. Documentation should not be older than 3 years.

ADMISSION INFORMATION FOR STUDENTS WITH LD/ADHD

College entrance tests required: Yes
Interview required: No
Essay recommended: Yes
What documentation required for LD: Psycho Ed evaluation to include: relevant historical info, instructional interventions, related services, age diagnosed, objective data (aptitude, achievement, info processing), test scores (standard, percentile and grade equivalents) and describe functional limitations.
With general application: No
To receive services after enrolling: Yes
What documentation required for ADHD: Diagnosis based on DSM-V; history of behaviors impairing functioning in academic setting; diagnostic interview; history of symptoms; evidence of ongoing behaviors.

With general application: No
Submitted to: Office of Learning Support Services
Special Ed. HS course work accepted: No
Specific course requirements of all applicants: Yes
Separate application required: No
# of LD applications submitted each year: NR
# of LD applications accepted yearly: NR
Total # of students receiving LD services: 150–160
Acceptance into program means acceptance into college: Students must be admitted to and enrolled in the university first and then request services.

ADMISSIONS

There is no special admissions process for students with learning disabilities. All applicants must submit the same general application and meet the same admission criteria. There is no minimum GPA required, though the average GPA is a 3.0. Courses required include 4 years of English, 3 years of math, 2 years of history, and 2–3 years of science. Personal statements and interviews are required. Admissions decisions are made by the Office of Admissions.

ADDITIONAL INFORMATION

Services provided through the Office of Learning Support Services include taped textbooks, taped lectures, readers, alternative testing, note-takers, tutors, computers with spell-check, reduced course loads, study skills and time management training, course accommodations, and assistance with course selection. Services and accommodations that may be appropriate for students with attention deficit hyperactivity disorder include testing accommodations, tape recording of lectures, assistance organizational skills, assistance with study skills, and access to adaptive technology. Services and accommodations that may be appropriate for students with learning disabilities include taped textbooks, readers, note-takers, tape recording of lectures, testing accommodations, reduced course load, assistance with study skills, assistance with organizational skills, and adaptive technology. Students experiencing academic difficulties may benefit from working one-on-one with an academic coach. Academic coaches help students put together a plan for success by focusing on each student's academic strengths and weaknesses. Academic coaches are available to help students address problems that impede academic progress, such as procrastination, time mismanagement, and related issues. Academic coaches develop plans to strengthen specific academic skills after an initial assessment. Tutoring is available for any Springfield College student who needs it. Faculty-approved tutors provide individual or small group sessions to students who are concerned about their academic performance.

LEARNING DISABILITY PROGRAMS OR SERVICES

Contact Information
Name of program or department: Student Support Services
  Telephone: 413-748-3768
  Fax: 413-748-3725

LEARNING DISABILITY SERVICES

Accommodations are decided upon an individual basis after a thorough review of appropriate, current documentation. The accommodations requested must be supported through the documentation provided and must be logically linked to the current impact of the condition on academic functioning.

Allowed in exams
  Calculator: Yes
  Dictionary: Yes
  Computer: Yes
  Spellchecker: Yes
Extended test time: Yes
Scribes: Yes
Proctors: Yes
Oral exams: Yes
Note-takers: Yes

Distraction-reduced environment: Yes
Tape recording in class: Yes
Electronic texts: Yes
Accommodations for students with
  ADHD: Yes
Kurzweil Reader: Yes
Other assistive technology: Yes
Priority registration: No

Added costs for services: No
LD specialists: Yes
Professional tutors: No
Peer tutors: No
Max. hours/wk. for services:
  Unlimited
How professors are notified of
  LD/ADHD: By both student and director

GENERAL ADMISSIONS INFORMATION

Office of Admission: 413-748-3136

ENTRANCE REQUIREMENTS

Academic units recommended: 4 English, 3 math, 3 science, 2 foreign language, 2 social studies, 4 academic electives. High school diploma is required, and GED is accepted. TOEFL required of all international applicants: minimum paper TOEFL 525.

Application deadline: 4/11
Notification: Rolling
Average GPA: NR
ACT Composite middle 50% range:
  NR

SAT Math middle 50% range:
  460–570
SAT Critical Reading middle 50%
  range: 450–540
SAT Writing middle 50% range: NR

Graduated top 10% of class: 14%
Graduated top 25% of class: 35%
Graduated top 50% of class: 76%

COLLEGE GRADUATION REQUIREMENTS

Course waivers allowed: Yes
In what course: Foreign language
Course substitutions allowed: Yes
In what course: Foreign language

ADDITIONAL INFORMATION

Environment: The campus is in a suburban area about 30 minutes north of Hartford.

Student Body
  Undergrad enrollment: 2,328
  Women: 47%
  Men: 53%
  Percent out-of-state: 72%

Cost Information
  Tuition: $30,660
  Room & board: $10,830
Housing Information
  University housing: Yes
  Percent living on campus: 85%

Greek System
  Fraternity: Yes
  Sorority: Yes
Athletics: Division III

U. OF MASSACHUSETTS—AMHERST

University Admissions Center, 37 Mather Drive, Amherst, MA 01003-9291
Phone: 413-545-0222 • Fax: 413-545-4312
E-mail: mail@admissions.umass.edu • Web: www.umass.edu
Support: CS • Institution type: 4-year public

PROGRAMS OR SERVICES FOR STUDENTS WITH LD

Disabilities Services (DS) supports all students with documented disabilities. Students must register with DS and provide documentation to receive services. Students are assigned to work with a professional Consumer Manager to work on three objectives for the entire academic year: understanding and obtaining accommodations needed, identifying and utilizing resources, and identifying and implementing learning strategies. DS also provides Learning Specialists are trained in disability-related learning issues who apply unique, specific expertise and knowledge to student's academic needs. Learning Specialists' seek to match student's specific disabilities and skills to their specific learning requirements through the use of individualized learning techniques, study skills, reading techniques, organizational techniques and other active learning skills

ADMISSION INFORMATION FOR STUDENTS WITH LD/ADHD

College entrance tests required: Yes
Interview required: No
Essay recommended: Yes
What documentation required for LD: Psycho Ed evaluation to include: relevant historical info, instructional interventions, related services, age diagnosed, objective data (aptitude, achievement, info processing), test scores (standard, percentile and grade equivalents) and describe functional limitations.
With general application: No
To receive services after enrolling: Yes
What documentation required for ADHD: Diagnosis based on DSM-V; history of behaviors impairing functioning in academic setting; diagnostic interview; history of symptoms; evidence of ongoing behaviors.

With general application: No
Submitted to: Both Admissions and Disability Services
Special Ed. HS course work accepted: No
Specific course requirements of all applicants: Yes
Separate application required: Yes
# of LD applications submitted each year: NR
# of LD applications accepted yearly: NR
Total # of students receiving LD services: 2,000+
Acceptance into program means acceptance into college: Students must be admitted to and enrolled in the university first and then request services.

ADMISSIONS

There are no special admissions criteria for students with disabilities. General admission requirements recommend include: Top 25% of their class with 3.5 GPA, SAT of 1140, or ACT of 24. Course requirements: 4 English, 3 math, 3 social studies, 2 sciences, and 2 foreign language (foreign language Current residents of MA with LD do not need to submit ACT//SAT. Essay and a personal statement are required. All admissions and support documents go to Admissions. Applicants who check the LD box are reviewed individually by LD specialists. There is no quota on the number of students with LD who admitted.

ADDITIONAL INFORMATION

Students and Consumer Managers prepare accommodation forms for professors for accommodations such as: extended test time on exams and/or assignments, alternate test formats, and note taking. Learning Specialists assigned to students work on average, one hour per week (more meeting times may be needed). The Learning Specialist works with students to facilitate obstacles being experienced. Students with relevant documented LD can petition to substitute a foreign language requirement with cultural courses (called a foreign language modification). DS operates several programs such as: Access Program, Communication Access Program and Information Access Program.

LEARNING DISABILITY PROGRAMS OR SERVICES

Contact Information
Name of program or department: Disability Services
  Telephone: 413-545-0892
  Fax: 413-577-0122

LEARNING DISABILITY SERVICES

Accommodations are decided upon an individual basis after a thorough review of appropriate, current documentation. The accommodations requested must be supported through the documentation provided and must be logically linked to the current impact of the condition on academic functioning.

Allowed in exams (Accommodations are specific to the individual and their documented needs in specific courses at the university level.)
  Calculator: Yes
  Dictionary: Yes
  Computer: Yes
  Spellchecker: Yes
Extended test time: Yes
Scribes: Yes
Proctors: Yes

Oral exams: Yes
Note-takers: Yes
Distraction-reduced environment: Yes
Tape recording in class: Yes
Electronic texts: Yes
Accommodations for students with ADHD: Yes
Kurzweil Reader: Yes
Other assistive technology: Yes
Priority registration: No

Added costs for services: No
LD specialists: Yes
Professional tutors: Yes
Peer tutors: Yes
Max. hours/wk. for services: 1–2
How professors are notified of LD/ADHD: By student and electronic accommodation notification form

GENERAL ADMISSIONS INFORMATION

Office of Admission: 413-545-0222

ENTRANCE REQUIREMENTS

Academic units required: 4 English, 3 math, 2 science (2 science labs), 2 foreign language, 2 social studies, 2 academic electives. High school diploma is required, and GED is accepted. ACT without Writing component accepted. TOEFL required of all international applicants: minimum score of 80 or better on the internet-based TOEFL (iBT) or 213 or better on the computer-based TOEFL is required. An IELTS score of 6.5 or higher is also acceptable. Applicants with strong SAT/ACT scores may receive a TOEFLS/IELTS waiver.

Application deadline: 1/15
Notification: Rolling
Average GPA: 3.5
ACT Composite middle 50% range: NR

SAT Math middle 50% range: 540–640
SAT Critical Reading middle 50% range: 510–620
SAT Writing middle 50% range: NR

Graduated top 10% of class: 23%
Graduated top 25% of class: 58%
Graduated top 50% of class: 94%

COLLEGE GRADUATION REQUIREMENTS

Course waivers allowed: No
Course substitutions allowed: Yes
In what course: The Colleges of Arts and Sciences require foreign language. This requirement is never waived; however, if documented disabilities prevent a student from learning a foreign language, a student can request a foreign language modification with support from the Disability Services Office.

ADDITIONAL INFORMATION

Environment: The university is located on 1,405 acres in a small town 90 miles west of Boston.

Student Body
  Undergrad enrollment: 21,373
  Women: 50%
  Men: 50%
  Percent out-of-state: 22%

Cost Information
  In-state tuition: $11,732
  Out-of-state tuition: $23,628
  Room & board: $8,814
Housing Information
  University housing: Yes
  Percent living on campus: 62%

Greek System
  Fraternity: Yes
  Sorority: Yes
Athletics: Division I

WHEATON COLLEGE (MA)

Office of Admission, Norton, MA 02766
Phone: 508-286-8251 • Fax: 508-286-8271
E-mail: admission@wheatoncollege.edu • Web: http://wheatoncollege.edu
Support: S • Institution: 4-year private

PROGRAMS OR SERVICES FOR STUDENTS WITH LD

Wheaton College encourages life-long learning by assisting students to become self-advocates and independent learners. The college does not have a special program for students with LD. The Assistant Dean for College Skills serves as the 504/ADA coordinator. Students with LD can access services through the dean. The Academic Advising Center houses the Dean of Academic Advising who holds drop-in office hours and assists students with petitions to the Committee on Admissions and Academic Standing, Orientation, and Probation; general advising; and incomplete grade resolution. The advising staff can assist with pressing advising questions. Students also have access to tutors, peer advisors, and preceptors who offer assistance with study strategies. All students have access to these services.

ADMISSION INFORMATION FOR STUDENTS WITH LD/ADHD

College entrance tests required: No
Interview required: No
Essay recommended: No
What documentation required for LD: Psycho Ed evaluation to include: relevant historical info, instructional interventions, related services, age diagnosed, objective data (aptitude, achievement, info processing), test scores (standard, percentile and grade equivalents) and describe functional limitations.
With general application: No
To receive services after enrolling: Yes
What documentation required for ADHD: Diagnosis based on DSM-V; history of behaviors impairing functioning in academic setting; diagnostic interview; history of symptoms; evidence of ongoing behaviors.

With general application: No
Submitted to: Academic Support Services
Special Ed. HS course work accepted: Yes
Specific course requirements of all applicants: NR
Separate application required: No
# of LD applications submitted each year: NR
# of LD applications accepted yearly: NR
Total # of students receiving LD services: 120
Acceptance into program means acceptance into college: Students must be admitted to and enrolled in the university first and then request services.

ADMISSIONS

All applicants must meet the same admission standards. Students with LD may choose to meet with the Assistant Dean for College Skills. Wheaton College does not require the ACT/SAT for admission. It is strongly suggested that students take 4 years of English, 3–4 years of math, 3–4 years of a foreign language, 2 years of social studies, and 3–4 years of science. Students are encouraged to take AP and honors courses and courses in visual/performing arts. Wheaton will accept courses taken in the special education department. Students with LD are encouraged to self-disclose and provide current documentation. All LD testing information should be sent to both admissions and support services.

ADDITIONAL INFORMATION

Services for students with LD can include classroom accommodations, college skills workshops, course tutoring program, general advising, and study strategy tutoring as well as strategy workshops. Reasonable accommodations are available for students with appropriate documentation. There is a summer program available for students who wish to participate. Proctors are not offered because Wheaton has an honor code for exams.

LEARNING DISABILITY PROGRAMS OR SERVICES

Contact Information
Name of program or department: Academic Support Services
 Telephone: 508-286-8215
 Fax: 508-286-5621

LEARNING DISABILITY SERVICES

Accommodations are decided upon an individual basis after a thorough review of appropriate, current documentation. The accommodations requested must be supported through the documentation provided and must be logically linked to the current impact of the condition on academic functioning.

Allowed in exams
 Calculator: Yes
 Dictionary: Yes
 Computer: Yes
 Spellchecker: Yes
Extended test time: Yes
Scribes: Yes
Proctors: No
Oral exams: Yes
Note-takers: Yes

Distraction-reduced environment: Yes
Tape recording in class: Yes
Electronic texts: Yes
Accommodations for students with ADHD: Yes
Kurzweil Reader: Yes
Other assistive technology: Yes
Priority registration: No

Added costs for services: No
LD specialists: No
Professional tutors: 7
Peer tutors: N/A
Max. hours/wk. for services: Unlimited
How professors are notified of LD/ADHD: By student

GENERAL ADMISSIONS INFORMATION

Office of Admission: 508-286-8251

ENTRANCE REQUIREMENTS

Academic units recommended: 4 English, 4 math, 3 science (2 science labs), 4 foreign language, 2 social studies, 2 history. High school diploma is required, and GED is accepted. TOEFL required of all international applicants: minimum paper TOEFL 550, minimum computer TOEFL 213.

Application deadline: 1/15
Notification: 4/1
Average GPA: 3.50
ACT Composite middle 50% range: 26–29

SAT Math middle 50% range: 580–670
SAT Critical Reading middle 50% range: 580–680
SAT Writing middle 50% range: NR

Graduated top 10% of class: 53%
Graduated top 25% of class: 83%
Graduated top 50% of class: 99%

COLLEGE GRADUATION REQUIREMENTS

Course waivers allowed: No
Course substitutions allowed: Yes
In what course: Foreign language

ADDITIONAL INFORMATION

Environment: The college is located 35 miles from Boston and 15 miles from Providence, Rhode Island.

Student Body
 Undergrad enrollment: 1,655
 Women: 62%
 Men: 38%
 Percent out-of-state: 71%

Cost Information
 Tuition: $41,600
 Room & board: $10,670
Housing Information
 University housing: Yes
 Percent living on campus: 96%

Greek System
 Fraternity: No
 Sorority: No
Athletics: Division III

WHEELOCK COLLEGE

200 The Riverway, Boston, MA 02215
Phone: 617-879-2206 • Fax: 617-879-2449
E-mail: undergrad@wheelock.edu • Web: www.wheelock.edu
Support: CS • Institution type: 4-year private

PROGRAMS OR SERVICES FOR STUDENTS WITH LD

The Disability Services Program at Wheelock College ensures that students with disabilities can participate in all facets of college life. They also provide and coordinate support services and programs that will enable students to maximize their educational potential. Students are encouraged to be independent individuals who know their strengths and develop compensatory skills for academic success. When working with students, the two major goals are to help with becoming independent and assisting in developing self-advocacy skills. Students with LD are encouraged to self-disclose to Disability Services. Students are required to provide documentation from a qualified professional. Disability Services will assist in identifying appropriate accommodations based on the documentation provided.

ADMISSION INFORMATION FOR STUDENTS WITH LD/ADHD

College entrance tests required: Yes
Interview required: N/A
Essay recommended: NR
What documentation required for LD: Psycho Ed evaluation to include: relevant historical info, instructional interventions, related services, age diagnosed, objective data (aptitude, achievement, info processing), test scores (standard, percentile and grade equivalents) and describe functional limitations.
With general application: No
To receive services after enrolling: Yes
What documentation required for ADHD: Diagnosis based on DSM-V; history of behaviors impairing functioning in academic setting; diagnostic interview; history of symptoms; evidence of ongoing behaviors.

With general application: No
Submitted to: Disability Services Program
Special Ed. HS course work accepted: Yes
Specific course requirements of all applicants: Yes
Separate application required: N/A
# of LD applications submitted each year: NR
# of LD applications accepted yearly: NR
Total # of students receiving LD services: 95
Acceptance into program means acceptance into college: Students must be admitted to and enrolled in the university first and then request services.

ADMISSIONS

There is no special admissions process for students with LD and ADHD. All applicants are expected to meet the general admission criteria. All students should have 4 years of English, 1 year of U.S. history and additional social studies, 3 years of college-prep math, and at least 1 year of science lab. Substitutions are not allowed for entrance requirements. Wheelock will accept courses in high school that were taken in the Special Education Department. Students should feel free to self-disclose their disabilities in the application process. Students must submit a copy of a graded paper written within the past year. It should be a minimum of 250 words and can be on any subject. Some examples are an English composition, a history thesis, a psychology report, or a literary critique.

ADDITIONAL INFORMATION

With appropriate documentation, students may be eligible for the following services or accommodations: priority registration, letters informing the instructors of the disability and what reasonable accommodations the student will need, individual sessions with a learning specialist to help with time management, academic, and organizational skills support. The Writing Center is available for all students interested in assistance with writing skills, and peer tutors work one-on-one with the students. Students may request referrals for peer tutors, and study groups are available. In addition, workshops on the following topics are offered throughout the academic year: academic survival skills, reading skills, and evaluation of students' learning styles. Other academic support services include academic advising, and referrals for diagnostic testing.

LEARNING DISABILITY PROGRAMS OR SERVICES

Contact Information
Name of program or department: Disability Services
Telephone: 617-879-2030
Fax: 617-879-2163

LEARNING DISABILITY SERVICES

Accommodations are decided upon an individual basis after a thorough review of appropriate, current documentation. The accommodations requested must be supported through the documentation provided and must be logically linked to the current impact of the condition on academic functioning.

Allowed in exams	**Distraction-reduced environment:** Yes	**Added costs for services:** No
Calculator: No	**Tape recording in class:** Yes	**LD specialists:** Yes
Dictionary: No	**Electronic texts:** Yes	**Professional tutors:** No
Computer: No	**Accommodations for students with**	**Peer tutors:** 25
Spellchecker: Yes	**ADHD:** Yes	**Max. hours/wk. for services:** 2–3
Extended test time: Yes	**Kurzweil Reader:** Yes	**How professors are notified of**
Scribes: Yes	**Other assistive technology:** Yes	**LD/ADHD:** By student
Proctors: Yes	**Priority registration:** Yes	
Oral exams: No		
Note-takers: Yes		

GENERAL ADMISSIONS INFORMATION

Office of Admission: 617-879-2206

ENTRANCE REQUIREMENTS

Academic units required: 4 English, 3 math, 2 science (1 science lab), 2 social studies. High school diploma is required, and GED is accepted. ACT with or without Writing component accepted. TOEFL required of all international applicants: minimum paper TOEFL 500, minimum computer TOEFL 173.

Application deadline: None	**SAT Math middle 50% range:**	**Graduated top 10% of class:** 11%
Notification: Rolling	420–530	**Graduated top 25% of class:** 30%
Average GPA: 3.0	**SAT Critical Reading middle 50%**	**Graduated top 50% of class:** 73%
ACT Composite middle 50% range:	**range:** 440–520	
18–23	**SAT Writing middle 50% range:**	
	430–540	

COLLEGE GRADUATION REQUIREMENTS

Course waivers allowed: No
Course substitutions allowed: No

ADDITIONAL INFORMATION

Environment: Wheelock College is located in the Fenway area of Boston, two miles from downtown.

Student Body	**Cost Information**	**Greek System**
Undergrad enrollment: 871	**Tuition:** $29,860	**Fraternity:** No
Women: 92%	**Room & board:** $12,800	**Sorority:** No
Men: 8%	**Housing Information**	**Athletics:** Division III
Percent out-of-state: 48%	**University housing:** Yes	
	Percent living on campus: 70%	

ADRIAN COLLEGE

110 South Madison Street, Adrian, MI 49221
Phone: 517-265-5161 • Fax: 517-264-3331
E-mail: admissions@adrian.edu • Web: www.adrian.edu
Support: CS • Institution: 4-year private

PROGRAMS OR SERVICES FOR STUDENTS WITH LD

Adrian College has extensive academic support services for all students with disabilities. The more the students are mainstreamed in high school, the greater their chances of success at Adrian. There is no special or separate curriculum for students with learning disabilities.

ADMISSION INFORMATION FOR STUDENTS WITH LD/ADHD

College entrance tests required: Yes
Interview required: No
Essay required: N/A
What documentation required for LD: Psycho Ed evaluation to include: relevant historical info, instructional interventions, related services, age diagnosed, objective data (aptitude, achievement, info processing), test scores (standard, percentile and grade equivalents) and describe functional limitations.
With general application: No
To receive services after enrolling: Yes
What documentation required for ADHD: Diagnosis based on DSM-V; history of behaviors impairing functioning in academic setting; diagnostic interview; history of symptoms; evidence of ongoing behaviors.

With general application: No
Submitted to: Support Program/Services
Special Ed. HS course work accepted: Yes
Specific course requirements for all applicants: NR
Separate application required for program services: Yes
# of LD applications submitted each year: 10
# of LD applications accepted yearly: NR
Total # of students receiving LD services: 37
Acceptance into program means acceptance into college: Separate application required after student has enrolled

ADMISSIONS

Students with learning disabilities must meet regular admission criteria. Students should demonstrate the ability to do college-level work through an acceptable GPA in college-preparatory classes (average 3.22) including four years English, three years math, social studies, science and language, ACT (average 19–24) or SAT, and a psychological report. Furthermore, by their senior year in high school, students should, for the most part, be mainstreamed. Courses taken in special education will be considered for admission. The applications of students who self-disclose are reviewed by Academic Services staff, not to determine admissions, but to start a documentation file. There is a special admissions program designed for students who demonstrate academic potential. This Adrian College Enrichment Program (ACE) requires students to sign a contract and maintain a certain GPA each of the first two semesters.

ADDITIONAL INFORMATION

Course adaptations help to make courses more understandable. Skills classes are available in reading, math, study skills, and research paper writing, and students are granted credit toward their GPA. Support services and accommodations are available if appropriate in the following areas: extended time on tests; distraction-free testing environment; scribes; note-takers; proctors; use of computers in exams; taped textbooks; scanners and voice-recognition software. Tutorial assistance is available for all students.

PROGRAM FOR DISABILITY SERVICES

Contact Information
Name of program or department: ACCESS, Academic Services
  Telephone: 517-265-5161, ext. 4093
  Fax: 517-264-3331

LEARNING DISABILITY SERVICES

Accommodations are decided upon an individual basis after a thorough review of appropriate, current documentation. The accommodations requested must be supported through the documentation provided and must be logically linked to the current impact of the condition on academic functioning.

Allowed in exams
  Calculator: No
  Dictionary: Yes
  Computer: Yes
  Spellchecker: Yes
Extended test time: Yes
Scribes: Yes
Proctors: Yes
Oral exams: Yes
Note-takers: Yes

Distraction-reduced environment: Yes
Tape recording in class: Yes
Electronic texts: Yes
Accommodations for students with ADHD: Yes
Kurzweil Reader: Yes, 1000 and 3000
Other assistive technology: Braille capabilities
Priority registration: No

Added costs for services: No
LD specialists: Yes
Professional tutors: NR
Peer tutors: 100–110
Max. hours/wk. for services:
How professors are notified of LD/ADHD: Both student and director

GENERAL ADMISSIONS INFORMATION

Office of Admission: 517-265-5161

ENTRANCE REQUIREMENTS

Academic units recommended: 4 English, 3 mathematics, 2 science, (1 science labs), 2 foreign language, 1 social studies, 1 history, 2 academic electives. High school diploma is required and GED is accepted. SAT or ACT required; ACT recommended; TOEFL required of all international applicants; minimum paper TOEFL 500, minimum computer TOEFL 173.

Application deadline: None
Notification: Rolling
Average GPA: 3.22
ACT Composite middle 50% range: 19–24

SAT Math middle 50% range: NR
SAT Critical Reading middle 50% range: NR
SAT Writing middle 50% range: NR

Graduated top 10% of class: 14%%
Graduated top 25% of class: 35%%
Graduated top 50% of class: 72%

COLLEGE GRADUATION REQUIREMENTS

Course waivers allowed: No
Course substitutions allowed: No

ADDITIONAL INFORMATION

Environment: The school is located on 100 acres in a residential section of Michigan 35 miles northeast of Ann Arbor.

Student Body
  Undergrad enrollment: 1,650
  Women: 50%
  Men: 50%
  Percent out-of-state: 22%

Cost Information
  Tuition: $27,050
  Room and board: $8,346
Housing Information
  University housing: Yes
  Percent living on campus: 86%

Greek System
  Fraternity: Yes
  Sorority: Yes
Athletics: Division III

CALVIN COLLEGE

3201 Burton Street Southeast, Grand Rapids, MI 49546
Phone: 616-526-6106 • Fax: 616-526-6777
E-mail: admissions@calvin.edu • Web: www.calvin.edu
Support: CS • Institution type: 4-year private

PROGRAMS OR SERVICES FOR STUDENTS WITH LD

The mission of Student Academic Services is to ensure that otherwise qualified students are able to benefit from a distinctly Christian education based on liberal arts. The Coaching Program is for students with learning disabilities and/or ADHD and other students who specifically need help with time management and study skills. The coaches give suggestions and feedback as well as encouragement on how to manage academics with other areas of life. First-year students are encouraged to apply for the Coaching Program at the beginning of the fall semester. Once admitted, the student with a learning disability or ADHD may take advantage of all academic services. The student must understand, however, that academic standards at Calvin are rigorous. By taking advantage of appropriate services and by means of individual effort, it is assumed that academic progress will be made. The student and the disability coordinator maintain open communication with the appropriate faculty members to ensure academic integrity as well as reasonable expectations.

ADMISSION INFORMATION FOR STUDENTS WITH LD/ADHD

College entrance tests required: Yes
Interview required: No
Essay recommended: No
What documentation required for LD: Psycho Ed evaluation to include: relevant historical info, instructional interventions, related services, age diagnosed, objective data (aptitude, achievement, info processing), test scores (standard, percentile and grade equivalents) and describe functional limitations.
With general application: No
To receive services after enrolling: Yes
What documentation required for ADHD: Diagnosis based on DSM-V; history of behaviors impairing functioning in academic setting; diagnostic interview; history of symptoms; evidence of ongoing behaviors.

With general application: No
Submitted to: Student Academic Services
Special Ed. HS course work accepted: No
Specific course requirements of all applicants: Yes
Separate application required: No
# of LD applications submitted each year: NR
# of LD applications accepted yearly: NR
Total # of students receiving LD services: 246
Acceptance into program means acceptance into college: Students must be admitted to and enrolled in the university first and then request services.

ADMISSIONS

There are no special admissions criteria for students with LD. Applicants are expected to have an ACT of 20 (19 English and 20 Math) or SAT of 940 (470 Critical Reading and 470 Math). The mid 50 percent for ACT is 23–25, and for SAT, it is 1090–1320. Courses required include: 3 English, 1 algebra, 1 geometry, and a minimum of 2 in any two of the following fields: social science, language, or natural science; one of the foreign language, math, social science, and natural science fields must include at least 3 years of study. The mid 50 percent GPA is 3.3–3.9. The Access Program provides an alternate entry track for first-time students who show promise of being successful at Calvin, but who cannot meet all of the admissions standards. The students are provided with placement testing in math and/or English, special advising, and enrollment in a college thinking and learning course during their first semester at Calvin. Depending on the outcome of the placement testing, additional developmental courses may be required as a condition of admission. The Access Program helps students develop new approaches, methods, and skills for learning by means of placement testing, academic advising, Academic Services Courses (ASC), and consultation with students' professors.

ADDITIONAL INFORMATION

The Office of Student Academic Services is a learning center is open to all students. SAS provides tutoring in most core and upper-level courses by trained upperclass students. Tutors meet with students each week to assist them in learning course content and in developing good approaches to learning. Classes are available in English, math, and study skills. These classes may be taken for college credit. The Coaching Program is an interactive relationship with another student who learns about the student's disability and learning style and then provides direction and strategies for the student. The program provides support in the areas of education and self-advocacy, time management and avoiding procrastination, note-taking, providing environments for studying, taking tests, and general organizational skills. Services and accommodations are offered to undergraduate and graduate students. Students who self-disclose and are admitted to the college are then reviewed for services.

LEARNING DISABILITY PROGRAMS OR SERVICES

Contact Information
Name of program or department: Student Academic Services
  Telephone: 616-526-6113
  Fax: 616-526-7066

LEARNING DISABILITY SERVICES

Accommodations are decided upon an individual basis after a thorough review of appropriate, current documentation. The accommodations requested must be supported through the documentation provided and must be logically linked to the current impact of the condition on academic functioning.

Allowed in exams	**Distraction-reduced environment:** Yes	**Added costs for services:** No
Calculator: Yes	**Tape recording in class:** Yes	**LD specialists:** Yes
Dictionary: No	**Electronic texts:** Yes	**Professional tutors:** 0
Computer: Yes	**Accommodations for students with**	**Peer tutors:** 100+
Spellchecker: Yes	**ADHD:** Yes	**Max. hours/wk. for services:**
Extended test time: Yes	**Kurzweil Reader:** No	Unlimited
Scribes: Yes	**Other assistive technology:** Yes	**How professors are notified of**
Proctors: Yes	**Priority registration:** Yes	**LD/ADHD:** By student
Oral exams: No		
Note-takers: Yes		

GENERAL ADMISSIONS INFORMATION

Office of Admission: 616-526-6106

ENTRANCE REQUIREMENTS

Academic units required: 3 English, 3 math, 2 science, 2 social studies, 3 academic electives. **Academic units recommended:** 4 English, 3 math, 2 science (1 science lab), 2 foreign language, 3 social studies, 3 academic electives. High school diploma is required, and GED is accepted. ACT with or without Writing component accepted. TOEFL required of all international applicants: minimum paper TOEFL 550, minimum computer TOEFL 213.

Application deadline: 8/15	**SAT Math middle 50% range:**	**Graduated top 10% of class:** 26%
Notification: Rolling	550–670	**Graduated top 25% of class:** 54%
Average GPA: 3.57	**SAT Critical Reading middle 50%**	**Graduated top 50% of class:** 80%
ACT Composite middle 50% range:	**range:** 530–660	
23–29	**SAT Writing middle 50% range:** NR	

COLLEGE GRADUATION REQUIREMENTS

Course waivers allowed: No
Course substitutions allowed: Yes
In what course: Foreign language with documentation

ADDITIONAL INFORMATION

Environment: The college is located on a 370-acre campus in a suburban area seven miles southeast of Grand Rapids.

Student Body	**Cost Information**	**Greek System**
Undergrad enrollment: 4,021	**Tuition:** $25,340	**Fraternity:** No
Women: 54%	**Room & board:** $8,760	**Sorority:** No
Men: 46%	**Housing Information**	**Athletics:** Division III
Percent out-of-state: 43%	**University housing:** Yes	
	Percent living on campus: 58%	

FERRIS STATE UNIVERSITY

1201 South State St., Center for Student Services, Big Rapids, MI 49307
Phone: 231-591-2100 • Fax: 231-591-3944
E-mail: admissions@ferris.edu • Web: www.ferris.edu
Support: CS • Institution type: 4-year public

PROGRAMS OR SERVICES FOR STUDENTS WITH LD

Ferris State University is committed to a policy of equal opportunity for qualified students. The mission of Disabilities Services is to serve and advocate for students with disabilities, empowering them for self-reliance and independence. Ferris State does not have a program for students with learning disabilities, but does provide a variety of support services and accommodations for students with documented learning disabilities that interfere with the learning process. Ferris State does not, however, attempt to rehabilitate learning disabilities. To obtain support services, students need to meet with a counselor in the Educational Counseling and Disability Services. Students will complete a request for services application and a copy of the documentation of the disability. Documentation for LD/ADHD must be current and be submitted by a qualified professional. Professional development is offered to faculty and staff.

ADMISSION INFORMATION FOR STUDENTS WITH LD/ADHD

College entrance tests required: Yes
Interview required: No
Essay recommended: No
What documentation required for LD: Psycho Ed evaluation to include: relevant historical info, instructional interventions, related services, age diagnosed, objective data (aptitude, achievement, info processing), test scores (standard, percentile and grade equivalents) and describe functional limitations.
With general application: No
To receive services after enrolling: Yes
What documentation required for ADHD: Diagnosis based on DSM-V; history of behaviors impairing functioning in academic setting; diagnostic interview; history of symptoms; evidence of ongoing behaviors.

With general application: No
Submitted to: Disabilities Services
Special Ed. HS course work accepted: Yes
Specific course requirements of all applicants: NR
Separate application required: Yes
# of LD applications submitted each year: 60–75
# of LD applications accepted yearly: 60–75
Total # of students receiving LD services: NR
Acceptance into program means acceptance into college: No

ADMISSIONS

Students with learning disabilities must submit the general application form and should meet the same entrance criteria as all students. Qualified persons with disabilities may not be denied or subjected to discrimination in admission. There is no limit on the number of students admitted with disabilities. ACT scores are used for placement only and may not have an adverse effect on applicants with disabilities. No pre-admission inquiry regarding a possible disability can be made. Therefore, students with LD/ADHD are encouraged to self-disclose and provide information as to the extent of the disability. Sometimes a pre-admission interview is required if the GPA is questionable. In general, students should have a 2.0 GPA, but some programs require a higher GPA and specific courses. Diverse curricula offerings and a flexible admissions policy allow for the admission of most high school graduates and transfer students. Some programs are selective in nature and require the completion of specific courses and/or a minimum GPA.

ADDITIONAL INFORMATION

Disability Services provides services and accommodations to students with LD or ADHD with appropriate documentation. These could include the Kurzweil Reading System; calculators for exams; Dragon Naturally Speaking extended testing times electronic text; spellchecker for essay tests or exams; note-takers; word processing for essay tests; use of student supplied recording device in class; quiet areas; educational counseling; and Kurtzweil/JAWS. The Academic Support Center offers tutoring for most courses. Flex tutoring is for in-depth clarification and review of subject material, and workshop tutoring is for short-term, walk-in assistance. The Collegiate Skills Program is designed to help academically underprepared students succeed in college by offering assistance in reading, writing, and study skills. Students also have an opportunity to develop skills in goal setting, decision making, and time management. The Academic Support Center offers special instruction to assist students in improving their academic performance.

LEARNING DISABILITY PROGRAMS OR SERVICES

Contact Information
Name of program or department: Disabilities Services
  Telephone: 231-591-3772
  Fax: 231-591-5398

LEARNING DISABILITY SERVICES

Accommodations are decided upon an individual basis after a thorough review of appropriate, current documentation. The accommodations requested must be supported through the documentation provided and must be logically linked to the current impact of the condition on academic functioning.

Allowed in exams
  Calculator: Yes
  Dictionary: Yes
  Computer: Yes
  Spellchecker: Yes
Extended test time: Yes
Scribes: Yes
Proctors: Yes
Oral exams: Yes
Note-takers: Yes

Distraction-reduced environment: Yes
Tape recording in class: Yes
Electronic texts: Yes
Accommodations for students with
  ADHD: Yes
Kurzweil Reader: Yes
Other assistive technology: Yes
Priority registration: Yes

Added costs for services: No
LD specialists: No
Professional tutors: NR
Peer tutors: 100
Max. hours/wk. for services: NR
How professors are notified of
  LD/ADHD: Form given to student

GENERAL ADMISSIONS INFORMATION

Office of Admission: 800-433-7747

ENTRANCE REQUIREMENTS

Academic units recommended: 4 English, 4 math, 3 science (2 science lab), 2 foreign language, 2 social studies, 2 history, 3 academic electives. High school diploma is required, and GED is accepted. ACT with or without Writing component accepted. TOEFL required of all international applicants: minimum paper TOEFL 500, minimum computer TOEFL 61.

Application deadline: 8/1
Notification: Rolling
Average GPA: 3.20
ACT Composite middle 50% range:
  18–23

SAT Math middle 50% range: NR
SAT Critical Reading middle 50%
  range: NR
SAT Writing middle 50% range: NR

Graduated top 10% of class: NR
Graduated top 25% of class: NR
Graduated top 50% of class: NR

COLLEGE GRADUATION REQUIREMENTS

Course waivers allowed: No
Course substitutions allowed: No

ADDITIONAL INFORMATION

Environment: The university is located on 600 acres 50 miles north of Grand Rapids.

Student Body
  Undergrad enrollment: 13,350
  Women: 51%
  Men: 49%
  Percent out-of-state: 4%

Cost Information
  In-state tuition: $10,440
  Out-of-state tuition: $15,666
  Room & board: $9,344
Housing Information
  University housing: Yes
  Percent living on campus: 29%

Greek System
  Fraternity: Yes
  Sorority: Yes
Athletics: Division II

FINLANDIA UNIVERSITY

601 Quincy Street, Hancock, MI 49930
Phone: 906-487-7274 • Fax: 906-487-7383
E-mail: admissions@finlandia.edu • Web: www.finlandia.edu
Support: SP • Institution: 4-year private

PROGRAMS OR SERVICES FOR STUDENTS WITH LD

Through Finlandia's Disability Student Services, students will receive individual counseling, tutoring, academic advising, and career counseling, but most importantly, students get an enormous amount of support and encouragement. Finlandia's DSS is designed for students needing personalized attention, additional support and reasonable accommodations. Careful academic planning is performed by the DSS Director to ensure that students carry a reasonable credit load that is sequential and well-balanced with attention to reading, written assignments, and other course requirements. The faculty is supportive, and written and verbal communication between the director and faculty is frequent. Student performance is monitored and there are weekly scheduled meetings. The director is the advisor and support person overseeing and coordinating each individual's program. Self-advocacy and compensatory skills are goals, rather than remediation.

ADMISSION INFORMATION FOR STUDENTS WITH LD/ADHD

College entrance tests required: No
Interview required: No
What documentation required for LD: Psycho Ed evaluation to include: relevant historical info, instructional interventions, related services, age diagnosed, objective data (aptitude, achievement, info processing), test scores (standard, percentile and grade equivalents) and describe functional limitations.
With general application: Yes if requested as part of Structured Program application
To receive services after enrolling: Yes
What documentation required for ADHD: Diagnosis based on DSM-V; history of behaviors impairing functioning in academic setting; diagnostic interview; history of symptoms; evidence of ongoing behaviors.

With general application: Yes if requested as part of Structured Program application
To receive services after enrolling: Yes
Submitted to: Support Program/Services
Special Ed. HS course work accepted: Yes
Specific course requirements for all applicants: NR
Separate application required for program services: No
# of LD applications submitted each year: NR
# of LD applications accepted yearly: NR
Total # of students receiving LD services: 10–15
Acceptance into program means acceptance into college: No

ADMISSIONS
General admission requirements must be met by all applicants. In addition, students with learning disabilities should submit an evaluation, within the last three years, documenting the learning disability; an IEP; and a handwritten essay by the student describing the learning disability. Sometimes a telephone interview or visitation is requested to help determine eligibility for the program. An applicant must have the academic ability and background for work on a college level. Each applicant is evaluated individually by the DSS Director and the admissions staff.

ADDITIONAL INFORMATION
The program director provides professors with a disability data sheet to request accommodations and also meets individually with faculty regarding student needs. Special services offered include alternative testing; individual counseling; career counseling; auxiliary aids and services; academic advising; computer-based instruction; support from the Teaching and Learning Center; and support from TRiO/Student Support Services. The Director of the program will help them set up a plan for growth in areas that are challenging. Students will meet with their advisor once a week for as much or as little time as is needed.

LEARNING DISABILITY PROGRAMS OR SERVICES

Contact Information
Name of program or department: Disability Student Services
  Telephone: 906-487-7276
  Fax: 906-487-7535

LEARNING DISABILITY SERVICES

Accommodations are decided upon an individual basis after a thorough review of appropriate, current documentation. The accommodations requested must be supported through the documentation provided and must be logically linked to the current impact of the condition on academic functioning.

Allowed in exams
  Calculator: Yes
  Dictionary: Yes
  Computer: Yes
  Spellchecker: Yes
Extended test time: Yes
Scribes: Yes
Proctors: Yes
Oral exams: Yes
Note-takers: Yes

Distraction-reduced environment: Yes
Tape recording in class: Yes
Electronic texts: Yes
Accommodations for students with ADHD: Yes
Kurzweil Reader: Yes
Other assistive technology: No
Priority registration: No

Added costs for services: No
LD specialists: Yes
Professional tutors: 7
Peer tutors: 5
Max. hours/wk. for services: Unlimited
How professors are notified of LD/ADHD: By both student and director

GENERAL ADMISSIONS INFORMATION

Office of Admission: 877-202-5491

ENTRANCE REQUIREMENTS

High school diploma or GED accepted. Applicants must have the academic ability and background to work on a college level. ACT/SAT not required. TOEFL required of all international applicants, minimum paper TOEFL 400, minimum computer TOEFL 97.

Application deadline: 8/25
Notification: Rolling
Average GPA: 2.8
ACT Composite middle 50% range: NR

SAT Math middle 50% range: NR
SAT Critical Reading middle 50% range: NR
SAT Writing middle 50% range: NR

Graduated top 10% of class: 15%
Graduated top 25% of class: 33%
Graduated top 50% of class: 70%

COLLEGE GRADUATION REQUIREMENTS

Course waivers allowed: No
Course substitutions allowed: Yes
In what course: Math

ADDITIONAL INFORMATION

Environment: The school is located in a beautiful and rugged area of the Upper Peninsula of Michigan.

Student Body
  Undergrad enrollment: 673
  Women: 64%
  Men: 36%
  Percent out-of-state: 19%

Cost Information
  Tuition: $19,980
  Room & board: $6,900
Housing Information
  University housing: Yes
  Percent living on campus: 45%

Greek System
  Fraternity: No
  Sorority: No
Athletics: Intramural and varsity sports

GRAND VALLEY STATE UNIVERSITY

One Campus Drive, Allendale, MI 49401
Phone: 616-331-2025 • Fax: 616-331-2000
E-mail: go2gvsu@gvsu.edu • Web: www.gvsu.edu
Support: S • Institution type: 4-year public

PROGRAMS OR SERVICES FOR STUDENTS WITH LD

The Office of Academic Support at Grand Valley State University provides academic support services and accommodations that enhance the learning environment for students with disabilities and helps educate the university community on disability issues. In addition to the regular services the university offers student skill assessment, academic and career advising, specialized tutoring, textbooks on tape, note-taking assistance, alternative test-taking assistance, peer mentoring, and counseling. OAS provides students with memoranda documenting their disability. The documentation will contain information on the nature of the disability and what academic accommodations the student may need.

ADMISSION INFORMATION FOR STUDENTS WITH LD/ADHD

College entrance tests required: Yes
Interview required: No
Essay recommended: No
What documentation required for LD: Psycho Ed evaluation to include: relevant historical info, instructional interventions, related services, age diagnosed, objective data (aptitude, achievement, info processing), test scores (standard, percentile and grade equivalents) and describe functional limitations.
With general application: No
To receive services after enrolling: Yes
What documentation required for ADHD: Diagnosis based on DSM-V; history of behaviors impairing functioning in academic setting; diagnostic interview; history of symptoms; evidence of ongoing behaviors.

With general application: No
Submitted to: Office of Academic Support
Special Ed. HS course work accepted: Yes
Specific course requirements of all applicants: Yes
Separate application required: Yes
# of LD applications submitted each year: 20–55
# of LD applications accepted yearly: 11
Total # of students receiving LD services: 263
Acceptance into program means acceptance into college: Students must be admitted to and enrolled in the university first and then request services.

ADMISSIONS

Students are given the opportunity to provide documentation of their LD or ADHD. Information is reviewed by the Office of Academic Support and Admissions. Students interested in special accommodations need to submit both the regular admissions application and a separate application for the program. An evaluation report should include the summary of a comprehensive diagnostic interview. Standardized tests are required for admission. General admission requirements include 4 years of English, 3 years of math, 3 years of social science, and 2 years of science. The average ACT score is 23 or 1050–1080 SAT Reasoning and a 2.8 GPA.

ADDITIONAL INFORMATION

Once admitted into the program students may request that an instructor progress report be sent to each of their professors. The purpose of this report is to inform students of their current academic standing in a class. Academic Support staff provide the following services: working with students to help them improve their academic weaknesses and increase their areas of strength; academic and career advising; specialized tutoring in addition to the general tutoring available for all students; seminars on reading textbooks, note-taking, time management, and test-taking strategies; tape recording of texts not available through RFBD; alternative test-taking; peer mentoring; and counseling. There is also the Organization for the Achievement of Disabled Students, which is a student organization whose goal is to advance the educational and career goals of students with disabilities.

LEARNING DISABILITY PROGRAMS OR SERVICES

Contact Information
Name of program or department: Academic Support (OAS)
  Telephone: 616-331-2490
  Fax: 616-331-3440

LEARNING DISABILITY SERVICES

Accommodations are decided upon an individual basis after a thorough review of appropriate, current documentation. The accommodations requested must be supported through the documentation provided and must be logically linked to the current impact of the condition on academic functioning.

Allowed in exams	**Distraction-reduced environment:** Yes	**Added costs for services:** No
Calculator: Yes	**Tape recording in class:** Yes	**LD specialists:** No
Dictionary: Yes	**Electronic texts:** No	**Professional tutors:** No
Computer: Yes	**Accommodations for students with**	**Peer tutors:** 140
Spellchecker: Yes	**ADHD:** Yes	**Max. hours/wk. for services:** 4
Extended test time: Yes	**Kurzweil Reader:** No	**How professors are notified of**
Scribes: Yes	**Other assistive technology:** Yes	**LD/ADHD:** By student
Proctors: Yes	**Priority registration:** Yes	
Oral exams: Yes		
Note-takers: Yes		

GENERAL ADMISSIONS INFORMATION

Office of Admission: 616-331-2025

ENTRANCE REQUIREMENTS

Academic units required: 4 English, 3 math, 2 science (1 science lab), 2 foreign language, 3 social studies.
Academic units recommended: 4 English, 4 math, 4 science (2 science labs), 2 foreign language, 3 social studies, 1 computer science, 1 fine arts. High school diploma is required, and GED is accepted. ACT without Writing component accepted. TOEFL required of all international applicants: minimum paper TOEFL 550, minimum computer TOEFL 213.

Application deadline: 5/1	**SAT Math middle 50% range:**	**Graduated top 10% of class:** 21%
Notification: Rolling	510–630	**Graduated top 25% of class:** 55%
Average GPA: 3.53	**SAT Critical Reading middle 50%**	**Graduated top 50% of class:** 90%
ACT Composite middle 50% range:	**range:** 480–600	
22–26	**SAT Writing middle 50% range:**	
	480–600	

COLLEGE GRADUATION REQUIREMENTS

Course waivers allowed: No
Course substitutions allowed: No

ADDITIONAL INFORMATION

Environment: The campus is located 12 miles from Grand Rapids, Michigan.

Student Body	**Cost Information**	**Greek System**
Undergrad enrollment: 20,986	**In-state tuition:** $9,716	**Fraternity:** Yes
Women: 60%	**Out-of-state tuition:** $14,030	**Sorority:** Yes
Men: 40%	**Room & board:** $7,624	**Athletics:** Division II
Percent out-of-state: 4%	**Housing Information**	
	University housing: Yes	
	Percent living on campus: 27%	

MICHIGAN STATE UNIVERSITY

250 Administration Building, East Lansing, MI 48824-1046
Phone: 517-355-8332 • Fax: 517-353-1647
E-mail: admis@msu.edu • Web: www.msu.edu
Support: CS • Institution: 4-year public

PROGRAMS OR SERVICES FOR STUDENTS WITH LD

MSU is serious in its commitment to helping students no matter what the disability. The RCPD (Resource Center for Persons with Disabilities) mission is to be an advocate for the inclusion of students with disabilities into the total university experience. The RCPD purpose is to respond to the needs of students by providing resources that equalize their chances for success, support their full participation in all university programs, and act as a resource for the university community and the community at large. Students must provide recent documentation and history in the form of a school report, psychologist's assessment, or certification by other recognized authority and must contain a clearly stated diagnosis. Staff specialists focus on freshmen and transfer students during their transition and adjustment to the university environment. As students learn to utilize appropriate accommodations and strategies, a greater sense of independence is achieved, although classroom accommodations may still be necessary.

ADMISSION INFORMATION FOR STUDENTS WITH LD/ADHD

College entrance tests required: Yes
Interview required: No
Essay required: N/A
What documentation required for LD: Psycho Ed evaluation to include: relevant historical info, instructional interventions, related services, age diagnosed, objective data (aptitude, achievement, info processing), test scores (standard, percentile and grade equivalents) and describe functional limitations.
With general application: No
To receive services after enrolling: Yes
What documentation required for ADHD: Diagnosis based on DSM-V; history of behaviors impairing functioning in academic setting; diagnostic interview; history of symptoms; evidence of ongoing behaviors.

With general application: No
Submitted to: RCPD
Special Ed. HS course work accepted: No
Specific course requirements for all applicants: Yes
Separate application required for program services: No
# of LD applications submitted each year: NR
# of LD applications accepted yearly: NR
Total # of students receiving LD services: 600
Acceptance into program means acceptance into college: Students must be admitted to and enrolled in the university first and then request services.

ADMISSIONS

Admission for students with learning disabilities to the university is based on the same criteria used for all other students. College Achievement Admissions Program (CAAP) is an alternative admissions procedure for students who have academic potential but who would be unable to realize that potential without special support services due to their economic, cultural, or educational background. Students with learning disabilities should not send any documentation to the Office of Admissions. All documentation should be sent to RCPD.

ADDITIONAL INFORMATION

Specialists are available by appointment to provide information to students. Accommodations include: E-text; study strategy tutoring; voice output computers; taping of lectures; extended time on tests; reader/scribe; quiet room for tests; scribes; advocacy assistance from specialists and letters to professors; support groups through RCPD; and consultation with service providers. Various other resources on campus such as Learning Resource Center; Office of Supportive Services; MSU Counseling Center; and Undergraduate University Division of Academic Advising. The Learning Resource Center works with students with learning characteristics on an individual basis to help the student learn to utilize appropriate learning strategies and to mediate their learning environment.

PROGRAM FOR DISABILITY SERVICES

Contact Information
Name of program or department: Resource Center for Persons with Disabilities
  Telephone: 517-884-RCPD (7273)
  Fax: 517-438-3191

LEARNING DISABILITY SERVICES

Accommodations are decided upon an individual basis after a thorough review of appropriate, current documentation. The accommodations requested must be supported through the documentation provided and must be logically linked to the current impact of the condition on academic functioning.

Allowed in exams
  Calculator: Decision
  Dictionary: No
  Computer: Decision
  Spellchecker: N/A
Extended test time: Yes
Scribes: Yes
Proctors: Yes
Oral exams: Yes
Note-takers: Yes

Distraction-reduced environment: Yes
Tape recording in class: Yes
Electronic texts: Yes
Accommodations for students with
  ADHD: Yes
Kurzweil Reader: Yes
Other assistive technology: Dragon
  Dictate, etc.
Priority registration: Yes

Added costs for services: No
LD specialists: Yes
Professional tutors: 3
Peer tutors: 10
Max. hours/wk. for services:
  Unlimited
How professors are notified of
  LD/ADHD: Student

GENERAL ADMISSIONS INFORMATION

Office of Admission: 517-355-8332

ENTRANCE REQUIREMENTS
Academic units required: 4 English, 3 mathematics, 2 science, 2 foreign language, 2 social studies, 1 history.
Academic units recommended: (2 science labs), 2 foreign language, 2 social studies, 2 history. High school diploma is required and GED is accepted. SAT or ACT required; ACT with Writing component required. TOEFL required of all international applicants; minimum paper TOEFL 550, minimum computer TOEFL 213, minimum web-based TOEFL 80.

Application deadline: None
Notification: Rolling
Average GPA: 3.61
ACT Composite middle 50% range:
  23–28

SAT Math middle 50% range:
  540–670
SAT Critical Reading middle 50%
  range: 440–600
SAT Writing middle 50% range:
  450–600

Graduated top 10% of class: 28%
Graduated top 25% of class: 68%
Graduated top 50% of class: 96%

COLLEGE GRADUATION REQUIREMENTS

Course waivers allowed: No
Course substitutions allowed: No
In what course: Individual consideration

ADDITIONAL INFORMATION

Environment: Michigan State is located one hour from Ann Arbor and one and a half hours from Detroit.

Student Body
  Undergrad enrollment: 36,675
  Women: 52%
  Men: 48%
  Percent out-of-state: 12%

Cost Information
  In-state tuition: $12,822
  Out-of-state tuition: $31,692
  Room and board: $8,204
Housing Information
  University housing: Yes
  Percent living on campus: 42%

Greek System
  Fraternity: Yes
  Sorority: Yes
Athletics: Division I

NORTHERN MICHIGAN UNIVERSITY

1401 Presque Isle Avenue, Marquette, MI 49855
Phone: 906-227-2650 • Fax: 906-227-1747
E-mail: admiss@nmu.edu • Web: www.nmu.edu
Support: S • Institution type: 4-year public

PROGRAMS OR SERVICES FOR STUDENTS WITH LD

Disability Services (DS) provides services and accommodations to all students with disabilities. The goal of DS is to meet the individual needs of students. Student Support Services is a multifaceted educational support project designed to assist students in completing their academic programs at NMU. The Student Support Services professional staff, peer tutors, mentors, and peer advisors provide program participants with individualized attention. Disability Services provides assistance and accommodations to students who have documented disabilities. Accommodation request are reviewed on an individual basis. Student are required to complete the Application for DS; provide appropriate documentation, which includes a diagnosis, symptoms of the disability, test scores and data that support the diagnosis, and recommendations regarding classroom accommodations; and schedule an appointment with the Disability Coordinator. Students with ADHD must provide appropriate documentation through a written report submitted by a medical doctor, psychiatrist, psychologist, counselor, or school psychologist to receive appropriate accommodations.

ADMISSION INFORMATION FOR STUDENTS WITH LD/ADHD

College entrance tests required: No
Interview required: No
Essay recommended: No
What documentation required for LD: Psycho Ed evaluation to include: relevant historical info, instructional interventions, related services, age diagnosed, objective data (aptitude, achievement, info processing), test scores (standard, percentile and grade equivalents) and describe functional limitations.
With general application: No
To receive services after enrolling: Yes
What documentation required for ADHD: Diagnosis based on DSM-V; history of behaviors impairing functioning in academic setting; diagnostic interview; history of symptoms; evidence of ongoing behaviors.

With general application: No
Submitted to: Disability Services
Special Ed. HS course work accepted: Yes
Specific course requirements of all applicants: No
Separate application required: No
# of LD applications submitted each year: NR
# of LD applications accepted yearly: 150
Total # of students receiving LD services: 150
Acceptance into program means acceptance into college: Students must be admitted to and enrolled in the university first and then request services.

ADMISSIONS

There are no special admissions for students with learning disabilities. All students submit the same general application and are expected to have an ACT of 19 or higher and a high school GPA of at least 2.25. There are no specific high school courses required for admissions, though the university recommends 4 years English, 4 years math, 3 years history/social studies, 3 years science, 3 years foreign language, 2 years fine or performing arts, and 1 year computer instruction. Applicants not meeting all of the criteria will be fully considered by the Admission Review Committee. Applicants may be asked to take a pre-admission test or supply further information. A review of the applicant's academic background and potential for success may result in admission into the applicant's program of choice or admission on probation or into the College Transitions Program. Students will be asked to agree to certain conditions as part of their enrollment. Applicants denied admission may appeal to the Admissions Review Committee. Appeal letters should be submitted to the Director of Admissions.

ADDITIONAL INFORMATION

The coordinator of DS works one-on-one with students as needed, and will also meet with students who do not have specific documentation if they request assistance. Skill classes are offered in reading, writing, math, study skills, sociocultural development, and interpersonal growth. No course waivers are granted for graduation requirements from NMU. Substitutions, however, are granted when appropriate. Student Support Services provides each student with an individual program of educational support services, including academic advising; basic skill building in reading, math, and writing; counseling; career advisement; developmental skill building; mentoring; support groups and study groups; tutoring from paraprofessionals; specialized tutors; group tutoring or supplemental instruction; and workshops on personal development and study skills improvement.

LEARNING DISABILITY PROGRAMS OR SERVICES

Contact Information
Name of program or department: Disability Services
  Telephone: 906-227-1700
  Fax: 906-227-1714

LEARNING DISABILITY SERVICES

Accommodations are decided upon an individual basis after a thorough review of appropriate, current documentation. The accommodations requested must be supported through the documentation provided and must be logically linked to the current impact of the condition on academic functioning.

Allowed in exams
  Calculator: Yes
  Dictionary: Yes
  Computer: Yes
  Spellchecker: Yes
Extended test time: Yes
Scribes: Yes
Proctors: Yes
Oral exams: Yes
Note-takers: Yes

Distraction-reduced environment: Yes
Tape recording in class: Yes
Electronic texts: Yes
Accommodations for students with ADHD: Yes
Kurzweil Reader: No
Other assistive technology: Yes
Priority registration: No

Added costs for services: No
LD specialists: No
Professional tutors: No
Peer tutors: Yes
Max. hours/wk. for services: 2–4
How professors are notified of LD/ADHD: By student

GENERAL ADMISSIONS INFORMATION

Office of Admission: 800-682-9797

ENTRANCE REQUIREMENTS

Academic units recommended: 4 English, 4 math, 3 science, 3 foreign language, 3 social studies. High school diploma is required, and GED is accepted. ACT with or without Writing component accepted. TOEFL required of all international applicants: minimum paper TOEFL 500, minimum computer TOEFL 173.

Application deadline: None
Notification: Rolling
Average GPA: 3.14
ACT Composite middle 50% range: 19–25

SAT Math middle 50% range: NR
SAT Critical Reading middle 50% range: NR
SAT Writing middle 50% range: NR

Graduated top 10% of class: NR
Graduated top 25% of class: NR
Graduated top 50% of class: NR

COLLEGE GRADUATION REQUIREMENTS

Course waivers allowed: No
Course substitutions allowed: Yes
In what course: Substitutions permitted to fulfill graduation requirements with appropriate documentation.

ADDITIONAL INFORMATION

Environment: The campus is located in an urban area about 300 miles north of Milwaukee, Wisconsin.

Student Body
  Undergrad enrollment: 8,615
  Women: 54%
  Men: 46%
  Percent out-of-state: 18%

Cost Information
  In-state tuition: $8,350
  Out-of-state tuition: $13,078
  Room & board: $8,174
Housing Information
  University housing: Yes
  Percent living on campus: 37.9%

Greek System
  Fraternity: Yes
  Sorority: Yes
Athletics: Division II; Hockey–Division I

UNIVERSITY OF MICHIGAN

1220 Student Activities Building, Ann Arbor, MI 48109-1316
Phone: 734-764-7433 • Fax: 734-936-0740
E-mail: • Web: www.umich.edu
Support: CS • Institution: 4-year public

PROGRAMS OR SERVICES FOR STUDENTS WITH LD

The philosophy of Services for Students with Disabilities (SSD) is based on the legal actions described in Section 504 of the Rehabilitation Act of 1973. SSD services are dependent on self-advocacy of the students and are "non-intrusive," giving the students the responsibility to seek out assistance. SSD offers selected student services that are not provided by other University of Michigan offices or outside organizations. SSD assists students in negotiating disability-related barriers to the pursuit of their education; strives to improve access to university programs, activities, and facilities; and promotes increased awareness of disability issues on campus. SSD encourages inquiries for information and will confidentially discuss concerns relating to a potential or recognized disability and, if requested, provide appropriate referrals for further assistance.

ADMISSION INFORMATION FOR STUDENTS WITH LD/ADHD

College entrance tests required: Yes
Interview required: No
Essay required: N/A
What documentation required for LD: Psycho Ed evaluation to include: relevant historical info, instructional interventions, related services, age diagnosed, objective data (aptitude, achievement, info processing), test scores (standard, percentile and grade equivalents) and describe functional limitations.
With general application: No
To receive services after enrolling: Yes
What documentation required for ADHD: Diagnosis based on DSM-V; history of behaviors impairing functioning in academic setting; diagnostic interview; history of symptoms; evidence of ongoing behaviors.

With general application: No
Submitted to: Support Program/Services
Special Ed. HS course work accepted: No
Specific course requirements for all applicants: Yes
Separate application required for program services: No
# of LD applications submitted each year: NR
# of LD applications accepted yearly: NR
Total # of students receiving LD services: 755
Acceptance into program means acceptance into college: Students must be admitted to and enrolled in the university first and then request services.

ADMISSIONS

Students with learning disabilities are expected to meet the same admission requirements as their peers. Courses required include: four years English, two years foreign language (four years recommended), three years math (four years recommended including algebra, trigonometry, and geometry), two years biological and physical sciences (three years recommended), three years history and the social sciences (two years history recommended, including one year of U.S. history), one year hands-on computer study is strongly recommended, as is one year in the fine or performing arts, or equivalent preparation. Score range for the ACT is 25–29 and SAT 1170–1340. There is no set minimum GPA as it is contingent on several other factors. For students with learning disabilities, the admissions office will accept letters of recommendation from LD specialists. When applying for admission to the University of Michigan, students with learning disabilities are encouraged to self-identify on the application form or by writing a cover letter.

ADDITIONAL INFORMATION

All accommodations are based on documented needs by the student. Services for students with learning disabilities include volunteer readers; volunteer tutors; referral for psychoeducational assessments; selected course book loans for taping; Franklin Spellers; free cassette tapes; APH 4-track recorders; advocacy and referral; advocacy letters to professors; limited scholarships; newsletters; volunteer note-takers; carbonized notepaper; free photocopying of class notes; free course notes service for some classes; many students eligible for assisted earlier registration; adaptive technology; and library reading rooms. SSD also provides appropriate services for students with "other health related disabilities" such as ADHD. There is a special summer program at the university for high school students with learning disabilities. Services and accommodations are available for undergraduates and graduates.

PROGRAM FOR DISABILITY SERVICES

Contact Information
Name of program or department: Services for Students with Disabilities (SSD)
  Telephone: 734-763-3000
  Fax: 734-936-3947

LEARNING DISABILITY SERVICES

Accommodations are decided upon an individual basis after a thorough review of appropriate, current documentation. The accommodations requested must be supported through the documentation provided and must be logically linked to the current impact of the condition on academic functioning.

Allowed in exams
  Calculator: Yes
  Dictionary: Yes
  Computer: Yes
  Spellchecker: Yes
Extended test time: Yes
Scribes: Yes
Proctors: No
Oral exams: No
Note-takers: Yes

Distraction-reduced environment: Yes
Tape recording in class: Yes
Electronic texts: Yes
Accommodations for students with ADHD: Yes
Kurzweil Reader: Yes
Other assistive technology: Yes
Priority registration: No

Added costs for services: No
LD specialists: Yes
Professional tutors: Yes, Academic coach
Peer tutors: No
Max. hours/wk. for services: NR
How professors are notified of LD/ADHD: Student

GENERAL ADMISSIONS INFORMATION

Office of Admission: 734-764-7433

ENTRANCE REQUIREMENTS
Academic units required: 4 English, (1 science labs), 3 social studies, 3 history, 1 academic electives. **Academic units recommended:** 4 English, 4 mathematics, 4 science, (1 science labs), 4 foreign language, 3 social studies, 3 history, 2 visual/performing arts, 1 computer science, 1 academic electives. High school diploma is required and GED is accepted. SAT or ACT required; ACT with Writing component required. TOEFL required of all international applicants; minimum paper TOEFL 570, minimum computer TOEFL 230, minimum web-based TOEFL 88.

Application deadline: 2/1
Notification: Rolling
Average GPA: 3.79
ACT Composite middle 50% range: 28–32

SAT Math middle 50% range: 650–750
SAT Critical Reading middle 50% range: 6000–700
SAT Writing middle 50% range: 620–720

Graduated top 10% of class: 92%
Graduated top 25% of class: 99%
Graduated top 50% of class: 100%

COLLEGE GRADUATION REQUIREMENTS

Course waivers allowed: No
Course substitutions allowed: Yes
In what course: Foreign language

ADDITIONAL INFORMATION

Environment: The campus is located in a suburban area about 30 miles west of Detroit.

Student Body
  Undergrad enrollment: 27,407
  Women: 49%
  Men: 51%
  Percent out-of-state: 36%

Cost Information
  In-state tuition: $11,648
  Out-of-state tuition: $37,588
  Room and board: $9,468
Housing Information
  University housing: Yes
  Percent living on campus: 37%

Greek System
  Fraternity: Yes
  Sorority: Yes
Athletics: Division I

AUGSBURG COLLEGE

2211 Riverside Avenue South, Minneapolis, MN 55454
Phone: 612-330-1001 • Fax: 612-330-1590
E-mail: admissions@augsburg.edu • Web: www.augsburg.edu
Support: SP • Institution: 4-year private

PROGRAMS OR SERVICES FOR STUDENTS WITH LD

CLASS illustrates its commitment to student success at Augsburg College by providing those academic services needed to accommodate individuals with learning, attentional, psychiatric, or other cognitive disabilities. (For information about services for a physical disability, please contact the Access Center.) The foundation of CLASS, however, is deeply rooted in the promotion of student independence and the personal realization of one's full potential. Augsburg students who are eligible to receive CLASS services, once admitted, will work one-on-one with a CLASS Disability Specialist. The Specialist will work to provide academic guidance and service-related assistance whenever appropriate. No additional or supplemental fee is required for CLASS services.

ADMISSION INFORMATION FOR STUDENTS WITH LD/ADHD

College entrance tests required: Yes
Interview required: Yes
Essay required: N/A
What documentation required for LD: Psycho Ed evaluation to include: relevant historical info, instructional interventions, related services, age diagnosed, objective data (aptitude, achievement, info processing), test scores (standard, percentile and grade equivalents) and describe functional limitations.
With general application: Yes if requested as part of Structured Program application
To receive services after enrolling: Yes
What documentation required for ADHD: Diagnosis based on DSM-V; history of behaviors impairing functioning in academic setting; diagnostic interview; history of symptoms; evidence of ongoing behaviors.

With general application: Yes if requested as part of Structured Program application
To receive services after enrolling: Yes
Submitted to: Support Program/Services
Special Ed. HS course work accepted: N/A
Specific course requirements for all applicants: Yes
Separate application required for program services: Yes
# of LD applications submitted each year: 140–160
# of LD applications accepted yearly: 70–90
Total # of students receiving LD services: 50–70
Acceptance into program means acceptance into college: Separate application required after student has enrolled

ADMISSIONS

Applicants with learning disabilities must first complete the Augsburg application form. Students with a 2.5 GPA who rank in top half of their class or scored at least 20 on the ACT are automatically admissable. Courses required include four years of English, three years of math, three years of science, two years of a foreign language, and three years of social studies (four recommended). Students submit LD documentation directly to CLASS. The written diagnostic report must contain a definite statement that an LD is present. Specific recommendations about accommodations and academic strenghths and weaknesses are valuable. A formal interview will be scheduled to allow the students to provide information and receive more details about accommodations at Augsburg. Students admitted on probation or as high-risk students must take a study skills class and earn a 2.0 GPA for the first year.

ADDITIONAL INFORMATION

Students admitted into CLASS are given individual assistance from application through graduation by learning specialists. Academic support may include assistance with registration and advising, guidance with course work, assistance with writing, instruction in learning strategies and compensatory techniques, help improving basic skills, and advocacy. Accommodations may include testing arrangements, access to computers and training, taped texts, allowing the use of Kurzweil software, assistance in securing note-takers, assistance in obtaining tutors, and foreign language alternatives. There are also many community resources available. Currently, there are 170 students receiving services and accommodations. Undergraduates and graduates can access support services.

PROGRAM FOR DISABILITY SERVICES

Contact Information
Name of program or department: Center for Learning and Adaptive Student Services (CLASS)
   Telephone: 612-330-1053
   Fax: 612-330-1137

LEARNING DISABILITY SERVICES

Accommodations are decided upon an individual basis after a thorough review of appropriate, current documentation. The accommodations requested must be supported through the documentation provided and must be logically linked to the current impact of the condition on academic functioning.

Allowed in exams
   Calculator: Yes
   Dictionary: Yes
   Computer: Yes
   Spellchecker: Yes
Extended test time: Yes
Scribes: Yes
Proctors: Yes
Oral exams: Yes
Note-takers: Yes

Distraction-reduced environment: Yes
Tape recording in class: Yes
Electronic texts: No
Accommodations for students with ADHD: Yes
Kurzweil Reader: Yes
Other assistive technology: Voice-recognition software
Priority registration: No

Added costs for services: No
LD specialists: Yes
Professional tutors: 0
Peer tutors: 40–80
Max. hours/wk. for services: NR
How professors are notified of LD/ADHD: Student

GENERAL ADMISSIONS INFORMATION

Office of Admission: 612-330-1001

ENTRANCE REQUIREMENTS
Academic units required: 4 English, 3 mathematics, 3 science, 2 foreign language, 2 social studies. **Academic units recommended:** 4 social studies, 2 history. High school diploma is required and GED is accepted. SAT or ACT recommended; TOEFL required of all international applicants; minimum paper TOEFL 550, minimum computer TOEFL 213.

Application deadline: 8/1
Notification: Rolling
Average GPA: 3.04
ACT Composite middle 50% range: 20–25

SAT Math middle 50% range: 500–640
SAT Critical Reading middle 50% range: 510–640
SAT Writing middle 50% range: 480–600

Graduated top 10% of class: 11%
Graduated top 25% of class: 37%
Graduated top 50% of class: 65%

COLLEGE GRADUATION REQUIREMENTS

Course waivers allowed: No
In what course:
Course substitutions allowed: Yes
In what course: Foreign language

ADDITIONAL INFORMATION

Environment: The college is located on 25 acres near downtown Minneapolis.

Student Body
   Undergrad enrollment: 3,065
   Women: 51%
   Men: 49%
   Percent out-of-state: 15%

Cost Information
   Tuition: $29,802
   Room and board: $7,850
Housing Information
   University housing: Yes
   Percent living on campus: 52%

Greek System
   Fraternity: No
   Sorority: No
Athletics: Division III

MINNESOTA STATE U. MOORHEAD

Owens Hall, MSU Moorhead, Moorhead, MN 56563
Phone: 218-477-2161 • Fax: 218-477-4374
E-mail: admissions@mnstate.edu • Web: www.mnstate.edu
Support: S • Institution type: 4-year public

PROGRAMS OR SERVICES FOR STUDENTS WITH LD

The university is committed to ensuring that all students have equal access to programs and services. The office of Disability Services (DS) addresses the needs of students who have disabilities. The purpose of DS is to provide services and accommodations to students with documented disabilities, work closely with faculty and staff in an advisory capacity, assist in the development of reasonable accommodations for students, and provide equal access for otherwise qualified individuals with disabilities. A student with a documented learning disability may be eligible for services. DS will assist in the development of reasonable accommodations for students with disabilities. To be eligible to receive services, students must provide appropriate documentation. This documentation should identify the nature and extent of the disability and provide information on the functional limitations as related to the academic environment. The documentation should provide recommended reasonable accommodations. Requests that would alter the academic standards are not granted. Students are responsible for monitoring their progress with faculty, requesting assistance, and meeting university standards.

ADMISSION INFORMATION FOR STUDENTS WITH LD/ADHD

College entrance tests required: Yes
Interview required: No
Essay recommended: No
What documentation required for LD: Psycho Ed evaluation to
  include: relevant historical info, instructional interventions,
  related services, age diagnosed, objective data (aptitude,
  achievement, info processing), test scores (standard, percentile
  and grade equivalents) and describe functional limitations.
With general application: No
To receive services after enrolling: Yes
What documentation required for ADHD: Diagnosis based
  on DSM-V; history of behaviors impairing functioning in
  academic setting; diagnostic interview; history of symptoms;
  evidence of ongoing behaviors.

With general application: No
Submitted to: Director, Disability Services
Special Ed. HS course work accepted: Yes
Specific course requirements of all applicants: Yes
Separate application required: NR
# of LD applications submitted each year: NR
# of LD applications accepted yearly: NR
Total # of students receiving LD services: 25–50
**Acceptance into program means acceptance into
  college:** Students must be admitted to and enrolled in the
  university first and then request services.

ADMISSIONS

To be automatically admitted to Minnesota State University Moorhead, you must have graduated from high school or earned a GED and meet the following requirements: An ACT (preferred) composite score of 21 or SAT score of 1000 or above in Critical Reading and Math SAT admissions tests, OR rank in the top 50% of your high school graduating class AND achieve a minimum score of 17 on the ACT or 830 on the SAT (Critical Reading and Math). If you are interested in MSU Moorhead and do not meet the above requirements, you are still encouraged to apply. Applications are reviewed based on such factors as strength of college preparation coursework, grade point average, academic progression, class rank, test scores, and probability of success. Additional information may be requested to help facilitate an admission decision. Visit msum.com for more information.

ADDITIONAL INFORMATION

Examples of general accommodations or services include the following: extended test times, reduced distraction testing environments, taped texts, note-taking, assistive technology, scribes, readers, tape-recording lectures, faculty liaisons, strategy development, priority registration, and individual support. Study skills courses are offered and students may earn credits for these courses. Services and accommodations are available for undergraduate and graduate students.

LEARNING DISABILITY PROGRAMS OR SERVICES

Contact Information
Name of program or department: Disability Services
  Telephone: 218-477-4318
  Fax: 218-477-2420

LEARNING DISABILITY SERVICES

Accommodations are decided upon an individual basis after a thorough review of appropriate, current documentation. The accommodations requested must be supported through the documentation provided and must be logically linked to the current impact of the condition on academic functioning.

Allowed in exams	**Tape recording in class:** Yes	**Added costs for services:** No
Calculator: Yes	**Electronic texts:** Yes	**LD specialists:** No
Dictionary: Yes	**Accommodations for students with**	**Professional tutors:** No
Computer: Yes	**ADHD:** Yes	**Peer tutors:** Yes
Spellchecker: Yes	**Kurzweil Reader:** Yes	**Max. hours/wk. for services:** 1
Extended test time: Yes	**Other assistive technology:** Yes	**How professors are notified of**
Scribes: Yes	**Priority registration:** Yes	**LD/ADHD:** By both student and
Proctors: Yes		director
Oral exams: Yes		
Note-takers: Yes		
Distraction-reduced environment: Yes		

GENERAL ADMISSIONS INFORMATION

Office of Admission: 218-477-2161

Application deadline: 8/1	**SAT Math middle 50% range:**	**Graduated top 10% of class:** 7%
Notification: Rolling	500–610	**Graduated top 25% of class:** 24%
Average GPA: NR	**SAT Critical Reading middle 50%**	**Graduated top 50% of class:** 57%
ACT Composite middle 50% range:	**range:** 440–570	
20–24	**SAT Writing middle 50% range:** NR	

COLLEGE GRADUATION REQUIREMENTS

Course waivers allowed: Yes
In what course: Depends on the disability and requirements of the student's major
Course substitutions allowed: Yes
In what course: Depends on the disability and requirements of the student's major

ADDITIONAL INFORMATION

Environment: The university has a suburban campus 240 miles northwest of Minneapolis.

Student Body	**Cost Information**	**Greek System**
Undergrad enrollment: 7,012	**In-state tuition:** $6,568	**Fraternity:** Yes
Women: 57%	**Room & board:** $6,468	**Sorority:** Yes
Men: 43%	**Housing Information**	**Athletics:** Division II
Percent out-of-state: 45%	**University housing:** Yes	
	Percent living on campus: 24%	

SAINT CATHERINE UNIVERSITY

2004 Randolph Avenue, St. Paul, MN 55105
Phone: 651-690-8850 • Fax: 651-690-8824
E-mail: admissions@stkate.edu • Web: www.stkate.edu
Support: CS • Institution type: 4-year private

PROGRAMS OR SERVICES FOR STUDENTS WITH LD

The Resources for Disabilities office is located within the O'Neill Center for Academic Development. Students with disabilities work in concert with Access Consultants to identify any barriers to the student's access to curricular and/or co-curricular programs. Accommodations are made on an individual basis and the process is guided by each student's history and experiences.

ADMISSION INFORMATION FOR STUDENTS WITH LD/ADHD

College entrance tests required: Yes, ACT or SAT
Interview required: No
Essay recommended: Yes
What documentation required for LD: Psycho Ed evaluation preferred along with educational history provided during meeting with an Access Consultant
With general application: No
To receive services after enrolling: Yes
What documentation required for ADHD: Diagnosis based on DSM-V; history of behaviors impairing functioning in academic setting; diagnostic interview; history of symptoms; evidence of ongoing behaviors.

With general application: No
Submitted to: Resources for Disabilities
Special Ed. HS course work accepted: Yes
Specific course requirements of all applicants: NR
Separate application required: No
# of LD applications submitted each year: NR
# of LD applications accepted yearly: NR
Total # of students receiving LD services: 110 (LD, AD/HD)
Acceptance into program means acceptance into college: Students must be admitted to and enrolled in the university first and then request services.

ADMISSIONS

There is no special admission procedure for students with learning disabilities, though the college tends to give special consideration if students self-disclose this information. Disclosure can help explain test scores, difficulties with certain course work, and so on. Saint Catherine University does not discriminate on the basis of disability in admission. A student may be accepted on a conditional basis, to a program which provides special advising, limited course lad and a course in strategies for success.

ADDITIONAL INFORMATION

To access services, the student and Access Consultant discuss the anticipated demands of the courses for which the student is registered and develop accommodation letters. The letters identify the learning strategies and accommodations that will be used. For example, texts in alternative formats, testing accommodations, and note-takers are some of the more frequently offered accommodations. The specific nature of the disability is not addressed the student delivers the accommodation letters to her professors. Some students meet with Access Consultants on a weekly basis for time-management and study strategies. Within the O'Neill Center, a student may access assistance in writing, math and science courses.

LEARNING DISABILITY PROGRAMS OR SERVICES

Contact Information
Name of program or department: O'Neill Learning Center
  Telephone: 651-590-6563
  Fax: 651-690-6718

LEARNING DISABILITY SERVICES

Accommodations are decided upon an individual basis after a thorough review of appropriate, current documentation. The accommodations requested must be supported through the documentation provided and must be logically linked to the current impact of the condition on academic functioning.

Allowed in exams
  Calculator: Yes
  Dictionary: Yes
  Computer: Yes
  Spellchecker: Yes
Extended test time: Yes
Scribes: Yes
Proctors: Yes
Oral exams: Rarely
Note-takers: Yes
Distraction-reduced environment: Yes

Tape recording in class: Yes
Electronic texts: Yes
Accommodations for students with ADHD: Yes
Kurzweil Reader: Yes
Other assistive technology: Yes
Priority registration: Yes

Added costs for services: No
LD specialists: Yes
Professional tutors: No
Peer tutors: 25–35 for Writing, Math, Science—available to all students, not just those with disabilities
Max. hours/wk. for services: Unlimited
How professors are notified of LD/ADHD: By both student and director

GENERAL ADMISSIONS INFORMATION

Office of Admission: 651-690-8850

ENTRANCE REQUIREMENTS

Academic units recommended: 4 English, 3 math, 2 natural science, 4 foreign language, 2 social science. High school diploma is required, and GED is accepted. ACT with or without Writing component accepted. TOEFL required of all international applicants: minimum paper TOEFL 500, minimum computer TOEFL 173.

Application deadline: None
Notification: Rolling
Average GPA: 3.4
ACT Composite middle 50% range: 22–26

SAT Math middle 50% range: 495–650
SAT Critical Reading middle 50% range: 518–660
SAT Writing middle 50% range: NR

Graduated top 10% of class: 34%
Graduated top 25% of class: 75%
Graduated top 50% of class: 95%

COLLEGE GRADUATION REQUIREMENTS

Course waivers allowed: No
Course substitutions allowed: Yes
In what course: Math, foreign language

ADDITIONAL INFORMATION

Environment: The college is located on 110 acres in an urban area in central St. Paul, Minnesota.

Student Body
  Undergrad enrollment: 3,636
  Women: 97%
  Men: 3%
  Percent out-of-state: 40%

Cost Information
  Tuition: $31,360
  Room & board: $8,002 (avg.)
Housing Information
  University housing: Yes
  Percent living on campus: 37%

Greek System
  Fraternity: No
  Sorority: Yes
Athletics: Division III

ST. OLAF COLLEGE

1520 St. Olaf Avenue, Northfield, MN 55057
Phone: 507-786-3025 • Fax: 507-786-3832
E-mail: admissions@stolaf.edu • Web: www.stolaf.edu
Support: S • Institution: 4-year private

PROGRAMS OR SERVICES FOR STUDENTS WITH LD

The goal of the services at St. Olaf is to provide equal access to a St. Olaf education for all students with disabilities. The purpose is to create and maintain an environment in which students may achieve their fullest potential, limited to the least extent possible by individual disabilities. All faculty, staff, and students of the college are expected to adhere to this philosophy of equal access to educational opportunity and assume broad responsibility for its implementation. In order to receive services through Student Disability Services, students must provide a clear statement of diagnosed disability.

ADMISSION INFORMATION FOR STUDENTS WITH LD/ADHD

College entrance tests required: Yes
Interview required: N/A
Essay required: N/A
Documentation required for LD: Clear statement of
   diagnosed disability with results from appropriate assessment
   instruments. Student Disability Services will work individually
   with students to determine whether documentation presented
   is sufficient.
Documentation required for ADHD: Same documentation
   required for LD.
Submitted to: Support Program/Services
Special Ed. HS course work accepted: N/A

Specific course requirements for all applicants: Yes
Separate application required for program services: No
# of LD applications submitted each year: N/A
# of LD applications accepted yearly: N/A
Total # of students receiving LD services: 100
**Acceptance into program means acceptance into
   college:** N/A

ADMISSIONS

All applicants must meet the same competitive admission criteria. There is no separate application process for students with learning disabilities or attention deficit disorder. The mid 50 percent scroe range for the ACT is 26–31 and for the SAT it is 1210–1390. It's recommended that students have a strong academic curriculum with four years English, three to four years math, four years social studies, three to four years science, and two to four years foreign language. High school diploma is required and the GED is accepted. The TOEFL is required of all international applicants with a minimum score of 550. Once admitted, students with documented disabilities should have their current documentation sent to the Student Disability Services Office.

ADDITIONAL INFORMATION

All students have access to tutoring, math clinics, writing centers, study skills assistance, and regular meetings with a Student Disability Services Specialist, if necessary. Other accommodations and services are available with appropriate documentation, including: extended testing time; distraction-free testing environment; use of a calculator, spellchecker or computer for exams; scribes; readers; note-takers; smart pens/recording devices; and alternate format texts.

PROGRAM FOR DISABILITY SERVICES

Contact Information
Name of program or department: Student Disability Services
  Telephone: 507-786-3288
  Fax: 507-786-3923

LEARNING DISABILITY SERVICES

Accommodations are decided upon an individual basis after a thorough review of appropriate, current documentation. The accommodations requested must be supported through the documentation provided and must be logically linked to the current impact of the condition on academic functioning.

Allowed in exams	**Distraction-reduced environment:** Yes	**Added costs for services:** No
Calculator: Yes	**Tape recording in class:** Yes	**LD specialists:** No
Dictionary: Yes	**Electronic texts:** Yes	**Professional tutors:** No
Computer: Yes	**Accommodations for students with**	**Peer tutors:** 200–250
Spellchecker: Yes	**ADHD:** Yes	**Max. hours/wk. for services:** none
Extended test time: Yes	**Kurzweil Reader:** Yes	**How professors are notified of**
Scribes: Yes	**Other assistive technology:** High	**LD/ADHD:** Student
Proctors: N/A	Speed Scanner Kurzweil license to go	
Oral exams: Yes	Dragon Naturally Speaking Inspiration	
Note-takers: Yes	Pulse Smart Pen	
	Priority registration: Yes	

GENERAL ADMISSIONS INFORMATION

Office of Admission: 800-800-3025

ENTRANCE REQUIREMENTS

Academic units recommended: 4 English, 4 mathematics, 4 science, (2 science labs), 4 foreign language, 4 social studies. High school diploma is required and GED is accepted. SAT or ACT required; TOEFL required of all international applicants; minimum paper TOEFL 550, minimum computer TOEFL 213.

Application deadline: 1/15	**SAT Math middle 50% range:**	**Graduated top 10% of class:** 60%
Notification: Rolling	590–710	**Graduated top 25% of class:** 82%
Average GPA: 3.65	**SAT Critical Reading middle 50%**	**Graduated top 50% of class:** 98%
ACT Composite middle 50% range:	range: 590–700	
27–31	**SAT Writing middle 50% range:**	
	580–680	

COLLEGE GRADUATION REQUIREMENTS

Course waivers allowed: No
Course substitutions allowed: Yes
In what course: Alternatives are rarely considered. A subcommittee must recommend substitutions and a faculty committee makes the decision. Most often a student is required to try a language with support from department, tutors, labs and study groups first.

ADDITIONAL INFORMATION

Environment: The college is located on 350 acres in a small town near Minneapolis.

Student Body	**Cost Information**	**Greek System**
Undergrad enrollment: 3,179	**Tuition:** $38,150	**Fraternity:** No
Women: 56%	**Room & board:** $8,800	**Sorority:** No
Men: 44%	**Housing Information**	**Athletics:** Division III
Percent out-of-state: 50%	**University housing:** Yes	
	Percent living on campus: 96%	

UNIVERSITY OF ST. THOMAS (MN)

2115 Summit Avenue, Mail #32F, St. Paul, MN 55105-1096
Phone: 651-962-6150 • Fax: 651-962-6160
E-mail: admissions@stthomas.edu • Web: www.stthomas.edu
Support: S • Institution type: 4-year private

PROGRAMS OR SERVICES FOR STUDENTS WITH LD

The mission of the Enhancement Program – Disability Services at the University of St. Thomas is to make reasonable effort to provide all qualified students with disabilities equal access to all university courses, services, programs, employment and facilities. Our goal is to enable students with disabilities to maximize their educational potential and to develop their independence and self-advocacy skills to the fullest extent possible within the standard university curriculum. Comprehensive support services and accommodations are offered that will allow the student equal access to all the university programs and facilities. Students qualify for services through the Enhancement Program once they have self-disclosed their disability and presented appropriate documentation of a disability. Reasonable accommodations are arranged on an individual basis based on the student's disability and the requirements of a particular course. For students to be eligible for these services, documentation from a licensed professional is required.

ADMISSION INFORMATION FOR STUDENTS WITH LD/ADHD

College entrance tests required: Yes
Interview required: No
Essay recommended: No
What documentation required for LD: Psycho Ed evaluation to include: relevant historical info, instructional interventions, related services, age diagnosed, objective data (aptitude, achievement, info processing), test scores (standard, percentile and grade equivalents) and describe functional limitations.
With general application: No
To receive services after enrolling: Yes
What documentation required for ADHD: Diagnosis based on DSM-V; history of behaviors impairing functioning in academic setting; diagnostic interview; history of symptoms; evidence of ongoing behaviors.

With general application: No
Submitted to: Enhancement Program
Special Ed. HS course work accepted: Yes
Specific course requirements of all applicants: Yes
Separate application required: No
# of LD applications submitted each year: NR
# of LD applications accepted yearly: NR
Total # of students receiving LD services: 500
Acceptance into program means acceptance into college: Students must be admitted to and enrolled in the university and then request services.

ADMISSIONS

There are general requirements for admission; some exceptions are made on a case-by-case basis. The general requirements include an ACT score of 20–21, a GPA of 3.0, or a rank within the top 35–40 percent of a student's class; recommendations; and an essay. If it is known that a student has a disability, the Office of Admissions may ask the Director of the Enhancement Program to assess the documentation. The Office of Admissions has the final decision, but the Director of the Enhancement Program may be asked to provide information and recommendations. Students can be admitted on a probationary status. They will be required to develop an academic contract with a counselor and meet with that person regularly throughout the semester. Students cannot get an F in any of their classes. They must maintain this for two semesters, and if they do, they are then admitted unconditionally.

ADDITIONAL INFORMATION

Comprehensive services are available through a collaborative effort of the Enhancement Program director, the Accommodations Coordinator, and student employees. Academic and personal counseling pertaining to the student's specific disability is offered. Reasonable accommodations such as note-takers, readers, and scribes; alternate format texts; alternate testing arrangements; and course/program modifications are offered, if appropriate.

LEARNING DISABILITY PROGRAMS OR SERVICES

Contact Information
Name of program or department: Enhancement Program—Disability Services
Telephone: 651-962-6315
Fax: 651-962-5965

LEARNING DISABILITY SERVICES

Accommodations are decided upon an individual basis after a thorough review of appropriate, current documentation. The accommodations requested must be supported through the documentation provided and must be logically linked to the current impact of the condition on academic functioning.

Allowed in exams
 Calculator: Yes
 Dictionary: Yes
 Computer: Yes
 Spellchecker: Yes
Extended test time: Yes
Scribes: Yes
Proctors: Yes
Oral exams: Yes
Note-takers: Yes

Distraction-reduced environment: Yes
Tape recording in class: Yes
Electronic texts: Yes
**Accommodations for students with
 ADHD:** Yes
Kurzweil Reader: Yes
Other assistive technology: Yes
Priority registration: Yes

Added costs for services: No
LD specialists: No
Professional tutors: No
Peer tutors: Yes
Max. hours/wk. for services:
 Unlimited
**How professors are notified of
 LD/ADHD:** By both student and
director

GENERAL ADMISSIONS INFORMATION

Office of Admission: 651-962-6151

ENTRANCE REQUIREMENTS

Academic units required: 3 math. **Academic units recommended:** 4 English, 4 math, 2 science, 4 foreign language, 2 social science/history. High school diploma is required, and GED is accepted. ACT with or without Writing component accepted. TOEFL required of all international applicants: minimum paper TOEFL 550, minimum computer TOEFL 213.

Application deadline: None
Notification: Rolling
Average GPA: 3.56
ACT Composite middle 50% range:
 23–28

SAT Math middle 50% range:
 530–640
**SAT Critical Reading middle 50%
 range:** 500–620
SAT Writing middle 50% range: NR

Graduated top 10% of class: 27%
Graduated top 25% of class: 56%
Graduated top 50% of class: 87%

COLLEGE GRADUATION REQUIREMENTS

Course waivers allowed: No
Course substitutions allowed: Yes
In what course: Students may petition to have their math or foreign language requirement substituted.

ADDITIONAL INFORMATION

Environment: The University of St. Thomas is located five miles from downtown St. Paul.

Student Body
 Undergrad enrollment: 6,270
 Women: 48%
 Men: 52%
 Percent out-of-state: 16%

Cost Information
 Tuition: $32,073
 Room & board: $8,924
Housing Information
 University housing: Yes
 Percent living on campus: 41%

Greek System
 Fraternity: No
 Sorority: No
Athletics: Division III

WINONA STATE UNIVERSITY

Office of Admissions/Maxwell Hall, Winona State Uni, Winona, MN 55987
Phone: 507-457-5100 • Fax: 507-457-5620
E-mail: admissions@winona.edu • Web: www.winona.edu
Support: S • Institution: 4-year public

PROGRAMS OR SERVICES FOR STUDENTS WITH LD

Winona State University is a public four-year liberal arts university located in Winona, Minnesota. WSU's current enrollment is over 8,000 students. Faculty to student ratio is 1:21. WSU is a laptop university in which all students lease a laptop. WSU has been recogized as "America's 100 Best College Buys." The oldest member of the Minnesota State Colleges and Universities System, Winona State offers 80 undergraduate, pre-professional, licensure and graduate programs on its three campuses: the original Main Campus in Winona, the West Campus in Winona, and Winona State University—Rochester Center.

ADMISSION INFORMATION FOR STUDENTS WITH LD/ADHD

College entrance tests required: Yes
Interview required: No
Essay required: N/A
What documentation required for LD: Psycho Ed evaluation to include: relevant historical info, instructional interventions, related services, age diagnosed, objective data (aptitude, achievement, info processing), test scores (standard, percentile and grade equivalents) and describe functional limitations.
With general application: No
To receive services after enrolling: Yes
What documentation required for ADHD: Diagnosis based on DSM-V; history of behaviors impairing functioning in academic setting; diagnostic interview; history of symptoms; evidence of ongoing behaviors.

With general application: No
Submitted to: Disability Services
Special Ed. HS course work accepted: N/A
Specific course requirements for all applicants: Yes
Separate application required for program services: Yes
# of LD applications submitted each year: NR
# of LD applications accepted yearly: NR
Total # of students receiving LD services: 50–75
Acceptance into program means acceptance into college: Separate application required after student has been accepted

ADMISSIONS
Winona State University Admissions requirements: ACT score of 21 or better with class rank in top 2/3 of high school class OR Top 50 % of graduating class with an ACT score of 18 or better. The students academic transcript will be reviewed to see that they have completed the Minnesota State University Preparation Requirements. Admissions decisions are processed in 15 to 20 days. Upon admission, student should make an appointment with the Disability Service Coordinator.

ADDITIONAL INFORMATION
WSU is consistently ranked among the nation's top regional universities, which offers all the advantages of a comprehensive public institution. Some of our great strengths include highly regarded academic programs in more than 80 disciplines, an institutional commitment to technology, national research endeavors, faculty experts, and exceptional facilities that include a state-of-the art library and a new $30 million science laboratory building. Disability Services provides academic accommodations for students who present qualifying documentation. Some of these accommodations include extended time on tests, low distraction, exams in auditory format, notetaker, scribe, accessible classrooms and labs.

PROGRAM FOR DISABILITY SERVICES

Contact Information
Name of program or department: Disability Services
  Telephone: 507-457-5878
  Fax: 507-457-2957

LEARNING DISABILITY SERVICES

Accommodations are decided upon an individual basis after a thorough review of appropriate, current documentation. The accommodations requested must be supported through the documentation provided and must be logically linked to the current impact of the condition on academic functioning.

Allowed in exams
  Calculator: Yes
  Dictionary: Yes
  Computer: Yes
  Spellchecker: Yes
Extended test time: Yes
Scribes: Yes
Proctors: Yes
Oral exams: Yes
Note-takers: Yes

Distraction-reduced environment: Yes
Tape recording in class: Yes
Electronic texts: Yes
Accommodations for students with ADHD: Yes
Kurzweil Reader: NoTiger printer, JAWS, TestTalker, Dragon Naturally Speaking, Natural Reader
Priority registration: Yes

Added costs for services: No
LD specialists: No
Professional tutors: 1–4
Peer tutors: 45–50
Max. hours/wk. for services: 1–4
How professors are notified of LD/ADHD: Online

GENERAL ADMISSIONS INFORMATION

Office of Admission: 507-457-5100

ENTRANCE REQUIREMENTS
Academic units required: 4 English, 3 mathematics, 3 science, (3 science labs), 2 foreign language, 2 social studies, 1 history, 1 academic electives. High school diploma is required and GED is accepted. SAT or ACT required; TOEFL required of all international applicants; minimum paper TOEFL 520, minimum computer TOEFL 190, minimum web-based TOEFL 68.

Application deadline: 45 days prior to beginning of term
Notification: Rolling
Average GPA: 3.26
ACT Composite middle 50% range: 21–24

SAT Math middle 50% range: 490–610
SAT Critical Reading middle 50% range: 440–580
SAT Writing middle 50% range: NR
Graduated top 10% of class: 10%

Graduated top 25% of class: 33%
Graduated top 50% of class: 73%

COLLEGE GRADUATION REQUIREMENTS

Course waivers allowed: No
Course substitutions allowed: Yes
In what course: Course substitutions are more likely, depending on the documentation. Decisions are made on a case-by-case situation.

ADDITIONAL INFORMATION

Environment: The campus is located 90 miles south of Minneapolis.

Student Body
  Undergrad enrollment: 8,435
  Women: 60%
  Men: 40%
  Percent out-of-state: 33%

Cost Information
  In-state tuition: $8,502
  Out-of-state tuition: $13,931
  Room & board: $7,330
Housing Information
  University housing: Yes
  Percent living on campus: 31%

Greek System
  Fraternity: Yes
  Sorority: Yes
Athletics: Division II

U. OF SOUTHERN MISSISSIPPI

118 College Drive, #5166, Hattiesburg, MS 39406
Phone: 601-266-5000 • Fax: 601-266-5148
E-mail: admissions@usm.edu • Web: www.usm.edu
Support: S • Institution type: 4-year public

PROGRAMS OR SERVICES FOR STUDENTS WITH LD

The philosophy of USM is to provide services to students with learning disabilities and give them the maximum opportunity to complete a college education. The Office for Disability Accommodations (ODA) is USM's designated office to verify eligibility for accommodations under the American with Disabilities Act and develop and coordinate plans for the provision of such accommodations. After receiving documentation of a student's disability, ODA works with the student to develop a plan for the provision of reasonable accommodations that are specific to his or her disabilities.

ADMISSION INFORMATION FOR STUDENTS WITH LD/ADHD

College entrance tests required: Yes
Interview required: No
Essay recommended: No
What documentation required for LD: Psycho Ed evaluation to include: relevant historical info, instructional interventions, related services, age diagnosed, objective data (aptitude, achievement, info processing), test scores (standard, percentile and grade equivalents) and describe functional limitations.
With general application: No
To receive services after enrolling: Yes
What documentation required for ADHD: Diagnosis based on DSM-V; history of behaviors impairing functioning in academic setting; diagnostic interview; history of symptoms; evidence of ongoing behaviors.

With general application: No
Submitted to: Office of Disability Accommodations
Special Ed. HS course work accepted: NR
Specific course requirements of all applicants: Yes
Separate application required: No
# of LD applications submitted each year: NR
# of LD applications accepted yearly: NR
Total # of students receiving LD services: NR
Acceptance into program means acceptance into college: Students must be admitted and enrolled prior to requesting services.

ADMISSIONS

There is no special application for students with learning disabilities. Freshmen applicants have specific curriculum, GPA and ACT/SAT test scores requirements.. Course requirements include: 4 years English (with substantial writing components), 3 years math (Algebra I and II, Geometry or higher math), 3 sciences, 3 social studies (including ½ year American Government and ½ year economics or geography), 2 years electives chosen from foreign language, geography, math above Algebra II, or a science. (One year must be a foreign language or geography), and ½ year of computer application. Courses taken prior to high school will be accepted for admission provided the course content is the same as the high school course. Full admission will be granted to students: 1) who complete the college prep curriculum with a minimum 3.2 GPA in these courses and the submission of ACT/SAT or 2) who complete the college prep curriculum with a minimum 2.5 GPA in these courses or a class rank in the top 50%, as well as a score of 16 or higher on the ACT or 760 SAT (Critical reading and math) or 3) complete the college prep curriculum with a minimum 2.0 GPA in these courses and a score of 18 or higher on the ACT or 860 SAT or 4) students who satisfy the National Collegiate Athletic Association (NCAA) standards for student-athletes who are full qualifiers under Division 1 guidelines.

ADDITIONAL INFORMATION

To receive reasonable accommodations for a disability, students must file an application with OSS and provide current documentation of a disability. After an application is filed, students schedule an appointment with the OSS coordinator, complete an intake form, and establish a plan for reasonable accommodations and services. The OSS helps students locate tutors, note-takers, and other ancillary aids for their classwork. The office works with vocational rehabilitation to pay for these services. The office staff works with students on a one-on-one basis to determine how they learn best. There are remedial programs in math, writing, and reading.

LEARNING DISABILITY PROGRAMS OR SERVICES

Contact Information
Name of program or department: Office for Disability Accommodations
 Telephone: 601-266-5024
 Fax: 601-266-6035

LEARNING DISABILITY SERVICES

Accommodations are decided upon an individual basis after a thorough review of appropriate, current documentation. The accommodations requested must be supported through the documentation provided and must be logically linked to the current impact of the condition on academic functioning.

Allowed in exams
 Calculator: Case-by-case
 Dictionary: Case-by-case
 Computer: Case-by-case
 Spellchecker: NR
Extended test time: Yes
Scribes: Yes
Proctors: Yes
Oral exams: Yes
Note-takers: Yes

Distraction-reduced environment: Yes
Tape recording in class: Yes
Electronic texts: Yes
Accommodations for students with ADHD: Yes
Kurzweil Reader: Yes
Other assistive technology: Yes
Priority registration: Yes

Added costs for services: No
LD specialists: No
Professional tutors: No
Peer tutors: No
Max. hours/wk. for services: Varies
How professors are notified of LD/ADHD: By student

GENERAL ADMISSIONS INFORMATION

Office of Admission: 601-266-5000

ENTRANCE REQUIREMENTS

Academic units required: 4 English, 3 math, 3 science, 3 social studies, 2 advanced electives, 0.5 computer applications. TOEFL required of all international applicants: minimum paper TOEFL 525. TOEFL required of all international applicants: minimum paper TOEFL 525.

Application deadline: None
Notification: Rolling
Average GPA: NR
ACT Composite middle 50% range: NR

SAT Math middle 50% range: NR
SAT Critical Reading middle 50% range: NR
SAT Writing middle 50% range: NR

Graduated top 10% of class: NR
Graduated top 25% of class: NR
Graduated top 50% of class: NR

COLLEGE GRADUATION REQUIREMENTS

Course waivers allowed: No
Course substitutions allowed: Yes

ADDITIONAL INFORMATION

Environment: The university is located on 840 acres in a small city 90 miles southeast of Jackson.

Student Body
 Undergrad enrollment: 13,618
 Women: 62%
 Men: 38%
 Percent out-of-state: 12%

Cost Information
 In-state tuition: $5,834
 Out-of-state tuition: $13,790
 Room & board: $5,648 (avg.)
Housing Information
 University housing: Yes
 Percent living on campus: N/A

Greek System
 Fraternity: Yes
 Sorority: Yes
Athletics: Division I

EVANGEL UNIVERSITY

111 North Glenstone, Springfield, MO 65802
Phone: 417-865-2811 • Fax: 417-865-9599
E-mail: admissions@evangel.edu • Web: www.evangel.edu
Support: CS • Institution type: 4-year private

PROGRAMS OR SERVICES FOR STUDENTS WITH LD

The Academic Support Center supports the needs of all students at Evangel College. The center focuses on assisting students with improving academic skills so that they remain successful in college. The center offers study skills assistance, tutorial services, and individual college planning. Group and individual support counseling is also available. Classes covering study skills are offered for credit.

ADMISSION INFORMATION FOR STUDENTS WITH LD/ADHD

College entrance tests required: Yes
Interview required: No
Essay recommended: No
What documentation required for LD: Psycho Ed evaluation to include: relevant historical info, instructional interventions, related services, age diagnosed, objective data (aptitude, achievement, info processing), test scores (standard, percentile and grade equivalents) and describe functional limitations.
With general application: No
To receive services after enrolling: Yes
What documentation required for ADHD: Diagnosis based on DSM-V; history of behaviors impairing functioning in academic setting; diagnostic interview; history of symptoms; evidence of ongoing behaviors.

With general application: No
Submitted to: Academic Support Center
Special Ed. HS course work accepted: Yes
Specific course requirements of all applicants: Yes
Separate application required: No
# of LD applications submitted each year: NR
# of LD applications accepted yearly: NR
Total # of students receiving LD services: 35
Acceptance into program means acceptance into college: Students must be admitted to and enrolled in the university first and then request services.

ADMISSIONS

There is no special application for students with learning disabilities. All students must meet the same admission criteria. Evangel College looks at the completed application. ACT test scores are required. Students should have at least a 2.0 GPA, a pastor's recommendation, and a high school recommendation. Course requirements include 3 years of English, 2 years of math, 2 years of social science, and 1 year of science. Students with documented LD can request a substitute for specific courses if their disability impacts their ability to learn that particular subject. Special admission to the SOAR Program is offered to students with ACT scores between 14–17. These students will be enrolled in study skills as well as other proficiency classes.

ADDITIONAL INFORMATION

Some study skills classes are required for students who are admitted conditionally. The Academic Support Center offers tutoring, at no cost, in a variety of courses. The center offers resources in such topics as personal growth, goal setting, self-concept enrichment, stress management, memory and concentration, test-taking, underlining, note-taking, outlining, reading a textbook, research, writing term papers, time scheduling, reading efficiency, and vocabulary. Additional resources include the design and implementation of individualized programs with an instructor, personal professional counseling at no charge, career counseling with the Director of Career Development Services, reading labs for increased reading speed, and tutoring in other classes at no charge. SOAR is designed to assist selected provisionally admitted students during the first two semesters of college. SOAR courses focus on specific modules such as assessment and skills review in reading, math, and writing; study skills application; and career planning.

LEARNING DISABILITY PROGRAMS OR SERVICES

Contact Information
Name of program or department: Academic Development Center
  Telephone: 417-865-2811
  Fax: 417-865-9599

LEARNING DISABILITY SERVICES

Accommodations are decided upon an individual basis after a thorough review of appropriate, current documentation. The accommodations requested must be supported through the documentation provided and must be logically linked to the current impact of the condition on academic functioning.

Allowed in exams	**Distraction-reduced environment:** Yes	**Added costs for services:** No
Calculator: Yes	**Tape recording in class:** Yes	**LD specialists:** Yes
Dictionary: Yes	**Electronic texts:** Yes	**Professional tutors:** 1
Computer: Yes	**Accommodations for students with**	**Peer tutors:** 5
Spellchecker: Yes	**ADHD:** Yes	**Max. hours/wk. for services:**
Extended test time: Yes	**Kurzweil Reader:** Yes	Unlimited
Scribes: Yes	**Other assistive technology:** Yes	**How professors are notified of**
Proctors: Yes	**Priority registration:** No	**LD/ADHD:** By both student and
Oral exams: Yes		director
Note-takers: Yes		

GENERAL ADMISSIONS INFORMATION

Office of Admission: 1-800-EVANGEL

ENTRANCE REQUIREMENTS

Academic units recommended: 3 English, 2 math, 1 science (1 science lab), 2 foreign language, 2 social studies, 3 academic electives. High school diploma is required, and GED is accepted. TOEFL required of all international applicants: minimum paper TOEFL 490.

Application deadline: 8/1	**SAT Math middle 50% range:** NR	**Graduated top 10% of class:** NR
Notification: Rolling	**SAT Critical Reading middle 50%**	**Graduated top 25% of class:** NR
Average GPA: 3.4	**range:** NR	**Graduated top 50% of class:** NR
ACT Composite middle 50% range:	**SAT Writing middle 50% range:** NR	
20–26		

COLLEGE GRADUATION REQUIREMENTS

Course waivers allowed: No
Course substitutions allowed: Yes
In what course: Math

ADDITIONAL INFORMATION

Environment: The college is located on 80 acres in an urban area 225 miles west of St. Louis.

Student Body	**Cost Information**	**Greek System**
Undergrad enrollment: 1,718	**Tuition:** $17,930	**Fraternity:** No
Women: 58%	**Room & board:** $6,640	**Sorority:** No
Men: 42%	**Housing Information**	**Athletics:** Division II
Percent out-of-state: 60%	**University housing:** Yes	
	Percent living on campus: 75%	

KANSAS CITY ART INSTITUTE

4415 Warwick Boulevard, Kansas City, MO 64111-1762
Phone: 816-474-5225 • Fax: 816-802-3309
E-mail: admiss@kcai.edu • Web:www.kcai.edu
Support: CS • Institution type: 4-year private

PROGRAMS OR SERVICES FOR STUDENTS WITH LD

The Academic Resource Center (ARC) is committed to the educational development of students at the Kansas City Art Institute. A recognition of the individual cognitive and creative styles of students of art and design is reflected in the comprehensive support service offered. The goal is to foster independent thinking and problem solving, resourcefulness, and personal responsibility. All KCAI students are invited to take advantage of the services provided by the ARC. Services are aimed at enhancing a student's experience throughout his or her academic career. The staff takes a holistic approach and is committed to the educational, personal, and evolving professional development of all students. Students with formal documentation of a disability are encouraged to contact the ARC for assistance in arranging accommodations or developing self-advocacy strategies.

ADMISSION INFORMATION FOR STUDENTS WITH LD/ADHD

College entrance tests required: Yes
Interview required: No
Essay recommended: No
What documentation required for LD: Psycho Ed evaluation to include: relevant historical info, instructional interventions, related services, age diagnosed, objective data (aptitude, achievement, info processing), test scores (standard, percentile and grade equivalents) and describe functional limitations.
With general application: No
To receive services after enrolling: Yes
What documentation required for ADHD: Diagnosis based on DSM-V; history of behaviors impairing functioning in academic setting; diagnostic interview; history of symptoms; evidence of ongoing behaviors.

With general application: No
Submitted to: Both the Admissions Office and the Academic Resource Center
Special Ed. HS course work accepted: Yes
Specific course requirements of all applicants: NR
Separate application required: No
# of LD applications submitted each year: NR
# of LD applications accepted yearly: NR
Total # of students receiving LD services: NR
Acceptance into program means acceptance into college: Students must be admitted to and enrolled in the university first and then request services.

ADMISSIONS

Students with learning disabilities must demonstrate art ability through a portfolio review and meet a combination of academic criteria, like all other applicants, but with a more specialized evaluation. Admitted students should have a minimum ACT of 20 or SAT of 1500 and a 2.5 GPA. Students must have had at least 4 years of high school English. If the criteria are not met, applicants are considered in depth via an Admissions Committee. An interview is recommended.

ADDITIONAL INFORMATION

Students are given assistance in the ARC on an individual basis. Students will consult with their academic advisors each semester about progress in their academic degree program. Advisors help assess progress toward a degree and provide guidance in course selection. Peer advisors are also available. The learning specialist helps students gain a more complete understanding of their individual learning styles, skills, strengths, and weaknesses to cope with the great demands of college courses. Assistance is available through study groups and one-on-one tutoring sessions to improve reading, writing, study, testing, and time management skills.

LEARNING DISABILITY PROGRAMS OR SERVICES

Contact Information
Name of program or department: Academic Resource Center (ARC)
  Telephone: 816-802-3485
  Fax: 816-802-3480

LEARNING DISABILITY SERVICES

Accommodations are decided upon an individual basis after a thorough review of appropriate, current documentation. The accommodations requested must be supported through the documentation provided and must be logically linked to the current impact of the condition on academic functioning.

Allowed in exams
  Calculator: Yes
  Dictionary: Yes
  Computer: Yes
  Spellchecker: Yes
Extended test time: Yes
Scribes: Yes
Proctors: Yes
Oral exams: Yes
Note-takers: Yes

Distraction-reduced environment: Yes
Tape recording in class: Yes
Electronic texts: Yes
Accommodations for students with ADHD: Yes
Kurzweil Reader: No
Other assistive technology: Yes
Priority registration: Yes

Added costs for services: No
LD specialists: Yes
Professional tutors: 1
Peer tutors: As needed
Max. hours/wk. for services: Unlimited
How professors are notified of LD/ADHD: By both student and director

GENERAL ADMISSIONS INFORMATION

Office of Admission: 816-802-3304

ENTRANCE REQUIREMENTS

Academic units recommended: 4 English, 3 math, 3 science, 3 social studies, 3 academic electives, 4 fine arts. High school diploma is required, and GED is accepted. TOEFL required of all international applicants: minimum paper TOEFL 550, minimum computer TOEFL 213.

Application deadline: None
Notification: Rolling
Average GPA: 3.30
ACT Composite middle 50% range: 20–25

SAT Math middle 50% range: 450–530
SAT Critical Reading middle 50% range: 450–590
SAT Writing middle 50% range: 430–550

Graduated top 10% of class: 11%
Graduated top 25% of class: 33%
Graduated top 50% of class: 65%

COLLEGE GRADUATION REQUIREMENTS

Course waivers allowed: No
Course substitutions allowed: No

ADDITIONAL INFORMATION

Environment: The campus is located in an urban area in Kansas City.

Student Body
  Undergrad enrollment: 746
  Women: 57%
  Men: 43%
  Percent out-of-state: 75%

Cost Information
  Tuition: $31,992
  Room & board: $9,466
  Housing Information
    University housing: Yes
    Percent living on campus: 20%

Greek System
  Fraternity: No
  Sorority: No
  Athletics: None

MISSOURI STATE UNIVERSITY

901 South National, Springfield, MO 65897
Phone: 417-836-5517 • Fax: 417-836-6334
E-mail: info@missouristate.edu • Web: www.missouristate.edu
Support: SP • Institution type: 4-year public

PROGRAMS OR SERVICES FOR STUDENTS WITH LD

The Learning Diagnostic Clinic (LDC) is an academic support facility to assist students with learning disabilities. The staff includes psychologists and learning specialists. The LDC provides two levels of academic support to qualified individuals: One level comprises basic accommodations guaranteed to the qualified students with disabilities under the law; offered at no cost. The second level is called Project Success, an academic support program for college students with learning disabilities who desire more comprehensive services. This program provides academic and emotional support that will help to ease the student's transition to higher learning and the opportunity to function independently. Students applying to Project Success are required to have a psychoeducational evaluation by the LDC staff to ensure that the program is suitable for their needs and able provide appropriate accommodations. The fee for testing is $500. If background and documentation do not support a diagnosis of LD, alternatives and suggestions are discussed with the student. If the student wishes to appeal a decision not to provide services, he or she is referred to the ADA/504 compliance officer.

ADMISSION INFORMATION FOR STUDENTS WITH LD/ADHD

College entrance tests required: Yes
Interview required: Yes
Essay recommended: NR
What documentation required for LD: Psycho Ed evaluation to include: relevant historical info, instructional interventions, related services, age diagnosed, objective data (aptitude, achievement, info processing), test scores (standard, percentile and grade equivalents) and describe functional limitations.
With general application: Yes if requested as part of Structured Program application
To receive services after enrolling: Yes
What documentation required for ADHD: Diagnosis based on DSM-V; history of behaviors impairing functioning in academic setting; diagnostic interview; history of symptoms; evidence of ongoing behaviors.

With general application: Yes if requested as part of Structured Program application
To receive services after enrolling: Yes
Submitted to: Learning Diagnostic Clinic
Special Ed. HS course work accepted: No
Specific course requirements of all applicants: Yes
Separate application required: Yes
# of LD applications submitted each year: NR
# of LD applications accepted yearly: NR
Total # of students receiving LD services: 200
Acceptance into program means acceptance into college: Students must be admitted and enrolled at the university first and then may request an application to LDC or Project Success.

ADMISSIONS

Students with LD must meet the same requirements for admission as all other applicants. There is a special application to be completed as well as a required evaluation fee for students requesting special services. Eligibility for admissions is based on a sliding scale determined by ACT scores and class rank. Course requirements include 4 English, 3 math, 3 social studies, 2 science, and 1 visual and performing arts, plus 3 additional core courses. Computer science may also be used. Procedure for Project Success: (1) acceptance to the university, (2) self-identify and request an application at LDC, (3) submit application and information, and (4) personal interview and testing. The student is accepted or offered alternative suggestions. The university admits a limited number of students who do not meet the above requirements but who demonstrate an academic potential not reflected in their standard performance measures. Students who wish to be considered for admission as an exception to the policy should contact Admissions for information on the appeal process. Students are encouraged to request this information before submitting their application.

ADDITIONAL INFORMATION

Students must self-identify to request accommodations. Appropriate accommodations are determined by the director and the student. The student is assigned to a graduate assistant who maintains contact, monitors progress, and assesses the effectiveness of accommodations. Project Success staff provides intensive remediation, focusing on written language and mathematics strategies. Caseworkers provide assistance with advocacy skills. Tutors trained by the LDC are available to students enrolled in the Project Success program; the fee for this level of accommodations is $1,500 per semester. Basic services from the LDC may include assistance in obtaining recorded textbooks, testing accommodations, counseling, advisement, and note-taking assistance; there is no fee for these basic services.

LEARNING DISABILITY PROGRAMS OR SERVICES

Contact Information
Name of program or department: Learning Diagnostic Clinic (LDC)
  Telephone: 417-836-4787
  Fax: 417-836-5475

LEARNING DISABILITY SERVICES

Accommodations are decided upon an individual basis after a thorough review of appropriate, current documentation. The accommodations requested must be supported through the documentation provided and must be logically linked to the current impact of the condition on academic functioning.

Allowed in exams
  Calculator: Yes
  Dictionary: Yes
  Computer: Yes
  Spellchecker: Yes
Extended test time: Yes
Scribes: Yes
Proctors: Yes
Oral exams: Yes
Note-takers: Yes

Distraction-reduced environment: Yes
Tape recording in class: Yes
Electronic texts: Yes
Accommodations for students with ADHD: Yes
Kurzweil Reader: Yes
Other assistive technology: Yes
Priority registration: Yes

Added costs for services: No
LD specialists: Yes
Professional tutors: No
Peer tutors: Yes
Max. hours/wk. for services: N/A
How professors are notified of LD/ADHD: By both student and director

GENERAL ADMISSIONS INFORMATION

Office of Admission: 417-836-5517

ENTRANCE REQUIREMENTS

Academic units required: 4 English, 3 math, 2 science (1 science lab), 3 social studies, 3 academic electives. High school diploma is required, and GED is accepted. ACT with or without Writing component accepted. TOEFL required of all international applicants: minimum paper TOEFL 500, minimum computer TOEFL 173.

Application deadline: 7/20
Notification: Rolling
Average GPA: NR
ACT Composite middle 50% range: 21–27

SAT Math middle 50% range: NR
SAT Critical Reading middle 50% range: NR
SAT Writing middle 50% range: NR

Graduated top 10% of class: 22%
Graduated top 25% of class: 49%
Graduated top 50% of class: 81%

COLLEGE GRADUATION REQUIREMENTS

Course waivers allowed: No
Course substitutions allowed: Yes
In what course: Varies

ADDITIONAL INFORMATION

Environment: The 200-acre rural campus is located 170 miles from Kansas City and 120 miles from St. Louis.

Student Body
  Undergrad enrollment: 17,205
  Women: 55%
  Men: 45%
  Percent out-of-state: 10%

Cost Information
  In-state tuition: $6,598
  Out-of-state tuition: $12,418
  Room & board: $6,582
Housing Information
  University housing: Yes
  Percent living on campus: 24%

Greek System
  Fraternity: Yes
  Sorority: Yes
Athletics: Division I

UNIVERSITY OF MISSOURI—COLUMBIA

230 Jesse Hall, Columbia, MO 65211
Phone: 573-882-7786 • Fax: 573-882-7887
E-mail: MU4U@missouri.edu • Web: www.missouri.edu
Support: CS • Institution type: 4-year public

PROGRAMS OR SERVICES FOR STUDENTS WITH LD

Reasonable accommodations, auxiliary aids, and support services are provided by the Office of Disability Services (ODS) to ensure that any student with a disability will have equal access to the educational programs and activities at the university. MU does not have a stand-alone program oriented to students with specific learning disabilities; all students with disabilities are supported through ODS. Students with disabilities (including specific learning disabilities or ADD/ADHD) are required to adhere to the same academic standards as other students at the university. As in any higher education setting, students with disabilities have the responsibility to self-identify and are encouraged to request accommodations through ODS as early as possible. In most instances, students will be expected to provide documentation of disability; for learning disabilities this will likely be in the form of a diagnostic report, as well as documented evidence of having received accommodations previously. For entering freshmen, contacting ODS in advance of the start of their first semester is strongly encouraged.

ADMISSION INFORMATION FOR STUDENTS WITH LD/ADHD

College entrance tests required: Yes
Interview required: No
Essay recommended: No
What documentation required for LD: Psycho Ed evaluation to include: relevant historical info, instructional interventions, related services, age diagnosed, objective data (aptitude, achievement, info processing), test scores (standard, percentile and grade equivalents) and describe functional limitations.
With general application: No
To receive services after enrolling: Yes
What documentation required for ADHD: Diagnosis based on DSM-V; history of behaviors impairing functioning in academic setting; diagnostic interview; history of symptoms; evidence of ongoing behaviors.

With general application: No
Submitted to: Office of Disability Services
Special Ed. HS course work accepted: Yes
Specific course requirements of all applicants: Yes
Separate application required: No
# of LD applications submitted each year: NR
# of LD applications accepted yearly: NR
Total # of students receiving LD services: 476
Acceptance into program means acceptance into college: Students must be admitted to and enrolled in the university first and then request services.

ADMISSIONS

There are no special admissions for students with learning disabilities. General admission is based on high school curriculum, ACT scores, and class rank. Applicants must have 4 years of English, 4 years of math, 3 years of social studies, 3 years of science, 2 years of a foreign language, and 1 unit of fine arts. Math, science, and foreign language requirements may be satisfied by completion of courses in middle school, junior high, or senior high. Any student with an ACT of 24 with the required courses is automatically admissible. Students with 23 ACT or 1050–1090 SAT need to rank within the top 52 percent of their graduating class. Students with 22 ACT or 1010–1040 SAT need to rank within the top 46 percent of their class. Students with 21 ACT or 970–1000 SAT need to rank within the top 31 percent of their class. Students with 19 ACT or 890–920 SAT need to rank within the top 22 percent of their class. Students with 18 ACT or 840–880 SAT need to rank within the top 14 percent of their class. Students with 17 ACT or 800–830 SAT need to rank within the top 6 percent of their class; ACT below 17 or SAT below 800 does not meet regular admission standards. Graduates of Missouri high schools who do not meet the standards for regular admission may be admitted on a conditional basis through a summer session program.

ADDITIONAL INFORMATION

Auxiliary aids and classroom accommodations include note-takers, lab assistants, readers, and assistive technology. Testing accommodations include time extensions, distraction-reduced environments, readers, scribes, or adaptive equipment. Coordinators can offer support and counseling in the areas of time management, study skills, learning styles, and other academic and social issues. Group support is also available. The Learning Center works cooperatively with ODS to provide individual tutoring free of charge. Other services include writing assistance, math assistance, test reviews, help with reading comprehension, and study skills training.

LEARNING DISABILITY PROGRAMS OR SERVICES

Contact Information
Name of program or department: Office of Disability Services (ODS)
  Telephone: 573-882-4696
  Fax: 573-884-5002

LEARNING DISABILITY SERVICES

Accommodations are decided on an individual basis after a thorough review of appropriate, current documentation, as well as an interview with an ODS Coordinator. The accommodations requested must be supported through the documentation provided and must be logically linked to the current impact of the condition on academic functioning.

Allowed in exams
  Calculator: Yes
  Dictionary: Yes
  Computer: Yes
  Spellchecker: Yes
Extended test time: Yes
Scribes: Yes
Proctors: Yes
Oral exams: Yes
Note-takers: Yes

Distraction-reduced environment: Yes
Tape recording in class: Yes
Electronic texts: Yes
Accommodations for students with ADHD: Yes
Kurzweil Reader: Yes
Other assistive technology: Yes
Priority registration: Yes

Added costs for services: No
LD specialists: No
Professional tutors: 7
Peer tutors: 120
Max. hours/wk. for services: Unlimited
How professors are notified of LD/ADHD: By student

GENERAL ADMISSIONS INFORMATION

Office of Admission: 573-882-7786

ENTRANCE REQUIREMENTS

Academic units required: 4 English, 4 math, 3 science (1 science lab), 2 foreign language, 3 social studies, 1 fine arts. High school diploma is required, and GED is accepted. ACT with or without Writing component accepted. TOEFL required of all international applicants: minimum paper TOEFL 500, minimum computer TOEFL 173.

Application deadline: None
Notification: Rolling
Average GPA: 3.05
ACT Composite middle 50% range: 23–28

SAT Math middle 50% range: 530–650
SAT Critical Reading middle 50% range: 540–650
SAT Writing middle 50% range: NR

Graduated top 10% of class: 25%
Graduated top 25% of class: 46%
Graduated top 50% of class: 86%

COLLEGE GRADUATION REQUIREMENTS

Course waivers allowed: No
Course substitutions allowed: Yes

ADDITIONAL INFORMATION

Environment: The university is located on 1,350 acres in a small town.

Student Body
  Undergrad enrollment: 24,901
  Women: 52%
  Men: 48%
  Percent out-of-state: 19%

Cost Information
  In-state tuition: $8,989
  Out-of-state tuition: $21,784
  Room & board: $8,643
Housing Information
  University housing: Yes
  Percent living on campus: 37%

Greek System
  Fraternity: Yes
  Sorority: Yes
Athletics: Division I

WASHINGTON U. IN ST. LOUIS

Campus Box 1089, One Brookings Drive, St. Louis, MO 63130-4899
Phone: 314-935-6000 • Fax: 314-935-4290
E-mail: admissions@wustl.edu • Web: www.wustl.edu
Support: CS • Institution type: 4-year private

PROGRAMS OR SERVICES FOR STUDENTS WITH LD

The Disability Resources (DR), a unit within Cornerstone: The Center for Advanced Learning at Washington University-St. Louis, recognizes that there are many types of disabilities that can hinder a student in achieving his or her true academic ability. It is the goal of DR to treat students with disabilities as individuals with specific needs and provide services responsive to those needs. DR provides a wide range of services and accommodations to help remove barriers posed by the students' disabilities. Students are encouraged to be their own advocates and have the major responsibility for securing services and accommodations. Reasonable accommodations will be made to assist students in meeting their individual needs. It is the goal of DR to incorporate students with disabilities into the mainstream of the university community. Any student who has a permanent or temporary psychological or physical disability is eligible for services. Students must self-identify and provide current documentation. The assistant director(s) of DR will work with the student to identify appropriate accommodations and services based on documentation and previous experiences. Most accommodations result from communication and agreements between the students and the classroom instructors.

ADMISSION INFORMATION FOR STUDENTS WITH LD/ADHD

College entrance tests required: Yes
Interview required: No
Essay recommended: No
What documentation required for LD: Psycho Ed evaluation to include: relevant historical info, instructional interventions, related services, age diagnosed, objective data (aptitude, achievement, info processing), test scores (standard, percentile and grade equivalents) and describe functional limitations.
With general application: No
To receive services after enrolling: Yes
What documentation required for ADHD: Diagnosis based on DSM-V; history of behaviors impairing functioning in academic setting; diagnostic interview; history of symptoms; evidence of ongoing behaviors.

With general application: No
Submitted to: Disability Resources
Special Ed. HS course work accepted: NR
Specific course requirements of all applicants: NR
Separate application required: Yes
# of LD applications submitted each year: NR
# of LD applications accepted yearly: NR
Total # of students receiving LD services: 159
Acceptance into program means acceptance into college: Students must be admitted to and enrolled in the university first and then request services.

ADMISSIONS

Washington University gives full consideration to all applicants for admission. There is no special admissions process for students with learning disabilities. Students may choose to voluntarily identify themselves as learning disabled in the admissions process. If they chose to self-identify, details of the history and treatment of their disability, of how they have met different academic requirements in light of the disability, and the relationship between the disability and the students' academic record help the university to understand more fully the applicants' profiles. This information can be helpful in the application process to explain, for example, lower grades in certain subjects. Washington University is a competitive school and looks for students with rigorous academic preparation, including 4 years of English, 3-4 years of math, 3-4 years of science, and 3-4 years of social studies. Two years of a foreign language are preferred but not required.

ADDITIONAL INFORMATION

Cornerstone: The Center for Advanced Learning provides support services to help the students to succeed academically. These include: essential study and test-taking skills, access to peer mentors, executive functioning, and time management and study techniques, etc. Common DR services and accommodations include, but are not limited to, readers or scribes, note-takers, assistance in obtaining accommodations for professional exams, referral for disability evaluation, audio taping class lectures, extra time to complete exams, alternative exam formats, and distraction-reduced exam sites. Services and accommodations are available for undergraduate and graduate students.

LEARNING DISABILITY PROGRAMS OR SERVICES

Contact Information
Name of program or department: Disability Resources
  Telephone: 314-935-4153
  Fax: 314-935-7559

LEARNING DISABILITY SERVICES

Accommodations are decided upon an individual basis after a thorough review of appropriate, current documentation. The accommodations requested must be supported through the documentation provided and must be logically linked to the current impact of the condition on academic functioning.

Allowed in exams
  Calculator: Yes
  Dictionary: Yes
  Computer: Yes
  Spellchecker: Yes
Extended test time: Yes
Scribes: Yes
Proctors: Yes
Oral exams: Yes
Note-takers: Yes

Distraction-reduced environment: Yes
Tape recording in class: Yes
Electronic texts: Yes
Accommodations for students with
  ADHD: Yes
Kurzweil Reader: Yes
Other assistive technology: Yes
Priority registration: Yes (early registration)

Added costs for services: No
LD specialists: No
Professional tutors: No
Peer tutors: No
Max. hours/wk. for services: Unlimited
How professors are notified of LD/ADHD: By the DR Coordinator

GENERAL ADMISSIONS INFORMATION

Office of Admission: 314-935-6000

ENTRANCE REQUIREMENTS

Academic units recommended: 4 English, 4 math, 4 science (4 science labs), 2 foreign language, 4 social studies, 4 history. High school diploma is required. ACT with or without Writing component accepted. TOEFL required of all international applicants: minimum paper TOEFL 550, minimum computer TOEFL 213.

Application deadline: 1/15
Notification: 4/1
Average GPA: NR
ACT Composite middle 50% range: 31–34

SAT Math middle 50% range: 700–780
SAT Critical Reading middle 50% range: 680–760
SAT Writing middle 50% range: NR

Graduated top 10% of class: 95%
Graduated top 25% of class: 100%
Graduated top 50% of class: 100%

COLLEGE GRADUATION REQUIREMENTS

Course waivers allowed: No
Course substitutions allowed: Yes
In what course: Foreign language and math are not required for most majors.

ADDITIONAL INFORMATION

Environment: The Washington University campus is located on 169 acres seven miles west of St. Louis.

Student Body
  Undergrad enrollment: 7,284
  Women: 50%
  Men: 50%
  Percent out-of-state: 90%

Cost Information
  Tuition: $40,950
  Room & board: $12,674
Housing Information
  University housing: Yes
  Percent living on campus: 72%

Greek System
  Fraternity: Yes
  Sorority: Yes
Athletics: Division III

WESTMINSTER COLLEGE

Admissions, 501 Westminster Ave, Westminster College, Fulton, MO 65251
Phone: 573-592-5251 • Fax: 573-592-5255
E-mail: admissions@westminster-mo.edu • Web: www.westminster-mo.edu
Support: SP • Institution: 4-year private

PROGRAMS OR SERVICES FOR STUDENTS WITH LD

The goal of the Learning Disabilities Program is to give students with learning disabilities the special attention they need to succeed in basically the same academic program as that pursued by other admitted students. Westminster offers the students a supportive environment, small classes, and professors who are readily accessible. The LD staff offers intensive instruction in reading, writing, and study skills. Much of the instruction is conducted on a one-on-one basis and is directed to the student's specific problem. Close supervision of the curriculum is essential in the student's freshman year, and the student's progress is monitored for any difficulties that may arise. The staff is LD certified, and faculty members have the specific role of providing LD support.

ADMISSION INFORMATION FOR STUDENTS WITH LD/ADHD

College entrance tests required: Yes
Interview required: Yes
Essay recommended: Yes
What documentation required for LD: Psycho Ed evaluation to include: relevant historical info, instructional interventions, related services, age diagnosed, objective data (aptitude, achievement, info processing), test scores (standard, percentile and grade equivalents) and describe functional limitations.
With general application: Yes if requested as part of Structured Program application
To receive services after enrolling: Yes
What documentation required for ADHD: Diagnosis based on DSM-V; history of behaviors impairing functioning in academic setting; diagnostic interview; history of symptoms; evidence of ongoing behaviors.

With general application: Yes if requested as part of Structured Program application
To receive services after enrolling: Yes
Submitted to: Admissions
Special Ed. HS course work accepted: No
Specific course requirements of all applicants: Yes
Separate application required: Yes
# of LD applications submitted each year: 40–60
# of LD applications accepted yearly: 14–17
Total # of students receiving LD services: 50–55
Acceptance into program means acceptance into college: Students are admitted to the college seperate from the program.

ADMISSIONS

There is a special application and admissions procedure for students with learning disabilities. Students submit a completed Westminster College application form and a separate application form for the LD program; results of an eye and hearing exam, WAIS, WJ-III, and achievement tests; SAT scores of 900-plus or ACT scores of 19-plus; two copies of their high school transcript; recent reports from school counselors, learning specialists, psychologists, or physicians who have diagnosed the disability; four recommendations from counselors or teachers familiar with their performance; and an evaluation from an educational specialist. An on-campus interview is required. Following the interview and a review of the file, the Professional Academic Staff confer and reach an admission decision usually within 1 week after the visit. Students are admitted directly into the college and then reviewed for LD services.

ADDITIONAL INFORMATION

Students are mainstreamed and need a solid college-prep background in high school. There is a fee of $4,800 for the first year of the program and $2,800 each year thereafter. Students have access to unlimited tutoring. Learning resources include audio tapes of textbooks; self-instructional materials; special classes in study, reading, and listening skills; test-taking, time management, and English composition strategies; and word processors to assist in writing instruction. There is also the Academic Resource Center, which is a learning center that is open to all students.

PROGRAM FOR DISABILITY SERVICES

Contact Information
Name of program or department: Learning Opportunity Center
  Telephone: 573-592-5304
  Fax: 573-592-5995

LEARNING DISABILITY SERVICES

Accommodations are decided upon an individual basis after a thorough review of appropriate, current documentation. The accommodations requested must be supported through the documentation provided and must be logically linked to the current impact of the condition on academic functioning.

Allowed in exams	**Distraction-reduced environment:** Yes	**Added costs for services:** Yes
Calculator: Yes	**Tape recording in class:** Yes	**LD specialists:** Yes
Dictionary: No	**Electronic texts:** Yes	**Professional tutors:** 3.5
Computer: Yes	**Accommodations for students with**	**Peer tutors:** 45
Spellchecker: Yes	**ADHD:** Yes	**Max. hours/wk. for services:** 6–8
Extended test time: Yes	**Kurzweil Reader:** Yes (but limited)	**How professors are notified of**
Scribes: Yes	**Other assistive technology:** NR	**LD/ADHD:** Both student and director
Proctors: Yes	**Priority registration:** No	
Oral exams: Yes		
Note-takers: Yes		

GENERAL ADMISSIONS INFORMATION

Office of Admission: 800-475-3361

ENTRANCE REQUIREMENTS
Academic units required: 4 English, 3 mathematics, 2 science, (2 science labs). **Academic units recommended:** 2 foreign language, 2 social studies, 2 academic electives. High school diploma is required and GED is accepted. SAT or ACT required; TOEFL required of all international applicants; minimum paper TOEFL 550, minimum computer TOEFL 213.

Application deadline: None	**SAT Math middle 50% range:**	**Graduated top 10% of class:** 22%
Notification: Rolling	500–620	**Graduated top 25% of class:** 50%
Average GPA: 3.44	**SAT Critical Reading middle 50%**	**Graduated top 50% of class:** 85%
ACT Composite middle 50% range:	range: 480–610	
23–27	**SAT Writing middle 50% range:**	
	470–610	

COLLEGE GRADUATION REQUIREMENTS

Course waivers allowed: No
Course substitutions allowed: Yes
In what course: Students can petition the academic dean for substitute courses in any area.

ADDITIONAL INFORMATION

Environment: The 250-acre college campus is located in a small town 20 miles east of Columbia, Missouri.

Student Body	**Cost Information**	**Greek System**
Undergrad enrollment: 1,180	**Tuition:** $19,750	**Fraternity:** Yes
Women: 44%	**Room and board:** $7,990	**Sorority:** Yes
Men: 56%	**Housing Information**	**Athletics:** Division III
Percent out-of-state: 37%	**University housing:** Yes	
	Percent living on campus: 84%	

MONTANA STATE U.—BILLINGS

1500 University Drive, Billings, MT 59101
Phone: 406-657-2158 • Fax: 406-657-2051
E-mail: cjohannes@msubillings.edu • Web: www.msubillings.edu
Support: S • Institution type: 4-year public

PROGRAMS OR SERVICES FOR STUDENTS WITH LD

The DSS mission statement is: Disability Support Services assists in creating an accessible university community where students with documented disabilities have an equal opportunity to fully participate in all aspects of the educational environment. We coordinate the provision of reasonable accommodations, advocate for an accessible and amenable learning environment, and promote self-determination for the students we serve.

ADMISSION INFORMATION FOR STUDENTS WITH LD/ADHD

College entrance tests required: Yes
Interview required: No
Essay recommended: No
What documentation required for LD: Psycho Ed evaluation to include: relevant historical info, instructional interventions, related services, age diagnosed, objective data (aptitude, achievement, info processing), test scores (standard, percentile and grade equivalents) and describe functional limitations.
With general application: No
To receive services after enrolling: Yes
What documentation required for ADHD: Diagnosis based on DSM-V; history of behaviors impairing functioning in academic setting; diagnostic interview; history of symptoms; evidence of ongoing behaviors.

With general application: No
Submitted to: Disability Support Services
Special Ed. HS course work accepted: Yes
Specific course requirements of all applicants: Yes
Separate application required: No
# of LD applications submitted each year: NR
# of LD applications accepted yearly: NR
Total # of students receiving LD services: NR
Acceptance into program means acceptance into college: Students must be admitted to and enrolled in the university first and then request services.

ADMISSIONS
There is no special admission process for students with learning disabilities. All students must meet the same admission criteria. Freshmen applicants must meet one of the following conditions: ACT of 22 or SAT of 920, a 2.5 GPA; or rank in the top half of the class. Students must have 4 years of English, 3 years of math (students are encouraged to take math in their senior year), 3 years of social studies, 2 years of science lab (1 year must be earth science, biology, chemistry, or physics), and 2 years chosen from foreign language, computer science, visual/performing arts, and/or vocational education that meet the Office of Public Instruction guidelines. Students not meeting the college-preparatory requirements have four options: They can (1) apply for an exemption by writing a letter and addressing their special needs, talents, or other reasons; (2) enroll part-time in a summer session; (3) enroll as a part-time student with seven or fewer credits the first semester; or (4) attend a community college or other college and attempt at least 12 credits or make up any deficiency.

ADDITIONAL INFORMATION
Students must request services, provide documentation specifying a learning disability or ADHD, make an appointment for an intake with DSS, meet with professors at the beginning of each semester, and work closely with DSS. DSS must keep documentation and intake on file, make a determination of accommodations, issue identification cards to qualified students, and serve as a resource and a support system. Services include course and testing accommodations, alternative testing, priority scheduling, technical assistance, liaison and referral services, taped textbooks, and career, academic, and counseling referrals. The use of a computer, calculator, dictionary, or spellchecker is at the discretion of the individual professor and based on the documented needs of the student. Services and accommodations are available for undergraduate and graduate students.

LEARNING DISABILITY PROGRAMS OR SERVICES

Contact Information
Name of program or department: Disability Support Services (DSS)
  Telephone: 406-657-2283
  Fax: 406-657-2187

LEARNING DISABILITY SERVICES

Accommodations are decided upon an individual basis after a thorough review of appropriate, current documentation. The accommodations requested must be supported through the documentation provided and must be logically linked to the current impact of the condition on academic functioning.

Allowed in exams
  Calculator: Yes
  Dictionary: No
  Computer: Yes
  Spellchecker: Yes
Extended test time: Yes
Scribes: Yes
Proctors: Yes
Oral exams: No
Note-takers: Yes

Distraction-reduced environment: Yes
Tape recording in class: Yes
Electronic texts: Yes
Accommodations for students with
  ADHD: Yes
Kurzweil Reader: Yes
Other assistive technology: Yes
Priority registration: Yes

Added costs for services: No
LD specialists: No
Professional tutors: 1
Peer tutors: 10–20
Max. hours/wk. for services:
  Unlimited
How professors are notified of
  LD/ADHD: By student

GENERAL ADMISSIONS INFORMATION

Office of Admission: 406-657-2880

ENTRANCE REQUIREMENTS

Academic units required: 4 English, 3 math, 2 science (2 science labs), 3 social studies, 2 foreign language, visual/performing arts, or computer science. High school diploma is required, and GED is accepted. ACT without Writing component accepted. TOEFL required of all international applicants: minimum paper TOEFL 500, minimum computer TOEFL 173.

Application deadline: None
Notification: Rolling
Average GPA: 3.10
ACT Composite middle 50% range:
  19–24

SAT Math middle 50% range:
  470–560
SAT Critical Reading middle 50%
  range: 430–570
SAT Writing middle 50% range: NR

Graduated top 10% of class: 8%
Graduated top 25% of class: 25%
Graduated top 50% of class: 63%

COLLEGE GRADUATION REQUIREMENTS

Course waivers allowed: Yes
In what course: In foreign language and math under strict guidelines
Course substitutions allowed: Yes
In what course: In foreign language and math under strict guidelines

ADDITIONAL INFORMATION

Environment: The campus is in an urban area in Billings, Montana.

Student Body
  Undergrad enrollment: 4,789
  Women: 64%
  Men: 36%
  Percent out-of-state: 8%

Cost Information
  In-state tuition: $5,206
  Out-of-state tuition: $14,647
  Room & board: $5,620
Housing Information
  University housing: Yes
  Percent living on campus: 11%

Greek System
  Fraternity: No
  Sorority: No
Athletics: Division II

MONTANA TECH OF THE U. OF MT

1300 West Park Street, Butte, MT 59701
Phone: 406-496-4178 • Fax: 406-496-4710
E-mail: admissions@mtech.edu • Web: www.mtech.edu
Support: CS • Institution type: 4-year public

PROGRAMS OR SERVICES FOR STUDENTS WITH LD

All persons with disabilities have the right to participate fully and equally in the programs and services of Montana Tech. Tech is committed to making the appropriate accommodations. Montana Tech's student life counselors are resources for students with disabilities. The counselors are a general resource for all students who may need assistance. Availability of services from Disability Services is subject to a student's eligibility for these and any other services. Students must provide appropriate and current documentation prior to requesting and receiving services or accommodations. All faculty and staff at the college are responsible for assuring access by providing reasonable accommodations. The Montana Tech Learning Center offers a variety of services to help students achieve their full academic potential. Tutors are available to help all students with course work in an assortment of subject areas. The Learning Center addresses the importance of developing basic college success skills.

ADMISSION INFORMATION FOR STUDENTS WITH LD/ADHD

College entrance tests required: Yes
Interview required: No
Essay recommended: No
What documentation required for LD: Psycho Ed evaluation to include: relevant historical info, instructional interventions, related services, age diagnosed, objective data (aptitude, achievement, info processing), test scores (standard, percentile and grade equivalents) and describe functional limitations.
With general application: No
To receive services after enrolling: Yes
What documentation required for ADHD: Diagnosis based on DSM-V; history of behaviors impairing functioning in academic setting; diagnostic interview; history of symptoms; evidence of ongoing behaviors.

With general application: No
Submitted to: Disability Services
Special Ed. HS course work accepted: No
Specific course requirements of all applicants: Yes
Separate application required: No
# of LD applications submitted each year: NR
# of LD applications accepted yearly: NR
Total # of students receiving LD services: NR
Acceptance into program means acceptance into college: Students must be admitted to and enrolled in the university first and then request services.

ADMISSIONS

There is no special admission process for students with LD or ADHD. Applicants must have a 22 ACT or 1540 SAT Reasoning, or be in the upper 50 percent of their high school class, or have a 2.5 GPA. The GED is accepted. Students must have 14 academic high school credits, including 4 years of English, 2 years of science, 3 years of math, 3 years of social studies, and 2 years from other academic areas, including foreign language, computer science, visual/performing arts, and vocational education. Interviews are not required, and special education courses in high school are not accepted. Students who do not meet any of the general admission criteria may ask to be evaluated considering other factors. Students with LD/ADHD are encouraged to self-disclose in the admissions process.

ADDITIONAL INFORMATION

The following types of services are offered to students with disabilities: responses to requests for accommodation, assistance in working with faculty members, text accommodation in concert with instructors, access to assistive technology, note-taking, and career services. Documentation to receive services should be sent directly to Disability Services. Montana Tech offers compensatory classes for students with LD in both math and English. Services and accommodations are available for undergraduate and graduate students.

LEARNING DISABILITY PROGRAMS OR SERVICES

Contact Information
Name of program or department: Disability Services
  Telephone: 406-496-4129
  Fax: 406-496-4757

LEARNING DISABILITY SERVICES

Accommodations are decided upon an individual basis after a thorough review of appropriate, current documentation. The accommodations requested must be supported through the documentation provided and must be logically linked to the current impact of the condition on academic functioning.

Allowed in exams
  Calculator: Yes
  Dictionary: NR
  Computer: Yes
  Spellchecker: Yes
Extended test time: Yes
Scribes: Yes
Proctors: Yes
Oral exams: Yes
Note-takers: Yes

Distraction-reduced environment: Yes
Tape recording in class: Yes
Electronic texts: Yes
Accommodations for students with ADHD: Yes
Kurzweil Reader: Yes
Other assistive technology: Yes
Priority registration: Yes

Added costs for services: No
LD specialists: Yes
Professional tutors: NR
Peer tutors: 0–12
Max. hours/wk. for services: Unlimited
How professors are notified of LD/ADHD: By both student and counselors

GENERAL ADMISSIONS INFORMATION

Office of Admission: 406-469-4632

ENTRANCE REQUIREMENTS
Academic units required: 4 English, 3 math, 2 science (2 science labs), 3 social studies, 2 years combined of a foreign language, visual/performing arts, computer science, or vocational education units. **Academic units recommended:** 4 English, 4 math, 4 science (2 science labs), 2 foreign language. High school diploma is required, and GED is accepted. ACT with Writing component required. TOEFL required of all international applicants: minimum paper TOEFL 525, minimum computer TOEFL 195.

Application deadline: None
Notification: Rolling
Average GPA: 3.20
ACT Composite middle 50% range: 22–27

SAT Math middle 50% range: 500–630
SAT Critical Reading middle 50% range: 480–590
SAT Writing middle 50% range: 450–580

Graduated top 10% of class: 22%
Graduated top 25% of class: 47%
Graduated top 50% of class: 79%

COLLEGE GRADUATION REQUIREMENTS

Course waivers allowed: No
Course substitutions allowed: No

ADDITIONAL INFORMATION

Environment: The campus is located 65 miles from Helena.

Student Body
  Undergrad enrollment: 2,651
  Women: 41%
  Men: 59%
  Percent out-of-state: 13%

Cost Information
  In-state tuition: $6,175
  Out-of-state tuition: $17,269
  Room & board: $7,266
Housing Information
  University housing: Yes
  Percent living on campus: 11%

Greek System
  Fraternity: No
  Sorority: No
  Athletics: NAIA

ROCKY MOUNTAIN COLLEGE

1511 Poly Drive, Billings, MT 59102-1796
Phone: 406-657-1128 • Fax: 406-657-1189
E-mail: admissions@rocky.edu • Web: www.rocky.edu
Support: CS • Institution type: 4-year private

PROGRAMS OR SERVICES FOR STUDENTS WITH LD

Rocky Mountain College is committed to providing courses, programs, and services for students with disabilities. Services for Academic Success (SAS) provides a comprehensive support program for students with LD. To be eligible, participants must meet one of the primary criteria: come from a low-income family, be a first-generation college student, or have a physical or learning disability. Participants must also be U.S. citizens and have an academic need for the program. Students are responsible for identifying themselves, providing appropriate documentation, and requesting reasonable accommodations. The program tailors services to meet the needs of the individuals. SAS welcomes applications from students who are committed to learning and who are excited about meeting the challenges of college with the support provided by the SAS staff. The SAS program is supported by a grant from the U.S. Department of Education and funds from Rocky Mountain College. The small size of the college, together with the caring attitude of the faculty and an excellent support program, make Rocky a learning disability-friendly college.

ADMISSION INFORMATION FOR STUDENTS WITH LD/ADHD

College entrance tests required: Yes
Interview required: No
Essay recommended: No
What documentation required for LD: Psycho Ed evaluation to include: relevant historical info, instructional interventions, related services, age diagnosed, objective data (aptitude, achievement, info processing), test scores (standard, percentile and grade equivalents) and describe functional limitations.
With general application: No
To receive services after enrolling: Yes
What documentation required for ADHD: Diagnosis based on DSM-V; history of behaviors impairing functioning in academic setting; diagnostic interview; history of symptoms; evidence of ongoing behaviors.

With general application: No
Submitted to: Services for Academic Success
Special Ed. HS course work accepted: No
Specific course requirements of all applicants: Yes
Separate application required: Yes
# of LD applications submitted each year: 10–20
# of LD applications accepted yearly: 10–20
Total # of students receiving LD services: 30–40
Acceptance into program means acceptance into college: Students must be admitted to and enrolled in the university first and then request services.

ADMISSIONS

There is no special admissions application for students with learning disabilities. All applicants must meet the same criteria, which include an ACT of 21 or SAT of 1000, a GPA of 2.5, and courses in English, math, science, and social studies. There is the opportunity to be considered for a conditional admission if scores or grades are below the cutoffs. To identify and provide necessary support services as soon as possible, students with disabilities are encouraged to complete a Services for Academic Success application when they are accepted. Recommended courses for admissions include 4 years of English, 3 years of math, 3 years of social science, 2 years of science lab, and 2 years of a foreign language.

ADDITIONAL INFORMATION

SAS provides a variety of services tailored to meet a student's individual needs. Services are free to participants and include developmental course work in reading, writing, and mathematics, study skills classes, tutoring in all subjects, academic, career, and personal counseling, graduate school counseling, accommodations for students with learning disabilities, alternative testing arrangements, taping of lectures or textbooks, cultural and academic enrichment opportunities, and advocacy. SAS staff meets with each student to talk about the supportive services the student needs and then develop a semester plan. Skills classes for college credit are offered in math, English, and studying techniques.

LEARNING DISABILITY PROGRAMS OR SERVICES

Contact Information
Name of program or department: Services for Academic Success (SAS)
  Telephone: 406-657-1128
  Fax: 406-259-9751

LEARNING DISABILITY SERVICES

Accommodations are decided upon an individual basis after a thorough review of appropriate, current documentation. The accommodations requested must be supported through the documentation provided and must be logically linked to the current impact of the condition on academic functioning.

Allowed in exams
  Calculator: Yes
  Dictionary: Yes
  Computer: Yes
  Spellchecker: Yes
Extended test time: Yes
Scribes: Yes
Proctors: Yes
Oral exams: Yes
Note-takers: Yes

Distraction-reduced environment: Yes
Tape recording in class: Yes
Electronic texts: Yes
Accommodations for students with
  ADHD: Yes
Kurzweil Reader: No
Other assistive technology: Yes
Priority registration: No

Added costs for services: No
LD specialists: Yes
Professional tutors: 2
Peer tutors: 30
Max. hours/wk. for services:
  Unlimited
How professors are notified of
  LD/ADHD: By both student and director

GENERAL ADMISSIONS INFORMATION

Office of Admission: 406-657-1026

ENTRANCE REQUIREMENTS

Academic units required: 4 English, 2 math, 2 science (1 science lab), 1 foreign language, 2 social studies, 2 history. **Academic units recommended:** 4 English, 3 math, 2 science (2 science lab), 2 foreign language, 2 social studies, 2 history. High school diploma is required, and GED is accepted. ACT with Writing component required. TOEFL required of all international applicants: minimum paper TOEFL 525, minimum computer TOEFL 197.

Application deadline: None
Notification: Rolling
Average GPA: 3.34
ACT Composite middle 50% range:
  19–24

SAT Math middle 50% range:
  450–570
SAT Critical Reading middle 50%
  range: 460–590
SAT Writing middle 50% range: NR

Graduated top 10% of class: 21%
Graduated top 25% of class: 43%
Graduated top 50% of class: 78%

COLLEGE GRADUATION REQUIREMENTS

Course waivers allowed: No
Course substitutions allowed: Yes

ADDITIONAL INFORMATION

Environment: The campus is located in a small town over 500 miles north of Denver, Colorado.

Student Body
  Undergrad enrollment: 936
  Women: 52%
  Men: 48%
  Percent out-of-state: 42%

Cost Information
  Tuition: $21,684
  Room & board: $6,595
Housing Information
  University housing: Yes
  Percent living on campus: 51%

Greek System
  Fraternity: No
  Sorority: No
  Athletics: NAIA

UNIVERSITY OF MONTANA

Lommasson Center 103, Missoula, MT 59812
Phone: 406-243-6266 • Fax: 406-243-5711
E-mail: admiss@umontana.edu • Web: www.umt.edu
Support: S • Institution type: 4-year public

PROGRAMS OR SERVICES FOR STUDENTS WITH LD

Disability Services for Students (DSS) ensures equal access to university students with disabilities. DSS is a stand-alone student affairs office at the university. It is staffed by more than ten full-time professionals. Students with learning disabilities have the same set of rights and responsibilities and the same set of services and reasonable program modifications, which are offered to other students with disabilities. Written documentation from a qualified diagnostician containing the diagnosis and functional limitations of the learning disability must be provided to DSS. However, the DSS office gives just as much weight to a student's self-report on how the disability impacts learning as the office does on a diagnostician's report. It should be noted that DSS does not operate in the same way that many special education programs in secondary schools do. At the university level, students have a right to access education, not a right to education. This means that DSS treats students as adults who either succeed or fail on their own merits. DSS assigns a coordinator to each student. The Coordinator and the student collaborate to address barriers in the university program that may deny or limit full and equal program access. Students are encouraged to secure their rights through the student-coordinator relationship.

ADMISSION INFORMATION FOR STUDENTS WITH LD/ADHD

College entrance tests required: Yes
Interview required: No
Essay recommended: No
Documentation required for LD: A current and comprehensive diagnostic report or comparable documentation
Documentation required for ADHD: A current and comprehensive diagnostic report or comparable documentation
Submitted to: Disability Services for Students

Special Ed. HS course work accepted: N/A
Specific course requirements of all applicants: Yes
Separate application required: Yes
# of LD applications submitted each year: NR
# of LD applications accepted yearly: NR
Total # of students receiving LD services: 1,300 (total number of students registered with DSS)
Acceptance into program means acceptance into college: Students must be admitted to and enrolled in the university first and then request services.

ADMISSIONS

Admissions criteria are the same for all applicants. However, consideration will be given to students who do not meet the general admissions criteria. General admission criteria include 22 on the ACT or 1540 on the SAT; ranking in the upper half of the class; and a 2.5 GPA, and successful completion of college prep program requirements. Disability Services will act as an advocate for students with learning disabilities during the admission process. Applicants not meeting admission criteria may request and receive a review of their eligibility by an Admissions Committee. Students should send documentation verifying the disability directly to the DSS office. The documentation should be written by a qualified professional and must include a diagnostic statement identifying the disability, a description of the diagnostic methodology, and the current functional limitations of the disability, the severity and longevity of the condition, and recommended modifications.

ADDITIONAL INFORMATION

Campus resources include academic and career advising, a study skill course, tutoring, math and writing centers, honors college, Student Fitness Center and outdoor programs, financial aid, housing, leadership development, diversity programs, health services including counseling, dental, and medical, and dietary and nutrition services.

LEARNING DISABILITY PROGRAMS OR SERVICES

Contact Information
Name of program or department: Disability Services for Students
 Telephone: 406-243-2243
 Fax: 406-243-5330

LEARNING DISABILITY SERVICES

Request for the following services/accommodations are evaluated individually based on appropriate and current documentation.

Allowed in exams
 Calculator: Yes
 Dictionary: Yes
 Computer: Yes
 Spellchecker: Yes
Extended test time: Yes
Scribes: Yes
Proctors: Yes
Oral exams: No
Note-takers: Yes

Distraction-reduced environment: Yes
Tape recording in class: Yes
Electronic texts: Yes
Accommodations for students with ADHD: Yes
Kurzweil Reader: Yes
Other assistive technology: Yes
Priority registration: Yes

Added costs for services: No
LD specialists: No
Professional tutors: Yes
Peer tutors: Yes
Max. hours/wk. for services: N/A
How professors are notified of LD/ADHD: By student

GENERAL ADMISSIONS INFORMATION

Office of Admission: 406-243-6266 or 800-462-8636

ENTRANCE REQUIREMENTS

Academic units required: 4 English, 3 math, 2 science (2 science labs), 3 social studies, 2 history, 2 academic electives, and choice of 2 units in foreign language, computer science, visual/performing arts, or vocational education. **Academic units recommended:** 2 foreign language. High school diploma is required, and GED is accepted. ACT with Writing component accepted. TOEFL required of all international applicants: minimum paper TOEFL 500, minimum computer TOEFL 173.

Application deadline: None
Notification: Rolling
Average GPA: 3.3
ACT Composite middle 50% range: 21–26

SAT Math middle 50% range: 480–600
SAT Critical Reading middle 50% range: 490–610
SAT Writing middle 50% range: 470–580

Graduated top 10% of class: 16%
Graduated top 25% of class: 39%
Graduated top 50% of class: 71%

COLLEGE GRADUATION REQUIREMENTS

Course waivers allowed: No
Course substitutions allowed: Yes
In what course: Determined case-by-case

ADDITIONAL INFORMATION

Environment: The university's urban campus is 200 miles from Spokane.

Student Body
 Undergrad enrollment: 15,641
 Women: 53%
 Men: 47%
 Percent out-of-state: 37%

Cost Information
 In-state tuition: $5,775
 Out-of-state tuition: $19,612
 Room & board: $7,500
Housing Information
 University housing: Yes
 Percent living on campus: 29%

Greek System
 Fraternity: Yes
 Sorority: Yes
Athletics: Division I

UNIVERSITY OF MONTANA—WESTERN

710 South Atlantic, Dillon, MT 59725
Phone: 406-683-7331 • Fax: 406-683-7493
E-mail: admissions@umwestern.edu • Web: www.umwestern.edu
Support: S • Institution type: 4-year public

PROGRAMS OR SERVICES FOR STUDENTS WITH LD

Western Montana College strives to accommodate all students with special needs. These needs may be physical, social, and/or academic. Almost all services are free to the student. The Associate Dean of Students is in charge of making special accommodations available to students with learning disabilities. If an applicant has a documented learning disability and requests special accommodations for a class, he or she must contact the Associate Dean of Students so that arrangements can be made. The professor of the class, the Associate Dean, and the student will meet to set up an IEP for that class, and documentation will be kept on file in the Student Life Office.

ADMISSION INFORMATION FOR STUDENTS WITH LD/ADHD

College entrance tests required: Yes
Interview required: No
Essay recommended: No
What documentation required for LD: Psycho Ed evaluation to include: relevant historical info, instructional interventions, related services, age diagnosed, objective data (aptitude, achievement, info processing), test scores (standard, percentile and grade equivalents) and describe functional limitations.
With general application: No
To receive services after enrolling: Yes
What documentation required for ADHD: Diagnosis based on DSM-V; history of behaviors impairing functioning in academic setting; diagnostic interview; history of symptoms; evidence of ongoing behaviors.

With general application: No
Submitted to: Disability Services
Special Ed. HS course work accepted: Yes
Specific course requirements of all applicants: Yes
Separate application required: No
# of LD applications submitted each year: NR
# of LD applications accepted yearly: NR
Total # of students receiving LD services: 21
Acceptance into program means acceptance into college: Students must be admitted to and enrolled in the university first and then request services.

ADMISSIONS

The college has no special requirements other than those outlined by the state Board of Regents: a valid high school diploma or GED. Criteria for general admission includes 4 years of English, 3 years of math, 3 years of science, 3 years of social studies, and 2 years from foreign language, computer science, visual/performing arts, or vocational education; a 2.5 GPA (minimum 2.0 for students with learning disabilities); a 20 ACT or 960 SAT; and ranking within the top 50 percent of the applicant's class. Students with documented learning disabilities may request waivers or substitutions in courses affected by the disability. Because Western Montana is a small university, each individual can set up an admissions plan. There is a 15 percent window of exemption for some students who do not meet admission requirements. These students can be admitted provisionally if they provide satisfactory evidence that they are prepared to pursue successfully the special courses required.

ADDITIONAL INFORMATION

Students who present appropriate documentation may be eligible for some of the following services or accommodations: the use of calculators, dictionaries, computers, or spellcheckers during tests; extended time on tests; distraction-free environments for tests; proctors; scribes; oral exams; note-takers; tape recorders in class; books on tape; and priority registration. The Learning Center offers skill-building classes in reading, writing, and math. These classes do not count toward a student's GPA, but they do for athletic eligibility. Students whose ACT or entrance tests show that they would profit from such instruction will be placed in courses that will best meet their needs and ensure a successful college career. Free tutoring is available in most areas on a drop-in basis and/or at prescribed times. Services and accommodations are available for undergraduate and graduate students.

LEARNING DISABILITY PROGRAMS OR SERVICES

Contact Information
Name of program or department: Disability Services
 Telephone: 406-683-7565
 Fax: 406-683-7570

LEARNING DISABILITY SERVICES

Accommodations are decided upon an individual basis after a thorough review of appropriate, current documentation. The accommodations requested must be supported through the documentation provided and must be logically linked to the current impact of the condition on academic functioning.

Allowed in exams
 Calculator: Yes
 Dictionary: Yes
 Computer: Yes
 Spellchecker: Yes
Extended test time: Yes
Scribes: Yes
Proctors: Yes
Oral exams: Yes
Note-takers: Yes

Distraction-reduced environment: Yes
Tape recording in class: Yes
Electronic texts: Yes
Accommodations for students with ADHD: Yes
Kurzweil Reader: No
Other assistive technology: No
Priority registration: Yes

Added costs for services: No
LD specialists: No
Professional tutors: 3
Peer tutors: 6
Max. hours/wk. for services: Unlimited
How professors are notified of LD/ADHD: By both student and director

GENERAL ADMISSIONS INFORMATION

Office of Admission: 406-683-7450

ENTRANCE REQUIREMENTS

Academic units required: 4 English, 3 math, 3 science (2 science labs), 3 social studies, 4 academic electives. High school diploma is required, and GED is accepted. ACT with Writing component required. TOEFL required of all international applicants: minimum paper TOEFL 500, minimum computer TOEFL 173.

Application deadline: None
Notification: Rolling
Average GPA: 2.99
ACT Composite middle 50% range: 16–21

SAT Math middle 50% range: 400–520
SAT Critical Reading middle 50% range: 390–500
SAT Writing middle 50% range: NR

Graduated top 10% of class: 5%
Graduated top 25% of class: 18%
Graduated top 50% of class: 49%

COLLEGE GRADUATION REQUIREMENTS

Course waivers allowed: Yes
In what course: General education courses
Course substitutions allowed: Yes
In what course: General education courses

ADDITIONAL INFORMATION

Environment: The college is located on 20 acres in a small town about 60 miles south of Butte, Montana.

Student Body
 Undergrad enrollment: 1,365
 Women: 55%
 Men: 45%
 Percent out-of-state: 27%

Cost Information
 In-state tuition: $3,945
 Out-of-state tuition: $13,778
 Room & board: $5,620
Housing Information
 University housing: Yes
 Percent living on campus: 30%

Greek System
 Fraternity: No
 Sorority: No
 Athletics: NAIA

UNION COLLEGE (NE)

3800 South Forty-eighth Street, Lincoln, NE 68506-4300
Phone: 402-486-2600 • Fax: 402-486-2895
E-mail: ucinfo@ucollege.edu • Web: www.ucollege.edu
Support: CS • Institution type: 4-year private

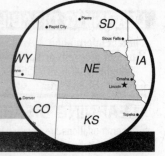

PROGRAMS OR SERVICES FOR STUDENTS WITH LD

The Teaching Learning Center (TLC) is a specialized program serving the Union College student with learning disabilities/dyslexia and has now expanded to serve all students with disabilities. The TLC offers assistance to the serious, capable student with learning disabilities who seeks to earn an undergraduate degree in a Christian environment. To qualify for accommodations, a student must have an IQ commensurate with college achievement; have a diagnosis based on current data, which will be reviewed by the TLC staff; complete admission procedures to Union College; take the ACT or SAT; apply to the TLC and provide needed information; and arrange for a 2-day visit to campus to complete diagnostic/prescriptive testing to determine needed accommodations and remediation. Students with LD in the program enroll in regular college classes, though a light load is initially recommended.

ADMISSION INFORMATION FOR STUDENTS WITH LD/ADHD

College entrance tests required: Yes
Interview required: No
Essay recommended: No
What documentation required for LD: Psycho Ed evaluation to include: relevant historical info, instructional interventions, related services, age diagnosed, objective data (aptitude, achievement, info processing), test scores (standard, percentile and grade equivalents) and describe functional limitations.
With general application: No
To receive services after enrolling: Yes
What documentation required for ADHD: Diagnosis based on DSM-V; history of behaviors impairing functioning in academic setting; diagnostic interview; history of symptoms; evidence of ongoing behaviors.

With general application: No
Submitted to: Teaching Learning Center
Special Ed. HS course work accepted: Yes
Specific course requirements of all applicants: Yes
Separate application required: Yes
# of LD applications submitted each year: 60–70
# of LD applications accepted yearly: NR
Total # of students receiving LD services: 80–90
Acceptance into program means acceptance into college: Students are admitted to the Teaching Learning Center program and the college jointly.

ADMISSIONS

There is no special admission process for students with LD. All applicants are expected to meet the same admission criteria, including 2.5 GPA, 18-plus on the ACT, and the course requirements listed on the following page. Students with course deficiencies can be admitted and make up the deficiencies in college. The staff from the Teaching Learning Center may review documentation from some applicants and provide a recommendation to Admissions regarding an admission decision. The final decision for admission into the program is made by the TLC. Applicants who do not meet the published admission requirements will be considered by the Admissions Committee, which may request further statements and other evidence indicating the likelihood of the applicant's success. If accepted by committee action, the applicant may be required to enroll in an appropriate fee-based program offered through the Teaching Learning Center (TLC).

ADDITIONAL INFORMATION

Accommodations may include texts on tape, oral testing, individual testing, extended time/alternate assignments, note-takers, remediation, academic tutoring (additional fee), counseling, instruction in word processing, and assistance with term papers. Skills classes for college credit are offered in reading, spelling, math, and writing. The Technology Resource Center for learning disabilities provides information on available technology such as: Audionotetaker (software program used to record lectures, type notes, upload powerpoint presentations), Language Master 600 (voice powered, hand-held dictionary, thesaurus, and word games), Calcu-Talk (scientific and financial talking calculator), plus laser printer, character recognition scanner, and two personal computers with screen filters. Software includes DragonNaturally Speaking (control computer by voice), Kurzweil (combines with scanner to convert written test to spoken word), and Inspiration (allows the visual person to organize thoughts in outline and cluster form).

LEARNING DISABILITY PROGRAMS OR SERVICES

Contact Information
Name of program or department: Teaching Learning Center (TLC)
  Telephone: 402.486.2506
  Fax: 402.486.2691

LEARNING DISABILITY SERVICES

Accommodations are decided upon an individual basis after a thorough review of appropriate, current documentation. The accommodations requested must be supported through the documentation provided and must be logically linked to the current impact of the condition on academic functioning.

Allowed in exams	**Distraction-reduced environment:** Yes	**Added costs for services:** Yes
Calculator: Yes	**Tape recording in class:** Yes	**LD specialists:** Yes
Dictionary: Yes	**Electronic texts:** Yes	**Professional tutors:** 3
Computer: Yes	**Accommodations for students with**	**Peer tutors:** 15–25
Spellchecker: Yes	**ADHD:** Yes	**Max. hours/wk. for services:** 5
Extended test time: Yes	**Kurzweil Reader:** Yes	**How professors are notified of**
Scribes: Yes	**Other assistive technology:** Yes	**LD/ADHD:** By both student and
Proctors: Yes	**Priority registration:** No	director
Oral exams: Yes		
Note-takers: Yes		

GENERAL ADMISSIONS INFORMATION

Office of Admission: 402-486-2051

ENTRANCE REQUIREMENTS

Academic units required: 3 English, 2 math, 2 science (1 science lab), 1 social studies, 2 history, 3 academic electives. **Academic units recommended:** 4 English, 3 math, 3 science, 2 social sciences. High school diploma is required, and GED is accepted. ACT with or without Writing component accepted. TOEFL required of all international applicants: minimum paper TOEFL 550, minimum internet-based TOEFL 80.

Application deadline: None	**SAT Math middle 50% range:** NR	**Graduated top 10% of class:** 17%
Notification: Rolling	**SAT Critical Reading middle 50%**	**Graduated top 25% of class:** 14%
Average GPA: NR	**range:** NR	**Graduated top 50% of class:** 57%
ACT Composite middle 50% range: 20–25	**SAT Writing middle 50% range:** NR	

COLLEGE GRADUATION REQUIREMENTS

Course waivers allowed: No
Course substitutions allowed: No

ADDITIONAL INFORMATION

Environment: The college has a suburban campus near Lincoln.

Student Body	**Cost Information**	**Greek System**
Undergrad enrollment: 838	**Tuition:** $18,990	**Fraternity:** No
Women: 57%	**Room & board:** $6,220	**Sorority:** No
Men: 43%	**Housing Information**	**Athletics:** Division III
Percent out-of-state: 86%	**University housing:** Yes	
	Percent living on campus: 58%	

UNIVERSITY OF NEBRASKA—LINCOLN

1410 Q Street, Lincoln, NE 68588-0256
Phone: 402-472-2023 • Fax: 402-472-0670
E-mail: admissions@unl.edu • Web: www.unl.edu
Support: S • Institution: 4-year public

PROGRAMS OR SERVICES FOR STUDENTS WITH LD

Services for Students with Disabilities (SSD) office provides special assistance to students with disabilities through individualized help and counseling. Because adjustment to college life and its academic demands is a new experience and there are special challenges confronting disabled students, SSD is committed to providing students with the support that will help them to reach their academic goals. SSD coordinates and delivers the services required to accommodate a disability. All accommodation requests are initiated at the SSD office with appropriate documentation.

ADMISSION INFORMATION FOR STUDENTS WITH LD/ADHD

College entrance tests required: Yes
Interview required: No
Essay required: N/A
What documentation required for LD: Psycho Ed evaluation to
 include: relevant historical info, instructional interventions,
 related services, age diagnosed, objective data (aptitude,
 achievement, info processing), test scores (standard, percentile
 and grade equivalents) and describe functional limitations.
With general application: No
To receive services after enrolling: Yes
What documentation required for ADHD: Diagnosis based
 on DSM-V; history of behaviors impairing functioning in
 academic setting; diagnostic interview; history of symptoms;
 evidence of ongoing behaviors.

With general application: No
Submitted to: Support Program/Services
Special Ed. HS course work accepted: N/A
Specific course requirements for all applicants: NR
Separate application required for program services: No
# of LD applications submitted each year: NR
# of LD applications accepted yearly: NR
Total # of students receiving LD services: NR
**Acceptance into program means acceptance into
 college:** Separate application required after student has
 enrolled

ADMISSIONS

All students applying for admission to UNL must meet the admission criterea. There is no special admission process for students with disabilities. The following is the current admission requirement: ACT composite score of 20 or higher, or an SAT total score (Critical Reading and Math only) of 950 or higher, or rank in the top half of graduating class along with meeting the following core requirements: 4 units of English (all units must include intensive reading & writing experiences), 4 units of math (algebra, algebra II & geometry are requred for student seeking admission, and one additional unit that builds on a knowledge of algebra), 3 units of social sciences (1 unit drawn from American and/or world history; 1 additional unit drawn from history, American government and/or geography; and a third unit drawn from any social science discipline), 3 units of natural sciences (At least 2 units selected from biology, chemistry, physics, and earth sciences. One of the above units must include laboratory instruction.), and 2 units of foreign language (both units must be in the same language). There is an appeal process for students with disabilities that are deferred admission.

ADDITIONAL INFORMATION

Accommodations are provided in an individualized manner for all students. Reasonable accommodations include: extended time on exams, a quiet distraction-reduced test environment, a reader, a scribe, an interpreter, Braille or large print exams, spelling assistance, the use of a computer or other adaptive equipment for exams, classroom notes, assistive notetaking device, transcriptionist in the classroom, and material in alternative formats which include Braille, and electronic texts. Other services provided include intercampus transportation coordination, priority registration, and assistance with advocacy.

Nebraska

PROGRAM FOR DISABILITY SERVICES

Contact Information
Name of program or department: Services for Students with Disabilities
  Telephone: 402-472-3787
  Fax: 402-472-0080

LEARNING DISABILITY SERVICES

The university has an obligation to confirm that students receiving services/accommodations have verified disabilities. Disability documentation is required to develop an accommodation plan/receive services..

Allowed in exams
  Calculator: Yes
  Dictionary: No
  Computer: Yes
  Spellchecker: Yes
Extended test time: Yes
Scribes: Yes
Proctors: Yes
Oral exams: Yes
Note-takers: Yes

Distraction-reduced environment: Yes
Tape recording in class: Yes
Electronic texts: Yes
Accommodations for students with ADHD: Yes
Kurzweil Reader: No
Other assistive technology: JAWS, Zoomtext, Optetec Reader, Dragon Naturally Speaking
Priority registration: Yes

Added costs for services: No
LD specialists: No
Professional tutors: No
Peer tutors: No
Max. hours/wk. for services: N/A
How professors are notified of LD/ADHD: SSD Office & Student

GENERAL ADMISSIONS INFORMATION

Office of Admission: 402-472-2023

ENTRANCE REQUIREMENTS
Academic units required: 4 English, 4 mathematics, 3 science, (1 science labs), 2 foreign language, 3 social studies.
Academic units recommended: High school diploma is required and GED is accepted. SAT or ACT required; TOEFL or IETS and UNL English placement exam required of all international applicants.

Application deadline: 5/1
Notification: Rolling
Average GPA: NR
ACT Composite middle 50% range: 22–28

SAT Math middle 50% range: NR
SAT Critical Reading middle 50% range: NR
SAT Writing middle 50% range: NR

Graduated top 10% of class: 27%
Graduated top 25% of class: 53%
Graduated top 50% of class: 83%

COLLEGE GRADUATION REQUIREMENTS

Course waivers allowed: No
Course substitutions allowed: Yes
In what course: Foreign Language

ADDITIONAL INFORMATION

Environment: The University of Nebraska is located in Lincoln, which is the capital and the second largest city in the state.

Student Body
  Undergrad enrollment: 24,640
  Women: 47%
  Men: 53%
  Percent out-of-state: 28%

Cost Information
  In-state tuition: $7,224
  Out-of-state tuition: $19,932
  Room & board: $8,648
Housing Information
  University housing: Yes
  Percent living on campus: 35%

Greek System
  Fraternity: Yes
  Sorority: Yes
Athletics: Division I

WAYNE STATE COLLEGE

1111 Main Street, Wayne, NE 68787
Phone: 402-375-7234 • Fax: 402-375-7204
E-mail: admit1@wsc.edu • Web: www.wsc.edu
Support: S • Institution: 4-year public

PROGRAMS OR SERVICES FOR STUDENTS WITH LD

At Wayne State College students with learning disabilities and ADHD are provided an individualized, cooperatively planned program of accommodations and services that are structured yet integrated within existing college services and programs. Accommodations are matched to the individual student's needs and are provided free of charge by the Counseling Center. In addition, WSC has a TRIO Student Support Services program known on campus as STRIDE. STRIDE (Students Taking Responsibility In Development and Education) is a program of student support services that includes individual attention, academic and personal support. STRIDE services help new students adjust more quickly and fully to college life. Students with disabilities are one of the populations eligible for STRIDE. STRIDE expects students to place a high priority on academic performance, invest the time and effort needed for college level learning, and take advantage of the services and programs available. Students with LD or ADD must complete a special application for STRIDE and submit written information, which verifies the disability diagnosis.

ADMISSION INFORMATION FOR STUDENTS WITH LD/ADHD

College entrance tests required: Yes
Interview required: No
Essay required: N/A
What documentation required for LD: Psycho Ed evaluation to include: relevant historical info, instructional interventions, related services, age diagnosed, objective data (aptitude, achievement, info processing), test scores (standard, percentile and grade equivalents) and describe functional limitations.
With general application: No
To receive services after enrolling: Yes
What documentation required for ADHD: Diagnosis based on DSM-V; history of behaviors impairing functioning in academic setting; diagnostic interview; history of symptoms; evidence of ongoing behaviors.

With general application: No
Submitted to: Support Program/Services
Special Ed. HS course work accepted: Yes
Specific course requirements for all applicants: NR
Separate application required for program services: No
# of LD applications submitted each year: NR
# of LD applications accepted yearly: NR
Total # of students receiving LD services: 25
Acceptance into program means acceptance into college: Students must be admitted to and enrolled in the university first and then request services.

ADMISSIONS
Admission to Wayne State College is open to all high school graduates or students with a GED or equivalent. The college recommends that students take four years of English, three years of math, three years of social studies, and two years of science. Foreign language is not an entrance or graduation requirement. High school special education courses are accepted.

ADDITIONAL INFORMATION
Through the STRIDE Program students have access to the following personal support services: a summer STRIDE pre-college experience, STRIDE peer mentor program, academic, and personal and career counseling; and academic support services including: academic advising and course selection guidance, a Succeeding in College course, one-on-one peer tutoring, writing skills, professional tutoring, individual study skills assistance in time management and organization, note-taking, study techniques and test taking strategies. The Counseling Center Office provides a cooperatively planned program of disability-related services and accommodations, which include: assistance in arranging accommodations, tape recorded textbooks and materials, and alternative exam arrangements.

PROGRAM FOR DISABILITY SERVICES

Contact Information
Name of program or department: Counseling Center
  Telephone: 402-375-7321
  Fax: 402-375-7058

LEARNING DISABILITY SERVICES

Accommodations are decided upon an individual basis after a thorough review of appropriate, current documentation. The accommodations requested must be supported through the documentation provided and must be logically linked to the current impact of the condition on academic functioning.

Allowed in exams
  Calculator: Yes
  Dictionary: Yes
  Computer: Yes
  Spellchecker: Yes
Extended test time: Yes
Scribes: Yes
Proctors: Yes
Oral exams: Yes
Note-takers: Yes

Distraction-reduced environment: Yes
Tape recording in class: Yes
Electronic texts: Yes
Accommodations for students with ADHD: Yes
Kurzweil Reader: Yes
Other assistive technology: Kurzweil Program
Priority registration: Yes

Added costs for services: No
LD specialists: No
Professional tutors: No
Peer tutors: 35
Max. hours/wk. for services: Unlimited
How professors are notified of LD/ADHD: Student

GENERAL ADMISSIONS INFORMATION

Office of Admission: 402 375-7234

ENTRANCE REQUIREMENTS

Academic units recommended: 4 English, 3 mathematics, 2 science, 2 foreign language, 3 social studies, 2 visual/performing arts, 2 computer science. High school diploma is required and GED is accepted. TOEFL required of all international applicants; minimum paper TOEFL 550, minimum computer TOEFL 213.

Application deadline: 8/20
Notification: Rolling
Average GPA: 3.24
ACT Composite middle 50% range: 18–24

SAT Math middle 50% range: NR
SAT Critical Reading middle 50% range: NR
SAT Writing middle 50% range: NR

Graduated top 10% of class: 11%
Graduated top 25% of class: 32%
Graduated top 50% of class: 62%

COLLEGE GRADUATION REQUIREMENTS

Course waivers allowed: No
In what course: No foreign language requirement.
Course substitutions allowed: No
In what course:

ADDITIONAL INFORMATION

Environment: The college is located in a rural area 45 miles southwest of Sioux City, Iowa.

Student Body
  Undergrad enrollment: 2,994
  Women: 54%
  Men: 46%
  Percent out-of-state: 14%

Cost Information
  In-state tuition: $4,057
  Out-of-state tuition: $8,115
  Room & board: $5,740
Housing Information
  University housing: Yes
  Percent living on campus: 46%

Greek System
  Fraternity: Yes
  Sorority: Yes
Athletics: Division II

UNIVERSITY OF NEVADA—LAS VEGAS

4505 Maryland Parkway, Box 451021, Las Vegas, NV 89154-1021
Phone: 702-774-8658 • Fax: 702-774-8008
E-mail: Undergraduate.Recruitment@ccmail.nevada.edu
Web: www.unlv.edu • Support: CS • Institution: 4-year public

PROGRAMS OR SERVICES FOR STUDENTS WITH LD

The Disability Resource Center (DRC) provides academic accommodations for students with documented disabilities who are otherwise qualified for university programs. Compliance with Section 504 requires that reasonable academic accommodations be made for students with disabilities. These accommodations might include note-taking, testing accommodations, books on tape, readers, assistive technology, housing adjustments and dietary adjustments. To establish services, students will need to provide DRC with appropriate documentation of their disability. Appropriate accommodations will be determined after both a review of the reporting student's documentation of a disability as well as a discussion with that student to clarify his or her disability related needs.

ADMISSION INFORMATION FOR STUDENTS WITH LD/ADHD

College entrance tests required: No
Interview required: No
Essay required: N/A
Documentation required for LD: Pyscho-educational
   evaluation (no more than three years old or done as an adult)
Documentation required for ADHD: Same as above.
Submitted to: Support Program/Services
Special Ed. HS course work accepted: No
Specific course requirements for all applicants: Yes

Separate application required for program services: No
# of LD applications submitted each year: NR
# of LD applications accepted yearly: NR
Total # of students receiving LD services: 96 LD; 76 ADHD
Acceptance into program means acceptance into
   college: Any student attending classes at UNLV who has a
   documented disability may apply for accommodations
   through the Learning Enhancement Services.

ADMISSIONS

All applicants are expected to meet the same admission criteria.. Freshmen applicants should have a weighted 3.0 grade point average (GPA) in the following high school academic courses: 4 years English, 3 years math, 3 years social science, and 3 years natural science with a total of 13 unites. If a student has completed the 13 core high school courses but does not have a 3.0 GPA the student may fulfill any of the following admission requirements to be admissible to UNLV: Have a combined score from the SAT Critical Reading and Math sections of at least 1040, or an ACT composite score of at least 22, or a Nevada Advanced High School Diploma. If the applicant does not satisfy the minimum admission requirements the student may still be eligible for admission.

ADDITIONAL INFORMATION

The Disability Resource Center offers help to all students on campus who have a diagnosed disability. Following their evaluation students meet with DRC specialists to develop a plan for services. Psychological services are available through the Counseling and Psychological Services Office. Assistance is provided year round to active students. Students remain active by requesting service each semester. Services are available to undergraduate, graduate, and continuing education students.

PROGRAM FOR DISABILITY SERVICES

Contact Information
Name of program or department: Disability Resource Center (DRC)
  Telephone: 702-895-0866
  Fax: 702-895-0651

LEARNING DISABILITY SERVICES

Accommodations are decided upon an individual basis after a thorough review of appropriate, current documentation. The accommodations requested must be supported through the documentation provided and must be logically linked to the current impact of the condition on academic functioning.

Allowed in exams
 Calculator: Yes
 Dictionary: Yes
 Computer: Yes
 Spellchecker: Yes
Extended test time: Yes
Scribes: Yes
Proctors: Yes
Oral exams: Yes
Note-takers: Yes

Distraction-reduced environment: Yes
Tape recording in class: Yes
Electronic texts: Yes
Accommodations for students with ADHD: Yes
Kurzweil Reader: Yes
Other assistive technology: Yes
Priority registration: Yes

Added costs for services: No
LD specialists: Yes
Professional tutors: No
Peer tutors: No
Max. hours/wk. for services: N/A
How professors are notified of LD/ADHD: Student

GENERAL ADMISSIONS INFORMATION

Office of Admission: 702-774-8658

ENTRANCE REQUIREMENTS
Academic units required: 4 English, 3 mathematics, 3 science, (2 science labs), 3 social studies. **Academic units recommended:** 4 English, 3 mathematics, 3 science, (2 science labs), 3 social studies. High school diploma is required and GED is accepted. SAT or ACT recommended; TOEFL required of all international applicants; minimum paper TOEFL 500.

Application deadline: None
Notification: Rolling
Average GPA: NR
ACT Composite middle 50% range: NR

SAT Math middle 50% range: NR
SAT Critical Reading middle 50% range: NR
SAT Writing middle 50% range: NR

Graduated top 10% of class: NR
Graduated top 25% of class: NR
Graduated top 50% of class: NR

COLLEGE GRADUATION REQUIREMENTS

Course waivers allowed: No
Course substitutions allowed: Yes
In what course: Foreign language is only required for English majors; substitutions are available. Math is required for graduation. All requests go to Academic Standards Committee after initial approval from the College Advisor, Chair of the Department, and Dean.

ADDITIONAL INFORMATION
Environment: The university is located on 355 acres in an urban area minutes from downtown Las Vegas.

Student Body
 Undergrad enrollment: 29,069
 Women: 55%
 Men: 45%
 Percent out-of-state: 18%

Cost Information
 In-state tuition: $5,645
 Out-of-state tuition: $18,255
 Room & board: $10,456
Housing Information
 University housing: Yes
 Percent living on campus: 7%

Greek System
 Fraternity: Yes
 Sorority: Yes
Athletics: Division I

UNIVERSITY OF NEVADA—RENO

Mail Stop 120, Reno, NV 89557
Phone: 775-784-4700 • Fax: 775-784-4283
E-mail: asknevada@unr.edu • Web: www.unr.edu
Support: CS • Institution type: 4-year public

PROGRAMS OR SERVICES FOR STUDENTS WITH LD

The Disability Resource Center was created to meet the unique educational needs of students with disabilities. The purpose of the DRC is to ensure that students with disabilities have equal access to participate in, contribute to, and benefit from all university programs. Their goal is to act as a catalyst for elimination of barriers and increase awareness of students with disabilities attending the university. The DRC staff is available to provide students with sensitive and individualized assistance at the student's request. Students who wish to request academic accommodations must provide the DRC with documentation of a verified disability. Appropriate services are determined and provided based on the student's specific disability and the academic requirements of the appropriate department.

ADMISSION INFORMATION FOR STUDENTS WITH LD/ADHD

College entrance tests required: No
Interview required: No
Essay recommended: No
What documentation required for LD: Psycho Ed evaluation to include: relevant historical info, instructional interventions, related services, age diagnosed, objective data (aptitude, achievement, info processing), test scores (standard, percentile and grade equivalents) and describe functional limitations.
With general application: No
To receive services after enrolling: Yes
What documentation required for ADHD: Diagnosis based on DSM-V; history of behaviors impairing functioning in academic setting; diagnostic interview; history of symptoms; evidence of ongoing behaviors.

With general application: No
Submitted to: Disability Resource Center
Special Ed. HS course work accepted: No
Specific course requirements of all applicants: Yes
Separate application required: Yes
# of LD applications submitted each year: NR
# of LD applications accepted yearly: NR
Total # of students receiving LD services: NR
Acceptance into program means acceptance into college: Students must be admitted to and enrolled in the university first and then request services.

ADMISSIONS

There is no special admission process for students with LD or attention deficit hyperactivity disorder. However, students with LD/ADHD are encouraged to self-disclose if they do not meet general admission requirements and to provide documentation. Admissions will consult with the DRC director during the admission process. General admission criteria include a 3.0 GPA, SAT 1040, or ACT 22; 4 years of English, 3 years of math, 3 years of social studies, 3 years of natural science. Students may appeal to use a substitute course for one of the required courses for admission.

ADDITIONAL INFORMATION

DRC provides accommodations and services tailored to the individual needs of each student. When appropriate, reasonable accommodations can include the following: electronic textbooks, note-taking services; alternative testing accommodations, proctors, and scribes; adaptive computer equipment access; accommodations counseling; registration assistance; faculty liaisons; learning strategies instruction; course substitutions; Math 019/119 (a two-semester course equivalent to Math 120); referrals to campus and community services; and other appropriate services as necessary. There is also a Writing Center, tutorial program, Math Lab, Counseling Center.

LEARNING DISABILITY PROGRAMS OR SERVICES

Contact Information
Name of program or department: Disability Resource Center
  Telephone: 775-784-6000
  Fax: 775-784-6955

LEARNING DISABILITY SERVICES

Accommodations are decided upon an individual basis after a thorough review of appropriate, current documentation. The accommodations requested must be supported through the documentation provided and must be logically linked to the current impact of the condition on academic functioning.

Allowed in exams	**Distraction-reduced environment:** Yes	**Added costs for services:** No
Calculator: Yes	**Tape recording in class:** Yes	**LD specialists:** Yes
Dictionary: Yes	**Electronic texts:** Yes	**Professional tutors:** No
Computer: Yes	**Accommodations for students with**	**Peer tutors:** 50
Spellchecker: Yes	**ADHD:** Yes	**Max. hours/wk. for services:** NR
Extended test time: Yes	**Kurzweil Reader:** Yes	**How professors are notified of**
Scribes: Yes	**Other assistive technology:** Yes	**LD/ADHD:** By student
Proctors: Yes	**Priority registration:** No	
Oral exams: Yes		
Note-takers: Yes		

GENERAL ADMISSIONS INFORMATION

Office of Admission: 775-784-4700

ENTRANCE REQUIREMENTS

Academic units required: 4 English, 3 math, 3 science (2 science labs), 3 social studies. High school diploma is required, and GED is not accepted.

Application deadline: 6/1	**SAT Math middle 50% range:**	**Graduated top 10% of class:** NR
Notification: Rolling	470–590	**Graduated top 25% of class:** NR
Average GPA: 3.36	**SAT Critical Reading middle 50%**	**Graduated top 50% of class:** NR
ACT Composite middle 50% range:	**range:** 460–580	
20–25	**SAT Writing middle 50% range:**	
	470–570	

COLLEGE GRADUATION REQUIREMENTS

Course waivers allowed: No
Course substitutions allowed: Yes
In what course: Foreign language (depending on declared major)

ADDITIONAL INFORMATION

Environment: In an urban area 200 miles east of San Francisco

Student Body	**Cost Information**	**Greek System**
Undergrad enrollment: 17,000	**In-state tuition:** $4,841	**Fraternity:** Yes
Women: 53%	**Out-of-state tuition:** $19,155	**Sorority:** Yes
Men: 47%	**Room & board:** $9,765	**Athletics:** Division I
Percent out-of-state: 15%	**Housing Information**	
	University housing: Yes	
	Percent living on campus: 14%	

COLBY-SAWYER COLLEGE

541 Main Street, New London, NH 03257-7835
Phone: 603-526-3700 • Fax: 603-526-3452
E-mail: admissions@colby-sawyer.edu • Web: www.colby-sawyer.edu
Support: CS • Institution type: 4-year private

PROGRAMS OR SERVICES FOR STUDENTS WITH LD

The mission of Access Resources (AR) is to provide qualified students with equal access to the curriculum, services, and activities of the college. AR collaborates with faculty and staff to foster a welcoming environment and implement reasonable accommodations to ensure that all students benefit from opportunities available to them. Students with disabilities can meet with a learning specialist on a weekly basis to support their needs. These Learning Specialists collaborate with other support services including counselors, advisors, tutors, and mentors. Tutors are trained through a College Reading and Learning Association approved program and are skilled at providing support to students with a wide range of abilities.

ADMISSION INFORMATION FOR STUDENTS WITH LD/ADHD

College entrance tests required: Yes
Interview required: No
Essay recommended: Yes
Documentation required for LD: Psychoeducational evaluation—aptitude and achievement results
Documentation required for ADHD: Diagnostic interview and substantiation and statement of diagnosis
Submitted to: Academic Development Center
Special Ed. HS course work accepted: Yes

Specific course requirements of all applicants: Yes
Separate application required: No
# of LD applications submitted each year: NR
# of LD applications accepted yearly: NR
Total # of students receiving LD services: 75
Acceptance into program means acceptance into college: Students must be admitted to and enrolled in the university first and then request services.

ADMISSIONS

There is no special admissions process for students with learning disabilities. Students must submit one recommendation from their counselor and one from a teacher. An essay is also required. It is recommended that students have at least 15 units of college-preparatory courses. Students with documented learning disabilities may substitute courses for math or foreign language if those are the areas of deficit. Students' GPA is evaluated in terms of factors that may have affected GPA.

ADDITIONAL INFORMATION

Colby-Sawyer College understands that students with disabilities enhance the culture of the college and contribute diverse perspectives to the academic community. Colby-Sawyer College provides resources for students in many areas of Academic and Student Life. The Academic Advising program creates collaborative relationships between students and faculty/staff. The process encourages students to become more self-directed and take responsibility for their own adjustment to college life and academic expectations. The Academic Development Center offers educational support for all Colby-Sawyer students. The center's goal is to assist you in achieving your academic goals through tutorial assistance in writing, reading, study skills and specific courses. The ADC also provides support services to students with documented learning disabilities. The Guide to Access Resources assists students in learning about resources available to them on campus and beyond, and to educate themselves about issues related to learning disabilities.

LEARNING DISABILITY PROGRAMS OR SERVICES

Contact Information
Name of program or department: Academic Development Center
  Telephone: 603-526-3711
  Fax: 603-526-3115

LEARNING DISABILITY SERVICES

Accommodations are decided upon an individual basis after a thorough review of appropriate, current documentation. The accommodations requested must be supported through the documentation provided and must be logically linked to the current impact of the condition on academic functioning.

Allowed in exams
  Calculator: Yes
  Dictionary: Yes
  Computer: Yes
  Spellchecker: Yes
Extended test time: Yes
Scribes: Yes
Proctors: Yes
Oral exams: No
Note-takers: Yes

Distraction-reduced environment: Yes
Tape recording in class: Yes
Electronic texts: Yes
Accommodations for students with ADHD: Yes
Kurzweil Reader: Yes
Other assistive technology: Yes
Priority registration: No

Added costs for services: No
LD specialists: Yes
Professional tutors: 3–4
Peer tutors: 15–20
Max. hours/wk. for services: 1 hour per class per week plus 3 writing consultations per paper
How professors are notified of LD/ADHD: By student

GENERAL ADMISSIONS INFORMATION

Office of Admission: 603-526-3700

ENTRANCE REQUIREMENTS

Academic units required: 4 English, 3 math, 2 science (2 science labs), 2 foreign language, 3 social studies. High school diploma is required, and GED is accepted. TOEFL required of all international applicants: minimum paper TOEFL 500, minimum computer TOEFL 173.

Application deadline: 4/1
Notification: Rolling
Average GPA: 3.17
ACT Composite middle 50% range: NR

SAT Math middle 50% range: NR
SAT Critical Reading middle 50% range: NR
SAT Writing middle 50% range: NR

Graduated top 10% of class: NR
Graduated top 25% of class: NR
Graduated top 50% of class: NR

COLLEGE GRADUATION REQUIREMENTS

Course waivers allowed: No
Course substitutions allowed: No

ADDITIONAL INFORMATION

Environment: The college has an 80-acre campus in a small town.

Student Body
  Undergrad enrollment: 1,239
  Women: 68%
  Men: 32%
  Percent out-of-state: 66%

Cost Information
  Tuition: $34,110
  Room & board: $11,700
Housing Information
  University housing: Yes
  Percent living on campus: 80%

Greek System
  Fraternity: No
  Sorority: No
Athletics: Division III

NEW ENGLAND COLLEGE

26 Bridge Street, Henniker, NH 03242
Phone: 603-428-2223 • Fax: 603-428-3155
E-mail: admission@nec.edu • Web: www.nec.edu
Support: CS • Institution type: 4-year private

PROGRAMS OR SERVICES FOR STUDENTS WITH LD

Pathways Services provides services for all students in a welcoming and supportive environment. Students come to the center with a variety of academic needs. Some want help writing term papers. Some feel they read too slowly. Others are confused and anxious about their ability to perform as college students. Some students may have learning disabilities. The center provides individual or small group tutoring, academic counseling, and referral services. Tutoring is available in most subject areas. The center focuses primarily on helping students make a successful transition to New England College while supporting all students in their effort to become independent and successful learners. The support services meet the needs of students who do not require a formal, structured program, but who can find success when offered support and advocacy by a trained and experienced staff in conjunction with small classes and personal attention by faculty. Typically, these students have done well in mainstream programs in high school when given assistance. Students with learning disabilities are encouraged to visit NEC and Pathways Services to determine whether the support services will adequately meet their academic needs.

ADMISSION INFORMATION FOR STUDENTS WITH LD/ADHD

College entrance tests required: No
Interview required: As requested
Essay recommended: Required
What documentation required for LD: Psycho Ed evaluation to include: relevant historical info, instructional interventions, related services, age diagnosed, objective data (aptitude, achievement, info processing), test scores (standard, percentile and grade equivalents) and describe functional limitations.
With general application: No
To receive services after enrolling: Yes
What documentation required for ADHD: Diagnosis based on DSM-V; history of behaviors impairing functioning in academic setting; diagnostic interview; history of symptoms; evidence of ongoing behaviors.

With general application: No
Submitted to: Disability Services
Special Ed. HS course work accepted: College prep courses
Specific course requirements of all applicants: Yes
Separate application required: No
# of LD applications submitted each year: NR
# of LD applications accepted yearly: NR
Total # of students receiving LD services: 20%
Acceptance into program means acceptance into college: Students must be admitted to and enrolled in the university first and then request services. No special program.

ADMISSIONS

Students with learning disabilities submit the general New England College application. Students should have a 2.0 GPA. SAT/ACT results are optional. Course requirements include 4 years of English, 2 years of math, 2 years of science, and 2 years of social studies. Documentation of the learning disability should be submitted. An interview is recommended. Successful applicants have typically done well in mainstream programs in high school when given tutorial and study skills assistance.

ADDITIONAL INFORMATION

Students may elect to use the Pathways Services with regular appointments or only occasionally in response to particular or difficult assignments. The center provides tutoring in content areas; computer facilities; study skills instruction; time management strategies; writing support in planning, editing, and proofreading; referrals to other college services; and one-on-one writing support for first-year students taking WR 101–102. Students are encouraged to use the word processors to generate writing assignments and to use the tutors to help plan and revise papers. The writing faculty works closely with the center to provide coordinated and supportive learning for all students. Professional tutors work with students individually and in small groups. These services are provided in a secure and accepting atmosphere. Currently, 20 percent of the student body has a diagnosed LD, and 10 percent have a diagnosed ADHD.

LEARNING DISABILITY PROGRAMS OR SERVICES

Contact Information
Name of program or department: Pathways Services
  Telephone: 603-428-2218
  Fax: 603-428-2433

LEARNING DISABILITY SERVICES

Accommodations are decided upon an individual basis after a thorough review of appropriate, current documentation. The accommodations requested must be supported through the documentation provided and must be logically linked to the current impact of the condition on academic functioning.

Allowed in exams
  Calculator: Yes
  Dictionary: No
  Computer: Yes
  Spellchecker: Yes
Extended test time: Yes
Scribes: Yes
Proctors: Yes
Oral exams: Yes
Note-takers: Lecture notes

Distraction-reduced environment: Yes
Tape recording in class: Yes
Electronic texts: Yes
Accommodations for students with ADHD: Some
Kurzweil Reader: No
Other assistive technology: No
Priority registration: No

Added costs for services: No
LD specialists: Yes
Professional tutors: 7–10
Peer tutors: 5–7
Max. hours/wk. for services: 3
How professors are notified of LD/ADHD: Student provides professor with form.

GENERAL ADMISSIONS INFORMATION

Office of Admission: 603-428-2223

ENTRANCE REQUIREMENTS

Academic units required: 4 English, 2 math, 2 science (1 science lab), 2 social studies. **Academic units recommended:** 4 English, 3 math, 3 science (2 science labs), 2 foreign language, 3 social studies. High school diploma is required, and GED is accepted. TOEFL required of all international applicants: minimum paper TOEFL 550, minimum computer TOEFL 213.

Application deadline: 9/1
Notification: Rolling, beginning 11/1
Average GPA: 2.63
ACT Composite middle 50% range: 18–23

SAT Math middle 50% range: 400–540
SAT Critical Reading middle 50% range: 400–530
SAT Writing middle 50% range: 400–520

Graduated top 10% of class: 3%
Graduated top 25% of class: 12%
Graduated top 50% of class: 37%

COLLEGE GRADUATION REQUIREMENTS

Course waivers allowed: No
Course substitutions allowed: No

ADDITIONAL INFORMATION

Environment: The college is located in the town of Henniker on 212 acres 17 miles west of Concord.

Student Body
  Undergrad enrollment: 961
  Women: 47%
  Men: 53%
  Percent out-of-state: 59%

Cost Information
  Tuition: $30,100
  Room & board: $11,959
Housing Information
  University housing: Yes
  Percent living on campus: 55%

Greek System
  Fraternity: Yes
  Sorority: Yes
Athletics: Division III

RIVIER COLLEGE

420 South Main Street, Nashua, NH 03060
Phone: 603-897-8219 • Fax: 603-891-1799
E-mail: rivadmit@rivier.edu • Web: www.rivier.edu
Support: S • Institution type: 4-year private

PROGRAMS OR SERVICES FOR STUDENTS WITH LD

Rivier College recognizes that learning styles differ from person to person. The college is committed to providing supports that allow all otherwise qualified individuals with disabilities an equal educational opportunity. Disability Services provides the opportunity for all individuals who meet academic requirements to be provided auxiliary services, facilitating their earning of a college education. To be eligible for support services, students are required to provide appropriate documentation of their disabilities to the coordinator of Disability Services. This documentation shall be provided from a professional in the field of psychoeducational testing or a physician and shall be current (completed within the past 3 to 5 years). This information will be confidential and is kept in the coordinator's office for the purpose of planning appropriate support services. To access services, students must contact the coordinator of Disability Services before the start of each semester to schedule an appointment and provide documentation; together the coordinator and the student will discuss and arrange for support services specifically related to the disability.

ADMISSION INFORMATION FOR STUDENTS WITH LD/ADHD

College entrance tests required: Yes
Interview required: No
Essay recommended: Yes
What documentation required for LD: Psycho Ed evaluation to include: relevant historical info, instructional interventions, related services, age diagnosed, objective data (aptitude, achievement, info processing), test scores (standard, percentile and grade equivalents) and describe functional limitations.
With general application: No
To receive services after enrolling: Yes
What documentation required for ADHD: Diagnosis based on DSM-V; history of behaviors impairing functioning in academic setting; diagnostic interview; history of symptoms; evidence of ongoing behaviors.

With general application: No
Submitted to: Disability Services
Special Ed. HS course work accepted: NR
Specific course requirements of all applicants: NR
Separate application required: No
# of LD applications submitted each year: NR
# of LD applications accepted yearly: NR
Total # of students receiving LD services: NR
Acceptance into program means acceptance into college: Students must be admitted to and enrolled in the university first and then request services.

ADMISSIONS

There is no special admissions process for students with LD. All applicants must meet the same criteria. Students should have a combined SAT of 820, a GPA in the top 80 percent of their graduating class, and take college-prep courses in high school. Courses required include 4 years of English, 2 years of a foreign language (though this may be substituted), 1 year of science, 3 years of math, 2 years of social science, and 4 years of academic electives. Applicants not meeting the general admission requirements may inquire about alternative admissions. The college offers a probational admit option that requires students to maintain a minimum 2.0 GPA their first semester.

ADDITIONAL INFORMATION

Services available include academic, career, and personal counseling; preferential registration; classroom accommodations including tape recording of lectures, extended times for test completion, testing free from distractions, and note-takers; student advocacy; a writing center for individualized instruction in writing; and individualized accommodations as developed by the coordinator of Disability Services with the student. Services and accommodations are available for undergraduate and graduate students.

LEARNING DISABILITY PROGRAMS OR SERVICES

Contact Information
Name of program or department: Disability Services
 Telephone: 603-897-8497
 Fax: 603-897-8887

LEARNING DISABILITY SERVICES

Accommodations are decided upon an individual basis after a thorough review of appropriate, current documentation. The accommodations requested must be supported through the documentation provided and must be logically linked to the current impact of the condition on academic functioning.

Allowed in exams
 Calculator: Yes/No
 Dictionary: No
 Computer: Yes
 Spellchecker: Yes/No
Extended test time: Yes
Scribes: Yes
Proctors: Yes
Oral exams: Yes
Note-takers: Yes

Distraction-reduced environment: Yes
Tape recording in class: Yes
Electronic texts: Yes
Accommodations for students with
 ADHD: Yes
Kurzweil Reader: Yes
Other assistive technology: Yes
Priority registration: Yes

Added costs for services: No
LD specialists: No
Professional tutors: No
Peer tutors: Yes
Max. hours/wk. for services: N/A
How professors are notified of
 LD/ADHD: By both student and director

GENERAL ADMISSIONS INFORMATION

Office of Admission: 603-897-8219

ENTRANCE REQUIREMENTS

Academic units recommended: 4 English, 3 math, 1 science (1 science lab), 2 foreign language, 2 social studies, 1 history, 4 academic electives. High school diploma is required, and GED is accepted. ACT without Writing component accepted. TOEFL required of all international applicants: minimum paper TOEFL 500, minimum computer TOEFL 173.

Application deadline: None
Notification: Rolling
Average GPA: 3.0
ACT Composite middle 50% range:
 17–21

SAT Math middle 50% range:
 410–510
SAT Critical Reading middle 50% range: 410–510
SAT Writing middle 50% range:
 420–520

Graduated top 10% of class: 6%
Graduated top 25% of class: 27%
Graduated top 50% of class: 71%

COLLEGE GRADUATION REQUIREMENTS

Course waivers allowed: No
Course substitutions allowed: Yes
In what course: Each course subtitution is looked at individually.

ADDITIONAL INFORMATION

Environment: The college is located on 60 acres in a suburban area 40 miles north of Boston.

Student Body
 Undergrad enrollment: 1,482
 Women: 84%
 Men: 16%
 Percent out-of-state: 38%

Cost Information
 Tuition: $25,410
 Room & board: $9,798
Housing Information
 University housing: Yes
 Percent living on campus: 43%

Greek System
 Fraternity: No
 Sorority: No
Athletics: Division III

UNIVERSITY OF NEW HAMPSHIRE

3 Garrison Avenue, Durham, NH 03824
Phone: 603-862-1360 • Fax: 603-862-0077
E-mail: admissions@unh.edu • Web: www.unh.edu
Support: CS • Institution type: 4-year public

PROGRAMS OR SERVICES FOR STUDENTS WITH LD

The University of New Hampshire and Disability Services for Students (DSS) take great pride in promoting the development of student self-reliance and the personal independence necessary to succeed in a university climate. DSS seeks to create a comprehensively accessible environment where students are viewed on a basis of ability, not disability. The University of New Hampshire believes that students have the right and also the responsibility to determine whether or not to use support services. In keeping with this objective, students are expected and encouraged to utilize the resources of DSS to the degree they determine necessary. Therefore, it is the prerogative of the student to disclose or not disclose their disability to the University. There is not a specific LD program at this time. Services and accommodations are based on student self-disclosure and providing documentation as appropriate to the student's disability. Documentation guidelines can be viewed at http://www.unh.edu/disabilityservices/unh-guidelines. Disability Services for Students (DSS) is where students with documented disabilities can receive those accommodations and academic services that offer them equal access to the classroom. All students with LD/ADHD must provide current and appropriate documentation to qualify for services. Through one to one meetings with DSS staff or a variety of workshops provided across campus, students can learn and further develop their self-advocacy skills, notetaking skills, exam preparation skills, organization and time management. DSS recently added a new Assistive Technology (AT) Lab. Students with LD/ADHD may benefit from using some of the AT available. Trainings are available for students who have had no prior experience with a particular piece of AT.

ADMISSION INFORMATION FOR STUDENTS WITH LD/ADHD

College entrance tests required: Yes
Interview required: No
Essay recommended: Recommended
What documentation required for LD: Complete
  neuropsychological or psychoeducational evaluation
With general application: No
To receive services after enrolling: Yes
What documentation required for ADHD: Complete
  neuropsychological or psychoeducational evaluation
With general application: No

Submitted to: Disabilities Services for Students (DSS)
Special Ed. HS course work accepted: NR
Specific course requirements of all applicants: Yes
Separate application required: No
# of LD applications submitted each year: Varies
# of LD applications accepted yearly: Varies
Total # of students receiving LD services: 327
**Acceptance into program means acceptance into
  college:** Students must be an admitted UNH student in order
  to be eligible to be registered with DSS.

ADMISSIONS

Admissions criteria are the same for all applicants. Typically, students who are admitted to the university are in the top 30 percent of their class, have a B average in college-preparatory courses, and have taken 4 years of college-prep math, 3–4 years of a science lab, and 3–4 years of a foreign language and 3–4 years of social sciences; SAT average range is 1500–1800, ACT average 24, but there are no cutoffs (or equivalent ACT). There are no alternative options for admissions. DSS has no involvement in any admissions decision. However, there is a member of the admissions staff with a background in special education.

ADDITIONAL INFORMATION

The Center for Academic Resources offers academic support to all UNH undergraduate students who are matriculated in 4-year degree programs. They support students in their development of the cognitive-skills and academic-strategies needed to succeed in college. For students with a demonstrated academic need who meet income or disability criteria (as specified in their federal TRIO SSS grant) free peer subject-area tutoring and other learning and enrichment services may be available.

LEARNING DISABILITY PROGRAMS OR SERVICES

Contact Information
Name of program or department: Disabilities Services for Students (DSS)
   Telephone: 603-862-2607
   Fax: 603-862-4043

LEARNING DISABILITY SERVICES

Accommodations are decided upon an individual basis after a thorough review of appropriate, current documentation. The accommodations requested must be supported through the documentation provided and must be logically linked to the current impact of the condition on academic functioning.

Allowed in exams
   Calculator: Yes
   Dictionary: Yes
   Computer: Yes
   Spellchecker: Yes
Extended test time: Yes
Scribes: Yes
Proctors: Yes
Oral exams: Yes
Note-takers: Yes

Distraction-reduced environment: Yes
Tape recording in class: Yes
Electronic texts: Yes
Accommodations for students with ADHD: Yes
Kurzweil Reader: Yes, mainly use Read White & Gold
Other assistive technology: Yes
Priority registration: Yes

Added costs for services: No
LD specialists: No
Professional tutors: No
Peer tutors: Not through DSS
Max. hours/wk. for services: Varies
How professors are notified of LD/ADHD: By student

GENERAL ADMISSIONS INFORMATION

Office of Admission: 603-862-1360

ENTRANCE REQUIREMENTS

Academic units required: 4 English, 3 math, 3 lab sciences, 2 foreign language, 3 social studies. **Academic units recommended:** 4 English, 4 math, 3 lab sciences, 3 foreign language, 3 social studies. High school diploma is required, and GED is accepted. ACT with Writing component required. TOEFL required of all international applicants: minimum paper TOEFL 550, minimum computer TOEFL 213, minimum internet TOEFL 80.

Application deadline: 2/1
Notification: 4/15
Average GPA: 3.0
ACT Composite middle 50% range: 24

SAT Math middle 50% range: 520–600
SAT Critical Reading middle 50% range: 500–580
SAT Writing middle 50% range: 510–590

Graduated top 10% of class: 22%
Graduated top 25% of class: 59%
Graduated top 50% of class: 96%

COLLEGE GRADUATION REQUIREMENTS

Course waivers allowed: No
Course substitutions allowed: Yes
In what course: In foreign language on a case-by-case basis by a petition process.

ADDITIONAL INFORMATION

Environment: The university is located in a rural area about 1 hour north of Boston.

Student Body
   Undergrad enrollment: 12,485
   Women: 55%
   Men: 45%
   Percent out-of-state: 58%

Cost Information
   In-state tuition: $15,250
   Out-of-state tuition: $28,570
   Room & board: $9,452
Housing Information
   University housing: Yes
   Percent living on campus: 59%

Greek System
   Fraternity: Yes
   Sorority: Yes
Athletics: Division I

CALDWELL COLLEGE

120 Bloomfield Avenue, Caldwell, NJ 07006-6195
Phone: 973-618-3500 • Fax: 973-618-3600
E-mail: admissions@caldwell.edu • Web: www.caldwell.edu
Support: CS • Institution type: 4-year private

PROGRAMS OR SERVICES FOR STUDENTS WITH LD

The Office of Disability Services at Caldwell College is a dedicated office for students with documented disabilities that arranges for reasonable and appropriate accommodations for eligible students. Caldwell College ensures that all students will have equal access to all services, programs and activities. Students with documentation of a disability are fully integrated into college degree programs of study. Academic Support Services such as tutoring and academic coaching are available for all students. The mission of the Office of Disability Services (ODS) is to provide a full range of reasonable and appropriate accommodations and support services to students with disabilities in order to ensure compliance with Section 504 of the Rehabilitation Act of 1973 and the Americans with Disabilities Act (1990).

ADMISSION INFORMATION FOR STUDENTS WITH LD/ADHD

College entrance tests required: Yes
Interview required: No
Essay recommended: No
What documentation required for LD: Psycho Ed evaluation to include: relevant historical info, instructional interventions, related services, age diagnosed, objective data (aptitude, achievement, info processing), test scores (standard, percentile and grade equivalents) and describe functional limitations.
With general application: No
To receive services after enrolling: Yes
What documentation required for ADHD: Diagnosis based on DSM-V; history of behaviors impairing functioning in academic setting; diagnostic interview; history of symptoms; evidence of ongoing behaviors.

With general application: No
Submitted to: Office of Disability Services
Special Ed. HS course work accepted: Yes
Specific course requirements of all applicants: Yes
Separate application required: No
# of LD applications submitted each year: NR
# of LD applications accepted yearly: NR
Total # of students receiving LD services: NR
Acceptance into program means acceptance into college: Students must be admitted to and enrolled in the university first and then request services.

ADMISSIONS

The mid 50 percent SAT score for general admissions is 830–1020. Additionally, students generally have a minimum GPA of 2.0 and have 16 high school academic units including 4 English, 2 years of a foreign language, 2 years of math, 2 years of science, and 1 year of history. With appropriate documentation, applicants with LD may request to substitute some of the required courses with other high school courses.

ADDITIONAL INFORMATION

There is one disabilities specialist on staff and there is no charge for registering with the office or using additional resources, such as tutoring or academic coaching. Individual academic coaching is available to help students improve organizational and time management skills, while one-on-one peer tutoring is available to assist students with content areas. Professional tutoring is available for writing and math, at no additional charge. Caldwell College offers an Assistive Technology Lab equipped with computers and various software programs, such as Kurzweil, Inspiration and ZoomText. The college also has a Writing Center where students can receive assistance with all areas of the writing process. Caldwell College administers a placement test to all incoming freshman. The test assesses skills in reading comprehension, mathematics and computers. The results of these tests are used to determine placement into courses such as Math, English and Computers.

LEARNING DISABILITY PROGRAMS OR SERVICES

Contact Information
Name of program or department: Office of Disability Services/Learning Center
  Telephone: 973-618-3645
  Fax: 973-618-3488

LEARNING DISABILITY SERVICES

Accommodations are decided upon an individual basis after a thorough review of appropriate, current documentation. The accommodations requested must be supported through the documentation provided and must be logically linked to the current impact of the condition on academic functioning.

Allowed in exams
  Calculator: Yes
  Dictionary: Yes
  Computer: Yes
  Spellchecker: Yes
Extended test time: Yes
Scribes: Yes
Proctors: Yes
Oral exams: Yes
Note-takers: Yes

Distraction-reduced environment: Yes
Tape recording in class: Yes
Electronic texts: Yes
Accommodations for students with ADHD: Yes
Kurzweil Reader: Yes
Other assistive technology: Yes
Priority registration: No

Added costs for services: No
LD specialists: Yes
Professional tutors: 5
Peer tutors: 30–40
Max. hours/wk. for services: Unlimited
How professors are notified of LD/ADHD: By both student and director

GENERAL ADMISSIONS INFORMATION

Office of Admission: 973-618-3500

ENTRANCE REQUIREMENTS

Academic units required: 4 English, 2 math, 2 science (1 science lab), 2 foreign language, 1 history, 5 academic electives. High school diploma is required, and GED is accepted. TOEFL required of all international applicants: minimum paper TOEFL 500.

Application deadline: None
Notification: Rolling
Average GPA: 3.09
ACT Composite middle 50% range: NR

SAT Math middle 50% range: 410–570
SAT Critical Reading middle 50% range: 420–510
SAT Writing middle 50% range: NR

Graduated top 10% of class: 7%
Graduated top 25% of class: 15%
Graduated top 50% of class: 33%

COLLEGE GRADUATION REQUIREMENTS

Course waivers allowed: No
Course substitutions allowed: Yes
In what course: Students may receive substitutions in foreign language if documentation supports the need for it.

ADDITIONAL INFORMATION

Environment: The campus is located 10 miles from Newark, New Jersey and 20 miles from New York City.

Student Body
  Undergrad enrollment: 1,668
  Women: 68%
  Men: 32%
  Percent out-of-state: 7%

Cost Information
  Tuition: $25,990
  Room & board: $9,440
Housing Information
  University housing: Yes
  Percent living on campus: 26%

Greek System
  Fraternity: No
  Sorority: No
Athletics: Division II

FAIRLEIGH DICKINSON UNIVERSITY— FLORHAM CAMPUS

285 Madison Avenue, Madison, NJ 07940
Phone: 800-338-8803 • Fax: 973-443-8088
E-mail: globaleducation@fdu.edu • Web: www.fdu.edu
Support: SP • Institution type: 4-year private

PROGRAMS OR SERVICES FOR STUDENTS WITH LD

The Regional Center for College Students with LD offers a structured plan of intensive advisement, academic support, and counseling services that is tailored to the unique needs of students with language-based learning disabilities. The goal is to provide a framework within which college students with LD will develop the confidence to succeed in their studies and the independence to do their best. Planning, learning strategies, professional tutors, counseling, and accommodations are the cornerstones of the Regional Center. Staffed by professionals with services at both the Teaneck and the Madison campus, the LD program and special services are free of charge. Assistance to students is intensive, and the program is fully integrated into the course work. Performance data are routinely reviewed to identify students in need of more intensive help. Upon admission, students are invited to attend a summer orientation session. During this time, students meet with center staff to develop an academic plan to develop a class schedule with the right balance.

ADMISSION INFORMATION FOR STUDENTS WITH LD/ADHD

College entrance tests required: Yes
Interview required: No
Essay recommended: No
What documentation required for LD: Psycho Ed evaluation to include: relevant historical info, instructional interventions, related services, age diagnosed, objective data (aptitude, achievement, info processing), test scores (standard, percentile and grade equivalents) and describe functional limitations.
With general application: Yes if requested as part of Structured Program application
To receive services after enrolling: Yes
What documentation required for ADHD: Diagnosis based on DSM-V; history of behaviors impairing functioning in academic setting; diagnostic interview; history of symptoms; evidence of ongoing behaviors.

With general application: Yes if requested as part of Structured Program application
To receive services after enrolling: Yes
Submitted to: Support Program/Services
Special Ed. HS course work accepted: Yes
Specific course requirements of all applicants: Yes
Separate application required: Yes
# of LD applications submitted each year: 250
# of LD applications accepted yearly: 50
Total # of students receiving LD services: 150
Acceptance into program means acceptance into college: Students musty first be admitted to the University before a regional center application is reviewed for admission to the program.

ADMISSIONS

Admissions decisions are made independently by the Admissions Office and the LD program admissions director. Criteria include documentation of LD made by licensed professionals dated within 24 months of the application, IQ in the average to above-average range, evidence of adequate performance in mainstream college-prep high school courses, and evidence of motivation as reflected in recommendations. Students enrolled in all special education high school classes are usually not admissible. Lower level mainstream classes are acceptable from high schools offering different levels in the same subjects. ACT/SAT required. Grades are the best predictors for success. General admissions require a class rank in top 40% or B average and an 850 SAT. If applicants have below a 2.5 GPA and an 850 SAT, they may be referred to Petrocelli College Program, a two-year college located on the Teaneck campus that requires an 18 ACT or 600 SAT.

ADDITIONAL INFORMATION

Edward Williams College, a two-year liberal arts college on the Teaneck campus, offers services and accommodations to students with learning disabilities who are not admissible to Fairleigh Dickinson. Skills class for no college credit are offered in math and writing. Tutorial sessions incorporate a variety of teaching techniques. Support sessions are small, individualized, and flexible. In their sophomore year, students can request tutoring for three courses. Students with disabilities are entitled to priority registration. Most students are seen by 3–4 different LD specialists who regularly exchange views on academic and counseling issues. Services include recorded textbooks, extended testing times and other class support, technological support, and supervised study to meet with specialists.

LEARNING DISABILITY PROGRAMS OR SERVICES

Contact Information
Name of program or department: Regional Center for College Students with LD
  Telephone: 973-443-8935
  Fax: 973-443-8932

LEARNING DISABILITY SERVICES

Accommodations are decided upon an individual basis after a thorough review of appropriate, current documentation. The accommodations requested must be supported through the documentation provided and must be logically linked to the current impact of the condition on academic functioning.

Allowed in exams	**Distraction-reduced environment:** Yes	**Added costs for services:** No
Calculator: Yes	**Tape recording in class:** Yes	**LD specialists:** Yes
Dictionary: No	**Electronic texts:** No	**Professional tutors:** 8
Computer: Yes	**Accommodations for students with**	**Peer tutors:** No
Spellchecker: Yes	**ADHD:** No	**Max. hours/wk. for services:** NR
Extended test time: Yes	**Kurzweil Reader:** Yes	**How professors are notified of**
Scribes: No	**Other assistive technology:** Yes	**LD/ADHD:** By both student and
Proctors: Yes	**Priority registration:** Yes	director
Oral exams: Yes		
Note-takers: No		

GENERAL ADMISSIONS INFORMATION

Office of Admission: 800-338-8803

ENTRANCE REQUIREMENTS

Academic units required: 4 English, 3 math, 2 science (2 science labs), 2 foreign language, 2 social studies, 2 history, 3 academic electives. **Academic units recommended:** 3 math, 3 science (3 science labs), 2 foreign language, 2 social studies, 2 history, 3 academic electives. High school diploma is required, and GED is accepted. ACT with or without Writing component accepted. TOEFL required of all international applicants: minimum paper TOEFL 550, minimum computer TOEFL 213.

Application deadline: None	**SAT Math middle 50% range:**	**Graduated top 10% of class:** 15%
Notification: Rolling	460–570	**Graduated top 25% of class:** 40%
Average GPA: 3.11	**SAT Critical Reading middle 50%**	**Graduated top 50% of class:** 76%
ACT Composite middle 50% range:	**range:** 450–560	
NR	**SAT Writing middle 50% range:**	
	450–560	

COLLEGE GRADUATION REQUIREMENTS

Course waivers allowed: No
Course substitutions allowed: Yes
In what course: Mathematics and foreign language substitutions may be granted if candidate qualifies per university policy.

ADDITIONAL INFORMATION

Environment: FDU's College at Florham is in Morris County, New Jersey, bridging the towns of Florham Park and Madison.

Student Body	**Cost Information**	**Greek System**
Undergrad enrollment: 2,401	**Tuition:** $34,082	**Fraternity:** Yes
Women: 52%	**Room & board:** $11,058	**Sorority:** Yes
Men: 48%	**Housing Information**	**Athletics:** Division III
Percent out-of-state: 16%	**University housing:** Yes	
	Percent living on campus: 61%	

FAIRLEIGH DICKINSON UNIVERSITY— METROPOLITAN CAMPUS

1000 River Road, H-DH3-10, Teaneck, NJ 07666-1966
Phone: 201-692-2553 • Fax: 201-692-7319
E-mail: globaleducation@fdu.edu • Web: www.fdu.edu
Support: SP • Institution: 2-year, 4-year private

PROGRAMS OR SERVICES FOR STUDENTS WITH LD

The Regional Center for College Students with LD offers a structured plan of intensive advisement, academic support, and counseling services tailored to the unique needs of students with language-based disabilities. The goal is to provide a framework within which college students identified with "Specific Learning Disabilities" will develop the confidence to succeed in their studies and the independence to do their best. Planning, learning strategies, professional tutors, counseling, and accommodations are the cornerstones of the Regional Center. Staffed by professionals at the Metropolitan Campus and the Campus of Florham, the LD program and special services are free. Assistance is intensive and the program fully integrated into the course work. Performance data is routinely reviewed to identify students in need of more intensive help. Upon admission students are invited to attend a summer orientation session.

ADMISSION INFORMATION FOR STUDENTS WITH LD/ADHD

College entrance tests required: Yes
Interview required: No
What documentation required for LD: Psycho Ed evaluation to include: relevant historical info, instructional interventions, related services, age diagnosed, objective data (aptitude, achievement, info processing), test scores (standard, percentile and grade equivalents) and describe functional limitations.
With general application: Yes if requested as part of Structured Program application
To receive services after enrolling: Yes
What documentation required for ADHD: Diagnosis based on DSM-V; history of behaviors impairing functioning in academic setting; diagnostic interview; history of symptoms; evidence of ongoing behaviors.

With general application: Yes if requested as part of Structured Program application
To receive services after enrolling: Yes
Submitted to: Support Program/Services
Special Ed. HS course work accepted: Yes
Specific course requirements for all applicants: Yes
Separate application required for program services: Yes
# of LD applications submitted each year: 250
# of LD applications accepted yearly: 50
Total # of students receiving LD services: 150
Acceptance into program means acceptance into college: Students must forst be admitted to the University before a Regional Center application is reviewed for admission to the program.

ADMISSIONS

Admissions decisions are made independently by FDU Admissions and the LD Program Admissions Directors. Students must be admitted to the university before applications can be reviewed by the Regional Center. Criteria include documentation of a primary diagnosis of a language-based learning disability made by licensed professionals dated within 24 months of the application; evidence of adequate performance in mainstream college-prep high school courses; and evidence of motivation as reflected in recommendations. Students enrolled solely in special education high school classes are usually not admissible. Lower level mainstream classes are acceptable from high schools offering different levels in the same subjects. ACT/SAT required but are secondary to the above criteria. Previous school achievement and positive recommendations are viewed as the best predictors for success. Students with a 2.5 GPA and 850 SAT can be accepted. General admissions require performance in the top two-fifths of class or B average. If applicants have a GPA below a 2.5, they may be referred to the Petrocelli College Program, which maintains a two-year associate's degree program on the Metropolitan Campus in Teaneck.

ADDITIONAL INFORMATION

Fairleigh Dickinson University maintains two campuses in New Jersey: The Metropolitan Campus situated in Bergen County,less than 10 miles from New York City; and The College at Florham, located in suburban Morris County, New Jersey. Both campuses offer the services of the Regional Center. There is an additional opportunity for students desiring a two-year degree via the Petrocelli College Program at the Metropoitan Campus. Support sessions are small, individualized, and flexible. Students have priority registration. Students may also participate in math and writing workshops.

PROGRAM FOR DISABILITY SERVICES

Contact Information
Name of program or department: Office of the Provost
  E-Mail: mourton@fdu.edu
  Telephone: 201-692-2460

LEARNING DISABILITY SERVICES

Accommodations are decided upon an individual basis after a thorough review of appropriate, current documentation. The accommodations requested must be supported through the documentation provided and must be logically linked to the current impact of the condition on academic functioning.

Allowed in exams	**Distraction-reduced environment:** Yes	**Added costs for services:** No
Calculator: Yes	**Tape recording in class:** Yes	**LD specialists:** Yes
Dictionary: No	**Electronic texts:** No	**Professional tutors:** 10
Computer: Yes	**Accommodations for students with**	**Peer tutors:** No
Spellchecker: Yes	**ADHD:** Yes	**Max. hours/wk. for services:** 8
Extended test time: Yes	**Kurzweil Reader:** Yes	**How professors are notified of**
Scribes: No	**Other assistive technology:** Through	**LD/ADHD:** Both student and director
Proctors: Yes	the Regional Center, students have	
Oral exams: Yes	access to innovative assistive	
Note-takers: No	technologies. The university library has	
	also begun to loan students Kindles	
	and other portable reading devices.	
	Priority registration: N/A	

GENERAL ADMISSIONS INFORMATION

Office of Admission: 201-692-2460

ENTRANCE REQUIREMENTS
Academic units required: 4 English, 3 mathematics, 2 science, (2 science labs), 2 foreign language, 2 social studies, 2 history, 3 academic electives. **Academic units recommended:** 3 mathematics, 3 science, (3 science labs), 2 foreign language, 2 social studies, 2 history, 3 academic electives. High school diploma is required and GED is accepted. SAT or ACT required; TOEFL required of all international applicants; minimum paper TOEFL 550, minimum computer TOEFL 213, minimum web-based TOEFL 79.

Application deadline: None	**SAT Critical Reading middle 50%**	**Graduated top 10% of class:** 17%
Notification: Rolling	**range:** 440–530	**Graduated top 25% of class:** 43%
Average GPA: 3.18	**SAT Math middle 50% range:**	**Graduated top 50% of class:** 81%
ACT Composite middle 50% range:	460–560	
NR	**SAT Writing middle 50% range:**	
	440–540	

COLLEGE GRADUATION REQUIREMENTS

Course waivers allowed: No
In what course: Math and foreign language substitutions may be granted if candidate qualifies per university policy.
Course substitutions allowed: Yes
In what course: Math and foreign language

ADDITIONAL INFORMATION

Environment: To learn more about each campus visit the website www.fdu.edu.

Student Body	Cost Information	Greek System
Undergrad enrollment: 6,636	**Tuition:** $31,618	**Fraternity:** Yes
Women: 58%	**Room & board:** $11,482	**Sorority:** Yes
Men: 42%	**Housing Information**	**Athletics:** Division I
Percent out-of-state: 14%	**University housing:** Yes	
	Percent living on campus: 20%	

GEORGIAN COURT UNIVERSITY

900 Lakewood Avenue, Lakewood, NJ 08701-2697
Phone: 732-987-2200 • Fax: 732-987-2000
E-mail: admissions@georgian.edu • Web: www.georgian.edu
Support: SP • Institution type: 4-year private

PROGRAMS OR SERVICES FOR STUDENTS WITH LD

The Learning Center (TLC) is an assistance program designed to provide an environment for students with mild to moderate learning disabilities who desire a college education. The program is not one of remediation, but it is an individualized support program to assist candidates in becoming successful college students. Emphasis is placed on developing self-help strategies and study techniques. To be eligible for the TLC program, all applicants must submit the following: documentation of a learning disability by a certified professional within a school system or state-certified agency; the documentation must be current, having been completed within the past 3 years and must include the identification and description of the learning disability, including the student's level of academic performance and the effect the disabilty has on the student's learning; a recent IEP; other evaluations or recommendations from professionals who have recently provided services to the student; and additional documentation on request. All applicants must have a personal interview.

ADMISSION INFORMATION FOR STUDENTS WITH LD/ADHD

College entrance tests required: Yes
Interview required: Yes
Essay recommended: No
What documentation required for LD: Psycho Ed evaluation to include: relevant historical info, instructional interventions, related services, age diagnosed, objective data (aptitude, achievement, info processing), test scores (standard, percentile and grade equivalents) and describe functional limitations.
With general application: Yes if requested as part of Structured Program application
To receive services after enrolling: Yes
What documentation required for ADHD: Diagnosis based on DSM-V; history of behaviors impairing functioning in academic setting; diagnostic interview; history of symptoms; evidence of ongoing behaviors.

With general application: Yes if requested as part of Structured Program application
To receive services after enrolling: Yes
Submitted to: Both Admissions and the Learning Center
Special Ed. HS course work accepted: No
Specific course requirements of all applicants: Yes
Separate application required: No
# of LD applications submitted each year: Numerous
# of LD applications accepted yearly: Numerous
Total # of students receiving LD services: Varies each semester
Acceptance into program means acceptance into college: Students are simultaneously admitted into The Learning Center and Georgian Court College.

ADMISSIONS

Applicants must meet the following criteria: 16 academic units that include 4 years of English, 2 years of a foreign language, 2 years of math, 1 year of science lab, 1 year history, and electives. The class rank and transcript should give evidence of the ability to succeed in college. Students must submit SAT scores. Conditional admission may be offered to some applicants. The Associate Director of Admissions is the liaison between the admissions staff and the TLC.

ADDITIONAL INFORMATION

College graduation requirements are not waived for TLC students. Reduced course load is recommended for students with learning disabilities, and program completion may take longer than 4 years. A social worker and counselor are on the staff of the TLC to help students as well. The TLC offers the following: an individualized support program; scheduled tutorial sessions with a learning disabilities specialist; faculty liaisons; academic counseling; priority registration; organizational skills training in time management, test-taking, note-taking, and outlining; study techniques; memory and concentration techniques; techniques for planning and writing research papers; and content tutoring if needed.

LEARNING DISABILITY PROGRAMS OR SERVICES

Contact Information
Name of program or department: The Learning Center (TLC)
  Telephone: 732-987-2650 or 732-987-2659
  Fax: 732-987-2026

LEARNING DISABILITY SERVICES

Accommodations are decided upon an individual basis after a thorough review of appropriate, current documentation. The accommodations requested must be supported through the documentation provided and must be logically linked to the current impact of the condition on academic functioning.

Allowed in exams		
Calculator: Yes	**Distraction-reduced environment:** Yes	**Added costs for services:** Yes
Dictionary: Yes	**Tape recording in class:** Yes	**LD specialists:** Yes
Computer: Yes	**Electronic texts:** No	**Professional tutors:** 3
Spellchecker: Yes	**Accommodations for students with**	**Peer tutors:** No
Extended test time: Yes	**ADHD:** Yes	**Max. hours/wk. for services:** Varies
Scribes: Yes	**Kurzweil Reader:** Yes	**How professors are notified of**
Proctors: Yes	**Other assistive technology:** Yes	**LD/ADHD:** By both student and
Oral exams: Yes	**Priority registration:** Yes	director
Note-takers: Yes		

GENERAL ADMISSIONS INFORMATION

Office of Admission: 732-364-2200

ENTRANCE REQUIREMENTS

Academic units required: 4 English, 2 math, 1 science (1 science lab), 2 foreign language, 1 history, 6 academic electives. High school diploma is required, and GED is accepted. ACT with or without Writing component accepted. TOEFL required of all international applicants: minimum paper TOEFL 550, minimum computer TOEFL 213.

Application deadline: 8/1	**SAT Math middle 50% range:** NR	**Graduated top 10% of class:** 9%
Notification: Rolling	**SAT Critical Reading middle 50%**	**Graduated top 25% of class:** 29%
Average GPA: 3.22	**range:** NR	**Graduated top 50% of class:** 68%
ACT Composite middle 50% range: NR	**SAT Writing middle 50% range:** NR	

COLLEGE GRADUATION REQUIREMENTS

Course waivers allowed: No
Course substitutions allowed: Yes
In what course: Foreign language, if applicable

ADDITIONAL INFORMATION

Environment: Georgian Court College is a small private institution centrally located in New Jersey.

Student Body	Cost Information	Greek System
Undergrad enrollment: 1,772	**Tuition:** $24,932	**Fraternity:** No
Women: 94%	**Room & board:** $9,855	**Sorority:** No
Men: 6%	**Housing Information**	**Athletics:** Division II
Percent out-of-state: 4%	**University housing:** Yes	
	Percent living on campus: 25%	

KEAN UNIVERSITY

PO Box 411, 1000 Morris Avenue, Union, NJ 07083-0411
Phone: 908-737-7100 • Fax: 908-737-7105
E-mail: admitme@kean.edu • Web: www.kean.edu
Support: CS • Institution type: 4-year public

PROGRAMS OR SERVICES FOR STUDENTS WITH LD

Kean University believes qualified students with difficulties processing oral and written material have the potential to earn a college degree if they are provided with certain individualized support services. These services are designed to help students develop skills to be independent, involved, responsible learners and use their own assets to become successful learners. Students with LD attend the same classes and meet the same academic requirements as their peers. Once admitted to Kean University, students who choose to register with Project Excel may do so by providing complete documentation of a diagnosed disability. Students are asked to complete a Project Excel application after admission to Kean and answer questions such as: in what academic areas are you most and least successful; describe how the LD affects your academic work; what support services are needed for success; describe any past special services received; identify high school mainstream courses; and when was your LD diagnosed.

ADMISSION INFORMATION FOR STUDENTS WITH LD/ADHD

College entrance tests required: Yes
Interview required: No
Essay recommended: No
What documentation required for LD: Psycho Ed evaluation to include: relevant historical info, instructional interventions, related services, age diagnosed, objective data (aptitude, achievement, info processing), test scores (standard, percentile and grade equivalents) and describe functional limitations.
With general application: No
To receive services after enrolling: Yes
What documentation required for ADHD: Diagnosis based on DSM-V; history of behaviors impairing functioning in academic setting; diagnostic interview; history of symptoms; evidence of ongoing behaviors.

With general application: No
Submitted to: Project Excel
Special Ed. HS course work accepted: No
Specific course requirements of all applicants: Yes
Separate application required: No
# of LD applications submitted each year: 30–35
# of LD applications accepted yearly: 30–33
Total # of students receiving LD services: 150–160
Acceptance into program means acceptance into college: Students must be admitted and enrolled in the university first and then may request services through Project Excel.

ADMISSIONS

There is no special admissions process for students with LD. It is recommended that students self-disclose in the admissions process. All applicants must meet the same admission criteria, which include 4 years of English, 3 years of math, 2 years of social studies, 2 years of science, and 5 elective credits. Courses taken in special education may be considered. SAT/ACT results are required, and the average SAT range is 1000–1020. The minimum GPA is 2.8. The student must be highly motivated, able to do college work, be of at least average intelligence, have a documented learning disability, have areas of academic strength, and make a commitment to work responsibly and attend classes, tutoring, workshops, and counseling sessions. Students are encouraged to apply by early March.

ADDITIONAL INFORMATION

Project Excel does not provide remedial or developmental instruction. A number of services are available through Project Excel: diagnostic assessments; academic, career, and personal advisement and counseling; development of a college education plan (CEP) for the individual student; student advocacy with faculty; and referral to other college services as appropriate such as tutoring in basic skills and course materials. All information about the student's LD is held in strict confidence. Information shared on- or off-campus is only done with the student's signed consent. LD assessments are available for a fee of $550 for a professional assessment and $150 for an assessment from a student intern. All students in Project Excel select from the same schedule of classes and attend with all other students in the college.

LEARNING DISABILITY PROGRAMS OR SERVICES

Contact Information
Name of program or department: Project Excel
  Telephone: 908-737-5400
  Fax: 908-737-5405

LEARNING DISABILITY SERVICES

Accommodations are decided upon an individual basis after a thorough review of appropriate, current documentation. The accommodations requested must be supported through the documentation provided and must be logically linked to the current impact of the condition on academic functioning.

Allowed in exams
  Calculator: Yes
  Dictionary: Yes
  Computer: Yes
  Spellchecker: Yes
Extended test time: Yes
Scribes: Yes
Proctors: Yes
Oral exams: Yes
Note-takers: No

Distraction-reduced environment: Yes
Tape recording in class: Yes
Electronic texts: No
Accommodations for students with
  ADHD: Yes
Kurzweil Reader: Yes
Other assistive technology: Yes
Priority registration: Yes

Added costs for services: No
LD specialists: Yes
Professional tutors: Yes
Peer tutors: Yes
Max. hours/wk. for services: NR
How professors are notified of
  LD/ADHD: By student

GENERAL ADMISSIONS INFORMATION

Office of Admission: 908-737-7109

ENTRANCE REQUIREMENTS

Academic units required: 4 English, 3 math, 2 science (2 science labs), 2 history, 5 academic electives.
Academic units recommended: 2 foreign language, 2 social studies. High school diploma is required, and GED is accepted. ACT with or without Writing component accepted.

Application deadline: 5/31
Notification: Rolling
Average GPA: 3.0
ACT Composite middle 50% range:
  NR

SAT Math middle 50% range:
  420–520
SAT Critical Reading middle 50%
  range: 400–500
SAT Writing middle 50% range: NR

Graduated top 10% of class: 7%
Graduated top 25% of class: 27%
Graduated top 50% of class: 68%

COLLEGE GRADUATION REQUIREMENTS

Course waivers allowed: No
Course substitutions allowed: No

ADDITIONAL INFORMATION

Environment: The college is located on 151 acres in a suburban area 20 miles west of New York City.

Student Body
  Undergrad enrollment: 13,462
  Women: 60%
  Men: 40%
  Percent out-of-state: 3%

Cost Information
  In-state tuition: $10,200
  Out-of-state tuition: $16,012
  Room & board: $13,528
Housing Information
  University housing: Yes
  Percent living on campus: 15%

Greek System
  Fraternity: Yes
  Sorority: Yes
Athletics: Division III

MONMOUTH UNIVERSITY (NJ)

Admissions, 400 Cedar Avenue, West Long Branch, NJ 07764-1898
Phone: 732-571-3456 • Fax: 732-263-5166
E-mail: admission@monmouth.edu • Web: www.monmouth.edu
Support: CS • Institution type: 4-year private

PROGRAMS OR SERVICES FOR STUDENTS WITH LD

Monmouth University recognizes the special needs of students with disabilities who are capable, with appropriate assistance, of excelling in a demanding college environment. Coordinated support services and a nurturing environment contribute to their success. Monmouth's commitment is to provide a learning process and atmosphere that allows students to pursue their educational goals, realize their full potential, contribute actively to their community and society, and determine the direction of their lives. Students are enrolled in regular courses and are not isolated from the rest of the student body in any manner. Students with documented disabilities may request reasonable accommodations, or auxiliary aids. It is important that students disclose their disability and provide the required documentation to DDS. Much of their success has to do with individual recognition of their specific learning needs combined with supportive faculty. Monmouth is very proud of the many important contributions of students with learning disabilities to life at the university.

ADMISSION INFORMATION FOR STUDENTS WITH LD/ADHD

College entrance tests required: Yes

Interview required: No
Essay recommended: No
What documentation required for LD: Psycho Ed evaluation to include: relevant historical info, instructional interventions, related services, age diagnosed, objective data (aptitude, achievement, info processing), test scores (standard, percentile and grade equivalents) and describe functional limitations.
With general application: No
To receive services after enrolling: Yes
What documentation required for ADHD: Diagnosis based on DSM-V; history of behaviors impairing functioning in academic setting; diagnostic interview; history of symptoms; evidence of ongoing behaviors.

With general application: No
Submitted to: Department of Disability Services
Special Ed. HS course work accepted: No
Specific course requirements of all applicants: Yes
Separate application required: No
# of LD applications submitted each year: NR
# of LD applications accepted yearly: NR
Total # of students receiving LD services: 208
Acceptance into program means acceptance into college: Students are accepted and can then register with DDS.

ADMISSIONS

There is no special admissions process for students with diagnosed learning disabilities. General admission requirements include 4 years of English, 3 years of math, 2 years of social science, 2 years of science, and 5 electives from English, math, science, social studies, and/or a foreign language. Courses taken in the special education department may be accepted. The minimum GPA is 2.25.

ADDITIONAL INFORMATION

Students with documented disabilities may request reasonable accommodations or auxiliary aids that will enable them to participate in and benefit from postsecondary educational programs and activities. These may include extended time on tests, reader assistance, and note-takers.

LEARNING DISABILITY PROGRAMS OR SERVICES

Contact Information
Name of program or department: Department of Disability Services for Students (DDS)
   Telephone: 732-571-3460
   Fax: 732-263-5126

LEARNING DISABILITY SERVICES

Accommodations are decided upon an individual basis after a thorough review of appropriate, current documentation. The accommodations requested must be supported through the documentation provided and must be logically linked to the current impact of the condition on academic functioning.

Allowed in exams
   Calculator: Yes
   Dictionary: No
   Computer: Yes
   Spellchecker: Yes
Extended test time: Yes
Scribes: Yes
Proctors: Yes
Oral exams: No
Note-takers: Yes

Distraction-reduced environment: Yes
Tape recording in class: Yes
Electronic texts: Yes
Accommodations for students with ADHD: Yes
Kurzweil Reader: No
Other assistive technology: Yes
Priority registration: No

Added costs for services: No
LD specialists: Yes
Professional tutors: No
Peer tutors: No
Max. hours/wk. for services: Unlimited
How professors are notified of LD/ADHD: Student

GENERAL ADMISSIONS INFORMATION

Office of Admission: 732-571-3456

ENTRANCE REQUIREMENTS

Academic units required: 4 English, 3 math, 2 science (1 science lab), 2 history, 5 academic electives. **Academic units recommended:** English, social science, science, humanities, foreign languages, or mathematics. High School diploma is required, and GED is accepted. SAT or ACT with Writing component required. TOEFL required of all non-English speaking applicants; minimum paper TOEFL 550, minimum computer TOEFL 213, minimum Internet TOEFL 79.

Application deadline: 3/1
Notification: 4/1
Average GPA: 3.40
ACT Composite middle 50% range: 22–25

SAT Math middle 50% range: 500–580
SAT Critical Reading middle 50% range: 480–560
SAT Writing middle 50% range: 500–580

Graduated top 10% of class: 20%
Graduated top 25% of class: 55%
Graduated top 50% of class: 87%

COLLEGE GRADUATION REQUIREMENTS

Course waivers allowed: No
Course substitutions allowed: No

ADDITIONAL INFORMATION

Environment: The college is located on 125 acres in a suburb 60 miles south of New York City.

Student Body
   Undergrad enrollment: 4,700
   Women: 58%
   Men: 42%
   Percent out-of-state: 14%

Cost Information
   Tuition: $28,000
   Room & board: $10,500
Housing Information
   University housing: Yes
   Percent living on campus: 46%

Greek System
   Fraternity: Yes
   Sorority: Yes
   Athletics: Division I

NEW JERSEY CITY UNIVERSITY

2039 Kennedy Boulevard, Jersey City, NJ 07305
Phone: 888-441-6528 • Fax: 201-200-2044
E-mail: admissions@njcu.edu • Web: www.njcu.edu
Support: SP • Institution type: 4-year public

PROGRAMS OR SERVICES FOR STUDENTS WITH LD

Students with Disabilities are served by the Office of Specialized Services for Student with Disabilities at New Jersey City University. The Office of Specialized Services (OSS) provides NJCU students with disabilities equal access to college programs. The OSS serves as a resource for students with mobility, vision, hearing, learning, and other disabilities that are in need of campus accommodations. The OSS assists students, on an individual basis, in securing reasonable accommodations, including, but not limited to alternate testing arrangements, adaptive technology, and assistance in arranging other support services (e.g., sign language interpreters, books on tape, and note-taking support) supported by documentation. It is the student's responsibility to self-identify and request services. Students requesting academic adjustments are required to submit appropriate and recent documentation of their disability. Students wishing to obtain accommodations may do so by contacting the OSS Director. Reasonable accommodations are then determined after consultation between the student and the Director.

ADMISSION INFORMATION FOR STUDENTS WITH LD/ADHD

College entrance tests required: NR
Interview required: NR
Essay recommended: NR
What documentation required for LD: Psycho Ed evaluation to include: relevant historical info, instructional interventions, related services, age diagnosed, objective data (aptitude, achievement, info processing), test scores (standard, percentile and grade equivalents) and describe functional limitations.
With general application: NR
To receive services after enrolling: NR
What documentation required for ADHD: Diagnosis based on DSM-V; history of behaviors impairing functioning in academic setting; diagnostic interview; history of symptoms; evidence of ongoing behaviors.

With general application: NR
To receive services after enrolling: NR
Submitted to: NR
Special Ed. HS course work accepted: NR
Specific course requirements of all applicants: NR
Separate application required: No
# of LD applications submitted each year: NR
# of LD applications accepted yearly: NR
Total # of students receiving LD services: NR
Acceptance into program means acceptance into college: Must be admitted and enrolled, and then request accommodations

ADMISSIONS

There is no separate application for students with disabilities. All applicants are expected to meet the same admission standards. Applicants must submit 2 letters of recommendations. Students may also write an essay to describe aspirations and motivations. ACT or SAT required. Courses required include: 4 English, 3 math, 4 science, 2 social studies, and 5 electives.

ADDITIONAL INFORMATION

The Center for Student Success (CSS) offers access to peer and professional tutoring services and academic resources, enabling all NJCU students to attain the necessary skills, strategies, and behaviors necessary to improve their academic standing and to identify appropriate career objectives. The CSS provides: Individual and small group peer tutoring in basic English and math; Study halls in basic English and math; Workshops on study skills, learning styles, information literacy, financial literacy, and success strategies; Access to computer-based learning skills materials and resources; Referrals to on-campus academic and personal assistance programs; Co-curricular transcript application; Learning and study skills strategies; and Exposure to leadership opportunities.

LEARNING DISABILITY PROGRAMS OR SERVICES

Contact Information
Name of program or department:
  Telephone: 201-200-2091
  Fax: 201-200-3083

LEARNING DISABILITY SERVICES

Accommodations are decided upon an individual basis after a thorough review of appropriate, current documentation. The accommodations requested must be supported through the documentation provided and must be logically linked to the current impact of the condition on academic functioning.

Allowed in exams
  Calculator: Yes
  Dictionary: Yes
  Computer: Yes
  Spellchecker: Yes
Extended test time: Yes
Scribes: Yes
Proctors: Yes
Oral exams: Yes
Note-takers: Yes

Distraction-reduced environment: Yes
Tape recording in class: Yes
Electronic texts: Yes
Accommodations for students with ADHD: Yes
Kurzweil Reader: No
Other assistive technology: Yes
Priority registration: NR

Added costs for services: No
LD specialists: NR
Professional tutors: NR
Peer tutors: Yes
Max. hours/wk. for services: Unlimited
How professors are notified of LD/ADHD: By both student and director

GENERAL ADMISSIONS INFORMATION

Office of Admission: 201-200-3234

ENTRANCE REQUIREMENTS

Academic units required: 4 English, 3 math, 2 science labs, 2 social studies, 5 electives. High school diploma is required, and GED is accepted. Official SAT or ACT scores if you have been out of high school fewer than 5 years. Two letters of recommendation from your high school guidance counselor, teacher or principal regarding your character and readiness for college-level work.

Application deadline: 4/1
Notification: Rolling
Average GPA: 2.7
ACT Composite middle 50% range: NR

SAT Math middle 50% range: 430–510
SAT Critical Reading middle 50% range: 420–500
SAT Writing middle 50% range: 410–500

Graduated top 10% of class: 8%
Graduated top 25% of class: 24%
Graduated top 50% of class: 62%

COLLEGE GRADUATION REQUIREMENTS

Course waivers allowed: No
Course substitutions allowed: Yes
In what course: Each case is reviewed on an individual basis.

ADDITIONAL INFORMATION

Environment: The college is located on 150 acres in a suburban area 20 miles west of New York City.

Student Body
  Undergrad enrollment: 6,639
  Women: 61%
  Men: 39%
  Percent out-of-state: 1%

Cost Information
  In-state tuition: $10,021
  Out-of-state tuition: $17,893
  Room & board: $9,738
Housing Information
  University housing: Yes
  Percent living on campus: 4%

Greek System
  Fraternity: Yes
  Sorority: Yes
  Athletics: Division III

RIDER UNIVERSITY

2083 Lawrenceville Road, Lawrenceville, NJ 08648-3099
Phone: 609-896-5042 • Fax: 609-895-6645
E-mail: admissions@rider.edu • Web: www.rider.edu
Support: CS • Institution: 4-year private

PROGRAMS OR SERVICES FOR STUDENTS WITH LD

Services for Students with Disabilities offer a range of services to help students with documented LD obtain appropriate accommodations. These services include screening and referral, informal assessment, and support services. The goal of the services is to assist students in becoming more independent and efficient learners. A learning disability specialist meets individually with students who have learning disabilities and/or attention deficit disorder. Students must initiate the request for this meeting and must supply documentation of the disability. These learning disability specialists conduct an intake interview and, based on the information resulting from this interview, refer students to appropriate support services. They also determine the appropriate academic adjustments.

ADMISSION INFORMATION FOR STUDENTS WITH LD/ADHD

College entrance tests required: Yes
Interview required: No
Essay required: Yes
What documentation required for LD: Psycho Ed evaluation to include: relevant historical info, instructional interventions, related services, age diagnosed, objective data (aptitude, achievement, info processing), test scores (standard, percentile and grade equivalents) and describe functional limitations.
With general application: No
To receive services after enrolling: Yes
What documentation required for ADHD: Diagnosis based on DSM-V; history of behaviors impairing functioning in academic setting; diagnostic interview; history of symptoms; evidence of ongoing behaviors.

With general application: No
Submitted to: Support Program/Services
Special Ed. HS course work accepted: No
Specific course requirements for all applicants: Yes
Separate application required for program services: No
# of LD applications submitted each year: NR
# of LD applications accepted yearly: NR
Total # of students receiving LD services: NR
Acceptance into program means acceptance into college: Students must be admitted to and enrolled in the university first and then request services.

ADMISSIONS
There is no special admissions process for students with learning disabilities. All students must submit the general university application. Admissions criteria are based on the following: high school academic record and GPA of 2.5 or better; SAT or ACT test results; and a college writing sample (essay). Courses required include 16 acceptable units from a college-prep curriculum: four years English, three years math, and the remaining in sciences, foreign language, social science, and humanities. The Rider Achievement Program is for academically admissible students who are just below the admissions criteria for the regularly admitted student. The Educational Opportunity Fund Program is the state-funded program for academically disadvantaged or economically disadvantaged students.

ADDITIONAL INFORMATION
The Writing Lab provides individual and small group tutoring in writing, reading comprehension, and study strategies. The staff offers study strategy workshops and students have access to computers. The Mathematics Skill Lab provides a math course for students who do not meet the placement criteria for college level math. The course is taught via individual tutoring, structured workshops, and computer-assisted instruction. The MSL staff offers weekly tutorial sessions for Finite Math, helps students prepare for the Algebra & Trig Qualifying Exam, and provides tutoring for other courses. The Student Success Center provides a peer tutoring program for students needing extra help. Courses in College Reading and Introduction to Academic Reading are available.

PROGRAM FOR DISABILITY SERVICES

Contact Information
Name of program or department: Services for Students with Disabilities)
 Telephone: 609-895-5492
 Fax: 609-895-5507

LEARNING DISABILITY SERVICES

Accommodations are decided upon an individual basis after a thorough review of appropriate, current documentation. The accommodations requested must be supported through the documentation provided and must be logically linked to the current impact of the condition on academic functioning.

Allowed in exams
  Calculator: Yes
  Dictionary: Yes
  Computer: Yes
  Spellchecker: Yes
Extended test time: Yes
Scribes: Yes
Proctors: Yes
Oral exams: Yes
Note-takers: Yes

Distraction-reduced environment: Yes
Tape recording in class: Yes
Electronic texts: Yes
Accommodations for students with ADHD: Yes
Kurzweil Reader: Yes
Other assistive technology: Digital book players, mini tape recorders, Kurzweil, Alpha Neo Smart
Priority registration: Yes

Added costs for services: No
LD specialists: Yes
Professional tutors: 3–5
Peer tutors: 100–125
Max. hours/wk. for services: 3
How professors are notified of LD/ADHD: Student

GENERAL ADMISSIONS INFORMATION

Office of Admission: 609-896-5042

ENTRANCE REQUIREMENTS
Academic units required: 4 English, 3 mathematics. **Academic units recommended:** 4 mathematics, 4 science, (2 science labs), 2 foreign language, 2 social studies, 2 history. High school diploma is required and GED is accepted. SAT or ACT required; ACT with Writing component required. TOEFL required of all international applicants; minimum paper TOEFL 550, minimum computer TOEFL 213, minimum web-based TOEFL 80.

Application deadline: None
Notification: Rolling
Average GPA: 3.27
ACT Composite middle 50% range: 18–24

SAT Math middle 50% range: 470–570
SAT Critical Reading middle 50% range: 470–560
SAT Writing middle 50% range: 460–570

Graduated top 10% of class: 16%
Graduated top 25% of class: 45%
Graduated top 50% of class: 79%

COLLEGE GRADUATION REQUIREMENTS

Course substitutions allowed: Yes
In what course: Substitutions are considered on a case-by-case basis only and may be considered for foreign language and math. The common practice is for students to accomplish the courses with academic support and accommodations.

ADDITIONAL INFORMATION

Environment: The college is located on a 353-acre campus between Princeton and Trenton, New Jersey.

Student Body
  Undergrad enrollment: 4,743
  Women: 61%
  Men: 39%
  Percent out-of-state: 25%

Cost Information
  Tuition: $29,870
  Room and board: $12,780
Housing Information
  University housing: Yes
  Percent living on campus: 56%

Greek System
  Fraternity: Yes
  Sorority: Yes
  Athletics: Division I

SETON HALL UNIVERSITY

Enrollment Services, 400 South Orange, South Orange, NJ 07079
Phone: 973-761-9332 • Fax: 973-275-2040
E-mail: thehall@shu.edu • Web: www.shu.edu
Support: CS • Institution: 4-year private

PROGRAMS OR SERVICES FOR STUDENTS WITH LD

The mission of Disability Support Services (DSS) is to provide students with disabilities equal access to all university programs and activities, while raising campus-wide awareness of issues impacting this student population. DSS works collaboratively with academic departments and student affairs offices to engage and support the intellectual and social development of students with disabilities. To this end, DSS employs policies and programming to promote academic excellence, the development of self-advocacy skills, and increased student leadership opportunities. Accommodations are provided based on submission of appropriate documentation, which is reviewed by DSS staff in compliance with university policy, Section 504 of the Rehabilitation Act, the Americans with Disabilities Act (ADA), and the New Jersey Law against Discrimination (NJLAD).

ADMISSION INFORMATION FOR STUDENTS WITH LD/ADHD

College entrance tests required: Yes
Interview required: No
Essay required: N/A
Documentation required for LD: Psychoeducational evaluation. Please visit the DSS website for information on documentation criteria: www.shu.edu/offices/disability-support-services-index.cfm.
Documentation required for ADHD: Yes
Submitted to: Disability Support Services
Special Ed. HS course work accepted: No

Specific course requirements for all applicants: Yes
Separate application required for program services: No
# of LD applications submitted each year: NR
# of LD applications accepted yearly: NR
Total # of students receiving LD services: 200

ADMISSIONS

There is no special admission process for students with learning disabilities, and all applicants must meet the same admission criteria. Courses required include 4 years of English, 3 years of math, 1 year of science lab, 2 years of a foreign language, 2 years of social studies, and 4 electives. If students have been waived from a world language via their IEP, the requirement will be waived if it is not a core requirement of a particular program. The minimum SAT is 900. Students need to rank in the top 40 percent of their class, and a minimum 2.5 GPA is preferred.

ADDITIONAL INFORMATION

In coordinating its activities with other departments of the university (such as Residence Life and Academic Services), Student Support Services works to assure that the university remains in compliance with all federal laws and regulations. The DSS office provides the following services to individuals with LD (with appropriate documentation): reduced course load, extended time to complete assignments, tape recorders, note-taking, taped texts, readers, extended time for in class assignments, assistive technology (calculator, word processor, etc.), extended time for testing, and a distraction-reduced environment.

PROGRAM FOR DISABILITY SERVICES

Contact Information
Name of program or department: Disability Support Services (DSS)
  Telephone: 973-313-6003
  Fax: 973-761-9185

LEARNING DISABILITY SERVICES

Accommodations are decided upon an individual basis after a thorough review of appropriate, current documentation. The accommodations requested must be supported through the documentation provided and must be logically linked to the current impact of the condition on academic functioning.

Allowed in exams	**Distraction-reduced environment:** Yes	**Added costs for services:** No
Calculator: Yes	**Tape recording in class:** Yes	**LD specialists:** Yes
Dictionary: Yes	**Electronic texts:** Yes	**Professional tutors:** Yes
Computer: Yes	**Accommodations for students with**	**Peer tutors:** Yes
Spellchecker: Yes	**ADHD:** Yes	**Max. hours/wk. for services:**
Extended test time: Yes	**Kurzweil Reader:** Yes	**How professors are notified of**
Scribes: Yes	**Other assistive technology:** Assistive	**LD/ADHD:** Student
Proctors: Yes	Technology (hardware and software) is	
Oral exams: Yes	allocated based on each student's	
Note-takers: Yes	individual needs.	
	Priority registration: No	

GENERAL ADMISSIONS INFORMATION

Office of Admission: 973-275-2498

ENTRANCE REQUIREMENTS
Academic units required: 4 English, 3 mathematics, 1 science, (1 science labs), 2 foreign language, 2 social studies, 4 academic electives. High school diploma is required and GED is accepted. SAT or ACT required; ACT with Writing component required. TOEFL required of all international applicants; minimum paper TOEFL 550, minimum computer TOEFL 213.

Application deadline: None	**SAT Math middle 50% range:**	**Graduated top 10% of class:** 22%
Notification: Rolling	470–580	**Graduated top 25% of class:** 50%
Average GPA: 3.13	**SAT Critical Reading middle 50%**	**Graduated top 50% of class:** 83%
ACT Composite middle 50% range:	**range:** 470–570	
20–25	**SAT Writing middle 50% range:**	
	480–580	

COLLEGE GRADUATION REQUIREMENTS

Course waivers allowed: Yes
In what course: Course substitutions for mathematics and world languages are available as long as they are not core courses required for the student's major. These determinations are based on documented need.
Course substitutions allowed: Yes
In what course: Students may request course substitutions through the DSS office for mathematics and world languages. DSS's recommendation is then submitted to the Dean of each school or college for review and approval.

ADDITIONAL INFORMATION

Environment: The university is located on 58 acres in a suburban area 14 miles west of New York City.

Student Body	**Cost Information**	**Greek System**
Undergrad enrollment: 5,301	**Tuition:** $33,490	**Fraternity:** No
Women: 58%	**Room and board:** $12,412	**Sorority:** No
Men: 42%	**Housing Information**	**Athletics:** Division I
Percent out-of-state: 25%	**University housing:** Yes	
	Percent living on campus: 43%	

New Mexico Institute of Mining and Technology

Campus Station, 801 Leroy Place, Socorro, NM 87801
Phone: 575-835-5424 • Fax: 575-835-5989
E-mail: admission@admin.nmt.edu • Web: www.nmt.edu
Support: S • Institution type: 4-year public

PROGRAMS OR SERVICES FOR STUDENTS WITH LD

New Mexico Tech does not have a specific program for students with LD. Services for students with disabilities are available in the Counseling and Student Health Center. Students must present recent documentation completed within the previous 3 years. The documentation should be sent to Office for Counseling and Disability Services. New Mexico Tech sends a letter to all admitted students asking those with disabilities to contact Office for Counseling and Disability Services. There is a special application required after admission and enrollment to receive services or accommodations. The counseling staff works with students with disabilities on an individual basis to accommodate their special needs. Students may also use the counseling service to reduce their stress, think through problems or difficulties, clarify options, and express and explore feelings.

ADMISSION INFORMATION FOR STUDENTS WITH LD/ADHD

College entrance tests required: Yes
Interview required: No
Essay recommended: No
What documentation required for LD: Psycho Ed evaluation to include: relevant historical info, instructional interventions, related services, age diagnosed, objective data (aptitude, achievement, info processing), test scores (standard, percentile and grade equivalents) and describe functional limitations.
With general application: No
To receive services after enrolling: Yes
What documentation required for ADHD: Diagnosis based on DSM-V; history of behaviors impairing functioning in academic setting; diagnostic interview; history of symptoms; evidence of ongoing behaviors.

With general application: No
Submitted to: Office for Counseling and Disability Services
Special Ed. HS course work accepted: NR
Specific course requirements of all applicants: Yes
Separate application required: Yes
# of LD applications submitted each year: NR
# of LD applications accepted yearly: NR
Total # of students receiving LD services: 24
Acceptance into program means acceptance into college: Students must be admitted to and enrolled in the university first and then request services.

ADMISSIONS

There is no special admission process for students with LD. The minimum GPA is a 2.5. The college requires an ACT composite score of 21 or higher or an SAT score of 970 or higher. The college will accept the SAT, but prefers the ACT. The GED is accepted with a score of 50 or higher. High school course requirements include 4 years of English, 2 years of science (including biology, physics, chemistry, and earth science), 3 years of math, and 3 years of social science, of which one must be history. Students are encouraged to self-disclose their disability during the admission process.

ADDITIONAL INFORMATION

Students will work with staff to determine appropriate accommodations or services. These services may include coordinating academic accommodations, extended time for tests, calculators in exams, skills classes in study strategies and time management, and tutorial services available for all students on campus.

LEARNING DISABILITY PROGRAMS OR SERVICES

Contact Information
Name of program or department: Office for Counseling and Disability Services
  Telephone: 575-835-5443
  Fax: 575-835-5959

LEARNING DISABILITY SERVICES

Accommodations are decided upon an individual basis after a thorough review of appropriate, current documentation. The accommodations requested must be supported through the documentation provided and must be logically linked to the current impact of the condition on academic functioning.

Allowed in exams
  Calculator: Yes
  Dictionary: No
  Computer: Yes
  Spellchecker: Yes
Extended test time: Yes
Scribes: Yes
Proctors: Yes
Oral exams: Yes
Note-takers: Yes

Distraction-reduced environment: Yes
Tape recording in class: Yes
Electronic texts: Yes
Accommodations for students with ADHD: Yes
Kurzweil Reader: No
Other assistive technology: Yes
Priority registration: Yes

Added costs for services: No
LD specialists: No
Professional tutors: No
Peer tutors: 50
Max. hours/wk. for services: Unlimited
How professors are notified of LD/ADHD: By both student and director

GENERAL ADMISSIONS INFORMATION

Office of Admission: 575-835-5424

ENTRANCE REQUIREMENTS
Academic units required: 4 English, 3 math, 2 science (2 science labs), 2 social studies, 1 history, 3 academic electives. **Academic units recommended:** 4 English, 4 math, 4 science (3 science labs), 2 foreign language, 3 social studies, 1 history. High school diploma is required, and GED is accepted. ACT with or without Writing component accepted. TOEFL required of all international applicants: minimum paper TOEFL 540, minimum computer TOEFL 207.

Application deadline: 8/1
Notification: Rolling
Average GPA: 3.60
ACT Composite middle 50% range: 23–28

SAT Math middle 50% range: 570–680
SAT Critical Reading middle 50% range: 540–660
SAT Writing middle 50% range: NR

Graduated top 10% of class: 40%
Graduated top 25% of class: 67%
Graduated top 50% of class: 90%

COLLEGE GRADUATION REQUIREMENTS

Course waivers allowed: No
Course substitutions allowed: No

ADDITIONAL INFORMATION

Environment: The campus is located 75 miles from Albuquerque.

Student Body
  Undergrad enrollment: 1,454
  Women: 32%
  Men: 68%
  Percent out-of-state: 17%

Cost Information
  In-state tuition: $4,643
  Out-of-state tuition: $15,095
  Room & board: $6,108
Housing Information
  University housing: Yes
  Percent living on campus: 53%

Greek System
  Fraternity: No
  Sorority: No
Athletics: Intramural

NEW MEXICO STATE UNIVERSITY

PO Box 30001, MSC 3A, Las Cruces, NM 88003-8001
Phone: 505-646-3121 • Fax: 505-646-6330
E-mail: admissions@nmsu.edu • Web: www.nmsu.edu
Support: S • Institution type: 4-year public

PROGRAMS OR SERVICES FOR STUDENTS WITH LD

Services for Students with Disabilities is a component of the Office of Student Development. The staff are committed to providing information and services that assist students with disabilities in personal and academic adjustment to the university community. Services for Students with Disabilities provides assistance with procuring auxiliary aids, coordinating services and resources, and discussing special needs and accommodations, and the staff serve as consultants regarding questions about various accommodations. They work with students to ensure that they have access to all of the programs and services that will affect their full participation in the campus community. Students are encouraged to contact Services for Students with Disabilities to discuss their needs and to register for the program. Students should complete the petition for Services for Students with Disabilities and return it with the appropriate documentation for evaluation and review. A review committee will determine their eligibility and the specific services and accommodations to be provided, and students will be notified by a coordinator. This process takes time, and students are encouraged to start the process as soon as possible.

ADMISSION INFORMATION FOR STUDENTS WITH LD/ADHD

College entrance tests required: Yes
Interview required: No
Essay recommended: No
What documentation required for LD: Psycho Ed evaluation to include: relevant historical info, instructional interventions, related services, age diagnosed, objective data (aptitude, achievement, info processing), test scores (standard, percentile and grade equivalents) and describe functional limitations.
With general application: No
To receive services after enrolling: Yes
What documentation required for ADHD: Diagnosis based on DSM-V; history of behaviors impairing functioning in academic setting; diagnostic interview; history of symptoms; evidence of ongoing behaviors.

With general application: No
Submitted to: Services for Students with Disabilities
Special Ed. HS course work accepted: Yes
Specific course requirements of all applicants: Yes
Separate application required: No
# of LD applications submitted each year: NR
# of LD applications accepted yearly: NR
Total # of students receiving LD services: 90
Acceptance into program means acceptance into college: Students must be admitted to and enrolled in the university first and then request services.

ADMISSIONS
Admission criteria are the same for all students. Admission can be granted on a regular status or provisional status. Regular admission requires high school GPA of 2.5 and 21 ACT or 970 SAT. Course requirements include 4 years of English, 2 years of science, 3 years of math, and 3 years of social studies (1 must be history). Provisional status is possible for students who have a high school GPA of 2.1 and 18 ACT. Students admitted provisionally must take at least 6, but not more than 12, credits in a regular semester and at least 3, but not more than 6, credits in a summer session.

ADDITIONAL INFORMATION
The Center for Learning Assistance offers students the skills they need to excel in college. Students work with learning facilitators to develop or maximize the skills needed for college success. Assistance is offered in time management, concentration, memory, test preparation, test-taking, listening/note-taking, textbook-reading techniques, math and science study skills, reasoning skills, writing, spelling, and grammar. Student Support Services is a program of academic and personal support with the goal of improving the retention and graduation of undergraduate students with disabilities. A mentor is provided for all participants to help motivate them, and tutors help with study skills in specific subjects. Students may have tutors in two subjects and can meet weekly. Other services available are early registration, note-taking services, readers, and test accommodations including extended time, a quiet location, scribes, readers, or other assistance with exams. All services are free.

LEARNING DISABILITY PROGRAMS OR SERVICES

Contact Information
Name of program or department: Services for Students with Disabilities (SSD)
 Telephone: 505-646-6840
 Fax: 505-646-5222

LEARNING DISABILITY SERVICES

Accommodations are decided upon an individual basis after a thorough review of appropriate, current documentation. The accommodations requested must be supported through the documentation provided and must be logically linked to the current impact of the condition on academic functioning.

Allowed in exams	**Distraction-reduced environment:** Yes	**Added costs for services:** No
Calculator: Yes	**Tape recording in class:** Yes	**LD specialists:** No
Dictionary: No	**Electronic texts:** Yes	**Professional tutors:** No
Computer: Yes	**Accommodations for students with**	**Peer tutors:** 50
Spellchecker: Yes	**ADHD:** Yes	**Max. hours/wk. for services:**
Extended test time: Yes	**Kurzweil Reader:** Yes	Unlimited
Scribes: Yes	**Other assistive technology:** Yes	**How professors are notified of**
Proctors: Yes	**Priority registration:** Yes	**LD/ADHD:** By both student and
Oral exams: Yes		director
Note-takers: Yes		

GENERAL ADMISSIONS INFORMATION

Office of Admission: 505-646-3121

ENTRANCE REQUIREMENTS

Academic units required: 4 English, 3 math, 2 science (2 science labs), 1 foreign language. High school diploma is required, and GED is accepted. TOEFL required of all international applicants: minimum paper TOEFL 500.

Application deadline: None	**SAT Math middle 50% range:**	**Graduated top 10% of class:** 17%
Notification: Rolling	430–560	**Graduated top 25% of class:** 44%
Average GPA: 3.40	**SAT Critical Reading middle 50%**	**Graduated top 50% of class:** 76%
ACT Composite middle 50% range:	**range:** 430–560	
18–24	**SAT Writing middle 50% range:**	
	430–550	

COLLEGE GRADUATION REQUIREMENTS

Course waivers allowed: Yes
In what course: Students need to negotiate with the college in which they are majoring.
Course substitutions allowed: Yes
In what course: Students need to negotiate with the college in which they are majoring.

ADDITIONAL INFORMATION

Environment: The university is located on 5,800 acres in a suburban area 40 miles north of El Paso, Texas.

Student Body	**Cost Information**	**Greek System**
Undergrad enrollment: 14,794	**In-state tuition:** $5,827	**Fraternity:** Yes
Women: 55%	**Out-of-state tuition:** $18,268	**Sorority:** Yes
Men: 45%	**Room & board:** $6,620	**Athletics:** Division I
Percent out-of-state: 21%	**Housing Information**	
	University housing: Yes	
	Percent living on campus: 16%	

SANTA FE U. OF ART & DESIGN

1600 St. Michaels Drive, Santa Fe, NM 87505-7634
Phone: 505-473-6133 • Fax: 505-473-6129
E-mail: admissions@csf.edu • Web: www.santafeuniversity.edu
Support: S • Institution type: 4-year private

PROGRAMS OR SERVICES FOR STUDENTS WITH LD

The Academic Resource Center (ARC) houses support services programs designed to assist eligible students to graduate from Santa Fe University. There is no formal disabilities program at the university, but the students do have access to many services and accommodations. Students may receive services in basic skills instruction for reading, study strategies, writing, math, humanities, and science. Students work with the professional staff to set up a support program that meets their specific needs. The initial meeting is during registration. To be eligible for services, students with learning disabilities must provide a current psychoeducational evaluation that identifies their learning disability. Once this documentation is on file with the Academic Resource Center, students may meet with staff to identify the necessary accommodations and services needed to be successful in college.

ADMISSION INFORMATION FOR STUDENTS WITH LD/ADHD

College entrance tests required: Yes
Interview required: Yes
Essay recommended: Yes
What documentation required for LD: Psycho Ed evaluation to include: relevant historical info, instructional interventions, related services, age diagnosed, objective data (aptitude, achievement, info processing), test scores (standard, percentile and grade equivalents) and describe functional limitations.
With general application: No
To receive services after enrolling: Yes
What documentation required for ADHD: Diagnosis based on DSM-V; history of behaviors impairing functioning in academic setting; diagnostic interview; history of symptoms; evidence of ongoing behaviors.

With general application: No
Submitted to: Academic Resource Center
Special Ed. HS course work accepted: Yes
Specific course requirements of all applicants: Yes
Separate application required: No
# of LD applications submitted each year: NR
# of LD applications accepted yearly: NR
Total # of students receiving LD services: NR
Acceptance into program means acceptance into college: Students are admitted to the college and to the Academic Resource Center after applying for services.

ADMISSIONS

There is no separate admission process for students with LD/ADHD. Students with LD/ADHD are required to meet the general admission criteria. This includes course requirements of 3 years of English, 2 years of math, 2 years of science, 2 years of social science, and a recommendation of 2 years of a foreign language. Each applicant is evaluated individually. All traditional first-time candidates for admission are required to go through an on-campus interview process. If students are unable to come to campus because of distance or time, the college will arrange a telephone interview. If admitted, students with a GPA inconsistent with their level of ability arrange for academic support from the Academic Resource Center. Copies of diagnostic examinations not more than 3 years old must document the student's learning disability or ADHD. The results of these tests are sent to the Academic Resource Center after the student is admitted.

ADDITIONAL INFORMATION

Throughout the academic year, the Disabilities Service Office works to support the needs of students with disabilities by providing an initial interview, assessment of accommodation needs, and ongoing support. Services provided by the college could include, but are not limited to, the following: alternative testing, specialized tutoring, academic advisement and career planning, note-takers, interpreters for the hearing impaired, screen-reader software, other assistive technology, peer tutoring, resource information, and referrals. ARC offers students free tutoring in most subjects taught at Santa Fe University of Art & Design. Tutoring helps students more fully understand course material and develop academic strategies helpful in all courses. Individual tutoring is available from professional staff as well as peer tutors. Peer tutors are Santa Fe University students who have excellent academic records, have taken the courses they tutor, and have been trained to work with students with a wide range of needs and learning styles. Tutors also facilitate study groups for many courses offered at the university. These groups provide opportunities to discuss course content, compare notes with other students, and develop success strategies. Accommodations are provided on an individual basis.

LEARNING DISABILITY PROGRAMS OR SERVICES

Contact Information
Name of program or department: Academic Resource Center
  Telephone: 505-473-6570
  Fax: 505-473-6286

LEARNING DISABILITY SERVICES

Accommodations are decided upon an individual basis after a thorough review of appropriate, current documentation. The accommodations requested must be supported through the documentation provided and must be logically linked to the current impact of the condition on academic functioning.

Allowed in exams
  Calculator: Yes
  Dictionary: Yes
  Computer: Yes
  Spellchecker: Yes
Extended test time: Yes
Scribes: Yes
Proctors: Yes
Oral exams: Yes
Note-takers: Yes

Distraction-reduced environment: Yes
Tape recording in class: Yes
Electronic texts: Yes
Accommodations for students with
  ADHD: Yes
Kurzweil Reader: Yes
Other assistive technology: Yes
Priority registration: No

Added costs for services: No
LD specialists: No
Professional tutors: 2
Peer tutors: 5–15
Max. hours/wk. for services: 3
How professors are notified of
  LD/ADHD: By both student and
  director

GENERAL ADMISSIONS INFORMATION

Office of Admission: 505-473-6133

ENTRANCE REQUIREMENTS

Academic units required: 3 English, 2 math, 2 science (2 science labs), 2 social studies, 6 academic electives.
Academic units recommended: 4 English, 3 math, 3 science (2 science labs), 2 foreign language, 2 social studies, 2 history, 4 academic electives. High school diploma is required, and GED is accepted. ACT with Writing component required. TOEFL required of all international applicants: minimum paper TOEFL 550, minimum computer TOEFL 213.

Application deadline: Rolling
Notification: Rolling
Average GPA: 2.98
ACT Composite middle 50% range:
  18–25

SAT Math middle 50% range:
  460–600
SAT Critical Reading middle 50%
  range: 400–510
SAT Writing middle 50% range:
  490–550

Graduated top 10% of class: NR
Graduated top 25% of class: NR
Graduated top 50% of class: NR

COLLEGE GRADUATION REQUIREMENTS

Course waivers allowed: Yes
In what course: This is done on an individual basis, depending on the experience of the individual student.
Course substitutions allowed: Yes
In what course: Again, it is done on a case-by-case basis, but substitution is common for all students here.

ADDITIONAL INFORMATION

Environment: The college is located on 60 acres in a suburban area of Santa Fe.

Student Body
  Undergrad enrollment: 400
  Women: 51%
  Men: 49%
  Percent out-of-state: 68%

Cost Information
  Tuition: $27,996
  Room & board: $8,984
Housing Information
  University housing: Yes
  Percent living on campus: 60%

Greek System
  Fraternity: No
  Sorority: No
  Athletics: No

ADELPHI UNIVERSITY

Levermore Hall 114, One South Avenue, Garden City, NY 11530
Phone: 516-877-3050 • Fax: 516-877-3039
E-mail: admissions@adelphi.edu • Web: www.adelphi.edu
Support: SP • Institution type: 4-year private

PROGRAMS OR SERVICES FOR STUDENTS WITH LD

The approach of the Learning Disabilities Program at Adelphi is to provide an atmosphere where students with LD/ADHD can realize their potential. The program is specially designed for students unable to process oral and written materials in conventional ways, but who excel in other ways. Each student is provided with the support of an interdisciplinary team of experienced professionals in tutoring and counseling. All instruction, counseling, and assessment are provided by more than 17 professionals with advanced degrees in special education and social work. Students meet individually with an educator and a counselor who work as a team. There is a mandatory summer program prior to freshman year. Students attend tutoring sessions two times a week, participate in all the program's services, and sign an agreement acknowledging their academic commitment. Students attend classes in their chosen major and meet standard academic requirements. The goal is independence in the academic and the real world.

ADMISSION INFORMATION FOR STUDENTS WITH LD/ADHD

College entrance tests required: Yes, by Admissions
Interview required: Yes
Essay recommended: Yes
Documentation required for LD: WAIS–IV, WJ–III, and specific LD diagnosis with psychoeducational evaluation
Documentation required for ADHD: Comprehensive evaluation with written interpretive report or ADHD certification, WAIS-IV, Achievement Testing
Submitted to: Learning Disabilities Program
Special Ed. HS course work accepted: No

Specific course requirements of all applicants: NR
Separate application required: Yes
# of LD applications submitted each year: 400–450
# of LD applications accepted yearly: 75–100
Total # of students receiving LD services: 125
Acceptance into program means acceptance into college: Yes.

ADMISSIONS

The Admissions Committee reviews all submitted materials for a total picture of strengths and disabilities. Applicants with LD who show an ability to succeed academically are invited to interview. They must submit a high school transcript, documentation of LD, ACT/SAT scores, and recent testing. The director of the program is actively involved in the admissions decision and conducts a highly individualized assessment of each applicant and their documentation. Motivation, college-prep courses, average or higher IQ (WAIS–IV), interview, documentation, and a recommendation from an LD specialist are factors that are used in making an admission decision. Prior to applying, applicants should attend an information session conducted by the program. The program seeks highly motivated and socially mature individuals with average to superior intelligence that are capable of handling full academic schedules. Judgment of the professional staff will determine the applicant's eligibility for the program.

ADDITIONAL INFORMATION

Students receive intensive academic tutoring and individual counseling that begin in the summer program. Course content and requirements are never compromised for students with learning disabilities, but program procedures do help to ease the way in the classroom. For example, in individual tutorials, professional special educators teach how to get the most of studies; instructors are privately notified if program students are in their classes; and deal with stress, frustration, and other issues of transition. Approximately 25 percent of these students make the dean's list.

LEARNING DISABILITY PROGRAMS OR SERVICES

Contact Information
Name of program or department: Learning Disabilities Program
 Telephone: 516-877-4710
 Fax: 516-877-4711

LEARNING DISABILITY SERVICES

Accommodations are decided upon an individual basis after a thorough review of appropriate, current documentation. The accommodations requested must be supported through the documentation provided and must be logically linked to the current impact of the condition on academic functioning.

Allowed in exams	**Distraction-reduced environment:** Yes	**Added costs for services:** Yes
Calculator: Yes	**Tape recording in class:** Yes	**LD specialists:** Yes
Dictionary: Yes	**Electronic texts:** Yes	**Professional tutors:** No
Computer: Yes	**Accommodations for students with**	**Peer tutors:** No
Spellchecker: Yes	**ADHD:** Yes	**Max. hours/wk. for services:** 3–5
Extended test time: Yes	**Kurzweil Reader:** Yes	**How professors are notified of**
Scribes: Yes	**Other assistive technology:** Yes	**LD/ADHD:** By both student and
Proctors: Yes	**Priority registration:** Yes	program
Oral exams: Yes		
Note-takers: Yes		

GENERAL ADMISSIONS INFORMATION

Office of Admission: 516-877-3050

ENTRANCE REQUIREMENTS

Academic units recommended: 4 English, 3 math, 3 science, 2 foreign language, 4 electives from social studies, history, English, math, science, or foreign language. High school diploma is required, and GED is accepted. ACT with Writing component required. TOEFL required of all international applicants: minimum paper TOEFL 550, minimum computer TOEFL 213.

Application deadline: None	**SAT Math middle 50% range:**	**Graduated top 10% of class:** 22%
Notification: Rolling	500–600	**Graduated top 25% of class:** 54%
Average GPA: 3.40	**SAT Critical Reading middle 50%**	**Graduated top 50% of class:** 91%
ACT Composite middle 50% range:	**range:** 480–580	
21–26	**SAT Writing middle 50% range:**	
	500–600	

COLLEGE GRADUATION REQUIREMENTS

Course waivers allowed: No
Course substitutions allowed: No

ADDITIONAL INFORMATION

Environment: The university is located on a 75-acre campus 20 miles from New York City.

Student Body	**Cost Information**	**Greek System**
Undergrad enrollment: 5,021	**Tuition:** $28,460	**Fraternity:** Yes
Women: 70%	**Room & board:** $11,420	**Sorority:** Yes
Men: 30%	**Housing Information**	**Athletics:** Division II
Percent out-of-state: 8%	**University housing:** Yes	
	Percent living on campus: 24%	

COLGATE UNIVERSITY

13 Oak Drive, Hamilton, NY 13346
Phone: 315-228-7401 • Fax: 315-228-7544
E-mail: admission@mail.colgate.edu • Web: www.colgate.edu
Support: CS • Institution type: 4-year private

PROGRAMS OR SERVICES FOR STUDENTS WITH LD

Colgate provides for a small student body a liberal arts education that will expand individual potential and ability to participate effectively in society's affairs. There are many resources available for all students. Colgate's goal is to offer resources and services within the campus-wide support system that are responsive to the various talents, needs, and preferences of students with disabilities. For the university to understand and prepare for the accommodations that may be requested, students are asked to complete a confidential self-assessment questionnaire and provide appropriate documentation about their disability. The Director of Academic Support and Disability Services works with students and faculty to assure that the needs of students with disabilities are met, serves as clearinghouse for information about disabilities, provides training and individual consultation for all members of the Colgate community, and provides academic counseling and individualized instruction. Seeking help early and learning to be a self-advocate are essential to college success.

ADMISSION INFORMATION FOR STUDENTS WITH LD/ADHD

College entrance tests required: Yes
Interview required: No
Essay recommended: No
What documentation required for LD: Psycho Ed evaluation to include: relevant historical info, instructional interventions, related services, age diagnosed, objective data (aptitude, achievement, info processing), test scores (standard, percentile and grade equivalents) and describe functional limitations.
With general application: No
To receive services after enrolling: Yes
What documentation required for ADHD: Diagnosis based on DSM-V; history of behaviors impairing functioning in academic setting; diagnostic interview; history of symptoms; evidence of ongoing behaviors.

With general application: No
Submitted to: Academic Support
Special Ed. HS course work accepted: No
Specific course requirements of all applicants: Yes
Separate application required: No
# of LD applications submitted each year: NR
# of LD applications accepted yearly: NR
Total # of students receiving LD services: NR
Acceptance into program means acceptance into college: Students must be admitted to and enrolled in the university first and then request services.

ADMISSIONS
There is no special admission process for students with learning disabilities. The Office of Admissions reviews the applications of all candidates for admission. The admissions staff looks for evidence of substantial achievement in a rigorous secondary school curriculum, one counselor recommendation, standardized testing, a personalized essay, and extracurricular involvement. Also valued are qualities such as curiosity, originality, thoughtfulness, and persistence. Admission is very competitive. Criteria include 16 courses in a college-preparatory program (20 recommended): 4 years of English, 3–4 years of math, 3–4 years of science, 3–4 years of social studies, and 3 years of a foreign language. The ACT average is 29 or the SAT Reasoning Test average is 1348. Three SAT Subject Tests of the applicant's choice are required if the applicant submits the SAT Reasoning Test. However, SAT Subject Tests are not required if the applicant submits the ACT.

ADDITIONAL INFORMATION
Students are encouraged to seek help early; meet with professors at the beginning of each semester to discuss approaches and accommodations that will meet their needs; and seek assistance from the Director of Academic Support and Disability Services, administrative advisor, and faculty advisor. Modifications in the curriculum are made on an individual basis. Colgate provides services in support of academic work on an as-needed basis, such as assistance with note-takers, tape-recorded lectures, tutors, readers, and assistive technology. There is a Writing and Speaking Center and tutoring, and skills help is available in writing, reading, and study strategies. Services and accommodations are available for undergraduate and graduate students.

LEARNING DISABILITY PROGRAMS OR SERVICES

Contact Information
Name of program or department: Academic Program Support and Disability Services
 Telephone: 315-228-7375
 Fax: 315-228-7831

LEARNING DISABILITY SERVICES

Accommodations are decided upon an individual basis after a thorough review of appropriate, current documentation. The accommodations requested must be supported through the documentation provided and must be logically linked to the current impact of the condition on academic functioning.

Allowed in exams
 Calculator: Yes
 Dictionary: Yes
 Computer: Yes
 Spellchecker: Yes
Extended test time: Yes
Scribes: Yes
Proctors: Yes
Oral exams: Yes
Note-takers: Yes

Distraction-reduced environment: Yes
Tape recording in class: Yes
Electronic texts: Yes
**Accommodations for students with
 ADHD:** Yes
Kurzweil Reader: Yes
Other assistive technology: Yes
Priority registration: Yes

Added costs for services: No
LD specialists: Yes
Professional tutors: No
Peer tutors: Yes
Max. hours/wk. for services:
 Unlimited
**How professors are notified of
 LD/ADHD:** By student

GENERAL ADMISSIONS INFORMATION

Office of Admission: 315-228-7401

ENTRANCE REQUIREMENTS

Academic units required: 4 English, 3 math, 3 science (2 science labs), 3 foreign language, 3 social studies, 1 history. **Academic units recommended:** 4 English, 4 math, 4 science (3 science labs), 4 foreign language, 4 social studies, 3 history. High school diploma is required, and GED is accepted. ACT with or without Writing component accepted. TOEFL required of all international applicants: minimum paper TOEFL 600, minimum computer TOEFL 250.

Application deadline: 1/15
Notification: 4/1
Average GPA: 3.62
ACT Composite middle 50% range:
 29–32

SAT Math middle 50% range:
 640–740
**SAT Critical Reading middle 50%
 range:** 630–720
SAT Writing middle 50% range: NR

Graduated top 10% of class: 64%
Graduated top 25% of class: 90%
Graduated top 50% of class: 98%

COLLEGE GRADUATION REQUIREMENTS

Course waivers allowed: Yes
Course substitutions allowed: Yes
In what course: Foreign language—all requests are considered case-by-case.

ADDITIONAL INFORMATION

Environment: The university is located in a small town about 45 miles from Syracuse.

Student Body
 Undergrad enrollment: 2,884
 Women: 52%
 Men: 48%
 Percent out-of-state: 74%

Cost Information
 Tuition: $42,625
 Room & board: $10,650
Housing Information
 University housing: Yes
 Percent living on campus: 91%

Greek System
 Fraternity: Yes
 Sorority: Yes
Athletics: Division I

CONCORDIA COLLEGE (NY)

171 White Plains Road, Bronxville, NY 10708
Phone: 914-337-9300 • Fax: 914-395-4636
E-mail: admission@concordia-ny.edu • Web: www.concordia-ny.edu
Support: CS • Institution type: 4-year private

PROGRAMS OR SERVICES FOR STUDENTS WITH LD

Concordia Connection is a program for students with LD who have demonstrated the potential to earn a college degree. Their commitment is to provide an intimate, supportive, and caring environment where students with special learning needs can experience college as a successful and rewarding endeavor. This is a mainstream program. Students are fully integrated into the college. During the fall and spring semesters, students are registered for four or five classes. Additionally, students are registered for a one-credit independent study, which incorporates a weekly, 1-hour group session with the director and staff that focuses on the development of individualized learning strategies. Progress is monitored, and an assessment of learning potential and academic levels is provided. The program's Director coordinates support services and works with the assigned freshman advisor to assure an optimal course plan each semester. A one summer orientation and academic seminar is required for all new Concordia Connection students.

ADMISSION INFORMATION FOR STUDENTS WITH LD/ADHD

College entrance tests required: Yes
Interview required: No
Essay recommended: Yes
What documentation required for LD: Psycho Ed evaluation to include: relevant historical info, instructional interventions, related services, age diagnosed, objective data (aptitude, achievement, info processing), test scores (standard, percentile and grade equivalents) and describe functional limitations.
With general application: No
To receive services after enrolling: Yes
What documentation required for ADHD: Diagnosis based on DSM-V; history of behaviors impairing functioning in academic setting; diagnostic interview; history of symptoms; evidence of ongoing behaviors.

With general application: No
Submitted to: Admissions
Special Ed. HS course work accepted: No
Specific course requirements of all applicants: Yes
Separate application required: No
# of LD applications submitted each year: 30–45
# of LD applications accepted yearly: 10–16
Total # of students receiving LD services: 32–50
Acceptance into program means acceptance into college: Students must be admitted to and enrolled in the university first and then request services. Some are reviewed by the LD program, which provides a recommendation to the Admissions Office.

ADMISSIONS

Students wishing to apply should submit the following documents to the Admissions Office: a Concordia application and the student's current transcript; SAT/ACT scores; documentation of LD, which must minimally include a WAIS–IV profile with subtest scores that was completed within the past year and the student's most recent IEP; recommendations from an LD specialist and a guidance counselor; and an essay describing the nature of the LD, the effect on learning patterns, and the student's reason for pursuing college. Visits are encouraged. Applicants must be high school graduates, have a diagnosed LD, have college-prep courses, and be committed to being successful. General admissions criteria include a B average, ACT/SAT scores (used to assess strengths and weaknesses rather than for acceptance or denial), and college-preparatory courses in high school (foreign language is recommended but not required). Students with LD who self-disclose and provide documentation will be reviewed by the Admissions Office and the Director of Concordia Connection.

ADDITIONAL INFORMATION

The Concordia Connection provides services to all students. These include test-taking modifications, taped text books, computer access, and tutoring. Although there are no charges for students requesting peer tutoring, there is a $3,000 per semester charge for program services. Skills courses for credit are offered in time management, organizational skills, and study skills. The 1-day summer orientation helps students get acquainted with support services, get exposure to academic expectations, review components and requirements of the freshman year, develop group cohesion, and explore individualized needs and strategies for seeking assistance.

LEARNING DISABILITY PROGRAMS OR SERVICES

Contact Information
Name of program or department: The Concordia Connection Program
 Telephone: 914-337-9300, ext. 2361
 Fax: 914-395-4500

LEARNING DISABILITY SERVICES

Accommodations are decided upon an individual basis after a thorough review of appropriate, current documentation. The accommodations requested must be supported through the documentation provided and must be logically linked to the current impact of the condition on academic functioning.

Allowed in exams	**Distraction-reduced environment:** Yes	**Added costs for services:** Yes
Calculator: Yes	**Tape recording in class:** Yes	**LD specialists:** Yes
Dictionary: Yes	**Electronic texts:** No	**Professional tutors:** 3–6
Computer: Yes	**Accommodations for students with**	**Peer tutors:** 10–20
Spellchecker: Yes	**ADHD:** Yes	**Max. hours/wk. for services:** 10
Extended test time: Yes	**Kurzweil Reader:** No	**How professors are notified of**
Scribes: Yes	**Other assistive technology:** No	**LD/ADHD:** By both student and
Proctors: Yes	**Priority registration:** Yes	director
Oral exams: Yes		
Note-takers: Yes		

GENERAL ADMISSIONS INFORMATION

Office of Admission: 914-337-9300

ENTRANCE REQUIREMENTS

Academic units required: 4 English, 3 math, 2 science (2 science labs), 2 foreign language, 2 social studies, 2 history. High school diploma is required, and GED is accepted. ACT without Writing component accepted. TOEFL required of all international applicants: minimum paper TOEFL 550, minimum computer TOEFL 213.

Application deadline: 3/15	**SAT Math middle 50% range:**	**Graduated top 10% of class:** 4%
Notification: Rolling	410–500	**Graduated top 25% of class:** 21%
Average GPA: 2.82	**SAT Critical Reading middle 50%**	**Graduated top 50% of class:** 50%
ACT Composite middle 50% range:	**range:** 410–490	
18-21	**SAT Writing middle 50% range:**	
	410–480	

COLLEGE GRADUATION REQUIREMENTS

Course waivers allowed: No
Course substitutions allowed: Yes
In what course: Substitution of American Sign Language for foreign language

ADDITIONAL INFORMATION

Environment: The college is in a suburban area approximately 15 miles north of New York City.

Student Body	**Cost Information**	**Greek System**
Undergrad enrollment: 820	**Tuition:** $25,650	**Fraternity:** Yes
Women: 65%	**Room & board:** $9,365	**Sorority:** Yes
Men: 35%	**Housing Information**	**Athletics:** Division II
Percent out-of-state: 26%	**University housing:** Yes	
	Percent living on campus: 68%	

CORNELL UNIVERSITY

Undergraduate Admissions, 410 Thurston Avenue, Ithaca, NY 14850
Phone: 607-255-5241 • Fax: 607-255-0659
E-mail: admissions@cornell.edu • Web: www.cornell.edu
Support: S • Institution type: 4-year private

PROGRAMS OR SERVICES FOR STUDENTS WITH LD

Cornell University strives to be an accessible community where students with disabilities have an equitable opportunity to fully participate in all aspects of university life. Students with disabilities must submit requests for disability services to the Student Disability Services (SDS) office. The SDS staff is responsible for determining appropriate and effective federally mandated support services for eligible students. The University provides support services for a broad range of disabilities. There is not a specific program designed for students with learning disabilities. Once a student has been approved for disability services, many units across campus are responsible for fulfilling access needs. Students are directly involved in the process of arranging accommodations with instructors and for following established procedures for using disability services.

ADMISSION INFORMATION FOR STUDENTS WITH LD/ADHD

College entrance tests required: Yes
Interview required: No
Essay recommended: No
What documentation required for LD: Psycho Ed evaluation to include: relevant historical info, instructional interventions, related services, age diagnosed, objective data (aptitude, achievement, info processing), test scores (standard, percentile and grade equivalents) and describe functional limitations.
With general application: No
To receive services after enrolling: Yes
What documentation required for ADHD: Diagnosis based on DSM-V; history of behaviors impairing functioning in academic setting; diagnostic interview; history of symptoms; evidence of ongoing behaviors.

With general application: No
Submitted to: Student Disability Services
Special Ed. HS course work accepted: Yes
Specific course requirements of all applicants: Yes
Separate application required: No
# of LD applications submitted each year: NR
# of LD applications accepted yearly: NR
Total # of students receiving LD services: 135–160
Acceptance into program means acceptance into college: Students must be admitted to and enrolled in the university first and then request services.

ADMISSIONS

Cornell does not have a special admissions process for students with learning disabilities. All students applying to Cornell are expected to meet admissions criteria. General admission requirements include 16 units of English, math, science, social studies, and foreign language. Each of the seven undergraduate colleges has its own specific requirements. Admission is very competitive and most of the admitted students rank in the top 10 percent of the class, at least, and have taken AP and honors courses in high school. Disability documentation should not be sent along with the admissions application, but should be sent directly to Student Disability Services after acceptance to Cornell.

ADDITIONAL INFORMATION

Students are encouraged to complete a disability self-identification form that is included on the New Students website. Once Student Disability Services has received current and complete documentation of a disability, the staff will work with students to determine effective and reasonable accommodations. Diagnostic testing, remedial courses, and tutors specifically selected to work with students with LD are not available at Cornell. The Learning Strategies Center provides general supportive services including classes and workshops in reading comprehension, organizational skills, note-taking, and exam preparation. The Learning Strategies Center is available to all students.

LEARNING DISABILITY PROGRAMS OR SERVICES

Contact Information
Name of program or department: Student Disability Services
  Telephone: 607-254-4545
  Fax: 607-255-1562

LEARNING DISABILITY SERVICES

Disability services and accommodations are provided in order to afford equitable opportunity to participate in Cornell's courses and program. Decisions regarding services are determined on an individual basis using relevant information including: a) the student's skills and abilities; b) the impact of the disability on a major life activity; c) the sufficiency of the documentation provided; c) available, effective and reasonable accommodations. An SDS Counselor is assigned to each student. The Counselor and student meet to discuss the information above and decide together on an accommodation plan. The accommodations listed below are an example of those approved for a student after an individualized assessment.

Allowed in exams	**Distraction-reduced environment:** Yes	**Added costs for services:** No
Calculator: Yes	**Tape recording in class:** Yes	**LD specialists:** No
Dictionary: Yes	**Electronic texts:** Yes	**Professional tutors:** No
Computer: Yes	**Accommodations for students with**	**Peer tutors:** Yes
Spellchecker: Yes	**ADHD:** Yes	**Max. hours/wk. for services:**
Extended test time: Yes	**Kurzweil Reader:** No	Unlimited
Scribes: Yes	**Other assistive technology:** Yes	**How professors are notified of**
Proctors: Yes	**Priority registration:** No	**LD/ADHD:** By student
Oral exams: No		
Note-takers: Yes		

GENERAL ADMISSIONS INFORMATION

Office of Admission: 607-255-5241

ENTRANCE REQUIREMENTS

Academic units required: 4 English, 3 math. **Academic units recommended:** 3 science (3 science labs), 3 foreign language, 3 social studies, 3 history. High school diploma or equivalent is not required. ACT with Writing component required. TOEFL required of all international applicants: minimum paper TOEFL 550, minimum computer TOEFL 250.

Application deadline: 1/2	**SAT Math middle 50% range:**	**Graduated top 10% of class:** 89%
Notification: early April	670–770	**Graduated top 25% of class:** 98%
Average GPA: NR	**SAT Critical Reading middle 50%**	**Graduated top 50% of class:** 99%
ACT Composite middle 50% range:	**range:** 630–730	
29–33	**SAT Writing middle 50% range:** NR	

COLLEGE GRADUATION REQUIREMENTS

Course waivers allowed: No
Course substitutions allowed: Yes
In what course: Foreign language

ADDITIONAL INFORMATION

Environment: Cornell is located 45 minutes from Syracuse on the southern end of Cayuga Lake in the Finger Lakes region.

Student Body	**Cost Information**	**Greek System**
Undergrad enrollment: 14,167	**Tuition:** $43,413	**Fraternity:** Yes
Women: 50%	**Room & board:** $13,678	**Sorority:** Yes
Men: 50%	**Housing Information**	**Athletics:** Division I
Percent out-of-state: 65%	**University housing:** Yes	
	Percent living on campus: 57%	

DOWLING COLLEGE

Idle Hour Boulevard, Oakdale, NY 11769-1999
Phone: 800-369-5464 • Fax: 631-563-3827
E-mail: admissions@dowling.edu • Web: www.dowling.edu
Support: SP • Institution type: 4-year private

PROGRAMS OR SERVICES FOR STUDENTS WITH LD

Dowling College's Program for Potentially Gifted College Students (it is still a program devoted to students with learning disabilities; however, as one recent graduate noted, "We learn differently, we do not have a disability") is a small, individualized program that provides for cognitive development. The college is looking for students who are committed to life-long learning who have taken academically demanding courses in high school. They seek students who are eager and willing to persevere to achieve their goals. Additionally, students need to be interested and involved in community and extracurricular activities. There is a fee of approximately $2,000 per semester for services from the LD program. Students must submit a recent psychoevaluation and an IEP to be eligible to receive services or accommodations. Students are encouraged to make sure that their IEPs include all of the necessary accommodations. Students sign a contract promising to attend tutoring sessions and all of their classes. Services are available all four years; additionally, for those who have completed an undergraduate program at Dowling, a graduate program is now offered.

ADMISSION INFORMATION FOR STUDENTS WITH LD/ADHD

College entrance tests required: Yes
Interview required: Yes, after acceptance into Dowling
Essay recommended: No
What documentation required for LD: Psycho Ed evaluation to include: relevant historical info, instructional interventions, related services, age diagnosed, objective data (aptitude, achievement, info processing), test scores (standard, percentile and grade equivalents) and describe functional limitations.
With general application: Yes if requested as part of Structured Program application
To receive services after enrolling: Yes
What documentation required for ADHD: Diagnosis based on DSM-V; history of behaviors impairing functioning in academic setting; diagnostic interview; history of symptoms; evidence of ongoing behaviors.

With general application: Yes if requested as part of Structured Program application
To receive services after enrolling: Yes
Submitted to: Admissions
Special Ed. HS course work accepted: NR
Specific course requirements of all applicants: NR
Separate application required: Yes
# of LD applications submitted each year: 20
# of LD applications accepted yearly: 6–11
Total # of students receiving LD services: 25
Acceptance into program means acceptance into college: Students must be admitted to and enrolled in the university first and then request services.

ADMISSIONS

Students must be admitted to Dowling College first and then may request an application to the Program for Potentially Gifted College Students. Applicants to Dowling College are encouraged to submit either the ACT or SAT. Students should have 16 academic courses in high school, including four years of English. Students must have an interview. Once a student with LD has been admitted to the college, s/he may submit an application to the LD program. Both student and parent are required to complete an application. Students must submit their most recent IEP and psychoeducational evaluation. An interview is required, and the director of Dowling's Program for Potentially Gifted College Students looks for students with tenacity and motivation. Approximately 25 students are admitted to the program each year.

ADDITIONAL INFORMATION

The Program for Potentially Gifted College Students offers support services, and a liaison between professors and students, weekly writing workshops and early individualized class selection. In addition, students who have specific discipline needs will visit the student service center. The Program will concentrate on developing individualized academic strategies for success; tutors are trained to provide academic support. This is a lab school at which students with learning disabilities receive tutoring at least twice a week in learning strategies. Students are eligible to receive all accommodations or services that are listed in their most recent IEP. For students who will not be serviced in Dowling's Program for Potentially Gifted College Students, there is the Hausman Center.

LEARNING DISABILITY PROGRAMS OR SERVICES

Contact Information
Name of program or department: Program for Potentially Gifted College Students
  Telephone: 631-244-3306
  Fax: 631-244-5036

LEARNING DISABILITY SERVICES

Accommodations are decided upon an individual basis after a thorough review of appropriate, current documentation. The accommodations requested must be supported through the documentation provided and must be logically linked to the current impact of the condition on academic functioning.

Allowed in exams
  Calculator: Yes
  Dictionary: Yes
  Computer: Yes
  Spellchecker: Yes
Extended test time: Yes
Scribes: Yes
Proctors: Yes
Oral exams: Yes
Note-takers: Yes

Distraction-reduced environment: Yes
Tape recording in class: Yes
Electronic texts: Yes
Accommodations for students with
  ADHD: Yes
Kurzweil Reader: Yes
Other assistive technology: Yes
Priority registration: Yes

Added costs for services: Yes
LD specialists: Yes
Professional tutors: 25
Peer tutors: No
Max. hours/wk. for services:
  Unlimited
How professors are notified of
  LD/ADHD: By director

GENERAL ADMISSIONS INFORMATION

Office of Admission: 631-244-3436

ENTRANCE REQUIREMENTS

Academic units recommended: 4 English, 3 math, 2 science, 3 social studies, 4 electives. High school diploma is required, and GED is accepted.

Application deadline: None
Notification: Rolling
Average GPA: NR
ACT Composite middle 50% range: NR

SAT Math middle 50% range: NR
SAT Critical Reading middle 50% range: NR
SAT Writing middle 50% range: NR

Graduated top 10% of class: NR
Graduated top 25% of class: NR
Graduated top 50% of class: NR

COLLEGE GRADUATION REQUIREMENTS

Course waivers allowed: Yes
In what course: Foreign language
Course substitutions allowed: Yes
In what course: Foreign language

ADDITIONAL INFORMATION

Environment: The university is located 50 miles from New York City.

Student Body
  Undergrad enrollment: 3,402
  Women: 56%
  Men: 44%
  Percent out-of-state: 7%

Cost Information
  Tuition: $24,118
  Room & board: $10,770
Housing Information
  University housing: Yes
  Percent living on campus: 17%

Greek System
  Fraternity: No
  Sorority: No
  Athletics: Division II

HOFSTRA UNIVERSITY

Admissions Center, Bernon Hall, Hempstead, NY 11549
Phone: 516-463-6700 • Fax: 516-463-5100
E-mail: admitmission@hofstra.edu • Web: www.hofstra.edu
Support: SP • Institution type: 4-year private

PROGRAMS OR SERVICES FOR STUDENTS WITH LD

The Program for Academic Learning Skills (PALS) seeks candidates who have been diagnosed with Specific Learning Disabilities and/or ADHD and who show above average intellectual ability and emotional stability. The program concentrates on identifying qualified applicants for entrance to the University and on enhancing the independent learning skills that will help students achieve academic success. The PALS program is administered by Services for Students with Disabilities (SSD) and consists of one-to-one support and services over and above the accommodations afforded to any qualified student with a disability. Each participant in the PALS program will meet weekly with their assigned learning specialist with the goal of developing more effective learning, organizational and time-management strategies. These weekly meetings are mandatory during the first year and optional thereafter.

ADMISSION INFORMATION FOR STUDENTS WITH LD/ADHD

College entrance tests required: No
Interview required: Yes
Essay recommended: No
What documentation required for LD: Psycho Ed evaluation to include: relevant historical info, instructional interventions, related services, age diagnosed, objective data (aptitude, achievement, info processing), test scores (standard, percentile and grade equivalents) and describe functional limitations.
With general application: Yes if requested as part of Structured Program application
To receive services after enrolling: Yes
What documentation required for ADHD: Diagnosis based on DSM-V; history of behaviors impairing functioning in academic setting; diagnostic interview; history of symptoms; evidence of ongoing behaviors.

With general application: Yes if requested as part of Structured Program application
To receive services after enrolling: Yes
Submitted to: Admissions
Special Ed. HS course work accepted: NR
Specific course requirements of all applicants: Yes
Separate application required: No
# of LD applications submitted each year: 287
# of LD applications accepted yearly: 42
Total # of students receiving LD services: 30
Acceptance into program means acceptance into college: Students who are admitted to PALS are automatically admitted to the university.

ADMISSIONS

Students applying to PALS must meet the same admission criteria as other University applicants. All application materials and disability documentation should be submitted for review prior to scheduling an interview for the PALS program. Students who do not meet University admissions criteria may be referred to Hofstra's School for University Studies. The interview is very important, as admissions decisions are often made jointly by Services for Students with Disabilities and the Office of Admissions. Although PALS is intended for first-time first year students, on occasion, transfer students with less than 30 transferrable credit hours are considered for the program.

ADDITIONAL INFORMATION

Accommodations for all qualified students with LD and/or ADHD (including those not enrolled in PALS) include extended time and a separate location for exams, use of assistive technology including alternate format texts, screen reading or voice activating software, and note-taking assistance. Currently, content area tutoring is not available through PALS, but is available for all students through the University Tutorial Program (UTP).

LEARNING DISABILITY PROGRAMS OR SERVICES

Contact Information
Name of program or department: Program for Academic Learning Skills (PALS)
  Telephone: 516-463-7075
  Fax: 516-463-7074

LEARNING DISABILITY SERVICES

Accommodations are decided upon an individual basis after a thorough review of appropriate, current documentation. The accommodations requested must be supported through the documentation provided and must be logically linked to the current impact of the condition on academic functioning.

Allowed in exams
  Calculator: Yes
  Dictionary: Yes
  Computer: Yes
  Spellchecker: Yes
Extended test time: Yes
Scribes: Yes
Proctors: Yes
Oral exams: Yes
Note-takers: Yes

Distraction-reduced environment: Yes
Tape recording in class: Yes
Electronic texts: Yes
Accommodations for students with ADHD: Yes
Kurzweil Reader: Yes
Other assistive technology: Yes
Priority registration: No

Added costs for services: Yes (for PALS services)
LD specialists: Yes
Professional tutors: No
Peer tutors: No
Max. hours/wk. for services: 1
How professors are notified of LD/ADHD: Student

GENERAL ADMISSIONS INFORMATION

Office of Admission: 516-463-6700

ENTRANCE REQUIREMENTS
Academic units required: 4 English, 3 math, 3 science (1 science lab), 2 foreign language, 3 social studies.
Academic units recommended: 4 math, 4 science (2 science labs), 3 foreign language, 4 social studies. High school diploma is required, and GED is accepted. ACT with Writing component required. TOEFL required of all international applicants: minimum paper TOEFL 550, minimum computer TOEFL 213.

Application deadline: None
Notification: Rolling
Average GPA: 3.51
ACT Composite middle 50% range: 23–27

SAT Math middle 50% range: 550–630
SAT Critical Reading middle 50% range: 530–620
SAT Writing middle 50% range: NR

Graduated top 10% of class: 25%
Graduated top 25% of class: 56%
Graduated top 50% of class: 87%

COLLEGE GRADUATION REQUIREMENTS

Course waivers allowed: No
Course substitutions allowed: Yes
In what course: Students requesting accommodations for foreign language requirements must meet with the PALS director soon after beginning their first semester.

ADDITIONAL INFORMATION

Environment: Hempstead is a residential community in Long Island just outside New York City.

Student Body
  Undergrad enrollment: 7,183
  Women: 53%
  Men: 47%
  Percent out-of-state: 45%

Cost Information
  Tuition: $33,100
  Room & board: $11,940
Housing Information
  University housing: Yes
  Percent living on campus: 47%

Greek System
  Fraternity: Yes
  Sorority: Yes
Athletics: Division I

IONA COLLEGE

715 North Avenue, New Rochelle, NY 10801
Phone: 914-633-2502 • Fax: 914-633-2642
E-mail: icad@iona.edu • Web: www.iona.edu
Support: SP • Institution type: 4-year private

PROGRAMS OR SERVICES FOR STUDENTS WITH LD

The College Assistance Program (CAP) offers comprehensive support and services for students with LD/ADHD. CAP is designed to encourage success by providing instruction tailored to individual strengths and needs. Students take standard full-time course requirements to ensure the level of quality education expected of all degree candidates. Professional tutors teach individually appropriate strategies that cross disciplines. CAP staff encourages students to become involved members of the college community. All CAP freshmen must participate in a 2-week summer orientation. During the orientation, the staff instructs and guides students in intensive writing instruction and study and organizational and time management skills; students are oriented to the college and services; individual learning styles are explored; opportunities are provided for the students to practice self-advocacy; several workshops are offered in areas that meet the student's specific needs; and individual fall classes are developed. Semester services include supplementary advisement, counseling, regularly scheduled weekly skill-based tutoring with an LD professional, study groups, skills workshops, and provision of appropriate documented accommodations.

ADMISSION INFORMATION FOR STUDENTS WITH LD/ADHD

College entrance tests required: Yes
Interview required: Yes
Essay recommended: No
What documentation required for LD: Psycho Ed evaluation to include: relevant historical info, instructional interventions, related services, age diagnosed, objective data (aptitude, achievement, info processing), test scores (standard, percentile and grade equivalents) and describe functional limitations.
With general application: Yes if requested as part of Structured Program application
To receive services after enrolling: Yes
What documentation required for ADHD: Diagnosis based on DSM-V; history of behaviors impairing functioning in academic setting; diagnostic interview; history of symptoms; evidence of ongoing behaviors.

With general application: Yes if requested as part of Structured Program application
To receive services after enrolling: Yes
Submitted to: College Assistance Program
Special Ed. HS course work accepted: No
Specific course requirements of all applicants: Yes
Separate application required: No
# of LD applications submitted each year: 150–250
# of LD applications accepted yearly: 20
Total # of students receiving LD services: 8095
Acceptance into program means acceptance into college: Students must be admitted to the college and also admitted to CAP (simultaneously).

ADMISSIONS

All applicants must meet the same admission criteria, which include 4 years of English, 1 year of American history, 1 year of social studies, 2 years of a foreign language (waivers granted), 1 year of natural science, and 3 years of math. Students should send the following to the CAP office: a complete psychological evaluation conducted within the past 2 years that includes the WAIS or WAIS subtest scores, a comprehensive report, a copy of the most recent IEP, and two letters of recommendation (one from an LD instructor). A personal interview is required. CAP is designed for students with LD and ADHD who have been mainstreamed in their academic courses in high school. Students should be average or above average in intellectual ability, socially mature, emotionally stable, and motivated to work hard.

ADDITIONAL INFORMATION

CAP services include a freshman summer college transition program, supplementary academic advising and program planning based on each student's learning style, priority registration, 2 hours per week of scheduled skill-based individual tutoring with a professional learning specialist (additional tutoring sessions are possible), small group tutoring and workshops, testing accommodations, alternative testing procedures, special equipment, self-advocacy training, referrals to additional services on campus, and counseling services. The CAP director works with faculty to help them understand the problems faced by students with LD and explore creative ways to support the learning process. The Samuel Rudin Academic Resource Center (ARC) offers free services to all students who wish to improve their learning skills or who want academic support. ARC provides free reasonable services to all students with documented LD/ADHD.

LEARNING DISABILITY PROGRAMS OR SERVICES

Contact Information
Name of program or department: College Assistance Program (CAP)
   Telephone: 914-633-2159
   Fax: 914-633-2011

LEARNING DISABILITY SERVICES

Accommodations are decided upon an individual basis after a thorough review of appropriate, current documentation. The accommodations requested must be supported through the documentation provided and must be logically linked to the current impact of the condition on academic functioning.

Allowed in exams
   Calculator: Yes
   Dictionary: Yes
   Computer: Yes
   Spellchecker: Yes
Extended test time: Yes
Scribes: Yes
Proctors: Yes
Oral exams: No
Note-takers: Yes

Distraction-reduced environment: Yes
Tape recording in class: Yes
Electronic texts: Yes
Accommodations for students with ADHD: Yes
Kurzweil Reader: Yes
Other assistive technology: Yes
Priority registration: Yes

Added costs for services: Yes
LD specialists: Yes
Professional tutors: 10–15
Peer tutors: No
Max. hours/wk. for services: Unlimited
How professors are notified of LD/ADHD: By student

GENERAL ADMISSIONS INFORMATION

Office of Admission: 914-633-2120

ENTRANCE REQUIREMENTS
Academic units required: 4 English, 3 math, 2 science (2 science labs), 2 foreign language, 1 social studies, 1 history, 1 academic elective. **Academic units recommended:** 4 English, 4 math, 3 science (2 science labs), 2 foreign language, 2 social studies, 2 history, 3 academic electives. High school diploma is required, and GED is accepted. ACT with or without Writing component accepted. TOEFL required of all international applicants: minimum paper TOEFL 550, minimum computer TOEFL 213.

Application deadline: 2/15
Notification: 3/20
Average GPA: 3.40
ACT middle 50% range: 19–24

SAT Math middle 50% range: 450–540
SAT Critical Reading middle 50% range: 440–540
SAT Writing middle 50% range: NR

Graduated top 10% of class: 14%
Graduated top 25% of class: 36%
Graduated top 50% of class: 73%

COLLEGE GRADUATION REQUIREMENTS

Course waivers allowed: No
Course substitutions allowed: Yes
In what course: Foreign language

ADDITIONAL INFORMATION

Environment: The college is located on 56 acres 20 miles northeast of New York City.

Student Body
   Undergrad enrollment: 3,189
   Women: 54%
   Men: 45%
   Percent out-of-state: 23%

Cost Information
   Tuition: $29,490
   Room & board: $12,488
Housing Information
   University housing: Yes
   Percent living on campus: 39%

Greek System
   Fraternity: Yes
   Sorority: Yes
Athletics: Division I

KEUKA COLLEGE

Office of Admissions, Keuka Park, NY 14478-0098
Phone: 315-279-5254 • Fax: 315-536-5386
E-mail: admissions@mail.keuka.edu • Web: www.keuka.edu
Support: CS • Institution: 4-year private

PROGRAMS OR SERVICES FOR STUDENTS WITH LD

The Academic Success at Keuka Program will assist students in becoming competent, independent learners able to achieve their maximum potential in academic endeavors. Students with documented disabilities who are admitted and enrolled are encouraged to request services either in advance of the new semester or immediately at the beginning of the semester. Every effort is made to provide services and accommodations as quickly and appropriately as possible. It is the student's responsibility to contact the Academic Success at Keuka office. The Director will meet with the student and review the documentation to create a plan of services and accommodations. The provision of services will be based on the specific diagnoses and recommendations of the professional performing the assessments. Students are encouraged to ensure that the diagnoses and all recommendations for accommodations are clearly stated within the report. Students who are eligible for testing accommodations will be required to make these arrangements with the professor prior to EVERY test of the semester, as well as signing up for each test with the Academic Success at Keuka Program Office.

ADMISSION INFORMATION FOR STUDENTS WITH LD/ADHD

College entrance tests required: No
Interview required: No
What documentation required for LD: Psycho Ed evaluation
  to include: relevant historical info, instructional interventions,
  related services, age diagnosed, objective data (aptitude,
  achievement, info processing), test scores (standard,
  percentile and grade equivalents) and describe functional
  limitations.
With general application: No
To receive services after enrolling: Yes
What documentation required for ADHD: Diagnosis based
  on DSM-V; history of behaviors impairing functioning in
  academic setting; diagnostic interview; history of symptoms;
  evidence of ongoing behaviors.

With general application: No
Submitted to: Support Program/Services
Special Ed. HS course work accepted: Yes
Specific course requirements for all applicants: NR
Separate application required for program services: No
# of LD applications submitted each year: NR
# of LD applications accepted yearly: NR
Total # of students receiving LD services: 115
Acceptance into program means acceptance into
  college: Students must be admitted to and enrolled in the
  university first and then request services.

ADMISSIONS

There is no special admissions process available and all students are expected to meet the general admission criteria. Students are expected to rank in the top 50 percent of their high school class and have a minimum 2.8 GPA. Course requirements include four years of English, three years of history, one year of social studies, two to three years of math and science, and two years of foreign language. An essay is required and a campus visit with an interview is recommended.

ADDITIONAL INFORMATION

The provision of support is based on the specific diagnosis and recommendations of the professional performing the assessments. Examples of some support services offered by the Academic Support Program are: testing accommodations, tutors (group and individual), individual appointments with professional staff members, and alternative texts. Workshops for all students are offered in note-taking strategies, testing strategies, time management and study skills.

PROGRAM FOR DISABILITY SERVICES

Contact Information
Name of program or department: Academic Success at Keuka
   Telephone: 315-279-5636
   Fax: 315-279-5626

LEARNING DISABILITY SERVICES

Accommodations are decided upon an individual basis after a thorough review of appropriate, current documentation. The accommodations requested must be supported through the documentation provided and must be logically linked to the current impact of the condition on academic functioning.

Allowed in exams	**Distraction-reduced environment:** Yes	**Added costs for services:** No
Calculator: Yes	**Tape recording in class:** Yes	**LD specialists:** Yes
Dictionary: Yes	**Electronic texts:** Yes	**Professional tutors:** 4
Computer: Yes	**Accommodations for students with**	**Peer tutors:** 40
Spellchecker: Yes	ADHD: Yes	**Max. hours/wk. for services:** No
Extended test time: Yes	**Kurzweil Reader:** No	**How professors are notified of**
Scribes: Yes	**Other assistive technology:** Dragon	**LD/ADHD:** Student
Proctors: Yes	Naturally Speaking; Read Please 2000;	
Oral exams: Yes	text scanner	
Note-takers: Yes	**Priority registration:** Yes	

GENERAL ADMISSIONS INFORMATION

Office of Admission: 315-279-5262

ENTRANCE REQUIREMENTS

Academic units recommended: 4 English, 3 mathematics, 3 science, (2 science labs), 3 foreign language, 3 social studies, 2 history. High school diploma is required and GED is accepted. TOEFL required of all international applicants; minimum paper TOEFL 500, minimum computer TOEFL 300.

Application deadline: None	**SAT Math middle 50% range:**	**Graduated top 10% of class:** 13%
Notification: Rolling	420–520	**Graduated top 25% of class:** 34%
Average GPA: 3.11	**SAT Critical Reading middle 50%**	**Graduated top 50% of class:** 73%
ACT Composite middle 50% range:	**range:** 420–520	
19–23	**SAT Writing middle 50% range:**	
	410–500	

COLLEGE GRADUATION REQUIREMENTS

Course waivers allowed: No
Course substitutions allowed: Yes
In what course: When appropiate and agreed upon by student,instructor, division chair, and registrar.

ADDITIONAL INFORMATION

Environment: The college is located 50 miles from Rochester, New York.

Student Body	**Cost Information**	**Greek System**
Undergrad enrollment: 1,702	Tuition: $25,110	Fraternity: No
Women: 75%	Room and board: $9,880	Sorority: No
Men: 25%	**Housing Information**	Athletics: Division III
Percent out-of-state: 6%	University housing: Yes	
	Percent living on campus: 82%	

LE MOYNE COLLEGE

1419 Salt Springs Rd., Syracuse, NY 13214-1301
Phone: 315-445-4300 • Fax: 315-445-4711
E-mail: admission@lemoyne.edu • Web: www.lemoyne.edu
Support: S • Institution: 4-year private

PROGRAMS OR SERVICES FOR STUDENTS WITH LD

Le Moyne College welcomes people with disabilities and, in compliance with Section 504 of the Rehabilitation Act of 1973, as amended, and the Americans with Disabilities Act of 1990, supports students' entitlements and does not discriminate on the basis of disability. Academic support services for students with disabilities are coordinated by the Director of Disability Support Services in the Academic Support Center.

Students with Special Needs have access to the same support services provided to all students–individual sessions with professionals in the Academic Support Center (ASC) regarding study skills and learning strategies, ASC Workshops provided each fall semester, and individual and small-group tutoring in writing, mathematics, foreign languages, economics, and the natural sciences. In addition, students with disabilities receive individualized services through the ASC. Our goal is to create collaborative partnerships that put students in the driver's seat of their education to enhance their chances for academic success.

ADMISSION INFORMATION FOR STUDENTS WITH LD/ADHD

College entrance tests required: Yes
Interview required: No
Essay required: Yes
What documentation required for LD: Psycho Ed evaluation
   to include: relevant historical info, instructional interventions,
   related services, age diagnosed, objective data (aptitude,
   achievement, info processing), test scores (standard,
   percentile and grade equivalents) and describe functional
   limitations.
With general application: No
To receive services after enrolling: Yes
What documentation required for ADHD: Diagnosis based
   on DSM-V; history of behaviors impairing functioning in
   academic setting; diagnostic interview; history of symptoms;
   evidence of ongoing behaviors.

With general application: No
Submitted to: Support Program/Services
Special Ed. HS course work accepted: No
Specific course requirements for all applicants: NR
Separate application required for program services: No
# of LD applications submitted each year: NR
# of LD applications accepted yearly: NR
Total # of students receiving LD services: NR
Acceptance into program means acceptance into
   college: NR

ADMISSIONS

Admissions to Le Moyne College is the same for all applicants. Besides a general college-prep program, it is recommended that all potential students visits the campus and interviews. For the student with learning disabilities there is an essay that is required and an interview that is recommended.The high school record is very important. Class rank, recommendations, standardized test scores, and the essay are used in the admissions process to assess the applicant. Foreign language requirement may be substituted dependent on the documentation presented by the applicant.

ADDITIONAL INFORMATION

The office provides and arranges accommodations for students with special needs due to learning, emotional, and temporary or permanent diagnostic referrals, review of previously administered diagnostic tests, informal academic advising, presentation of self-advocacy skills for students, and liaison and advocacy measures with faculty and staff. If applicable you will also need to connect with appropriate adult services agencies

Students with documented disabilities may be eligible for one or more of the following services:note-takers, recorded texts, access to adaptive technologies ,time extensions for exams and alternative testing sites.

PROGRAM FOR DISABILITY SERVICES

Contact Information
Name of program or department: Disability Support Services
  Telephone: 315-445-4118
  Fax: 315-445-6014

LEARNING DISABILITY SERVICES

Accommodations are decided upon an individual basis after a thorough review of appropriate, current documentation. The accommodations requested must be supported through the documentation provided and must be logically linked to the current impact of the condition on academic functioning.

Allowed in exams	**Distraction-reduced environment:** Yes	**Added costs for services:** NR
Calculator: Yes	**Tape recording in class:** Yes	**LD specialists:** No
Dictionary: Yes	**Electronic texts:** Yes	**Professional tutors:** Yes
Computer: Yes	**Accommodations for students with**	**Peer tutors:** Yes
Spellchecker: Yes	**ADHD:** Yes	**Max. hours/wk. for services:** NR
Extended test time: Yes	**Kurzweil Reader:** Yes	**How professors are notified of**
Scribes: N/A	**Other assistive technology:** Yes	**LD/ADHD:** Student
Proctors: Yes	**Priority registration:** Yes	
Oral exams: N/A		
Note-takers: Yes		

GENERAL ADMISSIONS INFORMATION

Office of Admission: 315-445-4300

ENTRANCE REQUIREMENTS
Academic units required: 4 English, 3 mathematics, 3 science, 3 foreign language, 4 social studies. **Academic units recommended:** 4 mathematics, 4 science, (3 science labs). High school diploma is required and GED is accepted. SAT or ACT required; TOEFL required of all international applicants; minimum paper TOEFL 550, minimum computer TOEFL 213, minimum web-based TOEFL 79.

Application deadline: None	**SAT Math middle 50% range:**	**Graduated top 10% of class:** 22%
Notification: Rolling	500–610	**Graduated top 25% of class:** 53%
Average GPA: 3.37	**SAT Critical Reading middle 50%**	**Graduated top 50% of class:** 88%
ACT Composite middle 50% range:	**range:** 480–590	
21–26	**SAT Writing middle 50% range:** NR	

COLLEGE GRADUATION REQUIREMENTS

Course waivers allowed: N/A
Course substitutions allowed: Yes
In what course: Course substitutions are provided on a case-by-case basis. American Sign Language may be accepted by some majors.

ADDITIONAL INFORMATION

Environment: The college is located on 161 acres in a city environment.

Student Body	**Cost Information**	**Greek System**
Undergrad enrollment: 2,786	**Tuition:** $28,380	**Fraternity:** No
Women: 60%	**Room and board:** $10,890	**Sorority:** No
Men: 40%	**Housing Information**	**Athletics:** Division II
Percent out-of-state: 6%	**University housing:** Yes	
	Percent living on campus: 50%	

LONG ISLAND U.—C.W. POST

720 Northern Boulevard, Brookville, NY 11548
Phone: 516-299-2900 • Fax: 516-299-2137
E-mail: enroll@cwpost.liu.edu • Web: www.liu.edu
Support: SP • Institution type: 4-year private

PROGRAMS OR SERVICES FOR STUDENTS WITH LD

The Academic Resource Program (ARP), is housed in our Learning Support Center, is a comprehensive, structured, fee-for-service support program designed to meet the needs of students certified as having a LD and/or ADHD. Students are provided with one-on-one sessions with a trained learning assistant; an up-to-date computer lab with assistive technology; weekly meetings with an ARP administrator; and as needed, sessions with our social worker, time management counselor, and/or Bridges to Post counselor. The staff is committed to working with each individual student enrolled in the program to help students learn the strategies and skills needed to transition and succeed in college. The staff provides each student with the opportunity, structure, and support necessary to help him or her develop the academic, social, problem-solving, and strategic skills to achieve goals. This is accomplished through a structured program and an approach that is designed to assist the individual student. The key ingredient is, of course, the student and the student's desire to succeed and willingness to be actively involved in the program.

ADMISSION INFORMATION FOR STUDENTS WITH LD/ADHD

College entrance tests required: Yes
Interview required: Yes
Essay recommended: Yes
What documentation required for LD: Psycho Ed evaluation to include: relevant historical info, instructional interventions, related services, age diagnosed, objective data (aptitude, achievement, info processing), test scores (standard, percentile and grade equivalents) and describe functional limitations.
With general application: Yes if requested as part of Structured Program application
To receive services after enrolling: Yes
What documentation required for ADHD: Diagnosis based on DSM-V; history of behaviors impairing functioning in academic setting; diagnostic interview; history of symptoms; evidence of ongoing behaviors.

With general application: Yes if requested as part of Structured Program application
To receive services after enrolling: Yes
Submitted to: Academic Resource Program
Special Ed. HS course work accepted: Yes
Specific course requirements of all applicants: NR
Separate application required: Yes
# of LD applications submitted each year: 100
# of LD applications accepted yearly: 30–50
Total # of students receiving LD services: 65–75
Acceptance into program means acceptance into college: Students must be admitted to the University first and then request an application for the program.

ADMISSIONS

Admission to the ARP is separate and distinct from admission to the University. Upon receipt of an acceptance letter from the Office of Admissions, prospective students should contact the Learning Support Center at 516-299-3057 to request an application for the Academic Resource Program. The student must submit the completed Academic Resource Program application, together with the required essay, and a Diagnostic Evaluation conducted within the past three years. Upon receipt of the completed application essay, and required psychological-educational evaluations, the staff will contact eligible candidates to schedule a personal interview, which is an integral part of the admission to ARP process. For fall admission to the Academic Resource Program, the deadline for receipt of the application and required documentation is July 15th. For spring admission, the deadline is November 15th.

ADDITIONAL INFORMATION

Learning assistants help freshmen make the transition from high school to college. They assist all Academic Resource Program students in time management, organizational skills, note-taking techniques, study skills, and other necessary learning strategies. Each student is responsible for his or her attendance and participation in these sessions. Freshmen and sophomores meet with a learning assistant for two hours per week. Students are welcome to schedule more hours if necessary. Juniors and seniors are given the opportunity to schedule and contract more flexible hours with the Academic Resource Program staff. Ancillary Services available to the Academic Resource Program students include: note-takers for class lectures, proctors for extended-time exams and other reasonable test accommodations as supported by the students' documentation, assistance with textbooks in audio and/or alternate format, assistance with planning and scheduling of classes, guidance to direct students to supplemental services on campus, instruction on using computers including speech-to-text and text-to-speech programs, and workshops.

LEARNING DISABILITY PROGRAM OR SERVICES

Contact Information
Name of program or department: Academic Resource Center
  Telephone: 516-299-3057
  Fax: 516-299-2126

LEARNING DISABILITY SERVICES

After a thorough review of the documentation and interview conducted with the student, ARP administrators decide upon the appropriate reasonable accommodations. All approved reasonable accommodations will be discussed with the student and will be listed on the student's Accommodations Form.

Allowed in exams
  Calculator: Yes
  Dictionary: Yes
  Computer: Yes
  Spellchecker: Yes
Extended test time: Yes
Scribes: Yes
Proctors: Yes
Oral exams: NR
Note-takers: Yes

Distraction-reduced environment: Yes
Tape recording in class: Yes
Electronic texts: Yes
Accommodations for students with
  ADHD: Yes
Kurzweil Reader: Yes
Other assistive technology: Yes
Priority registration: No

Added costs for services: Yes
LD specialists: Yes
Professional tutors: 10–15
Peer tutors: 10
Max. hours/wk. for services:
  Unlimited
How professors are notified of
  LD/ADHD: By student with
  appropriate Accommodations Form

GENERAL ADMISSIONS INFORMATION

Office of Admission: 516-299-2900

ENTRANCE REQUIREMENTS

Academic units required: 4 English, 2 math, 2 science (2 science labs), 2 foreign language, 3 social studies, 1 academic elective. **Academic units recommended:** 4 English, 4 math, 4 science (4 science labs), 4 foreign language, 4 social studies. High school diploma is required, and GED is accepted. TOEFL required of all international applicants: minimum paper TOEFL 500.

Application deadline: None
Notification: Rolling
Average GPA: 3.00
ACT Composite middle 50% range:
  NR

SAT Math middle 50% range:
  440–550
SAT Critical Reading middle 50%
  range: 440–530
SAT Writing middle 50% range: NR

Graduated top 10% of class: 10%
Graduated top 25% of class: 26%
Graduated top 50% of class: 61%

COLLEGE GRADUATION REQUIREMENTS

Course waivers allowed: Yes
In what course: A specific computer course can be taken to staisfy the core math requirement. English 7 and 8 (anthology courses) can be taken instead of a foreign language. These are for core requirements only.
Course substitutions allowed: Yes
In what course: A specific computer course can be taken to staisfy the core math requirement. English 7 and 8 (anthology courses) can be taken instead of a foreign language. These are for core requirements only.

ADDITIONAL INFORMATION

Environment: The college is located in Long Island, about 30 minutes from New York City.

Student Body
  Undergrad enrollment: 4,925
  Women: 62%
  Men: 38%
  Percent out-of-state: 13%

Cost Information
  Tuition: $30,046
  Room & board: $11,840
Housing Information
  University housing: Yes
  Percent living on campus: 37%

Greek System
  Fraternity: Yes
  Sorority: Yes
Athletics: Division II

MANHATTANVILLE COLLEGE

2900 Purchase Street, Admissions Office, Purchase, NY 10577
Phone: 914-323-5464 • Fax: 914-694-1732
E-mail: admissions@mville.edu • Web: www.mville.edu
Support: SP • Institution type: 4-year private

PROGRAMS OR SERVICES FOR STUDENTS WITH LD

The Higher Education Learning Program (H.E.L.P.) serves as a center of support for students with documented learning disabilities. It is designed to assist students to successfully meet the academic challenges of the college curriculum. H.E.L.P. offers a range of services that are individualized to meet the needs of each student. Professionals are trained and experienced working with this population to provide instruction. No separate application is required for the H.E.L.P. Center. Students must register with the ODS first before accessing the H.E.L.P. Center. The Academic Resource Center (ARC) offers academic support free of charge to all students. At the ARC students may receive support, individually and in groups and the emphasis is on learning and gaining independence. The ARC has professional mathematics instructors available every day. In addition there are peer tutors and Supplemental Instructors for many subjects. Students are encouraged to look for the SI leaders who may be assigned to their courses, and take advantage of this opportunity to enhance their academic success.

ADMISSION INFORMATION FOR STUDENTS WITH LD/ADHD

College entrance tests required: Yes
Interview required: No
Essay recommended: No
Documentation required for LD: Current documentation of disability by a qualified professional is required.
Documentation required for ADHD: Current documentation of disability by a qualified professional is required.
Submitted to: Director of Disability Services
Special Ed. HS course work accepted: NR

Specific course requirements of all applicants: Yes
Separate application required: No
# of LD applications submitted each year: NR
# of LD applications accepted yearly: NR
Total # of students receiving LD services: 150
Acceptance into program means acceptance into college: No

ADMISSIONS

All applicants must meet the general admission requirements. The criteria includes: 3.0 GPA and 4 years of English, 3 years of math, 2 years of science, 2 years of history and 5 academic electives. The college is test optional. Students are not required to submit standardized test scores with their applications for admission to the College, except international and home-schooled applicants. Teacher and counselor recommendation is required plus a personal essay. Interviews are encouraged. Some students may be admitted as a Transitional students under the premise that they may need additional support in order to be successful in college. The overall goals and objectives of the program are to: provide to develop connections with other students and key staff from many resource centers; encourage the development of personal goals and plan for college and for life learning; and to enable students to recognize components of a successful college experience including health and wellness issues, time management, and study skills. Students admitted through the Transitional Acceptance Program fall under the oversight of the Center for Academic Success during their first semester. Students are required to attend a series of workshops through the Student Enrichment Program to ease their transition. Students must also successfully complete 12 credits with at least a 2.0 grade point average by the end of their first semester. Although 12 credits must be successfully completed by the end of the first semester, we recommend that students register for no fewer than 15 to 16 credits per semester. If these criteria are met, the student will no longer be considered a transitional student. If these criteria are not met, the student could be placed on academic probation or dismissed from the college.

ADDITIONAL INFORMATION

The H.E.L.P. Center offers a wide range of academic support services designed to fit the individual needs of each student. These services include: one-to one tutoring, study skills instruction, reading strategies, writing support, organizational skills, time management technique, All instruction is provided by a professional tutorial staff of certified teachers. All services are customized to match each student's learning style. During freshman year, students meet with their assigned tutor to work on time management skills, completion of all assignments, and to take responsibility for their own learning. Upperclassmen may meet with their tutors for either two or three hours per week, continuing to receive strategy-based instruction to address their specific needs. ARC provides instruction, enhancement, and ongoing support. And serves students at all levels who wish to work with a professional tutor on strategies in math, science, or study skills.

LEARNING DISABILITY PROGRAM OR SERVICES

Contact Information
Name of program or department: Office of Disability Services and HELP Center
  Telephone: 914-323-7127 (Disability Services) or 914-323-5313 (HELP
  Fax: 914-323-7218

LEARNING DISABILITY SERVICES

Accommodations are determined on an individual basis with thorough review of appropriate documentation and an intake interview. The accommodations requested must be supported by the documentation provided and linked to the current impact on academic functioning. The accommodations listed below are available to those for whom they are appropriate.

Allowed in exams
  Calculator: Yes
  Dictionary: No
  Computer: Yes
  Spellchecker: Yes (on computer)
Extended test time: Yes
Scribes: Yes
Proctors: Yes
Oral exams: Yes
Note-takers: Limited volunteers

Distraction-reduced environment: Yes
Tape recording in class: Yes
Electronic texts: Yes
Accommodations for students with ADHD: Yes
Kurzweil Reader: Yes
Other assistive technology: Yes
Priority registration: No

Added costs for services: HELP only
LD specialists: HELP only
Professional tutors: 8–10 in HELP center
Peer tutors: Yes for all students
Max. hours/wk. for services: 3 for HELP
How professors are notified of LD/ADHD: Letter sent by ODS Director

GENERAL ADMISSIONS INFORMATION

Office of Admission: 914-323-5464

ENTRANCE REQUIREMENTS

Academic units required: 4 English, 3 math, 2 science, 2 history, 5 academic electives. High school diploma is required, and GED is accepted. TOEFL or IELTS required of all international applicants: minimum paper TOEFL 550, minimum internet based TOEFL 80.

Application deadline: 3/1
Notification: Rolling
Average GPA: 3.0
ACT Composite middle 50% range: 21–24

SAT Math middle 50% range: 490–610
SAT Critical Reading middle 50% range: 500–610
SAT Writing middle 50% range: 500–610

Graduated top 10% of class: NR
Graduated top 25% of class: NR
Graduated top 50% of class: NR

COLLEGE GRADUATION REQUIREMENTS

Course waivers allowed: No
Course substitutions allowed: Yes by application

ADDITIONAL INFORMATION

Environment: The college is located on a 100-acre campus in a suburban area 30 miles north of New York City.

Student Body
  Undergrad enrollment: 1,723
  Women: 66%
  Men: 34%
  Percent out-of-state: 37%

Cost Information
  Tuition: $35,370
  Room & board: $14,520
Housing Information
  University housing: Yes
  Percent living on campus: 80%

Greek System
  Fraternity: No
  Sorority: No
  Athletics: Division III

MARIST COLLEGE

3399 North Road, Poughkeepsie, NY 12601-1387
Phone: 845-575-3226 • Fax: 845-575-3215
E-mail: admissions@marist.edu • Web: www.marist.edu
Support: SP • Institution type: 4-year private

PROGRAMS OR SERVICES FOR STUDENTS WITH LD

Marist College believes that bright, motivated students with specific learning disabilities are more similar than they are different from other college students and can achieve a higher education. Marist offers a program of support for students with learning disabilities through the Learning Disabilities Program. Students receive a complement of academic services designed to meet individual needs. The program focuses on the development and use of strategies to promote independence and personal success. The philosophy of the program does not emphasize remediation but rather the development of compensatory strategies. Each student is enrolled in credit-bearing courses and completes the same degree requirements as all students. Program staff work closely with faculty and administration, and students are encouraged to discuss their learning disabilities with faculty. Participation in the program is available on a continual basis for as long as the LD specialist and the student agree is necessary.

ADMISSION INFORMATION FOR STUDENTS WITH LD/ADHD

College entrance tests required: No
Interview required: Yes
Essay required: Yes
What documentation required for LD: Psycho Ed evaluation to include: relevant historical info, instructional interventions, related services, age diagnosed, objective data (aptitude, achievement, info processing), test scores (standard, percentile and grade equivalents) and describe functional limitations.
With general application: Yes if requested as part of Structured Program application
To receive services after enrolling: Yes
What documentation required for ADHD: Diagnosis based on DSM-V; history of behaviors impairing functioning in academic setting; diagnostic interview; history of symptoms; evidence of ongoing behaviors.

With general application: Yes if requested as part of Structured Program application
To receive services after enrolling: Yes
Submitted to: Learning Disabilities Support Program
Special Ed. HS course work accepted: No
Specific course requirements of all applicants: Yes
Separate application required: Yes
# of LD applications submitted each year: 325+
# of LD applications accepted yearly: 50
Total # of students receiving LD services: 90
Acceptance into program means acceptance into college: Students are admitted jointly into the college and the LD program.

ADMISSIONS

Students with LD must submit an application for admission and all required materials to the Office of Admissions. A supplementary application for the LD support program must also be completed and sent directly to the OSS. A copy of the transcript and recommendations is also required. Additionally, students must submit to the OSS the results of the WAIS–IV, including subtest scores; their calculated IQ and an accompanying narrative; achievement testing with current levels of functioning in reading, mathematics, and written language; an essay describing what the student thinks is important about them as a person; and a $25 fee. ACT/SAT scores are optional. Those most qualified and suited to the program will be invited to interview. Students accepted into the program should have an acceptance and understanding of their LD; know their academic strengths and weaknesses; have taken college-prep courses; provide recommendations that communicate strengths, motivation to succeed, and willingness to accept and access supports; and have sound study skills and work habits. Admission to the program is competitive, and students are encouraged to apply early.

ADDITIONAL INFORMATION

Upon enrollment, students complete a comprehensive survey of their abilities and attitudes toward academics. This survey is combined with diagnostic evaluations and the comprehensive record of students' performance to develop an individual support service plan. Students meet an LD specialist two times a week and typically concentrate on writing skills, note-taking, organizational skills, study skills, and testing strategies. Accommodations may include accommodated testing procedures, note-takers, scribes, readers, alternative texts, and use of adaptive equipment/software. A program fee is charged only for the services of the learning specialist. Students in the program also have access to content tutors and a counselor who can address academic, career, and personal issues. Services and accommodations are available for undergraduate and graduate students.

LEARNING DISABILITY PROGRAM OR SERVICES

Contact Information
Name of program or department: Office of Special Services(OSS)/ Learning Disabilities Program
Telephone: 845-575-3274
Fax: 845-575-3011

LEARNING DISABILITY SERVICES

Accommodations are decided upon an individual basis after a thorough review of appropriate, current documentation. The accommodations requested must be supported through the documentation provided and must be logically linked to the current impact of the condition on academic functioning.

Allowed in exams
 Calculator: Yes
 Dictionary: Yes
 Computer: Yes
 Spellchecker: Yes
Extended test time: Yes
Scribes: Yes
Proctors: Yes
Oral exams: Yes
Note-takers: Yes

Distraction-reduced environment: Yes
Tape recording in class: Yes
Electronic texts: Yes
Accommodations for students with
 ADHD: Yes
Kurzweil Reader: Yes
Other assistive technology: Yes
Priority registration: Yes

Added costs for services: Yes
LD specialists: Yes
Professional tutors: 4
Peer tutors: 60
Max. hours/wk. for services: 1.5
How professors are notified of
 LD/ADHD: By student

GENERAL ADMISSIONS INFORMATION

Office of Admission: 845-575-3226

ENTRANCE REQUIREMENTS

Academic units required: 4 English, 3 math, 3 science (2 science labs), 2 foreign language, 2 social studies, 1 history, 2 academic electives. **Academic units recommended:** 4 math, 4 science (3 science labs), 3 foreign language. High school diploma is required, and GED is accepted. ACT with Writing component required. TOEFL required of all international applicants: minimum paper TOEFL 550, minimum computer TOEFL 213.

Application deadline: 2/15
Notification: 3/30
Average GPA: 3.30
ACT Composite middle 50% range:
 24–28

SAT Math middle 50% range:
 560–640
SAT Critical Reading middle 50%
 range: 540–630
SAT Writing middle 50% range:
 550–640

Graduated top 10% of class: 32%
Graduated top 25% of class: 70%
Graduated top 50% of class: 95%

COLLEGE GRADUATION REQUIREMENTS

Course waivers allowed: Yes
In what course: Substitutions are made in math.
Course substitutions allowed: Yes
In what course: Substitutions are made in math.

ADDITIONAL INFORMATION

Environment: The college is located on 120 acres in upstate New York, 75 miles from New York City.

Student Body
 Undergrad enrollment: 5,442
 Women: 59%
 Men: 41%
 Percent out-of-state: 44%

Cost Information
 Tuition: $28,800
 Room & board: $12,100
Housing Information
 University housing: Yes
 Percent living on campus: 67%

Greek System
 Fraternity: Yes
 Sorority: Yes
 Athletics: Division I

MARYMOUNT MANHATTAN COLLEGE

221 East Seventy-first Street, New York, NY 10021
Phone: 212-517-0430 • Fax: 212-517-0448
E-mail: admissions@mmm.edu • Web: www.mmm.edu
Support: SP • Institution type: 4-year private

PROGRAMS OR SERVICES FOR STUDENTS WITH LD

Marymount Manhattan College's Program for Academic Access includes a full range of support services that center on academic and personal growth for students with learning disabilities. Students admitted are required to demonstrate commitment to overcoming learning difficulties through regular attendance and tutoring. Academic advisement and counseling is provided to assist in developing a program plan suited to individual needs. The college looks for highly motivated students with a commitment to compensate for their LD and fully participate in the tutoring program. Once admitted, students receive a program plan suited to their needs, based on a careful examination of the psychoeducational evaluations. Students sign a contract to regularly attend tutoring provided by professionals experienced within the field of LD. In addition to assisting students in the development of skills and strategies for their course work, LD specialists coach participants in the attitudes and behavior necessary for college success. Professors assist learning specialists in carefully monitoring students' progress throughout the academic year and arranging for accommodations. Students must submit a current and complete psychoeducational evaluation that provides clear and specific evidence of the disability and its limitations on academic functioning in the diagnosis summary statement. Students with ADHD must have a licensed physician, psychiatrist, or psychologist provide a complete and current documentation of the disorder.

ADMISSION INFORMATION FOR STUDENTS WITH LD/ADHD

College entrance tests required: No
Interview required: No
Essay recommended: Yes
What documentation required for LD: Psycho Ed evaluation to include: relevant historical info, instructional interventions, related services, age diagnosed, objective data (aptitude, achievement, info processing), test scores (standard, percentile and grade equivalents) and describe functional limitations.
With general application: Yes if requested as part of Structured Program application
To receive services after enrolling: Yes
What documentation required for ADHD: Diagnosis based on DSM-V; history of behaviors impairing functioning in academic setting; diagnostic interview; history of symptoms; evidence of ongoing behaviors.

With general application: Yes if requested as part of Structured Program application
To receive services after enrolling: Yes
Submitted to: Program for Academic Access
Special Ed. HS course work accepted: NR
Specific course requirements of all applicants: Yes
Separate application required: Yes, see website
# of LD applications submitted each year: 85
# of LD applications accepted yearly: 8–12
Total # of students receiving LD services: 48
Acceptance into program means acceptance into college: Students must be admitted to the College before applying to the Program for Academic Access.

ADMISSIONS

Admission to Marymount Manhattan College's Program for Academic Access is based on a diagnosis of dyslexia, ADHD, or other primary learning disability; intellectual potential within the average to superior range; and a serious commitment in attitude and work habits to meeting the program and college academic requirements. Prospective students submit a high school transcript and ACT or SAT scores. Results of a recent complete psychoeducational evaluation and letters of recommendation from teachers, tutors, or counselors are also required. There is no fixed deadline for the application; however, there are a limited number of slots available.

ADDITIONAL INFORMATION

There are seven LD professionals associated with the program. Six learning specialists and one Academic Coach are scheduled for 2 hours of tutoring per week. Skills classes are offered in study skills, reading, and vocabulary development, and workshops in overcoming procrastination are also available. The following services are offered to students with appropriate documentation: the use of calculators, computers; extended time on tests; proctors; oral exams; distraction-free testing environments; tape recorders in class; books on tape; separate and alternative forms of testing; and priority registration. The program fee is $5,000 per academic year above tuition.

LEARNING DISABILITY PROGRAM OR SERVICES

Contact Information
Name of program or department: Program for Academic Access
 Telephone: 212-774-0724
 Fax: 212-774-4875

LEARNING DISABILITY SERVICES

Accommodations are decided upon an individual basis after a thorough review of appropriate, current documentation. The accommodations requested must be supported through the documentation provided and must be logically linked to the current impact of the condition on academic functioning.

Allowed in exams	Distraction-reduced environment: Yes	Added costs for services: Yes
Calculator: Yes	Tape recording in class: Yes	LD specialists: Yes
Dictionary: No	Electronic texts: Yes	Professional tutors: No
Computer: Yes	Accommodations for students with	Peer tutors: No
Spellchecker: NR	ADHD: Yes	Max. hours/wk. for services: 2
Extended test time: Yes	Kurzweil Reader: Yes	How professors are notified of
Scribes: No	Other assistive technology: Yes	LD/ADHD: By the Academic Access
Proctors: Yes	Priority registration: Yes	Program
Oral exams: Yes		
Note-takers: Yes		

GENERAL ADMISSIONS INFORMATION

Office of Admission: 212-517-0430

ENTRANCE REQUIREMENTS

Academic units required: 4 English, 3 math, 2 science, 3 social studies, 4 academic electives. **Academic units recommended:** 3 science, 2 foreign language. High school diploma is required, and GED is accepted. ACT without Writing component accepted. TOEFL required of all international applicants: minimum paper TOEFL 550, minimum computer TOEFL 213.

Application deadline: None	SAT Math middle 50% range:	Graduated top 10% of class: NR
Notification: Rolling	500–550	Graduated top 25% of class: NR
Average GPA: 3.2	SAT Critical Reading middle 50%	Graduated top 50% of class: NR
ACT Composite middle 50% range:	range: 500–550	
23	SAT Writing middle 50% range: NR	

COLLEGE GRADUATION REQUIREMENTS

Course waivers allowed: No
Course substitutions allowed: No

ADDITIONAL INFORMATION

Environment: The campus is located on the upper east side of Manhattan.

Student Body	Cost Information	Greek System
Undergrad enrollment: 2,000	Tuition: $23,610	Fraternity: No
Women: 75%	Room & board: $13,416	Sorority: No
Men: 25%	Housing Information	Athletics: NR
Percent out-of-state: 60%	University housing: Yes	
	Percent living on campus: 65%	

NEW YORK UNIVERSITY

665 Broadway, 11th Floor, New York, NY 10012
Phone: 212-998-4500 • Fax: 212-995-4902
E-mail: admissions@nyu.edu • Web: www.nyu.edu
Support: S • Institution: 4-year private

PROGRAMS OR SERVICES FOR STUDENTS WITH LD

The Henry and Lucy Moses Center for Students with Disabilities (CSD) works with students with a documented disability or disabilities who register with the office to obtain appropriate accommodations and services. This process is designed to encourage independence, backed by a strong system of supports. Each student who is approved through CSD works with a staff specialist to develop an individualized and reasonable accommodation plan. Reasonable accommodations are adjustments to policy, practice, and programs that "level the playing field" for students with disabilities and provide equal access to NYU's programs and activities. Accommodation plans and other related services are based on each student's disability documentation and NYU program requirements and are therefore determined on a case-by-case basis.

ADMISSION INFORMATION FOR STUDENTS WITH LD/ADHD

College entrance tests required: No
Interview required: No
Essay required: Yes
What documentation required for LD: Psycho Ed evaluation to include: relevant historical info, instructional interventions, related services, age diagnosed, objective data (aptitude, achievement, info processing), test scores (standard, percentile and grade equivalents) and describe functional limitations.
With general application: No
To receive services after enrolling: Yes
What documentation required for ADHD: Diagnosis based on DSM-V; history of behaviors impairing functioning in academic setting; diagnostic interview; history of symptoms; evidence of ongoing behaviors.

With general application: No
Submitted to: Moses Center for Students with Disabilities
Special Ed. HS course work accepted: Yes
Specific course requirements for all applicants: Yes
Separate application required for program services: No
# of LD applications submitted each year: NR
# of LD applications accepted yearly: NR
Total # of students receiving LD services: NR
Acceptance into program means acceptance into college: Separate application required after student has enrolled

ADMISSIONS

When choosing a new class, the NYU Admissions Committee reviews each application holistically, considering and carefully evaluating many significant factors, including the following: the Common Application and NYU Supplement, School Report (including a letter from a student's guidance counselor and a transcript), a combination of standardized test scores the student chooses to submit (e.g., SAT, ACT, SAT Subject Test, AP, IB, or other national examination scores), one Teacher Evaluation, audition or portfolio submissions for art and music applicants to the Steinhardt School of Culture, Education, and Human Development and all applicants to the Tisch School of the Arts. The committee also takes into account each applicant's unique talents, personal attributes, accomplishments, and goals. For more information about the admissions process, visit www.admissions.nyu.edu.

ADDITIONAL INFORMATION

In addition to academic accommodations, CSD provides academic support services to registered students. Students may meet with a learning consultant on a restricted basis and may attend several academic strategy based workshops throughout the semester.

PROGRAM FOR DISABILITY SERVICES

Contact Information
Name of program or department: Henry and Lucy Moses Center for Students with Disabilities
Telephone: 212-998-4980
Fax: 212-995-4114

LEARNING DISABILITY SERVICES

Accommodations are determined through a careful review of appropriate and current documentation. The accommodations requested must be supported by the documentation provided and must be linked to the current impact on academic functioning. Reasonable accommodations do not negate requirements for successful completion of a program, course, or services or adherence to acceptable standard or behavior. It is important to note that some accommodations are not appropriate in all courses.

Allowed in exams
  Calculator: Yes
  Dictionary: Yes
  Computer: Yes
  Spellchecker: Yes
Extended test time: Yes
Scribes: Yes
Proctors: Yes
Oral exams: No
Note-takers: Yes

Distraction-reduced environment: Yes
Tape recording in class: Yes
Electronic texts: Yes
Accommodations for students with ADHD: Yes
Kurzweil Reader: Yes
Other assistive technology: Yes
Priority registration: Yes
Added costs for services: No
LD specialists: Yes

Professional tutors: Yes (NYU Writing Center)
Peer tutors: Yes (University Learning Center)
Max. hours/wk. for services: Students may schedule one session per week at the Writing Center; tutoring at the College Learning Center is determined by subject area and schedule.
How professors are notified of LD/ADHD: Student

GENERAL ADMISSIONS INFORMATION

Office of Admission: 212-998-4500

ENTRANCE REQUIREMENTS
Academic units recommended: 4 years of English with a heavy emphasis on writing; 3–4 years of history/social studies; 3–4 years of mathematics; 3–4 years of laboratory sciences; and 3–4 years of a foreign language. Results from one of the following testing options: SAT; or ACT (with Writing Test); or 3 SAT Subject Test scores; or 3 AP exam scores; or the International Baccalaureate Diploma; or 3 IB higher-level exam scores (if you are not an IB Diploma candidate); or students may instead elect to submit results from a nationally accredited exam that is considered locally to signify the completion of secondary education and is administered independently of the student's school.

Application deadline: 1/1
Notification: 4/1
Average GPA: A–
ACT Composite middle 50% range: 29–31

SAT Math middle 50% range: 650–750
SAT Critical Reading middle 50% range: 630–730
SAT Writing middle 50% range: 660–750

Graduated top 10% of class: 77%
Graduated top 25% of class: 96%
Graduated top 50% of class: NA

COLLEGE GRADUATION REQUIREMENTS

Course waivers allowed: No
Course substitutions allowed: Yes
In what course: Determined by the student's Office of the Dean on a case-by-case basis.

ADDITIONAL INFORMATION

Environment: The university has an urban campus in New York City.

Student Body
  Undergrad enrollment: 22,097
  Women: 61%
  Men: 39%
  Percent out-of-state: 65%

Cost Information
  Tuition: $41,614
  Room & board: $15,181
Housing Information
  University housing: Yes
  Percent living on campus: 48%

Greek System
  Fraternity: Yes
  Sorority: Yes
Athletics: Division III

ROCHESTER INST. OF TECHNOLOGY

60 Lomb Memorial Drive, Rochester, NY 14623-5604
Phone: 585-475-6631 • Fax: 585-475-7424
E-mail: admissions@rit.edu • Web: www.rit.edu
Support: SP • Institution type: 4-year private

PROGRAMS OR SERVICES FOR STUDENTS WITH LD

There is no separate academic program exclusively for students with disabilities; all students apply to a Rochester Institute of Technology degree program and major. Students with disabilities who require academic and/or residential accommodations should submit a request and relevant documentation to the RIT Disability Services Office. Currently about 700 students with disabilities are registered with the office, the majority of whom have learning disabilities and/or attention deficit disorders. The office also offers support with time management, organization, and study skills strategies to registered students upon request. Please see www.rit.edu/dso for information. RIT is home to the National Technical Institute for the Deaf; please see www.ntid.rit.edu for more information.

ADMISSION INFORMATION FOR STUDENTS WITH LD/ADHD

College entrance tests required: Yes
Interview required: No
Essay recommended: No
Documentation required for LD: Recent comprehensive psychological evaluation
Documentation required for ADHD: Diagnosis by qualified professional
Submitted to: Disability Services Office
Special Ed. HS course work accepted: NR

Specific course requirements of all applicants: NR
Separate application required: No
# of LD applications submitted each year: NR
# of LD applications accepted yearly: NR
Total # of students receiving LD services: NR
Acceptance into program means acceptance into college: Students must be admitted to the University, they then request accommodations (as needed)

ADMISSIONS

There is no special admissions process for students with learning disabilities. However, students with learning disabilities may include a supporting essay. Although an interview is not required, it is recommended. The required scores on the SAT or ACT will depend on the program the student is applying to within RIT. It is also helpful to identify compensatory strategies used in high school and what will be needed for success in college. The admission decision is made jointly by the program chairperson and Director of Admissions. Applicants are encouraged to indicate a second and third program choice. If RIT is unable to offer an admission to the first choice program, an applicant may be qualified for admission to one of the alternative choices. Factors considered in a general admission decision include, but are not limited to: overall GPA and rank in class, rigor of course work, grades in content courses, appropriateness of courses for academic major, competitiveness of high school, standardized test(s), recommendation from school counselor, recommendations from those familiar with the student's academic performance, and an essay.

ADDITIONAL INFORMATION

The RIT Academic Support Center offers a range of learning supports to all students, including time management and organization support through the Structured Monitoring program, math and physics tutoring, study skills strategies, and weekly academic success workshops. Please see www.rit.edu/asc for more information. RIT offers a "Spectrum Support Program" for interested students with autism spectrum disorders (www.rit.edu/ssp) and TRiO Student Support Services for qualified students (www.rit.edu/trio).

LEARNING DISABILITY PROGRAM OR SERVICES

Contact Information
Name of program or department: Disability Services Office
 Telephone: 585-475-6988
 Fax: 585-475-2215

LEARNING DISABILITY SERVICES

Accommodations are decided upon an individual basis after a thorough review of appropriate, current documentation. The accommodations requested must be supported through the documentation provided and must be logically linked to the current impact of the condition on academic functioning.

Allowed in exams	**Distraction-reduced environment:** NR	**Added costs for services:** NR
Calculator: NR	**Tape recording in class:** NR	**LD specialists:** NR
Dictionary: NR	**Electronic texts:** NR	**Professional tutors:** NR
Computer: NR	**Accommodations for students with**	**Peer tutors:** NR
Spellchecker: NR	**ADHD:** NR	**Max. hours/wk. for services:** NR
Extended test time: NR	**Kurzweil Reader:** NR	**How professors are notified of**
Scribes: NR	**Other assistive technology:** NR	**LD/ADHD:** By student
Proctors: NR	**Priority registration:** NR	
Oral exams: NR		
Note-takers: NR		

GENERAL ADMISSIONS INFORMATION

Office of Admission: 585-475-6631

ENTRANCE REQUIREMENTS

Academic units required: 4 English, 2 math, 2 science (1 science lab), 4 social studies, 10 academic electives.
Academic units recommended: 4 English, 3 math, 3 science (2 science labs), 3 foreign language, 4 social studies, 5 academic electives. High school diploma is required, and GED is accepted. ACT with or without Writing component accepted. TOEFL required of all international applicants: minimum paper TOEFL 550, minimum computer TOEFL 215.

Application deadline: None	**SAT Math middle 50% range:**	**Graduated top 10% of class:** 37%
Notification: 3/15	570–680	**Graduated top 25% of class:** 68%
Average GPA: 3.7	**SAT Critical Reading middle 50%**	**Graduated top 50% of class:** 93%
ACT Composite middle 50% range:	range: 530–650	
25–30	**SAT Writing middle 50% range:**	
	520–630	

COLLEGE GRADUATION REQUIREMENTS

Course waivers allowed: No
Course substitutions allowed: No
In what course: Courses may be substituted depending on documentation and for nonrequired courses only.

ADDITIONAL INFORMATION

Environment: RIT is located on a 1,300-acre campus five miles south of the city of Rochester, the third largest city in New York State.

Student Body	**Cost Information**	**Greek System**
Undergrad enrollment: 14,653	**Tuition:** $32,037	**Fraternity:** Yes
Women: 33%	**Room & board:** $10,413	**Sorority:** Yes
Men: 67%	**Housing Information**	**Athletics:** Division III
Percent out-of-state: 49%	**University housing:** Yes	
	Percent living on campus: 68%	

ST. BONAVENTURE UNIVERSITY

PO Box D, St. Bonaventure, NY 14778
Phone: 716-375-2400 • Fax: 716-375-4005
E-mail: admissions@sbu.edu • Web: www.sbu.edu
Support: CS • Institution type: 4-year private

PROGRAMS OR SERVICES FOR STUDENTS WITH LD

St. Bonaventure does not operate a specialized LD program but does provide services to students with identified disabilities. In the spirit of the federal mandates, reasonable accommodations are made for otherwise qualified students with disabilities. St. Bonaventure's Teaching and Learning Center is an intrinsic element of the university's goal of academic excellence. The credo is to assist, not do. Once authentic, current documentation has been received, a careful review of the records will be conducted and an evaluation of appropriate accommodations will be made. Students who wait to identify themselves until after registration may find that some accommodations are not immediately available. Students with learning disabilities/attention deficit hyperactivity disorder who wish to request accommodations must meet with the coordinator of Services for Students with Disabilities. It is the student's responsibility to deliver accommodation letters to professors after accommodations have been arranged. Accommodations are arranged each semester. Students are encouraged to discuss the disability with professors and arrange for specific accommodations for test-taking and other course requirements. Students must contact the coordinator of Services for Students with Disabilities to request a course substitution. The students need to accept responsibility for their own academic excellence, and assistance will be provided.

ADMISSION INFORMATION FOR STUDENTS WITH LD/ADHD

College entrance tests required: Yes
Interview required: No
Essay recommended: No
What documentation required for LD: Psycho Ed evaluation
  to include: relevant historical info, instructional interventions,
  related services, age diagnosed, objective data (aptitude,
  achievement, info processing), test scores (standard,
  percentile and grade equivalents) and describe functional
  limitations.
With general application: No
To receive services after enrolling: Yes
What documentation required for ADHD: Diagnosis based
  on DSM-V; history of behaviors impairing functioning in
  academic setting; diagnostic interview; history of symptoms;
  evidence of ongoing behaviors.

With general application: No
Submitted to: Services for Students with Disabilities
Special Ed. HS course work accepted: Yes
Specific course requirements of all applicants: Yes
Separate application required: No
# of LD applications submitted each year: NR
# of LD applications accepted yearly: NR
Total # of students receiving LD services: 50–100
**Acceptance into program means acceptance into
  college:** Students must be admitted to and enrolled in the
  university first and then request services.

ADMISSIONS

Students with learning disabilities must meet regular admission standards and complete the same admissions process as all applicants. The mid 50 percent ACT score range is 23–24, and for SAT it is 1070–1110. The minimum GPA is a 3.0. Course requirements include 4 years of English, 4 years of social studies, 3 years of math, 3 years of science, and 2 years of a foreign language. Special education courses may be considered. It is recommended that students self-disclose their disability in a personal statement. Once students are accepted and have enrolled, they are encouraged to self-disclose their learning disability, if this has not already been done, and provide appropriate documentation to the Office of Services for Students with Disabilities. Documentation is reviewed and appropriate accommodations are arranged.

ADDITIONAL INFORMATION

Students with LD may obtain assistance with assessing learning strengths and weaknesses and consult one-on-one or in groups to acquire a greater command of a subject, get help with a specific assignment, or discuss academic challenges. Services might include, but are not limited to: alternative testing arrangements, taped texts and classes, access to word processors/spellchecker, note-takers, tutors, peer mentors, time management and study skills training, and weekly individual appointments. Assistance can be offered in requesting books on tape. Tutoring services are available to all students and are not intended to be a substitute for independent study or preparation.

LEARNING DISABILITY PROGRAM OR SERVICES

Contact Information
Name of program or department: Services for Students with Disabilities
  Telephone: 716-375-2065
  Fax: 716-375-2072

LEARNING DISABILITY SERVICES

Accommodations are decided upon an individual basis after a thorough review of appropriate, current documentation. The accommodations requested must be supported through the documentation provided and must be logically linked to the current impact of the condition on academic functioning.

Allowed in exams	**Distraction-reduced environment:** Yes	**Added costs for services:** No
Calculator: Yes	**Tape recording in class:** Yes	**LD specialists:** Yes
Dictionary: Yes	**Electronic texts:** Yes	**Professional tutors:** 1
Computer: Yes	**Accommodations for students with**	**Peer tutors:** 60–100
Spellchecker: Yes	**ADHD:** Yes	**Max. hours/wk. for services:**
Extended test time: Yes	**Kurzweil Reader:** Yes	Unlimited
Scribes: Yes	**Other assistive technology:** Yes	**How professors are notified of**
Proctors: Yes	**Priority registration:** No	**LD/ADHD:** By both student and
Oral exams: Yes		director
Note-takers: Yes		

GENERAL ADMISSIONS INFORMATION

Office of Admission: 716-375-2400

ENTRANCE REQUIREMENTS

Academic units required: 4 English, 3 math, 3 science, 2 foreign language, 4 social studies. **Academic units recommended:** 4 English, 3 math, 3 science (3 science labs), 2 foreign language, 4 social studies. High school diploma is required, and GED is accepted. ACT with or without Writing component accepted. TOEFL required of all international applicants: minimum paper TOEFL 550, minimum computer TOEFL 213.

Application deadline: Rolling	**SAT Math middle 50% range:**	**Graduated top 10% of class:** 20%
Notification: Rolling	475–590	**Graduated top 25% of class:** 45%
Average GPA: 3.18	**SAT Critical Reading middle 50%**	**Graduated top 50% of class:** 74%
ACT Composite middle 50% range:	**range:** 475–585	
20–26	**SAT Writing middle 50% range:**	
	450–570	

COLLEGE GRADUATION REQUIREMENTS

Course waivers allowed: No
Course substitutions allowed: Yes
In what course: Foreign languages with appropriate documentation

ADDITIONAL INFORMATION

Environment: The university is located on 600 acres in a rural area 70 miles southeast of Buffalo.

Student Body	**Cost Information**	**Greek System**
Undergrad enrollment: 1,996	**Tuition:** $27,890	**Fraternity:** No
Women: 52%	**Room & board:** $10,342	**Sorority:** No
Men: 48%	**Housing Information**	**Athletics:** Division I
Percent out-of-state: 75%	**University housing:** Yes	
	Percent living on campus: 76%	

ST. LAWRENCE UNIVERSITY

Payson Hall, Canton, NY 13617
Phone: 315-229-5261 • Fax: 315-229-5818
E-mail: admissions@stlawu.edu • Web: www.stlawu.edu
Support: S • Institution type: 4-year private

PROGRAMS OR SERVICES FOR STUDENTS WITH LD

The Office of Academic Services for Students with Special Needs provides services to members of the university who either have identified themselves or believe they may have some type of learning disability. The office has several purposes: to serve students who are learning-challenged by documented disabilities; help students get the academic help that they need; put students in touch with other people on campus who can help; advise and counsel students; and educate everyone on campus about special needs. The office works with students in developing IEPs for the purpose of receiving reasonable accommodations in their educational and residential life concerns. The service will also make referrals and advocate at several on-campus services, and if necessary, connect with state or regional support agencies. There is a Writing Center for help with writing assignments, peer tutors for general assistance with academic work, and a Counseling Center and Health Center. As appropriate to the disability, documentation should include a diagnostic statement identifying the disability, date of the current diagnostic evaluation, and the date of the original diagnosis; a description of the diagnostic criteria and/or diagnostic test used; a description of the current functional impact of the disability; treatments, medications, and assistive devices/services currently prescribed or in use; a description of the expected progression or stability of the impact of the disability over time; and the credentials of the diagnosing professionals. Recommendations from professionals with a history of working with the individual provide valuable information for the review process. They will be included in the evaluation of requests for accommodation and/or auxiliary aids.

ADMISSION INFORMATION FOR STUDENTS WITH LD/ADHD

College entrance tests required: Yes
Interview required: No
Essay recommended: No
What documentation required for LD: Psycho Ed evaluation to include: relevant historical info, instructional interventions, related services, age diagnosed, objective data (aptitude, achievement, info processing), test scores (standard, percentile and grade equivalents) and describe functional limitations.
With general application: No
To receive services after enrolling: Yes
What documentation required for ADHD: Diagnosis based on DSM-V; history of behaviors impairing functioning in academic setting; diagnostic interview; history of symptoms; evidence of ongoing behaviors.

With general application: No
Submitted to: Office of Special Needs
Special Ed. HS course work accepted: Yes
Specific course requirements of all applicants: NR
Separate application required: No
# of LD applications submitted each year: NR
# of LD applications accepted yearly: NR
Total # of students receiving LD services: 130–141
Acceptance into program means acceptance into college: Students must be admitted to and enrolled in the university first and then request services.

ADMISSIONS
There is no special admissions process for students with learning disabilities. All applicants must meet the same admission criteria, which include recommended courses of 4 years of English, 3 years of math, 3 years of science, 3 years of a foreign language, and 3 years of social studies, test optional for the SAT/ACT (middle 50% SAT 1750–1940). An interview is recommended and can be done off campus with an alumni representative. Counselor and 2 teacher recommendations.

ADDITIONAL INFORMATION
Students need to be self-starters (to seek out the service early and follow through). As soon as possible, students should provide the official documents that describe the learning disability, the office helps develop the IEP—and notify the professors about the learning disability. Academic requirements required for graduation are waived. Services and accommodations are available for undergraduate and graduate students.

LEARNING DISABILITY PROGRAM OR SERVICES

Contact Information
Name of program or department: Office of Academic Services for Students with Special Needs
   Telephone: 315-229-5104
   Fax: 315-229-7453

LEARNING DISABILITY SERVICES

Accommodations are decided upon an individual basis after a thorough review of appropriate, current documentation. The accommodations requested must be supported through the documentation provided and must be logically linked to the current impact of the condition on academic functioning.

Allowed in exams	**Distraction-reduced environment:** Yes	**Added costs for services:** No
Calculator: Yes	**Tape recording in class:** Yes	**LD specialists:** No
Dictionary: Yes	**Electronic texts:** No	**Professional tutors:** No
Computer: Yes	**Accommodations for students with**	**Peer tutors:** 75
Spellchecker: Yes	**ADHD:** Yes	**Max. hours/wk. for services:**
Extended test time: Yes	**Kurzweil Reader:** Yes	Unlimited
Scribes: Yes	**Other assistive technology:** Yes	**How professors are notified of**
Proctors: Yes	**Priority registration:** Yes	**LD/ADHD:** By both student and
Oral exams: No		director
Note-takers: Yes		

GENERAL ADMISSIONS INFORMATION

Office of Admission: 315-229-5261

ENTRANCE REQUIREMENTS

Academic units recommended: 4 English, 3 math, 3 science, 3 foreign language, 3 social studies, 2 history. High school diploma is required, and GED is accepted. ACT/SAT test optional. TOEFL required of all international applicants: minimum paper TOEFL 600, minimum computer TOEFL 250.

Application deadline: 2/1	**SAT Math middle 50% range:**	**Graduated top 10% of class:** 44%
Notification: 3/31	570–640	**Graduated top 25% of class:** 76%
Average GPA: 3.49	**SAT Critical Reading middle 50%**	**Graduated top 50% of class:** 95%
ACT Composite middle 50% range:	**range:** 570–640	
25–29	**SAT Writing middle 50% range:**	
	560–650	

COLLEGE GRADUATION REQUIREMENTS

Course waivers allowed: No
Course substitutions allowed: No

ADDITIONAL INFORMATION

Environment: The university is located on 1,000 acres in a rural area 80 miles south of Ottawa, Canada.

Student Body	**Cost Information**	**Greek System**
Undergrad enrollment: 2,300	**Tuition:** $42,420	**Fraternity:** Yes
Women: 55%	**Room & board:** $11,005	**Sorority:** Yes
Men: 45%	**Housing Information**	**Athletics:** Division III
Percent out-of-state: 55%	**University housing:** Yes	
	Percent living on campus: 99%	

ST. THOMAS AQUINAS COLLEGE

125 Route 340, Sparkill, NY 10976
Phone: 845-398-4100 • Fax: 845-398-4114
E-mail: admissions@stac.edu • Web: www.stac.edu
Support: SP • Institution: 4-year private

PROGRAMS OR SERVICES FOR STUDENTS WITH LD

The mission of Pathways is to facilitate the academic performance of bright college students with LD and ADHD so that they may demonstrate their knowledge and abilities. Pathways program services are comprehensive and specialized. Pathways has an emphasis on individualized services. We focus on the development of effective learning strategies and attitudes by critically evaluating and educating students about their specific needs and abilities. The aim is to break the pattern of helplessness often created in students with learning deficits, foster a spirit of active learning, to teach students to maximize strengths in order to compensate for weaknesses, and to inspire confidence in the students' own abilities. At the heart of the program are mentoring sessions. Students meet twice weekly with a professional mentor in one-to-one sessions tailored to meet specific needs. Mentors are not tutors, but guides who help students develop learning strategies, improve organizational and editing skills, understand course concepts, and negotiate academic life. Incoming freshmen must attend a four-day residential summer program.

ADMISSION INFORMATION FOR STUDENTS WITH LD/ADHD

College entrance tests required: Yes
Interview required: Yes
What documentation required for LD: Psycho Ed evaluation to include: relevant historical info, instructional interventions, related services, age diagnosed, objective data (aptitude, achievement, info processing), test scores (standard, percentile and grade equivalents) and describe functional limitations.
With general application: Yes if requested as part of Structured Program application
To receive services after enrolling: Yes
What documentation required for ADHD: Diagnosis based on DSM-V; history of behaviors impairing functioning in academic setting; diagnostic interview; history of symptoms; evidence of ongoing behaviors.

With general application: Yes if requested as part of Structured Program application
To receive services after enrolling: Yes
Submitted to: Support Program/Services
Special Ed. HS course work accepted: Yes
Specific course requirements for all applicants: Yes
Separate application required for program services: Yes
# of LD applications submitted each year: 90–120
# of LD applications accepted yearly: 20–25
Total # of students receiving LD services: 70–80
Acceptance into program means acceptance into college: Separate application is part of admissions process

ADMISSIONS

Pathways has a separate application and admissions process from the college itself. Admission to Pathways is extremely competitive. Students must be accepted by the college before their Pathways application is evaluated; however, students should apply to the college and to Pathways at the same time. (SAT or ACT scores are required for regular college admission.) The following must be submitted to Pathways: a completed Pathways application; high school transcripts (college transcripts for transfers); a letter of recommendation from a teacher; most recent IEP if available; and a comprehensive diagnostic assessment including an adult intelligence test (WAIS-IV), measures of achievement, and the specific effects of the LD/ADHD on the student's current academic performance. Reports are required; scores on an IEP are insufficient documentation. Students must also have a personal interview with Pathways staff. Transfer applications are accepted.

ADDITIONAL INFORMATION

Pathways has a director, associate director, and trained staff of mentors. Mentors are professionals with post-college education and experience in some aspect of teaching. The director and assistant director also provide mentoring. Students come to mentoring sessions having already attended classes and prepared initial course work. Pathways students are required to attend regularly scheduled sessions with their own mentor and are encouraged to drop-in for additional help as needed. Study groups in specific skills and content areas are offered dependent upon student need and staff expertise. Pathways students are also provided with academic counseling, course advisement, and priority registration. The required summer program for incoming Pathways freshmen is designed to learn the specific needs of each student, to begin preparing them for academic rigors of higher education, and to build a sense of trust and community within the group.

PROGRAM FOR DISABILITY SERVICES

Contact Information
Name of program or department: Pathways
 Telephone: 845-398-4230
 Fax: 845-398-4229

LEARNING DISABILITY SERVICES

Accommodations are decided upon an individual basis after a thorough review of appropriate, current documentation. The accommodations requested must be supported through the documentation provided and must be logically linked to the current impact of the condition on academic functioning.

Allowed in exams	**Distraction-reduced environment:** Yes	**Added costs for services:** Yes
Calculator: Yes	**Tape recording in class:** Yes	**LD specialists:** Yes
Dictionary: No	**Electronic texts:** No	**Professional tutors:** 9
Computer: Yes	**Accommodations for students with**	**Peer tutors:** N/A
Spellchecker: Yes	**ADHD:** Yes	**Max. hours/wk. for services:**
Extended test time: Yes	**Kurzweil Reader:** Yes	Unlimited
Scribes: Yes	**Other assistive technology:** Various	**How professors are notified of**
Proctors: Yes	computer software; reading pens,	**LD/ADHD:** Student
Oral exams: Yes	voice activation, foreign language	
Note-takers: Yes	tutorials, etc.	
	Priority registration: Yes	

GENERAL ADMISSIONS INFORMATION

Office of Admission: 845-398-4100

ENTRANCE REQUIREMENTS
Academic units required: 4 English, 3 mathematics, 3 science, (2 science labs), 2 foreign language, 4 social studies. High school diploma is required and GED is accepted. SAT or ACT required; TOEFL required of all international applicants; minimum paper TOEFL 530, minimum computer TOEFL 173, minimum internet TOEFL 60 (with no section below 15).

Application deadline: None	**SAT Math middle 50% range:**	**Graduated top 10% of class:** 5%
Notification: Rolling	400–530	**Graduated top 25% of class:** 35%
Average GPA: 3.0	**SAT Critical Reading middle 50%**	**Graduated top 50% of class:** 50%
ACT Composite middle 50% range:	**range:** 420–510	
16–23	**SAT Writing middle 50% range:**	
	410–510	

COLLEGE GRADUATION REQUIREMENTS

Course substitutions allowed: Yes
In what course: Foreign language, only with appropriate documentation; two (2) culture course substitutions from approved list are then required. Speech, only with appropriate documentation; one (1) communications course substitution from approved list is then required.

ADDITIONAL INFORMATION

Environment: The school is located on 48 acres in a suburban area 15 miles from New York City

Student Body	**Cost Information**	**Greek System**
Undergrad enrollment: 1,852	**Tuition:** $24,610	**Fraternity:** No
Women: 55%	**Room and board:** $11,000	**Sorority:** No
Men: 45%	**Housing Information**	**Athletics:** NCAA Division II
Percent out-of-state: 30%	**University housing:** Yes	
	Percent living on campus: 45%	

STATE UNIVERSITY OF NEW YORK— ALFRED STATE

Hunter Student Development Center, Alfred, NY 14802
Phone: 607-587-4215 • Fax: 607-587-4299
E-mail: admissions@alfredstate.edu • Web: www.alfredstate.edu
Support: S • Institution type: 2 and 4-year public

PROGRAMS OR SERVICES FOR STUDENTS WITH LD

The goal of the Office of Student Disability Services (SDS) is to ensure that students with disabilities and appropriate documentation have equal access to programs, activities, and services offered to other students. Once students present appropriate documentation, services are provided depending on individual needs. The Learning Center has a team of dedicated professionals committed to fostering the personal and academic growth of all students. The centralized nature of the center allows for an important link among college supportive services dedicated to maximizing student growth and student success. Students should contact the Learning Center and must provide adequate documentation before accommodations/services will be provided. The Services for Students with Disabilities counselor determines the extent of services provided.

ADMISSION INFORMATION FOR STUDENTS WITH LD/ADHD

College entrance tests required: Yes
Interview required: No
Essay recommended: No
What documentation required for LD: Psycho Ed evaluation to include: relevant historical info, instructional interventions, related services, age diagnosed, objective data (aptitude, achievement, info processing), test scores (standard, percentile and grade equivalents) and describe functional limitations.
With general application: No
To receive services after enrolling: Yes
What documentation required for ADHD: Diagnosis based on DSM-V; history of behaviors impairing functioning in academic setting; diagnostic interview; history of symptoms; evidence of ongoing behaviors.

With general application: No
Submitted to: Services for Students with Disabilities
Special Ed. HS course work accepted: Yes
Specific course requirements of all applicants: NR
Separate application required: No
# of LD applications submitted each year: NR
# of LD applications accepted yearly: NR
Total # of students receiving LD services: 222
Acceptance into program means acceptance into college: Students must be admitted to and enrolled in the university first and then request services.

ADMISSIONS

There is no special admission process for students with learning disabilities. All applicants must meet the same admission criteria. The minimum core courses that are preferred include 4 years of English, 3 years of math, 3 years of science, 3 years of social science, 2 years of a foreign language, and 1 year of art. The minimum GPA is 74 percent. ASOP allows students to take 3 years to complete a 2-year program.

ADDITIONAL INFORMATION

Services available through SSD include individual academic skills development, note-takers and scribes, readers, peer tutors, taped texts, testing accommodations, extended curricular programs, referral to other offices and agencies, specialized equipment loans, advocacy, and registration assistance. ASOP provides counseling, extensive advising, and tutoring. Peer and professional tutors are available by appointment and provide course-specific assistance such as answers to questions, clarification of information, and drill and/or review for exams. Academic Skills Assistance for reading improvement, student success, and study skills can be provided through individual appointments, small group seminars, classroom instruction, or computer tutorials.

LEARNING DISABILITY PROGRAM OR SERVICES

Contact Information
Name of program or department: Services for Students with Disabilities (SSD)
　Telephone: 607-587-4122
　Fax: 607-587-3210

LEARNING DISABILITY SERVICES

Accommodations are decided upon an individual basis after a thorough review of appropriate, current documentation. The accommodations requested must be supported through the documentation provided and must be logically linked to the current impact of the condition on academic functioning.

Allowed in exams	**Distraction-reduced environment:** Yes	**Added costs for services:** No
Calculator: Yes	**Tape recording in class:** Yes	**LD specialists:** No
Dictionary: Yes	**Electronic texts:** No	**Professional tutors:** 2
Computer: Yes	**Accommodations for students with**	**Peer tutors:** 75
Spellchecker: Yes	**ADHD:** Yes	**Max. hours/wk. for services:** As
Extended test time: Yes	**Kurzweil Reader:** Yes	needed
Scribes: Yes	**Other assistive technology:** Yes	**How professors are notified of**
Proctors: Yes	**Priority registration:** Yes	**LD/ADHD:** By SDS coordinator
Oral exams: No		
Note-takers: Yes		

GENERAL ADMISSIONS INFORMATION

Office of Admission: 800-4-Alfred

ENTRANCE REQUIREMENTS

Academic units recommended: 4 English, 4 math, 4 science, 4 social studies, 2 foreign language, 1 art. High school diploma is required, and GED is accepted. ACT with or without Writing component accepted. TOEFL required of all international applicants: minimum paper TOEFL 500, minimum computer TOEFL 173.

Application deadline: None	**SAT Math middle 50% range:**	**Graduated top 10% of class:** NR
Notification: Rolling	430–540	**Graduated top 25% of class:** NR
Average GPA: 2.80	**SAT Critical Reading middle 50%**	**Graduated top 50% of class:** NR
ACT Composite middle 50% range:	**range:** 410–420	
NR	**SAT Writing middle 50% range:**	
	290–490	

COLLEGE GRADUATION REQUIREMENTS

Course waivers allowed: No
Course substitutions allowed: No

ADDITIONAL INFORMATION

Environment: The university has a rural campus 70 miles from Rochester.

Student Body	**Cost Information**	**Greek System**
Undergrad enrollment: 3,617	**In-state tuition:** $5,570	**Fraternity:** Yes
Women: 38%	**Out-of-state tuition:** $10,714	**Sorority:** Yes
Men: 62%	**Room & board:** $10,450	**Athletics:** Division III
Percent out-of-state: 6%	**Housing Information**	
	University housing: Yes	
	Percent living on campus: 74%	

STATE UNIVERSITY OF NEW YORK AT BINGHAMTON

PO Box 6001, Binghamton, NY 13902-6001
Phone: 607-777-2171 • Fax: 607-777-4445
E-mail: admit@binghamton.edu • Web: www.binghamton.edu
Support: CS • Institution type: 4-year public

PROGRAMS OR SERVICES FOR STUDENTS WITH LD

The Services for Students with Disabilities office provides assistance to students with physical or learning disabilities. They operate on the philosophy that the individuals they serve are students first and their disabilities are secondary. Support services assist students in taking advantage of the opportunities at Binghamton and in making their own contributions to the university community.

ADMISSION INFORMATION FOR STUDENTS WITH LD/ADHD

College entrance tests required: Yes
Interview required: No
Essay recommended: Yes
What documentation required for LD: Psycho Ed evaluation to include: relevant historical info, instructional interventions, related services, age diagnosed, objective data (aptitude, achievement, info processing), test scores (standard, percentile and grade equivalents) and describe functional limitations.
With general application: No
To receive services after enrolling: Yes
What documentation required for ADHD: Diagnosis based on DSM-V; history of behaviors impairing functioning in academic setting; diagnostic interview; history of symptoms; evidence of ongoing behaviors.

With general application: No
Submitted to: SSD
Special Ed. HS course work accepted: NR
Specific course requirements of all applicants: NR
Separate application required: No
# of LD applications submitted each year: NR
# of LD applications accepted yearly: NR
Total # of students receiving LD services: 79
Acceptance into program means acceptance into college: Students must be admitted to and enrolled in the university first and then request services.

ADMISSIONS

Binghamton University welcomes applications from all qualified individuals. While there are no special admissions procedures or academic programs expressly for students with disabilities, the Services for Students with Disabilities Office provides a wide range of support services to enrolled students. Diagnostic tests are not required for admissions, but students are encouraged to meet with the director of Services for Students with Disabilities and provide documentation to determine appropriate accommodations. Through nonmatriculated enrollment, students can take courses but are not enrolled in a degree program. If they do well, they may then apply for matriculation, using credits earned toward their degree. General admission criteria includes 4 years of English, 2.5 years of math, 2 years of social science, 2 years of science, and 2 years of 2 foreign languages or 3 years of 1 foreign language. The mid 50 percent score range on the SAT is 1100–1330.

ADDITIONAL INFORMATION

Students with LD/ADHD may use all campus-wide services, plus receive accommodations and services through SSD. Accommodations that are available for students with appropriate documentation include extended testing times; low-distraction environments for tests; scribes; proctors; use of calculators, dictionaries, computers, and spellchecker during exams; and assistive technology including voice recognition software, screen readers software, print enlargement, assistive listening devices, and variable speed tape recorders on loan. Tutorial services are provided for 4 hours per week to undergraduate students at no charge. However, SSD can arrange for more than 4 hours per week at the student's expense. The university's Center for Academic Excellence provides peer tutoring to any student at no cost. The university has offered courses in college study, coping skills, and applying study skills to career research. Availability of these courses each year is dependent on staffing. Students are provided memos of reasonable accommodation written by the SSD director or learning disabilities specialist to be given to their professors. Services and accommodations are available for undergraduate and graduate students.

LEARNING DISABILITY PROGRAM OR SERVICES

Contact Information
Name of program or department: Services for Students with Disabilities (SSD)
  Telephone: 607-777-2686
  Fax: 607-777-6893

LEARNING DISABILITY SERVICES

Accommodations are decided upon an individual basis after a thorough review of appropriate, current documentation. The accommodations requested must be supported through the documentation provided and must be logically linked to the current impact of the condition on academic functioning.

Allowed in exams
  Calculator: Yes
  Dictionary: Yes
  Computer: Yes
  Spellchecker: Yes
Extended test time: Yes
Scribes: Yes
Proctors: Yes
Oral exams: Yes
Note-takers: Yes

Distraction-reduced environment: Yes
Tape recording in class: Yes
Electronic texts: Yes
Accommodations for students with
  ADHD: Yes
Kurzweil Reader: Yes
Other assistive technology: Yes
Priority registration: Yes

Added costs for services: No
LD specialists: Yes
Professional tutors: No
Peer tutors: Yes
Max. hours/wk. for services: 5
How professors are notified of
  LD/ADHD: By student

GENERAL ADMISSIONS INFORMATION

Office of Admission: 607-777-2171

ENTRANCE REQUIREMENTS

Academic units required: 4 English, 3 math, 2 science, 3 foreign language, 2 social studies. **Academic units recommended:** 4 math, 4 science, 3 foreign language, 3 history. High school diploma is required, and GED is accepted. ACT with Writing component required. TOEFL required of all international applicants: minimum paper TOEFL 550, minimum computer TOEFL 213.

Application deadline: None
Notification: Rolling
Average GPA: 3.70
ACT Composite middle 50% range:
  26–29

SAT Math middle 50% range:
  610–690
SAT Critical Reading middle 50%
  range: 580–660
SAT Writing middle 50% range: NR

Graduated top 10% of class: 49%
Graduated top 25% of class: 84%
Graduated top 50% of class: 98%

COLLEGE GRADUATION REQUIREMENTS

Course waivers allowed: No
Course substitutions allowed: Yes
In what course: Varies, depending on the nature and severity of the student's disability, the student's current and comprehensive diagnostic documentation, and the student's major of study.

ADDITIONAL INFORMATION

Environment: The university has a suburban campus near Binghamton.

Student Body
  Undergrad enrollment: 11,787
  Women: 48%
  Men: 52%
  Percent out-of-state: 14%

Cost Information
  In-state tuition: $6,939
  Out-of-state tuition: $15,349
  Room & board: $11,886
Housing Information
  University housing: Yes
  Percent living on campus: 56%

Greek System
  Fraternity: Yes
  Sorority: Yes
Athletics: Division I

STATE UNIVERSITY OF NEW YORK—CANTON

French Hall, SUNY Canton, Canton, NY 13617
Phone: 315-386-7123 • Fax: 315-386-7929
E-mail: admissions@canton.edu • Web: www.canton.edu
Support: S • Institution Type: 2-year public

PROGRAMS OR SERVICES FOR STUDENTS WITH LD

At the State University of New York at Canton, College of Technology, the Accommodative Services Office is equipped to help students with learning disabilities make a smooth transaction to college and receive necessary accommodations to ensure their academic success. The mission of the Office of Accommodative Services is to create a comprehensively accessible environment where individuals are viewed on the basis of ability, not disability. This supports the mission of SUNY Canton, a technical college, offering 2- and 4-year degrees to a diverse student body. Prospective students are welcome to contact the Accommodative Services office with any questions. Although students with learning disabilities may register at the office at any time during their stay at SUNY Canton, they are encouraged to do so as early as possible. Students may register at the office to obtain the special resources and services. It is the student's responsibility to self-disclose, provide appropriate documentation, and request accommodations.

ADMISSION INFORMATION FOR STUDENTS WITH LD/ADHD

College entrance tests required: No
Interview required: No
Essay recommended: Yes
What documentation required for LD: Psycho Ed evaluation to include: relevant historical info, instructional interventions, related services, age diagnosed, objective data (aptitude, achievement, info processing), test scores (standard, percentile and grade equivalents) and describe functional limitations.
With general application: No
To receive services after enrolling: Yes
What documentation required for ADHD: Diagnosis based on DSM-V; history of behaviors impairing functioning in academic setting; diagnostic interview; history of symptoms; evidence of ongoing behaviors.

With general application: No
Submitted to: Accommodative Services
Special Ed. HS course work accepted: No
Specific course requirements of all applicants: NR
Separate application required: No
# of LD applications submitted each year: NR
# of LD applications accepted yearly: NR
Total # of students receiving LD services: average of 200 per semester
Acceptance into program means acceptance into college: Students must be admitted to and enrolled in the university first and then request services.

ADMISSIONS

All students follow the same admissions procedure and are evaluated similarly for specific course placement. The Office of Accommodative Services is not directly involved in the admission process, but will usually meet with students (and families) during admissions interviews. There are no specific course requirements as the requirements vary per curriculum, and foreign language is not required for admission. All students must have a high school diploma or the GED equivalent. No ACT/SAT tests are required for admission to the 2-year programs. However, ACT or SAT is required for the 4-year bachelor programs. Accuplacer test are used for placement. A student may be required to take our accuplacer exam for placement in English. Students are exempt if they achieve a minimum NYS English Regents score of 75, achieve a minimum SAT verbal score of 420, or achieve a minimum ACT score of 17 on the English and Reading sections.

ADDITIONAL INFORMATION

A number of support services are offered on campus: an Academic Advisement Center, Counseling Center, Educational Opportunity Program, Math Lab, Writing Center, Science Learning & Tutoring Center, Curriculum tutoring labs, and general tutoring for courses not covered through existing tutoring labs. Services or accommodations could include testing accommodations; scribes; proctors; notetakers; books in alternate format; assistive technology; use of calculators, dictionaries, computers, or spellcheckers in exams; distraction-reduced environments for tests; and priority registration. Acceptance into the university ensures that students will receive the services they request when they provide appropriate documentation.

LEARNING DISABILITY PROGRAM OR SERVICES

Contact Information
Name of program or department: Accommodative Services (AS)
   Telephone: 315-386-7392
   Fax: 315-379-3877

LEARNING DISABILITY SERVICES

Accommodations are decided upon an individual basis after a thorough review of appropriate, current documentation. The accommodations requested must be supported through the documentation provided and must be logically linked to the current impact of the condition on academic functioning.

Allowed in exams	**Distraction-reduced environment:** Yes	**Added costs for services:** No
Calculator: Yes	**Tape recording in class:** Yes	**LD specialists:** No
Dictionary: Yes	**Electronic texts:** Yes	**Professional tutors:** Yes
Computer: Yes	**Accommodations for students with**	**Peer tutors:** Yes
Spellchecker: Yes	**ADHD:** Yes	**Max. hours/wk. for services:** As
Extended test time: Yes	**Kurzweil Reader:** Yes	needed
Scribes: Yes	**Other assistive technology:** Yes	**How professors are notified of**
Proctors: Yes	**Priority registration:** Yes	**LD/ADHD:** By director
Oral exams: Yes		
Note-takers: Yes		

GENERAL ADMISSIONS INFORMATION

Office of Admission: 315-386-7123

ENTRANCE REQUIREMENTS

Academic units recommended: 4 English, 2 math, 2 science, 4 social studies. High school diploma is required, and GED is accepted. TOEFL required of all international applicants: minimum paper TOEFL 550, minimum computer TOEFL 213.

Application deadline: None	**SAT Math middle 50% range:** NR	**Graduated top 10% of class:** NR
Notification: Rolling	**SAT Critical Reading middle 50%**	**Graduated top 25% of class:** NR
Average GPA: 82	range: NR	**Graduated top 50% of class:** NR
ACT Composite middle 50% range: NR	**SAT Writing middle 50% range:** NR	

COLLEGE GRADUATION REQUIREMENTS

Course waivers allowed: No
In what course: NR
Course substitutions allowed: Yes
In what course: Depends on disability

ADDITIONAL INFORMATION

Environment: The 550-acre campus is 135 miles northeast of Syracuse.

Student Body	**Cost Information (Associates)**	**Greek System**
Undergrad enrollment: 3,800	**In-state tuition:** $6,990	**Fraternity:** Yes
Women: 51%	**Out-of-state tuition:** $13,380	**Sorority:** Yes
Men: 49%	**Room & board:** $10,340	**Athletics:** Division III
Percent out-of-state: 3%	**Housing Information**	
	University housing: Yes	
	Percent living on campus: 41%	

STATE UNIVERSITY OF NEW YORK— DELHI

Bush Hall, Two Main Street, Delhi, NY 13753
Phone: 607-746-4550 • Fax: 607-746-4104
E-mail: enroll@Delhi.edu • Web: www.delhi.edu
Support: CS • Institution type: 2-year public

PROGRAMS OR SERVICES FOR STUDENTS WITH LD

SUNY—Delhi provides students with learning disabilities with academic support services and equipment, including tutors, exams in distraction-free environments, and enlarged-video-display computer terminals. The Coordinator of Services often confers with students regarding their unique learning, study, and time management needs.

ADMISSION INFORMATION FOR STUDENTS WITH LD/ADHD

College entrance tests required: No
Interview required: No
Essay recommended: No
What documentation required for LD: Psycho Ed evaluation to include: relevant historical info, instructional interventions, related services, age diagnosed, objective data (aptitude, achievement, info processing), test scores (standard, percentile and grade equivalents) and describe functional limitations.
With general application: No
To receive services after enrolling: Yes
What documentation required for ADHD: Diagnosis based on DSM-V; history of behaviors impairing functioning in academic setting; diagnostic interview; history of symptoms; evidence of ongoing behaviors.

With general application: No
Submitted to: The Coordinator of Students with Disabilities
Special Ed. HS course work accepted: NR
Specific course requirements of all applicants: Yes
Separate application required: No
# of LD applications submitted each year: NR
# of LD applications accepted yearly: NR
Total # of students receiving LD services: NR
Acceptance into program means acceptance into college: Students must be admitted to and enrolled in the university first and then request services.

ADMISSIONS

The admission requirements are the same for all students. It is always helpful if students with learning disabilities present themselves as confident, independent, goal-oriented, and self-directed learners. The minimum GPA and course requirements depend on the major. Admissions counselors will refer students to the coordinator if the student provides information about a disability. To be eligible for services, students must disclose information about their learning disability/attention deficit hyperactivity disorder and meet with the coordinator of Services for Students with Disabilities.

ADDITIONAL INFORMATION

The Coordinator of Services for Students with Learning Disabilities is available to answer any questions regarding academic and non-academic matters. The coordinator also serves as a campus referral service. There are writing, tutoring, and computer labs available for all students. Services and accommodations available with appropriate documentation include extended testing times for exams; distraction-free environments; use of calculators, dictionaries, computers, and spellchecker during exams; scribes; proctors; note-takers; electronic books and assistive technology. Additionally, there are computer stations with built-in software to read tests independently, electronic books for qualified students, and a Writing and Math Center.

LEARNING DISABILITY PROGRAM OR SERVICES

Contact Information
Name of program or department: The Resnick Learning Center
  Telephone: 607-746-4593
  Fax: 607-746-4368

LEARNING DISABILITY SERVICES

Accommodations are decided upon an individual basis after a thorough review of appropriate, current documentation. The accommodations requested must be supported through the documentation provided and must be logically linked to the current impact of the condition on academic functioning.

Allowed in exams
  Calculator: Yes
  Dictionary: Yes
  Computer: Yes
  Spellchecker: Yes
Extended test time: Yes
Scribes: Yes
Proctors: Yes
Oral exams: Yes
Note-takers: Yes

Distraction-reduced environment: Yes
Tape recording in class: Yes
Electronic texts: No
Accommodations for students with
  ADHD: Yes
Kurzweil Reader: Yes
Other assistive technology: Yes
Priority registration: No

Added costs for services: No
LD specialists: Yes
Professional tutors: Yes
Peer tutors: Yes
Max. hours/wk. for services: 2 per course
How professors are notified of LD/ADHD: By student

GENERAL ADMISSIONS INFORMATION

Office of Admission: 607-746-4550

ENTRANCE REQUIREMENTS

Academic units required: 4 English, 1 math, 1 science, 3 social studies, 1 history. **Academic units recommended:** 2 math, 2 science (1 science lab). High school diploma is required, and GED is accepted.

Application deadline: None
Notification: Rolling
Average GPA: NR
ACT Composite middle 50% range: NR

SAT Math middle 50% range: NR
SAT Critical Reading middle 50% range: NR
SAT Writing middle 50% range: NR

Graduated top 10% of class: NR
Graduated top 25% of class: NR
Graduated top 50% of class: NR

COLLEGE GRADUATION REQUIREMENTS

Course waivers allowed: No
Course substitutions allowed: Yes
In what course: Math and foreign language

ADDITIONAL INFORMATION

Environment: The university is on 1,100 acres in a small town setting in upstate New York.

Student Body
  Undergrad enrollment: 2,751
  Women: 44%
  Men: 56%
  Percent out-of-state: 2%

Cost Information
  In-state tuition: $5,270
  Out-of-state tuition: $14,320
  Room & board: $10,120
Housing Information
  University housing: Yes
  Percent living on campus: 70%

Greek System
  Fraternity: Yes
  Sorority: Yes
Athletics: Division III

STATE UNIVERSITY OF NEW YORK— FARMINGDALE

Admissions Office, 2350 Broadhollow Road, Farmingdale, NY 11735
Phone: 631-420-2200 • Fax: 631-420-2633
E-mail: admissions@farmingdale.edu • Web: www.farmingdale.edu
Support: CS • Institution type: 4-year public

PROGRAMS OR SERVICES FOR STUDENTS WITH LD

There is no learning disabilities program at the college, but the Disability Services Center is dedicated to the principle that equal opportunity to realize one's full potential should be available to all students. In keeping with this philosophy, the staff offers services to students with disabilities in accordance with their needs. Students may be able to meet individually with a learning disability specialist or in group meetings. Services include academic remediation with emphasis on compensatory strategies, study skills strategies training, test accommodations, time management instruction, tutoring, and self-understanding of disability. The services offered strive to instill independence, self-confidence, and self-advocacy skills.

ADMISSION INFORMATION FOR STUDENTS WITH LD/ADHD

College entrance tests required: Yes
Interview required: Yes
Essay recommended: No
What documentation required for LD: Psycho Ed evaluation to include: relevant historical info, instructional interventions, related services, age diagnosed, objective data (aptitude, achievement, info processing), test scores (standard, percentile and grade equivalents) and describe functional limitations.
With general application: No
To receive services after enrolling: Yes
What documentation required for ADHD: Diagnosis based on DSM-V; history of behaviors impairing functioning in academic setting; diagnostic interview; history of symptoms; evidence of ongoing behaviors.

With general application: No
Submitted to: Office of Support Services
Special Ed. HS course work accepted: Yes
Specific course requirements of all applicants: Yes
Separate application required: No
# of LD applications submitted each year: NR
# of LD applications accepted yearly: NR
Total # of students receiving LD services: 145–155
Acceptance into program means acceptance into college: Students must be admitted and enrolled in the university first (they can appeal a denial) and then request services.

ADMISSIONS

There is no special admissions procedure for applicants with learning disabilities. Students should self-identify on the application. Admission decisions are made by the Office of Admissions. Students are required to take the SAT/ACT. The university has rolling admissions. Almost all of the programs accept students throughout the year. The minimum GPA is 80% and SAT 1000 or ACT 21.

ADDITIONAL INFORMATION

Students begin the process to receive support services by disclosing their disability to the Disability Services Center (DSC). Documentation providing diagnosis and how it impacts learning is required. Additional documentation may be required depending on specific disability. Services and accommodations available with appropriate documentation may include extended testing times; distraction-free environments; use of calculators, computers, and spellchecker; note-takers; scribes; proctors; assistive technology; tutors; and recording in classes.

LEARNING DISABILITY PROGRAM OR SERVICES

Contact Information
Name of program or department: Disability Services Center
  Telephone: 631-420-2411
  Fax: 631-794-6173

LEARNING DISABILITY SERVICES

Accommodations are decided upon an individual basis after a thorough review of appropriate, current documentation. The accommodations requested must be supported through the documentation provided and must be logically linked to the current impact of the condition on academic functioning.

Allowed in exams
  Calculator: Yes
  Dictionary: No
  Computer: Yes
  Spellchecker: Yes
Extended test time: Yes
Scribes: Yes
Proctors: Yes
Oral exams: Yes
Note-takers: Yes

Distraction-reduced environment: Yes
Tape recording in class: Yes
Electronic texts: Yes
Accommodations for students with
  ADHD: Yes
Kurzweil Reader: Yes
Other assistive technology: Yes
Priority registration: No

Added costs for services: No
LD specialists: Yes
Professional tutors: No
Peer tutors: Yes
Max. hours/wk. for services:
  Unlimited
How professors are notified of
  LD/ADHD: By student

GENERAL ADMISSIONS INFORMATION

Office of Admission: 631-420-2200

ENTRANCE REQUIREMENTS

Academic units required: 4 English, 2 math, 1 science (1 science lab), 4 social studies. **Academic units recommended:** 4 English, 4 math, 3 science (3 science labs), 4 social studies. High school diploma is required, and GED is accepted. TOEFL required of all international applicants: minimum paper TOEFL 520, minimum computer TOEFL 190.

Application deadline: None
Notification: Rolling
Average GPA: NR
ACT Composite middle 50% range:
  NR

SAT Math middle 50% range:
  450–550
SAT Critical Reading middle 50%
  range: 430–530
SAT Writing middle 50% range:
  420–500

Graduated top 10% of class: NR
Graduated top 25% of class: NR
Graduated top 50% of class: NR

COLLEGE GRADUATION REQUIREMENTS

Course substitutions allowed: Yes
In what course: Foreign language

ADDITIONAL INFORMATION

Environment: Farmingdale is in the suburbs with easy access to New York City.

Student Body
  Undergrad enrollment: 7,600
  Women: 42%
  Men: 58%
  Percent out-of-state: 1%

Cost Information
  In-state tuition: $6,444
  Out-of-state tuition: $14,320
  Room & board: $11,618
Housing Information
  University housing: Yes
  Percent living on campus: 10%

Greek System
  Fraternity: No
  Sorority: No
Athletics: Division III

STATE UNIVERSITY OF NEW YORK— POTSDAM

44 Pierrepont Avenue, Potsdam, NY 13676
Phone: 315-267-2180 • Fax: 315-267-2163
E-mail: admissions@potsdam.edu • Web: www.potsdam.edu
Support: S • Institution type: 4-year public

PROGRAMS OR SERVICES FOR STUDENTS WITH LD

The State University of New York College—Potsdam is committed to the full inclusion of all individuals who can benefit from educational opportunities. Accommodative Services provides academic accommodations for all qualified students who have documented learning, emotional, and/or physical disabilities and a need for accommodations. The ultimate goal is to promote individuals' independence within the academic atmosphere of the university. Students are assisted in this process by the support services and programs available to all Potsdam students. Students must submit (written) documentation of the disability and the need for accommodations. After forwarding documentation, students are encouraged to make an appointment to meet with the coordinator to discuss accommodations. All accommodations are determined on an individual basis. Accommodative Services makes every effort to ensure access to academic accommodations.

ADMISSION INFORMATION FOR STUDENTS WITH LD/ADHD

College entrance tests required: Yes
Interview required: No
Essay recommended: No
What documentation required for LD: Psycho Ed evaluation to include: relevant historical info, instructional interventions, related services, age diagnosed, objective data (aptitude, achievement, info processing), test scores (standard, percentile and grade equivalents) and describe functional limitations.
With general application: No
To receive services after enrolling: Yes
What documentation required for ADHD: Diagnosis based on DSM-V; history of behaviors impairing functioning in academic setting; diagnostic interview; history of symptoms; evidence of ongoing behaviors.

With general application: No
Submitted to: Support Services
Special Ed. HS course work accepted: No
Specific course requirements of all applicants: Yes
Separate application required: No
# of LD applications submitted each year: NR
# of LD applications accepted yearly: NR
Total # of students receiving LD services: 45–50
Acceptance into program means acceptance into college: Students must be admitted to and enrolled in the university first and then request services.

ADMISSIONS
Students with learning disabilities must meet the same admission criteria as all applicants to the university. General admissions requirements include an ACT of 20-plus or SAT of 960, 3.0 GPA, and 17 core courses including 3 years of math, 2 years of science, 4 years of social studies, 4 years of English, 3 years of a foreign language, and 1 year of fine or performing arts. There is no conditional or probational admission plan. Students are encouraged to self-disclose their disability and provide appropriate documentation to Accommodative Services.

ADDITIONAL INFORMATION
Accommodations available through Accommodative Services include note-takers; test readers/books on tape; alternative testing such as extended time and/or distraction-reduced environment, exam readers/scribes, and use of word processor with spellchecker; and lending of some equipment. Additional services can include special registration and academic advising. Accommodative Services will assist students requesting non-academic auxiliary aids or services in locating the appropriate campus resources to address the request. The College Counseling Center provides psychological services. The early warning system asks each instructor to indicate at midpoint in each semester if a student is making unsatisfactory academic progress. Results of this inquiry are sent to the student and advisor. Student Support Services provides academic support, peer mentoring, and counseling. Tutoring is available for all students one-on-one or in small groups.

LEARNING DISABILITY PROGRAM OR SERVICES

Contact Information
Name of program or department: Student Support Services
  Telephone: 315-267-3267
  Fax: 315-267-3268

LEARNING DISABILITY SERVICES

Accommodations are decided upon an individual basis after a thorough review of appropriate, current documentation. The accommodations requested must be supported through the documentation provided and must be logically linked to the current impact of the condition on academic functioning.

Allowed in exams
  Calculator: Yes
  Dictionary: Yes
  Computer: Yes
  Spellchecker: Yes
Extended test time: Yes
Scribes: Yes
Proctors: Yes
Oral exams: Yes
Note-takers: Yes

Distraction-reduced environment: Yes
Tape recording in class: Yes
Electronic texts: Yes
Accommodations for students with ADHD: Yes
Kurzweil Reader: Yes
Other assistive technology: Yes
Priority registration: Yes

Added costs for services: No
LD specialists: No
Professional tutors: No
Peer tutors: 180
Max. hours/wk. for services: 3
How professors are notified of LD/ADHD: By student

GENERAL ADMISSIONS INFORMATION

Office of Admission: 315-267-2180

ENTRANCE REQUIREMENTS
Academic units required: 4 English, 3 math, 2 science (1 science lab), 4 social studies, 1 fine arts. **Academic units recommended:** 4 English, 4 math, 4 science (2 science labs), 4 foreign language, 4 social studies, 1 fine arts. High school diploma is required, and GED is accepted. ACT with or without Writing component accepted. TOEFL required of all international applicants: minimum paper TOEFL 550, minimum computer TOEFL 213.

Application deadline: None
Notification: Rolling
Average GPA: 3.20
ACT Composite middle 50% range:
  20–25

SAT Math middle 50% range:
  470–580
SAT Critical Reading middle 50% range: 470–570
SAT Writing middle 50% range: NR

Graduated top 10% of class: 13%
Graduated top 25% of class: 35%
Graduated top 50% of class: 70%

COLLEGE GRADUATION REQUIREMENTS

Course waivers allowed: Yes
In what course: Waivers only done on an individual basis
Course substitutions allowed: Yes
In what course: Substitutions only done on an individual basis

ADDITIONAL INFORMATION

Environment: The university is located on 240 acres in a rural area.

Student Body
  Undergrad enrollment: 3,902
  Women: 57%
  Men: 43%
  Percent out-of-state: 4%

Cost Information
  In-state tuition: $6,790
  Out-of-state tuition: $14,600
  Room & board: $9,630
Housing Information
  University housing: Yes
  Percent living on campus: 54%

Greek System
  Fraternity: Yes
  Sorority: Yes
Athletics: Division III

STATE UNIVERSITY OF NEW YORK— STONY BROOK UNIVERSITY

Office of Admissions, Stony Brook, NY 11794-1901
Phone: 631-632-6868 • Fax: 631-632-9898
E-mail: enroll@stonybrook.edu • Web: www.stonybrook.edu
Support: CS • Institution type: 4-year public

PROGRAMS OR SERVICES FOR STUDENTS WITH LD

Disability Support Services (DSS) coordinates advocacy and support services for students with disabilities. These services assist integrating students' needs with the resources available at the university to eliminate physical or programmatic barriers and ensure an accessible academic environment. All information and documentation of student disabilities is confidential. Students are responsible for identifying and documenting their disabilities through the DSS office. Students receive assistance with special housing and transportation, recruitment of readers, interpreters, note-takers, test accommodations, and counseling. A learning disabilities specialist is available to refer students for diagnostic testing and educational programming, meet accommodation needs, and provide in-service training to the university community. A Supported Education Program offering individual counseling and group sessions is available for students with psychological disabilities. Students who anticipate requiring assistance should contact Disability Support Services as early as possible to allow time for implementing recommended services.

ADMISSION INFORMATION FOR STUDENTS WITH LD/ADHD

College entrance tests required: Yes
Interview required: No
Essay recommended: No
What documentation required for LD: Psycho Ed evaluation to include: relevant historical info, instructional interventions, related services, age diagnosed, objective data (aptitude, achievement, info processing), test scores (standard, percentile and grade equivalents) and describe functional limitations.
With general application: No
To receive services after enrolling: Yes
What documentation required for ADHD: Diagnosis based on DSM-V; history of behaviors impairing functioning in academic setting; diagnostic interview; history of symptoms; evidence of ongoing behaviors.

With general application: No
Submitted to: DSS
Special Ed. HS course work accepted: No
Specific course requirements of all applicants: Yes
Separate application required: No
# of LD applications submitted each year: NR
# of LD applications accepted yearly: NR
Total # of students receiving LD services: 165
Acceptance into program means acceptance into college: Students must be admitted to and enrolled in the university first and then request services.

ADMISSIONS

Admission decisions are based on grades, GPA and/or class rank, and ACT/SAT. There is no separate or special admission because there are no developmental or remedial classes. However, each applicant who is identified as having a disability is given the special consideration of being reviewed by an admissions counselor and a DSS staff member jointly. All special circumstances are taken into consideration. Students are encouraged to self-disclose their disability in the application process. The Director of Disabilities Services will review documentation from students with learning disabilities and provide a recommendation to the Office of Admissions. Courses required for admission include 4 units of English, 4 units of social studies, 3 units of mathematics (4 units required for engineering), 3 units of science (4 units required for engineering), and 2 or 3 units of a foreign language. The average high school GPA is 91.

ADDITIONAL INFORMATION

Types of services and accommodations available are pre-registration advisement, liaisoning with faculty and staff, taped texts, learning strategies and time management training, assistance in locating tutors, assistance in arranging for note-takers and readers, tutorial computer programs, proctoring and/or modified administration of exams, support groups, referrals to appropriate campus resources, peer advising, and aid in vocational decision making. Services and accommodations are available to undergraduate and graduate students. No skills classes are offered.

LEARNING DISABILITY PROGRAM OR SERVICES

Contact Information
Name of program or department: Disabilities Support Services (DSS)
  Telephone: 631-632-6748
  Fax: 631-632-6747

LEARNING DISABILITY SERVICES

Accommodations are decided upon an individual basis after a thorough review of appropriate, current documentation. The accommodations requested must be supported through the documentation provided and must be logically linked to the current impact of the condition on academic functioning.

Allowed in exams	**Distraction-reduced environment:** Yes	**Added costs for services:** No
Calculator: NR	**Tape recording in class:** Yes	**LD specialists:** Yes
Dictionary: No	**Electronic texts:** No	**Professional tutors:** No
Computer: Yes	**Accommodations for students with**	**Peer tutors:** No
Spellchecker: Yes	**ADHD:** Yes	**Max. hours/wk. for services:** N/A
Extended test time: Yes	**Kurzweil Reader:** Yes	**How professors are notified of**
Scribes: Yes	**Other assistive technology:** Yes	**LD/ADHD:** By student
Proctors: Yes	**Priority registration:** Yes	
Oral exams: No		
Note-takers: Yes		

GENERAL ADMISSIONS INFORMATION

Office of Admission: 631-632-6868

ENTRANCE REQUIREMENTS

Academic units required: 4 English, 3 math, 3 science, 2 foreign language, 4 social studies. **Academic units recommended:** 4 math, 4 science, 3 foreign language. High school diploma is required, and GED is accepted. ACT with Writing component required. TOEFL required of all international applicants: minimum paper TOEFL 550, minimum computer TOEFL 213.

Application deadline: None	**SAT Math middle 50% range:** 590–690	**Graduated top 10% of class:** 38%
Notification: Rolling	**SAT Critical Reading middle 50%**	**Graduated top 25% of class:** 72%
Average GPA: 3.60	**range:** 540–640	**Graduated top 50% of class:** 95%
ACT Composite middle 50% range: 25–29	**SAT Writing middle 50% range:** 530–640	

COLLEGE GRADUATION REQUIREMENTS

Course waivers allowed: No
Course substitutions allowed: Yes
In what course: Subsitutions possible for foreign language

ADDITIONAL INFORMATION

Environment: The university is located on 1,100 acres in a suburban area on Long Island, 60 miles from New York City.

Student Body	**Cost Information**	**Greek System**
Undergrad enrollment: 16,342	**In-state tuition:** $5,488	**Fraternity:** Yes
Women: 49%	**Out-of-state tuition:** $14,388	**Sorority:** Yes
Men: 51%	**Room & board:** $9,590	**Athletics:** Division I
Percent out-of-state: 10%	**Housing Information**	
	University housing: Yes	
	Percent living on campus: 52%	

STATE UNIVERSITY OF NEW YORK— UNIVERSITY AT ALBANY

University at Albany—SUNY, 1400 Washington Ave., Albany, NY 12222
Phone: 518-442-5435 • Fax: 518-442-5383
E-mail: ugadmissions@albany.edu • Web: www.albany.edu
Support: S • Institution: 4-year public

PROGRAMS OR SERVICES FOR STUDENTS WITH LD

The University at Albany—State University of New York, in response to a growing population of successful students with learning disabilities and/or attention deficit disorder, created an Office of Learning Disabled Student Services. This Office is now part of the newly created Disability Resource Center. The mission of the Disability Resource Center is to empower individual students, using appropriate supportive services, as well as acting as an expert resource for the university community. This includes assisting the student in developing the skills necessary to be a successful, independent learner, organizing class assignments, workload, social life, and developing appropriate academic accommodations for classes as well as increasing campus awareness of the issues surrounding students with disabilities.

ADMISSION INFORMATION FOR STUDENTS WITH LD/ADHD

College entrance tests required: Yes
Interview required: No
Essay required: N/A
What documentation required for LD: Psycho Ed evaluation to include: relevant historical info, instructional interventions, related services, age diagnosed, objective data (aptitude, achievement, info processing), test scores (standard, percentile and grade equivalents) and describe functional limitations.
With general application: No
To receive services after enrolling: Yes
What documentation required for ADHD: Diagnosis based on DSM-V; history of behaviors impairing functioning in academic setting; diagnostic interview; history of symptoms; evidence of ongoing behaviors.

With general application: No
Submitted to: Disability Resource Center
Special Ed. HS course work accepted: N/A
Specific course requirements for all applicants: Yes
Separate application required for program services: N/A
# of LD applications submitted each year: NR
# of LD applications accepted yearly: NR
Total # of students receiving LD services: 150–250
Acceptance into program means acceptance into college: Students must be admitted and enrolled in the university first and then request services.

ADMISSIONS
There is no special application for applicants with learning disabiities and/or attention deficit disorder. For regular admissions, a student needs to have a high school average of 85 percent or higher, be in the top third of their class, and obtain an acceptable standardized test score. The University does have a Talented Student Admissions program for those students that do not fit the standard profile. The minimum academic criteria for consideration has been set at an eleventh grade cumulative average of 80 and rank in the top half of the high school class at the end of eleventh grade, as well as having an ACT/SAT scores deemed acceptable by the University.

ADDITIONAL INFORMATION
Students visiting the University at Albany are encouraged to schedule an appointment to meet with the a staff member of the Disability Resource Center while they are on campus. The Disability Resource Center provides individual appointments to discuss academic concerns, develop study strategies, rehearse self-advocacy scenarios, and provide a "reality check" on the student's academic progress. The office receives and reviews documentation supplied by the student in regards to their disability. Appropriate academic accommodations are then developed based on the documentation supplied. The student and the Director or Associate Director discuss the academic accommodations that are developed and the mechanisms involved to receive the accommodation.

PROGRAM FOR DISABILITY SERVICES

Contact Information
Name of program or department: Disability Resource Center
  Telephone: 518-442-5490
  Fax: 518-442-5400

LEARNING DISABILITY SERVICES

Accommodations are decided upon an individual basis after a thorough review of appropriate, current documentation. The accommodations requested must be supported through the documentation provided and must be logically linked to the current impact of the condition on academic functioning.

Allowed in exams	**Distraction-reduced environment:** Yes	**Added costs for services:** No
Calculator: Yes	**Tape recording in class:** Yes	**LD specialists:** Yes
Dictionary: No	**Electronic texts:** Yes,, student must	**Professional tutors:** Rare
Computer: Yes	have software.	**Peer tutors:** Yes
Spellchecker: Yes	**Accommodations for students with**	**Max. hours/wk. for services:**
Extended test time: Yes	**ADHD:** Yes	Unlimited
Scribes: Yes	**Kurzweil Reader:** Yes	**How professors are notified of**
Proctors: Yes	**Other assistive technology:** Yes	**LD/ADHD:** Student
Note-takers: Yes	**Priority registration:** Yes	

GENERAL ADMISSIONS INFORMATION

Office of Admission: 518-442-5490

ENTRANCE REQUIREMENTS
Academic units required: 4 English, 2 mathematics, 2 science, (2 science labs), 1 foreign language, 3 social studies, 2 history, 4 academic electives. **Academic units recommended:** 4 mathematics, 3 science, (3 science labs), 3 foreign language. High school diploma is required and GED is accepted. SAT or ACT required; ACT with Writing component required. TOEFL required of all international applicants; minimum paper TOEFL 550, minimum computer TOEFL 213, minimum web-based TOEFL 79.

Application deadline: 3/1	**SAT Reading %Math composite:**	**Graduated top 10% of class:** NR
Notification: Rolling	1110–1250	**Graduated top 25% of class:** NR
		Graduated top 50% of class: NR

COLLEGE GRADUATION REQUIREMENTS

Course waivers allowed: No
In what course: Substitutions may be considered, but waivers of courses may change the graduation requirements/criteria for the major—case-by-case and specific documentation needed to support any request for substitution.
Course substitutions allowed: Yes
In what course: Determined on a case-by-case basis with supporting documentation.

ADDITIONAL INFORMATION

Environment: The university has an urban campus on 515 acres located on the fringe of the state capital.

Student Body	**Cost Information**	**Greek System**
Undergrad enrollment: 12,959	**In-state tuition:** $6,830	**Fraternity:** Yes
Women: 49%	**Out-of-state tuition:** $15,240	**Sorority:** Yes
Men: 51%	**Room and board:** $10,958	**Athletics:** Division I
Percent out-of-state: 8%	**Housing Information**	
	University housing: Yes	
	Percent living on campus: 57%	

SYRACUSE UNIVERSITY

200 Crouse-Hinds Hall, Office of Admissions, Syracuse, NY 13244-2130
Phone: 315-443-3611 • Fax: 315-443-4226
E-mail: orange@syr.edu • Web: www.syracuse.edu
Support: CS • Institution type: 4-year private

PROGRAMS OR SERVICES FOR STUDENTS WITH LD

The Office of Disability Services provides an integrated network of academic support, counseling, and advising services to meet the individual needs of students with diagnosed learning disabilities. Every student with learning disabilities who is accepted to the university is eligible for services and must provide diagnostic information from which appropriate academic accommodations are determined. Services are provided by a professional staff to assist students in developing a sense of independence as they learn to advocate for themselves and become involved in their college education.

ADMISSION INFORMATION FOR STUDENTS WITH LD/ADHD

College entrance tests required: Yes
Interview required: Yes
Essay recommended: Yes
What documentation required for LD: Psycho Ed evaluation to include: relevant historical info, instructional interventions, related services, age diagnosed, objective data (aptitude, achievement, info processing), test scores (standard, percentile and grade equivalents) and describe functional limitations.
With general application: No
To receive services after enrolling: Yes
What documentation required for ADHD: Diagnosis based on DSM-V; history of behaviors impairing functioning in academic setting; diagnostic interview; history of symptoms; evidence of ongoing behaviors.

With general application: No
Submitted to: Office of Disability Services
Special Ed. HS course work accepted: No
Specific course requirements of all applicants: Yes
Separate application required: No
# of LD applications submitted each year: NR
# of LD applications accepted yearly: NR
Total # of students receiving LD services: 450
Acceptance into program means acceptance into college: Students must be admitted to and enrolled in the university first and then request services.

ADMISSIONS

All students must meet regular admission standards and submit the general application form. General admission criteria include 4 years of English, 3–4 years of math, 3–4 years of science, 3–4 years of social studies, and 2 years of a foreign language; an ACT of 25 or SAT of 1100-plus; and a B average (80 percent or a 3.0 GPA). However, consideration will be given to standardized testing scores in light of the disability. Students with learning disabilities may request substitutions for high school math or foreign language if documentation can substantiate a disability in any one of these areas. Students should include current testing and documentation. Students can write an accompanying letter describing their learning disability, their goals, and the services needed. Students' grades should show an upward trend. In the event that an applicant is denied admission to a specific course of study, an alternative offer may be suggested.

ADDITIONAL INFORMATION

Students with identified learning disabilities are provided with an integrated network of academic and counseling services to meet their individual needs. Services include note-takers, proofreaders, readers for exams alternate format (electronic text) of textbooks, tutors, counseling, and advising. Accommodations include time extensions for exams, and alternative testing methods. The Office of Disability Services provides each student with an accommodation letter to be used when the students meet with instructors to verify their LD status. To take advantage of these support services, diagnosed students must submit recent documentation of their learning disability. Services are offered to undergraduate and graduate students.

LEARNING DISABILITY PROGRAM OR SERVICES

Contact Information
Name of program or department: Office of Disability Services
 Telephone: 315-443-4498
 Fax: 315-443-1312

LEARNING DISABILITY SERVICES

Accommodations are decided upon an individual basis after a thorough review of appropriate, current documentation. The accommodations requested must be supported through the documentation provided and must be logically linked to the current impact on academic functioning.

Allowed in exams
 Calculator: With instructor approval
 Dictionary: With instructor approval
 Computer: With instructor approval
 Spellchecker: With instructor approval
Extended test time: Yes
Scribes: Yes
Proctors: With instructor approval
Oral exams: Yes

Note-takers: Yes
Distraction-reduced environment: Yes
Tape recording in class: Yes
Electronic texts: Yes
Accommodations for students with ADHD: Yes
Kurzweil Reader: Yes
Other assistive technology: Yes
Priority registration: No

Added costs for services: No
LD specialists: Yes
Professional tutors: No
Peer tutors: Yes
Max. hours/wk. for services: N/A
How professors are notified of LD/ADHD: By student

GENERAL ADMISSIONS INFORMATION

Office of Admission: 315-443-3611

ENTRANCE REQUIREMENTS

Academic units required: 4 English, 3 math, 3 science (3 science labs), 2 foreign language, 3 social studies, 5 academic electives. **Academic units recommended:** 4 English, 3 math, 3 science (3 science labs), 3 foreign language, 3 social studies, 5 academic electives. High school diploma is required, and GED is accepted. ACT with Writing component required. TOEFL required of all international applicants: minimum paper TOEFL 560, minimum computer TOEFL 217.

Application deadline: 1/1
Notification: Rolling
Average GPA: 3.60
ACT Composite middle 50% range: 23–28

SAT Math middle 50% range: 540–650
SAT Critical Reading middle 50% range: 510–620
SAT Writing middle 50% range: 520–630

Graduated top 10% of class: 40%
Graduated top 25% of class: 73%
Graduated top 50% of class: 95%

COLLEGE GRADUATION REQUIREMENTS

Course waivers allowed: No
Course substitutions allowed: Yes
In what course: Students can petition for substitutions for math or foreign language. Substitutions must be approved by each college.

ADDITIONAL INFORMATION

Environment: The school is located on 200 acres set on a hill overlooking the city of Syracuse.

Student Body
 Undergrad enrollment: 14,671
 Women: 56%
 Men: 44%
 Percent out-of-state: 54%

Cost Information
 Tuition: $36,300
 Room & board: $13,254
Housing Information
 University housing: Yes
 Percent living on campus: 75%

Greek System
 Fraternity: Yes
 Sorority: Yes
 Athletics: Division I

UTICA COLLEGE

1600 Burrstone Road, Utica, NY 13502-4892
Phone: 315-792-3006 • Fax: 315-792-3003
E-mail: admiss@utica.edu • Web: www.utica.edu
Support: CS • Institution: 4-year private

PROGRAMS OR SERVICES FOR STUDENTS WITH LD

The Office of Learning Services provides academic support and advisement to students who identify themselves as disabled and who provide appropriate supporting documentation. Accommodations are determined on a case-by-case basis based on supportive documentation provided by the student. Students are responsible for initiating a request for accommodations; for providing documentation of a disability; and for contacting the Office of Learning Services as early as possible upon admission. The Office of Learning Services professional staff members determine eligibility for services based on documentation; consult with students about appropriate accommodations; assist students in self-monitoring the effectiveness of the accommodations; coordinate auxiliary services; provide information regarding rights and responsibilities of students; provide individualized educational advising; and serve as advocates for the student.

ADMISSION INFORMATION FOR STUDENTS WITH LD/ADHD

Interview required: Recommended
Essay required: N/A
What documentation required for LD: Psycho Ed evaluation
  to include: relevant historical info, instructional interventions,
  related services, age diagnosed, objective data (aptitude,
  achievement, info processing), test scores (standard,
  percentile and grade equivalents) and describe functional
  limitations.
With general application: No
To receive services after enrolling: Yes
What documentation required for ADHD: Diagnosis based
  on DSM-V; history of behaviors impairing functioning in
  academic setting; diagnostic interview; history of symptoms;
  evidence of ongoing behaviors.

With general application: No
Submitted to: Office of Learning Services
Special Ed. HS course work accepted: N/A
Specific course requirements for all applicants: Yes
Separate application required for program services: No
# of LD applications submitted each year: NR
# of LD applications accepted yearly: NR
Total # of students receiving LD services: NR
**Acceptance into program means acceptance into
  college:** Students must be admitted to and enrolled in the
  college first and then request services.

ADMISSIONS
Utica College requires standardized test scores (such as SAT and ACT) for specific programs. Students are evaluated on an individualized basis. Students should have four years of English, three years of social studies, three years of math, three years of science, and two years of foreign language. Students with disabilities are strongly encouraged to schedule an interview. Documentation of a disability should be sent to the Office of Learning Services. Students are not required to self-disclose the disability during the admission process.

ADDITIONAL INFORMATION
The Office of Learning Services provides accommodations to students with disabilities based on appropriate and current documentation. Documentation would be a written evaluation completed by an appropriate professional which states the specific disability, what functional limitations the student has because of the disability, and which offers recommendations for academic accommodations. Services may include priority registration, specific skill remediation, learning and study strategy development, referrals for diagnostic evaluation, time management strategies, professional tutoring. Accommodations may include such items as: use of a tape recorder; time extensions for tests and/or alternative testing methods; note-takers; and separate location for tests. An accommodation letter is generated for each student stating what accommodations are appropriate in each individual case. It is the responsibility of the students to meet with their instructors to discuss their disability and their accommodations.

PROGRAM FOR DISABILITY SERVICES

Contact Information
Name of program or department: Office of Learning Services
 Telephone: 315-792-3032
 Fax: 315-223-2504

LEARNING DISABILITY SERVICES

Accommodations are decided upon an individual basis after a thorough review of appropriate, current documentation. The accommodations requested must be supported through the documentation provided and must be logically linked to the current impact of the condition on academic functioning.

Allowed in exams
 Calculator: *
 Dictionary: *
 Computer: *
 Spellchecker: *
Extended test time: *
Scribes: No
Proctors: No
Oral exams: *
Note-takers: *

Distraction-reduced environment: *
Tape recording in class: *
Electronic texts: *
Accommodations for students with ADHD: Yes
Kurzweil Reader: No
Other assistive technology: Dragon Naturally Speaking JAWS
Priority registration: Yes

Added costs for services: No
LD specialists: Yes
Professional tutors: No
Peer tutors: From the College
Max. hours/wk. for services: N/A
How professors are notified of LD/ADHD: Student

*Per accommodation determination

GENERAL ADMISSIONS INFORMATION

Office of Admission: 315-792-3006

ENTRANCE REQUIREMENTS
Academic units required: 4 English, 3 mathematics, 3 science, 2 foreign language, 3 social studies, 1 academic electives. High school diploma is required and GED is accepted. TOEFL required of all international applicants; minimum paper TOEFL 525, minimum computer TOEFL 195.

Application deadline: None
Notification: Rolling
Average GPA: 3.01
ACT Composite middle 50% range: 16–24

SAT Math middle 50% range: 440–540
SAT Critical Reading middle 50% range: 430–510
SAT Writing middle 50% range: 410–510

Graduated top 10% of class: 8%
Graduated top 25% of class: 30%
Graduated top 50% of class: 70%

COLLEGE GRADUATION REQUIREMENTS

Course substitutions allowed: Yes
In what course: Foreign language substitutions are determined individually based on documentation, and only if the course is not an essential component of the major.

ADDITIONAL INFORMATION

Environment: The school has a suburban campus located 50 miles east of Syracuse.

Student Body
 Undergrad enrollment: 2,406
 Women: 58%
 Men: 42%
 Percent out-of-state: 17%

Cost Information
 Tuition: $29,496
 Room & board: $11,650
Housing Information
 University housing: Yes
 Percent living on campus: 48%

Greek System
 Fraternity: Yes
 Sorority: Yes
Athletics: Division III

APPALACHIAN STATE UNIVERSITY

Office of Admissions, ASU Box 32004, Boone, NC 28608-2004
Phone: 828-262-2120 • Fax: 828-262-3296
E-mail: admissions@appstate.edu • Web: www.appstate.edu
Support: CS • Institution type: 4-year public

PROGRAMS OR SERVICES FOR STUDENTS WITH LD

The University Learning Disability Program is part of a larger academic support service called the Learning Assistance Program. The LD program is designed to provide academic services for students who self-identify on a voluntary basis and attend regular classes. Students with learning disabilities are totally integrated throughout the university community. Students are expected to communicate with their instructors regarding their specific needs. The Coordinator of Services works with students and faculty to implement needed services and accommodations. The needs of each student are considered and treated individually in consultation with the student and are based on current documentation of the learning disability.

ADMISSION INFORMATION FOR STUDENTS WITH LD/ADHD

College entrance tests required: Yes
Interview required: No
Essay recommended: No
What documentation required for LD: Psycho Ed evaluation to include: relevant historical info, instructional interventions, related services, age diagnosed, objective data (aptitude, achievement, info processing), test scores (standard, percentile and grade equivalents) and describe functional limitations.
With general application: No
To receive services after enrolling: Yes
What documentation required for ADHD: Diagnosis based on DSM-V; history of behaviors impairing functioning in academic setting; diagnostic interview; history of symptoms; evidence of ongoing behaviors.

With general application: No
Submitted to: Disabiltity Services
Special Ed. HS course work accepted: No
Specific course requirements of all applicants: Yes
Separate application required: Yes
# of LD applications submitted each year: 100
# of LD applications accepted yearly: 100
Total # of students receiving LD services: 234
Acceptance into program means acceptance into college: Students must be accepted and enrolled at the university first and then must identify and provide documentation to be eligible for assistance.

ADMISSIONS

Students with learning disabilities are admitted to the university through the regular admission procedure. The minimum admissions requirements include 4 years of English, 3 years of math, 3 years of science (1 in biology and 1 in a physical science), 2 years of social science. Two years of a foreign language and 1 course in math and foreign language in the student's senior year are recommended. Applicants may self-disclose on their applications. This information would support their application for admission. A personal statement, letters of recommendations, and school activities provide additional useful information. Once students have been accepted by the university, a form is provided with which the students can identify their disabilities. This identification process is necessary for the students to have access to the services of the LD program. Students not regularly admissible may request a review of their application with additional or updated information.

ADDITIONAL INFORMATION

Tutoring is provided on a one-on-one basis for assistance with course content, as well as guidance in developing or improving learning skills. Tutors are trained in working with each student. Basic skills courses are available in memory skills, oral presentation, and note-taking strategies, reading textbooks, written language, math, time management techniques, and study strategies. Skills courses for no credit are offered in English and math. LD/ADHD coaching is available through the Office of Disability Services (ODS). Coaching is provided by ODS graduate assistants and consists of one-on-one meetings to minimize the frustrations of ADHD/LD and maximize your ability using feedback, guidance, and an ongoing partnership. Skills addressed include establishing and achieving semester goals, study and test strategies, time management and organizational planning, note-taking tips, and planning projects. Services and accommodations are available for undergraduates and graduates.

LEARNING DISABILITY PROGRAM OR SERVICES

Contact Information
Name of program or department: Office of Disability Services
  Telephone: 828-262-2291
  Fax: 828-262-6834

LEARNING DISABILITY SERVICES

Accommodations are decided upon an individual basis after a thorough review of appropriate, current documentation. The accommodations requested must be supported through the documentation provided and must be logically linked to the current impact of the condition on academic functioning.

Allowed in exams	**Distraction-reduced environment:** Yes	**Added costs for services:** No
Calculator: Yes	**Tape recording in class:** Yes	**LD specialists:** Yes
Dictionary: Yes	**Electronic texts:** No	**Professional tutors:** 2
Computer: Yes	**Accommodations for students with**	**Peer tutors:** 150
Spellchecker: Yes	**ADHD:** Yes	**Max. hours/wk. for services:**
Extended test time: Yes	**Kurzweil Reader:** Yes	Unlimited
Scribes: Yes	**Other assistive technology:** Yes	**How professors are notified of**
Proctors: Yes	**Priority registration:** Yes	**LD/ADHD:** By student
Oral exams: Yes		
Note-takers: Yes		

GENERAL ADMISSIONS INFORMATION

Office of Admission: 828-262-2120

ENTRANCE REQUIREMENTS

Academic units required: 4 English, 4 math, 3 science (1 science lab), 2 foreign language, 2 social studies, 1 history. High school diploma is required, and GED is not accepted. ACT with Writing component required. TOEFL required of all international applicants: minimum paper TOEFL 500.

Application deadline: None	**SAT Math middle 50% range:**	**Graduated top 10% of class:** 16%
Notification: Rolling	550–630	**Graduated top 25% of class:** 50%
Average GPA: 3.74	**SAT Critical Reading middle 50%**	**Graduated top 50% of class:** 87%
ACT Composite middle 50% range:	**range:** 530–620	
22–26	**SAT Writing middle 50% range:**	
	510–600	

COLLEGE GRADUATION REQUIREMENTS

Course waivers allowed: No
Course substitutions allowed: No

ADDITIONAL INFORMATION

Environment: The university has a 255-acre campus in a small town 90 miles northwest of Winston-Salem.

Student Body	**Cost Information**	**Greek System**
Undergrad enrollment: 15,137	**In-state tuition:** $5,742	**Fraternity:** Yes
Women: 51%	**Out-of-state tuition:** $17,790	**Sorority:** Yes
Men: 49%	**Room & board:** $5,940	**Athletics:** Division I
Percent out-of-state: 14%	**Housing Information**	
	University housing: Yes	
	Percent living on campus: 38%	

BREVARD COLLEGE

One Brevard College Drive, Brevard, NC 28712
Phone: 828-884-8300 • Fax: 828-884-8293
E-mail: admissions@brevard.edu
Support: CS • Institution: 4-year private

PROGRAMS OR SERVICES FOR STUDENTS WITH LD

Brevard College welcomes students who learn differently. Although the College does not offer a special program or curriculum for such students, the college has an excellent disabilities support service, as well as the Academic Enrichment Center, where any student can receive such services as counseling on academic matters, tutoring in a specific subject, advice on organizing work and/or managing time, assistance with reading skills, study skills, test taking skills, and arrange note-taking. The Director of the Office for Students with Special Needs and Disabilities reviews student documentation and identifies academic accommodations which are adjustments to course policies. The Director works with students to determine what would be useful to use in a particular course, and what the student must do in order to obtain these accommodations. The Director can also assist students with talking to their professors about the learning disability and accommodations.

ADMISSION INFORMATION FOR STUDENTS WITH LD/ADHD

College entrance tests required: Yes
Interview required: No
Essay required: N/A
What documentation required for LD: Psycho Ed evaluation to include: relevant historical info, instructional interventions, related services, age diagnosed, objective data (aptitude, achievement, info processing), test scores (standard, percentile and grade equivalents) and describe functional limitations.
With general application: No
To receive services after enrolling: Yes
What documentation required for ADHD: Diagnosis based on DSM-V; history of behaviors impairing functioning in academic setting; diagnostic interview; history of symptoms; evidence of ongoing behaviors.

With general application: No
Submitted to: Office for Students with Special Needs & Disabilities
Special Ed. HS course work accepted: Yes
Specific course requirements for all applicants: NR
Separate application required for program services: No
# of LD applications submitted each year: NR
# of LD applications accepted yearly: NR
Total # of students receiving LD services: 45
Acceptance into program means acceptance into college: NR

ADMISSIONS

There is no special admission process for students with LD. Brevard asks for quite a bit of information from applicants and from those who know the applicants and their learning style. If applicants are aware of a learning disability, they are encouraged to provide the Office for Students with Special Needs & Disabilities with as much information as possible, for example, counseling testing and reports, recommendations, and assessments. Applicants must provide official transcripts, letters of recommendation from college counselor or dean, a teacher of English, and one other teacher or adult who has worked with the student and knows the student well. Brevard requires official SAT or ACT scores. However, there is no "cut-off" point on these tests relative to admission. Brevard looks for strong verbal ability as represented in an applicant's writing sample(s). This gives the college a chance to know what the student struggles with, what the student feels confident about, what the student wants to achieve by earning a degree. Conditional admission status is available for students who display some, but not all, of the indicators of success as a post-secondary liberal arts student.

ADDITIONAL INFORMATION

Brevard College has a variety of achievement resources. As the central academic resource and support center on campus, the Academic Enrichment Center is designed to enrich the academic life of all students by providing strong academic support services and enrichment programming. The AEC services are offered on the premise that all students who are successful in college are those who have learned to take charge of their own learning and to utilize available resources to attain their academic goals. A major goal of the AEC is to supplement the classroom experience by offering a variety of support programs to both faculty and students. The AEC provides a variety of spaces for both individual and group study, one-on-one academic counseling, and peer tutors in a variety of subjects. The AEC also houses the Math Lab and the Writing Lab. In addition, the Office for Students with Special Needs and Disabilities, the Office for Career Exploration and Development, the Freshman Year Program, and the Honors Program are a part of the AEC. Brevard College also provides developmental courses in math, computers, study skills, and reading for students in need of a better academic foundation.

PROGRAM FOR DISABILITY SERVICES

Contact Information
Name of program or department: Office for Students with Special Needs and Disabilities
Telephone: 828-884-8131
Fax: 828-884-8293

LEARNING DISABILITY SERVICES

Accommodations are decided on an individual basis after a thorough review of appropriate, current documentation. The accommodations requested must be logically linked to the current impact of the condition on academic functioning.

Allowed in exams
 Calculator: Yes
 Dictionary: Yes
 Computer: Yes
 Spellchecker: Yes
Extended test time: Yes
Scribes: Yes
Proctors: Yes
Oral exams: Yes
Note-takers: Yes

Distraction-reduced environment: Yes
Tape recording in class: Yes
Electronic texts: Yes
Accommodations for students with ADHD: Yes
Kurzweil Reader: Yes
Other assistive technology: Auxiliary aids such as digital recorders, etc., can be signed out. The Kurzweil 3000 software is available for loan, as well as being available in certain computer labs.
Priority registration: Yes

Added costs for services: No
LD specialists: Yes
Professional tutors: 5–15
Peer tutors: 5–10
Max. hours/wk. for services: NR
How professors are notified of LD/ADHD: Student

GENERAL ADMISSIONS INFORMATION

Office of Admission: 828-884-8332

ENTRANCE REQUIREMENTS

Academic units recommended: 4 English, 3 mathematics, 3 science, (1 science labs), 2 foreign language, 4 social studies, 1 history, 4 academic electives. High school diploma is required and GED is accepted. SAT or ACT required; TOEFL required of all international applicants; minimum paper TOEFL 537, minimum computer TOEFL 203.

Application deadline: None
Notification: Rolling
Average GPA: 2.96
ACT Composite middle 50% range: 18–22

SAT Math middle 50% range: 410–520
SAT Critical Reading middle 50% range: 440–520
SAT Writing middle 50% range: NR

Graduated top 10% of class: 5%
Graduated top 25% of class: 20%
Graduated top 50% of class: 55%

COLLEGE GRADUATION REQUIREMENTS

Course waivers allowed: No
In what course: Substitutions are done on a case-by-case basis.
Course substitutions allowed: Yes
In what course: Substitutions are done on a case-by-case basis. Foreign language is not required for graduation.

ADDITIONAL INFORMATION

Environment: Brevard College is a residential campus located in a small town 33 miles from Asheville, North Carolina.

Student Body
 Undergrad enrollment: 644
 Women: 41%
 Men: 59%
 Percent out-of-state: 48%

Cost Information
 Tuition: $22,700
 Room & board: $7,950
Housing Information
 University housing: Yes
 Percent living on campus: 79%

Greek System
 Fraternity: No
 Sorority: No
 Athletics: Division II

DAVIDSON COLLEGE

PO Box 7156, Davidson, NC 28035-5000
Phone: 704-894-2230 • Fax: 704-894-2016
E-mail: admission@davidson.edu • Web: www.davidson.edu
Support: CS • Institution type: 4-year private

PROGRAMS OR SERVICES FOR STUDENTS WITH LD

Students enroll in Davidson with a proven record of academic achievement and the ability to utilize resources, persevere, and excel. The college provides services and accommodations to allow students an opportunity to continue to be successful. Special procedures have been developed for students handicapped by learning disabilities. Students who seek adapted instruction on the basis of a learning disability undergo an evaluation by college-designated learning specialists, usually at the student's expense. The results of the evaluation, made available to the college with the student's permission, may include recommendations for compensatory learning strategies to be used by the student and recommendations for services and accommodations to be provided by the college. Using these recommendations as a guide, the Student Learning Support Committee works with the student to develop a learning plan that enhances learning strengths and compensates for learning difficulties. If the learning plan recommends adjustment to academic requirements, the recommendation is considered by the Curriculum Requirements Committee and may result in the approval of the recommendation or the substitution of the academic requirement. All students seeking accommodations on the basis of an LD must provide recent documentation. The Dean of Students, with the student's permission, will notify professors of an individual student's need for adaptations. Accommodations are not universal in nature but are designed to meet the specific need of the individual to offset a specific disability.

ADMISSION INFORMATION FOR STUDENTS WITH LD/ADHD

College entrance tests required: Yes
Interview required: No
Essay recommended: No
What documentation required for LD: Psycho Ed evaluation to include: relevant historical info, instructional interventions, related services, age diagnosed, objective data (aptitude, achievement, info processing), test scores (standard, percentile and grade equivalents) and describe functional limitations.
With general application: No
To receive services after enrolling: Yes
What documentation required for ADHD: Diagnosis based on DSM-V; history of behaviors impairing functioning in academic setting; diagnostic interview; history of symptoms; evidence of ongoing behaviors.

With general application: No
Submitted to: Dean of Student Services
Special Ed. HS course work accepted: No
Specific course requirements of all applicants: Yes
Separate application required: No
# of LD applications submitted each year: NR
# of LD applications accepted yearly: NR
Total # of students receiving LD services: 54
Acceptance into program means acceptance into college: Students must be admitted to and enrolled in the university first and then request services.

ADMISSIONS

There is no special admission process for students with LD, though the Admissions Office may seek comments from support staff knowledgeable about LD. Students are encouraged to self-disclose their ADHD. The admission process is very competitive, and the disclosure can help the Admissions Office more fairly evaluate the transcript. This disclosure could address any specific academic issues related to the LD, such as no foreign language in high school because of the specific LD or lower grades in math as a result of a math disability. The GPA is recalculated to reflect rigor with 97 percent of the accepted students having a recalculated GPA of 3.0. Students have completed at least 4 years of English, 3 years of math, 2 years of the same foreign language, 2 years of science, and 2 years of history/social studies. Courses taken in special education are not accepted. The mid 50 percent of students have an ACT between 28 and 31 or SAT between 1240 and 1420. Interviews are not required but are recommended.

ADDITIONAL INFORMATION

Support services and accommodations available include, but are not limited to: referrals for appropriate diagnostic evaluation; individual coaching and instruction in compensatory strategies and study skills; consultation with faculty and staff; student support groups as requested; classroom accommodations such as extra test-taking time, taped texts, note-takers, use of tape recorders, use of computers with spellcheckers, and individual space for study or test-taking; reduced course loads; and course substitutions or waivers (rarely). There are a Math Center, Writing Lab, peer tutoring, and skill class in time management available for all students. There is one full-time and one part-time LD specialist on staff and peer tutoring for all students as needed.

LEARNING DISABILITY PROGRAM OR SERVICES

Contact Information
Name of program or department: Dean of Students Office
  Telephone: 704-894-2225
  Fax: 704-894-2849

LEARNING DISABILITY SERVICES

Accommodations are decided upon an individual basis after a thorough review of appropriate, current documentation. The accommodations requested must be supported through the documentation provided and must be logically linked to the current impact of the condition on academic functioning.

Allowed in exams
  Calculator: Yes
  Dictionary: Yes
  Computer: Yes
  Spellchecker: Yes
Extended test time: Yes
Scribes: Yes
Proctors: Yes
Oral exams: No
Note-takers: Yes

Distraction-reduced environment: Yes
Tape recording in class: Yes
Electronic texts: No
Accommodations for students with ADHD: Yes
Kurzweil Reader: No
Other assistive technology: No
Priority registration: No

Added costs for services: No
LD specialists: Yes
Professional tutors: No
Peer tutors: 100
Max. hours/wk. for services: Unlimited
How professors are notified of LD/ADHD: By both student and director

GENERAL ADMISSIONS INFORMATION

Office of Admission: 704-894-2230

ENTRANCE REQUIREMENTS
Academic units required: 4 English, 3 math, 2 science, 2 foreign language, 2 social studies and history.
Academic units recommended: 4 math, 4 science, 4 foreign language, 4 social studies and history. High school diploma is required, and GED is not accepted. ACT with or without Writing component accepted. TOEFL required of all international applicants: minimum paper TOEFL 600, minimum computer TOEFL 250.

Application deadline: 1/2
Notification: 4/1
Average GPA: 3.9
ACT Composite middle 50% range: 28–32

SAT Math middle 50% range: 640–730
SAT Critical Reading middle 50% range: 630–730
SAT Writing middle 50% range: 630–730

Graduated top 10% of class: 79%
Graduated top 25% of class: 97%
Graduated top 50% of class: 99%

COLLEGE GRADUATION REQUIREMENTS

Course waivers allowed: No
Course substitutions allowed: Yes
In what course: Substitutions in any appropriate course

ADDITIONAL INFORMATION

Environment: The campus is located 20 miles from Charlotte, North Carolina.

Student Body
  Undergrad enrollment: 1,742
  Women: 51%
  Men: 49%
  Percent out-of-state: 81%

Cost Information
  Tuition: $38,481
  Room & board: $10,857
Housing Information
  University housing: Yes
  Percent living on campus: 91%

Greek System
  Fraternity: Yes
  Sorority: No
Athletics: Division I

DUKE UNIVERSITY

2138 Campus Drive, Box 90586, Durham, NC 27708-0586
Phone: 919-684-3214 • Fax: 919-681-8941
E-mail: undergrad-admissions@duke.edu• Web: www.admissions.duke.edu
Support: CS • Institution type: 4-year private

PROGRAMS OR SERVICES FOR STUDENTS WITH LD

Duke University does not provide a formal, highly structured program for students with LD. The university does provide, however, significant academic support services for students through the Academic Resource Center (ARC). Students who submit appropriate documentation of their learning disability to the ARC clinical director are eligible for assistance in obtaining reasonable academic adjustments and auxiliary aids. In addition, the ARC clinical director and instructors can provide individualized instruction in academic skills and learning strategies, academic support counseling, and referrals for other services. Students with learning disabilities voluntarily access and use the services of the ARC, just as they might access and use other campus resources. Student interactions with the ARC staff are confidential. The goals of the support services for students with learning disabilities are in keeping with the goals of all services provided through the ARC: to help students achieve their academic potential within the context of a competitive university setting, promote a disciplined approach to study, and foster active, independent learners.

ADMISSION INFORMATION FOR STUDENTS WITH LD/ADHD

College entrance tests required: Yes
Interview required: No
Essay recommended: No
What documentation required for LD: Psycho Ed evaluation to include: relevant historical info, instructional interventions, related services, age diagnosed, objective data (aptitude, achievement, info processing), test scores (standard, percentile and grade equivalents) and describe functional limitations.
With general application: No
To receive services after enrolling: Yes
What documentation required for ADHD: Diagnosis based on DSM-V; history of behaviors impairing functioning in academic setting; diagnostic interview; history of symptoms; evidence of ongoing behaviors.

With general application: No
Submitted to: ARC
Special Ed. HS course work accepted: No
Specific course requirements of all applicants: NR
Separate application required: No
# of LD applications submitted each year: 30
# of LD applications accepted yearly: 20
Total # of students receiving LD services: 40–60
Acceptance into program means acceptance into college: Students must be admitted to and enrolled in the university first and then request services.

ADMISSIONS

There is no special admission process for students with LD. All applicants must meet the general Duke admission criteria. Most applicants are in the top 10% of their class and have completed a demanding curriculum including many AP and honors courses. The ACT with Writing OR SAT Reasoning and 2 Subject tests are required. Duke considers the highest ACT composite score and highest sub scores on each section, regardless of test date, but will not recalculate the composite score. Students who take the ACT are not required to submit SAT or SAT Subject Tests. Duke uses the highest available SAT Critical Reading, Writing, and Math sub scores, plus the two highest subject test sub scores, regardless of the date those tests were taken. Students may elect "Score Choice" when releasing their SAT scores. Students must submit two teacher and one counselor recommendation.. Applicants may also submit one optional personal recommendation from a coach, a director, a teacher from an elective course, a family member, or anyone else who knows the student well and will.. This optional information will be considered in understanding the student as a person, but will not be formally evaluated as part of the application. Some students choose to disclose a disability in their application because it is an important element of their experiences or to share how they dealt with an obstacle. Duke considers this information in understanding a student's achievements and evaluates accomplishments within the context of opportunities or challenges presented to that student. Duke does not use information to deny admission to a student.

ADDITIONAL INFORMATION

The Student Disability Access Office (SDAO) considers requests for accommodations and services when presented with appropriate documentation and the submission of a Request Form. Documentation must support the request. Students must meet with SDAO each semester. Assistance is available as needed from the student's academic dean and the clinical director of ARC. Students are encouraged to consult with their faculty advisor and the ARC well in advance of registration to determine the appropriate measures for particular courses. Students may also receive peer tutoring in introductory-level courses in several disciplines through the ARC peer tutoring program. Students work out reasonable accommodations with each professor.

LEARNING DISABILITY PROGRAM OR SERVICES

Contact Information
Name of program or department: Student Disability Access Office/Academic Resource Center (ARC)
   Telephone: 919-684-5917
   Fax: 919-684-5917

LEARNING DISABILITY SERVICES

Accommodations are decided upon an individual basis after a thorough review of appropriate, current documentation. The accommodations requested must be supported through the documentation provided and must be logically linked to the current impact of the condition on academic functioning.

Allowed in exams
   Calculator: No
   Dictionary: Yes
   Computer: Yes
   Spellchecker: No
Extended test time: Yes
Scribes: Yes
Proctors: Yes
Oral exams: Yes
Note-takers: Yes

Distraction-reduced environment: Yes
Tape recording in class: Yes
Electronic texts: Yes
Accommodations for students with ADHD: Yes
Kurzweil Reader: No
Other assistive technology: Yes
Priority registration: No

Added costs for services: No
LD specialists: Yes
Professional tutors: No
Peer tutors: 80
Max. hours/wk. for services: Unlimited
How professors are notified of LD/ADHD: By both student and director

GENERAL ADMISSIONS INFORMATION

Office of Admission: 919-684-3214

ENTRANCE REQUIREMENTS

Academic units recommended: 4 English, 4 math, 4 science, 4 foreign language, 4 social studies. High school diploma is required, and GED is not accepted.

Application deadline: 1/2
Notification: 4/1
Average GPA: NR
ACT Composite middle 50% range: 29–34

SAT Math middle 50% range: 680–780
SAT Critical Reading middle 50% range: 660–760
SAT Writing middle 50% range: 660–760

Graduated top 10% of class: 90%
Graduated top 25% of class: 98%
Graduated top 50% of class: 100%

COLLEGE GRADUATION REQUIREMENTS

Course waivers allowed: No
Course substitutions allowed: No

ADDITIONAL INFORMATION

Environment: The university is on 8,500 acres in a suburban area 285 miles southwest of Washington, DC.

Student Body
   Undergrad enrollment: 6,500
   Women: 49%
   Men: 51%
   Percent out-of-state: 85%

Cost Information
   Tuition: $41,900
   Room & board: $11,900
Housing Information
   University housing: Yes
   Percent living on campus: 82%

Greek System
   Fraternity: Yes
   Sorority: Yes
Athletics: Division I

EAST CAROLINA UNIVERSITY

Office of Undergraduate Admissions, 106 Whichard Building,
Greenville, NC 27858-4353 • Phone: 252-328-6131 • Fax: 252-328-6945
E-mail: admis@ecu.edu • Web: www.ecu.edu
Support: CS • Institution type: 4-year public

PROGRAMS OR SERVICES FOR STUDENTS WITH LD

Through the Department for Disability Support Services, the university seeks to meet individual needs by coordinating and implementing internal policy regarding programs, services, and activities for individuals with disabilities. The department functions as a source of information and advice and as a communication link among individuals with disabilities, faculty and staff members, state rehab agencies, and the community at large. The overall purpose of the university's program for students with learning disabilities is to provide auxiliary support services, so they may derive equal benefits from all that East Carolina University has to offer. Individuals with learning disabilities and attention deficit hyperactivity disorder are required to provide the department with proper documentation of their disability. An acceptable psychoeducational evaluation administered within the past 3 years must be submitted to qualify for services. Students should schedule a meeting with the department well in advance of the beginning of their first semester to prevent delays in the planning of services. Students with LD or ADHD will receive a letter describing the services required to give to their instructors. With the exception of tutorial services for personal use, academic support services are provided at no cost.

ADMISSION INFORMATION FOR STUDENTS WITH LD/ADHD

College entrance tests required: Yes
Interview required: No
Essay recommended: No
What documentation required for LD: Psycho Ed evaluation to include: relevant historical info, instructional interventions, related services, age diagnosed, objective data (aptitude, achievement, info processing), test scores (standard, percentile and grade equivalents) and describe functional limitations.
With general application: No
To receive services after enrolling: Yes
What documentation required for ADHD: Diagnosis based on DSM-V; history of behaviors impairing functioning in academic setting; diagnostic interview; history of symptoms; evidence of ongoing behaviors.

With general application: No
Submitted to: Disability Support Services
Special Ed. HS course work accepted: Yes
Specific course requirements of all applicants: Yes
Separate application required: No
# of LD applications submitted each year: NR
# of LD applications accepted yearly: NR
Total # of students receiving LD services: 100–150
Acceptance into program means acceptance into college: Students must be admitted to and enrolled in the university first and then request services.

ADMISSIONS

A student with a disability applies for admission and is considered for admission in the same manner as any other applicant. Neither the nature nor the severity of one's disability is used as a criterion for admission. Students with learning disabilities are admitted solely on academic qualifications. Out-of-state students must present slightly higher GPAs and test scores, but the minimum is 2.0 depending on the SAT score. Test scores vary, but the minimum out-of-state ACT is 19 and in-state is 17, and the average ACT is 21. The minimum SAT out-of-state is 1000 and in-state is 900, and the average SAT is 1030. Students must have taken 4 years of English, 2 years of social science, and 3 years of science (1 year biology and 1 year physical science); 3 years of math and 2 years of a foreign language are recommended.

ADDITIONAL INFORMATION

Once admitted to the university, students must self-identify and register with the Department for Disability Support Services. Students must show official verification of their disability. Students will be assigned to academic advisors from the department. Once students enter their major fields of study, the department will still be available to provide advising assistance but never to the exclusion of the individual's assigned academic advisor. Alternative testing accommodations may include extended time, a noise-free environment, reader-assisted test-taking, and other arrangements that satisfy the needs of the student. A maximum of double time can be allowed for students to complete a test or an exam. The university offers a modified language sequence for students enrolled in Spanish. There are several laboratories available, including a Writing Center, a Reading Center, a Mathematics Center, an Academic Support Center, and a computer lab. Students pay for private tutoring. Skills classes for any student are available in time management, test-taking and anxiety study strategies, and academic motivation.

LEARNING DISABILITY PROGRAM OR SERVICES

Contact Information
Name of program or department: Department for Disability Support Services
  Telephone: 252-737-1016
  Fax: 252-737-1025

LEARNING DISABILITY SERVICES

Accommodations are decided upon an individual basis after a thorough review of appropriate, current documentation. The accommodations requested must be supported through the documentation provided and must be logically linked to the current impact of the condition on academic functioning.

Allowed in exams
  Calculator: Yes
  Dictionary: Yes
  Computer: Yes
  Spellchecker: Yes
Extended test time: Yes
Scribes: Yes
Proctors: Yes
Oral exams: Yes
Note-takers: Yes

Distraction-reduced environment: Yes
Tape recording in class: Yes
Electronic texts: Yes
Accommodations for students with ADHD: Yes
Kurzweil Reader: Yes
Other assistive technology: Yes
Priority registration: Yes

Added costs for services: No
LD specialists: Yes
Professional tutors: No
Peer tutors: 2
Max. hours/wk. for services: Unlimited
How professors are notified of LD/ADHD: By student

GENERAL ADMISSIONS INFORMATION

Office of Admission: 252-328-6131

ENTRANCE REQUIREMENTS

Academic units required: 4 English, 4 math, 3 science (1 science lab), 2 foreign language, 2 social studies, 4 academic electives. **Academic units recommended:** 1 fine arts; 1 social studies (must be U.S. History). High school diploma is required, and GED is accepted. TOEFL required of all international applicants: minimum paper TOEFL 550, minimum computer TOEFL 213.

Application deadline: 3/15
Notification: Rolling
Average GPA: 3.42
ACT Composite middle 50% range: 19–23

SAT Math middle 50% range: 470–570
SAT Critical Reading middle 50% range: 450–540
SAT Writing middle 50% range: 440–530

Graduated top 10% of class: 11%
Graduated top 25% of class: 37%
Graduated top 50% of class: 75%

COLLEGE GRADUATION REQUIREMENTS

Course waivers allowed: No
Course substitutions allowed: No

ADDITIONAL INFORMATION

Environment: The school is located on over 370 acres within the city of Greenville, 85 miles from Raleigh.

Student Body
  Undergrad enrollment: 21,663
  Women: 58%
  Men: 42%
  Percent out-of-state: 16%

Cost Information
  In-state tuition: $4,327
  Out-of-state tuition: $15,161
  Room & board: $7,500
Housing Information
  University housing: Yes
  Percent living on campus: 24%

Greek System
  Fraternity: Yes
  Sorority: Yes
Athletics: Division I

ELON UNIVERSITY

100 Campus Drive, 2700 Campus Box, Elon, NC 27244-2010
Phone: 336-278-3566 • Fax: 336-278-7699
E-mail: admissions@elon.edu • Web: www.elon.edu
Support: S • Institution type: 4-year private

PROGRAMS OR SERVICES FOR STUDENTS WITH LD

Elon University is committed to the principle of equal opportunity. We assist students with disabilities in finding approaches and accommodations that provide them an opportunity to benefit from the many programs offered on campus. Faculty, staff, administrators, and students work together to find approaches and accommodations that enable students to benefit from the wide variety of programs and activities on campus.

ADMISSION INFORMATION FOR STUDENTS WITH LD/ADHD

College entrance tests required: Yes
Interview required: No
Essay recommended: No
What documentation required for LD: Psycho Ed evaluation to include: relevant historical info, instructional interventions, related services, age diagnosed, objective data (aptitude, achievement, info processing), test scores (standard, percentile and grade equivalents) and describe functional limitations.
With general application: No
To receive services after enrolling: Yes
What documentation required for ADHD: Diagnosis based on DSM-V; history of behaviors impairing functioning in academic setting; diagnostic interview; history of symptoms; evidence of ongoing behaviors.

With general application: No
Submitted to: Disability Services
Special Ed. HS course work accepted: No
Specific course requirements of all applicants: Yes
Separate application required: No
# of LD applications submitted each year: NR
# of LD applications accepted yearly: NR
Total # of students receiving LD services: NR
Acceptance into program means acceptance into college: Students must be admitted and enrolled prior to requesting services.

ADMISSIONS

Students with disabilities must meet the same admissions criteria as other applicants. There is no special admission process. Most important factors in admissions are academic rigor, grades, ACT (with writing) or SAT and counselor recommendation, activities, involvement and essay. GPA is converted to 4.0 scale, and then Elon gives weight to honors, AP or IB courses. Courses required include 4 years English, 3 years math, 2 years foreign language, 3 years social studies, and 3 years science. Students may be admitted with one deficiency. Disclosing a disability is totally up to the applicant.

ADDITIONAL INFORMATION

Students must provide current documentation to request accommodations. They are encouraged to be proactive and develop an ongoing conversation with their professors and service providers. Every student is assigned an advisor, a professor or an administrator who helps students get information regarding programs, tutors and special needs. All students have access to The Tutoring Center ad Writing Center. Waivers for foreign language or math courses are never approved. However, students may request a foreign language substitution. Documentation is required that demonstrates the presence of deficits that make learning a foreign language extremely difficult, as well as, a history of poor grades in the subject. Students who have never taken such classes will be asked to enroll; performance will be evaluated before the end of the drop/add period and a decision will be made regarding the substitution.

LEARNING DISABILITY PROGRAM OR SERVICES

Contact Information
Name of program or department: Disabilities Services
 Telephone: 336-278-6500
 Fax: 336-278-6514

LEARNING DISABILITY SERVICES

Accommodations are decided upon an individual basis after a thorough review of appropriate, current documentation. The accommodations requested must be supported through the documentation provided and must be logically linked to the current impact of the condition on academic functioning.

Allowed in exams	**Distraction-reduced environment:** Yes	**Added costs for services:** No
Calculator: Yes	**Tape recording in class:** Yes	**LD specialists:** No
Dictionary: Yes	**Electronic texts:** Yes	**Professional tutors:** No
Computer: Yes	**Accommodations for students with**	**Peer tutors:** 100
Spellchecker: Yes	**ADHD:** Yes	**Max. hours/wk. for services:**
Extended test time: Yes	**Kurzweil Reader:** Yes	Unlimited
Scribes: Yes	**Other assistive technology:** No	**How professors are notified of**
Proctors: NR	**Priority registration:** Yes	**LD/ADHD:** By both student and
Oral exams: No		director
Note-takers: Yes		

GENERAL ADMISSIONS INFORMATION

Office of Admission: 336-278-3566

ENTRANCE REQUIREMENTS

Academic units required: 4 English, 3 math, 3 science (1 science lab), 2 foreign language, 1 social studies, 1 history. **Academic units recommended:** 4 math, 3 foreign language, 3 social studies. High school diploma is required, and GED is accepted. ACT with Writing component required. TOEFL required of all international applicants: minimum paper TOEFL 550, minimum computer TOEFL 213.

Application deadline: 1/10	**SAT Math middle 50% range:**	**Graduated top 10% of class:** 32%
Notification: 3/15	560–660	**Graduated top 25% of class:** 67%
Average GPA: 3.96	**SAT Critical Reading middle 50%**	**Graduated top 50% of class:** 94%
ACT Composite middle 50% range:	**range:** 560–660	
25–29	**SAT Writing middle 50% range:**	
	560–660	

COLLEGE GRADUATION REQUIREMENTS

Course waivers allowed: No
Course substitutions allowed: Yes
In what course: Not generally, but on a case-by-case basis—rarely in foreign language and even more rarely in math, especially if the course is required in the student's major. Students will need sufficient documentation.

ADDITIONAL INFORMATION

Environment: The campus is on a 575-acre campus located in the Piedmont Triad area of North Carolina.

Student Body	**Cost Information**	**Greek System**
Undergrad enrollment: 5,255	**Tuition:** $28,981	**Fraternity:** Yes
Women: 59%	**Room & board:** $9,480	**Sorority:** Yes
Men: 41%	**Housing Information**	**Athletics:** Division I
Percent out-of-state: 75%	**University housing:** Yes	
	Percent living on campus: 60%	

GUILFORD COLLEGE

5800 West Friendly Avenue, Greensboro, NC 27410
Phone: 336-316-2100 • Fax: 336-316-2954
E-mail: admission@guilford.edu • Web: www.guilford.edu
Support: S • Institution type: 4-year private

PROGRAMS OR SERVICES FOR STUDENTS WITH LD

The Learning Commons (LC) serves the learning needs of a diverse campus by providing professional and peer tutoring, workshops, advocacy, and realistic encouragement. The focus is on self-advocacy and the articulation of both strengths and weaknesses. Faculty tutors work one-on-one with students on time management, study skills, test-taking, reading, and writing. A large student tutoring service offers course-specific tutoring. The center sponsors workshops on subjects pertaining to academic success. Faculty allow the usual accommodations requested by students: extra time, permission to use a computer for in-class work, testing in a less distracting environment, tape-recording classes, and so on.

ADMISSION INFORMATION FOR STUDENTS WITH LD/ADHD

College entrance tests required: No
Interview required: No
Essay recommended: Yes
What documentation required for LD: Psycho Ed evaluation to include: relevant historical info, instructional interventions, related services, age diagnosed, objective data (aptitude, achievement, info processing), test scores (standard, percentile and grade equivalents) and describe functional limitations.
With general application: No
To receive services after enrolling: Yes
What documentation required for ADHD: Diagnosis based on DSM-V; history of behaviors impairing functioning in academic setting; diagnostic interview; history of symptoms; evidence of ongoing behaviors.

With general application: No
Submitted to: Disability Resources
Special Ed. HS course work accepted: Yes
Specific course requirements of all applicants: NR
Separate application required: N/A
# of LD applications submitted each year: NR
# of LD applications accepted yearly: NR
Total # of students receiving LD services: NR
Acceptance into program means acceptance into college: Students must be admitted to and enrolled in the college first and then request services.

ADMISSIONS

Students with LD must meet the same criteria as other students. The general admission criteria include the mid 50 percent range for the ACT of 21–26 (or the SAT, 950–1210) and a 2.8–3.4 GPA. Typically, admitted students have 4 years of English, 3 years of math, 3–4 years natural science, 3 years of social studies, and 2 years of a foreign language. With appropriate documentation, students with LD can substitute some high school courses in areas that impact their ability to learn. The Disability Resources Committee reviews files to make certain that the college can provide appropriate support services.

ADDITIONAL INFORMATION

Guilford is a writing-intensive place. The writing program is revision-driven and utilizes peer-editing and response groups. The LC offers individualized professional tutoring in writing as well as opportunities to work with trained student writing tutors. The LC offers other services, including professional tutors to work one-on-one with students on time management, study skills, test-taking, and reading, math. A large student tutoring service offers course-specific tutoring. The center also sponsors workshops and seminars on subjects pertaining to academic success. Students are encouraged to speak with professors early concerning particular needs. Guilford waives the foreign language requirement if students submit appropriate documentation and petition through Disability Resources.

LEARNING DISABILITY PROGRAM OR SERVICES

Contact Information
Name of program or department: Disability Resources
 Telephone: 336-316-2253
 Fax: 336-316-2946

LEARNING DISABILITY SERVICES

Accommodations are decided upon an individual basis after a thorough review of appropriate, current documentation. The accommodations requested must be supported through the documentation provided and must be logically linked to the current impact of the condition on academic functioning.

Allowed in exams	**Distraction-reduced environment:** Yes	**Added costs for services:** No
Calculator: Yes	**Tape recording in class:** Yes	**LD specialists:** Yes
Dictionary: Yes	**Electronic texts:** Yes	**Professional tutors:** 2
Computer: Yes	**Accommodations for students with**	**Peer tutors:** 20–40
Spellchecker: Yes	**ADHD:** Yes	**Max. hours/wk. for services:** NR
Extended test time: Yes	**Kurzweil Reader:** Yes	**How professors are notified of**
Scribes: Yes	**Other assistive technology:** Yes	**LD/ADHD:** By student
Proctors: No	**Priority registration:** No	
Oral exams: Yes		
Note-takers: Yes		

GENERAL ADMISSIONS INFORMATION

Office of Admission: 336-316-2100

ENTRANCE REQUIREMENTS

Academic units recommended: 4 English, 3 math, 3 science, 3 social studies, 2 foreign language. High school diploma is required, and GED is accepted. ACT with or without Writing component accepted. TOEFL required of all international applicants: minimum paper TOEFL 550, minimum computer TOEFL 213, Internet based (IBT) 80 min.

Application deadline: 2/15	**SAT Math middle 50% range:**	**Graduated top 10% of class:** 14%
Notification: Rolling	480–590	**Graduated top 25% of class:** 41%
Average GPA: 3.12	**SAT Critical Reading middle 50%**	**Graduated top 50% of class:** 81%
ACT Composite middle 50% range:	**range:** 470–620	
21–26	**SAT Writing middle 50% range:**	
	460–600	

COLLEGE GRADUATION REQUIREMENTS

Course waivers allowed: Quantitative Literacy may be waived with approval from Disability Resources.
Course substitutions allowed: Yes
In what course: Foreign language

ADDITIONAL INFORMATION

Environment: The college is located on a suburban campus in a culturally diverse city in Greensboro, North Carolina.

Student Body	**Cost Information**	**Greek System**
Undergrad enrollment: 2,739	**Tuition:** $38,700	**Fraternity:** No
Women: 58%	**Room & Board:** $8,270	**Sorority:** No
Men: 42%	**Housing Information**	**Athletics:** Division III
Percent out-of-state: 56%	**University housing:** Yes	
	Percent living on campus: 76%	

NORTH CAROLINA STATE UNIVERSITY

Box 7103, Raleigh, NC 27695
Phone: 919-515-2434 • Fax: 919-515-5039
E-mail: undergrad_admissions@ncsu.edu • Web: http://www.ncsu.edu/
Support: CS • Institution: 4-year public

PROGRAMS OR SERVICES FOR STUDENTS WITH LD

Services for students with learning disabilities are handled by the LD coordinator through the Disability Services Office. The functions of the coordinator include identifying students with learning disabilities, helping to accommodate and interpret the needs of these students to the faculty, and providing services to students according to their individual needs. The purpose of the services is to ensure that students with documented learning disabilities receive appropriate accomodations to equalize their opportunities while studying at NCSU.

ADMISSION INFORMATION FOR STUDENTS WITH LD/ADHD

College entrance tests required: Yes
Interview required: No
Essay required: N/A
What documentation required for LD: Psycho Ed evaluation to include: relevant historical info, instructional interventions, related services, age diagnosed, objective data (aptitude, achievement, info processing), test scores (standard, percentile and grade equivalents) and describe functional limitations.
With general application: No
To receive services after enrolling: Yes
What documentation required for ADHD: Diagnosis based on DSM-V; history of behaviors impairing functioning in academic setting; diagnostic interview; history of symptoms; evidence of ongoing behaviors.

With general application: No
Submitted to: Disability Support Services
Specific course requirements for all applicants: Yes
Separate application required for program services: Yes
# of LD applications submitted each year: NR
# of LD applications accepted yearly: NR
Total # of students receiving LD services: 260–300
Acceptance into program means acceptance into college: Separate application required after student has enrolled

ADMISSIONS

Admission to the university for students with learning disabilities is determined on the basis of academic qualifications,and they are considered in the same manner as any other applicant. There is no pre-admission question regarding a learning disability. A cover letter from applicants, stating that a learning disability exists,alerts the admission staff to consider that there may be unusual circumstances. Self-disclosure of the learning disability could explain the high school record, such as late diagnosis and onset of LD accommodations or difficulty in particular subjects. General admission criteria include a minimum ACT 24 or SAT 1100. Over 75 percent of the students have at least a 3.5 GPA; minimum course requirements include four years English, three years math (including algebra I, algebra II, and geometry), two years social studies (including U.S. History), three years science (including one life science, one physical science, and one laboratory science), and two years of the same foreign language.

ADDITIONAL INFORMATION

All enrolled students may receive services and accommodations through the coordinator of learning disabilities of the DSO if they present appropriate documentation. The documentation should include a written report with a statement specifying areas of learning disabilities. Services and accommodations available with appropriate documentation include extended testing times for exams; reduced distraction testing environments; use of calculators, dictionaries, computers, or spellcheckers during exams; proctors; scribes; note-takers; audio format; assistive technology; and priority registration. If new needs are identified, services are modified or developed to accommodate them.

PROGRAM FOR DISABILITY SERVICES

Contact Information
Name of program or department: Disability Services Office (DSO)
  Telephone: 919-515-7653
  Fax: 919-513-2840

LEARNING DISABILITY SERVICES

Accommodations are decided upon an individual basis after a thorough review of appropriate, current documentation. The accommodations requested must be supported through the documentation provided and must be logically linked to the current impact of the condition on academic functioning.

Allowed in exams		
Calculator: Yes	**Distraction-reduced environment:** Yes	**Added costs for services:** No
Dictionary: Yes	**Tape recording in class:** Yes	**LD specialists:** Yes
Computer: Yes	**Electronic texts:** Yes	**Professional tutors:** No
Spellchecker: Yes	**Accommodations for students with**	**Peer tutors:** 20–25
Extended test time: Yes	**ADHD:** Yes	**Max. hours/wk. for services:**
Scribes: Yes	**Kurzweil Reader:** Yes	Unlimited
Proctors: Yes	**Other assistive technology:** Yes	**How professors are notified of**
Oral exams: Yes	**Priority registration:** Yes	**LD/ADHD:** Both student and director
Note-takers: Yes		

GENERAL ADMISSIONS INFORMATION

Office of Admission: 919-515-2434

ENTRANCE REQUIREMENTS
Academic units required: 4 English, 4 mathematics, 3 science, (1 science labs), 2 foreign language, 1 social studies, 1 history, 1 academic electives. **Academic units recommended:** 4 English, 4 mathematics, 4 science, (2 science labs), 2 foreign language, 1 social studies, 1 history, 4 academic electives. High school diploma is required and GED is not accepted. SAT or ACT required; ACT with Writing component required. TOEFL required of all international applicants; minimum paper TOEFL 550, minimum computer TOEFL 213.

Application deadline: 2/1	**SAT Math middle 50% range:**	**Graduated top 10% of class:** 43%
Notification: 3/30	560–660	**Graduated top 25% of class:** 83%
Average GPA: 4.28	**SAT Critical Reading middle 50%**	**Graduated top 50% of class:** 99%
ACT Composite middle 50% range:	**range:** 530–620	
23–28	**SAT Writing middle 50% range:**	
	510–610	

COLLEGE GRADUATION REQUIREMENTS

Course waivers allowed: No
Course substitutions allowed: Yes
In what course: Students may apply to substitute courses to satisfy the foreign lanuage proficiency requirement.

ADDITIONAL INFORMATION

Environment: The university sits on 623 acres in the central part of the state and has an adjacent 900-acre research campus.

Student Body	Cost Information	Greek System
Undergrad enrollment: 25,246	**In-state tuition:** $7,018	**Fraternity:** Yes
Women: 44%	**Out-of-state tuition:** $19,852	**Sorority:** Yes
Men: 56%	**Room & board:** $8,536	**Athletics:** Division I
Percent out-of-state: 8%	**Housing Information**	
	University housing: Yes	
	Percent living on campus: 32%	

ST. ANDREWS PRESBYTERIAN COLLEGE

1700 Dogwood Mile, Laurinburg, NC 28352
Phone: 910-277-5555 • Fax: 910-277-5087
E-mail: admissions@sapc.edu • Web: www.sapc.edu
Support: CS • Institution type: 4-year private

PROGRAMS OR SERVICES FOR STUDENTS WITH LD

St. Andrews Presbyterian College acknowledges its responsibility, both legally and educationally, to serve students with learning disabilities by providing reasonable accommodations. These services do not guarantee success, but endeavor to assist students in pursuing a quality postsecondary education. The Office of Disability Services and The Center for Academic Success at St. Andrews offer a range of support services for students with disabilities. These services are meant to help students devise strategies for meeting college demands and to foster independence, responsibility, and self-advocacy. The Office of Disability Services responds to each request for services and helps students develop a viable plan for personal success. The Office of Disability Services at St. Andrews Presbyterian College is committed to ensuring that all student information remains confidential.

ADMISSION INFORMATION FOR STUDENTS WITH LD/ADHD

College entrance tests required: Yes
Interview required: No
Essay recommended: SAT/ACT writing required
What documentation required for LD: Psycho Ed evaluation to include: relevant historical info, instructional interventions, related services, age diagnosed, objective data (aptitude, achievement, info processing), test scores (standard, percentile and grade equivalents) and describe functional limitations.
With general application: No
To receive services after enrolling: Yes
What documentation required for ADHD: Diagnosis based on DSM-V; history of behaviors impairing functioning in academic setting; diagnostic interview; history of symptoms; evidence of ongoing behaviors.

With general application: No
Submitted to: Office of Disability Services
Special Ed. HS course work accepted: Only as accepted for regular college entrance
Specific course requirements of all applicants: Yes
Separate application required: Yes
# of LD applications submitted each year: NR
# of LD applications accepted yearly: NR
Acceptance into program means acceptance into college: Students must be admitted to and enrolled in the university first and then request services.

ADMISSIONS

Each application is reviewed on an individual basis. Factors considered are an SAT minimum of 800 or ACT minimum of 17 and students' high school profiles and courses attempted, as well as a minimum GPA of 2.5; an essay and counselor and/or teacher recommendations are optional but strongly recommended. Courses recommended include 3 credits of college prep English, 3 credits of math including Algebra II and Geometry, 3 credits of science, 3 credits of social studies, and 1 years of a foreign language. Prospective students are strongly encouraged to visit the campus. Students with learning disabilities complete the regular admissions application. Students with a diagnosis of attention deficit hyperactivity disorder are required to show achievement and ability testing (adult version) that validates the DSM–IV diagnosis. All students must meet the same admissions criteria. For the Admissions Committee to make the most informed decision, students are encouraged to self-disclose the existence of a learning disability in their personal statement. Any other personal information indicating the student's ability to succeed in college should also be included with the application. All documentation of a specific learning disability should be sent separately with an application for services to the Office of Disability Services at St. Andrews. Application forms for disability services are on the college website.

ADDITIONAL INFORMATION

All accommodations are based on the submitted current documentation. Each case is reviewed individually. Disability Services reserves the right to determine eligibility for services based on the quality of the submitted documentation. The services and accommodations include note-taking, extended time on tests, alternative test formats, separate locations for tests, books on tape through Recordings for the Blind and Dyslexic or from readers, and content tutoring through individual departments. Franklin Language Masters and audiotape equipment are available for loan. All computers in computer labs are equipped with spellchecker and there are two Kurzweil Readers in the Center for Academic Success.

LEARNING DISABILITY PROGRAM OR SERVICES

Contact Information
Name of program or department: Office of Disability Services and Center for Academic Success
  Telephone: 910-277-5667
  Fax: 910-277-5746

LEARNING DISABILITY SERVICES

Accommodations are decided upon an individual basis after a thorough review of appropriate, current documentation. The accommodations requested must be supported through the documentation provided and must be logically linked to the current impact of the condition on academic functioning.

Allowed in exams	**Distraction-reduced environment:** Yes	**Added costs for services:** No
Calculator: Yes	**Tape recording in class:** Yes	**LD specialists:** Yes
Dictionary: Yes	**Electronic texts:** Yes	**Professional tutors:** NR
Computer: Yes	**Accommodations for students with**	**Peer tutors:** 5–15
Spellchecker: Yes	**ADHD:** Yes	**Max. hours/wk. for services:** As
Extended test time: Yes	**Kurzweil Reader:** Yes	needed
Scribes: Yes	**Other assistive technology:** Yes	**How professors are notified of**
Proctors: Yes	**Priority registration:** No	**LD/ADHD:** By student
Oral exams: Yes		
Note-takers: Yes		

GENERAL ADMISSIONS INFORMATION

Office of Admission: 910-277-5555

ENTRANCE REQUIREMENTS

Academic units recommended: 4 English, 3 math, 3 science, 1 foreign language, 3 social studies. High school diploma is required, and GED is accepted. ACT with Writing component accepted. TOEFL required of all international applicants.

Application deadline: None	**SAT Math middle 50% range:**	**Graduated top 10% of class:** NR
Notification: Rolling	430–530	**Graduated top 25% of class:** NR
Average GPA: NR	**SAT Critical Reading middle 50%**	**Graduated top 50% of class:** NR
ACT Composite middle 50% range:	**range:** 440–560	
18–23	**SAT Writing middle 50% range:**	
	430–530	

COLLEGE GRADUATION REQUIREMENTS

Course waivers allowed: No
Course substitutions allowed: Yes
In what course: Foreign language

ADDITIONAL INFORMATION

Environment: The college is located on 600 acres in a small town 40 miles southwest of Fayetteville, NC, and 30 miles south of Pinehurst, NC.		
Student Body	**Cost Information**	**Greek System**
Undergrad enrollment: 623	**Tuition:** $21,614	**Fraternity:** No
Women: 60%	**Room & board:** $8,938	**Sorority:** No
Men: 40%	**Housing Information**	**Athletics:** Division II
Percent out-of-state: 65%	**University housing:** Yes	
	Percent living on campus: 92%	

THE UNIVERSITY OF NORTH CAROLINA at CHAPEL HILL

Jackson Hall 153A—Campus Box #2200, Chapel Hill, NC 27599-2200
Phone: 919-966-3621 • Fax: 919-962-3045
E-mail: unchelp@admissions.unc.edu • Web: www.unc.edu
Support: CS • Institution type: 4-year public

PROGRAMS OR SERVICES FOR STUDENTS WITH LD

The Academic Success Program, or ASP (www.unc.edu/asp), is one of the many programs within the Learning Center. We provide accommodations and services for undergraduate, professional and graduate students who have a documented learning disability and/or attention-deficit/hyperactivity disorder (AD/HD). The staff determines legally mandated accommodations and collaborates with the Department of Disability Services in providing them. The staff also provides a variety of services to eligible students, including learning strategy sessions and coaching.

ADMISSION INFORMATION FOR STUDENTS WITH LD/ADHD

College entrance tests required: Yes
Interview required: No
Essay recommended: Yes
What documentation required for LD: Psycho Ed evaluation to
  include: relevant historical info, instructional interventions,
  related services, age diagnosed, objective data (aptitude,
  achievement, info processing), test scores (standard, percentile
  and grade equivalents) and describe functional limitations.
With general application: No
To receive services after enrolling: Yes
What documentation required for ADHD: Diagnosis based
  on DSM-V; history of behaviors impairing functioning in
  academic setting; diagnostic interview; history of symptoms;
  evidence of ongoing behaviors.

With general application: No
Submitted to: Admissions
Special Ed. HS course work accepted: Yes
Specific course requirements of all applicants: Yes
Separate application required: No
# of LD applications submitted each year: NR
# of LD applications accepted yearly: NR
Total # of students receiving LD services: 450
**Acceptance into program means acceptance into
  college:** No, students must be admitted to and enrolled in
  the university first and then request services.

ADMISSIONS

All applicants must meet the same admission criteria. Teacher recommendation and counselor statement are required. Students must submit either the SAT or ACT with writing. There is one long and one short essay required. UNC does not use formulas or cutoffs for admission. They look for and celebrate diversity of interests, backgrounds, and aspirations. UNC focuses forst on academics using courses, GPA tests, recommendations, and essays. Rigor of courses is very important. Beyond academics they look at leadership and service, and character.

ADDITIONAL INFORMATION

Coaching is a creative partnership between students and their coach. Accommodations provided include note-takers, taped textbooks, tutors in math or foreign languages, extended time on tests, distraction-free test environments, readers during exams, scribes to write dictated test answers, and computers for writing test answers. Using the student's current course work, LDS can teach a range of strategies, including how to plan, draft, and edit papers; how to take lecture notes and reading notes; how to read critically and efficiently; how to manage time; and how to prepare for and take exams. Group experiences are available to students each semester based on their expressed interests. These can include support groups that promote understanding, acceptance, and pride; academic workshops that allow students to help one another learn specific skills; seminars that provide topical information from campus experts as well as other students; and panel discussions between students and university personnel.

LEARNING DISABILITY PROGRAM OR SERVICES

Contact Information
Name of program or department: Learning Disabilities Services (LDS)
 Telephone: 919-962-7227
 Fax: 919-962-3674

LEARNING DISABILITY SERVICES

Accommodations are decided upon an individual basis after a thorough review of appropriate, current documentation. The accommodations requested must be supported through the documentation provided and must be logically linked to the current impact of the condition on academic functioning.

Allowed in exams
 Calculator: Yes
 Dictionary: Yes
 Computer: Yes
 Spellchecker: Yes
Extended test time: Yes
Scribes: Yes
Proctors: Yes
Oral exams: Yes
Note-takers: Yes

Distraction-reduced environment: Yes
Tape recording in class: Yes
Electronic texts: Yes
Accommodations for students with
 ADHD: Yes
Kurzweil Reader: Yes
Other assistive technology: Yes
Priority registration: Yes

Added costs for services: No
LD specialists: Yes
Professional tutors: No
Peer tutors: Referral
Max. hours/wk. for services: 2
How professors are notified of
 LD/ADHD: By director

GENERAL ADMISSIONS INFORMATION

Office of Admission: 919-966-3621

ENTRANCE REQUIREMENTS

Academic units required: 4 English, 3 math, 3 science (1 science lab), 2 foreign language, 2 social studies, 2 academic electives, 1 U.S. history. **Academic units recommended:** 4 English, 4 math, 4 science (1 science lab), 4 foreign language, 3 social studies. High school diploma is required, and GED is not accepted. ACT with Writing component required. TOEFL required of all international applicants: minimum paper TOEFL 600, minimum computer TOEFL 250.

Application deadline: 1/15
Notification: 1/15, 3/20
Average GPA: 4.37
ACT Composite middle 50% range:
 26–31

SAT Math middle 50% range:
 620–700
SAT Critical Reading middle 50%
 range: 590–690
SAT Writing middle 50% range:
 590–690

Graduated top 10% of class: 76%
Graduated top 25% of class: 96%
Graduated top 50% of class: 99%

COLLEGE GRADUATION REQUIREMENTS

Course waivers allowed: No
Course substitutions allowed: No

ADDITIONAL INFORMATION

Environment: The university is located in a suburban town near Raleigh.

Student Body
 Undergrad enrollment: 18,579
 Women: 59%
 Men: 41%
 Percent out-of-state: 16%

Cost Information
 In-state tuition: $6,666
 Out-of-state tuition: $25,280
 Room & board: $9,306
Housing Information
 University housing: Yes
 Percent living on campus: 44%

Greek System
 Fraternity: Yes
 Sorority: Yes
Athletics: Division I

THE UNIVERSITY OF NORTH CAROLINA AT CHARLOTTE

9201 University City Boulevard, Charlotte, NC 28223-0001
Phone: 704-687-2213 • Fax: 704-687-6483
E-mail: unccadm@uncc.edu • Web: www.uncc.edu
Support: S • Institution type: 4-year public

PROGRAMS OR SERVICES FOR STUDENTS WITH LD

The mission of Disability Services reflects the university's commitment to diversity by ensuring access to educational opportunities for persons with disabilities. The professional staff in Disability Services assists students with disabilities, including learning disabilities, through an interactive process based on their individual needs.

ADMISSION INFORMATION FOR STUDENTS WITH LD/ADHD

College entrance tests required: Yes
Interview required: No
Essay recommended: No
What documentation required for LD: Psycho Ed evaluation to include: relevant historical info, instructional interventions, related services, age diagnosed, objective data (aptitude, achievement, info processing), test scores (standard, percentile and grade equivalents) and describe functional limitations.
With general application: No
To receive services after enrolling: Yes
What documentation required for ADHD: Diagnosis based on DSM-V; history of behaviors impairing functioning in academic setting; diagnostic interview; history of symptoms; evidence of ongoing behaviors.

With general application: No
Submitted to: Admissions and Disability Services
Special Ed. HS course work accepted: No
Specific course requirements of all applicants: Yes
Separate application required: No
# of LD applications submitted each year: NR
# of LD applications accepted yearly: NR
Total # of students receiving LD services: NR
Acceptance into program means acceptance into college: Students must be admitted to and enrolled in the university first and then request services.

ADMISSIONS

All applicants must meet the general admissions requirements and any special requirements for acceptance into a particular program of study. Students go through the regular application process. Courses required include 4 years English, 4 years math (1 beyond algebra II) 3 years science, 2 years foreign language, 2 years social studies (1 history recommended), and 2 years of electives. The university reserves the right to withhold the admission of any applicant who fails to meet any of the requirements for admission. Once students have been admitted and enrolled they may request the necessary services. The mid 50% of the admitted students have a GPA of ¾-4/0. SAT 1480-1730 and ACT 21-26.

ADDITIONAL INFORMATION

Services offered are based on the student's disability documentation, the functional impact of the disability upon the student and an interactive process between the student and the Disability Services counselor. UNC Charlotte has a Tutoring Center and a Writing Center available to all students. Academic Services at UNC Charlotte enriches the academic community by offering a broad range of initiatives promoting student success, ensuring access, and enhancing the educational experience of all students. Through transition programs, learning communities, support for student-athletes, academic advising, career services, experiential learning, university-wide honors programs, disability services, tutorial programs, and initiatives for underrepresented students, Academic Services cultivates life skills critical to successful graduation and global citizenship. Advocating for the needs of a diverse student population, Academic Services utilizes an integrated student-centered approach that reinforces rigorous academic expectations and encourages student engagement from the time of enrollment through graduation.

LEARNING DISABILITY PROGRAM OR SERVICES

Contact Information
Name of program or department: Disability Services
  Telephone: 704-687-4355
  Fax: 704-687-3226

LEARNING DISABILITY SERVICES

Accommodations are decided upon an individual basis after a thorough review of appropriate, current documentation. The accommodations requested must be supported through the documentation provided and must be logically linked to the current impact of the condition on academic functioning.

Allowed in exams
  Calculator: Yes
  Dictionary: No
  Computer: Yes
  Spellchecker: No
Extended test time: Yes
Scribes: No
Proctors: No
Oral exams: No
Note-takers: Yes

Distraction-reduced environment: Yes
Tape recording in class: Yes
Electronic texts: No
Accommodations for students with ADHD: Yes
Kurzweil Reader: Yes
Other assistive technology: Yes
Priority registration: No

Added costs for services: No
LD specialists: No
Professional tutors: No
Peer tutors: Yes
Max. hours/wk. for services: N/A
How professors are notified of LD/ADHD: By student

GENERAL ADMISSIONS INFORMATION

Office of Admission: 704-687-2213

ENTRANCE REQUIREMENTS
Academic units required: 4 English, 3 math, 3 science (1 science lab), 2 foreign language, 2 social studies.
Academic units recommended: 1 foreign language. High school diploma is required, and GED is accepted. ACT with Writing component required. TOEFL required of all international applicants: minimum paper TOEFL 507, minimum computer TOEFL 180.

Application deadline: 7/1
Notification: Rolling
Average GPA: 3.66
ACT Composite middle 50% range: 19–29

SAT Math middle 50% range: 450–670
SAT Critical Reading middle 50% range: 420–640
SAT Writing middle 50% range: 410–650

Graduated top 10% of class: 19%
Graduated top 25% of class: 53%
Graduated top 50% of class: 89%

COLLEGE GRADUATION REQUIREMENTS

Course waivers allowed: No
Course substitutions allowed: Yes
In what course: Foreign language substitution if supported by documentation and only done on a case-by-case basis.

ADDITIONAL INFORMATION

Environment: The University is located on 1,000 acres 8 miles northeast of Charlotte.

Student Body
  Undergrad enrollment: 20,283
  Women: 52%
  Men: 48%
  Percent out-of-state: 7%

Cost Information
  In-state tuition: $5,440
  Out-of-state tuition: $17,205
  Room & board: $7,962
Housing Information
  University housing: Yes
  Percent living on campus: 25%

Greek System
  Fraternity: Yes
  Sorority: Yes
Athletics: Division I

THE UNIVERSITY OF NORTH CAROLINA AT GREENSBORO

1400 Spring Garden Street, Greensboro, NC 27402-6170
Phone: 336-334-5243 • Fax: 336-334-4180
E-mail: admissions@uncg.edu • Web: www.uncg.edu
Support: CS • Institution type: 4-year public

PROGRAMS OR SERVICES FOR STUDENTS WITH LD

The University of North Carolina—Greensboro is committed to equality of educational opportunities for qualified students with disabilities. The goal of Disabled Student Services is to provide a full range of academic accommodations. Students who need tests offered in a nontraditional format may request this service. Modifications may include extended test times, private rooms, readers, scribes, or the use of word processors for essay examinations. Documentation must verify the use of special accommodations. The Disability Services Office provides a handbook for students to use as a helpful guide in making their experience at UNCG a positive one.

ADMISSION INFORMATION FOR STUDENTS WITH LD/ADHD

College entrance tests required: Yes
Interview required: No
Essay recommended: No
What documentation required for LD: Psycho Ed evaluation to include: relevant historical info, instructional interventions, related services, age diagnosed, objective data (aptitude, achievement, info processing), test scores (standard, percentile and grade equivalents) and describe functional limitations.
With general application: No
To receive services after enrolling: Yes
What documentation required for ADHD: Diagnosis based on DSM-V; history of behaviors impairing functioning in academic setting; diagnostic interview; history of symptoms; evidence of ongoing behaviors.

With general application: No
Submitted to: Disabled Student Services
Special Ed. HS course work accepted: NR
Specific course requirements of all applicants: Yes
Separate application required: No
# of LD applications submitted each year: NR
# of LD applications accepted yearly: NR
Total # of students receiving LD services: 200
Acceptance into program means acceptance into college: Students must be admitted to and enrolled in the university first and then request services.

ADMISSIONS

There is no special admissions process for students with learning disabilities. Admission is competitive and based on academic qualifications. Students with learning disabilities must submit the regular application and are considered for admission in the same manner as any other applicant. No pre-admission inquiry regarding the learning disability is made. It is highly recommended that the SAT or ACT be taken with accommodations (if eligible) if this gives a better estimate of the student's ability.

ADDITIONAL INFORMATION

Trained staff members are available for counseling to assist students with academic and/or personal problems. Voluntary note-takers are solicited through DSS, and photocopying is available. Students will meet with their faculty advisor to discuss courses that need to be taken, and DSS will stamp the students' registration cards to verify that they are registered with DSS and warrant priority registration. Assistance in securing taped textbooks through Recording for the Blind is provided, and a file of available readers is available for instances when materials are not available through RFB. Students are provided with information regarding campus tutorials and labs. Individual tutors are provided when it seems necessary. Students can receive help with study skills and time management techniques.

LEARNING DISABILITY PROGRAM OR SERVICES

Contact Information
Name of program or department: Disabled Student Services
Telephone: 336-334-5440
Fax: 336-334-4412

LEARNING DISABILITY SERVICES

Accommodations are decided upon an individual basis after a thorough review of appropriate, current documentation. The accommodations requested must be supported through the documentation provided and must be logically linked to the current impact of the condition on academic functioning.

Allowed in exams
Calculator: Yes
Dictionary: Yes
Computer: Yes
Spellchecker: Yes
Extended test time: Yes
Scribes: Yes
Proctors: Yes
Oral exams: Yes
Note-takers: Yes

Distraction-reduced environment: Yes
Tape recording in class: Yes
Electronic texts: Yes
Accommodations for students with ADHD: Yes
Kurzweil Reader: Yes
Other assistive technology: Yes
Priority registration: Yes

Added costs for services: No
LD specialists: Yes
Professional tutors: No
Peer tutors: Yes
Max. hours/wk. for services: Depends on needs
How professors are notified of LD/ADHD: By both student and director

GENERAL ADMISSIONS INFORMATION

Office of Admission: 336-334-5243

ENTRANCE REQUIREMENTS

Academic units required: 4 English, 4 math, 3 science (1 science lab), 2 foreign language, 1 social studies, 1 history. High school diploma is required, and GED is not accepted. ACT with Writing component required. TOEFL required of all international applicants: minimum paper TOEFL 550, minimum computer TOEFL 213.

Application deadline: 3/1
Notification: Rolling
Average GPA: 3.59
ACT Composite middle 50% range: NR

SAT Math middle 50% range: 460–560
SAT Critical Reading middle 50% range: 460–560
SAT Writing middle 50% range: 440–550

Graduated top 10% of class: 18%
Graduated top 25% of class: 48%
Graduated top 50% of class: 86%

COLLEGE GRADUATION REQUIREMENTS

Course waivers allowed: No
Course substitutions allowed: Yes
In what course: Decided on a case-by-case basis in foreign language (an extreme exception rather than the rule). All substitutions must be approved by a faculty committee. Currently, the univeristy offers a modified foreign language program.

ADDITIONAL INFORMATION

Environment: The university is located on 178 acres in an urban area in Greensboro.

Student Body
Undergrad enrollment: 15,714
Women: 67%
Men: 33%
Percent out-of-state: 7%

Cost Information
In-state tuition: $5,275
Out-of-state tuition: $17,800
Room & board: $6,840
Housing Information
University housing: Yes
Percent living on campus: 29%

Greek System
Fraternity: Yes
Sorority: Yes
Athletics: Division I

THE UNIVERSITY OF NORTH CAROLINA

WILMINGTON

601 South College Road, Wilmington, NC 28403-5904
Phone: 910-962-3243 • Fax: 910-962-3038
E-mail: admissions@uncw.edu • Web: www.uncw.edu
Support: CS • Institution type: 4-year public

PROGRAMS OR SERVICES FOR STUDENTS WITH LD

The university's goal is to provide access to all of its academic programs, support services, and extracurricular activities and enrich students' academic and vocational experiences while in college. The coordinator of Disability Services (DS) meets with the student to appraise special needs, make referrals, and arrange for special accommodations. The university has devoted much time and energy to meeting the requirements of Section 504 and the ADA. This effort is exemplified by the accommodating services offered through DS for students with learning disabilities and by special cooperation of the faculty. As the number of students with learning disabilities attending UNCW increases, so does the university's commitment to making facilities and programs more accessible.

ADMISSION INFORMATION FOR STUDENTS WITH LD/ADHD

College entrance tests required: Yes
Interview required: No
Essay recommended: Yes
What documentation required for LD: Psycho Ed evaluation to include: relevant historical info, instructional interventions, related services, age diagnosed, objective data (aptitude, achievement, info processing), test scores (standard, percentile and grade equivalents) and describe functional limitations.
With general application: No
To receive services after enrolling: Yes
What documentation required for ADHD: Diagnosis based on DSM-V; history of behaviors impairing functioning in academic setting; diagnostic interview; history of symptoms; evidence of ongoing behaviors.

With general application: No
Submitted to: Disability Services
Special Ed. HS course work accepted: No
Specific course requirements of all applicants: Yes
Separate application required: N/A
# of LD applications submitted each year: NR
# of LD applications accepted yearly: NR
Total # of students receiving LD services: 250
Acceptance into program means acceptance into college: Students must be admitted to and enrolled in the university first and then request services.

ADMISSIONS

Students with learning disabilities must meet the same entrance requirements as all other applicants. Course requirements include 4 years of English, 3 years of math, 3 years of science, 2 years of social studies, and 2 years of a foreign language. UNCW requires one recommendation from a guidance counselor or a core academic teacher. Most students admitted to UNCW have SAT test scores between 1160 and 1230 or, ACT scores between 26 and 28, and the average GPA is 3.68. The university prefers that students respond to the essay question posed by UNCW rather than sending an essay they have prepared for another institution.

ADDITIONAL INFORMATION

Services are provided based on individual needs as assessed through recent diagnostic information and a personal interview. As new needs are identified, services may be modified or developed to accommodate them. Newly accepted students interested in services should complete and sign the disclosure form that is included with the letter of acceptance. This information should then be forwarded to the Disability Services. Current documentation must be sent to the Director of DS after acceptance to the university. Diagnostic testing must be conducted by a licensed professional, and an adequate report must include specific educational recommendations. There are no special classes or programs designed just for students with learning disabilities. Services and accommodations are offered to undergraduate and graduate students.

LEARNING DISABILITY PROGRAM OR SERVICES

Contact Information
Name of program or department: Disability Services (DS)
  Telephone: 910-962-7555
  Fax: 910-962-7556

LEARNING DISABILITY SERVICES

Accommodations are decided upon an individual basis after a thorough review of appropriate, current documentation. The accommodations requested must be supported through the documentation provided and must be logically linked to the current impact of the condition on academic functioning.

Allowed in exams	**Distraction-reduced environment:** Yes	**Added costs for services:** No
Calculator: Yes	**Tape recording in class:** Yes	**LD specialists:** Yes
Dictionary: No	**Electronic texts:** Yes	**Professional tutors:** No
Computer: Yes	**Accommodations for students with**	**Peer tutors:** Yes
Spellchecker: Yes	**ADHD:** Yes	**Max. hours/wk. for services:** Depends
Extended test time: Yes	**Kurzweil Reader:** Yes	on needs
Scribes: Yes	**Other assistive technology:** Yes	**How professors are notified of**
Proctors: Yes	**Priority registration:** Yes	**LD/ADHD:** By student
Oral exams: Yes		
Note-takers: Yes		

GENERAL ADMISSIONS INFORMATION

Office of Admission: 910-962-3243

ENTRANCE REQUIREMENTS

Academic units required: 4 English, 3 math, 3 science (1 science lab), 2 foreign language, 2 social studies, 1 history. High school diploma is required, and GED is accepted. SAT or ACT with Writing component required. TOEFL required of all international applicants: minimum paper TOEFL 550, minimum computer TOEFL 213.

Application deadline: 11/1 for Early Action; 2/1 for regular decision	**SAT Math middle 50% range:** NR	**Graduated top 10% of class:** 22%
Notification: 1/20; 4/1	**SAT Critical Reading middle 50% range:** NR	**Graduated top 25% of class:** 62%
Average GPA: 3.71–4.33	**SAT Writing middle 50% range:** NR	**Graduated top 50% of class:** 92%
ACT Composite middle 50% range: 23–28		

COLLEGE GRADUATION REQUIREMENTS

Course waivers allowed: No
Course substitutions allowed: Yes
In what course: Determined strictly on a case-by-case basis

ADDITIONAL INFORMATION

Environment: The university is located on a 660-acre urban campus.

Student Body	**Cost Information**	**Greek System**
Undergrad enrollment: 12,000	**In-state tuition:** $5,672	**Fraternity:** Yes
Women: 59%	**Out-of-state tuition:** $17,472	**Sorority:** Yes
Men: 41%	**Room & board:** $7,900	**Athletics:** Division I
Percent out-of-state: 15%	**Housing Information**	
	University housing: Yes	
	Percent living on campus: 35%	

WAKE FOREST UNIVERSITY

PO Box 7305, Reynolda Station, Winston-Salem, NC 27109
Phone: 336-758-5201 • Fax: 336-758-4324
E-mail: admissions@wfu.edu • Web: www.wfu.edu
Support: CS • Institution type: 4-year private

PROGRAMS OR SERVICES FOR STUDENTS WITH LD

The Learning Assistance Center (LAC) offers support for academic success. For students with documented disabilities, the program director will work with the student and members of the faculty to help implement any approved course accommodations. The students with learning disabilities have a series of conferences with staff members who specialize in academic skills and who help design an overall study plan to improve scholastic performance in those areas needing assistance. If special course accommodations are needed, the LAC staff will serve as an advocate for the students with members of the faculty.

ADMISSION INFORMATION FOR STUDENTS WITH LD/ADHD

College entrance tests required: No
Interview required: No
Essay recommended: Yes
What documentation required for LD: Psycho Ed evaluation to
  include: relevant historical info, instructional interventions,
  related services, age diagnosed, objective data (aptitude,
  achievement, info processing), test scores (standard, percentile
  and grade equivalents) and describe functional limitations.
With general application: No
To receive services after enrolling: Yes
What documentation required for ADHD: Diagnosis based
  on DSM-V; history of behaviors impairing functioning in
  academic setting; diagnostic interview; history of symptoms;
  evidence of ongoing behaviors.

With general application: No
Submitted to: LAC
Special Ed. HS course work accepted: No
Specific course requirements of all applicants: Yes
Separate application required: No
# of LD applications submitted each year: NR
# of LD applications accepted yearly: NR
Total # of students receiving LD services: 221
**Acceptance into program means acceptance into
  college:** Students must be admitted to and enrolled in the
  university first and then request services.

ADMISSIONS

There are no special admissions procedures for students with learning disabilities. Students with LD submit the general Wake Forest University application and are expected to meet the same admission criteria as all applicants. Wake Forest does not accept the ACT. The mid 50 percent range for the SAT is 1240–1360. Course requirements include 4 years of English, 3 years of math, 1 year of science, 2 years of social studies, and 2 years of a foreign language. Students should self-disclose to the Learning Assistance Center after admission. Services are available to all enrolled students with documentation on file. Students are encouraged to provide a recent psychoeducational evaluation.

ADDITIONAL INFORMATION

The Learning Assistance Program staff will assist students with learning disabilities to learn new approaches to studying and methods for improving reading comprehension, note-taking, time management, study organization, memory, motivation, and self-modification. The LAC offers peer tutoring services. In addition to one-on-one tutoring in many academic subjects, the LAC provides collaborative learning groups comprised of two to five students. The LAC also assists students who present special academic needs. Accommodations are determined based on appropriate documentation. All students with or without learning disabilities are eligible for group or individual tutoring in basic academic subjects. The tutors are advanced undergraduates or graduate students who have demonstrated mastery of specific subject areas and are supervised by the LAC staff for their tutoring activities. The LAC also offers all students individual academic counseling to help develop study, organization, and time management strategies that are important for successful college-level learning.

LEARNING DISABILITY PROGRAM OR SERVICES

Contact Information
Name of program or department: Learning Assistance Center (LAC)
 Telephone: 336-758-5929
 Fax: 336-758-1991

LEARNING DISABILITY SERVICES

Accommodations are decided upon an individual basis after a thorough review of appropriate, current documentation. The accommodations requested must be supported through the documentation provided and must be logically linked to the current impact of the condition on academic functioning.

Allowed in exams
 Calculator: No
 Dictionary: Yes
 Computer: Yes
 Spellchecker: Yes
Extended test time: Yes
Scribes: No
Proctors: No
Oral exams: No
Note-takers: No

Distraction-reduced environment: Yes
Tape recording in class: Yes
Electronic texts: No
Accommodations for students with
 ADHD: Yes
Kurzweil Reader: No
Other assistive technology: No
Priority registration: No

Added costs for services: No
LD specialists: Yes
Professional tutors: No
Peer tutors: 150
Max. hours/wk. for services: NR
How professors are notified of
 LD/ADHD: By both student and letter
 from Director

GENERAL ADMISSIONS INFORMATION

Office of Admission: 336-758-5201

ENTRANCE REQUIREMENTS

Academic units required: 4 English, 3 math, 1 science, 2 foreign language, 2 social studies. **Academic units recommended:** 4 English, 4 math, 4 science, 4 foreign language, 4 social studies. High school diploma is required, and GED is accepted. ACT with Writing component required. TOEFL required of all international applicants: minimum paper TOEFL 600, minimum computer TOEFL 250.

Application deadline: 1/15
Notification: 4/1
Average GPA: NR
ACT Composite middle 50% range:
 27–31

SAT Math middle 50% range:
 600–700
SAT Critical Reading middle 50%
 range: 580–690
SAT Writing middle 50% range: NR

Graduated top 10% of class: 75%
Graduated top 25% of class: 89%
Graduated top 50% of class: 99%

COLLEGE GRADUATION REQUIREMENTS

Course waivers allowed: No
Course substitutions allowed: Yes
In what course: Foreign language only. If there is a documented language-based LD and a good faith effort has been made by the student to learn a foreign language without success, then two courses from an approved list of classics and humanities courses may be substituted.

ADDITIONAL INFORMATION

Environment: The 550-acre campus is located in the Piedmont region of North Carolina.

Student Body
 Undergrad enrollment: 4,591
 Women: 51%
 Men: 49%
 Percent out-of-state: 74%

Cost Information
 Tuition: $41,100
 Room & board: $11,410
Housing Information
 University housing: Yes
 Percent living on campus: 70%

Greek System
 Fraternity: Yes
 Sorority: Yes
 Athletics: Division I

WESTERN CAROLINA UNIVERSITY

242 HFR Administration, Cullowhee, NC 28723
Phone: 828-227-7317 • Fax: 828-227-7319
E-mail: admiss@E-mail.wcu.edu • Web: www.wcu.edu
Support: CS • Institution type: 4-year public

PROGRAMS OR SERVICES FOR STUDENTS WITH LD

The Office of Disability Services attempts to respond to the needs of students with learning disabilities by making services and assistive technologies available as needed.

ADMISSION INFORMATION FOR STUDENTS WITH LD/ADHD

College entrance tests required: Yes
Interview required: No
Essay recommended: No
What documentation required for LD: Psycho Ed evaluation to include: relevant historical info, instructional interventions, related services, age diagnosed, objective data (aptitude, achievement, info processing), test scores (standard, percentile and grade equivalents) and describe functional limitations.
With general application: No
To receive services after enrolling: Yes
What documentation required for ADHD: Diagnosis based on DSM-V; history of behaviors impairing functioning in academic setting; diagnostic interview; history of symptoms; evidence of ongoing behaviors.

With general application: No
Submitted to: Office of Disability Services (ODS)
Special Ed. HS course work accepted: No
Specific course requirements of all applicants: Yes
Separate application required: No
# of LD applications submitted each year: NR
# of LD applications accepted yearly: NR
Total # of students receiving LD services: 100–120
Acceptance into program means acceptance into college: Students must be admitted to and enrolled in the university first and then request services.

ADMISSIONS

Students with learning disabilities are admitted under the same standards as students who do not have learning disabilities. WCU does not have a strict minimum GPA, but the average GPA for enrolled students in fall of 2011 was a 3.54 and the course requirements include 4 years of English, 4 years of math, 3 years of science, 3 years of social studies, and 2 years of a foreign language. The non-standardized ACT/SAT is acceptable. Students not admissible through the regular admission process may be offered a probationary admission and must begin in the summer prior to freshman year. The admission decision is made by the Admissions Office.

ADDITIONAL INFORMATION

To qualify for services, students must be enrolled at the university and have updated medical documentation. The following are examples of services or accommodations are available for students with appropriate documentation: the use of calculators, dictionaries, computers, or spellcheckers during exams; extended time on tests; quiet environments; scribes; proctors; oral exams; note-takers; tape recorders in class; text in alternate format; and priority registration. All students have access to tutoring, writing and math centers, a Technology Assistance Center, and counseling and psychological services. Admitted students should maintain good class attendance, strive for good grades, cooperate with counselors and advisors, set realistic career goals, and meet with the Office of Disability Services to arrange accommodations. Services and accommodations are available for all enrolled students.

LEARNING DISABILITY PROGRAM OR SERVICES

Contact Information
Name of program or department: Office of Disability Dervices (ODS)
  Telephone: 828-227-7234
  Fax: 828-227-7036

LEARNING DISABILITY SERVICES

Accommodations are decided upon an individual basis after a thorough review of appropriate, current documentation. The accommodations requested must be supported through the documentation provided and must be logically linked to the current impact of the condition on academic functioning.

Allowed in exams
  Calculator: Yes
  Dictionary: Yes
  Computer: Yes
  Spellchecker: Yes
Extended test time: Yes
Scribes: Yes
Proctors: Yes
Oral exams: Yes
Note-takers: Yes

Distraction-reduced environment: Yes
Tape recording in class: Yes
Electronic texts: Yes
Accommodations for students with
  ADHD: Yes
Kurzweil Reader: Yes
Other assistive technology: Yes
Priority registration: Yes

Added costs for services: No
LD specialists: Yes
Professional tutors: Varies
Peer tutors: 20–50
Max. hours/wk. for services: NR
How professors are notified of
  LD/ADHD: By student

GENERAL ADMISSIONS INFORMATION

Office of Admission: 877-WCU-4-YOU

ENTRANCE REQUIREMENTS

Academic units required: 4 English, 4 math, 3 science, 2 foreign language, 2 social studies,
1 history, 5 academic electives. **Academic units recommended:** 4 English, 4 math, 3 science (3 science labs),
2 foreign language, 2 social studies, 1 history, 7 academic electives. High school diploma is required, and GED is accepted. ACT with Writing component required. TOEFL required of all international applicants: minimum paper TOEFL 550, minimum computer TOEFL 213.

Application deadline: 4/1
Notification: Rolling
Average GPA: 3.61
ACT Composite middle 50% range:
  20–24

SAT Math middle 50% range:
  470–590
SAT Critical Reading middle 50%
  range: 450–540
SAT Writing middle 50% range:
  430–520

Graduated top 10% of class: 13%
Graduated top 25% of class: 36%
Graduated top 50% of class: 70%

COLLEGE GRADUATION REQUIREMENTS

Course waivers allowed: Yes
In what course: Individually considered
Course substitutions allowed: Yes
In what course: Individually considered

ADDITIONAL INFORMATION

Environment: The university is located on 400 acres in a rural area 50 miles southwest of Asheville.

Student Body
  Undergrad enrollment: 6,301
  Women: 56%
  Men: 44%
  Percent out-of-state: 12%

Cost Information
  In-state tuition: $6,367
  Out-of-state tuition: $15,964
  Room & board: $8,126
Housing Information
  University housing: Yes
  Percent living on campus: 42%

Greek System
  Fraternity: Yes
  Sorority: Yes
Athletics: Division I

DAKOTA COLLEGE AT BOTTINEAU

105 Simrall Boulevard, Bottineau, ND 58318
Phone: 800-542-6866 • Fax: 701-288-5499
E-mail: ken.grosz@dakotacollege.edu • Web: www.misu-b.nodak.edu
Support: CS • Institution type: 2-year public

PROGRAMS OR SERVICES FOR STUDENTS WITH LD

The Learning Center provides a variety of academic support services to eligible students with LD. The Learning Center also provides individualized or small group instruction in English, algebra, biology, basic computer use, and other areas. Individuals are also provided with services that best meet their needs. In addition, study skills and reading improvement classes are offered for credit. An LD specialist/math instructor and an English/social studies instructor provide assistance in this program. Students planning to enroll at Dakota College at Bottineau should send documentation of their disability that is no more than 3 years old to the Learning Center. The documentation should include an intelligence assessment (preferably the WAIS–R), achievement testing (such as the Woodcock-Johnson psychoeducational battery), and education recommendations such as accommodations provided in high school and a recent IEP. Students should visit the Learning Center as soon as they arrive on campus. Students will be asked to complete an application, and the Learning Center instructor will review the students' class schedules and arrange for tutoring if deemed necessary.

ADMISSION INFORMATION FOR STUDENTS WITH LD/ADHD

College entrance tests required: Yes
Interview required: No
Essay recommended: No
What documentation required for LD: Psycho Ed evaluation to include: relevant historical info, instructional interventions, related services, age diagnosed, objective data (aptitude, achievement, info processing), test scores (standard, percentile and grade equivalents) and describe functional limitations.
With general application: No
To receive services after enrolling: Yes
What documentation required for ADHD: Diagnosis based on DSM-V; history of behaviors impairing functioning in academic setting; diagnostic interview; history of symptoms; evidence of ongoing behaviors.

With general application: No
Submitted to: Learning Center
Special Ed. HS course work accepted: Yes
Specific course requirements of all applicants: NR
Separate application required: No
# of LD applications submitted each year: NR
# of LD applications accepted yearly: NR
Total # of students receiving LD services: 10–20
Acceptance into program means acceptance into college: Students must be admitted to and enrolled in the university first and then request services.

ADMISSIONS
Dakota College at Bottineau has an open admission policy. Applicants must present a high school diploma or equivalent such as a GED. Standardized tests are not required. Students are encouraged to self-disclose their disability during the application process so that the university may provide information about accessing support once enrolled. All students who enroll are asked to complete a questionnaire that asks them to identify academic support services that they feel they may need once on campus.

ADDITIONAL INFORMATION
The Learning Center offers free tutoring and is open to all students. Sessions are adapted to fit a student's schedule. Individual tutoring is available. Students may receive accommodations that include class scheduling, though priority registration is not offered. Skills courses are offered in note-taking strategies, test-taking tips, and memory aids. There is a one-credit reading improvement course that helps improve reading comprehension. Additional accommodations based on appropriate documentation could include extended testing times, note-takers, distraction-free testing environments, tape recorders in class, and e-text versions of textbooks.

LEARNING DISABILITY PROGRAM OR SERVICES

Contact Information
Name of program or department: Learning Center
  Telephone: 701-228-5479
  Fax: 701-228-5614

LEARNING DISABILITY SERVICES

Accommodations are decided upon an individual basis after a thorough review of appropriate, current documentation. The accommodations requested must be supported through the documentation provided and must be logically linked to the current impact of the condition on academic functioning.

Allowed in exams
  Calculator: Yes
  Dictionary: Yes
  Computer: Yes
  Spellchecker: Yes
Extended test time: Yes
Scribes: NR
Proctors: NR
Oral exams: Yes
Note-takers: Yes

Distraction-reduced environment: Yes
Tape recording in class: Yes
Electronic texts: Yes
Accommodations for students with ADHD: Yes
Kurzweil Reader: No
Other assistive technology: Yes
Priority registration: No

Added costs for services: No
LD specialists: Yes
Professional tutors: 2
Peer tutors: 2–5
Max. hours/wk. for services: Varies
How professors are notified of LD/ADHD: By both student and director

GENERAL ADMISSIONS INFORMATION

Office of Admission: 800-542-6866

ENTRANCE REQUIREMENTS
High school diploma is required, and GED is accepted.

Application deadline: None
Notification: Rolling
Average GPA: 3.1
ACT Composite middle 50% range: 19–24

SAT Math middle 50% range: N/A
SAT Critical Reading middle 50% range: N/A
SAT Writing middle 50% range: N/A

Graduated top 10% of class: NR
Graduated top 25% of class: NR
Graduated top 50% of class: NR

COLLEGE GRADUATION REQUIREMENTS

Course waivers allowed: No
Course substitutions allowed: No

ADDITIONAL INFORMATION

Environment: The campus is located in a small town 80 miles from Minot, North Dakota.

Student Body
  Undergrad enrollment: 812
  Women: 48%
  Men: 52%
  Percent out-of-state: 26%

Cost Information
  In-state tuition: $3,856
  Out-of-state tuition: $5,416
  Room & board: $4,950
Housing Information
  University housing: Yes
  Percent living on campus: N/A

Greek System
  Fraternity: No
  Sorority: No
Athletics: NAIA

NORTH DAKOTA STATE UNIVERSITY

PO Box 5454, Fargo, ND 58105
Phone: 701-231-8643 • Fax: 701-231-8802
E-mail: ndsu.admission@ndsu.edu • Web: www.ndsu.edu
Support: S • Institution type: 4-year public

PROGRAMS OR SERVICES FOR STUDENTS WITH LD

The mission of NDSU Disability Services is to ensure equal access to educational opportunities for students with disabilities to fully participate in the university environment. Disability Services (DS) assists both students with disabilities, and faculty and staff working with students with disabilities. DS staff members can provide individual consultation regarding the possible presence of a disability, making referrals when appropriate; determine eligibility for accommodations and services, explain how to access services, provide assistance when arranging accommodations; consult with students, faculty and staff and partner with NDSU personnel to implement appropriate accommodations; and make referrals to other available support services. Disability Services staff members work to promote equal access to academic programs, promote self-awareness and advocacy skill development, educate campus community about disability-related issues and collaborate with various support services.

ADMISSION INFORMATION FOR STUDENTS WITH LD/ADHD

College entrance tests required: Yes
Interview required: N/A
Essay recommended: N/A
What documentation required for LD: Psycho Ed evaluation to include: relevant historical info, instructional interventions, related services, age diagnosed, objective data (aptitude, achievement, info processing), test scores (standard, percentile and grade equivalents) and describe functional limitations.
With general application: No
To receive services after enrolling: Yes
What documentation required for ADHD: Diagnosis based on DSM-V; history of behaviors impairing functioning in academic setting; diagnostic interview; history of symptoms; evidence of ongoing behaviors.

With general application: No
Submitted to: Disability Services
Special Ed. HS course work accepted: N/A
Specific course requirements of all applicants: Yes
Separate application required: No
# of LD applications submitted each year: NR
# of LD applications accepted yearly: NR
Total # of students receiving LD services: NR
Acceptance into program means acceptance into college: Students must be admitted to and enrolled in the university first and then request services.

ADMISSIONS

Students with learning disabilities submit the general application form and are expected to meet the same admission standards as all other applicants. The ACT range is 20-22, and the minimum GPA is 2.5. Applicants are expected to have taken high school courses in math, including algebra; English; science labs; and social studies. Students with learning disabilities may include a self-disclosure or information explaining or documenting their disability.

ADDITIONAL INFORMATION

Skills courses are offered. A technology lab/resource room is available for student use. Individual, career, and academic counseling along with support groups are available through the NDSU Counseling Center. TRIO-Student Support Services Program provides tutoring and small group instruction in study strategies, reading, computers, math, and science. The Academic Collegiate Experience (ACE) offers group tutoring. Individuals with learning disabilities or attention deficit hyperactive disorder may utilize these services. Students need to apply and qualify for TRIO-Student Support Services.

LEARNING DISABILITY PROGRAM OR SERVICES

Contact Information
Name of program or department: Disability Services
   Telephone: 701-231-8463
   Fax: 701-231-5205

LEARNING DISABILITY SERVICES

Accommodations are decided on an individual, case-by-case basis after a thorough review of appropriate, current documentation and a student intake. The accommodations requested must be supported by the documentation provided and are based on the functional limitations of the disability.

Allowed in exams	**Distraction-reduced environment:** Yes	**Added costs for services:** No
Calculator: Yes	**Tape recording in class:** Yes	**LD specialists:** No
Dictionary: NR	**Electronic texts:** Yes	**Professional tutors:** No
Computer: NR	**Accommodations for students with**	**Peer tutors:** 20–50
Spellchecker: NR	**ADHD:** Yes	**Max. hours/wk. for services:**
Extended test time: Yes	**Kurzweil Reader:** Yes	Unlimited
Scribes: Yes	**Other assistive technology:** Yes	**How professors are notified of**
Proctors: Yes	**Priority registration:** Yes	**LD/ADHD:** By student
Oral exams: Yes		
Note-takers: Yes		

GENERAL ADMISSIONS INFORMATION

Office of Admission: 701-231-8643

ENTRANCE REQUIREMENTS

Academic units required: 4 English, 3 math, 3 science (3 science labs), 3 social studies. **Academic units recommended:** 2 foreign language. High school diploma is required, and GED is accepted. ACT with or without Writing component accepted. TOEFL required of all international applicants: minimum paper TOEFL 525, minimum computer TOEFL 193.

Application deadline: 8/15	**SAT Math middle 50% range:**	**Graduated top 10% of class:** 16%
Notification: Rolling	510–670	**Graduated top 25% of class:** 40%
Average GPA: 3.39	**SAT Critical Reading middle 50%**	**Graduated top 50% of class:** 74%
ACT Composite middle 50% range:	range: 480–660	
20–25	**SAT Writing middle 50% range:** NR	

COLLEGE GRADUATION REQUIREMENTS

Course waivers allowed: No
Course substitutions allowed: No

ADDITIONAL INFORMATION

Environment: The university is located in a small city 250 miles from Minneapolis, Sioux Falls, and Winnipeg, Canada.

Student Body	**Cost Information**	**Greek System**
Undergrad enrollment: 11,977	**In-state tuition:** $7,175	**Fraternity:** Yes
Women: 43%	**Out-of-state tuition:** $17,421	**Sorority:** Yes
Men: 57%	**Room & board:** $6,722	**Athletics:** Division I
Percent out-of-state: 65%	**Housing Information**	
	University housing: Yes	
	Percent living on campus: 30%	

BOWLING GREEN STATE UNIVERSITY

110 McFall Center, Bowling Green, OH 43403
Phone: 419-372-2478 • Fax: 419-372-6955
E-mail: admissions@bgsu.edu • Web: www.bgsu.edu
Support: S • Institution type: 4-year public

PROGRAMS OR SERVICES FOR STUDENTS WITH LD

The philosophy of the university is to level the playing field for students with LD and/or ADHD through the provision of appropriate accommodations and advocacy. The Office of Disability Services (ODS) is evidence of BGSU's commitment to provide people a support system that assists in conquering obstacles that persons with disabilities may encounter as they pursue their educational goals and activities. ODS provides services on an as-needed basis. The Study Skills Lab is open to all BGSU students, and the extent of participation is determined by the student. No grades are given in the lab, participation is voluntary, and the program is individualized. The lab is not a tutorial service, but students will be shown efficient techniques for studying, reading textbooks, taking notes, and time management and strategies for effective test-taking and test preparation.

ADMISSION INFORMATION FOR STUDENTS WITH LD/ADHD

College entrance tests required: Yes
Interview required: No
Essay recommended: No
What documentation required for LD: Psycho Ed evaluation to include: relevant historical info, instructional interventions, related services, age diagnosed, objective data (aptitude, achievement, info processing), test scores (standard, percentile and grade equivalents) and describe functional limitations.
With general application: No
To receive services after enrolling: Yes
What documentation required for ADHD: Diagnosis based on DSM-V; history of behaviors impairing functioning in academic setting; diagnostic interview; history of symptoms; evidence of ongoing behaviors.

With general application: No
Submitted to: Office of Disability Services
Special Ed. HS course work accepted: Yes
Specific course requirements of all applicants: Yes
Separate application required: No
# of LD applications submitted each year: NR
# of LD applications accepted yearly: NR
Total # of students receiving LD services: 325–350
Acceptance into program means acceptance into college: Students must be admitted to and enrolled in the university first and then request services.

ADMISSIONS

There is no special application or special admissions process. Core courses preferred include 4 years of English, 3 years of math, 3 years of science, 3 years of social studies, 2 years of a foreign language, and 1 year of art. Students with LD may substitute foreign language with another core course. The minimum GPA is approximately 2.0. Average ACT 22. Students with LD submit the regular application and are encouraged to self-disclose their LD and arrange an interview with ODS to allow staff to discuss any documentation they may require and any concerns of the student. Additional information such as school or medical history that describes specific strengths and weaknesses is helpful in determining the services necessary once the student is admitted. Applicants who do not meet the academic standards for admission may be offered admission to the University Program for Academic Success.

ADDITIONAL INFORMATION

Students admitted to the University Program for Academic Success can enroll in courses and receive academic support group and individual tutoring and academic advising is offered, as well as mentoring and individualized academic assistance. General services include priority registration; advising by sharing information on instructor's teaching and testing styles; a writing lab for effective strategies; a study skills center for effective study skills, test-taking strategies, time management techniques, and textbook-reading skills; a math lab, a walk-in lab for understanding basic and advanced concepts; computerized technology; note-takers, readers, and scribes; letters to professors explaining the disability and modifications needed; advocacy; and books on tape. To be eligible for test accommodations, students are required to provide documentation that provides a clear indication/recommendation for the need requested. Staff works with the student to reach a consensus on the type of accommodation to be provided. Test accommodations may include extended time, oral exams, take-home exams, open-book exams, readers, scribes, computers and spellcheckers or grammar checkers, calculators, scratch paper, speller's dictionaries, question clarification, modification of test response format, and quiet rooms.

LEARNING DISABILITY PROGRAM OR SERVICES

Contact Information
Name of program or department: Office of Disability Services
 Telephone: 419-372-8495
 Fax: 419-372-8496

LEARNING DISABILITY SERVICES

Accommodations are decided upon an individual basis after a thorough review of appropriate, current documentation. The accommodations requested must be supported through the documentation provided and must be logically linked to the current impact of the condition on academic functioning.

Allowed in exams
 Calculator: Yes
 Dictionary: Yes
 Computer: Yes
 Spellchecker: Yes
Extended test time: Yes
Scribes: Yes
Proctors: Yes
Oral exams: Yes
Note-takers: Yes

Distraction-reduced environment: Yes
Tape recording in class: Yes
Electronic texts: Yes
Accommodations for students with
 ADHD: Yes
Kurzweil Reader: Yes
Other assistive technology: Yes
Priority registration: Yes

Added costs for services: No
LD specialists: No
Professional tutors: No
Peer tutors: Yes
Max. hours/wk. for services:
 Unlimited
How professors are notified of
 LD/ADHD: By student

GENERAL ADMISSIONS INFORMATION

Office of Admission: 419-372-BGSU

ENTRANCE REQUIREMENTS

Academic units required: 4 English, 3 math, 3 science (2 science labs), 2 foreign language, 3 social studies, 1 visual/performing arts. **Academic units recommended:** 4 English, 3 math, 3 science (2 science labs), 2 foreign language, 3 social studies, 1 visual/performing arts. High school diploma is required, and GED is accepted. ACT with or without Writing component accepted. TOEFL required of all international applicants: minimum paper TOEFL 500, minimum computer TOEFL 173.

Application deadline: 7/15
Notification: Rolling
Average GPA: 3.23
ACT Composite middle 50% range:
 19–24

SAT Math middle 50% range:
 450–550
SAT Critical Reading middle 50%
 range: 440–560
SAT Writing middle 50% range:
 440–540

Graduated top 10% of class: 14%
Graduated top 25% of class: 36%
Graduated top 50% of class: 70%

COLLEGE GRADUATION REQUIREMENTS

Course waivers allowed: Yes
In what course: Primarily foreign language; other requests will be considered.
Course substitutions allowed: Yes
In what course: Primarily foreign language; other requests will be considered.

ADDITIONAL INFORMATION

Environment: The 1,250-acre campus is in a small town 25 miles south of Toledo.

Student Body
 Undergrad enrollment: 18,000
 Women: 53%
 Men: 47%
 Percent out-of-state: 12%

Cost Information
 In-sate tuition: $9,700
 Out-of-state: $17,000
 Room & board: $7,800
Housing Information
 University housing: Yes
 Percent living on campus: 43%

Greek System
 Fraternity: Yes
 Sorority: Yes
Athletics: NCAA Division I

CASE WESTERN RESERVE UNIVERSITY

103 Tomlinson Hall, 10900 Euclid Avenue, Cleveland, OH 44106-7055
Phone: 216-368-4450 • Fax: 216-368-5111
E-mail: admission@case.edu • Web: www.case.edu
Support: S • Institution type: 4-year private

PROGRAMS OR SERVICES FOR STUDENTS WITH LD

The goals of Educational Support Services (ESS) are to provide reasonable accommodations and serve as an advocate for individuals with diagnosed learning disabilities. ESS ensures that students with disabilities have access to services and accommodations needed to make the college experience a positive and successful one. ESS provides academic support, special accommodations, and personal encouragement. The associate director of Disability Resources will work closely with students and design an individual plan for accommodations. Included in that plan are strategies for disclosure to professors as well as identifying specific accommodations that will be needed for each course.

ADMISSION INFORMATION FOR STUDENTS WITH LD/ADHD

College entrance tests required: Yes
Interview required: No
Essay recommended: Ye
What documentation required for LD: Psycho Ed evaluation to include: relevant historical info, instructional interventions, related services, age diagnosed, objective data (aptitude, achievement, info processing), test scores (standard, percentile and grade equivalents) and describe functional limitations.
With general application: No
To receive services after enrolling: Yes
What documentation required for ADHD: Diagnosis based on DSM-V; history of behaviors impairing functioning in academic setting; diagnostic interview; history of symptoms; evidence of ongoing behaviors.

With general application: No
Submitted to: Educational Support Services
Special Ed. HS course work accepted: No
Specific course requirements of all applicants: Yes
Separate application required: No
# of LD applications submitted each year: NR
# of LD applications accepted yearly: NR
Total # of students receiving LD services: 52
Acceptance into program means acceptance into college: Students must be admitted to and enrolled in the university first and then request services.

ADMISSIONS

Students with learning disabilities are encouraged to apply to CWRU. Admission is highly competitive, but all applicants are evaluated on an individual basis. Students who feel additional information would be helpful to the Admissions Committee are encouraged to provide diagnostic information about their individual situation. General admission criteria include 4 years of English, 3 years of math, 3 years of social science, 1 year of science, and 2–4 years of a foreign language. Students must also submit a writing sample and are encouraged to have an interview. Most admitted students rank in the top 20 percent of their class and have an SAT Reasoning score of 1180–1380 or an ACT score of 27–31.

ADDITIONAL INFORMATION

Skills courses are offered in study and learning strategies, time management, and reading. It is helpful for students to provide information regarding the nature of their disability so that services may be accommodated to their needs. High-performing students do well with the peer tutors available through ESS. These tutors are students who have successfully completed the appropriate course work and have been approved by faculty. Special arrangements are made by ESS for students to have alternative testing such as additional time and proctored examinations in alternative settings. Students with LD are eligible for books on tape through RFBD. The ESS center has reading improvement software, word processing, and all network applications. A reading strategies tutorial program for 1 credit and taught by a graduate student is also available for students with LD.

LEARNING DISABILITY PROGRAM OR SERVICES

Contact Information
Name of program or department: Disability Services in Educational Support Services (ESS)
  Telephone: 216-368-5230
  Fax: 216-368-8826

LEARNING DISABILITY SERVICES

Accommodations are decided upon an individual basis after a thorough review of appropriate, current documentation. The accommodations requested must be supported through the documentation provided and must be logically linked to the current impact of the condition on academic functioning.

Allowed in exams
  Calculator: Yes
  Dictionary: No
  Computer: Yes
  Spellchecker: Yes
Extended test time: Yes
Scribes: Yes
Proctors: Yes
Oral exams: Yes
Note-takers: Yes

Distraction-reduced environment: Yes
Tape recording in class: Yes
Electronic texts: Yes
Accommodations for students with ADHD: Yes
Kurzweil Reader: Yes
Other assistive technology: Yes
Priority registration: Yes

Added costs for services: No
LD specialists: No
Professional tutors: No
Peer tutors: NR
Max. hours/wk. for services: Unlimited
How professors are notified of LD/ADHD: By student

GENERAL ADMISSIONS INFORMATION

Office of Admission: 216-368-4450

ENTRANCE REQUIREMENTS

Academic units required: 4 English, 3 math, 3 science (1 science lab), 2 foreign language, 3 social studies.
Academic units recommended: 4 math, (2 science labs), 3 foreign language, 4 social studies. High school diploma is required, and GED is accepted. ACT with Writing component required. TOEFL required of all international applicants: minimum paper TOEFL 550, minimum computer TOEFL 213.

Application deadline: 1/15
Notification: 4/1
Average GPA: NR
ACT Composite middle 50% range: 28–32

SAT Math middle 50% range: 650–750
SAT Critical Reading middle 50% range: 600–690
SAT Writing middle 50% range: 590–690

Graduated top 10% of class: NR
Graduated top 25% of class: NR
Graduated top 50% of class: NR

COLLEGE GRADUATION REQUIREMENTS

Course waivers allowed: No
Course substitutions allowed: No

ADDITIONAL INFORMATION

Environment: The university is located on 128 acres four miles east of downtown Cleveland.

Student Body
  Undergrad enrollment: 4,267
  Women: 47%
  Men: 53%
  Percent out-of-state: 55%

Cost Information
  Tuition: $38,760
  Room & board: $11,940
Housing Information
  University housing: Yes
  Percent living on campus: 79%

Greek System
  Fraternity: Yes
  Sorority: Yes
Athletics: Division III

CENTRAL OHIO TECHNICAL COLLEGE

1179 University Drive, Newark, OH 43055-1767
Phone: 740-366-9222 • Fax: 740-364-9531
E-mail: thoudesh@cotc.edu • Web: www.cotc.edu
Support: CS • Institution type: 2-year public

PROGRAMS OR SERVICES FOR STUDENTS WITH LD

The goals of Disability Services (DS) are to foster self-advocacy and independence. Disability Services provides counseling and accommodations for students with learning disabilities. Placement tests are given after admissions. The tutoring program and Disability Services are the academic support units. They provide programs and services to students desiring to strengthen their academic skills. Students should self-identify before scheduling classes. Early notice is needed for some services, such as alternate testing and recorded textbooks. The college advocates meeting the unique needs of students with disabilities. Accommodations provided allow for equal access to higher education. This permanent disorder does not impair the normally average to above-average IQ of these students, but it does mean that different teaching/learning strategies may be needed. A student with a diagnosed learning disability who has been to DS will present an authorized accommodation form signed by a DS staff member to a faculty member. The faculty member and student then arrange to meet the accommodations.

ADMISSION INFORMATION FOR STUDENTS WITH LD/ADHD

College entrance tests required: No
Interview required: No
Essay recommended: No
What documentation required for LD: Psycho Ed evaluation to include: relevant historical info, instructional interventions, related services, age diagnosed, objective data (aptitude, achievement, info processing), test scores (standard, percentile and grade equivalents) and describe functional limitations.
With general application: No
To receive services after enrolling: Yes
What documentation required for ADHD: Diagnosis based on DSM-V; history of behaviors impairing functioning in academic setting; diagnostic interview; history of symptoms; evidence of ongoing behaviors.

With general application: No
Submitted to: Disability Services
Special Ed. HS course work accepted: No
Specific course requirements of all applicants: No
Separate application required: No
# of LD applications submitted each year: NR
# of LD applications accepted yearly: NR
Total # of students receiving LD services: NR
Acceptance into program means acceptance into college: Students must be admitted and enrolled at the college, and then their requests for supportive services will be reviewed.

ADMISSIONS

Admission is open to all applicants with a high school diploma or the GED, except in health programs. There are no specific course requirements. ACT/SAT tests are not required. The application process is the same for all students. There is no requirement to provide disability-related information to the Admissions Office. Documentation of your disability should be sent directly to DS. Eligibility for services/accommodations from DS is a separate process from admissions. All prospective students are encouraged to contact DS in the early stages of their college planning. Preadmission services include information about academic support services, transition issues, admission requirements, and appropriate documentation and meetings with staff disability professionals.

ADDITIONAL INFORMATION

The Tutoring Center and the Assistive Technology Lab are for students with learning disabilities and ADHD. All students are automatically eligible for services. The tutoring program includes peer tutoring in almost any course, scheduled at the student's convenience for 2 hours each week per course. The Assistive Technology Lab has resources to improve reading, math, and language skills; word processing; and study aids for some courses and national tests. The Study Skills Workshop Series provides assistance in improving study skills and 50-minute workshops on time management, learning styles/memory, test preparation and taking, reading textbooks effectively, and note-taking. Students also have access to proctors, individualized instruction designed to meet special needs, advocacy assistance, diagnosis counseling, coaching, and assistance with accommodations.

LEARNING DISABILITY PROGRAM OR SERVICES

Contact Information
Name of program or department: Office for Disability Services (DS)
 Telephone: 740-366-9441
 Fax: 740-364-9646

LEARNING DISABILITY SERVICES

Accommodations are decided upon an individual basis after a thorough review of appropriate, current documentation. The accommodations requested must be supported through the documentation provided and must be logically linked to the current impact of the condition on academic functioning.

Allowed in exams
 Calculator: Yes
 Dictionary: No
 Computer: Yes
 Spellchecker: No
 Extended test time: Yes
 Scribes: Yes
 Proctors: Yes
 Oral exams: No
 Note-takers: Yes

Distraction-reduced environment: Yes
Tape recording in class: Yes
Electronic texts: Yes
Accommodations for students with ADHD: Yes
Kurzweil Reader: No
Other assistive technology: Yes, Read & Write Gold
Priority registration: No

Added costs for services: No
LD specialists: 1
Professional tutors: 15
Peer tutors: 25–40
Max. hours/wk. for services: Unlimited
How professors are notified of LD/ADHD: By student

GENERAL ADMISSIONS INFORMATION

Office of Admission: 740-366-9222

ENTRANCE REQUIREMENTS

Open admissions. High school diploma or GED accepted. ACT score of 14 on the English section and 15 on the Math section. Some programs have additional requirements.

Application deadline: None
Notification: Rolling
Average GPA: NR
ACT Composite middle 50% range: NR

SAT Math middle 50% range: NR
SAT Critical Reading middle 50% range: NR
SAT Writing middle 50% range: NR

Graduated top 10% of class: NR
Graduated top 25% of class: NR
Graduated top 50% of class: NR

COLLEGE GRADUATION REQUIREMENTS

Course waivers allowed: No
Course substitutions allowed: Yes
In what course: Varies, on case-by-case basis

ADDITIONAL INFORMATION

Environment: The campus is located in a small town with easy access to Columbus.

Student Body
 Undergrad enrollment: 4,700
 Women: 71%
 Men: 29%
 Percent out-of-state: 2%

Cost Information
 In-state tuition: $1,989 per semester
 Out-of-state tuition: $3,676.50 per semester
 Room & board: $3,262.50
Housing Information
 University housing: Yes
 Percent living on campus: <1%

Greek System
 Fraternity: No
 Sorority: No
 Athletics: ORCC

COLLEGE OF MOUNT ST. JOSEPH

5701 Delhi Road, Cincinnati, OH 45233
Phone: 513-244-4623 • Fax: 513-244-4629
E-mail: admission@mail.msj.edu • Web: www.msj.edu
Support: SP • Institution type: 4-year private

PROGRAMS OR SERVICES FOR STUDENTS WITH LD

Project EXCEL is a comprehensive academic support program for students with learning disabilities enrolled in the college. The program's goals are to assist students in the transition from a secondary program to a college curriculum and promote the development of learning strategies and compensatory skills that will enable students to achieve success in a regular academic program. The structure of the program and supportive environment at the Mount give Project EXCEL its singular quality. Project EXCEL offers students individualized attention and a variety of support services to meet specific needs, including supervised tutoring by professional tutors; monitoring of student progress; instruction in learning strategies, time management; and academic advising with attention to students' specific learning needs.

ADMISSION INFORMATION FOR STUDENTS WITH LD/ADHD

College entrance tests required: Yes
Interview required: Yes
Essay recommended: Yes
Documentation required for LD: Psychoeducational evaluation that less than 3 years old
Documentation required for ADHD: Yes
Submitted to: Project EXCEL
Special Ed. HS course work accepted: No

Specific course requirements of all applicants: Yes
Separate application required: Yes
# of LD applications submitted each year: 60
# of LD applications accepted yearly: 32
Total # of students receiving LD services: 92
Acceptance into program means acceptance into college: After admission to the college, students may apply to Project EXCEL.

ADMISSIONS

Upon acceptance to the College, students can choose to receive services from one of two available options: the structured program (Project EXCEL) or the services model (Disability Services). Acceptance into Project EXCEL is a multi-step process and includes the following: completed Project EXCEL forms (Applicant Form, General Information Form, and School Record Form), psycho-educational evaluation, a letter of recommendation, and an interview with the director. The application is reviewed by the director and the Project EXCEL Admissions Committee. The diagnostic evaluation must indicate the presence of specific LD and/or ADD/ADHD.

ADDITIONAL INFORMATION

Project EXCEL students are assisted with course and major selection. Students are offered individualized attention and a variety of support services to meet specific needs, including supervised professional tutoring, monitoring of student progress, instruction in learning strategies, time management and organizational skills training, and academic advising with attention to specific learning needs. Professional tutors offer help in writing, reading, and study skills based on the individual needs of the students. The program director serves as a student advisor. There are fees for the various levels in Project EXCEL.

LEARNING DISABILITY PROGRAM OR SERVICES

Contact Information
Name of program or department: Project EXCEL
  Telephone: 513-244-4623
  Fax: 513-244-4629

LEARNING DISABILITY SERVICES

Accommodations are decided upon an individual basis after a thorough review of appropriate, current documentation. The accommodations requested must be supported through the documentation provided and must be logically linked to the current impact of the condition on academic functioning.

Allowed in exams
  Calculator: Yes
  Dictionary: Yes
  Computer: Yes
  Spellchecker: Yes
Extended test time: Yes
Scribes: Yes
Proctors: Yes
Oral exams: Yes
Note-takers: Yes

Distraction-reduced environment: Yes
Tape recording in class: Yes
Electronic texts: Yes
Accommodations for students with
  ADHD: Yes
Kurzweil Reader: Yes
Other assistive technology: Yes
Priority registration: No

Added costs for services: Yes
LD specialists: Yes
Professional tutors: 15
Peer tutors: No
Max. hours/wk. for services:
  Unlimited
How professors are notified of
  LD/ADHD: By both student and
  director

GENERAL ADMISSIONS INFORMATION

Office of Admission: 513-244-4531

ENTRANCE REQUIREMENTS

Academic units required: 4 English, 2 math, 2 science (1 science lab), 2 foreign language, 1 social studies, 1 history, 1 academic elective, 1 fine arts. **Academic units recommended:** 4 English, 4 math, 4 science (2 science labs), 2 foreign language, 2 social studies, 2 history, 1 academic elective, 2 fine arts. High school diploma is required, and GED is accepted. ACT with or without Writing component accepted. TOEFL required of all international applicants: minimum paper TOEFL 510, minimum computer TOEFL 180.

Application deadline: 2 weeks before
  semester begins
Notification: Rolling
Average GPA: 3.22
ACT Composite middle 50% range:
  20–25

SAT Math middle 50% range:
  450–560
SAT Critical Reading middle 50%
  range: 450–540
SAT Writing middle 50% range: NR

Graduated top 10% of class: 9%
Graduated top 25% of class: 33%
Graduated top 50% of class: 71%

COLLEGE GRADUATION REQUIREMENTS

Course waivers allowed: No
Course substitutions allowed: No

ADDITIONAL INFORMATION

Environment: The Mount is a Catholic, coeducational, liberal arts college located approximately 15 miles from downtown
  Cincinnati.

Student Body
  Undergrad enrollment: 2,056
  Women: 65%
  Men: 35%
  Percent out-of-state: 17%

Cost Information
  Tuition: $24,400
  Room & board: $7,746 (varies)
Housing Information
  University housing: Yes
  Percent living on campus: 32%

Greek System
  Fraternity: No
  Sorority: No
Athletics: Division III

HOCKING COLLEGE

3301 Hocking Parkway, Nelsonville, OH 45764
Phone: 740-753-3591 • Fax: 740-753-1452
E-mail: admissions@hocking.edu • Web: www.hocking.edu
Support: CS • Institution type: 2-year public

PROGRAMS OR SERVICES FOR STUDENTS WITH LD

The Access Center Office of Disability Support Services (ACODS) is dedicated to serving the various needs of individuals with disabilities. The educational coordinator for students with disabilities helps all students with learning disabilities successfully adjust to college life by finding the right fit between the instructional offerings of Hocking College and their own individualized learning and personal needs. This is accomplished in part by working with assessment and counseling professionals to assist students in identifying individualized programs of study and means for success by more closely aligning interests and abilities with instructors and program effectiveness. The accommodation process is one of collaboration between students and instructors with support from ACODS. Eligibility is determined on the basis of the disability and a need for services and accommodations documentation, the student's experience with services and accommodations that have been effective in the past, and ACODS professional judgment.

ADMISSION INFORMATION FOR STUDENTS WITH LD/ADHD

College entrance tests required: Yes
Interview required: No
Essay recommended: No
What documentation required for LD: Psycho Ed evaluation to include: relevant historical info, instructional interventions, related services, age diagnosed, objective data (aptitude, achievement, info processing), test scores (standard, percentile and grade equivalents) and describe functional limitations.
With general application: No
To receive services after enrolling: Yes
What documentation required for ADHD: Diagnosis based on DSM-V; history of behaviors impairing functioning in academic setting; diagnostic interview; history of symptoms; evidence of ongoing behaviors.

With general application: No
Submitted to: ACODS
Special Ed. HS course work accepted: N/A
Specific course requirements of all applicants: No
Separate application required: Yes
# of LD applications submitted each year: NR
# of LD applications accepted yearly: NR
Total # of students receiving LD services: 171
Acceptance into program means acceptance into college: Students must be admitted to and enrolled in the university first and then request services.

ADMISSIONS

The college has open enrollment for any student with a high school diploma or equivalent. Students are not required to take any specific courses or have any specific test score on the ACT/SAT. Students requesting accommodations or services for learning disabilities must be admitted and enrolled, and then they may request services. Current documentation should be submitted.

ADDITIONAL INFORMATION

ACODS staff and the student work together to identify individual needs and then determine which of the support services and accommodations would enable the student to achieve academic potential. Strategies used to assist students with disabilities include assistance with instructional and supportive needs; aligning interests and abilities with instructors and program effectiveness; assuring individual program implementation consistent with the identified needs of the student; evaluating problematic situations regarding modes of presentation that affect student performance and potential for success; assisting on course assignments, troubleshooting learning problems, and assisting in solutions to situations that inhibit success; helping to obtain tutoring services; priority scheduling; liaising with community agencies; and serving as an advocate. For those who qualify, the Access Center staff can assist with advising, tutoring, and test-taking and also arrange for campus transportation and classroom access. In addition, the Access Center can link students with other college services and external service agencies. Eligibility is determined on the basis of the presence of a disability and a need for services and accommodations to support an equal educational opportunity. Documentation of the disability is required as well as the student's stated experience with services and accommodations that have been effective in the past. Quest for Success is a program designed especially for new students to help them prepare to start technical classes in the fall. Additional services include professional tutors in some mathematics and communications courses, Compu-Lenz to enlarge type on a computer screen and reduce glare, academic advising, and an educational coordinator to act as a liaison with college instructors and community agencies.

LEARNING DISABILITY PROGRAM OR SERVICES

Contact Information
Name of program or department: Office of Disability Services (ACODS)
  Telephone: 740-753-7107
  Fax: 740-753-6082

LEARNING DISABILITY SERVICES

Accommodations are decided upon an individual basis after a thorough review of appropriate, current documentation. The accommodations requested must be supported through the documentation provided and must be logically linked to the current impact of the condition on academic functioning.

Allowed in exams
  Calculator: Yes
  Dictionary: No
  Computer: Yes
  Spellchecker: Yes
Extended test time: Yes
Scribes: Yes
Proctors: Yes
Oral exams: Yes
Note-takers: Yes

Distraction-reduced environment: Yes
Tape recording in class: Yes
Electronic texts: Yes
Accommodations for students with ADHD: Yes
Kurzweil Reader: Yes
Other assistive technology: Yes
Priority registration: No

Added costs for services: No
LD specialists: Yes
Professional tutors: 3
Peer tutors: 25–40
Max. hours/wk. for services: Unlimited
How professors are notified of LD/ADHD: By student

GENERAL ADMISSIONS INFORMATION

Office of Admission: 740-753-7049

ENTRANCE REQUIREMENTS

Academic Units Recommended: 4 English, 3 math, 3 science, 4 social studies, 2 foreign language. Open admissions. High school diploma or GED accepted. Specific ACT or SAT scores are not required.

Application deadline: None
Notification: Rolling
Average GPA: NR
ACT Composite middle 50% range: NR

SAT Math middle 50% range: NR
SAT Critical Reading middle 50% range: NR
SAT Writing middle 50% range: NR

Graduated top 10% of class: NR
Graduated top 25% of class: NR
Graduated top 50% of class: NR

COLLEGE GRADUATION REQUIREMENTS

Course waivers allowed: NR
Course substitutions allowed: Yes
In what course: Any with an appropriate substitution

ADDITIONAL INFORMATION

Environment: The college is located on 150 acres in a rural area with easy access to Columbus.

Student Body
  Undergrad enrollment: 4,235
  Women: 50%
  Men: 50%
  Percent out-of-state: 2%

Cost Information
  In-state tuition: $3,669
  Out-of-state tuition: $7,338
  Room & board: $6,300
Housing Information
  University housing: Yes
  Percent living on campus: 10%

Greek System
  Fraternity: Yes
  Sorority: Yes
Athletics: Intramural

KENT STATE UNIVERSITY

161 Michael Schwartz Center, Kent, OH 44242-0001
Phone: 330-672-2444 • Fax: 330-672-2499
E-mail: admissions@kent.edu • Web: www.kent.edu
Support: CS • Institution type: 4-year public

PROGRAMS OR SERVICES FOR STUDENTS WITH LD

The goals and philosophy of the Student Accessibility Services (SAS) program are to promote student independence and self-advocacy at the college level. The university believes that the ability to do college work is highly correlated with grades in high school. Students with learning disabilities who receive accommodations in high school and who are academically successful are most likely to be successful at KSU. Students should meet with an SAS staff member approximately 6 months before enrollment to discuss needs and accommodations.

ADMISSION INFORMATION FOR STUDENTS WITH LD/ADHD

College entrance tests required: Yes
Interview required: Yes
Essay recommended: No
What documentation required for LD: Psycho Ed evaluation to include: relevant historical info, instructional interventions, related services, age diagnosed, objective data (aptitude, achievement, info processing), test scores (standard, percentile and grade equivalents) and describe functional limitations.
With general application: No
To receive services after enrolling: Yes
What documentation required for ADHD: Diagnosis based on DSM-V; history of behaviors impairing functioning in academic setting; diagnostic interview; history of symptoms; evidence of ongoing behaviors.

With general application: No
Submitted to: Student Accessibility Services
Special Ed. HS course work accepted: No
Specific course requirements of all applicants: NR
Separate application required: No
# of LD applications submitted each year: NR
# of LD applications accepted yearly: NR
Total # of students receiving LD services: NR
Acceptance into program means acceptance into college: Students must be admitted to and enrolled in the university prior to receiving services.

ADMISSIONS

Students with LD must meet the same admission criteria as all other applicants. There is no special admissions procedure for students with LD. Documentation of the student's disability is required. In addition to having completed standard college preparatory courses, applicants should be able to type or use a computer and a calculator and have skills in performing addition, subtraction, multiplication, and division using natural numbers, integers, fractions, and decimals. Students should also have highly developed study skills based on their specific strengths. The students most likely to be admitted and succeed are those who have completed the recommended college preparatory curriculum in high school, who have achieved a cumulative high school grade point average of 2.6 or higher, and whose composite ACT score is 21 or better (combined SAT score of 980 in critical reading and math).

ADDITIONAL INFORMATION

It is recommended that all documentation be submitted prior to enrolling, although students are welcome to register with the office at any time during the academic year. All students with documentation of a learning disability may utilize the academic and counseling services, such as academic advising; developmental education courses for freshmen students with deficits in reading, writing, and math; individual and small group tutoring; support groups; and individual and group study skills help through the Academic Success Center. The peer mentoring program, through the Academic Success Center, matches a student with a personal study coach—someone who can help them acquire the skills and motivation necessary for academic success. Supplemental Instruction (SI) is a national program that offers peer-facilitated group study sessions for students enrolled in large, high-risk liberal arts and science courses. (High-risk courses are courses that have a D, F, or withdrawal rate of at least 30 percent.) The basic difference between SI and other tutoring services offered at the Academic Success Center is that SI leaders actually attend classes along with the students they are tutoring. Each SI leader has already taken the course and earned an A or a B. The writing tutoring program is designed to help all students strengthen their writing skills and develop gradually as independent writers. Writing sessions at the Academic Success Center are process oriented. Services and accommodations are available for undergraduate and graduate students (graduate students are not eligible for services from the Academic Success Center).

LEARNING DISABILITY PROGRAM OR SERVICES

Contact Information
Name of program or department: Student Accessibility Services
Telephone: 330-672-3391

LEARNING DISABILITY SERVICES

Accommodations are determined on an individual basis after a thorough review of appropriate, current documentation and an intake interview with the student. The accommodations requested must be supported through the documentation provided and must be logically linked to the current impact of the condition on academic functioning.

Allowed in exams	**Distraction-reduced environment:** Yes	**Added costs for services:** No
Calculator: Yes	**Tape recording in class:** Yes	**LD specialists:** Yes
Dictionary: Yes	**Electronic texts:** Yes	**Professional tutors:** 3
Computer: Yes	**Accommodations for students with**	**Peer tutors:** 50
Spellchecker: Yes	**ADHD:** Yes	**Max. hours/wk. for services:** 4
Extended test time: Yes	**Kurzweil Reader:** No	**How professors are notified of**
Scribes: Yes	**Other assistive technology:** Yes	**LD/ADHD:** By student
Proctors: Yes	**Priority registration:** Yes	
Oral exams: No		
Note-takers: Yes		

GENERAL ADMISSIONS INFORMATION

Office of Admission: 330-672-2444

ENTRANCE REQUIREMENTS

Academic units recommended: 4 English, 3 math, 3 science (2 science labs), 3 foreign language, 3 social studies, 1 art. High school diploma is required, and GED is accepted. The Writing component of the ACT is required. TOEFL required of all international applicants: minimum paper TOEFL 525, minimum computer TOEFL 197.

Application deadline: 5/1	**SAT Math middle 50% range:**	**Graduated top 10% of class:** 13%
Notification: Rolling	450–580	**Graduated top 25% of class:** 36%
Average GPA: 3.22	**SAT Critical Reading middle 50%**	**Graduated top 50% of class:** 71%
ACT Composite middle 50% range:	**range:** 440–570	
20–25	**SAT Writing middle 50% range:**	
	430–560	

COLLEGE GRADUATION REQUIREMENTS

Course waivers allowed: No
Course substitutions allowed: Possibly
In what course: Decisions are made by individual colleges, and they depend on the student's major.

ADDITIONAL INFORMATION

Environment: The university is a residential campus located on 1,200 acres 45 miles southeast of Cleveland.

Student Body	**Cost Information**	**Greek System**
Undergrad enrollment: 22,260	**In-state tuition:** $9,346	**Fraternity:** Yes
Women: 59%	**Out-of-state tuition:** $17,306	**Sorority:** Yes
Men: 41%	**Room & board:** $8,830	**Athletics:** Division I
Percent out-of-state: 11%	**Housing Information**	
	University housing: Yes	
	Percent living on campus: 29%	

MIAMI UNIVERSITY

301 South Campus Avenue, Oxford, OH 45056
Phone: 513-529-2531 • Fax: 513-529-1550
E-mail: admission@muohio.edu • Web: www.muohio.edu
Support: CS • Institution type: 4-year public

PROGRAMS OR SERVICES FOR STUDENTS WITH LD

The Learning Disabilities Services staff coordinates university and community resources to meet the academic and personal needs of students with LD; assist faculty in understanding the characteristics and needs of these students; and provide services on an individual basis to students with appropriate documentation. All students with LD or ADHD are ultimately responsible for their own academic adjustment. Appropriate services and accommodations are determined through a flexible, interactive process that involves the student and the coordinator and are arranged through dialogue with faculty and staff responsible for implementing many of these services or accommodations. Decisions about services and accommodations for students with LD are made on the basis of the disability documentation and the functional limitations caused by the disability, as well as the current needs of the student. Students with ADHD must meet with the LD coordinator to initiate services after discussing disability-related needs and providing documentation of the disability and its impact on learning.

ADMISSION INFORMATION FOR STUDENTS WITH LD/ADHD

College entrance tests required: Yes
Interview required: No
Essay recommended: No
Documentation required for LD: Psychoeducational evaluation
Documentation required for ADHD: Psychoeducational evaluation
Submitted to: Admission Office
Special Ed. HS course work accepted: NR

Specific course requirements of all applicants: NR
Separate application required: No
# of LD applications submitted each year: NR
# of LD applications accepted yearly: NR
Total # of students receiving LD services: NR
Acceptance into program means acceptance into college: Students must be admitted to and enrolled in the university first and then request services.

ADMISSIONS

Students with LD are admitted to Miami through the regular admission process; therefore, it is important to ensure that the information in the application accurately reflects a student's academic ability and potential. Students with academic deficiencies may still be qualified for admission. Students may choose to self-disclose LD or ADHD on their application, either through a personal essay or the extenuating circumstances statement. Also, students may voluntarily choose to submit other information that may help the Admission Office to understand their unique learning strengths and needs.

ADDITIONAL INFORMATION

Support services for students with LD include priority registration; classroom accommodations such as test modifications, extended exam times, and so on; liaison with faculty; campus advocacy; counseling; and career awareness. In addition, students with LD can utilize services through the Rinella Learning Center, which works with students encountering academic difficulties. Its tutorial assistance program provides peer tutors. The Bernard B. Rinella Jr. Learning Center has special services designed to help students experiencing academic problems. In meeting with a learning specialist, students' existing learning strategies will be assessed, and new effective strategies will be introduced. Topics of time management, note-taking, test-taking, writing, and organization will be covered. New study strategies will be reinforced through individual conferences with a learning specialist, peer mentoring, and/or tutoring.

LEARNING DISABILITY PROGRAM OR SERVICES

Contact Information
Name of program or department: Office of Disability Resources
 Telephone: 513-529-1541
 Fax: 513-529-8799

LEARNING DISABILITY SERVICES

Accommodations are decided upon an individual basis after a thorough review of appropriate, current documentation. The accommodations requested must be supported through the documentation provided and must be logically linked to the current impact of the condition on academic functioning.

Allowed in exams	**Distraction-reduced environment:** Yes	**Added costs for services:** No
Calculator: TBD	**Tape recording in class:** Yes	**LD specialists:** Yes
Dictionary: TBD	**Electronic texts:** Yes	**Professional tutors:** No
Computer: TBD	**Accommodations for students with**	**Peer tutors:** 100–220
Spellchecker: TBD	**ADHD:** Yes	**Max. hours/wk. for services:** TBD
Extended test time: Yes	**Kurzweil Reader:** Yes	**How professors are notified of**
Scribes: TBD	**Other assistive technology:** Yes	**LD/ADHD:** By student
Proctors: TBD	**Priority registration:** Yes	
Oral exams: TBD		
Note-takers: TBD		

GENERAL ADMISSIONS INFORMATION

Office of Admission: 513-529-2531

ENTRANCE REQUIREMENTS

Academic units recommended: 4 English, 3 math, 3 science, 2 foreign language, 3 social sciences, 1 fine arts. High school diploma is required, and GED is accepted. ACT or SAT required. TOEFL or IELTS required of all international applicants: minimum paper TOEFL 540–543, minimum computer TOEFL 207.

Application deadline: 2/1	**SAT Math middle 50% range:**	**Graduated top 10% of class:** 32%
Notification: 3/15	560–660	**Graduated top 25% of class:** 68%
Average GPA: 3.65	**SAT Critical Reading middle 50%**	**Graduated top 50% of class:** 95%
ACT Composite middle 50% range:	**range:** 530–620	
24–29	**SAT Writing middle 50% range:** NR	

COLLEGE GRADUATION REQUIREMENTS

Course waivers allowed: No
Course substitutions allowed: Yes
In what course: Foreign language and math only if it is determined not to be an essential component of the curriculum and/or major.

ADDITIONAL INFORMATION

Environment: The university is in a small town northwest of Cincinnati.

Student Body	**Cost Information**	**Greek System**
Undergrad enrollment: 14,872	In-state tuition: $12,625	Fraternity: Yes
Women: 52%	Out-of-state tuition: $27,797	Sorority: Yes
Men: 48%	Room & board: $10,640	Athletics: Division I
Percent out-of-state: 30%	**Housing Information**	
	University housing: Yes	
	Percent living on campus: 48%	

MUSKINGUM UNIVERSITY

163 Stormont Drive, New Concord, OH 43762
Phone: 614-826-8137 • Fax: 614-826-8100
E-mail: adminfo@muskingum.edu • Web: www.muskigum.edu
Support: SP • Institution type: 4-year private

PROGRAMS OR SERVICES FOR STUDENTS WITH LD

The PLUS Program provides college students who have learning disorders with the opportunity to reach their academic potential. The Program is built upon a proven model of Embedded Learning Strategies Instruction blended with a Learning Conversation approach. This model facilitates life-long learning, essential to success in college, work, and life pursuits. Through Learning Strategy Instruction, Learning Consultants assist students by providing systematic and explicit instruction in learning strategies that are embedded in course content. Learning strategy instruction areas include time and materials management, organization, test-taking, note-taking, reading, writing, memory and study skills, among others. Through Learning Conversations, Learning Consultants provide the context within which students may appreciate that they can succeed, recognize the factors that influence their success, develop a possibility perspective, improve self-confidence, and understand their unique learning profile and what it means for their learning. The success of students can be attributed in part to the highly qualified, professional adult Learning Consultants who engage students in academic support services. Students participating in the Full PLUS Program receive an average of one contact hour per week for each eligible course for an average total of 3-4 hours per week. Maintenance PLUS Program students receive one half hour of PLUS tutorial services per week for each eligible course. Both levels of service are provided with additional services, including a Primary Learning Consultant who acts as liaison to home, faculty, and others; guidance to promote favorable number of courses; optimal course selection and balanced course load; continuum of services to provide a range of individual support for short term needs.

ADMISSION INFORMATION FOR STUDENTS WITH LD/ADHD

College entrance tests required: Yes
Interview required: Yes
Essay recommended: Yes
Documentation required for LD: Yes
Documentation required for ADHD: Yes
Submitted to: PLUS Program
Special Ed. HS course work accepted: Yes

Specific course requirements of all applicants: Yes
Separate application required: No
# of LD applications submitted each year: Varies
# of LD applications accepted yearly: 60–70
Total # of students receiving LD services: 130–160
Acceptance into program means acceptance into college: Joint admission to Muskingham University and PLUS Program

ADMISSIONS
The PLUS Program reflects the university's commitment to the ultimate success of its students. Course and graduate requirements are not compromised for PLUS students. Each applicant is evaluated by a committee for the potential to complete degree requirements and succeed in the campus residential environment. Students should have a university preparatory curriculum. Generally 4 years of English, Algebra I and II, and Geometry; at least 2 years of science with lab and social sciences are recommended for admissions. To apply to the PLUS Program, an applicant should complete all materials required for regular admission to the University. In addition, PLUS applicants should submit a recent comprehensive evaluation, which includes aptitude testing, achievement testing, and a diagnostic summary. Admission to the university and the PLUS Program are based upon application materials and a personal interview. Rolling admissions apply. Due to the great demand for the PLUS Program services, early application is strongly advised.

ADDITIONAL INFORMATION
Muskingum University offers the First Step Transition Program, a two-week summer transition program to help bridge the gap between high school and university life.

LEARNING DISABILITY PROGRAM OR SERVICES

Contact Information
Name of program or department: PLUS Program, Center for Advancement of Learning
 Telephone: 740-826-8284
 Fax: 740-826-8285

LEARNING DISABILITY SERVICES

The Disability Education Office provides federally mandated accommodations to qualified students at no charge. Individuals seeking these services must self-identify and provide specific documentation to the DEO. Accommodations are provided at no charge and are coordinated with or without PLUS Program services.

Allowed in exams	**Distraction-reduced environment:** Yes	**Added costs for services:** Yes for
Calculator: Yes	**Tape recording in class:** Yes	PLUS Program
Dictionary: Yes	**Electronic texts:** Yes	**LD specialists:** Yes
Computer: Yes	**Accommodations for students with**	**Professional tutors:** Yes
Spellchecker: Yes	**ADHD:** Yes	**Peer tutors:** No
Extended test time: Yes	**Kurzweil Reader:** Yes	**Max. hours/wk. for services:** 3–4
Scribes: Yes	**Other assistive technology:** Yes	**How professors are notified of**
Proctors: Yes	**Priority registration:** Yes	**LD/ADHD:** NR
Oral exams: Yes		
Note-takers: Yes		

GENERAL ADMISSIONS INFORMATION

Office of Admission: 740-826-8137

ENTRANCE REQUIREMENTS
Academic units required: 4 English, 2 math, 2 science (1 science lab), 2 foreign language, 1 social studies, 2 history. **Academic units recommended:** 4 English, 3 math, 3 science (2 science labs), 2 foreign language, 1 social studies, 2 history. High school diploma is required, and GED is accepted. ACT with or without Writing component accepted.

Application deadline: Rolling	**SAT Math middle 50% range:**	**Graduated top 10% of class:** 25%
Notification: Rolling	440–580	**Graduated top 25% of class:** 45%
Average GPA: 3.20	**SAT Critical Reading middle 50%**	**Graduated top 50% of class:** 72%
ACT Composite middle 50% range:	**range:** 440–560	
19–25	**SAT Writing middle 50% range:**	
	420–530	

COLLEGE GRADUATION REQUIREMENTS

Course waivers allowed: No
Course substitutions allowed: No

ADDITIONAL INFORMATION

Environment: The college is located on 215 acres in a rural area 70 miles east of Columbus.

Student Body	**Cost Information**	**Greek System**
Undergrad enrollment: 1,749	**Tuition:** $21,962	**Fraternity:** Yes
Women: 52%	**Room & board:** $9,282	**Sorority:** Yes
Men: 48%	**Housing Information**	**Athletics:** Division III
Percent out-of-state: 9%	**University housing:** Yes	
	Percent living on campus: 70%	

NOTRE DAME COLLEGE

4545 College Road, South Euclid, OH 44121
Phone: 216-373-5355 • Fax: 216-373-5278
E-mail: admissions@ndc.edu • Web: NotreDameCollege.edu
Support: SP • Institution type: 4-year private

PROGRAMS OR SERVICES FOR STUDENTS WITH LD

The Mission of the Academic Support Center (ASC) is to provide quality educational opportunities and support services above and beyond those required by law to individuals with documented learning disabilities, a group that is traditionally under-served in postsecondary education. The mission of the Academic Support Center parallels the mission of Notre Dame College, which is to educate a diverse population in the liberal arts for personal, professional, and global responsibility. The services provided by the ASC are structured and comprehensive, thus enabling a student with a documented learning disability to succeed in college. Prior to being admitted to the Center, the student must meet the admission requirements of Notre Dame College. To participate in the ASC, the student must submit documentation of a learning disability. This documentation must include a psychoeducational evaluation that has been conducted within the past 3 years. Refer to Web link on documentation.

ADMISSION INFORMATION FOR STUDENTS WITH LD/ADHD

College entrance tests required: Yes
Interview required: No
Essay recommended: Yes
What documentation required for LD: Psycho Ed evaluation to include: relevant historical info, instructional interventions, related services, age diagnosed, objective data (aptitude, achievement, info processing), test scores (standard, percentile and grade equivalents) and describe functional limitations.
With general application: Yes if requested as part of Structured Program application
To receive services after enrolling: Yes
What documentation required for ADHD: Diagnosis based on DSM-V; history of behaviors impairing functioning in academic setting; diagnostic interview; history of symptoms; evidence of ongoing behaviors.

With general application: Yes if requested as part of Structured Program application
To receive services after enrolling: Yes
Submitted to: ASC
Special Ed. HS course work accepted: N/A
Specific course requirements of all applicants: NR
Separate application required: No
# of LD applications submitted each year: 175–200
# of LD applications accepted yearly: 60–70
Total # of students receiving LD services: 115
Acceptance into program means acceptance into college: Students must be admitted and enrolled prior to requesting services.

ADMISSIONS

In fulfilling its mission, Notre Dame College seeks to attract students of diverse religious, racial, educational, and socioeconomic backgrounds and those of various ages and personal experiences. Notre Dame College admits students who demonstrate potential for success in rigorous academic work. The credentials of each applicant are individually evaluated with consideration to a combination of academic record, entrance examination performance, and evidence of potential for success in college studies. The following distribution of courses is considered to be standard academic preparation: 4 units of English, 3 units of math (including Algebra I, Geometry, and Algebra II), 3 units of science with laboratory experience, 3 units of social studies, 2 units of a foreign language, and 1 unit of fine arts.

ADDITIONAL INFORMATION

Services offered through the Academic Support Center include a fall orientation program, support group meetings, individual tutoring geared to subject matter, individual tutoring sessions with a writing specialist, academic advising, training and use of adaptive equipment, workshops on study skills, workshops on organizational skills, accommodations based on documentation, summer programs, and books on tape. Additionally, the Dwyer Learning Center provides free educational support to all Notre Dame students to help them achieve academic success.

LEARNING DISABILITY PROGRAM OR SERVICES

Contact Information
Name of program or department: Academic Support Center for Students with Learning Differences
  Telephone: 216-373-5185
  Fax: 216-373-5287

LEARNING DISABILITY SERVICES

Accommodations are decided upon an individual basis after a thorough review of appropriate, current documentation. The accommodations requested must be supported through the documentation provided and must be logically linked to the current impact of the condition on academic functioning.

Allowed in exams	**Distraction-reduced environment:** Yes	**Added costs for services:** Yes
Calculator: Yes	**Tape recording in class:** Yes	**LD specialists:** Yes
Dictionary: Yes	**Electronic texts:** Yes	**Professional tutors:** 35–40
Computer: Yes	**Accommodations for students with**	**Peer tutors:** N/A
Spellchecker: Yes	**ADHD:** Yes	**Max. hours/wk. for services:** N/A
Extended test time: Yes	**Kurzweil Reader:** Yes	**How professors are notified of**
Scribes: Yes	**Other assistive technology:** Yes	**LD/ADHD:** By student
Proctors: Yes	**Priority registration:** Yes	
Oral exams: Yes		
Note-takers: Yes		

GENERAL ADMISSIONS INFORMATION

Office of Admission: 216-373-5176

ENTRANCE REQUIREMENTS

Academic units recommended: 4 English, 3 math, 3 science (3 science labs), 2 foreign language, 3 social studies, 1 fine arts. High school diploma is required, and GED is accepted. ACT with or without Writing component accepted. TOEFL required of all international applicants: minimum paper TOEFL 550, minimum computer TOEFL 213.

Application deadline: None	**SAT Math middle 50% range:**	**Graduated top 10% of class:** 4%
Notification: Rolling	420–550	**Graduated top 25% of class:** 22%
Average GPA: 3.18	**SAT Critical Reading middle 50%**	**Graduated top 50% of class:** 62%
ACT Composite middle 50% range:	**range:** 410–520	
17–22	**SAT Writing middle 50% range:** NR	

COLLEGE GRADUATION REQUIREMENTS

Course waivers allowed: Yes
In what course: To be determined on an individual basis
Course substitutions allowed: Yes
In what course: Logic may be substituted for math with proper documentation. NDC does not require a foreign language.

ADDITIONAL INFORMATION

Environment: Notre Dame College is located in South Euclid, Ohio, a suburb under 30 minutes east of downtown Cleveland, Ohio. The college sits on a wooded 53-acre campus.

Student Body	**Cost Information**	**Greek System**
Undergrad enrollment: 1,800	**Tuition:** $24,652	**Fraternity:** No
Women: 45%	**Room & board:** $8,054	**Sorority:** No
Men: 55%	**Housing Information**	**Athletics:** NCAA II
Percent out-of-state: 15%	**University housing:** Yes	
	Percent living on campus: 48%	

OBERLIN COLLEGE

101 North Professor Street, Oberlin College, Oberlin, OH 44074
Phone: 440-775-8411 • Fax: 440-775-6905
E-mail: college.admissions@oberlin.edu • Web: www.oberlin.edu
Support: CS • Institution type: 4-year private

PROGRAMS OR SERVICES FOR STUDENTS WITH LD

Personnel from the Office of Services for Students with Disabilities (OSSD) provide services, as well as coordinate accommodations, to meet the needs of students who have disabilities. Their goal is to maximize the student's entire educational potential while helping him or her develop and maintain independence. The program philosophy is one that encourages self-advocacy. Students who are diagnosed by OSSD personnel as having LD, as well as those who can provide documentation of a current diagnosis of LD, are eligible for services. To verify a previously diagnosed LD, a student must provide a psychological assessment, educational test results, and a recent copy of an IEP that specifies placement in a learning disabilities program. These documents will be reviewed by personnel from OSSD to determine eligibility. Students requesting services are interviewed by a learning disability counselor before a service plan is developed or initiated.

ADMISSION INFORMATION FOR STUDENTS WITH LD/ADHD

College entrance tests required: Yes
Interview required: No
Essay recommended: No
What documentation required for LD: Psycho Ed evaluation to include: relevant historical info, instructional interventions, related services, age diagnosed, objective data (aptitude, achievement, info processing), test scores (standard, percentile and grade equivalents) and describe functional limitations.
With general application: No
To receive services after enrolling: Yes
What documentation required for ADHD: Diagnosis based on DSM-V; history of behaviors impairing functioning in academic setting; diagnostic interview; history of symptoms; evidence of ongoing behaviors.

With general application: No
Submitted to: SSD
Special Ed. HS course work accepted: Yes
Specific course requirements of all applicants: Yes
Separate application required: No
# of LD applications submitted each year: NR
# of LD applications accepted yearly: NR
Total # of students receiving LD services: 200
Acceptance into program means acceptance into college: Students must be admitted to and enrolled in the university first and then request services.

ADMISSIONS

There is no special admissions procedure for students with LD. All applicants must meet the same admission requirements. Courses required include 4 years of English and math and at least 3 years of social science and science. The average GPA is typically a B average or better. ACT scores range between 25 and 30; SAT Reasoning test scores range between 1100 and 1320, and SAT Subject Test scores range between 560 and 680 on each Subject Test. Students who self-disclose and provide documentation may have their files read by OSSD personnel, who will provide a recommendation to the Office of Admissions. Students who can provide valid and recent documentation of a psychoeducational diagnosis of LD may receive services.

ADDITIONAL INFORMATION

A Learning Resource Center and an Adaptive Technology Center are available for all students. Skills classes are offered for college credit in reading, study skills, and writing. OSSD can arrange one or all of the following services for students with learning disabilities: quiet space for exams; extended examination times, up to twice the time typically allotted, based on diagnosis; oral exams; scribes; individual academic, personal, and vocational counseling; computer resources for additional academic skill development and assistance; alternate text; priority academic scheduling; peer tutoring; new student orientation assistance; and faculty/staff consultation. In addition, OSSD can provide information about other support services sponsored by the college.

LEARNING DISABILITY PROGRAM OR SERVICES

Contact Information
Name of program or department: Office of Disability Services
 Telephone: 440-775-8464
 Fax: 440-775-5589

LEARNING DISABILITY SERVICES

Accommodations are decided upon an individual basis after a thorough review of appropriate, current documentation. The accommodations requested must be supported through the documentation provided and must be logically linked to the current impact of the condition on academic functioning.

Allowed in exams
 Calculator: Yes
 Dictionary: Yes
 Computer: Yes
 Spellchecker: Yes
Extended test time: Yes
Scribes: Yes
Proctors: Yes
Oral exams: Yes
Note-takers: Yes

Distraction-reduced environment: Yes
Tape recording in class: Yes
Electronic texts: Yes
Accommodations for students with
 ADHD: Yes
Kurzweil Reader: Yes
Other assistive technology: Yes
Priority registration: Yes

Added costs for services: No
LD specialists: Yes
Professional tutors: No
Peer tutors: 38
Max. hours/wk. for services:
 Unlimited
How professors are notified of
 LD/ADHD: By both student and
 director

GENERAL ADMISSIONS INFORMATION

Office of Admission: 440-775-8411

ENTRANCE REQUIREMENTS

Academic units required: 4 English, 4 math, 3 science, 3 foreign language, 3 social studies. High school diploma is required, and GED is accepted. ACT with Writing component required. TOEFL required of all international applicants: minimum paper TOEFL 600, minimum computer TOEFL 200.

Application deadline: 1/15
Notification: 4/1
Average GPA: 3.61
ACT Composite middle 50% range:
 NR

SAT Math middle 50% range: NR
SAT Critical Reading middle 50%
 range: NR
SAT Writing middle 50% range:
 640–730

Graduated top 10% of class: 68%
Graduated top 25% of class: 90%
Graduated top 50% of class: 100%

COLLEGE GRADUATION REQUIREMENTS

Course waivers allowed: No
Course substitutions allowed: Yes
In what course: Case-by-case

ADDITIONAL INFORMATION

Environment: The college is located on 440 acres in a small town 35 miles southwest of Cleveland.

Student Body
 Undergrad enrollment: 2,959
 Women: 55%
 Men: 45%
 Percent out-of-state: 92%

Cost Information
 Tuition: $42,842
 Room & board: $11,550
Housing Information
 University housing: Yes
 Percent living on campus: 88%

Greek System
 Fraternity: No
 Sorority: No
Athletics: Division III

THE OHIO STATE UNIVERSITY—COLUMBUS

Undergraduate Admissions 110 Enarson Hall, 154 W. 12th Avenue,
Columbus, OH 43210 • Phone: 614-292-3980 • Fax: 614-292-4818
E-mail: askabuckeye@osu.edu • Web: www.osu.edu
Support: S • Institution: 4-year public

PROGRAMS OR SERVICES FOR STUDENTS WITH LD

The Office for Disability Services (ODS) at Ohio State University offers a variety of services for students with documented disabilities, including learning disabilities, hearing or visual impairments, attention deficit disorders, and psychiatric or medical disabilities. The mission of ODS is to provide and coordinate support services and programs that enable students with disabilities to maximize their educational potential. ODS serves as a resource to all members of the university community so that students with disabilities can freely and actively participate in all facets of university life.

ADMISSION INFORMATION FOR STUDENTS WITH LD/ADHD

College entrance tests required: Yes
Interview required: No
Essay required: N/A
What documentation required for LD: Psycho Ed evaluation to include: relevant historical info, instructional interventions, related services, age diagnosed, objective data (aptitude, achievement, info processing), test scores (standard, percentile and grade equivalents) and describe functional limitations.
With general application: No
To receive services after enrolling: Yes
What documentation required for ADHD: Diagnosis based on DSM-V; history of behaviors impairing functioning in academic setting; diagnostic interview; history of symptoms; evidence of ongoing behaviors.

With general application: No
Submitted to: Support Program/Services
Special Ed. HS course work accepted: No
Specific course requirements for all applicants: Yes
Separate application required for program services: No
# of LD applications submitted each year: NR
# of LD applications accepted yearly: NR
Total # of students receiving LD services: 278
Acceptance into program means acceptance into college:

ADMISSIONS

A variety of staff members provide different functions. Some of the functions include: assistive technology, counseling, testing accommodations and scribes/readers. All eligible students are assigned to a disability counselor who coordinates services and accommodations. The counselor collaborates on issues such as learning strategies, advocacy, and transition issues.

ADMISSIONS

Students with LD are admitted under the same criteria as regular applicants. However, consideration can be given to students with LD with support from ODS in instances where the student's rank, GPA, or lack of courses, such as foreign language, have affected performance in high school. Applicants interested in services should submit a general application for admission; complete the section under optional personal statement that gives students the opportunity to provide information if they feel that their high school performance was adversely affected by special circumstances; and submit documentation of the disability to ODS, including the latest IEP and the results of the last psychoeducational testing. In some cases, ODS will be asked to consider supporting an appeal of an admissions decision. ODS will review the application, look at course work and deficiencies, review services received in high school and determine if the student's needs can be met at OSU if the student is not normally admissible, look at when a diagnosis was made and at the IEP, and make a recommendation to the Admissions Office. Students exceeding the minimum curriculum in math, natural resources, or foreign language will be given additional consideration. Other factors considered include the competitiveness of the high school, accelerated courses taken, if the applicant is a first-generation college student, or the student's cultural, economic, racial, or geographic diversity; outstanding talents; extracurricular activities; significant work experiences; or leadership positions.

PROGRAM FOR DISABILITY SERVICES

Contact Information
Name of program or department: Office for Disability Services (ODS)
  Telephone: 614-292-3307
  Fax: 614-292-4190

LEARNING DISABILITY SERVICES

Accommodations are decided upon an individual basis after a thorough review of appropriate, current documentation. The accommodations requested must be supported through the documentation provided and must be logically linked to the current impact of the condition on academic functioning.

Allowed in exams
  Calculator: Yes
  Dictionary: Yes
  Computer: Yes
  Spellchecker: Yes
Extended test time: Yes
Scribes: Yes
Proctors: Yes
Oral exams: No
Note-takers: Yes

Distraction-reduced environment: Yes
Tape recording in class: Yes
Electronic texts: Yes
Accommodations for students with ADHD: Yes
Kurzweil Reader: No
Other assistive technology: Open Book, Zoomtext, JAWS, Read and Write Gold, Kurweil, voice recognition software (Dragon, Smart Nav)
Priority registration: Yes

Added costs for services: No
LD specialists: Yes
Professional tutors: No
Peer tutors: Yes
Max. hours/wk. for services: N/A
How professors are notified of LD/ADHD: Student

GENERAL ADMISSIONS INFORMATION

Office of Admission: 614-247-6281

ENTRANCE REQUIREMENTS
Academic units required: 4 English, 3 mathematics, 2 science, (2 science labs), 2 foreign language, 2 social studies, 1 visual/performing arts, 1 academic electives. **Academic units recommended:** 4 English, 4 mathematics, 3 science, (3 science labs), 3 foreign language, 3 social studies, 1 visual/performing arts, 1 academic electives. High school diploma is required and GED is accepted. SAT or ACT required; ACT with Writing component required. TOEFL required of all international applicants; minimum paper TOEFL 527, minimum computer TOEFL 197, minimum web-based TOEFL 71.

Application deadline: 2/1
Notification: Rolling
Average GPA: NR
ACT Composite middle 50% range: 26–30

SAT Math middle 50% range: 600–700
SAT Critical Reading middle 50% range: 540–660
SAT Writing middle 50% range: 550–650

Graduated top 10% of class: 55%
Graduated top 25% of class: 89%
Graduated top 50% of class: 99%

COLLEGE GRADUATION REQUIREMENTS

Course substitutions allowed: Yes
In what course: On a case-by-case basis and with appropriate supporting disability documentation, some students can petition for a substitution of the foreign language if it is not essential for the major. Math substitutions are rare.

ADDITIONAL INFORMATION

Environment: The campus is in and urban area four miles from downtown Columbus.

Student Body
  Undergrad enrollment: 42,196
  Women: 46%
  Men: 54%
  Percent out-of-state: 12%

Cost Information
  In-state tuition: $9,735
  Out-of-state tuition: $24,759
  Room & board: $10,215
Housing Information
  University housing: Yes
  Percent living on campus: 23%

Greek System
  Fraternity: Yes
  Sorority: Yes
Athletics: Division I

OHIO UNIVERSITY

120 Chubb Hall, Athens, OH 45701
Phone: 740-593-4100 • Fax: 740-593-0560
E-mail: admissions@ohio.edu • Web: www.ohio.edu
Support: S • Institution type: 4-year public

PROGRAMS OR SERVICES FOR STUDENTS WITH LD

The Office of Disability Services facilitates requests for accommodations in accordance with the Americans with Disabilities Act and Section 504 of the Rehabilitation Act. Each student who provides documentation of disability and makes request for accommodation will be assigned a Disability Services Advisor. It is the role of the DS Advisor to assist the student in transition to college through determination of reasonable accommodations, referral to pertinent resources to support student success, assist students in developing self-advocacy skills, and to serve as a central point of contact for navigating the college experience. DS Advisors are available and willing to meet upon a student's request; however progress is not formally monitored by the Office. There is not a separate support program to which a student applies for admission; rather all admitted students with a disability may request accommodation through the Office of Disability Services.

ADMISSION INFORMATION FOR STUDENTS WITH LD/ADHD

College entrance tests required: N/A
Interview required: N/A
Essay recommended: N/A
What documentation required for LD: Psycho Ed evaluation to include: relevant historical info, instructional interventions, related services, age diagnosed, objective data (aptitude, achievement, info processing), test scores (standard, percentile and grade equivalents) and describe functional limitations.
With general application: No
To receive services after enrolling: Yes
What documentation required for ADHD: Diagnosis based on DSM-V; history of behaviors impairing functioning in academic setting; diagnostic interview; history of symptoms; evidence of ongoing behaviors.

With general application: No
Submitted to: Disability Student Services
Special Ed. HS course work accepted: Yes
Specific course requirements of all applicants: Yes
Separate application required: No
# of LD applications submitted each year: N/A
# of LD applications accepted yearly: N/A
Total # of students receiving LD services: NR
Acceptance into program means acceptance into college: N/A

ADMISSIONS

Applicants with learning disabilities are expected to meet the same admission criteria as all other applicants. General admission requires applicants to be in the top 30 percent of their class with 21 ACT or 990 SAT, or top 50 percent with 23 ACT or 1060 SAT. The mid 50 percent range for the ACT is 22–26, and for the SAT it is 1030–1200. Students taking the ACT must submit the optional Writing section. Course requirements include 4 years of English, 3 years of science and social studies, 3 years of math, and 2 years of a foreign language. Students can be admitted with deficiencies. Applicants with learning disabilities who meet the criteria should send documentation to special services after admission. Those students not meeting the admission criteria are encouraged to self-disclose by writing a narrative explaining the impact of the disability condition on their academic career as well as sending relevant documentation. This disclosure and accompanying documentation will be reviewed by admissions. Students, in general, must demonstrate the ability to perform in a mainstream academic setting where support is available when needed. Counselor recommendations are very helpful for students who do not meet the traditional criteria.

ADDITIONAL INFORMATION

Accommodations through the Office of Disability Services are provided in accordance with the Americans with Disabilities Act and Section 504 of the Rehabilitation Act and are not part of a distinct support program. General services provided include advising referrals, academic adjustments and classroom accommodations, priority scheduling, free tutoring (as available) through the Academic Advancement Center (4 hours per course per week), and tutoring in writing and reading skills. Skills classes are offered in learning strategies, college reading skills, reading, speed, and vocabulary. Accommodations are available to undergraduate and graduate students.

LEARNING DISABILITY PROGRAM OR SERVICES

Contact Information
Name of program or department: Office for Institutional Equity/Disability Student Services
 Telephone: 740-593-2620
 Fax: 740-593-0790

LEARNING DISABILITY SERVICES

Accommodations are decided upon an individual basis after a thorough review of appropriate, current documentation. The accommodations requested must be supported through the documentation provided and must be logically linked to the current impact of the condition on academic functioning.

Allowed in exams
 Calculator: Yes
 Dictionary: Yes
 Computer: Yes
 Spellchecker: Yes
Extended test time: Yes
Scribes: Yes
Proctors: No
Oral exams: Yes
Note-takers: No

Distraction-reduced environment: Yes
Tape recording in class: Yes
Electronic texts: Yes
**Accommodations for students with
 ADHD:** Yes
Kurzweil Reader: Yes
Other assistive technology: Yes
Priority registration: Yes

Added costs for services: No
LD specialists: No
Professional tutors: No
Peer tutors: Yes
Max. hours/wk. for services: N/A
**How professors are notified of
 LD/ADHD:** By student

GENERAL ADMISSIONS INFORMATION

Office of Admission: 740-593-4100

ENTRANCE REQUIREMENTS

Academic units required: 4 English, 3 math, 3 science, 2 foreign language, 3 social studies, 1 visual/performing arts. High school diploma is required, and GED is accepted. ACT with Writing component recommended.

Application deadline: 2/1
Notification: Rolling
Average GPA: 3.33
ACT Composite middle 50% range:
 21–26

SAT Math middle 50% range:
 480–590
**SAT Critical Reading middle 50%
 range:** 480–600
SAT Writing middle 50% range:
 470–570

Graduated top 10% of class: 15%
Graduated top 25% of class: 39%
Graduated top 50% of class: 77%

COLLEGE GRADUATION REQUIREMENTS

Course waivers allowed: No
Course substitutions allowed: Yes
In what course: Any substitution would be specific to each individual and his or her learning disability. This is not done as a general rule.

ADDITIONAL INFORMATION

Environment: The university is in a small town southeast of Columbia, Ohio.

Student Body
 Undergrad enrollment: 21,936
 Women: 58%
 Men: 42%
 Percent out-of-state: 14%

Cost Information
 In-state tuition: $9,936
 Out-of-state tuition: $18,900
 Room & board: $9,753
Housing Information
 University housing: Yes
 Percent living on campus: 44%

Greek System
 Fraternity: Yes
 Sorority: Yes
Athletics: Division I

UNIVERSITY OF CINCINNATI

PO Box 210091, Cincinnati, OH 45221-0091
Phone: 513-556-1100 • Fax: 513-556-1105
E-mail: admissions@uc.edu • Web: www.uc.edu
Support: CS • Institution: 4-year public

PROGRAMS OR SERVICES FOR STUDENTS WITH LD

The University of Cincinnati does not have a specific or separate learning disability program. However, students with learning disabilities who use academic accommodations and support services available through the Disability Services and other resources of the university find they can be successful in achieving their academic objectives. The goal of Disability Services is to provide the necessary accommodations to students in order for them to become successful and independent learners. Remedial/ developmental courses are available along with campus-wide tutoring. To receive support services, students must submit documentation from a licensed professional to the Disability Services Office (DSO). DSO staff will work with students and faculty to accommodate special needs.

ADMISSION INFORMATION FOR STUDENTS WITH LD/ADHD

College entrance tests required: Yes
Interview required: N/A
Essay required: N/A
What documentation required for LD: Psycho Ed evaluation to include: relevant historical info, instructional interventions, related services, age diagnosed, objective data (aptitude, achievement, info processing), test scores (standard, percentile and grade equivalents) and describe functional limitations.
With general application: No
To receive services after enrolling: Yes
What documentation required for ADHD: Diagnosis based on DSM-V; history of behaviors impairing functioning in academic setting; diagnostic interview; history of symptoms; evidence of ongoing behaviors.

With general application: No
Submitted to: Disability Services Office
Special Ed. HS course work accepted: Yes
Specific course requirements for all applicants: Yes
Separate application required for program services: N/A
# of LD applications submitted each year: NR
# of LD applications accepted yearly: NR
Total # of students receiving LD services: NR
Acceptance into program means acceptance into college: No

ADMISSIONS

There is no special admission procedure for students with learning disabilities. All students submit the university's general application form. Requests for substitutions/waivers of admission requirements should be made to the admissions office. The University of Cincinnati expects all baccalaureate students to have completed the following articulation requirements: four units of college-prep English, three units of college-prep math, two units of science, two units of social science, two units of a single foreign language, one unit of fine arts, two additional units of any of these. ACT/SAT scores are also required for baccalaureate programs. Branch campuses require a high school diploma or GED for admission. ACT/SAT scores are recommended but not required.

ADDITIONAL INFORMATION

Disabilities Services provides support services and accommodations including but not limited to: note-taking, tutors, readers, taped textbooks, testing accommodations, scribes, loan of equipment, and library disability services. Peer tutoring is available to all students at no cost. Students with appropriate documentation may request course substitutions in math or foreign language. Skill development classes are offered for all students in areas such as time management, organizational skills, and study skills. Developmental courses are also available on the branch campuses.

PROGRAM FOR DISABILITY SERVICES

Contact Information
Name of program or department: Disability Services
  Telephone: 513-556-6823
  Fax: 513-556-1383

LEARNING DISABILITY SERVICES

Accommodations are decided upon an individual basis after a thorough review of appropriate, current documentation. The accommodations requested must be supported through the documentation provided and must be logically linked to the current impact of the condition on academic functioning.

Allowed in exams
  Calculator: Yes
  Dictionary: Yes
  Computer: Yes
  Spellchecker: Yes
Extended test time: Yes
Scribes: Yes
Proctors: Yes
Oral exams: Yes
Note-takers: Yes

Distraction-reduced environment: Yes
Tape recording in class: Yes
Electronic texts: Yes
Accommodations for students with ADHD: Yes
Kurzweil Reader: Yes
Other assistive technology: voice activated software, screen reader software
Priority registration: Yes

Added costs for services: No
LD specialists: No
Professional tutors: No
Peer tutors: 15–25
Max. hours/wk. for services: Unlimited
How professors are notified of LD/ADHD: Student

GENERAL ADMISSIONS INFORMATION

Office of Admission: 513-556-1100

ENTRANCE REQUIREMENTS
Academic units required: 4 English, 3 mathematics, 2 science, 2 foreign language, 2 social studies, 2 academic electives. **Academic units recommended:** 4 mathematics, 3 science, 1 history. High school diploma is required and GED is accepted. SAT or ACT required; ACT with Writing component required. TOEFL required of all international applicants; minimum paper TOEFL 515.

Application deadline: 12/1 for scholarship consideration
Notification: Rolling
Average GPA: 3.4
ACT Composite middle 50% range: 22–27

SAT Math middle 50% range: 520–640
SAT Critical Reading middle 50% range: 500–610
SAT Writing middle 50% range: 490–600

Graduated top 10% of class: 22%
Graduated top 25% of class: 50%
Graduated top 50% of class: 65%

COLLEGE GRADUATION REQUIREMENTS

Course waivers allowed: No
Course substitutions allowed: Yes
In what course: math, foreign lanuage

ADDITIONAL INFORMATION

Environment: The university is located on 392 acres in downtown Cincinnati.

Student Body
  Undergrad enrollment: 22,893
  Women: 51%
  Men: 49%
  Percent out-of-state: 9.4%

Cost Information
  In-state tuition: $10,419
  Out-of-state tuition: $24,942
  Room and board: $9,780
Housing Information
  University housing: Yes
  Percent living on campus: 20%

Greek System
  Fraternity: Yes
  Sorority: Yes
Athletics: Division I

UNIVERSITY OF DAYTON

300 College Park, Dayton, OH 45469-1300
Phone: 937-229-4411 • Fax: 937-229-4729
E-mail: admission@udayton.edu • Web: www.udayton.edu
Support: CS • Institution: 4-year private

PROGRAMS OR SERVICES FOR STUDENTS WITH LD

The University of Dayton is: one of the nation's ten largest Catholic universities and Ohio's largest private university, with undergraduate and graduate programs; a university founded in 1850 by the Society of Mary (Marianists), a Roman Catholic teaching order of priests and brothers; a residential learning community with more than 70 academic programs in arts and sciences, business administration, education and allied professions, engineering and law; a diverse community committed to educating the whole person and to linking learning and scholarship with leadership and service; a vibrant living-learning environment, where modern campus housing blurs the line between living and learning.

ADMISSION INFORMATION FOR STUDENTS WITH LD/ADHD

College entrance tests required: Yes
Interview required: No
Essay required: N/A
What documentation required for LD: Psycho Ed evaluation to include: relevant historical info, instructional interventions, related services, age diagnosed, objective data (aptitude, achievement, info processing), test scores (standard, percentile and grade equivalents) and describe functional limitations.
With general application: No
To receive services after enrolling: Yes
What documentation required for ADHD: Diagnosis based on DSM-V; history of behaviors impairing functioning in academic setting; diagnostic interview; history of symptoms; evidence of ongoing behaviors.

With general application: No
Submitted to: Support Program/Services
Special Ed. HS course work accepted: N/A
Specific course requirements for all applicants: Yes
Separate application required for program services: No
# of LD applications submitted each year: NR
# of LD applications accepted yearly: NR
Total # of students receiving LD services: NR
Acceptance into program means acceptance into college: Students must be admitted and enrolled prior to requesting services.

ADMISSIONS

Applications for admission are reviewed for specific academic majors or, when applicable, for undeclared status in an academic division. Five factors are considered when we assess your preparation for a chosen field of study: your selection of courses in preparation for college, your grade record and pattern throughout high school, your class standing or ranking, results of either the SAT or ACT, and your character and record of leadership and service. Balanced consideration is given to all aspects of your college-preparation. While no minimum grade point average, class rank, or standardized test score is specified, these measures must provide evidence of your readiness for college studies in your chosen academic program.

ADDITIONAL INFORMATION

Because the university recognizes that students have individually unique academic and personal strengths and weaknesses, the Office of Learning Resources (OLR) provides support services to students such as drop-in tutoring (peer-facilitated), with additional support models (Supplemental Instruction) linked to specific classes, and writing support across the curriculum. All OLR support services are provided free of charge. OLR services are most effective if the student takes advantage of them before he or she falls too far behind or receives too many low grades. Every individual student with a disability is guaranteed equal access to all educational programs and services at the University of Dayton. OLR serves qualified students with disabilities after they have been accepted to the University of Dayton and registered with OLR. Students with disabilities must submit appropriate, current documentation of their disability (see website for specific requirements) and participate in the interactive process. There is no obligation for any student to identify a disability; however, students who wish to receive reasonable accommodations must submit proper documentation, participate in an interactive assessment interview with the OLR Disabilities Staff, request in writing the need for specific services following established published guidelines and deadlines. The Ryan C. Harris Adaptive Learning Lab is specifically designed with assistive technology for students with various physical and cognitive disabilities. Staff members provide technical assistance and proctored testing.

PROGRAM FOR DISABILITY SERVICES

Contact Information
Name of program or department: Office of Learning Resources
  Telephone: 937-229-2066
  Fax: 937-229-3270

LEARNING DISABILITY SERVICES

Accommodations are decided upon an individual basis after a thorough review of appropriate, current documentation and participation in an interactive assessment interview with the OLR Disabilities Staff. The accommodations requested must be supported and logically linked to the current impact of the student's condition in an academic and/or residential setting.

Allowed in exams	**Distraction-reduced environment:** Yes	**Added costs for services:** No
Calculator: Yes	**Tape recording in class:** Yes	**LD specialists:** Yes
Dictionary: Yes	**Electronic texts:** Yes	**Professional tutors:** No
Computer: Yes	**Accommodations for students with**	**Peer tutors:** Yes
Spellchecker: Yes	**ADHD:** Yes	**Max. hours/wk. for services:** Varies
Extended test time: Yes	**Kurzweil Reader:** No	**How professors are notified of**
Scribes: Yes	**Other assistive technology:** Yes	**LD/ADHD:** Student
Proctors: Yes	**Priority registration:** Yes	
Oral exams: Yes		
Note-takers: Yes		

GENERAL ADMISSIONS INFORMATION

Office of Admission: 937-229-4411

ENTRANCE REQUIREMENTS
Academic units required: 2 units of foreign language are required for admission to the College of Arts and Sciences.
Academic units recommended: 4 English, 3 mathematics, 2 science, (1 science labs), 3 social studies, 4 academic electives. High school diploma is required and GED is accepted. SAT or ACT required; TOEFL required of all international applicants; minimum paper TOEFL 523, minimum computer TOEFL 193, minimum web-based TOEFL 70.

Application deadline: None	**SAT Math middle 50% range:**	**Graduated top 10% of class:** 26%
Notification: Rolling	520–640	**Graduated top 25% of class:** 56%
Average GPA: 3.6	**SAT Critical Reading middle 50%**	**Graduated top 50% of class:** 88%
ACT Composite middle 50% range:	range: 510–610	
24–29	**SAT Writing middle 50% range:**	
	510–610	

COLLEGE GRADUATION REQUIREMENTS

Course waivers allowed: No
In what course: Each student's request would be reviewed on a case-by-case basis to discuss a course substitution, if applicable.
Course substitutions allowed: Yes
In what course: Each student's request would be reviewed on a case-by-case basisto discuss a course substitution, if applicable.

ADDITIONAL INFORMATION

Environment: The university of Dayton is an urban campus in Dayton, Ohio.

Student Body	**Cost Information**	**Greek System**
Undergrad enrollment: 7,843	Tuition: $31,640	Fraternity: Yes
Women: 49%	Room & board: $9,950	Sorority: Yes
Men: 51%	**Housing Information**	Athletics: Division I
Percent out-of-state: 41%	University housing: Yes	
	Percent living on campus: 73%	

UNIVERSITY OF TOLEDO

2801 West Bancroft, Toledo, OH 43606
Phone: 419-530-8888
E-mail: enroll@utoledo.edu • Web: www.utoledo.edu
Support: S • Institution type: 4-year public

PROGRAMS OR SERVICES FOR STUDENTS WITH LD

The Office of Accessibility at The University of Toledo is governed by Section 504 of the Rehabilitation Act of 1973 (non-discrimination) and Americans with Disabilities Act (equal access) and works with faculty and staff to offer academic accommodations to students with documented disabilities as defined by ADA. Accommodations are determined through an interactive interview process and on a case by case basis. Accommodations may include: access to adaptive computer software and instruction, advocacy and support, electronic textbooks, testing services, assistance accessing class notes, special housing eligibility, and third party scholarship opportunities.

ADMISSION INFORMATION FOR STUDENTS WITH LD/ADHD

College entrance tests required: Yes
Interview required: No
Essay recommended: No
What documentation required for LD: Psycho Ed evaluation to include: relevant historical info, instructional interventions, related services, age diagnosed, objective data (aptitude, achievement, info processing), test scores (standard, percentile and grade equivalents) and describe functional limitations.
With general application: No
To receive services after enrolling: Yes
What documentation required for ADHD: Diagnosis based on DSM-V; history of behaviors impairing functioning in academic setting; diagnostic interview; history of symptoms; evidence of ongoing behaviors.

With general application: No
Submitted to: Office of Accessibility
Special Ed. HS course work accepted: Yes
Specific course requirements of all applicants: Yes
Separate application required: No
# of LD applications submitted each year: NR
# of LD applications accepted yearly: Unlimited
Total # of students receiving LD services: NR
Acceptance into program means acceptance into college: Students must be admitted to and enrolled in the university. After receipt of documentation, those found eligible must complete an intake appointment prior to requesting academic accommodation.

ADMISSIONS

There is no separate admissions process for students with learning disabilities. All students must meet the same admission criteria. In-State: All students are required to submit an ACT or SAT score. Requirements vary by college. Also required: 4 years of English, 3 years of social science, 3 years of natural science, and 3 years of math. Students not admitted into their desired program will be admitted into the Gateway Transition program. Out-Of-State: GPA of 2.0 and 21 ACT/ 990 SAT. If these requirements are not met, students can appeal and will be reviewed on an individual basis. GED scores are accepted when students must submit an official copy of their GED certificate.

ADDITIONAL INFORMATION

Students are accepted into the Office of Accessibility once they are admitted to the University and provide appropriate disability documentation and have completed their intake appointment. The following academic accommodations are provided if supported by documentation: e-text, extension of time for quizzes, tests and exams, test proctors to help with reading or/and writing; note-taking; secondary academic advising, Faculty Advocacy/Notification memos; liaison with students and professors; priority registration; scholarship opportunities; and adaptive technology.

LEARNING DISABILITY PROGRAM OR SERVICES

Contact Information
Name of program or department: Office of Accessibility
  Telephone: 419-530-4981
  Fax: 419-530-6137

LEARNING DISABILITY SERVICES

Academic accommodations are decided upon through an interactive process. Accommodations are provided on an individual basis after a thorough review of appropriate, current documentation and an interview intake appointment with an Accessibility Specialist. The accommodations requested must be supported by the documentation provided and must be logically linked to the current impact of the condition on academic functioning.

Allowed in exams
  Calculator: Yes
  Dictionary: Yes
  Computer: Yes
  Spellchecker: Yes
Extended test time: Yes
Scribes: Yes
Proctors: Yes
Oral exams: Yes
Note-takers: Yes
Distraction-reduced environment: Yes

Tape recording in class: Yes
Electronic texts: No
Accommodations for students with
  ADHD: Yes
Kurzweil Reader: No
Other assistive technology: Yes
Priority registration: Yes
Added costs for services: No
LD specialists: No

Professional tutors: No. Tutoring offered through other campus resources.
Peer tutors: No. Tutoting offered through other campus resources.
Max. hours/wk. for services: Unlimited
How professors are notified of LD/ADHD: Faculty Advocacy/Notification Memos

GENERAL ADMISSIONS INFORMATION

Office of Admission: 419-530-5720

ENTRANCE REQUIREMENTS

Academic units required: 4 English, 3 math, 3 science, 3 social studies, 2 foreign language. **Academic units recommended:** 4 English, 3 math, 3 science (1 science lab), 3 social studies, 1 history. High school diploma is required, and GED is accepted. SAT or ACT with Writing component required. TOEFL required of all international applicants: minimum paper TOEFL 500, minimum computer TOEFL 173.

Application deadline: None
Notification: Rolling
Average GPA: 3.08
ACT Composite middle 50% range: 19–24

SAT Math middle 50% range: 460–590
SAT Critical Reading middle 50% range: 440–560
SAT Writing middle 50% range: 430–550

Graduated top 10% of class: 16%
Graduated top 25% of class: 37%
Graduated top 50% of class: 64%

COLLEGE GRADUATION REQUIREMENTS

Course waivers allowed: No
Course substitutions allowed: Yes
In what course: Foreign language if considered appropriate. Each case is decided on an individualized basis.

ADDITIONAL INFORMATION

Environment: The University of Toledo is located on a 305-acre campus in Toledo, Ohio.

Student Body
  Undergrad enrollment: 18,130
  Women: 49%
  Men: 51%
  Percent out-of-state: 10%

Cost Information
  In-state tuition: $8,204
  Out-of-state tuition: $17,016
  Room & board: $9,660
Housing Information
  University housing: Yes
  Percent living on campus: 18%

Greek System
  Fraternity: Yes
  Sorority: Yes
Athletics: Division I

URSULINE COLLEGE

2550 Lander Road; Pepper Pike, OH 44124-4398
Phone: 440-449-4203 • Fax: 440-684-6138
E-mail: admission@ursuline.edu • Web: www.ursuline.edu
Support: SP• Institution type: 4-year private

PROGRAMS OR SERVICES FOR STUDENTS WITH LD

Ursuline College is a small, private, Catholic college committed to helping students with learning disabilities maintain the FOCUS needed to succeed in their courses and become well-rounded, independent learners. The FOCUS program at Ursuline College is a voluntary mentoring and coaching service aimed at helping students with learning disabilities achieve collegiate success. The main goals of this one-on-one program include providing a smooth transition to college life and coaching students on appropriate learning strategies and self-advocacy skills. To be eligible to participate in the FOCUS program, applicants must have a current psycho-educational or neurological evaluation or other qualifying documentation and must meet all of the standards admissions requirements of Ursuline College.

ADMISSION INFORMATION FOR STUDENTS WITH LD/ADHD

College entrance tests required: Yes
Interview required: Yes
Essay recommended: No
Documentation required for LD: Current psychoeducational or neurological evaluation
Documentation required for ADHD: Same as LD
Submitted to: FOCUS
Special Ed. HS course work accepted: Yes

Specific course requirements of all applicants: Yes
Separate application required: No
# of LD applications submitted each year: Varies
# of LD applications accepted yearly: 12
Total # of students receiving LD services: Varies
Acceptance into program means acceptance into college: Students must be admitted to and enrolled in the university first and then request services.

ADMISSIONS

To be eligible to participate in the FOCUS program, students must first meet the requirements for clear or conditional admittance to the college by applying to the Admissions Office and completing all regular admissions procedures. Students with Learning Disabilities must meet the same requirements for admission to the college as all other students. Please refer to the admissions website at www.ursuline.edu/admission for more information. Once accepted to Ursuline College, students are then eligible to apply for FOCUS. To participate in the FOCUS program, students must meet with the Learning Disabilities Specialist once accepted to the college to determine if the program is suitable for them. Interested participants may also meet with the Learning Disability Specialist prior to being accepted if they desire.

ADDITIONAL INFORMATION

In addition, the FOCUS program features a separate orientation that provides FOCUS students the opportunity to tour the class locations on campus, become acquainted with other FOCUS students as well as valuable resources on campus, and introduce students to the adaptive technology the center provides. During each semester, students meet with a Learning Disability Specialist on a weekly or bi-weekly basis to review academic goals and coordinate assignments and tutoring appropriately. The Learning Disabilities Specialist also works with students on developing time management, test taking, and note-taking strategies as needed. FOCUS students also have guaranteed one-hour weekly sessions with a college writing specialist who helps students develop skills in writing effective sentences, paragraphs, and essays and to think critically about writing assignments. The Learning Disabilities Specialist also continues to provide ongoing support for FOCUS students that foster learning in coping skills, developing self-advocacy skills, discussing concerns in the classroom, and academic course advising.

LEARNING DISABILITY PROGRAM OR SERVICES

Contact Information
Name of program or department: Disability Services
  Telephone: 440-646-8123
  Fax: 440-644-6114

LEARNING DISABILITY SERVICES

Accommodations are decided upon an individual basis after a thorough review of appropriate, current documentation. The accommodations requested must be supported through the documentation provided and must be logically linked to the current impact of the condition on academic functioning.

Allowed in exams	**Distraction-reduced environment:** Yes	**Added costs for services:** No, unless
Calculator: Yes	**Tape recording in class:** Yes	enrolling in FOCUS
Dictionary: Yes	**Electronic texts:** Yes	**LD specialists:** Yes
Computer: Yes	**Accommodations for students with**	**Professional tutors:** Varies
Spellchecker: Yes	**ADHD:** Yes	**Peer tutors:** 1
Extended test time: Yes	**Kurzweil Reader:** Yes	**Max. hours/wk. for services:** Varies
Scribes: Yes	**Other assistive technology:** Yes	**How professors are notified of**
Proctors: Yes	**Priority registration:** Yes	**LD/ADHD:** By student
Oral exams: Yes		
Note-takers: Yes		

GENERAL ADMISSIONS INFORMATION

Office of Admission: 440-449-4203

ENTRANCE REQUIREMENTS

Academic units recommended: 4 English, 3 math, 3 science (2 science labs), 2 foreign language, 3 social studies, 1 fine/performing arts, 1 physical education/health. High school diploma is required, and GED is accepted. ACT with or without Writing component accepted. TOEFL required of all international applicants: minimum paper TOEFL 500, minimum computer TOEFL 173.

Application deadline: None	**SAT Math middle 50% range:**	**Graduated top 10% of class:** 11%
Notification: Within 3 weeks of	490–520	**Graduated top 25% of class:** 36%
completed application	**SAT Critical Reading middle 50%**	**Graduated top 50% of class:** 76%
Average GPA: 3.16	**range:** 400–500	
ACT Composite middle 50% range:	**SAT Writing middle 50% range:**	
18–23	350–430	

COLLEGE GRADUATION REQUIREMENTS

Course waivers allowed: Yes
In what course: Waiving of courses is done on an individual basis.
Course substitutions allowed: No

ADDITIONAL INFORMATION

Environment: The college is located in a suburban area about 20 miles from Cleveland.

Student Body	**Cost Information**	**Greek System**
Undergrad enrollment: 1,022	**Tuition:** $26,304	**Fraternity:** No
Women: 94%	**Room & board:** $8,288	**Sorority:** No
Men: 6%	**Housing Information**	**Athletics:** NAIA
Percent out-of-state: 3%	**University housing:** Yes	
	Percent living on campus: 17%	

WRIGHT STATE UNIVERSITY

3640 Colonel Glenn Highway, Dayton, OH 45435
Phone: 937-775-5700 • Fax: 937-775-5795
E-mail: admissions@wright.edu • Web: www.wright.edu
Support: CS • Institution type: 4-year public

PROGRAMS OR SERVICES FOR STUDENTS WITH LD

Students with disabilities are encouraged to participate in all facets of university life according to their abilities and interests and to develop independence and responsibility to the fullest extent possible. The philosophy of the university is intended to stimulate students to pursue the career of study regardless of their learning disability. Through the Office of Disability Services, the university provides a comprehensive array of services on a campus with a long history of commitment to students with physical, visual, and/or learning disabilities. A pre-service interview is required of all prospective students to discuss service needs. Eligibility for services is determined after documentation is received and the student has an individual interview.

ADMISSION INFORMATION FOR STUDENTS WITH LD/ADHD

College entrance tests required: Yes
Interview required: Yes
Essay recommended: No
What documentation required for LD: Psycho Ed evaluation to include: relevant historical info, instructional interventions, related services, age diagnosed, objective data (aptitude, achievement, info processing), test scores (standard, percentile and grade equivalents) and describe functional limitations.
With general application: No
To receive services after enrolling: Yes
What documentation required for ADHD: Diagnosis based on DSM-V; history of behaviors impairing functioning in academic setting; diagnostic interview; history of symptoms; evidence of ongoing behaviors.

With general application: No
Submitted to: Office of Disability Services
Special Ed. HS course work accepted: No
Specific course requirements of all applicants: Yes
Separate application required: Yes
# of LD applications submitted each year: 55–75
# of LD applications accepted yearly: NR
Total # of students receiving LD services: 175
Acceptance into program means acceptance into college: Students must be admitted to and enrolled in the university first and then request services.

ADMISSIONS

The university has an open admission policy for in-state students. ACT/SAT is used for placement, not admission. The mid 50 percent range for the ACT is 18–24, and for the SAT, it is 990–1140. Students with LD must meet the same criteria as all applicants and must be accepted to the university prior to requesting services. However, out-of-state students are encouraged to self-disclose their learning disability and submit documentation to the Office of Disability Services prior to applying to the university if they would like to discuss eligibility for admission and services available on campus and determine if Wright State is a good fit for them. It is recommended that students self-disclose the LD if GPA or test scores are low and the student feels that LD disclosure is important in explaining academic or testing information. The Director of Disability Services encourages students and their families to visit and interview. Admissions will ask ODS to review documentation, transcripts, and so on, and meet with the student to determine readiness for college. Students with a college-prep curriculum in high school have been more successful at Wright State than those who took a general curriculum. The final decision rests with the Admissions Office.

ADDITIONAL INFORMATION

Wright State Office of Disability Services offers testing accommodations, counseling, math learning center and tutoring services for all students. Develomental courses are offered in writing and math. Supplemental instruction helps students review course concepts, improve study habits, and be better prepared for exams and assignments. A trained supplemental instructor student leader works with a professor in consultation to provide group study sessions.

LEARNING DISABILITY PROGRAM OR SERVICES

Contact Information
Name of program or department: Office of Disability Services (ODS)
Telephone: 937-775-5680
Fax: 937-775-5699

LEARNING DISABILITY SERVICES

Accommodations are decided upon an individual basis after a thorough review of appropriate, current documentation. The accommodations requested must be supported through the documentation provided and must be logically linked to the current impact of the condition on academic functioning.

Allowed in exams
Calculator: Yes
Dictionary: Yes
Computer: Yes
Spellchecker: Yes
Extended test time: Yes
Scribes: Yes
Proctors: Yes
Oral exams: Yes
Note-takers: Yes

Distraction-reduced environment: Yes
Tape recording in class: Yes
Electronic texts: Yes
Accommodations for students with ADHD: Yes
Kurzweil Reader: No (Wynn Reader)
Other assistive technology: Yes
Priority registration: No

Added costs for services: No
LD specialists: Yes
Professional tutors: No
Peer tutors: 40–50
Max. hours/wk. for services: 10
How professors are notified of LD/ADHD: By student

GENERAL ADMISSIONS INFORMATION

Office of Admission: 937-775-5700

ENTRANCE REQUIREMENTS

Academic units required: 4 English, 3 math, 3 science (3 science labs), 2 foreign language, 3 social studies. High school diploma is required, and GED is accepted. ACT with or without Writing component accepted. TOEFL required of all international applicants: minimum paper TOEFL 500, minimum computer TOEFL 173.

Application deadline: None
Notification: Rolling
Average GPA: 3.02
ACT Composite middle 50% range: 18–24

SAT Math middle 50% range: 430–570
SAT Critical Reading middle 50% range: 440–570
SAT Writing middle 50% range: NR

Graduated top 10% of class: 14%
Graduated top 25% of class: 33%
Graduated top 50% of class: 61%

COLLEGE GRADUATION REQUIREMENTS

Course waivers allowed: Yes
In what course: Math
Course substitutions allowed: Yes
In what course: Foreign language

ADDITIONAL INFORMATION

Environment: The university is located on 645 acres 8 miles northeast of Dayton.

Student Body
Undergrad enrollment: 19,600
Women: 55%
Men: 45%
Percent out-of-state: 4%

Cost Information
In-state tuition: $8,070
Out-of-state tuition: $15,633
Room & board: $8,386
Housing Information
University housing: Yes
Percent living on campus: 14%

Greek System
Fraternity: Yes
Sorority: Yes
Athletics: Division I

XAVIER UNIVERSITY (OH)

3800 Victory Parkway, Cincinnati, OH 45207-5131
Phone: 513-745-3000 • Fax: 513-745-4319
E-mail: xuadmit@xavier.edu • Web: www.xavier.edu
Support: CS • Institution type: 4-year private

PROGRAMS OR SERVICES FOR STUDENTS WITH LD

The Learning Assistance Center (LAC) provides support services to facilitate learning. The LAC has two main purposes: tutoring and disability services. Our tutoring services are available to all Xavier students and include subject specific tutoring, drop-in sessions, study skills assistance and Supplemental Instruction (SI). For students with documented disabilities, our disability services provides accommodations such as extended time on exams, reduced distraction testing environment, note taking assistance, and assistive technology. We provide these services in a positive and encouraging environment which promotes appreciation for diversity and Cura Personalis.

ADMISSION INFORMATION FOR STUDENTS WITH LD/ADHD

College entrance tests required: Yes
Interview required: No
Essay recommended: Yes
What documentation required for LD: Psycho Ed evaluation to include: relevant historical info, instructional interventions, related services, age diagnosed, objective data (aptitude, achievement, info processing), test scores (standard, percentile and grade equivalents) and describe functional limitations.
With general application: No
To receive services after enrolling: Yes
What documentation required for ADHD: Diagnosis based on DSM-V; history of behaviors impairing functioning in academic setting; diagnostic interview; history of symptoms; evidence of ongoing behaviors.

With general application: No
Submitted to: LAC
Special Ed. HS course work accepted: Yes
Specific course requirements of all applicants: Yes
Separate application required: No
# of LD applications submitted each year: NR
# of LD applications accepted yearly: NR
Total # of students receiving LD services: 160
Acceptance into program means acceptance into college: Students must be admitted to and enrolled in the university first and then request services.

ADMISSIONS

There is no special admissions process for students with disabilities. The middle 50 percent GPA is 3.20–3.88; the middle 50 percent class rank is 62–89 percent; the middle 50 percent ACT score is 23–28; and the middle 50 percent SAT score is 1060–1230.

ADDITIONAL INFORMATION

All students have access to the Math Lab, Writing Center, and Tutoring Center. Accommodations and services are available for undergraduates and graduates. Documentation required for a student with LD is a copy of the last IEP and results of the last psychoeducational test battery. Students with ADHD should submit a copy of a recent diagnostic report that states the DSM–IV diagnosis, symptoms, instruments and procedures used to make the diagnosis, and the dosage, type and frequency of your current medication. In addition to this documentation, students must fill out paperwork and sign a release form at the beginning of each semester. This enables the staff at the Learning Assistance Center to contact professors and arrange for accommodations.

LEARNING DISABILITY PROGRAM OR SERVICES

Contact Information
Name of program or department: Learning Assistance Center (LAC)
 Telephone: 513-745-3280
 Fax: 513-745-3387

LEARNING DISABILITY SERVICES

Accommodations are decided upon an individual basis after a thorough review of appropriate, current documentation. The accommodations requested must be supported through the documentation provided and must be logically linked to the current impact of the condition on academic functioning.

Allowed in exams	**Distraction-reduced environment:** Yes	**Added costs for services:** No
Calculator: Yes	**Tape recording in class:** Yes	**LD specialists:** Yes
Dictionary: Yes	**Electronic texts:** Yes	**Professional tutors:** No
Computer: Yes	**Accommodations for students with**	**Peer tutors:** 80
Spellchecker: Yes	**ADHD:** Yes	**Max. hours/wk. for services:**
Extended test time: Yes	**Kurzweil Reader:** Yes	Unlimited
Scribes: Yes	**Other assistive technology:** Yes	**How professors are notified of**
Proctors: Yes	**Priority registration:** Yes	**LD/ADHD:** Accommodations
Oral exams: Yes		described in letter
Note-takers: Yes		

GENERAL ADMISSIONS INFORMATION

Office of Admission: 513-745-3301

ENTRANCE REQUIREMENTS

Academic units recommended: 4 English, 3 math, 3 science, 2 foreign language, 3 social studies, 5 academic electives, 1 health/physical education. High school diploma is required, and GED is accepted. ACT with or without Writing component accepted. TOEFL required of all international applicants: minimum paper TOEFL 530, minimum computer TOEFL 197.

Application deadline: 2/1	**SAT Math middle 50% range:**	**Graduated top 10% of class:** 22%
Notification: Rolling	500–610	**Graduated top 25% of class:** 54%
Average GPA: 3.5	**SAT Critical Reading middle 50%**	**Graduated top 50% of class:** 85%
ACT Composite middle 50% range:	**range:** 480–600	
22–27	**SAT Writing middle 50% range:**	
	470–600	

COLLEGE GRADUATION REQUIREMENTS

Course waivers allowed: No
Course substitutions allowed: Yes
In what course: Only substitutions are offered. These are usually in math and foreign language. Students are encouraged to petition the Deans Committee on course substitutions early in the Xavier careers. Documentation must support substitutions.

ADDITIONAL INFORMATION

Environment: The university is located 5 miles from downtown Cincinatti.

Student Body	**Cost Information**	**Greek System**
Undergrad enrollment: 4,540	**Tuition:** $30,230	**Fraternity:** No
Women: 54%	**Room & board:** $10,130	**Sorority:** No
Men: 46%	**Housing Information**	**Athletics:** Division I
Percent out-of-state: 49%	**University housing:** Yes	
	Percent living on campus: 50%	

OKLAHOMA STATE UNIVERSITY

219 Student Union, Stillwater, OK 74078
Phone: 405-744-5358 • Fax: 405-744-7092
E-mail: admissions@okstate.edu • Web: http://osu.okstate.edu/welcome/
Support: S • Institution: 4-year public

PROGRAMS OR SERVICES FOR STUDENTS WITH LD

Oklahoma State University does not have a formal learning disabilities program but uses a service-based model to assist the students in obtaining the necessary accommodations for specific learning disabilities. Students with learning disabilities may request priority enrollment and a campus orientation to assist in scheduling classes. Other services developed in coordination with the faculty work to minimize the students' difficulties in relation to course work. These services could include test accommodations, course substitutions, and independent study. The underlying philosophy of this program is to provide assistance to students to facilitate their academic progress. Student Disability Services (SDS) also acts as a resource for faculty and staff.

ADMISSION INFORMATION FOR STUDENTS WITH LD/ADHD

College entrance tests required: Yes
Interview required: No
Essay required: N/A
What documentation required for LD: Psycho Ed evaluation to include: relevant historical info, instructional interventions, related services, age diagnosed, objective data (aptitude, achievement, info processing), test scores (standard, percentile and grade equivalents) and describe functional limitations.
With general application: No
To receive services after enrolling: Yes
What documentation required for ADHD: Diagnosis based on DSM-V; history of behaviors impairing functioning in academic setting; diagnostic interview; history of symptoms; evidence of ongoing behaviors.

With general application: No
Submitted to: Support Program/Services
Special Ed. HS course work accepted: No
Specific course requirements for all applicants: Yes
Separate application required for program services: No
# of LD applications submitted each year: NR
# of LD applications accepted yearly: NR
Total # of students receiving LD services: 60–70
Acceptance into program means acceptance into college: Separate application required after student has enrolled

ADMISSIONS

There is no special admissions policy for students with LD. However, if ability to meet admission criteria was impacted by a disability (such as late identification, no accommodations, or high school courses waived), students should include a personal statement with their application and contact Disability Services. General admission requirements include minimum ACT 24 or SAT 1090 or a 3.0 GPA and rank in the top third of the class. Course requirements include four units English, three units math, two units lab science, three units history & citizenship skills (economics, geography, government, or non-western culture), and three units from previous areas and/or computer science and/or foreign language. Students with appropriate documentation may be allowed to substitute courses for math or foreign language. Students not meeting admission requirements may qualify for admission through (1) Alternative Admission for students whose high school achievement is slightly below the standards and/or deficient in no more than one curricular unit (2) Summer Provision Program for students who meet all the curricular requiremetns and have a GPA of 2.5 or above, or ACT of 18 or above or SAT of 870 or above. These students may enter in the summer on probation and may be required to take placement tests prior to a final acceptance.

ADDITIONAL INFORMATION

There is a math lab and a writing center for all students. All students with LD/ADHD requesting accommodations or services must provide appropriate and current documentation. All diagnostic testing and documentation should be sent to Student Disability Services. There are currently 100 students with learning disabilities and 40 with ADHD receiving services on campus. The university also operates the Oklahoma City Technical Institute, which offers two-year, career-oriented programs.

LEARNING DISABILITY PROGRAM OR SERVICES

Contact Information
Name of program or department: Student Disability Services (SDS)
   Telephone: 405-744-7116
   Fax: 405-744-8380

LEARNING DISABILITY SERVICES

Accommodations are decided upon an individual basis after a thorough review of appropriate, current documentation. The accommodations requested must be supported through the documentation provided and must be logically linked to the current impact of the condition on academic functioning.

Allowed in exams
   Calculator: Yes
   Dictionary: Yes
   Computer: Yes
   Spellchecker: Yes
Extended test time: Yes
Scribes: Yes
Proctors: Yes
Oral exams: Yes
Note-takers: Yes

Distraction-reduced environment: Yes
Tape recording in class: Yes
Electronic texts: Yes
Accommodations for students with ADHD: Yes
Kurzweil Reader: Yes
Other assistive technology: WYNN software, Open Book, JAWS, MAGic, Dragon Naturally Speaking, CCTV, Braille printer
Priority registration: Yes

Added costs for services: No
LD specialists: No
Professional tutors: NR
Peer tutors: No
Max. hours/wk. for services: Unlimited
How professors are notified of LD/ADHD: Both student and director

GENERAL ADMISSIONS INFORMATION

Office of Admission: 405-744-3087

ENTRANCE REQUIREMENTS
Academic units required: 4 English, 3 mathematics, 2 science, (2 science labs), 2 social studies, 1 history, 3 academic electives. **Academic units recommended:** 2 foreign language, 1 computer science. High school diploma is required and GED is accepted. SAT or ACT required; TOEFL required of all international applicants; minimum paper TOEFL 500, minimum computer TOEFL 173, minimum web-based TOEFL 61.

Application deadline: None
Notification: Rolling
Average GPA: 3.52
ACT Composite middle 50% range: 22–27

SAT Math middle 50% range: 500–620
SAT Critical Reading middle 50% range: 480–600
SAT Writing middle 50% range: NR

Graduated top 10% of class: 27%
Graduated top 25% of class: 55%
Graduated top 50% of class: 86%

COLLEGE GRADUATION REQUIREMENTS

Course substitutions allowed: Yes
In what course: Math, foreign language

ADDITIONAL INFORMATION

Environment: The 415-acre campus is located in a small city 65 miles north of Oklahoma City.

Student Body
   Undergrad enrollment: 18,197
   Women: 48%
   Men: 52%
   Percent out-of-state: 22%

Cost Information
   In-state tuition: $4,103
   Out-of-state tuition: $14,925
   Room and board: $6,750
Housing Information
   University housing: Yes
   Percent living on campus: 39%

Greek System
   Fraternity: No
   Sorority: No
Athletics: Division I

UNIVERSITY OF OKLAHOMA

1000 Asp Aveune, Norman, OK 73019-4076
Phone: 405-325-2252 • Fax: 405-325-7124
E-mail: admrec@ou.edu • Web: www.ou.edu
Support: S • Institution: 4-year public

PROGRAMS OR SERVICES FOR STUDENTS WITH LD

The Disability Resource Center provides support services and is committed to the goal of achieving equal educational opportunity and full participation for students with disabilities. In many cases, these services are developed in response to expressed student needs. There are no special LD or remedial classes. Students are encouraged to be self-advocates in making requests for reasonable academic accommodations. Assistance is to be used to support the accomplishment of educational goals. The Center Director sponsors the OU Association for Disabled Students, a student organization that provides a recognized forum for support, regular meetings, and social and recreational activities. Students should provide comprehensive evaluations documenting learning disabilities in order to receive services. The evaluation should include full-scale, performance, and verbal I.Q. scores; scores from aptitude-achievement comparisons; and a summary and recommendations.

ADMISSION INFORMATION FOR STUDENTS WITH LD/ADHD

College entrance tests required: Yes
Interview required: No
Essay required: N/A
Documentation required for LD: Comprehensive report that is reasonably current using adult norms that measures aptitude, academic achievement and information processing.
Documentation required for ADHD: Comprehensive report that is reasonably current using adult norms that measures aptitude, academic achievement and information processing, DSM–IV diagnosis, medication and side effects if any.
Submitted to: Disability Resource Center
Special Ed. HS course work accepted: No

Specific course requirements for all applicants: Yes
Separate application required for program services: No
# of LD applications submitted each year: NR
# of LD applications accepted yearly: NR
Total # of students receiving LD services: 296 (includes AD/HD)
Acceptance into program means acceptance into college: Students must be admitted and enrolled in the university first and then request services.

ADMISSIONS

Admissions requirements for students with LD are the same for all other students. For further information regarding admissions to the University of Oklahoma please go to: www.ou.edu/admissions/home.html. Students must self-identify and submit documentation in accordance with Documentation Guidelines. The DRC staff will review the documentation, once admitted to the university, and will let the student know their eligibility. Students can expect to receive a response within 15 business days of the Center's receipt of the appropriate documents.

ADDITIONAL INFORMATION

After receiving academic advisement from the college, the student should make an appointment with the Disability Resource Center Staff. The office will also provide a personal campus orientation upon request. Services offered, based on individual needs, include alternative testing, readers, scribes, note-takers (who are volunteers), tutors, electronic texts, and library assistance. Services are available for undergraduate and graduate students.

LEARNING DISABILITY PROGRAM OR SERVICES

Contact Information
Name of program or department: Disability Resource Center
  Telephone: 405-325-3852
  Fax: 405-325-4491

LEARNING DISABILITY SERVICES

Accommodations are decided upon an individual basis after a thorough review of appropriate, current documentation. The accommodations requested must be supported through the documentation provided and must be logically linked to the current impact of the condition on academic functioning. Accommodations must not alter fundemental nature of the program.

Allowed in exams
  Calculator: Yes
  Dictionary: Yes
  Computer: Yes
  Spellchecker: Yes
Extended test time: Yes
Scribes: Yes
Proctors: Yes
Oral exams: NR
Note-takers: Yes

Distraction-reduced environment: Yes
Tape recording in class: Yes
Electronic texts: Yes
Accommodations for students with ADHD: Yes
Reader: Yes
Other assistive technology: OCR Scanners, Large Print software, speech synthesis and speech recognition software and hardware
Priority registration: Yes

Added costs for services: No
LD specialists: No
Professional tutors: No
Peer tutors: No
Max. hours/wk. for services: As needed
How professors are notified of LD/ADHD: Director

GENERAL ADMISSIONS INFORMATION

Office of Admission: 405-325-2252

ENTRANCE REQUIREMENTS
Academic units required: 4 English, 3 mathematics, 3 science, (3 science labs), 2 social studies, 1 history, 2 academic electives. **Academic units recommended:** 2 foreign language, 1 computer science, 4 mathematics. High school diploma is required and GED is accepted. SAT or ACT required; TOEFL required of all applicants for whom English is a second language; minimum paper TOEFL 550, minimum web-based TOEFL 79.

Application deadline: 4/1
Notification: Rolling
Average GPA: 3.63
ACT Composite middle 50% range: 23–29

SAT Math middle 50% range: 530–660
SAT Critical Reading middle 50% range: 530–660
SAT Writing middle 50% range: NR

Graduated top 10% of class: 36%
Graduated top 25% of class: 70%
Graduated top 50% of class: 95%

COLLEGE GRADUATION REQUIREMENTS

Course waivers allowed: N/A
Course substitutions allowed: Yes
In what course: Students may petition degree-granting college for a foreign language substitution.

ADDITIONAL INFORMATION

Environment: The University of Oklahoma is located in the city of Norman, which is 17 miles south of Oklahoma City.

Student Body
  Undergrad enrollment: 20,892
  Women: 50%
  Men: 50%
  Percent out-of-state: 32%

Cost Information
  In-state tuition: $7,124.50
  Out-of-state tuition: $18,077.50
  Room and board: $8,060
Housing Information
  University housing: Yes
  Percent living on campus: 35%

Greek System
  Fraternity: Yes
  Sorority: Yes
Athletics: Division I

THE UNIVERSITY OF TULSA

800 South Tucker Drive, Tulsa, OK 74104
Phone: 918-631-2307 • Fax: 918-631-5003
E-mail: admission@utulsa.edu • Web: www.utulsa.edu
Support: CS • Institution type: 4-year private

PROGRAMS OR SERVICES FOR STUDENTS WITH LD

The Center for Student Academic Support offers a comprehensive range of academic support services and accommodations to students with disabilities. The goal is to provide services which will, in combination with the resources and talents of the student, maximize the students' independence for full participation in the curriculum and provide an opportunity to achieve career goals. The policy of the University of Tulsa, in keeping with the Americans with Disabilities Act, is to provide reasonable accommodations for students with disabilities, including students with learning disabilities. Students who have specific disabilities that might impact their full access and participation in university programs are urged to provide the relevant documentation and make an appointment with the Director of the Center for Student Academic Support.

ADMISSION INFORMATION FOR STUDENTS WITH LD/ADHD

College entrance tests required: Yes
Interview required: No
Essay recommended: Yes
What documentation required for LD: Psycho Ed evaluation to include: relevant historical info, instructional interventions, related services, age diagnosed, objective data (aptitude, achievement, info processing), test scores (standard, percentile and grade equivalents) and describe functional limitations.
With general application: No
To receive services after enrolling: Yes
What documentation required for ADHD: Diagnosis based on DSM-V; history of behaviors impairing functioning in academic setting; diagnostic interview; history of symptoms; evidence of ongoing behaviors.

With general application: No
Submitted to: Center for Student Academic Support
Special Ed. HS course work accepted: Yes
Specific course requirements of all applicants: Yes
Separate application required: Yes
# of LD applications submitted each year: 130
# of LD applications accepted yearly: 123
Total # of students receiving LD services: 123
Acceptance into program means acceptance into college: Student must be admitted and enrolled in the university first and then request services.

ADMISSIONS

All students must meet the general admissions requirements. Students with disabilities are not required to disclose information about the disability, but may voluntarily disclose or request information from CSAS. The university does not consider disabilities in the decision-making process, even if there is knowledge of the disability, without a request and disclosure by the applicant. Students may provide verification of the disability that should be submitted directly to CSAS. General admission requirements include: 4 years of English, 3 years of math, 4 years of science, and 2 years of foreign language. No course substitutions are allowed. The average ACT is above 21 and for the SAT is 1080–1140. Students applying to the nursing or athletic training programs must submit a special application. Conditional admission is available for freshmen and probational admission is an option for transfer students. The student with learning disabilities also needs to complete the application form and intake sheet. Also required is documentation presented from a doctor stating diagnostic material and diagnosis of the disorder.

ADDITIONAL INFORMATION

Accommodations students might qualify for depending upon their documentation and needs include: extended time on tests, priority registration, testing in self-contained environment, use of spelling aids on written exams, texts on tape, note-takers, preferential seating, tests given orally, and enlarged print tests. Concerns regarding requests for a referral for evaluation of a learning disability should be directed to the Coordinator of the Center for Student Academic Support. Students with LD must provide documentation that includes tests of intellect and of achievement administered by a professional. Students with documented ADHD must provide behavior checklist (one completed by a doctor), a test of intellect, a test of attention, and a clinical interview that includes a history of the ADHD.

LEARNING DISABILITY PROGRAM OR SERVICES

Contact Information
Name of program or department: Center for Student Academic Support
  Telephone: 918-631-2315
  Fax: 918-631-3459

LEARNING DISABILITY SERVICES

Accommodations are decided upon an individual basis after a thorough review of appropriate, current documentation. The accommodations requested must be supported through the documentation provided and must be logically linked to the current impact of the condition on academic functioning.

Allowed in exams	**Distraction-reduced environment:** Yes	**Added costs for services:** No
Calculator: Yes	**Tape recording in class:** Yes	**LD specialists:** Yes
Dictionary: Yes	**Electronic texts:** Yes	**Professional tutors:** 9
Computer: Yes	**Accommodations for students with**	**Peer tutors:** 63
Spellchecker: Yes	**ADHD:** Yes	**Max. hours/wk. for services:**
Extended test time: Yes	**Kurzweil Reader:** Yes	Unlimited
Scribes: Yes	**Other assistive technology:** Yes	**How professors are notified of**
Proctors: Yes	**Priority registration:** Yes	**LD/ADHD:** Center provides letter of
Oral exams: NR		accommodation to faculty
Notetakers: Yes		

GENERAL ADMISSIONS INFORMATION

Office of Admission: 918-631-2307

ENTRANCE REQUIREMENTS

Academic units required: 4 English, 3 math, 4 science (2 science labs), 2 foreign language, 1 social studies, 2 history, 1 academic elective. High school diploma is required, and GED is accepted. ACT with or without Writing component accepted. TOEFL required of all international applicants, minimum paper TOEFL 500, minimum computer TOEFL 173.

Application deadline: None	**SAT Math middle 50% range:**	**Graduated top 10% of class:** 71%
Notification: Rolling	550–700	**Graduated top 25% of class:** 89%
Average GPA: 3.80	**SAT Critical Reading middle 50%**	**Graduated top 50% of class:** 97%
ACT Composite middle 50% range:	**range:** 540–700	
25–31	**SAT Writing middle 50% range:**	
	NR	

COLLEGE GRADUATION REQUIREMENTS

Course waivers allowed: Yes
In what course: Depends on the nature of the disability
Course substitutions allowed: Yes
In what course: Depends on the nature of the disability

ADDITIONAL INFORMATION

Environment: The campus is in an urban area.

Student Body	**Cost Information**	**Greek System**
Undergrad enrollment: 3,105	**Tuition:** $30,866	**Fraternity:** Yes
Women: 48%	**Room & board:** $9,464	**Sorority:** Yes
Men: 52%	**Housing Information**	**Athletics:** NCAA Division I
Percent out-of-state: 48%	**University housing:** Yes	
	Percent living on campus: 80%	

OREGON STATE UNIVERSITY

104 Kerr Administration Building, Corvallis, OR 97331-2106
Phone: 541-737-4411 • Fax: 541-737-2482
E-mail: osuadmit@oregonstate.edu • Web: http://oregonstate.edu
Support: S • Institution: 4-year public

PROGRAMS OR SERVICES FOR STUDENTS WITH LD

OSU is committed to providing equal opportunity for higher education to academically qualified students without regard to disability. Disability Access Services (DAS) strives to be sensitive to the individual needs of students by offering a variety of services. Services rendered are dependent on the type of learning disability. Services are provided to ensure an equal opportunity to succeed but do not guarantee success. Self-advocacy and independence are promoted. DAS is available for all students who need extra services. The Educational Opportunities Program (EOP) offers students who are learning disabled, economically disadvantaged, or first-generation college-bound a variety of remedial courses for credit. EOP tries to provide tutoring for any undergraduate class if tutors are available. To be recognized as a person with a learning disability, students are required to submit documentation from a qualified educational evaluator. Preferred diagnostic testing would include at least one test in each of the following categories: cognitive, achievement, and processing. Other documentation specifying a learning disability without testing in the three categories mentioned must include an in-depth valid assessment of the disability by a qualified professional.

ADMISSION INFORMATION FOR STUDENTS WITH LD/ADHD

College entrance tests required: Yes
Interview required: No
What documentation required for LD: Psycho Ed evaluation to
  include: relevant historical info, instructional interventions,
  related services, age diagnosed, objective data (aptitude,
  achievement, info processing), test scores (standard, percentile
  and grade equivalents) and describe functional limitations.
With general application: No
To receive services after enrolling: Yes
What documentation required for ADHD: Diagnosis based
  on DSM-V; history of behaviors impairing functioning in
  academic setting; diagnostic interview; history of symptoms;
  evidence of ongoing behaviors.

With general application: No
Submitted to: Support Program/Services
Special Ed. HS course work accepted: No
Specific course requirements for all applicants: Yes
Separate application required for program services: No
# of LD applications submitted each year: 80
# of LD applications accepted yearly: NR
Total # of students receiving LD services: 179
**Acceptance into program means acceptance into
  college:** Separate application required after student has
  enrolled

ADMISSIONS

All students must submit the general application for admission. If a student does not meet admissions requirements, admission will be denied. Enclosed with the notification, the student will receive information regarding petitioning for special admission. Students who want to petition their admission on the basis of a learning disability must submit all information required in the petition. Petitioning students must utilize the services of EOP. The director of DAS helps to make admission decisions and may recommend EOP for the student with LD. Regular admission requires a 3.0 GPA and special admit for students with 2.5. Students requesting services should self-identify; submit documentation of their LD, including educational history and diagnostic testing administered by professionals; and include information describing cognitive strengths and weaknesses, recommendations for accommodations or services, and any other additional information in the form of a family history. Students must also submit a handwritten 1–2 page statement outlining educational goals and explaining motivation to succeed at OSU. Students admitted through the EOP Program must start in the summer and attend a required DAS orientation in the beginning of fall. EOP admission decision is made jointly between Admissions and EOP.

ADDITIONAL INFORMATION

Students with LD, whether admitted regularly or as special admits, are encouraged to apply for additional assistance from EOP, which can provide special counseling, tutoring, and intensive practice in study skills. Accommodations in instruction and related academic work may include alternative test methods such as extended testing time and use of resources such as calculators. Accommodations are negotiated with instructors, academic departments, and the college as appropriate. Personal counseling is available through the Counseling Center. The director acts as a liaison between students and faculty.

LEARNING DISABILITY PROGRAM OR SERVICES

Contact Information
Name of program or department: Disability Access Services (DAS)
Telephone: 541-737-4098
Fax: 541-737-7354

LEARNING DISABILITY SERVICES

Accommodations are decided upon an individual basis after a thorough review of appropriate, current documentation. The accommodations requested must be supported through the documentation provided and must be logically linked to the current impact of the condition on academic functioning.

Allowed in exams
Calculator: Yes
Dictionary: No
Computer: Yes
Spellchecker: Yes
Extended test time: Yes
Scribes: Yes
Proctors: Yes
Oral exams: Yes
Note-takers: Yes

Distraction-reduced environment: Yes
Tape recording in class: Yes
Electronic texts: Yes
Accommodations for students with ADHD: Yes
Kurzweil Reader: Yes
Other assistive technology: Assistive Listening Devices
Priority registration: Yes

Added costs for services: No
LD specialists: No
Professional tutors: NR
Peer tutors: Available at Academic Success Center
Max. hours/wk. for services: N/A
How professors are notified of LD/ADHD: Both student and director

GENERAL ADMISSIONS INFORMATION

Office of Admission: 800-291-4192

ENTRANCE REQUIREMENTS
Academic units required: 4 English, 3 mathematics, 2 science, (1 science labs), 2 foreign language, 3 social studies.
Academic units recommended: (2 science labs). High school diploma is required and GED is accepted. SAT or ACT required; ACT with Writing component required. TOEFL required of all international applicants; minimum paper TOEFL 550, minimum computer TOEFL 213.

Application deadline: 9/1
Notification: Rolling
Average GPA: 3.51
ACT Composite middle 50% range: 21–26

SAT Math middle 50% range: 490–610
SAT Critical Reading middle 50% range: 460–590
SAT Writing middle 50% range: 450–560

Graduated top 10% of class: 10%
Graduated top 25% of class: 51%
Graduated top 50% of class: 87%

COLLEGE GRADUATION REQUIREMENTS

Course waivers allowed: No
Course substitutions allowed: Yes
In what course: On a case-by-case basis, dependent on the major selected, and documentation.

ADDITIONAL INFORMATION

Environment: The university is located on 530 acres in a small town 85 miles south of Portland.

Student Body
Undergrad enrollment: 19,559
Women: 47%
Men: 53%
Percent out-of-state: 17%

Cost Information
In-state tuition: $7,518
Out-of-state tuition: $21,294
Room & board: $9,444
Housing Information
University housing: Yes
Percent living on campus: 21%

Greek System
Fraternity: Yes
Sorority: Yes
Athletics: Division I

UNIVERSITY OF OREGON

1217 University of Oregon, Eugene, OR 97403-1217
Phone: 541-346-3201 • Fax: 541-346-5815
E-mail: uoadmit@uoregon.edu • Web: www.uoregon.edu
Support: CS • Institution type: 4-year public

PROGRAMS OR SERVICES FOR STUDENTS WITH LD

At the University of Oregon, the Accessible Education Center (AEC) promotes inclusive teaching strategies and coordinates services and support to students with currently documented learning disabilities and Attention Deficit Hyperactivity Disorder. During university orientation programs students discuss their needs, challenges, educational goals, and available services. Accommodations are determined on a case-by-case basis after admission and an individual appointment. A faculty notification letter outlining suggested accommodations is provided when requested, and is shared at the students' discretion. The university is actively engaged in universal design instructional strategies to minimize the need for individualized accommodations when possible. Successful students are motivated, hardworking, and able to articulate their strengths and challenges.

ADMISSION INFORMATION FOR STUDENTS WITH LD/ADHD

College entrance tests required: Yes
Interview required: No
Essay recommended: Yes
What documentation required for LD: Psycho Ed evaluation to include: relevant historical info, instructional interventions, related services, age diagnosed, objective data (aptitude, achievement, info processing), test scores (standard, percentile and grade equivalents) and describe functional limitations.
With general application: No
To receive services after enrolling: Yes
What documentation required for ADHD: Diagnosis based on DSM-V; history of behaviors impairing functioning in academic setting; diagnostic interview; history of symptoms; evidence of ongoing behaviors.

With general application: No
Submitted to: Both Admissions and Disability Services
Special Ed. HS course work accepted: Yes
Specific course requirements of all applicants: Yes
Separate application required: No
# of LD applications submitted each year: NR
# of LD applications accepted yearly: NR
Total # of students receiving LD services: 350
Acceptance into program means acceptance into college: Student must be admitted and enrolled in the university first and then request services.

ADMISSIONS

Students with learning disabilities must meet the same admission criteria as all other applicants. Courses recommended for admission include: 4 years of English, 3 years of math including Algebra II, 3 years of science, 2 years of a second language, and 3 years of social studies. The average SAT is 1117 and the average GPA is 3.59. Students not meeting the regular admission requirements who have extenuating circumstances due to a learning disability may request additional consideration of their application by a special committee. A completed application form, a graded writing sample, two letters of recommendation, and documentation of the disability with information about how it has influenced the student's ability to meet minimum admission requirements are required for special admission consideration based on disability.

ADDITIONAL INFORMATION

Students are encouraged to take an active role in registering for and utilizing services. Once admitted, students should meet with AEC to review documentation and discuss educational goals. Typical support includes modification of testing procedures, including additional testing time, dictation of responses, text to speech formats, and distraction reduced testing environments; permission to record lectures, access to instructor or classmate notes; Assistive Technology Program with alternate print formats; faculty liaison to assist in communicating needs to instructors and to help negotiate reasonable accommodations or inclusive design strategies in courses and programs. For graduation the University requires two terms of writing classes for all degrees. The BS degree requires one year of college math, and the BA degree requires two years of a second language (American Sign Language is accepted). Writing and math labs are available on campus.

LEARNING DISABILITY PROGRAM OR SERVICES

Contact Information
Name of program or department: Accessible Education Center
   Telephone: 541-346-1155
   Fax: 541-346-6013

LEARNING DISABILITY SERVICES

Accommodations are determined an individual basis after a thorough review of appropriate, current documentation and an individual meeting with the student. The accommodations requested must be supported through the documentation provided and must be logically linked to the current impact of the condition on academic functioning.

Allowed in exams
   Calculator: Yes
   Dictionary: Yes
   Computer: Yes
   Spellchecker: Yes
Extended test time: Yes
Scribes: Yes
Proctors: Yes
Oral exams: Yes
Notetakers: Yes

Distraction-reduced environment: Yes
Tape recording in class: Yes
Electronic texts: Yes
**Accommodations for students with
   ADHD:** Yes
Kurzweil Reader: Yes
Other assistive technology: Yes
Priority registration: Yes

Added costs for services: Yes
LD specialists: Yes
Professional tutors: Yes
Peer tutors: Yes
Max. hours/wk. for services: NR
**How professors are notified of
   LD/ADHD:** By student and notification
letter

GENERAL ADMISSIONS INFORMATION

Office of Admission: 541-346-3201

ENTRANCE REQUIREMENTS

Academic units required: 4 English, 3 math, 3 science, 2 second language, 3 social studies. **Academic units recommended:** 1 science lab, 2 additional units in required college preparatory areas recommended. High school diploma is required, and GED is accepted. TOEFL required of all international applicants, minimum paper TOEFL 500, minimum internet TOEFL 61.

Application deadline: 1/15
Notification: Rolling
Average GPA: 3.59
ACT Composite middle 50% range:
   22–27

SAT Math middle 50% range:
   500–610
**SAT Critical Reading middle 50%
   range:** 490–610
SAT Writing middle 50% range:
   NR

Graduated top 10% of class: 23%
Graduated top 25% of class: 56%
Graduated top 50% of class: 89%

COLLEGE GRADUATION REQUIREMENTS

Course waivers allowed: No
Course substitutions allowed: Yes
In what course: In extreme cases with appropriate documentation.

ADDITIONAL INFORMATION

Environment: The university is located on 295 acres in an urban area of Eugene.

Student Body
   Undergrad enrollment: 20,631
   Women: NR
   Men: NR
   Percent out-of-state: 35%

Cost Information
   In-state tuition: $8,883
   Out-of-state tuition: $27,738
   Room & board: $9,501
Housing Information
   University housing: Yes
   Percent living on campus: 19%

Greek System
   Fraternity: Yes
   Sorority: Yes
Athletics: Division I

WESTERN OREGON UNIVERSITY

345 North Monmouth Avenue, Monmouth, OR 97361
Phone: 503-838-8211 • Fax: 503-838-8067
E-mail: wolfgram@wou.edu • Web: www.wou.edu
Support: S • Institution type: 4-year public

PROGRAMS OR SERVICES FOR STUDENTS WITH LD

The mission of the Office of Disability Services (ODS) is to remove barriers to learning for students with disabilities and to help ensure that these students access the tools and processes they need to create a successful experience at Western and beyond. These goals are realized by providing support services and information to help students develop skills such as self-advocacy, independence, identification and use of resources, appropriate use of problem-solving techniques, and accepting responsibility for one's actions. ODS strives to meet the individual needs of students with disabilities. The Student Enrichment Program (SEP) is designed to help students find success in college. The program's goals are to help SEP students develop writing, math, learning, and critical-thinking skills; maintain the necessary GPA to achieve individual goals; develop interpersonal communication skills; and achieve autonomy and maintain a sense of self-worth. Students who could benefit from SEP are those who enter the university without being completely prepared. SEP staff focuses on working with individual needs. Eligibility is based on federal guidelines determined by first-generation college-bound, financial need, or physical or learning disability; additionally, the student must have demonstrated academic need for the program.

ADMISSION INFORMATION FOR STUDENTS WITH LD/ADHD

College entrance tests required: No
Interview required: No
Essay recommended: No
What documentation required for LD: Psycho Ed evaluation to include: relevant historical info, instructional interventions, related services, age diagnosed, objective data (aptitude, achievement, info processing), test scores (standard, percentile and grade equivalents) and describe functional limitations.
With general application: No
To receive services after enrolling: Yes
What documentation required for ADHD: Diagnosis based on DSM-V; history of behaviors impairing functioning in academic setting; diagnostic interview; history of symptoms; evidence of ongoing behaviors.

With general application: No
Submitted to: Office of Disability Services
Special Ed. HS course work accepted: No
Specific course requirements of all applicants: Yes
Separate application required: Yes
# of LD applications submitted each year: NR
# of LD applications accepted yearly: NR
Total # of students receiving LD services: 60–70
Acceptance into program means acceptance into college: Student must be admitted and enrolled in the university first and then request services.

ADMISSIONS

General admission requires a 2.75 GPA and ACT/SAT scores, which are used only as alternatives to the required GPA. Applicants with a 2.50–2.74 are admissible with 21 ACT or 1000 SAT. Course requirements include 4 years of English, 3 years of math, 3 years of science, 3 years of social science, and 2 years of the same foreign language ("C-" or better in courses). Alternatives to course requirements require either a score of 470 or above on three SAT Subject Tests. A limited number of students who do not meet the regular admission requirements, alternatives, or exceptions may be admitted through special action of an Admissions Committee. Submit a letter of petition stating why they don't meet the admission requirements and what they are doing to make up deficiencies, and three letters of recommendation from school and community members.

ADDITIONAL INFORMATION

Skills classes are offered in academic survival strategies (no credit) and critical thinking (college credit). Other services include advocacy, computer stations, note-takers, readers and taping services, alternative testing, advisement, and assistance with registration. CEP offers counseling; basic math courses; advising; individualized instruction in reading, study skills, writing, and critical thinking; monitor programs; and workshops on study skills, research writing, math anxiety, rapid reading, note-taking, and time management. Services and accommodations are available for undergraduate and graduate students.

LEARNING DISABILITY PROGRAM OR SERVICES

Contact Information
Name of program or department: Office of Disability Services
  Telephone: 503-838-8250
  Fax: 503-838-8721

LEARNING DISABILITY SERVICES

Accommodations are decided upon an individual basis after a thorough review of appropriate, current documentation. The accommodations requested must be supported through the documentation provided and must be logically linked to the current impact of the condition on academic functioning.

Allowed in exams
  Calculator: Yes
  Dictionary: Yes
  Computer: Yes
  Spellchecker: Yes
Extended test time: Yes
Scribes: Yes
Proctors: Yes
Oral exams: Yes
Notetakers: Yes

Distraction-reduced environment: Yes
Tape recording in class: Yes
Electronic texts: No
Accommodations for students with
  ADHD: Yes
Kurzweil Reader: No
Other assistive technology: Yes
Priority registration: Yes

Added costs for services: No
LD specialists: No
Professional tutors: No
Peer tutors: Yes
Max. hours/wk. for services: N/A
How professors are notified of
  LD/ADHD: By both student and
  director

GENERAL ADMISSIONS INFORMATION

Office of Admission: 877-877-1593

ENTRANCE REQUIREMENTS

Academic units required: 4 English, 3 math, 3 science, 2 foreign language, 3 social studies, 1 history. **Academic units recommended:** 1 science lab. High school diploma is required, and GED is accepted. SAT Reasoning test or ACT with Writing component required. TOEFL required of all international applicants, minimum paper TOEFL 500, minimum computer TOEFL 180.

Application deadline: None
Notification: Rolling
Average GPA: 3.20
ACT Composite middle 50% range:
  17–22

SAT Math middle 50% range:
  430–530
SAT Critical Reading middle 50% range: 420–530
SAT Writing middle 50% range:
  470–560

Graduated top 10% of class: 13%
Graduated top 25% of class: 36%
Graduated top 50% of class: 73%

COLLEGE GRADUATION REQUIREMENTS

Course waivers allowed: No
Course substitutions allowed: Yes
In what course: Decisions are made on a case-by-case basis.

ADDITIONAL INFORMATION

Environment: The university is located on 134 acres in a rural area 15 miles west of Salem.

Student Body
  Undergrad enrollment: 5,318
  Women: 57%
  Men: 43%
  Percent out-of-state: 13%

Cost Information
  In-state tuition: $7,428
  Out-of-state tuition: $19,905
  Room & board: $8,622
Housing Information
  University housing: Yes
  Percent living on campus: 26%

Greek System
  Fraternity: No
  Sorority: No
Athletics: Division II

CLARION U. OF PENNSYLVANIA

Admissions Office, 840 Wood Street, Clarion, PA 16214
Phone: 814-393-2306 • Fax: 814-393-2030
E-mail: admissions@clarion.edu • Web: www.clarion.edu
Support: CS • Institution: 4-year public

PROGRAMS OR SERVICES FOR STUDENTS WITH LD

Clarion does not have a special admissions policy for students with learning disabilities nor does it offer a structured LD program. The Office of Disability Support Services works to ensure educational parity for students with learning disabilities within a mainstream setting. Academic accommodations and support focuses on minimizing the effects of the disability. The Center for Academic Enrichment is the university's primary vehicle for providing a Tutoring Center and is available to all students but especially beneficial for students with learning disabilities. These services are free of charge and include extensive peer tutoring, study skills workshops, and individual "learning to learn" activities.

ADMISSION INFORMATION FOR STUDENTS WITH LD/ADHD

College entrance tests required: Yes
Interview required: Yes
Essay recommended: No
What documentation required for LD: Psycho Ed evaluation to include: relevant historical info, instructional interventions, related services, age diagnosed, objective data (aptitude, achievement, info processing), test scores (standard, percentile and grade equivalents) and describe functional limitations.
With general application: No
To receive services after enrolling: Yes
What documentation required for ADHD: Diagnosis based on DSM-V; history of behaviors impairing functioning in academic setting; diagnostic interview; history of symptoms; evidence of ongoing behaviors.

With general application: No
Submitted to: Disability Support Services
Special Ed. HS course work accepted: Yes
Specific course requirements of all applicants: Yes
Separate application required: No
# of LD applications submitted each year: NR
# of LD applications accepted yearly: NR
Total # of students receiving LD services: 110
Acceptance into program means acceptance into college: Student must be admitted and enrolled in the university first and then request services.

ADMISSIONS

Students with learning disabilities who wish to be admitted to the university must meet regular admission requirements. Course requirements include 4 years of English, 2 years of math (4 recommended), 3 years of science (4 recommended), 2 years of a foreign language (recommended), and 4 years of social studies. Students not meeting the general admission criteria may be admitted by either the Academic Support Acceptance (these students are referred to Student Support Services) or Pre-College Experience Program (probationary admittance).

ADDITIONAL INFORMATION

The Disability Support Services staff serve as liaisons between students and faculty to provide special considerations when appropriate. Accommodations are based on documentation,for example, psychoeducational evaluations for students with learning disabilities. The nature of the student's disability, as well as the student's functional limitation, is considered when accommodations are determined. Accommodations could include extended time for exams, reader for exams, scribes for exams, word processor for exams, alternate test location, objective exams (when possible), essay exams (when possible), oral exams (when possible), word processor for written assignments, extended time for in-class assignments, taped lectures, tapes of textbooks, note-taking assistance, assistive technology, priority registration, and liaising with agencies. Services and accommodations are available to undergraduate and graduate students.

LEARNING DISABILITY PROGRAM OR SERVICES

Contact Information
Name of program or department: Disability Support Services
 Telephone: 814-393-2095
 Fax: 814-393-2368

LEARNING DISABILITY SERVICES

Accommodations are decided upon an individual basis after a thorough review of appropriate, current documentation. The accommodations requested must be supported through the documentation provided and must be logically linked to the current impact of the condition on academic functioning.

Allowed in exams
 Calculator: NR
 Dictionary: NR
 Computer: NR
 Spellchecker: NR
Extended test time: Yes
Scribes: Yes
Proctors: Yes
Oral exams: Yes
Notetakers: Yes

Distraction-reduced environment: Yes
Tape recording in class: Yes
Electronic texts: Yes
Accommodations for students with
 ADHD: Yes
Kurzweil Reader: Yes
Other assistive technology: Yes
Priority registration: Yes

Added costs for services: No
LD specialists: Yes
Professional tutors: 0
Peer tutors: 20
Max. hours/wk. for services: 1
How professors are notified of
 LD/ADHD: By student

GENERAL ADMISSIONS INFORMATION

Office of Admission: 800-672-7171

ENTRANCE REQUIREMENTS

Academic units required: 4 English, 3 math, 3 science, 3 social studies. **Academic units recommended:** 4 English, 4 math, 4 science (1 science lab), 2 foreign language, 4 social studies. High school diploma is required, and GED is accepted. ACT with or without Writing component accepted. TOEFL required of all international applicants, minimum paper TOEFL 500, minimum computer TOEFL 173.

Application deadline: None
Notification: Rolling
Average GPA: 3.2
ACT Composite middle 50% range:
 NR

SAT Math middle 50% range:
 420–530
SAT Critical Reading middle 50%
 range: 410–520
SAT Writing middle 50% range:
 400–500

Graduated top 10% of class: 6%
Graduated top 25% of class: 22%
Graduated top 50% of class: 52%

COLLEGE GRADUATION REQUIREMENTS

Course waivers allowed: Yes
In what course: Determined case-by-case
Course substitutions allowed: Yes
In what course: Determined case-by-case

ADDITIONAL INFORMATION

Environment: The university is located on 100 acres in a small town 85 miles northeast of Pittsburgh.

Student Body
 Undergrad enrollment: 6,223
 Women: 60%
 Men: 40%
 Percent out-of-state: 4%

Cost Information
 In-state tuition: $5,554
 Out-of-state tuition: $11,108
 Room & board: $6,390
Housing Information
 University housing: Yes
 Percent living on campus: 33%

Greek System
 Fraternity: Yes
 Sorority: Yes
Athletics: Division II

DREXEL UNIVERSITY

3141 Chestnut Street, 81-210, Philadelphia, PA 19104-2875
Phone: 215-895-1401 • Fax: 215-895-1402
E-mail: disability@drexel.edu • Web: www.drexel.edu/ODR
Support: CS • Institution type: 4-year private

PROGRAMS OR SERVICES FOR STUDENTS WITH LD

Drexel University does not have a specific learning disability program, but services are provided through the Office of Disability Resources (ODR). The professional staff works closely with the students who have special needs to ensure that they have the opportunity to participate fully in Drexel University's programs and activities. Drexel's ODR offers an individualized transition program for students with disabilities upon request. Students need to contact the ODR.

ADMISSION INFORMATION FOR STUDENTS WITH LD/ADHD

College entrance tests required: Yes
Nonstandardized tests accepted: Yes
Interview required: No
Essay required: No
What documentation required for LD: Psycho Ed evaluation to include: relevant historical info, instructional interventions, related services, age diagnosed, objective data (aptitude, achievement, info processing), test scores (standard, percentile and grade equivalents) and describe functional limitations.
With general application: No
To receive services after enrolling: Yes
What documentation required for ADHD: Diagnosis based on DSM-V; history of behaviors impairing functioning in academic setting; diagnostic interview; history of symptoms; evidence of ongoing behaviors.

With general application: No
Submitted to: Office of Disability Resources (ODR)
Special Ed. HS course work accepted: No
Specific course requirements of all applicants: Yes
Separate application required for services: No
# of LD applications submitted early: N/A
# of LD applications accepted yearly: N/A
Total # receiving LD/ADHD services: 270
Acceptance into program means acceptance into college: Students must be admitted and enrolled at the university first, then they may request services.

ADMISSIONS

The regular admission requirements are the same for all students, and there is no special process for students with learning disabilities or any other type of disability. Students are encouraged to self-disclose and provide current documentation of their disabilities to the ODR. General admission criteria include recommended courses of 4 years of English, 3 years of math, 1 year of science, 1 year of social studies, 7 electives (chosen from English, math, science, social studies, foreign language, history, or mechanical drawing). The average SAT score is 1180, and the average GPA is 3.4; an interview is recommended. For additional information, contact the Admissions Office at Drexel University directly.

ADDITIONAL INFORMATION

Accommodations may be provided, if appropriate and reasonable, and may include extra time for exams, adaptive technologies, note-takers, priority scheduling, instruction modifications, reduced course loads, and course substitutions. All accommodation eligibility is determined on a case-by-case basis. Tutors are not an accommodation in college, but are available for all students at Drexel through the Learning Centers. Currently there are nearly 270 students with LD eligible for services and accommodations.

LEARNING DISABILITY PROGRAM OR SERVICES

Contact Information
Name of program or department: Office of Disability Resources
  Phone: 215-895-1401
  Fax: 215-895-1402

LEARNING DISABILITY SERVICES

Accommodations are decided upon an individual basis after a thorough review of appropriate, current documentation. The accommodations requested must be supported through the documentation provided and must be logically linked to the current impact of the condition on academic functioning.

Allowed in Exams	**Distraction-reduced environment:** Yes	**Added costs:** No
Calculator: Yes	**Tape recording in class:** Yes	**LD Specialists:** 1
Dictionary: Yes	**Books on tape from RFBD:** Yes	**Professional tutors:** Yes
Computer: Yes	**Electronic texts:** Yes	**Peer tutors:** Yes
Spellchecker: Yes	**Accommodations for students with**	**Max hrs for serv:** Varies
Extended test time: Yes	**ADHD:** Yes	**How professors are notified of**
Scribes: Yes	**Kurzweil Reader:** Yes	**LD/ADHD:** By the student
Proctors: Yes	**Other assistive technology:** Yes	
Oral exams: Yes	**Priority registration:** Yes	
Note-takers: Yes		

GENERAL ADMISSIONS INFORMATION

Office of Admission: 215-895-2400

ENTRANCE REQUIREMENTS

Academic units required: 3 math, 1 science (1 science lab). **Academic units recommended:** 4 English, 3 math, 1 science (1 science lab), 1 foreign language, 1 social studies, 7 electives. High school diploma or GED is required. Minimum TOEFL is 550 written or 213 computer-based. TOEFL required of all international applicants.

Application deadline: 3/1	**SAT Math middle 50% range:**	**Graduated top 10%:** 32%
Notification: Rolling	570–670	**Graduated top 25%:** 64%
Average GPA: 3.41	**SAT Critical Reading middle 50%**	**Graduated top 50%:** 89%
ACT Composite middle 50% range:	**range:** 540–640	
23–28	**SAT Writing middle 50% range:**	
	520–630	

ADDITIONAL INFORMATION

Environment: The campus is located on 38 acres near the center of Philadelphia.

Student Body	**Cost Information**	**Greek System**
Undergrad enrollment: 13,980	**Tuition:** $34,405 (5-year)	**Fraternity:** Yes
Women: 45%	**Room & board:** $13,395	**Sorority:** Yes
Men: 55%	**Housing Information**	**Athletics:** Division I
Out-of-state: 50%	**University housing:** Yes	
	Percent living campus: 28%	

EAST STROUDSBURG U. OF PA

200 Prospect Street, East Stroudsburg, PA 18301-2999
Phone: 570-422-3542 • Fax: 570-422-3933
E-mail: undergrads@po-box.esu.edu • Web: www.esu.edu
Support: S • Institution: 4-year public

PROGRAMS OR SERVICES FOR STUDENTS WITH LD

There is no special program for students with learning disabilities at East Stroudsburg University. However, the university is committed to supporting otherwise qualified students with learning disabilities in their pursuit of an education. Disability Services offers students with academic accommodation recommendations assistive technology training and academic support and acts as their advocate on campus. Students who request accommodations or academic adjustments are responsible for providing required documentation to the Office of Disability Services and for requesting those accommodations or academic adjustments. East Stroudsburg University will need documentation of the disability, which consists of an evaluation by an appropriate professional and describes the current impact of the disability as it relates to the accommodation request. To receive services, students with disabilities must identify that they have a disability, submit appropriate documentation, and request services.

ADMISSION INFORMATION FOR STUDENTS WITH LD/ADHD

College entrance tests required: Yes
Interview required: No
Essay recommended: Yes
Documentation required for LD: Psychoeducational evaluation; reevaluation done within 3 years; must have been completed no earlier than 10th grade and functional limitation impact on learning.
Documentation required for ADHD: Psychoeducational evaluation and/or medical evaluation that includes medical history, diagnostic assessment instruments, diagnosis, and functional limitations.
Submitted to: Disability Services

Special Ed. HS course work accepted: Yes
Specific course requirements of all applicants: Yes
Separate application required: No
# of LD applications submitted each year: 0
# of LD applications accepted yearly: 0
Total # of students receiving LD services: 190
Acceptance into program means acceptance into college: Student must be admitted and enrolled in the university first and then request services.

ADMISSIONS

Students with LD file the general application and are encouraged to complete the section titled "Disabilities Information" and forward documentation of their disability to the Office of Disability Services. For general admission, academic achievement is the primary factor considered in the selection process. ESU looks for a good match between what each applicant can contribute to the university and how the university can meet each applicant's expectations through a whole-person assessment. ESU is interested in student contributions to their school and community, activities and achievements, aspirations, and anything else that would help evaluate potential success at ESU. SAT or ACT are used as a common yardstick to help in the selection process. SAT Subject Tests are not required.

ADDITIONAL INFORMATION

Students with learning disabilities may work individually or in groups with the disabilities specialist. All students enrolled in the university have the opportunity to take skills classes in reading, composition, and math. Other services include workshops in time management and test-taking strategies that are offered to all students. The Learning Center provides individual and group tutoring by peer tutors free of charge to ESU students. Tutors are assigned on a first-come, first-served basis, and students must complete and submit a request form in order to receive tutoring. East Stroudsburg University is the home of the Alpha Chapter of Delta Alpha Pi International Honor Society, an international honor society for students with disabilities who have achieved academic success. Services and accommodations are available for undergraduate and graduate students.

LEARNING DISABILITY PROGRAM OR SERVICES

Contact Information
Name of program or department: Office of Disability Services
Telephone: 570-422-3954
Fax: 717-422-3898

LEARNING DISABILITY SERVICES

Accommodations are decided upon an individual basis after a thorough review of appropriate, current documentation. The accommodations requested must be supported through the documentation provided and must be logically linked to the current impact of the condition on academic functioning.

Allowed in exams
  Calculator: Yes
  Dictionary: No
  Computer: Yes
  Spellchecker: Yes
Extended test time: Yes
Scribes: Yes
Proctors: No
Oral exams: Yes
Note-takers: Yes

Distraction-reduced environment: Yes
Tape recording in class: Yes
Electronic texts: Yes
Accommodations for students with ADHD: Yes
Kurzweil Reader: Yes
Other assistive technology: Yes
Priority registration: Yes

Added costs for services: No
LD specialists: No
Professional tutors: 20
Peer tutors: 70
Max. hours/wk. for services: 2
How professors are notified of LD/ADHD: By student

GENERAL ADMISSIONS INFORMATION

Office of Admission: 570-422-3542

ENTRANCE REQUIREMENTS

Academic units recomended: 4 English, 4 math, 3 science (2 science labs), 2 foreign language, 3 social studies, 3 history. High school diploma is required, and GED is accepted. ACT with or without Writing component accepted. TOEFL required of all international applicants, minimum paper TOEFL 500, minimum computer TOEFL 173.

Application deadline: 4/1
Notification: Rolling
Average GPA: NR
ACT Composite middle 50% range:
  NR

SAT Math middle 50% range:
  460–550
SAT Critical Reading middle 50% range: 440–530
SAT Writing middle 50% range:
  440–530

Graduated top 10% of class: 7%
Graduated top 25% of class: 30%
Graduated top 50% of class: 72%

COLLEGE GRADUATION REQUIREMENTS

Course waivers allowed: No
Course substitutions allowed: No

ADDITIONAL INFORMATION

Environment: The 813-acre campus is set in the foothills of the Pocono Mountains.

Student Body
  Undergrad enrollment: 6,372
  Women: 55%
  Men: 45%
  Percent out-of-state: 25%

Cost Information
  In-state tuition: $14,436
  Out-of-state tuition: $23,260
  Room & board: $6,758
Housing Information
  University housing: Yes
  Percent living on campus: 42%

Greek System
  Fraternity: Yes
  Sorority: Yes
Athletics: Division II

EDINBORO U. OF PENNSYLVANIA

200 East Normal Street, Edinboro, PA 16444
Phone: 814-732-2761 • Fax: 814-732-2420
E-mail: eup_admissions@edinboro.edu • Web: www.edinboro.edu
Support: CS • Institution: 4-year public

PROGRAMS OR SERVICES FOR STUDENTS WITH LD

Edinboro is actively involved in providing services for students with learning disabilities. The Office for Students with Disabilities (OSD) provides services that are individually directed by the program staff according to expressed needs. There are different levels of services offered depending on the student's needs. Level 1 offers supervised study sessions with trained peer advisors up to 10 hours per week; writing specialist by appointment one to two hours weekly; required appointment every two weeks with professional staff to review progress; and all services in Basic Service. Level 2 includes peer advising up to three hours weekly and all services in Basic Service. Basic Service provides assistance in arranging academic accommodations, including alternate test arrangements; priority scheduling; consultation with staff; and an alternate format of textbooks. Level 1 and 2 are fee-for-service levels.

ADMISSION INFORMATION FOR STUDENTS WITH LD/ADHD

College entrance tests required: Yes
Interview required: No
Essay required: N/A
Documentation required for LD: Psychoeducational
  evaluation
Documentation required for ADHD: Yes
Submitted to: Support Program/Services
Special Ed. HS course work accepted: Yes

Specific course requirements for all applicants: NR
Separate application required for program services: No
# of LD applications submitted each year: 40–100
# of LD applications accepted yearly: 40–60
Total # of students receiving LD services: 285
Acceptance into program means acceptance into
  college: Students must be admitted and enrolled in the
  university first and then request services.

ADMISSIONS

Students with LD submit the general application form. Upon receipt of the application by the Admissions Office, it is suggested that students identify any special services that may be required and contact the OSD so that a personal interview may be scheduled. Occasionally, OSD staff are asked for remarks on certain files, but it is not part of the admission decision. Students must provide a multifactored educational assessment; grade-level scores in reading, vocabulary and comprehension, math, and spelling; an individual intelligence test administered by a psychologist, including a list of the tests given; and a list of recommended accommodations. Evaluations submitted must have been completed recently (recommend within 3 years) and should meet the guidelines as published College Board, www.collegeboard.org. Students are reviewed for academic promise, motivation, and positive attitude.

ADDITIONAL INFORMATION

Students with LD are paired with peer advisors who help them with study skills, organizational skills, and time management skills. Students are recommended for different levels of services based on their needs. Students are not required to select a particular level, but OSD strongly recommends that students enroll for Level 1 if they have less than a 2.5 GPA. Specific academic scheduling needs may be complex, but students working through the OSD are given priority in academic scheduling. Tutoring is available for all students through Academic Support Services.

PROGRAM FOR DISABILITY SERVICES

Contact Information
Name of program or department: Office for Students with Disabilities (OSD)
 Telephone: 814-732-2462
 Fax: 814-732-2866

LEARNING DISABILITY SERVICES

Accommodations are decided upon an individual basis after a thorough review of appropriate, current documentation. The accommodations requested must be supported through the documentation provided and must be logically linked to the current impact of the condition on academic functioning. requested accommodations must not alter curriculum.

Allowed in exams
 Calculator: Yes
 Dictionary: Yes
 Computer: Yes
 Spellchecker: Yes
Extended test time: Yes
Scribes: Yes
Proctors: Yes
Oral exams: No
Note-takers: No

Distraction-reduced environment: Yes
Tape recording in class: Yes
Electronic texts: Yes
Accommodations for students with ADHD: Yes
Kurzweil Reader: Yes
Other assistive technology: We have an Assistive Tech Center on campus for evaluations and training of Assistive equipment.
Priority registration: Yes

Added costs for services: Yes
LD specialists: Yes
Professional tutors: 1
Peer tutors: 80–100
Max. hours/wk. for services: 12
How professors are notified of LD/ADHD: Student

GENERAL ADMISSIONS INFORMATION

Office of Admission: 1-888-846-2676

ENTRANCE REQUIREMENTS

Academic units recommended: 4 English, 3 mathematics, 3 science, 2 foreign language, 4 social studies, 1 computer science. High school diploma is required and GED is accepted. Requires ACT or SAT. TOEFL required of all international applicants; minimum paper TOEFL 500, minimum computer TOEFL 173, minimum web-based TOEFL 61.

Application deadline: None
Notification: Rolling
Average GPA: 3.30
ACT Composite middle 50% range:
 16–21

SAT Math middle 50% range:
 420–530
SAT Critical Reading middle 50% range: 420–520
SAT Writing middle 50% range: NR

Graduated top 10% of class: 5%
Graduated top 25% of class: 20%
Graduated top 50% of class: 51%

COLLEGE GRADUATION REQUIREMENTS

Course waivers allowed: No
In what course: Case-by-case basis only for substitutions
Course substitutions allowed: Yes
In what course: Case-by-case basis; request reviewed by committee

ADDITIONAL INFORMATION

Environment: Edinboro University is located on 600 acres in a small town 20 miles south of Erie.

Student Body
 Undergrad enrollment: 6,649
 Women: 56%
 Men: 44%
 Percent out-of-state: 14%

Cost Information
 In-state tuition: $6,240
 Out-of-state tuition: $9,360
 Room and board: $8,068
Housing Information
 University housing: Yes
 Percent living on campus: 29%

Greek System
 Fraternity: Yes
 Sorority: Yes
Athletics: Division II

GANNON UNIVERSITY

University Square, Erie, PA 16541
Phone: 814-871-7240 • Fax: 814-871-5803
E-mail: admissions@gannon.edu • Web: www.gannon.edu
Support: SP • Institution type: 4-year private

PROGRAMS OR SERVICES FOR STUDENTS WITH LD

Gannon's Program for Students with Learning Disabilities (PSLD) provides special support services for students who have been diagnosed with either LD or ADHD who are highly motivated for academic achievement. PSLD faculty are committed to excellence and strive to offer each student individually designed instruction. Students in the program may select any academic major offered by the university. Freshman-year support includes weekly individual sessions with instructor-tutors and a writing specialist. They also provide an advocacy seminar course that includes participation in small group counseling. Students should check the appropriate box on the admissions application if this service applies.

ADMISSION INFORMATION FOR STUDENTS WITH LD/ADHD

College entrance tests required: Yes
Interview required: No
Essay recommended: No
What documentation required for LD: Psycho Ed evaluation to include: relevant historical info, instructional interventions, related services, age diagnosed, objective data (aptitude, achievement, info processing), test scores (standard, percentile and grade equivalents) and describe functional limitations.
With general application: Yes if requested as part of Structured Program application
To receive services after enrolling: Yes
What documentation required for ADHD: Diagnosis based on DSM-V; history of behaviors impairing functioning in academic setting; diagnostic interview; history of symptoms; evidence of ongoing behaviors.

With general application: Yes if requested as part of Structured Program application
To receive services after enrolling: Yes
Submitted to: PSLD Director
Special Ed. HS course work accepted: No
Specific course requirements of all applicants: Yes
Separate application required: No
# of LD applications submitted each year: 45
# of LD applications accepted yearly: unlimited
Total # of students receiving LD services: 40–60
Acceptance into program means acceptance into college: The Director of PSLD accepts students into the PSLD program. For students who are otherwise qualified for general admission to the university.

ADMISSIONS

Admissions is based on several factors including academic courses, grades, rank in class, and counselor recommendation. ACT/SAT test required. The minimum GPA and test scores required very based on the academic program and the university will notify the applicant s if they do not meet the minimum requirements. Personal statement/essay is optional but recommended as it assists the university in evaluating eligibility beyond test scores and academic record. Courses required include 16 units of which 4 must be in English. Students diagnosed with a learning disability and who are interested in the Hannon's PSLD Program will also need: personal letters of recommendation from teachers, counselor or school administrators, WAIS/WISC scores and sub scores (abbreviate WISC/WAIS scores are not accepted). The WAIS/WISC are not required if the primary diagnosis is ADHD. Records from any professional with whom the student has worked, such as psychologist, physician, reading specialist or math specialist. Students admitted conditionally must enter as undeclared majors until they can achieve a 2.0 GPA.

ADDITIONAL INFORMATION

Specific features of the program include biweekly or more as needed, tutoring sessions with the program instructors and tutors to review course material, and focus on specific needs; weekly sessions with the writing specialist for reviewing, editing, and brainstorming. Additional services available are taping of classes, extended time on exams, scribes as prescribed. Basic services are free, and there is a $600 yearly fee for support services.

LEARNING DISABILITY PROGRAM OR SERVICES

Contact Information
Name of program or department: Program for Students with Learning Disabilities (PSLD)
  Telephone: 814-871-5360
  Fax: 814-871-7499

LEARNING DISABILITY SERVICES

Accommodations are decided upon an individual basis after a thorough review of appropriate, current documentation. The accommodations requested must be supported through the documentation provided and must be logically linked to the current impact of the condition on academic functioning.

Allowed in exams
  Calculator: No
  Dictionary: No
  Computer: Yes
  Spellchecker: No
Extended test time: Yes
Scribes: Yes, as recommended
Proctors: Yes
Oral exams: Yes, as recommended
Notetakers: Yes, as recommended

Distraction-reduced environment: Yes
Tape recording in class: Yes
Electronic texts: Yes
Accommodations for students with ADHD: Yes
Kurzweil Reader: No
Other assistive technology: Intel Reader
Priority registration: N/A

Added costs for services: No fee for basic accommodations, $600 per year for expanded services
LD specialists: Yes
Professional tutors: Yes
Peer tutors: Yes
Max. hours/wk. for services: 5+
How professors are notified of LD/ADHD: By student with letter from program director

GENERAL ADMISSIONS INFORMATION

Office of Admission: 814-871-5759

ENTRANCE REQUIREMENTS

Academic units required: 4 English, 12 combination of remaining academic units based on planned major. High school diploma is required, and GED is accepted. ACT. TOEFL required of all international applicants, minimum paper TOEFL 500, minimum computer TOEFL 173.

Application deadline: None
Notification: Rolling
Average GPA: 3.26
ACT Composite middle 50% range: 20–25

SAT Math middle 50% range: 460–580
SAT Critical Reading middle 50% range: 450–570
SAT Writing middle 50% range: NR

Graduated top 10% of class: 22%
Graduated top 25% of class: 52%
Graduated top 50% of class: 80%

COLLEGE GRADUATION REQUIREMENTS

Course waivers allowed: No
Course substitutions allowed: Yes
In what course: Substitutions for foreign language and mathematics in certain circumstances.

ADDITIONAL INFORMATION

Environment: The university is located on 13 acres in Erie, an urban area 135 miles north of Pittsburgh.

Student Body
  Undergrad enrollment: 2,925
  Women: 60%
  Men: 40%
  Percent out-of-state: 40%

Cost Information
  Tuition: $37,000
  Room & Board: $9,480
Housing Information
  University housing: Yes
  Percent living on campus: 60%

Greek System
  Fraternity: Yes
  Sorority: Yes
Athletics: Division II

KUTZTOWN U. OF PENNSYLVANIA

Admissions Office, PO Box 730, Kutztown, PA 19530-0730
Phone: 610-683-4060 • Fax: 610-683-1375
E-mail: admission@kutztown.edu • Web: www.kutztown.edu
Support: CS • Institution type: 4-year public

PROGRAMS OR SERVICES FOR STUDENTS WITH LD

The philosophy of the university is to provide equal opportunity to all individuals. The Disability Services Office provides reasonable accommodations while fostering independence in the students. The accommodations provided are in accordance with the needs of the students and the academic integrity of the institution. The office acts as an information and referral resource, provides direct services, coordinates services provided by other departments/agencies, and serves as a liaison between students with disabilities and university personnel working with students. Since information regarding a student's disability is not obtained through the admission process, it is the student's responsibility upon acceptance to the university to identify him or herself to the program. Students are encouraged to do this as early as possible upon admission. This will provide an opportunity to assess the university's capability of responding to special needs and the services available at the university. The Director of Disability Services works together with all university offices to help provide specific accommodations as warranted by appropriate documentation, as well as provide creative solutions to problems with which students with disabilities are confronted.

ADMISSION INFORMATION FOR STUDENTS WITH LD/ADHD

College entrance tests required: Yes
Interview required: No
Essay recommended: No
What documentation required for LD: Psycho Ed evaluation to include: relevant historical info, instructional interventions, related services, age diagnosed, objective data (aptitude, achievement, info processing), test scores (standard, percentile and grade equivalents) and describe functional limitations.
With general application: No
To receive services after enrolling: Yes
What documentation required for ADHD: Diagnosis based on DSM-V; history of behaviors impairing functioning in academic setting; diagnostic interview; history of symptoms; evidence of ongoing behaviors.

With general application: No
Submitted to: Disability Services Office
Special Ed. HS course work accepted: Yes
Specific course requirements of all applicants: Yes
Separate application required: No
# of LD applications submitted each year: NR
# of LD applications accepted yearly: NR
Total # of students receiving LD services: 300
Acceptance into program means acceptance into college: Students must be admitted to and enrolled in the university first and then request accommodations.

ADMISSIONS

Kutztown University uses a rolling admissions process to review applications, which means that applications are reviewed and decisions made as soon as the application is complete and as long as space is available. The application is complete when the university receives the $35 application fee, HS transcript, and SAT or ACT results. The focus of freshmen application review is the high school course curriculum, grade point average and class rank along with results from the standardized test scores from SAT or ACT. A favorable admission decision is based upon the student's qualifications at the time of the offer and is contingent upon the maintenance of those standards through graduation from high school. An Admissions Exceptions Committee considers applications that may warrant exceptions to the general admission standards.

ADDITIONAL INFORMATION

The Director of Disability Services is the initial resource person and record keeper who validates the existence of a disability and the need for any specific accommodations, and contacts faculty and other individuals who have reason to receive information. Academic assistance is provided through the Tutoring Center. Students with LD are eligible to receive services and accommodations prescribed in the psychoeducational evaluation, extended time on exams, use of tape recorder, use of calculator, testing in a separate location, readers, spellchecker and grammar check on written assignments, scribes, alternate text, tutorial assistance, early advisement and pre-registration, computer assistive technology, and referrals. Tutors are available to all students, and arrangements are made at no cost to the student.

LEARNING DISABILITY PROGRAM OR SERVICES

Contact Information
Name of program or department: Disability Services Office
Telephone: 610-683-4108
Fax: 610-683-1520

LEARNING DISABILITY SERVICES

Accommodations are decided upon an individual basis after a thorough review of appropriate, current documentation. The accommodations requested must be supported through the documentation provided and must be logically linked to the current impact of the condition on academic functioning.

Allowed in exams
Calculator: Yes
Dictionary: N/A
Computer: Yes
Spellchecker: Yes
Extended test time: Yes
Scribes: Yes
Proctors: Yes
Oral exams: Yes
Note-takers: Yes

Distraction-reduced environment: Yes
Tape recording in class: Yes
Electronic texts: Yes
Accommodations for students with
  ADHD: Yes
Kurzweil Reader: N/A
Other assistive technology: Yes
Priority registration: Yes

Added costs for services: No
LD specialists: One
Professional tutors: No
Peer tutors: Yes
Max. hours/wk. for services:
  Unlimited
How professors are notified of
  LD/ADHD: By both student and
  director

GENERAL ADMISSIONS INFORMATION

Office of Admission: 610-683-4060

ENTRANCE REQUIREMENTS

Academic units recommended: 4 English, 4 math, 4 science, 2–4 foreign language, 4 social studies. High school diploma is required, and GED is accepted. SAT, ACT with or without Writing component accepted. TOEFL required of all international applicants: minimum paper TOEFL 550, minimum iBT TOEFL 79.

Application deadline: None
Notification: Rolling
Average GPA: 3.10
ACT Composite middle 50% range:
  17–21

SAT Math middle 50% range:
  430–530
SAT Critical Reading middle 50%
  range: 430–530
SAT Writing middle 50% range:
  420–520

Graduated top 10% of class: 6%
Graduated top 25% of class: 24%
Graduated top 50% of class: 63%

COLLEGE GRADUATION REQUIREMENTS

Course waivers allowed: No
Course substitutions allowed: Yes
In what course: Only with strong diagnostic recommendation through the Undergraduate Exceptions Committee, foreign language and math.

ADDITIONAL INFORMATION

Environment: The university is located on 289 acres in a rural area 90 miles north of Philadelphia.

Student Body
Undergrad enrollment: 9,726
Women: 57%
Men: 43%
Percent out-of-state: 11%

Cost Information
In-state tuition: $7,398
Out-of-state tuition: $17,897
Room & board: $8,536
Housing Information
University housing: Yes
Percent living on campus: 48%

Greek System
Fraternity: Yes
Sorority: Yes
Athletics: Division II

LEHIGH UNIVERSITY

27 Memorial Drive West, Bethlehem, PA 18015
Phone: 610-758-3100 • Fax: 610-758-4361
E-mail: admissions@lehigh.edu • Web: www.lehigh.edu
Support: CS • Institution type: 4-year private

PROGRAMS OR SERVICES FOR STUDENTS WITH LD

Lehigh University is committed to ensuring reasonable accommodations to students who are substantially limited by a diagnosed disability. Students requesting academic accommodations are required to submit for review current documentation of their disability. If a student is not certain whether he or she has a learning disability, the Director of Academic Support Services can conduct a comprehensive intake interview and screening process. If a complete diagnostic evaluation seems appropriate, the student will be provided with referrals to community-based professionals who can perform a comprehensive evaluation at the student's expense. The ultimate goal is to ensure that students with disabilities have an opportunity to grow independently to their fullest potential at a competitive university. It is the responsibility of students with disabilities to identify themselves to the appropriate university contact person and provide the required documentation to receive accommodations. Given the specific nature of each person's disability, reasonable accommodations will be determined on an individual basis by the appropriate university contact person. Students who are eligible for accommodations must sign a professor notification and accommodation form at the beginning of each semester that students are requesting accommodations.

ADMISSION INFORMATION FOR STUDENTS WITH LD/ADHD

College entrance tests required: Yes
Interview required: No
Essay recommended: No
What documentation required for LD: Psycho Ed evaluation to include: relevant historical info, instructional interventions, related services, age diagnosed, objective data (aptitude, achievement, info processing), test scores (standard, percentile and grade equivalents) and describe functional limitations.
With general application: No
To receive services after enrolling: Yes
What documentation required for ADHD: Diagnosis based on DSM-V; history of behaviors impairing functioning in academic setting; diagnostic interview; history of symptoms; evidence of ongoing behaviors.

With general application: No
Submitted to: Office of Academic Support Services
Special Ed. HS course work accepted: No
Specific course requirements of all applicants: Yes
Separate application required: No
# of LD applications submitted each year: NR
# of LD applications accepted yearly: 30
Total # of students receiving LD services: 95
Acceptance into program means acceptance into college: Students must be admitted and enrolled prior to requesting services.

ADMISSIONS

There is no special admission process for students with learning disabilities. All applicants must meet the same admission criteria. Applicants must submit either the SAT Reasoning Test or the ACT with the optional Writing section. An on-campus interview is recommended. Applicants' evaluations are based on many factors, including a challenging college-prep curriculum that included AP and honors courses.

ADDITIONAL INFORMATION

The Peer Mentor Program assists first-year students with the transition from high school to a competitive university. The peer mentors are composed of upperclass students who have a diagnosed learning disability or attention deficit hyperactivity disorder. Each mentor has demonstrated leadership capability and has been academically successful at Lehigh University. First-year students are matched with a peer mentor by college and/or major. The rationale for matching students in this manner is because upperclass students of the same major and/or college have most likely taken the same courses and professors and have experienced the same challenges as the freshman with whom they have been matched. The first-year students who have participated in the Peer Mentor Program and who have worked with the Office of Academic Support Services have traditionally performed significantly better than students who have not participated in support services. Program participation is voluntary, and students may choose to withdraw from the program at any time. The Center for Writing and Math provides assistance with any writing assignments, including brainstorming, rough-draft preparations, and critiques of final draft and assistance in calculus and other math courses. The Center for Academic Success has peer tutors available in most freshman- and sophomore-level courses. Ten free hours of tutoring per course per semester are provided. The tutors provide assistance with study skills, note-taking skills, and time management techniques.

LEARNING DISABILITY PROGRAM OR SERVICES

Contact Information
Name of program or department: Office of Academic Support Services
Telephone: 610-758-4152
Fax: 610-758-5293

LEARNING DISABILITY SERVICES

Accommodations are decided upon an individual basis after a thorough review of appropriate, current documentation. The accommodations requested must be supported through the documentation provided and must be logically linked to the current impact of the condition on academic functioning.

Allowed in exams	**Distraction-reduced environment:** No	**Added costs for services:** No
Calculator: No	**Tape recording in class:** Yes	**LD specialists:** Yes
Dictionary: No	**Electronic texts:** Yes	**Professional tutors:** 3
Computer: Yes	**Accommodations for students with**	**Peer tutors:** 30
Spellchecker: No	**ADHD:** Yes	**Max. hours/wk. for services:** NR
Extended test time: Yes	**Kurzweil Reader:** Yes	**How professors are notified of**
Scribes: Yes	**Other assistive technology:** No	**LD/ADHD:** By both student and
Proctors: Yes	**Priority registration:** No	director
Oral exams: No		
Note-takers: Yes		

GENERAL ADMISSIONS INFORMATION

Office of Admission: 610-758-3100

ENTRANCE REQUIREMENTS

Academic units required: 4 English, 3 math, 2 science (2 science labs), 2 foreign language, 2 social studies, 3 academic electives. High school diploma or equivalent is not required. ACT with Writing component required. TOEFL required of all international applicants: minimum paper TOEFL 570, minimum computer TOEFL 230.

Application deadline: 1/1	**SAT Math middle 50% range:**	**Graduated top 10% of class:** 95.5%
Notification: 4/1	640–720	**Graduated top 25% of class:** 99%
Average GPA: NR	**SAT Critical Reading middle 50%**	**Graduated top 50% of class:** 100%
ACT Composite middle 50% range:	range: 590–680	
28–31	**SAT Writing middle 50% range:** NR	

COLLEGE GRADUATION REQUIREMENTS

Course waivers allowed: No
Course substitutions allowed: No

ADDITIONAL INFORMATION

Environment: Lehigh is located 60 miles north of Philadelphia and 80 miles southwest of New York City.

Student Body	**Cost Information**	**Greek System**
Undergrad enrollment: 4,869	Tuition: $40,660	Fraternity: Yes
Women: 42%	Room & board: $10,840	Sorority: Yes
Men: 58%	**Housing Information**	Athletics: Division I
Percent out-of-state: 75%	University housing: Yes	
	Percent living on campus: 75%	

MARYWOOD UNIVERSITY

2300 Adams Avenue, Scranton PA 18509
Phone: 570-348-6211 • Fax: 570-961-4763
E-mail: yourfuture@marywood.edu • Web: www.marywood.edu
Support: S • Institution Type: 4-year private

PROGRAMS OR SERVICES FOR STUDENTS WITH LD

Marywood University is committed to providing an environment that is accessible to all students, regardless of disability type. Through the Office of Disability Services, we have helped facilitate the education of students who have disabilities by coordinating a variety of services that support the unique academic needs of permanently and temporarily disabled students. The Office of Disability Services also works to ensure policies, procedures, and practices within the university environment do not discriminate against students because they have a disability. The Office of Disability Services provides individualized support to all qualified students with disabilities. This support includes academic advising, advocacy, awareness, and accommodations.

ADMISSION INFORMATION FOR STUDENTS WITH LD/ADHD

College entrance tests required: Yes
Interview required: No
Essay required: No
Documentation required for LD: Complete psychoeducational report; IEP/504 service plan suggested, no more than 3 years old.
Documentation required for ADD: Complete psychoeducational report; IEP/504 service plan suggested, no more than 3 years old.

Specific course requirements of all applicants: Yes
Submitted to: Admissions and Disability Services
Special Ed. HS course work accepted: Yes
Separate application required for program services: No
# of LD applications submitted each year: NR
# of LD applications accepted each year: NR
Total # of students receiving LD services: N/A
Acceptance into program means acceptance into college: Students must be admitted based upon standard acceptance criteria with allowance for accommodations.

ADMISSIONS

All applicants must meet the same admission criteria. There is an extensive application process, including official high school transcripts (and college if applicable), letters of recommendation, SAT/ACT and a review by the Admissions Office/Committee. Admissions requirements include approximately top 50 percent of high school class or high school 6-semester overall GPA of 2.25 or equivalent, 900 or higher SAT (CR+M only), or 19 ACT composite score. High school units required include 4 units of English, 3 units of social science, 2 units of math, 1 unit of lab science, and 6 additional units to fulfill graduation requirements. Marywood University makes all efforts to avoid any possible prejudice in the admissions process. Students with disabilities may choose to self-disclose and request an interview with the Office of Disability Services. The disability services provider can then make an informed recommendation to the Admissions Office/Committee regarding a student's ability to succeed at Marywood.

ADDITIONAL INFORMATION:

Students with disabilities may also find the services provided through the Tutoring Program to be helpful. These services are available for all Marywood students, and supports them in their efforts to become excellent learners and provides dynamic learning assistance services to increase student achievement and foster active involvement in the learning process. Services include tutoring, college-level study skill information, and a Writing Center staffed by both peer tutors and a professional writing tutor.

LEARNING DISABILITY PROGRAM OR SERVICES

Contact Information
Name of program or department: Office of Disability Services
   Telephone: 570-340-6045
   Fax: 570-340-6028

LEARNING DISABILITY SERVICES

Accommodations are decided upon an individual basis after a thorough review of appropriate, current documentation. The accommodations requested must be supported through the documentation provided and must be logically linked to the current impact of the condition on academic functioning.

Allowed in exams
   Calculator: Yes
   Dictionary: Yes
   Computer: Yes
   Spellchecker: Yes
Extended test time: Yes
Scribes: Yes
Proctors: No
Oral Exams: Yes
Note-takers: Yes

Distraction reduced environment: Yes
Tape recording in class: Yes
Electronic texts: Yes
Accommodations for students with ADD: Yes
Kurzweil Reader: Yes
Other assistive technology: Yes
Priority registration: Yes

Added costs for services: No
LD specialists: No
Professional tutors: 1
Peer tutors: 120
Max. hours/wk. for services: Unlimited
How professors are notified of LD/ADD: By both student and coordinator

GENERAL ADMISSIONS INFORMATION

Office of Admission: 570-348-6234

ENTRANCE REQUIREMENTS
Academic units required: 4 English, 3 social science, 2 math, 1 science lab, 6 additional units.
High school Diploma is required, and GED is accepted. SAT is preferred, and ACT is accepted. TOEFL is required of all international applicants.

Application Deadline: None
Notification: Rolling
Average GPA: 3.21
ACT Composite middle 50% range: NR

SAT Math middle 50% range: 480–570
SAT Critical Reading middle 50% range: 470–560
SAT Writing middle 50% range: 460–560

Graduated top 10% of class: 20%
Graduated top 25% of class: 54%
Graduated top 50% of class: 83%

COLLEGE GRADUATION REQUIREMENTS

Course waivers allowed: No
Course substitutions allowed: Yes
In what courses: Foreign Language, math and others on case-by-case basis

ADDITIONAL INFORMATION

Environment: Situated on a hill top, Marywood's scenic 122-acre campus is part of an attractive residential area of the city of Scranton in northeastern Pennsylvania.

Student Body
   Undergraduate enrollment: 2,267
   Women: 69%
   Men: 31%
   Percent out-of-state: 37%

Cost Information:
   Tuition: $26,000
   Room & board: $12,172
Housing Information:
   University housing: Yes
   Percent living on campus: 73%

Greek System:
   Fraternity: No
   Sorority: Yes
   Athletics: NCAA Division III

MERCYHURST UNIVERSITY

Admissions, 501 East Thirty-eighth Street, Erie, PA 16546
Phone: 814-824-2202 • Fax: 814-824-2071
E-mail: admissions@mercyhurst.edu • Web: www.mercyhurst.edu
Support: SP • Institution type: 4-year private

PROGRAMS OR SERVICES FOR STUDENTS WITH LD

The Learning Differences Program is a specialized program at Mercyhurst University, which is currently celebrating 25 years of experience in working with and advocating for students with learning disabilities and attention deficit disorder. Recently, programming was expanded to include the Asperger Initiative at Mercyhurst (AIM) designed for students with autism spectrum disorders (ASD). There are three levels of services available. For students with LD or ADHD, Mercryhurst offers a Level I (compliance/basic service) program which is free of charge as well as a Level II (structured) program. The Level III program, which includes both academic and social skills assistance, is designed for students on the autism spectrum. These programs consist of a structured, individualized set of experiences designed to assist students to gain maximum value from their educational potential. Students who select the Level II or III program must pay an additional fee for service. All students must submit documentation that completed within the last three years. Students who choose the Level II or III programs have the option of attending two different summer transition programs.

ADMISSION INFORMATION FOR STUDENTS WITH LD/ADHD

College entrance tests required: Yes
Interview required: Yes
Essay recommended: Yes
What documentation required for LD: Psycho Ed evaluation to include: relevant historical info, instructional interventions, related services, age diagnosed, objective data (aptitude, achievement, info processing), test scores (standard, percentile and grade equivalents) and describe functional limitations.
With general application: Yes if requested as part of Structured Program application
To receive services after enrolling: Yes
What documentation required for ADHD: Diagnosis based on DSM-V; history of behaviors impairing functioning in academic setting; diagnostic interview; history of symptoms; evidence of ongoing behaviors.

With general application: Yes if requested as part of Structured Program application
To receive services after enrolling: Yes
Submitted to: Admissions Office
Special Ed. HS course work accepted: No
Specific course requirements of all applicants: Yes
Separate application required: Yes
# of LD applications submitted each year: 120
# of LD applications accepted yearly: 50
Total # of students receiving LD services: 162
Acceptance into program means acceptance into college: Students must be admitted to and enrolled in the university first and then request services.

ADMISSIONS

To be eligible for any of the services at Mercyhurst, students with learning disabilities must adhere to the regular admission requirements and meet the regular admission criteria. General admission criteria include a 2.5 GPA; ACT 19-plus or SAT 900-plus; and 4 English, 2 social science, 3 math, 2 science, and 2 foreign language (waivers and substitutions are determined on an individual basis). Students who do not meet the regular admissions standards are referred to Mercyhurst—McAuley and/or Mercyhurst—Northeast for consideration into the 2-year division. Some students may be admitted on probation pending the completion of developmental course work. The college reserves the right to reject any student not meeting admission standards. The admission decisions are made jointly by the director of Programs for Students with Learning Differences and the Office of Admissions. Upon acceptance to the college, if the student wishes special services, he or she must self identify to Admissions and, at that time, choose to receive services available to students with documented learning differences. These programs are a structured program and a basic service program.

ADDITIONAL INFORMATION

The Structured Program for Students with Learning Differences provides special services that go beyond what is required by law. These fee-based programs include an invitation to a 3-week Summer transition program prior to the freshmen year, weekly meetings with a learning disabilities specialist, an advisory board, alternative testing, access to alternative textbooks through Kurzweil Reader, midterm progress reports, note-takers, peer tutoring, professional advising/priority registration. The Asperger Initiative at Mercyhurst (AIM) is designed for students on the autism spectrum who require academic as well as social skills competencies.

LEARNING DISABILITY PROGRAM OR SERVICES

Contact Information
Name of program or department: Program for Students with Learning Differences
 Telephone: 814-824-2450
 Fax: 814-824-2436

LEARNING DISABILITY SERVICES

Accommodations are decided upon an individual basis after a thorough review of appropriate, current documentation. The accommodations requested must be supported through the documentation provided and must be logically linked to the current impact of the condition on academic functioning.

Allowed in exams	Distraction-reduced environment: Yes	Added costs for services: Yes
Calculator: Yes	Tape recording in class: Yes	LD specialists: Yes
Dictionary: Yes	Electronic texts: Yes	Professional tutors: No
Computer: Yes	Accommodations for students with	Peer tutors: 30
Spellchecker: Yes	ADHD: Yes	Max. hours/wk. for services:
Extended test time: Yes	Kurzweil Reader: Yes	Unlimited
Scribes: Yes	Other assistive technology: Yes	How professors are notified of
Proctors: Yes	Priority registration: Yes	LD/ADHD: By both student and
Oral exams: Yes		director
Note-takers: Yes		

GENERAL ADMISSIONS INFORMATION

Office of Admission: 814-824-2202

ENTRANCE REQUIREMENTS

Academic units recommended: 4 English, 3 math, 3 science (1 science lab), 2 foreign language, 2 social studies, 2 history. High school diploma is required, and GED is accepted. ACT without Writing component accepted. TOEFL required of all international applicants: minimum paper TOEFL 550, minimum computer TOEFL 300.

Application deadline: None	SAT Math middle 50% range:	Graduated top 10% of class: 18%
Notification: Rolling	460–580	Graduated top 25% of class: 43%
Average GPA: 3.40	SAT Critical Reading middle 50%	Graduated top 50% of class: 79%
ACT Composite middle 50% range:	range: 470–570	
20–25	SAT Writing middle 50% range:	
	450–570	

COLLEGE GRADUATION REQUIREMENTS

Course waivers allowed: Yes
In what course: Foreign language
Course substitutions allowed: Any
In what course: With permission of Dean's office and faculty chair

ADDITIONAL INFORMATION

Environment: The 80-acre campus of Mercyhurst overlooks Lake Erie.

Student Body	Cost Information	Greek System
Undergrad enrollment: 4,014	Tuition: $29,247	Fraternity: No
Women: 57%	Room & board: $9,738	Sorority: No
Men: 43%	Housing Information	Athletics: Division II
Percent out-of-state: 55%	University housing: Yes	
	Percent living on campus: 58%	

MESSIAH COLLEGE

PO Box 3005, One College Avenue, Grantham, PA 17027
Phone: 717-691-6000 • Fax: 717-691-2307
E-mail: bwaltman@messiah.edu • Web: www.messiah.edu
Support: S • Institution: 4-year private

PROGRAMS OR SERVICES FOR STUDENTS WITH LD

Messiah College is a Christian college committed to providing reasonable accommodations to qualified students with disabilities. Students who feel they may qualify for services should meet with the Office of Disability Service's (ODS) staff. At that meeting, ODS staff will discuss the documentation process, services available, and their educational goals. Services and accommodations rendered will be based on the individualized needs of the students. Such services/accommodations are granted to create an equal opportunity for student success, but do not in any way waive class expectations. Therefore, classroom success is not guaranteed. To be recognized as a student with a disability, students are required to submit documentation from a qualified educational evaluator stating their diagnosis, how such a diagnosis creates a "substantial impairment" and in which life activities, and a list of accommodations that will be needed by the student in order to benefit from the program. Students who do not have documentation but who think they may have a disability may seek assistance from ODS by locating screening services. Any costs incurred for an evaluation are the responsibility of the student. ODS finds most students registered with the office to be motivated, hardworking, and interested and willing to meet their educational goals.

ADMISSION INFORMATION FOR STUDENTS WITH LD/ADHD

College entrance tests required: Yes
Interview required: No
Documentation required for LD: Complete psychoeducational report from a qualified examiner, to include all test details; IEP/504 service plan suggested with few exceptions, report should be less than three years old.
Documentation required for ADHD: Same as for LD
Submitted to: Office of Disability Services
Special Ed. HS course work accepted: Yes

Specific course requirements for all applicants: Yes
Separate application required for program services: No
# of LD applications submitted each year: NR
# of LD applications accepted yearly: NR
Total # of students receiving LD services: 25–30
Acceptance into program means acceptance into college: Student must be admitted to college first and may then request services.

ADMISSIONS

All applicants must meet the same admission criteria. There is an extensive application process including: letters of recommendation; ACT/SAT; high school transcript; essays, and a review by the Admissions officer/committee. Admission requirements include a high school transcript, SAT or ACT scores, and four English, two math, two natural sciences, two social studies, and six electives (prefer that two of these be in foreign language), and a Christian life recommendation. Messiah College makes all efforts to avoid any possible prejudice in the admission process. Students with disabilities are encouraged to self-disclose and request an interview with the ODS Director, but not to include documentation of the disability in the actual admissions packet.

ADDITIONAL INFORMATION

Documentation should include a recent multi-disciplinary evaluation appropriate to the disability claimed. Neither an IEP nor a written 504 plan is sufficient to determine eligibility, but may be helpful when included along with a comprehensive evaluation report. Commonly provided accommodations by the Office of Disability Services include: extended time for test-taking; proctored exams in an alternate location; assistance with getting notes; disability coaching support; advocacy with instructors; alternate format textbooks;transition services; peer tutoring; referral source for other required services. Other accommodations are considered on an individual basis. Additionally, The Learning Center offers assistance with time management, motivation, goal setting, reading skills, note-taking, learning theory, and taking exams, in addition to providing a range of tutorial services through trained peer tutors. The Writing Center provides peer tutors for written projects. Other supports include math tutors and Supplemental Instruction, primarily in the sciences. Personal counseling is available through the Engle Health Center. The staff at ODS encourages and develops students self advocacy, but may act as a liaison between students and faculty when needed.

PROGRAM FOR DISABILITY SERVICES

Contact Information
Name of program or department: Office of Disability Services
  Telephone: 717-796-5382
  Fax: 717-796-5217

LEARNING DISABILITY SERVICES

Accommodations are determined on an individual basis after a thorough review of appropriate, current documentation. The accommodations requested will be granted if they are supported by documentation that logically links to the current impact of the condition on academic functioning and does not fundamentally alter the nature of the course.

Allowed in exams
  Calculator: Yes
  Dictionary: Yes
  Computer: Yes
  Spellchecker: Yes
Extended test time: Yes
Scribes: Yes
Proctors: Yes
Oral exams: Yes
Note-takers: Yes

Distraction-reduced environment: Yes
Tape recording in class: Yes
Electronic texts: Yes
Accommodations for students with
  ADHD: Yes
Kurzweil Reader: No
Other assistive technology: Yes
Priority registration: Yes

Added costs for services: No
LD specialists: No
Professional tutors: No
Peer tutors: 16
Max. hours/wk. for services:
  Unlimited
How professors are notified of
  LD/ADHD: Student

GENERAL ADMISSIONS INFORMATION

Office of Admission: 717-691-6000

ENTRANCE REQUIREMENTS
Academic units required: 4 English, 2 mathematics, 2 science, (2 science labs), 2 foreign language, 2 social studies, 0 history, 4 academic electives. **Academic units recommended:** 4 English, 3 mathematics, 3 science, (3 science labs), 2 foreign language, 2 social studies, 2 history, 4 academic electives. High school diploma is required and GED is accepted. TOEFL required of all international applicants; minimum paper TOEFL 550, minimum computer TOEFL 213, minimum web-based TOEFL 80.

Application deadline: None
Notification: Rolling
Average GPA: 3.71
ACT Composite middle 50% range:
  22–29

SAT Math middle 50% range:
  520–640
SAT Critical Reading middle 50%
  range: 520–630
SAT Writing middle 50% range:
  500–620

Graduated top 10% of class: 39%
Graduated top 25% of class: 68%
Graduated top 50% of class: 91%

COLLEGE GRADUATION REQUIREMENTS

Course substitutions allowed: Yes
In what course: Foreign language substitutions from approved list of courses.

ADDITIONAL INFORMATION

Environment: The college is located on a hilly 400-acre campus within a 15-minute drive to Harrisburg.

Student Body
  Undergrad enrollment: 2,805
  Women: 61%
  Men: 39%
  Percent out-of-state: 42%

Cost Information
  Tuition: $27,536
  Room and board: $8,420
Housing Information
  University housing: Yes
  Percent living on campus: 88%

Greek System
  Fraternity: No
  Sorority: No
Athletics: Division III

MISERICORDIA UNIVERSITY

301 Lake Street, Dallas, PA 18612
Phone: 570-674-6454 • Fax: 570-674-3026
E-mail: tcoveney@misericordia.edu • Web: www.misericordia.edu
Support: SP • Institution: 4-year private

PROGRAMS OR SERVICES FOR STUDENTS WITH LD

All students who participate in the Alternate Learners Project (ALP) are enrolled in regular college classes. Students who participate in ALP are supported by an assortment of services delivered by a specially trained full-time staff. Services include "Learning Strategies," which are designed to make students more efficient, and accommodations designed to work around student's disabilities whenever possible. Upon entry each student develops a Program of Accomodation (POA) and participates in weekly meetings with a Program Coordinator. The ultimate goal of ALP is to help students with learning disabilities succeed independently in college.

ADMISSION INFORMATION FOR STUDENTS WITH LD/ADHD

College entrance tests required: Yes
Interview required: Yes
Essay recommended: Yes
What documentation required for LD: Psycho Ed evaluation to include: relevant historical info, instructional interventions, related services, age diagnosed, objective data (aptitude, achievement, info processing), test scores (standard, percentile and grade equivalents) and describe functional limitations.
With general application: Yes if requested as part of Structured Program application
To receive services after enrolling: Yes
What documentation required for ADHD: Diagnosis based on DSM-V; history of behaviors impairing functioning in academic setting; diagnostic interview; history of symptoms; evidence of ongoing behaviors.

With general application: Yes if requested as part of Structured Program application
To receive services after enrolling: Yes
Submitted to: ALP office
Special Ed. HS course work accepted: No
Specific course requirements of all applicants: Yes
Separate application required: Yes
# of LD applications submitted each year: 75
# of LD applications accepted yearly: variable
Total # of students receiving LD services: variable
Acceptance into program means acceptance into college: Applications are reviewed simultaneously by Admissions and ALP

ADMISSIONS

Misericordia University's experience with students with learning disabilities is that students who are highly motivated and socially mature have an excellent chance to be successful. Each applicant has to submit a standard application to the Admissions Office. In addition, students must send a written cover letter to the ALP Manager summarizing the learning disability, and indicate a desire to participate in the ALP. Additionally, a copy of the psychoeducational report should be submitted along with the high school transcript and three letters of recommendation (one should be written by a special education professional). Class rank is usually above the top 60 percent. Although ACT/SAT scores are required by the university for traditional admissions, they are not used in the ALP Admissions decision. Students and their parents will be invited to interviews. This interview is very important. The ALP specialist reviews all information and notifies the student directly regarding admission to the program.

ADDITIONAL INFORMATION

The ALP helps students to successfully complete their course requirements by offering: participation in the BRIDGE Program. This program provides incoming first-year ALP students the opportunity to arrive on campus early (one week prior to the start of the fall semester) and features a series of assessments and workshops designed to assist students in identifying both strengths and needs in their learning styles. They receive training in the use of the Learning Strategies Curriculum. They receive training in the use of the Learning Strategies Curriculum, designed to help students become more effective and efficient learners., Prior to the start of each semester the ALP staff works with students to establish their Program of Accommodations, which includes a list of courses to be taken, the names of the professors, and a list of accommodations the students should use during the semester. Supplemental services for ALP students also include:: case management by academic specialists, writing support including assistance with editing and transcription, planning and selecting courses in collaboration with department advisors, communicating with faculty and administration, dedicated study room with access to technology, and time management support.

LEARNING DISABILITY PROGRAM OR SERVICES

Contact Information
Name of program or department: Alternative Learners Project (ALP)
  Telephone: 570-674-8126
  Fax: 570-674-3026

LEARNING DISABILITY SERVICES

Accommodations are decided upon an individual basis after a thorough review of appropriate, current documentation. The accommodations requested must be supported through the documentation provided and must be logically linked to the current impact of the condition on academic functioning.

Allowed in exams
  Calculator: Yes
  Computer: Yes
  Spellchecker: Yes
Extended test time: Yes
Scribes: Yes
Proctors: Yes
Oral exams: Yes
Notetakers: Yes

Distraction-reduced environment: Yes
Tape recording in class: Yes
Electronic texts: Yes
Accommodations for students with
  ADHD: Yes
Kurzweil Reader: Yes
Other assistive technology: Yes
Priority registration: No

Added costs for services: Yes
LD specialists: Yes
Professional tutors: N/A
Peer tutors: 100
Max. hours/wk. for services: 3
How professors are notified of
  LD/ADHD: By Program Coordinators

GENERAL ADMISSIONS INFORMATION

Office of Admission: 570-674-6434

ENTRANCE REQUIREMENTS

Academic units required: High school diploma is required, and GED is accepted. ACT with or without Writing component accepted. TOEFL required of all international applicants.

Application deadline: None
Notification: Rolling
Average GPA: 3.2
ACT Composite middle 50% range:
  21–26

SAT Math middle 50% range:
  470–570
SAT Critical Reading middle 50%
  range: 460–560
SAT Writing middle 50% range:
  NR

Graduated top 10% of class: NR
Graduated top 25% of class: NR
Graduated top 50% of class: NR

COLLEGE GRADUATION REQUIREMENTS

Course waivers allowed: No
In what course: N/A
Course substitutions allowed: No
In what course: N/A

ADDITIONAL INFORMATION

Environment: The college is located on a 123-acre campus in a suburban small town 9 miles north of Wilkes-Barre.

Student Body
  Undergrad enrollment: 2,830
  Women: 71%
  Men: 29%
  Percent out-of-state: 23%

Cost Information
  Tuition: $24,700
  Room & board: $10,760
Housing Information
  University housing: Yes
  Percent living on campus: 50–60%

Greek System
  Fraternity: No
  Sorority: No
Athletics: Division III

PENN. STATE U.—UNIVERSITY PARK

201 Shields Building, Box 3000, University Park, PA 16802-3000
Phone: 814-865-5471 • Fax: 814-863-7590
E-mail: admissions@psu.edu • Web: www.psu.edu
Support: S • Institution type: 4-year public

PROGRAMS OR SERVICES FOR STUDENTS WITH LD

The goal of Penn State's academic support services for students with learning disabilities is to ensure that students receive appropriate accommodations so that they can function independently and meet the academic demands of a competitive university. Students with learning disabilities should be able to complete college-level courses with the help of support services and classroom accommodations. To receive any of the support services, students must submit documentation of their learning disability to the learning disability specialist in the Office for Disability Services (ODS). Documentation should be a psychoeducational report from a certified or licensed psychologist completed within the past 3 years. The report should include measures of intellectual functioning and measures of achievement that describe current levels of functioning in reading, mathematics, and written language. Students with ADHD should have the professional who diagnosed them complete the ADHD Verification Form and submit it to the Office for Disability Services.

ADMISSION INFORMATION FOR STUDENTS WITH LD/ADHD

College entrance tests required: Yes
Interview required: No
Essay recommended: No
What documentation required for LD: Psycho Ed evaluation to include: relevant historical info, instructional interventions, related services, age diagnosed, objective data (aptitude, achievement, info processing), test scores (standard, percentile and grade equivalents) and describe functional limitations.
With general application: No
To receive services after enrolling: Yes
What documentation required for ADHD: Diagnosis based on DSM-V; history of behaviors impairing functioning in academic setting; diagnostic interview; history of symptoms; evidence of ongoing behaviors.

With general application: No
Submitted to: Office for Disability Services
Special Ed. HS course work accepted: Yes
Specific course requirements of all applicants: NR
Separate application required: No
# of LD applications submitted each year: NR
# of LD applications accepted yearly: NR
Total # of students receiving LD services: NR
Acceptance into program means acceptance into college: Students must be admitted to and enrolled in the university first and then request services.

ADMISSIONS

There is no special application process for students with learning disabilities or attention deficit hyperactivity disorder, and these students are considered for admission on the same basis as other applicants. The minimum 50 percent of admitted students have a GPA between 3.52 and 3.97 and an ACT score between 26 and 30 or an SAT score between 1750 and 1990. Course requirements include 4 years of English, 3 years of math, 3 years of science, 2 years of a foreign language, and 3 years of social studies. If the applicant's high school grades and test scores are low, students may submit a letter explaining why their ability to succeed in college is higher than indicated by their academic records. The Admissions Office will consider this information as it is voluntarily provided. The acceptable ACT or SAT score will depend on the high school grades and class rank of the student. Two-thirds of the evaluation is based on high school grades and one-third on test scores. Once admitted, students must submit documentation of their learning disability to receive support services. Students may seek admission as a provisional or nondegree student if they do not meet criteria required for admission as a degree candidate. Any student may enroll as a nondegree student.

ADDITIONAL INFORMATION

Students with LD are encouraged to participate in the Buddy Program; incoming students are matched with a senior buddy who is a current student with a disability and is available to share experiences with a junior buddy. Other services include providing audiotaped textbooks, arranging course substitutions with academic departments (when essential requirements are not involved), providing test accommodations, and providing individual counseling. Assistance with note-taking is offered through the ODS. Services are offered in a mainstream setting. The Learning Assistance Center operates a Math Center, Tutoring Center, Writing Center, and Computer Learning Center. Students may receive academic help either individually or in small groups for a number of different courses. One-on-one academic assistance is available through the Office of Disability Services. Graduate clinicians provide individual assistance with study skills, time management, and compensatory learning strategies.

LEARNING DISABILITY PROGRAM OR SERVICES

Contact Information
Name of program or department: Office for Disability Services (ODS)
  Telephone: 814-863-1807
  Fax: 814-863-3217

LEARNING DISABILITY SERVICES

Accommodations are decided upon an individual basis after a thorough review of appropriate, current documentation. The accommodations requested must be supported through the documentation provided and must be logically linked to the current impact of the condition on academic functioning.

Allowed in exams	**Distraction-reduced environment:** Yes	**Added costs for services:** No
Calculator: Yes	**Tape recording in class:** Yes	**LD specialists:** No
Dictionary: No	**Electronic texts:** Yes	**Professional tutors:** No
Computer: Yes	**Accommodations for students with**	**Peer tutors:** Yes
Spellchecker: No	**ADHD:** Yes	**Max. hours/wk. for services:**
Extended test time: Yes	**Kurzweil Reader:** Yes	Unlimited
Scribes: Yes	**Other assistive technology:** Yes	**How professors are notified of**
Proctors: Yes	**Priority registration:** Yes	**LD/ADHD:** By student
Oral exams: Yes		
Note-takers: Yes		

GENERAL ADMISSIONS INFORMATION

Office of Admission: 814-865-5471

ENTRANCE REQUIREMENTS

Academic units required: 4 English, 3 math, 3 science, 2 foreign language, 3 social studies. High school diploma is required, and GED is accepted. ACT with or without Writing component accepted. TOEFL required of all international applicants: minimum paper TOEFL 550, minimum computer TOEFL 213.

Application deadline: None	**SAT Math middle 50% range:**	**Graduated top 10% of class:** 37%
Notification: Rolling	570–670	**Graduated top 25% of class:** 77%
Average GPA: 3.53	**SAT Critical Reading middle 50%**	**Graduated top 50% of class:** 98%
ACT Composite middle 50% range:	**range:** 530–630	
NR	**SAT Writing middle 50% range:** NR	

COLLEGE GRADUATION REQUIREMENTS

Course waivers allowed: No
Course substitutions allowed: Yes
In what course: Possibly foreign language if not essential to the major

ADDITIONAL INFORMATION

Environment: The school is located on more than 5,000 acres in a small city 90 miles west of Harrisburg.

Student Body	**Cost Information**	**Greek System**
Undergrad enrollment: 38,635	**In-state tuition:** $15,250	**Fraternity:** Yes
Women: 45%	**Out-of-state tuition:** $27,115	**Sorority:** Yes
Men: 55%	**Room & board:** $9,030	**Athletics:** Division I
Percent out-of-state: 34%	**Housing Information**	
	University housing: Yes	
	Percent living on campus: 38%	

SETON HILL UNIVERSITY

One Seton Hill Drive, Greensburg, PA 15601
Phone: 724-838-4255 • Fax: 724-830-1294
E-mail: admit@setonhill.edu • Web: www.setonhill.edu
Support: S • Institution type: private

PROGRAMS OR SERVICES FOR STUDENTS WITH LD

Students who are eligible for, and are requesting, accommodations under the Americans with Disabilities ACT are required to register with the Coordinator of Disabled Student Services. Students work individually with the disability services coordinator to determine what learning or environmental supports are needed based on the documentation and recommendations for accommodations in the report. An individualized plan of accommodation will be developed with the student. It is the student's responsibility to implement the plan. The student should advise the coordinator of Disability Services if they experience any difficulties with their accommodation plan.

ADMISSION INFORMATION FOR STUDENTS WITH LD/ADHD

College entrance tests required: Yes
Interview required: No
Essay recommended: No
What documentation required for LD: Psycho Ed evaluation to include: relevant historical info, instructional interventions, related services, age diagnosed, objective data (aptitude, achievement, info processing), test scores (standard, percentile and grade equivalents) and describe functional limitations.
With general application: No
To receive services after enrolling: Yes
What documentation required for ADHD: Diagnosis based on DSM-V; history of behaviors impairing functioning in academic setting; diagnostic interview; history of symptoms; evidence of ongoing behaviors.

With general application: No
Submitted to: Disability Services
Special Ed. HS course work accepted: NR
Specific course requirements of all applicants: Yes
Separate application required: No
# of LD applications submitted each year: NR
# of LD applications accepted yearly: NR
Total # of students receiving LD services: NR
Acceptance into program means acceptance into college: Students must be admitted to and enrolled in the university first and then request services.

ADMISSIONS

The admissions process is the same for all students. Those with documentation supporting a disability are given the option of meeting with the disability services coordinator. There is a summer program that targets English and study skills. These are required programs for students with weak transcripts or SAT/ACT scores who otherwise meet admissions standards. Students with documented learning disabilities may request course substitutions for deficiencies in entrance courses based on the LD. Preadmission interviews are not required but are recommended.

ADDITIONAL INFORMATION

Accommodations may include, but are not limited to, preferential seating, note-taking services, tape-recorded lectures, extended time for projects, extended time for quizzes and tests, testing in distraction-reduced environments, alternative testing formats, tutoring, counseling, course substitutions, use of assisted technologies (e.g., spellcheckers), computer-based programs, and scribe services. Students are responsible for notifying professors about their disability and requesting accommodations. Course substitution requests are reviewed and considered on an individual basis. Skills classes for college credit are offered in time management techniques, note-taking strategies, test-taking strategies, and text reading.

LEARNING DISABILITY PROGRAM OR SERVICES

Contact Information
Name of program or department: Disability Services
 Telephone: 724-838-4295
 Fax: 724-830-4233

LEARNING DISABILITY SERVICES

Accommodations are decided upon an individual basis after a thorough review of appropriate, current documentation. The accommodations requested must be supported through the documentation provided and must be logically linked to the current impact of the condition on academic functioning.

Allowed in exams	**Distraction-reduced environment:** Yes	**Added costs for services:** No
Calculator: Yes	**Tape recording in class:** Yes	**LD specialists:** No
Dictionary: Yes	**Electronic texts:** Yes	**Professional tutors:** No
Computer: Yes	**Accommodations for students with**	**Peer tutors:** 60
Spellchecker: Yes	**ADHD:** Yes	**Max. hours/wk. for services:**
Extended test time: Yes	**Kurzweil Reader:** Yes	Unlimited
Scribes: Yes	**Other assistive technology:** Yes	**How professors are notified of**
Proctors: Yes	**Priority registration:** No	**LD/ADHD:** By student
Oral exams: Yes		
Note-takers: Yes		

GENERAL ADMISSIONS INFORMATION

Office of Admission: 724-838-4255

ENTRANCE REQUIREMENTS

Academic units required: 4 English, 2 math, 1 science (1 science lab), 2 social studies, 4 academic electives.
Academic units recommended: 4 English, 2 math, 1 science (1 science lab), 2 foreign language, 2 social studies, 4 academic electives. High school diploma is required, and GED is accepted. ACT without Writing component accepted. TOEFL required of all international applicants: minimum paper TOEFL 550, minimum computer TOEFL 213.

Application deadline: 8/15	**SAT Math middle 50% range:**	**Graduated top 10% of class:** 19%
Notification: Rolling	450–570	**Graduated top 25% of class:** 47%
Average GPA: 3.45	**SAT Critical Reading middle 50%**	**Graduated top 50% of class:** 77%
ACT Composite middle 50% range:	**range:** 450–560	
19–26	**SAT Writing middle 50% range:**	
	440–550	

COLLEGE GRADUATION REQUIREMENTS

Course waivers allowed: Yes
In what course: All appropriate waivers are reviewed and considered. Essential elements of a students program of student cannot be waived.
Course substitutions allowed: Yes
In what course: All appropriate substitutions are reviewed and considered. Essential elements of a students program of student cannot be substituted.

ADDITIONAL INFORMATION

Environment: The campus is located 35 miles east of Pittsburgh.

Student Body	**Cost Information**	**Greek System**
Undergrad enrollment: 1,810	**Tuition:** $27,654	**Fraternity:** No
Women: 64%	**Room & board:** $9,126	**Sorority:** No
Men: 36%	**Housing Information**	**Athletics:** NCAA
Percent out-of-state: 21%	**University housing:** Yes	
	Percent living on campus: 55%	

UNIVERSITY OF PITTSBURGH

4227 Fifth Avenue, First Floor Alumni Hall, Pittsburgh, PA 15260
Phone: 412-624-7488 • Fax: 412-648-8815
E-mail: oafa@pitt.edu • Web: www.pitt.edu
Support: CS • Institution: 4-year public

PROGRAMS OR SERVICES FOR STUDENTS WITH LD

To access services, students must refer themselves to Disability Resource Services and submit documentation of their learning disability. Once eligibility is established, students meet regularly with a DRS disability specialist who will assist the student in accessing resources and developing an individualized, comprehensive educational plan. The objective of DRS is to work closely with students to empower them to plan and implement a successful academic experience.

ADMISSION INFORMATION FOR STUDENTS WITH LD/ADHD

College entrance tests required: Yes
Interview required: N/A
Essay required: N/A
What documentation required for LD: Psycho Ed evaluation to include: relevant historical info, instructional interventions, related services, age diagnosed, objective data (aptitude, achievement, info processing), test scores (standard, percentile and grade equivalents) and describe functional limitations.
With general application: No
To receive services after enrolling: Yes
What documentation required for ADHD: Diagnosis based on DSM-V; history of behaviors impairing functioning in academic setting; diagnostic interview; history of symptoms; evidence of ongoing behaviors.

With general application: No
Submitted to: Support Program/Services
Special Ed. HS course work accepted: No
Specific course requirements for all applicants: Yes
Separate application required for program services: No
# of LD applications submitted each year: NR
# of LD applications accepted yearly: NR
Total # of students receiving LD services: 225
Acceptance into program means acceptance into college: Students must be admitted to and enrolled in the university first and then request services.

ADMISSIONS

Students with learning disabilities must meet the same admission criteria established for all applicants.. It is important to have applications reviewed based on more than just the high school record and SAT/ACT scores. U Pitt recommends that students submit any supplemental information that they feel will help the committee get to know them better. The committee is looking for students who are well-rounded both in and out of the classroom. The Personal Essay is optional. However, applicants should definitely submit a personal essay if they want :scholarship consideration; consideration into the guaranteed admission to graduate/professional school; special consideration in the review process due to extenuating circumstances affecting a term or so of grades; and they would like the committee to review more than just the high school transcript and SAT/ACT scores. Likewise, while not required, letter(s) of recommendation from a person or people who knows the student well can help the admission office get to know the student better.

ADDITIONAL INFORMATION

DRS individually designs and recommends services to enhance the skills and personal development of the student. Services available may include: exam accommodations, use of calculators, computer or spell checker in exams, scribes, proctors, controlled environments, alternative format, instructional strategy assistance, and assistive technology. There are three disability specialists on staff.

PROGRAM FOR DISABILITY SERVICES

Contact Information
Name of program or department: Disability Resources and Services
  Telephone: 412-648-7890
  Fax: 412-624-3346

LEARNING DISABILITY SERVICES

Accommodations are decided upon an individual basis after a thorough review of appropriate, current documentation. The accommodations requested must be supported through the documentation provided and must be logically linked to the current impact of the condition on academic functioning.

Allowed in exams
  Calculator: Yes
  Dictionary: No
  Computer: Yes
  Spellchecker: Yes
Extended test time: Yes
Scribes: Yes
Proctors: Yes
Oral exams: No
Note-takers: No

Distraction-reduced environment: Yes
Tape recording in class: Yes
Electronic texts: Yes
Accommodations for students with ADHD: Yes
Kurzweil Reader: Available in campus labs
Other assistive technology: JAWS, Magic
Priority registration: No

Added costs for services: No
LD specialists: Yes
Professional tutors: No
Peer tutors: No
Max. hours/wk. for services: N/A
How professors are notified of LD/ADHD: Student

GENERAL ADMISSIONS INFORMATION

Office of Admission: 412-624-7488

ENTRANCE REQUIREMENTS
Academic units required: 4 English, 3 mathematics, 3 science, (3 science labs), 2 foreign language, 2 social studies, 3 academic electives. **Academic units recommended:** 4 English, 4 mathematics, 4 science, (4 science labs), 3 foreign language, 3 social studies, 5 academic electives. High school diploma is required and GED is not accepted. SAT or ACT required; TOEFL required of all international applicants; minimum paper TOEFL 550, minimum computer TOEFL 213, minimum web-based TOEFL 80.

Application deadline: None
Notification: Rolling
Average GPA: 3.94
ACT Composite middle 50% range: 25–30

SAT Math middle 50% range: 600–690
SAT Critical Reading middle 50% range: 570–690
SAT Writing middle 50% range: 560–660

Graduated top 10% of class: 54%
Graduated top 25% of class: 86%
Graduated top 50% of class: 99%

COLLEGE GRADUATION REQUIREMENTS

Course waivers allowed: No
Course substitutions allowed: Yes

ADDITIONAL INFORMATION

Environment: The university is located on a 132-acre urban campus.

Student Body
  Undergrad enrollment: 18,427
  Women: 51%
  Men: 49%
  Percent out-of-state: 24%

Cost Information
  Tuition: $32,148
  Room and board: $12,563
Housing Information
  University housing: Yes
  Percent living on campus: 45%

Greek System
  Fraternity: Yes
  Sorority: Yes
Athletics: Division I

WIDENER UNIVERSITY

One University Place, Chester, PA 19013
Phone: 610-499-4126 • Fax: 610-499-4676
E-mail: admissions.office@widener.edu • Web: www.widener.edu
Support: CS • Institution type: 4-year private

PROGRAMS OR SERVICES FOR STUDENTS WITH LD

Disabilities Services is a structured mainstream support service designed to assist students enrolled in one of Widener's standard academic programs. Students wishing to use Disabilities Services must submit documentation that describes the nature of the learning disability including relevant evaluations and assessments. Each student at Disabilities Services has the option of meeting once or twice a week with a learning specialist in our academic coaching program. Typically, academic coaching sessions focus on time management, study skills, social and emotional adjustment, and academic planning. Disabilities Services serves as a campus advocate for the needs of students with LD by making sure that accommodations are provided when appropriate. Participation in our services is included in the basic tuition charge. Thus, there is no extra fee.

ADMISSION INFORMATION FOR STUDENTS WITH LD/ADHD

College entrance tests required: Yes
Interview required: No
Essay recommended: Yes
What documentation required for LD: Psycho Ed evaluation to include: relevant historical info, instructional interventions, related services, age diagnosed, objective data (aptitude, achievement, info processing), test scores (standard, percentile and grade equivalents) and describe functional limitations.
With general application: No
To receive services after enrolling: Yes
What documentation required for ADHD: Diagnosis based on DSM-V; history of behaviors impairing functioning in academic setting; diagnostic interview; history of symptoms; evidence of ongoing behaviors.

With general application: No
Submitted to: Enable
Special Ed. HS course work accepted: Yes
Specific course requirements of all applicants: NR
Separate application required: No
# of LD applications submitted each year: NR
# of LD applications accepted yearly: NR
Total # of students receiving LD services: 200
Acceptance into program means acceptance into college: Students must be admitted to and enrolled in the university first and then request services.

ADMISSIONS

Students with learning disabilities submit the general application form. Admission decisions are made by the Office of Admissions. Students should submit their application, an essay, and recommendations. ACT scores range between 17 and 27 and SAT scores range between 750 and 1300. There are no specific course requirements for admissions. High school GPA range is 2.0–4.0.

ADDITIONAL INFORMATION

Disabilities Services is a personalized academic support and counseling service designed to help students with learning disabilities who meet university entrance requirements cope with the rigors of academic life. Students can sign up for academic coaching to meet with counselors who can help them understand and accept their disabilities; individualize learning strategies; teach self-advocacy; and link the students with the other Academic Support Services available at Widener. This office assures that professors understand which accommodations are needed. The Writing Center provides assistance with writing assignments and is staffed by professors. The Math Center offers individualized and group tutoring and is staffed by professors and experienced tutors. In addition, the Tutoring Office provides individual and group tutoring for the majority of undergraduate Widener courses.

LEARNING DISABILITY PROGRAM OR SERVICES

Contact Information
Name of program or department: Disability Services
  Telephone: 610-499-1266
  Fax: 610-499-1192

LEARNING DISABILITY SERVICES

Accommodations are decided upon an individual basis after a thorough review of appropriate, current documentation. The accommodations requested must be supported through the documentation provided and must be logically linked to the current impact of the condition on academic functioning.

Allowed in exams	**Distraction-reduced environment:** Yes	**Added costs for services:** No
Calculator: Yes	**Tape recording in class:** Yes	**LD specialists:** Yes
Dictionary: Yes	**Electronic texts:** Yes	**Professional tutors:** 1
Computer: Yes	**Accommodations for students with**	**Peer tutors:** Yes
Spellchecker: Yes	**ADHD:** Yes	**Max. hours/wk. for services:**
Extended test time: Yes	**Kurzweil Reader:** Yes	Unlimited
Scribes: Yes	**Other assistive technology:** Yes	**How professors are notified of**
Proctors: Yes	**Priority registration:** Yes	**LD/ADHD:** By student
Oral exams: Yes		
Note-takers: Yes		

GENERAL ADMISSIONS INFORMATION

Office of Admission: 610-499-4126

ENTRANCE REQUIREMENTS

Academic units required: 4 English, 3 math, 3 science, 2 foreign language, 3 social studies, 3 academic electives.
Academic units recommended: 4 English, 4 math, 4 science (2 science labs), 2 foreign language, 4 social studies, 3 academic electives. High school diploma is required, and GED is accepted. TOEFL required of all international applicants: minimum paper TOEFL 500, minimum computer TOEFL 173.

Application deadline: None	**SAT Math middle 50% range:**	**Graduated top 10% of class:** 12%
Notification: Rolling	450–550	**Graduated top 25% of class:** 37%
Average GPA: 3.37	**SAT Critical Reading middle 50%**	**Graduated top 50% of class:** 72%
ACT Composite middle 50% range:	**range:** 440–520	
NR	**SAT Writing middle 50% range:** NR	

COLLEGE GRADUATION REQUIREMENTS

Course waivers allowed: No
Course substitutions allowed: No

ADDITIONAL INFORMATION

Environment: The university's 105-acre campus is located 15 miles south of Philadelphia.

Student Body	**Cost Information**	**Greek System**
Undergrad enrollment: 3,347	**Tuition:** $34,224	**Fraternity:** Yes
Women: 54%	**Room & board:** $11,896	**Sorority:** Yes
Men: 46%	**Housing Information**	**Athletics:** Division III
Percent out-of-state: 40%	**University housing:** Yes	
	Percent living on campus: 50%	

BROWN UNIVERSITY

PO Box 1876, 45 Prospect Street, Providence, RI 02912
Phone: 401-863-2378 • Fax: 401-863-9300
E-mail: admission_undergraduate@brown.edu • Web: www.brown.edu
Support: CS • Institution type: 4-year private

PROGRAMS OR SERVICES FOR STUDENTS WITH LD

Student and Employee Accessibility Services (SEAS) coordinates accommodations and services for students with LD/ADHD.

ADMISSION INFORMATION FOR STUDENTS WITH LD/ADHD

College entrance tests required: Yes
Interview required: N/A
Essay recommended: N/A
Documentation required for LD: (After enrollment) A current, complete psychoeducational evaluation, WAIS, achievement testing such as the Woodcock-Johnson, and information processing testing as appropriate are required.
Documentation required for ADHD: Prefer same documentation we request to document a learning disability
Submitted to: SEAS
Special Ed. HS course work accepted: No

Specific course requirements of all applicants: NR
Separate application required: No
# of LD applications submitted each year: NR
# of LD applications accepted yearly: NR
Total # of students receiving LD services: 300
Acceptance into program means acceptance into college: Students must be admitted to and enrolled in the university first and then submit documentation and request services and accommodations.

ADMISSIONS

Admission is very competitive, and all students are required to submit the same application form and meet the same standards. Brown is a highly competitive university, and students have been enrolled in AP and honors courses in high school. If a student does disclose an area of disability, Brown admissions will carefully review any information submitted.

ADDITIONAL INFORMATION

Admitted students requesting accommodations and/or support services must provide documentation of the existence of an LD. With appropriate documentation, students may have access to the following services: note-takers; reduced distraction testing environments; tape recorders; books in alternate format; self-advocacy workshop; academic advising and study skills counseling; examination modifications as necessary, such as additional time, a quiet room, or use of a computer; extended deadlines for some paper assignments; the option of taking a reduced course load with a prorated tuition; referral to off-campus professional tutors; referral to off-campus neuropsychologists for diagnosis; and other assistive technology. Services and accommodations are available for undergraduate and graduate students.

LEARNING DISABILITY PROGRAM OR SERVICES

Contact Information
Name of program or department: Student and Employee Accessibility Services (SEAS)
  Telephone: 401-863-9588
  Fax: 401-863-1444

LEARNING DISABILITY SERVICES

Accommodations are decided upon an individual basis after a thorough review of appropriate, current documentation. The accommodations requested must be supported by the documentation provided and must be logically linked to the current impact of the condition on academic functioning.

Allowed in exams
  Calculator: Depends, but possible
  Dictionary: Depends, but possible
  Computer: Depends, but possible
  Spellchecker: Depends, but possible
Extended test time: Yes
Scribes: Yes
Proctors: Yes
Oral exams: Uncommon, but possible
Note-takers: Yes

Distraction-reduced environment: Yes
Tape recording in class: Yes
Electronic texts: Yes
Accommodations for students with ADHD: Yes
Kurzweil Reader: Yes
Other assistive technology: Yes
Priority registration: No

Added costs for services: No
LD specialists: Yes
Professional tutors: Yes
Peer tutors: Yes
Max. hours/wk. for services: Not restricted, but students may be referred to off-campus resources if needs exceed on campus programs.
How professors are notified of LD/ADHD: By student

GENERAL ADMISSIONS INFORMATION

Office of Admission: 401-863-2378

ENTRANCE REQUIREMENTS

Academic units required: 4 English, 3 math, 3 science (2 science labs), 3 foreign language, 2 history, 1 academic elective. **Academic units recommended:** 4 English, 4 math, 4 science (3 science labs), 4 foreign language, 2 history, 1 academic elective. High school diploma is required, and GED is not accepted. ACT with Writing component required. TOEFL required of all international applicants: minimum paper TOEFL 600, minimum computer TOEFL 250.

Application deadline: 1/1
Notification: 4/1
Average GPA: NR
ACT Composite middle 50% range: 29–33

SAT Math middle 50% range: 650–760
SAT Critical Reading middle 50% range: 630–710
SAT Writing middle 50% range: 640–750

Graduated top 10% of class: 80%
Graduated top 25% of class: 99%
Graduated top 50% of class: 100%

COLLEGE GRADUATION REQUIREMENTS

Course waivers allowed: No
Course substitutions allowed: Yes, but commonly because of specific general education requirement
In what course: Varies

ADDITIONAL INFORMATION

Environment: The university is located on 146 acres in the urban area of Providence, Rhode Island.

Student Body
  Undergrad enrollment: 6,380
  Women: 52%
  Men: 48%
  Percent out-of-state: 95%

Cost Information
  Tuition: $41,328
  Room & board: $10,906
Housing Information
  University housing: Yes
  Percent living on campus: 78%

Greek System
  Fraternity: Yes
  Sorority: Yes
Athletics: Division I

BRYANT UNIVERSITY

1150 Douglas Pike Ste 3, Smithfield, RI 02917-1285
Phone: 401-232-6100 • Fax: 401-232-6741
E-mail: admission@bryant.edu • Web: www.bryant.edu
Support: CS • Institution: 4-year private

PROGRAMS OR SERVICES FOR STUDENTS WITH LD

Bryant University offers services for students with learning disabilities. The Academic Center for Excellence (ACE)is dedicated to helping Bryant students achieve their goal of academic success. Basically, the center provides study skills training to help students become self-reliant, independent, and confident learners. This is achieved through an internationally accredited peer tutoring program and study skills instruction by professional staff. Group sessions as a mode of instruction are encouraged and the staff engages in a partnership with students to help them achieve their goals. The Learning Specialist provides support for students with LD. Consideration is given for reasonable modifications, accommodations, or auxiliary aids which will enable qualified students to have access to, participate in, and benefit from the full range of their educational programs and activities offered to all students. As a liaison among students, faculty, and administration, ACE encourages students with LD requiring special accommodations to schedule an appointment with a Learning Specialist as soon as they register for courses each semester.

ADMISSION INFORMATION FOR STUDENTS WITH LD/ADHD

College entrance tests required: Yes
Interview required: N/A
Essay required: N/A
What documentation required for LD: Psycho Ed evaluation to include: relevant historical info, instructional interventions, related services, age diagnosed, objective data (aptitude, achievement, info processing), test scores (standard, percentile and grade equivalents) and describe functional limitations.
With general application: No
To receive services after enrolling: Yes
What documentation required for ADHD: Diagnosis based on DSM-V; history of behaviors impairing functioning in academic setting; diagnostic interview; history of symptoms; evidence of ongoing behaviors.

With general application: No
Submitted to: Support Program/Services
Special Ed. HS course work accepted: N/A
Specific course requirements for all applicants: Yes
Separate application required for program services: No
# of LD applications submitted each year: NR
# of LD applications accepted yearly: NR
Total # of students receiving LD services: NR
Acceptance into program means acceptance into college: NR

ADMISSIONS

If students self-disclose during the admission process, the Office of Admissions will forward documentation to the Academic Center for Excellence. If students do not self-disclose, they must schedule an appointment at ACE to do so. Students may elect to self-disclose and provide current documentation that should be sent to admissions and to ACE. General admission criteria include an average GPA of 3.0 and 4 years of English, 2 years of social studies, at least 1 year of science lab, and 3 years of college-prep mathematics. Interviews are recommended. A probationary/conditional admission is available.

ADDITIONAL INFORMATION

Students with documented learning disabilities may receive accommodations and services based solely on the disability and appropriate services. Some of the accommodations might include: extended testing time, distraction-free environment, note sharers, use of calculators if applicable, and laptops with spell check. ACE provides learning specialists to assist students in college level study skill development. Learning Specialists also help students find out what learning and study strategies work best for them. The College Reading and Learning Association certifies the Peer Tutoring Program and one-on-one tutoring is available in a variety of subjects. Students can drop in to work with a specialist or peer tutor in the Learning Labs. Study Skills Workshops are offered covering topics such as time management, note-taking skills, test preparation, and combatting procrastination. The Writing Center provides one-on-one conferencing in writing for all subjects. There are writing consultants, writing specialists, ESL writing specialists, and writing workshops.

PROGRAM FOR DISABILITY SERVICES

Contact Information
Name of program or department: Academic Center for Excellence
 Telephone: 401-232-6746
 Fax: 401-232-6038

LEARNING DISABILITY SERVICES

Accommodations are decided upon an individual basis after a thorough review of appropriate, current documentation. The accommodations requested must be supported through the documentation provided and must be logically linked to the current impact of the condition on academic functioning.

Allowed in exams
 Calculator: Yes
 Dictionary: No
 Computer: Yes
 Spellchecker: Yes
 Extended test time: Yes
 Scribes: N/A
 Proctors: N/A
 Oral exams: N/A
 Note-takers: N/A

Distraction-reduced environment: Yes
Tape recording in class: Yes
Electronic texts: N/A
Accommodations for students with ADHD: Yes
Kurzweil Reader: Yes
Other assistive technology: N/A
Priority registration: No

Added costs for services: No
LD specialists: Yes
Professional tutors: 6
Peer tutors: 50
Max. hours/wk. for services: NR
How professors are notified of LD/ADHD: Both student and director

GENERAL ADMISSIONS INFORMATION

Office of Admission: 401-232-6100

ENTRANCE REQUIREMENTS
Academic units required: 4 English, 4 mathematics, 2 science, (2 science labs), 2 foreign language, 2 history.
Academic units recommended: 4 English, 4 mathematics, 3 science, (2 science labs), 3 foreign language, 3 history. High school diploma is required and GED is accepted. SAT or ACT required; TOEFL required of all international applicants; minimum paper TOEFL 550, minimum computer TOEFL 213, minimum web-based TOEFL 80.

Application deadline: 2/1
Notification: 3/21
Average GPA: 3.35
ACT Composite middle 50% range: 23–26

SAT Math middle 50% range: 510–630
SAT Critical Reading middle 50% range: 510–600
SAT Writing middle 50% range: 520–600

Graduated top 10% of class: 25%
Graduated top 25% of class: 58%
Graduated top 50% of class: 93%

COLLEGE GRADUATION REQUIREMENTS

Course waivers allowed: No
In what course: N/A
Course substitutions allowed: No
In what course: N/A

ADDITIONAL INFORMATION

Environment: The campus is located in a suburban area 12 miles from Providence.

Student Body
 Undergrad enrollment: 3,474
 Women: 43%
 Men: 57%
 Percent out-of-state: 86%

Cost Information
 Tuition: $34,624
 Room and board: $12,829
Housing Information
 University housing: Yes
 Percent living on campus: 83%

Greek System
 Fraternity: Yes
 Sorority: Yes
Athletics: Division II

JOHNSON & WALES UNIVERSITY

8 Abbott Park Place, Providence, RI 02903-3703
Phone: 401-598-2310 • Fax: 401-598-2948
E-mail: admissions.pvd@jwu.edu • Web: www.jwu.edu
Support: CS • Institution: 4-year private

PROGRAMS OR SERVICES FOR STUDENTS WITH LD

Johnson and Wales University is dedicated to providing reasonable accommodations to allow students with learning disabilities to succeed in their academic pursuits. While maintaining the highest academic integrity, the university strives to balance scholarship with support services that will assist special needs students to function in the post-secondary learning process. It is important that these students identify themselves and present the appropriate neurological, medical, and/or psychoeducational documentation as soon as possible. Recommendations for specific accommodations will be based on the student's individual needs and learning style. The goal of the Center for Academic Support is to support students in their efforts to develop their talents, empower them to direct their own learning, and lead them on the pathways of success.

ADMISSION INFORMATION FOR STUDENTS WITH LD/ADHD

College entrance tests required: No
Interview required: No
Essay required: No
What documentation required for LD: Psycho Ed evaluation to include: relevant historical info, instructional interventions, related services, age diagnosed, objective data (aptitude, achievement, info processing), test scores (standard, percentile and grade equivalents) and describe functional limitations.
With general application: No
To receive services after enrolling: Yes
What documentation required for ADHD: Diagnosis based on DSM-V; history of behaviors impairing functioning in academic setting; diagnostic interview; history of symptoms; evidence of ongoing behaviors.

With general application: No
Submitted to: Center for Academic Support
Special Ed. HS course work accepted: Yes
Specific course requirements for all applicants: Yes
Separate application required for program services: No
# of LD applications submitted each year: NR
# of LD applications accepted yearly: NR
Total # of students receiving LD services: 550
Acceptance into program means acceptance into college: No

ADMISSIONS

There is no special application process. Standardized tests are not required for admission, and foreign language is not required for admission. After the regular admissions process has been completed and the student is accepted, the student should self-identify and verify the learning disability with the appropriate neurological, medical, and/or psychoeducational documentation. This would include tests administered by the student's high school or private testing service within the past three years. Once admitted, a Special Needs Advisor will meet with the student, and recommendations for specific accommodations will be based on the student's individual needs and learning styles.

ADDITIONAL INFORMATION

Academic counselors establish initial contact with probational and conditional students. Counselors monitor and review grades and enforce academic policies. Accommodations could include decelerated course load, preferential scheduling, individualized exams, note-taker, audio recording in class, LD support group, individualized tutoring, and a special needs advisor. Career counselors and personal counselors are also available. The Center offers group and/or one-to-one tutoring, writing skills, culinary skills, grammar fundamentals, study groups, and supplemental instruction groups. Services and accommodations are available for undergraduate and graduate students.

PROGRAM FOR DISABILITY SERVICES

Contact Information
Name of program or department: Center for Academic Support
  Telephone: 401-598-4689
  Fax: 401-598-4657

LEARNING DISABILITY SERVICES

Accommodations are decided upon an individual basis after a thorough review of appropriate, current documentation. The accommodations requested must be supported through the documentation provided and must be logically linked to the current impact of the condition on academic functioning.

Allowed in exams	**Distraction-reduced environment:** Yes	**Added costs for services:** No
Calculator: Yes	**Audio recording in class:** Yes	**LD specialists:** Yes
Dictionary: Yes	**Electronic texts:** Yes	**Professional tutors:** 18
Computer: Yes	**Accommodations for students with**	**Peer tutors:** 10
Spellchecker: Yes	**ADHD:** Yes	**Max. hours/wk. for services:**
Extended test time: Yes	**Kurzweil Reader:** Yes	Unlimited
Scribes: Yes	**Other assistive technology:** Kurzweil	**How professors are notified of**
Proctors: Yes	3000, Braille Reader, FM System,	**LD/ADHD:** Student
Oral exams: Yes	Zoomtext, Dragon Dictate	
Note-takers: Yes	**Priority registration:** Yes	

GENERAL ADMISSIONS INFORMATION

Office of Admission: 401-598-2310

ENTRANCE REQUIREMENTS

Academic units recommended: 4 English, 3 mathematics, 3 science, 2 social studies. High school diploma is required and GED is accepted.

Application deadline: None	**SAT Math middle 50% range:**	**Graduated top 10% of class:** NR
Notification: Rolling	400–500	**Graduated top 25% of class:** NR
Average GPA: 2.0	**SAT Critical Reading middle 50%**	**Graduated top 50% of class:** NR
ACT Composite middle 50% range:	**range:** 410–520	
NR	**SAT Writing middle 50% range:** NR	

COLLEGE GRADUATION REQUIREMENT

Course waivers allowed: No
Course substitutions allowed: Yes
In what course: Foreign language, when appropriate

ADDITIONAL INFORMATION

Environment: The university is located on 100 acres with easy access to Boston.

Student Body	**Cost Information**	**Greek System**
Undergrad enrollment: 9,703	**Tuition:** $25,107	**Fraternity:** No
Women: 53%	**Room and board:** $9,603	**Sorority:** No
Men: 47%	**Housing Information**	**Athletics:** Division III
Percent out-of-state: 86%	**University housing:** Yes	
	Percent living on campus: 39%	

PROVIDENCE COLLEGE

Harkins 222, 1 Cunningham Sq., Providence, RI 02918
Phone: 401-865-2535 • Fax: 401-865-2826
E-mail: pcadmiss@providence.edu • Web: www.providence.edu
Support: CS • Institution: 4-year private

PROGRAMS OR SERVICES FOR STUDENTS WITH LD

The Director of the Office of Academic Services and the faculty of the college are very supportive and are diligent about providing comprehensive services. The goal of the college is to be available to assist students whenever help is requested. After admission, the Assistant Director for Disability Services meets with the learning disabled students during the summer, prior to entry, to help them begin planning for freshman year. Students are monitored for four years. The College makes every effort to provide "reasonable accommodations."

ADMISSION INFORMATION FOR STUDENTS WITH LD/ADHD

College entrance tests required: No
Interview required: N/A
Essay required: N/A
What documentation required for LD: Psycho Ed evaluation to include: relevant historical info, instructional interventions, related services, age diagnosed, objective data (aptitude, achievement, info processing), test scores (standard, percentile and grade equivalents) and describe functional limitations.
With general application: No
To receive services after enrolling: Yes
What documentation required for ADHD: Diagnosis based on DSM-V; history of behaviors impairing functioning in academic setting; diagnostic interview; history of symptoms; evidence of ongoing behaviors.

With general application: No
Submitted to: Support Program/Services
Special Ed. HS course work accepted: N/A
Specific course requirements for all applicants: Yes
Separate application required for program services: No
# of LD applications submitted each year: NR
# of LD applications accepted yearly: NR
Total # of students receiving LD services: NR
Acceptance into program means acceptance into college: Separate application required after student has enrolled

ADMISSIONS

There is no special admissions process for students with learning disabilities. However, an interview is highly recommended, during which individualized course work is examined. General course requirements include four years English, three years math, three years foreign language, two years lab science, two years social studies, and two years electives. Students with learning disabilities who have lower test scores but a fairly good academic record may be accepted. The admission committee has the flexibility to overlook poor test scores for students with learning disabilities. Those who have higher test scores and reasonable grades in college-prep courses (C-plus/B) may also gain admission. Students should self-identify as learning disabled on their application.

ADDITIONAL INFORMATION

The following services and accommodatations are available for students presenting appropriate documentation: the use of calculators, dictionaries and computers during exams; extended time on tests; distraction-free testing environment; scribes; proctors; oral exams; note-takers; tape recorders in class; assistive technology; and priority registration. Skills seminars, for no credit are offered in study techniques and test-taking strategies. All students have access to the Tutorial Center and Writing Center. Services and accommodations are available for undergraduate and graduate students.

PROGRAM FOR DISABILITY SERVICES

Contact Information
Name of program or department: Office of Academic Services - Disabilty Support Services
Telephone: 401-865-1121
Fax: 401-865-1219

LEARNING DISABILITY SERVICES

Accommodations are decided upon an individual basis after a thorough review of appropriate, current documentation. The accommodations requested must be supported through the documentation provided and must be logically linked to the current impact of the condition on academic functioning.

Allowed in exams	**Distraction-reduced environment:** Yes	**Added costs for services:** No
Calculator: Yes	**Tape recording in class:** Yes	**LD specialists:** Yes
Dictionary: Yes	**Electronic texts:** Yes	**Professional tutors:** No
Computer: Yes	**Accommodations for students with**	**Peer tutors:** 45–50
Spellchecker: Yes	**ADHD:** Yes	**Max. hours/wk. for services:**
Extended test time: Yes	**Kurzweil Reader:** No	Unlimited
Scribes: Yes	**Other assistive technology:** N/A	**How professors are notified of**
Proctors: Yes	**Priority registration:** Yes	**LD/ADHD:** Student
Oral exams: Yes		
Note-takers: Yes		

GENERAL ADMISSIONS INFORMATION

Office of Admission: 401-865-2535

ENTRANCE REQUIREMENTS
Academic units required: 4 English, 4 mathematics, 3 science, (2 science labs), 3 foreign language, 2 social studies, 2 history, 2 academic electives. **Academic units recommended:** 4 English, 4 mathematics, 4 science, (2 science labs), 3 foreign language, 2 social studies, 2 history, 0 academic electives. High school diploma is required and GED is not accepted. ACT with Writing component required. TOEFL required of all international applicants; minimum paper TOEFL 550, minimum computer TOEFL 215, minimum web-based TOEFL 80.

Application deadline: 1/15	**SAT Math middle 50% range:**	**Graduated top 10% of class:** 40%
Notification: 4/1	530–640	**Graduated top 25% of class:** 71%
Average GPA: 3.39	**SAT Critical Reading middle 50%**	**Graduated top 50% of class:** 95%
ACT Composite middle 50% range:	range: 520–620	
23–27	**SAT Writing middle 50% range:**	
	540–640	

COLLEGE GRADUATION REQUIREMENTS

Course waivers allowed: Yes
In what course: Depends on student's disability
Course substitutions allowed: Yes
In what course: Depends on student's disabilty

ADDITIONAL INFORMATION

Environment: Providence College has a 105-acre campus located in a small city 50 miles south of Boston.

Student Body	**Cost Information**	**Greek System**
Undergrad enrollment: 3,852	**Tuition:** $40,150	**Fraternity:** No
Women: 58%	**Room and board:** $12,140	**Sorority:** No
Men: 42%	**Housing Information**	**Athletics:** Division I
Percent out-of-state: 87%	**University housing:** Yes	
	Percent living on campus: 78%	

RHODE ISLAND COLLEGE

Undergrad. Admissions, 600 Mt. Pleasant Avenue, Providence, RI 02908
Phone: 401-456-2776 • Fax: 401-456-9525
E-mail: dsc@ric.edu • Web: www.ric.edu
Support: CS • Institution type: 4-year public

PROGRAMS OR SERVICES FOR STUDENTS WITH LD

Rhode Island College strives to create and promote an environment that is conducive to learning for all students. Necessary accommodations require that administration, faculty, and staff be consistent and use flexibility in making adaptations, and that the students be flexible in adapting to and using alternative modes of learning and instruction. Students with disabilities may self-identify at any point, but are encouraged to do so at admission. A registration card is sent to all new students. Filling out this card and returning it to the Office of Student Life starts the process. Faculty is responsible for stating at the beginning of each semester verbally or in writing that the instructor is available to meet individually with students who require accommodations. The college wants students to feel comfortable requesting assistance, and faculty and fellow students are encouraged to be friendly and supportive. The college feels that the presence of students with individual ways of learning and coping serves as a learning experience for the professor, student, and class.

ADMISSION INFORMATION FOR STUDENTS WITH LD/ADHD

College entrance tests required: Yes
Interview required: No
Essay recommended: No
What documentation required for LD: Psycho Ed evaluation to include: relevant historical info, instructional interventions, related services, age diagnosed, objective data (aptitude, achievement, info processing), test scores (standard, percentile and grade equivalents) and describe functional limitations.
With general application: No
To receive services after enrolling: Yes
What documentation required for ADHD: Diagnosis based on DSM-V; history of behaviors impairing functioning in academic setting; diagnostic interview; history of symptoms; evidence of ongoing behaviors.

With general application: No
Submitted to: Both Admissions Office and Office of Student Life
Special Ed. HS course work accepted: No
Specific course requirements of all applicants: NR
Separate application required: Yes
# of LD applications submitted each year: Yes
# of LD applications accepted yearly: NR
Total # of students receiving LD services: 177
Acceptance into program means acceptance into college: Students must be admitted to and enrolled in the university first and then request services.

ADMISSIONS

Admission requirements are the same for all applicants. Freshman requirements include 4 years of English, 2 years of a foreign language, 3 years of mathematics (Algebra I, Algebra II, and geometry), 2 years of social studies, 2 years of science (biology and chemistry or physics), 0.5 unit in the arts, and 4.5 additional college-preparatory units. Most accepted students rank in the upper 50 percent of their class. SAT or ACT scores required. Students with LD/ADHD should submit the general application for admission. If a student does not meet admission requirements and is considered as a conditional admit, this would be done regardless of having an LD or ADHD.

ADDITIONAL INFORMATION

The Student Life Office provides the following services for students with appropriate documentation: one-on-one consultation, note-taking arrangements, use of a tape recorders in class, readers/recorders, registration assistance, disability discussion groups, and assistive technology. The Office of Academic Support and Information Services provides the following for all students: academic advisement, an Academic Development Center, a Math Learning Center, tutorial services, and a Writing Center. Students may request substitutions in courses not required by their major.

LEARNING DISABILITY PROGRAM OR SERVICES

Contact Information
Name of program or department: Disability Services, Student Life Office
 Telephone: 401-456-8061
 Fax: 401-456-8702

LEARNING DISABILITY SERVICES

Accommodations are decided upon an individual basis after a thorough review of appropriate, current documentation. The accommodations requested must be supported through the documentation provided and must be logically linked to the current impact of the condition on academic functioning.

Allowed in exams
 Calculator: Yes
 Dictionary: Yes
 Computer: Yes
 Spellchecker: Yes
Extended test time: Yes
Scribes: Yes
Proctors: No
Oral exams: Yes
Note-takers: Yes

Distraction-reduced environment: Yes
Tape recording in class: Yes
Electronic texts: Yes
Accommodations for students with ADHD: Yes
Kurzweil Reader: Yes
Other assistive technology: Larger screen monitors, network printers, adjustable computer tables, a clearview optiplex enlarger and various specialized software
Priority registration: Yes

Added costs for services: No
LD specialists: Yes
Professional tutors: No
Peer tutors: Yes
Max. hours/wk. for services: Unlimited
How professors are notified of LD/ADHD: By both student and director

GENERAL ADMISSIONS INFORMATION

Office of Admission: 401-456-8234

ENTRANCE REQUIREMENTS

Academic units required: 4 English, 3 math, 2 science (2 science labs), 2 foreign language, 2 social studies, 4 academic electives, 1 art and computer literacy (0.5 each). High school diploma is required, and GED is accepted. TOEFL required of all international applicants: minimum paper TOEFL 550.

Application deadline: 3/1
Notification: Rolling
Average GPA: NR
ACT Composite middle 50% range: NR

SAT Math middle 50% range: NR
SAT Critical Reading middle 50% range: NR
SAT Writing middle 50% range: 430–530
Graduated top 10% of class: NR

Graduated top 25% of class: NR
Graduated top 50% of class: NR

COLLEGE GRADUATION REQUIREMENTS

Course waivers allowed: Yes
In what course: English and others if not required by student's major
Course substitutions allowed: Yes
In what course: English and others if not required by student's major

ADDITIONAL INFORMATION

Environment: The campus is located a few miles from downtown Providence.

Student Body
 Undergrad enrollment: 7,778
 Women: 68%
 Men: 32%
 Percent out-of-state: 20%

Cost Information
 In-state tuition: $7,268
 Out-of-state tuition: $17,554
 Room & board: $10,148
Housing Information
 University housing: Yes
 Percent living on campus: NR

Greek System
 Fraternity: Yes
 Sorority: Yes
Athletics: Division III

UNIVERSITY OF RHODE ISLAND

Undergrad. Admissions Office, 14 Upper College Road, Kingston, RI 02881
Phone: 401-874-7000 • Fax: 401-874-5523
E-mail: uriadmit@etal.uri.edu • Web: www.uri.edu
Support: CS • Institution type: 4-year public

PROGRAMS OR SERVICES FOR STUDENTS WITH LD

At the University of Rhode Island, Disability Services for Students recognizes disability as cultural diversity and equal opportunity. The DSS program fosters an inclusive environment for URI community members through education, awareness, and accessibility. They accomplish this mission by recommending and coordinating reasonable accommodations in a variety of domains (i.e. exams, courses, programs, housing, transportation and technology). Student development is encouraged through self-advocacy and personal decision making; the program supports student commitment to academic success and student retention; and the program provides information and training to faculty and administration that upholds inclusion of persons with disabilities, including students with learning disabilities. Students are expected to be leading and active partners in arranging for accommodations. For further information please see www.uri.edu/disability.

ADMISSION INFORMATION FOR STUDENTS WITH LD/ADHD

College entrance tests required: Yes
Interview required: No
Essay recommended: No
What documentation required for LD: Psycho Ed evaluation to include: relevant historical info, instructional interventions, related services, age diagnosed, objective data (aptitude, achievement, info processing), test scores (standard, percentile and grade equivalents) and describe functional limitations.
With general application: No
To receive services after enrolling: Yes.
What documentation required for ADHD: Diagnosis based on DSM-V; history of behaviors impairing functioning in academic setting; diagnostic interview; history of symptoms; evidence of ongoing behaviors.

With general application: No
Submitted to: Admissions Office
Special Ed. HS course work accepted: N/A
Specific course requirements of all applicants: Yes
Separate application required: No
# of LD applications submitted each year: NR
# of LD applications accepted yearly: NR
Total # of students receiving LD services: 500
Acceptance into program means acceptance into college: Students must be admitted to and enrolled in the university first and then request services.

ADMISSIONS

All applicants are expected to meet the general admission criteria. There is not a special process for students with LD/ADHD. General admission requirements expect students to rank in the upper 50 percent of their high school class and complete college-preparatory courses in English, math, social studies, science, and foreign language. If there is current documentation of a language-based LD, there is a waiver for the foreign language admissions requirement, but students must self-disclose during the admission process.

ADDITIONAL INFORMATION

Students need to provide the Disability Services for Students Office with current documentation of their disability that includes psychoeducational testing completed by a professional evaluator. DSS assists students in arranging for accommodations, help to facilitate communication between students and professors, work with students to develop effective coping strategies, assist students with identifying appropriate resources and provide referrals, and offer support groups for students with ADHD and a group working toward enhanced awareness of disability issues. Accommodations are based solely on documented disabilities, and eligible students have access to services such as priority registration, extended time on exams, permission to tape record lectures, and access to a note-taker.

LEARNING DISABILITY PROGRAM OR SERVICES

Contact Information
Name of program or department: Disability Services for Students
  Telephone: 401-874-2098
  Fax: 401-874-5574

LEARNING DISABILITY SERVICES

Accommodations are decided upon an individual basis after a thorough review of appropriate, current documentation. The accommodations requested must be supported through the documentation provided and must be logically linked to the current impact of the condition on academic functioning.

Allowed in exams
  Calculator: Yes
  Dictionary: Yes
  Computer: Yes
  Spellchecker: Yes
  Extended test time: Yes
  Scribes: Yes
  Proctors: No
  Oral exams: No
  Note-takers: Yes

Distraction-reduced environment: Yes
Tape recording in class: Yes
Electronic texts: Yes
Accommodations for students with ADHD: Yes
Kurzweil Reader: Yes
Other assistive technology: Yes
Priority registration: Yes

Added costs for services: No
LD specialists: Yes
Professional tutors: No
Peer tutors: Yes, other offices
Max. hours/wk. for services: N/A
How professors are notified of LD/ADHD: By both student and director

GENERAL ADMISSIONS INFORMATION

Office of Admission: 401-874-7100

ENTRANCE REQUIREMENTS

Academic units required: 4 English, 3 math, 2 science (1 science lab), 2 foreign language, 2 social studies, 5 academic electives. High school diploma is required, and GED is accepted. ACT with Writing component required. TOEFL required of all international applicants: minimum paper TOEFL 550, minimum computer TOEFL 213.

Application deadline: 2/1
Notification: 3/31
Average GPA: 3.4
ACT Composite middle 50% range: 21–26

SAT Math middle 50% range: 500–610
SAT Critical Reading middle 50% range: 490–590
SAT Writing middle 50% range: 490–590

Graduated top 10% of class: 18%
Graduated top 25% of class: 49%
Graduated top 50% of class: 87%

COLLEGE GRADUATION REQUIREMENTS

Course waivers allowed: No
Course substitutions allowed: Yes
In what course: On a case-by-case basis for eligible students

ADDITIONAL INFORMATION

Environment: The campus is located 30 miles from Providence.

Student Body
  Undergrad enrollment: 13,219
  Women: 55%
  Men: 45%
  Percent out-of-state: 38%

Cost Information
  In-state tuition: $9,824
  Out-of-state tuition: $25,912
  Room & board: $10,767
Housing Information
  University housing: Yes
  Percent living on campus: 43%

Greek System
  Fraternity: Yes
  Sorority: Yes
Athletics: Division I

CLEMSON UNIVERSITY

105 Sikes Hall, Box 345124, Clemson, SC 29634-5124
Phone: 864-656-2287 • Fax: 864-656-2464
E-mail: cuadmissions@clemson.edu • Web: www.clemson.edu
Support: S • Institution type: 4-year public

PROGRAMS OR SERVICES FOR STUDENTS WITH LD

Student Disability Services coordinates the provision of reasonable accommodations for students with disabilities. All reasonable accommodations are individualized, flexible, and confidential based on the nature of the disability and the academic environment. Students requesting accommodations must provide current documentation of the disability from a physician or licensed professional. High school IEP, 504 plan, and/or letter from a physician or other professional will not be sufficient to document some disabilities. While such documentation can be helpful in establishing the student's learning history, a recent (typically less than 3 years old) evaluation is still necessary to confirm current needs. Reasonable accommodations can be made in the instructional process to ensure full educational opportunities. The objective is to provide appropriate services to accommodate the student's learning differences, not to change scholastic requirements.

ADMISSION INFORMATION FOR STUDENTS WITH LD/ADHD

College entrance tests required: Yes
Interview required: No
Essay recommended: No
What documentation required for LD: Psycho Ed evaluation to include: relevant historical info, instructional interventions, related services, age diagnosed, objective data (aptitude, achievement, info processing), test scores (standard, percentile and grade equivalents) and describe functional limitations.
With general application: No
To receive services after enrolling: Yes
What documentation required for ADHD: Diagnosis based on DSM-V; history of behaviors impairing functioning in academic setting; diagnostic interview; history of symptoms; evidence of ongoing behaviors.

With general application: No
Submitted to: Student Disability Services
Special Ed. HS course work accepted: Yes
Specific course requirements of all applicants: Yes
Separate application required: No
# of LD applications submitted each year: NR
# of LD applications accepted yearly: NR
Total # of students receiving LD services: 135, ADHD
Acceptance into program means acceptance into college: Students must be admitted to and enrolled in the university first and then request services.

ADMISSIONS

All students must satisfy the same admission criteria for the university. There is no separate application process for students with disabilities. General admission requirements include an ACT score of 22–27 or an SAT Reasoning score of 1080–1260, and course requirements include 4 years of English, 3 years of math, 3 years of science lab, 3 years of a foreign language, and 3 years of social studies. Students may request a waiver of the foreign language requirement by submitting a request to the exception committee. It is recommended that students self-disclose their learning disability if they need to explain the lack of a foreign language in their background or other information that will help admissions to understand their challenges.

ADDITIONAL INFORMATION

Appropriate accommodations are discussed with each student individually and confidentially. Some of the accommodations offered are assistive technology; note-takers, readers, and transcribers; course substitutions; exam modifications, including computers, extended time, private and quiet rooms, readers, and scribes; priority registration; and recorded lectures. All students have access to peer tutoring, supplemental instruction, a writing lab, and departmental tutoring. Assistive technology available includes screen readers, and scanners. Study skills instruction is available in topics such as time management techniques and test strategies. Peer mentoring is available. There are currently 135 students with learning disabilities and 345 students with ADHD receiving services.

LEARNING DISABILITY PROGRAM OR SERVICES

Contact Information
Name of program or department: Student Disability Services
　Telephone: 864-656-6848
　Fax: 864-656-6849

LEARNING DISABILITY SERVICES

Accommodations are decided upon an individual basis after a thorough review of appropriate, current documentation. The accommodations requested must be supported through the documentation provided and must be logically linked to the current impact of the condition on academic functioning.

Allowed in exams
　Calculator: Yes
　Dictionary: Yes
　Computer: Yes
　Spellchecker: Yes
Extended test time: Yes
Scribes: Yes
Proctors: Yes
Oral exams: Yes
Note-takers: Yes

Distraction-reduced environment: Yes
Tape recording in class: Yes
Electronic texts: Yes
Accommodations for students with
　ADHD: Yes
Kurzweil Reader: Yes
Other assistive technology: Yes
Priority registration: Yes

Added costs for services: No
LD specialists: No
Professional tutors: No
Peer tutors: Yes
Max. hours/wk. for services:
　Unlimited
How professors are notified of
　LD/ADHD: Student

GENERAL ADMISSIONS INFORMATION

Office of Admission: 864-656-2287

ENTRANCE REQUIREMENTS

Academic units required: 4 English, 3 math, 3 science (3 science labs), 3 foreign language, 3 social studies, 1 history, 2 academic electives, 1 physical education or ROTC. **Academic units recommended:** 4 math, (4 science labs). High school diploma is required, and GED is accepted. ACT with Writing component required. TOEFL required of all international applicants: minimum paper TOEFL 550, minimum computer TOEFL 213.

Application deadline: 5/1
Notification: Rolling
Average GPA: 4.18
ACT Composite middle 50% range:
　25–30

SAT Math middle 50% range:
　590–680
SAT Critical Reading middle 50%
　range: 550–650
SAT Writing middle 50% range: NR

Graduated top 10% of class: 48%
Graduated top 25% of class: 80%
Graduated top 50% of class: 97%

COLLEGE GRADUATION REQUIREMENTS

Course waivers allowed: No
Course substitutions allowed: Yes
In what course: Math and foreign language, depending on program of study

ADDITIONAL INFORMATION

Environment: The university is located on 1,400 acres in a small town.

Student Body
　Undergrad enrollment: 15,836
　Women: 46%
　Men: 54%
　Percent out-of-state: 29%

Cost Information
　In-state tuition: $12,668
　Out-of-state tuition: $28,826
　Room & board: $7,228
Housing Information
　University housing: Yes
　Percent living on campus: 41%

Greek System
　Fraternity: Yes
　Sorority: Yes
Athletics: Division I

LIMESTONE COLLEGE

1115 College Drive, Gaffney, SC 29340-3799
Phone: 864-488-4549 • Fax: 864-487-8706
E-mail: admiss@limestone.edu • Web: www.limestone.edu
Support: SP • Institution: 4-year private

PROGRAMS OR SERVICES FOR STUDENTS WITH LD

In addition to free disability services offered by all institutions, the Program for Alternative Learning Styles (PALS) was developed to comprehensively service students with learning disabilities. Therefore, only students with documented learning disabilities are eligible to receive program services. For program purposes, LD refers to students with average to above average intelligence (above 90) who have a discrepancy between measured intelligence and achievement. PALS's biggest advantage is the follow-up system that is in place for the PALS students. Each student is very carefully monitored as to his or her progress in each course he or she takes. The students who are not successful are typically those students who do not take advantage of the system. Deliberate accountability helps students remain aware of their status and offers assistance to improve on negative reports. The tracking system is specifically designed to keep PALS personnel, the professors and the students informed about their progress toward a degree from Limestone College.

ADMISSION INFORMATION FOR STUDENTS WITH LD/ADHD

College entrance tests required: No
Interview required: Yes
Essay required: N/A
What documentation required for LD: Psycho Ed evaluation to include: relevant historical info, instructional interventions, related services, age diagnosed, objective data (aptitude, achievement, info processing), test scores (standard, percentile and grade equivalents) and describe functional limitations.
With general application: No
To receive services after enrolling: Yes
What documentation required for ADHD: Diagnosis based on DSM-V; history of behaviors impairing functioning in academic setting; diagnostic interview; history of symptoms; evidence of ongoing behaviors.

With general application: No
Submitted to: Disability Services
Special Ed. HS course work accepted: Yes
Specific course requirements for all applicants: Yes
Separate application required for program services: No
# of LD applications submitted each year: 50 (PALS)
# of LD applications accepted yearly: 25 (PALS)
Total # of students receiving LD services: 150 (PALS and LD)
Acceptance into program means acceptance into college: Yes

ADMISSIONS

Students who self-disclose their LD and want the services of PALS must first be admitted to Limestone College either fully or conditionally. Students must submit a high school transcript with a diploma or GED certificate, SAT or ACT scores (though a minimum score is not required to seek admission via PALS), and the general college application. The minimum GPA is a 2.0. To receive services through PALS, students must submit their most recent psychological report (completed within the past 3 years) documenting an LD. Only evaluations by certified school psychologists will be accepted. In addition, only intelligence test scores from the Stanford Binet and/or Wechsler Scales will be acceptable. All available information is carefully reviewed prior to acceptance. Students may be admitted provisionally via PALS, if approved by the PALS Admissions Committee and enrolled in PALS. Students interested in PALS must arrange for an interview with the director of PALS to learn what will be expected of the student and what the program will and will not do for the student. After the interview is completed, students will be notified of their eligibility for PALS and be given the opportunity to sign a statement indicating their wish to participate or not to participate.

ADDITIONAL INFORMATION

During the regular academic year, students will receive special instruction in the area of study skills. PALS personnel are in constant communication with students concerning grades, tutors, professors, accommodations, time management, and study habits. Tutorial services are provided on an individual basis so that all students can reach their maximum potential. Skills classes are offered in math and reading. Other services include counseling, time management skills, and screening for the best ways to make accommodations. All freshmen or new students are required to pay the full fee for the first year of services ($5,000). That fee will be reduced by 50 percent for all students who complete two consecutive semesters (with NO developmental courses) with a GPA of 2.0 or better.

PROGRAM FOR DISABILITY SERVICES

Contact Information
Name of program or department: Program for Alternative Learning Styles (PALS)
   Telephone: 864-488-8377
   Fax: 864-487-8706

LEARNING DISABILITY SERVICES

Accommodations are decided upon an individual basis after a thorough review of appropriate, current documentation and personal interview. The accommodations requested must be supported through the documentation provided and must be logically linked to the current impact of the condition on academic functioning. Accommodation may be include, but not limited to:

Allowed in exams
   Calculator: Yes
   Dictionary: Yes
   Computer: Yes
   Spellchecker: Yes
Extended test time: Yes
Scribes: Yes
Proctors: Yes
Oral exams: Yes
Note-takers: Yes

Distraction-reduced environment: Yes
Lecture recording: Yes
Electronic texts: Yes
Accommodations for students with ADHD: Yes
Universal Reader: Yes
Other assistive technology: Yes
Priority registration: No

Added costs for services: Yes
   (comprehensive PALS services)
LD specialists: Yes
Professional tutors: 4–8
Peer tutors: 18–24
Max. hours/wk. for services: Unlimited
How professors are notified of LD/ADHD: By PALS staff

GENERAL ADMISSIONS INFORMATION

Office of Admission: 864-488-4549

ENTRANCE REQUIREMENTS
Academic units required: 4 English, 3 mathematics, 2 science, (2 science labs), 3 social studies. High school diploma is required and GED is accepted. SAT or ACT required (no minimum score is required for PALS); TOEFL required of all international applicants; minimum paper TOEFL 500, minimum computer TOEFL 173.

Application deadline: 8/26
Notification: Rolling
Average GPA: 3.18
ACT Composite middle 50% range: 19–23

SAT Math middle 50% range: 480–560
SAT Critical Reading middle 50% range: 440–520
SAT Writing middle 50% range: NR

Graduated top 10% of class: 5%
Graduated top 25% of class: 18%
Graduated top 50% of class: 50%

COLLEGE GRADUATION REQUIREMENTS

Course waivers allowed: No
In what course: Foreign language is not required at Limestone!
Course substitutions allowed: No

ADDITIONAL INFORMATION

Environment: The campus is located Northeast of Greenville.

Student Body
   Undergrad enrollment: 858
   Women: 42%
   Men: 58%
   Percent out-of-state: 39%

Cost Information
   Tuition: $21,000
   Room and board: $7,500
Housing Information
   University housing: Yes
   Percent living on campus: 52%

Greek System
   Fraternity: No
   Sorority: No
   Athletics: Division II

SOUTHERN WESLEYAN UNIVERSITY

Wesleyan Drive, PO Box 1020, Central, SC 29630-1020
Phone: 864-644-5550 • Fax: 864-644-5972
E-mail: admissions@swu.edu • Web: www.swu.edu
Support: S • Institution: 4-year private

PROGRAMS OR SERVICES FOR STUDENTS WITH LD

Southern Wesleyan University offers services to students with disabilities by coordinating the efforts of faculty, staff, and the Center for Transformational Learning under the director of the Student Learning Services Coordinator and the Committee for Students with Disabilities. Supplemental Instruction (SI) is an academic assistance program designed to increase retention, improve student grades and increase graduation rates. SI accomplishes these goals by helping students learn to solve problems, organize classroom materials, develop effective study strategies and meet personal and faculty expectations. Supplemental Instruction is intended to be a semester-long series of weekly group study sessions led by an SI leader. The SI leader is an undergraduate who has successfully completed the course with an "A" average. All SI leaders are recommended by faculty. The SI leader attends the weekly lecture, takes notes, meets with the course instructor regularly, and then holds three study sessions weekly to provide support to students currently enrolled in the course.

ADMISSION INFORMATION FOR STUDENTS WITH LD/ADHD

College entrance tests required: Yes
Interview required: No
Essay required: N/A
What documentation required for LD: Psycho Ed evaluation to include: relevant historical info, instructional interventions, related services, age diagnosed, objective data (aptitude, achievement, info processing), test scores (standard, percentile and grade equivalents) and describe functional limitations.
With general application: No
To receive services after enrolling: Yes
What documentation required for ADHD: Diagnosis based on DSM-V; history of behaviors impairing functioning in academic setting; diagnostic interview; history of symptoms; evidence of ongoing behaviors.

With general application: No
Submitted to: Student Services Learning Coordinator
Specific course requirements for all applicants: Yes
Separate application required for program services: No
# of LD applications submitted each year: NR
# of LD applications accepted yearly: NR
Total # of students receiving LD services: 12
Acceptance into program means acceptance into college: Students are admitted directly into the university and to Services for Students with Disabilities with appropriate documentation.

ADMISSIONS

All applicants must meet the same admission criteria. Courses taken in high school should include at least: must have: 4 years of English, 2 years of science, 2 years of social studies, and 2 years of math. Applicants should have a GPA of 2.3 (or rank in upper half of your graduating class at time of acceptance) and a composite SAT score of 860 (based on the critical reading/verbal and math sections) or an ACT score of 18.

ADDITIONAL INFORMATION

Documentation of a disability goes to the student Learning Services Coordinator. The student must request services each semester by discussing with the coordinator what accommodations are appropriate and needed in each course. The coordinator sends a letter to the professor of each course the student has identified for needed accommodation. The student also receives a copy and arranges the logistics and details with professors. We emphasize that students must initiate the request and the arrangements. We encourage the student to develop the highest degree of independence possible during their college years and become prepared to compete successfully in their chosen career. There is a liaison person between faculty and students. Professors are available to students after class. Modifications can be made in test-taking, which could include extended time and a quiet place to take exams. Additionally, students may receive assistance with note-taking. All services are offered in response to students' requests.

PROGRAM FOR DISABILITY SERVICES

Contact Information
Name of program or department: Services to Students with Disabilities
  Telephone: 864-644-5036
  Fax: 864-644-5979

LEARNING DISABILITY SERVICES

Accommodations are decided upon an individual basis after a thorough review of appropriate, current documentation. The accommodations requested must be supported through the documentation provided and must be logically linked to the current impact of the condition on academic functioning.

Allowed in exams
  Calculator: Yes
  Dictionary: Yes
  Computer: Yes
  Spellchecker: Yes
Extended test time: Yes
Scribes: Yes
Proctors: Yes
Oral exams: Yes
Note-takers: Yes

Distraction-reduced environment: Yes
Tape recording in class: Yes
Electronic texts: N/A
Accommodations for students with ADHD: Yes
Kurzweil Reader: No
Other assistive technology: voice recognition program
Priority registration: No

Added costs for services: No
LD specialists: No
Professional tutors: 1
Peer tutors: 5–8
Max. hours/wk. for services: NR
How professors are notified of LD/ADHD: Both student and coordinator

GENERAL ADMISSIONS INFORMATION

Office of Admission: 864-644-5558

ENTRANCE REQUIREMENTS
Academic units required: 4 English, 2 mathematics, 2 science, 2 social studies. High school diploma is required and GED is accepted. SAT or ACT required; ACT with Writing component recommended. TOEFL required of all international applicants; minimum paper TOEFL 500, minimum computer TOEFL 173.

Application deadline: 8/1
Notification: Rolling
Average GPA: 3.6
ACT Composite middle 50% range: 18–22

SAT Math middle 50% range: 450–550
SAT Critical Reading middle 50% range: 460–550
SAT Writing middle 50% range: 430–530

Graduated top 10% of class: 13%
Graduated top 25% of class: 36%
Graduated top 50% of class: 75%

COLLEGE GRADUATION REQUIREMENTS

Course substitutions allowed: No
In what course: No

ADDITIONAL INFORMATION

Environment: The college is centrally located between Charlotte, North Carolina, and Atlanta, Georgia and within sight of the Blue Ridge Mountains.

Student Body
  Undergrad enrollment: 1,433
  Women: 62%
  Men: 38%
  Percent out-of-state: 15%

Cost Information
  Tuition: $20,850
  Room and board: $7,550
Housing Information
  University housing: Yes
  Percent living on campus: 25%

Greek System
  Fraternity: No
  Sorority: No
  Athletics: NAIA

THE UNIVERSITY OF SOUTH CAROLINA—COLUMBIA

Office of Undergraduate Admissions, Columbia, SC 29208
Phone: 803-777-7700 • Fax: 803-777-0101
E-mail: admissions@sc.edu • Web: www.sc.edu
Support: CS • Institution type: 4-year public

PROGRAMS OR SERVICES FOR STUDENTS WITH LD

The university's Office of Disability Services (ODS) provides educational support and assistance to students with LD who have the potential for success in a competitive university setting. The Office of Disability Services is specifically designed to empower them with the confidence to become self-advocates and to take an active role in their education. The university works with each student on an individualized basis to match needs with appropriate services. The services are tailored to provide educational support and assistance to students based on their specific needs. The Office of Disability Services recommends and coordinates support services with faculty, administrators, advisors, and deans. The nature and severity of LD may vary considerably. All requests are based on documented diagnostic information regarding each student's specific learning disability. The first step in accessing services from the Office of Disability Services is to self-disclose the disability and arrange an interview. During the interview, staff members will discuss the student's educational background and determine which services best fit his or her needs.

ADMISSION INFORMATION FOR STUDENTS WITH LD/ADHD

College entrance tests required: Yes
Interview required: Yes
Essay recommended: No
What documentation required for LD: Psycho Ed evaluation to include: relevant historical info, instructional interventions, related services, age diagnosed, objective data (aptitude, achievement, info processing), test scores (standard, percentile and grade equivalents) and describe functional limitations.
With general application: No
To receive services after enrolling: Yes
What documentation required for ADHD: Diagnosis based on DSM-V; history of behaviors impairing functioning in academic setting; diagnostic interview; history of symptoms; evidence of ongoing behaviors.

With general application: No
Submitted to: ODS
Special Ed. HS course work accepted: No
Specific course requirements of all applicants: Yes
Separate application required: No
# of LD applications submitted each year: NR
# of LD applications accepted yearly: NR
Total # of students receiving LD services: 500
Acceptance into program means acceptance into college: Students must be admitted and enrolled in the university first (they can appeal a denial) and then request services.

ADMISSIONS

There is no special application or admission process for students with LD. Required scores on the SAT and ACT vary with class rank. Applicants must have a cumulative C-plus average on defined college-preparatory courses, including 4 years of English, 3 years of math, 3 years of science, 2 years of the same foreign language, 4 years of electives, and 1 year of physical education, as well as a 1200 SAT or 27 ACT. If they are denied admission or feel they do not meet the required standards, students may petition the Admissions Committee for an exception to the regular admissions requirements. Once admitted, students should contact the Educational Support Services Center to arrange an interview to determine which services are necessary to accommodate their needs.

ADDITIONAL INFORMATION

Services are individually tailored to provide educational support and assistance. All requests are based on documented diagnostic information. The program is designed to provide educational support and assistance, including analysis of learning needs to determine appropriate interventions, consulting with the faculty about special academic needs, monitoring of progress by a staff member, study skills training, and tutorial referrals. Special program accommodations may include a reduced course load of 9–12 hours, waivers/substitutions for some courses, and expanded pass/fail options. Special classroom accommodations may include tape recorders, note-takers, and extended time on tests.

LEARNING DISABILITY PROGRAM OR SERVICES

Contact Information
Name of program or department: Office of Student Disability Services
  Telephone: 803-777-6142
  Fax: 803-777-6741

LEARNING DISABILITY SERVICES

Accommodations are decided upon an individual basis after a thorough review of appropriate, current documentation. The accommodations requested must be supported through the documentation provided and must be logically linked to the current impact of the condition on academic functioning.

Allowed in exams
  Calculator: Yes
  Dictionary: Yes
  Computer: Yes
  Spellchecker: Yes
Extended test time: Yes
Scribes: Yes
Proctors: Yes
Oral exams: No
Note-takers: Yes

Distraction-reduced environment: Yes
Tape recording in class: Yes
Electronic texts: Yes
Accommodations for students with
  ADHD: Yes
Kurzweil Reader: Yes
Other assistive technology: Yes
Priority registration: Yes

Added costs for services: No
LD specialists: Yes
Professional tutors: No
Peer tutors: No
Max. hours/wk. for services: 42.5
How professors are notified of
  LD/ADHD: By student

GENERAL ADMISSIONS INFORMATION

Office of Admission: 803-777-7700 or 800-868-5872

ENTRANCE REQUIREMENTS

Academic units required: 4 English, 3 math, 3 science (3 science labs), 2 foreign language, 2 social studies, 1 history, 4 academic electives, 1 physical education or ROTC. High school diploma is required, and GED is accepted. ACT with Writing component required. TOEFL required of all international applicants: minimum paper TOEFL 550, minimum computer TOEFL 210.

Application deadline: 12/1
Notification: Rolling
Average GPA: 3.90
ACT Composite middle 50% range:
  24–29

SAT Math middle 50% range:
  550–650
SAT Critical Reading middle 50%
  range: 540–640
SAT Writing middle 50% range: NR

Graduated top 10% of class: 28%
Graduated top 25% of class: 62%
Graduated top 50% of class: 91%

COLLEGE GRADUATION REQUIREMENTS

Course waivers allowed: Yes
In what course: Students with learning disabilities may petition their college for substitution of the required foreign language if the requirement is not an integral part of the degree program.
Course substitutions allowed: Yes
In what course: Students with learning disabilities may petition their college for substitution of the required foreign language if the requirement is not an intregal part of the degree program.

ADDITIONAL INFORMATION

Environment: The university is located on 242 acres in downtown Columbia.

Student Body
  Undergrad enrollment: 21,383
  Women: 55%
  Men: 45%
  Percent out-of-state: 30%

Cost Information
  In-state tuition: $10,168
  Out-of-state tuition: $26,352
  Room & board: $6,986
Housing Information
  University housing: Yes
  Percent living on campus: 40%

Greek System
  Fraternity: Yes
  Sorority: Yes
Athletics: Division I

BLACK HILLS STATE UNIVERSITY

1200 University Street, Spearfish, SD 57799
Phone: 605-642-6099 • Fax: 605-642-6024
E-mail: admissions@bhsu.edu • Web: www.bhsu.edu
Support: CS • Institution type: 2- and 4-year, public

PROGRAMS OR SERVICES FOR STUDENTS WITH LD

Student Support Services ensures equal access and opportunities to educational programs for students with learning disabilities. Within the program, the disabilities services coordinator arranges accommodations, counseling services, and campus awareness activities for students with disabilities. The algebra advisor, language/learning skills instructor, and academic and career advisor provide tutoring and advising services to encourage students with disabilities to achieve academic success.

ADMISSION INFORMATION FOR STUDENTS WITH LD/ADHD

College entrance tests required: Yes
Interview required: No
Essay recommended: No
What documentation required for LD: Psycho Ed evaluation to include: relevant historical info, instructional interventions, related services, age diagnosed, objective data (aptitude, achievement, info processing), test scores (standard, percentile and grade equivalents) and describe functional limitations.
With general application: No
To receive services after enrolling: Yes
What documentation required for ADHD: Diagnosis based on DSM-V; history of behaviors impairing functioning in academic setting; diagnostic interview; history of symptoms; evidence of ongoing behaviors.

With general application: No
Submitted to: Student Assistance Center
Special Ed. HS course work accepted: No
Specific course requirements of all applicants: Yes
Separate application required: Yes
# of LD applications submitted each year: NR
# of LD applications accepted yearly: NR
Total # of students receiving LD services: 70
Acceptance into program means acceptance into college: Students must be admitted to and enrolled in the university first and then request services.

ADMISSIONS

General admission requirements include a 2.0 GPA, and ACT of 18, or a rank in the upper 60% of graduation class. In addition, students must complete the following high school course work: 4 years of English, 3 years of science lab, 3 years of math, 3 years of social studies, and 1 year of fine arts. Transfer students must have a 2.0 cumulative GPA.

ADDITIONAL INFORMATION

Basic skills instruction is available in English and Math, and a university learning skills course provides an introduction to college-level studies. The Student Success Center and Black Hills State University is a student-centered, service-oriented office focused on ensuring student persistence and success. The center provides assistance and information to all students, faculty, and staff in an effort to facilitate academic success, student persistence, and student satisfaction with the university experience. Staff provides information and advisement on a number of topics related to study skills success and personal development. They use various valid and reliable inventories to assist students in identifying their academic strengths, personal interests, learning styles, and academic and career goals. They also draw up personal success plans with students early in the semester to clearly define goals, and they follow up on student progress throughout the semester to ensure that plans are put into action and monitored regularly. Testing services are available through Disability Services.

LEARNING DISABILITY PROGRAM OR SERVICES

Contact Information
Name of program or department: Disability Services
 Telephone: 605-642-6099
 Fax: 605-642-6024

LEARNING DISABILITY SERVICES

Accommodations are decided upon an individual basis after a thorough review of appropriate, current documentation. The accommodations requested must be supported through the documentation provided and must be logically linked to the current impact of the condition on academic functioning.

Allowed in exams
 Calculator: Yes
 Dictionary: Yes
 Computer: Yes
 Spellchecker: Yes
Extended test time: Yes
Scribes: Yes
Proctors: Yes
Oral exams: Yes
Note-takers: Yes

Distraction-reduced environment: Yes
Tape recording in class: Yes
Electronic texts: Yes
Accommodations for students with
 ADHD: Yes
Kurzweil Reader: Yes
Other assistive technology: Yes
Priority registration: No

Added costs for services: No
LD specialists: Yes
Professional tutors: 4
Peer tutors: 3–10
Max. hours/wk. for services: 40
How professors are notified of
 LD/ADHD: By both student and director

GENERAL ADMISSIONS INFORMATION

Office of Admission: 605-642-6343

ENTRANCE REQUIREMENTS

Academic units required: 4 English, 3 math, 3 science (3 science labs), 3 social studies, 1 fine arts. High school diploma is required, and GED is accepted. ACT with or without Writing component accepted. TOEFL required of all international applicants: minimum paper TOEFL 550 or IBT 79.

Application deadline: Rolling
Notification: Rolling
Average GPA: 3.14
ACT Composite middle 50% range:
 18–23

SAT Math middle 50% range: NR
SAT Critical Reading middle 50%
 range: NR
SAT Writing middle 50% range: NR

Graduated top 10% of class: 7%
Graduated top 25% of class: 28%
Graduated top 50% of class: 63%

COLLEGE GRADUATION REQUIREMENTS

Course waivers allowed: No
Course substitutions allowed: No

ADDITIONAL INFORMATION

Environment: The university is located on 123 acres in a small town 45 miles northwest of Rapid City.

Student Body
 Undergrad enrollment: 4,009
 Women: 65%
 Men: 35%
 Percent out-of-state: 22%

Cost Information
 In-state tuition: $7,424
 Out-of-state tuition: $9,252
 Room & board: $5,549
Housing Information
 University housing: Yes
 Percent living on campus: 16%

Greek System
 Fraternity: N/A
 Sorority: N/A
Athletics: NCAA

SOUTH DAKOTA STATE UNIVERSITY

SAD 200, BOX 2201, Brookings, SD 57007-0649
Phone: 605-688-4121 • Fax: 605-688-6891
E-mail: sdsu.admissions@sdstate.edu • Web: www.sdstate.edu
Support: S • Institution type: 4-year public

PROGRAMS OR SERVICES FOR STUDENTS WITH LD

South Dakota State University is committed to providing equal opportunities for higher education to academically qualified students with LDs. All students, including those with disabilities, have access to skill development courses in the areas of general academic success skills, English composition, and mathematics. Free tutoring is available for all students in a wide variety of subject areas.

ADMISSION INFORMATION FOR STUDENTS WITH LD/ADHD

College entrance tests required: Yes
Interview required: No
Essay recommended: No
Documentation required for LD: The Disability Services website is linked to the university's main page. On the DS site there are documentation forms that the student's medical/psychological professional is asked to complete.
Documentation required for ADHD: The Disability Services website is linked to the university's main page. On the DS site there are documentation forms that the student's medical/psychological professional is asked to complete.
Submitted to: DS
Special Ed. HS course work accepted: NR

Specific course requirements of all applicants: Yes
Separate application required: Students mus be admitted to university first and then apply
# of LD applications submitted each year: NR
# of LD applications accepted yearly: NR
Total # of students receiving LD services: NR
Acceptance into program means acceptance into college: Students must be admitted to and enrolled in the university first and then request services.

ADMISSIONS

Students with learning disabilities must meet the same admission criteria as all applicants. For admission to SDS they look for one of the following academic achievements: 1) An ACT composite score of 18 or higher (SAT of 870 or higher) 2) a high school cumulative GPA of 2.6 or higher or 3) rank in the top 60 percent of the class. Students should also complete the following core courses with a "C" average or above: 4 years of English (or ACT English sub-score of 18) 3 years of advanced math—Algebra I and higher (or ACT math sub-score of 20), 3 years of laboratory science (or ACT science reasoning sub-score of 17), 3 years of social science (or ACT reading sub-score of 17), 1 year of fine arts (includes vocal, instrumental and studio arts), and basic computer skills (students should have basic keyboarding, word processing, spreadsheet and internet skills).

ADDITIONAL INFORMATION

The Office of Disability Services provides assistance for students with a wide range of disabilities. The first step is to fill out the application for disability services. Along with this application, students need to send documentation of the disability. After that, ODS will set up an appointment to discuss services provided that will enhance the students learning experiences at SDSU. Some of the services include: alternative text formats, note taker, assistive technology, alternative accommodations for exams (for example, testing in a distraction-free environment or providing readers for exams), extended time for testing, and referrals to other resources. Tutoring and Supplemental Instruction (SI) is offered to all SDSU students through the Wintrode Tutoring & SI Program. They provide SI sessions, walk-in review sessions, and tutoring in select courses from peers who have been through the same classes.

LEARNING DISABILITY PROGRAM OR SERVICES

Contact Information
Name of program or department: Disability Services (DS)
  Telephone: 605-688-4504
  Fax: 605-688-4987

LEARNING DISABILITY SERVICES

Accommodations are decided upon an individual basis after a thorough review of appropriate, current documentation. The accommodations requested must be supported through the documentation provided and must be logically linked to the current impact of the condition on academic functioning.

Allowed in exams
  Calculator: Yes
  Dictionary: No
  Computer: Yes
  Spellchecker: Yes
Extended test time: Yes
Scribes: Yes
Proctors: Yes
Oral exams: Yes
Note-takers: Yes

Distraction-reduced environment: Yes
Tape recording in class: Yes
Electronic texts: Yes
Accommodations for students with ADHD: Yes
Kurzweil Reader: Yes
Other assistive technology: Yes
Priority registration: No

Added costs for services: No
LD specialists: No
Professional tutors: Yes
Peer tutors: 25–32
Max. hours/wk. for services: Unlimited
How professors are notified of LD/ADHD: Through accommodation letters student presents to professors. Disability not discussed, only accommodations being requested.

GENERAL ADMISSIONS INFORMATION

Office of Admission: 605-688-4121

ENTRANCE REQUIREMENTS

Academic units required: 4 English, 3 math, 3 science (3 science labs), 3 social studies, 0.5 fine arts. High school diploma is required, and GED is accepted. ACT with or without Writing component accepted. TOEFL required of all international applicants: minimum paper TOEFL 500, minimum computer TOEFL 1.

Application deadline: None
Notification: Rolling
Average GPA: 3.34
ACT Composite middle 50% range: 19–25

SAT Math middle 50% range: NR
SAT Critical Reading middle 50% range: NR
SAT Writing middle 50% range: NR

Graduated top 10% of class: 15%
Graduated top 25% of class: 39%
Graduated top 50% of class: 71%

COLLEGE GRADUATION REQUIREMENTS

Course waivers allowed: No
Course substitutions allowed: No

ADDITIONAL INFORMATION

Environment: The school is located on 220 acres in a rural area 50 miles north of Sioux Falls.

Student Body
  Undergrad enrollment: 11,062
  Women: 51%
  Men: 49%
  Percent out-of-state: 33%

Cost Information
  In-state tuition: $7,209
  Out-of-state tuition: $8,924
  Room & board: $5,992
Housing Information
  University housing: Yes
  Percent living on campus: NR

Greek System
  Fraternity: Yes
  Sorority: Yes
Athletics: Division I

THE UNIVERSITY OF SOUTH DAKOTA

414 East Clark, Vermillion, SD 57069
Phone: 605-677-5434 • Fax: 605-677-6323
E-mail: admissions@usd.edu • Web: www.usd.edu
Support: CS • Institution: 4-year public

PROGRAMS OR SERVICES FOR STUDENTS WITH LD

The University of South Dakota Disability Services (USDDS) operates on the premise that students at the university are full participants in the process of obtaining appropriate accommodations for their disabilities. Students are encouraged to make their own decisions and become self-advocates for appropriate accommodations or services. The three main goals are to (1) help students become self-advocates; (2) provide better transition services into and out of college; and (3) to provide better instructional and support services. The university strives to ensure that all individuals with legally defined disabilities have access to the full range of the university's programs, services, and activities.

ADMISSION INFORMATION FOR STUDENTS WITH LD/ADHD

College entrance tests required: Yes
Interview required: N/A
Essay required: N/A
What documentation required for LD: Psycho Ed evaluation to include: relevant historical info, instructional interventions, related services, age diagnosed, objective data (aptitude, achievement, info processing), test scores (standard, percentile and grade equivalents) and describe functional limitations.
With general application: No
To receive services after enrolling: Yes
What documentation required for ADHD: Diagnosis based on DSM-V; history of behaviors impairing functioning in academic setting; diagnostic interview; history of symptoms; evidence of ongoing behaviors.

With general application: No
Submitted to: Disability Services
Special Ed. HS course work accepted: Yes
Specific course requirements for all applicants: Yes
Separate application required for program services: Yes
# of LD applications submitted each year: NR
# of LD applications accepted yearly: NR
Total # of students receiving LD services: NR
Acceptance into program means acceptance into college: Separate registration required after student has enrolled

ADMISSIONS

For Freshmen Admission, students must have a minimum 2.6 GPA on a 4.0 scale in all high school courses, OR be in the top 50 percent of their high school graduating class, OR have a minimum 21 Composite Score on the ACT (minimum 990 SAT score), AND complete the following courses with a cumulative grade point average of a C or higher (2.0 on a 4.0 scale): four years of English, three years of advanced math (algebra I or higher), three years of social science, three years of lab science, and one year of fine arts. Other requirements apply for Transfer Admission and Non-Traditional Admission. Non-Traditional Admission requirements apply for students who are age 24 or over and for those who did not graduate from high school. Please contact the Office of Admissions at 1-877-COYOTES [1-877-269-6837] for more information.

ADDITIONAL INFORMATION

Services are individualized for each student's learning needs. USDDS staff provides the following activities: planning, developing, delivering, and evaluating direct service programs; meeting individually with students ensuring that students receive reasonable and appropriate accommodations that match their needs; consulting with faculty; and providing academic, career, and personal counseling referrals. Classroom accommodations include test modification, note-taking assistance, readers, books on tape, specialized computer facilities, and tutors.

LEARNING DISABILITY PROGRAM OR SERVICES

Contact Information
Name of program or department: Disability Services, Center for Disabilities, USDDS
   Telephone: 605-677-6389
   Fax: 605-677-3172

LEARNING DISABILITY SERVICES

Accommodations are decided upon an individual basis after a thorough review of appropriate, current documentation. The accommodations requested must be supported through the documentation provided and must be logically linked to the current impact of the condition on academic functioning.

Allowed in exams	**Distraction-reduced environment:** Yes	**Added costs for services:** No
Calculator: Yes	**Tape recording in class:** Yes	**LD specialists:** Yes
Dictionary: Yes	**Electronic texts:** Yes	**Professional tutors:** NR
Computer: Yes	**Accommodations for students with**	**Peer tutors:** Yes
Spellchecker: Yes	**ADHD:** Yes	**Max. hours/wk. for services:**
Extended test time: Yes	**Kurzweil Reader:** Yes	Unlimited
Scribes: Yes	**Other assistive technology:** N/A	**How professors are notified of**
Proctors: Yes	**Priority registration:** No	**LD/ADHD:** Student
Oral exams: Yes		
Note-takers: Yes		

GENERAL ADMISSIONS INFORMATION

Office of Admission: 605-677-5434

ENTRANCE REQUIREMENTS
Academic units required: 4 English, 3 mathematics, 3 science, (3 science labs), 3 social science, 1 fine arts.
Academic units recommended: 4 English, 4 mathematics, 4 science, (3 science labs), 2 foreign language, 3 social science, 1 fine arts. High school diploma is required and GED is accepted. SAT or ACT required; SAT and SAT Subject Tests or ACT required; TOEFL required of all international applicants; minimum paper TOEFL 530, minimum computer TOEFL 197, minimum web-based TOEFL 71.

Application deadline: None	**SAT Math middle 50% range:**	**Graduated top 10% of class:** 13%
Notification: Rolling	450–610	**Graduated top 25% of class:** 34%
Average GPA: 3.25	**SAT Critical Reading middle 50%**	**Graduated top 50% of class:** 69%
ACT Composite middle 50% range:	**range:** 470–660	
20–25	**SAT Writing middle 50% range:** NR	

COLLEGE GRADUATION REQUIREMENTS

Course waivers allowed: No
In what course: No courses will be waived for graduation based on disability.
Course substitutions allowed: No
In what course: No courses will be substituted for graduation based on disability.

ADDITIONAL INFORMATION

Environment: Located 35 miles from Sioux City		
Student Body	**Cost Information**	**Greek System**
Undergrad enrollment: 7,473	**In-state tuition:** $7,209	**Fraternity:** Yes
Women: 63%	**Out-of-state tuition:** $8,924	**Sorority:** Yes
Men: 37%	**Room and board:** $6,543	**Athletics:** Division I
Percent out-of-state: 32%	**Housing Information**	
	University housing: Yes	
	Percent living on campus: 30%	

LEE UNIVERSITY

PO Box 3450, Cleveland, TN 37320-3450
Phone: 423-614-8500 • Fax: 423-614-8533
E-mail: admissions@leeuniversity.edu • Web: www.leeuniversity.edu
Support: CS • Institution type: 4-year private

PROGRAMS OR SERVICES FOR STUDENTS WITH LD

Lee University provides an Academic Support Program for students. This service is free to students. It is the goal of the Lee University Academic Support Program to empower students to actualize all the academic potential that they can. The college offers a peer tutorial program that hires the best students on campus to share their time, experience, and insight in the course or courses that are most difficult for the students who need tutoring. In addition, the college provides direct assistance for any student to verify a learning disability. For these students, Lee University provides support teams, testing adjustments, classroom adjustments, tutoring, and personal monitoring. Students must initiate the request for special accommodations by applying at the Academic Support Program Office. Lee University is committed to the provision of reasonable accommodations for students with disabilities.

ADMISSION INFORMATION FOR STUDENTS WITH LD/ADHD

College entrance tests required: Yes
Interview required: No
Essay recommended: No
What documentation required for LD: Psycho Ed evaluation to include: relevant historical info, instructional interventions, related services, age diagnosed, objective data (aptitude, achievement, info processing), test scores (standard, percentile and grade equivalents) and describe functional limitations.
With general application: No
To receive services after enrolling: Yes
What documentation required for ADHD: Diagnosis based on DSM-V; history of behaviors impairing functioning in academic setting; diagnostic interview; history of symptoms; evidence of ongoing behaviors.

With general application: No
Submitted to: Both Admissions Office and Academic Support Program
Special Ed. HS course work accepted: Yes
Specific course requirements of all applicants: Yes
Separate application required: No
# of LD applications submitted each year: NR
# of LD applications accepted yearly: NR
Total # of students receiving LD services: NR
Acceptance into program means acceptance into college: Students must be admitted to and enrolled in the university first and then request services.

ADMISSIONS

Each applicant is reviewed on a case-by-case basis. Each student must be able to perform successfully with limited support. The ACT minimum is 17; for the SAT it is 860. The minimum required GPA is 2.0. There are no specific course requirements. Students who do not meet the college policy for entrance are referred to a special committee for possible probational acceptance.

ADDITIONAL INFORMATION

The Academic Support Program is staffed by a director, office manager, and several student assistants. The program provides readers and books on tape. Benefits included in the program are tutoring sessions with friendly and comfortable surroundings; 2 hours of tutoring per week per subject; and tutoring in most subjects, including biology, psychology, English, mathematics, religion, science, sociology, history, and foreign language. Freshmen are channeled into a gateway class, which provides study skills and time management skills.

LEARNING DISABILITY PROGRAM OR SERVICES

Contact Information
Name of program or department: Academic Support Program
  Telephone: 423-614-8181
  Fax: 423-614-8179

LEARNING DISABILITY SERVICES

Accommodations are decided upon an individual basis after a thorough review of appropriate, current documentation. The accommodations requested must be supported through the documentation provided and must be logically linked to the current impact of the condition on academic functioning.

Allowed in exams
  Calculator: Yes
  Dictionary: Yes
  Computer: Yes
  Spellchecker: No
Extended test time: Yes
Scribes: Yes
Proctors: Yes
Oral exams: Yes
Note-takers: Yes

Distraction-reduced environment: Yes
Tape recording in class: Yes
Electronic texts: No
Accommodations for students with
  ADHD: Yes
Kurzweil Reader: Yes
Other assistive technology: Yes
Priority registration: Yes

Added costs for services: No
LD specialists: Yes
Professional tutors: NR
Peer tutors: 100+
Max. hours/wk. for services: NR
How professors are notified of
  LD/ADHD: By student

GENERAL ADMISSIONS INFORMATION

Office of Admission: 423-614-8500

ENTRANCE REQUIREMENTS

Academic units required: 4 English, 3 math, 2 science, 1 foreign language, 2 social studies, 1 history. **Academic units recommended:** 4 English, 3 math, 2 science, 1 foreign language, 2 social studies, 1 history, 1 computer skills. High school diploma is required, and GED is accepted. ACT with or without Writing component accepted. TOEFL required of all international applicants: minimum paper TOEFL 450, minimum computer TOEFL 133.

Application deadline: 9/1
Notification: Rolling
Average GPA: 3.36
ACT Composite middle 50% range:
  20–27

SAT Math middle 50% range:
  460–580
SAT Critical Reading middle 50%
  range: 480–590
SAT Writing middle 50% range: NR

Graduated top 10% of class: 19%
Graduated top 25% of class: 46%
Graduated top 50% of class: 74%

COLLEGE GRADUATION REQUIREMENTS

Course waivers allowed: No
Course substitutions allowed: No

ADDITIONAL INFORMATION

Environment: The college is located on 40 acres in a small town 25 miles from Chattanooga.

Student Body
  Undergrad enrollment: 3,847
  Women: 56%
  Men: 44%
  Percent out-of-state: 64%

Cost Information
  Tuition: $12,680
  Room & board: $6,370
Housing Information
  University housing: Yes
  Percent living on campus: 45%

Greek System
  Fraternity: Yes
  Sorority: Yes
Athletics: NAIA

MIDDLE TENNESSEE STATE U.

Cope Administration Building 208, Murfreesboro, TN 37132
Phone: 615-898-2111 • Fax: 615-898-5478
E-mail: admissions@mtsu.edu • Web: www.mtsu.edu
Support: S • Institution: 4-year public

PROGRAMS OR SERVICES FOR STUDENTS WITH LD

The Learning Disabilities Program is a part of the Disabled Student Services office. The LD Program offers comprehensive support services for students diagnosed with LD and ADD. Eligibility for the program requires admission to MTSU and documentation of the disability. The LD Program is designed to ensure students have an equal opportunity to pursue an education. Students with LD are held to the same academic standards as all students; however, accommodations are available to assist meeting these requirements. Accommodations are determined on an individual basis considering the student's strengths, course requirements and documentation. To register with the LD program, students schedule an appointment with the coordinator, complete the registration form, and provide the most current documentation of the disability.

ADMISSION INFORMATION FOR STUDENTS WITH LD/ADHD

College entrance tests required: Yes
Interview required: No
Essay required: N/A
What documentation required for LD: Psycho Ed evaluation to include: relevant historical info, instructional interventions, related services, age diagnosed, objective data (aptitude, achievement, info processing), test scores (standard, percentile and grade equivalents) and describe functional limitations.
With general application: No
To receive services after enrolling: Yes
What documentation required for ADHD: Diagnosis based on DSM-V; history of behaviors impairing functioning in academic setting; diagnostic interview; history of symptoms; evidence of ongoing behaviors.

With general application: No
Submitted to: Support Program/Services
Special Ed. HS course work accepted: N/A
Specific course requirements for all applicants: Yes
Separate application required for program services: No
# of LD applications submitted each year: 50
# of LD applications accepted yearly: NR
Total # of students receiving LD services: 250–350
Acceptance into program means acceptance into college: Students must be admitted to and enrolled in the university first and then request services.

ADMISSIONS

There is no special admission process for students with LD. All students must meet the same general admission requirements. The minimum GPA is a 2.8 and/or ACT 20. Students should have four years of English, three years of math, two years of science, two years of social studies, two years of foreign language, and one year of visual/performing arts. Course substitutions are not allowed. The average ACT is 21 or 970 SAT. Students are encouraged to self-disclose a disability in a personal statement during the admission process, although this is not required.

ADDITIONAL INFORMATION

Students are encouraged to initiate contact with the LD program coordinator early in the semester to determine the necessary accommodations. Once enrolled in courses students schedule regular meetings with the coordinator in order to monitor progress and/or determine the need for adjustments to the accommodations. Services/resources provided include orientation to the LD Program; orientation to the Adaptive Technology Center; assistance with the admission process; advising and strategic scheduling of classes; early registration of classes; tutorial services; test accommodations; note-takers, readers, scribes, books on tape; exploration of time management/note-taking strategies; career planning and employment strategies; and resume preparation. The Adaptive Technology Center provides training support for students,with disabilities in the use of adaptive/assistive technology application and devices. All disability documentation is confidential and is not released without the consent of the student.

LEARNING DISABILITY PROGRAM OR SERVICES

Contact Information
Name of program or department: Disabled Student Services
  Telephone: 615-898-2783
  Fax: 615-898-4893

LEARNING DISABILITY SERVICES

Accommodations are decided upon an individual basis after a thorough review of appropriate, current documentation. The accommodations requested must be supported through the documentation provided and must be logically linked to the current impact of the condition on academic functioning.

Allowed in exams	**Distraction-reduced environment:** Yes	**Added costs for services:** No
Calculator: Yes	**Tape recording in class:** Yes	**LD specialists:** No
Dictionary: Yes	**Electronic texts:** Yes	**Professional tutors:** No
Computer: Yes	**Accommodations for students with**	**Peer tutors:** Yes
Spellchecker: Yes	**ADHD:** Yes	**Max. hours/wk. for services:**
Extended test time: Yes	**Kurzweil Reader:** Yes	Unlimited
Scribes: Yes	**Other assistive technology:** N/A	**How professors are notified of**
Proctors: Yes	**Priority registration:** Yes	**LD/ADHD:** Student
Oral exams: Yes		
Note-takers: Yes		

GENERAL ADMISSIONS INFORMATION

Office of Admission: 800-585-6781

ENTRANCE REQUIREMENTS
Academic units required: 4 English, 3 mathematics, 2 science, 2 foreign language, 1 social studies, 1 history, 1 visual/performing arts. High school diploma is required and GED is accepted. SAT or ACT required; TOEFL required of all international applicants; minimum paper TOEFL 500, minimum computer TOEFL 173.

Application deadline: 7/1	**SAT Math middle 50% range:**	**Graduated top 10% of class:** 17%
Notification: Rolling	450–580	**Graduated top 25% of class:** 51%
Average GPA: 2.96	**SAT Critical Reading middle 50%**	**Graduated top 50% of class:** 64%
ACT Composite middle 50% range:	range: 450–580	
19–24	**SAT Writing middle 50% range:** NR	

COLLEGE GRADUATION REQUIREMENTS

Course waivers allowed: N/A
In what course: On an individual basis
Course substitutions allowed: N/A
In what course: On an individual basis

ADDITIONAL INFORMATION

Environment: The university is located 32 miles from Nashville.

Student Body	**Cost Information**	**Greek System**
Undergrad enrollment: 23,300	**In-state tuition:** $7,100	**Fraternity:** No
Women: 52%	**Out-of-state tuition:** $21,400	**Sorority:** No
Men: 48%	**Room $ board:** $7,500	**Athletics:** Division I
Percent out-of-state: 1%	**Housing Information**	
	University housing: Yes	
	Percent living on campus: 12%	

THE UNIVERSITY OF MEMPHIS

101 Wilder Tower, Memphis, TN 38152
Phone: 901-678-2111 • Fax: 901-678-3053
E-mail: recruitment@memphis.edu • Web: www.memphis.edu
Support: CS • Institution: 4-year public

PROGRAMS OR SERVICES FOR STUDENTS WITH LD

The University's LD/ADHD/ASD Program is designed to enhance academic strengths, provide support for areas of weakness, and build skills to help students with Learning, ADHD, and Autism Spectrum Disorders compete in the college environment. The program encourages development of life-long learning skills as well as personal responsibility for academic success. Training in college survival skills and regular meetings with the staff are emphasized during the first year to aid in the transition to college. Specific services are tailored to individual needs, considering one's strengths, weaknesses, course requirements, and learning styles. Students are integrated into regular classes and are held to the same academic standards as other students; however, academic accommodations are available to assist them in meeting requirements. The LD/ADHD/ASD Program places responsibility on students to initiate services and follow through with services once they are arranged. Most students who use the appropriate services are successful in their academic pursuits.

ADMISSION INFORMATION FOR STUDENTS WITH LD/ADHD

College entrance tests required: Yes
Interview required: No
Essay required: N/A
What documentation required for LD: Psycho Ed evaluation to include: relevant historical info, instructional interventions, related services, age diagnosed, objective data (aptitude, achievement, info processing), test scores (standard, percentile and grade equivalents) and describe functional limitations.
With general application: No
To receive services after enrolling: Yes
What documentation required for ADHD: Diagnosis based on DSM-V; history of behaviors impairing functioning in academic setting; diagnostic interview; history of symptoms; evidence of ongoing behaviors.

With general application: No
Submitted to: LD/ADHD/ADD Coordinator
Special Ed. HS course work accepted: Yes
Specific course requirements for all applicants: Yes
Separate application required for program services: No
# of LD applications submitted each year: 150–200
# of LD applications accepted yearly: 120–200
Total # of students receiving LD/ADHD services: 500+
Acceptance into program means acceptance into college: Separate application required after student has been admitted

ADMISSIONS

The LD/ADHD/ASD services are open to any student admitted to the university who provides current, appropriate psychoeducational and other relevant medical information sufficient to establish the existence of a disability which causes substantial limitation.

ADDITIONAL INFORMATION

Some services are available to all students registered with SDS, however, academic services and accommodations are individually determined and are based on the student's current functional limitations outlined in the medical or professional documentation, the student's compensatory skills, and the requirements of a particular course or program. The following general services are available to all students registered with SDS: early registration; orientation to using disability services; assistance with strategic class scheduling to enhance academic success; semester plan for accommodations and services; memos to faculty about disability needs; advocacy relating to disability access issues; information and guidance on academic, social, career, and personal issues; orientation to and use of the Assistive Technology Lab; referral to other university departments and community agencies; liaison with state and federal rehabilitation agencies; and information about specific opportunities for students with disabilities. In addition to the general services available to all students registered with SDS, the following services may be available to students who have learning disabilities or attention deficit/hyperactivity disorder: special advising and strategic scheduling of classes; preferential classroom seating; permission to audio-record lectures; Kurzweil Readers; books on CD or e-text; access to voice recognition software; access to large screen monitors and screen enlargement; loaner equipment such as: CD Players; digital recorders; permission to audio-record lectures; note-taker service; assistance with developing study strategies for specific courses; assistance with organization and time management skills; weekly meetings with professional staff to monitor progress; coaching to deal with ADHD symptoms; tutor referral; test Accommodations such as extended time; low stimulus environment; computer; spell checker; calculator; reader; and alternative to scantron answer sheet.

LEARNING DISABILITY PROGRAM OR SERVICES

Contact Information
Name of program or department: Student Disability Services; LD/ADHD/ASD Program
    Telephone: 901-678-2880
    Fax: 901-678-3070

LEARNING DISABILITY SERVICES

Accommodations are decided upon an individual basis after a thorough review of appropriate, current documentation. The accommodations requested must be supported through the documentation provided and must be logically linked to the current impact of the condition on academic functioning.

Allowed in exams
    Calculator: Yes
    Dictionary: Yes
    Computer: Yes
    Spellchecker: Yes
Extended test time: Yes
Scribes: Yes
Proctors: Yes
Oral exams: N/A
Note-takers: Yes

Distraction-reduced environment: Yes
Tape recording in class: Yes
Electronic texts: Yes
Accommodations for students with ADHD: Yes
Kurzweil Reader: Yes
Other assistive technology: Scanners, voice recognition software, CCTVs, Large monitors and enlarged text, screen readers, Braille production equipment, digital recorders
Priority registration: Yes

Added costs for services: No
LD specialists: Yes
Professional tutors: 2
Peer tutors: 1–3
Max. hours/wk. for services: 6
How professors are notified of LD/ADHD: Student

GENERAL ADMISSIONS INFORMATION

Office of Admission: 901-678-2111

ENTRANCE REQUIREMENTS
Academic units required: 4 English, 3 mathematics, 2 science, (1 science labs), 2 foreign language, 2 social studies, 1 history, 1 visual/performing arts. High school diploma is required and GED is accepted. SAT or ACT required; TOEFL required of all international applicants; minimum paper TOEFL 500, minimum computer TOEFL 173, minimum web-based TOEFL 61.

Application deadline: 7/1
Notification: Rolling
Average GPA: 3.3
ACT Composite middle 50% range: 19–25

SAT Critical Reading middle 50% range: 420–555
SAT Math middle 50% range: 430–565
SAT Writing middle 50% range: 400–550

Graduated top 10% of class: 17%
Graduated top 25% of class: 45%
Graduated top 50% of class: 79%

COLLEGE GRADUATION REQUIREMENTS

Course waivers allowed: No
Course substitutions allowed: Yes
In what course: Mostly foreign language. Students with questions about specific course substitutions outside of foreign language should consult with their Coordinator.

ADDITIONAL INFORMATION

Environment: The university is located on 1,159 acres in an urban area.

Student Body
    Undergrad enrollment: 17,510
    Women: 58%
    Men: 42%
    Percent out-of-state: 10%

Cost Information
    In-state tuition: $7,700
    Out-of state tuition: $23,146
    Room & board: $6,300
Housing Information
    University housing: Yes
    Percent living on campus: NR

Greek System
    Fraternity: Yes
    Sorority: Yes
Athletics: Division I

THE U. OF TENNESSEE AT CHATTANOOGA

615 McCallie Avenue, 102 Frist Hall, Chattanooga, TN 37403
Phone: 423-425-4006 • Fax: 423-425-4006
E-mail: Michelle-Rigler@utc.edu • Web: www.utc.edu
Support: CS • Institution type: 4-year public

PROGRAMS OR SERVICES FOR STUDENTS WITH LD

Disability Resource Center (DRC) at The University of Tennessee at Chattanooga is committed to ensuring that each individual has equal access to all educational opportunities and maximizes their potential regardless of the impact of their disability. OSD is also committed to supporting the ongoing development of an accessible university that embraces diversity. This mission is accomplished by: creating a physically, programmatically and attitudinally accessible environment where people are accepted and expected to participate fully regardless of their disability, and encouraging the development of an educational culture that embraces and celebrates people's differences.

ADMISSION INFORMATION FOR STUDENTS WITH LD/ADHD

College entrance tests required: No
Interview required: No
Essay recommended: No
What documentation required for LD: Psycho Ed evaluation to include: relevant historical info, instructional interventions, related services, age diagnosed, objective data (aptitude, achievement, info processing), test scores (standard, percentile and grade equivalents) and describe functional limitations.
With general application: No
To receive services after enrolling: Yes
What documentation required for ADHD: Diagnosis based on DSM-V; history of behaviors impairing functioning in academic setting; diagnostic interview; history of symptoms; evidence of ongoing behaviors.

With general application: No
Submitted to: DRC
Special Ed. HS course work accepted: NR
Specific course requirements of all applicants: Yes
Separate application required: Yes
# of LD applications submitted each year: NR
# of LD applications accepted yearly: NR
Total # of students receiving LD services: 850
Acceptance into program means acceptance into college: Submit application to Admissions separate to DRC application.

ADMISSIONS

Students with disabilities submit a general application to the Admissions Office. Minimum admissions requirements are a 2.83 GPA (on a 4.0 scale) and an ACT composite score of 18(870 SAT) or 2.3 GPA and an ACT composite score of 21 (990 SAT); and 4 years of English, 3 years of math, 2 years of science lab, 1 year of American history, 1 year of European history, world history, or world geography, 2 years of a foreign language, and 1 year of fine arts. General applications are submitted online at http://www.utc.edu/Administration/Admissions/. Students may be admitted conditionally if they fall below these guidelines and have only 1 unit deficiency. If the course deficiency is due to impact of disability, an Appeals Committee will sometimes allow a probationary admittance if DRC works with prospective student to develop an accommodation plan. Students admitted on condition must earn at least a 2.0 GPA their first semester or suspension will result. The Dean of Admissions or Admission Committee may recommend conditions for acceptance. In order to receive accommodations in the classroom, students with disabilities need to submit application and documentation (listed above) to the Disability Resource Center. Application to the Disability Resource Center is a separate process and is not relevant to the admissions process.

ADDITIONAL INFORMATION

DRC does not, as a matter of policy, seek on a student's behalf a waiver of any course work. Students admitted conditionally may be required to carry a reduced course load, take specific courses, have a specific advisor, and take specific programs of developmental study. Social skills development activities may involve video and role-playing situations in group form as well as during informal gatherings. There is a monthly publication, *The CAPsule*, for CAP students and parents. UTC offers developmental math and English courses for institutional credit. Services and accommodations are available for undergraduate and graduate students.

LEARNING DISABILITY PROGRAM OR SERVICES

Contact Information
Name of program or department: College Access Program (CAP)
 Telephone: 423-425-4006
 Fax: 423-425-2288

LEARNING DISABILITY SERVICES

Accommodations are decided upon an individual basis after a thorough review of appropriate, current documentation. The accommodations requested must be supported through the documentation provided and must be logically linked to the current impact of the condition on academic functioning.

Allowed in exams	**Distraction-reduced environment:** Yes	**Added costs for services:** No
Calculator: Yes	**Tape recording in class:** Yes	**LD specialists:** Yes
Dictionary: NR	**Electronic texts:** NR	**Professional tutors:** No
Computer: Yes	**Accommodations for students with**	**Peer tutors:** No
Spellchecker: Yes	**ADHD:** Yes	**Max. hours/wk. for services:** NR
Extended test time: Yes	**Kurzweil Reader:** Yes	**How professors are notified of**
Scribes: NR	**Other assistive technology:** Yes	**LD/ADHD:** By student
Proctors: Yes	**Priority registration:** Yes	
Oral exams: NR		
Note-takers: Yes		

GENERAL ADMISSIONS INFORMATION

Office of Admission: 423-425-4662

ENTRANCE REQUIREMENTS

Academic units required: 4 English, 3 math, 2 science (2 science labs), 2 foreign language, 2 social studies, 2 history, 2 fine arts. High school diploma is required, and GED is accepted. ACT with or without Writing component accepted. TOEFL required of all international applicants: minimum paper TOEFL 500, minimum computer TOEFL 200.

Application deadline: 8/1	**SAT Math middle 50% range:**	**Graduated top 10% of class:** NR
Notification: Rolling	470–580	**Graduated top 25% of class:** 41%
Average GPA: 3.36	**SAT Critical Reading middle 50%**	**Graduated top 50% of class:** 81%
ACT Composite middle 50% range:	**range:** 470–600	
21–25	**SAT Writing middle 50% range:** NR	

COLLEGE GRADUATION REQUIREMENTS

Course waivers allowed: No
Course substitutions allowed: Yes

ADDITIONAL INFORMATION

Environment: The university is located on 60 acres in an urban area in Chattanooga.

Student Body	**Cost Information**	**Greek System**
Undergrad enrollment: 9,891	**In-state tuition:** $6,718	**Fraternity:** Yes
Women: 56%	**Out-of-state tuition:** $20,252	**Sorority:** Yes
Men: 44%	**Room & board:** $7,150	**Athletics:** Division I
Percent out-of-state: 5%	**Housing Information**	
	University housing: Yes	
	Percent living on campus: 31%	

THE U. OF TENNESSEE AT KNOXVILLE

320 Student Service Building, Circle Park Drive, Knoxville, TN 37996-0230
Phone: 865-974-2184 • Fax: 865-974-6341
E-mail: admissions@utk.edu • Web: www.utk.edu
Support: CS • Institution: 4-year public

PROGRAMS OR SERVICES FOR STUDENTS WITH LD

The mission of the Office of Disability Services is to provide each student with a disability an equal opportunity to participate in the university's programs and activities. Students who are requesting support services are required to submit documentation to verify eligibility under the ADA of 1990. The documentation must include medical or psychological information from a certified professional. It is each student's responsibility to meet the essential qualifications and institutional standards; disclose the disability in a timely manner to ODS; provide appropriate documentation; inform ODS of accommodation needs; talk with professors about accommodations in the classroom, as needed; inform ODS of barriers to a successful education; maintain and return borrowed equipment; keep all appointments with ODS staff members or call to cancel or reschedule; be involved in their academic planning and course selection; and monitor their own progress toward graduation.

ADMISSION INFORMATION FOR STUDENTS WITH LD/ADHD

College entrance tests required: Yes
Interview required: No
What documentation required for LD: Psycho Ed evaluation to include: relevant historical info, instructional interventions, related services, age diagnosed, objective data (aptitude, achievement, info processing), test scores (standard, percentile and grade equivalents) and describe functional limitations.
With general application: No
To receive services after enrolling: Yes
What documentation required for ADHD: Diagnosis based on DSM-V; history of behaviors impairing functioning in academic setting; diagnostic interview; history of symptoms; evidence of ongoing behaviors.

With general application: No
Submitted to: Support Program/Services
Special Ed. HS course work accepted: N/A
Specific course requirements for all applicants: Yes
Separate application required for program services: Yes
# of LD applications submitted each year: NR
# of LD applications accepted yearly: NR
Total # of students receiving LD services: NR
Acceptance into program means acceptance into college: Separate application required after student has enrolled

ADMISSIONS

There is no special admission process for students with learning disabilities. The Office of Admissions makes every attempt to judge each application on its academic merits. Applicants believe that their academic record does not accurately reflect their situation, do not include documentation with admission materials. Applicants feel more information is needed to compete at an equal level with others seeking admission, they consider voluntarily self-identifying the disability and the circumstances to the Admissions Office. Qualified candidates with a disability will not be denied admissions solely on the basis of their disability. Applicants are required to have 4 English; 4 math; 3 natural science, including at least 1 biology, chemistry, or physics; 3 social studies; 2 foreign language; and 1 year of visual and performing arts. ACT with writing or SAT and U Conn will super score..

ADDITIONAL INFORMATION

The goals of ODS are to provide access to appropriate accommodations and support services; provide referrals and information for a variety of campus resources, including transportation and housing; encourage and assist students with disabilities to develop greater independence; increase faculty and staff understanding of the various needs of students with disabilities; and assist the university in interpreting legal mandates that address students with disabilities. Disability Services works with each student on a case-by-case basis to determine and implement appropriate accommodations based on documentation. Services could include note-takers, alternative testing arrangements such as extra time, books on tape, computers with speech input, separate testing rooms, tape recorders, and foreign language substitutions. Content tutors are available on campus through different departments.

PROGRAM FOR DISABILITY SERVICES

Contact Information
Name of program or department: Office of Disability Services (ODS)
 Telephone: 865-974-6087
 Fax: 865-974-9552

LEARNING DISABILITY SERVICES

Accommodations are decided upon an individual basis after a thorough review of appropriate, current documentation. The accommodations requested must be supported through the documentation provided and must be logically linked to the current impact of the condition on academic functioning.

Allowed in exams
 Calculator: Yes
 Dictionary: Yes
 Computer: Yes
 Spellchecker: Yes
Extended test time: Yes
Scribes: Yes
Proctors: Yes
Oral exams: Yes
Note-takers: Yes

Distraction-reduced environment: Yes
Tape recording in class: Yes
Electronic texts: Yes
Accommodations for students with
 ADHD: Yes
Kurzweil Reader: Yes
Other assistive technology: Dragon Naturally Speaking, Kurzweil, Co-Writer, Write Out Loud, Brailler, Inspiration, Intellitools,Franklin Language Master, JAWS
Priority registration: Yes

Added costs for services: No
LD specialists: Yes
Professional tutors: No
Peer tutors: Yes
Max. hours/wk. for services: N/A
How professors are notified of
 LD/ADHD: Both student and director

GENERAL ADMISSIONS INFORMATION

Office of Admission: 865-974-2184

ENTRANCE REQUIREMENTS
Academic units required: 4 English, 4 mathematics, 3 science, (1 science labs), 2 foreign language, 4 social studies, 1 visual/performing arts. High school diploma is required and GED is accepted. SAT or ACT with writing required; TOEFL required of all international applicants; minimum paper TOEFL 523, minimum computer TOEFL 193, minimum web-based

TOEFL 70.
Application deadline: 12/1
Notification: Rolling
Average GPA: 3.78
ACT Composite middle 50% range: 24–29

SAT Math middle 50% range: 540–640
SAT Critical Reading middle 50% range: 530–630
SAT Writing middle 50% range: NR

Graduated top 10% of class: 39%
Graduated top 25% of class: 70%
Graduated top 50% of class: 92%

COLLEGE GRADUATION REQUIREMENTS

Course waivers allowed: No
Course substitutions allowed: Yes
In what course: Foreign languages and math, if appropriate

ADDITIONAL INFORMATION

Environment: The campus is located on a suburban acmpus in Knoxville.

Student Body
 Undergrad enrollment: 21,378
 Women: 50%
 Men: 50%
 Percent out-of-state: 13%

Cost Information
 In-state tuition: $8,456
 Out-of-state tuition: $5,298
 Room and board: $8,480
Housing Information
 University housing: Yes
 Percent living on campus: 26%

Greek System
 Fraternity: Yes
 Sorority: Yes
Athletics: Division I

THE U. OF TENNESSEE AT MARTIN

200 Hall-Moody, Administrative Building, Martin, TN 38238
Phone: 731-881-7020 • Fax: 731-881-7029
E-mail: admitme@utm.edu • Web: www.utm.edu
Support: SP • Institution type: 4-year public

PROGRAMS OR SERVICES FOR STUDENTS WITH LD

The university believes students with learning disabilities can achieve success in college without academic compromise and can become productive, self-sufficient members of society. A preliminary interview will include a review of previous assessments of the disability and the collection of background information. If the results of the PACE evaluation show that the academic and social needs of the student can be met by PACE services, the student will work with a learning disabilities specialist to develop an individually designed program. University staff who work with PACE students receive training in understanding learning disabilities and teaching strategies that meet the individual student's needs. Graduate supervisors coordinate support services. PACE is designed to complement and supplement existing university support services available for all students.

ADMISSION INFORMATION FOR STUDENTS WITH LD/ADHD

College entrance tests required: Yes
Interview required: No
Essay recommended: No
What documentation required for LD: Psycho Ed evaluation to include: relevant historical info, instructional interventions, related services, age diagnosed, objective data (aptitude, achievement, info processing), test scores (standard, percentile and grade equivalents) and describe functional limitations.
With general application: Yes if requested as part of Structured Program application
To receive services after enrolling: Yes
What documentation required for ADHD: Diagnosis based on DSM-V; history of behaviors impairing functioning in academic setting; diagnostic interview; history of symptoms; evidence of ongoing behaviors.

With general application: Yes if requested as part of Structured Program application
To receive services after enrolling: Yes
Submitted to: Admissions Office and PACE
Special Ed. HS course work accepted: No
Specific course requirements of all applicants: Yes
Separate application required: No
# of LD applications submitted each year: NR
# of LD applications accepted yearly: NR
Total # of students receiving LD services: NR
Acceptance into program means acceptance into college: Students must be admitted and enrolled prior to requesting services.

ADMISSIONS

Basically, applicants must meet regular admission criteria, including an ACT score of 16 and a 2.6 GPA, or an ACT score of 19 and a 2.2 GPA. Some applicants are considered through qualified admission with an ACT score of 14 and a 2.25 GPA. Course requirements include 4 years of English, 3 years of math, 2 years of science, 2 years of social studies, and 2 years of a foreign language. Each student is considered based on background, test scores, strengths/weaknesses, and motivation. Qualified students with learning disabilities should apply directly to both the PACE Center and the Office of Admissions. Students must complete all steps in both admission processes before an admission decision can be made. An interview is required for students applying to the PACE Program. Documentation should be sent to PACE. To be certain consideration is given to the learning disability, university decisions on acceptance are determined by both the PACE Center and the Admissions Office. Applicants are selected on the basis of intellectual potential (average to superior), motivation, academic preparation, and willingness to work hard.

ADDITIONAL INFORMATION

All freshmen students with LD selected to participate in PACE and admitted for fall semester must attend the second summer session program. Students take one selected university class in the mornings. In the afternoons, PACE staff teach learning strategies that can be applied to all future courses so that the students will have hands-on experience using the skills. The summer program will also address improvements in reading, spelling, written language, or math skills. Equally important are small group sessions to help students improve social skills. Students with ADHD must have comprehensive documentation to receive accommodations and services. There is a Math Lab and an English Writing Center. Students with appropriate documentation may be eligible to receive the following services: extended testing times; distraction-free testing environments; use of calculators, dictionaries, computers, and spellcheckers during exams; proctors; oral exams; note-takers; taper recorders in class; books of tape; and tutoring. Services and accommodations are provided to undergraduate and graduate students.

LEARNING DISABILITY PROGRAM OR SERVICES

Contact Information
Name of program or department: Program Access for College Enhancement (PACE)
  Telephone: 901-881,7195
  Fax: 901-587-7956

LEARNING DISABILITY SERVICES

Accommodations are decided upon an individual basis after a thorough review of appropriate, current documentation. The accommodations requested must be supported through the documentation provided and must be logically linked to the current impact of the condition on academic functioning.

Allowed in exams
  Calculator: NR
  Dictionary: NR
  Computer: NR
  Spellchecker: NR
Extended test time: Yes
Scribes: Yes
Proctors: Yes
Oral exams: Yes
Note-takers: Yes

Distraction-reduced environment: Yes
Tape recording in class: Yes
Electronic texts: Yes
Accommodations for students with ADHD: Yes
Kurzweil Reader: Yes
Other assistive technology: Yes
Priority registration: NR

Added costs for services: NR
LD specialists: Yes
Professional tutors: 2
Peer tutors: 20
Max. hours/wk. for services: Unlimited
How professors are notified of LD/ADHD: By student

GENERAL ADMISSIONS INFORMATION

Office of Admission: 731-881-7020

ENTRANCE REQUIREMENTS

Academic units required: 4 English, 3 math, 2 science (1 science lab), 2 foreign language, 2 history, 1 fine/performing arts. High school diploma is required, and GED is accepted. ACT with or without Writing component accepted. TOEFL required of all international applicants: minimum paper TOEFL 500, minimum computer TOEFL 173.

Application deadline: 8/1
Notification: Rolling
Average GPA: 3.34
ACT Composite middle 50% range: 20–25

SAT Math middle 50% range: NR
SAT Critical Reading middle 50% range: NR
SAT Writing middle 50% range: NR

Graduated top 10% of class: 20%
Graduated top 25% of class: 50%
Graduated top 50% of class: 85%

COLLEGE GRADUATION REQUIREMENTS

Course waivers allowed: No
Course substitutions allowed: No

ADDITIONAL INFORMATION

Environment: The university is located on a 200-acre campus in a small town 100 miles north of Memphis.

Student Body
  Undergrad enrollment: 7,947
  Women: 57%
  Men: 43%
  Percent out-of-state: 4%

Cost Information
  In-state: $6,718
  Out-of-state: $19,128
  Room & board: $5,424
Housing Information
  University housing: Yes
  Percent living on campus: 29%

Greek System
  Fraternity: Yes
  Sorority: Yes
Athletics: Division I

ABILENE CHRISTIAN UNIVERSITY

ACU Box 29000, Abilene, TX 79699
Phone: 325-674-2650 • Fax: 325-674-2130
E-mail: info@admissions.acu.edu • Web: www.acu.edu
Support: CS • Institution type: 4-year private

LEARNING DISABILITY PROGRAM OR SERVICES

Alpha Scholars Program is a Student Support Service Program funded under Title IV legislation governing TRIO programs. The program strives to assist students in programs that move them toward independence in learning and living. The staff is specially trained instructors, peer tutors, counselors, and administrators who focus on the problems encountered by college students. Staff members help qualifying students find and apply solutions to their problems. Students qualify for services if they are a first-generation college student, economically disadvantaged, or a student with disabilities. Alpha means one-on-one help, and the instruction and tutoring are tailored to the student's unique needs. Students with learning disabilities may receive special accommodation services to assist them in achieving success in their university studies. Documentation of the disability is required to receive disability accommodations. Students must make an appointment to determine if they qualify to receive services.

ADMISSION INFORMATION FOR STUDENTS WITH LD/ADHD

College entrance tests required: Yes
Interview required: Yes
Essay recommended: Yes
What documentation required for LD: Psycho Ed evaluation to include: relevant historical info, instructional interventions, related services, age diagnosed, objective data (aptitude, achievement, info processing), test scores (standard, percentile and grade equivalents) and describe functional limitations.
With general application: No
To receive services after enrolling: Yes
What documentation required for ADHD: Diagnosis based on DSM-V; history of behaviors impairing functioning in academic setting; diagnostic interview; history of symptoms; evidence of ongoing behaviors.

With general application: No
With general application: No
To receive services after enrolling: Yes
Submitted to: Both Admissions and Alpha Academic Services
Special Ed. HS course work accepted: Yes
Specific course requirements of all applicants: Yes
Separate application required: Yes
# of LD applications submitted each year: 60–70
# of LD applications accepted yearly: 45–55
Total # of students receiving LD services: 180–200
Acceptance into program means acceptance into college: Students must be admitted to and enrolled in the university first and then request services.

ADMISSIONS

All students must be admitted to the university and meet the same criteria for admission. There is no special admission process for students with learning disabilities. Regular admissions criteria include 20 ACT or 930-plus SAT; college-preparatory courses including 4 years of English, 3 years of math, 3 years of science, and 2 years of a foreign language; and no specific GPA. Some students not meeting the admission criteria may be admitted conditionally. Students admitted conditionally must take specified courses in a summer term and demonstrate motivation and ability. Freshman applicants need to take the SAT Reasoning Test or ACT with Writing component.

ADDITIONAL INFORMATION

Alpha Scholars Program provides opportunities for individual instruction in basic skills areas such as writing, math, or study skills; assessment of learning preferences, strengths, and weaknesses; instruction and tutoring designed to fit the student's particular learning preferences and strengths and academic needs; classroom help if needed such as readers, note-takers, alternative testing arrangements; personal, career, and academic counseling; and workshops on topics such as time management skills, resume writing, career placement, and study skills.

LEARNING DISABILITY PROGRAM OR SERVICES

Contact Information
Name of program or department: Alpha Scholars Program
 Telephone: 325-674-2275
 Fax: 325-674-6847

LEARNING DISABILITY SERVICES

Accommodations are decided upon an individual basis after a thorough review of appropriate, current documentation. The accommodations requested must be supported through the documentation provided and must be logically linked to the current impact of the condition on academic functioning.

Allowed in exams
 Calculator: Yes
 Dictionary: Yes
 Computer: Yes
 Spellchecker: Yes
Extended test time: Yes
Scribes: Yes
Proctors: Yes
Oral exams: Yes
Note-takers: Yes

Distraction-reduced environment: Yes
Tape recording in class: Yes
Electronic texts: Yes
Accommodations for students with ADHD: Yes
Kurzweil Reader: Yes
Other assistive technology: Yes
Priority registration: No

Added costs for services: No
LD specialists: Yes
Professional tutors: 3
Peer tutors: 12–20
Max. hours/wk. for services: Unlimited
How professors are notified of LD/ADHD: By student

GENERAL ADMISSIONS INFORMATION

Office of Admission: 325-674-2650

ENTRANCE REQUIREMENTS

Academic units recommended: 4 English, 3 math, 3 science (2 science labs), 2 foreign language. High school diploma is required, and GED is accepted. ACT without Writing component accepted. TOEFL required of all international applicants: minimum paper TOEFL 525, minimum computer TOEFL 197.

Application deadline: 8/1
Notification: Rolling
Average GPA: 3.56
ACT Composite middle 50% range: 22–28

SAT Math middle 50% range: 505–610
SAT Critical Reading middle 50% range: 490–620
SAT Writing middle 50% range: NR

Graduated top 10% of class: 25%
Graduated top 25% of class: 55%
Graduated top 50% of class: 84%

COLLEGE GRADUATION REQUIREMENTS

Course waivers allowed: No
Course substitutions allowed: Yes
In what course: As appropriate with petition to provost for reasonable substitute

ADDITIONAL INFORMATION

Environment: The campus is in a suburban area 150 miles from Fort Worth.

Student Body
 Undergrad enrollment: 3,681
 Women: 55%
 Men: 45%
 Percent out-of-state: 68%

Cost Information
 Tuition: $23,610
 Room & board: $8,316
Housing Information
 University housing: Yes
 Percent living on campus: 43%

Greek System
 Fraternity: Yes
 Sorority: Yes
Athletics: Division II

LAMAR UNIVERSITY

PO Box 10009, Beaumont, TX 77710
Phone: 409-880-8888 • Fax: 409-880-8463
E-mail: admissions@hal.lamar.edu • Web: www.lamar.edu
Support: S • Institution: 4-year public

PROGRAMS OR SERVICES FOR STUDENTS WITH LD

The Office of Services for Students with Disabilities (SSWD) assures qualified students access to Lamar University's academic activities, programs, resources, and services. Students with learning disabilities and/or ADHD could qualify for registration assistance, note-takers, and or testing accommodations. Students are encouraged to notify the director of SFSWD that specific disabilities exist, the modification needed, and a conference prior to registration will allow the appropriate accommodations to be made. Prior to registration, students are requested to notify the Director of Services for students with disabilities regarding assistance and/or accommodation they anticipate will be needed during the course of instruction for which they plan to register.

ADMISSION INFORMATION FOR STUDENTS WITH LD/ADHD

College entrance tests required: Yes
Interview required: N/A
Essay required: N/A
Documentation required for LD: Psychoeducational evaluation administered after sixteenth birthday; should contain relevant developmental, psychological, social, and educational history; cognitive abilities as well as achievement information.
Documentation required for ADHD: Psychoeducational evaluation administered after sixteenth birthday; should contain relevant developmental, psychological, social, and educational history; cognitive abilities as well as achievement information.
Submitted to: Support Program/Services
Special Ed. HS course work accepted: No

Specific course requirements for all applicants: Yes
Separate application required for program services: Yes
# of LD applications submitted each year: NR
# of LD applications accepted yearly: NR
Total # of students receiving LD services: 45
Acceptance into program means acceptance into college: Separate application required after student has enrolled

ADMISSIONS

Applicants with learning disabilities and/or ADHD must meet the general admission requirements. Services will be offered to enrolled students who notify the Director of Services for Students with Disabilities. Students must be in top half of their class and complete 14 "solid" credits to be admitted unconditionally, including four years English, three years math (algebra I–II and geometry or higher), two years science (physical science, biology, chemistry, physics, or geology), two and a half years social science, and two and a half years electives (foreign language is recommended). A very limited number of applicants not meeting the prerequisites may be admitted on "individual approval." Those not in the top half must achieve a minimum composite score of 1000 SAT/21 ACT. Some students may be considered on an Individual Approval basis if they fail to meet Unconditional Admission. These students are subject to mandatory advisement; six-credit limit in summer and 14 in fall term, and must successfully complete nine hours with 2.0 GPA; students must meet these provisions or leave for one year.

ADDITIONAL INFORMATION

SSWD offers a variety of services designed to assure qualified students access to the university's academic activities, programs, resources, and services. Services or accommodations could include priority registration; alternative testing accommodations; copying of class notes; classroom accommodations; note-takers; readers and textbooks on tape. Professional staff assist students with questions, problem solving, adjustment, decision making, goal planning, and testing. Skills classes in study skills are offered, including developmental writing, reading, and math for credit. Students are referred to other offices and personnel in accord with the needs and intents of the individual. Services and accommodations are available for undergraduate and graduate students.

PROGRAM FOR DISABILITY SERVICES

Contact Information
Name of program or department: Services for Students with Disabilities (SSWD)
 Telephone: 409-880-8347
 Fax: 409-880-2225

LEARNING DISABILITY SERVICES

Accommodations are decided upon an individual basis after a thorough review of appropriate, current documentation. The accommodations requested must be supported through the documentation provided and must be logically linked to the current impact of the condition on academic functioning.

Allowed in exams
 Calculator: Yes
 Dictionary: Yes
 Computer: Yes
 Spellchecker: Yes
Extended test time: Yes
Scribes: Yes
Proctors: Yes
Oral exams: Yes
Note-takers: Yes

Distraction-reduced environment: Yes
Tape recording in class: Yes
Electronic texts: Yes
Accommodations for students with
 ADHD: Yes
Kurzweil Reader: Yes
Other assistive technology: computer
 screen reader, screen enlarger; Braille
Priority registration: Yes

Added costs for services: No
LD specialists: No
Professional tutors: No
Peer tutors: Yes
Max. hours/wk. for services: 15
How professors are notified of
 LD/ADHD: Student

GENERAL ADMISSIONS INFORMATION

Office of Admission: 409-880-8888

ENTRANCE REQUIREMENTS

Academic units recommended: 4 English, 3 mathematics, 2 lab science, 2.5 social studies, 2.5 college preparatory electives. High school diploma is required and GED is not accepted. SAT or ACT required; TOEFL required of all international applicants; minimum paper TOEFL 500.

Application deadline: 8/1
Notification: Rolling
Average GPA: 2.0
ACT Composite middle 50% range:
 16–21

SAT Math middle 50% range:
 400–520
SAT Critical Reading middle 50%
 range: 400–510
SAT Writing middle 50% range:
 390–490

Graduated top 10% of class: 10%
Graduated top 25% of class: 27%
Graduated top 50% of class: 90%

COLLEGE GRADUATION REQUIREMENTS

Course waivers allowed: No
Course substitutions allowed: Yes
In what course: Appropriateness of a core course substitution is determined by the Coordinating Board of the State of Texas; other subsitutions are determined by student's academic department.

ADDITIONAL INFORMATION

Environment: The university is located on 200 acres in an urban area 90 miles east of Houston.

Student Body
 Undergrad enrollment: 9,941
 Women: 55%
 Men: 45%
 Percent out-of-state: 2%

Cost Information
 In-state tuition: $4,740
 Out-of-state tuition: $17,020
 Room and board: $7,682
Housing Information
 University housing: Yes
 Percent living on campus: 11%

Greek System
 Fraternity: Yes
 Sorority: Yes
Athletics: Division I

MIDWESTERN STATE UNIVERSITY

3410 Taft Boulevard, Wichita Falls, TX 76308-2099
Phone: 940-397-4334 • Fax: 940-397-4672
E-mail: admissions@mwsu.edu • Web: www.mwsu.edu
Support: S • Institution type: 4-year public

PROGRAMS OR SERVICES FOR STUDENTS WITH LD

In accordance with Section 504 of the Federal Rehabilitation Act of 1973 and the Americans with Disabilities Act of 1990, Midwestern State University endeavors to make reasonable adjustments in its policies, practices, services, and facilities to ensure equal opportunity for qualified persons with disabilities to participate in all educational programs and activities. Students requiring special accommodation or auxiliary aids must apply for such assistance through Disability Support Services, which focuses on helping students to negotiate all aspects of adapting to college life. These include academic, personal, career, and social concerns. To obtain services, students must be accepted for admission at MSU, complete an application form from Disability Support Services, and supply verification of the disability.

ADMISSION INFORMATION FOR STUDENTS WITH LD/ADHD

College entrance tests required: Yes
Interview required: No
Essay recommended: No
What documentation required for LD: Psycho Ed evaluation to include: relevant historical info, instructional interventions, related services, age diagnosed, objective data (aptitude, achievement, info processing), test scores (standard, percentile and grade equivalents) and describe functional limitations.
With general application: No
To receive services after enrolling: Yes
What documentation required for ADHD: Diagnosis based on DSM-V; history of behaviors impairing functioning in academic setting; diagnostic interview; history of symptoms; evidence of ongoing behaviors.

With general application: No
Submitted to: Disability Support Services
Special Ed. HS course work accepted: Yes
Specific course requirements of all applicants: Yes
Separate application required: Yes
# of LD applications submitted each year: NR
# of LD applications accepted yearly: NR
Total # of students receiving LD services: 50 (40 ADHD)
Acceptance into program means acceptance into college: Students must be admitted to and enrolled in the university first and then request services.

ADMISSIONS

Unconditional acceptance by the university is available to the student who graduates from an accredited high school with course work as follows: 4 years of English, 3 years of math, 2 years of science; a class rank within the top 60 percent; and an ACT of 20-plus or SAT score of 840-plus. Admission by review is an alternative admission with the same high school units as mentioned previously, but a high school rank 40–60 percent, an ACT score of 14–19, or an SAT score of 560–839. Students whose high school transcript does not reflect ranking must submit scores of 1110 on the SAT Reasoning Test or 24 composite on the ACT to be considered for unconditional admission.

ADDITIONAL INFORMATION

Disability Support Services arranges accommodations for students with disabilities. Assistance includes priority registration; testing arrangements; classroom accessibility; special equipment; and counseling for personal, academic, or vocational concerns. Skills courses for credit are offered in study skills and time management techniques.

LEARNING DISABILITY PROGRAM OR SERVICES

Contact Information
Name of program or department: Disability Support Services (DSS)
  Telephone: 940-397-4140
  Fax: 940-397-4180

LEARNING DISABILITY SERVICES

Accommodations are decided upon an individual basis after a thorough review of appropriate, current documentation. The accommodations requested must be supported through the documentation provided and must be logically linked to the current impact of the condition on academic functioning.

Allowed in exams
  Calculator: Yes
  Dictionary: Yes
  Computer: Yes
  Spellchecker: Yes
Extended test time: Yes
Scribes: Yes
Proctors: Yes
Oral exams: Yes
Note-takers: Yes

Distraction-reduced environment: Yes
Tape recording in class: Yes
Electronic texts: Yes
Accommodations for students with ADHD: Yes
Kurzweil Reader: Yes
Other assistive technology: Yes
Priority registration: Yes

Added costs for services: No
LD specialists: No
Professional tutors: No
Peer tutors: Yes
Max. hours/wk. for services: Yes
How professors are notified of LD/ADHD: By student, with DSS verification letters

GENERAL ADMISSIONS INFORMATION

Office of Admission: 940-397-4334

ENTRANCE REQUIREMENTS

Academic units required: 4 English, 3 math, 2 science, 6 academic electives. High school diploma is required, and GED is accepted. ACT with Writing component required. TOEFL required of all international applicants: minimum paper TOEFL 550, minimum computer TOEFL 213.

Application deadline: 8/7
Notification: Rolling
Average GPA: 3.41
ACT Composite middle 50% range: 18–23

SAT Math middle 50% range: 450–560
SAT Critical Reading middle 50% range: 440–550
SAT Writing middle 50% range: 440–540

Graduated top 10% of class: 12%
Graduated top 25% of class: 37%
Graduated top 50% of class: 73%

COLLEGE GRADUATION REQUIREMENTS

Course waivers allowed: No
Course substitutions allowed: Yes
In what course: Substitutions require an individual review by Disability Support Services, the chair of the department, and the Vice President of Academics.

ADDITIONAL INFORMATION

Environment: The campus is located 135 miles northwest of Dallas.

Student Body
  Undergrad enrollment: 5,607
  Women: 58%
  Men: 42%
  Percent out-of-state: 5%

Cost Information
  In-state: $7,238
  Out-of-state: $9,188
  Room & board: $6,220
Housing Information
  University housing: Yes
  Percent living on campus: 20%

Greek System
  Fraternity: Yes
  Sorority: Yes
Athletics: Division II

SCHREINER UNIVERSITY

2100 Memorial Boulevard, Kerrville, TX 78028-5697
Phone: 830-792-7217 • Fax: 830-792-7226
E-mail: admissions@schreiner.edu • Web: www.schreiner.edu
Support: SP • Institution type: 2- and 4-year private

LEARNING DISABILITY PROGRAM OR SERVICES

Students admitted to the Learning Support Services program must be highly motivated, have the intellectual potential for success in a rigorous academic program, and have the ability to meet the demands of college life. Extensive learning support is given to each student, and the ultimate goal is for students to be able to succeed without special help. The Learning Support Services (LSS) program is staffed by LD specialists and many tutors. Students with learning disabilities are enrolled in regular college courses and receive individual tutorial assistance in each subject. Students in the program are held to the same high standards and complete the same curriculum requirements as all other degree candidates. In addition to the LSS staff, the Schreiner University faculty is dedicated to helping students realize their full potential.

ADMISSION INFORMATION FOR STUDENTS WITH LD/ADHD

College entrance tests required: Yes
Interview required: Yes
Essay recommended: Yes
What documentation required for LD: Psycho Ed evaluation to include: relevant historical info, instructional interventions, related services, age diagnosed, objective data (aptitude, achievement, info processing), test scores (standard, percentile and grade equivalents) and describe functional limitations.
With general application: Yes if requested as part of Structured Program application
To receive services after enrolling: Yes
What documentation required for ADHD: Diagnosis based on DSM-V; history of behaviors impairing functioning in academic setting; diagnostic interview; history of symptoms; evidence of ongoing behaviors.

With general application: Yes if requested as part of Structured Program application
To receive services after enrolling: Yes
Submitted to: Admissions and Learning Support Services
Special Ed. HS course work accepted: No
Specific course requirements of all applicants: Yes
Separate application required: No
# of LD applications submitted each year: 110
# of LD applications accepted yearly: 30
Total # of students receiving LD services: 65
Acceptance into program means acceptance into college: Students admitted into the Learning Support Services program are automatically admitted into the college.

ADMISSIONS

Proof of high school diploma and all significant materials relevant to the specific learning disability must be submitted. Applicants should be enrolled in regular, mainstream English courses in high school. We recommend that students take a college-preparatory curriculum. However, admission would not be denied to a qualified candidate if some course work was not included. The Woodcock-Johnson Achievement Battery is preferred, but other tests are accepted. An interview is required and is an important part of the admissions decision. Applicants are considered individually and selected on the basis of their intellectual ability, motivation, academic preparation, and potential for success. For a candidate to be considered for admission, the following are required: all secondary school transcripts (transfer students must also supply transcripts of all attempted college work); medical or psychological statement of specific learning disability or attention deficit hyperactivity disorder; written report of the results of the WAIS-IV, including all subtest scores and verbal, performance, and full-scale IQ scores taken within 12 months of application for admission; current individual achievement test results showing level of proficiency in reading comprehension, word identification, word attack, spelling, writing (written language), math calculation, and applied mathematics; and a completed application with application fee must be submitted to the Office of Admissions. LSS students are admitted contingent on their participation in the program. Students admitted into LSS are automatically admitted into the college.

ADDITIONAL INFORMATION

The Learning Support Services Program is tailored to meet the needs of each participating student. Each LSS staff member is committed to helping students develop the independent study skills and strategies that are necessary for academic success. Individualized services may include study skills development; regularly scheduled tutoring for all classes; testing accommodations, including readers, scribes, and extended time; use of recorded textbooks; arrangements made for note-takers in lecture classes; and a freshman seminar class that addresses issues of specific concern to college students with learning disabilities. Individual skill development is available in study strategies, test-taking, note-taking, reading, math, and written language. There is a professional counselor on staff.

LEARNING DISABILITY PROGRAM OR SERVICES

Contact Information
Name of program or department: Learning Support Services (LSS)
 Telephone: 830-792-7257
 Fax: 830-792-7294

LEARNING DISABILITY SERVICES

Accommodations are decided upon an individual basis after a thorough review of appropriate, current documentation. The accommodations requested must be supported through the documentation provided and must be logically linked to the current impact of the condition on academic functioning.

Allowed in exams
 Calculator: No
 Dictionary: No
 Computer: Yes
 Spellchecker: Yes
 Extended test time: Yes
 Scribes: Yes
 Proctors: Yes
 Oral exams: Yes
 Note-takers: Yes

Distraction-reduced environment: Yes
Tape recording in class: Yes
Electronic texts: Yes
Accommodations for students with ADHD: Yes
Kurzweil Reader: Yes
Other assistive technology: No
Priority registration: No

Added costs for services: Yes
LD specialists: Yes
Professional tutors: 15
Peer tutors: No
Max. hours/wk. for services: Unlimited
How professors are notified of LD/ADHD: By both student and director

GENERAL ADMISSIONS INFORMATION

Office of Admission: 830-792-7217/800-343-4919

ENTRANCE REQUIREMENTS

Academic units recommended: 4 English, 3 math, 2 science (2 science labs), 2 social studies. High school diploma is required, and GED is accepted. ACT with Writing component required. TOEFL required of all international applicants: minimum paper TOEFL 550, minimum computer TOEFL 213.

Application deadline: 8/1
Notification: Rolling
Average GPA: 3.53
ACT Composite middle 50% range: 18–24

SAT Math middle 50% range: 440–550
SAT Critical Reading middle 50% range: 440–550
SAT Writing middle 50% range: 430–540

Graduated top 10% of class: 11%
Graduated top 25% of class: 40%
Graduated top 50% of class: 72%

COLLEGE GRADUATION REQUIREMENTS

Course waivers allowed: No
Course substitutions allowed: No

ADDITIONAL INFORMATION

Environment: The college is located on 175 acres in a rural wooded area 60 miles northwest of San Antonio.

Student Body
 Undergrad enrollment: 1,043
 Women: 57%
 Men: 43%
 Percent out-of-state: 1%

Cost Information
 Tuition: $20,354
 Room & board: $9,675
Housing Information
 University housing: Yes
 Percent living on campus: 54%

Greek System
 Fraternity: Yes
 Sorority: Yes
Athletics: Division III

SOUTHERN METHODIST UNIVERSITY

PO Box 750181, Dallas, TX 75275-0181
Phone: 214-768-3417 • Fax: 214-768-0202
E-mail: enrol_serv@smu.edu • Web: www.smu.edu
Support: CS • Institution: 4-year private

PROGRAMS OR SERVICES FOR STUDENTS WITH LD

The goal of Disability Accommodations & Success Strategies (DASS) is to provide students with documented disabilities services or reasonable accommodations in order to reduce the effects that a disability may have on their performance in a traditional academic setting. Services for Students with Disabilities provides individual attention and support for students needing assistance with various aspects of their campus experience such as notifying professors, arranging accommodations, referrals, and accessibility.

ADMISSION INFORMATION FOR STUDENTS WITH LD/ADHD

College entrance tests required: Yes
Interview required: No
Essay required: N/A
Documentation required for LD: A full psychoeducational assessment conducted in the last three years. Needs to use comprehensive measures of potential and achievement.
Documentation required for ADHD: Report from either a licensed psychologist or physician trained in diagnosing ADHD. Evaluation needs to be conducted within three years of the time student seeks accommodations. Documentation guidelines are posted on website.
Submitted to: Support Program/Services
Special Ed. HS course work accepted: N/A

Specific course requirements for all applicants: Yes
Separate application required for program services: No
# of LD applications submitted each year: NR
# of LD applications accepted yearly: NR
Total # of students receiving LD services: 428
Acceptance into program means acceptance into college: Separate application required after student has enrolled

ADMISSIONS

There is no special admission process for students with learning disabilities. In addition to GPA and SAT or ACT scores, our admission committee weighs many factors during the course of the application process, including classroom performance, rigor of high school curriculum, quality of essays and recommendations, extracurricular activities, talents, character and life experiences. But what's most important for you to know is that the students will be considered individually, on their own merit. Minimum high school course requirements include: 4 units of English, 3 units of math (algebra I, II, geometry), 3 units of social science, 3 units of science (of which 2 must be lab science), and 2 consecutive units of foreign language . Auditions are required for music, dance or theater.

ADDITIONAL INFORMATION

All students have access to tutoring, writing centers, study skills workshops, and classes to improve reading rate, comprehension, and vocabulary. Skills classes are offered in time management, test strategies, note-taking strategies, organizational skills, concentration, memory, and test anxiety. There are currently 428 students with learning disabilities and/or ADHD receiving services.

PROGRAM FOR DISABILITY SERVICES

Contact Information
Name of program or department: Disability Accommodations & Success Strategies (DASS)
 Telephone: 214-768-4557
 Fax: 214-768-1255

LEARNING DISABILITY SERVICES

Accommodations are decided upon an individual basis after a thorough review of appropriate, current documentation. The accommodations requested must be supported through the documentation provided and must be logically linked to the current impact of the condition on academic functioning. In addition to accommodations, DASS also provides academic coaching for undergraduates with LD/ADHD. See the website for additional resources, like the LD section ORACLE (study skills course) and the student support group, Students for New Learning (SNL). www.smu.edu/alec/dass

Allowed in exams
 Calculator: Yes
 Dictionary: Yes
 Computer: Yes
 Spellchecker: Yes
Extended test time: Yes
Scribes: Yes
Proctors: Yes
Oral exams: Yes
Note-takers: Yes

Distraction-reduced environment: Yes
Tape recording in class: Yes
Electronic texts: Yes
Accommodations for students with ADHD: Yes
Kurzweil Reader: Yes
Other assistive technology: Dragon Naturally Speaking
Priority registration: Yes

Added costs for services: No
LD specialists: Yes
Professional tutors: No
Peer tutors: 94
Max. hours/wk. for services: No maximum
How professors are notified of LD/ADHD: Both student and director

GENERAL ADMISSIONS INFORMATION

Office of Admission: 214-768-2058

ENTRANCE REQUIREMENTS
Academic units required: 4 English, 3 mathematics, 3 science, (2 science labs), 2 foreign language, 1 social studies, 2 history. **Academic units recommended:** 4 English, 4 mathematics, 4 science, (3 science labs), 3 foreign language, 2 social studies, 3 history. High school diploma is required and GED is not accepted. SAT or ACT required; TOEFL required of all international applicants; minimum paper TOEFL 550, minimum computer TOEFL 213.

Application deadline: 3/15
Notification: Rolling
Average GPA: 3.64
ACT Composite middle 50% range: 26–31

SAT Math middle 50% range: 600–690
SAT Critical Reading middle 50% range: 580–680
SAT Writing middle 50% range: 570–670

Graduated top 10% of class: 49%
Graduated top 25% of class: 78%
Graduated top 50% of class: 94%

COLLEGE GRADUATION REQUIREMENTS

Course waivers allowed: No
Course substitutions allowed: Yes
In what course: foreign language and math

ADDITIONAL INFORMATION

Environment: The university is located on a 210-acre suburban campus.

Student Body
 Undergrad enrollment: 6,221
 Women: 52%
 Men: 48%
 Percent out-of-state: 49%

Cost Information
 Tuition: $39,430
 Room and board: $13,539
Housing Information
 University housing: Yes
 Percent living on campus: 33%

Greek System
 Fraternity: Yes
 Sorority: Yes
Athletics: Division I

TEXAS A&M U.—COLLEGE STATION

Admissions Counseling, College Station, TX 77843-1265
Phone: 979-845-3741 • Fax: 979-847-8737
E-mail: admissions@tamu.edu • Web: www.tamu.edu
Support: S • Institution type: 4-year public

PROGRAMS OR SERVICES FOR STUDENTS WITH LD

The Department of Disability Services exists to promote an academic experience for all students that is fully inclusive and accessible. The philosophy of Disability Services is to empower students with the skills needed to act as their own advocate and succeed in the mainstream of the university environment. Services include accommodations counseling, evaluation referral, disability-related information, adaptive technology services, sign language interpreting, and transcription services for academically related purposes.

ADMISSION INFORMATION FOR STUDENTS WITH LD/ADHD

College entrance tests required: Yes
Interview required: No
Essay recommended: Yes
Documentation required for LD: Evaluation must both establish disability and provide adequate information on the functional impact of the disability so that effective accommodations can be identified.
Documentation required for ADHD: Evaluation must both establish disability and provide adequate information on the functional impact of the disability so that effective accommodations can be identified.
Submitted to: Disability Services

Special Ed. HS course work accepted: No
Specific course requirements of all applicants: Yes
Separate application required: Yes
# of LD applications submitted each year: NR
# of LD applications accepted yearly: NR
Total # of students receiving LD services: 480
Acceptance into program means acceptance into college: Students must be admitted to and enrolled in the university first and then request services.

ADMISSIONS

General application requirements require that students submit an essay, ACT (with optional essay) or new SAT scores, and have at least 4 years of English, 3.5 years of math (Algebra I and II, geometry, and 0.5 credit of advanced math), 3 years of science (2 must be in biology, chemistry, or physics), and recommend 2 years of the same foreign language. Students ranked in the top 10 percent of their class are automatically admissible if they have taken the required courses. Students not in the top 10 percent but ranked in the top 25 percent must have a 1300 on the SAT with a score of 600-plus in math and verbal or a 30 on the ACT and have the course requirements. Applicants with learning disabilities submit the general application form and are considered under the same guidelines as all applicants. Students may have their application reviewed by requesting special consideration based on their disability and by providing letters of recommendation from their high school counselor stating what accommodations are needed in college to be successful. Admissions will be affected by the student's record indicating success with provided accommodations along with any activities and leadership skills. Students not meeting academic criteria for automatic admission may be offered admission to a summer provisional program. These students must take 9–12 credits and receive a grade of C in each of the courses.

ADDITIONAL INFORMATION

Accommodations are provided on an individual basis as needs arise. Disability Services is a resource for information, including, but not limited to, tutoring services, study and time management skills training, community resources, disability awareness, and various university services. Skills classes in math, reading, and writing are offered to the entire student body though the Student Learning Center. Some of these classes may be taken for college credit. Services and accommodations are available for undergraduate and graduate students. Services include an adaptive technology laboratory equipped with state-of-the-art technology for students with disabilities, including text-to-speech scanning for personal use.

LEARNING DISABILITY PROGRAM OR SERVICES

Contact Information
Name of program or department: Disability Services
   Telephone: 979-845-1637
   Fax: 979-458-1214

LEARNING DISABILITY SERVICES

Accommodations are decided upon an individual basis after a thorough review of appropriate, current documentation. The accommodations requested must be supported through the documentation provided and must be logically linked to the current impact of the condition on academic functioning.

Allowed in exams
   Calculator: Yes
   Dictionary: Yes
   Computer: Yes
   Spellchecker: Yes
Extended test time: Yes
Scribes: Yes
Proctors: Yes
Oral exams: Yes
Note-takers: Yes

Distraction-reduced environment: Yes
Tape recording in class: Yes
Electronic texts: Yes
Accommodations for students with
   ADHD: Yes
Kurzweil Reader: Yes
Other assistive technology: Yes
Priority registration: Yes

Added costs for services: No
LD specialists: No
Professional tutors: No
Peer tutors: No
Max. hours/wk. for services: NR
How professors are notified of
   LD/ADHD: By student

GENERAL ADMISSIONS INFORMATION

Office of Admission: 979-458-0509

ENTRANCE REQUIREMENTS

Academic units required: 4 English, 3.5 math, 3 science (2 science labs), 2 foreign language, 2 social studies, 1 history. **Academic units recommended:** 4 English, 3 math, 3 science (2 science labs), 2 foreign language, 2 social studies, 1 history, 1 computer course. High school diploma is required, and GED is accepted. ACT with Writing component required. TOEFL required of all international applicants: minimum paper TOEFL 550.

Application deadline: 1/15
Notification: Rolling
Average GPA: NR
ACT Composite middle 50% range:
   25–30

SAT Math middle 50% range:
   570–670
SAT Critical Reading middle 50%
   range: 530–650
SAT Writing middle 50% range:
   510–620

Graduated top 10% of class: 55%
Graduated top 25% of class: 90%
Graduated top 50% of class: 99%

COLLEGE GRADUATION REQUIREMENTS

Course waivers allowed: Yes
In what course: Math and foreign language have been the only ones requested.
Course substitutions allowed: Yes
In what course: Math and foreign language courses are the only ones that have been requested. Courses are substituted, not waived.

ADDITIONAL INFORMATION

Environment: The school is located on more than 5,000 acres in a college town of 100,000 residents that is about 90 miles from Houston.

Student Body
   Undergrad enrollment: 39,867
   Women: 48%
   Men: 52%
   Percent out-of-state: 3%

Cost Information
   In-state tuition: $16,838
   Out-of-state tuition: $47,618
   Room & board: $8,200
Housing Information
   University housing: Yes

Percent living on campus: 13%
Greek System
   Fraternity: Yes
   Sorority: Yes
Athletics: Division I

TEXAS A&M U.—KINGSVILLE

MSC 105, Kingsville, TX 78363
Phone: 361-593-2315 • Fax: 361-593-2195
E-mail: ksossrx@tamuk.edu • Web: www.tamuk.edu
Support: S • Institution type: 4-year public

PROGRAMS OR SERVICES FOR STUDENTS WITH LD

The university is committed to providing an environment in which every student is encouraged to reach the highest level of personal and educational achievement. Students with disabilities may have special concerns and even special needs. Services vary according to the nature of the disability and are provided by the Center for Life Services and Wellness. Counseling services offer educational, vocational, and personal consultations, as well as tutoring, testing, and academic advising. Students with LD have access to note-takers, readers, writers, and other assistance that the university can provide. All students entering college as freshmen (or transfers with less than 30 hours) have the university's commitment to improve student achievement, retention, depth, and quality of instruction and services.

ADMISSION INFORMATION FOR STUDENTS WITH LD/ADHD

College entrance tests required: Yes
Interview required: Yes
Essay recommended: No
What documentation required for LD: Psycho Ed evaluation to include: relevant historical info, instructional interventions, related services, age diagnosed, objective data (aptitude, achievement, info processing), test scores (standard, percentile and grade equivalents) and describe functional limitations.
With general application: No
To receive services after enrolling: Yes
What documentation required for ADHD: Diagnosis based on DSM-V; history of behaviors impairing functioning in academic setting; diagnostic interview; history of symptoms; evidence of ongoing behaviors.

With general application: No
Submitted to: DRC
Special Ed. HS course work accepted: Yes
Specific course requirements of all applicants: Yes
Separate application required: No
# of LD applications submitted each year: NR
# of LD applications accepted yearly: NR
Total # of students receiving LD services: 190
Acceptance into program means acceptance into college: Students must be admitted to and enrolled in the university first and then request services.

ADMISSIONS

All applicants must meet the same general admission criteria. Admission is very similar to open door admissions, and thus, most applicants are admitted either conditionally or unconditionally or on probation. Average ACT scores are 16-plus; for the SAT, they are 610-plus. There are no specific courses required for entrance; however, it is recommended that students take 4 years of English, 3 years of math, 3 years of science, 4 years of social studies, 3 years of a foreign language, 0.5 year of health, 1.5 years of physical education, 1 year of computer science, 1 year of art/speech, and 3 years of electives. Students with LD are encouraged to self-disclose during the application process. There are two types of admission plans: conditional and unconditional. Unconditional admission is met by achieving 970-plus on the SAT. Conditional admission is achieved by scoring 810–960 on the SAT.

ADDITIONAL INFORMATION

Each freshman receives academic endorsement; developmental educational classes in writing, math, or reading (if necessary); access to tutoring or study groups; and academic rescue programs for students in academic jeopardy. Skills classes are offered for no credit in stress management and test anxiety. Letters are sent to faculty each semester, hand delivered by the student. DRC provides tutoring on a limited basis. Testing accommodations are available, but students are responsible for scheduling the tests. Accommodations include extended testing times, private rooms, scribes, and readers. DRC will also proctor the exam and return the test to the instructor. DRC relies on a volunteer program for note-takers. Services and accommodations are available to undergraduate and graduate students.

LEARNING DISABILITY PROGRAM OR SERVICES

Contact Information
Name of program or department: Disability Resource Center (DRC)
  Telephone: 361-593-3024
  Fax: 361-593-2006

LEARNING DISABILITY SERVICES

Accommodations are decided upon an individual basis after a thorough review of appropriate, current documentation. The accommodations requested must be supported through the documentation provided and must be logically linked to the current impact of the condition on academic functioning.

Allowed in exams
  Calculator: Yes
  Dictionary: Yes
  Computer: Yes
  Spellchecker: Yes
Extended test time: Yes
Scribes: Yes
Proctors: Yes
Oral exams: Yes
Note-takers: Yes

Distraction-reduced environment: Yes
Tape recording in class: Yes
Electronic texts: Yes
Accommodations for students with ADHD: Yes
Kurzweil Reader: No
Other assistive technology: Yes
Priority registration: Yes

Added costs for services: No
LD specialists: No
Professional tutors: No
Peer tutors: Yes
Max. hours/wk. for services: NR
How professors are notified of LD/ADHD: By student

GENERAL ADMISSIONS INFORMATION

Office of Admission: 361-593-2315

ENTRANCE REQUIREMENTS

Academic units recommended: 4 English, 3 math, 3 science, 3 foreign language, 4 social studies, 3 history, 0.5 health, 1.5 physical education, 1 computer science, 1 art/speech, 3 academic electives. High school diploma is required, and GED is accepted.

Application deadline: None
Notification: Rolling
Average GPA: NR
ACT Composite middle 50% range: 16–21

SAT Math middle 50% range: 410–540
SAT Critical Reading middle 50% range: 410–520
SAT Writing middle 50% range: NR

Graduated top 10% of class: NR
Graduated top 25% of class: NR
Graduated top 50% of class: NR

COLLEGE GRADUATION REQUIREMENTS

Course waivers allowed: Yes
In what course: Case-by-case decision made by provost
Course substitutions allowed: Yes
In what course: Case-by-case decision made by provost

ADDITIONAL INFORMATION

Environment: The 246-acre university campus is located 40 miles southwest of Corpus Christi.

Student Body
  Undergrad enrollment: 5,512
  Women: 50%
  Men: 50%
  Percent out-of-state: 1%

Cost Information
  In-state tuition: $6,640
  Out-of-state tuition: $16,030
  Room & board: $6,138
Housing Information
  University housing: Yes
  Percent living on campus: 30%

Greek System
  Fraternity: Yes
  Sorority: Yes
Athletics: Division I

TEXAS STATE U.—SAN MARCOS

429 North Guadalupe St., San Marcos, TX 78666
Phone: 512-245-2364 • Fax: 512-245-8044
E-mail: admissions@txstate.edu • Web: www.txstate.edu
Support: CS • Institution: 4-year public

PROGRAMS OR SERVICES FOR STUDENTS WITH LD

The mission of the Office of Disability Services (ODS) is to assist students with disabilities to independently achieve their educational goals and enhance their leadership development by ensuring equal access to all programs, activities, and services. This is accomplished through a decentralizing approach in providing education and awareness so that programs, activities, and services are conducted "in the most integrated setting appropriate." Students with learning disabilities are encouraged to self-identify and to submit documentation once admitted. By identifying and assessing student needs, ODS provides direct services and refers students to appropriate resources on and off campus. ODS also promotes awareness of the special needs and abilities of students with disabilities through educational events and outreach activities.

ADMISSION INFORMATION FOR STUDENTS WITH LD/ADHD

College entrance tests required: Yes
Interview required: No
Essay required: N/A
What documentation required for LD: Psycho Ed evaluation to include: relevant historical info, instructional interventions, related services, age diagnosed, objective data (aptitude, achievement, info processing), test scores (standard, percentile and grade equivalents) and describe functional limitations.
With general application: No
To receive services after enrolling: Yes
What documentation required for ADHD: Diagnosis based on DSM-V; history of behaviors impairing functioning in academic setting; diagnostic interview; history of symptoms; evidence of ongoing behaviors.

With general application: No
Submitted to: Support Program/Services
Specific course requirements for all applicants: Yes
Separate application required for program services: No
# of LD applications submitted each year: NR
# of LD applications accepted yearly: NR
Total # of students receiving LD services: 527
Acceptance into program means acceptance into college: No

ADMISSIONS

Students with LD must meet the same admission requirements as other applicants. A student whose educational and/or personal goals for success have been negatively impacted by a disability may address any challenges in the essay with their application for admission. This information may be considered during the application process. General admission requirements include: four years English, three years math, three years natural science, three years social science, one year computer science, and two years foreign language; freshman requirements are based on class rank and ACT/SAT scores; a second quarter class ranking would require an ACT score of 22 or SAT score of 1010. The ODS is available to review disability documentation for applicants for admission. This enables the ODS to inform the applicant as to whether or not they will qualify for accommodations at SWT based on the SWT disability guidelines, available from the ODS upon request. Freshmen applicants whose test scores do not meet the minimum requirements for their class rank are eligible for a PAS review if they rank in the top three-quarters of their class. Students in the fourth quarter are not eligible for this review. A limited number of students whose academic record demonstrates potential for academic success at SWT will be offered admission. Factors considered in the review process include specific class rank, size of the graduating class, quality and competitive level of high school courses taken and grades earned, and the applicant's individual verbal and math scores on ACT or SAT.

ADDITIONAL INFORMATION

Specialized support services are based on the individual student disability-based needs. Services available could include special groups registration, recorded textbooks, recording of textbooks not available on tape, arranging for special testing accommodations including extended time and reader services, assistance in accessing adaptive computer equipment, assistance in locating volunteer readers and note-takers, liaison and advocacy between students, faculty and staff, referral for tutoring, disability management counseling, and information and referral to on and off-campus resources.

PROGRAM FOR DISABILITY SERVICES

Contact Information
Name of program or department: Office of Disability Services (ODS)
 Telephone: 512-245-3451
 Fax: 512-245-3452

LEARNING DISABILITY SERVICES

Accommodations are decided upon an individual basis after a thorough review of appropriate, current documentation. The accommodations requested must be supported through the documentation provided and must be logically linked to the current impact of the condition on academic functioning.

Allowed in exams
 Calculator: Yes
 Dictionary: Yes
 Computer: Yes
 Spellchecker: Yes
Extended test time: Yes
Scribes: Yes
Proctors: Yes
Oral exams: Yes
Note-takers: Yes

Distraction-reduced environment: Yes
Tape recording in class: Yes
Electronic texts: Yes
**Accommodations for students with
 ADHD:** Yes
Kurzweil Reader: No
Other assistive technology: N/A
Priority registration: Yes

Added costs for services: No
LD specialists: Yes
Professional tutors: NR
Peer tutors: NR
Max. hours/wk. for services:
 Unlimited
**How professors are notified of
 LD/ADHD:** Student

GENERAL ADMISSIONS INFORMATION

Office of Admission: 512-245-2364

ENTRANCE REQUIREMENTS
Academic units required: 4 English, 3 mathematics, 3 science, (2 science labs), 2 foreign language, 1 visual/performing arts, 1 computer science, 3 PE 1.5, Eco.0.5, Health Ed. 0.5, Speech 0.5. **Academic units recommended:** 4 English, 4 mathematics, 4 science, (2 science labs), 3 foreign language, 1 visual/performing arts, 1 computer science, 3 PE 1.5, Eco.0.5, Health Ed. 0.5, Speech 0.5. High school diploma is required and GED is accepted. SAT recommended; SAT or ACT required; ACT recommended; ACT with Writing component required. TOEFL required of all international applicants; minimum paper TOEFL 550, minimum computer TOEFL 213, minimum web-based TOEFL 78.

Application deadline: 5/1
Notification: Rolling
Average GPA: NR
ACT Composite middle 50% range:
 21–25

SAT Math middle 50% range:
 490–590
**SAT Critical Reading middle 50%
 range:** 470–570
SAT Writing middle 50% range:
 460–560

Graduated top 10% of class: 13.9%
Graduated top 25% of class: 51.9%
Graduated top 50% of class: 91.9%

COLLEGE GRADUATION REQUIREMENTS

Course waivers allowed: No
Course substitutions allowed: Yes
In what course: Foreign language

ADDITIONAL INFORMATION

Environment: The 1,091-acre campus is located 30 miles south of Austin, and within easy access of San Antonio.

Student Body
 Undergrad enrollment: 27,448
 Women: 55%
 Men: 45%
 Percent out-of-state: 1%

Cost Information
 In-state tuition: $7,830
 Out-of-state tuition: $17,130
 Room and board: $7,310
Housing Information
 University housing: Yes
 Percent living on campus: 24%

Greek System
 Fraternity: Yes
 Sorority: Yes
Athletics: Division I

TEXAS TECH UNIVERSITY

PO Box 45005, Lubbock, TX 79409-5005
Phone: 806-742-1480 • Fax: 806-742-0062
E-mail: admissions@ttu.edu • Web: www.ttu.edu
Support: S • Institution type: 4-year public

PROGRAMS OR SERVICES FOR STUDENTS WITH LD

It is the philosophy of Texas Tech University to serve each student on a case-by-case basis. All services rendered are supported by adequate documentation. We firmly believe that all students should be and will become effective self-advocates. Students with disabilities attending Texas Tech will find numerous programs designed to provide services and promote access to all phases of university activity. Such programming is coordinated through the Dean of Students's Office with the assistance of an advisory committee of both disabled and non-disabled students, faculty, and staff. Services to disabled students are offered through a decentralized network of university and nonuniversity resources. This means that many excellent services are available, but it is up to the student to initiate them. Each student is encouraged to act as his or her own advocate and take the major responsibility for securing services and accommodations. The Disabled Student Services team, Dean of Students's Office, faculty, and staff are supportive in this effort.

ADMISSION INFORMATION FOR STUDENTS WITH LD/ADHD

College entrance tests required: Yes
Interview required: No
Essay recommended: No
What documentation required for LD: Psycho Ed evaluation to include: relevant historical info, instructional interventions, related services, age diagnosed, objective data (aptitude, achievement, info processing), test scores (standard, percentile and grade equivalents) and describe functional limitations.
With general application: No
To receive services after enrolling: Yes
What documentation required for ADHD: Diagnosis based on DSM-V; history of behaviors impairing functioning in academic setting; diagnostic interview; history of symptoms; evidence of ongoing behaviors.

With general application: No
Submitted to: PASS
Special Ed. HS course work accepted: Yes
Specific course requirements of all applicants: Yes
Separate application required: Yes
# of LD applications submitted each year: NR
# of LD applications accepted yearly: NR
Total # of students receiving LD services: 600
Acceptance into program means acceptance into college: Students must be admitted to and enrolled in the university first and then request services.

ADMISSIONS

There is no special admissions process for students with LD, and all applicants must meet the same criteria. All students must have 4 years of English, 3 years of math, 2.5 years of social studies, 2 years of science, and 3.5 years of electives. Any applicant who scores a 1200 on the SAT or a 29 on the ACT is automatically admitted regardless of class rank. Some students are admissible who do not meet the stated requirements, but they must have a 2.0 GPA for a provisional admission. After a student is admitted, Disabled Student Services requires documentation that provides a diagnosis and an indication of the severity of the disability and offers recommendations for accommodations for students to receive services.

ADDITIONAL INFORMATION

Support services through Disabled Student Services include academic support services, which can help students develop habits enabling them to get a good education. Students may receive academic support services in the PASS (Programs for Academic Support Services) Center, which is open to all students on campus. Services offered free of charge include tutor referral services (paid by student); study skills group; hour-long workshops that target a variety of subjects from overcoming math anxiety to preparing for finals; a self-help learning lab with videotapes; computer-assisted instruction; individual consultations assisting students with specific study problems; and setting study skills improvement goals. All students with LD are offered priority registration. Services and accommodations are available for undergraduate and graduate students.

LEARNING DISABILITY PROGRAM OR SERVICES

Contact Information
Name of program or department: Programs for Academic Support Services
　Telephone: 806-742-2405
　Fax: 806-742-4837

LEARNING DISABILITY SERVICES

Accommodations are decided upon an individual basis after a thorough review of appropriate, current documentation. The accommodations requested must be supported through the documentation provided and must be logically linked to the current impact of the condition on academic functioning.

Allowed in exams
　Calculator: Yes
　Dictionary: NR
　Computer: Yes
　Spellchecker: Yes
Extended test time: Yes
Scribes: Yes
Proctors: Yes
Oral exams: Yes
Note-takers: Yes

Distraction-reduced environment: Yes
Tape recording in class: Yes
Electronic texts: No
Accommodations for students with
　ADHD: Yes
Kurzweil Reader: Yes
Other assistive technology: Yes
Priority registration: Yes

Added costs for services: No
LD specialists: No
Professional tutors: No
Peer tutors: 25–35
Max. hours/wk. for services:
　Unlimited
How professors are notified of
　LD/ADHD: By student

GENERAL ADMISSIONS INFORMATION

Office of Admission: 806-742-1480

ENTRANCE REQUIREMENTS

Academic units required: 4 English, 3 math, 2 science (2 science labs), 2 foreign language. High school diploma is required, and GED is accepted. ACT with Writing component required. TOEFL required of all international applicants: minimum paper TOEFL 550, minimum computer TOEFL 213.

Application deadline: 5/1
Notification: Rolling
Average GPA: NR
ACT Composite middle 50% range:
　22–26

SAT Math middle 50% range:
　520–620
SAT Critical Reading middle 50%
　range: 490–590
SAT Writing middle 50% range:
　460–570

Graduated top 10% of class: 22%
Graduated top 25% of class: 54%
Graduated top 50% of class: 88%

COLLEGE GRADUATION REQUIREMENTS

Course waivers allowed: Yes
In what course: Possible in math or foreign language
Course substitutions allowed: Yes
In what course: Possible in math or foreign language

ADDITIONAL INFORMATION

Environment: The university is located on 1,839 acres in an urban area in Lubbock.

Student Body
　Undergrad enrollment: 25,462
　Women: 44%
　Men: 56%
　Percent out-of-state: 4%

Cost Information
　In-state tuition: $8,765
　Out-of-state tuition: $18,155
　Room & board: $8,095
Housing Information
　University housing: Yes
　Percent living on campus: 24%

Greek System
　Fraternity: Yes
　Sorority: Yes
Athletics: Division I

UNIVERSITY OF HOUSTON

Office of Admissions, 122 E. Cullen Building, Houston, TX 77204-2023
Phone: 713-743-1010 • Fax: 713-743-9633
E-mail: admissions@uh.edu • Web: www.uh.edu
Support: CS • Institution: 4-year public

PROGRAMS OR SERVICES FOR STUDENTS WITH LD

The Center for Students with DisABILITIES provides a wide variety of academic support services to students with all types of disabilities. Our goal is to help ensure that these otherwise qualified students are able to successfully compete with non-disabled students by receiving equal educational opportunities in college as mandated by law. Through advocacy efforts and a deliberate, ongoing, public education program, the staff strives to heighten the awareness of disability issues, educational rights, and abilities of persons who have disabilities.

ADMISSION INFORMATION FOR STUDENTS WITH LD/ADHD

College entrance tests required: Yes
Interview required: No
What documentation required for LD: Psycho Ed evaluation to include: relevant historical info, instructional interventions, related services, age diagnosed, objective data (aptitude, achievement, info processing), test scores (standard, percentile and grade equivalents) and describe functional limitations.
With general application: No
To receive services after enrolling: Yes
What documentation required for ADHD: Diagnosis based on DSM-V; history of behaviors impairing functioning in academic setting; diagnostic interview; history of symptoms; evidence of ongoing behaviors.

With general application: No
Submitted to: Support Program/Services
Special Ed. HS course work accepted: Yes
Specific course requirements for all applicants: Yes
Separate application required for program services: No
# of LD applications submitted each year: NR
# of LD applications accepted yearly: NR
Total # of students receiving LD services: 226
Acceptance into program means acceptance into college: Students must be admitted to and enrolled in the university first and then request services.

ADMISSIONS

Admission is automatic for Texas residents in the top 15 percent of the class. Other applicants must meet one of the following criteria: Top 16-25 percent of the class have an SAT score of 1000 or higher or an ACT score of 21 or higher; Top 26-50 percent class rank with an 1100 SAT score or higher or an ACT score of 24 or higher. Applicants who do not meet these admissions criteria will be reviewed in light of the applicant's academic rigor, community service, extracurricular activities, and surmounting obstacles to pursue higher education. Letters of reference from high school teachers, counselors, supervisors and activity leaders along with personal statements are welcome additions to an applicant's file.

ADDITIONAL INFORMATION

Students who come from an educationally and/or economically disadvantaged background may be eligible to participate in the UH 'Challenger Program' which is designed to provide intense support to students who face obstacles in their efforts to successfully complete college. Services to all students include: tutoring, counseling, financial aid advisement, and social enrichment. Remedial reading, writing, and study skills courses for three hours of non-college credit are offered. There are also remedial courses for credit in English and college algebra. Other services include assistance with petitions for course substitutions, peer support groups, free carbonized paper for note-taking, textbooks and class handouts put on tape by office staff or volunteer readers, and advocacy for student's legal rights to "reasonable and necessary accommodations" in their course work. Extended tutoring is available at the Learning Support Services and Math Lab.

PROGRAM FOR DISABILITY SERVICES

Contact Information
Name of program or department: Center for Students with Disabilities
 Telephone: 713-743-5400
 Fax: 713-743-5396

LEARNING DISABILITY SERVICES

Accommodations are decided upon an individual basis after a thorough review of appropriate, current documentation. The accommodations requested must be supported through the documentation provided and must be logically linked to the current impact of the condition on academic functioning.

Allowed in exams
 Calculator: Yes
 Dictionary: Yes
 Computer: Yes
 Spellchecker: Yes
Extended test time: Yes
Scribes: Yes
Proctors: Yes
Oral exams: Yes
Note-takers: Yes

Distraction-reduced environment: Yes
Tape recording in class: Yes
Electronic texts: Yes
Accommodations for students with ADHD: Yes
Kurzweil Reader: Yes
Other assistive technology: JAWS, Zoomtext, headmouse, Handiword, FmLoop, CCTV, voice activated software, etc.
Priority registration: Yes

Added costs for services: No
LD specialists: Yes
Professional tutors: No
Peer tutors: Yes
Max. hours/wk. for services: 4
How professors are notified of LD/ADHD: Student

GENERAL ADMISSIONS INFORMATION

Office of Admission: 713-743-1010

ENTRANCE REQUIREMENTS

Academic units required: 4 English, 4 mathematics, 4 science, 4 social studies. High school diploma is required and GED is accepted. SAT or ACT required; TOEFL required of all international applicants; minimum paper TOEFL 550, minimum computer TOEFL 213, minimum web-based TOEFL 79. **Academic units recommended:** 2 foreign language, 1 computer science, 1 visual/performance arts.

Application deadline: 4/1
Notification: Rolling
Average GPA: 3.33
ACT Composite middle 50% range: 19–24

SAT Math middle 50% range: 490–600
SAT Critical Reading middle 50% range: 460–570
SAT Writing middle 50% range: NR

Graduated top 10% of class: 21%
Graduated top 25% of class: 30%
Graduated top 50% of class: 81%

COLLEGE GRADUATION REQUIREMENTS

Course waivers allowed: Yes
In what course: Foreign language course waivers have been granted most recently.
Course substitutions allowed: Yes
In what course: Foreign language course substitutions have been granted most recently.

ADDITIONAL INFORMATION

Environment: The university is located on 594 acres in an urban area three miles from Houston.

Student Body
 Undergrad enrollment: 31,764
 Women: 50%
 Men: 50%
 Percent out-of-state: 1%

Cost Information
 In-state tuition: $9,211
 Out-of-state tuition: $18,601
 Room and board: $8,318
Housing Information
 University housing: Yes
 Percent living on campus: 15%

Greek System
 Fraternity: Yes
 Sorority: Yes
Athletics: Division I

UNIVERSITY OF NORTH TEXAS

PO Box 311277, Denton, TX 76203-1277
Phone: 940-565-2681 • Fax: 940-565-2408
E-mail: undergrad@unt.edu • Web: www.unt.edu
Support: CS • Institution type: 4-year public

PROGRAMS OR SERVICES FOR STUDENTS WITH LD

The goal of the Office of Disability Accommodations is to ensure that qualified students with disabilities have access to reasonable and appropriate services and learning resources needed to facilitate matriculation and successful completion of academic programs at the university. The office serves as a liaison to ensure that assistance and/or accommodation and adjustments are available for students with disabilities to enable them full access to the educational facilities and services at the university. The office provides consultation and assistance to academic and general service offices in making adaptations and adjustments for students with disabilities. It also provides alternative testing sites and proctors when the academic department is unable to provide assistance.

ADMISSION INFORMATION FOR STUDENTS WITH LD/ADHD

College entrance tests required: Yes
Interview required: No
Essay recommended: No
What documentation required for LD: Psycho Ed evaluation to include: relevant historical info, instructional interventions, related services, age diagnosed, objective data (aptitude, achievement, info processing), test scores (standard, percentile and grade equivalents) and describe functional limitations.
With general application: No
To receive services after enrolling: Yes
What documentation required for ADHD: Diagnosis based on DSM-V; history of behaviors impairing functioning in academic setting; diagnostic interview; history of symptoms; evidence of ongoing behaviors.

With general application: No
Submitted to: Office of Disability Accommodations
Special Ed. HS course work accepted: No
Specific course requirements of all applicants: Yes
Separate application required: No
# of LD applications submitted each year:
# of LD applications accepted yearly: NR
Total # of students receiving LD services: 225
Acceptance into program means acceptance into college: Students must be admitted and enrolled at the university first and then may request services. Students denied admission may appeal the decision.

ADMISSIONS

Students must apply directly to the Admissions Office and meet the current requirements. Course requirements include 4 years of English, 4 years of math, 3 years of science, 3 years of a foreign language, 4 years of social studies, and 3 years of electives. When a student makes a written request for waivers for admission requirements, the request is sent to an individual approval review committee for consideration. Students in the top 10 percent of their high school class must submit ACT/SAT scores, but no specific score is required; students in the remainder of top quarter need a minimum 920 SAT or 19 ACT; the second quarter need a minimum 1010 SAT or 21 ACT; the third quarter need a minimum 1100 SAT or 24 ACT; and the fourth quarter need a minimum 1180 SAT or 27 ACT. If a student is not accepted, there is an appeal process on the basis of the learning disability. These students may need letters of support, a statement of commitment from the student, and an evaluation of the documentation by the Disability Office. Admission decisions are made by the Office of Admissions and the Office of Disability Accommodations.

ADDITIONAL INFORMATION

The Center for Development Studies provides tutoring to build academic knowledge and skills in various subject areas, academic counseling to plan class schedules and evaluate areas of strengths and weaknesses, personal counseling to develop greater self-understanding and learn ways to cope with adjustments to college and the pressures of life, and study skills assessment for evaluating and improving academic performance. Skills courses for credit are offered in time management, career choice, and study skills. Students requesting a distraction-free environments for tests must provide the appropriate documentation. Calculators, dictionaries, computers, and spellcheckers are allowed with instructor's approval. Services and accommodations are available for undergraduate and graduate students.

LEARNING DISABILITY PROGRAM OR SERVICES

Contact Information
Name of program or department: Office of Disability Accommodations (ODA)
   Telephone: 940-565-4323
   Fax: 940-565-4376

LEARNING DISABILITY SERVICES

Accommodations are decided upon an individual basis after a thorough review of appropriate, current documentation. The accommodations requested must be supported through the documentation provided and must be logically linked to the current impact of the condition on academic functioning.

Allowed in exams
   Calculator: NR
   Dictionary: NR
   Computer: NR
   Spellchecker: NR
Extended test time: Yes
Scribes: Yes
Proctors: Yes
Oral exams: Yes
Note-takers: Yes

Distraction-reduced environment: Yes
Tape recording in class: Yes
Electronic texts: Yes
Accommodations for students with ADHD: Yes
Kurzweil Reader: Yes
Other assistive technology: Yes
Priority registration: Yes

Added costs for services: No
LD specialists: Yes
Professional tutors: No
Peer tutors: Yes
Max. hours/wk. for services: Unlimited
How professors are notified of LD/ADHD: By both student and director

GENERAL ADMISSIONS INFORMATION

Office of Admission: 940-565-2681

ENTRANCE REQUIREMENTS

Academic units required: 4 English, 4 math, 3 science, 3 foreign language, 4 social studies, 2 history, 3 academic electives. **Academic units recommended:** 4 English, 4 math, 3 science, 3 foreign language, 2 social studies, 2 history, 2 academic electives, 4.5 health, 1.5 physical education, 1 computer science, 1 fine arts. High school diploma is required, and GED is accepted. ACT with or without Writing component accepted. TOEFL required of all international applicants: minimum paper TOEFL 550, minimum computer TOEFL 213.

Application deadline: 8/1
Notification: Rolling, beginning 10/15
Average GPA: NR
ACT Composite middle 50% range: 21–26

SAT Math middle 50% range: 500–610
SAT Critical Reading middle 50% range: 490–600
SAT Writing middle 50% range: NR

Graduated top 10% of class: 23%
Graduated top 25% of class: 54%
Graduated top 50% of class: 90%

COLLEGE GRADUATION REQUIREMENTS

Course waivers allowed: Yes
In what course: This is looked at on an approval basis by each department. Approval is not automatic; it is dependent on the student's situation.
Course substitutions allowed: Yes
In what course: This is looked at on an approval basis by each department. Approval is not automatic; it is dependent on the student's situation.

ADDITIONAL INFORMATION

Environment: The university is located on 425 acres in an urban area 35 miles north of the Dallas/Fort Worth area.

Student Body
   Undergrad enrollment: 28,283
   Women: 54%
   Men: 46%
   Percent out-of-state: 3%

Cost Information
   In-state tuition: $6,184
   Out-of-state tuition: $15,574
   Room & board: $6,892
Housing Information
   University housing: Yes
   Percent living on campus: 19%

Greek System
   Fraternity: Yes
   Sorority: Yes
Athletics: Division I

THE UNIVERSITY OF TEXAS AT AUSTIN

P.O. Box 8058, Austin, TX 78713-8058
Phone: 512-475-7440 • Fax: 512-475-7475
E-mail: • Web: http://www.utexas.edu
Support: S • Institution: 4-year public

PROGRAMS OR SERVICES FOR STUDENTS WITH LD

Services for Students with Disabilities (SSD) provides a program of support and advocacy for students with LD. Services offered include assistance with learning strategies, note-takers for lectures, scribe/readers, and extended time for in-class work. There is also a Tutoring and Learning Center whose free services include study skill assistance, subject-area tutoring, life management skills, exam reviews, peer mentoring, and distance tutoring.

ADMISSION INFORMATION FOR STUDENTS WITH LD/ADHD

College entrance tests required: Yes
Interview required: No
Essay recommended: No
Documentation required for LD: Current diagnostic report, comprehensive and include aptitude and achievement testing, and specific evidence of a learning disability
Documentation required for ADHD: Information regarding onset, longevity, and severity of the symptoms; impact of ADHD on educational setting; medication history and current recommendations regarding medication, the exact DSM–IV diagnosis, and information concerning co-morbidity should also be included in the evaluation.
Submitted to: Services for Students with Disabilities (SSD)
Special Ed. HS course work accepted: Yes

Specific course requirements of all applicants: Yes
Separate application required: N/A
# of LD applications submitted each year: NR
# of LD applications accepted yearly: NR
Total # of students receiving LD services: 305
Acceptance into program means acceptance into college: Students must be admitted to and enrolled in the university first and then request services.

ADMISSIONS

There is no special admissions process for students with learning disabilities. General admission criteria requires students to have a high school diploma and ACT/SAT results, and they are not interested in class rank or GPA. Course requirements include 4 years of English, 3 years of math, 3 years of science, 4 years of social studies, 3 years of a foreign language, 0.5 year of health, 1 year of fine arts, 1.5 years of physical education, and 1 year of computer science. For students not otherwise eligible to enter due to grades or scores, a study skills class is required plus other courses from a course list.

ADDITIONAL INFORMATION

To receive services, students must meet an SSD coordinator. Students need to provide current documentation from an appropriate licensed professional. Services offered to students, when appropriate, assistance with learning strategies, and priority registration. Classroom accommodations include note-takers, assistive technology, scribes, readers, and extended testing times. In the Tutoring and Learning Center, students can access study skills assistance, subject area tutoring, life management skills assistance, and a special needs room with state of the art technology. Currently there are 305 students with LD and 745 with ADHD receiving services.

PROGRAM FOR DISABILITY SERVICES

Contact Information
Name of program or department: Services for Student with Disabilities
 Telephone: 512-471-6259
 Fax: 512-475-7730

LEARNING DISABILITY SERVICES

Accommodations are decided upon an individual basis after a thorough review of appropriate, current documentation. The accommodations requested must be supported through the documentation provided and must be logically linked to the current impact of the condition on academic functioning.

Allowed in exams
 Calculator: Yes
 Dictionary: Yes
 Computer: Yes
 Spellchecker: Yes
Extended test time: Yes
Scribes: Yes
Proctors: Yes
Oral exams: N/A
Note-takers: Yes

Distraction-reduced environment: Yes
Tape recording in class: Yes
Electronic texts: Yes
Accommodations for students with ADHD: Yes
Kurzweil Reader: Yes
Other assistive technology: Kurzweil 3000/1000, Dragon Naturally Speaking, JAWS, Zoomtext, high speed scanners, AT training
Priority registration: Yes

Added costs for services: No
LD specialists: Yes
Professional tutors: NR
Peer tutors: NR
Max. hours/wk. for services: NR
How professors are notified of LD/ADHD: Student

GENERAL ADMISSIONS INFORMATION

Office of Admission: 512-475-7399

ENTRANCE REQUIREMENTS
Academic units required: 4 English, 3 mathematics, 2 science, (2 science labs), 2 foreign language, 3 social studies.
Academic units recommended: 4 English, 4 mathematics, 4 science, (3 science labs), 3 foreign language, 3 social studies. High school diploma is required and GED is accepted. SAT or ACT required; ACT with Writing component required. TOEFL required of all international applicants; minimum paper TOEFL 550, minimum computer TOEFL 213, minimum web-based TOEFL 79.

Application deadline: 12/15
Notification: 4/1
Average GPA: NR
ACT Composite middle 50% range:
 25–31

SAT Math middle 50% range:
 580–710
SAT Critical Reading middle 50% range: 540–670
SAT Writing middle 50% range:
 540–680

Graduated top 10% of class: 73%
Graduated top 25% of class: 91%
Graduated top 50% of class: 98%

COLLEGE GRADUATION REQUIREMENTS

Course substitutions allowed: Yes
In what course: Varies depending on the nature of the disability and supportive documentation. Most course substitutions are for foreign language.

ADDITIONAL INFORMATION

Environment: NR

Student Body
 Undergrad enrollment: 38,437
 Women: 52%
 Men: 48%
 Percent out-of-state: 4%

Cost Information
 In-state tuition: $9,794
 Out-of-state tuition: $32,506
 Room and board: $10,422
 Housing Information
 University housing: Yes
 Percent living on campus: 20

Greek System
 Fraternity: Yes
 Sorority: Yes
 Athletics: Division I

UNIVERSITY OF TEXAS—EL PASO

500 West University Avenue, El Paso, TX 79968-0510
Phone: 915-747-5890 • Fax: 915-747-8893
E-mail: futureminer@utep.edu • Web: www.utep.edu
Support: S • Institution type: 4-year public

PROGRAMS OR SERVICES FOR STUDENTS WITH LD

The Center for Accommodations and Support Services (CASS) provides a program of support and advocacy for students with LD. Services offered include peer support group, assistance with learning strategies, note-takers for lectures, scribe/readers, extended time for in-class work, and altered test formats, such as oral exams. There is also a Tutoring and Learning Center whose free services include study skill assistance, subject-area tutoring, life management skills, exam reviews, peer mentoring, and distance tutoring.

ADMISSION INFORMATION FOR STUDENTS WITH LD/ADHD

College entrance tests required: Yes
Interview required: No
Essay recommended: No
What documentation required for LD: Psycho Ed evaluation to include: relevant historical info, instructional interventions, related services, age diagnosed, objective data (aptitude, achievement, info processing), test scores (standard, percentile and grade equivalents) and describe functional limitations.
With general application: No
To receive services after enrolling: Yes
What documentation required for ADHD: Diagnosis based on DSM-V; history of behaviors impairing functioning in academic setting; diagnostic interview; history of symptoms; evidence of ongoing behaviors.

With general application: No
Submitted to: The Center for Accommodations and Support Services (CASS)
Special Ed. HS course work accepted: Yes
Specific course requirements of all applicants: Yes
Separate application required: N/A
# of LD applications submitted each year: NR
# of LD applications accepted yearly: NR
Total # of students receiving LD services: 78
Acceptance into program means acceptance into college: Students must be admitted to and enrolled in the university first and then request services.

ADMISSIONS

There is no special admissions process for students with learning disabilities. General admission criteria requires students to have a high school diploma and ACT/SAT results, and they are not interested in class rank or GPA. Course requirements include 4 years of English, 3 years of math, 3 years of science, 4 years of social studies, 3 years of a foreign language, 0.5 year of health, 1 year of fine arts, 1.5 years of physical education, and 1 year of computer science. For students not otherwise eligible to enter due to grades or scores, a study skills class is required plus other courses from a course list.

ADDITIONAL INFORMATION

To receive services, students must meet with the staff of CASS. Students need to provide current documentation from an appropriate licensed professional. Services offered to students, when appropriate, are peer support group, assistance with learning strategies, and priority registration. Classroom accommodations include note-takers, assistive technology, scribes, readers, extended testing times, and exam modifications. Currently there are 78 students with LD and 8 with ADHD receiving services.

LEARNING DISABILITY PROGRAM OR SERVICES

Contact Information
Name of program or department: Disabled Student Services Office
  Telephone: 915-747-5648
  Fax: 915-747-6971

LEARNING DISABILITY SERVICES

Accommodations are decided upon an individual basis after a thorough review of appropriate, current documentation. The accommodations requested must be supported through the documentation provided and must be logically linked to the current impact of the condition on academic functioning.

Allowed in exams
  Calculator: Yes
  Dictionary: Yes
  Computer: Yes
  Spellchecker: Yes
Extended test time: Yes
Scribes: Yes
Proctors: Yes
Oral exams: Yes
Note-takers: Yes

Distraction-reduced environment: Yes
Tape recording in class: Yes
Electronic texts: Yes
**Accommodations for students with
  ADHD:** Yes
Kurzweil Reader: Yes
Other assistive technology: Yes
Priority registration: Yes

Added costs for services: No
LD specialists: No
Professional tutors: No
Peer tutors: No
Max. hours/wk. for services: 40
**How professors are notified of
  LD/ADHD:** By both student and
  director

GENERAL ADMISSIONS INFORMATION

Office of Admission: 915-747-5890

ENTRANCE REQUIREMENTS

Academic units recommended: 4 English, 4 math, 3 science, 3 foreign language, 4 social studies, 2 history. High school diploma is required, and GED is accepted.

Application deadline: 7/31
Notification: Rolling
Average GPA: 3.16
ACT Composite middle 50% range:
  17–22

SAT Math middle 50% range:
  420–530
**SAT Critical Reading middle 50%
  range:** 390–490
SAT Writing middle 50% range: NR

Graduated top 10% of class: 19%
Graduated top 25% of class: 41%
Graduated top 50% of class: 70%

COLLEGE GRADUATION REQUIREMENTS

Course waivers allowed: No
Course substitutions allowed: Yes
In what course: Math and foreign language

ADDITIONAL INFORMATION

Environment: The university is located on a 360-acre urban campus.

Student Body
  Undergrad enrollment: 18,975
  Women: 55%
  Men: 45%
  Percent out-of-state: 13%

Cost Information
  In-state tuition: $6,537
  Out-of-state tuition: $15,837
  Room & Board: $8,692
Housing Information
  University housing: Yes
  Percent living on campus: 3%

Greek System
  Fraternity: Yes
  Sorority: Yes
Athletics: Division I

UNIVERSITY OF TEXAS—
PAN AMERICAN

Admissions and New Student Services, 1201 West Univer, Edinburg, TX 78
Phone: 956-665-2999 • Fax:
E-mail: admissions@utpa.edu • Web: www.utpa.edu
Support: S • Institution: 4-year public

PROGRAMS OR SERVICES FOR STUDENTS WITH LD

Disability Services is a component of the Division of Student Affairs at the University of Texas—Pan American. It is designed and committed to providing support services to meet the educational, career, and personal needs of persons with disabilities attending or planning to attend the university. Students requesting accommodations must provide documentation from a professional who is qualified to diagnose and verify the particular disability; and the testing and documentation must be current. Disability Services will use the documentation to properly prepare an assistance plan for the student to use while enrolled at the university.

ADMISSION INFORMATION FOR STUDENTS WITH LD/ADHD

College entrance tests required: Yes
Interview required: No
Essay required: N/A
What documentation required for LD: Psycho Ed evaluation to include: relevant historical info, instructional interventions, related services, age diagnosed, objective data (aptitude, achievement, info processing), test scores (standard, percentile and grade equivalents) and describe functional limitations.
With general application: No
To receive services after enrolling: Yes
What documentation required for ADHD: Diagnosis based on DSM-V; history of behaviors impairing functioning in academic setting; diagnostic interview; history of symptoms; evidence of ongoing behaviors.

With general application: No
Submitted to: Support Program/Services
Special Ed. HS course work accepted: No
Specific course requirements for all applicants: NR
Separate application required for program services: Yes
# of LD applications submitted each year: NR
# of LD applications accepted yearly: NR
Total # of students receiving LD services: 66
Acceptance into program means acceptance into college: Separate application required after student has enrolled

ADMISSIONS

Students with learning disabilities must meet the same admission requirements as all other applicants. The admissions requirements for entering freshmen are: a) graduation in top ten percent of high school class; OR b) ACT Composite scores 18 or SAT Critical Reading and Math Composite of 860; c) recommended or higher graduation plan or GED certificate.

ADDITIONAL INFORMATION

Disability Services provides the following services: assessment for special needs; note-takers; readers and writers; advisement, counseling, and guidance; assistance with admissions, orientation, registration; referral services to other university units; interpreting services; liaison between students, faculty, staff, and others; resolution of problems/concerns; computer hardware and software; Kurzweil Reader; and Juliet Pro embosser. Services and accommodations are available for undergraduate and graduate students.

PROGRAM FOR DISABILITY SERVICES

Contact Information
Name of program or department: Disability Services
 Telephone: 956-665-7005
 Fax: 956-665-2450

LEARNING DISABILITY SERVICES

Accommodations are decided upon an individual basis after a thorough review of appropriate, current documentation. The accommodations requested must be supported through the documentation provided and must be logically linked to the current impact of the condition on academic functioning.

Allowed in exams
 Calculator: Yes
 Dictionary: Yes
 Computer: Yes
 Spellchecker: Yes
Extended test time: Yes
Scribes: Yes
Proctors: Yes
Oral exams: Yes
Note-takers: Yes

Distraction-reduced environment: Yes
Tape recording in class: Yes
Electronic texts: Yes
Accommodations for students with ADHD: Yes
Kurzweil Reader: Yes
Other assistive technology: JAWS, pocket talker, Braille format, readers, large print, etc.
Priority registration: No

Added costs for services: No
LD specialists: No
Professional tutors: No
Peer tutors: NR
Max. hours/wk. for services: 40
How professors are notified of LD/ADHD: Student

GENERAL ADMISSIONS INFORMATION

Office of Admission: 956-381-2482

ENTRANCE REQUIREMENTS
Academic units required: 4 English, 3 mathematics, 3 science, 2 foreign language. High school diploma is required and GED is accepted. SAT or ACT required; TOEFL required of all international applicants; minimum paper TOEFL 500, minimum computer TOEFL 173, minimum web-based TOEFL 61.

Application deadline: 8/11
Notification: Rolling
Average GPA: NR
ACT Composite middle 50% range: 18–22

SAT Math middle 50% range: 450–550
SAT Critical Reading middle 50% range: 420–520
SAT Writing middle 50% range: 410–500

Graduated top 10% of class: 23%
Graduated top 25% of class: 54%
Graduated top 50% of class: 84%

COLLEGE GRADUATION REQUIREMENTS

Course waivers allowed: Yes
In what course: It depends on the degree plan. Requests can be made through the Program Advisors, Department Chairs, and the VP for Academic Affairs. An appeal process is required.
Course substitutions allowed: Yes
In what course: On a case-by-case basis

ADDITIONAL INFORMATION

Environment: The campus is in a small town near the Mexican border.

Student Body
 Undergrad enrollment: 16,630
 Women: 45%
 Men: 55%
 Percent out-of-state: 1%

Cost Information
 In-state tuition: $5,978
 Out-of-state tuition: $15,368
 Room and board: $7,205
Housing Information
 University housing: Yes
 Percent living on campus: 10%

Greek System
 Fraternity: Yes
 Sorority: Yes
Athletics: Division I

BRIGHAM YOUNG UNIVERSITY

A-153 ASB, Provo, UT 84602-1110
Phone: 801-422-2507 • Fax: 801-422-0005
E-mail: admissions@byu.edu • Web: www.byu.edu
Support: C • Institution: 4-year private

PROGRAMS OR SERVICES FOR STUDENTS WITH LD

The University Accessibility Center works to provide individualized programs to meet the specific needs of each student with a disability, assisting in developing strengths to meet the challenges, and making arrangements for accommodations and special services as required.

ADMISSION INFORMATION FOR STUDENTS WITH LD/ADHD

College entrance tests required: Yes
Interview required: N/A
Essay required: N/A
What documentation required for LD: Psycho Ed evaluation to include: relevant historical info, instructional interventions, related services, age diagnosed, objective data (aptitude, achievement, info processing), test scores (standard, percentile and grade equivalents) and describe functional limitations.
With general application: No
To receive services after enrolling: Yes
What documentation required for ADHD: Diagnosis based on DSM-V; history of behaviors impairing functioning in academic setting; diagnostic interview; history of symptoms; evidence of ongoing behaviors.

With general application: No
Submitted to: Support Program/Services
Special Ed. HS course work accepted: N/A
Specific course requirements for all applicants: Yes
Separate application required for program services: Yes
# of LD applications submitted each year: 9,000
# of LD applications accepted yearly: 6,000
Total # of students receiving LD services: 110–130
Acceptance into program means acceptance into college:

ADMISSIONS
There is no special admission process for students with learning disabilities. Suggested courses include: four years English, three to four years math, two to three years science, two years history or government, two years foreign language, and two years of literature or writing. Evaluations are made on an individualized basis with a system weighted for college-prep courses and core classes.

ADDITIONAL INFORMATION
Non-credit workshops and a study skill class are offered for all student and often recommended to students with learning concerns. The following topics are some examples: math anxiety, memory, overcoming procrastination, self-appreciation, stress management, test-taking, textbook comprehension, time management, and communication. Additional services include counseling support and advising. Services and accommodations are available for undergraduate and graduate students.

PROGRAM FOR DISABILITY SERVICES

Contact Information
Name of program or department: University Accessibility Center
  Telephone: 801-422-2767
  Fax: 801-422-0174

LEARNING DISABILITY SERVICES

Accommodations are decided upon an individual basis after a thorough review of appropriate, current documentation. The accommodations requested must be supported through the documentation provided and must be logically linked to the current impact of the condition on academic functioning.

Allowed in exams
  Calculator: Yes
  Dictionary: Yes
  Computer: Yes
  Spellchecker: Yes
Extended test time: Yes
Scribes: Yes
Proctors: Yes
Oral exams: Yes
Note-takers: Yes

Distraction-reduced environment: Yes
Tape recording in class: Yes
Electronic texts: Yes
Accommodations for students with
  ADHD: Yes
Kurzweil Reader: Yes
Other assistive technology: N/A
Priority registration: Yes

Added costs for services: No
LD specialists: Yes
Professional tutors: 0
Peer tutors: 100
Max. hours/wk. for services:
How professors are notified of
  LD/ADHD: Both student and director

GENERAL ADMISSIONS INFORMATION

Office of Admission: 801-422-2507

ENTRANCE REQUIREMENTS
Academic units required: 4 English, 3 mathematics, 2 science, (2 science labs), 2 foreign language, 2 history, 2 literature or writing. **Academic units recommended:** 4 English, 4 mathematics, 3 science, (3 science labs), 4 foreign language. High school diploma is required and GED is accepted. ACT required; ACT with Writing component recommended. TOEFL required of all international applicants; minimum paper TOEFL 500, minimum computer TOEFL 173.

Application deadline: 2/1
Notification: Rolling
Average GPA: 3.8
ACT Composite middle 50% range:
  25–30

SAT Math middle 50% range:
  570–680
SAT Critical Reading middle 50%
  range: 550–660
SAT Writing middle 50% range: NR

Graduated top 10% of class: 51%
Graduated top 25% of class: 83%
Graduated top 50% of class: 98%

COLLEGE GRADUATION REQUIREMENTS

Course waivers allowed: No
In what course:
Course substitutions allowed: Yes
In what course: General education, foreign language, and/or math

ADDITIONAL INFORMATION

Environment: The university is located in a suburban area 45 miles south of Salt Lake City.

Student Body
  Undergrad enrollment: 30,912
  Women: 49%
  Men: 51%
  Percent out-of-state: 67%

Cost Information
  Tuition: $4,420
  Room and board: $7,310
Housing Information
  University housing: Yes
  Percent living on campus: 19%

Greek System
  Fraternity: No
  Sorority: No
Athletics: Division I

SOUTHERN UTAH UNIVERSITY

Southern Utah University, Admissions Off, 351 West Univeri, Cedar City, UT
Phone: 435-586-7740 • Fax: 435-865-8223
E-mail: adminfo@suu.edu • Web: www.suu.edu
Support: S • Institution: 4-year public

PROGRAMS OR SERVICES FOR STUDENTS WITH LD

The philosophy of the Office of Students with Disabilities is to promote self-sufficiency, achievement and support students with disabilities. OSD assists college students with developmental classes, skills courses, academic and tutorial support, and advisement. In particular, disabled students are encouraged and supported in advocating for themselves. The university provides a full variety of services and accommodations for all disabled students. The academic support coordinator assists students with enrollment in OSD and helps them identify academic areas where they feel a need to strengthen skills to assure college success.

ADMISSION INFORMATION FOR STUDENTS WITH LD/ADHD

College entrance tests required: Yes
Interview required: N/A
Essay required: N/A
What documentation required for LD: Psycho Ed evaluation to include: relevant historical info, instructional interventions, related services, age diagnosed, objective data (aptitude, achievement, info processing), test scores (standard, percentile and grade equivalents) and describe functional limitations.
With general application: No
To receive services after enrolling: Yes
What documentation required for ADHD: Diagnosis based on DSM-V; history of behaviors impairing functioning in academic setting; diagnostic interview; history of symptoms; evidence of ongoing behaviors.

With general application: No
Submitted to: Support Program/Services
Special Ed. HS course work accepted: No
Specific course requirements for all applicants: Yes
Separate application required for program services: No
# of LD applications submitted each year: NR
# of LD applications accepted yearly: NR
Total # of students receiving LD services: 94
Acceptance into program means acceptance into college: Students must be admitted to and enrolled in the university first and then request services.

ADMISSIONS

Students with learning disabilities submit the general application form. Students must have at least a 2.0 GPA and show competency in English, math, science, and social studies. The university uses an admissions index derived from the combination of the high school GPA and results of either the ACT or SAT. If students are not admissible through the regular process, special consideration by a Committee Review can be gained through reference letters and a personal letter. The university is allowed to admit 5 percent in "flex" admission. These applications are reviewed by a committee consisting of the Director of Support Services and representatives from the Admissions Office. Students are encouraged to self-disclose their learning disability and submit documentation.

ADDITIONAL INFORMATION

Students with disabilities are evaluated by the Office of Students with Disabilities to determine accommodations or services. The following accommodations or services may be available on a case-by-case basis for students with appropriate documentation: the use of calculators, dictionary, computer or spell checker in exams; extended testing time; scribes; proctors; oral exams; note-takers; distraction-free testing environments; tape recorders in class; books on tape; assistive technolgy; and priority registration. Tutoring is available in small groups or one-to-one, free of charge. Basic skills classes, for credit, are offered in English, reading, math, math anxiety, language, and study skills.

PROGRAM FOR DISABILITY SERVICES

Contact Information
Name of program or department: Office of Students with Disabilities
   Telephone: 435-865-8022
   Fax: 435-865-8235

LEARNING DISABILITY SERVICES

Accommodations are decided upon an individual basis after a thorough review of appropriate, current documentation. The accommodations requested must be supported through the documentation provided and must be logically linked to the current impact of the condition on academic functioning.

Allowed in exams
   Calculator: No
   Dictionary: Yes
   Computer: Yes
   Spellchecker: Yes
Extended test time: Yes
Scribes: Yes
Proctors: Yes
Oral exams: Yes
Note-takers: Yes

Distraction-reduced environment: Yes
Tape recording in class: Yes
Electronic texts: Yes
Accommodations for students with ADHD: Yes
Kurzweil Reader: Yes
Other assistive technology: We evaluate our students with disabilities population and depending who we serve and the need, we will make accommodations.
Priority registration: Yes

Added costs for services: No
LD specialists: No
Professional tutors: No
Peer tutors: No
Max. hours/wk. for services: N/A
How professors are notified of LD/ADHD: Both student and director, and by letter

GENERAL ADMISSIONS INFORMATION

Office of Admission: 435-586-7740

ENTRANCE REQUIREMENTS

Academic units recommended: 4 English, 3 mathematics, 3 science, (1 science labs), 2 foreign language, 3 social studies. High school diploma is required and GED is accepted. SAT or ACT required; TOEFL required of all international applicants; minimum paper TOEFL 500, minimum computer TOEFL 1.

Application deadline: 5/1 Fall; 12/1 Spring
Notification: Rolling
Average GPA: 3.0
ACT Composite middle 50% range: 18–25

SAT Math middle 50% range: NR
SAT Critical Reading middle 50% range: NR
SAT Writing middle 50% range: NR

Graduated top 10% of class: 26%
Graduated top 25% of class: 50.8%
Graduated top 50% of class: 80%

COLLEGE GRADUATION REQUIREMENTS

Course waivers allowed: No
Course substitutions allowed: No

ADDITIONAL INFORMATION

Environment: The university is in a small town 150 miles north of Las Vegas.

Student Body
   Undergrad enrollment: 8,024
   Women: 58%
   Men: 42%
   Percent out-of-state: 13%

Cost Information
   In-state tuition: $4,736
   Out-of-state tuition: $14,386
   Room & board: $9,247
Housing Information
   University housing: Yes
   Percent living on campus: 7%

Greek System
   Fraternity: Yes
   Sorority: Yes
Athletics: Division I

UNIVERSITY OF UTAH

201 South 1460 East, Room 250 S, Salt Lake City, UT 84112
Phone: 801-581-7281 • Fax: 801-585-7864
E-mail: admissions@sa.utah.edu • Web: www.utah.edu
Support: CS • Institution type: 4-year public

PROGRAMS OR SERVICES FOR STUDENTS WITH LD

The Center for Disability Services at the University of Utah provides accommodations and support for students with disabilities who have current physical or psychological documentation that qualifies them for services. The goal is to provide assistance to encourage and enhance student's independence, maintain ongoing cooperative efforts to develop and maintain an accessible physical environment, and provide educational efforts to create a supportive psychological environment for students to achieve their educational objectives. A cooperative relationship is maintained with relevant campus departments to ensure the University of Utah complies with federal and state regulations regarding students with disabilities.

ADMISSION INFORMATION FOR STUDENTS WITH LD/ADHD

College entrance tests required: Yes
Interview required: No
Essay recommended: No
What documentation required for LD: Psycho Ed evaluation to include: relevant historical info, instructional interventions, related services, age diagnosed, objective data (aptitude, achievement, info processing), test scores (standard, percentile and grade equivalents) and describe functional limitations.
With general application: No
To receive services after enrolling: Yes
What documentation required for ADHD: Diagnosis based on DSM-V; history of behaviors impairing functioning in academic setting; diagnostic interview; history of symptoms; evidence of ongoing behaviors.

With general application: No
Submitted to: Center for Disability Services
Special Ed. HS course work accepted: No
Specific course requirements of all applicants: Yes
Separate application required: No
# of LD applications submitted each year: NR
# of LD applications accepted yearly: NR
Total # of students receiving LD services: 300
Acceptance into program means acceptance into college: Students must be admitted to and enrolled in the university first and then request services.

ADMISSIONS

There is no special application process for students with learning disabilities. All applicants to the university must meet the general admission requirements. Students who do not meet the admission requirements as a direct result of their disability may be admitted on the condition that course deficiencies are filled prior to earning 30 semester hours at the university. Conditional admission is determined by the Center for Disability Services and the Admissions Office. Students must provide appropriate information regarding their disability and any services they received in high school due to their disability. Self-disclosure is recommended only if the student needs to inform the Admissions Office they are working with the Center for Disability Services to consider conditional admission. Otherwise disclosure is not recommended, but it is left to the student to make the decision.

ADDITIONAL INFORMATION

The University of Utah is committed to providing reasonable accommodations to students whose disabilities may limit their ability to function in the academic setting. To meet the needs of students and to make university activities, programs, and facilities accessible, the Center for Disability Services can provide the following services to students who provide documentation of a disability: assistance with admissions, registration, and graduation; orientation to the campus; referrals to campus and community services; guidelines for obtaining CDS services; general and academic advising related to disability; investigation of academic strengths and weaknesses; develop effective learning strategies; coordinate with academic and departmental advisors regarding program goals; coordinate reasonable accommodations of disability-related limitations with faculty and staff; liaison between student and faculty or staff; provide readers, scribes, note-takers, textbooks, and printed material recorded onto cassettes; and arrange for exam accommodations. The Center for Disability Services has the right to set procedures to determine whether the student qualifies for services and how the services will be implemented. Additionally, the center has the responsibility to adjust or substitute academic requirements that unfairly discriminate against the student with a disability and that are not essential to the integrity of a student's academic program. Students must provide appropriate documentation.

LEARNING DISABILITY PROGRAM OR SERVICES

Contact Information
Name of program or department: Center for Disability Services
 Telephone: 801-581-5020
 Fax: 801-581-5487

LEARNING DISABILITY SERVICES

Accommodations are decided upon an individual basis after a thorough review of appropriate, current documentation. The accommodations requested must be supported through the documentation provided and must be logically linked to the current impact of the condition on academic functioning.

Allowed in exams
 Calculator: No
 Dictionary: Yes
 Computer: Yes
 Spellchecker: Yes
Extended test time: Yes
Scribes: Yes
Proctors: Yes
Oral exams: Yes
Note-takers: Yes

Distraction-reduced environment: Yes
Tape recording in class: Yes
Electronic texts: Yes
Accommodations for students with
 ADHD: Yes
Kurzweil Reader: Yes
Other assistive technology: Yes
Priority registration: Yes

Added costs for services: No
LD specialists: Yes
Professional tutors: No
Peer tutors: 2
Max. hours/wk. for services: Varies
How professors are notified of
 LD/ADHD: By both student and
 director

GENERAL ADMISSIONS INFORMATION

Office of Admission: 801-581-6240

ENTRANCE REQUIREMENTS

Academic units required: 4 English, 2 math, 3 science (2 science labs), 2 foreign language, 1 history, 4 academic electives. High school diploma is required, and GED is accepted. ACT with or without Writing component accepted. TOEFL required of all international applicants: minimum paper TOEFL 500, minimum computer TOEFL 173.

Application deadline: 4/1
Notification: Rolling
Average GPA: 3.53
ACT Composite middle 50% range:
 21–27

SAT Math middle 50% range:
 513–650
SAT Critical Reading middle 50%
 range: 490–630
SAT Writing middle 50% range:
 490–610

Graduated top 10% of class: 21%
Graduated top 25% of class: 48%
Graduated top 50% of class: 80%

COLLEGE GRADUATION REQUIREMENTS

Course waivers allowed: Yes
In what course: Math requirement for general education for BS, and foreign language requirement for BA
Course substitutions allowed: Yes
In what course: Math and foreign language

ADDITIONAL INFORMATION

Environment: The university is located in Salt Lake City.

Student Body
 Undergrad enrollment: 24,297
 Women: 45%
 Men: 55%
 Percent out-of-state: 17%

Cost Information
 In-state tuition: $6,274
 Out-of-state tuition: $20,476
 Room & board: $6,699
Housing Information
 University housing: Yes
 Percent living on campus: 13%

Greek System
 Fraternity: Yes
 Sorority: Yes
Athletics: Division I

UTAH STATE UNIVERSITY

0160 Old Main Hill, Logan, UT 84322-0160
Phone: 435-797-1079 • Fax: 435-797-3708
E-mail: admit@usu.edu • Web: www.usu.edu
Support: CS • Institution: 4-year public

PROGRAMS OR SERVICES FOR STUDENTS WITH LD

The mission of the Disability Resource Center (DRC) is to provide qualified persons with disabilities equal access to University programs, services, and activities. This is accomplished by the provision of reasonable and appropriate accommodations and fostering an environment which supports the understanding and acceptance of persons with disabilities throughout the University community. The DRC works to individually tailor services to student's specific needs so they can reach their full educational potential.

ADMISSION INFORMATION FOR STUDENTS WITH LD/ADHD

College entrance tests required: Yes
Interview required: No
Essay required: N/A
What documentation required for LD: Psycho Ed evaluation to include: relevant historical info, instructional interventions, related services, age diagnosed, objective data (aptitude, achievement, info processing), test scores (standard, percentile and grade equivalents) and describe functional limitations.
With general application: No
To receive services after enrolling: Yes
What documentation required for ADHD: Diagnosis based on DSM-V; history of behaviors impairing functioning in academic setting; diagnostic interview; history of symptoms; evidence of ongoing behaviors.

With general application: No
Submitted to: Disability Resource Center
Special Ed. HS course work accepted: Yes
Specific course requirements for all applicants: Yes
Separate application required for program services: Yes
# of LD applications submitted each year: N/A
# of LD applications accepted yearly: N/A
Total # of students receiving LD services: 205 LD, 135 ADHD
Acceptance into program means acceptance into college: No, applications are completed independently of eachother

ADMISSIONS

All students must submit the regular application and meet the established admissions requirements. If they do not meet the minimum index score of 90 (usually a combination of at least a 2.5 GPA plus 18 ACT or 860 SAT) they may qualify for admission through the Regional Campus and Distance Education (RCDE) Program. Once the student completes 24 credits with a 2.5 GPA in the RCDE program, main campus classes will then be open to them. If a student does not meet the minimum requirements for either main campus or RCDE admission, they many still take classes through RCDE as a non-admitted student but financial aid will not be available.

ADDITIONAL INFORMATION

The Disability Resource Center provides the following services: registration assistance and priority registration, note-takers, textbooks in alternative formats, accommodations for exams, including extended time and distraction free rooms. Basic skills courses are offered to all students by the Academic Resource Center (ARC) in time management, learning strategies, reading, math, and study strategies. Tutoring in math and supplemental instruction for some classes are also offered free of charge to all students by the ARC. The DRC has developed an assistive technology lab with computers and adaptive equipment to promote independence in conducting research and completing class assignments.

PROGRAM FOR DISABILITY SERVICES

Contact Information
Name of program or department: Disability Resource Center (DRC)
  Telephone: 435-797-2444
  Fax: 435-797-0130

LEARNING DISABILITY SERVICES

Accommodations are decided upon an individual basis after a thorough review of appropriate, current documentation. The accommodations requested must be supported through the documentation provided and must be logically linked to the current impact of the condition on academic functioning.

Allowed in exams	**Distraction-reduced environment:** Yes	**Added costs for services:** No
Calculator: Depends upon level/course	**Tape recording in class:** Yes	**LD specialists:** Yes
Dictionary: Yes	**Electronic texts:** Yes	**Professional tutors:** No
Computer: Yes	**Accommodations for students with ADHD:** Yes	**Peer tutors:** Yes
Spellchecker: Yes	**Kurzweil Reader:** Yes	**Max. hours/wk. for services:** NR
Extended test time: Yes	**Other assistive technology:** Yes	**How professors are notified of LD/ADHD:** Counselor and/or student
Scribes: Yes	**Priority registration:** Yes	
Proctors: Yes		
Oral exams: Yes		
Note-takers: Yes		

GENERAL ADMISSIONS INFORMATION

Office of Admission: 435-797-1079

ENTRANCE REQUIREMENTS
Academic units required: High school diploma is required and GED is accepted. SAT or ACT required. TOEFL required of all international applicants, minimum paper TOEFL 500, minimum computer TOEFL 173. **Academic units recommended:** 2 foreign language, 4 English, 3 mathematics, 3 science, (1 science labs), 1 history, 4 academic electives.

Application deadline: 4/1 Fall; 10/1 Spring	**SAT Math middle 50% range:** 470–610	**Graduated top 10% of class:** 23.7%
Notification: Rolling	**SAT Critical Reading middle 50% range:** 470–600	**Graduated top 25% of class:** 49.4%
Average GPA: 3.54	**SAT Writing middle 50% range:** NR	**Graduated top 50% of class:** 82.2%
ACT Composite middle 50% range: 21–27		

COLLEGE GRADUATION REQUIREMENTS

Course waivers allowed: No
Course substitutions allowed: Yes
In what course: Case-by-case basis. Math substitution may be available depending upon requirements of major and/or licensure and proper documentation of a math disability.

ADDITIONAL INFORMATION

Environment: The university is located on 400 acres 81 miles north of Salt Lake City.

Student Body	**Cost Information**	**Greek System**
Undergrad enrollment: 16,000	**In-state tuition:** $7,343	**Fraternity:** Yes
Women: 54%	**Out-of-state tuition:** $21,500	**Sorority:** Yes
Men: 46%	**Room and board:** $5,070	**Athletics:** Division I
Percent out-of-state: 25%	**Housing Information**	
	University housing: Yes	
	Percent living on campus: 14%	

CHAMPLAIN COLLEGE

163 South Willard Street, PO Box 670, Burlington, VT 05402-0670
Phone: 802-860-2727 • Fax: 802-860-2767
E-mail: admission@champlain.edu • Web: www.champlain.edu
Support: S • Institution type: 4-year private

PROGRAMS OR SERVICES FOR STUDENTS WITH LD

Champlain College does not offer a special program for students with LD. Support services and academic accommodations are available when needed. Students with LD meet individually with a counselor at the start of the semester and are assisted in developing a plan of academic support. The counselor acts as liaison between the student and faculty. The College offers peer tutoring, writing assistance, accounting lab, math lab, and an oral communications lab. Mental health counseling is offered as is academic coaching. Students must provide documentation of the disability to the Office of Disability Services in the Counseling Department, which should include the most recent educational evaluation performed by a qualified individual, and a letter from any educational support service provider who has recently worked with the student would be most helpful. The letter should include information about the nature of the disability and the support services and/or program modifications provided.

ADMISSION INFORMATION FOR STUDENTS WITH LD/ADHD

College entrance tests required: Yes
Interview required: No
Essay recommended: Yes
What documentation required for LD: Psycho Ed evaluation to include: relevant historical info, instructional interventions, related services, age diagnosed, objective data (aptitude, achievement, info processing), test scores (standard, percentile and grade equivalents) and describe functional limitations.
With general application: No
To receive services after enrolling: Yes
What documentation required for ADHD: Diagnosis based on DSM-V; history of behaviors impairing functioning in academic setting; diagnostic interview; history of symptoms; evidence of ongoing behaviors.

With general application: No
Submitted to: Counseling Department
Special Ed. HS course work accepted: Yes
Specific course requirements of all applicants: Yes
Separate application required: No
# of LD applications submitted each year: NR
# of LD applications accepted yearly: NR
Total # of students receiving LD services: 200
Acceptance into program means acceptance into college: Students must be admitted to and enrolled in the university first and then request services.

ADMISSIONS

There is no special admissions procedure for students with LD. The admissions process is fairly competitive. The most important part of the application is the high school transcript. Upward grade trend and challenging course work are looked on favorably. Recommendations and college essay are required. Students are also required to take either the SAT or the ACT. Students may elect to self-disclose the LD during the admissions process, and the college will take this information into consideration when making admission decisions. The average ACT for applicants is a 24, and the average SAT for applicants is a 1650. The average GPA of an admitted student is a 3.3.

ADDITIONAL INFORMATION

Students with learning disabilities who self-disclose receive a special needs form after they have enrolled in college courses from the Counseling Department. The coordinator meets with each student during the first week of school. The first appointment includes a discussion about the student's disability and the academic accommodations that will be needed. Accommodations could include, but are not limited to, tutoring, extended time for tests, readers for tests, use of computers during exams, peer note-takers, tape recording lectures, and books on tape. With the student's permission, faculty members receive a letter discussing appropriate accommodations. The coordinators will continue to act as a liaison between students and faculty, consult with tutors, monitor students' academic progress, and consult with faculty as needed.

LEARNING DISABILITY PROGRAM OR SERVICES

Contact Information
Name of program or department: Support Services for Students with Disabilities
 Telephone: 802-865-6426
 Fax: 802-860-2764

LEARNING DISABILITY SERVICES

Accommodations are decided upon an individual basis after a thorough review of appropriate, current documentation. The accommodations requested must be supported through the documentation provided and must be logically linked to the current impact of the condition on academic functioning.

Allowed in exams
 Calculator: Yes
 Dictionary: Yes
 Computer: Yes
 Spellchecker: Yes
Extended test time: Yes
Scribes: Yes
Proctors: Yes
Oral exams: Yes
Note-takers: Yes

Distraction-reduced environment: Yes
Tape recording in class: Yes
Electronic texts: Yes
Accommodations for students with
 ADHD: Yes
Kurzweil Reader: Yes
Other assistive technology: Yes
Priority registration: No

Added costs for services: No
LD specialists: No
Professional tutors: Yes
Peer tutors: 30
Max. hours/wk. for services: N/A
How professors are notified of
 LD/ADHD: By student with a letter generated by the Disabilities Services Office

GENERAL ADMISSIONS INFORMATION

Office of Admission: 802-860-2727

ENTRANCE REQUIREMENTS

Academic units required: 4 English, 3 math, 3 science (2 science labs), 4 history, 2 foreign language. **Academic units recommended:** 4 math, 4 science (3 science labs), 2 foreign language, 2 social studies. High school diploma is required, and GED is accepted. ACT with or without Writing component accepted. TOEFL required of all international applicants: minimum paper TOEFL 550 or 173 with a minimum essay score of 4. ELPT: 950, IELTS: 5.

Application deadline: 11/15, 1/15, 2/1
Notification: 12/15, 2/15, 3/15
Average GPA: 3.3
ACT Composite middle 50% range: 23–27

SAT Math middle 50% range: NR
SAT Critical Reading middle 50% range: NR
SAT Writing middle 50% range: NR

Graduated top 10% of class: NR
Graduated top 25% of class: NR
Graduated top 50% of class: NR

COLLEGE GRADUATION REQUIREMENTS

Course waivers allowed: No
Course substitutions allowed: No

ADDITIONAL INFORMATION

Environment: The college is located on 16 acres in a small city surrounded by rural area mountains and Lake Champlain.

Student Body
 Undergrad enrollment: 2,067
 Women: 43%
 Men: 57%
 Percent out-of-state: 70%

Cost Information
 Tuition: $28,350
 Room & board: $12,620
Housing Information
 University housing: Yes
 Percent living on campus: 40%

Greek System
 Fraternity: No
 Sorority: No
 Athletics: Intramural

GREEN MOUNTAIN COLLEGE

One College Circle, Poultney, VT 05764-1199
Phone: 802-287-8000 • Fax: 802-287-8099
E-mail: admiss@greenmtn.edu • Web: www.greenmtn.edu
Support: CS • Institution type: 4-year private

PROGRAMS OR SERVICES FOR STUDENTS WITH LD

Green Mountain College provides accommodations for students with documented learning differences. The college believes that every student has the potential for academic success and strives to support students while teaching them independence and self-advocacy skills. The Calhoun Learning Center (CLC) functions as the primary source of information regarding academic issues relating to disabilities. Students seeking academic accommodations must self-identify and submit valid documentation of their learning needs. The CLC staff determines which students are eligible for academic accommodations and works with the student and staff to develop and implement an accommodation plan that will allow the student an opportunity to succeed at college. The CLC has six main functions: to provide academic support, primarily through one-on-one, small group, general content area tutoring; to serve as the campus Writing Center; to support courses specifically designed for underprepared students; to provide support for foreign students; to be the campus center for academic issues relating to disabilities; and to provide workshops and seminars and events with the goal of improving learning skills.

ADMISSION INFORMATION FOR STUDENTS WITH LD/ADHD

College entrance tests required: Yes
Interview required: No
Essay recommended: Yes
What documentation required for LD: Psycho Ed evaluation to include: relevant historical info, instructional interventions, related services, age diagnosed, objective data (aptitude, achievement, info processing), test scores (standard, percentile and grade equivalents) and describe functional limitations.
With general application: No
To receive services after enrolling: Yes
What documentation required for ADHD: Diagnosis based on DSM-V; history of behaviors impairing functioning in academic setting; diagnostic interview; history of symptoms; evidence of ongoing behaviors.

With general application: No
Submitted to: Support Program/Services
Special Ed. HS course work accepted: Yes
Specific course requirements of all applicants: Yes
Separate application required: No
# of LD applications submitted each year: NR
# of LD applications accepted yearly: NR
Total # of students receiving LD services: 70
Acceptance into program means acceptance into college: Students must be admitted and enrolled at the college and then reviewed for LC services.

ADMISSIONS

There is no special admissions process for students with learning disabilities. Students face the same admission criteria, which include: ACT score of 19 or SAT score of 900; 2.0 GPA; 4 years of English, 2–3 years of history/social studies, 2 years of science (with lab), 3 years of math, and 2 years of a foreign language. All applications are carefully considered with the best interest of both the student and the college in mind.

ADDITIONAL INFORMATION

The Learning Center provides support services to all students which include: academic counseling for students on an individual basis and, when appropriate, making referrals to related college departments; offering and facilitating group sessions for students experiencing similar academic concerns; coordinating the delivery of services for students with disabilities that impact academic performance including responding to requests for reasonable and appropriate accommodations; conducting educational workshops designed to facilitate the mastery of study strategies and learning skills and to improve overall academic performance; coordinating the college tutorial program in consultation with individual academic departments; and collaborating with existing college components. The tutoring program uses a three-tiered approach: a drop-in clinic for immediate but temporary academic assistance; individually scheduled tutoring; or a more extensive schedule of one, two, or three tutoring sessions per week for tutorial help throughout a course. All new students take placement tests to assess their achievement in mathematics. Students underprepared in math are advised to take Intro to College Math and tutoring is available.

LEARNING DISABILITY PROGRAM/SERVICES

Contact Information
Name of program or department: The Calhoun Learning Center (CLC)
 Telephone: 802-287-8287
 Fax: 802-287-8288

LEARNING DISABILITY SERVICES

Accommodations are decided upon an individual basis after a thorough review of appropriate, current documentation. The accommodations requested must be supported through the documentation provided and must be logically linked to the current impact of the condition on academic functioning.

Allowed in exams	**Distraction-reduced environment:** Yes	**Added costs for services:** No
Calculator: Yes	**Tape recording in class:** Yes	**LD specialists:** 1
Dictionary: Yes	**Electronic texts:** Yes	**Professional tutors:** 0
Computer: Yes	**Accommodations for students with**	**Peer tutors:** 18–20
Spellchecker: Yes	**ADHD:** Yes	**Max. hours/wk. for services:**
Extended test time: Yes	**Kurzweil Reader:** Yes	Unlimited
Scribes: Yes	**Other assistive technology:** Yes	**How professors are notified of**
Proctors: Yes	**Priority registration:** Yes	**LD/ADHD:** By both student and CLC
Oral exams: Yes		staff
Notetakers: Yes		

GENERAL ADMISSIONS INFORMATION

Office of Admission: 802-287-8207

ENTRANCE REQUIREMENTS

Academic units required: 4 English, 3 math, 3 science (2 science labs), 2 foreign language, 3 social studies, 1 history, 5 academic electives. Academic units recomended: 4 math, 4 science, 3 foreign language, 3 social studies, 2 history. High school diploma is required, and GED is accepted. ACT with or without Writing component accepted. TOEFL required of all international applicants: minimum paper TOEFL 500, minimum computer TOEFL 173.

Application deadline: None	**SAT Math middle 50% range:** NR	**Graduated top 10% of class:** NR
Notification: Rolling	**SAT Critical Reading middle 50%**	**Graduated top 25% of class:** NR
Average GPA: NR	**range:** NR	**Graduated top 50% of class:** NR
ACT Composite middle 50% range:	**SAT Writing middle 50% range:**	
NR	NR	

COLLEGE GRADUATION REQUIREMENTS

Course waivers allowed: No
Course substitutions allowed: By petition only

ADDITIONAL INFORMATION

Environment: The campus is in a small town near Rutland.

Student Body	**Cost Information**	**Greek System**
Undergrad enrollment: 710	**Tuition:** $29,316	**Fraternity:** No
Women: 52%	**Room & board:** $10,640	**Sorority:** No
Men: 48%	**Housing Information**	**Athletics:** Division III
Percent out-of-state: 89%	**University housing:** Yes	
	Percent living on campus: 82%	

JOHNSON STATE COLLEGE

337 College Hill, Johnson, VT 05656-9408
Phone: 802-635-1219 • Fax: 802-635-1230
E-mail: jscadmissions@jsc.edu • Web: www.jsc.edu
Support: CS • Institution: 4-year public

PROGRAMS OR SERVICES FOR STUDENTS WITH LD

Johnson State College provides services to students with disabilities through the Learning Specialist at the Academic Support Service Program. The fundamental purpose is to provide students with the appropriate services necessary to allow access to Johnson State College academic programs. Students with disabilities are integrated fully into the college community. In addition, students with disabilities may also be eligible for the TRiO program, which provides additional supports and services through the Learning Resource Center. The Learning Resource Center provides a friendly and supportive environment for any student who is academically struggling or underprepared to meet his or her educational goals. Services may include group and peer tutoring; professional tutoring in writing and math; and supplemental instruction in time management, study skills, organizational skills, and professional mentoring.

ADMISSION INFORMATION FOR STUDENTS WITH LD/ADHD

College entrance tests required: Yes
Interview required: No
Essay required: Yes
Documentation required for LD: Follow AHEAD Guidelines—cognitive measurement WAIS–R and achievement tests within three years. Additional testing for specific LD is recommended (e.g. Denny Reading Test) although not required. Documentation must include diagnostic information, test scores and interpretation, and functional impact of disability on major life activities. Guidelines for documenting LD can be found at http://www.jsc.edu/Academics/Academic Support/StudentsWithDisabilities.aspx.
Documentation required for ADHD: Follow ETS Guidelines for ADD documentation and forms to be completed by school personnel and diagnosing physician. Guidelines for documenting ADD can be found at http://www.jsc.edu/Academics/AcademicSupport/StudentsWithDisabilities.aspx.

Submitted to: Support Program/Services
Special Ed. HS course work accepted: N/A
Specific course requirements for all applicants: Yes
Separate application required for program services: No
# of LD applications submitted each year: NR
# of LD applications accepted yearly: NR
Total # of students receiving LD services: 50+
Acceptance into program means acceptance into college: Students must be admitted to and enrolled in the university first and then request services.

ADMISSIONS

Students with disabilities who demonstrate the academic ability to be successful at the post-secondary level are eligible for acceptance. Applicants with a disability are encouraged to contact the Admissions Office so that accommodations can be made available, where appropriate, throughout the admission process. Course requirements include four years of English, three years of college preparatory mathematics, three years of social sciences, and two years of science (one course with a lab).

ADDITIONAL INFORMATION

Academic Support Services provides tutoring, academic advising, personal counseling and mentoring, career exploration, college survival skills workshops, and assistance with establishing appropriate and reasonable accommodations. Students should be self-advocates and are responsible for notifying instructors to arrange for providing the approved accommodations.

PROGRAM FOR DISABILITY SERVICES

Contact Information
Name of program or department: Academic Support Services
  Telephone: 802-635-1259
  Fax: 802-635-1454

LEARNING DISABILITY SERVICES

Accommodations are determined on an individual basis after a thorough review of appropriate, current documentation. Accommodations must be substantiated by the documentation and must be logically linked to the current impact of the specific diagnosis(es) on academic functioning.

Allowed in exams
  Calculator: Yes
  Dictionary: Yes
  Computer: Yes
  Spellchecker: Yes
Extended test time: Yes
Scribes: Yes
Proctors: Yes
Oral exams: No
Note-takers: Yes

Distraction-reduced environment: Yes
Tape recording in class: Yes
Electronic texts: Yes
Accommodations for students with ADHD: Yes
Kurzweil Reader: Yes
Other assistive technology: Kurzweil 3000, Inspiration Mapping Software, Dragon Naturally-Speaking Text Help, Read and Write Gold, digital recorders, Victor Vibe, Smart Pen
Priority registration: No

Added costs for services: No
LD specialists: Yes
Professional tutors: 4–5
Peer tutors: 10–15
Max. hours/wk. for services: Unlimited
How professors are notified of LD/ADHD: Student

GENERAL ADMISSIONS INFORMATION

Office of Admission: 1-800-635-2536 or 802-635-1219

ENTRANCE REQUIREMENTS
Academic units required: 4 English, 2 mathematics, 2 science, (1 science lab), 0 foreign language, 3 social science.
Academic units recommended: 4 English, 3 mathematics, 3 science, (2 science labs), 1 foreign language, 3 social studies, 3 history. High school diploma is required and GED is accepted. SAT or ACT required; ACT with Writing component required. TOEFL required of all international applicants; minimum paper TOEFL 500, minimum web-based TOEFL 61.

Application deadline: None
Notification: Rolling
Average GPA: NR
ACT Composite middle 50% range: 20–28

SAT Math middle 50% range: 430–550
SAT Critical Reading middle 50% range: 430–550
SAT Writing middle 50% range: NR

Graduated top 10% of class: 34%
Graduated top 25% of class: 66%
Graduated top 50% of class: 68%

COLLEGE GRADUATION REQUIREMENTS

Course substitutions allowed: Yes
In what course: Lower math may be substituted for one of the two math requirements if there is a math LD only.

ADDITIONAL INFORMATION

Environment: The college is located in a rural area 45 miles northeast of Burlington.

Student Body
  Undergrad enrollment: 1,691
  Women: 59%
  Men: 41%
  Percent out-of-state: 28%

Cost Information
  In-state tuition: $8,568
  Out-of-state tuition: $19,008
  Room and board: $8,500
Housing Information
  University housing: Yes
  Percent living on campus: 38%

Greek System
  Fraternity: No
  Sorority: No
Athletics: Division III

LANDMARK COLLEGE

PO Box 820, Putney, VT 05346-0820
Phone: 802-387-6718 • Fax: 802-387-6868
E-mail: admissions@landmark.edu • Web: www.landmark.edu
Support: SP • Institution type: 2-year and 4-year private

PROGRAMS OR SERVICES FOR STUDENTS WITH LD

Landmark College is designed exclusively for high-potential students with dyslexia, specific learning disabilities, and/or ADHD. It is the first accredited college in the nation for students with LD/ADHD or ASD. More than 100 members of the faculty and professional staff devote their entire attention to providing the finest possible program for these students. The goal is to prepare students to enter or return to college. At Landmark, students do not bypass difficulties by using note-takers, taped books, or taking exams orally. Students must do their own work, and Landmark teaches them how. Landmark's approach is unique and includes very small classes, structured assignments, and an emphasis on constantly improving language and study skills. Coaching Services provides a specific and unique type of support. They are designed for students who struggle with the various aspects of academic work production known as "executive functioning." These include planning and prioritizing, organizing, remembering to do intended tasks, getting started, sustaining motivation, self-monitoring, managing multiple tasks, and following through to completion.

ADMISSION INFORMATION FOR STUDENTS WITH LD/ADHD

College entrance tests required: No
Interview required: Yes
Essay recommended: Yes
What documentation required for LD: Psycho Ed evaluation to include: relevant historical info, instructional interventions, related services, age diagnosed, objective data (aptitude, achievement, info processing), test scores (standard, percentile and grade equivalents) and describe functional limitations.
With general application: Yes if requested as part of Structured Program application
To receive services after enrolling: Yes
What documentation required for ADHD: Diagnosis based on DSM-V; history of behaviors impairing functioning in academic setting; diagnostic interview; history of symptoms; evidence of ongoing behaviors.

With general application: Yes if requested as part of Structured Program application
To receive services after enrolling: Yes
Submitted to: Admissions
Special Ed. HS course work accepted: Yes
Specific course requirements of all applicants: NR
Separate application required: No
# of LD applications submitted each year: 800
# of LD applications accepted yearly: 500
Total # of students receiving LD services: all enrolled students
Acceptance into program means acceptance into college: The program and the college are one and the same.

ADMISSIONS

Landmark College serves students whose academic skills have not been developed to a level equal to their intellectual capacity. Students must have average to superior intellectual potential; diagnosis of dyslexia, specific LD, ADHD or ASD; and high motivation. Applicants must have a willingness to undertake a rigorous academic program that does not provide bypass methods such as note-takers, books on tape, or oral exams. Focus instead is on individualized, intensive development and honing of academic skills. Qualified students must have a testing session and interview. An admission decision is made at this time. ACT/SAT are not required. There are no specific course requirements for admission, but students must take courses that lead to a high school diploma or the GED. Students may apply for admission for summer, fall, or spring semesters.

ADDITIONAL INFORMATION

Landmark College offers three summer programs: The High School Summer Program for rising juniors and seniors, the Transitions to College Program for first-time college freshman and the Summer Session for Visiting College Students. Students can get help with writing, reading, study skills, and understanding their own learning styles. Skills classes are offered to students on campus in study skills, math, written language, oral language, and content courses. In addition to the types of services found at typical institutions of higher learning, we have services that support any additional needs, due to learning disabilities or ADHD or ASD. Students can access support for skills development, coaching, class support, academic planning, advising, understanding their learning profile, and planning for future academic or professional goals. Typically, students work with your academic advisors to develop a plan. This determines which services students will access at any given time throughout the pursuit of their degree. All of these services are staffed by professional faculty and staff members.

LEARNING DISABILITY PROGRAM OR SERVICES

Contact Information
Name of program or department: Landmark College
 Telephone: 802-387-6718
 Fax: 802-387-6868

LEARNING DISABILITY SERVICES

Accommodations are decided upon an individual basis after a thorough review of appropriate, current documentation. The accommodations requested must be supported through the documentation provided and must be logically linked to the current impact of the condition on academic functioning.

Allowed in exams
 Calculator: Yes
 Dictionary: Yes
 Computer: Yes
 Spellchecker: Yes
Extended test time: Yes
Scribes: No
Proctors: No
Oral exams: Yes
Note-takers: No

Distraction-reduced environment: Yes
Tape recording in class: Yes
Electronic texts: Yes
Accommodations for students with ADHD: Yes
Kurzweil Reader: Yes
Other assistive technology: Yes
Priority registration: No

Added costs for services: No
LD specialists: Yes
Professional tutors: 20
Peer tutors: No
Max. hours/wk. for services: Unlimited
How professors are notified of LD/ADHD: N/A

GENERAL ADMISSIONS INFORMATION

Office of Admission: 802-387-6718

ENTRANCE REQUIREMENTS

High school diploma is required, and GED is accepted. TOEFL required of all international applicants: minimum paper TOEFL 550, minimum computer TOEFL 213, internet 79.

Application deadline: None
Notification: Rolling
Average GPA: NR
ACT Composite middle 50% range: NR

SAT Math middle 50% range: NR
SAT Critical Reading middle 50% range: NR
SAT Writing middle 50% range: NR

Graduated top 10% of class: NR
Graduated top 25% of class: NR
Graduated top 50% of class: NR

COLLEGE GRADUATION REQUIREMENTS

Course waivers allowed: No
Course substitutions allowed: No

ADDITIONAL INFORMATION

Environment: The college is located on 125 acres overlooking the Connecticut River Valley hills of Vermont and New Hampshire.

Student Body
 Undergrad enrollment: 488
 Women: 35%
 Men: 65%
 Percent out-of-state: 95%

Cost Information
 Tuition: $48,210
 Room & board: $8,620
Housing Information
 University housing: Yes
 Percent living on campus: 98%

Greek System
 Fraternity: No
 Sorority: No
 Athletics: No

NEW ENGLAND CULINARY INSTITUTE

56 College Street, Montpelier, VT 05602
Phone: 877-223-6324 • Fax: 802-225-3280
E-mail: admissions@neci.edu • Web: www.neci.edu
Support: CS • Institution type: 2- and 4-year private

PROGRAMS OR SERVICES FOR STUDENTS WITH LD

The New England Culinary Institute provides educational programs in the culinary arts, food and beverage management, basic cooking, and related areas that prepare students for employment and advancement in the hospitality industry. Students with LD/ADHD have found success at the institute, as the focus on hands-on learning and non-traditional academic curriculum often engage students who otherwise may dislike classroom learning environments. The AOS and BA programs available at NECI have an academic component in addition to the hands-on work, both of which require comprehension and retention of a great deal of new information. A strong work ethic and previous experience in the food industry are often precursors to a successful, meaningful learning experience. The Learning Services department coordinates support and accommodation services to all students, with a direct response from the Learning Services Coordinator available within 24 hours in most instances. The goal of the Learning Services Office is to provide support to maximize learning.

ADMISSION INFORMATION FOR STUDENTS WITH LD/ADHD

College entrance tests required: No
Interview required: No
Essay recommended: Required
What documentation required for LD: Psycho Ed evaluation to include: relevant historical info, instructional interventions, related services, age diagnosed, objective data (aptitude, achievement, info processing), test scores (standard, percentile and grade equivalents) and describe functional limitations.
With general application: No
To receive services after enrolling: Yes
What documentation required for ADHD: Diagnosis based on DSM-V; history of behaviors impairing functioning in academic setting; diagnostic interview; history of symptoms; evidence of ongoing behaviors.

With general application: No
Submitted to: Learning Services Coordinator
Special Ed. HS course work accepted: Yes
Specific course requirements of all applicants: NR
Separate application required: No
# of LD applications submitted each year: N/A
# of LD applications accepted yearly: N/A
Total # of students receiving LD services: Approximately 20–30 percent of active enrollment
Acceptance into program means acceptance into college: Students must be admitted to and enrolled at NECI prior to requesting services.

ADMISSIONS
There is no special admission process for students with LD/ADHD. General admissions information is available at the NECI website, at http://www.neci.edu. Applicants with LD/ADHD with appropriate documentation will be eligible to access accommodations upon acceptance into a program.

ADDITIONAL INFORMATION
Students with LD/ADHD requesting accommodations must provide appropriate documentation and meet with the Learning Services Coordinator to help determine appropriate supports. Upon receiving appropriate documentation, the Learning Services Coordinator will meet with the student to review requested accommodations, suggest any supports/accommodations that the student may find helpful, and collaboratively develop a plan of support that helps ensure the student's needs are met. Accommodations such as verbally proctored exams, untimed exams, alternate (non-classroom) testing locations, use of a dictionary during non-vocabulary tests, note-taking, individualized tutoring, use of calculators and computers, tape-recording of lectures, and paper writing assistance can be accessed through the Learning Services Department. These services also include one-on-one tutoring, small-group workshops, review sessions, opportunities to retake tests, computers, software to help with writing papers, reference books, and a quiet study/work space.

LEARNING DISABILITY PROGRAM OR SERVICES

Contact Information
Name of program or department: Learning Services Coordinator
  Telephone: 802-225-3327
  Fax: 802-225-3375

LEARNING DISABILITY SERVICES

Accommodations are determined on an individual basis after a thorough review of appropriate, current documentation. The accommodations requested must be supported through the documentation provided and must be logically linked to the current impact of the condition on academic functioning.

Allowed in exams
  Calculator: Yes
  Dictionary: Yes
  Computer: Yes
  Spellchecker: Yes
Extended test time: Yes
Scribes: Yes
Proctors: Yes
Oral exams: Yes
Note-takers: Yes

Distraction-reduced environment: Yes
Tape recording in class: Yes
Electronic texts: Yes
Accommodations for students with ADHD: Yes
Kurzweil Reader: No
Other assistive technology: Yes
Priority registration: No

Added costs for services: No
LD specialists: Yes
Professional tutors: Yes
Peer tutors: 10–25
Max. hours/wk. for services: Unlimited
How professors are notified of LD/ADHD: By both student and coordinator

GENERAL ADMISSIONS INFORMATION

Office of Admission: 877-223-6324

ENTRANCE REQUIREMENTS

Completed online or paper application, a high school diploma or GED, admissions interview, online Learning Readiness Survey, admissions essay, NECI Signature Page.

Application deadline: 1/1, 4/1, 7/1, 10/1
Notification: Rolling
Average GPA: NR
ACT Composite middle 50% range: NR

SAT Math middle 50% range: NR
SAT Critical Reading middle 50% range: NR
SAT Writing middle 50% range: NR

Graduated top 10% of class: NR
Graduated top 25% of class: NR
Graduated top 50% of class: NR

COLLEGE GRADUATION REQUIREMENTS

Course waivers allowed: No
Course substitutions allowed: If applicable
In what course: In applicable situations, to be determined upon review

ADDITIONAL INFORMATION

Environment: The institute is located in the city of Montpelier, 40 miles from Burlington.

Student Body
  Undergrad enrollment: 542
  Women: 37%
  Men: 63%
  Percent out-of-state: 76%

Cost Information
  Tuition: varies depending on program
  Room & board: varies depending on program
Housing Information
  University housing: Yes
  Percent living on campus: 67%

Greek System
  Fraternity: No
  Sorority: No
Athletics: Intramural

NORWICH UNIVERSITY

Admissions Office, 27 ID White Avenue, Northfield, VT 05663
Phone: 802-485-2001 • Fax: 802-485-2032
E-mail: nuadm@norwich.edu • Web: www.norwich.edu
Support: CS • Institution type: 4-year private

PROGRAMS OR SERVICES FOR STUDENTS WITH LD

The Academic Achievement Center (AAC) offers comprehensive support services in all areas of academic life. While Norwich does not have a formal program for students with learning disabilities, the university does offer support services on a voluntary basis. Students are instructed by the center staff in a wide range of study and college survival skills. The center's staff work closely with advisors and faculty members and are strong advocates for students with learning disabilities. The university stresses autonomy by providing a level of support that assists students with becoming responsible, thinking adults who are well acquainted with their own needs and able to articulate them. Services are provided by a staff of professionals that includes LD specialists, study skills/writing specialists, and a basic math specialist. The professional staff is supplemented by a trained, well-supervised student tutorial staff.

ADMISSION INFORMATION FOR STUDENTS WITH LD/ADHD

College entrance tests required: Yes
Interview required: No
Essay recommended: No
What documentation required for LD: Psycho Ed evaluation to
include: relevant historical info, instructional interventions,
related services, age diagnosed, objective data (aptitude,
achievement, info processing), test scores (standard, percentile
and grade equivalents) and describe functional limitations.
With general application: No
To receive services after enrolling: Yes
What documentation required for ADHD: Diagnosis based
on DSM-V; history of behaviors impairing functioning in
academic setting; diagnostic interview; history of symptoms;
evidence of ongoing behaviors.

With general application: No
Submitted to: Academic Achievement Center
Special Ed. HS course work accepted: No
Specific course requirements of all applicants: Yes
Separate application required: No
# of LD applications submitted each year: NR
# of LD applications accepted yearly: NR
Total # of students receiving LD services: NR
**Acceptance into program means acceptance into
college:** Students must be admitted to and enrolled in the
university first and then request services.

ADMISSIONS
Students with learning disabilities submit a general application. Admission criteria include high school GPA of a C or better; an SAT score of 850 or equivalent ACT; participation in activities; and strong college recommendations from teachers, counselors, or coaches. There are no course waivers for admission. The university is flexible on ACT/SAT test scores. If grades and other indicators are problematic is recommended that students provide detailed information to give a better understanding the disability. A complete psychodiagnostic evaluation is required. A small number of students who do not meet the general admission requirements may be admitted if they show promise. An interview is highly recommended. There are limited provisional admission slots.

ADDITIONAL INFORMATION
A telephone conversation or personal meeting with the LSC support personnel is encouraged prior to the start of college, so that work can begin immediately on preparing an individualized program. Students are responsible for meeting with each professor to discuss accommodations. Services begin with Freshman Placement Testing designed to assess each individual's level of readiness for college-level math. Other services include course advising with an assigned academic advisor and advocacy for academic petitions. Services and accommodations are available for undergraduate and graduate students.

LEARNING DISABILITY PROGRAM OR SERVICES

Contact Information
Name of program or department: Academic Achievement Center (AAC)
Telephone: 802-485-2130
Fax: 802-485-2684

LEARNING DISABILITY SERVICES

Accommodations are decided upon an individual basis after a thorough review of appropriate, current documentation. The accommodations requested must be supported through the documentation provided and must be logically linked to the current impact of the condition on academic functioning.

Allowed in exams	**Distraction-reduced environment:** Yes	**Added costs for services:** No
Calculator: Yes	**Tape recording in class:** Yes	**LD specialists:** Yes
Dictionary: Yes	**Electronic texts:** No	**Professional tutors:** 9
Computer: Yes	**Accommodations for students with**	**Peer tutors:** 30
Spellchecker: Yes	**ADHD:** Yes	**Max. hours/wk. for services:** N/A
Extended test time: Yes	**Kurzweil Reader:** No	**How professors are notified of**
Scribes: Yes	**Other assistive technology:** Yes	**LD/ADHD:** By both student and
Proctors: Yes	**Priority registration:** Limited	director
Oral exams: Yes		
Note-takers: No		

GENERAL ADMISSIONS INFORMATION

Office of Admission: 802-485-2001

ENTRANCE REQUIREMENTS

Academic units required: 4 English, 3 math, 2 science (2 science labs). **Academic units recommended:** 4 English, 4 math, 3 science (2 science labs), 2 foreign language. High school diploma is required, and GED is accepted. TOEFL required of all international applicants: minimum paper TOEFL 500, minimum computer TOEFL 1.

Application deadline: None	**SAT Math middle 50% range:**	**Graduated top 10% of class:** 11%
Notification: Rolling	500–640	**Graduated top 25% of class:** 37%
Average GPA: 3.12	**SAT Critical Reading middle 50%**	**Graduated top 50% of class:** 74%
ACT Composite middle 50% range:	range: 480–580	
21–26	**SAT Writing middle 50% range:**	
	460–620	

COLLEGE GRADUATION REQUIREMENTS

Course waivers allowed: No
Course substitutions allowed: Yes
In what course: Foreign language, only with proof of inability to successfully function and after having gone through a lengthy petition process.

ADDITIONAL INFORMATION

Environment: Two campuses in Northfield (traditional) and Montpelier (low residency), 50 miles southeast of Burlington.

Student Body	**Cost Information**	**Greek System**
Undergrad enrollment: 2,246	**Tuition:** $30,048	**Fraternity:** No
Women: 28%	**Room & board:** $10,976	**Sorority:** No
Men: 72%	**Housing Information**	**Athletics:** Division III
Percent out-of-state: 84%	**University housing:** Yes	
	Percent living on campus: 82%	

UNIVERSITY OF VERMONT

Admissions Office, 194 South Prospect Street, Burlington, VT 05401-3596
Phone: 802-656-3370 • Fax: 802-656-8611
E-mail: admissions@uvm.edu • Web: www.uvm.edu
Support: CS • Institution type: 4-year public

PROGRAMS OR SERVICES FOR STUDENTS WITH LD

Part of the Department of Academic Support Programs, ACCESS provides students with LD/ADD a comprehensive program. Each student is assigned to a Specialist who is a liaison to one or more schools/colleges within the University. Initially, a comprehensive assessment is completed to determine eligibility then identify students' strengths and recommended accommodations in relation to their diagnosis. This information is used to set up accommodations deemed reasonable and appropriate, as well as, foster techniques and strategies that enable successful academics. Advising involves the student's academic advisor, dean's office and their Specialist at ACCESS. The student works with these resources to review their tentative schedule balancing types of course work, course load, teaching methods and formats. ACCESS ensures they are aware of valuable campus resources such as The Learning Cooperative which offers many types of tutoring – individual/group, subject area, assistance with reading, writing, study skills, organization and time management strategies. ACCESS is an individualized educational support service program designed to equalize academic opportunities for students with disabilities.

ADMISSION INFORMATION FOR STUDENTS WITH LD/ADHD

College entrance tests required: Yes
Interview required: No
Essay recommended: No
What documentation required for LD: See
  www.uvm.edu/access/?page=docuguidelines.html
With general application: No
To receive services after enrolling: Yes
What documentation required for ADHD: See
  www.uvm.edu/access/?page=docuguidelines.html
With general application: No
Submitted to: ACCESS

Special Ed. HS course work accepted: Yes
Specific course requirements of all applicants: Yes
Separate application required: No
# of LD applications submitted each year: NR
# of LD applications accepted yearly: NR
Total # of students receiving LD services: NR
Acceptance into program means acceptance into college: Students must be admitted to and enrolled in the university first and then request services.

ADMISSIONS

Students submit a common application to admissions. Documentation of a student's disability is sent directly to ACCESS. Students are encouraged to voluntarily provide documentation of their disability. ACCESS reviews documentation and may consult with Admissions if/when necessary as to how a student's disability has affected their academic record. Upon request, if time and resources allow, students may request a review of their documentation to assess for eligibility and/or entrance requirements if they feel their disability has impacted them in such a way that they are missing a requirement such as Foreign Language. Students with LD/ADHD should submit a current educational evaluation that includes a comprehensive measure of both cognitive and achievement functioning. Course requirements include 4 years English, 3 years Social Science, 3 years Math, 2 years Physical Sciences and 2 years Foreign Language. Self-disclosing in the application is a matter of personal choice. At UVM, disclosing a disability will absolutely not have a negative impact on a student's admissibility.

ADDITIONAL INFORMATION

UVM provides a multidisciplinary program for students with LD /ADHD emphasizing development of advocacy and reasonable and appropriate use of academic accommodations including: note-taking, reduced course load, extended test time, alternative test and media formats, technology use, audio format, readers/scribes, computer/spellchecker, tutoring, reading and writing skill development, academic advising and course selection, priority registration, learning strategies and study skills training, LD/ADHD support via peer and community leadership building opportunities, faculty consultation, trainings, diagnostic screenings/info sessions and evaluation referral.

LEARNING DISABILITY PROGRAM OR SERVICES

Contact Information
Name of program or department: ACCESS
  Telephone: 802-656-7753
  Fax: 802-656-0739

LEARNING DISABILITY SERVICES

Accommodations are decided upon an individual basis after a thorough review of appropriate, current documentation. The accommodations requested must be supported through the documentation provided and must be logically linked to the current impact of the condition on academic functioning.

Allowed in exams	**Distraction-reduced environment:** Yes	**Added costs for services:** No
Calculator: Yes	**Tape recording in class:** Yes	**LD specialists:** Yes
Dictionary: Yes	**Electronic texts:** Yes	**Professional tutors:** For hire
Computer: Yes	**Accommodations for students with**	**Peer tutors:** 150
Spellchecker: Yes	**ADHD:** Yes	**Max. hours/wk. for services:** 1–2
Extended test time: Yes	**Kurzweil Reader:** Yes	**How professors are notified of**
Scribes: Yes	**Other assistive technology:** Yes	**LD/ADHD:** By both student and
Proctors: Yes	**Priority registration:** Yes	specialist
Oral exams: Yes		
Note-takers: Yes		

GENERAL ADMISSIONS INFORMATION

Office of Admission: 802-656-4667

ENTRANCE REQUIREMENTS

Academic units required: 4 English, 3 math, 2 science (1 science lab), 2 foreign language, 3 social studies. High school diploma is required, and GED is accepted. ACT with Writing component required. TOEFL required of all international applicants: minimum paper TOEFL 550, minimum computer TOEFL 213.

Application deadline: 1/15	**SAT Math middle 50% range:**	**Graduated top 10% of class:** 28%
Notification: 3/31	550–640	**Graduated top 25% of class:** 68%
Average GPA: NR	**SAT Critical Reading middle 50%**	**Graduated top 50% of class:** 96%
ACT Composite middle 50% range:	**range:** 540–640	
24–29	**SAT Writing middle 50% range:**	
	540–640	

COLLEGE GRADUATION REQUIREMENTS

Course waivers allowed: No
Course substitutions allowed: No

ADDITIONAL INFORMATION

Environment: The university is located on 425 acres by Lake Champlain 90 miles south of Montreal.

Student Body	**Cost Information**	**Greek System**
Undergrad enrollment: 11,482	**In-state tuition:** $12,900	**Fraternity:** Yes
Women: 56%	**Out-of-state tuition:** $32,600	**Sorority:** Yes
Men: 44%	**Room & board:** $9,708	**Athletics:** Division I
Percent out-of-state: 67%	**Housing Information**	
	University housing: Yes	
	Percent living on campus: 50%	

VERMONT TECHNICAL COLLEGE

PO Box 500, Randolph Center, VT 05061
Phone: 802-728-1242 • Fax: 802-728-1321
E-mail: Admissions@vtc.edu • Web: www.vtc.edu
Support: CS • Institution type: 2-year public

PROGRAMS OR SERVICES FOR STUDENTS WITH LD

The goal of Services for Students with Disabilities is to ensure equal access to all VTC programs for all qualified students with disabilities, to help students develop the necessary skills to be effective at VTC and beyond, and to further students' understanding of how their disabilities affect them in school, work, and social settings. The learning specialist at Vermont Technical College is responsible for coordinating services to ensure accessibility and usability of all programs, services, and activities of the college by people with disabilities and is a resource for information and advocacy toward their full participation in all aspects of campus life. The learning specialist collaborates with the entire campus community to provide services in the most appropriate setting to meet the access needs of the individual.

ADMISSION INFORMATION FOR STUDENTS WITH LD/ADHD

College entrance tests required: Yes
Interview required: Yes
Essay recommended: No
What documentation required for LD: Psycho Ed evaluation to include: relevant historical info, instructional interventions, related services, age diagnosed, objective data (aptitude, achievement, info processing), test scores (standard, percentile and grade equivalents) and describe functional limitations.
With general application: No
To receive services after enrolling: Yes
What documentation required for ADHD: Diagnosis based on DSM-V; history of behaviors impairing functioning in academic setting; diagnostic interview; history of symptoms; evidence of ongoing behaviors.

With general application: No
Submitted to: Services for Students with Disabilities
Special Ed. HS course work accepted: Yes
Specific course requirements of all applicants: Varies
Separate application required: No
# of LD applications submitted each year: NR
# of LD applications accepted yearly: NR
Total # of students receiving LD services: 70
Acceptance into program means acceptance into college: Students must be admitted to and enrolled in the university first and then request services.

ADMISSIONS

There is no special admissions process for students with learning disabilities. In general, students have a GPA of 80 percent or higher. There is no cutoff score for the SAT. The program director can make recommendations to waive certain admission criteria if they discriminate against a student with a learning disability and other evidence of a student's qualifications exist. General course requirements include Algebra I and II, geometry, and physics or chemistry for engineering programs. Many students meet with the disabilities coordinator during the application process to discuss their needs. The Summer Bridge Program, an alternative admission plan, is a 4-week math/physics and language arts program used as preparation for marginal freshmen who do not require the 3-year program option. The 3-year alternative admission option is for engineering students who need longer than 2 years to complete the program.

ADDITIONAL INFORMATION

The disabilities coordinator provides a variety of services, which include assessment of students' academic needs, coordination of tutoring to provide assistance with course material, and a disabilities forum for students to share experiences and academic strategies that they have learned with other students. Individual tutoring is provided in writing and study skills, such as time management, effective textbook reading, learning strategies, and stress management. Other accommodations could include individualized accommodations for test-taking, note-taking assistance, consultation and advocacy throughout the campus community, liaison with community-based disability service agencies, information and referral, academic adjustments, academic coaching, study skills instruction, assistive technology training, academic and career counseling, and coordination of accommodations. There is a Learning Center open to all students on campus.

LEARNING DISABILITY PROGRAM OR SERVICES

Contact Information
Name of program or department: Services for Students with Disabilities
  Telephone: 802-728-1278
  Fax: 802-728-1714

LEARNING DISABILITY SERVICES

Accommodations are decided upon an individual basis after a thorough review of appropriate, current documentation. The accommodations requested must be supported through the documentation provided and must be logically linked to the current impact of the condition on academic functioning.

Allowed in exams	**Distraction-reduced environment:** Yes	**Added costs for services:** No
Calculator: Yes	**Tape recording in class:** Yes	**LD specialists:** Yes
Dictionary: Yes	**Electronic texts:** Yes	**Professional tutors:** No
Computer: Yes	**Accommodations for students with**	**Peer tutors:** Yes
Spellchecker: Yes	**ADHD:** Yes	**Max. hours/wk. for services:**
Extended test time: Yes	**Kurzweil Reader:** Yes	Unlimited
Scribes: Yes	**Other assistive technology:** Yes	**How professors are notified of**
Proctors: Yes	**Priority registration:** Yes	**LD/ADHD:** By student
Oral exams: Yes		
Note-takers: Yes		

GENERAL ADMISSIONS INFORMATION

Office of Admission: 802-728-1242

ENTRANCE REQUIREMENTS

Admissions are based on a total picture of applicants, including transcript, ACT or SAT, recommendations, and activities. Courses required vary depending on major.

Application deadline: None	**SAT Math middle 50% range:**	**Graduated top 10% of class:** 10%
Notification: Rolling	430–540	**Graduated top 25% of class:** 29%
Average GPA: 3.01	**SAT Critical Reading middle 50%**	**Graduated top 50% of class:** 61%
ACT Composite middle 50% range:	**range:** 410–520	
17–22	**SAT Writing middle 50% range:**	
	400–500	

COLLEGE GRADUATION REQUIREMENTS

Course waivers allowed: No
Course substitutions allowed: No

ADDITIONAL INFORMATION

Environment: The college is located on 54 acres in a rural area.

Student Body	**Cost Information**	**Greek System**
Undergrad enrollment: 1,658	**In-state tuition:** $11,556	**Fraternity:** No
Women: 42%	**Out-of-state tuition:** $21,276	**Sorority:** No
Men: 58%	**Room & board:** $8,446	**Athletics:** Intramural and intercollegiate
Percent out-of-state: 12%	**Housing Information**	
	University housing: Yes	
	Percent living on campus: NR	

THE COLLEGE OF WILLIAM & MARY

Office of Admissions, P.O. Box 8795, Williamsburg, VA 23187-8795
Phone: 757-221-4223 • Fax: 757-221-1242
E-mail: admission@wm.edu • Web: www.wm.edu
Support: S • Institution: 4-year public

PROGRAMS OR SERVICES FOR STUDENTS WITH LD

Disability Services at the College of William and Mary are available to all students with disabilities. Reasonable accommodations upon request are evaluated on an individual and flexible basis. Program goals include fostering independence, encouraging self-determination, emphasizing accommodations over limitations, and creating an accessible environment to ensure that individuals are viewed on the basis of ability and not disability. Individual accommodations needs are considered on a case-by-case basis in consultation with the student. The staff works with students and faculty to implement reasonable supports. Students anticipating the need for academic support must provide pertinent documentation in a timely manner in order to facilitate the provision of the service. Additional documentation may be requested and accommodation requests can be denied if they do not seem to be substantially supported. Documentation for LD/ADHD must include a comprehensive report of psychoeducational or neuropsychological assessment. The documentation must demonstrate the impact of the disability on major life activities and support all the recommended accommodations.

ADMISSION INFORMATION FOR STUDENTS WITH LD/ADHD

College entrance tests required: Yes
Interview required: No
Essay required: N/A
What documentation required for LD: Psycho Ed evaluation
  to include: relevant historical info, instructional interventions,
  related services, age diagnosed, objective data (aptitude,
  achievement, info processing), test scores (standard,
  percentile and grade equivalents) and describe functional
  limitations.
With general application: No
To receive services after enrolling: Yes
What documentation required for ADHD: Diagnosis based
  on DSM-V; history of behaviors impairing functioning in
  academic setting; diagnostic interview; history of symptoms;
  evidence of ongoing behaviors.

With general application: No
Submitted to: Support Program/Services
Special Ed. HS course work accepted: No
Specific course requirements for all applicants: Yes
Separate application required for program services: No
# of LD applications submitted each year: NR
# of LD applications accepted yearly: NR
Total # of students receiving LD services: 235
**Acceptance into program means acceptance into
  college:** NR

ADMISSIONS
Students go through a regular admissions process. Students must take either the SAT or ACT and three SAT Subject Tests are recommended. Results of non-standardized test administrations and documentation of disability may be submitted in support of any application, but are not essential for full consideration. Once admitted, students are fully mainstreamed and are expected to maintain the same academic standards as all other students.

ADDITIONAL INFORMATION
The staff of Disability Services works with the student and the faculty to implement reasonable accommodations. The staff works closely with all college departments to identify appropriate options for accommodating students with disabilities.

LEARNING DISABILITY PROGRAM OR SERVICES

Contact Information
Name of program or department: Disability Services
  Telephone: 757-221-2510
  Fax: 757-221-2538

LEARNING DISABILITY SERVICES

Accommodations are decided upon an individual basis after a thorough review of appropriate, current documentation. The accommodations requested must be supported through the documentation provided and must be logically linked to the current impact of the condition on academic functioning.

Allowed in exams
  Calculator: N/A
  Dictionary: N/A
  Computer: Yes
  Spellchecker: N/A
Extended test time: Yes
Scribes: Yes
Proctors: N/A
Oral exams: No
Note-takers: Yes

Distraction-reduced environment: Yes
Tape recording in class: Yes
Electronic texts: N/A
Accommodations for students with ADHD: Yes
Kurzweil Reader: Yes
Other assistive technology: N/A
Priority registration: Yes

Added costs for services: No
LD specialists: No
Professional tutors: NR
Peer tutors: NR
Max. hours/wk. for services: NR
How professors are notified of LD/ADHD: Director

GENERAL ADMISSIONS INFORMATION

Office of Admission: 757-221-4223

ENTRANCE REQUIREMENTS
Academic units recommended: 4 English, 4 mathematics, 4 science, (3 science labs), 4 foreign language, 4 social studies. High school diploma or equivalent is not required. SAT or ACT required; TOEFL required of all international applicants; minimum paper TOEFL 600, minimum computer TOEFL 250, minimum web-based TOEFL 100.

Application deadline: 1/1
Notification: 4/1
Average GPA: 4
ACT Composite middle 50% range: 28–32

SAT Math middle 50% range: 620–720
SAT Critical Reading middle 50% range: 620–730
SAT Writing middle 50% range: 620–720

Graduated top 10% of class: 79%
Graduated top 25% of class: 96%
Graduated top 50% of class: 99%

COLLEGE GRADUATION REQUIREMENTS

Course waivers allowed: No
Course substitutions allowed: Yes
In what course: foreign language

ADDITIONAL INFORMATION

Environment: Located 50 miles from Richmond, Virginia.

Student Body
  Undergrad enrollment: 6,071
  Women: 55%
  Men: 45%
  Percent out-of-state: 32%

Cost Information
  In-state tuition: $13,132
  Out-of-state tuition: $35,409
  Room and Board: $8,772
  Housing Information
    University housing: Yes
    Percent living on campus: 73%

Greek System
  Fraternity: Yes
  Sorority: Yes
Athletics: Division I

FERRUM COLLEGE

PO Box 1000, Ferrum, VA 24088
Phone: 540-365-4290 • Fax: 540-365-4366
E-mail: admissions@ferrum.edu • Web: www.ferrum.edu
Support: CS • Institution type: 4-year private

PROGRAMS OR SERVICES FOR STUDENTS WITH LD

Ferrum College does not have a program for students with learning disabilities, but does provide services to students with disabilities documentation. Ferrum also does not offer a comprehensive program or monitoring services. Students motivated to accept the assistance and academic accommodations offered frequently find Ferrum's services to be excellent. The Academic Support Division combines library and media services with the Academic Resource Center and the first-year experience so that all academic support programs can function in unison and be housed under one roof. The division offers classes in academic skill development, Ferrum 101, mentoring, service-learning, and career development. Services offered include academic counseling, tutoring, assistance for the learning disabled, as well as traditional library, media, and information services.

ADMISSION INFORMATION FOR STUDENTS WITH LD/ADHD

College entrance tests required: Yes
Interview required: No
Essay recommended: Optional
What documentation required for LD: Psycho Ed evaluation to include: relevant historical info, instructional interventions, related services, age diagnosed, objective data (aptitude, achievement, info processing), test scores (standard, percentile and grade equivalents) and describe functional limitations.
With general application: No
To receive services after enrolling: Yes
What documentation required for ADHD: Diagnosis based on DSM-V; history of behaviors impairing functioning in academic setting; diagnostic interview; history of symptoms; evidence of ongoing behaviors.

With general application: No
Submitted to: Admissions Office and Office of Disability Services
Special Ed. HS course work accepted: N/A
Specific course requirements of all applicants: Yes
Separate application required: No
# of LD applications submitted each year: NR
# of LD applications accepted yearly: NR
Total # of students receiving LD services: NR
Acceptance into program means acceptance into college: Students must be admitted and enrolled at the university first and then may request services. Students denied admission may appeal the decision.

ADMISSIONS

Ferrum is proactive in terms of the admissions process for students with documentation of a disability. All students first go through the admissions process. If students are not admitted through the general admissions process, the committee can be requested to reconsider with the presentation of the documentation and a recommendation from the disability service provider. Those applicants who do not meet general admission criteria are encouraged to have an interview with the Office of Admissions. General admission criteria include 4 years of English, 1 year of math (3 recommended), 1 year of science (3 recommended), 2 years of a foreign language, and 3 years of social studies (recommended). The SAT/ACT is required (the average ACT is 18, and the average SAT is 1040); the average GPA is 2.6.

ADDITIONAL INFORMATION

The Office of Disability Services (ODS) is available for students with learning disabilities and ADHD as well as for other students with disabilities. Through our Academic Support Center, some tutoring is provided by professors, and tutoring is available through peer tutors. Accommodations are offered in accordance with the documentation submitted in cases where the student is 'otherwise qualified'. The most frequently used accommodations include extended time for testing, aural testing, testing in quieter area, and the use of adaptive equipment for testing, including word processors and Kurzwell software. Ferrum offers a summer program for pre-college freshmen that is encouraged for all students.

LEARNING DISABILITY PROGRAM OR SERVICES

Contact Information
Name of program or department: Office of Disability Services (ODS)
Telephone: 540-365-4529
Fax: 540-365-4271

LEARNING DISABILITY SERVICES

Accommodations are decided upon an individual basis after a thorough review of appropriate, current documentation. The accommodations requested must be supported through the documentation provided and must be logically linked to the current impact of the condition on academic functioning.

Allowed in exams
Calculator: Yes
Dictionary: Yes
Computer: Yes
Spellchecker: Yes
Extended test time: Yes
Scribes: Yes
Proctors: Yes
Oral exams: Yes
Note-takers: Yes

Distraction-reduced environment: Yes
Tape recording in class: Yes
Electronic texts: Yes
Accommodations for students with ADHD: Yes
Kurzweil Reader: Yes
Other assistive technology: Yes
Priority registration: No

Added costs for services: No
LD specialists: Yes
Professional tutors: No
Peer tutors: Yes
Max. hours/wk. for services: 10–15
How professors are notified of LD/ADHD: By both student and director

GENERAL ADMISSIONS INFORMATION

Office of Admission: 540-365-4290

ENTRANCE REQUIREMENTS

Academic units recommended: 4 English, 3 math, 2 science (1 science lab), 2 foreign language, 3 social studies, 2 academic electives. High school diploma is required, and GED is accepted. TOEFL required of all international applicants: minimum paper TOEFL 550.

Application deadline: None
Notification: Rolling
Average GPA: 2.64
ACT Composite middle 50% range: 16–20

SAT Math middle 50% range: 390–490
SAT Critical Reading middle 50% range: 400–480
SAT Writing middle 50% range: NR

Graduated top 10% of class: 6%
Graduated top 25% of class: 19%
Graduated top 50% of class: 46%

COLLEGE GRADUATION REQUIREMENTS

Course waivers allowed: No
Course substitutions allowed: Yes
In what course: Course substitution is discussed on a case-by-case basis and determined by the Academic Standards Committee.

ADDITIONAL INFORMATION

Environment: The college is located in a rural area south of Roanoke.

Student Body
Undergrad enrollment: 1,484
Women: 46%
Men: 54%
Percent out-of-state: 18%

Cost Information
Tuition: $26,375
Room & board: $8,530
Housing Information
University housing: Yes
Percent living on campus: 80%

Greek System
Fraternity: No
Sorority: No
Athletics: Division III

GEORGE MASON UNIVERSITY

Undergraduate Admissions Office, 4400 University Drive MSN 3A4,
Fairfax, VA 22030-4444 • Phone: 703-993-2400 • Fax: 703-993-2392
E-mail: admissions@gmu.edu • Web: www.gmu.edu
Support: S • Institution type: 4-year public

PROGRAMS OR SERVICES FOR STUDENTS WITH LD

The university does not maintain a specific program for students with LD. George Mason is, however, committed to providing appropriate services and accommodations to allow identified students with disabilities to access programs. The Office of Disabilities (ODS) strives to promote equal access in curricular and co-curricular activities with the university experience. ODS fosters partnerships with students, faculty and staff to create environments that are accessible, diverse, and inclusive. It also empowers students to fully participate in the university community.

ADMISSION INFORMATION FOR STUDENTS WITH LD/ADHD

College entrance tests required: Yes
Interview required: No
Essay recommended: No
What documentation required for LD: Psycho Ed evaluation
   to include: relevant historical info, instructional interventions,
   related services, age diagnosed, objective data (aptitude,
   achievement, info processing), test scores (standard,
   percentile and grade equivalents) and describe functional
   limitations.
With general application: No
To receive services after enrolling: Yes
What documentation required for ADHD: Diagnosis based
   on DSM-V; history of behaviors impairing functioning in
   academic setting; diagnostic interview; history of symptoms;
   evidence of ongoing behaviors.

With general application: No
Submitted to: Office of Disability Services
Special Ed. HS course work accepted: Yes
Specific course requirements of all applicants: Yes
Separate application required: No
# of LD applications submitted each year: NR
# of LD applications accepted yearly: NR
Total # of students receiving LD services: NR
**Acceptance into program means acceptance into
   college:** Students must be admitted to and enrolled in the
   university first and then request services.

ADMISSIONS
Students with LD must submit the general George Mason University undergraduate application and meet the same requirements as all other applicants. Students are encouraged to self-disclose and provide documentation of their disability. Students who have deficiencies in required courses may request a waiver of the requirement. These requests are considered on an individual basis. General admission criteria include 4 years of English, 3 years of math (4 recommended), 1 year of science (3 recommended), 3 years of a foreign language, 3 years of social studies (4 recommended), and 3–4 year of electives; an ACT/SAT score; and an interview.

ADDITIONAL INFORMATION
Students with LD may request extended testing times for exams, extended time for in-class writing assignments, note-takers, or use of a word processor for essay exams if documentation supports these modifications. Learning Services is a resource center for all students on campus. The center offers self-help skills classes in time management, organizational skills, and test-taking strategies. A freshman orientation class is offered for credit, and some sections of this class are geared toward academic skills. The staff at the Office of Disability Services collaborate with students individually to help choose the most effective reasonable accommodations; coordinate implementations of accommodations; act as a liaison between students and faculty/administration on concerns relating to accommodations, information is available for prospective students, community groups, and secondary education personnel interested in learning more about accommodations and services at George Mason.

LEARNING DISABILITY PROGRAM OR SERVICES

Contact Information
Name of program or department: Office of Disability Services
  Telephone: 703-993-2474
  Fax: 703-993-4306

LEARNING DISABILITY SERVICES

Accommodations are decided upon an individual basis after a thorough review of current comprehensive documentation. The accommodations requested must be supported through the documentation provided and must be logically linked to the current impact of the condition on academic functioning.

Allowed in exams
  Calculator: Yes
  Dictionary: Yes
  Computer: Yes
  Spellchecker: Yes
Extended test time: Yes
Scribes: Yes
Proctors: Yes
Oral exams: Yes
Note-takers: Yes

Distraction-reduced environment: Yes
Tape recording in class: Yes
Electronic texts: Yes
Accommodations for students with ADHD: Yes
Kurzweil Reader: Yes
Other assistive technology: Yes
Priority registration: Yes

Added costs for services: No
LD specialists: No
Professional tutors: No
Peer tutors: Yes
Max. hours/wk. for services: Unlimited
How professors are notified of LD/ADHD: By student

GENERAL ADMISSIONS INFORMATION

Office of Admission: 703-993-2400

ENTRANCE REQUIREMENTS

Academic units required: 4 English, 3 math, 1 science (1 science lab), 3 foreign language, 3 social studies, 3 academic electives. **Academic units recommended:** 4 English, 4 math, 3 science (3 science labs), 3 foreign language, 4 social studies, 4 academic electives. High school diploma is required, and GED is accepted. ACT with or without Writing component accepted. TOEFL required of all international applicants: minimum paper TOEFL 570, minimum computer TOEFL 230.

Application deadline: 1/15
Notification: 4/1
Average GPA: 3.65
ACT Composite middle 50% range: 23–28

SAT Math middle 50% range: 530–630
SAT Critical Reading middle 50% range: 520–620
SAT Writing middle 50% range: NR

Graduated top 10% of class: 23%
Graduated top 25% of class: 60%
Graduated top 50% of class: 93%

COLLEGE GRADUATION REQUIREMENTS

Course waivers allowed: No
Course substitutions allowed: Yes
In what course: Foreign language and, in some instances, analytical reasoning with specific documentation provided.

ADDITIONAL INFORMATION

Environment: The university is located on 682 acres in a suburban area 18 miles southwest of Washington, DC.

Student Body
  Undergrad enrollment: 20,782
  Women: 52%
  Men: 48%
  Percent out-of-state: 11%

Cost Information
  In-state tuition: $9,266
  Out-of-state tuition: $26,744
  Room & board: $9,050
Housing Information
  University housing: Yes
  Percent living on campus: 27%

Greek System
  Fraternity: Yes
  Sorority: Yes
Athletics: Division I

HAMPTON UNIVERSITY

Office of Admissions, Hampton University, Hampton, VA 23668
Phone: 757-727-5328 • Fax: 757-727-5095
E-mail: admit@hamptonu.edu • Web: www.hamptonu.edu
Support: S • Institution type: 4-year private

PROGRAMS OR SERVICES FOR STUDENTS WITH LD

Hampton University is committed to assisting students with disabilities. They seek to help students achieve academic potential within the academically competitive curriculum by providing a variety of accommodations. Accommodations provided for students are in accordance to what is necessary and reasonable for the specific documented disability.

ADMISSION INFORMATION FOR STUDENTS WITH LD/ADHD

College entrance tests required: Yes
Interview required: No
Essay recommended: No
What documentation required for LD: Psycho Ed evaluation to include: relevant historical info, instructional interventions, related services, age diagnosed, objective data (aptitude, achievement, info processing), test scores (standard, percentile and grade equivalents) and describe functional limitations.
With general application: No
To receive services after enrolling: Yes
What documentation required for ADHD: Diagnosis based on DSM-V; history of behaviors impairing functioning in academic setting; diagnostic interview; history of symptoms; evidence of ongoing behaviors.

With general application: No
Submitted to: Student Support Services
Special Ed. HS course work accepted: Yes
Specific course requirements of all applicants: Yes
Separate application required: No
# of LD applications submitted each year: NR
# of LD applications accepted yearly: NR
Total # of students receiving LD services: 30–40
Acceptance into program means acceptance into college: Students must be admitted to and enrolled in the university first and then request services.

ADMISSIONS

There is no special admission process for students with learning disabilities. Students are encouraged to send documentation directly to the Office of the Director of Compliance and Disability Services and not combine it with their application for admission to the University.

ADDITIONAL INFORMATION

Accommodations in the classroom could include permission to record lectures, use of calculators, extended time for assignments and note sharing. Accommodations in an examination could include reduced-distraction environment, extended time, alternative test formats, readers/scribes, printed copies of oral instructions, and oral proctors. A student who would like to receive accommodations must contact the Office of the Director of Compliance and Disability Services and provide documentation of the disability that is not older than 3 years. The Director is responsible for qualifying students with disabilities for reasonable academic accommodations within the university.

LEARNING DISABILITY PROGRAM·OR SERVICES

Contact Information
Name of program or department: Office of the Director of Compliance and Disability Services
 Telephone: 757-727-5493
 Fax: 757-727-4288

LEARNING DISABILITY SERVICES

Accommodations are available for students with supporting documentation. Documentation must be current no older than 3 years, and must clearly outline the disability, functional limitations and recommendations for accommodations in a competitive college environment.

Allowed in exams
 Calculator: Yes
 Dictionary: Yes
 Computer: Yes
 Spellchecker: Yes
Extended test time: Yes
Scribes: Yes
Proctors: Yes
Oral exams: Yes
Note-takers: Yes

Distraction-reduced environment: Yes
Tape recording in class: Yes
Electronic texts: No
Accommodations for students with
 ADHD: Yes
Kurzweil Reader: No
Other assistive technology: No
Priority registration: Yes

Added costs for services: No
LD specialists: No
Professional tutors: No
Peer tutors: Yes
Max. hours/wk. for services:
 Unlimited
How professors are notified of
 LD/ADHD: By student

GENERAL ADMISSIONS INFORMATION

Office of Admission: 757-727-5328

ENTRANCE REQUIREMENTS

Academic units required: 4 English, 3 math, 2 science (2 science labs), 2 social studies, 6 academic electives.
Academic units recommended: 2 foreign language. High school diploma is required, and GED is accepted. TOEFL required of all international applicants: minimum paper TOEFL 550, minimum computer TOEFL 214.

Application deadline: 3/1
Notification: Rolling
Average GPA: 3.20
ACT Composite middle 50% range:
 17–26

SAT Math middle 50% range:
 470–580
SAT Critical Reading middle 50%
 range: 470–620
SAT Writing middle 50% range: NR

Graduated top 10% of class: 20%
Graduated top 25% of class: 45%
Graduated top 50% of class: 90%

COLLEGE GRADUATION REQUIREMENTS

Course waivers allowed: determined on a case-by-case basis
Course substitutions allowed: determined on a case-by-case basis

ADDITIONAL INFORMATION

Environment: The university is located on 204 acres 15 miles west of Norfolk.

Student Body
 Undergrad enrollment: 4,565
 Women: 64%
 Men: 36%
 Percent out-of-state: 68%

Cost Information
 Tuition: $18,798
 Room & board: $8,370
Housing Information
 University housing: Yes
 Percent living on campus: 59%

Greek System
 Fraternity: Yes
 Sorority: Yes
Athletics: Division I

JAMES MADISON UNIVERSITY

Sonner Hall, MSC 0101, Harrisonburg, VA 22807
Phone: 540-568-5681 • Fax: 540-568-3332
E-mail: admissions@jmu.edu • Web: www.jmu.edu
Support: CS • Institution: 4-year public

PROGRAMS OR SERVICES FOR STUDENTS WITH LD

The mission of the Office of Disability Services (ODS) is to assist the university in creating an accessible community where students with disabilities have an equal opportunity to fully participate in their educational experience at JMU. Disability Services provides, coordinates, and facilitates accommodations, support services, and programs that afford students with disabilities an equal opportunity to participate in life at JMU. The program assists students in the developmental process as they transition to higher education, independence, and effective self-advocacy and self-determination. ODS also serves as a resource for faculty and the JMU community as they strive to create inclusive opportunities for diverse needs. In order to fully evaluate requests for accommodations or auxiliary aids, JMU's Disability Services will need documentation of the disability that consists of a comprehensive evaluation by an appropriate professional that describes the current impact of the disability as it relates to the accommodation(s) requested. All requests for accommodations—including substitutions—are considered on a case-by-case basis. Students must register with Disability Services if they are planning to request reasonable accommodations. Current documentation is required to register for services.

ADMISSION INFORMATION FOR STUDENTS WITH LD/ADHD

College entrance tests required: Yes
Interview required: No
What documentation required for LD: Psycho Ed evaluation
  to include: relevant historical info, instructional interventions,
  related services, age diagnosed, objective data (aptitude,
  achievement, info processing), test scores (standard,
  percentile and grade equivalents) and describe functional
  limitations.
With general application: No
To receive services after enrolling: Yes
What documentation required for ADHD: Diagnosis based
  on DSM-V; history of behaviors impairing functioning in
  academic setting; diagnostic interview; history of symptoms;
  evidence of ongoing behaviors.

With general application: No
Submitted to: Support Program/Services
Special Ed. HS course work accepted: Yes
Specific course requirements for all applicants: Yes
Separate application required for program services: No
# of LD applications submitted each year: NR
# of LD applications accepted yearly: NR
Total # of students receiving LD services: NR
**Acceptance into program means acceptance into
  college:** Separate application required after student has
  enrolled.

ADMISSIONS

During the admissions process, the admissions team at JMU is highly sensitive and knowledgeable concerning students with learning disabilities. Admission decisions are made without regard to disabilities and all prospective students are expected to present academic credentials that are competitive. After admission to JMU, the student should forward his or her documentation to ODS. Current recommendations for post-secondary accommodations are crucial for providing appropriate services in college. There are no specific courses required for admission into James Madison; however, students are expected to complete a solid college-prep curriculum. This would include four years of English, four years of mathematics (one year past algebra II), four years of social studies, three to five years of a foreign language and three years of laboratory sciences. The mid 50 percent range for the SAT is 1070–1230 and ACT is 24–28. Eighty-eight percent of the 2009–10 freshman class ranked in the top one-third of their high school class.

ADDITIONAL INFORMATION

The Office of Disability Services offers a number of services to students with disabilities including classroom accommodations such as extended time on tests, interpreters and other classroom accommodations for deaf and hard of hearing students, assistive technology labs; test proctoring; alternative texts and peer mentoring. Learning Strategies Instruction and Screening & Assessment services are available to all students, regardless of disability status. Additional on-campus services include: Learning Resource Centers (LRC). LRC consists of the following programs, tutoring and services available to all enrolled students: Communication Resource Center, Science & Math Learning Center, University Writing Center, Supplemental Instruction, Counseling and Student Development Center, and Career & Academic Planning.

PROGRAM FOR DISABILITY SERVICES

Contact Information
Name of program or department: Office of Disability Services
  Telephone: 540-568-6705
  Fax: 540-568-7099

LEARNING DISABILITY SERVICES

Accommodations are decided upon an individual basis after a thorough review of appropriate, current documentation. The accommodations requested must be supported through the documentation provided and must be logically linked to the current impact of the condition on academic functioning.

Allowed in exams	**Distraction-reduced environment:** Yes	**Added costs for services:** No
Calculator: Yes	**Tape recording in class:** Yes	**LD specialists:** Yes
Dictionary: Yes	**Electronic texts:** N/A	**Professional tutors:** No
Computer: Yes	**Accommodations for students with**	**Peer tutors:** 2
Spellchecker: Yes	**ADHD:** Yes	**Max. hours/wk. for services:** N/A
Extended test time: Yes	**Kurzweil Reader:** Yes	**How professors are notified of**
Scribes: Yes	**Other assistive technology:** Yes	**LD/ADHD:** Student
Proctors: Yes	**Priority registration:** Yes	
Oral exams: Yes		
Note-takers: Yes		

GENERAL ADMISSIONS INFORMATION

Office of Admission: 540-568-5681

ENTRANCE REQUIREMENTS
Academic units required: 4 English, 4 mathematics, 3 science, (3 science labs), 2 foreign language, 3 social studies.
Academic units recommended: 4 English, 4 mathematics, 4 science, (4 science labs), 3 foreign language, 4 social studies. High school diploma is required and GED is accepted. SAT or ACT required; TOEFL required of all international applicants; minimum paper TOEFL 550, minimum computer TOEFL 213.

Application deadline: 1/15	**SAT Math middle 50% range:**	**Graduated top 10% of class:** 28%
Notification: 4/1	540–630	**Graduated top 25% of class:** 72%
Average GPA: 3.8	**SAT Critical Reading middle 50%**	**Graduated top 50% of class:** 98%
ACT Composite middle 50% range:	**range:** 520–620	
22–26	**SAT Writing middle 50% range:**	
	520–620	

COLLEGE GRADUATION REQUIREMENTS

Course waivers allowed: No
In what course: All requests for waivers will be considered on a case-by-case basis.
Course substitutions allowed: Yes
In what course: All requests for substitutions will be considered on a case-by-case basis. American Sign Language can be approved as a substitution for the foreign language requirement if substitution is determined to be a reasonable accommodation.

ADDITIONAL INFORMATION

Environment: The university is located in the Shenandoah Valley surrounded by the Blue Ridge Mountains and the Allegheny Mountain Range, 120 miles from Washington, DC.

Student Body	**Cost Information**	**Greek System**
Undergrad enrollment: 17,655	**In-state tuition:** $8,448	**Fraternity:** Yes
Women: 60%	**Out-of-state tuition:** $21,738	**Sorority:** Yes
Men: 40%	**Room and board:** $8,340	**Athletics:** Division I
Percent out-of-state: 27%	**Housing Information**	
	University housing: Yes	
	Percent living on campus: 32%	

LIBERTY UNIVERSITY

1971 University Blvd, Lynchburg, VA 24502
Phone: 434-582-2000 • Fax: 800-628-7977
E-mail: admissions@liberty.edu • Web: www.liberty.edu
Support: CS • Institution: 4-year private

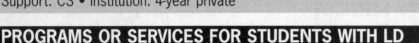

PROGRAMS OR SERVICES FOR STUDENTS WITH LD

The Bruckner Learning Center offers reading and study skills assistance to all students. The center provides individualized peer tutoring regularly or on a drop-in basis for English or math. There are five courses provided for students wishing to develop reading and study skills. Students with a disability who self-identify may be eligible for accommodations such as priority class registration, deaf interpreters, and confidential requests for classroom accommodations (additional time on tests, note-taking help, and so on).

ADMISSION INFORMATION FOR STUDENTS WITH LD/ADHD

College entrance tests required: Yes
Interview required: No
Essay required: N/A
What documentation required for LD: Psycho Ed evaluation to include: relevant historical info, instructional interventions, related services, age diagnosed, objective data (aptitude, achievement, info processing), test scores (standard, percentile and grade equivalents) and describe functional limitations.
With general application: No
To receive services after enrolling: Yes
What documentation required for ADHD: Diagnosis based on DSM-V; history of behaviors impairing functioning in academic setting; diagnostic interview; history of symptoms; evidence of ongoing behaviors.

With general application: No
Submitted to: Both Admissions and Support Program/Services
Special Ed. HS course work accepted: No
Specific course requirements for all applicants: Yes
Separate application required for program services: No
# of LD applications submitted each year: NR
# of LD applications accepted yearly: NR
Total # of students receiving LD services: 300
Acceptance into program means acceptance into college: Separate application required after student has enrolled

ADMISSIONS

All applicants must submit an official transcript from an accredited high school and/or college, an official copy of a state high school equivalency diploma, or an official copy of the GED test results. The minimum acceptable unweighted GPA is 2.0. Applicants who fail to meet the minimum required GPA will be evaluated using other indicators of collegiate ability and may be admitted on Academic Warning. All applicants must submit ACT or SAT prior to admission. The minimum acceptable scores are SAT 800 (Critical Reading & Math combined) or ACT 17 (composite).

ADDITIONAL INFORMATION

If a student's entrance test scores indicate a deficiency in English or math, then the student will enroll in a basic composition class or a fundamentals of math class. With the student's permission, instructors are provided with a written communication providing information about the student's specific disability and suggestions of appropriate accommodations. Students with a specific learning disability can be assigned to a faculty advisor who has had training in LD. This person acts as a liaison between instructors and students regarding classroom accommodations. The Bruckner Learning Center provides individualized peer tutoring in many subjects on a weekly or drop-in basis.

PROGRAM FOR DISABILITY SERVICES

Contact Information
Name of program or department: Office of Disability Academic Support
  Telephone: 434-582-2159
  Fax: 434-582-2297

LEARNING DISABILITY SERVICES

Accommodations are decided upon an individual basis after a thorough review of appropriate, current documentation. The accommodations requested must be supported through the documentation provided and must be logically linked to the current impact of the condition on academic functioning.

Allowed in exams	**Distraction-reduced environment:** Yes	**Added costs for services:** No
Calculator: Yes	**Tape recording in class:** Yes	**LD specialists:** Yes
Dictionary: Yes	**Electronic texts:** No	**Professional tutors:** No
Computer: No	**Accommodations for students with**	**Peer tutors:** 15
Spellchecker: Yes	**ADHD:** Yes	**Max. hours/wk. for services:**
Extended test time: Yes	**Kurzweil Reader:** Yes	Unlimited
Scribes: Yes	**Other assistive technology:** Yes	**How professors are notified of**
Proctors: Yes	**Priority registration:** Yes	**LD/ADHD:** Director
Oral exams: Yes		
Note-takers: Yes		

GENERAL ADMISSIONS INFORMATION

Office of Admission: 800-543-5317

ENTRANCE REQUIREMENTS

Academic units recommended: 4 English, 3 mathematics, 2 science, (2 science labs), 2 foreign language, 2 social studies, 4 academic electives. High school diploma is required and GED is accepted. SAT or ACT required; TOEFL required of all international applicants; minimum paper TOEFL 500, minimum computer TOEFL 173.

Application deadline: None	**SAT Math middle 50% range:**	**Graduated top 10% of class:** %
Notification: Rolling	420–530	**Graduated top 25% of class:** %
Average GPA: 3.23	**SAT Critical Reading middle 50%**	**Graduated top 50% of class:** %
ACT Composite middle 50% range:	**range:** 430–540	
18–23	**SAT Writing middle 50% range:** NR	

COLLEGE GRADUATION REQUIREMENTS

Course waivers allowed: No
Course substitutions allowed: Yes

ADDITIONAL INFORMATION

Environment: The 5,200-acre university ois located in a suburban area 45 miles east of Roanoke.

Student Body	**Cost Information**	**Greek System**
Undergrad enrollment: 34,625	**Tuition:** $19,154	**Fraternity:** No
Women: 53%	**Room and board:** $7,050–$8,380	**Sorority:** No
Men: 47%	**Housing Information**	**Athletics:** Division I
Percent out-of-state: 64%	**University housing:** Yes	
	Percent living on campus: 40%	

OLD DOMINION UNIVERSITY

108 Rollins Hall, 5115 Hampton Boulevard, Norfolk, VA 23529-0050
Phone: 757-683-3685 • Fax: 757-683-3255
E-mail: admissions@odu.edu • Web: www.odu.edu
Support: CS • Institution type: 4-year public

PROGRAMS OR SERVICES FOR STUDENTS WITH LD

The Office of Educational Accessibility at Old Dominion University advocates for all students with disabilities in the pursuit of their educational objectives and enhances their overall university experiences by providing services and accommodations. The office helps to ensure equal access to all campus facilities and activities. It fosters acceptance by designing opportunities which highlight respect, awareness, and understanding for individuals with disabilities. It empowers students to become self-advocates in fulfilling their collegiate goals so they can find success at ODU and in their future endeavors.

ADMISSION INFORMATION FOR STUDENTS WITH LD/ADHD

College entrance tests required: Yes
Interview required: No
Essay recommended: No
What documentation required for LD: Psycho Ed evaluation to include: relevant historical info, instructional interventions, related services, age diagnosed, objective data (aptitude, achievement, info processing), test scores (standard, percentile and grade equivalents) and describe functional limitations.
With general application: No
To receive services after enrolling: Yes
What documentation required for ADHD: Diagnosis based on DSM-V; history of behaviors impairing functioning in academic setting; diagnostic interview; history of symptoms; evidence of ongoing behaviors.

With general application: No
Submitted to: Office of Educational Accessibility
Special Ed. HS course work accepted: Yes
Specific course requirements of all applicants: Yes
Separate application required: No
# of LD applications submitted each year: 40–60
# of LD applications accepted yearly: 50
Total # of students receiving LD services: 275
Acceptance into program means acceptance into college: Students must be admitted to and enrolled in the university first and then request services.

ADMISSIONS

Admission to Old Dominion is based solely on the entrance requirements as described in the University Catalog. Disclosure of a disability during the admissions process is not required; neither the nature nor the severity of an individual's disability is used as criterion for admission. Recommended high school course work includes 4 years of English, 4 years of Mathematics, 3 years of Science, 3 years of Social Studies, and 3 years of Foreign Languages. For more information about the University and the admissions process, contact the Office of Admissions at (757) 683-3685.

ADDITIONAL INFORMATION

Counseling and advising; study skills instruction; reading, writing, and math instruction; and tutorial assistance are available. Program staff design support services that focus on students' learning styles and special needs. There is a special section of Spanish for students with learning disabilities to meet the foreign language requirements, as well as developmental math, reading, spelling, and writing classes.

LEARNING DISABILITY PROGRAM OR SERVICES

Contact Information
Name of program or department: Office of Educational Accessibility
  Telephone: 757-683-4655
  Fax: 757-683-5356

LEARNING DISABILITY SERVICES

Accommodations are decided upon an individual basis after a thorough review of appropriate, current documentation. The accommodations requested must be supported through the documentation provided and must be logically linked to the current impact of the condition on academic functioning.

Allowed in exams
  Calculator: Yes
  Dictionary: Yes
  Computer: Yes
  Spellchecker: Yes
Extended test time: Yes
Scribes: Yes
Proctors: Yes
Oral exams: Yes
Note-takers: Yes

Distraction-reduced environment: Yes
Tape recording in class: Yes
Electronic texts: Yes
Accommodations for students with
  ADHD: Yes
Kurzweil Reader: Yes
Other assistive technology: Yes
Priority registration: Yes

Added costs for services: No
LD specialists: Yes
Professional tutors: No
Peer tutors: N/A
Max. hours/wk. for services: NR
How professors are notified of
  LD/ADHD: By both student and director

GENERAL ADMISSIONS INFORMATION

Office of Admission: 757-683-3648

ENTRANCE REQUIREMENTS

Academic units recommended: 4 English, 4 math, 3 science, 3 foreign language, 3 social studies. High school diploma is required, and GED is accepted. ACT with Writing component required. TOEFL required of all international applicants: minimum paper TOEFL 550, minimum computer TOEFL 213.

Application deadline: 2/1
Notification: Rolling
Average GPA: 3.24
ACT Composite middle 50% range:
  19–24

SAT Math middle 50% range:
  460–560
SAT Critical Reading middle 50%
  range: 460–560
SAT Writing middle 50% range:
  440–540

Graduated top 10% of class: 10%
Graduated top 25% of class: 35%
Graduated top 50% of class: 81%

COLLEGE GRADUATION REQUIREMENTS

Course waivers allowed: No
Course substitutions allowed: Yes
In what course: All students must complete 3 credits in math. A special 1-year Spanish course is available for students registered with DS.

ADDITIONAL INFORMATION

Environment: The university is located on 46 acres in a suburban area of Norfolk.

Student Body
  Undergrad enrollment: 19,367
  Women: 53%
  Men: 47%
  Percent out-of-state: 6%

Cost Information
  In-state tuition: $7,890
  Out-of-state tuition: $22,230
  Room & board: $8,796
Housing Information
  University housing: Yes
  Percent living on campus: 24%

Greek System
  Fraternity: Yes
  Sorority: Yes
Athletics: Division I

University of Virginia

Office of Admissions, PO Box 400160, Charlottesville, VA 22906
Phone: 434-982-3200 • Fax: 434-924-3587
E-mail: undergradadmission@virginia.edu • Web: www.virginia.edu
Support: CS • Institution type: 4-year public

PROGRAMS OR SERVICES FOR STUDENTS WITH LD

The University of Virginia is committed to providing equal access to educational and social opportunities for all disabled students. The Learning Needs and Evaluation Center (LNEC) is housed within the university's Department of Student Health and serves as the coordinating agency for services to all students with disabilities. The LNEC assists students with disabilities to become independent self-advocates who are able to demonstrate their abilities both in the classroom and as members of the university community. The center provides a number of services, including review of documentation supporting the disability, determination of appropriate academic accommodations, and serving as a liaison with faculty and administrators. Information can be shared, with the student's permission, with university personnel who have an educational need to know. Once a learning disability is documented, the center assigns appropriate and reasonable accommodations and serves as a liaison with faculty and administrators. The center's primary purpose is to support the academic well-being of students with disabilities.

ADMISSION INFORMATION FOR STUDENTS WITH LD/ADHD

College entrance tests required: Yes
Interview required: No
Essay recommended: No
What documentation required for LD: Psycho Ed evaluation to include: relevant historical info, instructional interventions, related services, age diagnosed, objective data (aptitude, achievement, info processing), test scores (standard, percentile and grade equivalents) and describe functional limitations.
With general application: No
To receive services after enrolling: Yes
What documentation required for ADHD: Diagnosis based on DSM-V; history of behaviors impairing functioning in academic setting; diagnostic interview; history of symptoms; evidence of ongoing behaviors.

With general application: No
Submitted to: LNEC
Special Ed. HS course work accepted: NR
Specific course requirements of all applicants: Yes
Separate application required: No
# of LD applications submitted each year: NR
# of LD applications accepted yearly: NR
Total # of students receiving LD services: NR
Acceptance into program means acceptance into college: Students must be admitted to and enrolled in the university first and then request services.

ADMISSIONS

The students with learning disabilities go through the same admissions procedure as all incoming applicants. After admission to the university, students must contact the LNEC to receive services. Students with learning disabilities admitted to the university have qualified for admission because of their abilities. No criteria for admission are waived because of a disability. All applicants to UVA have outstanding grades, a high rank in their high school class, excellent performance in advanced placement and honor courses, superior performance on ACT/SAT Reasoning and SAT Subject Tests, extracurricular success, special talents, and interests and goals. Letters of recommendation are required.

ADDITIONAL INFORMATION

Following acceptance of an offer of admission to the university, students with an LD or ADHD are advised to contact the LNEC to identify their need for services. All students seeking accommodations while at the university must provide acceptable documentation of their disability, including, but not limited to, a neuropsychological or psychoeducational evaluation report, completed by a licensed clinical psychologist or clinical neuropsychologist, or other qualified provider that has been completed within 3 years of matriculation. Students are strongly encouraged to consult the Guidelines for Documentation of a Learning Disorder or ADHD available in the Information section of the LNEC's website: http://www.virginia.edu/studenthealth/lnec/infostudent.html. Services and accommodations are available for undergraduate and graduate students.

LEARNING DISABILITY PROGRAM OR SERVICES

Contact Information
Name of program or department: Learning Needs and Evaluation Center (LNEC)
  Telephone: 434-243-5181
  Fax: 434-243-5188

LEARNING DISABILITY SERVICES

Accommodations are decided upon an individual basis after a thorough review of appropriate, current documentation. The accommodations requested must be supported through the documentation provided and must be logically linked to the current impact of the condition on academic functioning.

Allowed in exams
  Calculator: Yes
  Dictionary: Yes
  Computer: Yes
  Spellchecker: Yes
Extended test time: Yes
Scribes: Yes
Proctors: Yes
Oral exams: Yes
Note-takers: Yes

Distraction-reduced environment: Yes
Tape recording in class: Yes
Electronic texts: Yes
Accommodations for students with ADHD: Yes
Kurzweil Reader: Yes
Other assistive technology: Yes
Priority registration: NR

Added costs for services: No
LD specialists: Yes
Professional tutors: No
Peer tutors: No
Max. hours/wk. for services: NR
How professors are notified of LD/ADHD: NR

GENERAL ADMISSIONS INFORMATION

Office of Admission: 434-982-3200

ENTRANCE REQUIREMENTS

Academic units required: 4 English, 4 math, 2 science, 2 foreign language, 1 social studies. **Academic units recommended:** 5 math, 4 science, 5 foreign language, 4 social studies. High school diploma is required, and GED is accepted. ACT with Writing component required. TOEFL required of all international applicants: minimum paper TOEFL 600, minimum computer TOEFL 250.

Application deadline: 1/2
Notification: 4/1
Average GPA: 4.19
ACT Composite middle 50% range: 28–32

SAT Math middle 50% range: 630–740
SAT Critical Reading middle 50% range: 610–720
SAT Writing middle 50% range: 620–720

Graduated top 10% of class: 91%
Graduated top 25% of class: 98%
Graduated top 50% of class: 100%

COLLEGE GRADUATION REQUIREMENTS

Course waivers allowed: No
Course substitutions allowed: Yes
In what course: Considerations of alternate courses for the foreign language requirement following an attempt by the student to complete standard language courses

ADDITIONAL INFORMATION

Environment: The 2,440-acre campus is located in a small city 70 miles northwest of Richmond.

Student Body
  Undergrad enrollment: 15,762
  Women: 55%
  Men: 45%
  Percent out-of-state: 26%

Cost Information
  In-state tuition: $11,786
  Out-of-state tuition: $36,780
  Room & board: $8,866
Housing Information
  University housing: Yes
  Percent living on campus: 42%

Greek System
  Fraternity: Yes
  Sorority: Yes
Athletics: Division I

VIRGINIA INTERMONT COLLEGE

1013 Moore Street, Bristol, VA 24201-4298
Phone: 276-466-7856 • Fax: 276-466-7855
E-mail: viadmit@vic.edu • Web: www.vic.edu
Support: CS • Institution type: 4-year private

PROGRAMS OR SERVICES FOR STUDENTS WITH LD

Student Support Services provides free supportive services to students who participate in the program. There are extensive services offered to those with LD. The objective of the services is to help students stay in school and graduate. Students work voluntarily with the staff as individuals or as a team to develop individual plans of support. Staff members act as advocates for students with faculty and administration and provide general faculty awareness and understanding of overall student needs without disclosure of confidentiality. Virginia Intermont staff and faculty have a commitment to the significance of the individual and to the value of personalizing education. The college provides quality education with extensive support services and accommodations, rather than altering admissions criteria or course requirements. Once admitted, students are encouraged to submit documentation of any special needs. This is usually in the form of psychoeducational test data and an IEP from high school. All accommodations are provided at the request of students with documentation.

ADMISSION INFORMATION FOR STUDENTS WITH LD/ADHD

College entrance tests required: Yes
Interview required: Recommended
Essay recommended: Yes
What documentation required for LD: Psycho Ed evaluation
   to include: relevant historical info, instructional interventions,
   related services, age diagnosed, objective data (aptitude,
   achievement, info processing), test scores (standard,
   percentile and grade equivalents) and describe functional
   limitations.
With general application: No
To receive services after enrolling: Yes
What documentation required for ADHD: Diagnosis based
   on DSM-V; history of behaviors impairing functioning in
   academic setting; diagnostic interview; history of symptoms;
   evidence of ongoing behaviors.

With general application: No
Submitted to: Student Support Services
Special Ed. HS course work accepted: No
Specific course requirements of all applicants: Yes
Separate application required: No
# of LD applications submitted each year: NR
# of LD applications accepted yearly: NR
Total # of students receiving LD services: 10–30
**Acceptance into program means acceptance into
   college:** Students must be admitted to and enrolled in the
   university first and then request services.

ADMISSIONS

There is no special admissions procedure for the student with a learning disability. Documentation related to a learning disability may be submitted to the Office of Admissions with the general application or may be submitted separately to the Office of Student Support Services. Testing done by a high school psychologist is acceptable, if current. The average ACT is 21; the average SAT is 970. The minimum GPA reuired is 2.5. Course requirements include a minimum of 15 units: 4 units of English, 3 units of math, 1 unit of science lab, 2 units of social science, and 5 units of electives. Virginia Intermont is more concerned with the student's quality of preparation than with the precise numerical distribution of requirements. A conditional admit may be offered if the high school GPA or SAT scores are below requirements. Students not having the proper high school preparation or not meeting the normal admissions criteria may be required, if admitted, to take developmental courses as needed in math, English, reading, and/or study strategies. These courses would not count toward graduation, and the student would be limited to 14 hours in the first semester.

ADDITIONAL INFORMATION

Students with LD will be offered appropriate accommodations recommended by Student Support Services based on the documentation. Accommodations and/or services available to eligible students include individual personal and academic counseling, freshman placement test accommodations, scribes, computer tests, extended time on tests, audio texts, peer and staff tutoring emphasizing unique techniques as needed, support groups, academic advising, liaison with faculty, tape recording of classes, assistance with course selection and registration, and optional reduced course load. A few accommodations require appointments, though generally there is an open door policy. Education 100 (1 credit), taught by Student Support Services staff, is designed for students interested in improving academic skills. Topics covered in this course are individual learning styles, time-study management, note-taking, textbook reading, memory strategies, test-taking strategies, and test anxiety reduction.

LEARNING DISABILITY PROGRAM OR SERVICES

Contact Information
Name of program or department: Student Support Services
  Telephone: 276-466-7906
  Fax: 276-645-6493

LEARNING DISABILITY SERVICES

Accommodations are decided upon an individual basis after a thorough review of appropriate, current documentation. The accommodations requested must be supported through the documentation provided and must be logically linked to the current impact of the condition on academic functioning.

Allowed in exams	Distraction-reduced environment: Yes	Added costs for services: No
Calculator: Yes	Tape recording in class: Yes	LD specialists: No
Dictionary: Yes	Electronic texts: Yes	Professional tutors: No
Computer: Yes	Accommodations for students with	Peer tutors: 12–30
Spellchecker: Yes	ADHD: Yes	Max. hours/wk. for services:
Extended test time: Yes	Kurzweil Reader: No	Unlimited
Scribes: Yes	Other assistive technology: No	How professors are notified of
Proctors: Yes	Priority registration: No	LD/ADHD: By both student and
Oral exams: Yes		director
Note-takers: Yes		

GENERAL ADMISSIONS INFORMATION

Office of Admission: 276-466-7867

ENTRANCE REQUIREMENTS

Academic units required: 4 English, 3 math, 1 science (1 science lab), 2 social studies, 5 academic electives, 2–3 science units recommended for science majors. High school diploma is required, and GED is accepted. ACT (with or without writing component) or SAT required. TOEFL required of all international applicants: minimum paper TOEFL 500, minimum computer TOEFL 173.

Application deadline: None	SAT Math middle 50% range:	Graduated top 10% of class: 11%
Notification: Rolling	420–520	Graduated top 25% of class: 30%
Average GPA: 3.20	SAT Critical Reading middle 50%	Graduated top 50% of class: 74%
ACT Composite middle 50% range:	range: 440–530	
18–23	SAT Writing middle 50% range:	
	440–520	

COLLEGE GRADUATION REQUIREMENTS

Course waivers allowed: No
Course substitutions allowed: Yes
In what course: Substitutions are rarely granted but must be considered by a committee.

ADDITIONAL INFORMATION

Environment: The college is located on a 16-acre campus in the Blue Ridge Mountains.

Student Body	Cost Information	Greek System
Undergrad enrollment: 591	Tuition: $24,542	Fraternity: No
Women: 71%	Room & board: $7,690	Sorority: No
Men: 29%	Housing Information	Athletics: NAIA
Percent out-of-state: 45%	University housing: Yes	
	Percent living on campus: 53%	

EASTERN WASHINGTON UNIVERSITY

526 Fifth Street, Cheney, WA 99004
Phone: 509-359-2397 • Fax: 509-359-6692
E-mail: admissions@mail.ewu.edu • Web: www.ewu.edu
Support: S • Institution type: 4-year public

PROGRAMS OR SERVICES FOR STUDENTS WITH LD

Although the university does not offer a specialized curriculum, personnel work with students to modify programs to meet individual needs. Disability Support Services (DSS) is dedicated to the coordination of appropriate and reasonable accommodations for students with disabilities. These accommodations are based on individual needs so that each student may receive an equal opportunity to learn to participate in campus life, to grow emotionally and socially, and to successfully complete a program of study that will enable him or her to be self-supporting and remain as independent as possible. This is facilitated through support services, information sharing, advisement, and referral when requested. Students who require services and support need to contact DSS so that the disability can be verified, specific needs determined, and timely accommodations made. In most cases, documentation by a professional service provider will be necessary. Information is kept strictly confidential. However, it is important to share information that will enable DSS staff to provide appropriate, reasonable, and timely services tailored to individual needs.

ADMISSION INFORMATION FOR STUDENTS WITH LD/ADHD

College entrance tests required: Yes
Interview required: No
Essay recommended: Yes
What documentation required for LD: Psycho Ed evaluation to include: relevant historical info, instructional interventions, related services, age diagnosed, objective data (aptitude, achievement, info processing), test scores (standard, percentile and grade equivalents) and describe functional limitations.
With general application: No
To receive services after enrolling: Yes
What documentation required for ADHD: Diagnosis based on DSM-V; history of behaviors impairing functioning in academic setting; diagnostic interview; history of symptoms; evidence of ongoing behaviors.

With general application: No
Submitted to: Admissions Office and DSS
Special Ed. HS course work accepted: Yes
Specific course requirements of all applicants: Yes
Separate application required: No
# of LD applications submitted each year: NR
# of LD applications accepted yearly: NR
Total # of students receiving LD services: 200
Acceptance into program means acceptance into college: Students must be admitted to and enrolled in the university first and then request services.

ADMISSIONS

Individuals with disabilities are admitted via the standard admissions criteria that apply to all students. General admissibility is based on an index using GPA and test scores. The minimum GPA accepted is a 2.0. Required courses include 4 years of English, 3 years of math, 3 years of social science, 2 years of science (1 year of lab), 2 years of a foreign language (American Sign Language accepted), and 1 year of arts or academic electives. Special education courses are acceptable if they are courses that are regularly taught in the high school. However, all applicants must complete the required core courses. Students who do not meet the grade and test score admission scale may provide additional information to the Admission Office and request consideration through the special talent admissions process.

ADDITIONAL INFORMATION

Examples of services for students with specific learning disabilities include alternative format textbooks; equipment loans; alternative testing arrangements such as oral exams, extended time on tests, relocation of testing site; note-takers; tutorial assistance (available to all students); referral to a Learning Skills Center, Writers' Center, and/or Mathematics Lab; accessible computer stations; and a Kurzweil Kurzweil Reader. Examples of services for students with ADHD are consultation regarding reasonable and effective accommodations with classroom professors; alternative testing; alternative format textbooks; note-takers; taped lectures; equipment loans; referrals to a Learning Skills Center, a Math Lab, a Writers' Center, and counseling and psychological services; information on ADHD; and informal counseling. Skills classes for credit are offered in math, reading, time management, study skills, and writing skills. FOCUS is a structured first-year experience for selected, provisionally admitted students. The experience includes advising; academic instruction in math, English, and study strategies; and professional mentoring. Services and accommodations are offered to undergraduate and graduate students.

LEARNING DISABILITY PROGRAM OR SERVICES

Contact Information
Name of program or department: Disability Support Services
  Telephone: 509-359-6871
  Fax: 509-359-7458

LEARNING DISABILITY SERVICES

Accommodations are decided upon an individual basis after a thorough review of appropriate, current documentation. The accommodations requested must be supported through the documentation provided and must be logically linked to the current impact of the condition on academic functioning.

Allowed in exams
  Calculator: Yes
  Dictionary: Yes
  Computer: Yes
  Spellchecker: Yes
Extended test time: Yes
Scribes: Yes
Proctors: Yes
Oral exams: Yes
Note-takers: Yes

Distraction-reduced environment: Yes
Tape recording in class: Yes
Electronic texts: Yes
Accommodations for students with
  ADHD: Yes
Kurzweil Reader: Yes
Other assistive technology: Yes
Priority registration: Yes

Added costs for services: No
LD specialists: No
Professional tutors: 7
Peer tutors: 33
Max. hours/wk. for services: NR
How professors are notified of
  LD/ADHD: By both student and
  director

GENERAL ADMISSIONS INFORMATION

Office of Admission: 509-359-2397

ENTRANCE REQUIREMENTS

Academic units required: 4 English, 3 math, 2 science (1 science lab), 2 foreign language, 3 social studies, 1 fine arts or another unit chosen from previously listed subjects. **Academic units recommended:** 4 English, 4 math, 3 science, 2 foreign language, 4 social studies, 1 fine arts or another unit chosen from previously listed subjects. High school diploma is required, and GED is accepted. ACT with Writing component required. TOEFL required of all international applicants: minimum paper TOEFL 525, minimum computer TOEFL 195.

Application deadline: 8/15
Notification: Rolling
Average GPA: 3.25
ACT Composite middle 50% range:
  18–24

SAT Math middle 50% range:
  440–540
SAT Critical Reading middle 50%
  range: 420–530
SAT Writing middle 50% range:
  410–520

Graduated top 10% of class: NR
Graduated top 25% of class: NR
Graduated top 50% of class: NR

COLLEGE GRADUATION REQUIREMENTS

Course waivers allowed: Yes
In what course: Possible waiver for foreign language. This must be supported by documentation.
Course substitutions allowed: Yes
In what course: Possible substitutions in math and foreign language. These must be supported by documentation.

ADDITIONAL INFORMATION

Environment: The university is located on 35 acres in a small town 18 miles southwest of Spokane.

Student Body
  Undergrad enrollment: 10,903
  Women: 55%
  Men: 45%
  Percent out-of-state: 6%

Cost Information
  In-state tuition: $7,422
    Out-of-state tuition: $17,100
  Room & board: $7,971
Housing Information
  University housing: Yes
  Percent living on campus: 20%

Greek System
  Fraternity: Yes
  Sorority: Yes
Athletics: Division I

THE EVERGREEN STATE COLLEGE

2700 Evergreen Pkwy NW, Office of Admissions, Olympia, WA 98505
Phone: 360-867-6170 • Fax: 360-867-5114
E-mail: admissions@evergreen.edu • Web: www.evergreen.edu
Support: S • Institution: 4-year public

PROGRAMS OR SERVICES FOR STUDENTS WITH LD

For almost 40 years, The Evergreen State College has consistently provided an integrated learning community for students. Instead of taking four or five separate, unrelated classes each quarter, students take one program that unifies these classes around a central theme, taught by two or three faculty members from different academic disciplines. Many programs continue for two or three consecutive quarters. This allows students to build specific skills to produce highly sophisticated work, even in introductory offerings. And, because learning is too important to be reduced to an arbitrary number or letter grade, students receive a narrative evaluation from the faculty. The student's accomplishments and achievements will be detailed to provide graduate schools and employers with a comprehensive overview of his or her undergraduate education.

ADMISSION INFORMATION FOR STUDENTS WITH LD/ADHD

College entrance tests required: Yes
Interview required: No
What documentation required for LD: Psycho Ed evaluation
  to include: relevant historical info, instructional interventions,
  related services, age diagnosed, objective data (aptitude,
  achievement, info processing), test scores (standard,
  percentile and grade equivalents) and describe functional
  limitations.
With general application: No
To receive services after enrolling: Yes
What documentation required for ADHD: Diagnosis based
  on DSM-V; history of behaviors impairing functioning in
  academic setting; diagnostic interview; history of symptoms;
  evidence of ongoing behaviors.

With general application: No
Submitted to: Support Program/Services
Special Ed. HS course work accepted: No
Specific course requirements for all applicants: Yes
Separate application required for program services: No
# of LD applications submitted each year: NR
# of LD applications accepted yearly: NR
Total # of students receiving LD services: NR
Acceptance into program means acceptance into
  college: Separate application required after student has
  enrolled

ADMISSIONS

Students entering Evergreen directly from high school will be considered for admission on the following basis: Completion of college-preparatory course work in high school; Grade point average (GPA) and ACT or SAT test scores. A 2.8 cumulative GPA is recommended; a 2.0 cumulative GPA is required for admission consideration. The SAT writing test and subject tests are not required; Good standing in any college-level work attempted while in high school or after high school graduation. The quality of the college work will be taken into consideration as well.

A personal statement is an important part of the application, too. This statement is desired from all applicants. However, Home School applicants must submit a personal statement. More information about the admission application process and the personal statement can be found on the web at admissions.evergreen.edu/application.

ADDITIONAL INFORMATION

The Evergreen State College is committed to providing equal access, accommodations, and educational support for qualified students with disabilities. It is our goal to invite and celebrate diversity within our campus community. Our approach is designed to be holistic and to empower by promoting: self reliance, effective problem solving skills, enhanced academic and personal development, and equal access to college programs and activities for qualified students with disabilities.

PROGRAM FOR DISABILITY SERVICES

Contact Information
Name of program or department: Access Services
  Telephone: 360-867-6364
  Fax: 360-867-6360

LEARNING DISABILITY SERVICES

Accommodations are decided upon an individual basis after a thorough review of appropriate, current documentation. The accommodations requested must be supported through the documentation provided and must be logically linked to the current impact of the condition on academic functioning.

Allowed in exams	**Distraction-reduced environment:** Yes	**Added costs for services:** No
Calculator: Yes	**Tape recording in class:** Yes	**LD specialists:** No
Dictionary: Yes	**Electronic texts:** Yes	**Professional tutors:** 6
Computer: Yes	**Accommodations for students with**	**Peer tutors:** 10
Spellchecker: Yes	**ADHD:** Yes	**Max. hours/wk. for services:** 5
Extended test time: Yes	**Kurzweil Reader:** Yes	**How professors are notified of**
Scribes: Yes	**Other assistive technology:** Yes	**LD/ADHD:** Both student and director
Proctors: Yes	**Priority registration:** No	
Oral exams: Yes		
Note-takers: Yes		

GENERAL ADMISSIONS INFORMATION

Office of Admission: 360-867-6170

ENTRANCE REQUIREMENTS
Academic units required: 4 English; 3 mathematics (algebra I and higher); 2 laboratory science and 1 credit in algebra-based biology, chemistry or physics; 2 foreign language (single language); 3 social studies; 1 arts or other college prep elective from the subjects identified here. A high school diploma is required and the GED is accepted. ACT or SAT required; the SAT writing test and subject tests are not required. TOEFL is required of all international applicants if English is not the native language. The minimum score on the TOEFL is 550 (paper), or 213 (computer) or 79 (web-based).

Application deadline: None	**SAT Math middle 50% range:**	**Graduated top 10% of class:** 11%
Notification: Rolling	460–580	**Graduated top 25% of class:** 28%
Average GPA: 3.01	**SAT Critical Reading middle 50%**	**Graduated top 50% of class:** 65%
ACT Composite middle 50% range:	**range:** 510–640	
21–26	**SAT Writing middle 50% range:**	
	470–610	

COLLEGE GRADUATION REQUIREMENTS

Course waivers allowed: N/A
In what course: Specific courses are not required to earn a B.A. If student is applying to graduate with a B.S. then a review of science, math, and computer science credits will be done to ensure that the student has met the B.S. criteria of 72 credits of science, math, or computer science.

ADDITIONAL INFORMATION

Environment: The campus is in Olympia, Washington—1 hour south of Seattle and 2 hours north of Portland, Oregon.

Student Body	**Cost Information**	**Greek System**
Undergrad enrollment: 4,489	**In-state tuition:** $8,610	**Fraternity:** No
Women: 55%	**Out-of-state tuition:** $18,070	**Sorority:** No
Men: 45%	**Room and board:** $9,000	**Athletics:** NAIA
Percent out-of-state: 26%	**Housing Information**	
	University housing: Yes	
	Percent living on campus: 20%	

WASHINGTON STATE UNIVERSITY

PO Box 641067, Pullman, WA 99164-1067
Phone: 509-335-5586 • Fax: 509-335-4902
E-mail: admissions@wsu.edu • Web: www.wsu.edu
Support: S • Institution type: 4-year public

PROGRAMS OR SERVICES FOR STUDENTS WITH LD

The Access Center (AC) assists students who have a disability by providing academic accommodations. The program may also refer students to other service programs that may assist them in achieving their academic goals. AC will help students overcome potential obstacles so that they may be successful in their area of study. All academic adjustments are authorized on an individual basis. The program offers academic coaching. To be eligible for assistance, students must be currently enrolled at Washington State University. They also must submit documentation of their disability. For a learning disability, the student must submit a written report that includes test scores and evaluation. It is the student's responsibility to request accommodations if desired. It is important to remember that even though two individuals may have the same disability, they may not necessarily need the same academic adjustments. AC works with students and instructors to determine and implement appropriate academic adjustments. Many adjustments are simple, creative alternatives for traditional ways of learning.

ADMISSION INFORMATION FOR STUDENTS WITH LD/ADHD

College entrance tests required: Yes
Interview required: No
Essay recommended: No
What documentation required for LD: Psycho Ed evaluation
  to include: relevant historical info, instructional interventions,
  related services, age diagnosed, objective data (aptitude,
  achievement, info processing), test scores (standard,
  percentile and grade equivalents) and describe functional
  limitations.
With general application: No
To receive services after enrolling: Yes
What documentation required for ADHD: Diagnosis based
  on DSM-V; history of behaviors impairing functioning in
  academic setting; diagnostic interview; history of symptoms;
  evidence of ongoing behaviors.

With general application: No
Submitted to: Access Center
Special Ed. HS course work accepted: Yes
Specific course requirements of all applicants: Yes
Separate application required: NR
# of LD applications submitted each year: NR
# of LD applications accepted yearly: NR
Total # of students receiving LD services: 125
**Acceptance into program means acceptance into
  college:** Students must be admitted and enrolled in the
  university first (they can appeal a denial) and then request
  services.

ADMISSIONS

All students must meet the general admission requirements. The university looks at the combination of scores on the ACT/SAT and the applicant's high school GPA. The standard admission criteria are based on an index score determined by 75 percent GPA and 25 percent SAT/ACT. Courses required include 4 years of English, 4 years of math, 2 years of science, 2 years of a foreign language, 3 years of social studies, 1 year of art. Only 15 percent of new admissions may be admitted under special admission. Documentation of the learning disability and diagnostic tests are required if requesting accommodations or services.

ADDITIONAL INFORMATION

General assistance to students with learning disabilities includes pre-admission counseling; information about disabilities; referral to appropriate community resources; academic, personal, and career counseling; information about accommodations; information about the laws pertaining to individuals with disabilities; and self-advocacy. Typical academic adjustments for students with learning disabilities may include note-takers and/or audiotape class sessions; alternative testing arrangements; alternate print (mp3 files or text files); extended time for exams; essay exams taken on computer; and use of computers with voice output and spellcheckers. Services and accommodations are available for undergraduate and graduate students.

LEARNING DISABILITY PROGRAM OR SERVICES

Contact Information
Name of program or department: Access Center (AC)
  Telephone: 509-335-3417
  Fax: 509-335-8511

LEARNING DISABILITY SERVICES

Accommodations are decided upon an individual basis after a thorough review of appropriate, current documentation. The accommodations requested must be supported through the documentation provided and must be logically linked to the current impact of the condition on academic functioning.

Allowed in exams
  Calculator: Yes
  Dictionary: Yes
  Computer: Yes
  Spellchecker: Yes
Extended test time: Yes
Scribes: Yes
Proctors: Yes
Oral exams: Yes

Note-takers: Yes
Distraction-reduced environment: Yes
Tape recording in class: Yes
Electronic texts: Yes
Accommodations for students with
  ADHD: Yes
Kurzweil Reader: Yes
Other assistive technology: Yes
Priority registration: Yes

Added costs for services: No
LD specialists: No
Professional tutors: No
Peer tutors: No
Max. hours/wk. for services: 5–10
How professors are notified of
  LD/ADHD: By student

GENERAL ADMISSIONS INFORMATION

Office of Admission: 509-335-5586

ENTRANCE REQUIREMENTS

Academic units required: 4 English, 4 math, 2 science (1 science lab), 2 foreign language, 3 social studies, 1 art.
Academic units recommended: 4 English, 4 math, 2 science (1 science lab), 2 foreign language, 2 social studies, 1 history, 1 academic elective. High school diploma is required, and GED is accepted. ACT with Writing component required. TOEFL required of all international applicants: minimum paper TOEFL 520, minimum computer TOEFL 190.

Application deadline: None
Notification: Rolling
Average GPA: 3.35
ACT Composite middle 50% range:
  20–26

SAT Math middle 50% range:
  480–600
SAT Critical Reading middle 50%
  range: 470–580
SAT Writing middle 50% range:
  460–560

Graduated top 10% of class: 26%
Graduated top 25% of class: 46%
Graduated top 50% of class: 78%

COLLEGE GRADUATION REQUIREMENTS

Course waivers allowed: No
Course substitutions allowed: Yes
In what course: Foreign language, math

ADDITIONAL INFORMATION

Environment: The university is located on 600 acres in a small town 80 miles south of Spokane.

Student Body
  Undergrad enrollment: 22,763
  Women: 51%
  Men: 49%
  Percent out-of-state: 9%

Cost Information
  In-state tuition: $10,798
  Out-of-state tuition: $22,076
  Room & board: $9,662
Housing Information
  University housing: Yes
  Percent living on campus: 25%

Greek System
  Fraternity: Yes
  Sorority: Yes
Athletics: Division I

DAVIS AND ELKINS COLLEGE

100 Campus Drive, Elkins, WV 26241
Phone: 304-637-1230 • Fax: 304-637-1800
E-mail: admiss@dewv.edu • Web: www.dewv.edu
Support: SP • Institution type: 4-year private

PROGRAMS OR SERVICES FOR STUDENTS WITH LD

Davis and Elkins offers a comprehensive support program for college students with learning disabilities. The goals blend with the college's commitment to diversity and providing a personalized education. The program goes well beyond accommodations or services by providing individualized instruction to meet each student's needs. The goal of the LD program is to enable students diagnosed with LD/ADHD to function to the best of their ability. To meet this goal, each student meets at least weekly for a regularly scheduled session with one of the three experienced learning disabilities specialists. The main focus of these meetings is to develop learning strategies and academic skills. Students may request extra assistance and use the lab as a study area. There is a fee per year. Applicants must submit complete and current documentation of their disability.

ADMISSION INFORMATION FOR STUDENTS WITH LD/ADHD

College entrance tests required: Yes
Interview required: Yes
Essay recommended: Yes
What documentation required for LD: Psycho Ed evaluation to include: relevant historical info, instructional interventions, related services, age diagnosed, objective data (aptitude, achievement, info processing), test scores (standard, percentile and grade equivalents) and describe functional limitations.
With general application: Yes if requested as part of Structured Program application
To receive services after enrolling: Yes
What documentation required for ADHD: Diagnosis based on DSM-V; history of behaviors impairing functioning in academic setting; diagnostic interview; history of symptoms; evidence of ongoing behaviors.

With general application: Yes if requested as part of Structured Program application
To receive services after enrolling: Yes
Submitted to: Supported Learning Program
Special Ed. HS course work accepted: No
Specific course requirements of all applicants: Yes
Separate application required: Yes
# of LD applications submitted each year: 30–50
# of LD applications accepted yearly: 15–20
Total # of students receiving LD services: 52
Acceptance into program means acceptance into college: Applications to the university and the LD program are separate. Must be accepted to the university before being accepted into the LD program.

ADMISSIONS

All applications are screened by the learning disabilities program director. Students must be admitted to Davis and Elkins College prior to being considered for the program. Students requesting admission to the program must meet admissions requirements; complete a separate application to the program; send current documentation completed within the past 2 years; provide recommendations for participation in the program by a counselor or a learning specialist; provide a copy of a recent IEP, if available; complete a handwritten essay requesting services and indicating why services are being requested; and have a personal interview with a member of the Supported Learning Program.

ADDITIONAL INFORMATION

Services include individual sessions with certified LD specialists, individualized programs focusing on improved writing skills, test-taking techniques, note-taking and textbook usage, and time management strategies. Specialists help students develop a personalized program focusing on improving written work, identifying class expectations and preparing work to that level of expectation, test-taking skills, using textbooks and taking notes, and managing time effectively. Students also receive advising and registration assistance based on assessment information. Personnel in the LD program also assist the students with course selection and registration; orientation to college life; monitoring of classes throughout the year and interpreting feedback from professors; coordinating of tutoring, additional counseling, and career planning; and modifying instructional programs as needed.

LEARNING DISABILITY PROGRAM OR SERVICES

Contact Information
Name of program or department: Supported Learning Program
  Telephone: 304-637-1384
  Fax: 304-637-1424

LEARNING DISABILITY SERVICES

Accommodations are decided upon an individual basis after a thorough review of appropriate, current documentation. The accommodations requested must be supported through the documentation provided and must be logically linked to the current impact of the condition on academic functioning.

Allowed in exams
  Calculator: Yes
  Dictionary: Yes
  Computer: Yes
  Spellchecker: Yes
Extended test time: Yes
Scribes: Yes
Proctors: Yes
Oral exams: Yes
Note-takers: Yes

Distraction-reduced environment: Yes
Tape recording in class: Yes, under discretion of instructor
Electronic texts: Yes
Accommodations for students with ADHD: Yes
Kurzweil Reader: Yes
Other assistive technology: Yes
Priority registration: N/A

Added costs for services: Yes
LD specialists: Yes
Professional tutors: No
Peer tutors: 25–50
Max. hours/wk. for services: Mandatory one hour meeting per week, and 5 hours supervised study hall
How professors are notified of LD/ADHD: By both student and director

GENERAL ADMISSIONS INFORMATION

Office of Admission: 304-637-1974

ENTRANCE REQUIREMENTS
Academic units required: 4 English, 3 science (1 science lab), 1 foreign language, 3 social studies, 2 math (must include Algebra I or II and geometry). High school diploma is required, and GED is accepted. ACT with Writing component required. TOEFL required of all international applicants: minimum paper TOEFL 450, minimum computer TOEFL 133.

Application deadline: None
Notification: Rolling
Average GPA: 3.06
ACT Composite middle 50% range: 18–23

SAT Math middle 50% range: 390–490
SAT Critical Reading middle 50% range: 380–490
SAT Writing middle 50% range: 390–490

Graduated top 10% of class: 12%
Graduated top 25% of class: 33%
Graduated top 50% of class: 71%

COLLEGE GRADUATION REQUIREMENTS

Course waivers allowed: Yes
In what course: Individual requests are reviewed by the dean.
Course substitutions allowed: Yes
In what course: Individual requests are reviewed by the dean.

ADDITIONAL INFORMATION

Environment: The college is located in a community of 10,000 residents in the foothills of the Allegheny Mountain Range.

Student Body
  Undergrad enrollment: 784
  Women: 56%
  Men: 44%
  Percent out-of-state: 31%

Cost Information
  Tuition: $22,320
  Room & board: $7,950
Housing Information
  University housing: Yes
  Percent living on campus: 49%

Greek System
  Fraternity: Yes
  Sorority: Yes
Athletics: NCAA, Division II

MARSHALL UNIVERSITY

One John Marshall Drive, Huntington, WV 25755
Phone: 304-696-3160 • Fax: 304-696-3135
E-mail: admissions@marshall.edu • Web: www.marshall.edu
Support: SP • Institution: 4-year public

PROGRAMS OR SERVICES FOR STUDENTS WITH LD

Higher Education for Learning Problems (H.E.L.P.) is a comprehensive and structured tutoring support program for college students who have a diagnosed Specific Learning Disability and/or Attention Deficit Disorder. Both academic and skills development tutoring is available. The academic tutoring is done by graduate assistants with expertise in the subject matter. The skills development tutoring is done by Learning Disabilities Specialists. Through the academic component, students receive tutoring in the classes they are taking as well as receiving the needed accommodations in testing. The skills development component addresses skills areas such as reading, written expression, math, study skills, time management and organizational skills. H.E.L.P. encourages a feeling of camaraderie among the students enrolled in the program. Students attend class with all other students at Marshall University and they must meet the same standards as all other students. The H.E.L.P. Program boasts a high success rate with students.

ADMISSION INFORMATION FOR STUDENTS WITH LD/ADHD

College entrance tests required: Yes
Interview required: Yes
Essay required: Yes
What documentation required for LD: Psycho Ed evaluation to include: relevant historical info, instructional interventions, related services, age diagnosed, objective data (aptitude, achievement, info processing), test scores (standard, percentile and grade equivalents) and describe functional limitations.
With general application: Yes if requested as part of Structured Program application
To receive services after enrolling: Yes
What documentation required for ADHD: Diagnosis based on DSM-V; history of behaviors impairing functioning in academic setting; diagnostic interview; history of symptoms; evidence of ongoing behaviors.

With general application: Yes if requested as part of Structured Program application
To receive services after enrolling: Yes
Submitted to: Support Program/Services
Special Ed. HS course work accepted: Yes
Specific course requirements for all applicants: Yes
Separate application required for program services: Yes
# of LD applications submitted each year: 200
# of LD applications accepted yearly: 30–40
Total # of students receiving LD services: 200
Acceptance into program means acceptance into college: Separate application is part of admissions process; separate application required after student has enrolled.

ADMISSIONS

Students must apply to both Marshall University and to the H.E.L.P. Program. Students applying to H.E.L.P. must have a diagnosed Specific Learning Disability and/or Attention Deficit Disorder. These students must submit: an application; updated psychological and educational evaluation; a one-page, handwritten statement by the student (no assistance) regarding why college is desirable; and two recommendations stating why the recommenders feel the student should attend college. An interview with H.E.L.P. is required. It is best if students apply to H.E.L.P. at least six months in advance of the proposed entry date to college. There is a required five-week summer H.E.L.P. Program for incoming freshmen. Marshall University admission requires minimum GPA of 2.0, ACT 19 or SAT 910, plus four years English, three years social studies, four years math (including algebra I and at least two higher units), and three years of laboratory science.

ADDITIONAL INFORMATION

The Summer Prep Learning Disabilities Program is offered through H.E.L.P. for our incoming freshmen. Students take one Marshall University class in the morning for credit, and receive one hour of tutoring daily for that class. In the afternoons, the students attend three hours of college-prep. Students are assigned to three, one-hour sessions based on their areas of greatest need. The areas covered are basic reading skills, reading comprehension, written expression, study skills, and math. The program is taught by Learning Disabilities Specialists. Students are taught in small groups, generally with five to six students per group. The cost for the Summer Prep Program is $1,000 for West Virginia residents, $1,400 for Metro area residents, and $2,200 for non-West Virginia residents. This does not include registration for classes students take through the university or housing. Students sign a release allowing H.E.L.P. to talk to professors and parents.

PROGRAM FOR DISABILITY SERVICES

Contact Information
Name of program or department: Higher Education for Learning Problems (H.E.L.P.)
Telephone: 304-696-6252
Fax: 304-696-3231

LEARNING DISABILITY SERVICES

Accommodations are decided on an individual basis after a thorough review of appropriate, current documentation. The accommodations requested must be supported through the documentation provided and must be logically linked to the current impact of the condition on academic functioning.

Allowed in exams
 Calculator: Yes
 Dictionary: Yes
 Computer: Yes
 Spellchecker: Yes
Extended test time: Yes
Scribes: Yes
Proctors: Yes
Oral exams: Yes
Note-takers: No

Distraction-reduced environment: Yes
Tape recording in class: Yes
Electronic texts: Yes
Accommodations for students with ADHD: Yes
Kurzweil Reader: Yes
Other assistive technology: Computer Programs,Kurzweil, Read and Write
Priority registration: Yes

Added costs for services: Yes
LD specialists: Yes
Professional tutors: 45
Peer tutors: No
Max. hours/wk. for services: Unlimited
How professors are notified of LD/ADHD: Documentation is sent to professor

GENERAL ADMISSIONS INFORMATION

Office of Admission: 304-696-3160

ENTRANCE REQUIREMENTS

Academic units required: 4 English, 4 mathematics, 3 science, (3 science labs), 2 foreign language, 3 social studies, 1 visual/performing arts. High school diploma is required and GED is accepted. SAT or ACT required; TOEFL required of all international applicants; minimum paper TOEFL 500, minimum computer TOEFL 173.

Application deadline: None
Notification: Rolling
Average GPA: 3.3
ACT Composite middle 50% range: 19–25

SAT Math middle 50% range: 440–560
SAT Critical Reading middle 50% range: 450–560
SAT Writing middle 50% range: 440–550

Graduated top 10% of class: %
Graduated top 25% of class: %
Graduated top 50% of class: %

COLLEGE GRADUATION REQUIREMENTS

Course waivers allowed: Yes
In what course: Math
Course substitutions allowed: Yes
In what course: Math, foreign language

ADDITIONAL INFORMATION

Environment: Marshall University has a 55-acre urban campus located 140 miles east of Lexington, Kentucky.

Student Body
 Undergrad enrollment: 10,018
 Women: 56%
 Men: 44%
 Percent out-of-state: 28%

Cost Information
 In-state tuition: $5,648
 Out-of-state tuition: $13,480
 Room and board: $8,710
Housing Information
 University housing: Yes
 Percent living on campus: NR

Greek System
 Fraternity: Yes
 Sorority: Yes
Athletics: Division I

WEST VIRGINIA UNIVERSITY

Admissions Office, PO Box 6009, Morgantown, WV 26506-6009
Phone: 304-293-2121 • Fax: 304-293-3080
E-mail: go2wvu@mail.wvu.edu • Web: www.wvu.edu
Support: S • Institution: 4-year public

PROGRAMS OR SERVICES FOR STUDENTS WITH LD

The Office of Disability Services is available to all students on the campus of West Virginia University. Services are provided to qualified students with disabilities. It is the student's responsibility to provide appropriate documentation for the diagnosis prior to receiving accommodations based upon that disability. Each student's academic accommodations will be determined by the University on an individual basis. In order to meet the adult criteria of "disability" under federal laws individuals must provide documentation of how the significant impairment substantially limits their academic functioning. A "significant impairment" means below average functioning. An IEP or a 504 plan from the public school system is not documentation of a disability for the purposes of providing accommodations at the college level.

ADMISSION INFORMATION FOR STUDENTS WITH LD/ADHD

College entrance tests required: Yes
Interview required: No
Essay required: No
What documentation required for LD: Psycho Ed evaluation to include: relevant historical info, instructional interventions, related services, age diagnosed, objective data (aptitude, achievement, info processing), test scores (standard, percentile and grade equivalents) and describe functional limitations.
With general application: No
To receive services after enrolling: Yes
What documentation required for ADHD: Diagnosis based on DSM-V; history of behaviors impairing functioning in academic setting; diagnostic interview; history of symptoms; evidence of ongoing behaviors.

With general application: No
Special Ed. HS course work accepted: No
Specific course requirements for all applicants: Yes
Separate application required for program services: Yes
# of LD applications submitted each year: 25–50
# of LD applications accepted yearly: 25–50
Total # of students receiving LD services: 575
Acceptance into program means acceptance into college: Separate application required after student has enrolled

ADMISSIONS

There is no special admissions process for students with LD and ADHD. Students must meet admissions requirements. In-state students must have a 2.0 GPA and out-of-state students must have a 2.25 GPA and either a composite ACT of 20 or a combined SAT score of 950 to be considered for admission. Additionally, all applicants must have four years of English, three years of social studies, four years of math, three years of lab science, two years of same foreign language and one year of fine art. Students are not encouraged to self-disclose a disability in a personal statement during the application process. Appropriate services/accommodations will be determined after the student is admitted.

ADDITIONAL INFORMATION

Requirements for the documentation of a LD include the following: a signed, dated comprehensive psychoeducational evaluation report indicating how the LD impacts academic performance and contributes to a "significant impairment" in academic functioning. The report should address Aptitude, Achievement, Processing, and should include the WAIS and full Woodcock-Johnson Battery. A description of the functional limitations, which impact against the educational effort, must be included in the diagnostic report. Additionally, a documented history of previous accommodations received should be included. Documentation of ADHD must be in the form of a signed and dated report, by either a psychiatrist, neuropsychologist or licensed psychologist trained in the differential diagnosis. Additional information is required. There are no LD specialists on staff; however, counselors are available to provide services to all students. Some accommodations that are available with appropriate documentation include: priority registration, extended testing time, note-takers, distraction-free environments, books on tape, and assistive technology.

PROGRAM FOR DISABILITY SERVICES

Contact Information
Name of program or department: Office of Disability Services
 Telephone: 304-293-5496
 Fax: 304-293-3861

LEARNING DISABILITY SERVICES

Accommodations are decided upon an individual basis after a thorough review of appropriate, current documentation. The accommodations requested must be supported through the documentation provided and must be logically linked to the current impact of the condition on academic functioning.

Allowed in exams
 Calculator: No
 Dictionary: Yes
 Computer: Yes
 Spellchecker: Yes
Extended test time: Yes
Scribes: Yes
Proctors: No
Oral exams: Yes
Note-takers: Yes

Distraction-reduced environment: Yes
Tape recording in class: Yes
Electronic texts: Yes
Accommodations for students with
 ADHD: Yes
Kurzweil Reader: Yes
Other assistive technology: As
 needed.
Priority registration: Yes

Added costs for services: Yes
LD specialists: Yes
Professional tutors: No
Peer tutors: 50–70
Max. hours/wk. for services: 5
How professors are notified of
 LD/ADHD: Student

GENERAL ADMISSIONS INFORMATION

Office of Admission: 304-293-4515

ENTRANCE REQUIREMENTS
Academic units required: 4 English, 4 mathematics, 3 science, (3 science labs), 2 foreign language, 3 social studies, 1 visual/performing arts. High school diploma is required and GED is accepted. SAT or ACT required; ACT with Writing component required. TOEFL required of all international applicants; minimum paper TOEFL 550, minimum computer TOEFL 173.

Application deadline: 8/1
Notification: Rolling
Average GPA: 3.3
ACT Composite middle 50% range:
 21–26

SAT Math middle 50% range:
 480–580
SAT Critical Reading middle 50%
 range: 470–560
SAT Writing middle 50% range: NR

Graduated top 10% of class: 19.3%
Graduated top 25% of class: 45.4%
Graduated top 50% of class: 76.8%

COLLEGE GRADUATION REQUIREMENTS

Course waivers allowed: Yes
In what course: Foreign Language substitutions
Course substitutions allowed: Yes
In what course: Foreign language substitution

ADDITIONAL INFORMATION

Environment: The campus is located 70 miles from Pittsburgh, Pennsylvania.

Student Body
 Undergrad enrollment: 22,711
 Women: 45%
 Men: 55%
 Percent out-of-state: 49%

Cost Information
 In-state tuition: $5,406
 Out-of-state tuition: $17,004
 Room and board: $8,120
Housing Information
 University housing: Yes
 Percent living on campus: 25%

Greek System
 Fraternity: Yes
 Sorority: Yes
Athletics: Division I

WEST VIRGINIA WESLEYAN COLLEGE

59 College Avenue, Buckhannon, WV 26201
Phone: 304-473-8510 • Fax: 304-473-8108
E-mail: admission@wvwc.edu • Web: www.wvwc.edu
Support: SP • Institution: 4-year private

PROGRAMS OR SERVICES FOR STUDENTS WITH LD

West Virginia Wesleyan College is strongly committed to providing excellent support to students with documented learning disabilities and attention difficulties. Our comprehensive program provides a solid foundational service delivered by master level professionals and two fee-based, optional programs assisting with the transition to college level academics. The Mentor Advantage Program provides an innovative, individualized support developed from research on the transition and persistence of post-secondary students with learning disabilities and from self-regulated learning theory. It is designed to create a bridge to academic regulation in the college environment. The program is composed of four elements: organizational mentoring, strategic content tutoring, weekly small group discussion, and evening check-in. In addition, Wesleyan offers an individualized clinical learning program that focuses on the improvement of reading and math skills and language comprehension. Although the program is not an official site certified and endorsed by Lindamood-Bell®, students work with instructors who have been trained in Lindamood-Bell® Learning Techniques. Consistent application with this approach will improve skills required for accurate decoding, quick word recognition, and comprehension for the increased volume of information facing today's college student. Test scores and improved academic performance have validated a record of success with our students.

ADMISSION INFORMATION FOR STUDENTS WITH LD/ADHD

College entrance tests required: Yes
Interview required: No
Essay required: No
What documentation required for LD: Psycho Ed evaluation to include: relevant historical info, instructional interventions, related services, age diagnosed, objective data (aptitude, achievement, info processing), test scores (standard, percentile and grade equivalents) and describe functional limitations.
With general application: Yes if requested as part of Structured Program application
To receive services after enrolling: Yes
What documentation required for ADHD: Diagnosis based on DSM-V; history of behaviors impairing functioning in academic setting; diagnostic interview; history of symptoms; evidence of ongoing behaviors.

With general application: Yes if requested as part of Structured Program application
To receive services after enrolling: Yes
Submitted to: Support Program/Services
Special Ed. HS course work accepted: Yes
Specific course requirements for all applicants: Yes
Separate application required for program services: No
# of LD applications submitted each year: 80–100
# of LD applications accepted yearly: 60–80
Total # of students receiving LD services: 40–45
Acceptance into program means acceptance into college: Students are admitted jointly into the college and SASS.

ADMISSIONS

The Director of the Learning Center reviews and decides the application outcome of students who disclose a disability. Applicants are encouraged to submit a psychoeducational evaluation if they believe it will help develop an accurate picture of student potential. An interview is encouraged but not required unless it is determined that it could help the College gain a better understanding of the applicant. General admission criteria include a GPA no lower than 2.0; four years English, three years math, two years science, two years social studies, one year history, and three years electives. No foreign language is required for admission. Submission of SAT or ACT testing is required.

ADDITIONAL INFORMATION

As part of ongoing assessment, during the spring of 2009, students who used the services of Wesleyan's Learning Center were asked to rate their level of satisfaction on eleven items using a scale ranging from 1 (never satisfied) to 5 (always satisfied). Three additional open-ended questions ask students to recommend improvements, identify strengths, and indicate whether participation in the services strengthened their learning. Results were positive. Forty eight (48) of seventy three (73) or 66 percent of the students participated in the assessment. The average satisfaction rating for the eleven items was 4.5. Perhaps the most important item was the open-ended question which asked: "Has your participation in the Learning Center helped you develop strategies to strengthen your learning? Eighty-seven percent (87%) of the respondents indicated an unequivocal "yes" to the question and all but two wrote explanations for their answer. The commitment and effectiveness of the program staff are exemplified in the comments of the students served.

PROGRAM FOR DISABILITY SERVICES

Contact Information
Name of program or department: Learning Center
  Telephone: 304-473-8563
  Fax: 304-473-8497

LEARNING DISABILITY SERVICES

Accommodations are decided upon an individual basis after a thorough review of appropriate, current documentation. The accommodations requested must be supported through the documentation provided and must be logically linked to the current impact of the condition on academic functioning.

Allowed in exams
  Calculator: Yes
  Dictionary: Yes
  Computer: Yes
  Spellchecker: Yes
Extended test time: Yes
Scribes: Yes
Proctors: Yes
Oral exams: Yes
Note-takers: Yes

Distraction-reduced environment: Yes
Tape recording in class: Yes
Electronic texts: Yes
Accommodations for students with ADHD: Yes
Kurzweil Reader: N/A
Other assistive technology: Yes
Priority registration: Yes

Added costs for services: Yes
LD specialists: Yes
Professional tutors: 9
Peer tutors: 14–18
Max. hours/wk. for services: 57
How professors are notified of LD/ADHD: Student

GENERAL ADMISSIONS INFORMATION

Office of Admission: 1800 722 9933

ENTRANCE REQUIREMENTS

Academic units recommended: 4 English, 2 mathematics, 2 science, (2 science labs), 1 foreign language, 2 social studies, 2 history, 1 visual/performing arts, 1 computer science. High school diploma is required and GED is accepted. SAT or ACT required; TOEFL required of all international applicants; minimum paper TOEFL 500, minimum computer TOEFL 200.

Application deadline: None
Notification: Rolling
Average GPA: 3.32
ACT Composite middle 50% range: 20–26

SAT Math middle 50% range: 430–550
SAT Critical Reading middle 50% range: 430–540
SAT Writing middle 50% range: 410–550

Graduated top 10% of class: 28%
Graduated top 25% of class: 59%
Graduated top 50% of class: 81%

COLLEGE GRADUATION REQUIREMENTS

Course waivers allowed: N/A
In what course: In any course where the request is appropriate. (There is no foreign language requirement.)We have only one math requirement and a student can fill this with a Math for the Liberal Arts class.
Course substitutions allowed: N/A
In what course: In any course where the request is appropriate. (There is no foreign language requirement.)

ADDITIONAL INFORMATION

Environment: The college is located on 80 acres 135 miles from Pittsburgh in the Appalachian foothills.

Student Body
  Undergrad enrollment: 1,331
  Women: 55%
  Men: 45%
  Percent out-of-state: 39%

Cost Information
  Tuition: $24,964
  Room and board: $7,390
Housing Information
  University housing: Yes
  Percent living on campus: 79%

Greek System
  Fraternity: Yes
  Sorority: Yes
Athletics: Division II

ALVERNO COLLEGE

3400 South 43rd Street, PO Box 343922, Milwaukee, WI 53234-3922
Phone: 414-382-6100 • Fax: 414-382-6354
E-mail: admissions@alverno.edu • Web: www.alverno.edu
Support: S • Institution type: 4-year private

PROGRAMS OR SERVICES FOR STUDENTS WITH LD

Alverno College is a small liberal arts college for women with approximately 12,400 students, undergraduate and graduate. The Instructional Services Center (ISC) provides academic support to Alverno students and assists Alverno applicants in meeting admissions requirements. ISC offers courses in reading, writing, math, and algebra to develop academic skills as required on the basis of new student assessment results. ISC also offers tutorial support, course-based study groups, and workshops to provide an opportunity for small groups of students to study together under the direction of a peer tutor or an ISC teacher. There is also a Student Accessibility Coordinator who assists the student to meet her academic potential by understanding of her learning needs, developing strategies and accommodations to maximize her strengths, and developing of self-advocacy with faculty.

ADMISSION INFORMATION FOR STUDENTS WITH LD/ADHD

College entrance tests required: Yes
Interview required: No
Essay recommended: No
What documentation required for LD: Psycho Ed evaluation to include: relevant historical info, instructional interventions, related services, age diagnosed, objective data (aptitude, achievement, info processing), test scores (standard, percentile and grade equivalents) and describe functional limitations.
With general application: No
To receive services after enrolling: Yes
What documentation required for ADHD: Diagnosis based on DSM-V; history of behaviors impairing functioning in academic setting; diagnostic interview; history of symptoms; evidence of ongoing behaviors.

With general application: No
Submitted to: Student Accessibility
Special Ed. HS course work accepted: NR
Specific course requirements of all applicants: Yes
Separate application required: No
# of LD applications submitted each year: NR
# of LD applications accepted yearly: NR
Total # of students receiving LD services: 45
Acceptance into program means acceptance into college: Students must be admitted and enrolled in the university first (they can appeal a denial) and then request services.

ADMISSIONS

Admission criteria are the same for all students coming directly from high school. General admission requirements include 19-plus ACT; 17 academic credits in college-prep courses with recommendations, including 4 years of English, 2 years of a foreign language, 3 years of math, 3 years of science, and 3 years of social studies; a minimum GPA of 2.5; and a class rank within the top half of the applicant's graduating class. There is a college transition program for students who do not meet the admissions criteria but have academic potential.

ADDITIONAL INFORMATION

Classes are offered at a beginning level in reading, writing, math, and algebra. Students may not substitute courses for math courses required to graduate, but intensive assistance is provided. Tutoring is provided through ISC. The college has a Math Resource Center, a Science Resource Center, and a Writing Resource Center available for all students. Alverno's unique emphasis on learning the abilities needed to put knowledge to use—commonly called "ability-based education"—has gained national praise. Alverno College's faculty has developed and implemented ability-based undergraduate education, redefining education in terms of abilities needed for effectiveness in the worlds of work, family, and civic community. The distinctive feature of an ability-based approach is the expectation that students should be able to do something with what they know. The specific abilities identified by the faculty as central to the approach to liberal arts and professional education are communication, analysis, problem solving, valuing in decision making, social interaction, development of a global perspective, effective citizenship, and aesthetic engagement.

LEARNING DISABILITY PROGRAM OR SERVICES

Contact Information
Name of program or department: Student Accessibility
  Telephone: 414-382-6026
  Fax: 414-382-6354

LEARNING DISABILITY SERVICES

Accommodations are decided upon an individual basis after a thorough review of appropriate, current documentation. The accommodations requested must be supported through the documentation provided and must be logically linked to the current impact of the condition on academic functioning.

Allowed in exams
  Calculator: Yes
  Dictionary: Yes
  Computer: Yes
  Spellchecker: Yes
Extended test time: Yes
Scribes: Yes
Proctors: Yes
Oral exams: Yes
Note-takers: Yes

Distraction-reduced environment: Yes
Tape recording in class: Yes
Electronic texts: Yes
Accommodations for students with ADHD: Yes
Kurzweil Reader: Yes
Other assistive technology: Yes
Priority registration: No

Added costs for services: No
LD specialists: No
Professional tutors: 10
Peer tutors: 75
Max. hours/wk. for services: NR
How professors are notified of LD/ADHD: By both student and coordinator

GENERAL ADMISSIONS INFORMATION

Office of Admission: 414-382-6100

ENTRANCE REQUIREMENTS
Academic units required: 4 English, 3 math, 3 science, 3 social studies, 2 foreign language. High school diploma is required, and GED is accepted. ACT with or without Writing component accepted. TOEFL required of all international applicants: minimum paper TOEFL 520, minimum computer TOEFL 190.

Application deadline: None
Notification: Rolling
Average GPA: 3.04
ACT Composite middle 50% range: 17–22

SAT Math middle 50% range: NR
SAT Critical Reading middle 50% range: NR
SAT Writing middle 50% range: NR

Graduated top 10% of class: NR
Graduated top 25% of class: NR
Graduated top 50% of class: NR

COLLEGE GRADUATION REQUIREMENTS

Course waivers allowed: No
Course substitutions allowed: No

ADDITIONAL INFORMATION

Environment: The campus is located in a suburban area on the southwest side of Milwaukee.

Student Body
  Undergrad enrollment: 2,371
  Women: 100%
  Percent out-of-state: 4%

Cost Information
  Tuition: $21,063
  Room & board: $6,966
Housing Information
  University housing: Yes
  Percent living on campus: 9%

Greek System
  Fraternity: No
  Sorority: Yes
  Athletics: NCAA Div. III

BELOIT COLLEGE

700 College Street, Beloit, WI 53511
Phone: 608-363-2500 • Fax: 608-363-2075
E-mail: admiss@beloit.edu • Web: www.beloit.edu
Support: S • Institution type: 4-year private

PROGRAMS OR SERVICES FOR STUDENTS WITH LD

The Learning Enrichment and Disability Services office provides academic enrichment opportunities (i.e. tutoring, one-on-one assistance) and support for all Beloit College students. For students with documented disabilities, we ensure that appropriate accommodations are implemented while educating the campus community regarding disability related laws, issues and concerns. In addition, we work with students with academic challenges and concerns (i.e. alert slips, academic probation) to assist them in implementing appropriate strategies to achieve personal and academic success. To accomplish these goals, we collaborate with faculty, staff and students and operate with a philosophy of student self-advocacy.

ADMISSION INFORMATION FOR STUDENTS WITH LD/ADHD

College entrance tests required: Yes
Interview required: No
Essay recommended: Yes
What documentation required for LD: Psycho Ed evaluation to include: relevant historical info, instructional interventions, related services, age diagnosed, objective data (aptitude, achievement, info processing), test scores (standard, percentile and grade equivalents) and describe functional limitations.
With general application: No
To receive services after enrolling: Yes
What documentation required for ADHD: Diagnosis based on DSM-V; history of behaviors impairing functioning in academic setting; diagnostic interview; history of symptoms; evidence of ongoing behaviors.

With general application: No
Submitted to: Learning Enrichment and Disability Services
Special Ed. HS course work accepted: Yes
Specific course requirements of all applicants: Yes
Separate application required: No
# of LD applications submitted each year: NR
# of LD applications accepted yearly: NR
Total # of students receiving LD services: 25–30
Acceptance into program means acceptance into college: Students must be admitted to and enrolled in the college first and then request services.

ADMISSIONS

There is no special admissions procedure for students with learning disabilities. Each student is reviewed individually, and the final decision is made by the Office of Admissions. The college is competitive in admissions, but there are no absolute GPA or test scores. A minimum of sixteen academic courses are required for admission. Courses recommended include 4 years of English, 4 years of math, 3 years of laboratory science, 2 years of a foreign language, and 3 years of social science or history.

ADDITIONAL INFORMATION

Beloit College Learning Enrichment and Disability Services offers additional resources to all students in the areas of tutoring (most courses, including math and science), reading strategies, study strategies, time management, study groups, advising, mentoring, as well as assistance with computer usage and assistive technology. Improvement of writing and research skills as well as personal counseling, career guidance, and crisis intervention are also available at the College. Individual assistance and small group workshops are offered each semester.

LEARNING DISABILITY PROGRAM OR SERVICES

Contact Information
Name of program or department: Learning Enrichment and Disability Services
  Telephone: 608-363-2572
  Fax: 608-363-7059

LEARNING DISABILITY SERVICES

Accommodations are decided upon an individual basis after a thorough review of appropriate, current documentation. The accommodations requested must be supported through the documentation provided and must be logically linked to the current impact of the condition on academic functioning.

Allowed in exams
  Calculator: Yes
  Dictionary: Yes
  Computer: Yes
  Spellchecker: Yes
Extended test time: Yes
Scribes: Yes
Proctors: Yes
Oral exams: Yes
Note-takers: Yes

Distraction-reduced environment: Yes
Tape recording in class: Yes
Electronic texts: Yes
Accommodations for students with ADHD: Yes
Kurzweil Reader: N/A
Other assistive technology: Yes
Priority registration: Yes

Added costs for services: No
LD specialists: No
Professional tutors: No
Peer tutors: 70–95
Max. hours/wk. for services: N/A
How professors are notified of LD/ADHD: By student with director letter

GENERAL ADMISSIONS INFORMATION

Office of Admission: 608-363-2500 or 800-923-5648

ENTRANCE REQUIREMENTS

Academic units recommended: 4 English, 4 math, 3 laboratory science, 2 foreign language, 3 social science or history. High school diploma is required, and GED is accepted. ACT with or without Writing component accepted. TOEFL required of all international applicants: minimum paper TOEFL 550, minimum iBT 80.

Application deadline: Early action I–11/1, early action 2-12/1, regular decision-1/15
Notification: Early action I–12/15, early action 2-1/15, regular decision-Rolling
Average GPA: 3.40
ACT Composite middle 50% range: 25–30

SAT Math middle 50% range: 550–650
SAT Critical Reading middle 50% range: 560–690
SAT Writing middle 50% range: NR

Graduated top 10% of class: 36%
Graduated top 25% of class: 71%
Graduated top 50% of class: 97%

COLLEGE GRADUATION REQUIREMENTS

Course waivers allowed: Possible with appropriate documentation
Course substitutions allowed: Possible with appropriate documentation

ADDITIONAL INFORMATION

Environment: The college is located 50 miles south of Madison and 90 miles northwest of Chicago.

Student Body
  Undergrad enrollment: 1,397
  Women: 57%
  Men: 43%
  Percent out-of-state: 80%

Cost Information
  Tuition: $38,474
  Room & board: $7,862
Housing Information
  University housing: Yes
  Percent living on campus: 95%

Greek System
  Fraternity: Yes
  Sorority: Yes
Athletics: Division III

EDGEWOOD COLLEGE

1000 Edgewood College Drive, Madison, WI 53711-1997
Phone: 608-663-2294 • Fax: 608-663-2214
E-mail: admissions@edgewood.edu • Web: www.edgewood.edu
Support: S • Institution: 4-year private

PROGRAMS OR SERVICES FOR STUDENTS WITH LD

Sponsored by the Sinsinawa Dominicans, Edgewood College is a community of learners that affirms both its Catholic heritage and its respect for other religious traditions. The liberal arts are the foundation of all our curricular offerings in the humanities, arts, sciences, and professional programs. Committed to excellence in teaching and learning, we seek to develop intellect, spirit, imagination, and heart. We welcome women and men who reflect the rich diversity of the world's cultures and perspectives. We foster open, caring, thoughtful engagement with one another and an enduring commitment to service, all in an educational community that seeks truth, compassion, justice and partnership.

ADMISSION INFORMATION FOR STUDENTS WITH LD/ADHD

College entrance tests required: Yes
Interview required: No
Essay required: No
What documentation required for LD: Psycho Ed evaluation to include: relevant historical info, instructional interventions, related services, age diagnosed, objective data (aptitude, achievement, info processing), test scores (standard, percentile and grade equivalents) and describe functional limitations.
With general application: No
To receive services after enrolling: Yes

What documentation required for ADHD: Diagnosis based on DSM-V; history of behaviors impairing functioning in academic setting; diagnostic interview; history of symptoms; evidence of ongoing behaviors.
With general application: No
Submitted to: Support Program/Services
Special Ed. HS course work accepted: Yes
Specific course requirements for all applicants: No
Separate application required for program services: No (with the exception of the Cutting Edge Program—see below)
# of LD applications submitted each year:

ADMISSIONS
Edgewood College offers rolling admission between September 1 and the following August 1 for fall enrollment. Campus tours and special visit days are available throughout the year. During the admission process you will be connected with an admissions counselor who will help you through the admission, financial aid, and housing processes. Generous financial aid is available to help make the exceptional Edgewood College education affordable.

ADDITIONAL INFORMATION
Edgewood College allows for foreign language course substitutions. There are also developmental writing and math courses. Other services include Summer Pre-orientation/Bridge Program, Academic Skills classes, individual academic coaching and learning support, Math/Science Tutoring Lab, Writing Center, content area tutoring, assistive technology training and career development services. Students are also able to participate in social skills and life skills classes offered through the Cutting Edge Program. Edgewood College was the first college in Wisconsin to offer inclusion in college for adult learners with intellectual and developmental disabilities. The Cutting-Edge program offers an alternative admissions process into the college along with a higher level of supports. The program strives to give the Cutting-Edge students, to the greatest degree possible, a college experience of academic, residential, and social inclusion. Through the use of peer mentors, the Cutting-Edge program provides students the opportunity to "fit in" to college by enrolling in undergraduate courses, residing in student housing, engaging in student life events, and pursuing service learning, internships and employment. Since its inception in 2007, the Cutting-Edge offers a non-degree program that includes a combination of pre-college level courses, life skills and social skills classes, general education courses—audited and modified—and internships. The Cutting-Edge students take regular college courses either for credit or audit. The Cutting-Edge program also provides career counseling and person-centered internship experiences that allow students to build their resumes and obtain gainful employment. During its development phase the college has found an increase in the admissions of "qualified" students with disabilities who have academically benefitted from the additional supports provided by the Cutting-Edge program. The Cutting-Edge program is developing occupational certificates for students who are unable to earn a bachelor's degree but who want to take courses for degree credit, and work towards terminal credentials.

PROGRAM FOR DISABILITY SERVICES

Contact Information
Name of program or department: Accessibility Services for Students with Disabilities
   Telephone: 608-663-8347
   Fax: 608-663-2278

LEARNING DISABILITY SERVICES

Accommodations are decided upon an individual basis after a thorough review of appropriate, current documentation. The accommodations requested must be supported through the documentation provided and must be logically linked to the current impact of the condition on academic functioning.

Allowed in exams
   Calculator: Yes
   Dictionary: Yes
   Computer: Yes
   Spellchecker: Yes
Extended test time: Yes
Scribes: Yes
Proctors: Yes
Oral exams: Yes
Note-takers: Yes

Distraction-reduced environment: Yes
Tape recording in class: Yes
Electronic texts: Yes
Accommodations for students with ADHD: Yes
Kurzweil Reader: Yes
Priority registration: Yes

Added costs for services: No
LD specialists: Yes
Professional tutors: No
Peer tutors: Yes
Max. hours/wk. for services: None
How professors are notified of LD/ADHD: Both student and director

GENERAL ADMISSIONS INFORMATION

Office of Admission: 608-663-2294

ENTRANCE REQUIREMENTS
Academic units required: 4 English, 2 mathematics, 2 science, (1 science labs), 2 foreign language, 2 social studies, 1 history. **Academic units recommended:** 4 English, 2 mathematics, 2 science, (1 science labs), 2 foreign language, 2 social studies, 1 history. High school diploma is required and GED is accepted. SAT or ACT required; TOEFL required of all international applicants; minimum paper TOEFL 525, minimum computer TOEFL 197, minimum web-based TOEFL 72.

Application deadline: 8/26
Notification: Rolling
Average GPA: 3.3
ACT Composite middle 50% range: 20–25

SAT Math middle 50% range: 460–560
SAT Critical Reading middle 50% range: 470–590
SAT Writing middle 50% range: NR

Graduated top 10% of class: 9%
Graduated top 25% of class: 33%
Graduated top 50% of class: 78%

COLLEGE GRADUATION REQUIREMENTS

Course waivers allowed: No
Course substitutions allowed: Yes
In what course: Foreign language

ADDITIONAL INFORMATION

Environment: The campus is located in Madison, Wisconsin near the University of Wisconsin.

Student Body
   Undergrad enrollment: 1,951
   Women: 70%
   Men: 30%
   Percent out-of-state: 6%

Cost Information
   Tuition: $22,850
   Room and board: $8,113
Housing Information
   University housing: Yes
   Percent living on campus: 30%

Greek System
   Fraternity: No
   Sorority: No
   Athletics: NR

MARIAN UNIVERSITY

45 South National Avenue, Fond du Lac, WI 54935
Phone: 920-923-7600 or 800-2-MARIAN
E-mail: admissions@marian.edu • Web: www.marian.edu
Support: S • Institution type: 4-year private

PROGRAMS OR SERVICES FOR STUDENTS WITH LD

Marian University is committed to providing equal educational opportunities to students with learning disabilities and/or ADD/ADHD. The Coordinator for Disability Services and Academic Support is housed in the Center for Academic Support and Excellence, (CASE) Office. The Coordinator for Disability Services and Academic Support is dedicated to providing personal and academic support to students with disabilities from freshman year to graduation.

ADMISSION INFORMATION FOR STUDENTS WITH LD/ADHD

College entrance tests required: Yes
Interview required: No
Essay recommended: No
What documentation required for LD: Psycho Ed evaluation to include: relevant historical info, instructional interventions, related services, age diagnosed, objective data (aptitude, achievement, info processing), test scores (standard, percentile and grade equivalents) and describe functional limitations.
With general application: No
To receive services after enrolling: Yes
What documentation required for ADHD: Diagnosis based on DSM-V; history of behaviors impairing functioning in academic setting; diagnostic interview; history of symptoms; evidence of ongoing behaviors.

With general application: No
Submitted to: Disability Services
Special Ed. HS course work accepted: NR
Specific course requirements of all applicants: Yes
Separate application required: No
# of LD applications submitted each year: NR
# of LD applications accepted yearly: NR
Total # of students receiving LD services: NR
Acceptance into program means acceptance into college: Students must be admitted to and enrolled in the university first and then request services.

ADMISSIONS

There is no special application or admissions procedure for students with learning disabilities. Admission criteria include a 2.0 GPA, a class rank within top 50 percent, and an ACT score of 18. All students, not just those with LD, are asked to meet two-thirds of these criteria. Students who do not meet two-thirds may be admitted on probation through a program called EXCEL. Students will be asked to submit 3 letters of recommendation supporting their ability to succeed in college-level course work. Students also may be asked to schedule a visit to Marian for a pre-admission interview during which their skills, attitudes, motivation, and self-understanding will be informally assessed. Students admitted provisionally may be admitted with limited credit status and may be required to take a freshman seminar course. Special education course work is accepted, but students are encouraged to be fully mainstreamed by senior year with minimal monitoring. Students who self-disclose their disability are given information on services available through the Center for Academic Support and Excellence (CASE) office.

ADDITIONAL INFORMATION

Disability Services offers the following services and accommodations to students who disclose a disability and submit appropriate documentation: notetakers, audio books, audio players, scan and read software, distraction-free test environments, extended exam times, and test readers/scribes. The following support is also provided: organizational and study skills training, liaison with instructors/advisors, consultation, advocacy, referrals, and resource materials. The peer tutoring program helps students gain the confidence and skills necessary to successfully complete course work. Other services include information on community, state, and national
resources, and course scheduling. Calculators are allowed in exams for students with a documented disability in math. Assistance is determined for each individual based on assessment. All students have access to the tutoring program, and the Learning and Writing Center. Services are available for undergraduate and graduate students.

LEARNING DISABILITY PROGRAM OR SERVICES

Contact Information
Name of program or department: Disability Services
Telephone: 920-923-8951
Fax: 920-923-8135

LEARNING DISABILITY SERVICES

Accommodations are decided upon an individual basis after a thorough review of appropriate, current documentation. The accommodations requested must be supported through the documentation provided and must be logically linked to the current impact of the condition on academic functioning.

Allowed in exams	**Distraction-reduced environment:** Yes	**Added costs for services:** No
Calculator: Yes	**Tape recording in class:** Yes	**LD specialists:** No
Dictionary: No	**Electronic texts:** Yes	**Professional tutors:** Yes
Computer: Yes	**Accommodations for students with**	**Peer tutors:** Yes
Spellchecker: Yes	**ADHD:** Yes	**Max. hours/wk. for services:**
Extended test time: Yes	**Kurzweil Reader:** Yes	Unlimited
Scribes: Yes	**Other assistive technology:** Yes	**How professors are notified of**
Proctors: Yes	**Priority registration:** Yes	**LD/ADHD:** By Coordinator of Disability
Oral exams: Yes		Services and Academic Support
Note-takers: Yes		

GENERAL ADMISSIONS INFORMATION

Office of Admission: 920-923-7650

ENTRANCE REQUIREMENTS

Academic units required: 4 English, 2 math, 1 science (1 science lab), 1 history. **Academic units recommended:** 3 math, 2 science, 2 foreign language. High school diploma is required, and GED is accepted. ACT with or without Writing component accepted. TOEFL required of all international applicants: minimum paper TOEFL 525, minimum computer TOEFL 193.

Application deadline: None	**SAT Math middle 50% range:** NR	**Graduated top 10% of class:** 9%
Notification: Rolling	**SAT Critical Reading middle 50%**	**Graduated top 25% of class:** 29%
Average GPA: 3.05	**range:** NR	**Graduated top 50% of class:** 66%
ACT Composite middle 50% range:	**SAT Writing middle 50% range:** NR	
18–22		

COLLEGE GRADUATION REQUIREMENTS

Course waivers allowed: No
Course substitutions allowed: Yes
In what course: Foreign Language. Students must attempt the required course.

ADDITIONAL INFORMATION

Environment: Marian College is located on 50 acres in a suburb of Fond du Lac, 60 miles north of Milwaukee.

Student Body	**Cost Information**	**Greek System**
Undergrad enrollment: 1,903	**Tuition:** $21,140	**Fraternity:** Yes
Women: 75%	**Room & board:** $6,710	**Sorority:** Yes
Men: 25%	**Housing Information**	**Athletics:** Division III
Percent out-of-state: 9%	**University housing:** Yes	
	Percent living on campus: 29%	

MARQUETTE UNIVERSITY

PO Box 1881, Milwaukee, WI 53201-1881
Phone: 414-288-7302 • Fax: 414-288-3764
E-mail: admissions@marquette.edu • Web: www.marquette.edu
Support: S • Institution type: 4-year private

PROGRAMS OR SERVICES FOR STUDENTS WITH LD

The Office of Disability Services (ODS) is the designated office at Marquette University to coordinate accommodations for all students with identified and documented disabilities. Accommodations are determined on a case-by-case basis. To obtain educational opportunities, the student must seek assistance in a timely manner, preferably prior to the start of classes. Relevant documentation from an appropriate licensed professional that gives a diagnosis of the disability and how it impacts the student's participation in courses, programs, jobs, and activities at Marquette is important. The student and a staff member from ODS will discuss the student's disability and how it will impact the requirements of the student's courses. Based on this evaluation, the Associate Director of Disability Services provides a range of individualized accommodations.

ADMISSION INFORMATION FOR STUDENTS WITH LD/ADHD

College entrance tests required: Yes
Interview required: No
Essay recommended: No
What documentation required for LD: Psycho Ed evaluation
 to include: relevant historical info, instructional interventions,
 related services, age diagnosed, objective data (aptitude,
 achievement, info processing), test scores (standard,
 percentile and grade equivalents) and describe functional
 limitations.
With general application: No
To receive services after enrolling: Yes
What documentation required for ADHD: Diagnosis based
 on DSM-V; history of behaviors impairing functioning in
 academic setting; diagnostic interview; history of symptoms;
 evidence of ongoing behaviors.

With general application: No
Submitted to: Office of Disability Services
Special Ed. HS course work accepted: No
Specific course requirements of all applicants: Yes
Separate application required: No
# of LD applications submitted each year: NR
# of LD applications accepted yearly: NR
Total # of students receiving LD services: 56
Acceptance into program means acceptance into
 college: Students must be admitted to and enrolled in the
 university first and then request services.

ADMISSIONS

There is no special admissions process for students with LD and ADHD. All applicants for admission must meet the same admission criteria. Marquette requires applicants to rank in the top 50 percent of their high school class (most rank in the top 25 percent) and have 4 years of English, 2–4 years of math and science, 2–3 years of social studies, 2 years of a foreign language, and additional subjects. Freshman Frontier Program offers admission to a small number of incoming freshman who show potential, though they may have low ACT/SAT scores but a reasonable GPA.

ADDITIONAL INFORMATION

ODS provides a number of accommodations for students with LD and ADHD, including audio books from Learning Ally and alternative testing arrangements. If a student's disability requires a backup note-taker, ODS assists students in locating or hiring note-takers and will provide if necessary, non-carbon-required paper. Other methods of acquiring class material may include the use of a tape recorder in class for later transcription and photocopying class notes or copies of lecture notes. Advance notice of assignments, alternative ways of completing an assignment, computer technology, assistive listening devices, taped textbooks, and course or program modifications are also available. To assist students with reading-related disabilities, the Kurzweil Omni 3000 Education System is available. Students also have access to the Campus Writing Center, tutors, and general study skills assistance from the Office of Student Educational Services.

LEARNING DISABILITY PROGRAM OR SERVICES

Contact Information
Name of program or department: Office of Disability Services
  Telephone: 414-288-1645
  Fax: 414-288-5799

LEARNING DISABILITY SERVICES

Accommodations are decided upon an individual basis after a thorough review of appropriate, current documentation. The accommodations requested must be supported through the documentation provided and must be logically linked to the current impact of the condition on academic functioning.

Allowed in exams	**Distraction-reduced environment:** Yes	**Added costs for services:** No
Calculator: Yes	**Tape recording in class:** Yes	**LD specialists:** No
Dictionary: Yes	**Electronic texts:** Yes	**Professional tutors:** No
Computer: Yes	**Accommodations for students with**	**Peer tutors:** 35–55
Spellchecker: Yes	**ADHD:** Yes	**Max. hours/wk. for services:** NR
Extended test time: Yes	**Kurzweil Reader:** Yes	**How professors are notified of**
Scribes: Yes	**Other assistive technology:** Yes	**LD/ADHD:** By student
Proctors: Yes	**Priority registration:** No	
Oral exams: Yes		
Note-takers: Yes		

GENERAL ADMISSIONS INFORMATION

Office of Admission: 414-288-7004

ENTRANCE REQUIREMENTS

Academic units required: 4 English, 2 math, 2 science (2 science labs), 2 social studies, 2–5 academic electives.
Academic units recommended: 4 English, 4 math, 3 science (3 science labs), 2 foreign language, 3 social studies, 5 academic electives. High school diploma is required, and GED is accepted. ACT without Writing component accepted. TOEFL required of all international applicants: minimum paper TOEFL 580, minimum computer TOEFL 78.

Application deadline: 12/1	**SAT Math middle 50% range:**	**Graduated top 10% of class:** 33%
Notification: 1/31	530–650	**Graduated top 25% of class:** 63%
Average GPA: NR	**SAT Critical Reading middle 50%**	**Graduated top 50% of class:** 93%
ACT Composite middle 50% range:	**range:** 520–630	
24–29	**SAT Writing middle 50% range:**	
	520–630	

COLLEGE GRADUATION REQUIREMENTS

Course waivers allowed: Yes
In what course: Foreign language, math, and others as appropriate
Course substitutions allowed: Yes
In what course: Foreign language, math, and others as appropriate

ADDITIONAL INFORMATION

Environment: Marquette University located in Milwaukee, 1 hour south of Madison and 1 hour north of Chicago.

Student Body	**Cost Information**	**Greek System**
Undergrad enrollment: 8,387	**Tuition:** $31,822	**Fraternity:** Yes
Women: 52%	**Room & board:** $10,370	**Sorority:** Yes
Men: 48%	**Housing Information**	**Athletics:** Division I
Percent out-of-state: 61%	**University housing:** Yes	
	Percent living on campus: 54%	

RIPON COLLEGE

PO Box 248, Ripon, WI 54971
Phone: 920-748-8114 • Fax: 920-748-8335
E-mail: adminfo@ripon.edu • Web: www.ripon.edu
Support: S • Institution: 4-year private

PROGRAMS OR SERVICES FOR STUDENTS WITH LD

The Student Support Services (SSS) provides a wide variety of services on the campus, including academic and personal counseling, study skills information, and tutoring. Although the focus of the program is on first generation students, students of higher need, and students who are learning disabled, other students who feel they might qualify are encouraged to contact the SSS office. SSS is a voluntary program that has been in existence at Ripon College since 1974. For the many students who have used its services, SSS has provided a network of support for academic, financial, and personal concerns. A group of peer contacts serves SSS by meeting regularly with students to facilitate communication between SSS participants and the office staff. For students who qualify, SSS offers free tutoring in specific subject areas. (All-campus tutoring is also available.) The tutors are upperclass students who have been recommended by their professors and trained by the SSS staff. These tutors serve as a supplement to faculty assistance. The aim of the tutoring program is to help students develop independent learning skills and improve their course grades. Although federal guidelines require a restriction on who "qualifies," the door to SSS remains open to all eligible students.

ADMISSION INFORMATION FOR STUDENTS WITH LD/ADHD

College entrance tests required: Yes
Interview required: Yes
What documentation required for LD: Psycho Ed evaluation
   to include: relevant historical info, instructional interventions,
   related services, age diagnosed, objective data (aptitude,
   achievement, info processing), test scores (standard,
   percentile and grade equivalents) and describe functional
   limitations.
With general application: No
To receive services after enrolling: Yes
What documentation required for ADHD: Diagnosis based
   on DSM-V; history of behaviors impairing functioning in
   academic setting; diagnostic interview; history of symptoms;
   evidence of ongoing behaviors.

With general application: No
Submitted to: Support Program/Services
Special Ed. HS course work accepted: N/A
Specific course requirements for all applicants: Yes
Separate application required for program services: No
# of LD applications submitted each year: NR
# of LD applications accepted yearly: NR
Total # of students receiving LD services: 10
Acceptance into program means acceptance into
   college: Students must be admitted to and enrolled in the
   university first and then request services.

ADMISSIONS

Students with learning disabilities are screened by admissions and must meet the same admission criteria as all other applicants. There is no set GPA required; courses required include four years English, algebra and geometry, two years natural science, two years social studies, and seven additional units. Students with learning disabilities who self-disclose are referred to Student Support Services when making prospective visits to the campus in order to ascertain specific needs and abilities of the student.

ADDITIONAL INFORMATION

SSS provides tutoring in subject areas; skills classes for no credit in time management, note-taking, test-taking strategies, reading college texts, writing papers, studying for and taking exams, and setting goals; and counseling/guidance. Student Support Services provides intensive study groups, LD support and internships. SSS provides students with peer contacts who provide students with one-on-one support and is useful in helping students adjust to college life, to provide a contact for the student to go to with problems or issues, organize group tutoring, and to help students open their minds and see hope in their future.

PROGRAM FOR DISABILITY SERVICES

Contact Information
Name of program or department: Student Support Services
  Telephone: 920-748-8107
  Fax: 920-748-8382

LEARNING DISABILITY SERVICES

Accommodations are decided upon an individual basis after a thorough review of appropriate, current documentation. The accommodations requested must be supported through the documentation provided and must be logically linked to the current impact of the condition on academic functioning.

Allowed in exams
  Calculator: Yes
  Dictionary: No
  Computer: Yes
  Spellchecker: Yes
Extended test time: Yes
Scribes: Yes
Proctors: Yes
Oral exams: Yes
Note-takers: Yes

Distraction-reduced environment: Yes
Tape recording in class: Yes
Electronic texts: Yes
Accommodations for students with
  ADHD: Yes
Kurzweil Reader: Yes
Other assistive technology: Interactive computer technology speech recognition and Kurzweil Reading technology
Priority registration: No

Added costs for services: No
LD specialists: No
Professional tutors: No
Peer tutors: 75
Max. hours/wk. for services:
  3hrs/week/class
How professors are notified of
  LD/ADHD: Both student and director

GENERAL ADMISSIONS INFORMATION

Office of Admission: 920-748-8185

ENTRANCE REQUIREMENTS
Academic units required: 4 English, 2 mathematics, 2 science, 2 social studies. **Academic units recommended:** 4 mathematics, 4 science, 2 foreign language, 4 social studies. High school diploma is required and GED is accepted. SAT or ACT required; TOEFL required of all international applicants; minimum paper TOEFL 550, minimum computer TOEFL 213, minimum web-based TOEFL 79.

Application deadline: None
Notification: Rolling
Average GPA: 3.41
ACT Composite middle 50% range:
  22–27

SAT Math middle 50% range:
  490–580
SAT Critical Reading middle 50% range: 500–650
SAT Writing middle 50% range: NR

Graduated top 10% of class: 23%
Graduated top 25% of class: 54%
Graduated top 50% of class: 90%

COLLEGE GRADUATION REQUIREMENTS

Course waivers allowed: No
Course substitutions allowed: No

ADDITIONAL INFORMATION

Environment: The college is located in a small town north of Milwaukee.

Student Body
  Undergrad enrollment: 1,065
  Women: 50%
  Men: 50%
  Percent out-of-state: 25%

Cost Information
  Tuition: $28,414
  Room and board: $8,270
Housing Information
  University housing: Yes
  Percent living on campus: 91%

Greek System
  Fraternity: Yes
  Sorority: Yes
Athletics: Division III

U. OF WISCONSIN—EAU CLAIRE

105 Garfield Avenue, Schofield 112, Eau Claire, WI 54701
Phone: 715-836-5415 • Fax: 715-836-2409
E-mail: admissions@uwec.edu • Web: www.uwec.edu
Support: S • Institution: 4-year public

PROGRAMS OR SERVICES FOR STUDENTS WITH LD

The University of Wisconsin—Eau Claire is committed to providing all students with an equal opportunity to fully participate in all aspects of the university community. Services for Students with Disabilities will work with students, faculty, staff, and community partners in a cooperative manner to review policies and procedures and to facilitate the provision of services and accommodations that will ensure that university facilities, programs, and activities are universally accessible.

ADMISSION INFORMATION FOR STUDENTS WITH LD/ADHD

College entrance tests required: Yes
Interview required: No
Essay required: N/A
What documentation required for LD: Psycho Ed evaluation to include: relevant historical info, instructional interventions, related services, age diagnosed, objective data (aptitude, achievement, info processing), test scores (standard, percentile and grade equivalents) and describe functional limitations.
With general application: No
To receive services after enrolling: Yes
What documentation required for ADHD: Diagnosis based on DSM-V; history of behaviors impairing functioning in academic setting; diagnostic interview; history of symptoms; evidence of ongoing behaviors.

With general application: No
Submitted to: Support Program/Services
Special Ed. HS course work accepted: No
Specific course requirements for all applicants: Yes
Separate application required for program services: No
# of LD applications submitted each year: NR
# of LD applications accepted yearly: NR
Total # of students receiving LD services: NR
Acceptance into program means acceptance into college: Separate application required after student has enrolled

ADMISSIONS

Individuals with disabilities must complete the standard university application form. Applicants should carefully review the university's published admission criteria, including math and foreign language requirements. If an applicant with a disability wishes to request an exception to any admission requirements, s/he must: 1) include with the application a letter requesting the exception and explaining the rationale for the request, and 2) submit to the Services for Students with Disabilities Office appropriate documentation establishing both the existence of a disability and a resulting need for the exception being requested. Any information regarding a disability is treated as confidential information as defined by the Family and Educational Rights and Privacy Act (FERPA) at: http://www.ed.gov/offices/OII/fpco/ferpa/.

ADDITIONAL INFORMATION

Students must provide documentation prior to receiving appropriate accommodations. Some of the accommodations provided with appropriate documentation could include tutoring individually or in groups, readers, scribes, note-takers, taped textbooks, proofreaders, and exam accommodations, including extended time, readers, and separate testing rooms. The Academic Skills Center offers individualized tutoring in math preparation and background, composition, reading, and study skills. Many departments on campus provide tutors to help students with course content. Students take a form identifying appropriate accommodation requests completed by SSD staff to instructors. Students who are denied accommodations can appeal any denial by filing a complaint with the Affirmative Action Review Board. Services and accommodations are available to undergraduate and graduate students.

PROGRAM FOR DISABILITY SERVICES

Contact Information
Name of program or department: Services for Students with Disabilities (SSD)
  Telephone: 715-836-4542
  Fax: 715-836-3712

LEARNING DISABILITY SERVICES

Accommodations are decided upon an individual basis after a thorough review of appropriate, current documentation. The accommodations requested must be supported through the documentation provided and must be logically linked to the current impact of the condition on academic functioning.

Allowed in exams	**Distraction-reduced environment:** Yes	**Added costs for services:** No
Calculator: Yes	**Tape recording in class:** Yes	**LD specialists:** No
Dictionary: Yes	**Electronic texts:** Yes	**Professional tutors:** No
Computer: Yes	**Accommodations for students with**	**Peer tutors:** 40–50
Spellchecker: Yes	**ADHD:** Yes	**Max. hours/wk. for services:** NR
Extended test time: Yes	**Kurzweil Reader:** Yes	**How professors are notified of**
Scribes: Yes	**Other assistive technology:** Scanning	**LD/ADHD:** Student
Proctors: Yes	and reading device, video magnifier,	
Oral exams: Yes	screen reader, check-out laptop, voice	
Note-takers: Yes	activated computers, accessible	
	workstations	
	Priority registration: Yes	

GENERAL ADMISSIONS INFORMATION

Office of Admission: 715-836-5415

ENTRANCE REQUIREMENTS
Academic units required: 4 English, 3 mathematics, 3 science, 2 foreign language, 3 social studies, 2 academic electives. High school diploma is required and GED is accepted. SAT or ACT required; TOEFL required of all international applicants; minimum paper TOEFL 550, minimum computer TOEFL 213, minimum web-based TOEFL 79.

Application deadline: None	**SAT Math middle 50% range:**	**Graduated top 10% of class:** 29%
Notification: Rolling	550–650	**Graduated top 25% of class:** 61%
Average GPA: NR	**SAT Critical Reading middle 50%**	**Graduated top 50% of class:** 98%
ACT Composite middle 50% range:	**range:** 500–640	
23–26	**SAT Writing middle 50% range:**	
	490–620	

COLLEGE GRADUATION REQUIREMENTS

Course waivers allowed: Yes
In what course: If appropriate documentation is provided, waivers may be permitted in the area of foreign language.
Course substitutions allowed: Yes

ADDITIONAL INFORMATION

Environment: The 333-acre campus is in an urban setting 95 miles east of Minneapolis.

Student Body	**Cost Information**	**Greek System**
Undergrad enrollment: 10,784	**In-state tuition:** $7,406	**Fraternity:** Yes
Women: 59%	**Out-of-state tuition:** $14,982	**Sorority:** Yes
Men: 41%	**Room and board:** $5,830	**Athletics:** Division III
Percent out-of-state: 24%	**Housing Information**	
	University housing: Yes	
	Percent living on campus: 38%	

U. OF WISCONSIN—MADISON

702 West Johnson Street, Suite 1101, Madison, WI 53715-1007
Phone: 608-262-3961 • Fax: 608-262-7706
E-mail: onwisconsin@admissions.wisc.edu • Web: www.wisc.edu
Support: CS • Institution: 4-year public

PROGRAMS OR SERVICES FOR STUDENTS WITH LD

The McBurney Disability Resource Center provides students with disabilities equal access to the programs and activities of the University. Staff work with students, staff, and faculty to promote student independence and to ensure assessment of their abilities, not disabilities. Staff work with students to determine disability-related accommodations and academic services that will maximize a student's opportunity for equal access. Over 900 undergraduate and graduate students with disabilities are currently registered with the McBurney Center. Students with disabilities who tend to do well have graduated from competitive high school or college programs and are reasonably independent, proactive in seeking assistance, and use accommodations similar to those offered here. For complete information about the McBurney Center, please visit our web site at www.mcburney.wisc.edu.

ADMISSION INFORMATION FOR STUDENTS WITH LD/ADHD

College entrance tests required: Yes
Interview required: No
Essay required: N/A
What documentation required for LD: Psycho Ed evaluation
to include: relevant historical info, instructional interventions,
related services, age diagnosed, objective data (aptitude,
achievement, info processing), test scores (standard,
percentile and grade equivalents) and describe functional
limitations.
With general application: No
To receive services after enrolling: Yes
What documentation required for ADHD: Diagnosis based
on DSM-V; history of behaviors impairing functioning in
academic setting; diagnostic interview; history of symptoms;
evidence of ongoing behaviors.

With general application: No
Submitted to: Support Program/Services
Special Ed. HS course work accepted: No
Specific course requirements for all applicants: Yes
Separate application required for program services: No
# of LD applications submitted each year: NR
# of LD applications accepted yearly: NR
Total # of students receiving LD services: 167
Acceptance into program means acceptance into
college: Separate application required after student has
enrolled

ADMISSIONS

The admission review process is the same for all applicants. Factors in the review process may include self-disclosed disability information in the written statement, grades, rank, test scores, course requirements completed, and potential for success. Disclosure of disability will not have a negative effect on a student's admission application. If a student wishes to disclose a disability they may do so in the "additional statement" on the application. Suggested information to include is the date of diagnosis or the onset of the disability and the ramifications of the disability on course requirements, attendance, and academic performance. This information will be considered during the admission review by trained admission counselors. Any documentation about the disability should be submitted to the McBurney Disability Resource Center.

ADDITIONAL INFORMATION

The documentation must be completed by a professional qualified to diagnose an LD. The report must include results of a clinical interview and descriptions of the testing procedures; instruments used; test and subtest results reported in standard scores, as well as percentile rank and grade scores where useful; and interpretation and recommendations based on data gathered. It must be comprehensive and include test results where applicable in intelligence, reading, math, spelling, written language, language processing, and cognitive processing skills. Testing should carefully examine areas of concern/weakness, as well as areas of strengths; documentation should include a clear diagnostic statement based on the test results and personal history. Students may be eligible for advocacy/liaison with faculty and staff, alternative testing accommodations, curriculum modifications, disability management advising, learning skills training, liaison with vocational rehab, access to the McBurney Learning Resource Room, note-takers, peer support groups, priority registration, taped texts, and course materials.

PROGRAM FOR DISABILITY SERVICES

Contact Information
Name of program or department: McBurney Disability Resource Center
  Telephone: 608-263-2741
  Fax: 608-265-2998

LEARNING DISABILITY SERVICES

Accommodations are decided upon an individual basis after a thorough review of appropriate, current documentation. The accommodations requested must be supported through the documentation provided and must be logically linked to the current impact of the condition on academic functioning.

Allowed in exams	**Distraction-reduced environment:** Yes	**Added costs for services:** No
Calculator: Yes	**Tape recording in class:** N/A	**LD specialists:** Yes
Dictionary: N/A	**Electronic texts:** Yes	**Professional tutors:** No
Computer: Yes	**Accommodations for students with**	**Peer tutors:** Yes
Spellchecker: Yes	**ADHD:** Yes	**Max. hours/wk. for services:** .5
Extended test time: Yes	**Kurzweil Reader:** Yes	**How professors are notified of**
Scribes: Yes	**Other assistive technology:** Voice	**LD/ADHD:** Student
Proctors: Yes	recognition and screen reading	
Oral exams: Yes	software	
Note-takers: Yes	**Priority registration:** Yes	

GENERAL ADMISSIONS INFORMATION

Office of Admission: 608-262-3961

ENTRANCE REQUIREMENTS
Academic units required: 4 English, 3 mathematics, 3 science, 2 foreign language, 3 social studies, 2 academic electives. **Academic units recommended:** 4 English, 4 mathematics, 4 science, 4 foreign language, 4 social studies, 2 academic electives. High school diploma is required and GED is accepted. SAT or ACT required; ACT with Writing component required. TOEFL required of all international applicants; minimum paper TOEFL 550, minimum computer TOEFL 80.

Application deadline: 2/1	**SAT Math middle 50% range:**	**Graduated top 10% of class:** 58%
Notification: Rolling	620–740	**Graduated top 25% of class:** 94%
Average GPA: 3.69	**SAT Critical Reading middle 50%**	**Graduated top 50% of class:** 99%
ACT Composite middle 50% range:	**range:** 550–670	
26–30	**SAT Writing middle 50% range:**	
	590–680	

COLLEGE GRADUATION REQUIREMENTS

Course waivers allowed: No
Course substitutions allowed: Yes
In what course: Foreign language

ADDITIONAL INFORMATION

Environment: The university is located in an urban area in the state capital.

Student Body	**Cost Information**	**Greek System**
Undergrad enrollment: 30,555	**In-state tuition:** $9,671	**Fraternity:** Yes
Women: 52%	**Out-of-state tuition:** $25,421	**Sorority:** Yes
Men: 48%	**Room & board:** $7,780	**Athletics:** Division I
Percent out-of-state: 32%	**Housing Information**	
	University housing: Yes	
	Percent living on campus: 24%	

U. OF WISCONSIN—MILWAUKEE

PO Box 749, Milwaukee, WI 53201
Phone: 414-229-2222 • Fax: 414-229-6940
E-mail: uwmlook@uwm.edu • Web: www4.uwm.edu
Support: CS • Institution: 4-year public

PROGRAMS OR SERVICES FOR STUDENTS WITH LD

The Learning Disabilities Program at UW—Milwaukee, a component of the Student Accessibility Center, offers a wide range of academic support services to students with learning disabilities, attention deficit hyperactivity disorders, Autism Spectrum Disorders, and traumatic brain injuries. Our mission is to create an accessible university community for students with disabilities that fosters the development of each student's full potential. There are no waiting lists or caps on participation for the LD Program. This program is well suited for students who are fairly independent and willing to seek the support services they need. Recommended academic accommodations are based on documentation of disability and disability related needs. The accommodations may include but are not limited to: note-taking assistance, exam accommodations, electronic textbooks, priority registration, and progress reports. In addition the LD Program staff is available to meet individually with students to work on study strategies, time management issues, and organizational strategies. Tutoring is widely available for all students.

ADMISSION INFORMATION FOR STUDENTS WITH LD/ADHD

College entrance tests required: Yes
Interview required: No
What documentation required for LD: Psycho Ed evaluation to include: relevant historical info, instructional interventions, related services, age diagnosed, objective data (aptitude, achievement, info processing), test scores (standard, percentile and grade equivalents) and describe functional limitations.
With general application: No
To receive services after enrolling: Yes
What documentation required for ADHD: Diagnosis based on DSM-V; history of behaviors impairing functioning in academic setting; diagnostic interview; history of symptoms; evidence of ongoing behaviors.

With general application: No
Submitted to: Support Program/Services
Special Ed. HS course work accepted: No
Specific course requirements for all applicants: Yes
Separate application required for program services: Yes
# of LD applications submitted each year: 50
# of LD applications accepted yearly: 25–50
Total # of students receiving LD services: 150–225
Acceptance into program means acceptance into college: Separate application required after student has enrolled

ADMISSIONS
Admission into UWM is necessary for participation in the LD Program. Students apply directly to Enrollment Services or online. Online applications are encouraged. Apply online at http://apply.wisconsin.edu. Documentation should be sent directly to the LD Program. Students need to submit the standard application packet or apply online, including ACT scores and high school transcripts. Accommodations can be requested to take the placement tests by contacting the LD Program and submitting documentation of disability.

ADDITIONAL INFORMATION
Students who meet eligibility criteria receive individual counseling and guidance. In addition, students may be eligible for academic accommodations based upon specific disability-related needs. These accommodations may include but are not limited to: Priority registration; note-taking assistance; exam accommodations; electronic textbooks; use of computer; and progress reports. To use the Computer & Assistive Technology Lab, students must have an initial screening of the need for assistive technology. Specific, individualized recommendations for each student are evaluated. Eligible students will have portable, flexible access to technology. Assistive Technology is based on student need and there is training in the use of Assistive Technology.

PROGRAM FOR DISABILITY SERVICES

Contact Information
Name of program or department: Student Accessibility Center
  Telephone: 414-229-5822
  Fax: 414-229-2237

LEARNING DISABILITY SERVICES

Accommodations are determined on an individual basis after a thorough review of appropriate, current documentation. The accommodations requested must be supported through the documentation provided and must be logically linked to the current impact of the condition on academic functioning.

Allowed in exams
  Calculator: No
  Dictionary: Yes
  Computer: Yes
  Spellchecker: Yes
Extended test time: Yes
Scribes: Yes
Proctors: Yes
Oral exams: Yes
Note-takers: Yes

Distraction-reduced environment: Yes
Tape recording in class: Yes
Electronic texts: Yes
Accommodations for students with
  ADHD: Yes
Kurzweil Reader: Yes
Other assistive technology: Our center has an Assistive Technology Computer Lab.
Priority registration: Yes

Added costs for services: No
LD specialists: Yes
Professional tutors: No
Peer tutors: Yes
Max. hours/wk. for services: 3
How professors are notified of
  LD/ADHD: Student

GENERAL ADMISSIONS INFORMATION

Office of Admission: 414-229-2222

ENTRANCE REQUIREMENTS
Academic units required: 4 English, 3 mathematics, 3 science, (1 science labs), 3 social studies, 2 academic electives, 2 from the above areas, computer science, fine arts, or other appropriate courses. **Academic units recommended:** 4 English, 4 mathematics, 3 science, (1 science labs), 2 foreign language, 3 social studies, 2 academic electives, 2 from the above areas, computer science, fine arts, or other appropriate courses. High school diploma is required and GED is accepted. SAT or ACT required; TOEFL required of all international applicants; minimum paper TOEFL 500.

Application deadline: 7/1
Notification: Rolling
Average GPA: 3.06
ACT Composite middle 50% range:
  19–24

SAT Math middle 50% range: NR
SAT Critical Reading middle 50% range: NR
SAT Writing middle 50% range: NR

Graduated top 10% of class: 8%
Graduated top 25% of class: 26%
Graduated top 50% of class: 63%

COLLEGE GRADUATION REQUIREMENTS

Course substitutions allowed: Yes
In what course: On an individual basis, determinations will be made for course substitutions, generally in math and foreign language courses.

ADDITIONAL INFORMATION

Environment: The university is located on 90 acres in a residential area 90 miles north of Chicago.

Student Body
  Undergrad enrollment: 30,502
  Women: 51%
  Men: 49%
  Percent out-of-state: 2%

Cost Information
  In-state tuition: $8,681
  Out-of-state tuition: $18,409
  Room & board: $7,200
Housing Information
  University housing: Yes
  Percent living on campus: 16%

Greek System
  Fraternity: Yes
  Sorority: Yes
Athletics: Division I

UNIVERSITY OF WISCONSIN—OSHKOSH

Dempsey Hall 135, 800 Algoma Boulevard, Oshkosh, WI 54901
Phone: 920-424-0202 • Fax: 920-424-1098
E-mail: oshadmuw@uwosh.edu • Web: www.uwosh.edu
Support: SP • Institution type: 4-year public

PROGRAMS OR SERVICES FOR STUDENTS WITH LD

Project Success is a language remediation project that is based on mastering the entire sound structure of the English language. These students are academically able and determined to succeed, in spite of a pronounced problem in a number of areas. Help is offered in the following ways: direct remediation of deficiencies through the Orton-Gillingham Technique, one-on-one tutoring assistance, math and writing labs, guidance and counseling with scheduling course work and interpersonal relations, extended time, and by providing an atmosphere that is supportive. The goal is for students to become language independent in and across all of these major educational areas: math, spelling, reading, writing, comprehension, and study skills. As full-time university students, they will acquire language independence by mastering the entire phonetic structure of the American English language.

ADMISSION INFORMATION FOR STUDENTS WITH LD/ADHD

College entrance tests required: Yes
Interview required: No
Essay recommended: Yes
What documentation required for LD: Psycho Ed evaluation to include: relevant historical info, instructional interventions, related services, age diagnosed, objective data (aptitude, achievement, info processing), test scores (standard, percentile and grade equivalents) and describe functional limitations.
With general application: Yes if requested as part of Structured Program application
To receive services after enrolling: Yes
What documentation required for ADHD: Diagnosis based on DSM-V; history of behaviors impairing functioning in academic setting; diagnostic interview; history of symptoms; evidence of ongoing behaviors.

With general application: Yes if requested as part of Structured Program application
To receive services after enrolling: Yes
Submitted to: Admissions Office and Project Success
Special Ed. HS course work accepted: Yes
Specific course requirements of all applicants: Yes
Separate application required: Yes
# of LD applications submitted each year: 50–70
# of LD applications accepted yearly: 40
Total # of students receiving LD services: 350
Acceptance into program means acceptance into college: Students are accepted jointly to Project Success and the university; however, they must submit separate applications for the program and the university.

ADMISSIONS

Students may apply to Project Success in their junior year of high school. Applicants apply by writing a letter, in their own handwriting, indicating interest in the program and why they are interested. Applications are processed on a first-come, first-served basis. Those interested should apply at least 1 to 2 years prior to the student's desired entrance sememster. Students and parents will be invited to interview. The interview is used to assess family dynamics in terms of support for the student and reasons for wanting to attend college. The director is looking for motivation, stability, and the ability of the students to describe the disability. Acceptance into Project Success does not grant acceptance into the university. Admission to the university and acceptance into Project Success is a joint decision, but a separate process is required for each. General admissions procedures must be followed before acceptance into Project Success can be offered. ACT/SAT or GPA are not critical. Students who are admitted to UW—Oshkosh and Project Success not in full standing (all high school units completed, top 40 percent of graduating class, and ACT of 22-plus) must attend the Project Success summer program prior to freshman year.

ADDITIONAL INFORMATION

Incoming freshmen to Project Success must participate in an 6-week summer school program consisting of simultaneous multisensory instructional procedures (SMSIP). This program is used to teach study skills, reading, spelling, writing, and mathematical operations. The Project Success program offers the following remedial and support services for all students enrolled in its program: organizational tutors, mathematics courses/tutoring, remedial reading and spelling courses, English/written expression courses/tutoring, and content area tutoring. Additionally, students are eligible for extended time testing opportunities. Although Project Success does not offer taped texts, students are not prohibited from using them. Student requesting taped texts are referred to the UW—Oshkosh Disability Services office. Services and accommodations are available for undergraduate and graduate students.

LEARNING DISABILITY PROGRAM OR SERVICES

Contact Information
Name of program or department: Project Success
  Telephone: 920-424-3100
  Fax: 920-424-0858

LEARNING DISABILITY SERVICES

Accommodations are decided upon an individual basis after a thorough review of appropriate, current documentation. The accommodations requested must be supported through the documentation provided and must be logically linked to the current impact of the condition on academic functioning.

Allowed in exams
  Calculator: Yes
  Dictionary: Yes
  Computer: Yes
  Spellchecker: No
Extended test time: Yes
Scribes: No
Proctors: Yes
Oral exams: No
Note-takers: Yes

Distraction-reduced environment: Yes
Tape recording in class: Yes
Electronic texts: Yes
Accommodations for students with ADHD: Yes
Kurzweil Reader: Yes
Other assistive technology: Yes
Priority registration: Yes

Added costs for services: No
LD specialists: Yes
Professional tutors: No
Peer tutors: 80
Max. hours/wk. for services: NR
How professors are notified of LD/ADHD: By both student and director

GENERAL ADMISSIONS INFORMATION

Office of Admission: 920-424-0202

ENTRANCE REQUIREMENTS

Academic units required: 4 English, 3 math, 3 science (2 science labs), 3 social studies, 1 history, 4 academic electives. **Academic units recommended:** 4 math, 4 science (4 science labs). High school diploma is required, and GED is accepted. ACT with or without Writing component accepted. TOEFL required of all international applicants: minimum paper TOEFL 525, minimum computer TOEFL 197.

Application deadline: None
Notification: Rolling
Average GPA: 3.27
ACT Composite middle 50% range: 20–24

SAT Math middle 50% range: NR
SAT Critical Reading middle 50% range: NR
SAT Writing middle 50% range: NR

Graduated top 10% of class: 11%
Graduated top 25% of class: 39%
Graduated top 50% of class: 89%

COLLEGE GRADUATION REQUIREMENTS

Course waivers allowed: Yes
In what course: UW—Oshkosh has special accommodations in place relating to the foreign language requirement.
Course substitutions allowed: Yes
In what course: Foreign language and several others in select areas

ADDITIONAL INFORMATION

Environment: The campus is located 3 hours north of Chicago and 2 hours northeast of Madison.

Student Body
  Undergrad enrollment: 13,461
  Women: 59%
  Men: 41%
  Percent out-of-state: 3%

Cost Information
  In-state tuition: $7,278
  Out-of-state tuition: $14,999
  Room & board: $7,042
Housing Information
  University housing: Yes
  Percent living on campus: 25%

Greek System
  Fraternity: Yes
  Sorority: Yes
Athletics: Division III

U. OF WISCONSIN—STEVENS POINT

102 Student Services Center, Stevens Point, WI 54481
Phone: 715-346-2441 • Fax: 715-346-3296
E-mail: admiss@uwsp.edu • Web: www.uwsp.edu
Support: S • Institution: 4-year public

PROGRAMS OR SERVICES FOR STUDENTS WITH LD

The university does not have a formal program or a specialized curriculum for students with LD; rather, it provides all of the services appropriate to ensure equal access to all programs. Their philosophy is to provide what is mandated in order to enhance the student's academic success, and also to convey their concern for the student's total well-being. The coordinator is a strong advocate for students. Students are encouraged to meet with the coordinator prior to admissions for information about the services. A full range of accommodations are provided. The services provide a multisensory approach developing compensatory skills, not remediation, and utilize a developmental model for advising as well as psychosocial adjustment. Student success is contingent on many factors; some responsibilities belong to the student, others belong to the university, and others are shared by both. Students should make an appointment at the beginning of each semester; should not miss appointments; make their needs known; and be a self-advocate. Disability Services (DS) provides students with accommodations that are appropriate for the disability. Together, DS and the student can work toward effective accommodations and utilization of support services and establish a working relationship based on trust and communication.

ADMISSION INFORMATION FOR STUDENTS WITH LD/ADHD

College entrance tests required: Yes
Interview required: No
Essay required: N/A
Documentation required for LD: WAIS or WISC R, WJ, etc. as appropriate
Documentation required for ADHD: Medical documentation in the form of a report or statementf from a qualified professional verifying the disability.
Submitted to: Disability Services
Special Ed. HS course work accepted: No

Specific course requirements for all applicants: Yes
Separate application required for program services: No
# of LD applications submitted each year: 50
# of LD applications accepted yearly: 25–50
Total # of students receiving LD services: 100–125
Acceptance into program means acceptance into college: Students must be admitted to and enrolled in the university first and then request services.

ADMISSIONS

There is no separate admission procedure for students with learning disabilities. However, students are encouraged to make a pre-admission inquiry and talk to the director of DS.

ADDITIONAL INFORMATION

DS provides: accommodations that are appropriate to the disability, such as text-to-voice textbooks, note-takers, proctors and scribes, adaptive testing, assistive technology and advising, referral to tutoring and writing assistance, time management and study strategies training, notification to faculty/staff regarding necessary accommodations, referral for assessment for those not yet diagnosed, and a commitment to keeping scheduled appointments and a corresponding commitment to being timely. The Tutoring-Learning Center schedules one-on-one tutoring sessions and small-group tutoring; tutoring is free for students wanting help with reading or writing assignments. Tutoring in subject areas is done in groups and one-on-one in which there is a fee; however, for some students, the fee is covered by various support funding.

PROGRAM FOR DISABILITY SERVICES

Contact Information
Name of program or department: Disability Services (DS)
   Telephone: 715-346-3365
   Fax: 715-346-4143

LEARNING DISABILITY SERVICES

Accommodations are decided upon an individual basis after a thorough review of appropriate, current documentation. The accommodations requested must be supported through the documentation provided and must be logically linked to the current impact of the condition on academic functioning.

Allowed in exams	**Distraction-reduced environment:** Yes	**Added costs for services:** No
Calculator: Yes	**Tape recording in class:** Yes	**LD specialists:** No
Dictionary: Yes	**Electronic texts:** Yes	**Professional tutors:** 3
Computer: Yes	**Accommodations for students with**	**Peer tutors:** Yes
Spellchecker: Yes	**ADHD:** Yes	**Max. hours/wk. for services:** 2
Extended test time: Yes	**Kurzweil Reader:** Yes	**How professors are notified of**
Scribes: Yes	**Other assistive technology:** Yes	**LD/ADHD:** Student
Proctors: Yes	**Priority registration:** Yes	
Oral exams: Yes		
Note-takers: Yes		

GENERAL ADMISSIONS INFORMATION

Office of Admission: 715-346-2441

ENTRANCE REQUIREMENTS
Academic units required: 4 English, 3 mathematics, 3 science, 3 social studies, 4 academic electives; 4 additional: 2 units from English, mathematics, social sciences, sciences, or foreign language and 2 units from above areas or other academic areas. **Academic units recommended:** 4 mathematics, 4 science, 4 social studies, 4 Additional 2 units from English, mathematics, social sciences, sciences, or foreign language and 2 units from above areas or other academic areas. High school diploma is required and GED is accepted. SAT or ACT required; TOEFL required of all international applicants; minimum paper TOEFL 523, minimum computer TOEFL 193, minimum web-based TOEFL 70.

Application deadline: None	**SAT Math middle 50% range:**	**Graduated top 10% of class:** 15%
Notification: Rolling	460–610	**Graduated top 25% of class:** 46%
Average GPA: 3.4	**SAT Critical Reading middle 50%**	**Graduated top 50% of class:** 93%
ACT Composite middle 50% range:	**range:** 440–610	
21–25	**SAT Writing middle 50% range:**	
	440–640	

COLLEGE GRADUATION REQUIREMENTS

Course waivers allowed: No
Course substitutions allowed: Yes
In what course: Math and foreign language

ADDITIONAL INFORMATION

Environment: The University of Wisconsin at Stevens Point is located on 335 acres 110 miles north of Madison.

Student Body	**Cost Information**	**Greek System**
Undergrad enrollment: 9,500	**In-state tuition:** $7,146	**Fraternity:** Yes
Women: 53%	**Out-of-state tuition:** $14,719	**Sorority:** Yes
Men: 47%	**Room and board:** $6,302	**Athletics:** Division III
Percent out-of-state: 10%	**Housing Information**	
	University housing: Yes	
	Percent living on campus: 32%	

U. OF WISCONSIN—WHITEWATER

800 West Main Street, Whitewater, WI 53190-1791
Phone: 262-472-1440 • Fax: 262-472-1515
E-mail: uwwadmit@uww.edu • Web: www.uww.edu
Support: CS • Institution: 4-year public

PROGRAMS OR SERVICES FOR STUDENTS WITH LD

The University of Wisconsin—Whitewater Project ASSIST offers support services for students with learning disabilities and ADD/ADHD. The Project ASSIST Summer Transition Program is a four-week program in which students enroll in a three-credit study skills class, and a three credit Transitioning to College course. Areas addressed include learning strategies, comprehension concerns, written language skills, study habits, time management and self-advocacy skills. The philosophy of the program is that students with learning disabilities can learn strategies to become independent learners.

ADMISSION INFORMATION FOR STUDENTS WITH LD/ADHD

College entrance tests required: Yes
Interview required: No
Essay required: N/A
What documentation required for LD: Psycho Ed evaluation to include: relevant historical info, instructional interventions, related services, age diagnosed, objective data (aptitude, achievement, info processing), test scores (standard, percentile and grade equivalents) and describe functional limitations.
With general application: No
To receive services after enrolling: Yes
What documentation required for ADHD: Diagnosis based on DSM-V; history of behaviors impairing functioning in academic setting; diagnostic interview; history of symptoms; evidence of ongoing behaviors.

With general application: No
Submitted to: Support Program/Services
Special Ed. HS course work accepted: No
Specific course requirements for all applicants: Yes
Separate application required for program services: No
# of LD applications submitted each year: 80–100
# of LD applications accepted yearly: 60–70
Total # of students receiving LD services: 80–90
Acceptance into program means acceptance into college: Separate application required after student has enrolled

ADMISSIONS

All applicants must meet the same criteria for admission. Students should apply to both the university and the Center for Students with Disabilities. General criteria include: completion of 17 required high school units, rank in class, and GPA. Course requirements include four English, three social studies, three sciences, three math (algebra, geometry, advanced algebra). Students apply to the University Admissions and the Center for Students with Disabilities at the same time. Program staff review the documentation and application regarding eligibilty for academic accommodations and Project ASSIST. Conditional admission to a limited number of students may be possible depending on review of documentation and reason for admission denial.

ADDITIONAL INFORMATION

Tutoring serices are provided in a one-to-one setting where students work with tutors on study, math and written language strategies in the context of specific course work. In addition, organizational tutoring is offered to assist students with time managment and organization. Computer lab with assistive technology, small group support and academic advising are available. Study areas available for student use with daytime and evening hours. In addition, drop-in tutoring is available each weekday and early evening.

PROGRAM FOR DISABILITY SERVICES

Contact Information
Name of program or department: Center for Students with Disabilities
  Telephone: 262-472-4711
  Fax: 262-472-4865

LEARNING DISABILITY SERVICES

Accommodations are decided upon an individual basis after a thorough review of appropriate, current documentation. The accommodations requested must be supported through the documentation provided and must be logically linked to the current impact of the condition on academic functioning.

Allowed in exams	**Distraction-reduced environment:** Yes	**Added costs for services:** Yes
Calculator: Yes	**Tape recording in class:** Yes	**LD specialists:** Yes
Dictionary: Yes	**Electronic texts:** Yes	**Professional tutors:** No
Computer: Yes	**Accommodations for students with**	**Peer tutors:** 35–40
Spellchecker: Yes	**ADHD:** Yes	**Max. hours/wk. for services:**
Extended test time: Yes	**Kurzweil Reader:** Yes	Unlimited
Scribes: Yes	**Other assistive technology:** Kurzweil	**How professors are notified of**
Proctors: Yes	3000, TextHelp, Inspiration	**LD/ADHD:** Student
Oral exams: Yes	**Priority registration:** Yes	
Note-takers: Yes		

GENERAL ADMISSIONS INFORMATION

Office of Admission: 262-472-1440

ENTRANCE REQUIREMENTS
Academic units required: 4 English, 3 mathematics, 3 science, (1 science labs), 3 social studies, 4 academic electives. **Academic units recommended:** 4 mathematics, 4 science, 2 foreign language, 4 social studies. High school diploma is required and GED is accepted. SAT or ACT recommended; TOEFL required of all international applicants; minimum paper TOEFL 500, minimum computer TOEFL 214.

Application deadline: 5/1	**SAT Math middle 50% range:**	**Graduated top 10% of class:** 9%
Notification: Rolling	480–600	**Graduated top 25% of class:** 32%
Average GPA: NR	**SAT Critical Reading middle 50%**	**Graduated top 50% of class:** 77%
ACT Composite middle 50% range:	**range:** 470–610	
20–24	**SAT Writing middle 50% range:**	
	470–610	

COLLEGE GRADUATION REQUIREMENTS

Course waivers allowed: No
Course substitutions allowed:
In what course: Some math requirements

ADDITIONAL INFORMATION

Environment: The university is considered a medium-size campus and is located in close proximity to two major metropolitan areas—Milwaukee and Madison. The Chicago area is approximately two hours away.

Student Body	**Cost Information**	**Greek System**
Undergrad enrollment: 11,615	**In-state tuition:** $7,196	**Fraternity:** Yes
Women: 50%	**Out-of-state tuition:** $14,798	**Sorority:** Yes
Men: 50%	**Room and board:** $5,550	**Athletics:** Division III
Percent out-of-state: 8%	**Housing Information**	
	University housing: Yes	
	Percent living on campus: 40%	

LARAMIE COUNTY COMMUNITY COLLEGE

1400 East College Drive, Cheyenne, WY 82007 • Phone: 800-522-2993
E-mail: dss@lccc.wy.edu • Web: www.lccc.wy.edu
Support: CS • Institution type: 2-year public

PROGRAMS OR SERVICES FOR STUDENTS WITH LD

Disability Support Services at Laramie County Community College provides comprehensive, confidential services for LCCC students with documented disabilities. Services and adaptive equipment are available to reduce mobility, sensory, and perceptual concerns. Services are provided free of charge to LCCC students. High school students are encouraged to contact DSS during their junior year to gather information.

ADMISSION INFORMATION FOR STUDENTS WITH LD/ADHD

College entrance tests required: No
Interview required: No
Essay recommended: No
What documentation required for LD: Psycho Ed evaluation
  to include: relevant historical info, instructional interventions,
  related services, age diagnosed, objective data (aptitude,
  achievement, info processing), test scores (standard,
  percentile and grade equivalents) and describe functional
  limitations.
With general application: No
To receive services after enrolling: Yes
What documentation required for ADHD: Diagnosis based
  on DSM-V; history of behaviors impairing functioning in
  academic setting; diagnostic interview; history of symptoms;
  evidence of ongoing behaviors.

With general application: No
Submitted to: Disability Support Services Office
Special Ed. HS course work accepted: Yes
Specific course requirements of all applicants: NR
Separate application required: No
# of LD applications submitted each year: NR
# of LD applications accepted yearly: NR
Total # of students receiving LD services: 35
**Acceptance into program means acceptance into
  college:** Students must be admitted and enrolled prior to
  requesting services.

ADMISSIONS
Admission is open to all high school graduates or GED recipients. To register students for classes, LCCC needs to assess the student's skill level in three key areas (reading, English, and math). Admission to LCCC is not based on these scores. There are no specific course requirements.

ADDITIONAL INFORMATION
Students requesting services will be required to provide a copy of current documentation. Laramie County Community College has adopted documentation guidelines as developed by the Consortium of Support Programs for Students with Disabilities, representing the postsecondary institutions of Colorado and Wyoming. Examples of services available include testing accommodations, readers/taped tests, scribes, extended time on exams, quiet rooms, use of calculators, special seating, textbooks on tape, tape recording of lectures, note-takers, assistive listening devices, assistive technology equipment, hardware and software programs, and priority registration. Appropriate accommodations are determined on a case-by-case basis between the DSS staff and the student.

LEARNING DISABILITY PROGRAM OR SERVICES

Contact Information
Name of program or department: Disability Support Services
  Telephone: 307-778-1359
  Fax: 307-778-1262

LEARNING DISABILITY SERVICES

Accommodations are decided upon an individual basis after a thorough review of appropriate, current documentation. The accommodations requested must be supported through the documentation provided.

Allowed in exams
  Calculator: Yes
  Dictionary: Yes
  Computer: Yes
  Spellchecker: Yes
Extended test time: Yes
Scribes: Yes
Proctors: Yes
Oral exams: Yes
Note-takers: Yes

Distraction-reduced environment: Yes
Tape recording in class: Yes
Electronic texts: Yes
Accommodations for students with ADHD: Yes
Kurzweil Reader: Yes
Other assistive technology: Yes
Priority registration: Yes

Added costs for services: No
LD specialists: Yes
Professional tutors: 5–15
Peer tutors: 10–20
Max. hours/wk. for services: Unlimited
How professors are notified of LD/ADHD: Accommodation letters

GENERAL ADMISSIONS INFORMATION

Office of Admission: 307-778-1117

ENTRANCE REQUIREMENTS

Open admissions but selective for some majors. Interview is required for equine training. ACT/SAT not required. High school diploma or GED accepted.

Application deadline: None
Notification: Rolling
Average GPA: NR
ACT Composite middle 50% range: NR

SAT Math middle 50% range: NR
SAT Critical Reading middle 50% range: NR
SAT Writing middle 50% range: NR

Graduated top 10% of class: NR
Graduated top 25% of class: NR
Graduated top 50% of class: NR

COLLEGE GRADUATION REQUIREMENTS

Course waivers allowed: No
Course substitutions allowed: Yes
In what course: Decided on a case-by-case basis depending on the documented disability and the student's course of study.

ADDITIONAL INFORMATION

Environment: LCCC is 100 miles north of Denver, Colorado.

Student Body
  Undergrad enrollment: 5,600
  Women: 58%
  Men: 42%
  Percent out-of-state: 10%

Cost Information
  In-state tuition: $2,640
  Out-of-state tuition: $5,952
  Room & board: $6,742–$8,740
Housing Information
  University housing: Yes
  Percent living on campus: 4%

Greek System
  Fraternity: No
  Sorority: No
Athletics: NJCAA

UNIVERSITY OF WYOMING

1000 East University Avenue, Laramie, WY 82071
Phone: 307-766-5160 • Fax: 307-766-4042
E-mail: Why-Wyo@uwyo.edu • Web: www.uwyo.edu
Support: CS • Institution type: 4-year public

PROGRAMS OR SERVICES FOR STUDENTS WITH LD

University Disability Support Services (UDSS) offers academic support services to students with learning disabilities and physically handicapped students. Its goals are to promote the independence and self-sufficiency of students and encourage the provision of equal opportunities in education for students with disabilities. Any student enrolled at UW who has a documented disability is eligible for assistance. UDSS provides disability-related accommodations and services, technical assistance, consultations, and resource information. Recommended documentation includes a clear statement of the LD (documentation should be current, preferably having been completed within the past 3 years); a summary of assessment procedures and evaluation instruments used to make the diagnosis and a summary of the results, including standardized or percentile scores that support the diagnosis (LD testing must be comprehensive, including a measure of both aptitude and achievement in the areas of reading, mathematics, and written language); a statement of strengths and needs that will impact the student's ability to meet the demands of college; and suggestions of reasonable accommodations that may be appropriate. Accommodations are collaboratively determined by the student and the assigned disability support service coordinator.

ADMISSION INFORMATION FOR STUDENTS WITH LD/ADHD

College entrance tests required: Yes
Interview required: No
Essay recommended: No
What documentation required for LD: Psycho Ed evaluation to include: relevant historical info, instructional interventions, related services, age diagnosed, objective data (aptitude, achievement, info processing), test scores (standard, percentile and grade equivalents) and describe functional limitations.
With general application: No
To receive services after enrolling: Yes
What documentation required for ADHD: Diagnosis based on DSM-V; history of behaviors impairing functioning in academic setting; diagnostic interview; history of symptoms; evidence of ongoing behaviors.

With general application: No
Submitted to: University Disability Support Services
Special Ed. HS course work accepted: Yes
Specific course requirements of all applicants: Yes
Separate application required: Yes
# of LD applications submitted each year: 50–75
# of LD applications accepted yearly: NR
Total # of students receiving LD services: 120–140
Acceptance into program means acceptance into college: Students must be admitted to and enrolled in the university first and then request services.

ADMISSIONS

Students with learning disabilities must meet general admission requirements. If the students are borderline and have a documented learning disability, they are encouraged to self-identify to the director. Students who were diagnosed late in high school or began utilizing services late may be able to explain how this had an impact on academics. Students with learning disabilities who meet the general admission criteria request LD services after being admitted. Conditional admission is granted with a GPA of 2.5 or a GPA of 2.25 and an ACT score of 20 or an SAT score of 960. Students with learning disabilities not meeting admission criteria and not qualifying for assured or conditional admission may have their applications reviewed by the LD program director. The LD director will make a recommendation to the Office of Admissions.

ADDITIONAL INFORMATION

Services include priority registration, readers, assistance with study skills, note-taking, test preparation, word processing orientation, equipment loan assistance, tutor referral, and advocacy for students via the University Accessibility Committee. Auditory systems are also used to provide access to print mediums for persons with LD. Synthesized speech reinforces visual cues. Grammar-checking software is available to proof documents and improve writing skills; writing skills may also be improved through the use of word prediction software. Dragon Dictate, a voice recognition program, may benefit those students who have learning disabilities that affect written expression. All students must take one course in math or quantitative reasoning to graduate.

LEARNING DISABILITY PROGRAM OR SERVICES

Contact Information
Name of program or department: University Disability Support Services (UDSS)
 Telephone: 307-766-6189
 Fax: 307-766-4010

LEARNING DISABILITY SERVICES

Accommodations are decided upon an individual basis after a thorough review of appropriate, current documentation. The accommodations requested must be supported through the documentation provided or via other information provided by the student, and must be logically linked to the current impact of the condition on academic functioning.

Allowed in exams
 Calculator: Depends
 Dictionary: Depends
 Computer: Depends
 Spellchecker: Depends
Extended test time: Yes
Scribes: Yes
Proctors: Yes
Oral exams: Yes
Note-takers: Yes

Distraction-reduced environment: Yes
Tape recording in class: Yes
Electronic texts: Yes
Accommodations for students with
 ADHD: Yes
Kurzweil Reader: Yes
Other assistive technology: Yes
Priority registration: Yes

Added costs for services: No
LD specialists: Yes
Professional tutors: No
Peer tutors: Yes
Max. hours/wk. for services: NR
How professors are notified of
 LD/ADHD: By both student and UDSS
 coordinators

GENERAL ADMISSIONS INFORMATION

Office of Admission: 307-766-5160

ENTRANCE REQUIREMENTS

Academic units required: 4 English, 3 math, 3 science (3 science labs), 3 cultural context electives (recommended), 3 behavioral or social sciences, 3 visual/performing arts, 3 humanities or earth/space sciences. **Academic units recommended:** 4 English, 4 math, 4 science (3 science labs), 2 foreign language, 3 cultural context electives, 3 behavioral or social sciences, 3 visual/performing arts, 3 humanities or earth/space sciences. High school diploma is required, and GED is accepted. ACT with or without Writing component accepted. TOEFL required of all international applicants: minimum paper TOEFL 525, minimum computer TOEFL 197.

Application deadline: 8/10
Notification: Rolling.
Average GPA: 3.46
ACT Composite middle 50% range:
 22–27

SAT Math middle 50% range:
 490–630
SAT Critical Reading middle 50%
 range: 490–600
SAT Writing middle 50% range: NR

Graduated top 10% of class: 21%
Graduated top 25% of class: 51%
Graduated top 50% of class: 79%

COLLEGE GRADUATION REQUIREMENTS

Course waivers allowed: No
Course substitutions allowed: Yes
In what course: Substitutions are possible for foreign language and some math course requirements, depending on the student's major and the purpose of the language and/or math requirements for that major.

ADDITIONAL INFORMATION

Environment: The university is located on 785 acres in a small town 128 miles north of Denver.

Student Body
 Undergrad enrollment: 10,081
 Women: 52%
 Men: 48%
 Percent out-of-state: 29%

Cost Information
 In-state tuition: $4,125
 Out-of-state tuition: $12,855
 Room & board: $8,790
Housing Information
 University housing: Yes
 Percent living on campus: 21%

Greek System
 Fraternity: Yes
 Sorority: Yes
Athletics: Division I

SHERIDAN COLLEGE

3059 Cofeen Avenue, Sheridan, WY 82801
Phone: 307-674-6446 • Fax: 307-674-3384
E-mail: admmissions@sheridan.edu • Web: www.sheridanc.edu
Support: S • Institution type: 2-year public

PROGRAMS OR SERVICES FOR STUDENTS WITH LD

Sheridan College has limited services available for students with learning disabilities. Students who have been enrolled in special education classes in high school may find that the college does not have the extensive services necessary for them to be successful. Students need to be self-sufficient because the two advisor/counselors are able to allot only a small percentage of their time to work with students with disabilities. Students requesting accommodations must provide psychoeducational evaluations and have these sent to the Counseling/Testing Offices. The college reserves the right to evaluate if it can serve the needs of students.

ADMISSION INFORMATION FOR STUDENTS WITH LD/ADHD

College entrance tests required: No
Interview required: No
Essay recommended: No
What documentation required for LD: Psycho Ed evaluation to include: relevant historical info, instructional interventions, related services, age diagnosed, objective data (aptitude, achievement, info processing), test scores (standard, percentile and grade equivalents) and describe functional limitations.
With general application: No
To receive services after enrolling: Yes
What documentation required for ADHD: Diagnosis based on DSM-V; history of behaviors impairing functioning in academic setting; diagnostic interview; history of symptoms; evidence of ongoing behaviors.

With general application: No
Submitted to: Admissions Office
Special Ed. HS course work accepted: N/A
Specific course requirements of all applicants: No
Separate application required: Yes
# of LD applications submitted each year: 30
# of LD applications accepted yearly: all applicants
Total # of students receiving LD services: 30
Acceptance into program means acceptance into college: Students must be admitted to and enrolled in the university first and then request services.

ADMISSIONS

There are no special admission procedures or criteria for students with learning disabilities. The college has open admissions, and any student with a high school diploma or GED is eligible to attend. All students are treated the same and must submit the general college application for admission. Any information on learning disabilities provided is voluntarily given by the student. Students with learning disabilities must submit psychoeducational evaluations. The admission decision is made by the director of the program.

ADDITIONAL INFORMATION

The college offers tutoring, quiet places to take tests, readers, extended testing times, recorders, note-takers, and the availability of a few Franklin Spellers. Remediation courses are offered in arithmetic skills, spelling, vocabulary, reading, writing, and algebra. Other aids for students with learning disabilities include test-taking strategies training, books on tape, tutoring one-on-one or in small groups in the Learning Center, and GED preparation and testing. Support services include career testing and evaluation, peer counseling, and personal and career development.

LEARNING DISABILITY PROGRAM OR SERVICES

Contact Information
Name of program or department: Advising/Learning Center
  Telephone: 307-674-6446
  Fax: 307-674-3384

LEARNING DISABILITY SERVICES

Accommodations are decided upon an individual basis after a thorough review of appropriate, current documentation. The accommodations requested must be supported through the documentation provided and must be logically linked to the current impact of the condition on academic functioning.

Allowed in exams	**Distraction-reduced environment:** Yes	**Added costs for services:** No
Calculator: Yes	**Tape recording in class:** Yes	**LD specialists:** No
Dictionary: Yes	**Electronic texts:** Yes	**Professional tutors:** No
Computer: Yes	**Accommodations for students with**	**Peer tutors:** Yes
Spellchecker: Yes	**ADHD:** Yes	**Max. hours/wk. for services:**
Extended test time: Yes	**Kurzweil Reader:** No	Unlimited
Scribes: Yes	**Other assistive technology:** Yes	**How professors are notified of**
Proctors: Yes	**Priority registration:** No	**LD/ADHD:** By student
Oral exams: Yes		
Note-takers: Yes		

GENERAL ADMISSIONS INFORMATION

Office of Admission: 800-913-9139

ENTRANCE REQUIREMENTS

Open enrollment. Admissions does not require diploma or GED, but the financial aid office does to release federal aid.

Application deadline: 6/1	**SAT Math middle 50% range:** NR	**Graduated top 10% of class:** NR
Notification: NR	**SAT Critical Reading middle 50%**	**Graduated top 25% of class:** NR
Average GPA: NR	**range:** NR	**Graduated top 50% of class:** NR
ACT Composite middle 50% range:	**SAT Writing middle 50% range:** NR	
NR		

COLLEGE GRADUATION REQUIREMENTS

Course waivers allowed: Yes
In what course: Would have to be very particular circumstances
Course substitutions allowed: Yes
In what course: Would have to be very particular circumstances

ADDITIONAL INFORMATION

Environment: The college is located on 64 acres in Sheridan.

Student Body	**Cost Information**	**Greek System**
Undergrad enrollment: 3,500	**In-state tuition:** $2,578	**Fraternity:** No
Women: 66%	**Out-of-state tuition:** $5,986	**Sorority:** No
Men: 34%	**Room & board:** $5,880	**Athletics:** NJCAA
Percent out-of-state: 9%	**Housing Information**	
	University housing: Yes	
	Percent living on campus: 15%	

QUICK CONTACT REFERENCE LIST

ALABAMA

AAlabama St. U.	Montgomery, AL 36101	Learning Disabilities Program	334-229-5134
Auburn U.	Auburn U., AL 36849	Students w/ Disabilities	334-844-2096
Auburn U.	Montgomery, AL 36124-4023	Special Services	334-244-3754
Birmingham-Southern C.	Birmingham, AL 35254	Learning Disabilities Program	205-226-4696
Faulkner U.	Montgomery, AL 36109	Project Key	334-386-7185
Gadsden St. C.C.	Gadsden, AL 35999	Student Services	256-549-8200
Huntingdon C.	Montgomery, AL 36106-2148	Student Activities & Career Resources	334-833-4465
Jacksonville St. U.	Jacksonville, AL 36265	Academic Center for Excellence	256-782-8380
Judson C.	Marion, AL 36756	LD Services	334-683-5112
Miles C.	Birmingham, AL 35208	Student Support Services	205-929-1000
Samford U.	Birmingham, AL 35229	Counseling Services	205-726-4078
Spring Hill C.	Mobile, AL 36608	Student Academic Support	251-380-3470
Stillman C.	Tuscaloosa, AL 35403	Student Development Center	250-366-8894
Troy St. U.	Troy, AL 36082	Adaptive Needs Program	334-670-3221
Troy St. U.—Dothan	Dothan, AL 36304	Learning Disability Services	334-983-6556 ext. 221
Tuskegee U.	Tuskegee, AL 36088	Office of Student Life and Development	334-727-8837).
U. of Alabama—Birmingham	Birmingham, AL 35294-1150	Disability Support	205-934-4205
U. of Alabama—Huntsville	Huntsville, AL 35899	Disability Support Services	256-824-6203
U. of Alabama—Tuscaloosa	Tuscaloosa, AL 35487	Office of Disabilities Services	205-348-4285
U. of Montevallo	Montevallo, AL 35115	Services for Students w/ Disabilities	205-665-6250
U. of North Alabama	Florence, AL 35632	Disability Services	256-765-4214
U. of South Alabama	Mobile, AL 36688-0002	Special Student Services	251-460-7212
U. of West Alabama	Livingston, AL 35470	Learning Disabilities Services	205-652-3581

ALASKA

U. of Alaska—Anchorage	Anchorage, AK 99508-8046	Disability Support Services	907-786-4535
U. of Alaska—Fairbanks	Fairbanks, AK 99775-7480	Disability Services	907-474-5655
U. of Alaska—Southeast	Juneau, AK 99801-8681	Student Resource Center	907-796-6000

ARIZONA

Institution	Location	Program	Phone
Arizona St. U.	Tempe, AZ 85287-3202	Disability Resource Services	480-965-1234
Arizona St. U. West	Phoenix, AZ 85069-7100	Disability Research Center	602-543-8145
Coconino C.C.	Flagstaff, AZ 86004	Disability Resources	928-226-4243

Institution	Location	Service	Phone
Embry-Riddle Aero. U. AZ)	Prescott, AZ 86301-3720	Director Student Activities	843-767-8912
Gateway C.C.	Phoenix, AZ 85034	Special Services	602-286-8170
Mesa C.C.	Mesa, AZ 85202	Disability Resources and Services	480-461-7395
Northern Arizona U.	Flagstaff, AZ 86011-4084	Disability Support Services	928-523-8773
Phoenix C.	Phoenix, AZ 85013	Disability Resource Center	602-285-7962
Pima C.C.	Tucson, AZ 85702	Disabled Student Resources	520-206-7699
Prescott C.	Prescott, AZ 86301	Learning Disability Program	928-350-1009
U. of Arizona	Tucson, AZ 85921	SALT 520-621-1427	520-621-3268
U. of Phoenix	Phoenix, AZ 85040-1958	Office of Admissions	866.766.0766

ARKANSAS

Institution	Location	Service	Phone
Arkansas St. U.	Jonesboro, AR 72467	Disability Services	870-972-3964
Harding U.	Searcy, AR 72149	Student Support Services SSS)	501-279-4028
Henderson St. U.	Arkadelphia, AR 71999-0001	Disability Services	870-230-5475
Hendrix C.	Conway, AR 72032	Counseling Center	501-505-2945
John Brown U.	Siloam Springs, AR 72761	Disability Services	479-524-7217
Lyon C.	Batesville, AR72503-2317	Disability Services	870-307-7332
NW Arkansas C.C.	Bentonville, AR 72712	Learner Development Center	479-986-4076
Ouachita Baptist U.	Arkadelphia, AR 71998	Disability Services	870-245-5591
S. Arkansas U.	Magnolia, AR 71753-5000	Student Disability Special Services	870-235-4145
U. of Arkansas—Fayetteville	Fayetteville, AR 72701	Student Support Services	479-575-3104
U. of Arkansas—Little Rock	Little Rock, AR 72204	Disability Support Services	501-569-3143
U. of Arkansas—Pine Bluff	Pine Bluff, AR 71601-2799	Office of Veterans & Disability Services	870-575-8293
U. of Central Arkansas	Conway, AR 72035	Disability Services	501-450-5167
U. of the Ozarks	Clarksville, AR 72830	Jones Learning Center	479-979-1401
Williams Baptist C.	Walnut Ridge, AR 72476	Learning Disabilities	870-886-6741

CALIFORNIA

Institution	Location	Service	Phone
Alliant Intl. U.	San Diego, CA 92131	Disability Services	858-635-4471
Art Center C. of Design	Pasadena, CA 91103	Admissions	626-396-2373
Azusa Pacific U.	Azusa, CA 91702	Learning Enrichment Center	626-815-3849
Bakersfield C.	Bakersfield, CA 93305	Support Services Program	661-395-4334
Biola U.	La Mirada, CA 90639	Learning Center	562-906-4542

College	Location	Service	Phone
Butte C.C.	Oroville, CA 95965	Services for Students with Disabilities	530-895-2455
Cabrillo C.	Santa Cruz, CA 95060	Disabled Student Services	831-479-6379
Cabrillo C.	Aptos, CA 95003	Learning Skills Program	831-479-6220
California Baptist U.	Riverside, CA 92504	Disability Services	951-343-4962
California C. of Arts	Oakland, CA 94618-1426	Learning Resource Center	510-594-3756
California Institute of Arts	Valencia CA 91355	Dean of Students	661-253-7891
California Institute of Tech.	Pasadena, CA 91125	Disability Services	626-395-6351
California Lutheran U.	Thousand Oaks, CA 91360	Center for Academic & Accessibility	805-493-3878
California Polytechnic St. U.	San Luis Obispo, CA 93407	Disability Resource Center	805-756-5752
California St. Polytechnic U.	Pomona, CA 91768	Disabled Student Services	909-869-5257
California St. U.	Turlock, CA 95832	Disabled Student Services	209-667-3159
California St. U.—Bakersfield	Bakersfield, CA 93311	Services for Students with Disabilities	661-664-2011
California St. U.—Fullerton	Fullerton, CA 92634	Disabled Student Services	657-278-2515
California St. U.—Hayward	Hayward, CA 94542	Learning Disabled Resources	510-885-3868
California St. U.—Long Beach	Long Beach, CA 90840	Disabled Student Services	562-985-5401
California St. U.—Monterey Bay	Seaside, CA 93955-8001	Student Disability Resources	831-582-3357
California St. U.—Northridge	Northridge, CA 91328-	Students with Disabilities Resource	818-677-2578
California St. U.—Sacramento	Sacramento, CA 95819	Services for Students With LD	916-278-7239
Calif. St. U.—San Bernardino	San Bernardino, CA 92407	Services to Students with Disabilities	909-537-5238
California St. U.—San Marcos	San Marcos, CA 92096-	Disabled Student Services	760-750-4905
California St. U.—Stanislaus	Turlock, CA 95382	Disability Resource Center	209-667-3159
Cerritos C.C.	Norwalk, CA 90650	Disabled Students Programs & Svcs	562-860-2451 ext. 2334
Chapman U.	Orange, CA 92866	Center for Academic Success	714-744-7971
Charles R. Drew U. of Med	Los Angeles, CA 90059	Student Education Center	323-563-9351
Citrus C.C.	Glendora, CA 91741	Disabled Student Program	626-914-8677
City C. San Francisco	Orinda, CA 94563	Disabled Student Services	415-452-5481
Claremont McKenna C.	Claremont, CA 91711	Dean of Students	909-621-8114
C. of Redwoods	Crescent City, CA 95531	Disabled Student Spec.	707-465-2324
College of the Siskiyous	Weed, CA 96094	Disabled Student Services	530-938-5297
Columbia C.C.	Sonora, CA 95370	Disabled Student Programs & Services	209-588-5130
Concordia U.	Irvine, CA 92612-3299	Disability Services	949-854-8002 ext. 1836
Cuesta C.	San Luis Obispo, CA 93403	Academic Support	805-546-3100 ext 2149

Institution	Location	Service	Phone
De Anza C.	Sunnyvale, CA 94087	Disability Support Services	408-864-8959
Dominican U. of California	San Rafeal, CA 94901-2298	Tutoring and Disability Services	415-257-0187
East Los Angeles C.	Monterey Pk, CA 90025	DSPS	323-265-8787
El Camino C.	Torrance, CA 90506	Special Resource Center	310-532-3670
Evergreen Valley C.	San Jose, CA 95135	Disabled Students Program	408-223-6756
Foothill C.	Los Altos, CA 94022	STEP	650-949-7038
Fresno Pacific U.	Fresno, CA 93702	Student Development Program	559-453-2247
Grossmont C.	Ramona, CA 92065	Disabled Students Programs & Services	619-644-7112
Harvey Mudd C.	Claremont, CA 91711	Dean of Students	909-621-8125
Holy Names U.	Oakland, CA 94619	Disability Support Services	510-436-1658
Humboldt St. U.	Arcata, CA 95521-8299	Student Disability Resource Center	707-826-4678
Humphreys C.	Stockton, CA 95207	Disability Services	209-478-0800
John F. Kennedy U.	Orinda, CA 94563	Student Disability Services	925-969-3447
Lake Tahoe C.C.	So. Lake Tahoe, CA 96150	Disability Resource Center	530-541-4660 ext. 384
Laney College	El Sobrante, CA 94803	Disabled Student Program Services	510-464-3428
Life Pacific C.	San Dimas, CA 91773-3298	Life Challenges & PCS	909-599-5433 ext. 363
Long Beach City C.	Long Beach, CA 90808	Disabled Student Program Services	562-938-4111
Los Angeles City C.	Los Angeles, CA 90039	LD Services	323-953-4000 ext. 2273
Loyola Marymount U.	Los Angeles, CA 90045	Disability Support Services	310-338-4535
Master's C.	Newhall, CA 91322	Disability Services	661-259-3540
Menlo C.	Atherton, CA 94027	Academic Success Center	650-543-3917
Mills C.	Oakland, CA 94613	Disability Services	510-430-2130
Mount St. Mary's C.	Los Angeles, CA 90049	Disability Services	310-954-4141
Norte Dame de Namur U.	Belmont, CA 94002-1908	PASS	650-508-3613
Occidental C.	Los Angeles, CA 90041	Center for Academic Excellence	323-259-2545
Orange Coast C.	Costa Mesa, CA 92628	Learning Center	714-432-5535
Oxnard C.	Oxnard, CA 93033	Disabled Students Program & Services	805-986-5830
Pasadena City C.	Pasadena, CA 91106	Disabled Student Services	626-585-7127
Pacific Oaks C.	Pasadena, CA 31103	CARE Center	626-397-1338 ext 5
Pacific Union C.	Angwin, CA 94508	Disability Support Services	707-965-7688
Patten U.	Oakland, CA94601	Enrollment Services	510-261-8500 ext. 7783
Pepperdine U.	Malibu, CA 90263	Disability Services	310-506-6500
Pitzer C.	Claremont, CA 91711	Academic Support Services	909-607-3553

College	Location	Office	Phone
Reedley College	Reedley, CA 93654-2099	Disabled Students Programs & Services	559-638-0332
Pitzer C.	Claremont, CA 91711	Academic Support Services	909-607-3553
Point Loma Nazarene U.	San Diego, CA 92106	Disability Resource Center	619-849-2486
Pomona C.	Claremont, CA 91711	Disability Services	909)621-8017
Saddleback C.	Carlsbad, CA 92008	Special Services	949-582-4885
St. Mary's C. of CA	Moraga, CA 94556	Academic Support Center	925-631-4358
San Diego City C.	San Diego, CA 92101	Disabled Student Program & Service	619-388-3513
San Diego St. U.	San Diego, CA 92182	Disabled Student Services	619-594-6473
San Francisco Art Institute	San Francisco, CA 94133	Office of Academic Support	415-771-7020 ext. 4471
San Francisco St. U.	San Francisco, CA 94132	Disability Programs & Resource Center	415-338-2472
San Jose St. U.	San Jose, CA 95192	Disability Resource Center	408-924-6000
Santa Barbara City C.	Santa Barbara, CA 93109	Disabled Student Services	805-965-0581
Santa Clara U.	Santa Clara, CA 95053	Disability Resources	408-554-4111
Santa Monica C.	Santa Monica, CA 90405	Center for Students with Disabilities	310-434-4443
Santa Rosa Junior C.	Santa Rosa, CA 95401	Disability Resource Department	707-527-4278
Scripps C.	Claremont, CA 91711	Disability Services	909-607-1564
Sierra C.	Rocklin, CA 95677	Learning Opportunities Center	916-660-7450
Simpson U.	Redding, CA 96003-8606	Growth and Development	530-226-4179
Sonoma St. U.	Rohnert Park, CA 94928	Disabled Student Services	707-664-2677
Stanford U.	Stanford, CA 94305-3005	Office of Accessible Education	650-723-1066
Taft C.	Taft, CA 93268	Disabled Student Services	661-763-7866
U. of California—Berkeley	Berkeley, CA 94720-4250	Disabled Students' Program	510-642-0518
U. of California—Davis	Davis, CA 95616	Learning Disability Center	530-752-3184
U. of California—Irvine	Irvine, CA 92717	Office of Disability Services	949-824-7494
U. of California—Los Angeles	Los Angeles, CA 90095	Office for Students with Disabilities	310-825-1501
U. of California—Riverside	Riverside, CA 92521	Services for Students w/ Disabilities	951-827-4538
U. of California—San Diego	La Jolla, CA 92093-0337	Office for Students with Disabilities	858-534-4382
U. of California—Santa Barbara	Santa Barbara, CA 93106	Disabled Student Program	805-893-2182
U. of California—Santa Cruz	Santa Cruz, CA 95064	Disability Resource Center	831-459-2089
U. of Judaism	Bel Air, CA 90077	Director of Admission	310-440-1250
U. of La Verne	La Verne, CA 91750	Disability Services	909-593-3511 ext. 4441
U. of Redlands	Redlands, CA 92373-0999	Student Services	909-748-8108

Institution	Location	Service	Phone
U. of San Diego	San Diego, CA 92110-2492	Disabled Student Services	619-260-4655
U. of San Francisco	San Francisco, CA 94117	Student Disability Services	415-422-2613
U. of Southern California	Los Angeles, CA 90089	Disability Services & Programs	213-740-0776
U. of the Pacific	Stockton, CA 95211	Services for students with Disabilities	209-946-2879
Vanguard U. of Southern CA	Costa Mesa, CA 92626	Learning Skills	714-556-3610 ext2540
Westmont C.	Santa Barbara, CA 93108	Academic Resource Center	805-565-6159
Whittier C.	Whittier, CA 90608	Disability Services	562-907-4840
Woodbury C.	Burbank, CA 91510	Academic Advising	818-252-5122

COLORADO

Institution	Location	Service	Phone
Colorado Christian C.	Lakewood, CO 80226	Academic Services	303-963-3267
Colorado C.	Colorado Springs, CO 80903	Disability Services	719-227-8285
Colorado Mt. C.	Glenwood Springs, CO 81601	Developmental Education	970-870-4450
Colorado School of Mines	Golden, CO 80401-1869	Student Development & Career Center	303-273-3297
Colorado St. U.	Fort Collins, CO 80523	Resources for Disabled Students	970-491-6385
Mesa St. C.	Grand Junction, CO 81502-2647	Education Access Service	970-248-1826
Metropolitan St. C. of Denver	Denver, CO 80217-3362	Access Center	303-556-8387
Northeastern Junior C.	Sterling, CO 80751	Disability Services	970-521-6727
Regis U.	Denver, CO 80221-1099	Disability Services	303-458-4941
U. of Colorado—Boulder	Boulder, CO 80309-0107	Disability Services	303-492-8671
U. of Colorado—Col. Springs	Colorado Springs, CO 80933	Disability Services	719-255-3653
U. of Colorado—Denver	Denver, CO 80217	Disability Resources and Services	303-556-3450
U. of Denver	Denver, CO 80208	LEP	303-871-2372
U. of Northern Colorado	Greeley, CO 80639	Disability Access Center	970-351-2289
Colorado State U.—Pueblo	Pueblo, CO 81001	Disabilities Resources Office	719-549-2663
Western St. C. of Colorado	Gunnison, CO 81231	Academic Resource Center	970-943-7056

CONNECTICUT

Institution	Location	Service	Phone
Albertus Magnus C.	New Haven, CT 06511	Academic Development Center	203-773-8564
Briarwood C.	Southington, CT 06489	Services for Students with LD	860-628-4751 Ext. 40979
Central Connecticut St. U.	New Britain, CT 06050	Special Student Services	860-832-1957
Eastern Connecticut St. U.	Willimantic, CT 06226	Counseling for Students w/ Disabilities	860-465-5573
Fairfield U.	Fairfield, CT 06430-5195	Academic & Diability Support Services	203-254-4000 ext 2615
Housatonic C.	Bridgeport, CT 06608	Disability Support Services	203-332-5018

College	Location	Service	Phone
Mitchell C.	New London, CT 06320	Learning Resource Center	860-701-5071
Post U.	Waterbury, CT 06723	Disability Services	203-596-4508
Quinnipiac C.	Hamden, CT 06518	Learning Services	203-582-5390
Sacred Heart U.	Fairfield, CT 06825	Special Services	203-365-4730 ext 7
St. Joseph C.	West Hartford, CT 06117	Disability Services	860-231-5428
Southern Connecticut St. U.	New Haven, CT 06515	Disability Resource Office	203-392-6828
Trinity C.	Hartford, CT 06106	Disability Services	860-297-2018
U. of Bridgeport	Bridgeport, CT 06604	Disability Services	203-576-4454
U. of Connecticut	W. Hartford, CT 06117	Disability Support Services	860-570-9135
U. of Connecticut	Storrs, CT 06269	Univ. Program for College Students with LD	860-486-2020
U. of Hartford	West Hartford, CT 06117	Learning Plus	860.768.4312
U. of New Haven	West Haven, CT 06516	Disability Services & Resources	203-932-7332
Wesleyan U.	Middletown, CT 06459-0265	Learning Disabilities Services	860-685-2332
Western Connecticut St. U.	Danbury, CT 06810	Accessibility	203-837-8946
Yale U.	New Haven, CT 06520	Resource Office for Disabilities	203-432-2324

DELAWARE

Delaware St. U.	Dover, DE 19901	Academic Support Center	302-857-6388
Delaware Tech C.C.	Georgetown, DE 19947	Student Support Services	302-855-1681
U. of Delaware	Newark, DE 19716-6210	Academic Success Services	302-831-3025
Wesley C.	Dover, DE 19901-3875	Academic Support Services	302)736-2492

DISTRICT OF COLUMBIA

American U.	Washington, DC 20016	Academic Support Center	202-885-3360
Catholic U. of America, The	Washington, DC 20064-0001	Disability Support Services	202-319-5211
Corcoran C. of Art	Washington DC 20006-4804	Disability Services	202-639-1801
Gallaudet U.	Washington, DC 20002	Prog for Students w/ Other Disabilities	202-651-5256
George Washington U.	Washington, DC 20052	Disability Support Services	202-994-8250
Georgetown U.	Washington, DC 20057	Academic Resource Center	202-687-8354
Howard U.	Washington, DC	Special Student Services	202-238-2423
Trinity C. DC)	Washington, DC 20017-1094	Career Services	202-884-9636
U. of District of Columbia	Washington, DC 20008	Disability Resource Center	202-274-6412

FLORIDA

Institution	Location	Office	Phone
Baptist C. of Florida	Graceville, GL 32440	Disability Services	800-328-2660 ext 454
Barry U.	Miami Shores, FL 33161-6695	Clinical Center for Advanced Learning	305-899-3488
Beacon C.	Leesburg, FL 34748	Office of President	352-787-7660
Broward C.C.	Ft. Lauderdale, FL 33301	Disability Services	954-201-7655
Clearwater Christian C.	Clearwater, FL 33759-4595	Disability Services	727-726-1153 ext 262
Eckerd C.	St. Petersburg, FL 33711	Disability Support Services	727-864-8248
Edison C.C.	Fort Meyers, FL 33906	Learning Assistance	239-489-9427
Edward Waters C.	Jacksonville, FL 32009	Disability Services	904-470-8230
Embry-Riddle Aeronaut. U. FL)	Daytona Beach, FL 32114	Disability Services	386-226-7916
Flagler C.	St. Augustine, FL 32084	Services for Students w/ Disabilities	904-819-6460
Florida A&M U.	Tallahassee, FL 32307	Center for Disability Access and Resources	850-599-3180
Florida Atlantic U.	Boca Raton, FL 33431	Office for Students with Disabilities	561-297-3880
Florida Gulf Coast U.	Fort Myers, FL 33965-6565	Disability Services	239-590-7941
Florida Institute of Tech.	Melborne, FL 32901-6975	Academic Support Services	321-674-8080
Florida International U.	Miami, FL 33199	Disability Services	305-348-3532
Florida Memorial C.	Miami, FL 33054	Student Affairs	305-626-3711
Florida St. U.	Tallahassee, FL 32306	Student Disability Resource Center	850-644-9566
Gulf Coast C.C.	Panama City, FL 32401	Disability Support Services	850-872-3834
Hillsborough C.C.	Tampa, FL 33631-3127	Disabled Services	813-253-7914
Indian River C.C.	Fort Pierce, FL 34981	Disability Services	772-462-7782
Jacksonville U.	Jacksonville, FL 32211	Student Life	904-256-7067
Lynn U.	Boca Raton, FL 33431	Institute for Achievement & Learning	561-237-7013
Miami Int'l. U. of Art	Miami, FL 33132	StudentAffairs	305.428.5900
New C. of Florida	Sarasota, FL 34243-2197	Student Disability Services	941-487-4254
Northwood U.—Florida Campus	West Palm Beach, FL 33409	Learning Center	561-478-5585
Nova Southeastern U.	Ft. Lauderdale, FL 33314	Academic Services	954-262-7189
Pensacola Jr. C.	Pensacola, FL 32504	Disability Support Services	850-484-1637
Ringling School of Art	Sarasota, FL 34234-5895	Academic Resource Center	941.359.7627
Rollins C.	Winter Park, FL 32789-4499	Student Resources Center	407-646-2354
Saint Thomas U.	Miami, FL 33054	Academic Enhancement	651-9626315
Santa Fe C.C.	Gainsville, FL 32606	Disability Resource Center	352-395-4400

Seminole C.C.	Sanford, FL 32773	Disabled Support Services	407-708-4722
St. Leo U.	Saint Leo, FL 33574-6665	Academic Student Support Services	352-588-8462
St. Petersburg Jr. C.	St. Petersburg, FL 33733	Disability Services	727-341-3398
Southeastern U.	Lakeland, FL 33801	Student Life	863-667-5746
Stetson U.	Deland, FL 32723	Academic Resource Center	386-822-7127
Tallahassee CC	Tallahassee, FL 32340	Disability Support Services	850-201-8430
Trinity Baptist C.	Jacksonville, FL 32221	Disability Services	800-786-2206
U. of Central Florida	Orlando, FL 32816	Student Disability Services	407-823-2371
U. of Florida	Gainesville, FL 32611	Disability Resources Center	352-392-8565
U. of Miami	Coral Gables, FL 33146	Academic Resource Center	305-284-2374
U. of North Florida	Jacksonville, FL 32224-2645 Disability Resource Center		904-620-2769
U. of South Florida	Tampa, FL 33620	Student Disability Services	813-974-8135
U. of Tampa	Tampa, FL 33606-1490	Student Disability Services	813-257-3266
U. of West Florida	Pensacola, FL 32514-5750	Dean of Students	850-474-2161
Warner Southern C.	Lake Wales, FL 33859	Dean of Enrollment	863-638-7213

GEORGIA

Agnes Scott C.	Decatur, GA 30030	Academic Advising	404-471-6200
Andrew C.	Cuthbert, GA 31740	FOCUS	229-732-5908
Armstrong St. C.	Savannah, GA 31419	Disability Services	912-344-2744
Art Institute of Atlanta	Atlanta, GA 30328	Disability Services	770-689-4827
Augusta State U.	August, GA 30904-2200	Testing & Disability Services	706-737-1469
Berry C.	Mount Berry, GA 30149	Academic Support	706-233-4080
Brenau U.	Gainesville, GA 30501	Learning Center	770-534-6134
Brewton-Parker C.	Mt. Vernon, GA 30445	Disability Services	912-583-3219
Clark Atlanta U.	Atlanta, GA 30314	Student Assistance	404-880-8771
Clayton College & St. U.	Morrow, GA 30260	Disability Resource Center	678-466-5445
Columbus C.	Columbus, GA 31907	Disability Services	614-287-2570
Covenant C.	Lookout Mountain, GA 30750	Disability Services	706-419-1262
Darton C.	Albany, GA 31707	Disabled Student Services	229-317-6867
Georgia Perimeter College	Clarkston, GA 30021	Ctr. for Disability Services	678-891-3385
Emmanuel College	Franklin Springs, GA 30639	Counseling Services	706-245-2715
Emory U.	Atlanta, GA 30322	Disability Services	404-727-9877

Ft. Valley St. U.	Fort Valley, GA 31030-4313	Differently Abled Services	476-825-6744
Gainesville C.	Gainesville, GA 30503	Disability Services	678-717-3839
Georgia C. and St. U.	Milledgeville, GA 31061	Dept. of Special Ed. & Educational Leadership	478-445-4577
Georgia Institute of Tech.	Atlanta, GA 30332-0320	Disabled Student Services	404-894-2563
Georgia Southern U.	Statesboro, GA 30460	Disabled Student Services	912-478-1566
Georgia St. U.	Atlanta, GA 30302-4009	Disability Services	404-413-1560
Kennesaw St. U.	Kennesaw, GA 30144-5591	Disabled Student Services	770-423-6443
Life U.	Marietta, GA 30060	Academic Assistance Center	770-794-3035 x.1720
LaGrange C.	La Grange, GA 30240	Counseling Center	706-880-8313
Mercer U.	Macon, GA 31207-0003	Disability Services	478-301-2778
Morehouse C.	Atlanta, GA 30314	Counseling center	404-215-2636
North Georgia C. & St. U.	Dahlonega, GA 30597	Student Disability Resources	706-864-1819
Oglethorpe U.	Atlanta, GA 30319	Learning Resources Services	404-364-8869
Paine C.	Augusta, GA 30901-3182	Disability Services	706-821-8282
Piedmont C.	Demorest, GA 30535	Academic Support Services	706-776-0101
Reinhardt C.	Waleska, GA 30183	Academic Support Office	770-720-5549
Shorter C.	Rome, GA 301654898	Academic Support Center	706-233-7323
South U.—Georgia	Savannah, GA 33411	Disability Services	912-201-8170
Southern Polytechnic St. U.	Marietta, GA 30060	Counseling & Disability Services	678-915-7391
Spelman C.	Atlanta, GA 30314	Student Disability Services	404-270-5293
The Savannah C. of Art	Savannah, GA 31402-3146	Disability Services	912-525-6971
Truett-McConnell C.	Cleveland, GA 30528	Special Support Services	706-865-2134ext 172
U. of Georgia	Athens, GA 30602	Counseling Center	706-542-8719
U. of West Georgia	Carrolton, GA 30118	Disability Services	678-839-6428
Valdosta St. U.	Valdosta, GA 31698	Access Office for Students with Disabilities	229-245-2498
Wesleyan C.	Macon, GA 31210-4462	Academic Center	478-757-5219

HAWAII

Institution	Address	Service	Phone
Brigham Young U.	Laie Oahu, HI 96762-1294	Services for Students with Special Needs	808-293-3999
Chaminade U. of Honolulu	Honolulu, HI 96816	Student Affairs	808-375-1177
Hawaii C.C.	Hilo, HI 96720	Ha'awi Kokua Program	808-934-2725
Hawaii Pacific U.	Honolulu, HI 96813	Office of Admissions	808-544-0238

Institution	City, State ZIP	Office	Phone
U. of Hawaii—Hilo	Hilo, HI 96720-4091	Disability Services	808-933-0816
U. of Hawaii—Manoa	Honolulu, HI 96822	KOKUA Program	808-956-7511

IDAHO

Institution	City, State ZIP	Office	Phone
Albertson C. of Idaho	Caldwell, ID 83605	Disability Services	208-459-5683
Boise St. U.	Boise, ID 83725	Special Services	208-426-1583
Idaho St. U.	Pocatello, ID 83209-8270	ADA Disabilities Center	208-282-3599
Lewis-Clark St. C.	Lewiston, ID 83501	Disability Services	208-792-2211
Northwest Nazarene U.	Nampa, ID 83686	Academic Support Center	208-467-8669
U. of Idaho	Moscow, ID 83844-4140	Disability Support Services	208-885-6307

ILLINOIS

Institution	City, State ZIP	Office	Phone
Augustana C.	Rock Island, IL 61201-2296	Dean of Students Office	309-794-7533
Aurora U.	Aurora, IL 60506	Disability Services	630-844-5267
Benedictine U.	Lisle, IL 60532-0900	Academic Resource Center	630-829-6512
Blackburn C.	Carlinville, IL 62626	Counseling Office/Learning Center	800-233-3550
Bradley U.	Peoria, IL 61625	Disability Services	309-794-7533
Chicago St. U.	Chicago, IL 60628	Abilities Office	773-995-4401
C. of Du Page	Glen Ellyn, IL 60137	Special Student Services	630-942-2567
C. of Lake County	Grayslake, IL 60030	Disability Student Services	847-543-2055
Columbia C. (IL)	Chicago, IL 60605-1996	Services for Students with Disabilities	573-875-7626
Concordia U.	River Forest, IL 60305-1499	Learning Assistance	708-809-3042
DePaul University	Chicago, IL 60604	Dean of Students	773-325-7290
Eastern Illinois U.	Charleston, IL 61920-3099	Disability Services	217-581-6583
Elgin C.C.	Elgin, IL 60123	Disability Services	847-214-7220
Elmhurst C.	Elmhurst, IL 60126	Disability Services	630-617-3753
Eureka C.	Eureka, IL 61530-1500	Learning Center	309-467-6520
Governors St. U.	University Park, IL 60466	Disability Services	708-534-4508
Greenville C.	Greenville, IL 62246-0159	Student Success	618-664-6611
Harper C.	Palatine, IL 60067	Center for Students with Disabilities	847-925-6266
Illinois C.	Jacksonville, IL 62650-2299	Templeton Counseling Center	217-245-3073
Illinois Institute of Technology	Chicago, IL 60616	Academic Resource Center	312-567-7959

Institution	Location	Office	Phone
Illinois St. U.	Normal, IL 61790	Disability Concerns	309-438-5853
Illinois Wesleyan U.	Bloomington, IL 61702-2900	Associate Provost Office	309-556-3255
Ivy Tech St. C.	Evansville, IL 47710	Special Needs	812-429-1386
John Wood C.C.	Quincy, IL 62301	Support Services Center	217-641-4352
Joliet Junior C.	Joliet, IL 60436	Project Achieve	815-729-9020 ext. 2455
Kankakee C. C.	Kankakee, IL 60901	Special Population & Instruc. Support	800-526-0844
Knox C.	Galesburg, IL 61401	Center for Teaching and Learning	309-341-7151
Lake Forest C.	Lake Forest, IL 60045	Dean's Office	847-735-5240
Lakeland C.	Mattoon, IL 61938	Special Needs Office	217-234-5259
Lewis U.	Romeoville, IL 60446-2200	Disability Resources	815-836-5284
Lincoln C.	Lincoln, IL 62656	Disability Services	217-732-3155
Loyola U. of Chicago	Chicago, IL 60611	Services for Students with Disabilities	773-508-3197
MacMurray C.	Lebanon, IL 62254-1299	Disability Services	217-479-7176
McHenry C.C.	Crystal Lake, IL 60012	Special Needs	815-455-8676
McKendree C.	Lebanon, IL 62254-1299	Academic Support	618-537-6850
Millikin U.	Decatur, IL 62522-2084	Disability Services	217-424-3511
Monmouth C.	Monmouth, IL 61462	Student Affairs	309-457-2257
Morraine Valley C.C.	Palos Hills, IL 60465	Center for Disability Services	708-974-5711
Morton C.	Cicero, IL 60650	Special Needs	708-656-8000
National-Louis U.	Evanston, IL 60201	Center for Academic Development	800-443-5522 ext 3083
North Central C.	Naperville, IL 60566	Learning Disability Services	630-637-5266
North Park U.	Chicago, IL 60625-4895	Academic Services	773-244-5726
Northeastern Illinois U.	Chicago, IL 60625	HELP Program	773-442-5495
Northern Illinois U.	DeKalb, IL 60115	Ctr. for Access-Ability Resources	815-753-9734
Northwestern U.	Evanston, IL 60204	Services for Students with Disabilities	847-491-2960
Oakton Community C.	Des Plaines, IL 60116	ASSIST	847-635-1759
Olivet Nazarene U.	Bourbonnais, IL 60914	Disability Services	815-928-5150
Parkland C.	Champaign, IL 61821	Disability Services	217-351-2364
Quincy U.	Quincy, IL 62301	Disability Services	217-228-5432 x3350
Robert Morris C.	Chicago, IL 60605	Student Services	312-935-2003
Rockford C.	Rockford, IL 61108-2393	Disability Support Services	815-226-4083
Roosevelt U.	Chicago, IL 60605	Academic Success Center Director	312-341-3810

College	Location	Office	Phone
St. Francis Medical Center of Nurs.	Peoria, IL 61603	Disability Services	309-655-7100
Saint Xavier U.	Chicago, IL 60655	Student Success Director	773-298-3121
Schl. of Art Inst. of Chicago	Chicago, IL 60603	Learning Center	312-499-4278
Shimer C.	Waukegan, IL 60079-0500	Disability Services	312-235-3500
SIU-Carbondale	Carbondale, IL 62901-4710	Achieve Program	618-453-5738
SIU-Edwardsville	Edwardsville, IL 62026	Director, Disability Support Services	618-650-3782
St. Anthony C. of Nursing	Rockford, IL 61108-2468	Student Affairs Office	815-395-5100
Trinity Christian C.	Palos Heights, IL 60463	Director, Academic Support and Services	708-239-4765
Trinity International C.	Deerfield, IL	Dean of Students Office	847-317-4063
U. of Chicago	Chicago, IL 60637	Assistance for Disabled Students	773-702-5671
U. of Illinois—Chicago	Chicago, IL 60680	Disability Services	312-413-2183
U. of Illinois—Springfield	Springfield, IL 62703-5407	Disability Services	217-206-6666
U. of Ill.—Urbana-Champaign	Urbana, IL 61801	Disability Resources & Educational Services	217-333-4601
U. of St. Francis	Joliet, IL 60435	Office of Disability Services	815-740-3204
Waubonsee C.C.	Sugar Grove, IL 60554	Access Ctr. for Students w/ Disabilities	630-466-7900 x5702
Western Illinois U.	Macomb, IL 61455-1390	Disability Support Services	309-298-2512
Wheaton C.	Wheaton, IL 60187	Registrars Office	508.286.8215

INDIANA

College	Location	Office	Phone
Anderson U.	Anderson, IN 46012	Learning Assistance Program	765-641-4227
Ball St. U.	Muncie, IN 47306	Office of Disabled Students	765-285-5293
Bethel C.	Mishawaka, IN 46545	Academic Support Center	: 651.638.6833
Butler U.	Indianapolis, IN 46208	Student Disabilities Center	317-940-9308
Calumet C. of St. Joseph	Whiting, IN 46394	Student Support Services	219-473-4388
DePauw U.	Greencastle, IN 46135	Academic Services	765-658-6267
Earlham C.	Richmond, IN 47374	Center for Academic Enrichment	765-983-1341
Franklin C.	Franklin, IN 46131-2623	Academic Resource Center	317-738-8286
Goshen C.	Goshen, IN 46526-4794	Academic Support Center	574-535-7576
Grace C. and Seminary	Winona Lake, IN 46590	Academic Achievement Center	574-372-5100 ext. 6422
Hanover C.	Hanover, IN 47243	Disability Services	812-866-7215
Huntington C.	Huntington, IN 46750	Learning Center	260-359-4290
Indiana St. U.	Terre Haute, IN 47809	Student Support Services	812-237-2301
Indiana U. SE	New Albany, IN 47150	Disabilities Services	812-941-2243
Indiana U. East	Richmond, IN 47374-1289	Student Support Services	765-973-8302

Institution	Location	Service	Phone
Indiana U.—Bloomington	Bloomington, IN 47405-7700	Disabled Student Services	812-855-7578
Indiana U.—Kokomo	Kokomo, IN 46904-9003	Disability Services	765-455-9309
Indiana U.—Northwest	Gary, IN 46408	Counseling Services	219-980-6942
Indiana U.—Purdue Univ.	Indianapolis, IN 46202-5143	Adaptive Educational Services	317-274-3241
Indiana U.—South Bend	South Bend, IN 46634-7111	Division of Disabled Student Services	574-520-4832
Indiana Wesleyan U.	Marion, IN 46953-4999	Student Support Services	765-677-2257
IPFW-Ft. Wayne	Ft. Wayne, IN 46805	Services for Students with Disabilities(SSD)	260-481-6658
IVY Tech	Fort Wayne, IN 46805	Disability Services	812-298-2282
Manchester C.	N. Manchester, IN 46962	Health Services	260-982-5306
Marion C.	Indianapolis, IN 46222	Learning and Counseling Center	317-955-6150
Purdue U.—Calumet	Hammond, IN 46323-2094	Student Support Services	219-989-2920
Purdue U.—North Central	Westville, IL 46391	Disability Services	219-785-5374
Purdue U.—West Lafayette	West Lafayette, IN 47907	Adaptive Program	765-496-6168
Rose-Human Institute of Tech.	Terre Haute, IN 47803	Special Programs	812-877-8438
St. Joseph's C.	Rensselaer, IN 47978	Office for Student Development	219-866-6116
St. Mary-of-the-Wood C.	St. Mary-of-the-Wood, IN 47876	Learning Resource Center	812-535-5271
Taylor U.	Upland, IN 46989	Academic Support Services	765-998-5523
Tri-St. U.	Angola, IN 46703	Special Students	260-665-4172
U. of Evansville	Evansville, IN 47722	Counselling & Testing Center	812-479-2663
U. of Indianapolis	Indianapolis, IN 46227	BUILD	317-788-6167
U. of Notre Dame	Notre Dame, IN 46556	Office for Students w/ Disabilities	574-631-7157
U. of Saint Francis	Fort Wayne, IN 46808	Student Learning Center	260-434-7677
U. of Southern Indiana	Evansville, IN 47712	Counseling Center	812-464-1961
Valparaiso U.	Valparaiso, IN 46383	Disability Support Services	219-464-5456
Vincennes U.	Vincennes, IN 47591	STEP	812-888-4501
Wabash C.	Crawfordsville, IN 47933	Writing Center—Academic Support	765-361-6024

IOWA

Institution	Location	Service	Phone
Briar Cliff U.	Sioux City, IA 51104	Student Support Services	712-279-5232
Buena Vista U.	Storm Lake, IA 50588	Disability Services	712-749-1236
Central C.	Pella, IA 50219	Student Support Services	641-628-5247
Clarke C.	Dubuque, IA 52001	Learning Center	563-588-8107
Coe C.	Cedar Rapids, IA 52402	Academic Achievement Program	319-399-8547

College	Location	Office	Phone
Cornell C.	Mount Vernon, IA 52341	Dean's Office	319-895-4234
Des Moines Area C.C.	Ankeny, IA 50021	Disability Services Office	515-964-6850
Dordt C.	Sioux Center, IA	Academic Skill Center	712-722-6490
Drake U.	Des Moines, IA 50311	Disability Resource Center	515-271-1835
Faith Baptist & Theological Seminary	Ankeny, IA 50021	Office of Admissions	515-965-2025 ext. 233
Graceland U.	Lamoni, IA 50140	Student Support Services	641-784-5421
Grand View C.	Des Moines, IA 50316-1599	Academic Success	515-263-2971
Grinnell C.	Grinnell, IA 50112	Academic Advising Office	641-269-3702
Hawkeye C.C.	Waterloo, IA 50704	Student Development	319-296-4014
Indian Hills C.C.	Ottumwa, IA 52501	Academic Services	641-683-5218
Iowa Central C.C.	Ft. Dodge, IA 50501	Special Needs	515-574-1045
Iowa St. U.	Ames, IA 50011-2011	Student Disability Resources	515-294-7220
Iowa Wesleyan C.	Mount Pleasant, IA 52641	Academic Resource Center	319-385-6376
Iowa Western C.C.	Council Bluffs, IA 51502	Program Director	712-325-3479
Loras C.	Dubuque, IA 52001	Learning Disabilities Program	563-588-7134
Luther C.	Decorah, IA 52101-1045	Student Academic Support Services	563-387-1270
Morningside College	Sioux City, IA 51106-1751	Academic Support Center	800-831-0806 ext. 5166
Mount Mercy C.	Cedar Rapids, IA 52402	Disability Services	319-363-8213 ext. 1204
Mount Saint Clare C.	Clinton, IA 52733-2967	Student Affairs	563-242-4023
Northwestern C.	Orange City, IA 51041	Disabilities Office for Support Services	712-707-7446
Saint Ambrose U.	Davenport, IA 52803-2898	Services for Students with Disabilities	563-333-6275
Scott CC E. Iowa CC	Bettonderf, IA 52722	Student Support Services	563-336-5210
Simpson C.	Indianola, IA 50125	Academic Resource Center	515-961-1524
Southeastern C.C.	W. Burlington, IA 52655	Office for Students with Disabilities	319-752-2731 ext. 5157
U. of Dubuque	Dubuque, IA 52001-5050	Academic Support Center	563-589-3570
U. of Iowa	Iowa City, IA 52242	Student Disability Services	319-335-1462
U. of Northern Iowa	Cedar Falls, IA 5061	Counseling Center	319-273-2676
Waldorf C.	Forest City, IA 50436	Learning Disability Program	641-584-8207
Wartburg C.	Waverly, IA 50677	Student Life	800-772-2085
William Penn U.	Oskaloosa, IA 52577	Academic Resource Center	641-673-1102

KANSAS

Baker University	Baldwin City, KS 66006	Learning Resource Center	785-594-8349
Benedictine College	Atchison, KS 66002	Institutional Advancement	800-467-5340 ext.7418

Institution	Location	Service	Phone
Bethany C.	Lindsborg, KS 67456-1897	Academic Support Services	785-227-3380 x8151
Bethel C.	N. Newton, KS 67117	Center for Academic Development	800-522-1887, ext. 333
Butler City C.C.	Eldorado, KS 67042	Advising Center	316-322-3166 ext 4
Central Christian C. of Kansas	McPherson, KS 67460-5799	Guidence Center	620-241-0723 ext. 312
Colby CC.	Colby, KS 67701	Student Support Services	785-460-5510
Emporia St. U.	Emporia, KS 66801-5087	Cheer Programs	620-341-5097
Friends U.	Wichita, KS 67213	Student Affairs	316-295-5779
Hutchinson C.C.	Hutchison, KS 67502	Disability Services	620-665-3554
Johnson County C.C.	Overland Park, KS 66210	Student Access Center	913-469-8500 ext. 3974
Kansas City C.C.	Kansas City, KS 66112	Academic Resource Center	913-288-7670
Kansas St. U.	Manhattan, KS 66506	Disability Support Services	785-532-6441
Manhattan Christian C.	Manhattan, KS 66502	Student Development	877-246-4622
McPherson C.	McPherson, KS 67460	Disability Services	620-242-0507
MidAmerica Nazarene U.	Olathe, KS 66062	Learning Resources Center	913-971-3582
Newman University	Wichita, KS 67213	Student Support Services	316-942-4291
Pittsburg State U.	Pittsburg, KS 66762-5880	Learning Center	620-235-6584
Pratt C.C.	Pratt, KS 67124	Student Success	620-672-5641 ext. 215
U. of Kansas	Lawrence, KS 66045	Academic Achievement	785-864-4064
U. of St. Mary	Levenworth, KS 66048	Student Life	913-682-5151
Wichita St. U.	Wichita, KS 67260	Resource Center for Independence	316-978-3309

KENTUCKY

Institution	Location	Service	Phone
Bellarmine C.	Louisville, KY 40205	Office of Student Affairs	502-452-8070
Berea C.	Berea, KY 40404	Special Needs	859-985-3150
Bluegrass Comm. & Tech. College	Lexington, KY 40506-0235	Disability Support Services	859-246-6535
Brescia C.	Owensboro, KY 42301	Student Support Services	270-686-4259
Centre C.	Danville, KY 40422	Disability Services	859-238-5223
Cumberlands C.	Williamsburg, KY 40769	Academic Services	606-539-4214
Eastern Kentucky U.	Richmond, KY 40475	Project SUCCESS	859-622-2933
Georgetown C.	Georgetown, KY 40324	Counseling Center	502-863-7074
Kentucky Christian U.	Grayson, KY 41143	Special Student Services	606-474-3257
Kentucky Wesleyan C.	Owensboro, KY 42302	PLUS Center	270-852-3212
Lexington C.C.	Lexington, KY 40506-0235	Disability Support Services	859-246-6535
Lindsey Wilson C.	Columbia, KY 42728	Learning Disabilities	270-384-8080

College	Location	Office	Phone
Mid-Continent C.	Mayfield, KY 42066	A.C.E. Program	270-247-8521 ext. 354
Morehead St. U.	Morehead, KY 40351	Disability Services	606-783-5188
Murray St. U.	Murray, KY 42071	Office of Equal Opportunity	270-809-3155
Northern Kentucky U.	Highland Heights, KY 41099	Disability Services	859-572-5282
Southeast C.C.	Cumberland, KY 40823	Student Support Services	402-228-3468 ext. 1361
Thomas More C.	Crestview Hill, KY 41017	Student Support Services	859-344-3521
U. of Kentucky	Lexington, KY 40506	Disability Resource Center	859-257-2754
U. of Louisville	Louisville, KY 40292	Disability Resource Center	502-852-6938
Western Kentucky U.	Bowling Green, KY 42101	Student Disability Services	270-745-5004

LOUISIANA

Louisiana C.	Pineville, LA 71359-0560	PATH Program	318-487-7629
LSU—Baton Rouge	Baton Rouge, LA 70803	Office of Disability Services	225-578-4401
Loyola U. New Orleans	New Orleans, LA 70118	Acad. Enrichment and Disability Svcs.	504-865-2990
McNeese St. U.	Lake Charles, LA 70609	Services for Students with Disabilities	337-475-5916
Nicholls St. U.	Thibodaux, LA 70310	Office of Disability Services	985-448-4429
Northwestern St. U. of Louisiana	Natchitoches, LA 71497	Academic and Career Engagement Center	318-357-6950
Our Lady of Holy Cross C.	New Orleans, LA 70131	Enrollment Services	504-398-2165
Southeastern Louisiana U.	Hammond, LA 70402	Disability Services	985-549-2247
Southern U. & A&M C.	Baton Rouge, LA 70813	Special Education	225-771-3950
Southern U. of New Orleans	New Orleans, LA 70126	Student Support Services	504-286-5106
Tulane U.	New Orleans, LA 70118-5680	Disability Services	504-862-8433
U. of New Orleans	New Orleans, LA 70148	Student Affairs	504-280-6222
U. of Louisiana—Lafayette	Lafayette, LA 70504	Services for Students w/ Disabilities	337-482-5252
U. of Louisiana,—Monroe	Monroe, LA 71209	Dean of the Faculty's Office	318-342-5431

MAINE

Bates C.	Lewiston, ME 04240-9917	Dean's Office	207-786-6067
Bowdoin C.	Brunswick, ME 04011-8441	Dean's Office	207-725-3578
Colby C.	Waterville, ME 04901-8840	Dean's Office	207-859-4255
C. of Atlantic	Bar Harbor, ME 04609	Disability Services	207-288-5015
Eastern Maine Tech. C.	Bangor, ME 04401	Academic Support Center	207-974-4658
Husson C.	Bangor, ME 04401	Dean of Students Office	207-992-1934

Institution	Location	Service	Phone
Kennebec Valley Tech	Fairfield, ME 04937	Students With Disabilities	207-453-5019
Maine C. of Art	Portland, ME 04101	Student Affairs	207.699.5067
N. Maine Tech C.	Presque Isle, ME 04769	Student Affairs—TRIO	207-768-2747
St. Joseph's C.	Standish, ME 04054	Dean of College	207-893-6641
Southern Maine C. C.	South Portland, ME 04106	Disability Services	207-741-5629
Thomas C.	Waterville, ME 04901	Center for Academic Support	207-859-1214
Unity C.	Unity, ME 04988-0532	Learning Resource Center	207-948-3131 ext. 263
U. of Maine—Augusta	Bangor, ME 04401-4367	Cornerstone Program	207-621-3501
U. of Maine—Farmington	Farmington, ME 04938	Acad. Svcs. for Students w/ Disab.	207-778-7295
U. of Maine—Fort Kent	Fort Kent, ME 04743	Disability Services	207-834-7834
U. of Maine—Machias	Machias, ME 04654	Student Resources	207-255-1228
U. of Maine—Orono	Orono, ME 04469-5757	Onward Program/Disabilities	207-581-2325
U. of Maine—Presque Isle	Presque Isle, ME 04769	Student Support Services	207-768-9613
U. of New England	Biddeford, ME 04005	Disability Services	207-602-2815
U. of Southern Maine	Portland, ME 04104	Support for Students with Disabilities	207-780-4706

MARYLAND

Allegany C.	Cumberland, MD 21502	Student Success Center	301-784-5551
Anne Arundel C.C.	Arnold, MD 21012	Disabled Student Services	410-777-2306
Baltimore City C.C.	Baltimore, MD 21215	Disability Support Services Center	410-462-8589
Capitol C.	Laurel, MD 20708	Dean of Student's Office	301-369-2800 ext. 3046
Carroll C.C.	Westminster, MD 21157	Student Support Services	410-386-8329
Catonsville C.C.	Catonsville, MD 21228	Special Student Population	443-840-4718
Cecil C.C.	North East, MD 20901	Academic Advising	410-287-6060 ext556
C. of Norte Dame of Maryland	Baltimore, MD 21210	Disability Support Services	410-532-5379
C. of Southern MD—La Plata	La Plata, MD 20646	Academic Support Services	301-934-2251 ext. 7614
Columbia Union C.	Takoma Park, MD 20912	Center for Learning Resources	301-891-4184
Coppin St. U.	Baltimore, MD 21216-3698	Counseling Center	410-951-3510
Essex C.C.	Baltimore, MD 21237	Office of Special Services	443-840-1741
Frostburg St. U.	Frostburg, MD 21532	Disability Support Services	301-687-4738
Goucher C.	Baltimore, MD 21204-2794	Disability Specialist	410-337-6178
Harford C.C.	Bel Air, MD 21015	Learning Support Services	443-412-2414
Hood C.	Fredrick, MD 21701	Disability Services	301-696-3550
Howard C.C.	Columbia, MD 21044	Learning Assistance Center	410-772-4822

College	Office/Service	Location	Phone
John Hopkins U.		Baltimore, MD 21218	
Institutional Equity			410-516-8075
Loyola C. MD)	Center for Academic Services and Support	Baltimore, MD 21210	410-617-2663
McDaniel College	Academic Skills Center	Westminster, MD 21157	410-857-2504
Montgomery C.	Disability Support Services	Rockville, MD 20850	240-567-5058
Morgan St. U.	Counseling Center	Baltimore, MD 2125	443-885-3130
Mount St. Mary's U.	Learning Services	Emmitsburg, MD 21727	301-447-5006
Salisbury U.	Student Affairs	Salisbury, MD 21801	410-543-6080
Towson U.	Disability Support Services	Towson, MD 21252-0001	410-704-4425
U. of Baltimore	Disability Support Services	Baltimore, MD 21201	410-837-4775
U. of Maryland—C. Park		College Park, MD 20742-5235	
Disability Support Services			301-314-7682
U. of Maryland—Eastern Shore	Disabled Student Services	Princess Anne, MD 21853	410-651-6461
U. of Maryland—U. College	Disability Services	Adelphi, MD 20783	301.314.7682

MASSACHUSETTS

College	Office/Service	Location	Phone
American International C.	Supportive Learning Services	Springfield, MA 01109-3184	413-205-3430
Amherst C.	Dean of Students	Amherst, MA 01002	413-542-2529
Anna Maria C.	Learning Center	Paxton, MA 01612	508-849-3372
Art Institute of Boston—Lesley U.	Center for Academic Achievement	Boston, MA 02215-2598	617-582-4610
Assumption C.	Disabled Students Services	Worcester, MA 01615	508-767-7500
Babson C.	Office of Academic Services	Babson Park, MA 02157-0310	781-239-4075
Bay Path C.	Office of Disability Services	Longmeadow, MA 01106	413-565-1353
Becker C.	Center for Academic Success	Worchester, MA 01609	508-373-9704
Bentley C.	Counseling & Student Development	Waltham, MA 2452	781-891-2274
Berklee C. of Music	Advising Center	Boston, MA 02215	617-747-2310
Berkshire C.C.	Services for Disabled Students	Pittsfield, MA 01201	413-236-1605
Boston Architectural Center	Academic Services	Boston, MA 02115	617-585-0274
Boston C.	Academic Development Center	Chestnut Hill, MA 02167	617-552-9259
Boston U.	Learning Disability Support Services	Boston, MA 02215	617-353-3658
Brandeis U.	Dean's Office-Academic Affairs	Waltham, MA 02254	781-736-3470
Bridgewater St. C.	Office for Students with Disabilities	Bridgewater, MA 02325	508-531-1214
Clark U.	Academic Advising Center	Worcester, MA 01610-1477	508-793-7468
C. of the Holy Cross	Student Affairs	Worcester, MA 01610-2395	508-793-3693

Institution	Location	Service/Office	Phone
Curry C.	Milton, MA 02186	Program for Advancement of Learning	617-333-2385
Dean C.	Franklin, MA 02038	Disability Support Services	508-541-1764
Elms C.	Chicopee, MA 01013	Office of Students with Disabilities	413-265-2333
Emerson C.	Boston, MA 02116-1511	Disability Services Office	617-824-8592
Emmanuel C.	Boston, MA 02115	Disability Services	617-735-9923
Endicott C.	Beverly, MA 01915	Dean	978-232-2055
Fitchburg St. C.	Fitchburg, MA 01420-2697	Disability Services	978-665-3562
Framingham St. C.	Framingham, MA 01701	Academic Support	508-626-4906
Gordon C.	Wenham, MA 01984-1899	Academic Support	978-867-4746
Hampshire C.	Amherst, MA 01002	Center for Academic Support and Advising	413-559-5423
Harvard and Radcliffe C.s	Cambridge, MA 02318	Accessible Education Center	617-496-8707
Holyoke C.C.	Holyoke, MA 01040	College Disability Services	413-552-2417
Lasell C.	Newton, MA 02466	Academic Achievement Center	617-243-2306
Lesley C.	Cambridge, MA 02138	Disability Services	617-349-8194
Mass. C. of Liberal Arts	North Adams, MA 01247	Learning Services Center	413-662-5309
Mass. C. of Pharmacy & Health	Boston, MA 02115-5896	Academic Support Services	617-732-2860
Mass. Institute of Technology	Cambridge, MA 02139	Disability Services	617-253-1674
Mass. Maritime Academy	Bussards Bay, MA 02532-1803	Disability Resource	508-830-5000 x2208
Mass Bay C.C.	Wellesley Hills, MA 02181	Disability Services	781-239-2626
Massasoit C.C.	Brockton, MA 02402	Disability Services	508-588-9100 x1805
Merrimack C.	North Andover, MA 01845	Disability Services	978-837-5140
Montserrat C. of Art	Beverly, MA 01915	Academic Affairs	978-921-4242 ext. 1603
Mt. Holyoke C.	South Hadley, MA 01075	Disability Services	413-538-2550
Mt. Ida C.	Newton, MA 01259	Learning Opportunities Program	617-928-4648
Mt. Wachusett C.C.	Gardner, MA 01440	Students with Disabilities	978-630-9178
Nichols C.	Dudley, MA 01571	Advising Services	508-213-2212
Northeastern U.	Boston, MA 02115	Disability Resource Center	617-373-4428
N. Adams St. C.	N. Adams, MA 01247	Learning Center	413-662-5309
North Shore C.C.	Danvers, MA 01923	SSC—Disabilities Services	978-762-4000 ext. 4501
Pine Manor C.	Chestnut Hill, MA 02167	Learning Resource Center	617-731-7181
Quinsigamond C.C.	Worcester, MA 01606	Disabilities Services	508-854-4471
Regis C.	Weston, MA 02493-1571	Disability Services	781-768-7384
Simmons C.	Boston, MA 02115	Academic Support	617-521-2473

Smith C.	Northampton, MA 01063	Office of Disability Services	413-585-2071
Springfield C.	Springfield, MA 01109	Student Support Service	413-748-3768
Springfield Tech C.C.	Springfield, MA 01105	Office of Disability Services	413-755-4551
Stonehill C.	Easton, MA 02357-5610	Academic Services	508-565-1306
Suffolk U.	Boston, MA 02114-4280	Dean of Students Office	617-573-8239
Tufts U.	Medford, MA 02155	Academic Resource Center	617-627-4345
U. Mass.—Amherst	Amherst, MA 01003	Learning Disabilities Support Services	413-545-0892
U. Mass.—Boston	Boston, MA 02125-3393	Roth Center for Disability Services	617-287-7432
U. Mass.—Dartmouth	North Dartmouth, MA 02747	Disabled Student Services	508-999-8711
U. Mass.—Lowell	Lowell, MA 01854	Disability Services	978-934-4574
Wellesley C.	Wellesley, MA 02481	POTC	781-283-2641
Wentworth Institute of Technology	Boston, MA 02115-5998	Disability Services	617-989-4393
Western New England C.	Springfield, MA 01119	Student Disability Services	413-782-1257
Wheaton C. (MA)	Norton, MA 02766	Academic Support Services	508-286-3848
Wheelock C.	Boston, MA 02215	Disability Support Services	617-879-2030
Williams C.	Williamstown, MA 01267	Disability Support Services	413-597-4672
Worcester Poly. Institute	Worcester, MA 01609	Student Disability Services	508-831-5235
Worcester St. C.	Worcester, MA 01602-2597	Disability Services Office	508-929-8733

MICHIGAN

Adrian C.	Adrian, MI 49221-2575	Academic Service Office	517-265-5161 ext. 4413
Albion College	Albion, MI 49224	Disability Services	517-629-0825
Alma C.	Alma, MI 48801-1599	Counseling Center	989-463-7225
Andrews U.	Berrien Springs, MI 49104	Student Services	269-471-3227
Aquinas C.	Grand Rapids, MI 49506-1799	Academic Achievement Center	616-632-2166
Calvin C.	Grand Rapids, MI 49546	Student Academic Services	616-526-6613
Central Michigan U.	Mount Pleasant, MI 48859	Academic Assistance	989-774-7506
C. of Creative Studies	Detroit, MI 48202	Student Success Services	313-664-7680
Concordia U.	Ann Arbor, MI 48105	Disability Services	734-995-7479
Cornerstone U.	Grand Rapids, MI 49525	Learning Center	616-222-1596
Davenport U.	Grand Rapids, MI 49503	Disability Services	616-554-5687
Delta C.	Universal City, MI 48710	Learning Disabilities Services	989-686-9322
Eastern Michigan U.	Ypsilanti, MI 48197	Student Success	734-487-6694

College	Location	Service	Phone
Ferris St. U.	Big Rapids, MI 49307	Merwin Disabilities Services	231-591-3772
Finlandia U.	Hancock, MI 49930	Student Support Services	906-487-7346
Grand Rapids C.C.	Grand Rapids, MI 49503	Disability Support Services	616-234-4140
Grand Valley St. U.	Allendale, MI 49401	Academic Support (OAS)	616-331-2490
Hillsdale C.	Hillsdale, MI 49242	Health and Wellness	517-437-7341 ext. 2561
Hope C.	Holland, MI 49422-9000	Academic Support Center	616-395-7830
Itaska C.C.	Grand Rapids, MI 55744	Support Services	218-322-2430
Kalamazoo C.	Kalamazoo, MI 49006	Dean of Students	269-337-7209
Kellogg C.C.	Battle Creek, MI 49017	Support Services	269-965-3931 ext. 2627
Kettering U.	Flint, MI 48504	Wellness Center	810-762-9650
Kuyper C.	Grand Rapids, MI 49525	Academic Support	616-988-3688
Lansing C.C.	Lansing, MI 48901	Counseling Services	517-483-1904
Lawrence Tech. U.	Southfield, MI 48075	Disability Services	248-204-4119
Madonna U.	Livonia, MI 48150-1173	Educational Support Services	734-432-5641
Marygrove C.	Detroit, MI 48221	Support Services	313-927-1423
Michigan St. U.	East Lansing, MI 48824	Resource Center for Persons with Disabilities	517-884-1903
Michigan Tech U.	Houghton, MI 49931	Dean of Students	906-487-2212
North Central Michigan C.	Petoskey, MI 49770	Educational Opportunity Program	231-348-6687
Northern Michigan U.	Marquette, MI 49855	Disability Services	906-227-1737
Northwood U.—Midland	Midland, MI 48640	Special Needs Services	989-837-4213
Oakland C.C.	Auburn Hills, MI 48309	ACCESS	248-232-4081
Oakland U.	Rochester, MI 48309	Disability Support Services	248-370-3266
Olivet C.	Olivet, MI 49076	Disability Services	269-749-7702
Rochester C.	Rochester Hills, MI 48307	Student Support Center	248-218-2014
Saginaw Valley St. U.	University Ctr, MI 48152	Disability Services—Student Affairs	989-964-4168
Schoolcraft C.C.	Livonia, MI 48152	Learning Assistance Center	734-462-4436
SW Michigan C.	Dowagiac, MI 49047	Academic Support	269-782-1321
Spring Arbor U.	Spring Arbor, MI	Disability Center	517-750-6479 x1479
U. of Michigan—Ann Arbor	Ann Arbor, MI 48109	Services for Students with Disabilities	734-763-3000
U. of Michigan—Dearborn	Dearborn, MI 48128-1491	Counseling & Support Services	313-593-5430
U. of Michigan—Flint	Flint, MI 48502	Student Development Center	810-762-3456
Walsh C.	Troy, MI 48007-7006	Academic Advising	248-823-1386

College	Location	Service	Phone
Wayne St. U.	Detroit, MI 48202	Education Access Service	313-577-2356
Western Michigan U.	Kalamazoo, MI 49008	Disabled Student Resources and Services	269 387-2120

MINNESOTA

College	Location	Service	Phone
Augsburg C.	Minneapolis, MN 55454	CLASS Program	612-330-1218
Bethel U.	St. Paul, MN 55112	Disability Services	651-635-8759
Bimidji St. U.	Bimidji, MN 55601	Disability Services	218-755-3883
Carleton C.	Northfield, MN 55057	Support Services	507-222-4017
Century College	White Bear Lk, MN 55110	Access Center	651-779-3354
C. of Saint Benedict	Saint Joseph, MN 56374	Academic Advising	320-363-5687
C. of St. Catherine, The	Saint Paul, MN 55105	O'Neill Learning Center	651-590-6563
C. of St. Scholastica, The	Duluth, MN 55811-4199	Academic Support Services	218-723-6552
Concordia C.—Moorhead	Moorhead, MN 56562	Disability Counseling	218-299-3514
Concordia C.—Saint Paul	Saint Paul, MN 55104-5494	Students with Disabilities	651-641-8272
Crown C.	St. Bonifacius, MN 55375	Disability Counseling	952-446-4216
Fond du Lac C.C.	Cloquet, MN 55720	Office of Students with Disabilities	218-879-0805
Gustavus Adolphus C.	St. Peter, MN 56082	Academic Advising: Dean of Students	507-933-7027
Hamline U.	Saint Paul, MN 55104	Disability Services	651-523-2521
Hibbing C.C.	Hibbing, MN 55746	Disability Services	218-262-6712
Inver Hills C.C.	Inver Grove Hgts, MN 55076	Disabled Student Services	651-450-3628
Lake Superior C.	Duluth, MN 55811	Disability Services	218-733-7650
Macalester C.	St. Paul, MN 55105	Learning Center	651-696-6121
Mesabi C.C.	Virginia, MN 55792	Disability Services	218-749-0319
Minneapolis C.C.	Minneapolis, MN 55403	Office for Students with Disabilities	612-659-6733
Minnesota State U.—Mankato	Mankato, MN 56002	Center for Academic Success	507-389-1791
Minnesota State U.—Moorhead	Moorhead, MN 56563	Disability Services	218-477-2131
N. Hennepin C.C.	Brooklyn Pk, MN 55445	Disability Access Services	763-493-0556
Normandale C.C.	Bloomington, MN 55431	Office for Students with Disabilities	952-487-7035
North Central U.	Minneapolis, MN 55404	Disability Services	612-343-3510
Northwestern C.	St. Paul, MN 55113-1598	Disability Services	651-631-7446
Riverland C.C.	Austin, MN 55912	Student Success Center	507-433-0646
Rochester C.C.	Rochester, MN 55904	Disability Services	507-280-2968
Saint Cloud St. U.	Saint Cloud, MN 56301-4498	Student Disability Services	320-308-3117
Saint John's U.	Collegeville, MN 56321-7155	Academic Advising	320-363-5687

College	Location	Service	Phone
Saint Mary's U.	Winona, MN 55987-1399	Disability Services	507-457-1465
St. Olaf C.	Northfield, MN 55057-1098	Student Disability Service	507-786-3288
Southwest St. U.	Marshall, MN 56258	Learning Resources	507-537-7672
U. of Minnesota	Crookston, MN 56716	Office for Students w/ Disabilities	218-281-8587
U. of Minnesota—Duluth	Duluth, MN 55812-2496	Learning Disability Program	218-726-8727
U. of Minnesota—Morris	Morris, MN 56267	Disability Services	320-589-6163
U. of Minnesota—Twin Cities	Minneapolis, MN 55455-0213	Disability Services	612-626-1333
U. of St. Thomas	St. Paul, MN 55105-1096	Enhancement Program	651-962-6315
Winona St. U.	Winona, MN 55987	Disability Resource Center	507-457-5878

MISSISSIPPI

College	Location	Service	Phone
Belhaven C.	Jackson, MS 39202	Academic Support	601-968-8990
Blue Mountain C.	Blue Mountain, MS 38610-0160		662-685-4771
Jackson St. U	Jackson, MS 39217	Disability Services	601-979-3704
Millsaps C.	Jackson, MS 39210-0001	Disability Services	601-974-1228
Mississippi C.	Clinton, MS 39058	Counseling & Testing Center	601-325-3354
Mississippi St. U.	Mississippi, MS 39762	Student Support Services	662-325-3335
Mississippi U. for Women	Columbus, MS 39701	Academic Support Services	662-241-7138
Rust C.	Holy Springs, MS 38635	Disability Services	662-252-8000 ext. 4909
U. of Mississippi	University, MS 38677	Services for Students with Disabilities	662-915-7128
U. of Southern Mississippi	Hattiesburg, MS 39406	Office of Disability Accmmodations	601-266-5024
William Carey C.	Hattiesburg, MS 39401-5499	Student Support Services	601-318-6208

MISSOURI

College	Location	Service	Phone
Avila U.	Kansas City, MO 64145	Learning Center	816-501-3670
Barnes-Jewish C. of Nurs. & AH	St. Louis, MO 33132	Student Support Services	314-454-8686
Blue River C.C.	Blue Springs, MO 64015-7242	ACCESS Office	816-220-6651
Central Missouri St. U.	Warrensburg, MO 64093	Office of Accessibility	660-543-4421
C. of the Ozarks	Point Lookout, MO 65726	Academic Dean's Office	417-334-6411 ext. 2278
Columbia C.	Columbia, MO 65216	Student Support Center	573-875-7651
Culver-Stockton C.	Canton, MO 63435	Academic Support Services	573-288-6451
Drury C.	Springfield, MO 65802-9977	Assistive Student Services	417-873-6881
Evangel U.	Springfield, MO 65802	Academic Development Center	417-865-2811
Fontbonne C.	St. Louis, MO 63105	Academic Resource Center	314-719-3627

College	Location	Office	Phone
Hannibal-LaGrange C.	Hannibal, MO 63401	Academic Affairs	573-221-3675 ext. 253
Harris-Stowe St. C.	St. Louis, MO 63103	Disability Services	314-340-3648
Kansas City Art Institute	Kansas City, MO 64111-1762	Academic Resource Center	816-802-3485
Lincoln U.	Jefferson City, MO 65102-0029	Disability Services	573-681-5167
Lindenwood U.	St. Charles, MO 63301-1695	Disability Services	636-949-4784
Longview Comm. C.	Lee Summit, MO 64081-2105	ACCESS Office	816-672-2252
Maple Woods C.C.	Kansas City, MO 64156	ACCESS Office	816-437-3192
Maryville U. of St. Louis	St. Louis, MO 63141-7299	Academic Success Center	314-529-9374
Mineral Area C.	Park Hills, MO 63601	Special Services	573-518-2152
Missouri Southern St. C.	Joplin, MO 64801-1595	Learning Center	417-659-3725
Missouri State U.	Springfield, MO 65897	Learning Diagnostic Clinic	417-836-4192
Missouri Valley C.	Marshall, MO 65340	Learning Center	660-831-4226
Missouri Western St. U.	Saint Joseph, MO 64507	Disability Services	816-271-4330
Northwest Missouri St. U.	Maryville, MO 64468	Student Support Services	660-562-1259
Park U.	Parkville, Mo 64152	Academic Support Services	816-584-6332
Penn Valley C.C.	Kansas City, MO 64110	Access Office	816-759-4152
Saint Louis U.	Saint Louis, MO 63103	Student Disabilities Center	314-977-8885
Southwest Baptist U.	Bolivar, MO 65613	University Success Center	417-328-1425
Southwest Missouri St. U.	Springfield, MO 65804	Learning Diagnostic Clinic	417-836-4787
St. Charles City C.C.	St. Peters, MO 63376	Disabled Student Services	636-922-8247
St. Louis C C.—Florissant Valley	St. Louis, MO 63135	ACCESS Office	314-513-4551
St. Louis C.C.—Forest Park	St. Louis, MO 63110	ACCESS Office	314-644-9039
St. Louis C.C.—Meramec	St. Louis, MO 63122	ACCESS Office	314-984-7673
Stephens C.	Columbia, MO 65215	Student Services	573-876-7212
Three River C.C.	Poplar Bluff, MO 63901	Student Support Services	573-840-9650
Truman St. U.	Kirksville, MO 63501	Disability Services	660-785-4478
U. of Missouri—Columbia	Columbia, MO 65203	Office of Disability Services	573-882-4696
U. of Missouri—Kansas City	Kansas City, MO 64110-2499	Services for Students with Disabilities	816-235-5696
U. of Missouri—Rolla	Rolla, MO 65409	Disability Support Services	573-341-6655
U. of Missouri—Saint Louis	Saint Louis, MO 63121	Disability Access Services	314-516-6554
Washington U.	Saint Louis, MO 63130-4899	Disability Resource Center	314-935-4153
Webster U.	St. Louis, MO 63119	Academic Support Center	314-968-7495
Westminster C.	Fulton, MO 65251-1299	Learning Disabilities Program	573-592-5305

Institution	Location	Service	Phone
William Jewell C.	Liberty, MO 64068	Counseling and Testing	816-415-5946
William Woods U.	Fulton, MO 65251	Disability Services	573-592-1194

MONTANA

Institution	Location	Service	Phone
Carroll C.	Helena, MT 59625-0002	Academic Resource Center	406-447-4504
Montana St. U.	Billings, MT 59101-0298	Disability Support Services	406-657-2283
Montana St. U.	Bozeman, MT 59717	Disability Services	406-994-2824
Montana Tech. College	Butte, MT 59701	Disability Services	406-496-4129
Montana State U.—Northern	Harve, MT 59501	Assistant Dean of Students	406-265-4152
Rocky Mountain C.	Billings, MT 59102	Services for Academic Success	406-657-1128
U. of Great Falls	Great Falls, MT 59405	Center for Academic Excellence	406-791-5213
U. of Montana	Missoula, MT 59812	Disability Services for Students	406-243-2243
The U. of Montana—Western	Dillon, MT 59725	Disability Services	406-683-7900

NEBRASKA

Institution	Location	Service	Phone
Bellevue U.	Bellevue, NE 68005	Special Needs Services	402-557-7417
Concordia U.	Seward, NE 68434	Academic Support	402-643-7377
Creighton U.	Omaha, NE 68178	Disability Support Services	402-280-2166
Dana C.	Blair, NE 68008	Academic Support Services	402-426-7343
Doane C.	Crete, NE 68333	Academic Support	402-826-8554
Grace U.	Omaha, NE 68108-3629	Dean of Women	402-449-2849
Hastings C.	Hastings, NE 68901-7621	Disability Services	402-461-7386
Nebraska Methodist C.	Omaha, NE 68114	Student Development Services	402-354-7214
Metropolitan C.C.	Omaha, NE 68103	Special Needs Program	402-457-2580
Midland Lutheran C.	Fremont, NE 68025	Academic Support Center	402-941-6257
Southeast C.C.	Lincoln, NE 68510	Disability Services	402-437-2624
Union C.	Lincoln, NE 68506-4300	Teaching Learning Center	402-486-2506
U. of Nebraska—Kearney	Kearney, NE 68849	Academic Success	308-865-8988
U. of Nebraska—Lincoln	Lincoln, NE 68588-0417	Services for Students w/ Disabilities	402-472-0828
U. of Nebraska—Medical Center	Omaha, NE 68198-4265	Student Disability Services	402-559-5553
U. of Nebraska—Omaha	Omaha, NE 68182	Disability Services	402-554-2872
Wayne St. C.	Wayne, NE 68787	STRIDE	402-375-7321
West Nebraska C.C.	Scottsbluff, NE 69361-1899	Counseling Center	800-348-4435

NEVADA

Truckee Meadows C.C.	Reno, NV 89512	Disability Resource Center	775-673-7126
U. of Nevada—Las Vegas	Las Vegas, NV 89154	Disability Resource Center	702-895-0866
U. of Nevada—Reno	Reno, NV 89557	Disability Resource Center	775-784-6000
Western Nevada C.C.	Carson City, NV 89703	Disability Support Services	775-445-3275

NEW HAMPSHIRE

Colby-Sawyer C.	New London, NH 03257	Disability Resources	603-526-3712
Dartmouth C.	Hanover, NH 03755	Student Disabilities Center	603-646-2014
Franklin Pierce U.	Rindge, NH 03461-0060	Academic Services	603-899-4044
Keene St. C.	Keene, NH 03435	Office of Disability Services	603-358-2354
New England C.	Henniker, NH 03242	Academic Advising & Support Ctr.	603-428-2218
New Hampshire Tech	Concord, NH 03301	Support Services	603-271-7723
Plymouth St. U.	Plymouth, NH 03264-1595	Disability Services	603-535-2270
Rivier College	Nashua, NH 03060	Special Needs Services	603-897-8479
St. Anselm C.	Manchester, NH 03102	Academic Advisment	603-641-7465
Southern New Hampshire U.	Manchester, NH 03108	Disability Services	603-668-2211 x2386
U. of New Hampshire	Durham, NH 03824	Support for Students with Disabilities	603-862-2607

NEW JERSEY

Bergen C.C.	Paramus, NJ 07652	Office of Special Services	201-612-5273
Bloomfield C.	Bloomfield, NJ 07003	Learning Needs	973-748-9000 x654
Brookdale C.C.	Lincroft, NJ 07738	Director of Disability Services	732-224-2730
Caldwell College	Caldwell, NJ 07006-9165	Office of Disability Services	973-618-3645
Camden County C.	Blackwood, NJ 08012	PACS Program	856-227-7200 ext. 4430
Centenary C.	Hackettstown, NJ 07840	Disability Services	908-852-1400 ext. 2251
C. of New Jersey, The	Ewing, NJ 06628-0718	Office for Students w/ Differing Abilities	609-771-2571
C. of St. Elizabeth	Morristown, NJ 07960-6989	Disability Services	973-290-4261
County C. of Morris	Randolph, NJ 07869	Horizons Program	973-328-5284
Drew U.	Madison, NJ 07940	Disability Specialist	973-408-3962
Fairleigh Dickinson U.-Florham Campus		Reg. Ctr. for Coll. Students with LD	973-443-8734
Fairleigh Dickinson U.	Teaneck, NJ 07666	Reg. Ctr. for College Students with LD	201-692-2087
Georgian Court U.	Lakewood, NJ 08701	The Learning Center	732-987-2650
Kean U.	Union, NJ 07083-0411	Project Excel	908-737-5400

Institution	Location	Service	Phone
Middlesex C.C.	Edison, NJ 08818	Project Connections	732-906-2507
Monmouth U.	W. Long Branch, NJ 07764	Department of Disability Services for Students	732-571-3460
Mountclair St. U.	Montclair, NJ 07043	Disability Services	973-655-5431
New Jersey City U.	Jersey City, NJ 07305	Project Mentor	201-200-2091
New Jersey Institute of Tech.	Newark, NJ 070102-1982	Disability Services	973-596-3420
Ocean County C.	Toms River, NJ 08754	Disability Resource Center	732-255-0456
Princeton U.	Princeton, NJ 08544-0430	Disability Services	609-258-3061
Raritan Valley C.C.	Somerville, NJ 08876	Disability Services	908-526-1200 ext. 8418
Richard Stockton C. of NJ	Pomona, NJ 08240-0195	Learning Access Program	609-652-4988
Rider U.	Lawrenceville, NJ 08648	Student Support Services	609-895-5616
Rowan U.	Glassboro, NJ 08028	Academic Success Center	856-256-4234
Rutgers U.	Piscataway, NJ 08854-8097	Disability Services	973-353-5608
Rutgers U.	Newark, NJ 07102-1896	Dean's Office	973-353-5300
Salem C.C.	Carneys Point, NJ 08069	Center for Student Success	856-351-2700
Seton Hall U.	South Orange, NJ 07079	Disability Support Services	973-313-6003
St. Peter's C.	Jersey City, NJ 07306-5997	Special Needs Students	201-761-6032
Stevens Institute of Tech.	Hoboken, NJ 07030	Director of Counseling & Disability Services	201-216-5177
Sussex C.C.	Newton, NJ 07860	LD Program	973-300-2154
Thomas Edison St. C.	Trenton, NJ 08608-1176	Learners Services	609-984-1141 ext. 3415
Westminster Choir C. of Rider U.	Princeton, NJ 08540	Services for Students w/ Disabilities	609-896-5000 ext. 7365
William Paterson U. of NJ	Wayne, NJ 07470	Disability Services	973-720-2853

NEW MEXICO

Institution	Location	Service	Phone
C. of Santa Fe	Santa Fe, NM 84505	Center for Academic Excellence	505-473-6552
Eastern New Mexico U.	Portales, NM 88130	Services for Students with Disabilities	505-562-2280
New Mexico Highlands U.	Las Vegas, NM 87701	Disability & Testing Services	505-454-3252
New Mexico Junior C.	Hobbs, NM 88240	Special Needs Services	575-492-2574
N.M. Inst. of Mining & Tech.	Socorro, NM 87801	Services for Students with Disabilities	575.835.6619
New Mexico St. U.	Las Cruces, NM 88003	Services for Students with Disabilities	505-646-6840
Santa Fe C.C.	Santa Fe, NM 87502	TRIO Program	505-428-1446
U. of New Mexico	Albuquerque, NM 87131	Special Services Program	505-277-3506
U. of the Southwest	Hobbs, NM 88240	Office of Special Services	505-392-6564
Western New Mexico U.	Silver City, NM 88062	Special Needs Services	505-538-6498

College	Location	Service	Phone
Adelphi U.	Garden City, NY 11530	Learning Disabilities Program	516-877-3145
Bard C.	Annadale, NY 12504	Academic Resource Center	845-758-7051
Barnard C.	New York, NY 10027	Disability Services	212-854-4634
Canisius C.	Buffalo, NY 14208	Disabled Student Services	716-888-3748
CUNY—Baruch C.	New York, NY 10010	Disability Services	646-312-4590
CUNY—Bronx C.C.	Bronx, NY 10453	Disability Services	718-289-5874
CUNY—Brooklyn C.	Brooklyn, NY 11210	Services for Students with Disabilities	718-951-5538
CUNY—C. of Staten Island	Staten Island, NY 10314	Disability Services	718- 982-2510
CUNY—Hunter C.	New York, NY 10021	Office of Students with Disabilities	212-650-3449
CUNY—John Jay C	New York, NY 10019	Services for Individuals with Disabilities	212-237-8185
CUNY—Kingsborough C.C.	Brooklyn, NY 11235	Special Services	718-368-5175
CUNY—LaGuardia C.C.	Long Island City, NY 11101	Office for Students with Disabilities	718-482-5278
CUNY—Lehman C.	Bronx, NY 10468	Disability Issues	718-960-8441
CUNY—Medgar Evers C.	Brooklyn, NY 11225	Differently Abled Student Services	718-270-5027
CUNY—New York City C. of Tech.	Brooklyn, NY 11201	Student Support Services	718-260-5143
CUNY—York C.	Jamaica, NY 11451	Disability Services	718-262-2073
Clarkson U.	Potsdam, NY 13699	Accommodative Services	315-268-7643
Colgate U.	Hamilton, NY 13346	Academic Program Support	315-228-7375
C. of New Rochelle	New Rochelle, NY 10805-2339	Student Services	914-654-5364
C. of Saint Rose, The	Albany, NY 12203	Office of Students with Disabilities	518-337-2335
Columbia U.	New York, NY10027	Disability Services	212-854-2388
Concordia C. NY)	Bronxville, NY 10708	The Concordia Connection	914-337-9300 ext. 2361
Cooper Union	New York, NY 10003	Dean of Students	212-353-4115
Cornell U.	Ithaca, NY 14850	Student Disability Services	607-254-4545
Corning C.C.	Corning, NY 14830	Counseling for Students with Disabilities	607-962-9262
Culinary Institute of America	Hyde Park, NY 12538	The Learning Strategies Center	845-451-1219
Daemen C.	Amherst, NY 14226	The Learning Center	716-839-8228
Dominican C.	Orangeburg, NY 10692-1210	Disability Services	845-848-4035
Dowling C.	Oakdale, NY 11769-1999	College Students with Learning Disabilities	631-244-3306
D'Youville C.	Buffalo, NY 14201	Disability Services	716-829-7728
Eastman School of Music	Rochester, NY 14627	Dean of Academic Affairs	585-274-1020
Elmira C.	Elmira, NY 14901	Education Services	607-735-1857

Institution	Location	Service	Phone
Eugene Lang C. of New School U.	New York, NY 10011	Student Disability Services	212-229-5626
Fashion Institue of Technology	New York, NY 10001-5992	Disability Support Services	212-217-4090
Five Towns C.	Dix Hills, NY 11746-5871	Academic Support Services	631-656-2129
Fordham U.	New York, NY 10458	Disabled Student Services	718-817-0655
Hamilton C.	Clinton, NY 13323	Disabled Student Services	315-859-4021
Hartwick C.	Oneonta, NY 13820-4020	Academic Center for Excellence	607-431-4435
Hilbert C.	Hamburg, NY 14075-1597	Academic Services	716-649-7900 ext. 257
Hobart & William Smith C.	Geneva, NY 14456	Center for Teaching and Learning	315-781-3351
Hofstra U.	Hempstead, NY 11549	PALS Program	516-463-5761
Houghton C.	Houghton, NY 14744	Student Academic Services	716-567-9262
Iona C.	New Rochelle, NY 10801	College Assistance Program	914-633-2159
Ithaca C.	Ithaca, NY 14850-7020	Academic Support Services	607-274-1257
Keuka College	Keuka Park, NY 14478-0098	Academic Support Program	315-279-5636
Le Moyne C.	Syracuse, NY 13214	Academic Support Center	315-445-4118
Long Island U.—Brooklyn	Brooklyn, NY 11021	Special Educational Services	718-488-1219
Long Island U.—C.W. Post	Brookville, NY 11548-1300	Academic Resource Center	516-299-3057
Manhattan C.	Riverdale, NY 10471	Learning Disabilites Program	718-862-7101
Manhattan School of Music	New York, NY 10027	Dean of Students	212-749-2802 ext. 4036
Manhattanville C.	Purchase, NY 10577	Higher Education Learning Program	914-323-3186
Marist C.	Poughkeepsie, NY 12601-1387	Office of Special Services/LD Program	845-575-3274
Marymount Manhattan C.	New York, NY 10021	Disability Services	212-774-0724
Mercy C.	Dobbs Ferry, NY 10522	Support Services	914-674-7523
Molloy C.	Rockville Centre, NY 11570	Disability Support Services	516-678-5000 ext. 6381
NY Institute of Technology	Old Westbury, NY 11568-8000	Office of Counseling & Wellness	516-686-7683
New York U.	New York, NY 10011	Moses Center for Students with Disabilities	212-998-4980
Niagara U.	Niagara University, NY 14109	Office of Academic Support	716-286-8076
NYU Teaching & Learning Ctn.	New York, NY 10003	Para Educator for Young Adults	212-998-5185
Onondaga C.C.	Syracuse, NY 13215	Disability Services	315-498-2245
Paul Smith C.	Paul Smith's, NY 12970	Special Services	518-327-6358
Rensselaer Polytechnic Inst.	Troy, NY 12180	Disability Services	518-276-2746
Roberts Wesleyan C.	Rochester, NY 14624	Learning Center	585-594-6493
Rochester Inst. of Technology	Rochester, NY 14623	Learning Development Center	585-475-6988
Rockland C.C.	Suffern, NY 10901	Office of Disability Services	845-574-4541

College	Location	Service	Phone
Saint Bonaventure U.	St. Bonaventure, NY 14778	Services for Students with Disabilities	716-375-2065
Saint Francis C.	Brooklyn Heights, NY 11201	Student Health Services	718-489-5366
Saint John's U. NY)	Jamaica, NY 11439	Director of Student Services	718-990-6568
Saint Lawrence U.	Canton, NY 13617	Academic Svcs for Students with Special Needs	315-229-5104
Saint Thomas Aquinas C.	Sparkill, NY 10976	Pathways	845-398-4230
Schenectady C.C.	Schenectady, NY 12305	TRIO Student Support Services	518-381-1465
State University College at Buffalo	Buffalo, NY 14260	Office of Disability Services	716-645-2608
SUNY—Alfred State College	Alfred, NY 14802	Services for Students with Disabilities	607-587-4122
SUNY at Binghamton	Binghamton, NY 13902	Services for Student with Disabilities	607-777-2686
SUNY—Brockport	Brockport, NY 14420-2915	Office for Students with Disabilities	585-395-5409
SUNY—Broome C.C.	Binghamton, NY 134902	Learning Disabilities	607-778-5316
SUNY—Canton	Canton, NY 13617	Accommodative Services	315-386-7603
SUNY—Cayuga C.C.	Auburn, NY 13021	Office of Disability Services	315-255-1743 ext. 422
SUNY—C. of Technology	Cobelskill, NY 12043	Disability Support Services	518-255-5282
SUNY—Columbia Greene C.C.	Hudson, NY 12534	Dean of Students	518-828-4181 x3123
SUNY—Cortland	Cortland, NY 13045	Disabilities Services	607-753-2066
SUNY—Delhi	Delhi, NY 13753	Center for Academic Services	607-746-4593
SUNY—Farmingdale	Farmingdale, NY 11735	Support Svcs. for Stdnts. w/ Disabilities	631-420-2411
SUNY—Finger Lakes C.C.	Canandaigua, NY 14424	Services for Students w/Disabilities	585-394-3500 ext. 1390
SUNY—Fredonia	Fredonia, NY 14063	Disabled Student Support	716-673-3270
SUNY—Geneseo	Geneseo, NY 14454-1471	Disability Services	585-245-5112
SUNY—Hudson Valley C.C.	Troy, NY 12180	Disability Resource Center	518-266-8106
SUNY—Jamestown C.C.	Jamestown, NY 14702	Main Street Center	716-665-5220
SUNY—Jefferson C.C.	Watertown, NY 13601	Learning Skills Center	315-786-2335
SUNY—Mohawk Valley C.C.	Utica, NY 13501	Services for Students with Disabilities	315-792-5413
SUNY—Nassau C.C.	Garden City, NY 11530	Center for Students with Disabilities	516-572-7138
SUNY—New Paltz	New Paltz, NY 12561	Disability Resource Center	845-257-3020
SUNY—Old Westbury	Old Westbury, NY 11568	Disability Services	516-876-3009
SUNY—Oneonta	Oneonta, NY 13820	Learning Support Services	607-436-2137
SUNY—Oswego	Oswego, NY 13126	Office of Disabled Student Services	315-312-3358
SUNY—Plattsburgh	Plattsburgh, NY 12901-2681	Student Support Services	518-564-2810
SUNY—Potsdam	Potsdam, NY 13676	Student Support Services	315-267-3267
SUNY—Purchase	Purchase, NY 10577	Special Services	914-251-6390

Institution	Location	Service	Phone
SUNY—Stony Brook U.	Stony Brook, NY 11794	Disabilities Support Services	631-632-6748
SUNY—University at Albany	Albany, NY 12222	Learning Disabilities Resource Program	518-442-5490
SUNY—University at Buffalo	Buffalo, NY 14222-1095	Disability Services	716-878-4500
Syracuse U.	Syracuse, NY 13244	Center for Academic Acievement	315-443-1128
Tompkins Cortland C.C.	Dryden, NY 13035	Baker Center for Learning	607-844-8222 ext. 4283
U. of Rochester	Rochester, NY 14627-0251	Disability Resources	585-275-9125
Union C.	Schenectady, NY 12308	DEean of Students	518-388-6061
Utica C. of Syracuse U.	Utica, NY 13502-4892	Academic Support Services	315-223-2555
Vassar C.	Poughkeepsie, NY 12604	Office of Disability Services	845-437-7584
Vaughn C. of Aeronautics & Tech.	Flushing, NY 11369	Academic Support Services	718-429-6600
Wagner C.	Staten Island, NY 10301	Academic Advisement Center	718-390-3278
Wells C.	Aurora, NY 13026	Academic Advising	315-364-3401
Westchester C.C.	Valhalla, NY 10595	Disabled Students	914-606-6552
Yeshiva U.	New York, NY 10033	Disability Services	917-326-4828

NORTH CAROLINA

Institution	Location	Service	Phone
Appalachian St. U.	Boone, NC 28608	Office of Disability Services	828-262-3056
Asheville-Buncombe Tech.	Asheville, NC 28801	Special Needs	828-254-1921 ext. 141
Barton C.	Wilson, NC 27893	Disability Services	252-399-6587
Belmont Abbey C.	Belmont, NC 28012	Academic Assistance	704-461-6776
Bennett C.	Greensboro, NC 27401	Center for Teaching, Learning, and Technology	336-517-1567
Brevard College	Brevard, NC 28712	Office for Stnts w/Special Needs & Disabilities	828-884-8131
Campbell U.	Buies Creek, NC 27506	Student Support Services	910-814-4364
Catawba C.	Salisbury, NC 28144	Academic Resource Center	704-637-4410
Central Piedmont C.C.	Charlotte, NC 28235	Services for Students with Disabilities	704-330-2722 x7279
Chowan College	Murfreesboro, NC 27855	Learning Center	252-398-6356
Davidson C.	Davidson, NC 28036	Dean of Students Office	704-894-2225
Duke U.	Durham, NC 27708	Student Disability Access Office	919-668-1267
East Carolina U.	Greenville, NC 27858	Disability Support Services	252-737-1016
Elizabeth City State U.	Elizabeth City, NC 27909	Center for Special Needs Students	252-335-3527
Elon University	Elon, NC 27244	Disability Services	336-278-6500
Gardner-Webb U.	Boiling Springs, NC 28071	Disability Services	704-406-4271
Greensboro C.	Greensboro, NC 27401-1875	Disability Services	336-272-7102 ext. 591
Guilford C.	Greensboro, NC 27410	The Learning Commons	336-316-2451

Institution	Location	Service	Phone
Guilford Tech C.C.	Jamestown, NC 27282	Counseling Services	336-454-1126, ext. 50157
High Point U.	High Point, NC 27262-3598	Disability Services	336-841-9037
Johnson C. Smith U.	Charlotte, NC 28216	Student Support Services	708-378-1116
Lees-McRae C.	Banner Elk, NC 28604	Disability Services	828-898-2561
Lenoir-Rhyne U.	Hickory, NC 28603	Disability Services	828-328-7296
Livingstone C.	Salisbury, NC 28144	Empowering Scholars	704-216-6065
Mars Hill C.	Mars Hill, NC 28754	Special Education	828-689-1495
Meredith C.	Raleigh, NC 27607-5298	Disability Services	919-760-8427
Methodist C.	Fayetteville, NC 28311-1498	Disability Services	910-630-7402
Mt. Olive C.	Mount Olive, NC 28365	Teaching and Learning Center	919-658-2502 ext. 4013
Nash Community C.	Rocky Mount, NC 27804	Compensatory Education Dept.	252-451-8315
North Carolina School of the Arts	Winston-Salem, NC 27127-2189	Counseling Center	336-770-3288
North Carolina St. U.	Raleigh, NC 27695	Disability Services for Students	919-513-3768
Richmond C.C.	Hamlet, NC 28345	Student Development	910-410-1867
Rockingham C.C.	Wentworth, NC 27375	Student Development	336-342-4261 ext. 2243
St. Andrews Presbyterian C.	Laurinburg, NC 28352	Disability Services	910-277-5298
Southwestern C.C.	Sylva, NC 28779	Student Support Services	800.447.4091, ext. 4420
UNC at Chapel Hill, The	Chapel Hill, NC 27599	Learning Disabilities Services	919-962-7227
UNC at Charlotte, The	Charlotte, NC 28223-0001	Disability Services	704-687-4355
UNC at Greensboro, The	Greensboro, NC 27402-6170	Disabled Student Services	336-334-5440
UNC at Pembroke, The	Pembroke, NC 28372	Disability Support Services	910-521-6695
UNC at Wilmington, The	Wilmington, NC 28403	Disability Services	910-962-7555
Wake Forest U.	Winston-Salem, NC 27109	Learning Assistance Center	336-758-5929
Wake Tech C.C.	Raleigh, NC 27603	Disability Support Services	919-866-5668
Western Piedmont C.C.	Morgantown, NC 28655	Disabled Student Services	828-448-3153
Western Carolina U.	Cullowhee, NC 28723	Disability Services	828-227-2716
Wingate U.	Wingate, NC 28174	Disability Services	704-233-8269
Winston-Salem St. U.	Winston-Salem, NC 27110	Academic Resource Center	336-750-2138

NORTH DAKOTA

Institution	Location	Service	Phone
Bismarck St. C.	Bismarck, ND 58506	Disability Support Services	701-224-5554
Dickinson St. U.	Dickinson, ND 58601-4896	Student Support Services	701-483-2999
Jamestown C.	Jamestown, ND 58405	Office of Admissions	701-252-5512
Maryville St. U.	Maryville, ND 58257	Academic Support Services	701-788-4675

Institution	Location	Service	Phone
Minot St. U.	Minot, ND 58707	Extended Learning Center	701-858-3822
North Dakota St. C.	Wahpeton, ND 58076-0002	Study Svcs. for Students w/ Disabilities	701-671-2623
North Dakota St. U.	Fargo, ND 58105-5226	Disability Services	701-231-7198
United Tribes Tech C.	Bismarck, ND 58504	Student Support Services	701-255-3285 x1471
U. of Mary	Bismarck, ND 58504	Learning Skill Services	701-355-8264
U. of North Dakota—Grand Forks	Grand Forks, ND 58202	Disabled Student Support Services	701-777-3425
Valley City St. U.	Valley City, ND 58072	Student Academic Services	701-845-7298
Williston St. C.	Williston, ND 58801	Enrollment Services	1-888-863-9455 ext 4222

OHIO

Institution	Location	Service	Phone
Antioch C.	Yellow Spring, OH 45387	Academic Support Services	937-319-6082
Art Academy of Cincinnati	Cincinnati, OH 45202	Learning Assistance	513-562-6261
Ashland U.	Ashland, OH 44805	Disability Services	419-289-5953
Baldwin-Wallace C.	Berea, OH 44017	Svcs for Students w/ Disabilities	440-826-5936
Bowling Green St. U.	Bowling Green, OH 43403	Office of Disability Services	419-372-8495
Capital U.	Columbus, OH 43209	Disability Concerns	614-236-6327
Case Western Reserve U.	Cleveland, OH 44106	Disability Support Services	216-368-5230
Central Ohio Tech C.	Newark, OH 43055	Office for Disability Services	740-366-9441
Clark St. C.C.	Springfield, OH 45505	Office of Student Services	937-328-6084
Cleveland Institute of Art	Cleveland, OH 44106	Office of Academic Services	216-421-7462
Cleveland Institute of Music	Cleveland, OH 44106	Office of Admissions	216-795-3107
Cleveland St. U.	Cleveland, OH 44115	Disability Services	216-687-2015
C. of Mount Saint Joseph	Cincinnati, OH 45233-1630	Project Excel	513-244-4623
C. of Wooster	Wooster, OH 44691	Learning Center	330-263-2595
Columbus C. of Art and Design	Columbis, OH 43215	Disability Services	614-222-4004
Columbus St. C.C.	Columbus, OH 43216	Disability Services	614-227-2629
Cuyahoga C.C. Western	Parma, OH 44130	Access Office for Accommodation	216-987-5077
Denison U.	Granville, OH 43023	Office of Academic Support	740-587-6666
Franciscan U. of Seubenville	Stubenville, OH 43952-1763	Disability Services	740-284-5358
Franklin U.	Columbus, OH 43215-5399	Student Services	614-797-4700
Heidelburg C.	Tiffin, OH 44883	Learning Center	419-448-2301
Hiram C.	Hiram, OH 44234	Counseling	330-569-5952
Hocking C.	Nelsonville, OH 45764	Office of Disability Services	740-753-3591

College	Location	Office	Phone
John Carroll U.	University Heights, OH 44118	Services for Students with Disabilities	216-397-4967
Kent St. U.	Kent, OH 44242-0001	Student Accessibility Services	330-672-3391
Kenyon C.	Gambier, OH 43022	Academic Advising	740-427-5145
Lake Erie C.	Painesville, OH 44077	Student Success Center	440-375-7426
Lakeland C.C.	Kirtland, OH 44095	Services for Students with Disabilities	440-525-7245
Lorain County C.C.	Elyria, OH 44035	Office for Special Needs Services	440-366-4124
Lourdes C.	Sylvania, OH 43560	Disability Services	419-824-3834
Malone U.	Canton, OH 44709	Student Retention	330-471-8359
Marietta C.	Marietta, OH 45750	Counseling Center	740-376-4477
Miami U.—Hamilton	Hamilton, OH 45011	Special Services	513-785-3211
Miami U.	Oxford, OH 45056	Office of Disability Resources	513-529-1541
Mt. Union C.	Alliance, OH 44601	Disability Support Services	330-823-7372
Mt. Vernon Nazarene U.	Mount Vernon, OH 43050	Academic Support Services	740-392-6868
Muskingum C.	New Concord, OH 43762	PLUS Program	740-826-8280
North Central State C.	Mansfield, OH 44901	Disability Services	419-755-4727
Notre Dame C. of Ohio	Cleveland, OH 44121	Disability Services	216-373-5185
Oberlin C.	Oberlin, OH 44074	Off. of Serv. for Students w/ Disab.	440-775-5588
Ohio Dominican C.	Coumbus, OH 42319	Academic Development	614-251-4233
Ohio Northern U.	Ada, OH 45810	Disability Resources	419-772-2534
Ohio St. U.	Marion, OH 43302	Learning Disabilities Services	614-292-3307
Ohio St. U.—Columbus	Columbus, OH 43210-1200	Office for Disability Services	614-292-3307
Ohio St. U.—Newark	Newark, OH 43055	Learning Assistance Services	740-366-9441
Ohio U.—Athens	Athens, OH 45701	Office for Institutional Equity	740-593-2620
Ohio Wesleyan U.	Delaware, OH 43015	Academic Advising	740-368-3105
Otterbein C.	Westerville, OH 43081	Academic Support Center	614-823-1618
Owens C.C.	Toledo, OH 43699	Disability Resource Services	419-661-7010
Raymond Walters C.	Cincinnati, OH 45236	Disability Services	513-729-8625
Shawnee St. U.	Portsmouth, OH 45662	Student Succes Center	740-351-3276
Sinclair C.C.	Dayton, OH 45402	Disability Services	937-512-5337
Terra St. C.C.	Fremont, OH 43420	Disability Services	419-559-2208
Union Institute U.	Cincinnati, OH 45206	Disability Services	802-828-8740
U. of Akron	Akron, OH 44325-2001	Services for Students with Disabilities	330-972-7928

Institution	Location	Office	Phone
U. of Cincinnati	Cincinnati, OH 45221-0091	Disability Student Services	513-556-6823
U. of Dayton	Dayton, OH 45469-1611	Office of Students with Disabilities	937-229-2066
U. of Findlay	Findlay, OH 45840	Supporting Skills System	419-422-8313
U. of Rio Grande	Rio Grande, OH 45674	Disability Services	740-245-7339
U. of Toledo	Toledo, OH 43606-3390	Office of Accessibility	419-530-4981
Urbana U.	Urbana, OH 43078	Disability Services	937-484-1286
Ursuline C.	Pepper Pike, OH 44124-4398	Program for Students with LD	440-646-8123
Walsh U.	Canton, OH 44720	Academic Support Center	330-490-7234
Washington St. C.C.	Marietta, OH 45750	Student Development	740-374-8716
Wilmington C.	Wilmington, OH 45177	Disability Services	937-382-6661
Whittenberg U.	Springfield, OH 45501	Academic Services	937-327-7924
Wright St. U.	Dayton, OH 45435	Office of Disability Services	937-775-5680
Xavier U.	Cincinnati, OH 45207-2612	Learning Assistance Center	513-745-3214
Youngstown St. U.	Youngstown, OH 44555	Disability Services	330-941-1372

OKLAHOMA

Institution	Location	Office	Phone
Cameron U.	Lawton, OK 73505	Disability Services	580-581-2209
East Central U.	Ada, OK 74820	Disability Services	580-559-5677
Northeastern St. U.	Tahlequah, OK 74464	Student Affairs	918-456-5511 ext. 2120
Oklahoma Baptist U.	Shawnee, OK 74804	Student Services	405-878-2420
Oklahoma Christian U.	Oklahoma City, OK 73136-1100	Student Life	405-425-5907
Oklahoma City C.C.	Oklahoma City, OK 73159	Services to Students with Disabilities	405-682-7520
Oklahoma St. U.	Stillwater, OK 74078	Student Disability Services	405-744-7116
Oklahoma Wesleyan U.	Bartlesville, OK 74006	Disability Support Services	918.335.6200
Oral Roberts U.	Tulsa, OK 74171	Student Support Services	918495-7018
Southern Nazarene U.	Bethany, OK 73008	Student Support Services	405-491-6694
Southeastern Oklahoma St. U.	Durant, OK 74701-0609	Student Support Services	580-745-2394
St. Gregory's U.	Shawnee, OK 74804	Disability Support Services	405-878-5310
Tulsa Junior C.	Tulsa, OK 74119	Disabled Student Resource Center	918-595-7115
U. of Central Oklahoma	Edmound, OK 73034	Disability Support Services	405-974-2516
U. of Oklahoma	Norman, OK 73019	Office of Disability Services	405-325-3852
U. of Tulsa	Tulsa, OK 74104	Center for Student Academic Support	918-631-2315

OREGON

College	Location	Service	Phone
Blue Mountain C.C.	Pendleton, OR 97801	Services for Students with Disabilities	541-278-5934
Chemeketa C.C.	Salem, OR 97309	Office for Students with Disabilities	503-399-5192
Concordia U.	Portland, OR 97211	Couseling and Learning Services	503-493-6280
Corban C.	Salem, OR 97301	Career and Academic Services	503-375-7012
Eastern Oregon U.	La Grande, OR 97850	Learning Center	541-962-3081
George Fox U.	Newberg, OR 97132	Disability Services	503-554-2314
Lane C.C.	Eugene, OR 97405	Disability Resources	541-463-3010
Lewis & Clark C.	Portland, OR 97219-7899	Student Support Services	503-768-7156
Linfield C.	McMinnville, OR 97128-6894	Learning Support Services	503-883-2562
Linn-Benton C.C.	Albany, OR 97321	Disability Services	541-917-4789
Marylhurst U.	Marylhurst, OR 97036-0261	Disability Services	503-636-8141 ext. 3344
Mt. Hood C.C.	Gresham, OR 97030	Disability Services	503-491-6923
Northwest Christian C.	Eugene, OR 97401	Career Development & Service Learning	541-684-7345
Oregon Institute of Technology	Klamath Falls, OR 97601	Diasability Services	541-885-1129
Oregon St. U.	Corvallis, OR 97331-2133	Services for Students with Disabilities	541-737-4098
Pacific U.	Forest Grove, OR 97116	Learning Support Services	503-352-2107
Portland St. U.	Portland, OR 97207	Disability Resource Center	503-725-4150
Rogue C.C.	Grants Pass, OR 97527	Disability Services	541-956-7337
Southern Oregon St. U.	Ashland, OR 97520-5032	Disabled Student Services	541-552-6213
Umpqua C.C.	Roseburg, OR 97470	Disability Services	541-440-7655
U. of Oregon	Eugene, OR 97403-1217	Disability Services	541-346-1155
U. of Portland	Portland, OR 97203	Disability Services	503-943-7134
Warner Pacific C.	Portland, OR 97215	Career Services	503-517-1010
Western Oregon U.	Monmouth, OR 97361	Office of Disability Services	503-838-8250
Willamette U.	Salem, OR 97301	Disability Services	503-370-6471

PENNSYLVANIA

College	Location	Service	Phone
Albright C.	Reading, PA 19612	Learning Center - Academic Support	610-921-7662
Allegheny C.	Meadville, PA 16335	Learning Commons	814-332-2898
Alvernia C.	Reading, PA 19607-1799	Office of Admissions	610-790-1918
Arcadia U.	Glenside, PA 19038-3295	Learning Resource Network	215-572-4033
Bloomsburg U. of Pennsylvania	Bloomsburg, PA 17815	Accommodative Services	570-389-4491
Bryn Athyn C. of the New Church	Bryn Athyn, PA 19009	Disability Services	267-502-2637

College	Location	Service	Phone
Bryn Mawr C.	Bryn Mawr, PA 19010-2899	Access Services	610-526-7351
Bucknell U.	Lewisburg, PA 17837-9988	Services for Disabled Students	570-577-1301
Bucks County C.C.	Newton, PA 18940	Program for Students with Disabilities	215-968-8463
Cabrini C.	Randor, PA 19087	Disabilities Support Services	610-902-8572
California U. of Pennsylvania	California, PA 15419	Office for Students with Disabilities	724-938-5781
Carlow U.	Pittsburgh, PA 15213	Disability Services	412-578-6257
Carnegie Mellon U.	Pittsburgh, PA 15213	Equal Opportunity Services	412-268-2013
Cedar Crest C.	Allentown, PA 18104-6796	Academic Services	610-606-4628
Chatham U.	Pittsburgh, PA 15232	College Learning Center	412-365-1611
Chestnut Hill C.	Philadelphia, PA 19118-2693	Academic Advising	215-248-7199
Cheyney U. of PA	Cheyney, PA 19319	Academic Success Center	610-399-2217
Clarion U. of Pennsylvania	Clarion, PA 16214	Disability Support Services	814-393-2095
C. Misericordia	Dallas, PA 18612	Alternative Learning Project	570-674-8126
C.C. of Allegheny County	Pittsburgh, PA 15212	Support Svcs. for Stdnts. w/ Disabilities	412-237-4614
C.C. of Philadelphia	Philadelphia, PA 19130	Educational Support Services	215-751-8050
CCAC North	Pittsburgh, PA 15237	Support Services	412-369-3686
Delaware Valley C.	Doylestown, PA 18901	Learning Support Services	215-489-2490
DeSales U.	Center Valley, PA 18034	Academic Resource Center	610-282-1100
Drexel U.	Philadelphia, PA 19104	Office of Disability Services	215-895-1401
Duquesne U.	Pittsburgh, PA 15282	Learning Skills Center	412-396-6000
Eastern U.	St. Davids, PA 19087-3696	Cushing Center for Counseling	610-341-5837
East Stroudsburg U. of PA	East Stroudsburg, PA 18301-2999	Office of Disability Services	570-422-3954
Edinboro U. of Pennsylvania	Edinboro, PA 16444	Office for Students with Disabilities	814-732-2462
Elizabethtown C.	Elizabethtown, PA 17022-2298	Disability Services	717-361-1227
Franklin & Marshall C.	Lancaster, PA 17604-3003	Counseling Services	717-291-3989
Gannon U.	Erie, PA 16541	Program for Students w/ LD	814-871-5522
Geneva C.	Beaver Falls, PA 15010	ACCESS Center	724-847-5566
Gettysburg C.	Gettysburg, PA 17325	Academic Advising	717-337-6579
Grove City College	Grove City, PA 16127	Disability Services	724-458-2700
Gwynedd-Mercy C.	Gwyned Valley, PA 19437-0901	Disability Services	215-646-7300 ext. 427
Harcum Jr C.	Bryn Mawr, PA 19010	AccESS Development	610-526-6036
Haverford C.	Haverford, PA 19041-1392	Counseling & Psychological Services	610-896-1290

College	Location	Office	Phone
Holy Family U.	Philadelphia, PA 19114-2094	Disability Services	215-637-7700 ext. 3231
Immaculata U.	Immaculata, PA 19345-0702	Academic Success Services	610-647-4400 ext. 3876
Indiana U. of Penn	Indiana, PA 15705	Advising and Testing Center	724-357-4067
Juniata C.	Huntingdon, PA 16652	Academic Support	814-641-3152
King's C.	Wilkes-Baree, PA 18711	Academic Skills Center	570-208-5800
Kutztown U. of Pennsylvania	Kutztown, PA 19530	Services for Students with Disabilities	610-683-4000
LaRoche C.	Pittsburgh, PA 15327	Academic Enrichment	412-536-1117
LaSalle U.	Philadelphia, PA 19141-1199	Teaching and Learning Center	215-951-1014
Lebanon Valley College	Annville, PA 17003-0501	Office of Disability Services	717-867-6071
Lehigh U.	Bethlehem, PA 18015	Office of Academic Support Services	610-758-4152
Lincoln U.	Lincoln University, PA 19352	Student Support Services	484-365-7290
Lock Haven U. of Pennsylvania	Lock Haven, PA 17745	Student Support Services	570-484-2324
Luzerne County C.C.	Nanticoke, PA 18634	Learning Support Services	570-740-0406
Lycoming C.	Williamsport, PA 17701	Academic Resource Center	570-321-4294
Mansfield U. of PA	Mansfield, PA 16933	Disability Services	570-662-4798
Marywood U.	Scranton, PA 18509-1598	Office of Disability Services	570-348-6211
Messiah C.	Grantham, PA 17027-0800	Disability Services	717-796-5382
Millersville U. of PA	Millersville, PA 17551-0302	Learning Services	717-872-3178
Montgomery County C.C.	Blue Bell, PA 19422	Services for Students with Disabilities	215-641-6577
Moore C. of Art & Design	Philadelphia, PA 19103	Educational Support Services	215-965-4061
Moravian C.	Bethlehem, PA 18018	Learning Services	610-861-1510
Mount Aloysius C.	Cresson, PA 16630	Disability Services	814-886-6336
Muhlenberg C.	Allentown, PA 18104-5596	Disability Services	484-664-3825
Neumann C.	Aston, PA 19014-1298	Disability Services	610-361-5349
Northampton C.C.	Bethlehem, PA 18017	Services for Disabled Students	610-861-5342
Peirce C.	Philadelphia, PA 19102	Dean of Students	215-670-9251
Pennsylvania C. of Technology	Williamsport, PA 17701	Disability Support Services	570-327-4765
Penn St. U.—Delaware	Media, PA 19063-5596	Learning Center	610-892-1460
Penn St. U.—Erie, The Behrend C.	Erie, PA 16563	Services for Students with Disabilities	814-898-7101
Penn St. U.—Lehigh Valley	Fogelsville, PA 18051-9999	Disability Services	610-396-6410
Penn St. U.—Mont Alto	Mont Alto, PA 17237-9703	Learning Center	717-749-6045
Penn St. U.—Schuylkill	Schuylkill Haven, PA 17972-2208	Disability Services	570-385-6127
Pennsylvania St. U.—U. Park	Univ. Park, PA 16802-3000	Office for Disability Services	814-863-1807

Institution	Location	Service	Phone
Philadelphia Biblical U.	Langhorne, PA 19047-2990	Disability Services	215-702-4270
Philadelphia U.	Philadelphia, PA 19144	Disability Service Office	215-951-6830
Point Park U.	Pittsburg, PA 15222	Academic Success	412-392-3870
Robert Morris U.	Moon Township, PA 15108	Center For Student Success	412-397-4342
Rosemont C.	Rosemont, PA 19010-1699	Dean of Students	610-527-0200 ext. 2400
Saint Francis U. PA)	Loretto, PA 15940	Academic Center for Enrichment	814-472-3024
Saint Joseph's U. PA)	Philadelphia, PA 19131	Services for Students with Disabilities	610-660-1774
Saint Vincent C. PA)	Latrobe, PA 15650-2690	Disability Support Services	724-805-2371
Seton Hill University	Greensburg, PA 15601	Disability Services	724-838-4295
Shippensburg U. of Penn.	Shippensburg, PA 17257-2299	Office of Disability Services	717-477-1329
Slippery Rock U. of PA	Slippery Rock, PA 16057	Office for Students with Disabilities	724-738-4877
Susquehanna U.	Selinsgrove, PA 17870	Counseling Center	570-372-4751
Swarthmore C.	Swarthmore, PA 19081	Disability Services	610-690-5014
Thiel C.	Greenville, PA 16125	Office of Special Needs	724-589-2063
Thomas Jefferson U., Col. of Health	Philadelphia, PA 19107	Student Affairs	215-503-8189
U. of Arts, The	Philadelphia, PA 19102	Disability Services	215-717-6616
U. of Pennsylvania	Philadelphia, PA 19104	Student Disability Services	215-573-9235
U. of Pittsburg-Bradford	Bradford, PA 16701	Academic Success Center	814-362-7609
U. of Pittsburg-Greensburg	Greensburg, PA 15601	Disability Services	724-836-7098
U. of Pittsburg-Johnstown	Johnstown, PA 15904	Learning Resources Center	814-269-7062
U. of Pittsburgh-Pittsburgh	Pittsburgh, PA 15260	Disability Resources & Services	412-648-7890
U. of Scranton	Scranton, PA 18510-4699	Learning Enrich. Spclst-Learning Resources Cntr	570-941-4039
Ursinus C.	Collegeville, PA 19426	Disability Services	610-409-3687 x4329
Villanova U.	Villanova, PA 19085	Learning Support Services	610-519-5636
Washington & Jefferson C.	Washington, PA 15301	Student Resource Center	724-223-6008
Westminster C.	New Wilmington, PA 16172	Disability Support Services	724-946-7192
West Chester U. of PA	West Chester, PA 19383	Disability Services	610-436-3217
Widener U.	Chester, PA 19013-5792	Student Affairs	302-477-2173
Wilkes U.	Wilkes-Barre, PA 18766	Learning Center	570-408-4233
Wilson College	Chambersburg, PA 17201	Learning Resource Center	717-264-4141 x3351
York C. of PA	York, PA 17405-7199	Academic Advising	717-815-1531

RHODE ISLAND

Brown U.	Providence, RI 02912	Disability Support Services	401-863-9588
Bryant C.	Smithfield, RI 02917	Academic Center for Excellence	401-232-6746
C.C. of Rhode Island	Warwick, RI 02856	Student Access and Mentoring	401-825-2402
Johnson & Wales	Providence, RI 02903	Center for Academic Support	401-598-4689
Providence C.	Providence, RI 02918	Office of Academic Services	401-865-1121
Rhode Island College	Providence, RI 02908	Disability Services	401-456-8061
Roger Williams U.	Bristol, RI 02809	Center for Academic Development	401-254-3841
Salve Regina U.	Newport, RI 02840-4192	Disability Services	401-341-3150
U. of Rhode Island	Kingston, RI 02881	Disability Services for Students	401-874-2098

SOUTH CAROLINA

Anderson U.	Anderson, SC 29621	Cneter for Student Success	864-231-2107
Citadel, The	Charleston, SC 29409	Academic Support Special Services	843-953-5305
Clemson U.	Clemson, SC 29634	Student Disability Services	864-656-6848
Coastal Carolina U.	Conway, SC 29528-6054	Counseling Services	843-349-2307
Coker C.	Hartsville, SC 29550	Disability Services	843-383-8035
C. of Charleston	Charleston, SC 29424	Center for Disability Services	843-953-1431
Columbia International U.	Columbia, SC 29203	Academic Services	803-807-5612
Converse C.	Spartanburg, SC 29302	Academic Support	864-577-2028
Erskine C.	Due West, SC 29639	Student Services	864-379-8701
Francis Marion U.	Florence, SC 295001	Counseling & Testing	843-661-1840
Furman U.	Greenville, SC 29613	Disability Services	864-294-2322
Lander U.	Greenwood, SC 29649-2099	Student Support Services	864-388-8972
Limestone C.	Gaffney, SC 29340	Program for Alternative Learning Styles PALS)	864-488-8377
Newberry C.	Newberry, SC 29108	Institutional Research and Disabilities	803-321-5112
North Greeville C.	Tigerville, SC 29688	Learning Disability Services	800.468.6642
Presbyterian C.	Clinton, SC 29325	Office of Provost	864-833-8233
Southern Wesleyan U.	Central, SC 29630-1020	Services to Students with Disabilities	864-644-5133
USC—Lancaster	Lancaster, SC 29721	Academic Success Center	803-313-7113
USC—Aiken	Aiken, SC 29801	Disability Services	803-641-3609
USC—Columbia	Columbia, SC 29208	Office of Student Disability Services	803-777-4331
USC—Spartanburg	Spartanburg, SC 29303	Disability Services	864-503-5199
Winthrop U.	Rock Hill, SC 29733	Students with Disabilities Services	803-323-2233

Institution	Location	Office	Phone
Wofford C.	Spartanburg, SC 29303-3663	Health Services and Counseling	864-597-4371
York Tech C.	Clover, SC 29730	Disability Services—Special Resources Office	803-325-2894

SOUTH DAKOTA

Institution	Location	Office	Phone
Augustana C. SD)	Sioux Falls, SD 57197	Svcs. for Students with Special Needs	605-274-5503
Black Hills St. U.	Spearfish, SD 57799	Student Assistant Center	605-642-6099
Dakota St. U.	Madison, SD 57042	Academic Support	605-256-5049
Dakota Wesleyan U.	Mitchell, SD 57301-4398	Student Support Services	605-995-2901
Mount Marty C.	Yankton, SD 57078	Dean for Academic Affairs	605-668-1584
National American U.	Rapid City, SD 57709	HR Services	605-721-5214
Northern St. U.	Aberdeen, SD 57401	Office of Disability Services	605-626-2371
South Dakota Scl of Mines & Tech.	Rapid City, SD 57701	Disability Services	605-394-1924
South Dakota St. U.	Brookings, SD 57007-1198	Disability Services	605-688-4504
U. of Sioux Falls	Sioux Falls, SD 57105	Career Services	605-331-6740
U. of South Dakota—Vermillion	Vermillion, SD 57069	Disability Services	605-677-6389

TENNESSEE

Institution	Location	Office	Phone
Austin Peay St. U.	Clarksville, TN 37044	Office of Disability Services	931-221-6230
Chattanooga St. Tech C.C.	Chattanooga, TN 37406	Disability Services	423-697-3105
Christian Brothers U.	Memphis, TN 38104	Student Disability Services	901-321-3536
Cleveland St. CC.	Cleveland, TN 37320	Disabilities Support Services	423-478-6217
Crichton C.	Memphis, TN 38111-1375	Academic Affairs	901-320-9700
Cumberland U.	Lebanon, TN 37087-3408	Student Affairs	615-547-1225
East Tennessee St. U.	Johnson City, TN 37614-0731	Disability Services	423-439-8346
Lambuth U.	Jackson, TN 38301	Student Academic Support	731-425-2500
Lipscomb U.	Nashville, TN 37204-3951	Disability Services	615-966-1781
Lee U.	Cleveland, TN 37311	Academic Support Program	423-614-8181
Martin Methodist C.	Pulaski, TN 38472	Student Resources Center	931-363-9895
Maryville C.	Maryville, TN 37804-5907	Learning Center	865-981-8124
Middle Tennessee State U.	Murfreesboro, TN 37132	Disabled Student Services	615-898-2783
Milligan C.	Milligan College, TN 37682	Dean's Office	423-461-8720
Pellissippi St. Tech C.	Knoxville, TN 37933	Services for Students with Disabilities	865-539-7091
Rhodes C.	Memphis, TN 38112	Disability Services	901-843-3885
Southern Adventist U.	Collegeedale, TN 37315	Learning Success Services	423-236-2574

College	Location	Service	Phone
Tennessee St. U.	Nashville, TN 37209-1561	Disability Services	615-963-7438
Tennessee Tech U.	Cookeville, TN 38505	Disabled Services	931-372-6119
Tennessee Wesleyan C.	Athens, TN 37371-0040	Academic Success Center	423-746-5275
Trevecca Nazarene U.	Nashville, TN 37210	Academic Support	615-248-1346
Tusculum C.	Greenville, Tn 37743	Academic Resource Center	423-636-7300
Union U.	Jackson, TN 38305	Counseling Services	731-661-5322
U. of Memphis	Memphis, TN 38152-6687	LD/ADHD Program	901-587-7195
U. of Tenn. at Martin, The	Martin, TN 38238	Disability Services	731-881-7719
U. of Tenn. at Chattanooga, The	Chattanooga, TN 37403	College Access Program	423-425-4006
U. of Tenn. at Knoxville, The	Knoxville, TN 37996	Office of Disability Services	865-974-6087
Vanderbilt U.	Nashville, TN 37203-1700	Opportunity Development Center	615-322-4705

TEXAS

College	Location	Service	Phone
Abilene Christian U.	Abilene, TX 79699	Alpha Academic Services	325-674-2667
Amarillo C.	Amarillo, TX 79178	disAbility Services	806-371-5436
Angelo St. U.	San Angelo, TX 76909	Student Services	325-942-2169
Austin C.C.	Cedar Park, TX 78613	Students Services	512-223-2126
Baylor U.	Waco, TX 76798	Access & Learning Accomodations	254-710-3605
Central Texas C.	Killeen, TX 76540	Project PASS	254-526-1293
Dallas Baptist U.	Dallas, TX 75211-9299	Student Affairs	214-333-5101
East Texas Baptist U.	Marshall, TX 75670	Advising and Career Development	903-923-2079
El Paso C.C.	El Paso, TX 79998	Center for Students with Disabilities	915-831-2426
Hardin-Simmons U.	Abilene, TX 79698-1000	Disability Support Services	325-670-5842
Houston Baptist U.	Houston, TX 77074-3298	Academic Advising	281-649-3000
Howard Payne U.	Brownwood, TX 76801	Disabled Student Services	325-649-8052
Jarvis Christian U.	Hawkins, TX 75765-1470	Career Management Services	903-730-4890
Lamar U.	Beaumont, TX 77710	Services for Students with Disabilities	409-880-8347
Lamar U.—Orange	Orange, TX 77630	Disability Services	409-882-3379
Laredo C.C.	Laredo, TX 78040	Special Population	956-721-5137
LaTourneau U.	Longview, TX 75607-7001	Student Services	903-233-4460
Lee C.	Baytown, TX 77522	Disabilities Services	281-425-6384
Lubbock Christian U.	Lubbock, TX 79407	Disability Services	806-720-7486
McMurry U.	Abilene, TX 79697	Counseling and Testing	325-793-4880
Midwestern St. U.	Wichita Falls, TX 76308-2099	Office of Disability Accommodations	940-397-4140

Institution	Address	Service	Phone
Northwood U. Texas Campus	Cedar Hill, TX 75104	Academic Office	972-293-5480
Our Lady of the Lake U.	San Antonio, TX 78207-4689	Center for Academic Achivement	210-434-6711 ext. 2731
Prairie View A&M U.	Praire View, TX 77446	Disability Support Services	936-261-3585
Rice U.	Houston, TX 77251-1892	Disability Services	713-348-5841
Saint Edward's U.	Austin, TX 78704	Student Disability Office	512-448-8557
Sam Houston St. U.	Huntsville, Tx 77341	Counseling Center	936-294-1720
Schreiner U.	Kerrville, TX 78028-5697	Learning Support Services	830-792-7256
Southern Methodist U.	Dallas, TX 75275-0355	Services for Students with Disabilities	214-768-4557
Southwestern U.	Georgetown, TX 78627-0770	Academic Services	512-863-1286
St. Mary's U. of San Antonio	San Antonio, TX 78228	Student Life	210-436-3135
Stephen F. Austin St. U.	Nonacogdoches, TX 75962	Disability Services	936-468-3004
Texas A&M U.—Corpus Christi	Corpus Christi, TX 78412-5503	Services for Students with Disabilities	361-825-5816
Texas A&M U.—Galveston	Galveston, TX 77553-1675	Counseling Center	409-740-4736
Texas A&M U.—Kingsville	Kingsville, TX 78363	Services for Students with Disabilities	361-593-3421
Texas A&M U.—C. Station	College Station, TX 77843	Disability Services	979-845-1637
Texas Christian U.	Fort Worth, TX 76129	Student Disability Services	817-257-7486
Texas Lutheran U.	Seguin, TX 78156-5999	Disability Support Services	830-372-8009
Texas St. U.—San Marcos	San Marcos, TX 78666	Office of Disability Services	512-245-3451
Texas Tech U.	Lubbock, TX 79409-5005	Program for Academic Support Services	806-742-2405
Texas Wesleyan U.	Fort Worth, TX 76105-1536	Counseling Center	817-531-4468
Texas Woman's U.	Denton, TX 76204-5679	Disability Support Services	940-898-3835
Tyler Jr. C.	Tyler, TX 75711	Suport Services	903-510-2389
U. of Houston	Houston, TX 77204-3022	Center for Students with Disabilities	713-743-5400
U. of Houston—Downtown	Houston, TX 77002-1001	Disabled Student Services	713-226-5227
U of the Incarnate World	San Antonio, TX 78209-6397	Student Disability Services	210-829-3997
U. of Mary Hardin-Baylor	Belton, TX 76513	Counseling and Testing	254-295-4696
U. of North Texas	Denton, TX 76203-5358	Office of Disability Accommodations	940-565-4323
U. of St. Thomas	Houston, TX 77006-4696	Counceling Services	713-525-3162
U. of Texas—Arlington	Arlington, TX 76019-0111	Office for Students with Disabilities	817-272-3364
U. of Texas—Austin	Austin, TX 78712	Services for Students with Disabilities	512-471-6259
U. of Texas—Dallas	Richardson, TX 75083-0688	Disability Services	972-883-2098
Univesity of Texas—El Paso	El Paso, TX 79968	Disabled Student Services	915-747-5148
U. of Texas—Pan American	Edinburg, TX 78539	Off. of Serv. for Persons with Disabilities	956-381-2659

College	Location	Office	Phone
U. of Texas—Permian Basin	Odessa, TX 79762-0001	PASS Office	432-552-2630
U. of Texas—San Antonio	San Antonio, TX 78249-0617	Disability Services	210-458-4157
U. of Texas—Tyler	Tyler, TX 75799	Testing Center	903-566-7079
West Texas A&M U.	Canyon, TX 79016	Student Disability Services	806-651-2335
Wiley C.	Marshall, TX 75670	Academic Affairs	903-923-2474

UTAH

College	Location	Office	Phone
Brigham Young U. UT)	Provo, UT 84602-1110	University Accessibility Center	801-422-2767
C. of Eastern Utah	Price, UT 84501	Disability Support Services	435-613-5483
Snow C.	Ephraim, UT 84627	Student Support Services	435-283-7321
Southern Utah U.	Cedar City, UT 84720	Student Support Services	435-865-8022
U. of Utah	Salt Lake City, UT 84112	Center for Disability Services	801-581-5020
Utah St. U.	Logan, UT 84322	Disability Resource Center	435-797-2444
Utah Valley State College	Orem, UT 84058	Accessibility Services	801-863-8747
Weber St. U.	Ogden, UT 84408-1103	Disabilities Center	801-626-6413
Westminster C.	Salt Lake City, UT 84105-3697	START Center	801-832-2281

VERMONT

College	Location	Office	Phone
Bennington C.	Bennington, VT 05701	Dean of Studies	802-442-5401
Burlington C.	Burlington, VT 05401	Student Support Services	802-862-9616 ext. 124
Castleton St. C.	Castleton, VT 05735	Academic Support Center	802-468-1321
Champlain C.	Burlington, VT 05402-0670	Support Services for Students w/Disabilities	802-651-5961
C. of St. Joseph	Rutland, VT 05701	Project Success	802-773-5900 ext. 3239
Green Mountain C.	Poultney, VT 05764-1199	Learning Center	802-287-8812
Johnson St. C.	Johnson, VT 05656	Academic Support Services	802-635-1438
Landmark C.	Putney, VT 05346	Center for Academic Support	802-387-6839
Lyndon St. C.	Lyndonville, VT 05851	Student Support Services	802-626-6210
Marlboro C.	Marlboro, VT 05344	Disability Services	802-258-9335
Middlebury C.	Middlebury, VT 05753-6002	ADA Office	802-443-5936
New England Culinary School	Montpelier, VT 05602	Learning Services	802-595-9367
Norwich U.	Northfield, VT 05663	Learning Support Center	802-485-2130
Saint Michael's C.	Colchester, VT 05439	Dean's Office	802-654-2818
Southern Vermont C.	Bennington, VT 05201	Disabilities Support Program	802-447-6360
U. of Vermont	Burlington, VT 05401	ACCESS	802-656-7753
Vermont Technical C.	Randolph Center, VT 05061	Services for Students with Disabilities	802-728-1278

VIRGINIA

Institution	Location	Office	Phone
Averett U.	Danville, VA 24541	Dean of Admissions	434-791-7301
Blue Ridge C.C.	Weyers Cave, VA 24486	Disability Services	540-453-2298
Bridgewater C.	Bridgewater, VA 22812-1599	Disability Services	540-828-5370
Bluefield C.	Bluefield, VA 24605	ACE Program	276-326-4606
Christopher Newport U.	Newport News, VA 23606	Center for Career & Academic Planning	757-594-8887
C. of William & Mary, The	Williamsburg, VA 23187-8795	Disability Services	757-221-2510
Eastern Mennonite U.	Harrisonburg, VA 22801	Disability Support Services	540-432-4233
Emory & Henry C.	Emory, VA 24327	Academic Support Services	276-944-6145
Ferrum C.	Ferrum, VA 24088	Academic Resource Center	540-365-4262
George Mason U.	Fairfax, VA 22030-4444	Disability Resource Center	703-993-2474
Hampden-Sydney C.	Hampden-Sydney, VA 23943	Academic Success Center	434-223-6286
Hampton U.	Hampton, VA 23668	Student Support Services	757-727-5611
Hollins U.	Roanoke, VA 24020	Academic Affairs	540-362-6684
James Madison U.	Harrisonburg, VA 22807	Office of Disability Services	540-568-6705
Liberty U.	Lynchburg, VA 24502	Office of Disability Academic Support	434-582-2159
Longwood U.	Farmville, VA 23909	Office of Disability Support Services	434-395-4935
Lynchburg C.	Lynchburg, VA 24501	Academic Advising	434-544-8152
Mary Baldwin C.	Staunton, VA 24401	Learning Skills Center	540-887-7250
Mary Washington C.	Fredericksburg, VA 22401	Academic Services	540-654-1266
Marymount U.	Arlington, VA 22207	Disabled Student Services	703-284-1615
New River C.C.	Dublin, VA 24060	LEAP Center	540-674-3600 ext. 4358
Old Dominion U.	Norfolk, VA 23529-0050	Disability Services	757-683-4655
Patrick Henry C.C.	Martinsville, VA 24115	Student Support Services	276-656-0257
Radford U.	Radford, VA 24142	Disability Resouce Office	540-831-6350
Randolph-Macon C.	Ashland, VA 23005	Disability Support Services	804-752-7343
Roanoke C.	Salem, VA 24153-3794	Center for Learning & Teaching	540-375-2247
Saint Paul's C.	Lawrenceville, VA 23868	Student Support Services	651.846.1547
Shenandoah U.	Winchester, VA 22601	Academic Success Center	540-665-4928
Sweet Briar C.	Sweet Briar, VA 24595	Academic Resource Center	434-381-6100 x6278
Thomas Nelson C.C.	Hampton, VA 23670	Disabled Student Services	757-825-2833
Tidewater C.C.	Portsmouth, VA 23703	LD Services	757-822-1805

Institution	Location	Program	Phone
U. of Richmond	Richmond, VA 23173	Academic Skills Center	804-289-8626
U. of Virginia	Charlottesville, VA 22906	Learning Needs & Evaluation Center	434-243-5180
U. of Virginia—College at Wise	Wise, VA 24293	Student Support Services	276-328-0265
Virginia Commonwealth U.	Richmond, VA 23284	Disability Support Services	804-828-2253
Virginia Intermont College	Bristol, VA 24201-4298	Student Support Services	276-466-7905
Virginia Military Institute	Lexington, VA 24450-0304	Miller Academic Center	540-464-7421
Virginia St. U.	Petersburg, VA 23806	Students with Disabilities Program	804-524-5061
Virginia Tech	Blacksburg, VA 24061	Services for Students with Disabilities	540-231-0858
Virginia Union U.	Richmond, VA 23220	Academic Enpowerment Center	804-342-3885
Virginia Wesleyan C.	Norfolk, VA 23502-5599	Learning Center	757-455-3246
Virginia Western Comm. C.	Roanoke, VA 24038	Reach Student Support Services	540-857-7286
Washington and Lee U.	Lexington, VA 24450-0303	Student Academic Support	540-458-8746

WASHINGTON

Institution	Location	Program	Phone
Bates Tech C.	Tacoma, WA 98405	Special Needs	253-680-7010
Central Washington U.	Ellensburg, WA 98926-7463	Disability Support Services	509-963-2171
City U.	Bellevue, WA 98005	Disability Resource Center	1.800.426.5596 x5228
Cornish C. of the Arts	Seattle, WA 98121	Student Affairs Program	206-726-5098
Eastern Washington U.	Cheney, WA 99004	Disability Support Services	509-359-6871
Everett C.C.	Everette, WA 98201	Center for Disability Services	425-388-9273
Evergreen St. C., The	Olympia, WA 98505	Access Services	360-867-6364
Gonzaga U.	Spokane, WA 99258	Disabilities Support Services	509-313-4134
Heritage U.	Toppenish, WA 98948	Disability Services	509-865-8544
North Seattle C.C.	Seattle, WA 98103	Educational Access Center	206-527-3697
Northwest U.	Kirkland, WA 98083	Academic Success Center	425-889-7823
Pacific Lutheran U.	Tacoma, WA 98447-0003	Academic Assistance	253-535-7206
Pierce C.	Tacoma, WA 98446	Disability Support Services	253-964-6460
Saint Martin's U.	Lacey, WA 98503	Disability Support Services	360-438-4580
Seattle Pacific U.	Seattle, WA 98119	Center for Learning	206-281-2272
Seattle U.	Seattle, WA 98122	Student Learning Center	206-296-5744
Spokane Falls C.C.	Spokane, WA 99204	Support Services	509-533-7169
Tacoma C.C.	Tacoma, WA 98465	Services for Students with Disabilities	253-566-5328
U. of Puget Sound	Tacoma, WA 98416	Disability Services	253-879-2692
U. of Washington	Seattle, WA 98195-5840	Disabled Student Services	206-543-8924

Institution	Location	Service	Phone
Walla Walla C.	College Place, WA 99324-1198	Disability Support Services	509-527-2366
Washington St. U.	Pullman, WA 99164-4122	Disability Resource Center	509-335-3417
Western Washington U.	Bellingham, WA 98225	Disabled Student Services	360-650-3083
Whatcom C.C.	Bellingham, WA 98226	Disabled Student Services	360-383-3045
Whitman C.	Walla Walla, WA 99362-2083	Academic Resource Center	509-527-5111 x5213
Whitworth C.	Spokane, WA 99251	Disability Support Services	509-777-4534
Yakima Valley C.C.	Yakima, WA 98907	Disability Services	509-574-4968

WEST VIRGINIA

Institution	Location	Service	Phone
Bethany C.	Bethany, WV 26032	Disability Support Services	800-922-7611
Bluefield St. C.	Bluefield, WB 24701	Student Support Services	304-327-4098
Concord C.	Athens, WV 24712	Office of Disability Services	304-384-6086
Davis & Elkins C.	Elkins, WV 26241	Supported Learning Program	304-637-1384
Fairmount St. U.	Fairmont, WV 26554	Disability Services	304-367-4686
Glenville St. C.	Glenville, WV 26351	Academic Support Center	304-462-4118
Marshall U.	Huntington, WV 25755	HELP	304-696-6252
Mountain St. U.	Beckley, WV 25802	Student Affairs	304-929-1434
Ohio Valley U.	Vienna, WV 26105-8000	Academic Support	304-865-6127
Shepherd U.	Shepherdstown, WV 25443-3210	Disability Support Services	304-876-5453
U. of Charleston	Charleston, WV 25304	Learning Support Services	304-340-3738
West Liberty St. C.	West Liberty, WV 26074-0295	Center for Student Success	304-336-8018
West Virginia St. C.	Institute, WV 25112-1000	Collegiate Support Services	304-766-3168
West Virginia Tech	Montgomery, WV 25136	Student Support Services	304-442-3498
West Virginia U.	Morgantown, WV 26506-6009	Disability Services	304-293-5496
West Virginia Wesleyan C.	Buckhannon, WV 26201	Learning Center	304-473-8499
Wheeling Jesuit U.	Wheeling, WV 26003	Academic Resource Center	304-243-4484

WISCONSIN

Institution	Location	Service	Phone
Alverno C.	Milwaukee, WI 53234-3922	Student Accessibility	414-382-6026
Bellin C. of Nursing	Green Bay, WI 54305	Disability Support Services	920-433-6699
Beloit C.	Beloit, WI 53511	Learning Support Services Center	608-363-2572
Cardinal Stritch C.	Milwaukee, WI 53217-3985	Academic Support	414-410-4166
Carroll C. (WI)	Waukesha, WI 53186	Walter Young Center	262-524-7335
Carthage C.	Kenosha, WI 53140	Office of Academic Advising	262-551-5802

College	Location	Service	Phone
Concordia U. WI)	Mequon, WI 53097	Learning Resource Center	262-243-4535
Edgewood C.	Madison, WI 53711	Disability Services	608-663-2281
Gateway Technical C.	Kenosha, WI 53144	Special Needs	262-564-2320
Lawrence U.	Appleton, WI 54912-0599	Disability Services	920-832-6530
Marian C. of Fond Du Lac	Fond du Lac, WI 54935	Disability Services	920-923-8951
Marquette U.	Milwaukee, WI 53201-1881	Disability Services	414-288-1645
Milwaukee Inst. of Art & Des.	Milwaukee, WI 53202	Disability Services	414-847-3347
Milwaukee School of Eng.	Milwaukee, WI 53202-3109	Student Support Services	414-277-2476
Mount Mary C.	Milwaukee, WI 53222	Disability Services	414-258-4810
Northland C.	Ashland, WI 54806	Office of Special Needs	715-682-1230
Ripon C.	Ripon, WI 54971	Student Support Services	920-748-8394
Saint Norbert C.	De Pere, WI 54115	Academic Support Services	920-403-1326
Silver Lake C.	Manitowoc, WI 54220	Disability Services	920-686-6115
U of Wisc.—Baraboo/Sauk County	Baraboo, WI 53913	Student Services	608-355-5230
U. of Wisconsin—Eau Claire	Eau Claire, WI 54701	Services for Students with Disabilities	715-836-4542
U. of Wisconsin—Green Bay	Green Bay, WI 53411-7001	Disability Services	920-465-2841
U. of Wisconsin—LaCrosse	LaCrosse, WI 54601-3742	Disability Resource Services	608-785-6900
U. of Wisconsin—Madison	Madison, WI 53706	McBurney Disability Resource Center	608-263-2741
U. of Wisconsin—Milwaukee	Milwaukee, WI 53201	Learning Disabilities Program	414-229-6239
U. of Wisconsin—Oshkosh	Oshkosh, WI 54901-8662	Disability Services	920-424-3100
U. of Wisconsin—Parkside	Kenosha, WI 53141	Learning Disabilities Support Services	262-595-2610
U. of Wisconsin—Platteville	Platteville, WI 53818	Student Support Services	608-342-1818
U. of Wisconsin—River Falls	River Falls, WI 54022	Challenge Program	715-425-3531
U. of Wisconsin—Stevens Pt.	Stevens Point, WI 54481	Disability Services	715-346-3365
U. of Wisconsin—Stout	Menomonie, WI 54751	Disabilities Services	715-232-2995
U. of Wisconsin—Superior	Superior, WI 54880	Special Services	715-394-8580
U. of Wisconsin—Whitewater	Whitewater, WI 53190	Center for Students with Disabilities	262-472-1630
Viterbo U.	La Crosse, WI 54601	Learning Center	608-796-3194
West Wisconsin Tech. C.	La Crosse, WI 54602	Disability Services	608-785-9875

| Wisconsin Indianhead Tech. | Shell Lake, WI 54871 | Disability Services | 715-468-2815 ext. 5350 |
| Wisconsin Lutheran C. | Milwaukee, WI 53226 | Student Support | 414-443-8797 |

WYOMING

Central Wyoming C	Riverton, WY	Student Support Services	307-855-2227
Laramie County C.C.	Cheyenne, WY 82007	Disability Resource Center	307-778-1266
Sheridan C.	Sheridan, WY 82801	Learning Center	307-674-6446
U. of Wyoming	Laramie, WY 82071	University Disability Support Services	307-766-6189

CANADA

ALBERTA

Grace MacEwan C.C.	Edmonton, AB T51 2P2	Counseling & Special Services	780-497-5811
Lethbridge C.	Lethbridge, AB T1K 1L6	Support Services	403-320-3202 ext. 5400
N. Alberta Inst. Tech.	Edmonton AB T5G 2R1	Disabled Student Services	780-378-6133
S. Alberta Inst. Tech.	Calgary AB T2M OL4	Disability Support Services	403-284-8295
U. of Alberta	Edmonton AB T6G 2E8	Disabled Student Services	780-492-3381
U. of Calgary	Calgary AB T2N 1N4	Disability Resource Centre	403-220-8237

BRITISH COLUMBIA

Camosun C.	Victoria BC V8P 4X8	Adult Special Education	250-370-3325
Capilano C.	N. Vancouver BC V71 3H5	Disability Support Services	604-983-7526
C. of New Caledonia	Pr. George BC V2N 1P8	Disability Support Services	250-561-5848 ext. 5250
Kwantlen College	Surrey V3T BC 5H8	Services for Stud. With Disabilities	604-599-2003
Langara C.	Vancouver BC V5Y 2Z6	Disability Services	604-323-5509
Okanagan C.	Kelowna BC V1Y 4X8	Disability Services	250-762-5445 ext. 4119
Simon Fraser U.	Burnaaby BC V5A 1S6	Centre for Students with Disabilities	778-782-3313
U. of N. British Colum.	Prince Grge BC V2L 5P2	Disability Services	250-960-6355
U. of British Columbia	Vancouver BC V6T 1Z1	Disabilities Resource Center	604-822-5844
U. of Victoria	Victoria BC V8W 3P2	Student & Ancillary Services	250-721-8023

MANITOBA

| U. of Manitoba | Winnipeg MB R3T 2N2 | Disabilities Services | 204-474-6213 |
| U. of Winnipeg | Winnipeg MB R3B 2E9 | Disability Resource Center | 204-786-9973 |

NEW BRUNSWICK

School	Location	Service	Phone
Mt. Allison U.	Sackville NB E0A 3C0	Center for Learning Assistance	506-364-2527
U. of New Brunswick	Fredericton NB E3B 6E3	Disability Services	506-648-5680

NEWFOUNDLAND

School	Location	Service	Phone
Mem. U. Newfoundland	St. John's NF A1G 5S7	Centre for Students with Disabilities	709-737-2156

NOVA SCOTIA

School	Location	Service	Phone
Dalhousie U.	Halifax NS B3H 4J2	Student Accessibility Services	902-494-2836
NSCAD U.	Halifax NS B3J 3J6	Disability Resources	902-494-8313
St. Mary's U.	Halifax NS B3H 3C3	Support for Disabled Students	902-420-5449

ONTARIO

School	Location	Service	Phone
Algoma U. C.	S. Ste. Marie ON P6A 2G4	Learning Center	705-949-2301 ext. 4221
Cambrian C.	Sudbury ON P3A 3V8	Disability Services	705-566-8101 ext. 7793
Canadore C.	N. Bay ON P1B 8K9	Special Needs Services	705-474-7600 ext. 5213
Carleton U.	Ottawa ON K1S 5B6	P. Menton Cntr for Stnts w/ Disabilities	613-520-6608
Centennial C.	Scarborough ON M1K 5E9	Special Needs	416-289-5000 ext. 2254
Durham C.	Oshawa ON L1H 7L7	Special Needs—REACH)	905-721-3123
Fanshawe C.	London ON N5V 1W2	Counseling & Student Life	519-452-4282
George Brown C.	Toronto ON M5T 2T9	Special Needs	416-415-5000 ext. 6370
Humber College	Toronto ON M9W 5L7	Services for Students with Disabilities	416-675-5090
Lakehead U.	Thunder Bay ON P7B 5E1	Learning Assistance	807-343-8086
Loyalist College	Belleville ON K8N 5B9	Stnt Office for Alternative Resources	613-969-1913 ext. 2256
Mohawk College	Hamilton ON L8N 3T2	Disability Services	905-575-2389
Nippissing U.	N. Bay ON P1B 8L7	Disability Services	705-474-3450 ext. 4331
Ontario C. of Art	Toronto ON M5T 1W1	Services for Students with Disabilities	416-977-6000 ext. 288
Queen's U.	Kingston ON K7L 3N6	Disability Services	613-533-6666
Seneca College	N. York ON M2J 2X5	Special Needs	416-491-5050 ext. 3150
St. Clair C.	Windsor ON N9A 6S4	Disability Services	519-972-2727 ext. 4226
St. Lawrence C.	Brockville ON K6V 5X3	Disability Services	613-345-0660 ext. 3154
Sheridan C.	Oakville ON L6H 2L1	Enrollment Services	905-845-9430 x2530

Institution	Address	Service	Phone
Trent U.	Peterborough ON K9J 7B8	Special Needs	705-748-1281
U. of W. Ontario	London ON N6A 3K7	Services for Students with Disabilities SDC)	519-661-2147
U. of Waterloo	Waterloo ON N2L 3G1	Services for Disabled Persons	519-888-4567 ext. 35231
U. of Windsor	Windsor ON N9B 3P4	Special Needs Office	519-253-3000 ext. 3287
York U.	N. York ON M3J 1P3	LD Programs—Counseling & Dev. Cntr.	416-736-5297

PRINCE EDWARD ISLAND

Institution	Address	Service	Phone
Holland College	Charlottetown PE C1A 4Z1	Counseling	902-566-9525

QUEBEC

Institution	Address	Service	Phone
Concordia U.	Montreal PQ H4B 1R6	Office for Students with Disabilities	514-848-2424 ext. 3518
Dawson C.	Montreal PQ H3Z 1A4	Centre for Students with Disabilities	514-931-8731 ext. 1211
John Abbott C.	St. An. Belvue. PQ H9X 3L9	Special Needs Learning Center	514-457-6610
McGill U.	Montreal PQ H3A 1X1	Special Services	514-398-6009

SASKATCHEWAN

Institution	Address	Service	Phone
SIAST-Kelsey	Saskatoon SK S7K 6B1	Learning Services	306-659-4048
U. of Saskatchewan	Saskatoon SK S7N 0W0	Disabled Student Services	306-966-5673

YUKON

Institution	Address	Service	Phone
Yukon C.	Yukon YT Y1A 5K4	Learning Assistance Center	867-668-8785

PUERTO RICO

Institution	Address	Service	Phone
Pontifical Catholic U. of Puerto Rico	Ponce, PR 00717-0777	Disability Support Services	1.800.961.7696
U. of Puerto Rico—Humacao	Humacao, PR 00791-4300	SERPI	787-850-0000
U. of Puerto Rico—Mayaguez	Mayaguez, PR 00631-9000	Students with Disabilities	787-832-4040

UNITED KINGDOM

Institution	Address	Service	Phone
American International U.—Rich	Rich.-upon Thames TW10 6JP, Eng.	Disability Support Services	617-450-5617

ALPHABETICAL LIST OF COLLEGES BY LEVEL OF SUPPORT SERVICES

College/University	State	Support
Adelphi University	New York	SP
American International College	Massachusetts	SP
American University	District of Columbia	SP
Augsburg College	Minnesota	SP
Barry University	Florida	SP
Beacon College	Florida	SP
Brenau University	Georgia	SP
College Misericordia	Pennsylvania	SP
College of Mount St. Joseph	Ohio	SP
Curry College	Massachusetts	SP
Davis and Elkins College	West Virginia	SP
Dean College	Massachusetts	SP
Dowling College	New York	SP
Fairleigh Dickinson University—Florham Campus	New Jersey	SP
Fairleigh Dickinson University—Metropolitan Campus	New Jersey	SP
Finlandia University	Michigan	SP
Florida A&M University	Florida	SP
Gannon University	Pennsylvania	SP
Georgian Court College	New Jersey	SP
Hofstra University	New York	SP
Iona College	New York	SP
Landmark College	Vermont	SP
Long Island University—C.W. Post	New York	SP
Loras College	Iowa	SP
Louisiana College	Louisiana	SP
Lynn University	Florida	SP
Manhattanville College	New York	SP
Marist College	New York	SP
Marshall University	West Virginia	SP
Marymount Manhattan College	New York	SP
Mercyhurst College	Pennsylvania	SP
Misericordia University	Pennsylvania	SP
Missouri State University	Missouri	SP
Mitchell College	Connecticut	SP
Mount Ida College	Massachusetts	SP
Muskingum College	Ohio	SP
National-Louis University	Illinois	SP
New Jersey City University	New Jersey	SP
Norte Dame College	Ohio	SP
Northeastern University	Massachusetts	SP
Reinhardt College	Georgia	SP
Rochester Institute of Technology	New York	SP

College/University	State	Support
St. Thomas Aquinas College	New York	SP
Schreiner College	Texas	SP
Southern Illinois University—Carbondale	Illinois	SP
University of Arizona	Arizona	SP
University of Denver	Colorado	SP
University of Indianapolis	Indiana	SP
University of the Ozarks	Arkansas	SP
University of Tennessee at Martin, The	Tennessee	SP
University of Wisconsin—Oshkosh	Wisconsin	SP
Ursuline College	Ohio	SP
Vincennes University	Indiana	SP
Waldorf College	Iowa	SP
West Virginia Wesleyan College	West Virginia	SP
Westminster College	Missouri	SP

CS: COORDINATED SERVICES

College/University	State	Support
Abilene Christian University	Texas	CS
Adrian College	Michigan	CS
Anderson University	Indiana	CS
Appalachian State University	North Carolina	CS
Arizona State University	Arizona	CS
Black Hills State University	South Dakota	CS
Boston College	Massachusetts	CS
Boston University	Massachusetts	CS
Brevard College	North Carolina	CS
Brigham Young University	Utah	CS
Brown University	Rhode Island	CS
Bryant College	Rhode Island	CS
Caldwell College	New Jersey	CS
California Polytechnic State University—San Luis Obispo	California	CS
California State Polytechnic University—Pomona	California	CS
California State University—Chico	California	CS
California State University—Fullerton	California	CS
California State University—Long Beach	California	CS
California State University—Northridge	California	CS
California State University—San Bernardino	California	CS
Calvin College	Michigan	CS
Catholic University of America	District of Columbia	CS
Central Ohio Technical College	Ohio	CS
Clarion University of Pennsylvania	Pennsylvania	CS
Clark University	Massachusetts	CS
Colby-Sawyer College	New Hampshire	CS
Colgate University	New York	CS
College of St. Catherine, The	Minnesota	CS

College of the Siskiyous	California	CS
College of William and Mary, The	Virginia	CS
Concordia College	New York	CS
Davidson College	North Carolina	CS
DePaul University	Illinois	CS
Drexel University	Pennsylvania	CS
Duke University	North Carolina	CS
East Carolina University	North Carolina	CS
East Stroudsburg University of Pennsylvania	Pennsylvania	CS
Eastern Kentucky University	Kentucky	CS
Edinboro University of Pennsylvania	Pennsylvania	CS
Emerson College	Massachusetts	CS
Emory University	Georgia	CS
Evangel College	Missouri	CS
Fairfield University	Connecticut	CS
Ferris State University	Michigan	CS
Ferrum College	Virginia	CS
Florida Atlantic University	Florida	CS
Florida State University	Florida	CS
George Washington University	District of Columbia	CS
Georgia Southern University	Georgia	CS
Georgia State University	Georgia	CS
Grand View College	Iowa	CS
Harding University	Arkansas	CS
Hocking College	Ohio	CS
Illinois State University	Illinois	CS
Indiana University	Indiana	CS
Iowa State University	Iowa	CS
Jacksonville State University	Alabama	CS
James Madison University	Virginia	CS
Johnson & Wales University	Rhode Island	CS
Johnson State College	Vermont	CS
Kansas City Art Institute	Missouri	CS
Kansas State University	Kansas	CS
Kean University	New Jersey	CS
Kent State University	Ohio	CS
Keuka College	New York	CS
Kutztown University of Pennsylvania	Pennsylvania	CS
Laramie County Community College	Wyoming	CS
Lee University	Tennessee	CS
Lehigh University	Pennsylvania	CS
Lenoir-Rhyne College	North Carolina	CS
Liberty University	Virginia	CS
Limestone College	South Carolina	CS
Lincoln College	Illinois	CS

Louisiana State University	Louisiana	CS
Loyola University—Chicago	Illinois	CS
Manchester College	Indiana	CS
McDaniel College	Maryland	CS
Menlo College	California	CS
Miami University	Ohio	CS
Michigan State University	Michigan	CS
Minot State University—Bottineau	North Dakota	CS
Monmouth University	New Jersey	CS
Montana Tech of the University of Montana	Montana	CS
Morningside College	Iowa	CS
New England College	New Hampshire	CS
New England Culinary Institute	Vermont	CS
New York University	New York	CS
North Carolina State University	North Carolina	CS
Northern Illinois University	Illinois	CS
Northwestern University	Illinois	CS
Norwich University	Vermont	CS
Oberlin College	Ohio	CS
Ohio State University—Columbus	Ohio	CS
Old Dominion University	Virginia	CS
Pine Manor College	Massachusetts	CS
Pittsburg State University	Kansas	CS
Providence College	Rhode Island	CS
Reedley College	California	CS
Regis University	Colorado	CS
Rhode Island College	Rhode Island	CS
Rider University	New Jersey	CS
Rocky Mountain College	Montana	CS
Roosevelt University	Illinois	CS
Saint Ambrose University	Iowa	CS
St. Andrew's Presbyterian College	North Carolina	CS
San Diego State University	California	CS
San Francisco State University	California	CS
San Jose State University	California	CS
Santa Clara University	California	CS
Santa Monica College	California	CS
Santa Rosa Junior College	California	CS
Seton Hall University	New Jersey	CS
Sierra College	California	CS
Southern Connecticut State University	Connecticut	CS
Southern Illinois University—Edwardsville	Illinois	CS
Southern Methodist University	Texas	CS
Southwest Texas State University	Texas	CS
Springfield College	Massachusetts	CS

Stanford University	California	CS
SUNY—Delhi	New York	CS
SUNY—Stony Brook University	New York	CS
Syracuse University	New York	CS
Temple University	Pennsylvania	CS
Texa State University—San Marcos	Texas	CS
Towson University	Maryland	CS
Union College	Nebraska	CS
Unity College	Maine	CS
University of California—Berkeley	California	CS
University of California—Los Angeles	California	CS
University of California—San Diego	California	CS
University of California—Santa Barbara	California	CS
University of Central Florida	Florida	CS
University of Cincinnati	Ohio	CS
University of Colorado—Boulder	Colorado	CS
University of Colorado—Colorado Springs	Colorado	CS
University of Connecticut	Connecticut	CS
University of Dayton	Ohio	CS
University of Delaware	Delaware	CS
University of Dubuque	Iowa	CS
University of Florida	Florida	CS
University of Georgia	Georgia	CS
University of Hartford	Connecticut	CS
University of Houston	Texas	CS
University of Illinois at Urbana-Champaign	Illinois	CS
University of Iowa	Iowa	CS
University of Kansas	Kansas	CS
University of Kentucky	Kentucky	CS
University of Maryland—College Park	Maryland	CS
University of Maryland—Eastern Shore	Maryland	CS
University of Massachusetts—Amherst	Massachusetts	CS
University of Memphis, The	Tennessee	CS
University of Michigan	Michigan	CS
University of Missouri—Columbia	Missouri	CS
University of Nevada—Las Vegas	Nevada	CS
University of Nevada—Reno	Nevada	CS
University of New Hampshire	New Hampshire	CS
University of North Carolina at Chapel Hill, The	North Carolina	CS
University of North Carolina at Charlotte, The	North Carolina	CS
University of North Carolina at Greensboro, The	North Carolina	CS
University of North Carolina at Wilmington, The	North Carolina	CS
University of Oregon	Oregon	CS
University of Pittsburgh	Pennsylvania	CS
University of Rhode Island	Rhode Island	CS

College/University	State	Support
University of Saint Francis	Indiana	CS
University of San Francisco	California	CS
University of South Carolina—Columbia	South Carolina	CS
University of South Dakota, The	South Dakota	CS
University of Southern California	California	CS
University of Tennessee at Chattanooga, The	Tennessee	CS
University of Tennessee at Knoxville, The	Tennessee	CS
University of Tulsa, The	Oklahoma	CS
University of Utah	Utah	CS
University of Vermont	Vermont	CS
University of Virginia	Virginia	CS
University of Wisconsin—La Crosse	Wisconsin	CS
University of Wisconsin—Madison	Wisconsin	CS
University of Wisconsin—Milwaukee	Wisconsin	CS
University of Wisconsin—Whitewater	Wisconsin	CS
University of Wyoming	Wyoming	CS
Utah State University	Utah	CS
Utica College	New York	CS
Vermont Technical College	Vermont	CS
Virginia Intermont College	Virginia	CS
Wake Forest University	North Carolina	CS
Washington University in St. Louis	Missouri	CS
Western Carolina University	North Carolina	CS
Western Connecticut State University	Connecticut	CS
Western Illinois University	Illinois	CS
Western Kentucky University	Kentucky	CS
Wheelock College	Massachusetts	CS
Widener University	Pennsylvania	CS
Wingate University	North Carolina	CS
Wright State University	Ohio	CS
Xavier University	Ohio	CS

S: SERVICES

College/University	State	Support
Alfred State College	New York	S
Alverno College	Wisconsin	S
Beloit College	Wisconsin	S
Bluegrass Community and Technical College	Kentucky	S
Bowling Green State University	Ohio	S
Case Western Reserve University	Ohio	S
Champlain College	Vermont	S
Clemson University	South Carolina	S
College of Santa Fe	New Mexico	S
Colorado State University—Pueblo	Colorado	S
Cornell University	New York	S

Dickinson College	Pennsylvania	S
Drake University	Iowa	S
Eastern Illinois University	Illinois	S
Eastern Washington University	Washington	S
Edgewood College	Wisconsin	S
Elon University	North Carolina	S
Emory University	Georgia	S
Evergreen State College, The	Washington	S
Fitchburg State College	Massachusetts	S
Frostburg State University	Maryland	S
George Mason University	Virginia	S
Grand Valley State University	Michigan	S
Green Mountain College	Vermont	S
Grinnell College	Iowa	S
Guilford College	North Carolina	S
Hampton University	Virginia	S
Indian Hills Community College	Iowa	S
Indiana Wesleyan University	Indiana	S
Lamar University	Texas	S
Loyola Marymount University	California	S
Marian College of Fond du Lac	Wisconsin	S
Marquette University	Wisconsin	S
Marywood University	Pennsylvania	S
Messiah College	Pennsylvania	S
Middle Tennessee State University	Tennessee	S
Midwestern State University	Texas	S
Minnesota State University—Moorhead	Minnesota	S
Montana State University—Billings	Montana	S
New Mexico Institute of Mining and Technology	New Mexico	S
New Mexico State University	New Mexico	S
Nicholls State University	Louisiana	S
North Dakota State University	North Dakota	S
Northern Arizona University	Arizona	S
Northern Michigan University	Michigan	S
Occidental College	California	S
Ohio University	Ohio	S
Oklahoma State University	Oklahoma	S
Oregon State University	Oregon	S
Penn State University—University Park	Pennsylvania	S
Ripon College	Wisconsin	S
Rivier College	New Hampshire	S
St. Bonaventure University	New York	S
St. Lawrence University	New York	S
St. Olaf College	Minnesota	S
Seton Hill University	Pennsylvania	S

Sheridan College	Wyoming	S
Shimer College	Illinois	S
Smith College	Massachusetts	S
Sonoma State University	California	S
South Dakota State University	South Dakota	S
Southern Maine Comm. College	Maine	S
Southern Wesleyan University	South Carolina	S
Southern Utah University	Utah	S
SUNY—Alfred State College	New York	S
SUNY at Binghamton	New York	S
SUNY—Canton	New York	S
SUNY—Farmingdale	New York	S
SUNY—Potsdam	New York	S
SUNY—University at Albany	New York	S
Texas A&M University—College Station	Texas	S
Texas A&M University—Kingsville	Texas	S
Texas Tech University	Texas	S
Thomas More College	Kentucky	S
University of Alabama in Huntsville, The	Alabama	S
University of Alabama at Tuscaloosa, The	Alabama	S
University of Alaska—Anchorage	Alaska	S
University of Alaska—Fairbanks	Alaska	S
University of Arkansas–Fayetteville	Arkansas	S
University of Idaho	Idaho	S
University of Kansas	Kansas	S
University of Maine at Machias	Maine	S
University of Montana	Montana	S
University of Montana—Western	Montana	S
University of Nebraska—Lincoln	Nebraska	S
University of New England	Maine	S
University of New Haven	Connecticut	S
University of New Orleans	Louisiana	S
University of North Texas	Texas	S
University of Northern Colorado	Colorado	S
University of Northern Iowa	Iowa	S
University of Notre Dame	Indiana	S
University of Oklahoma	Oklahoma	S
University of Redlands	California	S
University of Saint Thomas (MN)	Minnesota	S
University of Southern Indiana	Indiana	S
University of Southern Mississippi	Mississippi	S
University of Texas—Austin	Texas	S
University of Texas—El Paso	Texas	S
University of Texas—Pan American	Texas	S
University of Toledo	Ohio	S

University of the Pacific	California	S
University of Wisconsin—Eau Claire	Wisconsin	S
University of Wisconsin—Stevens Point	Wisconsin	S
Washington State University	Washington	S
Wayne State College	Nebraska	S
West Virginia University	West Virginia	S
Western Oregon University	Oregon	S
Western State College of Colorado	Colorado	S
Wheaton College (MA)	Massachusetts	S
Whittier College	California	S
Winona State University	Minnesota	S

ADDENDUM: INDEPENDENT LIVING OPTIONS

The following programs are options for students who may have LD/ADHD or other disabilities, but who want to continue to pursue independent living skills and education beyond high school.

School	Program Overview	Contact Information
Anchor to Windward, Inc.	Structured living experience	Anchor to Windward, Inc. 600 Loring Avenue Salem, MA 09\1970 P.O. Box 813 Marblehead, MA 01945 978-740-0013 www.anchor-to-windward.com
Bancroft NeuroHealth	Various therapeutic services for children and adults with autism, and other neurological impairments.	Bancroft Admissions Office Haddonfield Campus 425 Kings Highway East P.O. Box 20 Haddonfield, NJ 08033-0018 Ph: 856-429-0010 www.bancroftneurohealth.org
Berkshire Hills Music Academy	Post-secondary school providing young adults with learning and developmental disabilities to live in a college setting while developing musical potential. Two-year certificate program.	Berkshire Hills Music Academy Mark Hudgik 48 Woodbridge Street South Hadley, MA 01075 Ph:413-540-9720 www.berkshirehills.org
Berkshire Center	College Internship Program and the Aspire Program—both are independent living experiences. Aspire for those with Asperger's and Non-verbal learning differences. (Also Brevard)	Caroline Wheeler Admissions Director 18 Park Street Lee, MA 01238 Ph: (877) Know-CIP http://www.berkshirecenter.org/academicsupport.html
Casa de Amma	Young adults who function independently but require assistance and structure in daily living. Life-long residential community.	Casa de Amma 27231 Calle Arroyo San Juan Capistrano, CA 92675 Ph: (949) 496-9901
Center for Adaptive Learning	18+ with a neurological disability, supportive living program.	Center for Adaptive Learning 3227 Clayton Road Concord, CA 94519 Ph: (925) 827-3863 www.centerforadaptivelearning.org

School	Program Overview	Contact Information
Chapel Haven	Residential program teaching independent living to young adults.	Judy Lefkowitz 1040 Whalley Avenue New Haven, CT 06151 Ph: (203) 397-1714 Ext 113 or 148 www.chapelhaven.org
Chapel Haven West	Residential program teaching independent living to young adults.	1701 N. Park Ave Tucson, Arizona 85719 University of Arizona Ph: 877-824-9378 Cdecarlo@chapelhaven.org http://chapelhavenwest.org/
College Excel	Support programs for young adults 18–27 years of age who are ready to begin or continue in college. Program provides college-accredited courses, skill development classes, tutoring, life skills education, and life coaching.	College Excel 86 SW Century Drive Box 199 Bend, OR 97702 Ph: 541-388-3043 http://www.collegeexcel.com/
College Internship Programs	Post-secondary academic, internship and independent living experiences for age 18–25 with Asperger's and non-verbal learning differences. Students participate in the College Internship Programs and can also attend classes at local colleges or community colleges.	CIP Bloomington Center 425 N. College Ave Bloomington, Indiana 47404 ph: 812-323-0600 X 22 http://www.cipbloomington.org lmanagrum@cipbloomington.org CIP Berkshire 40 Main St. Suite 3 Lee, MA 01238 Ph: (413) 243-2576 X34 lhubbard@cipberkshire.org www.cipberkshire.org CIP Brevard 3692 N. Wickham Road Melbourne, FL 32935 Ph: 321-259-1900 X11 sbrown@cipbrevard.org http://www.brevard.org CIP Berkeley Center 2020 Kittredge Street, Suite B Berkeley, CA 94704 Ph: 510-704-4476 X104 mpaul@cipberkeley.org www.cipberkeley.org

School	Program Overview	Contact Information
		CIP Amherst 4500 Harlem Rd Amherst, NY 14226 Ph: 716-839-2620 X 14 jcovert@cipamherst.org www.cipamherst.org
		CIP Long Beach 4510 E. Pacific Highway Long Beach, CA 90804 Ph: 562-961-9250 X 223
		CIP National Admissions Office 18 Park Street Lee, MA 01238 admissions@cipworldwide.org www.cipworldwide.org
College Living Experience	College program for students with autism spectrum disorders, Asperger's nonverbal learning disorder, ADD/ADHD and other learning disabilities.	National Admissions 7150 Columbus Gateway Suite J Columbia MD 21046 Ph: 800-486-5058
		CLE Fort Lauderdale 6555 Nova Drive Suite 300 Fort Lauderdale, FL 33317 Ph: (800) 486 – 5058 http://www.experiencecle.com/locations/ft_lauderdale.aspx
		CLE Austin TX 11801Stonehollow Dr. Suite 100 Austin, TZX 78758 Ph: 800-486-5058 http://www.cleinc.net/locations/austin.aspx
		CLE Denver CO 1391 Speer Blvd. Suite 400 Denver. CO 80204 Ph: 800-486-5058 http://www.cleinc.net/locations/denver.aspx

School	Program Overview	Contact Information
		CLE Monterey CA 787 Munras Ave. Suite 201 Montery, CA 93940 Ph: 800-486-5058 http://www.cleinc.net/locations/ monterey.aspx CLE Washington DC 401 North Washington St. Suite 420 Rockville Maryland 20850 http://www.cleinc.net/locations/ washington_dc.aspx CLE Costa Mesa, CA 2183 Fairview Road Suite 101 Costa Mesa, CA 92627 Ph: 800-486-5058 http://www.experiencecle.com/ locations/Costa_Mesa.aspx
Elmhurst Life Skills Academy ELSA	Program assists students with special needs in completing college and transitioning into independent adults. Locations in Florida, Colorado and Texas.	Elmhurst Life Skills Academy 190 Prospect Avenue Elmhurst, Illinois 60126 Ph: (630) 617-3752 http://public.elmhurst.edu/elsa
Evaluation & Development Center	Center provides services to anyone 16+ who is vocationally handicapped to attain greater productivity and self-sufficiency.	Evaluation & Development Center 500 C. Lewis Lane Carbondale, Il 62901 Ph: (618) 453-2331 rehab@siu.edu
Gersh College Experience at Daemen College	Post-secondary, undergraduate Mary E. Lawler, Director program for students with neuro-biological disorders, e.g. Asperger's ADHD, OCD, Tourette's Syndrome, Anxiety or Depression, Autism Spectrum and Nonverbal Learning disorders.	150 Broad Hollow Rd Suite 120 Mellville NY 11747 Ph: (631) 385-3342 http://www.gershacademy.org/ index.php/schools/the-gersh- experience
The Horizons School	Young adults with learning disabilities to live self-sufficient lives. Non-degree program focused on life and social skills and career development.	The Horizons School 2018 15th Ave. South Birmingham, AL 35205 Ph: (800)-822- 6242 www.horizonsschool.org

School	Program Overview	Contact Information
Independence Center	Young adults 18-30 transitional residential program.	Independence Center 3640 S. Sepulveda Blvd., Ste. 102 Los Angeles, CA 90034 Ph: (310) 202-7102 www.independencecenter.com
Lesley University	Threshold Program is a comprehensive two year non-degree campus-based program for highly motivated young adults with diverse learning disabilities and other special needs.	Threshold Program Lesley University 29 Everett Street Cambridge, MA 02138 – 2790 Ph: 617-868-9600 http://www.lesley.edu/threshold/ admissions.html
Life Development Institute	High school and post-secondary programs teaching independence.	Life Development Institute 18001 N. 79th Ave., E-71 Glendale, AZ 85308 Ph: (623) 773-2774 www.life-development-inst.org
LIFE Skills, Inc.	Young adults 18+ with developmental disabilities, brain injury or mental illness. Services to enhance higher levels of independence.	LIFE Skills, Inc. 483 Highway I West Iowa City, Iowa 52246-4205 Ph: (319) 354-2121 www.lifeskills-inc.com
Maplebrook School	11-21 residential and day school consisting of vocational and college programs.	Maplebrook School 5142 Route 22 Amenia, NY 12501 Ph: (845) 373-9511 Amenia, NY 12501 www.maplebrookschool.org
Minnesota Life College	Apartment living instructional program for young adults whose learning disabilities pose serious challenges to their independence. Must be 18+ and have completed K-12 education. Vocational skills and workforce readiness.	Minnesota Life College 7501 Logan Ave. South Suite 2A Richfield, MN 55423 Ph: (612) 869-4008 www.minnesotalifecollege.com
New York Institute of Technology Vocational Independence Program	18+ with significant learning disabilities and have received special education services during high school years. 3 year certificate program for vocational major or degree program.	VIP Program NY Institute of Technology Central Islip Campus 300 Carleton Avenue Central Islip, NY 11722-9029 Ph: (631) 348-3354 http://www.nyit.edu/vip/

School	Program Overview	Contact Information
OPTIONS at Brehm	Young adults with complex learning disabilities. Certificate. 2 year and 4 year degree programs.	OPTIONS at Brehm 1245 East Grand Avenue Carbondale, Il 62901 Ph: (618) 457-0371 www.brehm.org/options
PACE Program at National Louis University	18-30 years with cognitive and provides integrated services to empower students to become independent adults within the community.	PACE National Louis University 5202 Old Orchard Road Skokie, Il 60077 Ph: 224-233-2670 http://www.nl.edu/pace/
Pathway at UCLA	Two year certificate program for students with developmental disabilities providing a blend of educational, social and vocational experiences.	Pathway UCLA Extension 10995 Le Conte Avenue Suite 639 Los Angeles, CA 90024 Ph: (310) 794-1235 pathway@uclaextension.edu
Riverview School	Ages 12-20 in secondary program, 19-23 in post secondary program (GROW). Co-ed residential school for students with complex language, learning and cognitive disabilities.	Riverview School Admissions Office 551 Route 6A East Sandwich, MA 02537 Ph: (508) 888-0489 www.riverviewschool.org
University of Iowa	R.E.A.C.H Realizing Educational and Career Hopes A 2-year certificate for students with multiple learning and cognitive disabilities	N297 Lindquist Center The University of Iowa Iowa City, IA 52242-1529 319-384-2127 REACH@uiowa.edu
Vista Vocational & Life Skills Center	Three year post-secondary training program for 18+ with neurological disabilities.	Vista Vocational & Life Skills Center 1358 Old Clinton Road Westbrook, CT Ph: (800) 399-8080 www.vistavocational.org
Wellspring Foundation	Intensive residential treatment for various populations including girls 13-18 and adults. Highly structured programs designed to treat a wide range of emotional and behavioral problems including affective, personality, attachment, eating and traumatic stress disorders.	The Wellspring Foundation, Inc. 21 Arch Bridge Road P.O. Box 370 Bethlehem, CT 06751 Ph: (203) 266-8000 www.wellspring.org

RECOMMENDED WEBSITES

Independent Educational Consultants Association
www.IECAonline.com

LDA of America
www.ldanatl.org

Council for Exceptional Children
www.cec.sped.org

Council for Learning Disabilities
www.cldinternational.org

INDEX

ABOUT THE AUTHORS

Marybeth Kravets, M.A., retired in 2010 as the College Counselor at Deerfield High School, a public high school, in Deerfield, Illinois after 31 years. She is now the Chief Education Officer for Chicago Scholars, Chicago Illinois. Marybeth also has a private practice and provides educational and college consulting to high schools, colleges, families and other professionals. She received her BA in education from the University of Michigan in Ann Arbor, and her MA in Counseling from Wayne State University in Detroit, Michigan. She is a Past President of the National Association for College Admission Counseling (NACAC) and also served as the President of the Illinois Association for College Admission Counseling. In addition to co-authoring the K&W Guide, she has authored many articles and is a contributing author to The Fundamentals of College Admission Counseling: A Textbook for Graduate Students and Practicing Counselors, published by NACAC. She has been a guest on the NBC'S Today Show several times and has appeared on many other radio and television programs. She has been a keynote speaker and presenter at major conferences in the United States and Europe. For additional information or to contact Marybeth Kravets for consultation email or call:

Marybeth Kravets
847-212-3687- Cell
847-236-1985- voicemail/fax
Marybeth@kravets.net

Imy F. Wax, M.S.,LCPC,CEP is a psychotherapist and educational consultant. Imy is a member of several professional and parental organizations. She has presented at both professional and parental conferences on such topics as "The Emotional Expectations of Parenting a Child with Learning Disabilities," and has written numerous articles in professional and parental journals. Imy conducts workshops for parents on raising children with learning disabilities and/or attention deficit/hyperactivity disorder, as well as, for school districts all over the United States on the college process. She has been invited a number of times to speak at conferences and at schools in countries in Asia and South America. She has appeared as a guest on the NBC's Today Show, as well as, other television and radio shows. She is married to Howard Wax and has four children, two with learning disabilities and one who also has attention deficit/hyperactivity disorder. Her daughter was the inspiration for this book. For additional information or to contact Imy Wax for consultation or for presentations, email or call:

Imy Wax
847-945-0913
imy@imywax.com

NOTES

NOTES